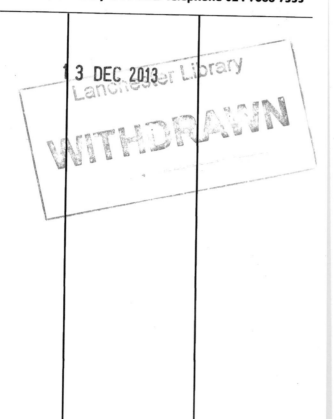

# Corporate
# Finance

## European Edition

# Corporate Finance

## First European Edition

David Hillier, Stephen Ross,
Randolph Westerfield,
Jeffrey Jaffe, Bradford Jordan

**McGraw-Hill
Higher Education**

London  Boston  Burr Ridge, IL  Dubuque, IA  Madison, WI  New York  San   Francisco
St. Louis  Bangkok  Bogotá  Caracas  Kuala Lumpur  Lisbon  Madrid  Mexico City  Milan
Montreal   New Delhi   Santiago   Seoul   Singapore   Sydney   Taipei   Toronto

*Corporate Finance*
David Hillier, Stephen Ross, Randolph Westerfield, Jeffrey Jaffe, Bradford Jordan
ISBN-13 978-0-07-712115-0
ISBN-10 0-07-712115-5

## McGraw-Hill
## Higher Education

Published by McGraw-Hill Education
Shoppenhangers Road
Maidenhead
Berkshire
SL6 2QL
Telephone: 44 (0) 1628 502 500
Fax: 44 (0) 1628 770 224
Website: www.mcgraw-hill.co.uk

**British Library Cataloguing in Publication Data**
A catalogue record for this book is available from the British Library

**Library of Congress Cataloguing in Publication Data**
The Library of Congress data for this book has been applied for from the Library
of Congress

Acquisitions Editor: Mark Kavanagh
Development Editor: Tom Hill
Marketing Manager: Vanessa Boddington
Head of Production: Beverley Shields

Text Design by Hard Lines
Cover design by Adam Renvoize
Printed and bound in Italy by Rotolito Lombarda S.p.A.

ISBN-13 978-0-07-712115-0
ISBN-10 0-07-712115-5

## Dedication

To Benjy, Danny, and Con

*In life, as in Finance, the past does not determine the future.*

# Brief Table of Contents

# Detailed Table of Contents

# Preface

I've been teaching Finance courses since 1994, first as a tutorial assistant in small group classes for masters and undergraduate students, all the way through to large lecture auditoriums of several hundred people. During that time, three books have formed the basis of all my teaching (Ross, Westerfield and Jaffe, *Corporate Finance*; Brealey, Myers and Allen, *Principles of Corporate Finance*; and Grinblatt and Titman, *Financial Markets and Corporate Strategy*). In fact, coming from a mathematics background, I initially learned about finance through these textbooks.

When McGraw-Hill approached me to work on *Corporate Finance*, I was at first reluctant. The book is an institution. What could I do to improve on a text that has gone through so many editions and been taught in so many places? On reflection, however, I knew that there were many areas where the book needed to be changed for an international readership. Like many other lecturers, I had slipped into the habit of recommending RWJ and BM, but then replacing more than half of the slides and examples so that the material was appropriate for my students. Differences in depreciation rules, taxes, accounting standards, and bankruptcy regulations, changed everything except the bare bones.

This book isn't just a reflection of my views on *Corporate Finance*. To make it as relevant as possible, we had a multi-stage review process. First, McGraw-Hill surveyed more than 80 finance academics on the textbook, its strengths, its weaknesses, and areas where improvement was most required. On that basis, I put together a proposal for a suite of changes for each chapter. Once that was agreed by McGraw-Hill, I began the epic process of the adaptation.

From the very beginning, I was absolutely determined that the adaptation was going to be more than a mere cut and paste job. From the initial survey, I knew I had a job on my hands and, as a result, have spent nearly twelve months on the rewrite. Each rewritten chapter has gone out to academics in the field, leading to extensive feedback and further significant improvements in the text. We also had a focus group meeting in Copenhagen with key lecturers. I can assure you that I was given face-to-face (and very frank!) views on the US version of the text and how it needed to be improved for an international readership.

On the basis of the reviewers' advice, comments, and suggestions, the new version is fully focused on an international environment and comprehensively updated with current research. The entire text has basically been reinvigorated and this hasn't been a cosmetic change. While the original engine is still there, the shell is completely international. Important improvements include the following:

- **Rewritten for an environment that follows fair value accounting and International Financial Reporting Standards** Nearly every chapter is affected and consequently, most chapters have a section at the end discussing the important accounting standards that affect the material.
- **International Tax System** Taxation affects the main sections of the book (Capital Budgeting and Capital Structure) and this is reflected in the examples and *end of chapter* questions of every chapter.
- **Bankruptcy Laws** Bankruptcy regulations have significant differences across countries.
- **International Corporate Governance** There is now a recognition of different governance systems across countries and their effect on corporate behaviour and decision-making.
- **Islamic Financing** A growing part of the global economy follows Islamic principles in its financing decisions. This is now discussed in the text with worked examples and *end of chapter* questions.
- **Business Practice across Countries** Companies in the US have quite different operational methods and strategies from those in Europe and the rest of the world. This is now reflected in the text and supported by research references.

- **Capital Raising** Similarly, the US capital raising environment is quite different to that of Europe and the rest of the world. Pre-emptive rights and other regulatory constraints introduce important differences in corporate financing.
- **Regulatory Differences** There is a range of regulatory differences that affect business decision-making. For example, illegality of poison pills in Europe have affected merger and acquisition activity. Moreover, there have been a number of harmonization laws within the European Union that have changed corporate finance practice. Examples are the Single Euro Payments Area for cash transactions (affects Chapters 26 to 28) and the Common Consolidated Tax Base (affects all cross-border business within Europe).

I also recognise that the readership and teaching styles are different across the world. As a result, the book is now broader in its approach:

- **Accounting Standards** Corporate Finance students who continue into an accounting profession now have a section devoted to the relevant international accounting standards in each chapter.
- **Additional Reading Lists** Many readers wish to specialise in a particular area. While discussion of more advanced material is beyond the scope of the text (Financial Markets and Corporate Strategy is more appropriate), it is necessary to have up-to-date and targeted reading lists. Consequently, most chapters have an additional reading list with the most recent important papers in each area.
- **Practical Case Studies** Most chapters now have practical case studies that require the use of data and independent research skills.
- **End of Chapter Questions** The questions have now been completely overhauled for an international readership.

The field of Corporate Finance is always changing and the book has been updated to reflect the newest developments in the field:

- **New Theories** New theories relating to capital structure (market timing) and dividend policy (catering theory).
- **New Fields** Market efficiency (behavioural finance), corporate governance, and Islamic finance.
- **New Understanding** Updated pricing of warrants and a variety of other changes.

I'm exceptionally honoured to be part of the RWJ history and very proud of the final book. I've thoroughly enjoyed writing the chapters and I sincerely hope you have the same enjoyment reading them.

David Hillier
1 October, 2009

# Guided Tour

## Chapter Opening Vignettes

The Chinese stock markets experienced explosive 2007, gaining 52 per cent and 216 per cent, Sept and 2007, respectively. Of course, that spectacular after the global credit crisis, when the Shanghai cent in 2008.

What caused the incredible growth in 2007, performance in 2008 for China? Even when the the Chinese economy still grew at more than 10 p been inflated because investors were irrationally positive media attention about the Chinese econo reverse their views so quickly? Did the Chinese s 'bubble' in prices, in which equity valuations wer other macroeconomic factors have been the root cuss the competing ideas, p for financial managers.

ncing Decisions Cr

howed how to evaluate proje titive one, where projects wit ugh hard work or through go ue from capital budgeting de

emand for a particular produ

Each chapter begins with a 'roadmap' that describes the objectives of the chapter. Real company examples that will be discussed are highlighted in these sections.

## Figures and Tables

This text makes extensive use of real data and presents them in various figures and tables. Explanations in the narrative, examples and end-of-chapter problems will refer to many of these exhibits.

## Examples

**EXAMPLE 12.4**

### Asset versus Equit

Consider a Swedish tree growing has a beta of 0.8. The firm has de two parts equity. Because the fir remain at 0.8. However, assuming a zero beta

$\beta_{\text{Equity}}$

1.2

If the firm had one part debt to one part equi

1.6

However, as long as it stayed in the same ind leverage, then, is to increase the equity beta.

Separate called-out examples using both real and hypothetical companies are integrated throughout the chapters. Each example illustrates an intuitive or mathematical application in a step-by-step format.

## 'In Their Own Words' Boxes

### In Their Own Words

#### In Professor Miller's Words . . .

The Modigliani–Miller results are not easy to understand fully. This point is related in a story told by Merton Miller.[*]

How difficult it is to summarize briefly the contribution of the [Modigliani–Miller] papers was brought home to me very clearly last October after Franco Modigliani was awarded the Nobel Prize in Economics in part – but, of course, only in part – for the work to finance. The television camera crews from our local stations in Chicago immediately descended upon me. 'We understand,' they said, 'that you worked with Modigliani some years back in developing these M and M theorems and we wonder if you could explain them briefly to our television viewers.'

'How briefly?' I asked.

'Oh, take ten seconds,' was the reply.

Ten seconds to explain the work of a lifetime! Ten seconds to describe two carefully reasoned articles, each running to more than thirty printed pages and each with sixty or so long footnotes! When they saw the look of dismay on my face, they said, 'You don't have to go into details. Just give us the main point in simple, commonsense terms.'

The main point of the first or cost-of-capital article was, in principle at least, simple enough to make. It said that in an economist's ideal world of complete and perfect capital markets and with full and symmetric information among all market participants, the total market value of all the securities issued by a firm was governed by the earning power and risk of its underlying real assets and was independent of how the mix of securities issued to finance it was divided between debt instruments and equity capital . . .

Such a summary, however, uses too many shorthand terms and concepts, like perfect capital markets, that are rich in connotations to economists but hardly so to the general public. So I thought, instead, of an analogy that we ourselves had invoked in the original paper . . .

'Think of the firm,' I said, 'as a gigantic tub of whole milk. The farmer can sell the whole milk as is. Or he can separate out the cream and sell it at a considerably higher price than the whole milk would bring. (That's the analogy of a firm selling low-yield and hence high-priced debt securities.) But, of course, what the farmer would have left would be skim milk with low butterfat content and that would sell for much less than whole milk. That corresponds to the levered equity. The M and M proposition says that if there were no costs of separation (and, of course, no government dairy support programmes), the cream plus the skim milk would bring the same price as the whole milk.'

The television people conferred among themselves and came back to inform me that it was too long, too complicated, and too academic.

'Don't you have anything simpler?' they asked. I thought of another way that the M and M proposition is presented these days, which emphasizes the notion of market complemen

▶

Located throughout the chapters, this unique series consists of articles written by distinguished scholars or practitioners about key topics in the text.

erating cash flows be managed? This question co e sheet. There is often a mismatch between the tim uring operating activities. Furthermore, the amount not known with certainty. Financial managers mu flow. From a balance sheet perspective, short-ter ted with a firm's **net working capital**. Net workin nus current liabilities. From a financial perspective, om the mismatching of cash inflows and outflows. e.

Group plc, a British motor insurer, announced i insurance companies earn income from receiving s money in the financial markets. They pay out or roughout the year. The assets of an insurance co that they can sell at any time, and the liabilities a thin a year. The figures, which come from the firm mple more accessible.
£7.7 million in tangible non-current assets and £6 t assets amounted to £793.6 million and curren 32.7 million. Admiral Group had no non-current plc is presented below.

## Key Terms

Highlighted in boldface type the first time they appear for easy referencing.

## Summary and Conclusions

This briefly reviews and reinforces the main topics you will have covered in each chapter to ensure you have acquired a solid understanding of the key topics.

**Summary and Conclusions**

This chapter discussed a number of practical ap

1 Though NPV is the best capital budgeting a practice for giving managers a false sense of varying assumptions, giving managers a be sensitivity analysis modifies only one varia vary together in the real world. Scenario an different scenarios (such as war breaking ou want to know how bad forecasts must be be calculates the sales figure at which the proj frequently performed on an accounting pr basis is more appropriate.

2 Monte Carlo simulation begins with a mod interactions between different variables an over time. Random sampling generates a di leading to a net present value calculation.

3 We analysed the hidden options in capital option to abandon, and timing options.

... represent an approach for

## Questions and Problems

Each chapter ends with up to 60 questions, graded by difficulty to test your knowledge of the chapter.

## Mini Cases

Most chapters end with a mini case which focus on common company situations. Each case presents a new scenario, data, and a dilemma. Several questions at the end of each case reinforce the material learned in that chapter.

**Exotic Cuisines Employee Share Options**

## Practical Case Studies

The majority of chapters have a practical case study that requires the use of data, and tests independent research skills.

**Practical Case Study**

1 Cash and Operating Cycles   Find th and Nokia. Calculate the cash and recent year. Are the numbers simila

2 Cash and Operating Cycles   Down for Rio Tinto plc. Calculate the oper last four quarters. Comment on any period.

**Relevant Accounting S**

The relevant accounting standards are statements and cash flow. These are IA *Statement of Cash Flows.*

## Relevant Accounting Standards and Additional Reading

Most chapters finish with a section dedicated to the relevant accounting standards, and highlights up-to-date further reading to aid students who wish to explore the topics in further detail.

**Relevant Accounting Standards**

**Additional Reading**

# Technology to Enhance Learning and Teaching

Visit **www.mcgraw-hill.co.uk/textbooks/hillier** today.

After completing each chapter, log on to the supporting Online Learning Centre website. Take advantage of the study tools offered to reinforce the material you have read in the text, and to develop your knowledge of finance in a fun and effective way.

**Resources for students include:**

- Chapter summaries
- Additional case studies

**Also available for lecturers:**

- PowerPoint® presentations
- Instructor's Manual
- Solutions Manual
- Test Bank
- Artwork

**Test Bank available in McGraw-Hill EZ Test Online**

A test bank of over 2000 questions is available to lecturers adopting this book for their module. A range of questions is provided for each chapter including multiple choice, true or false, and short answer or essay questions. The questions are identified by type, difficulty and topic to help you to select questions that best suit your needs, and are accessible through an easy-to-use online testing tool, **McGraw-Hill EZ Test Online**.

**McGraw-Hill EZ Test Online** is accessible to busy academics virtually anywhere – in their office, at home or while travelling – and eliminates the need for software installation. Lecturers can choose from question banks associated with their adopted textbook or easily create their own questions. They also have access to hundreds of banks and thousands of questions created for other McGraw-Hill titles. Multiple versions of tests can be saved for delivery on paper or online through WebCT, Blackboard and other course management systems. When created and delivered though EZ Test Online, students' tests can be immediately marked, saving lecturers' time and providing prompt results to students.

To register for this FREE resource, visit www.eztestonline.com

# Connect

 **|FINANCE**

## Students can connect to knowledge, connect to learning, connect to their futures.

**McGraw-Hill Connect Finance™** is a web-based assignment and assessment platform that gives you the power to create assignments, practice, tests, and quizzes online, while saving you time!

Connect Finance provides the problems directly from the end-of-chapter material in your McGraw-Hill textbook, so you can easily create assignments and tests and deliver them to your students. Connect Finance grades assignments automatically, provides instant feedback to students, and securely stores all student results. Detailed results let you see at a glance how each student performs, and easily track the progress of every student in your course.

### Create Assignments
With four easy steps, set up assignments using end-of-chapter questions from your McGraw-Hill textbook and deliver it to your students . . . all online.

### Students Take Assignments and Receive Instant Feedback
Connect Finance helps you close the feedback loop on students' homework and reduce the time you spend grading. Once an assignment is completed, students can see immediately how they've performed and receive feedback on each question.

### View Grades and Reports
Track each student's progress in your Connect Finance Grade Reports. Student results on each assignment automatically feed to the grade reports so you can track student or class progress on any concept. Learning objective tags help you track course outcomes and aid in Assurance of Learning.

Contact your local McGraw-Hill representative to learn more about Connect Finance.
Visit http://connectdemo.mcgraw-hill.com

# Custom Publishing Solutions: Let us help make our *content* your *solution*

At McGraw-Hill Education our aim is to help lecturers to find the most suitable content for their needs delivered to their students in the most appropriate way. Our **custom publishing solutions** offer the ideal combination of content delivered in the way that best suits lecturer and students.

Our custom publishing programme offers lecturers the opportunity to select just the chapters or sections of material they wish to deliver to their students from a database called Primis at www.primisonline.com

Primis contains over two million pages of content from:

- textbooks
- professional books
- case books – Harvard Articles, Insead, Ivey, Darden, Thunderbird and BusinessWeek
- Taking Sides – debate materials

Across the following imprints:

- McGraw-Hill Education
- Open University Press
- Harvard Business School Press
- US and European material

There is also the option to include additional material authored by lecturers in the custom product – this does not necessarily have to be in English.

We will take care of everything from start to finish in the process of developing and delivering a custom product to ensure that lecturers and students receive exactly the material needed in the most suitable way.

With a Custom Publishing Solution, students enjoy the best selection of material deemed to be the most suitable for learning everything they need for their courses – something of real value to support their learning. Teachers are able to use exactly the material they want, in the way they want, to support their teaching on the course.

Please contact your local McGraw-Hill representative with any questions or alternatively contact Warren Eels **e:** warren_eels@mcgraw-hill.com

# Make the grade!

  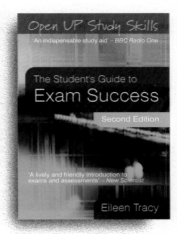

# Acknowledgements

I would like to acknowledge the following individuals who have all contributed in one way or another to the book.

First mention must go to Mark Kavanagh and Tom Hill, who thought up the idea of adapting the US text to an international audience. They carried out the original market research, and worked with me on the project from the beginning to end. This whole endeavour has been a complete team effort and they deserve as much credit as me in putting everything together.

The review process has been extensive and many individuals have given me extensive advice and suggestions on how to make the text much more relevant and current to its intended readership. Every chapter has been scrutinised by several reviewers, leading to a substantial improvement in the quality of the text.

The whole project has taken more than a year of exceptionally hard work and my family, friends, and colleagues have had to take a lot of the burden of supporting me through this intensive period. I would like to thank the following colleagues for standing in for me at various meetings, helping with deadlines, and other sundry support: Emanuele Bajo, Marco Bigelli, Charlie Cai, Iain Clacher, Dick Davies, Michelle Dickson, Joshua Doriye, Paul Draper, Jens Hagendorff, Allan Hodgson, Phil Holmes, Kevin Keasey, Suntharee Lhaopadchan, Helix Li, Andy Marshall, Patrick McColgan, Suleiman Mohamed, Krishna Paudyal, Julio Pindado, and Helen Short.

A year is such a long time (especially in my life!) and the following friends deserve a special mention for their advice, support, and good times during this time: Ronnie and Anne Convery, Philip and Pauline Church, David and Morena Devine, Martin Kemmitt, Paul and Clare Lombardi, Anne and Nicky McCluskey, Pete and Katherine McCudden, and Monsignor Tom Monaghan.

My family is the first, last, and always, and so I especially mention my children, Benjy, Danny, Con, Mia, Patrick, and Saoirse, my mother, Marion, my brothers, Joe and Chris, and my sister Margaret. Finally, other family members I would like to mention are Mary and Willie, Bonnie, Cathie, Ian, Liam, John, Patrick, Quentin, Julie, Con and Nan.

Finally, I wish to thank my wife, Mary-Jo, for everything.

David Hillier
1 October 2009

The author and publishers would like to pay special thanks to all those who participated in the text's development. Be it by completing one of our surveys, reviewing chapters, or attending our symposium, each has made a positive contribution to the final product.

Berndt Andersson, Karlstad University
Tony Appleyard, Newcastle University
Edel Barnes, University College Cork
Jan Bartholdy, University of Aarhus
Anthony Birts, University of Bath
Uwe-Wilhelm Bloos, Goethe University Frankfurt
Tor Brunzell, Stockholm University
Maria Carapeto, Cass Business School
Evert Carlsson, Göteborg University
James Collins, Galway, National University of Ireland
Barbara Cornelius, Umea University
Viet Dang, Manchester Business School
Bob Davidson, Glasgow Caledonian University
Graham Diggle, Oxford Brookes University
Peter de Goeij, Tilburg University

Arie de Wild, Hogeschool Rotterdam
Sveinn Eldon, Arcada Polytechnic
Dr Ahmed El-Masry, University of Plymouth
Twm Evans, Swansea University
Andre Farber, Université Libre de Bruxelles
Evangelos Giouvris, Royal Holloway, University of London
Jonas Grettve, Mid Sweden University
Kathleen Mary Grieve, University of Central England, Birmingham
Liang Han, University of Hull
Thomas Hartung, Universität der Bundeswehr München
Ulrich Hommel, European Business School
Ronald Huisman, Erasmus University
Andy Kilmister, Oxford Brookes University
Stefanie Kleimeier, Maastricht University
Johanna Koeter-Kant, VU University, Amsterdam
Marc M. Kramer, University of Groningen
Claes-Goran Larsson, Umea University
Mezianne Lasfer, Cass Business School
Chien-Hui Liao, University of Birmingham
Brian Lucey, Trinity College Dublin
Sushanta Mallick, Queen Mary University of London
Sophie Manigart, Ghent University
Patrick McColgan, University of Strathclyde
Dag Michalsen, BI, Norwegian School of Management
Arjen Mulder, Erasmus University
Claus Munk, University of Southern Denmark
Emil Numminen, Blekinge Institute of Technology
Bill Peng, University of Exeter
Urs Peyer, INSEAD
Igor Pouchkarev, Erasmus University
Giorgio Questa, Cass Business School
Antti Ilmari Rautiainen, University of Jyväskylä
Marian Rizov, Middlesex University Business School
Knut Sagmo, BI, Norwegian School of Management
Pascal Schnelle, University of Freiburg
Hendrik Scholz, Catholic University of Eichstaett-Ingolstadt
Moh Sherif, Heriot-Watt University
Espen Sirnes, University of Tromso
David Spencer, University College London
Charles Sutcliffe, Reading University
Isaac T. Tabner, University of Stirling
Heather Tarbert, Glasgow Caledonian University
Simon Torp, University of Aarhus
Ilias Tsiakas, University of Warwick
Mika Vaihekoski, Lappeenranta University of Technology
Chris Veld, University of Stirling
Niklas Wagner, Passau University
Wim Westerman, University of Groningen
Chendi Zhang, University of Warwick
Dayong Zhang, University of Leicester
Jianhua Zhang, Gothenburg University
Yin Zhang, University of Dundee

# About the Authors

**David Hillier** is Head of Accounting and Finance, Centenary Professor, and Ziff Chair in Financial Markets at Leeds University Business School in the University of Leeds, UK. He is on the editorial board of several journals including *Accounting and Finance*, *Journal of Business Finance and Accounting*, and *Review of Behavioral Finance*. Professor Hillier has taught across the range of his research interests and more general accounting and finance topics in a number of domestic and overseas locations, including Greece, Italy, Malaysia, the Netherlands, Spain, Tanzania and Thailand. He is an established teacher of executive programmes and has conducted courses for a variety of professional clients, including The World Bank and the UK National Health Service.

**Steven A. Ross** is the Franco Modigliani Professor of Financial Economics at the Sloan School of Management, Massachusetts Institute of Technology. One of the most widely published authors in finance and economics, Professor Ross is recognized for his work in developing the Arbitrage Pricing Theory, as well as for having made substantial contributions to the discipline through his research in signalling, agency theory, option pricing, and the theory of the term structure of interest rates, among other topics. A past president of the American Finance Association, he currently serves as an associate editor of several academic and practitioner journals. He is a trustee of CalTech.

**Randolph W. Westerfield** is Dean Emeritus of the University of Southern California's Marshall School of Business and is the Charles B. Thornton Professor of Finance. Professor Westerfield went to USC from the Wharton School, University of Pennsylvania, where he was the chairman of the finance department and member of the finance faculty for 20 years. He is a member of several public company boards of directors, including Health Management Associates, Inc., William Lyon Homes, and the Nicholas Applegate Growth Fund. His areas of expertise include corporate financial policy, investment management, and stock market price behaviour.

**Jeffrey F. Jaffe** has been a frequent contributor to the finance and economics literatures in such journals as the *Quarterly Economic Journal*, *The Journal of Finance*, *The Journal of Financial and Quantitative Analysis*, *The Journal of Financial Economics*, and *The Financial Analysts Journal*. His best-known work concerns insider trading, where he showed both that corporate insiders earn abnormal profits from their trades and that regulation has little effect on these profits. He has also made contributions concerning initial public offerings, regulation of utilities, the behavior of marketmakers, the fluctuation of gold prices, the theoretical effect of inflation on interest rates, the empirical effect of inflation on capital asset prices, the relationship between small-capitalization stocks and the January effect, and the capital structure decision.

**Bradford D. Jordan** is Professor of Finance and holder of the Richard W. and Janis H. Furst Endowed Chair in Finance at the University of Kentucky. Professor Jordan has published numerous articles on issues such as cost of capital, capital structure and the behaviour of security prices.

# Chapter 1

# Introduction to Corporate Finance

**KEY NOTATIONS**

*B*   Market value of debt
*S*   Market value of equity
*V*   Value of the firm

The business world experiences many events in the space of a year. However, sometimes major events that shake the confidence of corporate managers, regulators and investors come along to change the business environment permanently. Arguably, 2007 and 2008 experienced one of these events with the global credit crisis that has affected banks, corporations and consumers alike.

For many years, low inflation and buoyant economies led to a supply of very cheap money in the world's financial markets. China and India's economic growth, excessive consumption by individuals in the US and Europe, escalating property prices, and highly competitive economic conditions contributed to a fairly unique business environment. However, in the summer of 2007, the world was stunned when news reports announced major defaults in high-risk or subprime mortgages in the United States.

While the problem was confined largely to the US, the fallout from the mortgage defaults rippled through all developed economies. US banks, worried about further losses in the subprime mortgage market, reduced their credit facilities and lending to other banks. This led to a worldwide liquidity crunch, and in the following months, bank after bank announced massive losses resulting from worsening economic conditions.

The bad news was not just confined to the banking sector. In 2008, crude oil prices passed $100 a barrel and gold moved towards $1,000 an ounce, when just three years before they were valued at $49 and $430 respectively. As inflationary pressures grew, raw material costs increased and corporate profit margins eroded. To maintain their level of funding, many companies went to the Middle East and Asia to raise more capital, and more frequently, investors from this region have become the main investors.

Now, more than ever, corporate managers need to understand how to value investments accurately, choose the best funding mix for their operations, manage the risk of their short- and long-term capital, and satisfy the expectations of their investors. Understanding all of these issues and integrating them into a cohesive picture is the goal of this text. Understanding corporate decision-making first requires an understanding of what is meant by corporate finance and what a corporate entity looks like, all of which we discuss in this chapter.

## 1.1  What Is Corporate Finance?

Suppose you decide to start a firm to make tennis balls. To do this, you hire managers to buy raw materials, and you assemble a workforce that will produce and sell finished tennis balls. In the language of finance, you make an investment in assets such as inventory, machinery, land and labour. The amount of cash you invest in assets must be matched by an equal amount of cash raised by financing. When you begin to sell tennis balls, your firm will generate cash. This is the basis of value creation. The purpose of the firm is to create value for you, the owner. The value is reflected in the framework of the simple balance sheet model of the firm.

## The Balance Sheet Model of the Firm

Suppose we take a financial snapshot of the firm and its activities at a single point in time. Figure 1.1 shows a graphic conceptualization of the balance sheet, and it will help introduce you to corporate finance.

**Figure 1.1** The balance sheet model of the firm

The assets of the firm are on the left side of the balance sheet. These assets can be thought of as short-term (current) and long-term (non-current). *Non-current assets* are those that will last a long time, such as buildings. Some non-current assets are tangible, such as machinery and equipment. Other non-current assets are intangible, such as patents and trademarks. The other category of assets, *current assets*, comprises those that have short lives, such as inventory. The tennis balls that your firm has made, but has not yet sold, are part of its inventory. Unless you have overproduced, they will leave the firm shortly.

Before a company can invest in an asset, it must obtain financing, which means that it must raise the money to pay for the investment. The forms of financing are represented on the right side of the balance sheet. A firm will issue (sell) pieces of paper called *debt* (loan agreements) or *equity shares* (share certificates). Just as assets are classified as long-lived or short-lived, so too are liabilities. A short-term debt is called a *current liability*. Short-term debt represents loans and other obligations that must be repaid within one year. *Non-current liabilities* include debt that does not have to be repaid within one year. Shareholders' equity represents the difference between the value of the assets and the liabilities of the firm. In this sense, it is a residual claim on the firm's assets.

From the balance sheet model of the firm, it is easy to see why finance can be thought of as the study of the following three questions:

1   In what long-lived assets should the firm invest? This question concerns the left side of the balance sheet. Of course the types and proportions of assets the firm needs tend to be set by the nature of the business. We use the term capital budgeting to describe the process of making and managing expenditures on long-lived assets.

2   How can the firm raise cash for required capital expenditures? This question concerns the right side of the balance sheet. The answer to this question involves the firm's capital structure, which represents the proportions of the firm's financing from current and long-term debt and equity.

3  How should short-term operating cash flows be managed? This question concerns the upper portion of the balance sheet. There is often a mismatch between the timing of cash inflows and cash outflows during operating activities. Furthermore, the amount and timing of operating cash flows are not known with certainty. Financial managers must attempt to manage the gaps in cash flow. From a balance sheet perspective, short-term management of cash flow is associated with a firm's net working capital. Net working capital is defined as current assets minus current liabilities. From a financial perspective, short-term cash flow problems come from the mismatching of cash inflows and outflows. This is the subject of short-term finance.

**EXAMPLE 1.1**

On 4 March 2008, Admiral Group plc, a British motor insurer, announced its financial results for the year 2007. Insurance companies earn income from receiving insurance premiums and investing this money in the financial markets. They pay out on insurance claims that they receive throughout the year. The assets of an insurance company are generally financial securities that they can sell at any time, and the liabilities are generally insurance claims that will be paid out within a year. The figures, which come from the firm's financial accounts, are simplified to make the example more accessible.

At the end of 2007, the company had £7.7 million in tangible non-current assets and £69.0 million in intangible non-current assets. Current assets amounted to £793.6 million and current liabilities (liabilities due within one year) were £632.7 million. Admiral Group had no non-current liabilities. A balance sheet model for Admiral Group plc is presented below.

| | | | |
|---|---|---|---|
| Current assets £793.6 million | | Current liabilities £632.7 million | |
| | Net working capital: £793.6 million – £632.7 million = £160.9 million | | |
| Non-current assets Tangible: £7.7 million Intangible: £69.0 million | | Shareholders' equity: £237.6 million | |
| Total value of assets: £870.3 million | | Total value of firm to investors: £870.3 million | |

## Capital Structure

Financing arrangements determine how the value of the firm is sliced up. The people or institutions that buy debt from (i.e. lend money to) the firm are called *creditors*, *bondholders* or *debtholders*. The holders of equity shares are called *shareholders*.

Sometimes it is useful to think of the firm as a pie. Initially the size of the pie will depend on how well the firm has made its investment decisions. After a firm has made its investment decisions, it determines the value of its assets (e.g. its buildings, land, and inventories).

The firm can then determine its capital structure. The firm might initially have raised the cash to invest in its assets by issuing more debt than equity; now it can consider changing that mix by issuing more equity and using the proceeds to buy back (pay off) some of its debt. Financing decisions like this can be made independently of the original investment decisions. The decisions to issue debt and equity affect how the pie is sliced.

The pie we are thinking of is depicted in Fig. 1.2. The size of the pie is the value of the firm in the financial markets. We can write the value of the firm, $V$, as

$$V = B + S$$

where $B$ is the market value of the debt and $S$ is the market value of the equity. The pie diagrams consider two ways of slicing the pie: 50 per cent debt and 50 per cent equity, and 25 per cent debt and 75 per cent equity. The way the pie is sliced could affect its value. If so, the goal of the financial manager will be to choose the ratio of debt to equity that makes the value of the pie – that is, the value of the firm, $V$ – as large as it can be.

**FIGURE 1.2**

Capital structure 1          Capital structure 2

**Figure 1.2** Two pie models of the firm

**EXAMPLE 1.2**

In response to the €4.9 billion loss made from trading in the financial markets at the beginning of 2008, the French bank Société Générale announced that it would issue €5.5 billion of new shares to recover its funding levels. Société Générale could also have issued new debt securities for the same amount of money. If the funding ratio of debt to equity does not affect the value of the firm, the managers of Société Générale would have been indifferent between the two funding options, since the money raised would have been the same.

## The Financial Manager

In large firms, the finance activity is usually associated with a top officer of the firm, such as the vice-president or chief financial officer, and some lesser officers. Reporting to the chief financial officer are the treasurer and the controller. The treasurer is responsible for handling cash flows, managing capital expenditure decisions, and making financial plans. The controller handles the accounting function, which includes taxes, financial and management accounting, and information systems.

In smaller firms, many of the roles within an organization are combined into one job. Although each firm will be different, there will always be someone who is responsible for the duties of a financial manager. The most important job of a financial manager is to create value from the firm's capital budgeting, financing, and net working capital activities. How do financial managers create value? The answer is that the firm should:

(a)   try to buy assets that generate more cash than they cost;

(b)   sell bonds, shares, and other financial instruments that raise more cash than they cost.

Thus the firm must create more cash flow than it uses. The cash flows paid to bondholders and shareholders of the firm should be greater than the cash flows put into the firm by the bondholders and shareholders. To see how this is done, we can trace the cash flows from the firm to the financial markets and back again.

# In Their Own Words

## Skills Needed for a Chief Financial Officer

One needs only to read the employment opportunities section in the financial press to appreciate the skills that are required for someone to be a successful chief financial officer. Below is presented an advert that appeared in 2008 for a chief financial officer position based in Europe. The company is large and, as a result, the successful candidate would have needed extensive experience in the role. As a budding financial manager yourself, it is useful to keep in mind the CV you must build to become an appropriate candidate for this type of job. It seems an awful lot at the moment, but experience and study will bring you to your required level if you keep focused on your target. The name of the company has been changed to FM GmbH to ensure anonymity.

Company:  FM GmbH
Location:  Frankfurt, Germany

The Chief Financial Officer will be responsible for the internal and external financial and accounting reporting requirements of the company. This position requires an individual whose business acumen, financial aptitude and professional initiative enable them to improve the organization's performance and enhance the effectiveness of the individuals within. The CFO will need to be committed to results and have a strong sense of personal responsibility for how the company performs. Financial aptitude and analytical skills need to translate into insightful corrective actions and proactive business improvement. FM is of a size where the CFO will need to blend both strategic and tactical skills. The candidate will need to maintain a 'big picture' perspective but also have a strong attention to detail.

Primary responsibilities:

- Oversee financial management of corporate operations, to include developing financial and budget policies and procedures.
- Responsible for cash management, banking relationships and debt management, as well as heavy involvement in any merger and acquisition activities.
- Create, co-ordinate, and evaluate the financial programmes and supporting information systems of the company to include budgeting, tax planning, property, and conservation of assets.
- Ensure compliance with local and international budgetary reporting requirements.
- Oversee the approval and processing of revenue, expenditure, and position control documents, department budgets, mass salary updates, ledger, and account maintenance.
- Co-ordinate the preparation of financial statements, financial reports, special analyses and information reports.
- Manage an accounting department including a controller and accounting staff.
- Implement finance, accounting, billing and auditing procedures.
- Establish and maintain appropriate internal control safeguards.
- Interact with other managers to provide consultative support to planning initiatives through financial and management information analyses, reports and recommendations.
- Ensure records systems are maintained in accordance with internationally accepted auditing standards.
- Strategic thinker who has the ability to manage with an operational perspective.
- Approve and co-ordinate changes and improvements in automated financial and management information systems for the company.
- Analyse cash flow, cost controls and expenses to guide business leaders. Analyse financial statements to pinpoint potential weak areas.
- Establish and implement short- and long-range departmental goals, objectives, policies and operating procedures.
- Serve on planning and policy-making committees.

The interplay of the firm's activities with the financial markets is illustrated in Fig. 1.3. The arrows in Fig. 1.3 trace cash flow from the firm to the financial markets and back again. Suppose we begin with the firm's financing activities. To raise money, the firm sells debt (bonds) and equity (shares) to investors in the financial markets. This results in cash flows from the financial markets to the firm (A). This cash is invested in the investment activities (assets) of the firm (B) by the firm's management. The cash generated by the firm (C) is paid to shareholders and bondholders (F). The shareholders receive cash in the form of dividends; the bondholders who lent funds to the firm receive interest and, when the initial loan is repaid, principal. Not all of the firm's cash is paid out. Some is retained (E), and some is paid to the government as taxes (D).

Over time, if the cash paid to shareholders and bondholders (F) is greater than the cash raised in the financial markets (A), value will be created.

**FIGURE 1.3**

**Figure 1.3** Cash flows between the firm and the financial markets

**Identification of cash flows**  Unfortunately, it is not easy to observe cash flows directly. Much of the information we obtain is in the form of accounting statements, and much of the work of financial analysis is to extract cash flow information from accounting statements. The following example illustrates how this is done.

**EXAMPLE 1.3**

## Accounting Profit versus Cash Flows

Midland plc is an Irish firm that refines and trades gold. At the end of the year, it sold 2,500 ounces of gold for €1.67 million. The company had acquired the gold for €1 million at the beginning of the year. The company paid cash for the gold when it was purchased. Unfortunately it has yet to collect from the customer to whom the gold was sold. The following is a standard accounting of Midland's financial circumstances at year-end:

| The Midland plc Accounting view Income statement Year ended 31 December | |
|---|---|
| Sales | €1,670,000 |
| –Costs | –€1,000,000 |
| Profit | € 670,000 |

Under International Financial Reporting Standards (IFRS), the sale is recorded even though the customer has yet to pay. It is assumed that the customer will pay soon. From the accounting perspective, Midland seems to be profitable. However, the perspective of corporate finance is different. It focuses on cash flows:

| The Midland plc Financial view Income statement Year ended 31 December | |
|---|---|
| Cash inflow | € 0 |
| Cash outflow | –€1,000,000 |
| | –€1,000,000 |

The perspective of corporate finance is interested in whether cash flows are being created by the gold trading operations of Midland. Value creation depends on cash flows. For Midland, value creation depends on whether and when it actually receives €1.67 million.

**Timing of Cash Flows** The value of an investment made by a firm depends on the timing of cash flows. One of the most important principles of finance is that individuals prefer to receive cash flows earlier rather than later. One euro received today is worth more than one euro received next year.

<table>
<tr><td>EXAMPLE<br>1.4</td><td>

## Cash Flow Timing

The Italian firm Montana SpA is attempting to choose between two proposals for new products. Both proposals will provide additional cash flows over a four-year period and will initially cost €10,000. The cash flows from the proposals are as follows:

</td></tr>
</table>

| Year | New product A (€) | New product B (€) |
|---|---|---|
| 1 | 0 | 4,000 |
| 2 | 0 | 4,000 |
| 3 | 0 | 4,000 |
| 4 | 20,000 | 4,000 |
| Total | 20,000 | 16,000 |

At first it appears that new product A would be best. However, the cash flows from proposal B come earlier than those of A. Without more information, we cannot decide which set of cash flows would create the most value for the bondholders and shareholders. It depends on whether the value of getting cash from B up front outweighs the extra total cash from A. Bond and share prices reflect this preference for earlier cash, and we shall see how to use them to decide between A and B.

**Risk of Cash Flows** The firm must consider risk. The amount and timing of cash flows are not usually known with certainty. Most investors have an aversion to risk.

## Risk

**EXAMPLE 1.5**

The Norwegian firm Fjell ASA is considering expanding operations overseas, and it is evaluating the Netherlands and South Africa as possible sites. The Netherlands is considered to be relatively safe, whereas operating in South Africa is seen as considerably more risky. In both cases the company would close down operations after one year.

After undertaking a complete financial analysis, Fjell has come up with the following cash flows of the alternative plans for expansion under three scenarios – pessimistic, most likely, and optimistic:

|  | Pessimistic (NKr) | Most likely (NKr) | Optimistic (NKr) |
|---|---|---|---|
| Netherlands | 750,000 | 1,000,000 | 1,250,000 |
| South Africa | 0 | 1,500,000 | 2,000,000 |

If we ignore the pessimistic scenario, perhaps South Africa is the better alternative. When we take the pessimistic scenario into account, the choice is unclear. South Africa appears to be riskier, but it also offers a higher expected level of cash flow. What is risk, and how can it be defined? We must try to answer this important question. Corporate finance cannot avoid coping with risky alternatives, and much of our book is devoted to developing methods for evaluating risky opportunities.

## 1.2 The Goal of Financial Management

Assuming that we restrict our discussion to for-profit businesses, the goal of financial management is to make money or add value for the owners. This goal is a little vague, of course, so we examine some different ways of formulating it to come up with a more precise definition. Such a definition is important, because it leads to an objective basis for making and evaluating financial decisions.

### Possible Goals

If we were to consider possible financial goals, we might come up with some ideas like the following:

- Survive.
- Avoid financial distress and bankruptcy.
- Beat the competition.
- Maximize sales or market share.
- Minimize costs.
- Maximize profits.
- Maintain steady earnings growth.

These are only a few of the goals we could list. Furthermore, each of these possibilities, as a goal for the financial manager, presents problems.

For example, it's easy to increase market share or unit sales: all we have to do is lower our prices or relax our credit terms. Similarly, we can always cut costs, simply by doing away with things such as research and development. We can avoid bankruptcy by never borrowing any money or never taking any risks, and so on. It's not clear that any of these actions are in the shareholders' best interests.

Profit maximization would probably be the most commonly cited goal, but even this is not a precise objective. Do we mean profits this year? If so, then we should note that actions such as deferring maintenance, letting inventories run down, and taking other short-run cost-cutting measures will tend to increase profits now, but these activities aren't necessarily desirable.

The goal of maximizing profits may refer to some sort of 'long-run' or 'average' profits, but it's still unclear exactly what this means. First, do we mean something like accounting net income or earnings per share? As we shall see in more detail in Chapter 4, these accounting numbers may have little to do with what is good or bad for the firm. Second, what do we mean by the long run? As a famous economist once remarked, in the long run we're all dead!

More to the point, this goal doesn't tell us what the appropriate trade-off is between current and future profits.

The goals we've listed here are all different, but they tend to fall into two classes. The first of these relates to profitability. The goals involving sales, market share and cost control all relate, at least potentially, to different ways of earning or increasing profits. The goals in the second group, involving bankruptcy avoidance, stability and safety, relate in some way to controlling risk. Unfortunately, these two types of goal are somewhat contradictory. The pursuit of profit normally involves some element of risk, so it isn't really possible to maximize both safety and profit. What we need, therefore, is a goal that encompasses both factors.

## The Goal of Financial Management

The financial manager in a corporation makes decisions for the shareholders of the firm. So, instead of listing possible goals for the financial manager, we really need to answer a more fundamental question: from the shareholders' point of view, what is a good financial management decision?

If we assume that shareholders buy shares because they seek to gain financially, then the answer is obvious: good decisions increase the value of the company's shares, and poor decisions decrease the value of the shares.

From our observations, it follows that the financial manager acts in the shareholders' best interests by making decisions that increase the value of the company's shares. The appropriate goal for the financial manager can thus be stated quite easily:

**The goal of financial management is to maximize the share price of the company.**

The goal of maximizing the share price avoids the problems associated with the different goals we listed earlier. There is no ambiguity in the criterion, and there is no short-run versus long-run issue. We explicitly mean that our goal is to maximize the *current* share value.

If this goal seems a little strong or one-dimensional to you, keep in mind that the shareholders in a firm are residual owners. By this we mean that they are entitled only to what is left after employees, suppliers and creditors (and everyone else with legitimate claims) are paid their due. If any of these groups go unpaid, the shareholders get nothing. So if the shareholders are winning in the sense that the leftover, residual portion is growing, it must be true that everyone else is winning also.

Because the goal of financial management is to maximize the value of the equity, we need to learn how to identify investments and financing arrangements that favourably impact on the value of the shares. This is precisely what we shall be studying. In fact, we could have defined *corporate finance* as the study of the relationship between business decisions and the value of the shares in the business.

## A More General Goal

If our goal is as stated in the preceding section (to maximize the company's share price), an obvious question comes up: what is the appropriate goal when the firm has no traded shares? Corporations are certainly not the only type of business, and the shares in many corporations rarely change hands, so it's difficult to say what the value per share is at any particular time.

As long as we are considering for-profit businesses, only a slight modification is needed. The total value of the shares in a corporation is simply equal to the value of the owners' equity. Therefore, a more general way of stating our goal is as follows: maximize the market value of the existing owners' equity.

With this in mind, we don't care what the organizational form is, since good financial decisions increase the market value of the owners' equity, and poor financial decisions decrease it. In fact, although we choose to focus on corporations in the chapters ahead, the principles we develop apply to all forms of business. Many of them apply even to the not-for-profit sector.

Finally, our goal does not imply that the financial manager should take illegal or unethical actions in the hope of increasing the value of the equity in the firm. What we mean is that the financial manager best serves the owners of the business by identifying goods and services that add value to the firm because they are desired and valued in the free marketplace.

## 1.3 Financial Markets

When firms require cash to invest in new projects, they have to choose the most efficient and cost-effective financing option from a range of appropriate alternatives. First, they must choose whether to borrow money or give up a fraction of ownership of their firm. When borrowing, the company takes out a loan and agrees to later pay back the borrowed amount (principal), plus interest, to compensate the lender for giving the money to the borrower. If the firm decides to give up ownership, it sells a part of its company for a set cash amount. Irrespective, the firm will end up with the cash that it needs.

If a firm borrows funds, it can go to a bank for a loan, or it can issue *debt securities* in the financial markets. Debt securities are contractual obligations to repay corporate borrowing. If a firm gives up ownership, it can do this through private negotiation or a public sale. The public sale of ownership is undertaken through the marketing and sale of *equity securities*. Equity securities are shares (known as *ordinary shares* or *common stock*) that represent non-contractual claims on the residual cash flow of the firm. Issues of debt and equity that are publicly sold by the firm are then traded in the financial markets.

In many countries the financial markets are not nearly as well developed as in Europe. For example, in Africa, many stock exchanges are very small and only a handful of companies have equity or debt securities. For these firms, it is cheaper to get funding from banks and strategic investors.

The financial markets are composed of the money markets and the capital markets. Money markets are the markets for debt securities that will pay off in the short term (usually less than one year). Capital markets are the markets for long-term debt (with a maturity of over one year) and for equity shares.

The term *money market* applies to a group of loosely connected markets. They are dealer markets. Dealers are firms that make continuous quotations of prices for which they stand ready to buy and sell money market instruments for their own inventory and at their own risk. Thus the dealer is a principal in most transactions. This is different from a stockbroker acting as an agent for a customer in buying or selling shares on most stock exchanges; an agent does not actually acquire the securities.

**Figure 1.4** Comparison of dealer and agency markets

Figure 1.4 illustrates the major difference between dealer and agency markets. In both cases, Trader A wishes to sell to Trader B. Moreover, in each scenario, Trader A sells shares for £100 and Trader B buys shares for £110. So what is the difference between the market types? In the dealer market, the dealer bears the risk of holding the shares before he can find a counterparty to buy them. In Fig. 1.4, the dealer finds someone to buy the shares at £110. However, if they are unable to locate a counterparty, they may end up with shares that are less than the value at which they were purchased (£100). This is known as inventory risk, and constitutes a cost to the dealer. The difference between the dealer's buying and selling price is known as the *bid-ask spread*, which in this case is £10.

In an agency market, Trader A hires an agent or broker to find a counterparty. The broker will hopefully find someone and then take a commission on the sale price, which in this case is £10. At no time does the broker own the shares that she is trying to sell and, as a result, does not bear inventory risk.

At the core of the money markets are the money market banks (these tend to be large banks located in Frankfurt, London and New York), government securities dealers (some of which are the large banks), and many money brokers. Money brokers specialize in finding short-term money for borrowers and placing money for lenders. The financial markets can be classified further as the *primary market* and the *secondary markets*.

## The Primary Market: New Issues

The primary market is used when governments and public corporations initially sell securities. Corporations engage in two types of primary market sales of debt and equity: public offerings and private placements.

Most publicly offered corporate debt and equity come to the market underwritten by a syndicate of investment banking firms. The *underwriting* syndicate buys the new securities from the firm for the syndicate's own account and resells them at a higher price. Publicly issued debt and equity must be registered with the local regulatory authority. *Registration* requires the corporation to disclose any and all material information in a registration statement.

The legal, accounting and other costs of preparing the registration statement are not negligible. In part to avoid these costs, privately placed debt and equity are sold on the basis of private negotiations to large financial institutions, such as insurance companies and mutual funds, and other investors. Private placements tend not to be registered with regulatory authorities in the same way as public issues.

Every country has its own regulatory authority that deals with the registration of publicly traded securities. Corporations that wish to have traded securities in a country's securities exchange must register with the competent authority. Table 1.1 presents the names of regulators for a sample of countries.

## Secondary Markets

A secondary market transaction involves one owner or creditor selling to another. Therefore the secondary markets provide the means for transferring ownership of corporate securities. Although a corporation is directly involved only in a primary market transaction (when it sells securities to raise cash), the secondary markets are still critical to large corporations. The reason for this is that investors are much more willing to purchase securities in a primary market transaction when they know that those securities can later be resold if desired.

**Dealer versus Auction Markets**  There are two kinds of secondary markets: *dealer* markets and *auction* markets. Generally speaking, dealers buy and sell for themselves, at their own risk. A car dealer, for example, buys and sells automobiles. In contrast, brokers and agents match buyers and sellers, but they do not actually own the commodity that is bought or sold. An estate agent, for example, does not normally buy and sell houses.

Dealer markets in equities and long-term debt are called *over-the-counter* (OTC) markets. Most trading in debt securities takes place over the counter. The expression *over the counter* refers to days of old, when securities were literally bought and sold at counters in offices

**TABLE 1.1**

| Country | Regulator | Country | Regulator |
|---|---|---|---|
| Australia | Australian Securities and Investment Commission | Italy | Commissione Nazionale per le Società e la Borsa |
| Austria | Financial Market Authority | The Netherlands | The Netherlands Authority for the Financial Markets |
| Bahrain | Central Bank of Bahrain | Norway | Kredittilsynet |
| Belgium | Banking, Finance and Insurance Commission | Poland | Financial Supervision Authority |
| China | China Securities Regulatory Commission | Portugal | Comissão do Mercado de Valores Mobiliários |
| Denmark | Finanstilsynet | South Africa | Financial Services Board |
| Egypt | Capital Market Authority | Spain | Comisión Nacional del Mercado de Valores |
| Finland | Financial Supervision Authority | Sweden | Finansinspektionen |
| France | Autorité des Marchés Financiers | Switzerland | Commission fédérale des banques |
| Germany | Bundesanstalt für Finanzdienstleistungsaufsicht (BaFin) | Tanzania | Capital Markets and Securities Authority |
| Greece | Hellenic Republic Capital Market Commission | Thailand | Securities and Exchange Commission |
| India | Securities and Exchange Board of India | Turkey | Capital Markets Board |
| Ireland | Central Bank and Financial Services Authority | United Kingdom | Financial Services Authority |
| Israel | Israel Securities Authority | United States | Securities and Exchange Commission |

**Table 1.1** Corporate and financial regulators

around the country. Today a significant fraction of the market for equities and almost all of the market for long-term debt has no central location; the many dealers are connected electronically.

Auction markets differ from dealer markets in two ways. First, an auction market or exchange has a physical location (such as Wall Street in New York). Second, in a dealer market, most of the buying and selling is done by the dealer. The primary purpose of an auction market, on the other hand, is to match those who wish to sell with those who wish to buy. Dealers play a limited role.

**Trading in Corporate Securities**   The equity shares of most large firms trade in organized auction markets. The largest such market is the New York Stock Exchange (NYSE). Other auction exchanges include Euronext (Amsterdam, Brussels, Paris, and Lisbon Stock Exchanges) and London Stock Exchange (largest securities only).

In addition to the stock exchanges, there is a large OTC market for equities. The National Association of Securities Dealers Automated Quotation System (NASDAQ) in the US and most equity securities traded on the London Stock Exchange are both examples of OTC markets. The fact that OTC markets have no physical location means that national borders do not present a great barrier, and there is now a huge international OTC debt market. Because of globalization, financial markets have reached the point where trading in many investments never stops; it just travels around the world.

## Exchange Trading of Listed Companies

Auction markets are different from dealer markets in two ways. First, trading in a given auction exchange takes place at a single site on the floor of the exchange. Second, transaction prices of shares traded on auction exchanges are communicated almost immediately to the public by computer and other devices.

The London Stock Exchange is ideal for describing how shares are traded, since the dealer and auction systems operate simultaneously. As of the beginning of 2009 there were more than 2,700 equities traded on the London Stock Exchange. Out of this number, approximately 900 of the largest equities were traded on the exchange's auction system, SETS (Stock Exchange Trading System), and the rest were traded through dealers.

On SETS, traders are allowed to submit orders to buy or sell at a stated price within a reasonable time (limit order), or to buy or sell a stated number of shares immediately at the best price (market order). If a limit order cannot execute immediately (i.e. there are not enough shares at the stated price to fulfil the order), it will stay in the limit order book, which lists all outstanding limit orders.

Smaller companies are traded through a dealer system, called SEAQ (Stock Exchange Automated Quotation System). Dealers compete with each other by posting buy and sell quotes for a maximum number of shares through an electronic system that lists every dealer's quotes. The dealer that quotes the highest buy price and the lowest sell price is most likely to trade.

## Listing

Shares that trade on an organized exchange are said to be *listed* on that exchange. To be listed, firms must meet certain minimum criteria concerning, for example, asset size and number of shareholders. These criteria differ from one exchange to another. For example, Euronext has three main requirements for listing. First, a company must have at least 25 per cent of its shares listed on the exchange, and the value of these shares must be at least €5 million. Unlike other exchanges, Euronext does not have a minimum threshold for asset size. The second requirement is that the listing firm have at least three years of financial accounts filed with the regulator. Finally, all of the company's financial statements must follow recognized international financial reporting standards, also known as IFRS.

Table 1.2 gives the market value of stock exchanges around the world as at the beginning of 2008.

# 1.4 Corporate Finance in Action: The Case of Google

The verb 'to google' is defined in the *Concise Oxford English Dictionary* as 'to search for information on the Internet'. This integration into everyday language is just one signal of the exceptional success of the Internet search engine that was started in 1996 by two Stanford PhD students, Sergey Brin and Larry Page. Google is now worth in excess of $130 billion. During Google's massive growth, its management had to consider and deal with many issues, all of which are covered in this textbook over the next 30 chapters.

## Early Days

The foundation of any new business is the product or service idea. Through their research, Brin and Page believed they had a more efficient model of searching through Internet pages than the search engines that existed in 1996. Armed only with this idea and a few working algorithms, they approached several potential investors, and successfully attracted $100,000 from one of the founders of Sun Microsystems to develop their business concept. Within a year they had received a further $25 million from venture capitalists. To receive this financing, Brin and Page would have had to create a business plan and cash flow forecast that estimated their future costs and revenues. From business plans and cash flows, investors are able to arrive at a valuation of the future company. Valuation of companies and projects is covered in Part Two of this text.

| TABLE 1.2 | Exchange | Market value (£m) | Exchange | Market value (£m) |
|---|---|---|---|---|
| | NYSE Group | 7,825,416 | Athens Exchange | 132,480 |
| | Tokyo SE Group | 2,165,461 | American SE | 128,899 |
| | Euronext | 2,111,340 | Wiener Börse | 118,224 |
| | Nasdaq | 2,006,825 | Tel Aviv SE | 117,528 |
| | London SE | 1,925,853 | Santiago SE | 106,455 |
| | Shanghai SE | 1,847,174 | Osaka SE | 106,089 |
| | Hong Kong | 1,327,208 | Jakarta SE | 105,847 |
| | TSX Group | 1,093,275 | Warsaw SE | 105,502 |
| | Deutsche Börse | 1,052,599 | Thailand SE | 98,565 |
| | Bombay SE | 909,550 | Luxembourg SE | 83,047 |
| | BME Spanish Exch. | 890,566 | Irish SE | 71,953 |
| | NSE India | 830,048 | Cairo & Alexandria SE | 69,637 |
| | Sao Paulo SE | 684,856 | Philippine SE | 51,426 |
| | Australian SE | 649,158 | Colombia SE | 50,978 |
| | Swiss Exchange | 635,524 | Lima SE | 34,693 |
| | OMX Nordic SE | 621,289 | Buenos Aires SE | 28,535 |
| | Korea Exchange | 561,303 | New Zealand SE | 23,743 |
| | Borsa Italiana | 536,267 | Budapest SE | 23,048 |
| | JSE | 414,093 | Tehran SE | 21,943 |
| | Shenzhen SE | 392,259 | Cyprus SE | 14,737 |
| | Taiwan SE Corp. | 331,858 | Ljubljana SE | 14,397 |
| | Singapore SE | 269,588 | Mauritius SE | 3,960 |
| | Mexican Exchange | 198,862 | Colombo SE | 3,777 |
| | Oslo Børs | 176,677 | Malta SE | 2,817 |
| | Bursa Malaysia | 162,645 | Bermuda SE | 1,366 |
| | Istanbul SE | 143,286 | | |

**Table 1.2** Stock exchanges around the world

## The Google Share Issue

By 2004 Google had been so successful with its business model and grown so much that it needed significant injections of cash to capture the emerging business opportunities that were becoming available. To the two founders, Brin and Page, it was paramount that they retain control of the company, but they also knew that they would have to issue many shares to investors so as to receive adequate funding. As a solution, Google restructured its ownership to have two types of equity shares, A and B class. B class shares, which were predominantly owned by Brin and Page, awarded 10 votes at company meetings for every share certificate, whereas A class shares received one vote for every share certificate. This meant that even though the number of shares held by outside investors was much higher than those of the two founders put together, the number of votes of outsiders was lower. Issues relating to ownership structure and corporate governance in general are covered in the next chapter.

When Google was thinking of raising capital, it had two choices. It could borrow the money (through a bank loan or public debt markets) or issue equity (through the equity markets). In the end, it chose to raise all the money in the form of equity financing. Google actually has no long-term debt. There are a number of reasons for this, and there are many factors to take into consideration when a firm chooses its own debt-to-equity mix, which is also known as its *capital structure*. It may even choose to use more complex instruments such as options or warrants. Capital structure is covered in Part Four of this textbook, and complex funding securities are discussed in detail in Part Six.

The Google share issue was highly unusual in that it was organized wholly over the Internet. However, several fundamental issues had to be decided upon. First, what should the value of the new shares be? Should A class shares have a different value from B class shares? How risky were the shares? These questions are of huge importance to investors who are planning to invest their cash in any new investment. Assessing the risk of investments is covered in Part Three, and the process of issuing new securities is reviewed in Part Five.

## Google as a Business

Although Google is known as an Internet firm, its success and size make it quite similar to other large firms in more capital-intensive industries. As at the end of 2007 Google had over $4 billion invested in property, and nearly 17,000 employees. In fact, the Google management were so concerned that the firm was losing a lot of its early values and culture that they appointed a chief cultural officer, whose remit was to develop and maintain the early Google working environment. Like all other firms, Google needs to ensure that it has enough liquidity and cash available to pay off its creditors. Short-term financial planning is therefore crucial to its continued existence. This is covered in Part Seven of the text.

Finally, Google has undertaken over 30 acquisitions since 2001. Most notably, it bought YouTube ($1.65 billion) in 2006 and DoubleClick ($3.1 billion) in 2007. Its operations span many countries, making its global reach enormous. It is one of the biggest companies in the world, and will continue to evolve and develop in the future. The final part of this textbook deals with issues such as corporate restructuring, financial distress, and international finance. These are extremely important to all companies, and not just Google.

## So what Is Corporate Finance?

Many people who think of corporate finance tend to consider valuation as being most important. Others think of risk assessment and risk management, while many believe that capital structure should be emphasized. Hopefully, this section shows that for a business to be truly successful, the management of the firm and its shareholders must have a solid understanding of all corporate finance areas, and not just one or two topics. Google was a success, not just because it had a fantastic business idea, but also because it understands the fundamental basis of good business and corporate finance.

## Summary and Conclusions

This chapter introduced you to some of the basic ideas in corporate finance:

1    Corporate finance has three main areas of concern:

   (a)  *Capital budgeting:* What long-term investments should the firm take?

   (b)  *Capital structure:* Where will the firm get the long-term financing to pay for its investments? Also, what mixture of debt and equity should it use to fund operations?

   (c)  *Working capital management:* How should the firm manage its everyday financial activities?

2    The goal of financial management in a for-profit business is to make decisions that increase the value of the shares or, more generally, increase the market value of the equity.

Of the topics we've discussed thus far, the most important is the goal of financial management: maximizing share value. Throughout the text we shall be analysing many different financial decisions, but we shall always ask the same question: How does the decision under consideration affect the value of the equity?

## connect Questions and Problems

CONCEPT
1–6

1 **Corporate Finance**   Your grandmother sees you reading a fantastic book called *Corporate Finance*. She asks you, 'What does corporate finance mean?' Explain to her in a way that doesn't put her to sleep.

2 **Corporate Finance Decisions**   What are the three main types of decision a financial manager can make? For each decision, give a relevant example.

3 **Goal of the Firm**   Evaluate the following statement: 'Managers should not focus on the current share price, because doing so will lead to an overemphasis on short-term profits at the expense of long-term profits.'

4 **Goal of Financial Management**   Why is the goal of financial management to maximize the current share price? In other words, why isn't the goal to maximize the future share price?

5 **Financial Markets**   'The advantages of the corporate form are enhanced by the existence of financial markets. Financial markets function as both primary and secondary markets for corporate securities and can be organized as either dealer or auction markets.' Explain this statement.

6 **The Corporate Life Cycle**   Many companies view a stock market listing as an important objective. Why do you think this is the case? Why do you think Google listed on a stock exchange?

REGULAR
7–20

7 **Balance Sheet Equation**   The 2007 annual report for Anglo American plc, the world's leading global mining company, shows that the firm had $34.042 billion in non-current assets and $9.962 billion in current assets. It reported $11.480 billion in current liabilities and $8.665 billion in non-current liabilities. How much was the equity of Anglo American plc worth?

8 **Capital Structure**   Anglo American plc announces that it plans to increase its non-current assets by $10 billion. If the company wishes to maintain its ratio of total liabilities to equity, how much long-term debt should it issue?

9 **Accounting and Cash Flows**   You work for a private airport that has just purchased a new radar system from the UK for £3.5 billion. You have paid £100 million up front, with the rest to be paid in three months. Explain how these figures would appear on an accounting statement and cash flow statement.

10 **Timing of Cash Flows**   Your company has just purchased a forklift truck, and has two payment options. The first option is to pay 100,000 Swedish kroner every month for 12 months. The second option is to pay 1,200,000 Swedish kroner at the end of the year. Which option should you choose? Why?

11 **Risk of Cash Flows**   You are assessing the viability of two projects. Project A has a 25 per cent chance of losing €1,000,000, a 50 per cent chance of breaking even, and a 25 per cent chance of making €1,000,000 profit. Project B has a 25 per cent chance of losing €2,000,000, a 50 per cent chance of breaking even, and a 25 per cent chance of making €2,000,0000 profit. Which project should you choose? Why?

12 **Corporate Goals**   The global conglomerate, A.P. Moller-Maersk, states on its website that, 'At A.P. Moller-Maersk, our vision is to be a world-class group, known and highly respected. An attractive business partner and employer, and a good corporate citizen.' Is this consistent with the goals of financial management? Explain.

13 **Financing Goals**   Small firms tend to raise funds from private investors and venture capitalists. As these firms grow larger, they focus more on raising capital from the organized capital markets. Explain why this occurs.

14 **Financial Management Goals**   You have read the first chapter of this textbook and have taken over a company that you now discover is losing £100,000 a week. At the rate things are going, the company won't have any cash left in six months to pay its creditors. What are your goals as a financial manager? Is this consistent with what you have read in this chapter? Explain.

15 **Financial Management Goals**   If you are in charge of a private firm and it doesn't have a share price, what should be your goal as a financial manager? Explain.

16   **Financial Management Goals**   You have been manager of a small company for 20 years and have become great friends with your employees. In the last month, new Norwegian owners have bought out the company's founding owner and have told you that they need to cut costs in order to maximize the value of the company. One of the things they suggest is to lay off 40 per cent of the workforce. However, you believe that the workforce is the company's greatest asset. On what basis do you argue against the new owners' opinions?

17   **Goals of the Firm**   Your company's new owners suggest the following changes to maximize the value of the firm. Write a brief report responding to each point in turn:

(a)   Add a cost of living adjustment to the pensions of your retired employees.

(b)   It is expected that high oil prices will increase your revenues by 25 per cent. The company wishes to increase its exploration costs by 15 per cent and pay the rest of the profit out to shareholders (i.e. themselves) in the form of increased cash dividends.

(c)   Begin new research and development into more advanced but untried exploration techniques.

(d)   Lay off 15 per cent of the workforce to keep costs down.

18   **Dealer versus Agency Markets**   Explain the difference between dealer and agency markets. Why do you think both types of market exist? Is there one type of market that is the best? Explain.

19   **Balance Sheet**   If a firm is to cut costs as a result of falling revenues, how would this appear in the balance sheet? Explain.

20   **Dual Class Shares**   Your grandmother asks you why Google has two classes of shares. Explain to her, in a way she would understand and not put her to sleep, why Google structured its share issue in such a way.

21   **Balance Sheet Equation**   You have the following information for the British mining firm Antofagasta plc. All figures are in $ millions.

| | 31 Dec 2007 | 31 Dec 2006 | 31 Dec 2005 | 31 Dec 2004 | 31 Dec 2003 |
|---|---|---|---|---|---|
| Total current assets | 2,911 | 2,451 | 1,849 | 1,302 | 452 |
| Total non-current assets | 2,945 | 2,634 | 1,931 | 1,897 | 1,954 |
| **Total assets** | **5,856** | **5,085** | **3,780** | **3,199** | **2,406** |
| Total current liabilities | 367 | 514 | 389 | 405 | 309 |
| Total non-current liabilities | 1,424 | 1,416 | 1,349 | 1,328 | 1,191 |
| Total liabilities | 1,791 | 1,930 | 1,738 | 1,733 | 1,500 |
| Total equity | 4,065 | 3,155 | 2,042 | 1,466 | 906 |
| **Total liabilities and shareholders' equity** | **5,856** | **5,085** | **3,780** | **3,199** | **2,406** |

Give a brief interpretation of what you think Antofagasta plc did over the period 2003–2007. Do you think it is in a better position now than in 2003?

22   **Balance Sheet**   Assume that Antofagasta plc increased its non-current assets by $1,000 million in 2008 and at the same time reduced its current assets by $500 million. Review the ways in which Antofagasta would be able to finance this expansion.

23   **Balance Sheet**   Assume that, in 2009, Antofagasta purchased a new mine for $500 million. It paid this on credit, and won't be due to actually pay for the mine until 2011. The managers of Antofagasta state that, in the future, any increase in assets will be wholly funded by debt. What would the balance sheet look like at the end of 2009? At the end of 2011?

24   **Balance Sheet**   Assume that instead of financing the expansion fully with debt, the managers of Antofagasta say they wish to maintain the ratio of non-current liabilities to equity after the expansion. What would Antofagasta's balance sheet look like at the end of 2011?

**CHALLENGE**

**21 – 25**

25 **Financial Market Regulators** The UK's Financial Services Authority states that its objectives are to promote efficient, orderly, and fair markets, help retail consumers achieve a fair deal, and improve the country's business capacity and effectiveness. The German financial markets regulator, BaFin, states that 'The objective of securities supervision is to ensure the transparency and integrity of the financial market and the protection of investors.' Are the British and German objectives consistent with each other? Explain.

## Practical Case Study

A skill any financial manager must have is to be able to find and understand financial information. Visit the websites of Volkswagen AG, Daimler AG and Renault SA. Download their financial accounts for the most recent year. At first you may find it difficult to find these, but persevere, because the information is there.

1   For each firm, look at its statement of financial position and record the following:

 (a) Non-current assets

 (b) Current assets

 (c) Current liabilities

 (d) Non-current liabilities

 Construct the balance sheet for each firm and calculate the value of shareholders' equity. What do the figures say about each company?

2   Visit the Yahoo! Finance website and find the share price of each firm. What does the share price history tell you about each company?

3   On Yahoo! Finance read the news for each company. What does the news tell you about the fortunes of each company?

4   Combining all the information, which company do you think is the best investment? Explain.

## Additional Reading

The field of corporate finance is enormous, and evolves in conjunction with events in the global business environment. An interesting paper for readers who wish to delve further is given below. Admittedly, the paper was written in 2000, but the discussion is still highly relevant today. Furthermore, as you will discover in later chapters, corporate finance research has progressed a lot in the 10 years since the paper was published.

Zingales, L. (2000) 'In search of new foundations', *Journal of Finance*, vol. 55, no. 4, pp. 1623–1653.

Online
**Learning**Centre

To help you grasp the key concepts of this chapter check out the extra resources posted on the Online Learning Centre at **www.mcgraw-hill.co.uk/textbooks/hillier**

Among other helpful resources there are PowerPoint presentations, chapter outlines and mini-cases.

# Chapter 2

# Corporate Governance

In March 2008 HSBC, the large British bank, announced that a number of its independent directors were stepping down after very long tenures on its board. This was in response to criticisms by major shareholders that the individuals were associated with the company so long that they could no longer be perceived as independent. The bank also stated that it was considering the introduction of a new long-term incentive plan for senior executives that was linked to the return on the firm's equity, cost efficiency, capital ratios, and relative share price return in relation to their competitors.

In the same week, Marks and Spencer plc announced to investors that its chief executive officer, Sir Stuart Rose, would take over the chairmanship of the firm to become an executive chairman, which combines both roles. This is in opposition to the recommendations made by the UK Combined Code of Corporate Governance, which recommends separation of the roles so as to ensure that no one individual has too much power in a company.

While having two positions on a board for chief executive and chairman is common in the UK, it is less popular in other countries. In the US, for example, the ex-Federal Reserve chairman, Alan Greenspan, has said that 'Chief executive control and the authoritarianism it breeds are probably the only way to run an enterprise successfully.' Debate still rages on the best way to govern and run a corporation. Largely, this will be dependent on who owns the firm, the stage in the company's life cycle, its size, the industry in which the firm operates, the economic and financial development of the country from which the firm comes, and the political environment in which it operates.

*Source*: *Financial Times*, www.ft.com

## 2.1 The Corporate Firm

A firm is a way of organizing the economic activity of many individuals. A basic problem faced by a firm is how to raise cash. The corporate form of business – that is, organizing the firm as a corporation – is the standard method for solving problems encountered in raising large amounts of cash. However, businesses can take other forms. In this section we consider the three basic legal forms of organizing firms, and we see how firms go about the task of raising large amounts of money under each form.

### The Sole Proprietorship

A sole proprietorship is a business owned by one person. Suppose you decide to start a business to produce bagpipes. Going into business is simple: you announce to all who will listen, 'Today, I am going to build better bagpipes.'

A sole proprietorship is the most common form of business structure in the world. From London to Dar es Salaam, from Bangkok to Amsterdam, from Bahrain to Madrid, you will see people doing their business in the streets and roadsides. These are all businesses owned by one person. Possibly, you even come from a family with a sole proprietorship.

In many countries you need a business licence to run a sole proprietorship, but it is also common for sole proprietorships to be set up without any paperwork. Once started, a sole proprietorship can hire as many people as needed and borrow whatever money is required. At year-end, all the profits and losses will belong to the owner, and this becomes his or her salary.

Here are some factors that are important in considering a sole proprietorship:

- The sole proprietorship is the cheapest business to form. No formal charter, articles or memoranda of association are required. Very few government regulations must be satisfied for most industries.

- A sole proprietorship pays no corporate income taxes. All profits of the business are taxed as individual income.

- The sole proprietorship has unlimited liability for business debts and obligations. No distinction is made between personal and business assets. This means that if a sole proprietorship owes money to creditors and cannot pay, the owner's own possessions must be used to pay off the firm's debts.

- The life of the sole proprietorship is limited by the life of the sole proprietor.

- Because the only money invested in the firm is the proprietor's, the equity money that can be raised by the sole proprietor is limited to the proprietor's personal wealth.

## EXAMPLE 2.1 JonMac Builders

JonMac Builders is a Glasgow building contractor, owned as a sole proprietorship by John McAfee. It was started in 1987 by a fresh-looking 24-year-old with his own savings. John leased a small van for £200, used his own tools, and began working on jobs garnered through word of mouth. The firm still exists in 2010 as a sole proprietorship and now has four employees: Benjy (his nephew), JJ (his son), Danny (his other nephew and Benjy's brother), and Christie (Benjy's friend). All income from the company's activities are taxed at John's income tax rate, and the firm's liabilities are secured by John's personal assets, such as his house.

## The Partnership

Any two or more people can get together and form a partnership. Partnerships fall into two categories: (a) general partnerships, and (b) limited partnerships.

In a *general partnership* all partners agree to provide some fraction of the work and cash, and to share the profits and losses. Each partner is liable for all of the debts of the partnership. A partnership agreement specifies the nature of the arrangement. The partnership agreement may be an oral agreement, or a formal document setting forth the understanding.

*Limited partnerships* permit the liability of some of the partners to be limited to the amount of cash each has contributed to the partnership. Limited partnerships usually require that (a) at least one partner be a general partner, and (b) the limited partners do not participate in managing the business. Here are some things that are important when considering a partnership:

- Partnerships are usually inexpensive and easy to form. Written documents are required in complicated arrangements, including general and limited partnerships. Business licences and filing fees may be necessary.

- General partners have unlimited liability for all debts. The liability of limited partners is usually limited to the contribution each has made to the partnership. If one general partner is unable to meet his or her commitment, the shortfall must be made up by the other general partners.

- The general partnership is terminated when a general partner dies or withdraws (but this is not so for a limited partner). It is difficult for a partnership to transfer ownership without dissolving. Usually all general partners must agree. However, limited partners may sell their interest in a business.

- It is difficult for a partnership to raise large amounts of cash. Equity contributions are usually limited to a partner's ability and desire to contribute to the partnership. Many companies start life as a proprietorship or partnership, but at some point they choose to convert to corporate form.

- Income from a partnership is taxed as personal income to the partners.

- Management control resides with the general partners. Usually a majority vote is required on important matters, such as the amount of profit to be retained in the business.

It is difficult for large business organizations to exist as sole proprietorships or partnerships. The main advantage of a sole proprietorship or partnership is the cost of getting started. Afterwards, the disadvantages, which may become severe, are (a) unlimited liability, (b) limited life of the enterprise, and (c) difficulty of transferring ownership. These three disadvantages lead to (d) difficulty in raising cash.

## The Corporation

Of the forms of business enterprise, the corporation is by far the most important. It is a distinct legal entity. As such, a corporation can have a name and enjoy many of the legal powers of natural persons. For example, corporations can acquire and exchange property. Corporations can enter contracts, and may sue and be sued. For jurisdictional purposes the corporation is a citizen of its country of incorporation (it cannot vote, however).

Starting a corporation is more complicated than starting a proprietorship or partnership. The incorporators must prepare articles of incorporation and a memorandum of association. The articles of incorporation must include the following:

1   Name of the corporation

2   Intended life of the corporation (it may be for ever)

3   Business purpose

4   Number of shares that the corporation is authorized to issue, with a statement of limitations and rights of different classes of shares

5   Nature of the rights granted to shareholders

6   Number of members of the initial board of directors

The memorandum of association contains the rules to be used by the corporation to regulate its own existence, and they concern its shareholders, directors, and officers. The rules can range from the briefest possible statement of rules for the corporation's management to hundreds of pages of text.

A corporation will normally start off as a private limited corporation, in which the shares of the firm are not permitted to be traded or advertised in the public arena. The directors of the company will very likely also be the major shareholders. These companies are usually very small, with employee numbers ranging between three and several thousand. Families are regularly the major shareholders in private limited companies.

In closely held corporations with few shareholders there may be a large overlap among the shareholders, the directors, and the top management. However, in larger corporations the shareholders, directors and top management are likely to be distinct groups. At this point, the corporation will comprise four sets of distinct interests: the shareholders (the owners), the directors, the corporation officers (the top management), and the firm's stakeholders (e.g. lenders, employees, local community).

The senior executives of a corporation make up the board of directors. On the board, someone will have the chairperson's role, and is responsible for ensuring that the interests of shareholders are actively considered in corporate decision-making. The chairperson is the most senior member of a corporation, and leads all general meetings. The chief executive officer is the most senior manager of the corporation, and is in ultimate charge of the day-to-day running of the firm. In many companies the same person takes on the role of both chief executive and chairperson (see the opening vignette). The board also has other directors, and these are made up of two distinct categories. Executive directors are senior managers who work in the company on a day-to-day basis; non-executive directors are independent, and are not involved in management. Non-executives usually attend monthly board meetings, and will be individuals with significant business experience and possible political importance.

In countries (Belgium, Ireland, Italy, Portugal, Spain, Sweden, the UK and US) with single-tier, or unitary, board structures, the shareholders control the corporation's direction, policies and activities. The shareholders elect the board of directors, who in turn select top management. Members of top management serve as corporate officers, and manage the operations of the corporation in the best interests of the shareholders.

In countries with two-tier board structures, a corporation's management report to, and are elected by, a supervisory board, which may consist of major shareholders, creditors, trade union representatives, major lenders, and other important stakeholders. Countries with two-tier boards include Austria, Denmark, Germany and The Netherlands. Countries where both unitary and two-tier boards can exist include Finland, France, Norway and Switzerland. However, things are never straightforward, and there will always be country-specific differences. Belgium, for example, has a unitary board system, but banks and insurance companies are allowed to have two-tier board structures.

| TABLE 2.1 | | Corporation | Partnership |
|---|---|---|---|
| | Liquidity and marketability | Shares can be exchanged without termination of the corporation. Shares can be listed on a stock exchange. | Units are subject to substantial restrictions on transferability. There is usually no established trading market for partnership units. |
| | Voting rights | In single-tier board structures, usually each share of common stock entitles the holder to one vote per share on matters requiring a vote and on the election of the directors. Directors determine top management. | Some voting rights by limited partners. However, general partners have exclusive control and management of operations. |
| | Taxation | Corporations may have double taxation: Corporate income is taxable, and dividends to shareholders are also taxable. Each country has its own approach to how it deals with double taxation, and may give a full or partial rebate on the corporate tax payment. | Partnerships are not taxable. Partners pay personal taxes on partnership profits. |
| | Reinvestment and dividend payout | Corporations have broad latitude on dividend payout decisions. | Partnerships are generally prohibited from reinvesting partnership profits. All profits are distributed to partners. |
| | Liability | Shareholders are not personally liable for obligations of the corporation. | Limited partners are not liable for obligations of partnerships. General partners may have unlimited liability. |
| | Continuity of existence | Corporations may have a perpetual life. | Partnerships have limited life. |

**Table 2.1** A comparison of partnerships and corporations

The potential separation of ownership from management gives the corporation several advantages over proprietorships and partnerships:

1 Because ownership in a corporation is represented by shares of equity, it can readily be transferred to new owners. Because the corporation exists independently of those who own its shares, there is no limit to the transferability of shares as there is in partnerships.

2 The corporation has unlimited life. Because the corporation is separate from its owners, the death or withdrawal of an owner does not affect the corporation's legal existence. The corporation can continue on after the original owners have withdrawn.

3 The shareholders' liability is limited to the amount invested in the ownership shares. For example, if a shareholder purchased €1,000 in shares of a corporation, the potential loss would be €1,000. In a partnership, a general partner with a €1,000 contribution could lose the €1,000 plus any other indebtedness of the partnership.

Limited liability, ease of ownership transfer, and perpetual succession are the major advantages of the corporation form of business organization. These give the corporation an enhanced ability to raise cash.

There is, however, one great disadvantage to incorporation. Many countries tax corporate income in addition to the personal income tax that shareholders pay on dividend income they receive. Although there are normally tax rebates given to shareholders, this is in effect a double taxation when compared with taxation on proprietorships and partnerships. Table 2.1 summarizes our discussion of partnerships and corporations.

## A Corporation by Another Name . . .

The corporate form of organization has many variations around the world. The exact laws and regulations differ from country to country, of course, but the essential features of public ownership and limited liability remain. These firms are often called *joint stock companies*, *public limited companies*, or *limited liability companies*, depending on the specific nature of the firm and the country of origin.

Table 2.2 gives the names of a number of corporate abbreviations, their countries of origin, a translation of the abbreviation, and a description of its meaning.

The differences across corporate environments are very large, and the regulatory framework of a country can dramatically affect the way a corporation carries out its business and raises financing for investments. To explore the full range of environments is far beyond the scope of this text. However, one important characteristic is the strength of financial institutions in a country, and their effect on corporate behaviour.

## Bank-based versus Market-based Financial Systems

In a bank-based financial system, banks play a major role in facilitating the flow of money between investors with surplus cash and organizations that require funding. In market-based systems, financial markets take on the role of the main financial intermediary. Corporations in countries with very well-developed financial markets find it easier to raise money by issuing debt and equity to the public than through bank borrowing. Countries with bank-based systems have very strong banks, which actively monitor corporations and are often involved in long-term strategic decisions.

It has been argued that corporations in market-based countries have a shorter-term focus than in bank-based countries because of the emphasis on share price and market performance. When banks are the major source of funding to a company, managers may have longer investment horizons and be less willing to take risks. On the other hand, it has been argued that market-based systems are more efficient at funding companies than bank systems. There are many ways in which a country's financial system can be classified as bank- or market-based. Table 2.3 shows, for a number of countries, the level of domestic deposits in banks divided by stock market size. A country with a high ratio would be regarded as a bank-based financial system.

TABLE
2.2

| Type of corporation | Country of origin | In original language | Description |
|---|---|---|---|
| Pty Ltd | Australia | Proprietary Limited | Private limited |
| Limited | Australia | Limited | Publicly listed |
| AG | Austria, Germany | Aktiengesellschaft | Publicly listed |
| GmbH | Austria, Germany | Gesellschaft mit Beschränkter Haftung | Private limited |
| NV | Belgium, Netherlands | Naamloze Venootschap | Private/public |
| SA | Belgium, France, Luxembourg, Portugal, Spain | Société Anonyme/Sociedade Anónima | Publicly listed |
| AD | Bulgaria | акционерно дружество | Publicly listed |
| OOD | Bulgaria | дружество с ограничена отговорност | Private limited |
| 股份有限公司 | China Mainland | 股份有限公司 | Publicly listed |
| 有限公司 | China Mainland | 有限公司 | Private limited |
| ApS | Denmark | Anpartsselkab | Private limited |
| A/S | Denmark | Aktieselskab | Publicly listed |
| SE | European Union | Societas Europaea | Publicly listed |
| Oy | Finland | Osakeyhtiö | Private limited |
| Oyj | Finland | Julkinen Osakeyhtiö | Publicly listed |
| AB | Finland, Sweden | Aktiebolag | Private limited |
| Abp | Finland | Publikt Aktiebolag | Publicly listed |
| SARL | France, Luxembourg | Société à Responsibilité Limitée | Private limited |
| Ltd | Hong Kong | Limited | Private/public |
| Pvt. Ltd | India | Private Limited Company | Private limited |
| Plc | India, Ireland, Thailand, UK | Public Limited Company | Publicly listed |
| S.r.l. | Italy | Società a Responsabilità Limitata | Private limited |
| S.p.A. | Italy | Società per Azioni | Publicly listed |
| AS | Norway | Aksjeselskap | Private limited |
| ASA | Norway | Allmennaksjeselskap | Publicly listed |
| OOO | Russia | Общество с ограниченной ответственностью | Private limited |
| AO | Russia | Акционерное общество | Publicly listed |
| (Pty) Ltd | South Africa | Privaat Maatskappy | Private limited |
| LTD | South Africa | Publieke Maatskappy | Publicly listed |
| S.L. | Spain | Sociedad Limitada | Private limited |
| Ltd | Ireland, UK, US | Limited | Private limited |
| Inc., Corp. | US | Incorporated, Corporation | Publicly listed |

**Table 2.2** International corporations

TABLE
2.3

| Country | Domestic bank deposits/ Stock market capitalization | Country | Domestic bank deposits/ Stock market capitalization | Country | Domestic bank deposits/ Stock market capitalization |
|---|---|---|---|---|---|
| South Africa | 0.40 | Denmark | 1.40 | Finland | 2.71 |
| Malaysia | 0.41 | Thailand | 1.44 | Israel | 2.76 |
| Singapore | 0.70 | Netherlands | 1.63 | Greece | 2.78 |
| Hong Kong | 0.76 | Japan | 1.66 | France | 3.11 |
| Sweden | 0.86 | New Zealand | 1.73 | Belgium | 3.31 |
| United States | 0.91 | Kenya | 1.80 | Cyprus | 3.73 |
| United Kingdom | 1.03 | Switzerland | 1.80 | Italy | 4.45 |
| Australia | 1.08 | Nigeria | 1.88 | Iceland | 4.50 |
| Canada | 1.12 | Pakistan | 2.17 | Germany | 5.01 |
| India | 1.24 | Indonesia | 2.67 | Portugal | 5.84 |
| Turkey | 1.35 | Norway | 2.69 | Egypt | 6.10 |
| Ireland | 1.36 | Spain | 3.20 | Austria | 10.24 |

*Source*: Asli Demirguc-Kunt and Ross Levine, 'Bank-based and market-based financial systems: cross-country comparisons', World Bank Working Paper.

**Table 2.3** Bank-based versus market-based financial systems

There are other features of a corporate environment that can affect the way a firm makes financial decisions. Table 2.4 lists a number of characteristics that a corporate system may exhibit.

## 2.2 The Agency Problem and Control of the Corporation

We've seen in Chapter 1 that the financial manager acts in the best interests of the shareholders by taking actions that increase the share price of their company. However, in large corporations ownership can be spread over a huge number of investors. This dispersion of ownership arguably means that management effectively controls the firm. In this case, will management necessarily act in the best interests of the owners of the firm, the shareholders? Put another way, might not management pursue its own goals at the shareholders' expense? In the following pages we briefly consider some of the arguments relating to this question.

### Agency Relationships

The relationship between shareholders and management is called an *agency relationship*. Such a relationship exists whenever someone (the principal) hires another (the agent) to represent his or her interests. For example, you might hire someone (an agent) to sell a car that you own while you are away at university. In all such relationships there is a possibility of a conflict of interest between the principal and the agent. Such a conflict is called an agency problem.

Suppose you hire someone to sell your car, and you agree to pay that person a flat fee when he or she sells the car. The agent's incentive in this case is to make the sale, not necessarily to get you the best price. If you offer a commission of, say, 10 per cent of the sales price instead of a flat fee, then this problem might not exist. This example illustrates that the way in which an agent is compensated is one factor that affects agency problems.

TABLE
2.4

| The legal system | Shareholder legal protection | Law enforcement | Ownership structure |
|---|---|---|---|
| **Common law**: Law is developed through court rulings. Can change in response to court rulings. Example: UK | **Voting mechanisms**: Shareholders with small proportional holdings are able to influence board decisions. | **Regulatory enforcement**: A country may have strong regulation, but it could have weak enforcement of laws. | **Widely held firms**: No shareholder has a concentrated shareholding or controls the board through voting power. |
| Civil law: Law is based on code of principles. Does not change. Example: continental Europe. | **Pre-emptive rights**: Existing shareholders are given first opportunity to buy newly issued shares. | | **Closely held firms**: Families, the government or investor groups hold a significant proportion of a company's shares. |
| **Religious law**: Law is based on religious principles. Example: much of the Middle East. | **Extraordinary meetings**: Mechanism is in place to force extraordinary shareholder meetings. | | |

**Table 2.4** Differentiating features of corporate environments

## Management Goals

To see how management and shareholder interests might differ, imagine that a firm is considering a new investment. The new investment is expected to impact favourably on the share value, but it is also a relatively risky venture. The owners of the firm will wish to take the investment (because the share price will rise), but management may not, because there is the possibility that things will turn out badly and management jobs will be lost. If management does not take the investment, then the shareholders may lose a valuable opportunity. This is one example of an *agency cost*.

More generally, the term *agency costs* refers to the costs of the conflict of interest between shareholders and management. These costs can be indirect or direct. An indirect agency cost is a lost opportunity, such as the one we have just described.

Direct agency costs come in two forms. The first type is a corporate expenditure that benefits management but costs the shareholders. Perhaps the purchase of a luxurious and unneeded corporate jet would fall under this heading. The second type of direct agency cost is an expense that arises from the need to monitor management actions. Paying outside auditors to assess the accuracy of financial statement information could be one example.

It is sometimes argued that, left to themselves, managers would tend to maximize the amount of resources over which they have control or, more generally, corporate power or wealth. This goal could lead to an overemphasis on corporate size or growth. For example, cases in which management is accused of overpaying to buy up another company just to increase the size of the business, or to demonstrate corporate power, are not uncommon. Obviously, if overpayment does take place, such a purchase does not benefit the shareholders of the purchasing company.

Our discussion indicates that management may tend to overemphasize organizational survival to protect job security. Also, management may dislike outside interference, so independence and corporate self-sufficiency may be important goals.

EXAMPLE
2.2

# Conrad Black and Hollinger Inc.

A good example of direct agency costs being incurred by a company's shareholders is Hollinger Inc., the parent company of the Sun-Times Media Group. Conrad Black, the British/Canadian press baron who has a controlling stake in the company, started a six-and-a-half-year jail term in March 2008 in the US for mail fraud and obstruction of justice. Black's use of Hollinger's resources for personal expenses is well documented. The *Guardian* newspaper (16 March 2007) reported that he made the company pay £2,735 for his wife's handbags, opera tickets, and jogging gear. Other alleged payments included £20,000 for a holiday in Bora Bora and £45,000 to restore his antique car. Significantly more important, Hollinger paid Black and three colleagues £40 million in the form of 'non-competition payments', the nature of which was the beginning of his eventual downfall. Jeffrey Cramer, the assistant US attorney, used a great line in his opening statement when referring to Conrad Black and his associates:

'Bank robbers wear masks and use guns. Burglars wear dark clothing and use a crowbar. These four, three lawyers and an accountant, dressed in ties and wore a suit!'

Interestingly, although Black used his company's money to fund holidays, houses in many parts of the world, restaurant bills, club membership fees, and other non-corporate expenses, he was not found guilty of using money to subsidize his extravagant standard of living.

## Do Managers Act in the Shareholders' Interests?

Whether managers will, in fact, act in the best interests of shareholders depends on two factors. First, how closely are management goals aligned with shareholder goals? This question relates, at least in part, to the way managers are compensated. Second, can managers be replaced if they do not pursue shareholder goals? This issue relates to control of the firm. As we shall discuss, there are a number of reasons for thinking that, even in the largest firms, management has a significant incentive to act in the interests of shareholders.

**Managerial Compensation**  Management will frequently have a significant economic incentive to increase share value, for two reasons. First, managerial compensation, particularly at the top, is usually tied to financial performance in general, and often to share value in particular. For example, managers are frequently given the option to buy shares at a bargain price. The more the company's shares are worth, the more valuable is this option. In fact, options are often used to motivate employees of all types, not just top management.

The second incentive managers have relates to job prospects. Better performers within the firm will tend to get promoted. More generally, managers who are successful in pursuing shareholder goals will be in greater demand in the labour market and thus command higher salaries.

In fact, managers who are successful in pursuing shareholder goals can reap enormous rewards. For example, the best-paid executive in 2007 was Steve Jobs, the CEO of Apple: according to *Forbes* magazine he made about £323 million. By way of comparison, Jobs made quite a bit more than Ray Irani of Occidental Petroleum (£162 million), Oprah Winfrey (£130 million), and Steven Spielberg (£55 million).

**Control of the Firm**  In most countries, control of the firm ultimately rests with shareholders. They elect the board of directors, who in turn hire and fire management. In other countries, such as Germany and the Netherlands, management are elected by a supervisory board, which is made up of the company's most important stakeholders. The supervisory board contains not just major shareholders but also the main lenders to the company, and trade union representatives.

An important mechanism by which unhappy shareholders can replace existing management is called a *proxy fight*. A proxy is the authority to vote someone else's stock. A proxy fight develops when a group solicits proxies in order to replace the existing board and thereby replace existing management. For example, when Yahoo management turned down an offer from Microsoft to buy the company in early 2008, speculation raged amongst financial analysts that the next stage would be a proxy fight instigated by Microsoft.

Another way that management can be replaced is by takeover. Firms that are poorly managed are more attractive as acquisitions than well-managed firms, because a greater profit potential exists. Thus, avoiding a takeover by another firm gives management an incentive to act in the shareholders' interests.

The frequency of takeovers varies significantly across the world because of the way in which corporations are owned. In the US and UK most large companies do not have controlling shareholders and, as a result, corporations find it easier to successfully undertake acquisitions. In Italy and Spain many firms are controlled by family groups, who are very reticent about selling their shares to outside bidders. In Germany and the Netherlands takeovers must be accepted by a company's supervisory board, which tends to contain those groups, such as employee representatives, that do badly when a firm is taken over. Finally, in many countries, such as Russia and China, the government owns the majority of companies' shares and for political reasons is unwilling to sell its shareholdings.

**Conclusion**   The available theory and evidence are consistent with the view that shareholders control the firm, and that shareholder wealth maximization is the relevant goal of the corporation. Even so, there will undoubtedly be times when management goals are pursued at the expense of the shareholders, at least temporarily.

## Stakeholders

Our discussion thus far implies that management and shareholders are the only parties with an interest in the firm's decisions. This is an oversimplification, of course. Employees, customers, suppliers, and even the government all have a financial interest in the firm.

Taken together, these various groups are called stakeholders in the firm. In general, a stakeholder is someone other than a shareholder or creditor who potentially has a claim on the cash flows of the firm. Such groups will also attempt to exert control over the firm, perhaps to the detriment of the owners. In countries with two-tier boards, such as the Netherlands and Germany, stakeholders are formally included in the decision-making activities of a firm, through its supervisory board to which its management must report.

## 2.3  The Governance Structure of Corporations

In this section we review in more detail the different ways in which corporations can be governed. Because of cultural and regulatory differences, a large number of governance structures can be seen operating successfully in companies in many different countries. Moreover, company size is very important. The largest companies may have more than 10 directors, a chairman, a chief executive and other individuals on their executive board. Compare this with a private limited company, where the shareholders are also likely to be running the company, or, even more extreme, a sole proprietorship where the manager is the owner. Some firms may be run by a family with many family members involved in the firm's management, or they may be state-owned, with appointments made through political decisions.

In all businesses there are a number of duties or responsibilities that must be carried out by corporate executives. For example, a firm must know and form its long-term business strategy. It must be in control of its financial affairs, and actively seek out new and profitable investment opportunities. It should seek the most appropriate new financing when required, and ensure it has complied with all relevant regulation.

As companies grow, these respective responsibilities become too large to be undertaken by only one individual, and consequently must be delegated to a team, or even a large department. Executives need to know what is happening in every sphere of their company's business activities and ensure that all aspects of business are operating at peak efficiency. Corporate governance is concerned primarily with ensuring that businesses are operating well, that business decisions are made rationally, and that the appropriate individuals who make these decisions are held accountable when things go wrong.

Not all organizations are governed well. Just because a firm is listed on a stock exchange does not mean that correct business decisions are being made, or that shareholder wealth is being maximized. In many companies, governance culture lags behind the growth of the firm. Small, successful companies are likely to have governance structures that are very different from those of large successful firms in the same industry. In many countries, individuals with political links are placed on corporate boards and their objectives are very different from that of shareholders.

While it is impossible to cover all the governance structures that exist in the business world, it is useful to see examples of the way in which different firms are governed.

## The Sole Proprietorship

Let us return to JonMac Builders, the sole proprietorship that was introduced in Example 2.1. These types of firm are the easiest to understand, since all the business activities are concentrated in one individual – the owner/manager. Business decisions, long-term strategy, short-term cash management, and financing decisions are all made by John McAfee, the owner of JonMac Builders. John has no skill whatsoever in accounting, so he hires an accountant to draw up his financial accounts for the year. The main reason for hiring an accountant is to determine the amount of tax John has to pay, based on the company's profits.

With the exception of the accounting function, everything in JonMac Builders is done informally and on a day-to-day basis. In these types of organization there is no real need for formal governance structures, since there is nothing really to be governed. The only important formal aspect of the business, the financial accounting, has been outsourced to another company that specializes in the accounting function. It is hopefully clear that it is neither sensible nor cost-effective for JonMac builders to employ its own accountant, or to introduce formal governance structures within the firm. This is the general position for most sole proprietorships.

## Partnerships

A partnership is, in many ways, very similar to a sole proprietorship. Generally, partners will have unlimited liability, which means that they are personally liable for all of their firm's debts. Every partnership will have some form of partnership agreement that governs the financial affairs of the firm, such as apportioning of profits among partners. Senior partners may receive a higher proportion of the company's profits than junior partners, and this will be enshrined within the partnership agreement. Rules on partners resigning, new partners joining and major corporate decisions may also be included.

Partnership agreements need not be complicated or filled with legal jargon. They can also be quite short. Example 2.3 shows an actual partnership agreement for Twiga Export Partners, a partnership that sources materials, automobiles and electrical appliances from around the world and exports them to sub-Saharan Africa. There are five partners in the firm, all concerned with different aspects of the business. Three of the partners are based in East Africa and two are based in Europe.

---

**EXAMPLE 2.3**

## Partnership Agreement of Twiga Export Partners

This partnership agreement relates wholly, entirely and only to Twiga Export Partners, hereafter known as 'the business'. It does not convey rights or claim (partial, incidental or whole) towards any other activity or association to which any partner is involved.

This agreement applies as follows:

1   Each partner is due an equal share of all profits or losses accruing to the business. That is, each partner has claim to 20% of profits or losses in any financial period.

2   Any injection of loan funds into the business will result in interest being paid, amounting to 8% per annum compounded on an annual basis. Interest will be allocated against the partner's capital account.

3   Any withdrawal of funds from the business, not including any salary, will be charged interest at 8% per annum compounded on an annual basis. Interest on drawings will be charged against the partner's capital account.

4   Any capital contributed by a partner must be agreed upon by all partners beforehand.

5   A partner will be paid a salary only on agreement by all partners. The level of salary must be agreed upon by all partners.

6   Before admission of any new partners, agreement and consent must be reached by all partners in business.

7   Upon leaving or retiring from business, a partner will be paid in cash their total capital invested in business as well as any goodwill owned by partner. Goodwill will be calculated as 20% of average net profit over previous five years.

8   Changes in any of the points above must be agreed upon in writing by all partners.

Upon signing this document in the presence of two other partners, a partner will be deemed to accept the points in this document in full.

The partnership agreement deals only partially with the governance structure of a partnership. The firm must also have procedures in place for ensuring that all partners are carrying out their responsibilities fully. Normally, a partners' meeting will be held regularly to discuss business strategy and other long-term issues facing the business. The partners will also report on their own activity since the last partners' meeting. These may take place on a monthly basis, or more frequently. In the case of Twiga Export Partners, the meeting takes place every six months because of the geographical distance between partners. More regular meetings would not be cost-effective for Twiga – a trade-off that all companies must bear in mind when assessing the importance of better governance procedures.

Because the owners are also managers of the firm, partnerships do not normally require outside or independent individuals in the partners' meetings. In addition, they are also likely to appoint auditors and accountants to take care of the financial reporting of the firm.

## Corporations

Because a corporation is a separate legal entity, the informality that is common in sole proprietorships and partnerships is substituted by the formal corporate governance structures that are commonly seen in large organizations. Formal structures are necessary because the owners of the firm are less likely to be involved in management. As stated earlier, corporations must have articles of incorporation that govern the allocation and issuance of shares, the number of directors in the firm, and procedures for appointment and resignation from the board.

However, shareholders also require formal and explicit assurances that managers are running their company to maximize shareholder wealth. This is normally exhibited through the inclusion of external, non-executive and independent board members who attend all of the company's executive board meetings. In addition, there are usually a number of other governance structures ensuring that individuals do not have too much power within a firm, which may make them entrenched and less likely to pursue shareholder objectives over their own personal objectives.

Whereas regulatory requirements force board structures into a two-tier or unitary board structure, there are a number of principles to which all corporations are recommended to adhere, so as to minimize governance failures. Individual countries have their own specific approach to corporate governance, but all follow to a lesser or greater extent the 2004 OECD Principles of Corporate Governance, published by the Organization for Economic Co-operation and Development. The principles themselves are not legally binding, but are recommendations on best governance practice within corporate organizations.

## 2.4  The 2004 OECD Principles of Corporate Governance

The principles are centred around six major areas, and concern all aspects of corporate governance. These are detailed below.

### 1.  Ensuring the Basis for an Effective Corporate Governance Framework

**The corporate governance framework should promote transparent and efficient markets, be consistent with the rule of law and clearly articulate the division of responsibilities among different supervisory, regulatory and enforcement authorities.**

This principle emphasizes the need to take into account the fact that corporations are fundamentally geared towards making money, and corporate governance structures must be set up to ensure that this is not adversely affected. It also states that any governance regulation must be consistent with the legal and regulatory environment in which the firm operates. Finally, the principle argues that there should be a strict and transparent delineation of responsibilities in setting, monitoring and managing the governance of corporations.

### 2.  The Rights of Shareholders and Key Ownership Functions

**The corporate governance framework should protect and facilitate the exercise of shareholders' rights.**

The second principle focuses on the most important stakeholder of corporations – the shareholder. As owner, the shareholder is entitled to basic rights, such as being able to register ownership of their shares, selling their shares to other parties, having access to important information about the company, being able to participate at general shareholder meetings, being able to elect and remove members from the board of directors, and sharing in the profits of the corporation.

Shareholders should also be notified of, and participate in, their company's major decisions, such as increasing the long-term financing of the company through debt or equity offerings, or when the company management decide to sell off a major proportion of the company's assets. Giving shareholders power to influence the direction of their company is the basic rationale underlying this principle, and much of its discussion relates to putting in a framework that allows shareholders to vote and participate at general meetings. The principle recommends that structures should be put in place to allow shareholders to appoint the senior management, and stop them from pursuing business objectives that are not consistent with maximizing shareholder wealth.

The principle also encourages shareholder activism, especially for institutional shareholders, who can exert significant pressure on the incumbent management of corporations because of the size of their shareholdings. The institutions themselves are recommended to publish their own governance structures and policies on voting in general meetings. They are also encouraged to consult with each other on issues concerning their basic shareholder rights.

### 3.  The Equitable Treatment of Shareholders

**The corporate governance framework should ensure the equitable treatment of all shareholders, including minority and foreign shareholders. All shareholders should have the opportunity to obtain effective redress for violation of their rights.**

In many firms there is one shareholder or a group of shareholders who own a very large fraction of the outstanding shares. It is important that dominant, or controlling, shareholders do not run the company in their interests at the expense of minority shareholders. There are several ways in which this could be done. For example, the controlling shareholder may vote for personal friends or family to be on the corporate board. Given that minority shareholders are not strong enough to force their view at general meetings, majority shareholders will always get their way.

EXAMPLE
2.4

# British Sky Broadcasting plc

British Sky Broadcasting plc operates Sky Digital, the satellite television service. In 2003 the then chairman, Rupert Murdoch, announced that his 30-year-old son James would become the company's new chief executive. Rupert Murdoch did not personally hold any BSkyB shares, so how was he able to bring his son onto the board of one of the largest companies in the United Kingdom against the wishes of many of the firm's shareholders?

To understand Rupert Murdoch's power within BSkyB, one must look very carefully at the ownership structure of the corporation. Just under 40 per cent of BSkyB's shares are owned by News UK Nominees Limited, a private British corporation. News UK Nominees Limited is 100 per cent owned by News Corporation, a massive US and Australian media firm, which publishes newspapers all over the world. The Murdoch family is a major shareholder of News Corporation and holds just under 30 per cent of the company's shares. However, these shares are special voting shares, and they give the Murdoch family effective control of News Corporation.

So (breathe deeply!), the Murdoch family controls News Corporation, News Corporation controls News UK Nominees Limited, and News UK Nominees Limited has a powerful stake in BSkyB. This indirect link means that Rupert Murdoch effectively controls BSkyB, even though he does not personally hold any shares in the firm whatsoever.

The third OECD governance principle states that firms must ensure that minority shareholders are protected, and that policies introduced by the company do not penalise them. Processes must ensure that the voice of minority and foreign shareholders is heard at company general meetings.

Corporate executive behaviour is also addressed in principle III, where it is recommended that company insiders should be forbidden from trading when they have private specific and precise information that could be used to benefit themselves personally at the expense of other shareholders. This is known as *insider dealing*, and is illegal in most countries. Board members should also disclose to shareholders any conflicts of interest or material interests in corporate decisions.

## 4. The Role of Stakeholders in Corporate Governance

**The corporate governance framework should recognize the rights of stakeholders established by law or through mutual agreements and encourage active co-operation between corporations and stakeholders in creating wealth, jobs, and the sustainability of financially sound enterprises.**

Principle IV considers the other stakeholders of the corporation, such as employees and local communities. All rights of stakeholders that are enshrined in law should be respected by the corporation, and if a firm violates any stakeholder rights there should be a process or structure to allow those stakeholders to seek redress from the firm. The principle also encourages the development of employee share ownership schemes and other performance-enhancing schemes.

If any stakeholder group feels that the company is not performing to its expectations or meeting its responsibilities to its stakeholders, they should be able to communicate their concerns freely to the company and expect the firm to proactively consider the concerns. Firms should also have a framework for dealing with insolvency procedures (to be used if needed) and effective enforcement of creditor rights.

## 5. Disclosure and Transparency

**The corporate governance framework should ensure that timely and accurate disclosure is made on all material matters regarding the corporation, including the financial situation, performance, ownership, and governance of the company.**

Prompt disclosure of new information relating to the activities of a corporation is an absolute necessity for investors. If little is known about a company, it is almost impossible for outside shareholders to form an accurate estimate of the value of a firm, or evaluate the performance of its management. Principle V states the main types of information that companies should disclose to the market.

These include the following:

(a)   The main financial results, namely the profit and loss over the year, a statement of the firm's assets and liabilities (the balance sheet or statement of financial position), and the cash flow position of the firm

(b)   Corporate objectives

(c)   The main shareholders, and the various voting rights pertaining to different share classes

(d)   Information on the individuals that constitute the board of directors, their salaries and annual bonuses, and a statement on whether a director is independent or executive should be published regularly

(e)   Any trading of the company's shares undertaken by the firm's senior executives, their family, friends and other close associates

(f)   The major risks facing the firm's operations

(g)   Issues regarding employees and other stakeholders

(h)   The main governance structures and policies of the firm

The principle maintains that all information disclosed by the firm should be made as rigorous and informative as possible. This means that financial statements should be prepared by qualified accountants, and all the activities of a firm should be audited and assessed by an external professional firm, the auditor.

## 6.   The Responsibilities of the Board

**The corporate governance framework should ensure the strategic guidance of the company, the effective monitoring of management by the board, and the board's accountability to the company and the shareholders.**

The final OECD principle of corporate governance focuses on the corporate board itself. Board members are expected to make decisions on an informed and ethical basis, and always take the company and shareholder objectives into account. The board must take all shareholders into account and act in their best interests whether they are minority shareholders, foreign shareholders or other groups that have little combined power to influence management. All of the firm's major stakeholders (e.g. lenders, employees, local community, creditors) must also be taken into account when making corporate decisions.

The principle states that a corporate board must fulfil a set number of functions, including

(a)   Reviewing and guiding corporate strategy, major plans of action, risk policy, annual budgets and business plans; setting performance objectives; monitoring implementation and corporate performance; and overseeing major capital expenditures, acquisitions and divestitures

(b)   Monitoring the effectiveness of the company's governance practices and making changes as needed

(c)   Selecting, compensating, monitoring and, when necessary, replacing key executives and overseeing succession planning

(d)   Aligning key executive and board remuneration with the longer-term interests of the company and its shareholders

(e)   Ensuring a formal and transparent board nomination and election process

(f)   Monitoring and managing potential conflicts of interest between management, board members and shareholders, including misuse of corporate assets and abuse in related party transactions

| TABLE 2.5 | | |
|---|---|---|
| **Country** | **Code** | |
| Australia | Revised Corporate Governance Principles and Recommendations (2007) | |
| Austria | Austrian Code of Corporate Governance (2002, amended 2007) | |
| Belgium | Draft 2009 Belgian Code on Corporate Governance (2008) | |
| China | Provisional Code of Corporate Governance for Securities Companies (2004) | |
| Commonwealth | CACG: Principles for Corporate Governance in the Commonwealth (1999) | |
| Czech Republic | Corporate Governance Code (2004) | |
| Denmark | Revised Recommendations for Corporate Governance in Denmark (2008) | |
| Estonia | Corporate Governance Recommendations (2006) | |
| EU | Euroshareholders Corporate Governance Guidelines 2000 (2002) | |
| Finland | Finnish Corporate Governance Code (2008) | |
| France | The Corporate Governance of Listed Companies (2003) | |
| Germany | German Corporate Governance Code (2002, amended 2008) | |
| Greece | Principles of Corporate Governance (2001) | |
| Hong Kong | Hong Kong Code on Corporate Governance (2004) | |
| India | Report of the Kumar Mangalam Birla Committee on Corporate Governance (2000) | |
| Ireland | Corporate Governance, Share Option and Other Incentive Schemes (1999) | |
| Italy | Codice di Autodisciplina (2006) | |
| Japan | Principles of Corporate Governance for Listed Companies (2004) | |
| Kenya | Principles for Corporate Governance in Kenya (2002) | |
| Netherlands | SCGOP Handbook of Corporate Governance (2004) The Dutch Corporate Governance Code (The Tabaksblat Code) (2003) | |
| Norway | The Norwegian Code of Practice for Corporate Governance (2007) | |
| OECD | OECD Principles of Corporate Governance (2004) | |
| Poland | Code of Best Practice for WSE Companies (2007) | |
| Portugal | White Book on Corporate Governance in Portugal (2006) | |
| Romania | Bucharest Stock Exchange Corporate Governance Code (2009) | |
| Russia | The Russian Code of Corporate Conduct (2002) | |
| Singapore | Code of Corporate Governance 2005 (2005) | |
| Slovakia | Corporate Governance Code for Slovakia (2008) | |
| Slovenia | Corporate Governance Code (2005, amended 2007) | |
| South Africa | King Report on Corporate Governance for South Africa (King II Report) (2002) | |
| South Korea | Code of Best Practice for Corporate Governance (1999) | |
| Spain | Code of Ethics for Companies (2006) Draft Unified Code of Recommendations for Good Governance (2006) | |
| Sweden | Swedish Code of Corporate Governance (2008) | |
| Switzerland | Swiss Code of Best Practice for Corporate Governance (2008) | |
| Taiwan | Taiwan Corporate Governance Best-Practice Principles (2002) | |
| Thailand | The Principles of Good Corporate Governance for Listed Companies (2006) | |
| Turkey | Corporate Governance Principles (2003) | |
| Ukraine | Ukranian Corporate Governance Principles (2003) | |
| UK | The Combined Code on Corporate Governance (2008) | |
| US | Key Agreed Principles to Strengthen Corporate Governance for US Publicly Traded Corporations (2008) Final NYSE Corporate Governance Rules (2003) The Sarbanes-Oxley Act (2002) | |

**Table 2.5** Country codes of corporate governance

(g)   Ensuring the integrity of the corporation's accounting and financial reporting systems, including the independent audit, and ensuring that appropriate systems of control are in place – in particular, systems for risk management, financial and operational control, and compliance with the law and relevant standards

(h)   Overseeing the process of disclosure and communications

It is expected that corporate boards approach the job of running a corporation in an objective and independent fashion. When there are conflicts of interest, non-executives should be used to manage potentially problematic situations. Sub-committees of the board, such as an audit committee, nomination committee and remuneration committee, should also be established to deal effectively with conflicts of interest.

## Bringing it All Together

The basis of all good corporate finance decisions is a sound framework of corporate governance. This point can't be emphasized too much, because most of the problems that companies experience can usually be identified by failings in the way in which they are governed. When covering subjects in later chapters, the underlying assumption is that corporate executives are acting in the interests of shareholders, and that the firm is well governed.

When a company does not have strong corporate governance, it may make decisions that do not maximize share value. For example, a firm may choose to invest in projects that maximize managers' own wealth and not that of shareholders. It may also make financing decisions that minimize the risk of the firm for the management but not necessarily for the shareholders. This would lead it to make different investment and financing decisions from those that would be recommended in later chapters.

Transparency and timely information disclosure are major aspects of good governance. Without this, investors would find it extremely difficult to value a firm, or assess the risk of its operations. Part Three of the textbook assumes that share prices efficiently incorporate information about a company. However, if the management of a firm do not see transparency and disclosure as an important part of their responsibilities, share prices will be uninformative and risk assessment would be meaningless.

The 2004 OECD Principles of Corporate Governance set the basis by which individual countries set their own corporate governance codes. This has led to a proliferation of codes issued by regulators specific to individual countries. Table 2.5 lists the main corporate governance codes and their date of publication for different countries.

## 2.5   Corporate Governance in Action: Starbucks

Starbucks, the international coffee retailer chain, is frequently under scrutiny regarding its corporate governance policies. This is because much of its raw material (coffee beans) is created in very poor, developing countries. The scope for manipulation and exploitation of the coffee farmers is massive, and the company has to proactively ensure that one of its stakeholder groups (the farmers) is not adversely and unfairly treated by the board's strategic decisions.

To see how Starbucks adheres to the main OECD corporate governance principles, it is useful to examine its own principles and practices. A document of the company's corporate governance policy has been made publicly available, and details Starbucks' approach to corporate governance.

The document states that the Starbucks board

*"is responsible for overseeing the exercise of corporate powers and ensuring that the Company's business and affairs are managed to meet its stated goals and objectives. The Board recognizes its responsibility to engage, and provide for the continuity of, executive management that possesses the character, skills and experience required to attain the Company's goals and its responsibility to select nominees for the Board of Directors who possess appropriate qualifications and reflect a reasonable diversity of backgrounds and perspectives."*

Next in line is the board of directors, its composition and activities. The board consists of 12 members, including the chairman and chief executive officer. In addition, the majority of board members must be independent non-executive directors.

## Board Meetings

The board meets a minimum of five times per year, and one of these meetings is concerned solely with long-term strategic planning. The chairman and chief executive officer are responsible for distributing the agenda of each meeting beforehand in a timely manner. All members of the board are expected to make every effort to attend the board meetings.

## Authority and Responsibilities of the Board

Naturally, the company sees its shareholders as the main stakeholder group of the company. The fundamental responsibility of the board is to 'promote the best interests of the Company and its shareholders by overseeing the management of the Company's business and affairs'. This is the standard responsibility of a corporate board, and translates itself into two basic legal obligations:

1   the duty of care, which generally requires that Board members exercise appropriate diligence in making decisions and in overseeing management of the Company; and

2   the duty of loyalty, which generally requires that Board members make decisions based on the best interests of the Company and its shareholders, without regard to any personal interest.

## Policies and Practices

Starbucks is ahead of many other companies in that it has a corporate governance committee that reports directly to the board of directors. This places corporate governance at the same level of importance as the audit function, the remuneration of directors, and their nomination to the board, which all have their separate committees.

The corporate governance document sets out detailed procedures for selecting new directorial candidates and their appointment to the board. It also describes the process by which agenda items are set for each board meeting.

Non-executive directors have time at each board meeting to meet on their own without any executive directors present. This is to ensure that a balanced discussion of the company's strategy can be carried out without the interference of the managers who are actually implementing the strategy.

## Director Share Ownership

Starbucks insists that all its directors, whether they be executive or non-executive, hold shares in the company. This is important to the directors, as it ensures some convergence of objectives of directors and shareholders. The minimum shareholding for directors, as of 2008, is $240,000. New directors have four years from the date of appointment to purchase these shares, and must hold them for the period of appointment to the board.

## Assessing Board Performance

Starbucks carries out an annual evaluation of the directors' performance, the effectiveness of the board of directors, and all its subcommittees. An evaluation of the chairman and chief executive is also carried out.

> *"Each year the chair of the Nominating and Corporate Governance Committee (based on such committee's annual review) and the chair of the Compensation and Management Development Committee will conduct a formal evaluation of the performance of the chairman of the Board and the president and chief executive officer based on appropriate quantitative and qualitative*

*criteria. The Board believes that the compensation packages for the chairman of the Board and for the president and chief executive officer should consist of three components: (1) annual base salary; (2) incentive bonuses, the amount of which is dependent upon the Company's performance during the prior fiscal year; and (3) equity incentive awards designed to align their interests with those of the Company's shareholders. The independent members of the Board establish the objective performance measure upon which incentive bonuses are based, such as the achievement of an earnings per share target."*

All the business and financing decisions of Starbucks are framed by the company's main corporate governance principles. Because corporate governance is placed at the very forefront of the Starbucks philosophy, shareholders and stakeholders know that their financial and human investment is governed in an appropriate manner.

## Summary and Conclusions

All of the material in this textbook makes the assumption that firms are run properly, efficiently, and ethically. Unfortunately, in practice, this may not be the case. Corporate governance is concerned with the way in which a firm is managed. There are a number of basic principles that should be followed to minimize the danger of firms getting into difficulty solely because of the way they are managed. The budding financial manager must be aware of and familiar with the basic principles underlying the way in which his or her company should be run. Without this knowledge, he or she will not be in a position to make the best financial decisions for the company's shareholders.

## connect Questions and Problems

CONCEPT
1–6

1 **Private Limited and Publicly Listed Corporations** What are the main similarities and differences between private and public limited companies? Why are all firms not publicly listed?

2 **Macro Governance** Why do you think corporate behaviour in bank-based financial systems would be different from market-based financial systems? How do you think other differences in the macro environment can affect corporate objectives?

3 **Agency Problems** Suppose you own shares in a company. The current share price is £25. Another company has just announced that it wants to buy your company, and will pay £35 per share to acquire all the outstanding equity. Your company's management immediately begins fighting off this hostile bid. Is management acting in the shareholders' best interests? Why or why not?

4 **Corporate Governance** Why is corporate governance important to the shareholders of a firm? Should the same corporate governance rules be applied to all companies? Why or why not?

5 **Corporate Governance** Explain why the corporate governance of a sole proprietorship should be different from that for a partnership, which in turn should be different from a limited corporation.

6 **Corporate Governance across the World** Why is there no single code of corporate governance applied to all the countries of the world? Would emerging-market firms have different issues to consider?

REGULAR
7–19

7 **Sole Proprietorship** Sole proprietorships are the most common types of corporation throughout the world. Why do you think this is? What are the benefits of sole proprietorships over other corporate forms?

8 **Partnerships** What are the differences between a general partnership and a limited partnership? Why do firms choose to be partnerships instead of limited liability corporations?

9　**Organizations**　Review the differences between various corporate forms. Why would an owner move from being a sole owner, to a partner, to a controlling shareholder in a limited corporation?

10　**Corporate Governance Principles**　In your opinion what is the most important corporate governance principle? Explain your answer.

11　**Corporate Governance Principles**　Is it possible to improve one governance principle in a firm but weaken another at the same time? Use an illustration to explain your answer.

12　**Corporate Governance Policy**　Explain what is meant by 'corporate governance'. In your opinion, is this a necessary function of business? Describe Starbucks' approach to corporate governance. In your opinion, is Starbucks serious about corporate governance? Do you have any criticism about its approach? Explain.

13　**Government Ownership**　In recent years, governments have taken control of banks through buying their shares. What impact does this have on the lending culture of these banks? Is this consistent with shareholder maximization? Use an example to illustrate your answer.

14　**Principles of Good Governance**　In 2004 the OECD published its document 'Principles of Good Governance'. Discuss this report in detail, and the major principles that are contained in it. In your opinion, what is the most important (if any) principle? Use practical examples to illustrate your answer.

15　**Regulatory Governance**　You have been appointed as a consultant for a very poor country in Africa, with no corporate governance regulations, and have been asked to formulate an appropriate corporate governance framework for the country's fledgling banking sector. Propose and justify five governance structures or systems that you would recommend to the country's regulators.

16　**Stakeholders**　Discuss what is meant by a stakeholder. In what ways are stakeholders represented in two-tier board structures? How does this differ from companies with a unitary board structure? Use real examples to illustrate your answer.

17　**Institutional Shareholders**　Regulators have developed a number of new policies with respect to institutional shareholder involvement in the running of firms. Review the reasons why regulators would prefer more or less involvement of institutions in the running of corporations. In addition, discuss the proposals that have been put forward by regulators in your own country, and whether these are likely to be effective.

18　**Audit Committees**　The audit committee of a firm is an integral part of its corporate governance. Explain what an audit committee is, why it is important, what its main responsibilities are, and how you can evaluate the audit process within a company. Your answer should refer to real-life examples where the audit process was ineffective or flawed.

19　**Managerial Objectives**　Why would we expect managers of a corporation to pursue the objectives of shareholders? What about bondholders?

20　**Codes of Corporate Governance**　Download a set of country codes from the European Corporate Governance Institute website (www.ecgi.org), and identify any differences and similarities between your chosen country and the US codes. What are the main differences between your chosen country and the US's governance codes?

**CHALLENGE**

**20–22**

21　**Board of Directors**　You have been hired as a consultant to evaluate the performance of a board of directors. What things would you look for? Why would shareholders want to hire a consultant to do such a job, when the share price is supposed to give an accurate reflection of corporate performance?

22　**Managerial Ownership**　How do agency costs in a firm change as managers build up their shareholdings? What does it mean when we say that managers are entrenched? Provide some examples of real-life cases where managers have acted in a selfish fashion, even when they are shareholders in the firm.

## Practical Case Study

Finance executives need to know and understand the corporate governance environment in which they operate.

1   Visit the European Corporate Governance Institute website (www.ecgi.org) and download the appropriate corporate governance code for your country. If your country doesn't have a governance code, download the OECD Principles of Good Governance.

2   Read over the document, identify five aspects of corporate governance that have been highlighted in the document, and explain their importance for your country.

## Additional Reading

Corporate governance is one of the fastest-growing research areas in finance, and the number of top-quality papers that have been published over the last few years is enormous. The ownership structure and governance environment, as well as its impact on all aspects of financial decision-making, has rightly been recognized as crucial to understanding how corporations make decisions. Consequently, the number of papers listed below is necessarily large.

**Macro Governance**   Macro governance papers consider the impact of regulatory structures, culture and law on corporations. They normally examine more than one country, and compare different regulatory and governance environments. Important papers are as follows:

Aggarwal, R., I. Erel, R. Stulz and R. Williamson (2009) 'Differences in governance practices between US and foreign firms: measurement, causes, and consequences', *Review of Financial Studies* (forthcoming).

Andres, C. and E. Theissen (2008) 'Setting a fox to keep the geese: does the comply-or-explain principle work?', *Journal of Corporate Finance*, vol. 15, no. 3, pp. 289–301.

Atanassov, J. and E.H. Kim (2009) 'Labor and corporate governance: international evidence from restructuring decisions', *Journal of Finance*, vol. 64, no. 1, pp. 341–374.

Beck, T., A. Demirguc-Kunt and R. Levine (2003) 'Law, endowments, and finance', *Journal of Financial Economics*, vol. 70, no. 2, pp. 137–181.

Bortolotti, B. and M. Faccio (2009) 'Government control of privatized firms', *Review of Financial Studies* (forthcoming).

Carlin, W. and C. Mayer (2003) 'Finance, investment, and growth', *Journal of Financial Economics*, vol. 69, no. 1, pp. 191–226.

Doidge, C., G.A. Karolyi and R. Sultz (2007) 'Why do countries matter so much for corporate governance?', *Journal of Financial Economics*, vol. 86, no. 1, pp. 1–39.

Doidge, C., G.A. Karolyi, K.V. Lins, D.P. Miller and R. Sultz (2009) 'Private benefits of control ownership and the cross-listing decision', *Journal of Finance*, vol. 64, no. 1, pp. 425–466.

Donghui, L., F. Moshirian, P.K. Pham and J. Zein (2006) 'When financial institutions are large shareholders: the role of macro corporate governance environments', *Journal of Finance*, vol. 61, no. 6, pp. 2975–3007.

Dyck, A. and L. Zingales (2004) 'Private benefits of control: an international comparison', *Journal of Finance*, vol. 59, no. 2, pp. 537–600.

Goergen, M. and L. Renneboog (2008) 'Contractual corporate governance', *Journal of Corporate Finance*, vol. 15, no. 3, pp. 166–182.

Guiso, L., P. Sapienza and L. Zingales (2008) 'Trusting the stock market', *Journal of Finance*, vol. 63, no. 6, pp. 2557–2600.

John, K., L. Litov and B. Yeung (2008) 'Corporate governance and risk-taking', *Journal of Finance*, vol. 63, no. 4, pp. 1679–1728.

Kim, K.A., P. Kitsabunnarat-Chatjuthamard and J.R. Nofsinger (2007) 'Large shareholders, board independence, and minority shareholder rights: evidence from Europe', *Journal of Corporate Finance*, vol. 13, no. 5, pp. 859–880.

La Porta, L., F. Lopez-de-Silanes, A. Shliefer and R. Vishney (2000) 'Investor protection and corporate governance', *Journal of Financial Economics*, vol. 58, Nos. 1 and 2, pp. 3–27.

Laeven, L. and R. Levine (2008) 'Complex ownership structures and corporate valuations', *Review of Financial Studies*, vol. 21, no. 2, pp. 579–604.

Leuz, C., K.V. Lins and F.E. Warnock (2009) 'Do foreigners invest less in poorly governed firms?', *Review of Financial Studies* (forthcoming).

Nenova, T. (2003) 'The value of corporate voting rights and control: a cross-country analysis', *Journal of Financial Economics*, vol. 68, no. 3, pp. 325–351.

Stulz, R. and R. Williamson (2003) 'Culture, openness and finance', *Journal of Financial Economics*, vol. 70, no. 3, pp. 313–349.

There has also been a lot of research at the firm level in single countries. Researchers have examined a wide range of issues, but the general theme considers how governance structures or regulation affect the performance of firms and their strategic decisions. Another important area relates to ownership structure and how that affects a corporation. The listings below are categorised by general subject. The country of study is highlighted in bold.

## Board Characteristics

Bebchuk, L., A. Cohen and A. Ferrell (2009) 'What matters in corporate governance?', *Review of Financial Studies*, vol. 22, no. 2, pp. 783–827. **US**.

Bennedsen, M., H.C. Kongsted and K.M. Nielsen (2008) 'The causal effect of board size in the performance of small and medium sized firms', *Journal of Banking and Finance*, vol. 32, no. 6, pp. 1098–1109. **Denmark**.

Bhagat, S. and B. Bolton (2008) 'Corporate governance and firm performance', *Journal of Corporate Finance*, vol. 15, no. 3, pp. 257–273. **US**.

Chung, K.H., J. Elder and J.-C. Kim (2009) 'Corporate governance and liquidity', *Journal of Financial and Quantitative Analysis* (forthcoming). **US**.

Cremers, K.J.M. and V.B. Nair (2005) 'Governance mechanisms and equity prices', *Journal of Finance*, vol. 60, no. 6, pp. 2859–2894. **US**.

Dahya, J. and J.J. McConnell (2005) 'Outside directors and corporate board decisions', *Journal of Corporate Finance*, vol. 11, Nos 1 and 2, pp. 37–60. **UK**.

Dahya, J. and J.J. McConnell (2007) 'Board composition, corporate performance, and the Cadbury Committee recommendation', *Journal of Financial and Quantitative Analysis*, vol. 535–564. **UK**.

Dahya, J., J.J. McConnell and N.G. Travlos (2002) 'The Cadbury Committee, corporate performance, and top management turnover', *Journal of Finance*, vol. 57, no. 1, pp. 461–483. **UK**.

Doukas, J., M. Holmen and N. Travlos (2002) 'Diversification, ownership and control of Swedish corporations', *European Financial Management*, vol. 8, pp. 281–314. **Sweden**.

Fich, E.M. and A. Shivdasani (2006) 'Are busy boards effective monitors?', *Journal of Finance*, vol. 61, no. 2, pp. 689–724. **US**.

Guest, P.M. (2008) 'The determinants of board size and composition: evidence from the UK', *Journal of Corporate Finance*, vol. 15, no. 1, pp. 51–72. **UK**.

Hillier, D. and P. McColgan (2006) 'An analysis of changes in board structure during corporate governance reforms', *European Financial Management*, vol. 12, no. 4, pp. 575–607. **UK**.

Mura, R. (2007) 'Firm performance: do non-executive directors have minds of their own? Evidence from UK panel data', *Financial Management*, vol. 36, no. 3, pp. 81–112. **UK**.

## Ownership Structure and Shareholder Activism

Ang, J.S., R.A. Cole and J. Lin (2000) 'Agency costs and ownership structure', *Journal of Finance*, vol. 55, no. 1, pp. 81–106. **US**.

Barontini, R. and L. Caprio (2006) 'The effect of family control on firm value and performance: evidence from continental Europe', *European Financial Management*, vol. 12, no. 5, pp. 689–723. **Europe**.

Becht, M., J. Franks, C. Mayer and S. Rossi (2009) 'Returns to shareholder activism: evidence from a clinical study of the Hermes UK focus fund', *Review of Financial Studies* (forthcoming). **UK**.

Boubaker, S. and F. Labegorre (2008) 'Ownership structure, corporate governance and analyst following: a study of French listed firms', *Journal of Banking and Finance*, vol. 32, no. 6, pp. 961–976. **France.**

Davies, J.R., D. Hillier and P. McColgan (2005) 'Ownership structure, managerial behavior, and corporate value', *Journal of Corporate Finance*, vol. 11, no. 4, pp. 645–660. **UK.**

Faccio, M. and L.H.P. Lang (2002) 'The ultimate ownership of western European corporations', *Journal of Financial Economics*, vol. 65, no. 3, pp. 365–395. **Europe.**

Fauver, L. and M.E. Fuerst (2006) 'Does good corporate governance include employee representation? Evidence from German corporate boards', *Journal of Financial Economics*, vol. 82, no. 3, pp. 673–710. **Germany.**

Franks, J., C. Mayer and S. Rossi (2009) 'Ownership: evolution and regulation', *Review of Financial Studies* (forthcoming). **UK.**

Harbula, P. (2007) 'The ownership structure, governance, and performance of French companies', *Journal of Applied Corporate Finance*, vol. 19, no. 1, pp. 88–101. **France.**

Klein, A. and E. Zur (2009) 'Entrepreneurial shareholder activism: hedge funds and other private investors', *Journal of Finance*, vol. 64, no. 1, pp. 187–229. **US.**

Maury, B. (2006) 'Family ownership and firm performance: empirical evidence from western European corporations', *Journal of Corporate Finance*, vol. 12, no. 2, pp. 321–341. **Europe.**

## Executive Turnover and Managerial Succession

Cucculelli, M. and G. Micucci (2008) 'Family succession and firm performance: evidence from Italian family firms', *Journal of Corporate Finance*, vol. 15, no. 1, pp. 17–31. **Italy.**

Hillier, D., S.C. Linn and P. McColgan (2005) 'Equity issuance, CEO turnover, and corporate governance', *European Financial Management*, vol. 11, no. 4, pp. 515–538. **UK.**

Hillier, D. and P. McColgan (2009) 'Firm performance and managerial succession in family managed firms', *Journal of Business Finance and Accounting* (forthcoming). **UK.**

Volpin, P.F. (2002) 'Governance with poor investor protection: evidence from top executive turnover in Italy', *Journal of Financial Economics*, vol. 64, no. 1, pp. 61–90. **Italy.**

## Regulation and Environment

Bajo, E., M. Bigelli, D. Hillier and B. Petracci (2009) 'The determinants of regulatory compliance: an analysis of insider trading disclosures', *Journal of Business Ethics* (forthcoming). **Italy.**

Benfratello, L., F. Schiantarelli and A. Sembenelli (2008) 'Banks and innovation: micro-econometric evidence on Italian firms', *Journal of Financial Economics*, vol. 90, no. 2, pp. 197–217. **Italy.**

Cronqvist, H., F. Heyman, M. Nilsson, H. Svaleryd and J. Vlachos (2009) 'Do entrenched managers pay their workers more?', *Journal of Finance*, vol. 64, no. 1, pp. 309–339. **Sweden.**

Gorton, G. and F.A. Schmid (2000) 'Universal banking and the performance of German firms', *Journal of Financial Economics*, vol. 58, Nos 1 and 2, pp. 29–80. **Germany.**

Hillier, D. and A. Marshall (2002) 'Are trading bans effective? Exchange regulation and corporate insider trading', *Journal of Corporate Finance*, vol. 8, no. 4, pp. 393–410. **UK.**

Masulis, R.W., C. Wang and F. Xie (2009) 'Agency problems at dual-class companies', *Journal of Finance* (forthcoming). **US.**

To help you grasp the key concepts of this chapter check out the extra resources posted on the Online Learning Centre at **www.mcgraw-hill.co.uk/textbooks/hillier**

Among other helpful resources there are PowerPoint presentations, chapter outlines and mini-cases.

# Chapter 3

# Financial Statement Analysis and Long-Term Planning

## KEY NOTATIONS

| | |
|---|---|
| ACP | Average collection period |
| b | Ploughback (or retention) ratio |
| CF | Cash flow |
| EBIT | Earnings before interest and taxes |
| EBITD | Earnings before interest, taxes, and depreciation |
| EFN | External financing needed |
| EPS | Earnings per share |
| P/E | Price–earnings ratio |
| ROA | Return on assets |
| ROE | Return on equity |
| SIC | Standard Industrial Classification |
| TIE | Times interest earned ratio |

In April 2008 shares in food producer Associated British Foods (ABF) were trading for about £8.92. At that price, ABF had a price–earnings ratio, or P/E, of 19.11, meaning that investors were willing to pay £19.11 for every pound in income earned by ABF. At the same time (just after Terminal 5 at Heathrow Airport opened), investors were willing to pay only £6.32 for each pound earned by British Airways, but £38.23 and £3.48 for each pound earned by Carphone Warehouse and 3i Group, respectively. There were stocks such as Kofax, which, despite having no earnings (a loss actually), had a share price of about £2 per share. Meanwhile, the average equity in the FTSE 100 index, which contains 100 of the largest publicly traded companies in the United Kingdom, had a P/E ratio of about 11, so ABF was above average in this regard.

What do P/E ratios tell us, and why are they important? To find out, this chapter explores a variety of ratios and their use in financial analysis and planning. However, before examining price–earnings ratios, we need to spend some time on the source of this ratio – the company's financial statements.

## 3.1 The Statement of Financial Position

The **statement of financial position** or **balance sheet**[1] is an accountant's snapshot of a firm's accounting value on a particular date, as though the firm stood momentarily still. The statement of financial position has two sides: on the left are the *assets* and on the right are the *liabilities* and *shareholders' equity*. The statement of financial position states what the firm owns and how it is financed. The accounting definition that underlies the statement of financial position and describes the relationship is

$$\text{Assets} \equiv \text{Liabilities} + \text{Shareholders' equity}$$

We have put a three-line equality in the balance equation to indicate that it must always hold, by definition. In fact, the shareholders' equity is *defined* to be the difference between the assets and the liabilities of the firm. In principle, equity is what the shareholders would have remaining after the firm has discharged its obligations.

Table 3.1 gives the December 2007 statement of financial position for Ryanair, Europe's largest budget airline. The assets in the statement of financial position are listed in order by the length of

**TABLE 3.1**

| Ryanair Holdings plc and Subsidiaries Interim Statement of Financial Position as at December 2007 | (€m) | | (€m) |
|---|---|---|---|
| **Non-current assets** | | **Current liabilities** | |
| Property, plant and equipment | 3,252.192 | Trade payables | 55.727 |
| Intangible assets | 46.841 | Accrued expenses and other liabilities | 676.863 |
| Available for sale financial assets | 325.478 | Current maturities of debt | 194.834 |
| **Total non-current assets** | 3,624.511 | Derivative financial instruments | 94.621 |
| | | Current tax | 42.300 |
| **Current assets** | | **Total current liabilities** | 1,064.345 |
| Inventories | 2.777 | | |
| Other assets | 113.711 | **Non-current liabilities** | |
| Trade receivables | 24.519 | Provisions | 38.630 |
| Derivative financial instruments | 57.907 | Derivative financial instruments | 49.440 |
| Restricted cash | 171.728 | Deferred income tax liability | 153.824 |
| Financial assets: cash > 3 months | 419.667 | Other creditors | 113.218 |
| Cash and cash equivalents | 1,459.606 | Non-current maturities of debt | 1,874.165 |
| **Total current assets** | 2,249.915 | **Total non-current liabilities** | 2,229.277 |
| | | **Shareholders' equity** | |
| | | Issued share capital | 9.465 |
| | | Share premium account | 591.400 |
| | | Retained earnings | 2,059.991 |
| | | Other reserves | −80.052 |
| | | **Shareholders' equity** | 2,580.804 |
| **Total assets** | 5,874.426 | **Total liabilities and shareholders' equity** | 5,874.426 |

Source: Ryanair Holdings plc., www.ryanair.com

**Table 3.1** The statement of financial position of Ryanair Holdings plc

time it normally would take an ongoing firm to convert them into cash. The asset side depends on the nature of the business and how management chooses to conduct it. Management must make decisions about cash versus marketable securities, credit versus cash sales, whether to make or buy commodities, whether to lease or purchase items, the types of business in which to engage, and so on. The liabilities and the shareholders' equity are listed in the order in which they would typically be paid over time.

The liabilities and shareholders' equity side reflects the types and proportions of financing, which depend on management's choice of capital structure, as between debt and equity and between current debt and long-term debt.

When analysing a statement of financial position, the financial manager should be aware of three concerns: liquidity, debt versus equity, and value versus cost.

## Liquidity

*Liquidity* refers to the ease and rapidity with which assets can be converted into cash (without significant loss in value). *Current assets* are the most liquid, and include cash and assets that will be turned into cash within a year from the date of the statement of financial position.

*Trade receivables* are amounts not yet collected from customers for goods or services sold to them (after adjustment for potential bad debts). *Inventories* are composed of raw materials to be used in production, work in process, and finished goods. These are small for Ryanair, since the company focuses on the sales of tickets for flights across Europe. *Non-current assets* are the least liquid kind of assets. Tangible non-current assets include property, plant, and equipment. In Ryanair's case this will consist largely of airplanes themselves. These assets do not convert to cash from normal business activity, and they are not usually used to pay expenses such as payroll.

Some non-current assets are intangible. Intangible assets have no physical existence but can be very valuable. Examples of intangible assets are the value of a trademark or the value of a patent. The more liquid a firm's assets, the less likely the firm is to experience problems meeting short-term obligations. Thus the probability that a firm will avoid financial distress can be linked to the firm's liquidity. Unfortunately, liquid assets frequently have lower rates of return than non-current assets: for example, cash generates no investment income. To the extent that a firm invests in liquid assets, it sacrifices an opportunity to invest in more profitable investment vehicles.

## Debt versus Equity

*Liabilities* are obligations of the firm that require a payout of cash within a stipulated period. Many liabilities involve contractual obligations to repay a stated amount and interest over a period. Thus liabilities are debts, and are frequently associated with nominally fixed cash burdens, called *debt service*, that put the firm in default of a contract if they are not paid. *Shareholders' equity* is a claim against the firm's assets that is residual and not fixed. In general terms, when the firm borrows, it gives the bondholders first claim on the firm's cash flow. Bondholders can sue the firm if the firm defaults on its bond contracts. This may lead the firm to declare itself bankrupt. Shareholders' equity is the residual difference between assets and liabilities:

$$\text{Assets} - \text{Liabilities} \equiv \text{Shareholders' equity}$$

This is the shareholders' ownership of the firm stated in accounting terms. The accounting value of shareholders' equity increases when retained earnings are added. This occurs when the firm retains part of its earnings instead of paying them out as dividends.

## Value versus Cost

The accounting value of a firm's assets is frequently referred to as the *book value* of the assets. Firms in different countries use various accounting standards to report the value of their assets. Since 2005, all countries in the European Union have been required to use International Financial Reporting Standards (IFRS), whereas in the United States companies use what are known as Generally Accepted Accounting Principles (GAAP). The main difference between US accounting standards and IFRS is that under US GAAP the audited financial statements of firms value assets such as property, plant, and equipment at cost. In contrast, IFRS values assets at theoretically true market or fair values. *Market or fair value* is the price at which willing buyers and sellers would trade the assets. It would be only a coincidence if the book value under GAAP and IFRS were the same. Unfortunately, even with fair value accounting (IFRS), the tradable value of assets is likely to be different from their accounting value. This is because in many cases there is no liquid market that allows the calculation of an asset's accounting fair value. In these situations the financial manager must estimate a fair value from a similar asset or a theoretical model. In this book, we shall treat IFRS as the main accounting system.

## 3.2 The Income Statement

The income statement measures performance over a specific period – say a year. The accounting definition of income is

$$\text{Revenue} - \text{Expenses} \equiv \text{Income}$$

**TABLE 3.2**

| Ryanair Holdings plc Consolidated Income Statement for year ending 31 December 2007 | (€m) |
|---|---|
| **Operating revenues** | |
| Scheduled revenues | 1,761 |
| Ancillary revenues | 363 |
| **Total operating revenues: continuing operations** | 2,124 |
| **Operating expenses** | |
| Staff costs | 213 |
| Depreciation | 124 |
| Fuel and oil | 585 |
| Maintenance, materials and repairs | 41 |
| Marketing and distribution costs | 16 |
| Aircraft rentals | 55 |
| Route charges | 192 |
| Airport and handling charges | 303 |
| Other | 90 |
| **Total operating expenses** | 1,618 |
| **Operating profit: continuing operations** | 506 |
| Gain on disposal of property, plant and equipment | 14 |
| **Other income** | |
| Finance income | 63 |
| Finance expense | (70) |
| Foreign exchange gain/(losses) | (2) |
| **Total other income** | (9) |
| **Profit before tax** | 510 |
| Tax on profit on ordinary activities | (55) |
| **Profit for the period: all attributable to equity holders of parent** | 455 |

*Note:* There are 1.519 billion shares outstanding. Earnings per share can be calculated as follows:

$$\text{Earnings per share} = \frac{\text{Profit for the period attributable to equity holders}}{\text{Total shares outstanding}}$$
$$= \frac{\text{€455 million}}{\text{1,519 million}}$$
$$= \text{€0.30 per share}$$

*Source*: *Ryanair Holdings plc.*, www.ryanair.com

**Table 3.2** The income statement of Ryanair Holdings plc

If the statement of financial position is like a snapshot, the income statement is like a video recording of what the firm did between two snapshots. Table 3.2 presents Ryanair's income statement.

The income statement usually includes several sections. The operations section reports the firm's revenues and expenses from principal operations. One number of particular importance is earnings before interest and taxes (EBIT), which summarizes earnings before taxes and financing costs. Among other things, the non-operating section of the income statement includes all financing costs, such as interest expense. Usually a second section reports as a separate item the amount of taxes levied on income. The last item on the income statement is the bottom line, or net income. Net income is frequently expressed per share of equity – that is, earnings per share.

When analysing an income statement, the financial manager should keep in mind non-cash items, time, and costs.

## Non-Cash Items

The economic value of assets is naturally connected to their future incremental cash flows. However, cash flow does not appear on an income statement. There are several non-cash items, which are expenses against revenues but do not affect cash flow. The most important of these is *depreciation*. Depreciation reflects the accountant's estimate of the cost of equipment used up in the production process. For example, suppose an asset with a five-year life and no resale value is purchased for €1,000. According to accountants, the €1,000 cost must be expensed over the useful life of the asset. If straight-line depreciation is used, there will be five equal instalments, and €200 of depreciation expense will be incurred each year. From a finance perspective, the cost of the asset is the actual negative cash flow incurred when the asset is acquired (that is, €1,000, *not* the accountant's smoothed €200-per-year depreciation expense).

Another non-cash expense is *deferred taxes*. Deferred taxes result from differences between accounting income and true taxable income. Notice that the accounting tax shown on the income statement for Ryanair is €55 million. This can be broken down into current taxes and deferred taxes. The current tax portion is actually sent to the tax authorities. The deferred tax portion is not. However, the theory is that if taxable income is less than accounting income in the current year, it will be more than accounting income later on. Consequently, the taxes that are not paid today will have to be paid in the future, and they represent a liability of the firm. This shows up on the statement of financial position as deferred tax liability. From the cash flow perspective, though, deferred tax is not a cash outflow.

In practice, the difference between cash flows and accounting income can be quite dramatic, so it is important to understand the difference. For example, Ryanair made a total profit of €455 million during 2007. However, their cash increased by only €113 million. We look at financial cash flow in more detail in Section 3.5.

## Time and Costs

It is often useful to visualize all of future time as having two distinct parts: the *short run* and the *long run*. The short run is the period in which certain equipment, resources and commitments of the firm are fixed; but the time is long enough for the firm to vary its output by using more labour and raw materials. The short run is not a precise period that will be the same for all industries. However, all firms making decisions in the short run have some fixed costs – that is, costs that will not change because of fixed commitments. In real business activity, examples of fixed costs are bond interest, overhead, and property taxes. Costs that are not fixed are variable. Variable costs change as the output of the firm changes: some examples are raw materials, and wages for employees on the production line.

In the long run, all costs are variable. Accountants do not distinguish between variable costs and fixed costs. Instead, accounting costs usually fit into a classification that distinguishes product costs from period costs. Product costs are the total production costs incurred during a period – raw materials, direct labour, and manufacturing overheads – and are reported on the income statement as cost of goods sold. Both variable and fixed costs are included in product costs. Period costs are costs that are allocated to a time period: they are called *selling*, *general* and *administrative expenses*. One period cost would be the company chief executive's salary.

## 3.3 Taxes

Taxes can be one of the largest cash outflows a firm experiences. For example, for the nine months between 31 March and 31 December 2007, British Airways' profit before taxes was £788 million. Its tax bill for this period was £165 million, or about 20.9 per cent of its pre-tax

| TABLE 3.3 | Country | Corporation tax (%) | Country | Corporation tax (%) |
|---|---|---|---|---|
| | Australia | 30 | New Zealand | 33 |
| | Austria | 25 | Norway | 28 |
| | Belgium | 33.99 | Pakistan | 35 |
| | Brazil | 34 | Poland | 19 |
| | Canada | 36.10 | Portugal | 25 |
| | China | 25 | Russia | 24 |
| | Denmark | 28 | South Africa | 36.89 |
| | Finland | 26 | Spain | 32.50 |
| | France | 33.33 | Sweden | 28 |
| | Germany | 38.36 | Switzerland | 21.30 |
| | Greece | 25 | Taiwan | 25 |
| | India | 30 | Tanzania | 35 |
| | Ireland | 12.50 | Thailand | 30 |
| | Italy | 37.25 | Turkey | 20 |
| | Japan | 40.69 | United Kingdom | 28 |
| | Malaysia | 27 | United States | 40 |
| | Netherlands | 20/23.5/25.5 | | |

*Source*: Federation of International Trade Associations, KPMG.

**Table 3.3** Corporate tax rates around the world

earnings. The size of the tax bill is determined by the tax code, an often amended set of rules. In this section we examine corporate tax rates and how taxes are calculated.

If the various rules of taxation seem a little bizarre or convoluted to you, keep in mind that the tax code is the result of political, not economic, forces. As a result, there is no reason why it has to make economic sense. To put the complexity of corporate taxation into perspective, General Electric's (GE's) 2006 tax return required 24,000 pages!

## Corporate Tax Rates

An overview of corporate tax rates that were in effect for 2008 for a sample of countries is shown in Table 3.3. Corporate taxes are not normally a simple arithmetic deduction from profit before taxes. Almost all countries in the world allow firms to carry forward losses they've made in previous years to offset their tax bill in the future. This is what happened to British Airways in 2007. Although the corporate tax rate in the UK is much higher, British Airways paid only 20.9 per cent of its income in taxes because of previous losses.

The tax rates presented in Table 3.3 are average tax rates for the largest companies. Many countries apply differential taxation, depending on how much a company earns in any given year. In the UK, for example, there are two corporation tax bands. Firms that earn between £0 and £300,000 per annum have a tax rate of 22 per cent. Firms that earn above £1,500,000 must pay 28 per cent (as presented in the table). Firms that report annual turnover between £300,000 and £1,500,000 receive a rebate called *marginal tax relief*, which allows them to gradually transition their tax rates between the small companies' tax rate and the standard rate.

## Average versus Marginal Tax Rates

In making financial decisions, it is frequently important to distinguish between average and marginal tax rates. Your average tax rate is your tax bill divided by your taxable income – in other words, the percentage of your income that goes to pay taxes. Your marginal tax rate is the tax you would pay (in per cent) if you earned one more unit of currency. The percentage tax rates shown in Table 3.3 for the Netherlands are marginal rates. The first €25,000 earned by Dutch firms incurs 20 per cent tax. The next €35,000 of earnings is taxed at the higher rate of 23.5 per cent. Any extra earnings are charged 25.5 per cent tax. Put another way, marginal tax rates apply to the part of income in the indicated range only, not all income.

The difference between average and marginal tax rates can best be illustrated with a simple example. Suppose our Dutch corporation has a taxable income of €200,000. What is the tax bill? Using Table 3.3, we can figure our tax bill like this:

$$
\begin{aligned}
0.20 \times €25,000 &= €\ \ 5,000 \\
0.235 \times (€60,000 - 25,000) &= €\ \ 8,225 \\
0.255 \times (€200,000 - 60,000) &= \underline{€35,700} \\
&\phantom{=}\ \underline{€48,925}
\end{aligned}
$$

Our total tax is thus €48,925.

In our example, what is the average tax rate? We had a taxable income of €200,000 and a tax bill of €48,925, so the average tax rate is €48,925/200,000 = 24.46%. What is the marginal tax rate? If we made one more euro, the tax on that euro would be 25.5 cents, so our marginal rate is 25.5 per cent.

## Deep in the Heart of Taxes

**EXAMPLE 3.1**

Assume that TimTim, the Dutch satellite navigation firm, has a taxable income of €85,000. What is its tax bill? What is its average tax rate? What is its marginal tax rate?

From Table 3.3, we see that the tax rate applied to the first €25,000 is 20 per cent; the rate applied to the next €35,000 is 23.5 per cent, and the rate applied after that is 25.5 per cent. So TimTim must pay 0.20 × €25,000 + 0.235 × €35,000 + 0.255 × €(85,000 − 60,000) = €19,600. The average tax rate is thus €19,600/85,000 = 23.06%. The marginal rate is 25.5 per cent because TimTim's taxes would rise by 25.5 cents if it had another euro in taxable income.

With a *flat-rate* tax, there is only one tax rate, so the rate is the same for all income levels. With such a tax, the marginal tax rate is always the same as the average tax rate. As it stands now, corporate taxation in the United Kingdom is based on a modified flat-rate tax, which becomes a true flat rate for the highest incomes.

Normally, the marginal tax rate will be relevant for financial decision-making. The reason is that any new cash flows will be taxed at that marginal rate. Because financial decisions usually involve new cash flows or changes in existing ones, this rate will tell us the marginal effect of a decision on our tax bill.

## 3.4 Net Working Capital

Net working capital is current assets minus current liabilities. Net working capital is positive when current assets are greater than current liabilities. This means the cash that will become available over the next 12 months will be greater than the cash that must be paid out. The net working capital of Ryanair Holdings plc was €1,185.57 million in 2007 and €1,236.546 million in 2006:

|  | Current assets (€ millions) | − | Current liabilities (€ millions) | = | Net working capital (€ millions) |
|---|---|---|---|---|---|
| 2007 | 2,249.915 | − | 1,064.345 | = | 1,185.570 |
| 2006 | 2,354.276 | − | 1,117.730 | = | 1,236.546 |

In addition to investing in fixed assets (i.e. capital spending), a firm can invest in net working capital. This is called the change in net working capital. The change in net working capital in 2007 is the difference between the net working capital in 2007 and 2006 – that is, €1,185.57 million – €1,236.546 million = –€50.976 million. The change in net working capital is usually positive in a growing firm, but in Ryanair's case it is negative. Although both current assets and liabilities fell for Ryanair between 2006 and 2007, its current assets fell by much more.

## 3.5  Cash Flow

Perhaps the most important item that can be extracted from financial statements is the actual cash flow of the firm. An official accounting statement called the *statement of cash flows* helps to explain the change in accounting cash and equivalents, which for Ryanair was €113 million in 2007.

The first point we should mention is that cash flow is not the same as net working capital. For example, increasing inventory requires the use of cash. Because both inventories and cash are current assets, this does not affect net working capital. In this case, an increase in inventory is associated with decreasing cash flow.

Just as we established that the value of a firm's assets is always equal to the combined value of the liabilities and the value of the equity, the cash flows received from the firm's assets (that is, its operating activities), CF(*A*), must equal the cash flows to the firm's creditors, CF(*B*), and equity investors, CF(*S*):

$$CF(A) \equiv CF(B) + CF(S)$$

The first step in determining the cash flows of the firm is to figure out the *operating cash flow* or, more formally, *net cash provided by operating activities*. As can be seen in Table 3.4, operating cash flow is the cash flow generated by business activities, including sales of goods and services. Operating cash flow reflects tax payments, but not financing, capital spending, or changes in net working capital.

Another important component of cash flow involves *changes in cash flow from investing activities*. The net change in cash flow from investing activities equals the acquisition of non-current assets plus any security investments minus the sales of non-current assets. The result is the cash flow used for investment purposes. In Ryanair's cash flow statement, this is recorded under *Investing activities* and amounts to a net outflow of €243 million.

Cash flows also come from financing purposes, such as the firm buying back its own shares, issuing new shares to the market, and increasing or decreasing borrowing. In Ryanair in 2007, cash outflows from *Financing activities* were €84 million. This was because the company bought back nearly €300 million of its own shares at the same time as borrowing €207 million.

Total cash flows generated by the firm's assets are then equal to:

|  | (€ millions) |
|---|---|
| Net cash provided by operating activities | 441.485 |
| Net cash provided by investing activities | −243.634 |
| Net cash provided by financing activities | −84.664 |
| Increase in cash and cash equivalents | 113.187 |

Some important observations can be drawn from our discussion of cash flow:

1   Several types of cash flow are relevant to understanding the financial situation of the firm. Operating cash flow measures the cash generated from operations, not counting cash flows arising from investment expenditure or financing. It is usually positive; a firm is in trouble if operating cash flow is negative for a long time, because the firm is not generating enough cash to pay operating costs. Total cash flow of the firm includes adjustments for capital spending and new financing. It will frequently be negative. When a firm is growing at a rapid rate, spending on inventory and fixed assets can be higher than operating cash flow.

2   Profit is not cash flow. The profit made by Ryanair in 2007 was €455 million, whereas cash flow was €113 million. The two numbers are not usually the same. In determining the economic and financial condition of a firm, cash flow is more revealing.

TABLE
**3.4**

| Consolidated Cash Flow Statement of Ryanair Holdings plc for year ending 31 December 2007 | Period ended 31 Dec 2007 (€m) | Period ended 31 Dec 2006 (€m) |
|---|---|---|
| **Operating activities** | | |
| Profit before tax | **510.029** | 423.398 |
| **Adjustments to reconcile profits before tax to net cash provided by operating activities** | | |
| Depreciation | **123.600** | 108.242 |
| (Increase)/decrease in inventories | **−0.357** | 1.470 |
| (Increase)/decrease in trade receivables | **−1.107** | 9.141 |
| (Increase) in other current assets | **−13.780** | −25.776 |
| Increase/(decrease) in trade payables | **0.926** | −15.057 |
| (Decrease) in accrued expenses | **−165.654** | −40.618 |
| Increase in other creditors | **1.041** | 72.571 |
| Increase in maintenance provisions | **9.911** | 9.769 |
| (Gain) on disposal of property, plant and equipment | **−13.650** | 0 |
| (Increase)/decrease in interest receivable | **−4.857** | 1.221 |
| Increase in interest payable | **2.138** | 7.047 |
| Retirement costs | **0.985** | 0.494 |
| Share based payments | **10.162** | 2.747 |
| Income tax (paid)/refunded | **−17.902** | 0.236 |
| **Net cash provided by operating activities** | **441.485** | 554.885 |
| **Investing activities** | | |
| Capital expenditure (purchase of property, plant and equipment) | **−578.444** | −195.208 |
| Proceeds from sale of property, plant and equipment | **132.613** | 0 |
| Purchase of equities classified as available for sale | **−57.990** | −342.410 |
| Reduction/(investment) in restricted cash | **87.080** | −0.136 |
| Reduction/(investment) in financial assets: cash > 3 months | **173.107** | −198.158 |
| **Net cash used in investing activities** | **−243.634** | −735.912 |
| **Financing activities** | | |
| Cost associated with repurchase of shares | **−299.994** | 0 |
| Net proceeds from shares issued | **8.397** | 10.055 |
| Increase in long-term borrowings | **206.933** | 19.954 |
| **Net cash provided by financing activities** | **−84.664** | 30.009 |
| **Increase/(decrease) in cash and cash equivalents** | **113.187** | −151.018 |
| Cash and cash equivalents at beginning of the period | **1,346.419** | 1,439.004 |
| **Cash and cash equivalents at end of the period** | **1,459.606** | 1,287.986 |

*Source: Ryanair Holdings plc.*, www.ryanair.com

**Table 3.4** Cash flow of Ryanair Holdings plc

A firm's total cash flow sometimes goes by a different name, free cash flow. Of course, there is no such thing as 'free' cash. Instead, the name refers to cash that the firm is free to distribute to creditors and shareholders because it is not needed for working capital or investments. We shall stick with 'total cash flow of the firm' as our label for this important concept because, in practice, there is some variation in exactly how free cash flow is computed. Nonetheless, whenever you hear the phrase 'free cash flow', you should understand that what is being discussed is cash flow from assets or something quite similar.

## 3.6 Financial Statement Analysis

A good working knowledge of financial statements is desirable simply because such statements, and numbers derived from those statements, are the primary means of communicating financial information, both within the firm and outside the firm. In short, much of the language of business finance is rooted in the ideas we discuss in this chapter.

Clearly, one important goal of the accountant is to report financial information to the user in a form useful for decision-making. Ironically, the information frequently does not come to the user in such a form. In other words, financial statements don't come with a user's guide. This chapter is a first step in filling this gap.

### Standardizing Statements

One obvious thing we might want to do with a company's financial statements is compare them with those of other, similar companies. We would immediately have a problem, however. It's almost impossible to compare the financial statements for two companies directly because of differences in size.

For example, Aer Lingus and Air France-KLM are obviously serious rivals in the European flights market, but Air France-KLM is much larger (in terms of assets), so it is difficult to compare them directly. For that matter, it's difficult even to compare financial statements from different points in time for the *same* company if the company's size has changed. The size problem is compounded if we try to compare Air France-KLM with, say, British Airways. Since British Airways' financial statements are denominated in British pounds, we have size *and* currency differences.

To start making comparisons, one obvious thing we might try to do is to somehow standardize the financial statements. One common and useful way of doing this is to work with percentages instead of total monetary amounts. The resulting financial statements are called common-size statements. We consider these next.

### Common-Size Statements of Financial Position

For easy reference, we return to the statement of financial position for Ryanair as presented in Table 3.1. Using this, we construct a common-size statement of financial position by expressing each item as a percentage of total assets. Ryanair's 2007 common-size statement of financial position is shown in Table 3.5.

In this form, financial statements are relatively easy to read and compare. For example, just looking at the statement of financial position for Ryanair, we see that current assets were 38.3 per cent of total assets in 2007. Current liabilities were only 18.12 per cent of total liabilities and equity over that same time. Similarly, shareholders' equity comprised 43.93 per cent of total asset value.

### Common-Size Income Statements

A useful way of standardizing the income statement shown in Table 3.2 is to express each item as a percentage of total revenues, as illustrated for Ryanair in Table 3.6.

This income statement tells us what happens to each euro in revenues. For Ryanair, fuel and oil ate up €0.27 out of every euro made in revenues, and taxes took another €0.026. When all is said and done, €0.214 of each euro flows through to the bottom line (net income).

TABLE
**3.5**

| Ryanair Holdings plc and Subsidiaries Interim Common-Size Statement of Financial Position as at December 2007 | | | |
|---|---|---|---|
| | **%** | | **%** |
| **Non-current assets** | | **Current liabilities** | |
| Property, plant and equipment | 55.36 | Trade payables | 0.95 |
| Intangible assets | 0.80 | Accrued expenses and other liabilities | 11.52 |
| Available for sale financial assets | 5.54 | Current maturities of debt | 3.32 |
| **Total non-current assets** | **61.70** | Derivative financial instruments | 1.61 |
| | | Current tax | 0.72 |
| **Current assets** | | **Total current liabilities** | **18.12** |
| Inventories | 0.05 | | |
| Other assets | 1.94 | **Non-current liabilities** | |
| Trade receivables | 0.42 | Provisions | 0.66 |
| Derivative financial instruments | 0.99 | Derivative financial instruments | 0.84 |
| Restricted cash | 2.92 | Deferred income tax liability | 2.62 |
| Financial assets: cash > 3 months | 7.14 | Other creditors | 1.93 |
| Cash and cash equivalents | 24.85 | Non-current maturities of debt | 31.90 |
| **Total current assets** | **38.30** | **Total non-current liabilities** | **37.95** |
| | | **Shareholders' equity** | |
| | | Issued share capital | 0.16 |
| | | Share premium account | 10.07 |
| | | Retained earnings | 35.07 |
| | | Other reserves | −1.36 |
| | | **Shareholders' equity** | **43.93** |
| **Total assets** | **100.00** | **Total liabilities and shareholders' equity** | **100.00** |

*Source: Ryanair Holdings plc.*, www.ryanair.com

**Table 3.5** Financial position of Ryanair Holdings plc

These percentages are useful in comparisons. For example, a relevant figure is the cost percentage. For Ryanair, €0.762 of each €1.00 in revenues goes in expenses. It would be interesting to compute the same percentage for Ryanair's main competitors to see how Ryanair stacks up in terms of cost control.

## 3.7 Ratio Analysis

Another way of avoiding the problems involved in comparing companies of different sizes is to calculate and compare financial ratios. Such ratios are ways of comparing and investigating the relationships between different pieces of financial information. We cover some of the more common ratios next (there are many others we don't discuss here).

One problem with ratios is that different people and different sources frequently don't compute them in exactly the same way, and this leads to much confusion. The specific definitions we use here may or may not be the same as ones you have seen or will see elsewhere. If you are using ratios as tools for analysis, you should be careful to document how you calculate each one; and, if you are comparing your numbers with those of another source, be sure you know how their numbers are computed.

| TABLE 3.6 | Ryanair Holdings plc Consolidated Common-Size Income Statement Year ending 31 December 2007 | |
|---|---|---|
| | | % |
| **Operating revenues** | | |
| Scheduled revenues | | 82.90 |
| Ancillary revenues | | 17.10 |
| **Total operating revenues: continuing operations** | | **100.00** |
| **Operating expenses** | | |
| Staff costs | | 10.03 |
| Depreciation | | 5.82 |
| Fuel and oil | | 27.55 |
| Maintenance, materials and repairs | | 1.94 |
| Marketing and distribution costs | | 0.73 |
| Aircraft rentals | | 2.59 |
| Route charges | | 9.05 |
| Airport and handling charges | | 14.26 |
| Other | | 4.21 |
| **Total operating expenses** | | **76.19** |
| **Operating profit: continuing operations** | | **23.81** |
| Gain on disposal of property, plant and equipment | | 0.64 |
| **Other income** | | |
| Finance income | | 2.96 |
| Finance expense | | −3.30 |
| Foreign exchange gain/(losses) | | −0.09 |
| **Total other income** | | **−0.44** |
| **Profit before tax** | | **24.02** |
| Tax on profit on ordinary activities | | −2.60 |
| **Profit for the period: all attributable to equity holders of parent** | | **21.41** |

Source: Ryanair Holdings plc., www.ryanair.com

**Table 3.6** Ryanair Holdings plc consolidated common-size income statement

We shall defer much of our discussion of how ratios are used, and some problems that come up with using them, until later in the chapter. For now, for each ratio we discuss, several questions come to mind:

1   How is it computed?

2   What is it intended to measure, and why might we be interested?

3   What is the unit of measurement?

4   What might a high or low value be telling us? How might such values be misleading?

5   How could this measure be improved?

Financial ratios are traditionally grouped into the following categories:

• Short-term solvency, or liquidity, ratios

• Long-term solvency, or financial leverage, ratios

• Asset management, or turnover, ratios

- Profitability ratios

- Market value ratios

We shall consider each of these in turn. In calculating these numbers for Ryanair, we shall use the ending statement of financial position (2007) figures unless we explicitly say otherwise.

## Short-Term Solvency or Liquidity Measures

As the name suggests, short-term solvency ratios as a group are intended to provide information about a firm's liquidity, and these ratios are sometimes called *liquidity measures*. The primary concern is the firm's ability to pay its bills over the short run without undue stress. Consequently, these ratios focus on current assets and current liabilities.

For obvious reasons, liquidity ratios are particularly interesting to short-term creditors. Because financial managers are constantly working with banks and other short-term lenders, an understanding of these ratios is essential.

One advantage of looking at current assets and liabilities is that their book values and market values are likely to be similar. Often (though not always), these assets and liabilities just don't live long enough for the two to get seriously out of step. On the other hand, like any type of near-cash, current assets and liabilities can and do change fairly rapidly, so today's amounts may not be a reliable guide to the future.

**Current Ratio**   One of the best-known and most widely used ratios is the *current ratio*. As you might guess, the current ratio is defined as:

$$\text{Current ratio} = \frac{\text{Current assets}}{\text{Current liabilities}} \tag{3.1}$$

For Ryanair, the 2007 current ratio is

$$\text{Current ratio} = \frac{€2,250}{€1,064} = 2.11 \text{ times}$$

Because current assets and liabilities are, in principle, converted to cash over the following 12 months, the current ratio is a measure of short-term liquidity. The unit of measurement is either in monetary units (such as euros) or times. So, we could say Ryanair has €2.11 in current assets for every €1 in current liabilities, or we could say Ryanair has its current liabilities covered 2.11 times over.

To a creditor, particularly a short-term creditor such as a supplier, the higher the current ratio, the better. To the firm, a high current ratio indicates liquidity, but it also may indicate an inefficient use of cash and other short-term assets. Except for some extraordinary circumstances, we would expect to see a current ratio of at least 1; a current ratio of less than 1 would mean that net working capital (current assets less current liabilities) is negative. This would be unusual in a healthy firm, at least for most types of business.

The current ratio, like any ratio, is affected by various types of transaction. For example, suppose the firm borrows over the long term to raise money. The short-run effect would be an increase in cash from the issue proceeds and an increase in long-term debt. Current liabilities would not be affected, so the current ratio would rise.

<br>

| EXAMPLE 3.2 | ## Current Events |
| --- | --- |

Suppose a firm were to pay off some of its suppliers and short-term creditors. What would happen to the current ratio? Suppose a firm buys some inventory. What happens in this case? What happens if a firm sells some merchandise?

The first case is a trick question. What happens is that the current ratio moves away from 1. If it is greater than 1 (the usual case), it will get bigger, but if it is less than 1, it will get smaller. To see this, suppose the firm has £4 in current assets and £2 in current liabilities for a current ratio of 2. If we use £1 in cash to reduce current liabilities, the new current ratio is £(4 − 1)/(2 − 1) = 3. If we reverse the original situation to £2 in current assets and £4 in current liabilities, the change will cause the current ratio to fall to 1/3 from 1/2.

The second case is not quite as tricky. Nothing happens to the current ratio because cash goes down while inventory goes up; total current assets are unaffected.

In the third case the current ratio would usually rise, because inventory is normally shown at cost, and the sale would normally be at something greater than cost (the difference is the markup). The increase in either cash or receivables is therefore greater than the decrease in inventory. This increases current assets, and the current ratio rises.

Finally, note that an apparently low current ratio may not be a bad sign for a company with a large reserve of untapped borrowing power.

**Quick (or Acid-Test) Ratio**  Inventory is often the least liquid current asset. It's also the one for which the book values are least reliable as measures of market value, because the quality of the inventory isn't considered. Some of the inventory may later turn out to be damaged, or obsolete, or lost.

More to the point, relatively large inventories are often a sign of short-term trouble. The firm may have overestimated sales, and overbought or overproduced as a result. In this case the firm may have a substantial portion of its liquidity tied up in slow-moving inventory.

To further evaluate liquidity, the *quick*, or *acid-test*, *ratio* is computed just like the current ratio, except that inventory is included:

$$\text{Quick ratio} = \frac{\text{Current assets} - \text{Inventory}}{\text{Current liabilities}} \qquad (3.2)$$

Notice that using cash to buy inventory does not affect the current ratio, but it reduces the quick ratio. Again, the idea is that inventory is relatively illiquid compared with cash.

For Ryanair, this ratio in 2007 was

$$\text{Quick ratio} = \frac{€2,250 - 0.002}{€1,064} = 2.11 \text{ times}$$

For Ryanair, the quick ratio here tells virtually the same story as the current ratio, because inventory accounts for very little of Ryanair's current assets.

To give an example of current versus quick ratios, based on recent financial statements, Ryanair and CRH plc (the building materials group) had current ratios of 2.11 and 1.70, respectively. As we have seen, Ryanair carries very little inventory to speak of, whereas CRH, being involved in building materials, will have current assets that largely comprise inventory. As a result, CRH's quick ratio was only 1.14, and Ryanair's was 2.11 – the same as its current ratio.

**Cash Ratio**  A very short-term creditor might be interested in the *cash ratio*:

$$\text{Cash ratio} = \frac{\text{Cash and cash equivalents}}{\text{Current liabilities}} \qquad (3.3)$$

You can verify that this works out to be 1.37 times for Ryanair.

## Long-Term Solvency Measures

Long-term solvency ratios are intended to address the firm's long-run ability to meet its obligations or, more generally, its financial leverage. These ratios are sometimes called *financial leverage ratios* or just *leverage ratios*. We consider three commonly used measures and some variations.

**Total Debt Ratio**  The *total debt ratio* takes into account all debts of all maturities to all creditors. It can be defined in several ways, the easiest of which is

$$\text{Total debt ratio} = \frac{\text{Total assets} - \text{Total equity}}{\text{Total assets}}$$

$$= \frac{€5,874 - 2,581}{€5,874} \tag{3.4}$$

$$= 0.56 \text{ times}$$

In this case, an analyst might say that Ryanair uses 56 per cent debt. Whether this is high or low, or whether it even makes any difference, depends on whether capital structure matters, a subject we discuss in a later chapter.

Ryanair has €0.56 in debt for every €1 in assets. Therefore there is €0.44 in equity €(1 − 0.56) for every €0.56 in debt. With this in mind, we can define two useful variations on the total debt ratio: the *debt–equity ratio* and the *equity multiplier*:

$$\text{Debt–equity ratio} = \text{Total debt/Total equity}$$

$$= €0.56/€0.44 \tag{3.5}$$

$$= 1.27 \text{ times}$$

$$\text{Equity multiplier} = \text{Total assets/Total equity}$$

$$= €1/€0.44 \tag{3.6}$$

$$= 2.27 \text{ times}$$

The fact that the equity multiplier is 1 plus the debt–equity ratio is not a coincidence:

$$\text{Equity multiplier} = \text{Total assets/Total equity} = €1/€0.44 = 2.27 \text{ times}$$

$$= (\text{Total equity} + \text{Total debt})/\text{Total equity}$$

$$= 1 + \text{Debt–equity ratio} = 2.27 \text{ times}$$

The thing to notice here is that, given any one of these three ratios, you can immediately calculate the other two, so they all say exactly the same thing.

**Times Interest Earned** Another common measure of long-term solvency is the *times interest earned* (TIE) *ratio*. Once again, there are several possible (and common) definitions, but we'll stick with the most traditional. To calculate EBIT for Ryanair, you must calculate the operating profit plus any non-operating income. From Table 3.2, this would be equal to (€506 million + €14 million + €63 million − €2 million =) €581 million.

$$\text{Times interest earned ratio} = \frac{\text{EBIT}}{\text{Interest}}$$

$$= \frac{€581}{€70} \tag{3.7}$$

$$= 8.3 \text{ times}$$

As the name suggests, this ratio measures how well a company has its interest obligations covered, and it is often called the *interest coverage ratio*. For Ryanair, the interest bill is covered 8.3 times over.

**Cash Coverage** A problem with the TIE ratio is that it is based on EBIT, which is not really a measure of cash available to pay interest. The reason is that depreciation, a non-cash expense, has been deducted out. Because interest is most definitely a cash outflow (to creditors), one way to define the *cash coverage ratio* is

$$\text{Cash coverage ratio} = \frac{\text{EBIT} + \text{Depreciation}}{\text{Interest}}$$

$$= \frac{€581 + 124}{€70}$$

$$= \frac{€705}{70} \tag{3.8}$$

$$= 10.1 \text{ times}$$

The numerator here, EBIT plus depreciation, is often abbreviated to EBITD (earnings before interest, taxes and depreciation). It is a basic measure of the firm's ability to generate cash from operations, and it is frequently used as a measure of cash flow available to meet financial obligations.

## Asset Management or Turnover Measures

We next turn our attention to the efficiency with which Ryanair uses its assets. The measures in this section are sometimes called *asset management* or *utilization ratios*. The specific ratios we discuss can all be interpreted as measures of turnover. What they are intended to describe is how efficiently, or intensively, a firm uses its assets to generate sales. We first look at two important current assets: inventory and receivables.

**Inventory Turnover and Days' Sales in Inventory**    To calculate inventory turnover, one must first consider the cost of goods sold. This is the direct cost of earning the company's main revenues during the year. The costs should include materials used, labour costs, managerial salaries, and other costs of earning the revenues. Depreciation is included in the figure if it is being charged on assets directly related to the main revenue stream; otherwise it is left out. In Ryanair's case the depreciation would be charged for reduction in the value of their planes, and so this figure should be included in the figure for cost of goods sold.

For Ryanair, the concept of inventory turnover and days' sales in inventory is not appropriate, because the firm does not have any real inventories to speak of. You would, therefore, not consider these ratios for Ryanair.

Normally, *inventory turnover* can be calculated as

$$\text{Inventory turnover} = \frac{\text{Cost of goods sold}}{\text{Inventory}} \qquad (3.9)$$

As long as your company is not running out of stock and thereby forgoing sales, the higher this ratio is, the more efficient your company is at managing inventory.

For example, if we know that we turned our inventory over 3.2 times during the year, we can immediately figure out how long it took us to turn it over on average. The result is the average *days' sales in inventory*:

$$\begin{aligned}
\text{Days' sales in inventory} &= \frac{365 \text{ days}}{\text{Inventory turnover}} \\
&= \frac{365}{3.2} \qquad (3.10)\\
&= 114 \text{ days}
\end{aligned}$$

This tells us that, roughly speaking, inventory sits 114 days on average before it is sold. Alternatively, assuming we used the most recent inventory and cost figures, it will take about 114 days to work off our current inventory.

**Receivables Turnover and Days' Sales in Receivables**    Our inventory measures give some indication of how fast we can sell products. We now look at how fast we collect on those sales. The *receivables turnover* is defined in the same way as inventory turnover:

$$\begin{aligned}
\text{Receivables turnover} &= \frac{\text{Sales}}{\text{Trade receivables}} \\
&= \frac{\text{€}2,124}{\text{€}25} \qquad (3.11)\\
&= 84.96 \text{ times}
\end{aligned}$$

Loosely speaking, Ryanair collected its outstanding credit accounts and lent the money again 84.96 times during the year.

This ratio makes more sense if we convert it to days, so the *days' sales in receivables* is

$$\text{Days' sales in receivables} = \frac{365 \text{ days}}{\text{Receivables turnover}}$$

$$= \frac{365}{84.96} \quad (3.12)$$

$$= 4.30 \text{ days}$$

Therefore, on average, Ryanair collects on its credit sales in 4.3 days. For obvious reasons, this ratio is frequently called the *average collection period* (ACP). Also, note that if we are using the most recent figures, we can say that Ryanair has 4.3 days' worth of sales currently uncollected.

Unfortunately, this ratio illustrates the dangers of using financial ratios without really understanding their true meaning. The receivables turnover ratio and days' sales in receivables figures implicitly assume that all sales in a firm are credit sales. When this is not true, only credit sales figures should be used – not total sales. Ryanair's business model requires payment of air tickets immediately, and so credit sales will make up only a small proportion of total sales. If we had the data, we should have used only credit sales in the numerator of equation (3.11).

## EXAMPLE 3.3

## Payables Turnover

Here is a variation on the receivables collection period. How long, on average, does it take for Ryanair to *pay* its bills? To answer, we need to calculate the trade payables turnover rate using cost of goods sold. We shall assume that Ryanair purchases everything on credit. The cost of goods sold is €1,529 million, and trade payables are €56 million. The turnover is therefore €1,529/€56 = 27 times. So payables turned over about every 365/27 = 13.51 days. On average, then, Ryanair takes only 14 days to pay. As a potential creditor, we might take note of this fact.

**Total Asset Turnover**   Moving away from specific accounts such as inventory or receivables, we can consider an important 'big picture' ratio, the *total asset turnover* ratio. As the name suggests, total asset turnover is

$$\text{Total asset turnover} = \frac{\text{Sales}}{\text{Total assets}}$$

$$= \frac{€2,124}{€5,874} \quad (3.13)$$

$$= 0.36 \text{ times}$$

In other words, for every euro in assets, Ryanair generated €0.36 in sales.

## EXAMPLE 3.4

## More Turnover

Suppose you find that a particular company generates £0.40 in annual sales for every pound in total assets. How often does this company turn over its total assets?

The total asset turnover here is 0.40 times per year. It takes 1/0.40 = 2.5 years to turn assets over completely.

## Profitability Measures

The three measures we discuss in this section are probably the best-known and most widely used of all financial ratios. In one form or another, they are intended to measure how efficiently the firm uses its assets, and how efficiently the firm manages its operations. The focus in this group is on the bottom line: net income.

**Profit Margin**   Companies pay a great deal of attention to their *profit margin*:

$$\text{Profit margin} = \frac{\text{Net income}}{\text{Sales}}$$

$$= \frac{€455}{€2,124}$$

$$= 21.4\%$$

(3.14)

This tells us that Ryanair, in an accounting sense, generates a little more than 21 cents in profit for every euro in sales.

All other things being equal, a relatively high profit margin is obviously desirable. This situation corresponds to low expense ratios relative to sales. However, we hasten to add that other things are often not equal.

For example, lowering our sales price will usually increase unit volume but will normally cause profit margins to shrink. Total profit (or, more importantly, operating cash flow) may go up or down, so the fact that margins are smaller isn't necessarily bad.

Profit margins are very different for different industries. Grocery stores have a notoriously low profit margin, generally around 2 per cent. In contrast, the profit margin for the pharmaceutical industry is about 18 per cent. So, for example, it is not surprising that recent profit margins for Albertson's and Pfizer were about 1.2 per cent and 15.6 per cent, respectively.

**Return on Assets**   *Return on assets* (ROA) is a measure of profit per asset value. It can be defined in several ways, but the most common is

$$\text{Return on assets} = \frac{\text{Net income}}{\text{Total assets}}$$

$$= \frac{€455}{€5,874}$$

$$= 7.75\%$$

(3.15)

**Return on Equity**   *Return on equity* (ROE) is a measure of how the shareholders fared during the year. Because benefiting shareholders is our goal, ROE is, in an accounting sense, the true bottom-line measure of performance. ROE is usually measured as

$$\text{Return on equity} = \frac{\text{Net income}}{\text{Total equity}}$$

$$= \frac{€455}{€2,581}$$

$$= 17.63\%$$

(3.16)

Therefore, for every euro in equity, Ryanair generated nearly 18 cents in profit; but, again, this is correct only in accounting terms.

Because ROA and ROE are such commonly cited numbers, we stress that it is important to remember they are accounting rates of return. For this reason, these measures should properly be called *return on book assets* and *return on book equity*. Whatever it's called, it would be inappropriate to compare the result with, for example, an interest rate observed in the financial markets.

The fact that ROE exceeds ROA reflects Ryanair's use of financial leverage. We shall examine the relationship between these two measures in the next section.

## Market Value Measures

Our final group of measures is based, in part, on information not necessarily contained in financial statements – the share price. Obviously, these measures can be calculated directly only for publicly traded companies.

At the end of December 2007 Ryanair had 1,534 million shares outstanding, and its shares sold on the London Stock Exchange for €4.62. If we recall that Ryanair's net income was €455 million, then we can calculate that its earnings per share were

$$EPS = \frac{\text{Net income}}{\text{Shares outstanding}}$$
$$= \frac{€455}{1,534}$$
$$= €0.297$$

(3.17)

**Price–Earnings Ratio**   The first of our market value measures, the *price–earnings* or *P/E ratio* (or multiple), is defined as

$$PE \text{ ratio} = \frac{\text{Price per share}}{\text{Earnings per share}}$$
$$= \frac{€4.62}{€0.297}$$
$$= 15.58 \text{ times}$$

(3.18)

In the vernacular, we would say that Ryanair shares sell for nearly 16 times earnings, or we might say that Ryanair shares have, or 'carry', a P/E multiple of 15.58.

Because the P/E ratio measures how much investors are willing to pay per unit of current earnings, higher P/Es are often taken to mean that the firm has significant prospects for future growth. Of course, if a firm had no or almost no earnings, its P/E would probably be quite large; so, as always, care is needed in interpreting this ratio.

**Market-to-Book Ratio**   A second commonly quoted measure is the *market-to-book ratio*:

$$\text{Market-to-book ratio} = \frac{\text{Market value per share}}{\text{Book value per share}}$$
$$= \frac{€4.62}{€2,581/1,534}$$
$$= \frac{€4.62}{€1.68}$$
$$= 2.75 \text{ times}$$

(3.19)

Notice that book value per share is total equity (not just ordinary shares) divided by the total number of shares outstanding.

Book value per share is an accounting number that reflects historical costs. In a loose sense, the market-to-book ratio therefore compares the market value of the firm's investments with their cost. A value less than 1 could mean that the firm has not been successful overall in creating value for its shareholders.

This completes our definition of some common ratios. We could tell you about more of them, but these are enough for now. We'll leave it here and go on to discuss some ways of using these ratios instead of just how to calculate them. Table 3.7 summarizes the ratios we've discussed.

## 3.8 The Du Pont Identity

As we mentioned in discussing ROA and ROE, the difference between these two profitability measures reflects the use of debt financing or financial leverage. We illustrate the relationship between these measures in this section by investigating a famous way of decomposing ROE into its component parts.

### A Closer Look at ROE

To begin, let's recall the definition of ROE:

$$\text{Return on equity} = \frac{\text{Net income}}{\text{Total equity}}$$

**TABLE 3.7**

### (a) Short-term solvency, or liquidity, ratios

$$\text{Current ratio} = \frac{\text{Current assets}}{\text{Current liabilities}}$$

$$\text{Quick ratio} = \frac{\text{Current assets} - \text{Inventory}}{\text{Current liabilities}}$$

$$\text{Cash ratio} = \frac{\text{Cash}}{\text{Current liabilities}}$$

$$\text{Days' sales in receivables} = \frac{365 \text{ days}}{\text{Receivables turnover}}$$

$$\text{Total asset turnover} = \frac{\text{Sales}}{\text{Total assets}}$$

$$\text{Capital intensity} = \frac{\text{Total assets}}{\text{Sales}}$$

### (b) Long-term solvency, or financial leverage, ratios

$$\text{Total debt ratio} = \frac{\text{Total assets} - \text{Total equity}}{\text{Total assets}}$$

Debt–equity ratio = Total debt/Total equity

Equity multiplier = Total assets/Total equity

$$\text{Times interest earned ratio} = \frac{\text{EBIT}}{\text{Interest}}$$

$$\text{Cash coverage ratio} = \frac{\text{EBIT} + \text{Depreciation}}{\text{Interest}}$$

### (d) Profitability ratios

$$\text{Profit margin} = \frac{\text{Net income}}{\text{Sales}}$$

$$\text{Return on assets (ROA)} = \frac{\text{Net income}}{\text{Total assets}}$$

$$\text{Return on equity (ROE)} = \frac{\text{Net income}}{\text{Total equity}}$$

$$\text{ROE} = \frac{\text{Net income}}{\text{Sales}} \times \frac{\text{Sales}}{\text{Assets}} \times \frac{\text{Assets}}{\text{Equity}}$$

### (c) Asset utilization, or turnover, ratios

$$\text{Inventory turnover} = \frac{\text{Cost of goods sold}}{\text{Inventory}}$$

$$\text{Days' sales in inventory} = \frac{365 \text{ days}}{\text{Inventory turnover}}$$

$$\text{Receivables turnover} = \frac{\text{Sales}}{\text{Accounts receivable}}$$

### (e) Market value ratios

$$\text{Price–earnings ratio} = \frac{\text{Price per share}}{\text{Earnings per share}}$$

$$\text{Market-to-book ratio} = \frac{\text{Market value per share}}{\text{Book value per share}}$$

**Table 3.7** Common financial ratios

If we were so inclined, we could multiply this ratio by Assets/Assets without changing anything:

$$\begin{aligned}\text{Return on equity} &= \frac{\text{Net income}}{\text{Total equity}} \\ &= \frac{\text{Net income}}{\text{Total equity}} \times \frac{\text{Assets}}{\text{Assets}} \\ &= \frac{\text{Net income}}{\text{Assets}} \times \frac{\text{Assets}}{\text{Total equity}}\end{aligned}$$

Notice that we have expressed the ROE as the product of two other ratios – ROA and the equity multiplier:

$$\text{ROE} = \text{ROA} \times \text{Equity multiplier} = \text{ROA} \times (1 + \text{Debt–equity ratio})$$

Looking back at Ryanair, for example, we see that the debt–equity ratio was 1.27 and ROA was 7.75 per cent. Our work here implies that Ryanair's ROE, as we previously calculated, is

$$\text{ROE} = 7.75\% \times 2.27 = 17.6\%$$

The difference between ROE and ROA can be substantial, particularly for certain businesses. For example, before it was nationalized by the British government in 2008, the Royal Bank of Scotland Group plc had an ROA of only 0.79 per cent, which is low for a bank. Given that the Royal Bank of Scotland had borrowed a lot of money, its ROE was 17.17 per cent, implying an equity multiplier of 21.7.

We can further decompose ROE by multiplying the top and bottom by total sales:

$$\text{ROE} = \frac{\text{Sales}}{\text{Sales}} \times \frac{\text{Net income}}{\text{Assets}} \times \frac{\text{Assets}}{\text{Total equity}}$$

If we rearrange things a bit, ROE is

$$\text{ROE} = \underbrace{\frac{\text{Net income}}{\text{Sales}} \times \frac{\text{Sales}}{\text{Assets}}}_{\text{Return on assets}} \times \frac{\text{Assets}}{\text{Total equity}} \tag{3.20}$$

$$= \text{Profit margin} \times \text{Total asset turnover} \times \text{Equity multiplier}$$

What we have now done is partition ROA into its two component parts: profit margin and total asset turnover. The last expression of the preceding equation is called the **Du Pont identity**, after the Du Pont Corporation, which popularized its use.

We can check this relationship for Ryanair by noting that the profit margin was 21.4 per cent and the total asset turnover was 0.36. ROE should thus be

$$\begin{aligned} \text{ROE} &= \text{Profit margin} \times \text{Total asset turnover} \times \text{Equity multiplier} \\ &= 21.4\% \quad\quad \times \quad\quad 0.36 \quad\quad \times \quad\quad 2.27 \\ &= 17.6\% \end{aligned}$$

This 17.6 per cent ROE is exactly what we had before.

The Du Pont identity tells us that ROE is affected by three things:

1   Operating efficiency (as measured by profit margin)

2   Asset use efficiency (as measured by total asset turnover)

3   Financial leverage (as measured by the equity multiplier)

Weakness in either operating or asset use efficiency (or both) will show up in a diminished return on assets, which will translate into a lower ROE.

Considering the Du Pont identity, it appears that the ROE could be leveraged up by increasing the amount of debt in the firm. However, notice that increasing debt also increases interest expense, which reduces profit margins and acts to reduce ROE. More important, the use of debt financing has a number of other effects, and, as we discuss at some length in later chapters, the amount of leverage a firm uses is governed by its capital structure policy.

The decomposition of ROE we've discussed in this section is a convenient way of approaching financial statement analysis systematically. If ROE is unsatisfactory by some measure, then the Du Pont identity tells you where to start looking for the reasons.

General Motors provides a good example of how Du Pont analysis can be useful, and also illustrates why care must be taken in interpreting ROE values. In 1989, GM had an ROE of 12.1 per cent. By 1993 its ROE had improved dramatically, to 44.1 per cent. On closer inspection, however, we find that over the same period GM's profit margin declined from 3.4 to 1.8 per cent, and ROA declined from 2.4 to 1.3 per cent. The decline in ROA was moderated only slightly by an increase in total asset turnover from 0.71 to 0.73 over the period.

Given this information, how was it possible for GM's ROE to have climbed so sharply? From our understanding of the Du Pont identity, it must be the case that GM's equity multiplier increased substantially. In fact, what happened was that GM's book equity value was almost wiped out overnight in 1992 by changes in the accounting treatment of pension liabilities. If a company's equity value declines sharply, its equity multiplier rises. In GM's case, the multiplier went from 4.95 in 1989 to 33.62 in 1993. In sum, the dramatic 'improvement' in GM's ROE was almost entirely due to an accounting change that affected the equity multiplier, and doesn't really represent an improvement in financial performance at all.

# 3.9  Using Financial Statement Information

Our next task is to discuss in more detail some practical aspects of financial statement analysis. In particular, we shall look at how to go about getting benchmark information, and some of the problems that come up in the process.

## Choosing a Benchmark

Given that we want to evaluate a division or a firm based on its financial statements, a basic problem immediately comes up. How do we choose a benchmark, or a standard of comparison? We describe some ways of getting started in this section.

**Time Trend Analysis**   One standard we could use is history. Suppose we find that the current ratio for a particular firm is 2.4, based on the most recent financial statement information. Looking back over the last 10 years, we might find that this ratio has declined fairly steadily over that period.

Based on this, we might wonder whether the liquidity position of the firm has deteriorated. It could be, of course, that the firm has made changes that allow it to use its current assets more efficiently, that the nature of the firm's business has changed, or that business practices have changed. If we investigate, we might find any of these possible explanations behind the decline. This is an example of what we mean by management by exception – a deteriorating time trend may not be bad, but it does merit investigation.

**Peer Group Analysis**   The second means of establishing a benchmark is to identify firms similar in the sense that they compete in the same markets, have similar assets, and operate in similar ways. In other words, we need to identify a *peer group*. There are obvious problems with doing this: no two companies are identical. Ultimately, the choice of which companies to use as a basis for comparison is subjective.

One common way of identifying potential peers is based on Standard Industrial Classification (SIC) codes. In the UK these are called UK Standard Industrial Classification (SIC) Codes, and in the European Union they are called the Industrial Classification System or 'Nomenclature générale des activités économiques dans les Communautés européennes' (NACE). These are alphabetical categories subdivided by four-digit codes that are used for statistical reporting purposes. From 1 January 2008 SIC and NACE codes have become virtually identical. Firms with the same SIC or NACE code are frequently assumed to be similar.

In total there are 21 industry groups, categorized by alphabetical letter. The first digit in an SIC code establishes the general type of business. For example, firms engaged in finance, insurance and real estate have SIC codes beginning with 6. Each additional digit narrows the industry. Companies with SIC codes beginning with 64 are mostly banks and bank-like businesses, those with codes beginning with 64.19 are mostly commercial banks, and SIC code 64.11 is assigned to central banks. Table 3.8 lists selected two-digit codes (the first two digits of the four-digit SIC codes) and the industries they represent.

Industry classification codes are far from perfect. For example, suppose you were examining financial statements for Tesco plc, one of the largest retailers in Europe. Tesco is not just involved in supermarket retailing. It also has Tesco Telecom Services and Tesco Personal Finance, which includes credit cards and personal mortgages. Which industry code would Tesco plc have?

As this example illustrates, it is probably not appropriate to blindly use SIC codes as the basis for carrying out a peer analysis. Instead, analysts often identify a set of primary competitors with similar activities and then compute a set of averages based on just this group. Also, we may be more concerned with a group of the top firms in an industry, not similar firms. Such a group is called an *aspirant group* because we aspire to be like its members. In this case, a financial statement analysis reveals how far we have to go.

There are many sources of financial information on the Internet that an analyst can access: for example www.ft.com, Reuters, and Yahoo! Finance show a variety of ratios for publicly traded companies. On the next page we show a screenshot of some profitability ratios (called 'Management Effectiveness' on Reuters) for the German automobile firm, BMW, together with peer statistics ('TTM' stands for 'trailing twelve months').

TABLE
**3.8**

| A Agriculture, Forestry and Fishing | H Transportation and Storage |
|---|---|
| 01 Crop and animal production, hunting and related service activities | 49 Land transport and transport via pipelines |
| 02 Forestry and logging | 50 Water transport |
| 03 Fishing and aquaculture | 51 Air transport |
| **B Mining and Quarrying** | **I Accommodation and Food Service Activities** |
| 05 Mining of coal and lignite | 55 Accommodation |
| 06 Extraction of crude petroleum and natural gas | 56 Food and beverage service activities |
| 07 Mining of metal ores | |
| **C Manufacturing** | **K Financial and Insurance Activities** |
| 10 Manufacture of food products | 64 Financial service activities, except insurance and pension funding |
| 22 Manufacture of rubber and plastic products | 65 Insurance, reinsurance and pension funding, except compulsory social security |
| 24 Manufacture of basic metals | |
| **F Construction** | **M Professional, Scientific and Technical Services** |
| 41 Construction of buildings | 69 Legal and accounting activities |
| 42 Civil engineering | 72 Scientific research and development |
| 43 Specialized construction activities | 73 Advertising and market resarch |
| **G Wholesale and Retail Trade; Repair of Motor Vehicles and Motor Cycles** | **R Arts, Entertainment and Recreation** |
| 45 Wholesale and retail trade and repair of motor vehicles and motor cycles | 90 Creative arts and entertainment activities |
| 46 Wholesale trade, except for motor vehicles and motor cycles | 91 Libraries, archives, museums, and other cultural activities |
| 47 Retail trade, except for motor vehicles and motor cycles | 92 Gambling and betting activities |

**Table 3.8** Selected two-digit SIC codes

| MANAGEMENT EFFECTIVENESS | | | | |
|---|---|---|---|---|
| | Company | Industry | Sector | S&P 500 |
| Return on assets (TTM) | 3.73 | −2.64 | 4.61 | 8.72 |
| Return on assets: 5 yr. avg. | 3.50 | 1.63 | 4.25 | 8.15 |
| | | | | |
| Return on investment (TTM) | 5.93 | 5.24 | 7.25 | 12.41 |
| Return on investment: 5 yr. avg. | 5.43 | −4.17 | 6.45 | 11.79 |
| | | | | |
| Return on equity (TTM) | 15.30 | 21.81 | 15.96 | 20.59 |
| Retrun on equity: 5 yr. avg. | 14.35 | 13.42 | 13.11 | 19.66 |
| *Source*: Reuters | | | | |

In looking at numbers such as these, recall our caution about analysing ratios that you don't calculate yourself: different sources frequently do their calculations somewhat differently, even if the ratio names are the same.

## Problems with Financial Statement Analysis

We continue our chapter on financial statements by discussing some additional problems that can arise when using them. In one way or another, the basic problem with financial statement analysis is that there is no underlying theory to help us identify which quantities to look at and guide us in establishing benchmarks.

As we discuss in other chapters, there are many cases in which financial theory and economic logic provide guidance in making judgements about value and risk. Little such help exists with financial statements. This is why we can't say which ratios matter the most, or what a high or low value might be.

One particularly severe problem is that many firms are conglomerates, owning more or less unrelated lines of business. Anglo American plc is a well-known example. Anglo American was originally founded in South Africa as a mining firm but is now involved in packaging, paper, coal, and a variety of metal extraction activities. It is now listed on the London Stock Exchange and is commonly regarded as a metals conglomerate. Similar to Tesco plc, the consolidated financial statements of Anglo American don't really fit any neat industry category. More generally, the kind of peer group analysis we have been describing is going to work best when the firms are strictly in the same line of business, the industry is competitive, and there is only one way of operating.

Another problem that is becoming increasingly common is that major competitors and natural peer group members in an industry may be scattered around the globe. The automobile industry is an obvious example. The problem here is that financial statements in many countries do not necessarily conform to IFRS. For example, US firms follow US GAAP whereas European firms follow IFRS. The existence of different standards and procedures makes it difficult to compare financial statements across national borders.

Even companies that are clearly in the same line of business may not be comparable. For example, electric utilities engaged primarily in power generation are all classified in the same group. This group is often thought to be relatively homogeneous. However, most utilities operate as regulated monopolies, so they don't compete much with each other, at least not historically. Many have shareholders, and many are organized as co-operatives with no shareholders. There are several different ways of generating power, ranging from hydroelectric to nuclear, so the operating activities of these utilities can differ quite a bit. Finally, profitability is strongly affected by the regulatory environment, so utilities in different countries can be similar but show different profits.

Several other general problems frequently crop up. First, firms use different accounting procedures – for inventory, for example. This makes it difficult to compare statements. Second, firms end their fiscal years at different times. For firms in seasonal businesses (such as a retailer with a large Christmas season), this can lead to difficulties in comparing statements of financial positions because of fluctuations in accounts during the year. Finally, for any particular firm, unusual or transient events, such as a one-time profit from an asset sale, may affect financial performance. Such events can give misleading signals as we compare firms.

## 3.10 Long-Term Financial Planning

Long-term planning is another important use of financial statements. We can begin our discussion of long-term planning models with a relatively simple example. Computerfield plc's financial statements from the most recent year are shown on the next page.

Unless otherwise stated, the financial planners at Computerfield assume that all variables are tied directly to sales, and current relationships are optimal. This means that all items will grow at exactly the same rate as sales. This is obviously oversimplified, and we use this assumption only to make a point.

| Computerfield plc<br>Financial statements | | | | | |
|---|---|---|---|---|---|
| **Income statement (£)** | | **Statement of financial position (£)** | | | |
| Sales | 1,000 | Assets | 500 | Debt | 250 |
| Costs | 800 | | | Equity | 250 |
| Net income | 200 | Total | 500 | Total | 500 |

Suppose sales increase by 20 per cent, rising from £1,000 to £1,200. Planners would then also forecast a 20 per cent increase in costs, from £800 to £800 × 1.2 = £960. The income statement would thus look like this:

| Income statement (£) | |
|---|---|
| Sales | 1,200 |
| Costs | 960 |
| Net income | 240 |

The assumption that all variables will grow by 20 per cent lets us easily construct the statement of financial position as well:

| Statement of financial position | | | |
|---|---|---|---|
| **(£)** | | **(£)** | |
| Assets | 600 (+100) | Debt | 300 (+50) |
| | | Equity | 300 (+50) |
| Total | 600 (+100) | Total | 600 (+100) |

Notice we have simply increased every item by 20 per cent. The numbers in parentheses are the changes in value for the different items.

Now we have to reconcile these two statements. How, for example, can net income be equal to £240 and equity increase by only £50? The answer is that Computerfield must have paid out the difference of £240 − 50 = £190, possibly as a cash dividend. In this case dividends are the 'plug' variable.

Suppose Computerfield does not pay out the £190. In this case, the addition to retained earnings is the full £240. Computerfield's equity will thus grow to £250 (the starting amount) plus £240 (net income), or £490, and debt must be retired to keep total assets equal to £600.

With £600 in total assets and £490 in equity, debt will have to be £600 − 490 = £110. Because we started with £250 in debt, Computerfield will have to retire £250 − 110 = £140 in debt. The resulting statement of financial position would look like this:

| Statement of financial position | | | |
|---|---|---|---|
| **(£)** | | **(£)** | |
| Assets | 600 (+100) | Debt | 110 (−140) |
| | | Equity | 490 (+240) |
| Total | 600 (+100) | Total | 600 (+100) |

In this case, debt is the plug variable used to balance projected total assets and liabilities.

This example shows the interaction between sales growth and financial policy. As sales increase, so do total assets. This occurs because the firm must invest in net working capital and fixed assets to support higher sales levels. Because assets are growing, total liabilities and equity, which are on the right side of the statement of financial position, will grow as well.

The thing to notice from our simple example is that the way the liabilities and owners' equity change depends on the firm's financing policy and its dividend policy. The growth in assets requires that the firm decide on how to finance that growth. This is strictly a managerial decision. Note that in our example the firm needed no outside funds. This won't usually be the case, so we explore a more detailed situation in the next section.

## The Percentage of Sales Approach

In the previous section we described a simple planning model in which every item increased at the same rate as sales. This may be a reasonable assumption for some elements. For others, such as long-term borrowing, it probably is not: the amount of long-term borrowing is set by management, and it does not necessarily relate directly to the level of sales.

In this section we describe an extended version of our simple model. The basic idea is to separate the income statement and statement of financial position accounts into two groups: those that vary directly with sales, and those that do not. Given a sales forecast, we shall then be able to calculate how much financing the firm will need to support the predicted sales level.

The financial planning model we describe next is based on the percentage of sales approach. Our goal here is to develop a quick and practical way of generating predicted financial accounts. We defer discussion of some 'bells and whistles' to a later section.

**The Income Statement**   We start out with the most recent income statement for Rosengarten GmbH, as shown in Table 3.9. Notice that we have still simplified things by including costs, depreciation, and interest in a single cost figure.

Rosengarten has projected a 25 per cent increase in sales for the coming year, so we are anticipating sales of €1,000 × 1.25 = €1,250. To generate an income statement, we assume that total costs will continue to run at €800/1,000 = 80 per cent of sales. With this assumption, Rosengarten's pro forma income statement is as shown in Table 3.10. The effect here of assuming that costs are a constant percentage of sales is to assume that the profit margin is constant. To check this, notice that the profit margin was €132/1,000 =13.2 per cent. In our new income statement the profit margin is €165/1,250 = 13.2 per cent; so it is unchanged.

Next, we need to project the dividend payment. This amount is up to Rosengarten's management. We shall assume that Rosengarten has a policy of paying out a constant fraction of net income in the form of a cash dividend. For the most recent year, the dividend payout ratio was

$$\text{Dividend payout ratio} = \text{Cash dividends/Net income}$$
$$= €44/132 \qquad\qquad (3.21)$$
$$= 33\tfrac{1}{3}\%$$

We can also calculate the ratio of the addition to retained earnings to net income:

| TABLE 3.9 | Rosengarten GmbH Income Statement | | |
|---|---|---|---|
| | | (€) | (€) |
| Sales | | | 1,000 |
| Costs | | | 800 |
| Taxable income | | | 200 |
| Taxes (34%) | | | 68 |
| Net income | | | 132 |
| Dividends | | 44 | |
| Addition to retained earnings | | 88 | |

**Table 3.9** Rosengarten GmbH income statement

| TABLE 3.10 | Rosengarten GmbH Pro Forma Income Statement | (€) |
|---|---|---|
| Sales (projected) | | 1,250 |
| Costs (80% of sales) | | 1,000 |
| Taxable income | | 250 |
| Taxes (34%) | | 85 |
| Net income | | 165 |

**Table 3.10** Rosengarten GmbH pro forma income statement

$$\text{Addition to retained earnings/Net income} = €88/132$$
$$= 66\tfrac{2}{3}\%$$

This ratio is called the retention ratio or ploughback ratio, and it is equal to 1 minus the dividend payout ratio, because everything not paid out is retained. Assuming that the payout ratio is constant, the projected dividends and addition to retained earnings will be

$$\text{Projected dividends paid to shareholders} = €165 \times \tfrac{1}{3} = €\ 55$$
$$\text{Projected addition to retained earnings} = €165 \times \tfrac{2}{3} = €110$$
$$€165$$

**The Statement of Financial Position**  To generate a new statement of financial position, we start with the most recent statement, as shown in Table 3.11.

| TABLE 3.11 | Rosengarten GmbH Statement of Financial Position | | | | |
|---|---|---|---|---|---|
| | **Assets** | | **Liabilities and Owners' Equity** | | |
| | (€) | Percentage of sales (%) | | (€) | Percentage of sales % |
| **Current assets** | | | **Current liabilities** | | |
| Cash | 160 | 16 | Trade payables | 300 | 30 |
| Trade receivables | 440 | 44 | Notes payable | 100 | n/a |
| Inventory | 600 | 60 | | | |
| Total | 1,200 | 120 | Total | 400 | n/a |
| **Non-current assets** | | | **Non-current liabilities** | 800 | n/a |
| Net plant and equipment | 1,800 | 180 | **Owners' equity** | | |
| | | | Ordinary shares and paid-in surplus | 800 | n/a |
| | | | Retained earnings | 1,000 | n/a |
| | | | Total | 1,800 | n/a |
| **Total assets** | 3,000 | 300 | **Total liabilities and owners' equity** | 3,000 | n/a |

**Table 3.11** Rosengarten GmbH statement of financial position

In our statement of financial position, we assume that some items vary directly with sales and others do not. For those items that vary with sales, we express each as a percentage of sales for the year just completed. When an item does not vary directly with sales, we write 'n/a' for 'not applicable'.

For example, on the asset side, inventory is equal to 60 per cent of sales (€600/1,000) for the year just ended. We assume this percentage applies to the coming year, so for each €1 increase in sales, inventory will rise by €0.60. More generally, the ratio of total assets to sales for the year just ended is €3,000/1,000 = 3, or 300 per cent.

This ratio of total assets to sales is sometimes called the **capital intensity ratio**. It tells us the amount of assets needed to generate €1 in sales: the higher the ratio, the more capital intensive the firm is. Notice also that this ratio is just the reciprocal of the total asset turnover ratio we defined previously.

For Rosengarten, assuming that this ratio is constant, it takes €3 in total assets to generate €1 in sales (apparently Rosengarten is in a relatively capital-intensive business). Therefore, if sales are to increase by €100, Rosengarten will have to increase total assets by three times this amount, or €300.

On the liability side of the statement of financial position, we show trade payables varying with sales. The reason for this is that we expect to place more orders with our suppliers as sales volume increases, so payables will change 'spontaneously' with sales. Notes payable, on the other hand, represent short-term debt such as bank borrowing. This will not vary unless we take specific actions to change the amount, so we mark this item as 'n/a'.

Similarly, we use 'n/a' for non-current liabilities because they won't automatically change with sales. The same is true for ordinary shares and paid-in surplus. The last item on the right side, retained earnings, will vary with sales, but it won't be a simple percentage of sales. Instead, we shall explicitly calculate the change in retained earnings based on our projected net income and dividends.

We can now construct a partial statement of financial position for Rosengarten. We do this by using the percentages we have just calculated, wherever possible, to calculate the projected amounts. For example, non-current assets are 180 per cent of sales: so, with a new sales level of €1,250, the non-current asset amount will be 1.80 × €1,250 = €2,250, representing an increase of €2,250 − 1,800 = €450 in plant and equipment. It is important to note that for items that don't vary directly with sales, we initially assume no change and simply write in the original amounts. The result is shown in Table 3.12. Notice that the change in retained earnings is equal to the €110 addition to retained earnings we calculated earlier.

Inspecting our new statement of financial position, we notice that assets are projected to increase by €750. However, without additional financing, liabilities and equity will increase by only €185, leaving a shortfall of €750 − 185 = €565. We label this amount *external financing needed* (EFN).

Rather than create new financial statements, if we were so inclined, we could calculate EFN directly as follows:

$$\text{EFN} = \left( \frac{\text{Assets}}{\text{Sales}} \times \Delta\text{Sales} \right) - \left( \frac{\text{Spontaneous liabilities}}{\text{Sales}} \times \Delta\text{Sales} \right) \qquad \textbf{(3.22)}$$
$$- \left[ (PM \times \text{Projected sales}) \times (1 - d) \right]$$

In this expression, 'ΔSales' is the projected change in sales (in euros). In our example projected sales for next year are €1,250, an increase of €250 over the previous year, so ΔSales = €250. By 'Spontaneous liabilities', we mean liabilities that naturally move up and down with sales. For Rosengarten, the spontaneous liabilities are the €300 in trade payables. Finally, *PM* and *d* are the profit margin and dividend payout ratios, which we previously calculated as 13.2 per cent and 33 1/3 per cent, respectively. Total assets and sales are €3,000 and €1,000, respectively, so we have:

$$\text{EFN} = \left( \frac{€3,000}{1,000} \times €250 \right) - \left( \frac{€300}{1,000} \times €250 \right) - \left[ 0.132 \times €1,250 \times \left( 1 - \frac{1}{3} \right) \right] = €565$$

In this calculation, notice that there are three parts. The first part is the projected increase in assets, which is calculated using the capital intensity ratio. The second is the spontaneous increase in liabilities. The third part is the product of profit margin and projected sales, which

TABLE
3.12

| Rosengarten GmbH Partial Statement of Financial Position | | | | | |
|---|---|---|---|---|---|
| **Assets** | | | **Liabilities and Owners' Equity** | | |
| | Next year (€) | Change from current year (€) | | Next year (€) | Change from current year (€) |
| **Current assets** | | | **Current liabilities** | | |
| Cash | 200 | 40 | Trade payables | 375 | 75 |
| Trade receivables | 550 | 110 | Notes payable | 100 | 0 |
| Inventory | 750 | 150 | | | |
| Total | 1,500 | 300 | Total | 475 | 75 |
| **Non-current assets** | | | **Non-current liabilities** | 800 | 0 |
| Net plant and equipment | 2,250 | 450 | **Owners' equity** | | |
| | | | Ordinary shares and paid-in surplus | 800 | 0 |
| | | | Retained earnings | 1,110 | 110 |
| | | | Total | 1,910 | 110 |
| **Total assets** | 3,750 | 750 | **Total liabilities and owners' equity** | 3,185 | 185 |
| | | | External financing needed | 565 | 565 |

**Table 3.12** Rosengarten GmbH partial statement of financial position

is projected net income, multiplied by the retention ratio. Thus the third part is the projected addition to retained earnings.

**A Particular Scenario** Our financial planning model now reminds us of one of those good news–bad news jokes. The good news is we're projecting a 25 per cent increase in sales. The bad news is this isn't going to happen unless Rosengarten can somehow raise €565 in new financing.

This is a good example of how the planning process can point out problems and potential conflicts. If, for example, Rosengarten has a goal of not borrowing any additional funds and not selling any new equity, then a 25 per cent increase in sales is probably not feasible.

If we take the need for €565 in new financing as given, we know that Rosengarten has three possible sources: short-term borrowing, long-term borrowing, and new equity. The choice of some combination among these three is up to management; we shall illustrate only one of the many possibilities.

Suppose Rosengarten decides to borrow the needed funds. In this case, the firm might choose to borrow some over the short term and some over the long term. For example, current assets increased by €300 whereas current liabilities rose by only €75. Rosengarten could borrow €300 – 75 = €225 in short-term notes payable and leave total net working capital unchanged. With €565 needed, the remaining €565 – 225 = €340 would have to come from long-term debt. Table 3.13 shows the completed statement of financial position for Rosengarten.

We have used a combination of short- and long-term debt as the plug here, but we emphasize that this is just one possible strategy; it is not necessarily the best one by any means. We could (and should) investigate many other scenarios. The various ratios we discussed earlier come in handy here. For example, with the scenario we have just examined, we would surely want to examine the current ratio and the total debt ratio to see whether we were comfortable with the new projected debt levels.

TABLE
3.13

| | Rosengarten GmbH Statement of Financial Position | | | | |
|---|---|---|---|---|---|
| | **Assets** | | **Liabilities and Owners' Equity** | | |
| | Next year (€) | Change from current year (€) | | Next year (€) | Change from current year (€) |
| **Current assets** | | | **Current liabilities** | | |
| Cash | 200 | 40 | Trade payables | 375 | 75 |
| Trade receivables | 550 | 110 | Notes payable | 325 | 225 |
| Inventory | 750 | 150 | | | |
| Total | 1,500 | 300 | Total | 700 | 300 |
| **Non-current assets** | | | **Non-current liabilities** | 1,140 | 340 |
| Net plant and equipment | 2,250 | 450 | **Owners' equity** | | |
| | | | Ordinary shares and paid-in surplus | 800 | 0 |
| | | | Retained earnings | 1,110 | 110 |
| | | | Total | 1,910 | 110 |
| **Total assets** | 3,750 | 750 | **Total liabilities and owners' equity** | 3,750 | 750 |

Table 3.13 Rosengarten GmbH statement of financial position

## 3.11 External Financing and Growth

External financing needed and growth are obviously related. All other things staying the same, the higher the rate of growth in sales or assets, the greater will be the need for external financing. In the previous section we took growth rate as given, and then we determined the amount of external financing needed to support that growth. In this section we turn things round a bit. We shall take the firm's financial policy as given and then examine the relationship between that financial policy and the firm's ability to finance new investments, and thereby grow.

We emphasize that we are focusing on growth not because growth is an appropriate goal; instead, for our purposes, growth is simply a convenient means of examining the interactions between investment and financing decisions. In effect, we assume that the use of growth as a basis for planning is just a reflection of the very high level of aggregation used in the planning process.

### EFN and Growth

The first thing we need to do is establish the relationship between EFN and growth. To do this, we introduce the simplified income statement and statement of financial position for Paradise plc in Table 3.14. Notice that we have simplified the statement of financial position by combining short-term and long-term debt into a single total debt figure. Effectively, we are assuming that none of the current liabilities vary spontaneously with sales. This assumption isn't as restrictive as it sounds. If any current liabilities (such as trade payables) vary with sales, we can assume that any such accounts have been netted out in current assets. Also, we continue to combine depreciation, interest, and costs on the income statement.

**TABLE 3.14**

| Paradise plc Income Statement | (£) | (£) |
|---|---|---|
| Sales | | 500 |
| Costs | | 400 |
| Taxable income | | 100 |
| Taxes (28%) | | 28 |
| Net income | | 72 |
|    Dividends | 24 | |
|    Addition to retained earnings | 48 | |

| Statement of Financial Position | | | | | |
|---|---|---|---|---|---|
| **Assets** | | | **Liabilities and Owners' Equity** | | |
| | (£) | Percentage of sales (%) | | (£) | Percentage of sales (%) |
| Current assets | 200 | 40 | Total debt | 250 | n/a |
| Non-current assets | 300 | 60 | Owners' equity | 250 | n/a |
|   Total assets | 500 | 100 |   Total liabilities and owners' equity | 500 | n/a |

**Table 3.14** Paradise plc income statement and statement of financial position

Suppose Paradise plc is forecasting next year's sales level at £600, a £100 increase. Notice that the percentage increase in sales is £100/500 = 20 per cent. Using the percentage of sales approach and the figures in Table 3.14 we can prepare a new income statement and statement of financial position as in Table 3.15. As Table 3.15 illustrates, at a 20 per cent growth rate, Paradise needs £100 in new assets. The projected addition to retained earnings is £57.6, so the external financing needed, EFN, is £100 − £57.6 = £42.4.

Notice that the debt–equity ratio for Paradise was originally (from Table 3.15) equal to £250/250 = 1.0. We shall assume that Paradise plc does not wish to sell new equity. In this case, the £42.4 in EFN will have to be borrowed. What will the new debt–equity ratio be? From Table 3.15 we know that total owners' equity is projected at £307.6. The new total debt will be the original £250 plus £42.4 in new borrowing, or £292.4 total. The debt–equity ratio thus falls slightly from 1.0 to £292.4/307.6 = 0.95.

Table 3.16 shows EFN for several different growth rates. The projected addition to retained earnings and the projected debt–equity ratio for each scenario are also given (you should probably calculate a few of these for practice). In determining the debt–equity ratios, we assumed that any needed funds were borrowed, and we also assumed any surplus funds were used to pay off debt. Thus, for the zero growth case the debt falls by £48, from £250 to £202. In Table 3.16, notice that the increase in assets required is simply equal to the original assets of £500 multiplied by the growth rate. Similarly, the addition to retained earnings is equal to the original £48 plus £48 times the growth rate.

Table 3.16 shows that, for relatively low growth rates, Paradise will run a surplus, and its debt–equity ratio will decline. Once the growth rate increases to just over 10 per cent, however, the surplus becomes a deficit. Furthermore, as the growth rate exceeds approximately 25 per cent, the debt–equity ratio passes its original value of 1.0.

Figure 3.1 illustrates the connection between growth in sales and external financing needed by plotting asset needs and additions to retained earnings from Table 3.16 against the growth rates. As shown, the need for new assets grows at a much faster rate than the addition to

**TABLE 3.15**

| Paradise plc Income Statement | (£) | (£) |
|---|---|---|
| Sales (projected) | | 600.0 |
| Costs (80% of sales) | | 480.0 |
| Taxable income | | 120.0 |
| Taxes (28%) | | 33.6 |
| Net income | | 86.4 |
| Dividends | 28.8 | |
| Addition to retained earnings | 57.6 | |

| Statement of Financial Position | | | | | |
|---|---|---|---|---|---|
| **Assets** | | | **Liabilities and Owners' Equity** | | |
| | (£) | Percentage of sales (%) | | (£) | Percentage of sales (%) |
| Current assets | 240.0 | 40 | Total debt | 250.0 | n/a |
| Non-current assets | 360.0 | 60 | Owners' equity | 307.6 | n/a |
| Total assets | 600.0 | 100 | Total liabilities and owners' equity | 557.6 | n/a |
| | | | External financing needed | 42.4 | n/a |

**Table 3.15** Paradise plc income statement and statement of financial position

**TABLE 3.16**

| Projected sales growth (%) | Increase in assets required (£) | Addition to retained earnings (£) | External financing needed, EFN (£) | Projected debt–equity ratio |
|---|---|---|---|---|
| 0 | 0 | 48.0 | −48.0 | 0.68 |
| 5 | 25 | 50.4 | −25.4 | 0.75 |
| 10 | 50 | 52.4 | −2.8 | 0.82 |
| 15 | 75 | 55.2 | 19.8 | 0.88 |
| 20 | 100 | 57.6 | 42.4 | 0.95 |
| 25 | 125 | 60.0 | 65.0 | 1.02 |

**Table 3.16** Growth and projected EFN for Paradise plc

retained earnings, so the internal financing provided by the addition to retained earnings rapidly disappears.

As this discussion shows, whether a firm runs a cash surplus or deficit depends on growth. Microsoft is a good example. Its revenue growth in the 1990s was amazing, averaging well over 30 per cent per year for the decade. Growth slowed down noticeably over the 2000–2008 period, but, nonetheless, Microsoft's combination of growth and substantial profit margins led to enormous cash surpluses. In part because Microsoft paid few or no dividends, the cash really piled up: in 2007 Microsoft's cash hoard exceeded $23 billion.

FIGURE

**3.1**

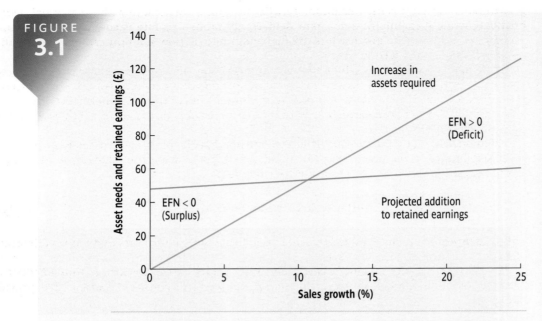

**Figure 3.1** Growth and related financing needed for Paradise plc

## Financial Policy and Growth

Based on our discussion just preceding, we see that there is a direct link between growth and external financing. In this section we discuss two growth rates that are particularly useful in long-range planning.

**The Internal Growth Rate**   The first growth rate of interest is the maximum growth rate that can be achieved with no external financing of any kind. We shall call this the internal growth rate because this is the rate the firm can maintain with internal financing only. In Fig. 3.1 this internal growth rate is represented by the point where the two lines cross. At this point, the required increase in assets is exactly equal to the addition to retained earnings, and EFN is therefore zero. We have seen that this happens when the growth rate is slightly more than 10 per cent. With a little algebra (see Problem 34 at the end of the chapter), we can define this growth rate more precisely as

$$\text{Internal growth rate} = \frac{\text{ROA} \times b}{1 - \text{ROA} \times b} \tag{3.23}$$

where ROA is the return on assets we discussed earlier, and $b$ is the ploughback, or retention, ratio also defined earlier in this chapter.

For Paradise plc, net income was £72 and total assets were £500. ROA is thus £72/500 = 14.4 per cent. Of the £72 net income, £48 was retained, so the ploughback ratio, $b$, is £48/72 = 2/3. With these numbers, we can calculate the internal growth rate as

$$\begin{aligned}
\text{Internal growth rate} &= \frac{\text{ROA} \times b}{1 - \text{ROA} \times b} \\
&= \frac{0.144 \times (2/3)}{1 - 0.144 \times (2/3)} \\
&= 10.62\%
\end{aligned}$$

Thus Paradise plc can expand at a maximum rate of 10.62 per cent per year without external financing.

**The Sustainable Growth Rate**   We have seen that if Paradise plc wishes to grow more rapidly than at a rate of 10.62 per cent per year, external financing must be arranged. The second growth rate of interest is the maximum growth rate a firm can achieve with no external *equity* financing while it maintains a constant debt–equity ratio. This rate is commonly called the sustainable growth rate because it is the maximum rate of growth a firm can maintain without increasing its financial leverage.

There are various reasons why a firm might wish to avoid equity sales. For example, new equity sales can be expensive because of the substantial fees that may be involved. Alternatively, the current owners may not wish to bring in new owners or contribute additional equity. Why a firm might view a particular debt–equity ratio as optimal is discussed in later chapters; for now, we shall take it as given.

Based on Table 3.16, the sustainable growth rate for Paradise plc is approximately 25 per cent because the debt–equity ratio is near 1.0 at that growth rate. The precise value can be calculated as follows (see Problem 34 at the end of the chapter):

$$\text{Sustainable growth rate} = \frac{\text{ROE} \times b}{1 - \text{ROE} \times b} \tag{3.24}$$

This is identical to the internal growth rate except that ROE, return on equity, is used instead of ROA.

For Paradise plc, net income was £72 and total equity was £250: ROE is thus £72/250 = 28.8 per cent. The ploughback ratio, $b$, is still 2/3, so we can calculate the sustainable growth rate as

$$\begin{aligned}
\text{Sustainable growth rate} &= \frac{\text{ROE} \times b}{1 - \text{ROE} \times b} \\
&= \frac{0.288 \times (2/3)}{1 - 0.288 \times (2/3)} \\
&= 23.76\%
\end{aligned}$$

Thus Paradise plc can expand at a maximum rate of 23.76 per cent per year without external equity financing.

## EXAMPLE 3.5
## Sustainable Growth

Suppose Paradise plc grows at exactly the sustainable growth rate of 23.76 per cent. What will the financial statements look like?

At a 23.76 per cent growth rate, sales will rise from £500 to £618.8. The new income statement will look like this:

| Paradise plc Income Statement | | |
|---|---|---|
| | (£) | (£) |
| Sales (projected) | | 618.8 |
| Costs (80% of sales) | | 495.0 |
| Taxable income | | 123.8 |
| Taxes (28%) | | 34.7 |
| Net income | | 89.1 |
| Dividends | 29.7 | |
| Addition to retained earnings | 59.4 | |

We construct the statement of financial position just as we did before. Notice, in this case, that owners' equity will rise from £250 to £309.4 because the addition to retained earnings is £59.4.

| Paradise plc  Statement of Financial Position | | | | | |
|---|---|---|---|---|---|
| **Assets** | | | **Liabilities and owners' equity** | | |
| | **(£)** | **Percentage of sales (%)** | | **(£)** | **Percentage of sales (%)** |
| Current assets | 247.5 | 40 | Total debt | 250.0 | n/a |
| Non-current assets | 371.3 | 60 | Owners' equity | 309.4 | n/a |
| Total assets | 618.8 | 100 | Total liabilities and owners' equity | 559.4 | n/a |
| | | | External financing needed | 59.4 | n/a |

As illustrated, EFN is £59.4. If Paradise borrows this amount, then total debt will rise to £309.4, and the debt–equity ratio will be exactly 1.0, which verifies our earlier calculation. At any other growth rate, something would have to change.

**Determinants of Growth**   Earlier in this chapter, we saw that the return on equity, ROE, could be decomposed into its various components using the Du Pont identity. Because ROE appears so prominently in the determination of the sustainable growth rate, it is obvious that the factors important in determining ROE are also important determinants of growth.

From our previous discussions, we know that ROE can be written as the product of three factors:

$$ROE = \text{Profit margin} \times \text{Total asset turnover} \times \text{Equity multiplier}$$

If we examine our expression for the sustainable growth rate, we see that anything that increases ROE will increase the sustainable growth rate by making the top bigger and the bottom smaller. Increasing the ploughback ratio will have the same effect.

Putting it all together, what we have is that a firm's ability to sustain growth depends explicitly on the following four factors:

1   *Profit margin*: An increase in profit margin will increase the firm's ability to generate funds internally and thereby increase its sustainable growth.

2   *Dividend policy*: A decrease in the percentage of net income paid out as dividends will increase the retention ratio. This increases internally generated equity and thus increases sustainable growth.

3   *Financial policy*: An increase in the debt–equity ratio increases the firm's financial leverage. Because this makes additional debt financing available, it increases the sustainable growth rate.

4   *Total asset turnover*: An increase in the firm's total asset turnover increases the sales generated for each unit in assets. This decreases the firm's need for new assets as sales grow, and thereby increases the sustainable growth rate. Notice that increasing total asset turnover is the same thing as decreasing capital intensity.

The sustainable growth rate is a very useful planning number. What it illustrates is the explicit relationship between the firm's four major areas of concern: its operating efficiency as measured by profit margin; its asset use efficiency as measured by total asset turnover; its dividend policy as measured by the retention ratio; and its financial policy as measured by the debt–equity ratio.

EXAMPLE
**3.6**

## Profit Margins and Sustainable Growth

Hage ASA has a debt–equity ratio of 0.5, a profit margin of 3 per cent, a dividend payout ratio of 40 per cent, and a capital intensity ratio of 1. What is its sustainable growth rate? If Hage desired a 10 per cent sustainable growth rate and planned to achieve this goal by improving profit margins, what would you think?

ROE is 0.03 × 1 × 1.5 = 4.5 per cent. The retention ratio is 1 − 0.40 = 0.60. Sustainable growth is thus 0.045(0.60)/[1 − 0.045(0.60)] = 2.77 per cent.

For the company to achieve a 10 per cent growth rate, the profit margin will have to rise. To see this, assume that sustainable growth is equal to 10 per cent and then solve for profit margin, PM:

$$0.10 = PM(1.5)(0.6)/[1 − PM(1.5)(0.6)]$$
$$PM = 0.1/0.99 = 10.1\%$$

For the plan to succeed, the necessary increase in profit margin is substantial, from 3 per cent to about 10 per cent. This may not be feasible.

Given values for all four of these, there is only one growth rate that can be achieved. This is an important point, so it bears restating:

**If a firm does not wish to sell new equity and its profit margin, dividend policy, financial policy, and total asset turnover (or capital intensity) are all fixed, then there is only one possible growth rate.**

One of the primary benefits of financial planning is that it ensures internal consistency among the firm's various goals. The concept of the sustainable growth rate captures this element nicely. Also, we now see how a financial planning model can be used to test the feasibility of a planned growth rate. If sales are to grow at a rate higher than the sustainable growth rate, the firm must increase profit margins, increase total asset turnover, increase financial leverage, increase earnings retention, or sell new shares.

The two growth rates, internal and sustainable, are summarized in Table 3.17.

**TABLE 3.17**

**(a) Internal growth rate**

$$\text{Internal growth rate} = \frac{\text{ROA} \times b}{1 − \text{ROA} \times b}$$

where
ROA = Return on assets = Net income/Total assets
$b$ = Ploughback (retention) ratio
= Addition to retained earnings/Net income

The internal growth rate is the maximum growth rate that can be achieved with no external financing of any kind.

**(b) Sustainable growth rate**

$$\text{Sustainable growth rate} = \frac{\text{ROE} \times b}{1 − \text{ROE} \times b}$$

where
ROE = Return on equity = Net income/Total equity
$b$ = Ploughback (retention) ratio
= Addition to retained earnings/Net income

The sustainable growth rate is the maximum growth rate that can be achieved with no external equity financing while maintaining a constant debt–equity ratio.

**Table 3.17** Summary of internal and sustainable growth rates

## A Note about Sustainable Growth Rate Calculations

Very commonly, the sustainable growth rate is calculated using just the numerator in our expression, ROE × b. This causes some confusion, which we can clear up here. The issue has to do with how ROE is computed. Recall that ROE is calculated as net income divided by total equity. If total equity is taken from an ending statement of financial position (as we have done consistently, and is commonly done in practice), then our formula is the right one. However, if total equity is from the beginning of the period, then the simpler formula is the correct one.

In principle, you'll get exactly the same sustainable growth rate regardless of which way you calculate it (as long as you match up the ROE calculation with the right formula). In reality, you may see some differences because of accounting-related complications. By the way, if you use the average of beginning and ending equity (as some advocate), yet another formula is needed. Also, all of our comments here apply to the internal growth rate as well.

## 3.12 Some Caveats regarding Financial Planning Models

Financial planning models do not always ask the right questions. A primary reason is that they tend to rely on accounting relationships and not financial relationships. In particular, the three basic elements of firm value tend to get left out – namely, cash flow size, risk, and timing.

Because of this, financial planning models sometimes do not produce output that gives the user many meaningful clues about what strategies will lead to increases in value. Instead, they divert the user's attention to questions concerning the association of, say, the debt–equity ratio and firm growth.

The financial model we used for Paradise plc was simple – in fact, too simple. Our model, like many in use today, is really an accounting statement generator at heart. Such models are useful for pointing out inconsistencies and reminding us of financial needs, but they offer little guidance concerning what to do about these problems.

In closing our discussion, we should add that financial planning is an iterative process. Plans are created, examined, and modified over and over. The final plan will be a result negotiated between all the different parties to the process. Upper-level management has a goal in mind, and it is up to the planning staff to rework and to ultimately deliver a feasible plan that meets that goal.

The final plan will therefore implicitly contain different goals in different areas, and also satisfy many constraints. For this reason, such a plan need not be a dispassionate assessment of what we think the future will bring; it may instead be a means of reconciling the planned activities of different groups, and a way of setting common goals for the future.

However financial planning is done, the important thing to remember is that it should not become a purely mechanical exercise. If it does, it will probably focus on the wrong things. Nevertheless, the alternative to planning is stumbling into the future.

## Summary and Conclusions

This chapter focuses on working with information contained in financial statements. Specifically, we studied standardized financial statements, ratio analysis, and long-term financial planning.

1   We explained that differences in firm size make it difficult to compare financial statements, and we discussed how to form common-size statements to make comparisons easier and more meaningful.

2   Evaluating ratios of accounting numbers is another way of comparing financial statement information. We defined a number of the most commonly used ratios, and we discussed the famous Du Pont identity.

3   We showed how pro forma financial statements can be generated and used to plan for future financing needs.

After you have studied this chapter, we hope that you have some perspective on the uses and abuses of financial statement information. You should also find that your vocabulary of business and financial terms has grown substantially.

# Questions and Problems

CONCEPT
1–12

1 **The Statement of Financial Position**  Under standard accounting rules, it is possible for a company's liabilities to exceed its assets. When this occurs, the owners' equity is negative. Can this happen with market values? Why or why not?

2 **The Income Statement**  Why might the revenue and cost figures shown on a standard income statement not represent the actual cash inflows and outflows that occurred during a period?

3 **Taxes**  Why are taxes relevant in corporate finance?

4 **Net Working Capital**  Why do you think current assets less current liabilities is known as net working capital? Explain your answer using some practical examples.

5 **Cash Flow**  Why is it not necessarily bad for the operating cash flow to be negative for a particular period?

6 **Financial Statement Analysis**  One tool of financial analysis is common-size financial statements. Why do you think common-size income statements and statements of financial position are used? Note that the accounting statement of cash flows is not converted into a common-size statement. Why do you think this is?

7 **Ratio Analysis**  In the chapter, we presented several ratios for BMW from www.reuters.com. One of the ratios was return on investment. Return on investment is calculated as net income divided by long-term liabilities plus equity. What do you think return on investment is intended to measure? What is the relationship between return on investment and return on assets?

8 **The Du Pont Identity**  Both ROA and ROE measure profitability. Which one is more useful for comparing two companies? Why?

9 **Using Financial Statement Information**  A financial ratio by itself tells us little about a company, because financial ratios vary a great deal across industries. There are two basic methods for analysing financial ratios for a company: time trend analysis and peer group analysis. Why might each of these approaches be useful? What does each tell you about the company's financial health?

10 **Long-Term Financial Planning**  Why do you think most long-term financial planning begins with sales forecasts? Put differently, why are future sales the key input?

11 **External Financing and Growth**  Clacher plc maintains a positive retention ratio and keeps its debt–equity ratio constant every year. When sales grow by 20 per cent, the firm has a negative projected EFN. What does this tell you about the firm's sustainable growth rate? Do you know, with certainty, if the internal growth rate is greater than or less than 20 per cent? Why? What happens to the projected EFN if the retention ratio is increased? What if the retention ratio is decreased? What if the retention ratio is zero?

12 **Weaknesses in Financial Planning Models**  What are the main weaknesses in financial planning models? Provide some examples.

REGULAR
13–30

13 **Building a Statement of Financial Position**  According to BAE Systems plc's financial statements as of 31 December 2008, the firm had current assets of £8.069 billion, non-current assets of £17.606 billion, current liabilities of £10.790 billion, and non-current liabilities of £7.651 billion. What is the value of the shareholders' equity for BAE Systems? How much is net working capital?

14 **Building an Income Statement**  In 2007 the British building firm Balfour Beatty plc had sales of £6,466 million, total operating expenses of £6,319 million, a tax allowance (rebate) of £12 million because of past losses, and zero depreciation. What is the net income for the firm? Balfour Beatty paid out £50 million in cash dividends. What is the addition to retained earnings?

15 **Market Values and Book Values**  Your company has just sealed a deal to sell a tract of land with accompanying warehouse for €3.2 million. This is significantly lower than the €7 million your firm paid when the plot was purchased at the height of the property boom. International Accounting Standards have been followed by your firm, and so you will not make an accounting loss on the sale (why?). The company has non-current assets of €4 million, non-current liabilities of €2.2 million, and net working capital (current assets less current liabilities) of €0.9 million. What impact does the sale have on your firm's statement of financial position?

16 **Calculating Taxes**  The Dutch firm Herrera NV had €273,000 in taxable income. Using Table 3.3, what is the company's average tax rate? What is its marginal tax rate?

17 **Calculating OCF**  For the year ending 31 March 2008 Cable & Wireless plc had net revenues of £220 million, and net non-cash expenses (including depreciation) were £238 million. Cash outflows from investing activities (including capital expenditures) were £327 million. Cable & Wireless paid a total cash dividend of £138 million, and net interest expense was £341 million. If the company made £4 million from foreign exchange transactions, what was the net change in cash for Cable & Wireless plc for the year ending 31 March 2008?

18 **Calculating Net Capital Spending**  Morena's Driving School's 2008 statement of financial position showed non-current assets of £4.2 million. One year later, the 2009 statement of financial position showed non-current assets of £4.7 million. The company's 2009 income statement showed a depreciation expense of £925,000. What was Morena's net capital spending for 2009?

19 **Building a Statement of Financial Position**  The following table presents the long-term debt and shareholders' equity of Tumbler SA one year ago:

|  | (€) |
|---|---|
| Long-term debt | 60,000,000 |
| Preference shares | 18,000,000 |
| Ordinary shares (€1 par value) | 25,000,000 |
| Capital surplus | 49,000,000 |
| Accumulated retained earnings | 89,000,000 |

During the past year, Tumbler issued 20 million shares at a total price of €52 million, and issued €16 million in new long-term debt. The company generated €14 million in net income and paid €8 million in dividends. Construct the current statement of financial position, reflecting the changes that occurred at Tumbler during the year.

20 **EFN**  The year ending 31 December 2008 financial statements for Cadbury plc are shown here:

| Income statement (£m) | | Statement of financial position (£m) | | | |
|---|---|---|---|---|---|
| Total revenue | 5,384 | Assets | 8,895 | Liabilities | 5,373 |
| Costs | 4,984 | | | Equity | 3,522 |
| Taxable income | 400 | Total | 8,895 | Total | 8,895 |
| Taxes | 36 | | | | |
| Net income | 364 | | | | |

Assets and costs are proportional to sales. Debt and equity are not. Total cash dividends of £295 million were paid, and assume that Cadbury wishes to maintain a constant payout ratio. Next year's revenues are projected to be £9,000 million. What external financing is needed?

21 **Sales and Growth**  The most recent financial statements for Fontenot A/S are shown here:

| Income statement | | Statement of financial position | | | |
|---|---|---|---|---|---|
| | **(DKK)** | | **(DKK)** | | **(DKK)** |
| Total revenue | 54,000 | Current assets | 26,000 | Total liabilities | 58,000 |
| Costs | 34,800 | Non-current assets | 105,000 | Equity | 73,000 |
| Taxable income | 19,200 | Total | 131,000 | Total | 131,000 |
| Taxes (28%) | 5,376 | | | | |
| Net income | 13,824 | | | | |

Assets and costs are proportional to sales. The company maintains a constant 30 per cent dividend payout ratio and a constant debt–equity ratio. What is the maximum increase in sales that can be sustained, assuming no new equity is issued?

22 **Ratios and Foreign Companies** In 2007 the French IT firm CapGemini had a net income of €440 million on revenues of €8,703 million. What was the company's profit margin? Does the fact that these figures are quoted in euros make any difference to a British investor? Why? In sterling, sales were £7,967 million. What was the net income in pounds?

23 **External Funds Needed** The Optical Scam Company has forecast a 20 per cent sales growth rate for next year. The current financial statements are shown here:

| Income statement | | |
|---|---|---|
| | **(£)** | **(£)** |
| Sales | | 38,000,000 |
| Costs | | 33,400,000 |
| Taxable income | | 4,600,000 |
| Taxes | | 1,288,000 |
| Net income | | 3,312,000 |
| Dividends | 1,324,800 | |
| Additions to retained earnings | 1,987,200 | |

| Statement of financial position | | | |
|---|---|---|---|
| **Assets** | | **Liabilities and equity** | |
| **(£)** | | **(£)** | |
| Current assets | 9,000,000 | Current liabilities | 8,000,000 |
| Non-current assets | 22,000,000 | Non-current liabilities | 6,000,000 |
| | | Ordinary shares | 4,000,000 |
| | | Accumulated retained earnings | 13,000,000 |
| | | Total equity | 17,000,000 |
| Total assets | 31,000,000 | Total liabilities and equity | 31,000,000 |

(a) Using the equation from the chapter, calculate the external funds needed for next year.

(b) Construct the firm's statement of financial position for next year, and confirm the external funds needed you calculated in part (a).

(c) Calculate the sustainable growth rate for the company.

(d) Can Optical Scam eliminate the need for external funds by changing its dividend policy? What other options are available to the company to meet its growth objectives?

24 **Days' Sales in Receivables** A company has net income of €173,000, a profit margin of 8.6 per cent, and a trade receivables balance of €143,200. Assuming 75 per cent of sales are on credit, what is the company's days' sales in receivables?

25 **Ratios and Fixed Assets** Le Verd SA has a ratio of long-term debt to total assets of 0.70 and a current ratio of 1.20. Current liabilities are €850, revenues are €4,310, profit margin is 9.5 per cent, and ROE is 21.5 per cent. What is the amount of the firm's non-current assets?

26 **Calculating the Cash Coverage Ratio** Titan SpA's net income for the most recent year was €7,850. The tax rate was 37.25 per cent. The firm paid €2,108 in total interest expense and deducted €1,687 in depreciation expense. What was Titan's cash coverage ratio for the year?

27 **Cost of Goods Sold** Guthrie plc has current liabilities of £340,000, a quick ratio of 1.8, inventory turnover of 4.2, and a current ratio of 3.3. What is the cost of goods sold for the company?

28 **Common-Size and Common-Base Year Financial Statements** In addition to common-size financial statements, common-base year financial statements are often used. Common-base year financial statements are constructed by dividing the current year account value by the base year account value. Thus the result shows the growth rate in the account. Using the following financial statements, construct the common-size statement of financial position and common-base year statement of financial position for the company. Use 2007 as the base year.

| Jarrow plc 2007 and 2008 Statement of financial positions | | | | | |
|---|---|---|---|---|---|
| **Assets** | | | **Liabilities and owners' equity** | | |
| | **2007** | **2008** | | **2007** | **2008** |
| | **(£)** | **(£)** | | **(£)** | **(£)** |
| Current assets | | | Current liabilities | | |
| Cash | 10,168 | 10,683 | Trade payables | 73,185 | 59,309 |
| Trade receivables | 27,145 | 28,613 | Notes payable | 39,125 | 48,168 |
| Inventory | 59,324 | 64,853 | Total | 112,310 | 107,477 |
| Total | 96,637 | 104,149 | Non-current liabilities | 50,000 | 62,000 |
| Non-current assets | | | Owners' equity | | |
| Net plant and equipment | 304,165 | 347,168 | Ordinary shares and paid-in surplus | 80,000 | 80,000 |
| | | | Retained earnings | 158,492 | 201,840 |
| | | | Total | 238,492 | 281,840 |
| Total assets | 400,802 | 451,317 | Total liabilities and owners' equity | 400,802 | 451,317 |

Use the following information for Problem 29:

The discussion of EFN in the chapter implicitly assumed that the company was operating at full capacity. Often, this is not the case. For example, assume that Rosengarten was operating at 90 per cent capacity. Full-capacity sales would be €1,000/0.90 = €1,111. If the statement of financial position shows €1,800 in fixed assets, the capital intensity ratio for the company is

Capital intensity ratio = Fixed assets/Full-capacity sales = €1,800/€1,111 = 1.62

This means that Rosengarten needs €1.62 in fixed assets for every euro in sales when it reaches full capacity. At the projected sales level of €1,250, it needs €1,250 ×1.62 = €2,025 in fixed assets, which is €225 lower than our projection of €2,250 in fixed assets. So, EFN is only €565 − 225 = €340.

29 **Calculating EFN** The most recent financial statements for Lapland Tours AG follow. Sales for 2010 are projected to grow by 20 per cent. Interest expense will remain constant; the tax rate and the dividend payout rate will also remain constant. Costs, other expenses, current assets, and accounts payable increase simultaneously with sales. If the firm is operating at full capacity and no new debt or equity is issued, what external financing is needed to support the 20 per cent growth rate in sales?

### LAPLAND TOURS AG
### 2009 Income statement

|  | (€) | (€) |
|---|---|---|
| Revenues |  | 800,000 |
| Costs |  | 710,000 |
| Other expenses |  | 12,000 |
| Income before interest and taxes |  | 78,000 |
| Interest paid |  | 19,700 |
| Taxable income |  | 58,300 |
| Taxes (35%) |  | 20,405 |
| Net income |  | 37,895 |
| Dividends | 15,158 |  |
| Addition to retained earnings | 22,737 |  |

### LAPLAND TOURS AG
### Statement of financial position as of 31 December 2009

| Assets | | Liabilities and owners' equity | |
|---|---|---|---|
| | (€) | | (€) |
| Current assets | | Current liabilities | |
| Cash | 25,000 | Trade payables | 65,000 |
| Trade receivables | 43,000 | Notes payable | 9,000 |
| Inventory | 76,000 | Total | 74,000 |
| Total | 144,000 | | |
| Non-current assets | | Non-current liabilities | 156,000 |
| | | Owners' equity | |
| Net plant and equipment | 364,000 | Ordinary shares and paid-in surplus | 21,000 |
| | | Retained earnings | 257,000 |
| Total assets | 508,000 | Total | 278,000 |
| | | Total liabilities and owners' equity | 508,000 |

30 **Capacity Usage and Growth** In the previous problem, suppose the firm was operating at only 80 per cent capacity in 2009. What is EFN now? Suppose the firm wishes to keep its debt–equity ratio constant. What is EFN now?

CHALLENGE 31–38

31 **Calculating the Du Pont Identity** Find the annual income statements and statements of financial position for the British companies Experian plc and First Group plc. Calculate the Du Pont identity for each company for the most recent three years. Comment on the changes in each component of the Du Pont identity for each company over this period, and compare the components between the two companies. Are the results what you expected? Why or why not?

32 **EFN and Internal Growth** Redo Problem 29 using sales growth rates of 15 and 25 per cent in addition to 20 per cent. Illustrate graphically the relationship between EFN and the growth rate, and use this graph to determine the relationship between them.

33   **EFN**   Define the following:

S = Previous year's sales
A = Total assets
D = Total debt
E = Total equity
g = Projected growth in sales
PM = Profit margin
b = Retention (ploughback) ratio

Show that EFN can be written as

$$EFN = -PM(S)b + [A - PM(S)b] \times g$$

*Hint*: Asset needs will equal A × g. The addition to retained earnings will equal PM(S)b × (1 + g).

34   **Sustainable Growth Rate**   Based on the results in Problem 33, show that the internal and sustainable growth rates can be calculated as shown in Eqs 3.23 and 3.24. *Hint:* For the internal growth rate, set EFN equal to zero and solve for g.

35   **Sustainable Growth Rate**   In the chapter, we discussed one calculation of the sustainable growth rate as

$$\text{Sustainable growth rate} = \frac{\text{ROE} \times b}{1 - \text{ROE} \times b}$$

In practice, probably the most commonly used calculation of the sustainable growth rate is ROE × b. This equation is identical to the sustainable growth rate equation presented in the chapter if the ROE is calculated using the beginning of period equity. Derive this equation from the equation presented in the chapter.

36   **Sustainable Growth Rate**   Use the sustainable growth rate equations from the previous problem to answer the following questions. No Return NV had total assets of €210,000 and equity of €165,000 at the beginning of the year. At the end of the year, the company had total assets of €250,000. During the year the company sold no new equity. Net income for the year was €80,000 and dividends were €49,000. What is the sustainable growth rate for the company? What is the sustainable growth rate if you calculate ROE based on the beginning of period equity?

For questions 37–38, consider the summarized financial statements for 2008 of Siemens AG:

| Summarized statement of income | 2008 (€m) |
|---|---|
| Revenue | 77,327 |
| Cost of goods sold | 56,284 |
| **Operating income** | **21,043** |
| Less: | |
| Depreciation | 2,130 |
| Other expenses | 16,039 |
| **Income from continuing operations before income taxes** | **2,874** |
| Income taxes | 1,015 |
| **Income from continuing operations** | **1,859** |
| Income from discontinued operations, net of taxes | 4,027 |
| **Net income** | **5,886** |

| Summarized statement of financial position | | | |
|---|---|---|---|
| **Assets** | **(€m)** | **Liabilities** | **(€m)** |
| **Current assets** | | **Current liabilities** | |
| Cash and cash equivalents | 6,893 | Trade payables | 8,860 |
| Trade and other receivables | 15,785 | Other current liabilities | 33,591 |
| Inventories | 14,509 | **Total current liabilities** | **42,451** |
| Other current assets | 6,055 | Long-term debt | 14,260 |
| **Total current assets** | **43,242** | Other non-current liabilities | 10,372 |
| Non-current assets | 51,221 | **Total liabilities** | **67,083** |
| | | Equity | 4,391 |
| | | Retained earnings | 22,989 |
| **Total assets** | **94,463** | **Total liabilities and equity** | **94,463** |

37 **Financial Ratios** Calculate all relevant financial ratios for Siemens AG.

38 **Financial Statement Analysis** What are the weaknesses in the Siemens examples for interpreting its financial well-being? Explain.

MINI CASE

# Ratios and Financial Planning at West Coast Yachts

Dan Ervin was recently hired by West Coast Yachts Ltd to assist the company with its short-term financial planning, and also to evaluate the company's financial performance. Dan graduated from university five years ago with a finance degree, and he has been employed in the treasury department of an FTSE 100 company since then.

West Coast Yachts was founded 10 years ago by Larissa Warren. The company's operations are located in a well-known marina, Inverkip, on the west coast of Scotland. The firm is structured as a private limited company. The company has manufactured custom midsize, high-performance yachts for clients over this period, and its products have received high reviews for safety and reliability. The company's yachts have also recently received the highest award for customer satisfaction. The yachts are purchased primarily by wealthy individuals for pleasure use. Occasionally, a yacht is manufactured for purchase by a company for business purposes.

The custom yacht industry is fragmented, with several manufacturers. As with any industry, there are market leaders, but the diverse nature of the industry ensures that no manufacturer dominates the market. The competition in the market, as well as the product cost, ensures that attention to detail is a necessity. For instance, West Coast Yachts will spend 80 to 100 hours on hand-buffing the stainless steel stem-iron, which is the metal cap on the yacht's bow that conceivably could collide with a dock or another boat.

To get Dan started with his analyses, Larissa has provided the following financial statements. Larissa has also gathered the industry ratios for the yacht manufacturing industry.

| West Coast Yachts 2008 Income statement | | |
|---|---|---|
| | **(£)** | **(£)** |
| Operating revenues | | 128,700,000 |
| Operating expenses | | 90,700,000 |
| Operating profit | | 38,000,000 |
| Depreciation | | 4,200,000 |
| Other non-operating expenses | | 15,380,000 |
| Interest | | 2,315,000 |

| West Coast Yachts<br>2008 Income statement | | |
|---|---|---|
| | **(£)** | **(£)** |
| Profit before taxes | | 16,105,000 |
| Taxes (28%) | | 4,509,400 |
| Profit for period attributable to equity holders | | 11,595,600 |
| Dividends | 6,957,360 | |
| Addition to retained earnings | 4,638,240 | |

| West Coast Yachts<br>Statement of financial position as of 31 December 2008 | | | |
|---|---|---|---|
| **Assets (£)** | | **Liabilities and equity (£)** | |
| Current assets | | Current liabilities | |
| Cash | 2,340,000 | Trade payables | 4,970,000 |
| Trade receivables | 4,210,000 | Notes payable | 10,060,000 |
| Inventory | 4,720,000 | | |
| Total | 11,270,000 | Total | 15,030,000 |
| | | | |
| Non-current assets | | Non-current liabilities | 25,950,000 |
| Net plant and equipment | 72,280,000 | | |
| | | Shareholders' equity | |
| | | Ordinary shares | 4,000,000 |
| | | Retained earnings | 38,570,000 |
| | | Total equity | 42,570,000 |
| Total assets | 83,550,000 | Total liabilities and equity | 83,550,000 |

| Yacht industry ratios | | | |
|---|---|---|---|
| | **Lower quartile** | **Median** | **Upper quartile** |
| Current ratio | 0.50 | 1.43 | 1.89 |
| Quick ratio | 0.21 | 0.38 | 0.62 |
| Total asset turnover | 0.68 | 0.85 | 1.38 |
| Inventory turnover | 4.89 | 6.15 | 10.89 |
| Receivables turnover | 6.27 | 9.82 | 14.11 |
| Debt ratio | 0.44 | 0.52 | 0.61 |
| Debt–equity ratio | 0.79 | 1.08 | 1.56 |
| Equity multiplier | 1.79 | 2.08 | 2.56 |
| Interest coverage | 5.18 | 8.06 | 9.83 |
| Profit margin | 4.05% | 6.98% | 9.87% |
| Return on assets | 6.05% | 10.53% | 13.21% |
| Return on equity | 9.93% | 16.54% | 26.15% |

1   Calculate all the ratios listed in the industry table for West Coast Yachts.

2   Compare the performance of West Coast Yachts with that of the industry as a whole. For each ratio, comment on why it might be viewed as positive or negative relative to the industry. Suppose you create an inventory ratio, calculated as inventory divided by current liabilities. How do you interpret this ratio? How does West Coast Yachts compare with the industry average?

3  Calculate the sustainable growth rate of West Coast Yachts. Calculate external funds needed (EFN) and prepare pro forma income statements and statement of financial positions assuming growth at precisely this rate. Recalculate the ratios in the previous question. What do you observe?

4  As a practical matter, West Coast Yachts is unlikely to be willing to raise external equity capital, in part because the owners don't want to dilute their existing ownership and control positions. However, West Coast Yachts is planning for a growth rate of 20 per cent next year. What are your conclusions and recommendations about the feasibility of West Coast's expansion plans?

5  Most assets can be increased as a percentage of sales. For instance, cash can be increased by any amount. However, non-current assets often must be increased in specific amounts, because it is impossible, as a practical matter, to buy part of a new plant or machine. In this case a company has a 'staircase' or 'lumpy' fixed cost structure. Assume that West Coast Yachts is currently producing at 100 per cent of capacity. As a result, to expand production, the company must set up an entirely new line at a cost of £25,000,000. Calculate the new EFN with this assumption. What does this imply about capacity utilization for West Coast Yachts next year?

## Practical Case Study

Choose a listed company from your own country. Download the financial accounts from its website and carry out a full financial statement analysis. You should calculate financial ratios for not only the most recent year but also past years as well. You should also consider the financial ratios of the company's competitors. Write a report on your analysis.

## Relevant Accounting Standards

Given that this chapter is concerned with interpreting financial statements, all international accounting standards are relevant. However, the most important ones are IAS1 *Presentation of Financial Statements*, IAS7 *Statement of Cash Flows*, IAS27 *Consolidated and Separate Financial Statements*, IAS33 *Earnings per Share*, and IFRS8 *Operating Segments*. For an excellent summary of these and other international accounting standards, visit the IASPlus website (www.iasplus.com).

## Additional Reading

The interested reader can find a whole range of readings to peruse in accounting journals such as *Journal of Accounting Research*, *The Accounting Review*, *Journal of Accounting and Economics*, *Journal of Business Finance and Accounting* and *Accounting and Business Research*. Two important recent papers that relate to corporate finance are:

Lewellen, J. (2004) 'Predicting returns with financial ratios', *Journal of Financial Economics*, vol. 74, no. 2, pp. 209–235.

Rountree, B., J.P. Weston and G. Allayannis (2008) 'Do investors value smooth performance?', *Journal of Financial Economics*, vol. 90, no. 3, pp. 237–251.

# Endnote

1 Accounting conventions can be confusing, and each country follows its own accounting standards. The most common one is published by the International Accounting Standards Board and is called the International Financial Reporting Standards (IFRS). This is used by over 100 countries, including countries in the European Union, which made the standards mandatory for all listed companies from 2005. Unlisted and private companies have more flexibility in their approach to presenting financial statements. A major change in financial statement presentation took place in January 2009, when IFRS dropped the term 'balance sheet' and replaced it with 'statement of financial position'. Given that the focus of this textbook is on listed companies, we shall adopt the conventions as laid out by the IASB.

To help you grasp the key concepts of this chapter check out the extra resources posted on the Online Learning Centre at **www.mcgraw-hill.co.uk/textbooks/hillier**

Among other helpful resources there are PowerPoint presentations, chapter outlines and mini-cases.

# Chapter 4

# Discounted Cash Flow Valuation

## KEY NOTATIONS

| | |
|---|---|
| APR | Annual percentage rate |
| $C_0$ | Cash to be invested at date 0 |
| $C_T$ | Cash flow at date $T$ |
| EAR | Effective annual rate |
| EAY | Effective annual yield |
| FV | Future value |
| $g$ | rate of growth |
| NPV | Net present value |
| PV | Present value |
| $r$ | Rate of return, or discount rate |
| $r^2$ | Interest on interest |
| $T$ | Number of periods |
| TCC | Total charge for credit |

When David Beckham left Real Madrid in 2007 to join L.A. Galaxy, his business representative, Simon Fuller, announced that Beckham would earn $250 million (£126/€160 million) over the five years he was at L.A. Galaxy. So how did Simon Fuller actually arrive at this number? If Beckham was paid the $250 million in basic salary over five years, his earnings would have been more than 10 times that of Kaka, the highest-paid footballer in Europe at the time.

In reality, the $250 million was expected income and not base salary. Beckham was paid $6.5 million in annual salary over his five years, which explains only $32.5 million of the $250 million. Herbalife, the sports nutrition firm, entered into a $25 million contract with Beckham to show their logo on his L.A. Galaxy jersey. Beckham also had existing corporate sponsorships and endorsements when he left Real Madrid, which amounted to approximately $20 million.

Because of his worldwide marketability, Beckham and AEG (the owner of L.A. Galaxy) entered into a profit-sharing deal that was directly linked to income generated through Beckham's association with L.A. Galaxy. This included football shirts (Reuters reported 250,000 sold at $80 each in his first season), merchandising, ticket sales, increased global television exposure, and other non-football related activities. One example that has been cited is the Spice Girls' reunion tour in 2007 and 2008. As a result of the marital relationship between Beckham and one of the group, the Spice Girls played throughout the US in venues owned by AEG, thereby increasing the income earned by AEG.

Much of the cash flow associated with the $250 million was risky, and depended on Beckham being a success in the United States. Unfortunately, he was injured very soon into his L.A. Galaxy career, and started only three games in his first season. He was also dropped from the England team for a period. This would have had a definite impact on Beckham's earnings because of the loss of international visibility. Moreover, because the payments were spread out over time, we must consider the time value of money, which means his earnings were worth less than reported. How much did Beckham really get? This chapter gives you the 'tools of knowledge' to answer this question, and possibly the reason for his wanting to return to Europe earlier than expected.

## 4.1 Valuation: The One-Period Case

Keith Vaughan is trying to sell a piece of undeveloped land in Wales. Yesterday he was offered £10,000 for the property. He was about ready to accept the offer when another individual offered him £11,424, to be paid a year from now. Keith has satisfied himself that both buyers are honest and financially solvent, so he has no fear that the offer he selects will fall through. These two offers are pictured as cash flows in Fig. 4.1. Which offer should Keith choose?

Mike Tuttle, Keith's financial adviser, points out that if Keith takes the first offer, he could invest the £10,000 in the bank at an insured rate of 12 per cent. At the end of one year he would have:

Alternative sale prices £10,000 £11,424

Year 0 1

**Figure 4.1** Cash flow for Keith Vaughan's sale

$$\underbrace{£10,000}_{\substack{\text{Return of}\\\text{principal}}} + \underbrace{(0.12 \times £10,000)}_{\text{Interest}} = £10,000 \times 1.12 = £11,200$$

Because this is less than the £11,424 Keith could receive from the second offer, Mike recommends that he take the latter. This analysis uses the concept of future value (FV) or compound value, which is the value of a sum after investing over one or more periods. The compound or future value of £10,000 at 12 per cent is £11,200.

An alternative method employs the concept of present value (PV). One can determine present value by asking the following question: How much money must Keith put in the bank today so that he will have £11,424 next year? We can write this algebraically as

$$PV \times 1.12 = £11,424$$

We want to solve for PV, the amount of money that yields £11,424 if invested at 12 per cent today. Solving for PV, we have

$$PV = \frac{£11,424}{1.12} = £10,200$$

The formula for PV can be written as follows:

$$\text{Present value of investment, } PV = \frac{C_1}{1+r} \qquad (4.1)$$

where $C_1$ is cash flow at date 1, and $r$ is the rate of return that Keith Vaughan requires on his land sale. It is sometimes referred to as the *discount rate*.

*Present value analysis* tells us that a payment of £11,424 to be received next year has a present value of £10,200 today. In other words, at a 12 per cent interest rate, Keith is indifferent between £10,200 today or £11,424 next year. If you gave him £10,200 today, he could put it in the bank and receive £11,424 next year.

Because the second offer has a present value of £10,200, whereas the first offer is for only £10,000, present value analysis also indicates that Keith should take the second offer. In other words, both future value analysis and present value analysis lead to the same decision. As it turns out, present value analysis and future value analysis must always lead to the same decision.

As simple as this example is, it contains the basic principles that we shall be working with over the next few chapters. We now use another example to develop the concept of net present value.

EXAMPLE
4.1

## Present Value

Lida Jennings, a financial analyst at Kaufman & Broad, a leading real estate firm, is considering recommending that Kaufman & Broad invest in a piece of land that costs €85,000. She is certain that next year the land will be worth €91,000, a sure €6,000 gain. Given that the guaranteed interest rate in the bank is 10 per cent, should Kaufman & Broad undertake the investment in land? Ms Jennings's choice is described in Fig. 4.2 with the cash flow time chart.

**Figure 4.2** Cash flows for land investment

A moment's thought should be all it takes to convince her that this is not an attractive business deal. By investing €85,000 in the land, she will have €91,000 available next year. Suppose, instead, that Kaufman & Broad puts the same €85,000 into the bank. At the interest rate of 10 per cent, this €85,000 would grow to

$$(1 + 0.10) \times €85,000 = €93,500$$

next year.

It would be foolish to buy the land when investing the same €85,000 in the financial market would produce an extra €2,500 (that is, €93,500 from the bank minus €91,000 from the land investment). This is a future value calculation.

Alternatively, she could calculate the present value of the sale price next year as

$$\text{Present value} = \frac{€91,000}{1.10} = €82,727.27$$

Because the present value of next year's sales price is less than this year's purchase price of €85,000, present value analysis also indicates that she should not recommend purchasing the property.

Frequently, businesspeople want to determine the exact *cost* or *benefit* of a decision. In Example 4.1, the decision to buy this year and sell next year can be evaluated as

$$-€2,273 = \underbrace{-€85,000}_{\substack{\text{Cost of land} \\ \text{today}}} + \underbrace{\frac{€91,000}{1.10}}_{\substack{\text{Present value} \\ \text{of next year's} \\ \text{sales price}}}$$

The formula for NPV can be written as follows:

$$\text{Net present value of investment, NPV} = -\text{Cost} + \text{PV} \tag{4.2}$$

Equation (4.2) says that the value of the investment is −€2,273, after stating all the benefits and all the costs as of date 0. We say that −€2,273 is the net present value (NPV) of the investment. That is, NPV is the present value of future cash flows minus the present value of the cost of the investment. Because the net present value is negative, Lida Jennings should not recommend purchasing the land.

Both the Vaughan and the Jennings examples deal with perfect certainty. That is, Keith Vaughan knows with perfect certainty that he could sell his land for £11,424 next year. Similarly, Lida Jennings knows with perfect certainty that Kaufman & Broad could receive €91,000 for selling its land. Unfortunately, businesspeople frequently do not know future cash flows. This uncertainty is treated in the next example.

EXAMPLE
**4.2**

## Uncertainty and Valuation

Professional Artworks plc is a firm that speculates in modern paintings. The manager is thinking of buying an original Picasso for £400,000, with the intention of selling it at the end of one year. The manager expects that the painting will be worth £480,000 in one year. The relevant cash flows are depicted in Fig. 4.3.

**Figure 4.3** Cash flows for investment in painting

Of course, this is only an expectation; the painting could be worth more or less than £480,000. Suppose the guaranteed interest rate granted by banks is 10 per cent. Should the firm purchase the piece of art?

Our first thought might be to discount at the interest rate, yielding

$$\frac{£480,000}{1.10} = £436,364$$

Because £436,364 is greater than £400,000, it looks at first glance as if the painting should be purchased. However, 10 per cent is the return one can earn on a riskless investment. Because the painting is quite risky, a higher discount rate is called for. The manager chooses a rate of 25 per cent to reflect this risk. In other words, he argues that a 25 per cent expected return is fair compensation for an investment as risky as this painting.

The present value of the painting becomes

$$\frac{£480,000}{1.25} = £384,000$$

Thus the manager believes that the painting is currently overpriced at £400,000, and does not make the purchase.

The preceding analysis is typical of decision-making in today's corporations, though real-world examples are, of course, much more complex. Unfortunately, any example with risk poses a problem not presented by a riskless example. In an example with riskless cash flows, the appropriate interest rate can be determined by simply checking with a few banks. The selection of the discount rate for a risky investment is quite a difficult task. We simply don't know at this point whether the discount rate on the painting in Example 4.2 should be 11 per cent, 25 per cent, 52 per cent, or some other percentage.

Because the choice of a discount rate is so difficult, we merely wanted to broach the subject here. We must wait until the specific material on risk and return is covered in later chapters before a risk-adjusted analysis can be presented.

## 4.2 Valuation: The Multi-Period Case

The previous section presented the calculation of future value and present value for one period only. We shall now perform the calculations for the multi-period case.

## Future Value and Compounding

Suppose an individual were to make a loan of £1. At the end of the first year, the borrower would owe the lender the principal amount of £1 plus the interest on the loan at the interest rate of $r$. For the specific case where the interest rate is, say, 9 per cent, the borrower owes the lender

$$£1 \times (1 + r) = £1 \times 1.09 = £1.09$$

At the end of the year, though, the lender has two choices. She can either take the £1.09 – or, more generally, $(1 + r)$ – out of the financial market, or she can leave it in and lend it again for a second year. The process of leaving the money in the financial market and lending it for another year is called **compounding**.

Suppose the lender decides to compound her loan for another year. She does this by taking the proceeds from her first one-year loan, £1.09, and lending this amount for the next year. At the end of next year, then, the borrower will owe her

$$£1 \times (1 + r) \times (1 + r) = £1 \times (1 + r)^2 = 1 + 2r + r^2$$
$$£1 \times (1.09) \times (1.09) = £1 \times (1.09)^2 = £1 + £0.18 + £0.0081 = £1.1881$$

This is the total she will receive two years from now by compounding the loan.

In other words, the capital market enables the investor, by providing a ready opportunity for lending, to transform £1 today into £1.1881 at the end of two years. At the end of three years, the cash will be £1 × $(1.09)^3$ = £1.2950.

The most important point to notice is that the total amount the lender receives is not just the £1 that she lent plus two years' worth of interest on £1:

$$2 \times r = 2 \times £0.09 = £0.18$$

The lender also gets back an amount $r^2$, which is the interest in the second year on the interest that was earned in the first year. The term $2 \times r$ represents **simple interest** over the two years, and the term $r^2$ is referred to as the *interest on interest*. In our example, this latter amount is exactly

$$r^2 = (£0.09)^2 = £0.0081$$

When cash is invested at **compound interest**, each interest payment is reinvested. With simple interest, the interest is not reinvested. The difference between compound interest and simple interest is illustrated in Fig. 4.4. In this example, the difference does not amount to much because the loan is for €1. If the loan were for €1 million, the lender would receive €1,188,100

*Note:* The green-shaded area indicates the difference between compound and simple interest. The difference is substantial over a period of many years.

**Figure 4.4** Simple and compound interest

in two years' time. Of this amount, €8,100 is interest on interest. The lesson is that those small numbers beyond the decimal point can add up to a lot when the transactions are for big amounts. In addition, the longer the loan lasts, the more important interest on interest becomes.

The general formula for an investment over many periods can be written as follows:

Future value of an investment:

$$FV = C_0 \times (1 + r)^T \tag{4.3}$$

where $C_0$ is the cash to be invested at date 0 (i.e. today), $r$ is the interest rate per period, and $T$ is the number of periods over which the cash is invested.

### EXAMPLE 4.3

## Interest on Interest

Suh-Pyng Ku has put £500 in a savings account at Barclays, a major bank. The account earns 7 per cent, compounded annually. How much will Ms Ku have at the end of three years? The answer is

$$£500 \times 1.07 \times 1.07 \times 1.07 = £500 \times (1.07)^3 = £612.52$$

Figure 4.5 illustrates the growth of Ms Ku's account.

**Figure 4.5** Suh-Pyng Ku's savings account

### EXAMPLE 4.4

## Compound Growth

Kevin Keasey invested £1,000 in the shares of SDH Ltd. The company pays a current dividend of £2, which is expected to grow by 20 per cent per year for the next two years. What will be the dividend of SDH Ltd after two years? A simple calculation gives

$$£2 \times (1.20)^2 = £2.88$$

Figure 4.6 illustrates the increasing value of SDH's dividends.

The two previous examples can be calculated in any one of several ways. The computations could be done by hand, by calculator, by spreadsheet, or with the help of a table. The appropriate table is Table A.3, which appears in the back of the text. This table presents *future value of £1 or €1 at the end of T periods*. The table is used by locating the appropriate interest rate on the horizontal and the appropriate number of periods on the vertical. For example, Suh-Pyng Ku would look at the following portion of Table A.3:

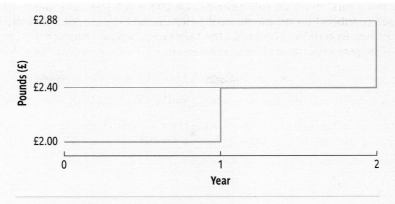

Figure 4.6 The growth of SDH dividends

|  | Interest rate | | |
| Period | 6% | 7% | 8% |
| --- | --- | --- | --- |
| 1 | 1.0600 | 1.0700 | 1.0800 |
| 2 | 1.1236 | 1.1449 | 1.1664 |
| 3 | 1.1910 | 1.2250 | 1.2597 |
| 4 | 1.2625 | 1.3108 | 1.3605 |

She could calculate the future value of her £500 as

$$£500 \times 1.2250 = £612.50$$

In the example concerning Suh-Pyng Ku, we gave you both the initial investment and the interest rate, and then asked you to calculate the future value. Alternatively, the interest rate could have been unknown, as shown in the following example.

## Finding the Rate

EXAMPLE 4.5

Carl Voigt, who recently won €10,000 in the lottery, wants to buy a car in five years. Carl estimates that the car will cost €16,105 at that time. His cash flows are displayed in Fig. 4.7.

Figure 4.7 Cash flows for purchase of Carl Voigt's car

What interest rate must he earn to be able to afford the car?
The ratio of purchase price to initial cash is

$$\frac{€16.105}{€10.000} = 1.6105$$

Thus he must earn an interest rate that allows €1 to become €1.6105 in five years. Table A.3 tells us that an interest rate of 10 per cent will allow him to purchase the car.

We can express the problem algebraically as

$$€10{,}000 \times (1 + r)^5 = €16{,}105$$

where $r$ is the interest rate needed to purchase the car. Because €16,105/€10,000 = 1.6105, we have

$$(1 + r)^5 = 1.6105$$
$$r = 10\%$$

Either the table or a calculator lets us solve for $r$.

## The Power of Compounding: A Digression

Most people who have had any experience with compounding are impressed with its power over long periods. Take equities, for example. The average annual return on the 100 largest companies in the UK has been 8.47 per cent since 1984. Now assume that this is the average return on companies on the London Stock Exchange since it opened in 1801. If your great-great-grandmother invested £1 in the Stock Exchange on the very first day of trading, it would have been worth £22,100,655 in 2008! This is 8.47 per cent compounded annually for 208 years – that is, $(1.0847)^{208} = £22{,}100{,}655$, ignoring a small rounding error.

The example illustrates the great difference between compound and simple interest. At 8.47 per cent, simple interest on £1 is 8.47 pence a year. Simple interest over 208 years is £17.62 (= 208 × £0.0847). That is, an individual withdrawing 8.47 pence every year would have withdrawn £17.62 (= 208 × £0.0847) over 208 years. This is quite a bit below the £22,100,655 that was obtained by reinvestment of all principal and interest.

### EXAMPLE 4.6

## How Much for that Island?

Some people have said that it was the best real estate deal in history. Peter Minuit, director general of New Netherlands, the Dutch West India Company's colony in North America, in 1626 allegedly bought Manhattan Island for 60 guilders' worth of trinkets from native Americans. By 1667 the Dutch were forced by the British to exchange it for Suriname (perhaps the worst real estate deal ever). This sounds cheap; but did the Dutch really get the better end of the deal? It is reported that 60 guilders was worth about $24 at the prevailing exchange rate. If the native Americans had sold the trinkets at a fair market value and invested the $24 at 5 per cent (tax free), it would now, about 380 years later, be worth more than $2.5 billion. Today, Manhattan is undoubtedly worth more than $2.5 billion, so at a 5 per cent rate of return the native Americans got the worst of the deal. However, if invested at 10 per cent, the amount of money they received would be worth about

$$\$24(1 + r)^T = 24 \times 1.1^{380} \cong \$129 \text{ quadrillion}$$

This is a lot of money. In fact, $129 quadrillion is more than all the real estate in the world is worth today. Note that no one in the history of the world has ever been able to find an investment yielding 10 per cent every year for 380 years.

## Present Value and Discounting

We now know that an annual interest rate of 9 per cent enables the investor to transform £1 today into £1.1881 two years from now. In addition, we would like to know the following:

How much would an investor need to lend today so that she could receive £1 two years from today?

Algebraically, we can write this as

$$PV \times (1.09)^2 = £1$$

In the preceding equation, PV stands for present value, the amount of money we must lend today to receive £1 in two years' time.

Solving for PV in this equation, we have

$$PV = \frac{£1}{1.1881} = £0.84$$

This process of calculating the present value of a future cash flow is called discounting. It is the opposite of compounding. To be certain that £0.84 is in fact the present value of £1 to be received in two years, we must check whether or not, if we lent £0.84 today and rolled over the loan for two years, we would get exactly £1 back. If this were the case, the capital markets would be saying that £1 received in two years' time is equivalent to having £0.84 today. Checking the exact numbers, we get

$$£0.84168 \times 1.09 \times 1.09 = £1$$

In other words, when we have capital markets with a sure interest rate of 9 per cent, we are indifferent between receiving £0.84 today or £1 in two years. We have no reason to treat these two choices differently from each other, because if we had £0.84 today and lent it out for two years, it would return £1 to us at the end of that time. The value 0.84 [= $1/(1.09)^2$] is called the present value factor. It is the factor used to calculate the present value of a future cash flow.

In the multi-period case, the formula for PV can be written as follows:

$$\text{Present value of investment, } PV = \frac{C_T}{(1 + r)^T} \tag{4.4}$$

Here, $C_T$ is the cash flow at date $T$ and $r$ is the appropriate discount rate.

## Multi-Period Discounting

EXAMPLE 4.7

Allan Hodgson will receive €10,000 three years from now. Allan can earn 8 per cent on his investments, so the appropriate discount rate is 8 per cent. What is the present value of his future cash flow? The answer is

$$PV = €10,000 \times \left(\frac{1}{1.08}\right)^3$$
$$= €10,000 \times 0.7938$$
$$= €7,938$$

Figure 4.8 illustrates the application of the present value factor to Allan's investment.

**Figure 4.8** Discounting Allan Hodgson's opportunity

When his investments grow at an 8 per cent rate of interest, Allan Hodgson is equally inclined towards receiving €7,938 now and receiving €10,000 in three years' time. After all, he could convert the €7,938 he receives today into €10,000 in three years by lending it at an interest rate of 8 per cent.

Allan Hodgson could have reached his present value calculation in one of several ways. The computation could have been done by hand, by calculator, with a spreadsheet, or with the help of Table A.1, which appears in the back of the text. This table presents the *present value of £1 or €1 to be received after T periods.* We use the table by locating the appropriate interest rate on the horizontal and the appropriate number of periods on the vertical.

The appropriate present value factor is 0.7938.

In the preceding example we gave both the interest rate and the future cash flow. Alternatively, the interest rate could have been unknown.

## Finding the Rate

**EXAMPLE 4.8**

A customer of Chaffkin GmbH wants to buy a tugboat today. Rather than pay immediately, he will pay €50,000 in three years. It will cost Chaffkin GmbH €38,610 to build the tugboat immediately. The relevant cash flows to Chaffkin GmbH are displayed in Fig. 4.9. At what interest rate would Chaffkin GmbH neither gain nor lose on the sale?

**Figure 4.9** Cash flows for tugboat

The ratio of construction cost (present value) to sale price (future value) is

$$\frac{€38,610}{€50,000} = 0.7722$$

We must determine the interest rate that allows €1 to be received in three years to have a present value of €0.7722. Table A.1 tells us that 9 per cent is that interest rate.

Frequently, an investor or a business will receive more than one cash flow. The present value of the set of cash flows is simply the sum of the present values of the individual cash flows. This is illustrated in the following example.

## Cash Flow Valuation

**EXAMPLE 4.9**

Paul Draper has won a crossword competition, and will receive the following set of cash flows over the next two years:

| Year | Cash flow |
|---|---|
| 1 | £2,000 |
| 2 | £5,000 |

Mr Draper can currently earn 6 per cent in his money market account, so the appropriate discount rate is 6 per cent. The present value of the cash flows is

| Year | Cash flow × Present value factor = Present value |
|------|--------------------------------------------------|
| 1 | $£2,000 \times \dfrac{1}{1.06} = £2,000 \times 0.943 = £1,887$ |
| 2 | $£5,000 \times \left(\dfrac{1}{1.06}\right)^{2} = £5,000 \times 0.890 = £4,450$ |
| | **Total** £6,337 |

In other words, Mr Draper is equally inclined towards receiving £6,337 today and receiving £2,000 and £5,000 over the next two years.

## NPV

**EXAMPLE 4.10**

Dratsel.com, an online broker based in Sweden, has an opportunity to invest in a new high-speed computer that costs SEK250,000. The computer will generate cash flows (from cost savings) of SEK125,000 one year from now, SEK100,000 two years from now, and SEK75,000 three years from now. The computer will be worthless after three years, and no additional cash flows will occur. Dratsel.com has determined that the appropriate discount rate is 7 per cent for this investment. Should Dratsel.com make this investment in a new high-speed computer? What is the net present value of the investment?

The cash flows and present value factors of the proposed computer are as follows:

| Year | Cash flows (SEK) | Present value factor |
|------|------------------|----------------------|
| 0 | −250,000 | $1 = 1$ |
| 1 | 125,000 | $\dfrac{1}{1.07} = 0.9346$ |
| 2 | 100,000 | $\left(\dfrac{1}{1.07}\right)^{2} = 0.8734$ |
| 3 | 75,000 | $\left(\dfrac{1}{1.07}\right)^{3} = 0.8163$ |

The present value of the cash flows is

| Year | Cash flows (SEK) × Present value factor | = | Present value (SEK) |
|------|-----------------------------------------|---|---------------------|
| 0 | −250,000 × 1 | = | −250,000 |
| 1 | 125,000 × 0.9346 | = | 116,825 |
| 2 | 100,000 × 0.8734 | = | 87,340 |
| 3 | 75,000 × 0.8163 | = | 61,225.5 |
| | Total | | 15,387.5 |

Dratsel.com should invest in the new high-speed computer because the present value of its future cash flows is greater than its cost. The NPV is SEK15,387.5.

## The Algebraic Formula

To derive an algebraic formula for the net present value of a cash flow, recall that the PV of receiving a cash flow one year from now is

$$PV = \frac{C_1}{1+r}$$

and the PV of receiving a cash flow two years from now is

$$PV = \frac{C_2}{(1+r)^2}$$

We can write the NPV of a $T$-period project as

$$\begin{aligned} NPV &= -C_0 + \frac{C_1}{1+r} + \frac{C_2}{(1+r)^2} + \cdots + \frac{C_T}{(1+r)^T} \\ &= -C_0 + \sum_{i=1}^{T} \frac{C_i}{(1+r)^i} \end{aligned} \qquad \textbf{(4.5)}$$

The initial flow, $-C_0$, is assumed to be negative because it represents an investment. The $\Sigma$ is shorthand for the sum of the series. We shall close this section by answering the question we posed at the beginning of the chapter concerning footballer David Beckham's contract. Remember that the contract called for an annual payment of $6.5 million over five years. Assume also that the $25 million sponsorship contract is spread over five years, as is the remainder of the corporate sponsorship deals, worth $20 million. We don't know full details of the profit sharing deal with AEG, so for just now we shall ignore this part of the salary. If 12 per cent is the appropriate interest rate, what is the present value of David Beckham's income?

To answer, we can calculate the present value by discounting each year's salary back to the present as follows (notice we assumed the future salaries will be paid at the end of the year):

| | |
|---|---|
| Year 1: $(6,500,000 + 5,000,000 + 4,000,000) = $13,839,286 | |
| Year 2: $15,500,000 × 1/1.12² | = $12,356,505 |
| ⋮                 ⋮ | ⋮ |
| Year 5: $15,500,000 × 1/1.12⁵ | = $8,795,116.3 |

If you fill in the missing rows and then add (do it for practice), you will see that Beckham's basic contract had a present value of about $55.87 million, or only about 70 per cent of the $77.5 (15,500,000 × 5 years) million reported value, but still pretty good.

## 4.3 Compounding Periods

So far, we have assumed that compounding and discounting occur yearly. Sometimes, compounding may occur more frequently than just once a year. For example, imagine that a bank pays a 10 per cent interest rate 'compounded semi-annually'. This means that a £1,000 deposit in the bank would be worth £1,000 × 1.05 = £1,050 after six months, and £1,050 × 1.05 = £1,102.50 at the end of the year.

The end-of-year wealth can be written as

$$£1,000\left(1 + \frac{0.10}{2}\right)^2 = £1,000 \times (1.05)^2 = £1,102.50$$

Of course, a £1,000 deposit would be worth £1,100 (£1,000 × 1.10) with yearly compounding. Note that the future value at the end of one year is greater with semi-annual compounding than with yearly compounding. With yearly compounding, the original £1,000 remains the investment base for the full year. The original £1,000 is the investment base only for the first six months with semi-annual compounding. The base over the second six months is £1,050. Hence one gets *interest on interest* with semi-annual compounding.

Because £1,000 × 1.1025 = £1,102.50, 10 per cent compounded semi-annually is the same as 10.25 per cent compounded annually. In other words, a rational investor could not care less whether she is quoted a rate of 10 per cent compounded semi-annually or a rate of 10.25 per cent compounded annually.

Quarterly compounding at 10 per cent yields wealth at the end of one year of

$$£1,000\left(1+\frac{0.10}{4}\right)^4 = £1,103.81$$

More generally, compounding an investment $m$ times a year provides end-of-year wealth of

$$C_0\left(1+\frac{r}{m}\right)^m \tag{4.6}$$

where $C_0$ is the initial investment and $r$ is the stated annual interest rate. The stated annual interest rate is the annual interest rate without consideration of compounding.

**EXAMPLE 4.11**

## EARs

What is the end-of-year wealth if Jane Christine receives a stated annual interest rate of 24 per cent compounded monthly on a €1 investment?

Using Eq. (4.6), her wealth is

$$€1\left(1+\frac{0.24}{12}\right)^{12} = €1 \times (1.02)^{12}$$
$$= €1.2682$$

The annual rate of return is 26.82 per cent. This annual rate of return is called either the effective annual rate (EAR) or the effective annual yield (EAY). Because of compounding, the effective annual interest rate is greater than the stated annual interest rate of 24 per cent. Algebraically, we can rewrite the effective annual interest rate as follows:

Effective annual rate:

$$\left(1+\frac{r}{m}\right)^m - 1 \tag{4.7}$$

Students are often bothered by the subtraction of 1 in Eq. (4.7). Note that end-of-year wealth is composed of both the interest earned over the year and the original principal. We remove the original principal by subtracting 1 in Eq. (4.7).

**EXAMPLE 4.12**

## Compounding Frequencies

If the stated annual rate of interest, 8 per cent, is compounded quarterly, what is the effective annual rate?

Using Eq. (4.7), we have

$$\left(1+\frac{r}{m}\right)^m - 1 = \left(1+\frac{0.08}{4}\right)^4 - 1 = 0.0824 = 8.24\%$$

Referring back to our original example, where $C_0 = £1,000$ and $r = 10\%$, we can generate the following table:

| $C_0$ (£) | Compounding frequency, $m$ | $C_1$ (£) | Effective annual rate $= \left(1+\dfrac{r}{m}\right)^m - 1$ |
|---|---|---|---|
| 1,000 | Yearly ($m = 1$) | 1,100.00 | 0.10 |
| 1,000 | Semi-annually ($m = 2$) | 1,102.50 | 0.1025 |
| 1,000 | Quarterly ($m = 4$) | 1,103.81 | 0.10381 |
| 1,000 | Daily ($m = 365$) | 1,105.16 | 0.10516 |

## Compounding over Many Years

Equation (4.6) applies for an investment over one year. For an investment over one or more (T) years, the formula becomes

Future value with compounding:

$$FV = C_0 \left(1 + \frac{r}{m}\right)^{mT}$$

(4.8)

---

EXAMPLE
**4.13**

## Multi-Year Compounding

Harry DeAngelo is investing €5,000 at a stated annual interest rate of 12 per cent per year, compounded quarterly, for five years. What is his wealth at the end of five years?

Using Eq. (4.8), his wealth is

$$
\begin{aligned}
€5,000 \times \left(1 + \frac{0.12}{4}\right)^{4 \times 5} &= €5,000 \times (1.03)^{20} \\
&= €5,000 \times 1.8061 \\
&= €9,030.50
\end{aligned}
$$

## The Annual Percentage Rate

Given the many different ways in which interest rates can be presented to the public, the European Union introduced a directive in 2004 that harmonized the way in which interest rates in any credit agreement for under €50,000 are presented. The UK extended the directive to all regulated loans, and the Netherlands uses it for mortgage loans. This harmonized interest rate is called the annual percentage rate (APR); it expresses the *total* cost of borrowing or investing as a percentage interest rate.

The reason for an APR is that a credit agreement may not just include interest payments, but also management fees, arrangement fees, and other sundry costs that will affect the total charge for credit (TCC). In addition, knowing the interest rate is still not enough to guarantee full comparability of different loans or investments. As shown above, the compounding frequency and the date when interest is charged will influence the effective annual rate of interest.

Under the EU directive, all providers of credit must prominently show the APR in any document or advertising material that promotes a particular type of loan or investment. To calculate APR, we use the standard present value formula. The main difference is in the cash flows that are included in the calculation.

$$
\begin{aligned}
PV &= C_0 + \frac{C_1}{1 + APR} + \frac{C_2}{(1 + APR)^2} + \cdots + \frac{C_T}{(1 + APR)^T} \\
&= C_0 + \sum_{i=1}^{T} \frac{C_i}{(1 + APR)^i}
\end{aligned}
$$

(4.9)

---

EXAMPLE
**4.14**

## APR

After much deliberation, Mary Moan decides to buy a new Mercedes Benz car for her family. The sale price of the car is £30,000. Mary arranges financing through the Mercedes dealer, who quotes a simple annual interest rate of 12 per cent on the original borrowed amount over three years, payable in 36 monthly instalments. This means that the lender will charge 12 per cent interest on the original loan of £30,000 every year for three years. Each year, the interest charge will be 12 per cent of £30,000 = £3,600, making a total interest payment of £10,800 over three years.

The regular monthly instalments that Mary must pay are

$$\text{Monthly instalment} = (£30,000 + £10,800)/36 = £1,133.33$$

In addition to the interest payments, the Mercedes dealer charges a £250 administration fee, which must be paid when the financing agreement is made. We now solve for APR in Eq. (4.9):

$$£30,000 = £250 + \frac{£1,133.33}{(1+APR)^{1/12}} + \frac{£1,133.33}{(1+APR)^{2/12}} + \cdots + \frac{£1,133.33}{(1+APR)^{36/12}}$$

This gives an annual percentage rate (APR) of 24.13%! The lender must also state the total amount paid at the end of the loan, which in this case is £41,049.88, and the total charge for credit is £11,049.88 (£41,049.88 − £30,000).

The definition used by the European Union for APR is very different from the formula used in the United States, and this can cause considerable confusion when European students read finance textbooks aimed at an American market. In the US the APR is simply the stated annual interest. Remember this if you ever plan to take out a loan overseas!

## Continuous Compounding

The previous discussion shows that we can compound much more frequently than once a year. We could compound semi-annually, quarterly, monthly, daily, hourly, each minute, or even more often. The limiting case would be to compound every infinitesimal instant, which is commonly called **continuous compounding**. Surprisingly, banks and other financial institutions sometimes quote continuously compounded rates, which is why we study them.

Though the idea of compounding this rapidly may boggle the mind, a simple formula is involved. With continuous compounding, the value at the end of $T$ years is expressed as

$$C_0 \times e^{rT} \tag{4.10}$$

where $C_0$ is the initial investment, $r$ is the stated annual interest rate, and $T$ is the number of years over which the investment runs. The number $e$ is a constant and approximately equal to 2.718. It is not an unknown like $C_0$, $r$ and $T$.

EXAMPLE
4.15

## Continuous Compounding

Linda DeFond invested £1,000 at a continuously compounded rate of 10 per cent for one year. What is the value of her wealth at the end of one year?

From Eq. (4.10) we have

$$£1,000 \times e^{0.10} = £1,000 \times 1.1052 = £1,105.20$$

This number can easily be read from Table A.5. We merely set $r$, the value on the horizontal dimension, to 10 per cent and $T$, the value on the vertical dimension, to 1. For this problem the relevant portion of the table is shown here:

| Period, T | Continuously compounded rate, r | | |
|---|---|---|---|
| | 9% | 10% | 11% |
| 1 | 1.0942 | 1.1052 | 1.1163 |
| 2 | 1.1972 | 1.2214 | 1.2461 |
| 3 | 1.3100 | 1.3499 | 1.3910 |

Note that a continuously compounded rate of 10 per cent is equivalent to an annually compounded rate of 10.52 per cent. In other words, Linda DeFond would not care whether her bank quoted a continuously compounded rate of 10 per cent or a 10.52 per cent rate, compounded annually.

EXAMPLE
**4.16**

# Continuous Compounding (continued)

Linda DeFond's brother, Mark, invested £1,000 at a continuously compounded rate of 10 per cent for two years.

The appropriate formula here is

$$£1,000 \times e^{0.10 \times 2} = £1,000 \times e^{0.20} = £1,221.40$$

Using the portion of the table of continuously compounded rates shown in the previous example, we find the value to be 1.2214.

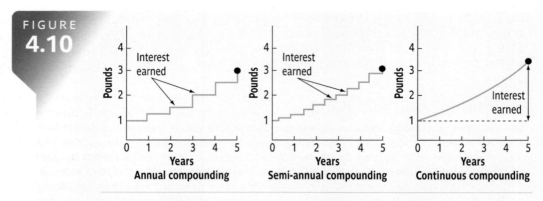

**Figure 4.10** Annual, semi-annual, and continuous compounding.

Figure 4.10 illustrates the relationship between annual, semi-annual, and continuous compounding. Semi-annual compounding gives rise to both a smoother curve and a higher ending value than does annual compounding. Continuous compounding has both the smoothest curve and the highest ending value of all.

EXAMPLE
**4.17**

# Present Value with Continuous Compounding

A crossword competition is going to pay you €1,000 at the end of four years. If the annual continuously compounded rate of interest is 8 per cent, what is the present value of this payment?

$$€1,000 \times \frac{1}{e^{0.08 \times 4}} = €1,000 \times \frac{1}{1.3771}$$
$$= €726.16$$

## 4.4 Simplifications

The first part of this chapter has examined the concepts of future value and present value. Although these concepts allow us to answer a host of problems concerning the time value of money, the human effort involved can be excessive. For example, consider a bank calculating the present value of a 20-year monthly mortgage. This mortgage has 240 (= 20 × 12) payments, so a lot of time is needed to perform a conceptually simple task.

Because many basic finance problems are potentially time-consuming, we search for simplifications in this section. We provide simplifying formulae for four classes of cash flow stream:

1   Perpetuity
2   Growing perpetuity
3   Annuity
4   Growing annuity

## Perpetuity

A perpetuity is a constant stream of cash flows without end. If you are thinking that perpetuities have no relevance to reality, it will surprise you that there is a well-known case of an unending cash flow stream: the British bonds called *consols*. An investor purchasing a consol is entitled to receive yearly interest from the British government for ever.

How can the price of a consol be determined? Consider a consol that pays a coupon of $C$ each year, and will do so for ever. Simply applying the PV formula gives us

$$PV = \frac{C}{1+r} + \frac{C}{(1+r)^2} + \frac{C}{(1+r)^3} + \cdots$$

where the dots at the end of the formula stand for the infinite string of terms that continues the formula. Series like the preceding one are called *geometric series*. It is well known that even though they have an infinite number of terms, the whole series has a finite sum because each term is only a fraction of the preceding term. Before turning to our calculus books, though, it is worth going back to our original principles to see if a bit of financial intuition can help us find the PV.

The present value of the consol is the present value of all of its future coupons. In other words, it is an amount of money that, if an investor had it today, would enable him to achieve the same pattern of expenditures that the consol and its coupons would. Suppose an investor wanted to spend exactly $C$ euros each year. If he had the consol, he could do this. How much money must he have today to spend the same amount? Clearly, he would need exactly enough so that the interest on the money would be $C$ euros per year. If he had any more, he could spend more than $C$ euros each year. If he had any less, he would eventually run out of money spending $C$ euros per year.

The amount that will give the investor $C$ euros each year, and therefore the present value of the consol, is simply

$$PV = \frac{C}{r} \tag{4.11}$$

To confirm that this is the right answer, notice that if we lend the amount $C/r$, the interest it earns each year will be

$$\text{Interest} = \frac{C}{r} \times r = C$$

which is exactly the consol payment. We have arrived at this formula for a consol:

Formula for present value of perpetuity:

$$PV = \frac{C}{1+r} + \frac{C}{(1+r)^2} + \frac{C}{(1+r)^3} + \cdots$$
$$= \frac{C}{r} \tag{4.12}$$

It is comforting to know how easily we can use a bit of financial intuition to solve this mathematical problem.

**EXAMPLE 4.18**

## Perpetuities

Consider a perpetuity paying £100 a year. If the relevant interest rate is 8 per cent, what is the value of the consol?

Using Eq. (4.11) we have

$$PV = \frac{£100}{0.08} = £1,250$$

Now suppose that interest rates fall to 6 per cent. Using Eq. (4.11) the value of the perpetuity is

$$PV = \frac{£100}{0.06} = £1,666.67$$

Note that the value of the perpetuity rises with a drop in the interest rate. Conversely, the value of the perpetuity falls with a rise in the interest rate.

## Growing Perpetuity

Imagine an apartment building where cash flows to the landlord after expenses will be €100,000 next year. These cash flows are expected to rise at 5 per cent per year. If one assumes that this rise will continue indefinitely, the cash flow stream is termed a growing perpetuity. The relevant interest rate is 11 per cent. Therefore, the appropriate discount rate is 11 per cent, and the present value of the cash flows can be represented as

$$PV = \frac{€100,000}{1.11} + \frac{€100,000(1.05)}{(1.11)^2} + \frac{€100,000(1.05)^2}{(1.11)^3} + \cdots$$
$$+ \frac{€100,000(1.05)^{N-1}}{(1.11)^N} + \cdots$$

Algebraically, we can write the formula as

$$PV = \frac{C}{1+r} + \frac{C \times (1+g)}{(1+r)^2} + \frac{C \times (1+g)^2}{(1+r)^3} + \cdots + \frac{C \times (1+g)^{N-1}}{(1+r)^N} + \cdots$$

where $C$ is the cash flow to be received one period hence, $g$ is the rate of growth per period, expressed as a percentage, and $r$ is the appropriate discount rate.

Fortunately, this formula reduces to the following simplification:

Formula for present value of growing perpetuity:

$$PV = \frac{C}{r-g} \tag{4.13}$$

From Eq. (4.13) the present value of the cash flows from the apartment building is

$$\frac{€100,000}{0.11 - 0.05} = €1,666,667$$

There are three important points concerning the growing perpetuity formula:

1   *The numerator*: The numerator in Eq. (4.13) is the cash flow one period hence, not at date 0.

2   *The discount rate and the growth rate*: The discount rate $r$ must be greater than the growth rate $g$ for the growing perpetuity formula to work. Consider the case in which the growth rate approaches the interest rate in magnitude. Then the denominator in the growing perpetuity formula gets infinitesimally small and the present value grows infinitely large. The present value is in fact undefined when $r$ is less than $g$.

3   *The timing assumption*: Cash generally flows into and out of real-world firms both randomly and nearly continuously. However, Eq. (4.13) assumes that cash flows are received and disbursed at regular and discrete points in time. In the example of the apartment, we assumed that the net cash flows of €100,000 occurred only once a year. In reality, rent is usually paid every month. Payments for maintenance and other expenses may occur any time within the year.

We can apply the growing perpetuity formula of Eq. (4.13) only by assuming a regular and discrete pattern of cash flows. Although this assumption is sensible, because the formula saves so much time, the user should never forget that it is an *assumption*. This point will be mentioned again in the chapters ahead.

## Paying Dividends

EXAMPLE
4.19

Pindado SA is *just about* to pay a dividend of €3.00 per share. Investors anticipate that the annual dividend will rise by 6 per cent a year for ever. The applicable discount rate is 11 per cent. What is the share price today?

The numerator in Eq. (4.13) is the cash flow to be received next period. Since the growth rate is 6 per cent, the dividend next year is €3.18 (= €3.00 × 1.06). The share price today is

$$€66.60 = \underbrace{€3.00}_{\text{Imminent dividend}} + \underbrace{\frac{€3.18}{0.11 - 0.06}}_{\substack{\text{Present value of all} \\ \text{dividends beginning} \\ \text{a year from now}}}$$

The price of €66.60 includes both the dividend to be received immediately and the present value of all dividends beginning a year from now. Eq. (4.13) makes it possible to calculate only the present value of all dividends beginning a year from now.

A few words should be said about terminology. Authors of financial textbooks generally use one of two conventions to refer to time. A minority of financial writers treat cash flows as being received on exact *dates* – for example date 0, date 1, and so forth. Under this convention, date 0 represents the present time. However, because a year is an interval, not a specific moment in time, the great majority of authors refer to cash flows that occur at the end of a year (or alternatively, the end of a *period*). Under this *end-of-the-year* convention, the end of year 0 is the present, the end of year 1 occurs one period hence, and so on. (The beginning of year 0 has already passed and is not generally referred to.)[1]

The interchangeability of the two conventions can be seen from the following chart:

| Date 0 | Date 1 | Date 2 | Date 3 | ... |
|---|---|---|---|---|
| = Now | | | | |
| End of year 0 | End of year 1 | End of year 2 | End of year 3 | ... |
| = Now | | | | |

We strongly believe that the *dates convention* reduces ambiguity. However, we use both conventions because you are likely to see the *end-of-year convention* in later courses. In fact, both conventions may appear in the same example for the sake of practice.

## Annuity

An **annuity** is a level stream of regular payments that lasts for a fixed number of periods. Not surprisingly, annuities are among the most common kinds of financial instruments. The pensions that people receive when they retire are often in the form of an annuity. Leases and mortgages are also often annuities.

To figure out the present value of an annuity we need to evaluate the following function:

$$\frac{C}{1+r} + \frac{C}{(1+r)^2} + \frac{C}{(1+r)^3} + \cdots + \frac{C}{(1+r)^T}$$

The present value of receiving the coupons for only $T$ periods must be less than the present value of a consol, but how much less? To answer this, we have to look at consols a bit more closely. Consider the following time chart:

| Date (or end of year) | Now | | | | | | | |
| | 0 | 1 | 2 | 3 | T | | (T+1) | (T+2) |
|---|---|---|---|---|---|---|---|---|
| Consol 1 | | C | C | C... | C | | C | C... |
| Consol 2 | | | | | | | C | C... |
| Annuity | | C | C | C... | C | | | |

Consol 1 is a normal consol with its first payment at date 1. The first payment of consol 2 occurs at date $T + 1$.

The present value of having a cash flow of $C$ at each of $T$ dates is equal to the present value of consol 1 minus the present value of consol 2. The present value of consol 1 is given by

$$PV = \frac{C}{r} \tag{4.14}$$

Consol 2 is just a consol with its first payment at date $T + 1$. From the perpetuity formula, this consol will be worth $C/r$ at date $T$.[2] However, we do not want the value at date $T$. We want the value now – in other words, the present value at date 0. We must discount $C/r$ back by $T$ periods. Therefore, the present value of consol 2 is

$$PV = \frac{C}{r} \left[ \frac{1}{(1 + r)^T} \right] \tag{4.15}$$

The present value of having cash flows for $T$ years is the present value of a consol with its first payment at date 1 minus the present value of a consol with its first payment at date $T + 1$. Thus the present value of an annuity is Eq. (4.14) minus Eq. (4.15). This can be written as

$$\frac{C}{r} - \frac{C}{r} \left[ \frac{1}{(1 + r)^T} \right]$$

This simplifies to the following:

Formula for present value of annuity:

$$PV = C \left[ \frac{1}{r} - \frac{1}{r(1 + r)^T} \right]$$

This can also be written as

$$PV = C \left[ \frac{1 - \dfrac{1}{(1 + r)^T}}{r} \right] \tag{4.16}$$

EXAMPLE
4.20

## Lottery Valuation

Mark Young has just won a competition paying £50,000 a year for 20 years. He is to receive his first payment a year from now. The competition organizers advertise this as the Million Pound Competition because £1,000,000 = £50,000 × 20. If the interest rate is 8 per cent, what is the true value of the prize?

Equation (4.16) yields

$$\text{Present value of million pound competition} = £50,000 \times \left[ \frac{1 - \dfrac{1}{(1.08)^{20}}}{0.08} \right]$$

$$
\begin{array}{ccc}
\text{Periodic payment} & \times & \text{Annuity factor} \\
= £50,000 & \times & 9.8181
\end{array}
$$

$$= £490,905$$

Rather than being overjoyed at winning, Mr Young sues the company for misrepresentation and fraud. His legal brief states that he was promised £1 million but received only £490,905.

The term we use to compute the present value of the stream of level payments, $C$, for $T$ years is called an annuity factor. The annuity factor in the current example is 9.8181. Because the annuity factor is used so often in PV calculations, we have included it in Table A.2 in the back of this book. The table gives the values of these factors for a range of interest rates, $r$, and maturity dates, $T$.

The annuity factor as expressed in the brackets of Eq. (4.16) is a complex formula. For simplification, we may from time to time refer to the annuity factor as

$$A_r^T$$

This expression stands for the present value of £1 or €1 a year for $T$ years at an interest rate of $r$.

We can also provide a formula for the future value of an annuity:

$$FV = C\left[\frac{(1+r)^T}{r} - \frac{1}{r}\right] = C\left[\frac{(1+r)^T - 1}{r}\right] \tag{4.17}$$

As with present value factors for annuities, we have compiled future value factors in Table A.3 in the back of this book.

## Retirement Investing

**EXAMPLE 4.21**

Suppose you put £3,000 per year into a cash investment savings account. The account pays 6 per cent interest per year, tax-free. How much will you have when you retire in 30 years?

This question asks for the future value of an annuity of £3,000 per year for 30 years at 6 per cent, which we can calculate as follows:

$$FV = C\left[\frac{(1+r)^T - 1}{r}\right]$$
$$= £3,000 \times \left[\frac{1.06^{30} - 1}{0.06}\right]$$
$$= £3,000 \times 79.0582$$
$$= £237,174.56$$

So you'll have close to a quarter of a million pounds in the account.

Our experience is that annuity formulae are not hard for the beginning student, but they are tricky.

We present four tricks next.

**Trick 1: A Delayed Annuity** One of the tricks in working with annuities or perpetuities is getting the timing exactly right. This is particularly true when an annuity or perpetuity begins at a date many periods in the future. We have found that even the brightest beginning student can make errors here. Consider the following example.

## Delayed Annuities

**EXAMPLE 4.22**

Danielle Caravello will receive a four-year annuity of €500 per year, beginning at date 6. If the interest rate is 10 per cent, what is the present value of her annuity? This situation can be graphed as follows:

The analysis involves two steps:

1 Calculate the present value of the annuity using Eq. (4.16).

Present value of annuity at date 5:

$$€500 \left[ \frac{1 - \frac{1}{(1.04)^4}}{0.10} \right] = €500 \times A_{0.10}^4$$
$$= €500 \times 3.1699$$
$$= €1,584.95$$

Note that €1,584.95 represents the present value at *date 5*.

Students frequently think that €1,584.95 is the present value at date 6 because the annuity begins at date 6. However, our formula values the annuity as of one period prior to the first payment. This can be seen in the most typical case, where the first payment occurs at date 1. The formula values the annuity as of date 0 in that case.

2 Discount the present value of the annuity back to date 0.

Present value at date 0:

$$\frac{€1,584.95}{(1.10)^5} = €984.13$$

Again, it is worth while mentioning that because the annuity formula brings Danielle's annuity back to date 5, the second calculation must discount over the remaining five periods.

**Trick 2: Annuity Due**   The annuity formula of Eq. (4.16) assumes that the first annuity payment begins a full period hence. This type of annuity is sometimes called an *annuity in arrears* or an *ordinary annuity*. What happens if the annuity begins today – in other words, at date 0?

## Annuity Due

EXAMPLE
**4.23**

In a previous example, Mark Young received £50,000 a year for 20 years from a competition. In that example, he was to receive the first payment a year from the winning date. Let us now assume that the first payment occurs immediately. The total number of payments remains 20.

Under this new assumption, we have a 19-date annuity with the first payment occurring at date 1 – plus an extra payment at date 0. The present value is

$$
\begin{array}{ccc}
£50,000 & + & £50,000 \times A_{0.08}^{19} \\
\text{Payment at date 0} & & \text{19-year annuity}
\end{array}
$$
$$= £50,000 + (£50,000 \times 9.6036)$$
$$= £530,180$$

£530,180, the present value in this example, is greater than £490,905, the present value in the earlier competition example. This is to be expected, because the annuity of the current example begins earlier. An annuity with an immediate initial payment is called an *annuity in advance* or, more commonly, an *annuity due*. Always remember that Eq. (4.16) and Table A.2 in this book refer to an *ordinary annuity*.

Trick 3: The Infrequent Annuity   The following example treats an annuity with payments occurring less frequently than once a year.

## Infrequent Annuities

EXAMPLE 4.24

Ann Chen receives an annuity of £450, payable once every two years. The annuity stretches out over 20 years. The first payment occurs at date 2 – that is, two years from today. The annual interest rate is 6 per cent.

The trick is to determine the interest rate over a two-year period. The interest rate over two years is

$$(1.06 \times 1.06) - 1 = 12.36\%$$

That is, £100 invested over two years will yield £112.36.

What we want is the present value of a £450 annuity over 10 periods, with an interest rate of 12.36 per cent per period:

$$£450 \left[ \frac{1 - \dfrac{1}{(1 + 0.1236)^{10}}}{0.1236} \right] = £450 \times A^{10}_{0.1236} = £2,505.57$$

Trick 4: Equating Present Value of Two Annuities   The following example equates the present value of inflows with the present value of outflows.

## Working with Annuities

EXAMPLE 4.25

Harold and Helen Nash are saving for the university education of their newborn daughter, Susan. The Nashes estimate that university expenses will be €30,000 per year when their daughter reaches university in 18 years. The annual interest rate over the next few decades will be 14 per cent. How much money must they deposit in the bank each year so that their daughter will be completely supported through four years of university?

To simplify the calculations, we assume that Susan is born today. Her parents will make the first of her four annual tuition payments on her 18th birthday. They will make equal bank deposits on each of her first 17 birthdays, but no deposit at date 0. This is illustrated as follows:

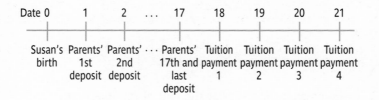

Mr and Mrs Nash will be making deposits to the bank over the next 17 years. They will be withdrawing €30,000 per year over the following four years. We can be sure they will be able to withdraw fully €30,000 per year if the present value of the deposits is equal to the present value of the four €30,000 withdrawals.

This calculation requires three steps. The first two determine the present value of the withdrawals. The final step determines yearly deposits that will have a present value equal to that of the withdrawals.

▶ 1 We calculate the present value of the four years at university using the annuity formula:

$$€30{,}000 \times \left[ \frac{1 - \frac{1}{(1.14)^4}}{0.14} \right] = €30.000 \times A_{0.14}^4$$

$$= €30{,}000 \times 2{,}9137$$
$$= €87{,}411$$

We assume that Susan enters university on her 18th birthday. Given our discussion in Trick 1, €87,411 represents the present value at date 17.

2 We calculate the present value of the university education at date 0 as

$$\frac{€87{,}411}{(1.14)^{17}} = €9{,}422.91$$

3 Assuming that Harold and Helen Nash make deposits to the bank at the end of each of the 17 years, we calculate the annual deposit that will yield a present value of all deposits of €9,422.91. This is calculated as

$$C \times A_{0.14}^{17} = €9{,}422.91$$

Because $A_{0.14}^{17} = 6.3729$

$$C = \frac{€9{,}422.91}{6.3729} = €1{,}478.59$$

Thus deposits of €1,478.59 made at the end of each of the first 17 years and invested at 14 per cent will provide enough money to make tuition payments of €30,000 over the following four years.

## Growing Annuity

Cash flows in business are likely to grow over time, either because of real growth or because of inflation. The growing perpetuity, which assumes an infinite number of cash flows, provides one formula to handle this growth. We now consider a *growing annuity*, which is a *finite* number of growing cash flows. Because perpetuities of any kind are rare, a formula for a growing annuity would be useful indeed. Here is the formula:

Formula for present value of growing annuity:

$$PV = C \left[ \frac{1}{r - g} - \frac{1}{r - g} \times \left( \frac{1 + g}{1 + r} \right)^T \right]$$

$$= C \left[ \frac{1 - \left( \frac{1 + g}{1 + r} \right)^T}{r - g} \right].$$

(4.18)

As before, $C$ is the payment to occur at the end of the first period, $r$ is the interest rate, $g$ is the rate of growth per period, expressed as a percentage, and $T$ is the number of periods for the annuity.

EXAMPLE
**4.26**

## Growing Annuities

Stuart Gabriel, a second-year MBA student, has just been offered a job at £80,000 a year. He anticipates his salary increasing by 9 per cent a year until his retirement in 40 years. Given an interest rate of 20 per cent, what is the present value of his lifetime salary?

We simplify by assuming he will be paid his £80,000 salary exactly one year from now, and that his salary will continue to be paid in annual instalments. The appropriate discount rate is 20 per cent. From Eq. (4.18), the calculation is

$$\text{Present value of Stuart's lifetime salary} = £80,000 \times \left[ 1 - \frac{\left(\frac{1.09}{1.20}\right)^{40}}{0.20 - 0.09} \right]$$
$$= £711,730.71$$

EXAMPLE
**4.27**

## More Growing Annuities

In our previous example, Helen and Harold Nash planned to make 17 identical payments to fund the university education of their daughter, Susan. Alternatively, imagine that they planned to increase their payments at 4 per cent per year. What would their first payment be?

The first two steps of the previous Nash family example showed that the present value of the college costs was €9,422.91. These two steps would be the same here. However, the third step must be altered. Now we must ask: How much should their first payment be so that, if payments increase by 4 per cent per year, the present value of all payments will be €9,422.91?

We set the growing annuity formula equal to €9,422.91 and solve for C:

$$C \left[ 1 - \frac{\left(\frac{1+g}{1+r}\right)^{T}}{r-g} \right] = C \left[ 1 - \frac{\left(\frac{1.04}{1.14}\right)^{17}}{0.14 - 0.04} \right]$$
$$= €9,422.91$$

Here, $C = €1,192.78$. Thus the deposit on their daughter's first birthday is €1,192.78. The deposit on the second birthday is €1,240.49 (= 1.04 × €1,192.78), and so on.

## 4.5 What Is a Firm Worth?

Suppose you are a business appraiser trying to determine the value of small companies. How can you determine what a firm is worth? One way to think about the question of how much a firm is worth is to calculate the present value of its future cash flows.

Let us consider the example of a firm that is expected to generate net cash flows (cash inflows minus cash outflows) of £5,000 in the first year and £2,000 for each of the next five years. The firm can be sold for £10,000 seven years from now. The owners of the firm would like to be able to make 10 per cent on their investment in the firm.

The value of the firm is found by multiplying the net cash flows by the appropriate present value factor. The value of the firm is simply the sum of the present values of the individual net cash flows.

The present value of the net cash flows is given next.

| The present value of the firm | | | |
|---|---|---|---|
| End of year | Net cash flow of the firm (£) | Present value factor (10%) | Present value of net cash flows (£) |
| 1 | 5,000 | 0.90909 | 4,545.45 |
| 2 | 2,000 | 0.82645 | 1,652.90 |
| 3 | 2,000 | 0.75131 | 1,502.62 |
| 4 | 2,000 | 0.68301 | 1,366.02 |

| The present value of the firm | | | |
| --- | --- | --- | --- |
| End of year | Net cash flow of the firm (£) | Present value factor (10%) | Present value of net cash flows (£) |
| 5 | 2,000 | 0.62092 | 1,241.84 |
| 6 | 2,000 | 0.56447 | 1,128.94 |
| 7 | 10,000 | 0.51316 | 5,131.58 |
| | | Present value of firm | 16,569.35 |

We can also use the simplifying formula for an annuity:

$$\frac{£5,000}{1.1} + \frac{2,000 \times A_{0.10}^5}{1.1} + \frac{10,000}{(1.1)^7} = £16,569.35$$

Suppose you have the opportunity to acquire the firm for £12,000. Should you acquire the firm? The answer is yes, because the NPV is positive:

$$NPV = PV - Cost$$
$$£4,569.35 = £16,569.35 - £12,000$$

The incremental value (NPV) of acquiring the firm is £4,569.35.

## Firm Valuation

EXAMPLE
**4.28**

Daniele's Pizza Company is contemplating investing €1 million in four new outlets in Italy. Massimiliano Barbi, the firm's chief financial officer (CFO), has estimated that the investments will pay out cash flows of €200,000 per year for nine years, and nothing thereafter. (The cash flows will occur at the end of each year, and there will be no cash flow after year 9.) Mr Barbi has determined that the relevant discount rate for this investment is 15 per cent. This is the rate of return that the firm can earn at comparable projects. Should Daniele make the investments in the new outlets?

The decision can be evaluated as follows:

$$NPV = -€1,000,000 + \frac{€200,000}{1.15} + \frac{€200,000}{(1.15)^2} + \cdots + \frac{€200,000}{(1.15)^9}$$
$$= -€1,000,000 + €200,000 \times A_{0.15}^9$$
$$= -€1,000,000 + €954,316.78$$
$$= -€45,683.22$$

The present value of the four new outlets is only €954,316.78. The outlets are worth less than they cost. Daniele should not make the investment, because the NPV is −€45,683.22. If Daniele requires a 15 per cent rate of return, the new outlets are not a good investment.

## Summary and Conclusions

1   Two basic concepts, *future value* and *present value*, were introduced at the beginning of this chapter. With a 10 per cent interest rate, an investor with £1 today can generate a future value of £1.10 in a year, £1.21 [= £1 × (1.10)²] in two years, and so on. Conversely, present value analysis places a current value on a future cash flow. With the same 10 per cent interest rate, £1 to be received in one year has a present value of £0.909 (= £1/1.10) in year 0. £1 to be received in two years has a present value of £0.826 [= £1/(1.10)²].

2   We commonly express an interest rate as, say, 12 per cent per year. However, we can speak of the interest rate as 3 per cent per quarter. Although the stated annual interest rate remains 12 per cent (= 3 per cent × 4), the effective annual interest rate is 12.55 per cent $[= (1.03)^4 \times 1]$. In other words, the compounding process increases the future value of an investment. The limiting case is continuous compounding, where funds are assumed to be reinvested every infinitesimal instant.

3   A basic quantitative technique for financial decision-making is net present value analysis. The net present value formula for an investment that generates cash flows $(C_i)$ in future periods is

$$NVP = -C_0 + \frac{C_1}{(1+r)} + \frac{C_2}{(1+r)^2} + \cdots + \frac{C_r}{(1+r)^T}$$
$$= -C_0 + \sum_{i=1}^{T} \frac{C_i}{(1+r)^i}$$

The formula assumes that the cash flow at date 0 is the initial investment (a cash outflow).

4   Frequently, the actual calculation of present value is long and tedious. The computation of the present value of a long-term mortgage with monthly payments is a good example of this. We presented four simplifying formulae:

Perpetuity:

$$PV = \frac{C}{r}$$

Growing perpetuity:

$$PV = \frac{C}{r-g}$$

Annuity:

$$PV = C \left[ \frac{1 - \frac{1}{(1+r)^T}}{r} \right]$$

Growing annuity:

$$PV = C \left[ \frac{1 - \left(\frac{1+g}{1+r}\right)^T}{r-g} \right]$$

5   We stressed a few practical considerations in the application of these formulae:

(a)  The numerator in each of the formulae, $C$, is the cash flow to be received *one full period hence*.

(b)  Cash flows are generally irregular in practice. To avoid unwieldy problems, assumptions to create more regular cash flows are made both in this textbook and in the real world.

(c)  A number of present value problems involve annuities (or perpetuities) beginning a few periods hence. Students should practise combining the annuity (or perpetuity) formula with the discounting formula to solve these problems.

(d)  Annuities and perpetuities may have periods of every two or every $n$ years, rather than once a year. The annuity and perpetuity formulae can easily handle such circumstances.

(e)  We frequently encounter problems where the present value of one annuity must be equated with the present value of another annuity.

# connect Questions and Problems

1   **Valuation: The One-Period Case**   Would you be willing to pay £500 today in exchange for £525 in one year? What would be the key considerations in answering yes or no? Would your answer depend on who is making the promise to repay?

2   **Valuation: The Multi-Period Case**   Students in the UK who take out student loans must start repaying their loan only when they earn over £15,000. Interest does not begin to accrue until repayment begins. If two students take out a loan at the same time, who receives a bigger subsidy, a first-year student or a third-year student? Explain.

3   **Compounding Periods**   As you increase the length of time involved, what happens to future values? What happens to present values? What happens to the future value of an annuity if you increase the rate $r$? What happens to the present value?

4   **Simplifications**   Can the simplified formulae provided in this chapter work for every valuation problem? Explain your answer with an illustration.

5   **What Is a Firm Worth?**   Can the techniques in this chapter be used to value firms? What are the main considerations in any firm valuation analysis?

6   **Interest**   You work for a jewellers and have sourced a good goldsmith who is able to sell you 100 ounces of gold for one million rand. You approach your two main customers. Mr Martyn says he will buy the gold from you in six months for R1,040,000, whereas Ms Kuchner tells you that she will be able to buy the gold from you in two years' time for R1,160,000. What is the annual percentage rate that Mr Martyn and Ms Kuchner are offering you? Which option should you go for?

7   **Calculating Future Values**   In the UK, every child born after 1 September 2002 receives a £250 voucher from the government that they cannot touch until they reach the age of 18. Assume that the growth rate on the funds is 3.5 per cent (this is what the British government suggests): how much will your child have at the age of 18?

8   **Calculating Present Values**   In 2008, British Airways had a pension liability of £330 million. Let's assume it must be paid in 30 years' time. To assess the value of the firm's shares, financial analysts want to discount this liability back to the present. If the relevant discount rate is 5.6 per cent, what is the present value of this liability?

9   **Calculating Rates of Return**   On 8 February 2009 John Madejski, chairman of Reading Football Club, sold the Edgar Degas bronze sculpture *Petite Danseuse de Quatorze Ans* at auction for a world record price of £13.3 million. He bought the statue in 2004 for £5 million. What was his annual rate of return on this sculpture?

10   **Perpetuities**   An investor purchasing a British consol is entitled to receive annual payments from the British government for ever. What is the price of a consol that pays £4 annually if the next payment occurs one year from today? The market interest rate is 3 per cent.

11   **Continuous Compounding**   A zero coupon bond that will pay €1,000 in 10 years is selling today at €422.41. What is the continuously compounded annual interest rate on the bond?

12   **Net Present Value**   FIFA rules regarding player contracts are very interesting. If a player wishes to break his contract, the purchasing club must pay the player's club four times the player's annual salary multiplied by the number of years left on the contract. The player must pay 10 per cent of this amount personally, and the agent must also pay 10 per cent of the amount from his own pocket. Consider the footballer Cristiano Ronaldo, who was widely rumoured to be leaving Manchester United for Real Madrid during the summer of 2008 (he actually joined in the summer of 2009). At that time Ronaldo was earning €120,000 a week, and had four years of his contract with Manchester United left.

(a)   Calculate how much Ronaldo would have personally had to pay Manchester United if he left with 4 years remaining, 3 years remaining, 2 years remaining, and 1 year remaining.

(b) If the appropriate annualized discount rate is 8 per cent, what is the present value to Ronaldo of breaking his contract with 4, 3, 2, 1 and 0 years remaining?

(c) Assume you are Ronaldo's agent and can personally earn €5 million today from getting Ronaldo to sign a pre-contract agreement to join Real Madrid in the future. Calculate the net present value to you if Ronaldo left with 4 years remaining, 3 years remaining, 2 years remaining, and 1 year remaining.

13 **Calculating Annuity Present Value** An investment offers €4,000 per year for 10 years, with the first payment occurring one year from now. If the required return is 9 per cent, what is the value of the investment? What would the value be if the payments occurred for 20 years? For 50 years? For ever?

14 **Calculating APR** Find the APR for the following five-year loan: a principal of £15,000 with a stated annual interest rate of 7 per cent on the original principal amount to be paid in 60 monthly instalments. The loan has a £250 arrangement fee, to be paid as soon as the contract is signed.

15 **Present Value** A 25-year fixed-rate mortgage has monthly payments of €717 per month and a mortgage interest rate of 6.14 per cent per year, compounded monthly. If a buyer purchases a home with the cash proceeds of the mortgage loan plus an additional 20 per cent deposit, what is the purchase price of the home?

16 **Future Value** What is the future value in four years of €1,000 invested in an account with a stated annual interest rate of 10 per cent:

(a) Compounded annually?

(b) Compounded semi-annually?

(c) Compounded monthly?

(d) Compounded continuously?

(e) Why does the future value increase as the compounding period shortens?

17 **Calculating Annuities** You are planning to save for retirement over the next 30 years. To do this, you will invest £500 a month in a share account and £500 a month in a bond account. The return of the share account is expected to be 7 per cent, and the bond account will pay 4 per cent. When you retire, you will combine your money into an account with a 6 per cent return. How much can you withdraw each month from your account, assuming a 25-year withdrawal period?

18 **Compounding** What is the annualized interest rate, compounded daily, that is equivalent to 12 per cent interest compounded semi-annually? What is the daily compounded rate that is equivalent to 12 per cent compounded continuously?

19 **Growing Perpetuities** Marcus Boruc has been working on a new hands-free telephone that clips into your ear. The new gadget has now been cleared for manufacture and development. Marcus anticipates his first annual cash flow from the phone to be €200,000, received two years from today. Subsequent annual cash flows will grow at 5 per cent in perpetuity. What is the present value of the phone if the discount rate is 10 per cent?

20 **Balloon Payments** Mario Guiglini has just sold his hotel and purchased a restaurant with the proceeds. The restaurant is on the Riccione seafront in northern Italy. The cost of the restaurant to Mario is €500,000, and the seller requires a 25 per cent up-front payment. Mario is able to pay the up-front payment from the proceeds of the hotel sale. He needs to take out a mortgage, and has been able to arrange one with Unicredit Bank that charges a 9 per cent APR. Mario will make equal monthly payments over the next 30 years. His first payment will be due one month from now. However, the mortgage has an eight-year balloon payment option, meaning that the balance of the loan could be paid off at the end of year 8. There were no other transaction costs or finance charges. How much will Mario's balloon payment be in eight years?

21 **Calculating Interest Expense** You receive a credit card application from Shady Banks plc offering an introductory rate of 1.90 per cent per year, compounded monthly for the

first six months, increasing thereafter to 16 per cent per year compounded monthly. Assuming you transfer the £4,000 balance from your existing credit card and make no subsequent payments, how much interest will you owe at the end of the first year?

22   **Growing Annuity**   Your job pays you only once a year for all the work you did over the previous 12 months. Today, 31 December, you just received your salary of £100,000, and plan to spend all of it. However, you have also decided to join the company's employee pension scheme. Under the very generous scheme your company contributes £2 for every £1 that you pay into the pension. You have decided that one year from today you will begin paying 2 per cent of your annual salary into the pension, in which you are guaranteed to earn 8 per cent per year. Your salary will increase at 4 per cent per year throughout your career. How much money will you have on the date of your retirement 40 years from today?

23   **Calculating APR**   A local finance company quotes a 14 per cent interest rate on one-year loans. So, if you borrow €20,000, the interest for the year will be €2,800. Because you must repay a total of €22,800 in one year, the finance company requires you to pay €22,800/12, or €1,900, per month over the next 12 months. Is this a 14 per cent loan? What rate would legally have to be quoted?

24   **Calculating Present Values**   A three-year annuity of six £5,000 semi-annual payments will begin 10 years from now, with the first payment coming 10.5 years from now. If the discount rate is 10 per cent compounded monthly, what is the value of this annuity five years from now? What is the value three years from now? What is the current value of the annuity?

25   **Calculating Annuities Due**   You want to lease a set of golf clubs from Pings Ltd. The lease contract is in the form of 36 equal monthly payments at a 14 per cent stated annual interest rate, compounded monthly. Because the clubs cost £4,000 retail, Pings wants the PV of the lease payments to equal £4,000. Suppose that your first payment is due immediately. What will your monthly lease payments be?

**CHALLENGE**
**26–32**

26   **Annuities**   Today, you have become a new mother, and the British government has given you £250 for your child's trust fund. You think it would be a great idea to use this as the basis for saving for your child's future. You believe in private schooling, and so you want to put aside a certain amount each year to pay for your child's primary schooling (ages 5–11), secondary schooling (ages 12–17), and university tuition (ages 18–22). Private primary schooling costs £7,000 per year and private secondary schooling costs £8,000 per year. If your child gets into university, the fees and maintenance will be in the region of £15,000 per year. Your child will start school five years from now, and you plan to deposit money every year in the trust fund, starting one year from now. The annual percentage rate you've been quoted by the government is 6.5 per cent. How much money must you deposit in an account each year to fund your child's education? You will make your last deposit when your child enters university.

27   **Balloon Payments**   On 1 September 2009 Susan Chao bought a motorcycle for £15,000. She paid £1,000 down, and financed the balance with a five-year loan at a stated annual interest rate of 9.6 per cent, compounded monthly. She started the monthly payments exactly one month after the purchase (i.e. 1 October 2009). Two years later, at the end of October 2011, Susan got a new job and decided to pay off the loan. If the bank charges her a 1 per cent prepayment penalty based on the loan balance, how much must she pay the bank on 1 November 2011?

28   **Calculating Annuity Values**   You are serving on a jury. A plaintiff is suing the city for injuries sustained after a freak doggie pooh accident. In the trial, doctors testified that it will be five years before the plaintiff is able to return to work. The jury has already decided in favour of the plaintiff. You are the foreperson of the jury and propose that the jury give the plaintiff an award to cover the following:

(a)   The present value of two years' back pay. The plaintiff's annual salary for the last two years would have been €25,000 and €28,000, respectively.

(b) The present value of five years' future salary. You assume the salary will be €28,000 per year.

(c) €100,000 for pain, suffering and humiliation.

(d) €20,000 for court costs.

Assume that the salary payments are equal amounts paid at the end of each month. If the interest rate you choose is 4 per cent APR, what is the size of the settlement? If you were the plaintiff, would you like to see a higher or lower interest rate?

29  **Annuities**  You've just read a life-enhancing book that tells you that if you believe things will happen, they will! You decide that you want to become a millionaire by the time you are 65. You have just turned 22, and you decide to play the stock market. Your fantastic corporate finance textbook leads you to believe that you can earn 11.8 per cent per annum from investing in equities. How much must you invest each year in order to realize your dream? You've decided that investing each year will be boring, and so you just want to invest an amount today and leave it in an account for 43 years. How much should you invest today?

30  **Ordinary Annuities and Annuities Due**  As discussed in the text, an annuity due is identical to an ordinary annuity, except that the periodic payments occur at the beginning of each period and not at the end of the period. Show that the relationship between the value of an ordinary annuity and the value of an otherwise equivalent annuity due is

$$\text{Annuity due value} = \text{Ordinary annuity value} \times (1 + r)$$

Show this for both present and future values.

31  **Present Value of a Growing Perpetuity**  What is the equation for the present value of a growing perpetuity with a payment of $C$ one period from today if the payments grow by $C$ each period?

32  **Rule of 72**  A useful rule of thumb for the time it takes an investment to double with discrete compounding is the 'Rule of 72'. To use the Rule of 72, you simply divide 72 by the interest rate to determine the number of periods it takes for a value today to double. For example, if the interest rate is 6 per cent, the Rule of 72 says it will take 72/6 = 12 years to double. This is approximately equal to the actual answer of 11.90 years. The Rule of 72 can also be applied to determine what interest rate is needed to double money in a specified period. This is a useful approximation for many interest rates and periods. At what rate is the Rule of 72 exact? A corollary to the Rule of 72 is the Rule of 69.3. The Rule of 69.3 is exactly correct except for rounding when interest rates are compounded continuously. Prove the Rule of 69.3 for continuously compounded interest.

# The MBA Decision

Ben Bates graduated from university six years ago with a finance undergraduate degree. Although he is satisfied with his current job, his goal is to become an investment banker. He feels that an MBA degree would allow him to achieve this goal. After examining schools, he has narrowed his choice to either Wilton University or Mount Perry University. Although internships are encouraged by both schools, to get class credit for the internship no salary can be paid. Other than internships, neither school will allow its students to work while enrolled in its MBA programme.

Ben currently works at the money management firm of Dewey and Louis. His annual salary at the firm is £50,000 per year, and his salary is expected to increase at 3 per cent per year until retirement. He is currently 28 years old and expects to work for 35 more years. His current job includes a fully paid health insurance plan, and his current average tax rate is 26 per cent. Ben has a savings account with enough money to cover the entire cost of his MBA programme.

The Draper College of Business at Wilton University is one of the top MBA programmes in the country. The MBA degree requires two years of full-time enrolment at the university. The annual tuition is £60,000, payable at the beginning of each school year. Books and other supplies are estimated to cost £2,500 per year. Ben expects that after graduation from Wilton he will receive a job offer for about £95,000 per year, with a £15,000 signing bonus. The salary at this job will increase at 4 per cent per year. Because of the higher salary, his average income tax rate will increase to 31 per cent.

The Bradley School of Business at Mount Perry University began its MBA programme 16 years ago. The Bradley School is smaller and less well known than the Draper College. Bradley offers an accelerated, one-year programme, with a tuition cost of £75,000 to be paid upon matriculation. Books and other supplies for the programme are expected to cost £3,500. Ben thinks that he will receive an offer of £78,000 per year upon graduation, with a £10,000 signing bonus. The salary at this job will increase at 3.5 per cent per year. His average tax rate at this level of income will be 29 per cent.

Both schools offer a discounted health insurance plan that will cost £3,000 per year, payable at the beginning of the year. Ben also estimates that room and board expenses will cost £20,000 per year at either school. The appropriate discount rate is 6.5 per cent.

1   How does Ben's age affect his decision to get an MBA?

2   What other, perhaps non-quantifiable factors affect Ben's decision to get an MBA?

3   Assuming all salaries are paid at the end of each year, what is the best option for Ben – from a strictly financial standpoint?

4   Ben believes that the appropriate analysis is to calculate the future value of each option. How would you evaluate this statement?

5   What initial salary would Ben need to receive to make him indifferent between attending Wilton University and staying in his current position?

6   Suppose, instead of being able to pay cash for his MBA, Ben must borrow the money. The current borrowing rate is 5.4 per cent. How would this affect his decision?

## Practical Case Study

1   In Yahoo! Finance, find the closing price for a company in your country. Find the price exactly four years before. What was your annual return over the last four years, assuming you purchased the equity at the closing price four years ago? (Assume no dividends were paid.) Using this same return, what price will the company sell for five years from now? Ten years from now? What if the share price increases at 11 per cent per year? Are these figures realistic? Explain.

2   Find the share price for a company in your country by visiting Yahoo! Finance. You find an analyst who projects the share price will increase 12 per cent per year for the foreseeable future. Based on the most recent share price, if the projection holds true, when will the share price be 10 times higher? When will it be 20 times higher?

## Endnotes

1   Sometimes, financial writers merely speak of a cash flow in year *x*. Although this terminology is ambiguous, such writers generally mean the *end of year x*.

2   Students frequently think that *C/r* is the present value at date *T* + 1 because the consol's first payment is at date *T* + 1. However, the formula values the consol as of one period prior to the first payment.

*Appendix 4A   Net Present Value: First Principles of Finance can be found on the OLC (www.mcgraw-hill.co.uk/textbooks/hillier)*

# Chapter 5

# How to Value Bonds and Shares

When the London Stock Exchange closed on 8 May 2008, the share price of the construction company Persimmon plc was £6.355. On that same day, Reuters Group closed at £6.31, while the advertising and marketing firm WPP closed at £6.315. Because the share prices of these three companies were so similar, you might expect they would be offering similar dividends to their shareholders, but you would be wrong. In fact, Persimmon's dividend was £0.372 per share, Reuters' was £0.05 per share, and WPP Group was even lower at £0.0432.

As we shall see in this chapter, the dividends currently being paid are one of the primary factors we look at when attempting to value the shares of a company. However, it is obvious from looking at Reuters and WPP that current dividends are not the end of the story, so this chapter explores dividends, share values, and the connection between the two.

## 5.1 Definition and Example of a Bond

A *bond* is a certificate showing that a borrower owes a specified sum. To repay the money, the borrower has agreed to make interest and principal payments on designated dates. For example, imagine that South African firm Kreuger Enterprises has just issued 100,000 bonds for 10,000 rand each, where the bonds have a coupon rate of 5 per cent and a maturity of two years. Interest on the bonds is to be paid yearly. This means that

1  R1 billion (= 100,000 × R10,000) has been borrowed by the firm.

2  The firm must pay interest of R50 million (= 5% × R1 billion) at the end of one year.

3  The firm must pay both R50 million of interest and R1 billion of principal at the end of two years.

There are many types of bond that exist in the capital markets, and issuers include corporations, private firms, banks, and governments. In fact, the government bond market is one of the largest and most liquid markets in the world. Governments use bonds to manage their long- and short-term cash flow requirements, and as a result almost every country will have government bonds. Corporate bonds are similar in structure to government bonds but, unlike governments, companies have the option to issue both debt and equity, and the corporate bond market is smaller.

FIGURE
**5.1**

| Borrower | Amount m. | Coupon % | Price | Maturity |
|---|---|---|---|---|
| ■ **US DOLLAR** | | | | |
| Korail | 300 | 5.375 | 99.637 | May 2013 |
| Network Rail | 1.25bn | 3.5 | 99.537 | Jun 2013 |
| NWB | 1bn | 3 | 99.949 | Jun 2010 |
| ■ **EUROS(e)** | | | | |
| Caixa Catalunya | 1.75bn | 5 | 99.877 | May 2010 |
| Eurohypo | 50 | FRN | undiscl | May 2009 |
| ■ **SWISS FRANC** | | | | |
| BNG | 50 | 4.875 | 99.992 | Apr 2010 |
| IBK | 250 | 2.25 | 100.72 | Jun 2012 |
| IBM Corp | 350 | 3.25 | 100.435 | May 2011 |
| IBM | 150 | 3.625 | 100.095 | May 2015 |
| UBS AG | 200 | 3.5 | 100.606 | Jun 2011 |
| ■ **HONG KONG DOLLAR** | | | | |
| NACF | 250 | 4.56 | 100 | May 2013 |
| ■ **KOREAN WO** | | | | |
| Hanjin Trans | 50bn | 6.21 | 100 | Nov 2011 |
| Hyundai Rotem | 100bn | 5.92 | 100 | May 2011 |
| Megamart | 30bn | 5.88 | 100 | May 2011 |
| ■ **NEW ZEALAND DOLLAR** | | | | |
| Deutsche Bank | 100 | 8 | 99.722 | May 2010 |
| ■ **SOUTH AFRICAN RAND** | | | | |
| IFC | 500 | 11 | 99 | Jul 2009 |
| ■ **SWEDISH KRONE** | | | | |
| EIB | 200 | 4.5 | 100.635 | Sep 2011 |

*Source*: www.ft.com, *Financial Times*, 8 May 2008.

**Figure 5.1** International bond issues. FRN denotes a bond with a floating coupon rate. Prices are quoted as a percentage of the face value

Figure 5.1 presents the bonds that were issued on 8 May 2008 across the world. Notice how the bond market is completely international. IBM, an American firm, issued new bonds in Switzerland, Deutsche Bank issued new bonds in New Zealand, and Network Rail, a British firm, issued new bonds in the United States. The bonds listed in Fig. 5.1 are all denominated in the currency of the country in which they were listed. 'Coupon %' is the coupon rate of the bond and 'Maturity' is the date the bond expires. For example, Fig. 5.1 shows that on 8 May 2008 IBM issued a seven-year bond in Switzerland that pays interest of 3.625 per cent per year.

## 5.2  How to Value Bonds

### Pure Discount Bonds

The **pure discount bond** is perhaps the simplest kind of bond. It promises a single payment, say £1, at a fixed future date. If the payment is one year from now, it is called a *one-year discount bond*; if it is two years from now, it is called a *two-year discount bond*, and so on.

The date when the issuer of the bond makes the last payment is called the **maturity date** of the bond, or just its *maturity* for short. The bond is said to mature or *expire* on the date of its final payment. The payment at maturity (£1 in this example) is termed the bond's **face** or **par value**.

Pure discount bonds are often called *zero coupon bonds* to emphasize the fact that the holder receives no cash payments until maturity. We shall use the terms *zero* and *discount* interchangeably to refer to bonds that pay no coupons.

FIGURE
**5.2**

**Figure 5.2** Different types of bond: $C$, coupon paid every 6 months; $F$, face value at year 4 (maturity for pure discount and coupon bonds)

The first row of Fig. 5.2 shows the pattern of cash flows from a four-year pure discount bond. Note that the face value, $F$, is paid when the bond expires in the 48th month. There are no payments of either interest or principal prior to this date.

In the previous chapter, we indicated that one discounts a future cash flow to determine its present value. The present value of a pure discount bond can easily be determined by the techniques of the previous chapter. For short, we sometimes speak of the *value* of a bond instead of its present value.

Consider a pure discount bond that pays a face value of $F$ in $T$ years, where the interest rate is $R$ in each of the $T$ years. (We also refer to this rate as the *market interest rate*.) Because the face value is the only cash flow that the bond pays, the present value of this face amount is calculated as follows:

Value of a pure discount bond:

$$PV = \frac{F}{(1 + R)^T}$$

The present value formula can produce some surprising results. Suppose that the interest rate is 10 per cent. Consider a bond with a face value of €1 million that matures in 20 years. Applying the formula to this bond, its PV is given by

$$PV = \frac{€1 \text{ million}}{(1.1)^{20}}$$
$$= €148,644$$

or only about 15 per cent of the face value.

## Level Coupon Bonds

Typical bonds issued either by governments or by corporations offer cash payments not just at maturity, but also at regular times in between. For example, payments on government issues and corporate bonds tend to be made every six months until the bonds mature. These payments are called the coupons of the bond. The middle row of Fig. 5.2 illustrates the case of a four-year, *level coupon bond*: the coupon, $C$, is paid every six months in most countries (although annual and quarterly payments are also common) and is the same throughout the life of the bond.

Note that the face value of the bond, $F$, is paid at maturity (end of year 4). $F$ is sometimes called the *principal* or the *denomination*. Bonds issued in the United Kingdom typically have face values of £100,000, and in the Eurozone bonds tend to have face values of €1,000. This isn't universally followed, and can vary with the type of bond.

As we mentioned before, the value of a bond is simply the present value of its cash flows. Therefore, the value of a level coupon bond is merely the present value of its stream of coupon payments plus the present value of its repayment of principal. Because a level coupon bond is just an annuity of $C$ each period, together with a payment at maturity of, say, €1,000, the value of a level coupon bond is calculated as follows:

Value of a level coupon bond:

$$PV = \frac{C}{1 + R} + \frac{C}{(1 + R)^2} + \cdots + \frac{C}{(1 + R)^T} + \frac{€1,000}{(1 + R)^T}$$

where $C$ is the coupon and the face value, $F$, is €1,000. The value of the bond can be rewritten like this:

Value of a level coupon bond:

$$PV = C \times A_R^T + \frac{€1,000}{(1 + R)^T}$$

As mentioned in the previous chapter, $A_R^T$ is the present value of an annuity of €1 per period for $T$ periods at an interest rate per period of $R$.

---

## Bond Prices

EXAMPLE
**5.1**

Consider the Caixa bond from Fig. 5.1 that was issued on 8 May 2008 in the Eurozone. The coupon is 5 per cent and the face value is €1,000, implying that the yearly coupon is €50 (= 5% × €1,000). Interest is paid each November and May, implying that the coupon every six months is €25 (= €50/2). The face value is paid out in May 2010, two years from the issue date. By this we mean that the purchaser obtains claims to the following cash flows:

| Nov 2008 | May 2009 | Nov 2009 | May 2010 |
|----------|----------|----------|----------|
| €25 | €25 | €25 | €25 + €1,000 |

If the stated annual interest rate in the market is 5.06 per cent per year, what is the present value of the bond?

Our work on compounding in the previous chapter showed that the interest rate over any six-month interval is half of the stated annual interest rate. In the current example, this semi-annual rate is 2.53 per cent (= 5.06%/2). Because the coupon payment in each six-month period is €25, and there are four of these six-month periods from May 2008 to May 2010, the present value of the bond is

$$\begin{aligned}
PV &= \frac{€25}{(1.0253)} + \frac{€25}{(1.0253)^2} + \frac{€25}{(1.0253)^3} + \frac{€25}{(1.0253)^4} + \frac{€1,000}{(1.0253)^4} \\
&= €25 \times A_{0.0253}^4 + €1,000/(1.0253)^4 \\
&= (€25 \times 3.759) + (€1,000 \times 0.905) \\
&= €93.98 + €904.89 \\
&= €998.87
\end{aligned}$$

This figure is almost exactly the same as the price quoted in Fig. 5.1. Traders will generally quote the bond as 99.887, indicating that it is selling at 99.887 per cent of the face value of €1,000.

At this point it is worth while to relate the preceding example of bond pricing to the discussion of compounding in the previous chapter. At that time, we distinguished between the stated annual interest rate and the effective annual interest rate. In particular, we pointed out that the effective annual interest rate is

$$(1 + R/m)^m - 1$$

where $R$ is the stated annual interest rate and $m$ is the number of compounding intervals. Because $R = 5.06\%$ and $m = 2$ (the bond makes semi-annual payments), the effective annual interest rate is

$$\begin{aligned}
[1 + (0.0506/2)]^2 - 1 &= (1.0253)^2 - 1 \\
&= 5.124\%
\end{aligned}$$

In other words, because the bond is paying interest twice a year, the bondholder earns a 5.124 per cent return when compounding is considered.

One final note concerning level coupon bonds: although the preceding example concerns corporate bonds, government bonds are identical in form. For example, the British government has a 5 per cent bond maturing in 2014. This means that the British government will make semi-annual payments of £2.50 (= 5%/2 × £100) between now and 2014 for each face value of £100.

## Consols

Not all bonds have a final maturity date. As we mentioned in the previous chapter, consols are bonds that never stop paying a coupon, have no final maturity date, and therefore never mature. Thus a consol is a perpetuity. In the 18th century the Bank of England issued such bonds, called 'English consols'. These were bonds that the Bank of England guaranteed would pay the holder a cash flow for ever! Through wars and depressions, the Bank of England continued to honour this commitment, and you can still buy such bonds in London today.

An important example of a consol, though, is called *preferred stock* or *preference shares*. Preference shares are shares that are issued by corporations and provide the holder with a fixed dividend in perpetuity. If there were never any question that the firm would actually pay the dividend on the preference shares, such securities would in fact be consols.

These instruments can be valued by the perpetuity formula of the previous chapter. For example, if the market-wide interest rate is 10 per cent, a consol with a yearly interest payment of €50 is valued at

$$\frac{€50}{0.10} = €500$$

## 5.3 Bond Concepts

We complete our discussion of bonds by considering two concepts concerning them. First we examine the relationship between interest rates and bond prices. Then we define the concept of yield to maturity.

### Interest Rates and Bond Prices

The discussion of level coupon bonds allows us to relate bond prices to interest rates. Consider the following example.

---

EXAMPLE **5.2**

## Bond Valuation

The interest rate is 10 per cent. A two-year bond with a 10 per cent coupon pays interest of £10 (= £100 × 10%). For simplicity we assume that the interest is paid annually. In this case we see that the bond is priced at its face value of £100:

$$£100 = \frac{£10}{1.10} + \frac{£100 + £10}{(1.10)^2}$$

If the interest rate unexpectedly rises to 12 per cent, the bond sells at

$$£96.62 = \frac{£10}{1.12} + \frac{£100 + £10}{(1.12)^2}$$

Because £96.62 is less than £100, the bond is said to sell at a discount. This is a sensible result. Now that the interest rate is 12 per cent, a newly issued bond with a 12 per cent coupon rate will sell at £100. This newly issued bond will have coupon payments of £12 (= 0.12 × £100). Because our bond has interest payments of only £10, investors will pay less than £100 for it.

If interest rates fell to 8 per cent, the bond would sell at

$$£103.567 = \frac{£10}{1.08} + \frac{£100 + £10}{(1.08)^2}$$

Because £103.567 is more than £100, the bond is said to sell at a premium.

Thus we find that bond prices fall with a rise in interest rates, and rise with a fall in interest rates. Furthermore, the general principle is that a level coupon bond sells in the following ways:

- At the face value if the coupon rate is equal to the market-wide interest rate
- At a discount if the coupon rate is below the market-wide interest rate
- At a premium if the coupon rate is above the market-wide interest rate

## Yield to Maturity

Let's now consider the previous example *in reverse*. If our bond is selling at £103.567, what return is a bondholder receiving? This can be answered by considering the following equation:

$$£103.567 = \frac{£10}{1 + y} + \frac{£100 + £10}{(1 + y)^2}$$

The unknown, $y$, is the discount rate that equates the price of the bond with the discounted value of the coupons and face value. Our earlier work implies that $y = 8\%$. Thus traders state that the bond is yielding an 8 per cent return. Bond traders also state that the bond has a yield to maturity of 8 per cent. The yield to maturity is frequently called the bond's *yield* for short. So, we would say the bond with its 10 per cent coupon is priced to yield 8 per cent at £103.567.

---

### The Present Value Formulae for Bonds

**Pure Discount Bonds**

$$PV = \frac{F}{(1 + R)^T}$$

**Level Coupon Bonds**

$$PV = C\left[\frac{1}{R} - \frac{1}{R \times (1 + R)^T}\right] + \frac{F}{(1 + R)^T}$$

$$= C \times A_R^T + \frac{F}{(1 + R)^T}$$

where $F$ is the face value.

**Consols**

$$PV = \frac{C}{R}$$

---

## 5.4 The Present Value of Equity

### Dividends versus Capital Gains

Our goal in this section is to value ordinary shares. We learned in the previous chapter that an asset's value is determined by the present value of its future cash flows. An equity provides two kinds of cash flow. First, equities often pay dividends on a regular basis. Second, the shareholder receives the sale price when selling the equity. Thus, to value equity, we need to answer an interesting question: Which of the following is the value of an equity equal to?

1   The discounted present value of the sum of next period's dividend plus next period's share price

2   The discounted present value of all future dividends

This is the kind of question that students would love to see in a multiple-choice exam: both (1) and (2) are right.

To see that (1) and (2) are the same, let's start with an individual who will buy the equity and hold it for one year. In other words, she has a one-year *holding period*. In addition, she is willing to pay $P_0$ for the share today. That is, she calculates

$$P_0 = \frac{\text{Div}_1}{1 + R} + \frac{P_1}{1 + R} \tag{5.1}$$

$\text{Div}_1$ is the dividend paid at year's end, and $P_1$ is the price at year's end. $P_0$ is the PV of the equity investment. The term in the denominator, $R$, is the appropriate discount rate for the equity.

That seems easy enough; but where does $P_1$ come from? $P_1$ is not pulled out of thin air. Rather, there must be a buyer at the end of year 1 who is willing to purchase the equity for $P_1$. This buyer determines price as follows:

$$P_1 = \frac{\text{Div}_2}{1 + R} + \frac{P_2}{1 + R} \tag{5.2}$$

Substituting the value of $P_1$ from Eq. (5.2) into Eq. (5.1) yields

$$P_0 = \frac{1}{1 + R}\left[\text{Div}_1 + \left(\frac{\text{Div}_2 + P_2}{1 + R}\right)\right]$$
$$= \frac{\text{Div}_1}{1 + R} + \frac{\text{Div}_2}{(1 + R)^2} + \frac{P_2}{(1 + R)^2} \tag{5.3}$$

We can ask a similar question for Eq. (5.3): Where does $P_2$ come from? An investor at the end of year 2 is willing to pay $P_2$ because of the dividend and share price at year 3. This process can be repeated *ad nauseam*. At the end, we are left with this:

$$P_0 = \frac{\text{Div}_1}{1 + R} + \frac{\text{Div}_2}{(1 + R)^2} + \frac{\text{Div}_3}{(1 + R)^3} + \cdots$$
$$= \sum_{t=1}^{\infty} \frac{\text{Div}_t}{(1 + R)^t}$$

Thus the value of a firm's equity to the investor is equal to the present value of all of the expected future dividends.

This is a very useful result. A common objection to applying present value analysis to equities is that investors are too short-sighted to care about the long-run stream of dividends. These critics argue that an investor will generally not look past his or her time horizon. Thus prices in a market dominated by short-term investors will reflect only near-term dividends. However, our discussion shows that a long-run dividend discount model holds even when investors have short-term time horizons. Although an investor may want to cash out early, she must find another investor who is willing to buy. The price this second investor pays is dependent on dividends *after* his date of purchase.

## Valuation of Different Types of Equity

The preceding discussion shows that the value of the firm is the present value of its future dividends. How do we apply this idea in practice? Equation (5.4) represents a very general model, and is applicable regardless of whether the level of expected dividends is growing, fluctuating, or constant. The general model can be simplified if the firm's dividends are expected to follow some basic patterns: (1) zero growth, (2) constant growth, and (3) differential growth. These cases are illustrated in Fig. 5.3.

**Figure 5.3** Zero growth, constant growth, and differential growth patterns

**Case 1 (Zero Growth)**   The value of an equity with a constant dividend is given by

$$P_0 = \frac{\text{Div}_1}{1 + R} + \frac{\text{Div}_2}{(1 + R)^2} + \cdots = \frac{\text{Div}_1}{R}$$

Here it is assumed that $\text{Div}_1 = \text{Div}_2 = \ldots = \text{Div}$. This is just an application of the perpetuity formula from a previous chapter.

**Case 2 (Constant Growth)**   Dividends grow at rate $g$, as follows:

End-of-year dividend:

| 1 | 2 | 3 | 4 | |
|---|---|---|---|---|
| $\text{Div}_1$ | $\text{Div}_1(1 + g)$ | $\text{Div}_1(1 + g)^2$ | $\text{Div}_1(1 + g)^3$ | $\cdots$ |

Note that $\text{Div}_1$ is the dividend at the end of the *first* period.

## Projected Dividends

EXAMPLE
5.3

Hampshire Products will pay a dividend of £4 per share a year from now. Financial analysts believe that dividends will rise at 6 per cent per year for the foreseeable future. What is the dividend per share at the end of each of the first five years? With 6 per cent growth we have this:

| End-of-year dividend | | | | |
|---|---|---|---|---|
| **1** | **2** | **3** | **4** | **5** |
| £4.00 | £4 × (1.06) = £4.24 | £4 × (1.06)$^2$ = £4.4944 | £4 × (1.06)$^3$ = £4.7641 | £4 × (1.06)$^4$ = £5.0499 |

The value of an ordinary share with dividends growing at a constant rate is

$$P_0 = \frac{\text{Div}_1}{1 + R} + \frac{\text{Div}_1(1 + g)}{(1 + R)^2} + \frac{\text{Div}_1(1 + g)^2}{(1 + R)^3} + \frac{\text{Div}_1(1 + g)^3}{(1 + R)^4} + \cdots$$

$$= \frac{\text{Div}_1}{R - g}$$

where $g$ is the growth rate. $\text{Div}_1$ is the dividend on the equity at the end of the first period. This is the formula for the present value of a growing perpetuity, which we derived in a previous chapter.

## Share Valuation

**EXAMPLE 5.4**

Suppose an investor is considering the purchase of a share of the Avila Mining Company. The equity will pay a €3 dividend a year from today. This dividend is expected to grow at 10 per cent per year ($g = 10\%$) for the foreseeable future. The investor thinks that the required return ($R$) on this equity is 15 per cent, given her assessment of Avila Mining's risk. (We also refer to $R$ as the discount rate for the equity.) What is the share price of Avila Mining Company?

Using the constant growth formula of case 2, we assess the value to be €60:

$$€60 = \frac{€3}{0.15 - 0.10}$$

$P_0$ is quite dependent on the value of $g$. If $g$ had been estimated to be 12.5 per cent, the share price would have been

$$€120 = \frac{€3}{0.15 - 0.125}$$

The share price doubles (from €60 to €120) when $g$ increases by only 25 per cent (from 10 per cent to 12.5 per cent). Because of $P_0$'s dependence on $g$, one must maintain a healthy sense of scepticism when using this constant growth of dividends model.

Furthermore, note that $P_0$ is equal to infinity when the growth rate, $g$, equals the discount rate, $R$. Because share prices do not grow infinitely, an estimate of $g$ greater than $R$ implies an error in estimation. More will be said about this point later.

**Case 3 (Differential Growth)**   In this case, an algebraic formula would be too unwieldy. Instead we present examples.

## Differential Growth

**EXAMPLE 5.5**

Consider the equity of Mint Drug Company, which has a new massage ointment and is enjoying rapid growth. The dividend per share a year from today will be €1.15. During the following four years the dividend will grow at 15 per cent per year ($g_1 = 15\%$). After that, growth ($g_2$) will equal 10 per cent per year. Can you calculate the present value of the equity if the required return ($R$) is 15 per cent?

Figure 5.4 displays the growth in the dividends. We need to apply a two-step process to discount these dividends. We first calculate the net present value of the dividends growing at 15 per cent per annum. That is, we first calculate the present value of the dividends at the end of each of the first five years. Second, we calculate the present value of the dividends that begin at the end of year 6.

**Calculate Present Value of First Five Dividends**   The present value of dividend payments in years 1–5 is as follows:

| Future year | Growth rate, $g_1$ | Expected dividend (€) | Present value (€) |
|---|---|---|---|
| 1 | 0.15 | 1.15 | 1 |
| 2 | 0.15 | 1.3225 | 1 |
| 3 | 0.15 | 1.5209 | 1 |
| 4 | 0.15 | 1.7490 | 1 |
| 5 | 0.15 | 2.0114 | 1 |
| Years 1–5 The present value of dividends = €5 | | | |

The growing annuity formula of the previous chapter could normally be used in this step. However, note that dividends grow at 15 per cent, which is also the discount rate. Because $g = R$, the growing annuity formula cannot be used in this example.

**Figure 5.4** Growth in dividends for Mint Drug Company

**Calculate Present Value of Dividends Beginning at End of Year 6** This is the procedure for deferred perpetuities and deferred annuities that we mentioned in the previous chapter. The dividends beginning at the end of year 6 are as follows:

| End-of-year dividend | | | |
|---|---|---|---|
| **6** | **7** | **8** | **9** |
| $Div_5 \times (1 + g_2)$ | $Div_5 \times (1 + g_2)^2$ | $Div_5 \times (1 + g_2)^3$ | $Div_5 \times (1 + g_2)^4$ |
| €2.0114 × (1.10) | €2.0114 × (1.10)² | €2.0114 × (1.10)³ | €2.0114 × (1.10)⁴ |
| = €2.2125 | = €2.4338 | = €2.6772 | = €2.9449 |

As stated in the previous chapter, the growing perpetuity formula calculates present value as of one year prior to the first payment. Because the payment begins at the end of year 6, the present value formula calculates present value as of the end of year 5.

The price at the end of year 5 is given by

$$P_5 = \frac{Div_6}{R - g_2} = \frac{€2.2125}{0.15 - 0.10} = €44.25$$

The present value of $P_5$ today is

$$\frac{P_5}{(1 + R)^5} = \frac{€44.25}{(1.15)^5} = €22$$

The present value of *all* dividends today is €27 (= €22 + 5).

## 5.5 Estimates of Parameters in the Dividend Growth Model

The value of the firm is a function of its growth rate, $g$, and its discount rate, $R$. How do we estimate these variables?

# Where Does $g$ Come From?

The previous discussion of equities assumed that dividends grow at the rate $g$. We now want to estimate this rate of growth. This section extends the discussion of growth contained in Chapter 3. Consider a business whose earnings next year are expected to be the same as earnings this year unless a *net investment* is made. This situation is likely to occur because net investment is equal to gross, or total, investment less depreciation. A net investment of zero occurs when *total investment* equals depreciation. If total investment is equal to depreciation, the firm's physical plant is maintained, consistent with no growth in earnings.

Net investment will be positive only if some earnings are not paid out as dividends – that is, only if some earnings are retained.[1] This leads to the following equation:

$$\begin{matrix} \text{Earnings} \\ \text{next} \\ \text{year} \end{matrix} = \begin{matrix} \text{Earnings} \\ \text{this} \\ \text{year} \end{matrix} + \underbrace{\begin{matrix} \text{Retained} \\ \text{earnings} \\ \text{this year} \end{matrix} \times \begin{matrix} \text{Return on} \\ \text{retained} \\ \text{earnings} \end{matrix}}_{\text{Increase in earnings}} \qquad (5.4)$$

The increase in earnings is a function of both the *retained earnings* and the *return on the retained earnings*.

We now divide both sides of Eq. (5.4) by earnings this year, yielding

$$\frac{\text{Earnings next year}}{\text{Earnings this year}} = \frac{\text{Earnings this year}}{\text{Earnings this year}} + \left( \frac{\text{Retained earnings this year}}{\text{Earnings this year}} \right) \times \text{Return on retained earnings} \qquad (5.5)$$

The left side of Eq. (5.5) is simply 1 plus the growth rate in earnings, which we write as $1 + g$. The ratio of retained earnings to earnings is called the retention ratio. Thus we can write

$$1 + g = 1 + (\text{Retention ratio} \times \text{Return on retained earnings}) \qquad (5.6)$$

It is difficult for a financial analyst to determine the return to be expected on currently retained earnings; the details on forthcoming projects are not generally public information. However, it is frequently assumed that the projects selected in the current year have an anticipated return equal to returns from projects in other years. Here we can estimate the anticipated return on current retained earnings by the historical return on equity or ROE. After all, ROE is simply the return on the firm's entire equity, which is the return on the cumulation of all the firm's past projects.

From Eq. (5.6), we have a simple way to estimate growth:

Formula for firm's growth rate:

$$g = \text{Retention ratio} \times \text{Return on retained earnings} \qquad (5.7)$$

Previously, $g$ referred to growth in dividends. However, the growth in earnings is equal to the growth rate in dividends in this context, because, as we shall presently see, the ratio of dividends to earnings is held constant. In fact, as you have probably figured out, $g$ is the sustainable growth rate we introduced in Chapter 3.

EXAMPLE
**5.6**

## Earnings Growth

Pagemaster plc just reported earnings of £2 million. It plans to retain 40 per cent of its earnings. The historical return on equity (ROE) has been 16 per cent, a figure that is expected to continue into the future. How much will earnings grow over the coming year? We first perform the calculation without reference to Eq. (5.7). Then we use Eq. (5.7) as a check.

▶ **Calculation without Reference to Eq. (5.7)**   The firm will retain £800,000 (= 40% × £2 million). Assuming that historical ROE is an appropriate estimate for future returns, the anticipated increase in earnings is

$$£800,000 \times 0.16 = £128,000$$

The percentage growth in earnings is

$$\frac{\text{Change in earnings}}{\text{Total earnings}} = \frac{£128,000}{£2 \text{ million}} = 0.064$$

This implies that earnings in one year will be £2,128,000 (= £2,000,000 × 1.064).

**Check Using Eq. (5.7)**   We use $g$ = Retention ratio × ROE. We have

$$g = 0.4 \times 0.16 = 0.064$$

## Where Does $\bar{R}$ Come From?

Thus far, we have taken the required return, or discount rate $R$, as given. We shall have quite a bit to say about this subject in later chapters. For now, we want to examine the implications of the dividend growth model for this required return. Earlier we calculated $P_0$ as follows:

$$P_0 = \frac{\text{Div}_1}{R - g}$$

If we rearrange this to solve for $R$, we get

$$R - g = \frac{\text{Div}_1}{P_0}$$
$$R = \frac{\text{Div}_1}{P_0} + g \tag{5.8}$$

This tells us that the total return, $R$, has two components. The first of these, $\text{Div}_1/P_0$, is called the dividend yield. Because this is calculated as the expected cash dividend divided by the current price, it is conceptually similar to the current yield on a bond, which is the annual coupon divided by the bond's price.

The second part of the total return is the growth rate, $g$. As we shall verify shortly, the dividend growth rate is also the rate at which the share price grows. Thus this growth rate can be interpreted as the capital gains yield – that is, the rate at which the value of the investment grows.

To illustrate the components of the required return, suppose we observe an equity selling for €20 per share. The next dividend will be €1 per share. You think that the dividend will grow by 10 per cent per year more or less indefinitely. What return does this equity offer you if this is correct?

The dividend growth model calculates total return as

$$R = \text{Dividend yield} + \text{Capital gains yield}$$
$$R = \text{Div}_1/P_0 \qquad + \qquad g$$

In this case, total return works out to be

$$R = €1/€20 + 10\%$$
$$= 5\% + 10\%$$
$$= 15\%$$

This equity therefore has an expected return of 15 per cent.

We can verify this answer by calculating the price in one year, $P_1$, using 15 per cent as the required return. Based on the dividend growth model, this price is

$$P_1 = \text{Div}_1 \times \frac{1+g}{R-g}$$
$$= \mathord{\in}1 \times \frac{1.10}{0.15 - 0.10}$$
$$= \mathord{\in}1.10/0.05$$
$$= \mathord{\in}22$$

Notice that this €22 is €20 × 1.1, so the share price has grown by 10 per cent as it should. If you pay €20 for the shares today, you will get a €1 dividend at the end of the year, and you will have a €22 – 20 = €2 gain. Your dividend yield is thus €1/20 = 5 per cent. Your capital gains yield is €2/20 = 10 per cent, so your total return would be 5 per cent + 10 per cent = 15 per cent.

To get a feel for actual numbers, consider that, according to Yahoo! Finance estimates, the dividends of Centrica, the British energy firm, were expected to grow from £0.134 per share in 2008 to £0.1504 in 2009. The share price at that time was about £2.875 per share. What is the return investors require on Centrica? Here, the dividend yield is 5.23 (= £0.1504/£2.875) per cent and the capital gains yield is 12.24 (= [£0.1504/£0.134] − 1) per cent, giving a total required return of 17.47 per cent on Centrica shares.

<table>
<tr><td>EXAMPLE<br>**5.7**</td><td>

## Calculating the Required Return

Pagemaster plc, the company examined in the previous example, has 1,000,000 shares outstanding. The equity is selling at £10. What is the required return on the shares?</td></tr>
</table>

Because the retention ratio is 40 per cent, the payout ratio is 60 per cent (= 1 − retention ratio). The payout ratio is the ratio of dividends/earnings. Because earnings one year from now will be £2,128,000 (= £2,000,000 × 1.064), dividends will be £1,276,800 (= 0.60 × £2,128,000). Dividends per share will be £1.28 (= £1,276,800/1,000,000). Given our previous result that $g = 0.064$, we calculate $R$ from Eq. (5.8) as follows:

$$0.192 = \frac{£1.28}{10.00} + 0.064$$

## A Healthy Sense of Scepticism

It is important to emphasize that our approach merely *estimates* $g$; our approach does not *determine* $g$ precisely. We mentioned earlier that our estimate of $g$ is based on a number of assumptions. For example, we assume that the return on reinvestment of future retained earnings is equal to the firm's past ROE. We assume that the future retention ratio is equal to the past retention ratio. Our estimate for $g$ will be off if these assumptions prove to be wrong.

Unfortunately, the determination of $R$ is highly dependent on $g$. For example, if $g$ is estimated to be 0 in our example, $R$ equals 12.8 per cent (= £1.28/£10.00). If $g$ is estimated to be 12 per cent, $R$ equals 24.8 per cent (= £1.28/£10.00 + 12%). Thus one should view estimates of $R$ with a healthy sense of scepticism.

Because of the preceding, some financial economists generally argue that the estimation error of $R$ for a single security is too large to be practical. Therefore they suggest calculating the average $R$ for an entire industry. This $R$ would then be used to discount the dividends of a particular equity in the same industry.

One should be particularly sceptical of two polar cases when estimating $R$ for individual securities. First, consider a firm currently paying no dividend. The share price will be above zero because investors believe that the firm may initiate a dividend at some point, or the firm may be acquired at some point. However, when a firm goes from no dividends to a positive number of dividends, the implied growth rate is *infinite*. Thus Eq. (5.8) must be used with extreme caution here, if at all – a point we emphasize later in this chapter.

Second, we mentioned earlier that the value of the firm is infinite when $g$ is equal to $R$. Because share prices do not grow infinitely, an analyst whose estimate of $g$ for a particular firm is equal to or above $R$ must have made a mistake. Most likely the analyst's high estimate for $g$ is correct for the next few years. However, firms simply cannot maintain an abnormally high growth rate *for ever*. The analyst's error was to use a short-run estimate of $g$ in a model requiring a perpetual growth rate.

## 5.6 Growth Opportunities

We previously spoke of the growth rate of dividends. We now want to address the related concept of growth opportunities. Imagine a company with a level stream of earnings per share in perpetuity. The company pays all of these earnings out to shareholders as dividends. Hence we have

$$EPS = Div$$

where EPS is *earnings per share* and Div is dividends per share. A company of this type is frequently called a *cash cow*.

The perpetuity formula of the previous chapter gives the value of a share of equity:

Value of a share of equity when a firm acts as a cash cow:

$$\frac{EPS}{R} = \frac{Div}{R}$$

where $R$ is the discount rate on the firm's equity.

This policy of paying out all earnings as dividends may not be the optimal one. Many firms have *growth* opportunities: opportunities to invest in profitable projects. Because these projects can represent a significant fraction of the firm's value, it would be foolish to forgo them in order to pay out all earnings as dividends.

Although firms frequently think in terms of a *set* of growth opportunities, let's focus on only one opportunity – that is, the opportunity to invest in a single project. Suppose the firm retains the entire dividend at date 1 to invest in a particular capital budgeting project. The net present value *per share* of the project as of date 0 is NPVGO, which stands for the *net present value (per share) of the growth opportunity*.

What is the share price at date 0 if the firm decides to take on the project at date 1? Because the per share value of the project is added to the original share price, the share price must now be this:

Share price after firm commits to new project:

$$\frac{EPS}{R} + NPVGO \tag{5.9}$$

Thus Eq. (5.9) indicates that the share price can be viewed as the sum of two different items. The first term (EPS/$R$) is the value of the firm if it rested on its laurels – that is, if it simply distributed all earnings to the shareholders. The second term is the *additional* value if the firm retains earnings to fund new projects.

---

EXAMPLE
**5.8**

## Growth Opportunities

Sarro Shipping plc expects to earn £1 million per year in perpetuity if it undertakes no new investment opportunities. There are 100,000 shares of equity outstanding, so earnings per share equal £10 (= £1,000,000/100,000). The firm will have an opportunity at date 1 to spend £1,000,000 on a new marketing campaign. The new campaign will increase earnings in every subsequent period by £210,000 (or £2.10 per share). This is a 21 per cent return per year on the project. The firm's discount rate is 10 per cent. What is the share price before and after deciding to accept the marketing campaign?

The share price of Sarro Shipping before the campaign is

Share price of Sarro when firm acts as a cash cow:

$$\frac{EPS}{R} = \frac{£10}{0.1} = £100$$

The value of the marketing campaign as of date 1 is

Value of marketing campaign at date 1:

$$-£1,000,000 + \frac{£210,000}{0.1} = £1,100,000 \tag{5.10}$$

Because the investment is made at date 1 and the first cash inflow occurs at date 2, Eq. (5.10) represents the value of the marketing campaign as of date 1. We determine the value at date 0 by discounting back one period as follows:

Value of marketing campaign at date 0:

$$\frac{£1,100,000}{1.1} = £1,000,000$$

Thus NPVGO per share is £10 (= £1,000,000/100,000).
   The share price is

$$EPS/R + NPVGO = £100 + 10 = £110$$

The calculation in our example can also be made on a straight net present value basis. Because all the earnings at date 1 are spent on the marketing effort, no dividends are paid to shareholders at that date. Dividends in all subsequent periods are £1,210,000 (= £1,000,000 + £210,000). In this case £1,000,000 is the annual dividend when Sarro is a cash cow. The additional contribution to the dividend from the marketing effort is £210,000. Dividends per share are £12.10 (= £1,210,000/100,000). Because these dividends start at date 2, the share price at date 1 is £121 (= £12.10/0.1). The share price at date 0 is £110 (= £121/1.1).

Note that value is created in this example because the project earned a 21 per cent rate of return when the discount rate was only 10 per cent. No value would have been created had the project earned a 10 per cent rate of return. The NPVGO would have been zero, and value would have been negative had the project earned a percentage return below 10 per cent. The NPVGO would be negative in that case.

Two conditions must be met in order to increase value:

1   Earnings must be retained so that projects can be funded.[2]

2   The projects must have positive net present value.

Surprisingly, a number of companies seem to invest in projects known to have *negative* net present values. For example, in the late 1970s oil companies and tobacco companies were flush with cash. Because of declining markets in both industries, high dividends and low investment would have been the rational action. Unfortunately, a number of companies in both industries reinvested heavily in what were widely perceived to be negative NPVGO projects.

Given that NPV analysis (such as that presented in the previous chapter) is common knowledge in business, why would managers choose projects with negative NPVs? One conjecture is that some managers enjoy controlling a large company. Because paying dividends in lieu of reinvesting earnings reduces the size of the firm, some managers find it emotionally difficult to pay high dividends.

## Growth in Earnings and Dividends versus Growth Opportunities

As mentioned earlier, a firm's value increases when it invests in growth opportunities with positive NPVGOs. A firm's value falls when it selects opportunities with negative NPVGOs. However, dividends grow whether projects with positive NPVs or negative NPVs are selected. This surprising result can be explained by the following example.

EXAMPLE
5.9

## NPV versus Dividends

Lane Supermarkets, a new firm, will earn €100,000 a year in perpetuity if it pays out all its earnings as dividends. However, the firm plans to invest 20 per cent of its earnings in projects that earn 10 per cent per year. The discount rate is 18 per cent. An earlier formula tells us that the growth rate of dividends is

$$g = \text{Retention ratio} \times \text{Return on retained earnings} = 0.2 \times 0.10 = 2\%$$

For example, in this first year of the new policy, dividends are €80,000 [= (1 − 0.2) × €100,000]. Dividends next year are €81,600 (= €80,000 × 1.02). Dividends the following year are €83,232 [= €80,000 × (1.02)³] and so on. Because dividends represent a fixed percentage of earnings, earnings must grow at 2 per cent a year as well.

However, note that the policy reduces value, because the rate of return on the projects of 10 per cent is less than the discount rate of 18 per cent. That is, the firm would have had a higher value at date 0 if it had a policy of paying all its earnings out as dividends. Thus a policy of investing in projects with negative NPVs rather than paying out earnings as dividends will lead to growth in dividends and earnings, but will reduce value.

## Dividends or Earnings: Which to Discount?

As mentioned earlier, this chapter applied the growing perpetuity formula to the valuation of equity. In our application, we discounted dividends, not earnings. This is sensible, because investors select shares for what they can get out of them. They get only two things out of shares: dividends and the ultimate sale price, which is determined by what future investors expect to receive in dividends.

The calculated share price would be too high were earnings to be discounted instead of dividends. As we saw in our estimation of a firm's growth rate, only a portion of earnings goes to the shareholders as dividends. The remainder is retained to generate future dividends. In our model, retained earnings are equal to the firm's investment. To discount earnings instead of dividends would be to ignore the investment a firm must make today to generate future returns.

## The No-Dividend Firm

Students frequently ask the following question: If the dividend discount model is correct, why aren't no-dividend shares selling at zero? This is a good question, and gets at the goals of the firm. A firm with many growth opportunities faces a dilemma. The firm can pay out dividends now, or it can forgo dividends now so that it can make investments that will generate even greater dividends in the future.[3] This is often a painful choice, because a strategy of dividend deferment may be optimal, yet unpopular among certain shareholders.

Many firms choose to pay no dividends – and these firms sell at positive prices. For example, most Internet firms, such as Amazon.com, Google and eBay, pay no dividends. Rational shareholders believe that either they will receive dividends at some point or they will receive something just as good. That is, the firm will be acquired in a merger, with the shareholders receiving either cash or shares of equity at that time.

Of course, the actual application of the dividend discount model is difficult for firms of this type. Clearly, the model for constant growth of dividends does not apply. Though the differential growth model can work in theory, the difficulties of estimating the date of first dividend, the growth rate of dividends after that date, and the ultimate merger price make application of the model quite difficult in reality.

Empirical evidence suggests that firms with high growth rates are likely to pay lower dividends, a result consistent with the analysis here. For example, consider McDonald's Corporation. The company started in the 1950s and grew rapidly for many years. It paid its first dividend in 1975, though it was a billion-dollar company (in both sales and market value of shareholders' equity) prior to that date. Why did it wait so long to pay a dividend? It waited because it had so many positive growth opportunities (additional locations for new outlets) to take advantage of.

## 5.7 The Dividend Growth Model and the NPVGO Model

This chapter has revealed that the share price is the sum of its price as a cash cow plus the per-share value of its growth opportunities. The Sarro Shipping example illustrated this formula using only one growth opportunity. We also used the growing perpetuity formula to price an equity security with a steady growth in dividends. When the formula is applied to shares, it is typically called the *dividend growth model*. A steady growth in dividends results from a continual investment in growth opportunities, not just investment in a single opportunity. Therefore it is worth while to compare the dividend growth model with the *NPVGO model* when growth occurs through continual investing.

We can use an example to illustrate the main points. Suppose Manama Books has EPS of €10 at the end of the first year, a dividend payout ratio of 40 per cent, a discount rate of 16 per cent, and a return on its retained earnings of 20 per cent. Because the firm retains some of its earnings each year, it is selecting growth opportunities each year. This is different from Sarro Shipping, which had a growth opportunity in only one year. We wish to calculate the price per share using both the dividend growth model and the NPVGO model.

### The Dividend Growth Model

The dividends at date 1 are $0.40 \times €10 = €4$ per share. The retention ratio is 0.60 (1 − 0.40), implying a growth rate in dividends of 0.12 (= 0.60 × 0.20).

From the dividend growth model, the price of a share today is

$$\frac{\text{Div}_1}{R - g} = \frac{€4}{0.16 - 0.12} = €100$$

### The NPVGO Model

Using the NPVGO model, it is more difficult to value a firm with growth opportunities each year (like Manama) than a firm with growth opportunities in only one year (like Sarro). To value according to the NPVGO model, we need to calculate on a per-share basis (1) the net present value of a single growth opportunity, (2) the net present value of all growth opportunities, and (3) the share price if the firm acts as a cash cow – that is, the value of the firm without these growth opportunities. The value of the firm is the sum of (2) + (3).

1  *Value per share of a single growth opportunity*: Out of the earnings per share of €10 at date 1, the firm retains €6 (= 0.6 × €10) at that date. The firm earns €1.20 (= €6 × 0.20) per year in perpetuity on that €6 investment. The NPV from the investment is calculated as follows:

Per-share NPV generated from investment of date 1:

$$-€6 + \frac{€1.20}{0.16} = €1.50 \tag{5.11}$$

That is, the firm invests €6 to reap €1.20 per year on the investment. The earnings are discounted at 16 per cent, implying a value per share from the project of €1.50. Because the investment occurs at date 1 and the first cash flow occurs at date 2, €1.50 is the value of the investment at *date 1*. In other words, the NPV from the date 1 investment has *not* yet been brought back to date 0.

2  *Value per share of all opportunities*: As pointed out earlier, the growth rate of earnings and dividends is 12 per cent. Because retained earnings are a fixed percentage of total earnings, retained earnings must also grow at 12 per cent a year. That is, retained earnings at date

2 are €6.72 (= €6 × 1.12), retained earnings at date 3 are €7.5264 [= €6 × (1.12)$^2$], and so on.

Let's analyse the retained earnings at date 2 in more detail. Because projects will always earn 20 per cent per year, the firm earns €1.344 (= €6.72 × 0.20) in each future year on the €6.72 investment at date 2.

Here is the NPV from the investment:

NPV per share generated from investment at date 2:

$$-€6.72 + \frac{€1.344}{0.16} = €1.68 \tag{5.12}$$

€1.68 is the NPV as of date 2 of the investment made at date 2. The NPV from the date 2 investment has *not* yet been brought back to date 0.

Now consider the retained earnings at date 3 in more detail. The firm earns €1.5053 (= €7.5264 × 0.20) per year on the investment of €7.5264 at date 3.
The NPV from the investment is thus

NPV per share generated from investment at date 3:

$$-€7.5264 + \frac{€1.5053}{0.16} = €1.882 \tag{5.13}$$

From Eqs (5.11), (5.12) and (5.13) the NPV per share of all of the growth opportunities, discounted back to date 0, is

$$\frac{€1.50}{1.16} + \frac{€1.68}{(1.16)^2} + \frac{€1.882}{(1.16)^3} + \cdots \tag{5.14}$$

Because it has an infinite number of terms, this expression looks quite difficult to compute. However, there is an easy simplification. Note that retained earnings are growing at 12 per cent per year. Because all projects earn the same rate of return per year, the NPVs in Eqs (5.11), (5.12) and (5.13) are also growing at 12 per cent per year. Hence we can write Eq. (5.14) as

$$\frac{€1.50}{1.16} + \frac{€1.50 \times 1.12}{(1.16)^2} + \frac{€1.50 \times (1.12)^2}{(1.16)^3} + \cdots$$

This is a growth perpetuity whose value is

$$\text{NPVGO} = \frac{€1.50}{0.16 - 0.12} = €37.50$$

Because the first NPV of €1.50 occurs at date 1, the NPVGO is €37.50 as of date 0. In other words, the firm's policy of investing in new projects from retained earnings has an NPV of €37.50.

3   *Value per share if the firm is a cash cow*: We now assume that the firm pays out all of its earnings as dividends. The dividends would be €10 per year in this case. Because there would be no growth, the value per share would be evaluated by the perpetuity formula:

$$\frac{\text{Div}}{R} = \frac{€10}{0.16} = €62.50$$

## Summation

Equation (5.9) states that share price is the value of a cash cow plus the value of the growth opportunities. This is

$$€100 = €62.50 + €37.50$$

Hence value is the same, whether calculated by a discounted dividend approach or a growth opportunities approach. The share prices from the two approaches must be equal because the approaches are different yet equivalent methods of applying concepts of present value.

## 5.8  Price – Earnings Ratio

We argued earlier that one should not discount earnings to determine the share price. Nevertheless, financial analysts frequently relate earnings and share price, as made evident by their heavy reliance on the price–earnings (or P/E) ratio.

Our previous discussion stated that

$$\text{Price per share} = \frac{\text{EPS}}{R} + \text{NPVGO}$$

Dividing by EPS yields

$$\frac{\text{Price per share}}{\text{EPS}} = \frac{1}{R} + \frac{\text{NPVGO}}{\text{EPS}}$$

The left side is the formula for the price–earnings ratio. The equation shows that the P/E ratio is related to the net present value of growth opportunities. As an example, consider two firms, each having just reported earnings per share of £1. However, one firm has many valuable growth opportunities, whereas the other firm has no growth opportunities at all. The firm with growth opportunities should sell at a higher price, because an investor is buying both current income of £1 and growth opportunities. Suppose that the firm with growth opportunities sells for £16 and the other firm sells for £8. The £1 earnings per share number appears in the denominator of the P/E ratio for both firms. Thus the P/E ratio is 16 for the firm with growth opportunities but only 8 for the firm without the opportunities.

This explanation seems to hold fairly well in the real world. Electronic and other high-tech shares generally sell at very high P/E ratios (or *multiples*, as they are often called) because they are perceived to have high growth rates. In fact, some technology shares sell at high prices even though the companies have never earned a profit. Conversely, railways, utilities and steel companies sell at lower multiples because of the prospects of lower growth. Table 5.1 contains P/E ratios in 2008 for different UK industries. Notice the variation across industries and how the P/E ratios are related to growth opportunities.

Of course, the market is merely pricing *perceptions* of the future, not the future itself. We shall argue later in the text that the stock market generally has realistic perceptions of a firm's prospects. However, this is not always true. In the late 1960s many electronics firms were selling at multiples of 200 times earnings. The high perceived growth rates did not materialize, causing great declines in share prices during the early 1970s. In earlier decades fortunes were made in equities such as IBM and Xerox because the high growth rates were not anticipated by investors. Most recently we have experienced the dot-com collapse, when many Internet stocks were trading at multiples of thousands of times annual earnings. In fact, most Internet stocks had no earnings.

**TABLE 5.1**

| Industry | P/E ratio | Industry | P/E ratio |
|---|---|---|---|
| Oil and gas | 10.88 | Utilities | 11.71 |
| Basic materials | 13.67 | Financials | 11.12 |
| Industrials | 15.41 | Non-financials | 12.85 |
| Consumer goods | 15.61 | Technology | 25.18 |
| Health care | 13.09 | Travel and leisure | 9.73 |
| Consumer services | 12.24 | Oil equipment and services | 29.71 |
| Telecommunications | 13.01 | General retailers | 10.04 |

*Source*: www.ft.com, *Financial Times*

**Table 5.1** Selected P/E ratios

There is an additional factor that explains the P/E ratio, and this is the discount rate, $R$. The previous formula shows that the P/E ratio is *negatively* related to the firm's discount rate. We have already suggested that the discount rate is positively related to the equity's risk or variability. Thus the P/E ratio is negatively related to the equity's risk. To see that this is a sensible result, consider two firms, A and B, behaving as cash cows. The stock market *expects* both firms to have annual earnings of €1 per share for ever. However, the earnings of firm A are known with certainty, whereas the earnings of firm B are quite variable. A rational investor is likely to pay more for a share of firm A because of the absence of risk. If a share of firm A sells at a higher price, and both firms have the same EPS, the P/E ratio of firm A must be higher.

## 5.9  Stock Market Reporting

If you visit Yahoo! Finance, Reuters, FT.com, or the Hemscott website, you will find information about a large number of equities in several different markets. Figure 5.5 reproduces a small section of a Yahoo! Finance page from 15 May 2008 for Enterprise Inns, which is listed on the London Stock Exchange. Information on most listed equities is reported in the same way.

The first line has the name of the firm plus its identifying code (ETI.L), which is also known as the 'ticker'. Last trade refers to the last trade in the shares prior to the time of the printout at 4pm. In this case the last trade was at 3.33pm. The table also shows that the price has fallen by £0.02 from the previous day's closing price of £4.76.

The opening price of £4.7375 is the price at which the equity started trading on 15 May 2008. The bid and ask prices are the prices at which an investor can sell and buy Enterprise Inns shares on the London Stock Exchange. '1y Target Est' is the mean forecast price that financial analysts expect Enterprise Inns will have in one year's time. Looking at the day's and year's variation in prices ('Day's Range' and '52wk Range') illustrates the extreme volatility of Enterprise shares in the year to 15 May 2008. At one point Enterprise Inns was worth only £3.5075, but on another day the price hit a high of £6.535.

Enterprise Inns is one of the largest companies in the UK, and on 15 May 2008 nearly 2 million shares were traded in the company on the London Stock Exchange. This was actually a lot lower than its three-month average daily trading volume of over 5.5 million shares. The total value of Enterprise Inns' shares was £2.40 billion.

Enterprise Inns plc leases pubs and restaurant chains in the UK, and would be included in the 'Travel and leisure' industry grouping shown in Table 5.1. A comparison of Enterprise Inns' P/E ratio (8.88) and that of firms in the same industry (9.73) suggests that the growth opportunities available to it are less than the average firm in the 'Travel and leisure' industry. There could be several reasons for this, and extra analysis would need to be undertaken to understand more fully the factors leading to the lower P/E ratio. The earnings per share of Enterprise Inns was £0.534 and the firm paid a dividend of £0.104 on 21 January 2008.

**FIGURE 5.5**

**ENTERPRISE INNS (LSE:ETI.L)**

| | | | |
|---|---|---|---|
| Last Trade: | **474.00 p** | Day's Range: | 469.75–480.00 |
| Trade Time: | 3:33PM | 52wk Range: | 350.75–653.50 |
| Change: | ↓ 2.00 (0.42%) | Volume: | 1,854,735 |
| Prev Close: | 476.00 | Avg Vol (3m): | 5,601,950 |
| Open: | 473.75 | Market Cap: | £2.40 B |
| Bid: | 473.75 | P/E: | 8.88 |
| Ask: | 474.00 | EPS: | 53.40p |
| 1y Target Est: | 548.83p | Dividend: | 10.40p (21-Jan-08) |

*Source*: *Yahoo! Finance*, www.uk.finance.yahoo.com

**Figure 5.5** Yahoo! Finance listing for Enterprise Inns at 4pm on 15 May 2008

# Summary and Conclusions

In this chapter we used general present value formulae from the previous chapter to price bonds and equities.

1   Pure discount bonds and perpetuities can be viewed as polar cases of bonds. The value of a pure discount bond (also called a zero coupon bond) is

$$PV = \frac{F}{(1 + R)^T}$$

The value of a perpetuity (also called a *consol*) is

$$PV = \frac{C}{R}$$

2   Level payment bonds can be viewed as an intermediate case. The coupon payments form an annuity, and the principal repayment is a lump sum. The value of this type of bond is simply the sum of the values of its two parts.

3   The yield to maturity on a bond is the single rate that discounts the payments on the bond to its purchase price.

4   An equity can be valued by discounting its dividends. We mentioned three types of situation:

   (a)   the case of zero growth of dividends;

   (b)   the case of constant growth of dividends;

   (c)   the case of differential growth.

5   An estimate of the growth rate of an equity is needed for the formulae for situations 4(b) or 4(c). A useful estimate of the growth rate is

$$g = \text{Retention ratio} \times \text{Return on retained earnings}$$

6   It is worth while to view a share as the sum of its worth if the company behaves like a cash cow (the company does no investing) and the value per share of its growth opportunities. We write the value of a share as

$$\frac{EPS}{R} + NPVGO$$

We showed that, in theory, the share price must be the same whether the dividend growth model or the formula here is used.

7   From accounting, we know that earnings are divided into two parts: dividends and retained earnings. Most firms continually retain earnings to create future dividends. One should not discount earnings to obtain the share price, because part of earnings must be reinvested. Only dividends reach the shareholders, and only they should be discounted to obtain share price.

8   We suggested that a firm's price–earnings ratio is a function of three factors:

   (a)   the per-share amount of the firm's valuable growth opportunities;

   (b)   the risk of the share price;

   (c)   the type of accounting method used by the firm.

# Questions and Problems

CONCEPT
1 – 9

1  **Definition of a Bond**  What are the main characteristics of a bond? Provide examples of different types of bond in terms of coupons, maturity and face value.

2  **Bond Valuation**  Show, using the simplified present value formulae from the previous chapter, how you would value a level coupon bond and a zero coupon bond. How would you value a bond with a changing coupon rate?

3  **Bond Concepts**  Explain the difference between a coupon rate and a yield to maturity. Show, using examples, how changing the coupon rate and yield to maturity affects the bond price.

4  **The Present Value of Equity**  Explain why the share price depends on dividends and capital gains.

5  **The Dividend Growth Model**  Under what two assumptions can we use the dividend growth model to determine the share price? Comment on the reasonableness of these assumptions.

6  **Growth Opportunities**  In the context of the dividend growth model, is it true that the growth rate in dividends and the growth rate in the share price are identical?

7  **Net Present Value of Growth Opportunities**  Explain what is meant by NPVGO. In what circumstances is calculating the NPVGO better than other methods of share valuation?

8  **Price–Earnings Ratio**  What are the three factors that determine a company's price–earnings ratio?

9  **Stock Market Reporting**  Why do you think investment websites provide so much information about shares? How would you use this information when valuing shares?

REGULAR
10 – 27

10  **Valuing Bonds**  In March 2009 the German freight company Deutsche Bahn issued a 10-year bond with face value of €1,000 and paying an annual coupon of 4.875 per cent. What is the price of the bond if the YTM is

(a)  4 per cent?

(b)  5 per cent?

(c)  10 per cent?

11  **Bond Yields**  In March 2009 the auto firm DaimlerChrysler, issued a 15-month bond with a face value of €1,000, and an annual coupon rate of 6.875 per cent, paid every quarter. The issue price was €999.7. What was its YTM?

12  **Share Values**  In 2009 DaimlerChrysler had just paid a dividend of €2 per share on its equity. The dividends are expected to grow at a constant rate of 5 per cent per year indefinitely. If investors require a 11 per cent return on DaimlerChrysler's equity, what is the current price? What will the price be in three years? In 15 years?

13  **Share Values**  The next dividend payment from French health food firm Danone will be €1.12 per share. The dividends are anticipated to maintain a 5 per cent growth rate for ever. If Danone shares currently sell for €35.00, what is the required return?

14  **Share Values**  Bless the Weather plc pays dividends that are expected to grow at 5 per cent each year. These will stop in year 5, at which point the company will pay out all its earnings as dividends. Next year's dividend is £10 and its EPS at the time will be £15. If the appropriate discount rate on Bless the Weather shares is 8 per cent, what is its share price today?

15  **Growth Opportunities**  If Bless the Weather plc were to distribute all its earnings, it could maintain a level dividend stream of £15 per share. How much is the market actually paying per share for growth opportunities?

16  **Equity Valuation**  Solid Air plc pays a constant £10 dividend on its equity. The company will maintain this dividend for the next six years, and will then cease paying dividends

for ever. If the required return on the company's equity is 10 per cent, what is the current share price?

17  **Bond Price Movements**   Consider the Deutsche Bahn bond in question 10(c), and the DaimlerChrysler bond in question 11. If yields remain unchanged, what do you expect the price of these bonds to be one year from now? In two years? What's going on here? Illustrate your answers by graphing bond prices against time to maturity.

18  **Bond Returns**   A six-year government bond makes annual coupon payments of 5 per cent and offers a yield of 3 per cent annually compounded. Suppose that one year later the bond still yields 3 per cent. What return has the bondholder earned over the 12-month period? Now suppose that the bond yields 2 per cent at the end of the year. What return would the bondholder earn in this case?

19  **Non-Constant Growth**   Dylan Bearings is a young start-up company. No dividends will be paid on the shares over the next nine years because the firm needs to plough back its earnings to fuel growth. The company will pay an £8 per share dividend in 10 years and will increase the dividend by 6 per cent per year thereafter. If the required return is 13 per cent, what is the current share price?

20  **Valuing Preference Shares**   Mark Bank just issued some new preference shares. The issue will pay a £5 annual dividend in perpetuity, beginning four years from now. If the market requires a 8 per cent return on this investment, how much do preference shares cost today?

21  **Non-Constant Growth**   The return on equity (ROE) of Sunday Child SA is 14 per cent, and it has a payout ratio of 0.5. Current book value per share is €50, and the book value will grow as the firm reinvests earnings. Assume that the ROE and payout ratio stay constant for the next four years. After that, competition forces ROE down to 11.5 per cent, and the payout ratio increases to 0.8. The appropriate discount rate is 11.5 per cent. What are Sunday Child's EPS and dividends next year? How will EPS and dividends grow in years 2, 3, 4, 5 and subsequent years? What is Sunday Child's share price? How does that value depend on the payout ratio and growth rate after year 4?

22  **Semi-Annual Dividends**   The Belgian food group Delhaize paid a dividend of €1.08 in 2008. This is paid in semi-annual instalments. The firm has a policy to pay out 75 per cent of its annual dividend after six months and the remaining amount at the end of the year. If the annual discount rate on Delhaize shares is 8 per cent and the dividend is expected to grow at 3 per cent per year, what is the current share price of Delhaize?

23  **Finding the Required Return**   Daltrey Ltd earned AS$10 million for the fiscal year ending yesterday. The firm also paid out 20 per cent of its earnings as dividends yesterday. The firm will continue to pay out 20 per cent of its earnings as annual, end-of-year dividends. The remaining 80 per cent of earnings is retained by the company for use in projects. The company has 1.25 million shares of equity outstanding. The current share price is AS$40. The historical return on equity (ROE) of 11 per cent is expected to continue in the future. What is the required rate of return on the equity?

24  **Price–Earnings Ratio**   Consider North Sea Energy plc and Highland Bluechips plc, both of which reported earnings of £1,800,000. Without new projects, both firms will continue to generate earnings of £1,800,000 in perpetuity. Assume that all earnings are paid as dividends, and that both firms require a 12 per cent rate of return.

(a)  What is the current P/E ratio for each company?

(b)  North Sea Energy plc has a new project that will generate additional earnings of £200,000 each year in perpetuity. Calculate the new P/E ratio of the company.

(c)  Highland Bluechips has a new project that will increase earnings by £400,000 in perpetuity. Calculate the new P/E ratio of the firm.

25  **Growth Opportunities**   Stambaugh Corporation currently has earnings per share of €4.00. The company has no growth, and pays out all earnings as dividends. It has a new project that will require an investment of €1.00 per share in one year. The project will

only last two years and will increase earnings in the two years following the investment by €1.90 and €2.10, respectively. Investors require a 12 per cent return on Stambaugh equity.

(a) What is the share price, assuming the firm does not undertake the investment opportunity?

(b) If the company does undertake the investment, what is the share price now?

(c) Again assume the company undertakes the investment. What will the share price be four years from today?

26 **Growth Opportunities** Yorkshire Property Ltd expects to earn £100 million per year in perpetuity if it does not undertake any new projects. The firm has an opportunity to invest £12 million today and £7 million in one year in real estate. The new investment will generate annual earnings of £10 million in perpetuity, beginning two years from today. The firm has 20 million shares outstanding, and the required rate of return on the equity is 15 per cent. Land investments are not depreciable. Ignore taxes.

(a) What is the share price if the firm does not undertake the new investment?

(b) What is the value of the investment?

(c) What is the share price if the firm undertakes the investment?

27 **Growth Opportunities** The annual earnings of Avalanche Skis will be 6 Swedish kroner per share in perpetuity if the firm makes no new investments. Under such a situation the firm would pay out all of its earnings as dividends. Assume the first dividend will be received exactly one year from now.

Alternatively, assume that three years from now, and in every subsequent year in perpetuity, the company can invest 25 per cent of its earnings in new projects. Each project will earn 40 per cent at year-end in perpetuity. The firm's discount rate is 14 per cent.

(a) What is the share price of Avalanche Skis today without the company making the new investment?

(b) If Avalanche announces that the new investment will be made, what will the share price be today?

**CHALLENGE**

**28 – 34**

28 **Components of Bond Returns** Bond P is a premium bond with an 11 per cent coupon. Bond D is a 5 per cent coupon bond currently selling at a discount. Both bonds make annual payments, have a YTM of 8 per cent, and have five years to maturity. What is the current yield for Bond P? For Bond D? If interest rates remain unchanged, what is the expected capital gains yield over the next year for Bond P? For Bond D? Explain your answers, and the interrelationships among the various types of yield.

29 **Holding Period Yield** The YTM on a bond is the interest rate you earn on your investment if interest rates don't change. If you actually sell the bond before it matures, your realized return is known as the holding period yield (HPY).

(a) Suppose that today you buy an 8 per cent annual coupon bond for €1,150. The bond has 10 years to maturity. What rate of return do you expect to earn on your investment?

(b) Two years from now, the YTM on your bond has declined by 1 per cent, and you decide to sell. What price will your bond sell for? What is the HPY on your investment? Compare this yield with the YTM when you first bought the bond. Why are they different?

30 **Valuing Bonds** Mallory plc has two different bonds currently outstanding. Bond M has a face value of £20,000 and matures in 20 years. The bond makes no payments for the first six years, then pays £1,200 every six months over the subsequent eight years, and finally pays £1,500 every six months over the last six years. Bond N also has a face value of £20,000 and a maturity of 20 years; it makes no coupon payments over the life of the bond. If the required return on both these bonds is 10 per cent compounded semi-annually, what is the current price of Bond M? Of Bond N?

31  **Capital Gains versus Income**  Consider four different equities, all of which have a required return of 15 per cent and a most recent dividend of £4.00 per share. Equities W, X and Y are expected to maintain constant rates in dividends for the foreseeable future of 10 per cent, 0 per cent and −5 per cent per year, respectively. Z is a growth stock that will increase its dividend by 20 per cent for the next two years and then maintain a constant 12 per cent growth rate thereafter. What is the dividend yield for each of these four equities? What is the expected capital gains yield? Discuss the relationship between the various returns that you find for each of these equities.

32  **Equity Valuation**  Most corporations pay semi-annual rather than annual dividends on their equity. Barring any unusual circumstances during the year, the board raises, lowers, or maintains the current dividend once a year, and then pays this dividend out in equal biannual instalments to its shareholders.

(a)  Suppose a company currently pays a €3.00 annual dividend on its equity in a single annual instalment, and management plans on raising this dividend by 6 per cent per year indefinitely. If the required return on this equity is 14 per cent, what is the current share price?

(b)  Now suppose that the company in (a) actually pays its annual dividend in equal six-monthly instalments: thus this company has just paid a £1.50 dividend per share, as it has in the previous six months. What is the current share price now? (*Hint:* Find the equivalent annual end-of-year dividend for each year.) Comment on whether you think that this model of share valuation is appropriate.

33  **Growth Opportunities**  Nakamura has earnings of £10 million and is projected to grow at a constant rate of 5 per cent for ever. Currently all earnings are paid out as dividends. The company plans to launch a new project two years from now that would be completely internally funded and require 20 per cent of the earnings that year. The project would start generating revenues one year after the launch of the project, and the earnings from the new project in any year are estimated to be constant at £5 million. The company has 10 million shares outstanding. Estimate the value of Nakamura. The discount rate is 10 per cent.

34  **Spreadsheets**  Write a spreadsheet program to construct a series of bond tables that show the price of a bond given the coupon rate, maturity, and yield to maturity. Assume that coupon payments are annual and yields are compounded semi-annually.

MINI CASE

# Equity Valuation at Ragan Thermal Systems

Ragan Thermal Systems plc was founded nine years ago by brother and sister Carrington and Genevieve Ragan. The company manufactures and installs commercial heating, ventilation and cooling (HVAC) units. Ragan has experienced rapid growth because of a proprietary technology that increases the energy efficiency of its systems. The company is owned equally by Carrington and Genevieve. The original agreement between the siblings gave each 50,000 shares. In the event that either wishes to sell the shares, they first have to be offered to the other at a discounted price.

Although neither sibling wants to sell any shares at present, they have decided they should value their holdings in the company for financial planning purposes. To accomplish this, they have gathered the following information about their main competitors.

| Ragan Thermal Systems plc Competitors | | | | | |
|---|---|---|---|---|---|
| | EPS (€) | DPS (€) | Share price (€) | ROE (%) | R (%) |
| Arctic Cooling Ltd | 0.82 | 0.16 | 15.19 | 11 | 10 |
| National Heating & Cooling | 1.32 | 0.52 | 12.49 | 14 | 13 |
| Expert HVAC plc | −0.47 | 0.54 | 48.60 | 14 | 12 |
| Industry Average | 0.56 | 0.41 | 25.43 | 13 | 11.67 |

Expert HVAC plc's negative earnings per share (EPS) were the result of an accounting write-off last year. Without the write-off, EPS for the company would have been €2.34.

Last year, Ragan had an EPS of €4.32 and paid a dividend to Carrington and Genevieve of €54,000 each. The company also had a return on equity of 25 per cent. The siblings believe a required return for the company of 20 per cent is appropriate.

1   Assuming the company continues its current growth rate, what is the share price of the company's equity?

2   To verify their calculations, Carrington and Genevieve have hired Josh Jobby as a consultant. Josh was previously an equity analyst, and he has covered the HVAC industry. Josh has examined the company's financial statements as well as those of its competitors. Although Ragan currently has a technological advantage, Josh's research indicates that Ragan's competitors are investigating other methods to improve efficiency. Given this, Josh believes that Ragan's technological advantage will last for only the next five years. After that period, the company's growth is likely to slow to the industry average. Additionally, Josh believes that the required return the company uses is too high. He believes the industry average required return is more appropriate. Under Josh's assumptions, what is the estimated share price?

3   What is the industry average price–earnings ratio? What is Ragan's price–earnings ratio? Comment on any differences and explain why they may exist.

4   Assume the company's growth rate declines to the industry average after five years. What percentage of the equity's value is attributable to growth opportunities?

5   Assume the company's growth rate slows to the industry average in five years. What future return on equity does this imply?

6   After discussions with Josh, Carrington and Genevieve agree that they would like to try to increase the value of the company equity. Like many small business owners, they want to retain control of the company and do not want to sell shares to outside investors. They also feel that the company's debt is at a manageable level and do not want to borrow more money. What steps can they take to increase the share price? Are there any conditions under which this strategy would not increase the share price?

## Practical Case Study

For these problems, use any web service that provides financial information. Good examples are Yahoo! Finance, Hemscott, Reuters, and FT.com. You can also go to the company's website and download financial accounts from there. Get used to accessing financial websites, as it is a basic skill required by all financial managers.

1   **Dividend Discount Model**   Choose any large company from your country and download its most recent statement of financial position and income statement. Using the financial figures in the accounts, calculate the sustainable growth rate for your company. Now go to Yahoo! Finance or any other financial website and find the closing share price for the same month as the financial accounts you used. What is the implied required return on your company according to the dividend growth model? Does this number make sense? Why or why not?

2   **Growth Opportunities**   Assume that investors require an 8 per cent return on the company you have studied in question 1. Using this share price and the EPS for the most recent year, calculate the NPVGO for your company. What is the appropriate P/E ratio for your company using these calculations? What is the P/E ratio on Yahoo! Finance? Can you explain the difference, if any?

## Relevant Accounting Standards

Accounting standards are very relevant for security valuation because you need to be able to interpret the correct growth rates from the accounting figures. Important standards relating to this chapter are IAS33 *Earnings per Share* and IAS39 *Financial Instruments: Recognition and Measurement*. IAS39 provides definitions for different types of financial securities. This can sometimes be problematic for an accountant because many securities have equity and bond-like features. Visit the IASPlus website (www.iasplus.com) for more information.

## Additional Reading

A major challenge in share and bond valuation is measuring growth rates. The following papers investigate this issue (country or region of study is given in bold).

Beck, T., A. Demirguc-Kunt and V. Maksimovic (2005) 'Financial and legal constraints to growth: does firm size matter?', *Journal of Finance*, vol. 60, no. 1, pp. 137–177. **International**.
Chen, L. (2009) 'On the reversal of return and dividend growth predictability: a tale of two periods', *Journal of Financial Economics* (forthcoming). **US**.
Claessens, S. and L. Laeven (2003) 'Financial development, property rights, and growth', *Journal of Finance*, vol. 58, no. 6, pp. 2401–2436. **International**.

The following papers are also of interest.
Bris, A., Y. Koskinen and M. Nilsson (2009) 'The euro and corporate valuations', *Review of Financial Studies* (forthcoming). **Europe**.
Penman, S. (2006) 'Handling valuation models', *Journal of Applied Corporate Finance*, vol. 18, no. 2, pp. 48–55. **Theoretical**.

## Endnotes

1  We ignore the possibility of the issuance of equities or bonds to raise capital. These possibilities are considered in later chapters.

2  Later in the text, we speak of issuing shares or debt to fund projects.

3  A third alternative is to issue equity so the firm has enough cash both to pay dividends and to invest. This possibility is explored in a later chapter.

**Online LearningCentre**

To help you grasp the key concepts of this chapter check out the extra resources posted on the Online Learning Centre at **www.mcgraw-hill.co.uk/textbooks/hillier**

Among other helpful resources such as PowerPoint presentations and chapter outlines there is the following:

• Appendix 5A The term structure of interest rates, spot rates, and yield to maturity.

# Chapter 6

# Net Present Value and Other Investment Rules

Irrespective of the state of the economy, companies need to invest to maintain existing operations or exploit new opportunities. For example, Tesco plc, the multinational food retailer, spent nearly £4 billion in 2007 and 2008 on new branches and the purchase of another company, Homever Stores.

Tesco's new branches are an example of a capital budgeting decision. Decisions such as these, with a price tag of many millions of pounds each, are obviously major undertakings, and the risks and rewards must be carefully weighed. In this chapter we discuss the basic tools used in making such decisions.

In Chapter 1 we saw that increasing the value of a company's equity is the goal of financial management. Thus we need to know how a particular investment will achieve that. This chapter considers a variety of techniques that are used in practice for this purpose. More important, it shows how many of these techniques can be misleading, and it explains why the net present value approach is the right one.

## 6.1 Why Use Net Present Value?

This chapter, as well as the next two, focuses on *capital budgeting*, the decision-making process for accepting or rejecting projects. We develop the basic capital budgeting methods, leaving much of the practical application to subsequent chapters. Fortunately, we don't have to develop these methods from scratch. In Chapter 4 we pointed out that one pound or euro received in the future is worth less than a pound or euro respectively received today. The reason, of course, is that today's money can be reinvested, yielding a greater amount in the future. And we showed in Chapter 4 that the exact worth of a pound or euro to be received in the future is its present value. Furthermore, Section 4.1 suggested calculating the *net present value* of any project. That is, the section suggested calculating the difference between the sum of the present values of the project's future cash flows and the initial cost of the project.

The net present value (NPV) method is the first one to be considered in this chapter. We begin by reviewing the approach with a simple example. Then we ask why the method leads to good decisions.

## Net Present Value

**EXAMPLE 6.1**

Alpha Corporation is considering investing in a riskless project costing £100. The project receives £107 in one year and has no other cash flows. The discount rate is 6 per cent.

The NPV of the project can easily be calculated as

$$£0.94 = -£100 + \frac{£107}{1.06} \tag{6.1}$$

From Chapter 4 we know that the project should be accepted, because its NPV is positive. Had the NPV of the project been negative, as would have been the case with an interest rate greater than 7 per cent, the project should be rejected.

The basic investment rule can be generalized thus:

**Accept a project if the NPV is greater than zero.**
**Reject a project if NPV is less than zero.**

We refer to this as the NPV rule.

Why does the NPV rule lead to good decisions? Consider the following two strategies available to the managers of Alpha Corporation:

1   Use £100 of corporate cash to invest in the project. The £107 will be paid as a dividend in one year.

2   Forgo the project and pay the £100 of corporate cash as a dividend today.

If strategy 2 is employed, the shareholder might deposit the dividend in a bank for one year. With an interest rate of 6 per cent, strategy 2 would produce cash of £106 (= £100 × 1.06) at the end of the year. The shareholder would prefer strategy 1, because strategy 2 produces less than £107 at the end of the year.

Our basic point is this: Accepting positive NPV projects benefits shareholders.

How do we interpret the exact NPV of £0.94? This is the increase in the value of the firm from the project. For example, imagine that the firm today has productive assets worth £V and has £100 of cash. If the firm forgoes the project, the value of the firm today would simply be

$$£V + £100$$

If the firm accepts the project, the firm will receive £107 in one year but will have no cash today. Thus the firm's value today would be

$$£V + \frac{£107}{1.06}$$

The difference between these equations is just £0.94, the present value of Eq. (6.1). Thus: The value of the firm rises by the NPV of the project.

Note that the value of the firm is merely the sum of the values of the different projects, divisions, or other entities within the firm. This property, called value additivity, is quite important. It implies that the contribution of any project to a firm's value is simply the NPV of the project. As we shall see later, alternative methods discussed in this chapter do not generally have this nice property.

One detail remains. We assumed that the project was riskless, a rather implausible assumption. Future cash flows of real-world projects are invariably risky. In other words, cash flows can only be estimated, rather than known. Imagine that the managers of Alpha *expect* the cash flow of the project to be £107 next year. That is, the cash flow could be higher, say £117, or lower, say £97. With this slight change, the project is risky. Suppose the project is about as risky as the stock market as a whole, where the expected return this year is perhaps

10 per cent. Then 10 per cent becomes the discount rate, implying that the NPV of the project would be

$$-£2.73 = -£100 + \frac{£107}{1.10}$$

Because the NPV is negative, the project should be rejected. This makes sense: a shareholder of Alpha receiving a £100 dividend today could invest it in the stock market, expecting a 10 per cent return. Why accept a project with the same risk as the market but with an expected return of only 7 per cent?

Conceptually, the discount rate on a risky project is the return that one can expect to earn on a financial asset of comparable risk. This discount rate is often referred to as an *opportunity cost*, because corporate investment in the project takes away the shareholder's opportunity to invest the dividend in a financial asset. If the actual calculation of the discount rate strikes you as extremely difficult in the real world, you are probably right. Although you can call a bank to find out the current interest rate, whom do you call to find the expected return on the market this year? And, if the risk of the project differs from that of the market, how do you make the adjustment? However, the calculation is by no means impossible. We forgo the calculation in this chapter, but we present it in later chapters of the text.

Having shown that NPV is a sensible approach, how can we tell whether alternative methods are as good as NPV? The key to NPV is its three attributes:

1   *NPV uses cash flows.* Cash flows from a project can be used for other corporate purposes (such as dividend payments, other capital budgeting projects, or payments of corporate interest). By contrast, earnings are an artificial construct. Although earnings are useful to accountants, they should not be used in capital budgeting because they do not represent cash.

2   *NPV uses all the cash flows of the project.* Other approaches ignore cash flows beyond a particular date: beware of these approaches.

3   *NPV discounts the cash flows properly.* Other approaches may ignore the time value of money when handling cash flows. Beware of these approaches as well.

## 6.2   The Payback Period Method

### Defining the Rule

One of the most popular alternatives to NPV is payback. Here is how payback works. Consider a project with an initial investment of –€50,000. Cash flows are €30,000, €20,000 and €10,000 in the first three years, respectively. These flows are illustrated in Fig. 6.1. A useful way of writing down investments such as the preceding is with the notation

$$(-€50,000, €30,000, €20,000, €10,000)$$

The minus sign in front of the €50,000 reminds us that this is a cash outflow for the investor, and the commas between the different numbers indicate that they are received – or if they are cash outflows, that they are paid out – at different times. In this example we are assuming that the cash flows occur one year apart, with the first one occurring the moment we decide to take on the investment.

The firm receives cash flows of €30,000 and €20,000 in the first two years, which add up to the €50,000 original investment. This means that the firm has recovered its investment within two years. In this case two years is the *payback period* of the investment.

The payback period rule for making investment decisions is simple. A particular cut-off date, say two years, is selected. All investment projects that have payback periods of two years or less are accepted, and all of those that pay off in more than two years – if at all – are rejected.

**Figure 6.1** Cash flows of an investment project

TABLE 6.1

| Year | A (£) | B (£) | C (£) |
|---|---|---|---|
| 0 | −100 | −100 | −100 |
| 1 | 20 | 50 | 50 |
| 2 | 30 | 30 | 30 |
| 3 | 50 | 20 | 20 |
| 4 | 60 | 60 | 60,000 |
| Payback period (years) | 3 | ·3 | 3 |

**Table 6.1** Expected cash flows for projects A, B and C

## Problems with the Payback Method

There are at least three problems with payback. To illustrate the first two problems, we consider the three projects in Table 6.1. All three projects have the same three-year payback period, so they should all be equally attractive – right?

Actually, they are not equally attractive, as can be seen by a comparison of different *pairs* of projects.

**Problem 1: Timing of Cash Flows within the Payback Period**   Let us compare project A with project B. In years 1 to 3 the cash flows of project A rise from £20 to £50, while the cash flows of project B fall from £50 to £20. Because the large cash flow of £50 comes earlier with project B, its net present value must be higher. Nevertheless, we just saw that the payback periods of the two projects are identical. Thus a problem with the payback method is that it does not consider the timing of the cash flows within the payback period. This example shows that the payback method is inferior to NPV because, as we pointed out earlier, the NPV method *discounts the cash flows properly.*

**Problem 2: Payments after the Payback Period**   Now consider projects B and C, which have identical cash flows within the payback period. However, project C is clearly preferred, because it has a cash flow of £60,000 in the fourth year. Thus another problem with the payback method is that it ignores all cash flows occurring after the payback period. Because of the short-term orientation of the payback method, some valuable long-term projects are likely to be rejected. The NPV method does not have this flaw because, as we pointed out earlier, this method *uses all the cash flows of the project.*

**Problem 3: Arbitrary Standard for Payback Period**   We do not need to refer to Table 6.1 when considering a third problem with the payback method. Capital markets help us estimate the discount rate used in the NPV method. The riskless rate, perhaps proxied by the yield on a Treasury instrument, would be the appropriate rate for a riskless investment. Later chapters of this textbook show how to use historical returns in the capital markets to estimate the discount rate for a risky project. However, there is no comparable guide for choosing the payback cut-off date, so the choice is somewhat arbitrary.

## Managerial Perspective

The payback method is often used by large, sophisticated companies when making relatively small decisions. The decision to build a small warehouse, for example, or to pay for a tune-up for a truck is the sort of decision that is often made by lower-level management. Typically, a manager might reason that a tune-up would cost, say, £200, and if it saved £120 each year in reduced fuel costs it would pay for itself in less than two years. On such a basis the decision would be made.

Although the treasurer of the company might not have made the decision in the same way, the company endorses such decision-making. Why would upper management condone or even encourage such retrograde activity in its employees? One answer would be that it is easy to make decisions using payback. Multiply the tune-up decision into 50 such decisions a month, and the appeal of this simple method becomes clearer.

The payback method also has some desirable features for managerial control. Just as important as the investment decision itself is the company's ability to evaluate the manager's decision-making ability. Under the NPV method a long time may pass before one decides whether a decision was correct. With the payback method we know in two years whether the manager's assessment of the cash flows was correct.

It has also been suggested that firms with good investment opportunities but no available cash may justifiably use payback. For example, the payback method could be used by small, privately held firms with good growth prospects but limited access to the capital markets. Quick cash recovery enhances the reinvestment possibilities for such firms.

Finally, practitioners often argue that standard academic criticisms of payback overstate any real-world problems with the method. For example, textbooks typically make fun of payback by positing a project with low cash inflows in the early years but a huge cash inflow right after the payback cut-off date. This project is likely to be rejected under the payback method, though its acceptance would, in truth, benefit the firm. Project C in our Table 6.1 is an example of such a project. Practitioners point out that the pattern of cash flows in these textbook examples is much too stylized to mirror the real world. In fact, a number of executives have told us that, for the overwhelming majority of real-world projects, payback and NPV both lead to the same decision. In addition, these executives indicate that if an investment like project C were encountered in the real world, decision-makers would almost certainly make ad hoc adjustments to the payback rule so that the project would be accepted.

Notwithstanding all of the preceding rationale, it is not surprising to discover that as the decisions grow in importance, which is to say when firms look at bigger projects, NPV becomes the order of the day. When questions of controlling and evaluating the manager become less important than making the right investment decision, payback is used less frequently. For big-ticket decisions, such as whether or not to buy a machine, build a factory, or acquire a company, the payback method is seldom used.

## Summary of Payback

The payback method differs from NPV and is therefore conceptually wrong. With its arbitrary cut-off date and its blindness to cash flows after that date, it can lead to some flagrantly foolish decisions if it is used too literally. Nevertheless, because of its simplicity, as well as its other mentioned advantages, companies often use it as a screen for making the myriad minor investment decisions they continually face.

Although this means that you should be wary of trying to change approaches such as the payback method when you encounter them in companies, you should probably be careful not to accept the sloppy financial thinking they represent. After this course, you would do your company a disservice if you used payback instead of NPV when you had a choice.

## 6.3 The Discounted Payback Period Method

Aware of the pitfalls of payback, some decision-makers use a variant called the **discounted payback period method**. Under this approach, we first discount the cash flows. Then we ask how long it takes for the discounted cash flows to equal the initial investment.

For example, suppose that the discount rate is 10 per cent and the cash flows on a project are given by

$$(-£100, £50, £50, £20)$$

This investment has a payback period of two years because the investment is paid back in that time.

To compute the project's discounted payback period, we first discount each of the cash flows at the 10 per cent rate. These discounted cash flows are

$$[-£100, £50/1.1, £50/(1.1)^2, £20/(1.1)^3] = (-£100, £45.45, £41.32, £15.03)$$

The discounted payback period of the original investment is simply the payback period for these discounted cash flows. The payback period for the discounted cash flows is slightly less than three years because the discounted cash flows over the three years are £101.80 (= £45.45 + 41.32 + 15.03). As long as the cash flows and discount rate are positive, the discounted payback period will never be smaller than the payback period because discounting reduces the value of the cash flows.

At first glance discounted payback may seem like an attractive alternative, but on closer inspection we see that it has some of the same major flaws as payback. Like payback, discounted payback first requires us to make a somewhat magical choice of an arbitrary cut-off period, and then it ignores all cash flows after that date.

If we have already gone to the trouble of discounting the cash flows, any small appeal to simplicity or to managerial control that payback may have has been lost. We might just as well add up all the discounted cash flows and use NPV to make the decision. Although discounted payback looks a bit like NPV, it is just a poor compromise between the payback method and NPV.

## 6.4 The Average Accounting Return Method

### Defining the Rule

Another attractive, but fatally flawed, approach to financial decision-making is the **average accounting return**. The average accounting return is the average project earnings after taxes and depreciation, divided by the average book value of the investment during its life. In spite of its flaws, the average accounting return method is worth examining because it is used frequently in the real world.

**EXAMPLE 6.2**

## Average Accounting Return

Consider a company that is evaluating whether to buy a store in a new shopping centre. The purchase price is £500,000. We shall assume that the store has an estimated life of five years, and will need to be completely scrapped or rebuilt at the end of that time. For simplicity's sake, the asset will be depreciated using straight-line depreciation (this does not occur in countries that use IFRS, but suits to illustrate the method). The projected yearly sales and expense figures are shown in Table 6.2.

| | Year 1 (£) | Year 2 (£) | Year 3 (£) | Year 4 (£) | Year 5 (£) |
|---|---|---|---|---|---|
| Revenue | 433,333 | 450,000 | 266,667 | 200,000 | 133,333 |
| Expenses | 200,000 | 150,000 | 100,000 | 100,000 | 100,000 |
| Before-tax cash flow | 233,333 | 300,000 | 166,667 | 100,000 | 33,333 |
| Depreciation | 100,000 | 100,000 | 100,000 | 100,000 | 100,000 |
| Profit before taxes | 133,333 | 200,000 | 66,667 | 0 | −66,667 |
| Taxes ($t_c = 0.25$)* | 33,333 | 50,000 | 16,667 | 0 | −16,667 |
| Net income | 100,000 | 150,000 | 50,000 | 0 | −50,000 |

$$\text{Average net income} = \frac{(£100{,}000 + 150{,}000 + 50{,}000 + 0 - 50{,}000)}{5} = £50{,}000$$

$$\text{Average investment} = \frac{£500{,}000 + 0}{2} = £250{,}000$$

$$\text{AAR} = \frac{£50{,}000}{£250{,}000} = 20\%$$

*Corporate tax rate = $t_c$. The tax rebate in year 5 of −£16,667 occurs if the rest of the firm is profitable. Here the loss in the project reduces the taxes of the entire firm.

**Table 6.2** Projected yearly revenue and costs for average accounting return

It is worth examining Table 6.2 carefully. In fact, the first step in any project assessment is a careful look at projected cash flows. First-year sales for the store are estimated to be £433,333. Before-tax cash flow will be £233,333. Sales are expected to rise and expenses are expected to fall in the second year, resulting in a before-tax cash flow of £300,000. Competition from other stores and the loss in novelty will reduce before-tax cash flow to £166,667, £100,000 and £33,333, respectively, in the next three years.

To compute the average accounting return (AAR) on the project, we divide the average net income by the average amount invested. This can be done in three steps.

**Step 1: Determining Average Net Income**    Net income in any year is net cash flow minus depreciation and taxes. Depreciation is *not* a cash outflow.[1] Rather, it is a charge reflecting the fact that the investment in the store becomes less valuable every year.

We assume the project has a useful life of five years, at which time it will be worthless. Because the initial investment is £500,000, and because it will be worthless in five years, we assume that it loses value at the rate of £100,000 each year. This steady loss in value of £100,000 is called *straight-line depreciation*. The method used in countries that employ IFRS is known as the *reducing-balance method*, which will be discussed in detail later. We subtract both depreciation and taxes from before-tax cash flow to derive net income, as shown in Table 6.2. Net income is £100,000 in the first year, £150,000 in year 2, £50,000 in year 3, zero in year 4, and −£50,000 in the last year. The average net income over the life of the project is therefore

Average net income:

$$[£100{,}000 + 150{,}000 + 50{,}000 + 0 + (-50{,}000)]/5 = £50{,}000$$

**Step 2: Determining Average Investment**    We stated earlier that, because of depreciation, the investment in the store becomes less valuable every year. Because depreciation is £100,000 per year, the value at the end of year zero is £500,000, the value at the end of year 1 is £400,000, and so on. What is the average value of the investment over the life of the investment?

The mechanical calculation is

Average investment:

$$(\pounds500,000 + 400,000 + 300,000 + 200,000 + 100,000 + 0)/6$$
$$= \pounds250,000 \tag{6.2}$$

We divide by 6, not 5, because £500,000 is what the investment is worth at the beginning of the five years and £0 is what it is worth at the beginning of the sixth year. In other words, there are six terms in the parentheses of Eq. (6.2).

**Step 3: Determining AAR**   The average return is simply

$$AAR = \frac{\pounds50,000}{\pounds250,000} = 20\%$$

If the firm had a targeted accounting rate of return greater than 20 per cent, the project would be rejected; if its targeted return were less than 20 per cent, it would be accepted.

## Analysing the Average Accounting Return Method

By now you should be able to see what is wrong with the AAR method.

The most important flaw with AAR is that it does not work with the right raw materials. It uses net income and book value of the investment, both of which come from the accounting figures. Accounting numbers are somewhat arbitrary. For example, certain cash outflows, such as the cost of a building, are depreciated under specific accounting rules. Other flows, such as maintenance, are expensed. In real-world situations, the decision to depreciate or expense an item involves judgement. Thus the basic inputs of the AAR method – income and average investment – are affected by the accountant's judgement. Conversely, the NPV method *uses cash flows*. Accounting judgements do not affect cash flow.

Second, AAR takes no account of timing. In the previous example, the AAR would have been the same if the £100,000 net income in the first year had occurred in the last year. However, delaying an inflow for five years would have lowered the NPV of the investment. As mentioned earlier in this chapter, the NPV approach *discounts properly*.

Third, just as payback requires an arbitrary choice of the cut-off date, the AAR method offers no guidance on what the right targeted rate of return should be. It could be the discount rate in the market. But then again, because the AAR method is not the same as the present value method, it is not obvious that this would be the right choice.

Given these problems, is the AAR method employed in practice? Like the payback method, the AAR (and variations of it) is frequently used as a 'backup' to discounted cash flow methods. Perhaps this is so because it is easy to calculate and uses accounting numbers readily available from the firm's accounting system. In addition, both shareholders and the media pay a lot of attention to the overall profitability of a firm. Thus some managers may feel pressured to select projects that are profitable in the near term, even if the projects come up short in terms of NPV. These managers may focus on the AAR of individual projects more than they should.

## 6.5  The Internal Rate of Return

Now we come to the most important alternative to the NPV method: the internal rate of return, universally known as the IRR. The IRR is about as close as you can get to NPV without actually being NPV. The basic rationale behind the IRR method is that it provides a single number summarizing the merits of a project. That number does not depend on the interest rate prevailing in the capital market. That is why it is called the internal rate of return; the

FIGURE
6.2

**Figure 6.2** Cash flows for a simple project

number is internal or intrinsic to the project and does not depend on anything except the cash flows of the project.

For example, consider the simple project (−£100, £110) in Fig. 6.2. For a given rate, the net present value of this project can be described as

$$\text{NPV} = -£100 + \frac{£110}{1 + R}$$

where $R$ is the discount rate. What must the discount rate be to make the NPV of the project equal to zero?

We begin by using an arbitrary discount rate of 0.08, which yields

$$£1.85 = -£100 + \frac{£110}{1.08}$$

Because the NPV in this equation is positive, we now try a higher discount rate, such as 0.12. This yields

$$-£1.79 = -£100 + \frac{£110}{1.12}$$

Because the NPV in this equation is negative, we try lowering the discount rate to 0.10. This yields

$$0 = -£100 + \frac{£110}{1.10}$$

This trial-and-error procedure tells us that the NPV of the project is zero when $R$ equals 10 per cent.[2] Thus we say that 10 per cent is the project's internal rate of return (IRR). In general, the IRR is the rate that causes the NPV of the project to be zero. The implication of this exercise is very simple. The firm should be equally willing to accept or reject the project if the discount rate is 10 per cent. The firm should accept the project if the discount rate is below 10 per cent. The firm should reject the project if the discount rate is above 10 per cent.

The general investment rule is clear:

**Accept the project if the IRR is greater than the discount rate. Reject the project if the IRR is less than the discount rate.**

We refer to this as the basic IRR rule. Now we can try the more complicated example (−€200, €100, €100, €100) in Fig. 6.3.

As we did previously, let's use trial and error to calculate the internal rate of return. We try 20 per cent and 30 per cent, yielding the following:

| Discount rate (%) | NPV (€) |
| --- | --- |
| 20 | 10.65 |
| 30 | −18.39 |

FIGURE
6.3

**Figure 6.3** Cash flows for a more complex project

After much more trial and error, we find that the NPV of the project is zero when the discount rate is 23.37 per cent. Thus the IRR is 23.37 per cent. With a 20 per cent discount rate, the NPV is positive and we would accept it. However, if the discount rate were 30 per cent, we would reject it.

Algebraically, IRR is the unknown in the following equation:[3]

$$0 = -€200 + \frac{€100}{1 + \text{IRR}} + \frac{€100}{(1 + \text{IRR})^2} + \frac{€100}{(1 + \text{IRR})^3}$$

FIGURE
6.4

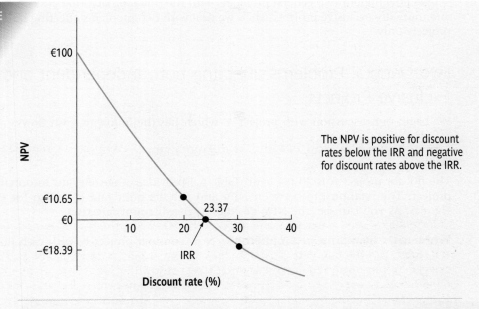

**Figure 6.4** Net present value (NPV) and discount rates for a more complex project

Figure 6.4 illustrates what the IRR of a project means. The figure plots the NPV as a function of the discount rate. The curve crosses the horizontal axis at the IRR of 23.37 per cent because this is where the NPV equals zero.

It should also be clear that the NPV is positive for discount rates below the IRR and negative for discount rates above the IRR. This means that if we accept projects like this one when the discount rate is less than the IRR, we shall be accepting positive NPV projects. Thus the IRR rule coincides exactly with the NPV rule.

If this were all there were to it, the IRR rule would always coincide with the NPV rule. This would be a wonderful discovery, because it would mean that just by computing the IRR for a project we would be able to tell where it ranks among all of the projects we are considering. For example, if the IRR rule really works, a project with an IRR of 20 per cent will always be at least as good as one with an IRR of 15 per cent.

Unfortunately, the world of finance is not so kind. The IRR rule and the NPV rule are the same only for examples like the one just discussed. Several problems with the IRR approach occur in more complicated situations.

## 6.6 Problems with the IRR Approach

### Definition of Independent and Mutually Exclusive Projects

An **independent project** is one whose acceptance or rejection is independent of the acceptance or rejection of other projects. For example, imagine that Starbucks is considering putting a coffee outlet on a remote island in the north of Scotland. Acceptance or rejection of this outlet is likely to be unrelated to the acceptance or rejection of any other coffee outlet in its system. The remoteness of the outlet in question ensures that it will not pull sales away from other outlets.

Now consider the other extreme, **mutually exclusive investments**. What does it mean for two projects, A and B, to be mutually exclusive? You can accept A or you can accept B, or you can reject both of them, but you cannot accept both of them. For example, A might be a decision to build a house on a corner plot that you own, and B might be a decision to build a movie theatre on the same plot.

We now present two general problems with the IRR approach that affect both independent and mutually exclusive projects. Then we deal with two problems affecting mutually exclusive projects only.

### Two General Problems affecting both Independent and Mutually Exclusive Projects

We begin our discussion with project A, which has the following cash flows:

$$(-£100, £130)$$

The IRR for project A is 30 per cent. Table 6.3 provides other relevant information about the project. The relationship between NPV and the discount rate is shown for this project in Fig. 6.5. As you can see, the NPV declines as the discount rate rises.

**Problem 1: Investing or Financing?**   Now consider project B, with cash flows of:

$$(£100, -£130)$$

| TABLE 6.3 | | Project A | | | Project B | | | Project C | | |
|---|---|---|---|---|---|---|---|---|---|---|
| **Dates:** | | **0** | **1** | **2** | **0** | **1** | **2** | **0** | **1** | **2** |
| Cash flows | | −£100 | £130 | | £100 | −£130 | | −£100 | £230 | −£132 |
| IRR | | | 30% | | | 30% | | 10% | and | 20% |
| NPV @10% | | | £18.2 | | | −£18.2 | | | 0 | |
| Accept if market rate | | | <30% | | | >30% | | >10% | but | <20% |
| Financing or investing | | | Investing | | | Financing | | | Mixture | |

**Table 6.3** The internal rate of return and net present value

**FIGURE 6.5**

**Project A** has a cash outflow at date 0 followed by a cash inflow at date 1. Its NPV is negatively related to the discount rate.
**Project B** has a cash inflow at date 0 followed by a cash outflow at date 1. Its NPV is positively related to the discount rate.
**Project C** has two changes of sign in its cash flows. It has an outflow at date 0, an inflow at date 1, and an outflow at date 2.
Projects with more than one change of sign can have multiple rates of return.

**Figure 6.5** Net present value and discount rates for projects *A*, *B*, and *C*

These cash flows are exactly the reverse of the flows for project A. In project B, the firm receives funds first and then pays out funds later. While unusual, projects of this type do exist. For example, consider a company conducting a seminar where the participants pay in advance. Because large expenses are frequently incurred at the seminar date, cash inflows precede cash outflows.

Consider our trial-and-error method to calculate IRR:

$$-\pounds 4 = +\pounds 100 - \frac{\pounds 130}{1.25}$$

$$\pounds 0 = +\pounds 100 - \frac{\pounds 130}{1.30}$$

$$\pounds 3.70 = +\pounds 100 - \frac{\pounds 130}{1.35}$$

As with project A, the internal rate of return is 30 per cent. However, notice that the net present value is *negative* when the discount rate is *below* 30 per cent. Conversely, the net present value is positive when the discount rate is above 30 per cent. The decision rule is exactly the opposite of our previous result. For this type of a project, the following rule applies:

**Accept the project when the IRR is less than the discount rate. Reject the project when the IRR is greater than the discount rate.**

This unusual decision rule follows from the graph of project B in Fig. 6.5. The curve is upward sloping, implying that NPV is *positively* related to the discount rate.

The graph makes intuitive sense. Suppose the firm wants to obtain £100 immediately. It can either (1) accept project B or (2) borrow £100 from a bank. Thus the project is actually a substitute for borrowing. In fact, because the IRR is 30 per cent, taking on project B is tantamount to borrowing at 30 per cent. If the firm can borrow from a bank at, say, only 25 per cent, it should reject the project. However, if a firm can borrow from a bank only at, say, 35 per cent, it should accept the project. Thus project B will be accepted if and only if the discount rate is *above* the IRR.[4]

This should be contrasted with project A. If the firm has £100 of cash to invest, it can either (1) accept project A or (2) lend £100 to the bank. The project is actually a substitute for lending. In fact, because the IRR is 30 per cent, taking on project A is tantamount to lending at 30 per cent. The firm should accept project A if the lending rate is below 30 per cent. Conversely, the firm should reject project A if the lending rate is above 30 per cent.

Because the firm initially pays out money with project A, but initially receives money with project B, we refer to project A as an *investing-type project* and project B as a *financing-type project*. Investing-type projects are the norm. Because the IRR rule is reversed for financing-type projects, be careful when using it with this type of project.

**Problem 2: Multiple Rates of Return**   Suppose the cash flows from a project are

$$(-£100, £230, -£132)$$

Because this project has a negative cash flow, a positive cash flow, and another negative cash flow, we say that the project's cash flows exhibit two changes of sign, or 'flip-flops'. Although this pattern of cash flows might look a bit strange at first, many projects require outflows of cash after receiving some inflows. An example would be a strip-mining project. The first stage in such a project is the initial investment in excavating the mine. Profits from operating the mine are received in the second stage. The third stage involves a further investment to reclaim the land and satisfy the requirements of environmental protection legislation. Cash flows are negative at this stage.

It is easy to verify that this project has not one but two IRRs, 10 per cent and 20 per cent.[5] In a case like this, the IRR does not make any sense. What IRR are we to use – 10 per cent or 20 per cent? Because there is no good reason to use one over the other, IRR simply cannot be used here.

Why does this project have multiple rates of return? Project C generates multiple internal rates of return because both an inflow and an outflow occur after the initial investment. In general, these flip-flops or changes in sign produce multiple IRRs. In theory, a cash flow stream with K changes in sign can have up to K sensible internal rates of return (IRRs above −100 per cent). Therefore, because project C has two changes in sign, it can have as many as two IRRs. As we pointed out, projects whose cash flows change sign repeatedly can occur in the real world.

**NPV Rule**   Of course, we should not be too worried about multiple rates of return. After all, we can always fall back on the NPV rule. Figure 6.5 plots the NPV of project C (−£100, £230, −£132) as a function of the discount rate. As the figure shows, the NPV is zero at both 10 per cent and 20 per cent, and negative outside the range. Thus the NPV rule tells us to accept the project if the appropriate discount rate is between 10 per cent and 20 per cent. The project should be rejected if the discount rate lies outside this range.

**The Guarantee against Multiple IRRs**   If the first cash flow of a project is negative (because it is the initial investment), and if all of the remaining flows are positive, there can only be a single, unique IRR, no matter how many periods the project lasts. This is easy to understand by using the concept of the time value of money. For example, it is simple to verify that project A in Table 6.3 has an IRR of 30 per cent, because using a 30-per cent discount rate gives

$$NPV = -£100 + £130/(1.3)$$
$$= £0$$

How do we know that this is the only IRR? Suppose we were to try a discount rate greater than 30 per cent. In computing the NPV, changing the discount rate does not change the value of the initial cash flow of −£100, because that cash flow is not discounted. But raising the discount rate can only lower the present value of the future cash flows. In other words, because the NPV is zero at 30 per cent, any increase in the rate will push the NPV into the negative range. Similarly, if we try a discount rate of less than 30 per cent, the overall NPV of the project will be positive. Though this example has only one positive flow, the above reasoning still implies a single, unique IRR if there are many inflows (but no outflows) after the initial investment.

If the initial cash flow is positive – and if all of the remaining flows are negative – there can only be a single, unique IRR. This result follows from similar reasoning. Both these cases have only one change of sign or flip-flop in the cash flows. Thus we are safe from multiple IRRs whenever there is only one sign change in the cash flows.

**General Rules**  The following chart summarizes our rules:

| Flows | Number of IRRs | IRR criterion | NPV criterion |
|---|---|---|---|
| First cash flow is negative and all remaining cash flows are positive. | 1 | Accept if IRR > R. Reject if IRR < R. | Accept if NPV > 0. Reject if NPV < 0. |
| First cash flow is positive and all remaining cash flows are negative. | 1 | Accept if IRR < R. Reject if IRR > R. | Accept if NPV > 0. Reject if NPV < 0. |
| Some cash flows after first are positive and some cash flows after first are negative. | May be more than 1. | No valid IRR. | Accept if NPV > 0. Reject if NPV < 0. |

Note that the NPV criterion is the same for each of the three cases. In other words, NPV analysis is always appropriate. Conversely, the IRR can be used only in certain cases.

## Problems Specific to Mutually Exclusive Projects

As mentioned earlier, two or more projects are mutually exclusive if the firm can accept only one of them. We now present two problems dealing with the application of the IRR approach to mutually exclusive projects. These two problems are quite similar, though logically distinct.

**The Scale Problem**  A professor we know motivates class discussions of this topic with the statement: 'Students, I am prepared to let one of you choose between two mutually exclusive 'business' propositions. Opportunity 1 – You give me €1 now and I'll give you €1.50 back at the end of the class period. Opportunity 2 – You give me €10 and I'll give you €11 back at the end of the class period. You can choose only one of the two opportunities. And you cannot choose either opportunity more than once. I'll pick the first volunteer.'

Which would you choose? The correct answer is opportunity 2. To see this, look at the following chart:

| | Cash flow at beginning of class (€) | Cash flow at end of class (90 minutes later) (€) | NPV[6] (€) | IRR (%) |
|---|---|---|---|---|
| Opportunity 1 | −1 | +1.50 | 0.50 | 50 |
| Opportunity 2 | −10 | +11.00 | 1.00 | 10 |

As we have stressed earlier in the text, one should choose the opportunity with the highest NPV. This is opportunity 2 in the example.

This business proposition illustrates a defect with the internal rate of return criterion. The basic IRR rule indicates the selection of opportunity 1 because the IRR is 50 per cent. The IRR is only 10 per cent for opportunity 2.

Where does IRR go wrong? The problem with IRR is that it ignores issues of *scale*. Although opportunity 1 has a greater IRR, the investment is much smaller. In other words, the high percentage return on opportunity 1 is more than offset by the ability to earn at least a decent return on a much bigger investment under opportunity 2.

Because IRR seems to be misguided here, can we adjust or correct it? We illustrate how in the next example.

EXAMPLE
**6.3**

# NPV versus IRR

Stanley Jaffe and Sherry Lansing have just purchased the rights to *Corporate Finance: The Motion Picture*. They will produce this major motion picture on either a small budget or a big budget. Here are the estimated cash flows:

| | Cash flow at date 0 ($) | Cash flow at date 1 ($) | NPV @25% ($) | IRR (%) |
|---|---|---|---|---|
| Small budget | −10 million | 40 million | 22 million | 300 |
| Large budget | −25 million | 65 million | 27 million | 160 |

Because of high risk, a 25 per cent discount rate is considered appropriate. Sherry wants to adopt the large budget because the NPV is higher. Stanley wants to adopt the small budget because the IRR is higher. Who is right?

For the reasons espoused in the classroom example, NPV is correct. Hence Sherry is right. However, Stanley is very stubborn where IRR is concerned. How can Sherry justify the large budget to Stanley using the IRR approach?

This is where *incremental IRR* comes in. Sherry calculates the incremental cash flows from choosing the large budget instead of the small budget as follows:

| | Cash flow at date 0 ($ millions) | Cash flow at date 1 ($ millions) |
|---|---|---|
| Incremental cash flows from choosing large budget instead of small budget | −25 − (−10) = −15 | 65 − 40 = 25 |

This chart shows that the incremental cash flows are −$15 million at date 0 and $25 million at date 1. Sherry calculates incremental IRR as follows:

Formula for calculating the incremental IRR:

$$0 = -\$15 \text{ million} + \frac{\$25 \text{ million}}{1 + \text{IRR}}$$

IRR equals 66.67 per cent in this equation, implying that the incremental IRR is 66.67 per cent. Incremental IRR is the IRR on the incremental investment from choosing the large project instead of the small project.

In addition, we can calculate the NPV of the incremental cash flows:

NPV of incremental cash flows:

$$-\$15 \text{ million} + \frac{\$25 \text{ million}}{1.25} = \$5 \text{ million}$$

We know the small-budget picture would be acceptable as an independent project because its NPV is positive. We want to know whether it is beneficial to invest an additional $15 million to make the large-budget picture instead of the small-budget picture. In other words, is it beneficial to invest an additional $15 million to receive an additional $25 million next year? First, our calculations show the NPV on the incremental investment to be positive. Second, the incremental IRR of 66.67 per cent is higher than the discount rate of 25 per cent. For both reasons, the incremental investment can be justified, so the large-budget movie should be made. The second reason is what Stanley needed to hear to be convinced.

In review, we can handle this example (or any mutually exclusive example) in one of three ways:

1   *Compare the NPVs of the two choices.* The NPV of the large-budget picture is greater than the NPV of the small-budget picture. That is, $27 million is greater than $22 million.

2   *Calculate the incremental NPV from making the large-budget picture instead of the small-budget picture.* Because the incremental NPV equals $5 million, we choose the large-budget picture.

3   *Compare the incremental IRR with the discount rate.* Because the incremental IRR is 66.67 per cent and the discount rate is 25 per cent, we take the large-budget picture.

All three approaches always give the same decision. However, we must *not* compare the IRRs of the two pictures. If we did, we would make the wrong choice. That is, we would accept the small-budget picture.

Although students frequently think that problems of scale are relatively unimportant, the truth is just the opposite. No real-world project comes in one clear-cut size. Rather, the firm has to *determine* the best size for the project. The movie budget of $25 million is not fixed in stone. Perhaps an extra $1 million to hire a bigger star or to film at a better location will increase the movie's gross revenues. Similarly, an industrial firm must decide whether it wants a warehouse of, say, 500,000 square feet or one of 600,000 square feet. And, earlier in the chapter, we imagined Starbucks opening an outlet on a remote island. If it does this, it must decide how big the outlet should be. For almost any project, someone in the firm has to decide on its size, implying that problems of scale abound in the real world.

One final note here. Students often ask which project should be subtracted from the other in calculating incremental flows. Notice that we are subtracting the smaller project's cash flows from the bigger project's cash flows. This leaves an *outflow* at date 0. We then use the basic IRR rule on the incremental flows.[7]

**The Timing Problem**   Next we illustrate another, quite similar problem with the IRR approach to evaluating mutually exclusive projects.

EXAMPLE
**6.4**

## Mutually Exclusive Investments

Suppose that Kaufold plc has two alternative uses for a warehouse. It can store toxic waste containers (investment A) or electronic equipment (investment B). The cash flows are as follows:

| | Cash flow (£) at year: | | | | NPV (£) | | | |
| --- | --- | --- | --- | --- | --- | --- | --- | --- |
| | **0** | **1** | **2** | **3** | **@ 0%** | **@ 10%** | **@ 15%** | **IRR (%)** |
| Investment A | −10,000 | 10,000 | 1,000 | 1,000 | 2,000 | 669 | 109 | 16.04 |
| Investment B | −10,000 | 1,000 | 1,000 | 12,000 | 4,000 | 751 | −484 | 12.94 |

We find that the NPV of investment B is higher with low discount rates, and the NPV of investment A is higher with high discount rates. This is not surprising if you look closely at the cash flow patterns. The cash flows of A occur early, whereas the cash flows of B occur later. If we assume a high discount rate, we favour investment A because we are implicitly assuming that the early cash flow (for example, £10,000 in year 1) can be reinvested at that rate. Because most of investment B's cash flows occur in year 3, B's value is relatively high with low discount rates.

Project A has an NPV of £2,000 at a discount rate of zero. This is calculated by simply adding up the cash flows without discounting them. Project B has an NPV of £4,000 at the zero rate. However, the NPV of project B declines more rapidly as the discount rate increases than does the NPV of project A. As we mentioned, this occurs because the cash flows of B occur later. Both projects have the same NPV at a discount rate of 10.55 per cent. The IRR for a project is the rate at which the NPV equals zero. Because the NPV of B declines more rapidly, B actually has a lower IRR.

As with the movie example, we can select the better project with one of three different methods:

1 *Compare NPVs of the two projects.* If the discount rate is below 10.55 per cent, we should choose project B because B has a higher NPV. If the rate is above 10.55 per cent, we should choose project A because A has a higher NPV.

2 *Compare incremental IRR to discount rate.* Method 1 employed NPV. Another way of determining that B is a better project is to subtract the cash flows of A from the cash flows of B and then to calculate the IRR. This is the incremental IRR approach we spoke of earlier.
Here are the incremental cash flows:

| | | | | | NPV of incremental cash flows | | | |
|---|---|---|---|---|---|---|---|---|
| Year: | 0 | 1 | 2 | 3 | Incremental IRR | @ 0% | @ 10% | @ 15% |
| B − A | 0 | −£9,000 | 0 | £11,000 | 10.55% | £2,000 | £83 | −£593 |

This chart shows that the incremental IRR is 10.55 per cent. In other words, the NPV on the incremental investment is zero when the discount rate is 10.55 per cent. Thus, if the relevant discount rate is below 10.55 per cent, project B is preferred to project A. If the relevant discount rate is above 10.55 per cent, project A is preferred to project B.[8]

3 *Calculate NPV on incremental cash flows.* Finally, we could calculate the NPV on the incremental cash flows. The chart that appears with the previous method displays these NPVs. We find that the incremental NPV is positive when the discount rate is either 0 per cent or 10 per cent. The incremental NPV is negative if the discount rate is 15 per cent. If the NPV is positive on the incremental flows, we should choose B. If the NPV is negative, we should choose A.

In summary, the same decision is reached whether we (1) compare the NPVs of the two projects, (2) compare the incremental IRR to the relevant discount rate, or (3) examine the NPV of the incremental cash flows. However, as mentioned earlier, we should *not* compare the IRR of project A with the IRR of project B.

We suggested earlier that we should subtract the cash flows of the smaller project from the cash flows of the bigger project. What do we do here when the two projects have the same initial investment? Our suggestion in this case is to perform the subtraction so that the *first* non-zero cash flow is negative. In the Kaufold plc example we achieved this by subtracting A from B. In this way, we can still use the basic IRR rule for evaluating cash flows.

The preceding examples illustrate problems with the IRR approach in evaluating mutually exclusive projects. Both the professor–student example and the motion picture example illustrate the problem that arises when mutually exclusive projects have different initial investments. The Kaufold plc example illustrates the problem that arises when mutually exclusive projects have different cash flow timing. When working with mutually exclusive projects, it is not necessary to determine whether it is the scale problem or the timing problem that exists. Very likely both will occur in any real-world situation. Instead, the practitioner should simply use either an incremental IRR or an NPV approach.

## Redeeming Qualities of IRR

IRR probably survives because it fills a need that NPV does not. People seem to want a rule that summarizes the information about a project in a single rate of return. This single rate gives people a simple way of discussing projects. For example, one manager in a firm might say to another, 'Remodelling the north wing has a 20 per cent IRR.'

To their credit, however, companies that employ the IRR approach seem to understand its deficiencies. For example, companies frequently restrict managerial projections of cash flows to be negative at the beginning and strictly positive later. Perhaps, then, the ability of the IRR approach to capture a complex investment project in a single number and the ease of communicating that number explain the survival of the IRR.

## A Test

To test your knowledge, consider the following two statements:

1  You must know the discount rate to compute the NPV of a project, but you compute the IRR without referring to the discount rate.

2  Hence the IRR rule is easier to apply than the NPV rule because you don't use the discount rate when applying IRR.

The first statement is true. The discount rate is needed to *compute* NPV. The IRR is *computed* by solving for the rate where the NPV is zero. No mention is made of the discount rate in the mere computation. However, the second statement is false. To *apply* IRR, you must compare the internal rate of return with the discount rate. Thus the discount rate is needed for making a decision under either the NPV or the IRR approach.

## 6.7 The Profitability Index

Another method used to evaluate projects is called the profitability index. It is the ratio of the present value of the future expected cash flows *after* initial investment divided by the amount of the initial investment. The profitability index can be represented like this:

$$\text{Profitability index (PI)} = \frac{\text{PV of cash flows } subsequent \text{ to initial investment}}{\text{Initial investment}}$$

## Profitability Index

### EXAMPLE 6.5

Hiram Finnegan Int. (HFI) applies a 12 per cent discount rate to two investment opportunities.

| Project | Cash flows (€m) | | | PV @ 12% of cash flows subsequent to initial investment (€m) | Profitability index | NPV @ 12% (€m) |
|---|---|---|---|---|---|---|
| | $C_0$ | $C_1$ | $C_2$ | | | |
| 1 | −20 | 70 | 10 | 70.5 | 3.53 | 50.5 |
| 2 | −10 | 15 | 40 | 45.3 | 4.53 | 35.3 |

## Calculation of Profitability Index

The profitability index is calculated for project 1 as follows. The present value of the cash flows *after* the initial investment is

$$€70.5 = \frac{€70}{1.12} + \frac{€10}{(1.12)^2}$$

The profitability index is obtained by dividing this result by the initial investment of €20. This yields

$$3.53 = \frac{€70.5}{€20}$$

**Application of the Profitability Index**   How do we use the profitability index? We consider three situations:

1  *Independent projects*: Assume that HFI's two projects are independent. According to the NPV rule, both projects should be accepted because NPV is positive in each case. The profitability index (PI) is greater than 1 whenever the NPV is positive. Thus, the PI *decision rule* is

(a) Accept an independent project if PI > 1.

(b) Reject it if PI < 1.

2 *Mutually exclusive projects*: Let us now assume that HFI can only accept one of its two projects. NPV analysis says accept project 1 because this project has the bigger NPV. Because project 2 has the higher PI, the profitability index leads to the wrong selection.

The problem with the profitability index for mutually exclusive projects is the same as the scale problem with the IRR that we mentioned earlier. Project 2 is smaller than project 1. Because the PI is a ratio, this index misses the fact that project 1 has a larger investment than project 2 has. Thus, like IRR, PI ignores differences of scale for mutually exclusive projects.

However, like IRR, the flaw with the PI approach can be corrected using incremental analysis. We write the incremental cash flows after subtracting project 2 from project 1 as follows:

| | Cash flows (€m) | | | PV @ 12% of cash flows subsequent to initial investment (€m) | Profitability index | NPV @ 12% (€m) |
| --- | --- | --- | --- | --- | --- | --- |
| Project | $C_0$ | $C_1$ | $C_2$ | | | |
| 1 – 2 | −10 | 55 | −30 | 25.2 | 2.52 | 15.2 |

Because the profitability index on the incremental cash flows is greater than 1.0, we should choose the bigger project – that is, project 1. This is the same decision we get with the NPV approach.

3 *Capital rationing*: The first two cases implicitly assumed that HFI could always attract enough capital to make any profitable investments. Now consider the case when the firm does not have enough capital to fund all positive NPV projects. This is the case of capital rationing.

Imagine that the firm has a third project, as well as the first two. Project 3 has the following cash flows:

| | Cash flows (€m) | | | PV @ 12% of cash flows subsequent to initial investment (€m) | Profitability index | NPV @ 12% (€m) |
| --- | --- | --- | --- | --- | --- | --- |
| Project | $C_0$ | $C_1$ | $C_2$ | | | |
| 3 | −10 | −5 | 60 | 43.4 | 4.34 | 33.4 |

Further, imagine that (a) the projects of Hiram Finnegan Int. are independent, but (b) the firm has only €20 million to invest. Because project 1 has an initial investment of €20 million, the firm cannot select both this project and another one. Conversely, because projects 2 and 3 have initial investments of €10 million each, both these projects can be chosen. In other words, the cash constraint forces the firm to choose either project 1 or projects 2 and 3.

What should the firm do? Individually, projects 2 and 3 have lower NPVs than project 1 has. However, when the NPVs of projects 2 and 3 are added together, the sum is higher than the NPV of project 1. Thus common sense dictates that projects 2 and 3 should be accepted.

What does our conclusion have to say about the NPV rule or the PI rule? In the case of limited funds, we cannot rank projects according to their NPVs. Instead we should rank them according to the ratio of present value to initial investment. This is the PI rule. Both project 2 and project 3 have higher PI ratios than does project 1. Thus they should be ranked ahead of project 1 when capital is rationed.

Note that the profitability index does not work if funds are also limited beyond the initial time period. For example, if heavy cash outflows elsewhere in the firm were to occur at date 1, project 3, which also has a cash outflow at date 1, might need to be rejected. In other words, the profitability index cannot handle capital rationing over multiple time periods.

In addition, what economists term *indivisibilities* may reduce the effectiveness of the PI rule. Imagine that HFI has €30 million available for capital investment, not just €20 million. The firm now has enough cash for projects 1 and 2. Because the sum of the NPVs of these two projects is greater than the sum of the NPVs of projects 2 and 3, the firm would be better served by accepting projects 1 and 2. But because projects 2 and 3 still have the highest profitability indexes, the PI rule now leads to the wrong decision. Why does the PI rule lead us astray here? The key is that projects 1 and 2 use up all of the €30 million, whereas projects 2 and 3 have a combined initial investment of only €20 million ( = €10 + 10). If projects 2 and 3 are accepted, the remaining €10 million must be left in the bank.

This situation points out that care should be exercised when using the profitability index in the real world. Nevertheless, while not perfect, the profitability index goes a long way towards handling capital rationing.

## 6.8 The Practice of Capital Budgeting

So far this chapter has asked 'Which capital budgeting methods should companies be using?' An equally important question is this: Which methods *are* companies using? Table 6.4 helps answer this question. As can be seen from the table, there is quite strong variation in the frequency with which different techniques are utilized. Other more advanced techniques, such as real options and sensitivity analysis, are covered in Chapter 8. The hurdle rate is known as the break-even approach and is also covered in Chapter 8. Most companies use the IRR and NPV methods. This is not surprising, given the theoretical advantages of these approaches. The most interesting point is that for the UK, Germany and France payback period is the most popular technique to appraise new projects, which is surprising, given the conceptual problems with this approach. However, the flaws of payback period, as mentioned in the current chapter, may be relatively easy to correct. For example, while the payback method ignores all cash flows after the payback period, an alert manager can make ad hoc adjustments for a project with back-loaded cash flows.

Capital expenditures by individual corporations can add up to enormous sums for the economy as a whole. For example, for the financial year 2008, BP announced that it had capital expenditure of just under $22 billion. About the same time, competitor Shell announced its capital expenditure of $26.6 billion.

The use of quantitative techniques in capital budgeting varies with industry. As one would imagine, firms that are better able to estimate cash flows are more likely to use NPV. For example, estimation of cash flow in certain aspects of the oil business is quite feasible. Because of this, energy-related firms were among the first to use NPV analysis. Conversely, the cash

| TABLE 6.4 | US | UK | The Netherlands | Germany | France |
|---|---|---|---|---|---|
| Net present value | 74.93 | 46.97 | 70.00 | 47.58 | 35.09 |
| Internal rate of return | 75.61 | 53.13 | 56.00 | 42.15 | 44.07 |
| Accounting rate of return | 20.29 | 38.10 | 25.00 | 32.17 | 16.07 |
| Profitability index | 11.87 | 15.87 | 8.16 | 16.07 | 37.74 |
| Payback period | 56.74 | 69.23 | 64.71 | 50.00 | 50.88 |
| Discounted payback | 29.45 | 25.40 | 25.00 | 30.51 | 11.32 |
| Hurdle rate | 56.94 | 26.98 | 41.67 | 28.81 | 3.85 |
| Sensitivity analysis | 51.54 | 42.86 | 36.73 | 28.07 | 10.42 |
| Real options | 26.56 | 29.03 | 34.69 | 44.04 | 53.06 |

*Source*: Table 2 from D. Brounen, A. de Jong and K. Koedijk, 'Corporate finance in Europe: confronting theory and practice', *Journal of Banking and Finance* (2006), vol. 30, no. 5, 1409–1442.

**Table 6.4** Percentage of firms in selected countries that use capital budgeting techniques flows in the motion picture business are very hard to project. The grosses of the great hits like *Titanic*, *Harry Potter* and *Star Wars* were far, far greater than anyone imagined. The big failures like *Alamo* and *Waterworld* were unexpected as well. Because of this, NPV analysis is frowned upon in the movie business.

## Summary and Conclusions

1   In this chapter we covered different investment decision rules. We evaluated the most popular alternatives to NPV: the payback period, the discounted payback period, the accounting rate of return, the internal rate of return, and the profitability index. In doing so we learned more about the NPV.

2   While we found that the alternatives have some redeeming qualities, when all is said and done, they are not the NPV rule: for those of us in finance, that makes them decidedly second-rate.

3   Of the competitors to NPV, IRR must be ranked above both payback and accounting rate of return. In fact, IRR always reaches the same decision as NPV in the normal case where the initial outflows of an independent investment project are followed only by a series of inflows.

4   We classified the flaws of IRR into two types. First, we considered the general case applying to both independent and mutually exclusive projects. There appeared to be two problems here:

   (a)   Some projects have cash inflows followed by one or more outflows. The IRR rule is inverted here: one should accept when the IRR is *below* the discount rate.

   (b)   Some projects have a number of changes of sign in their cash flows. Here, there are likely to be multiple internal rates of return. The practitioner must use either NPV or modified internal rate of return here.

5   Next, we considered the specific problems with the NPV for mutually exclusive projects. We showed that, owing to differences in either size or timing, the project with the highest IRR need not have the highest NPV. Hence the IRR rule should not be applied. (Of course, NPV can still be applied.)

   However, we then calculated incremental cash flows. For ease of calculation, we suggested subtracting the cash flows of the smaller project from the cash flows of the larger project. In that way the incremental initial cash flow is negative. One can always reach a correct decision by accepting the larger project if the incremental IRR is greater than the discount rate.

6   We described capital rationing as the case where funds are limited to a fixed monetary amount. With capital rationing the profitability index is a useful method of adjusting NPV.

## connect  Questions and Problems

**CONCEPT**
**1–8**

1   **Net Present Value**   List the main strengths of the net present value method. What do you think are the weaknesses of NPV in practical capital budgeting analysis?

2   **Payback Period**   List the main strengths of the payback period method. In comparison with net present value, what are its advantages and disadvantages?

3   **Discounted Payback Period**   Why would a manager use discounted payback period?

4   **Average Accounting Return**   Average accounting return is a popular method with accountants. Review the main strengths and weaknesses of the methodology for practical capital budgeting.

5 **Internal Rate of Return** In many countries internal rate of return is the most popular capital budgeting technique, yet in almost all academic textbooks NPV is put forward as the best method. Why do you think this is the case?

6 **Problems with IRR** Review the main problems that arise when one uses only IRR to evaluate potential projects.

7 **Profitability Index** Discuss the main applications of the profitability index in capital budgeting. When is it most useful, and what are its weaknesses?

8 **The Practice of Capital Budgeting** Why do you think certain capital budgeting techniques are used more often in some countries than in others? If NPV is theoretically the best methodology, and most managers of large European corporations have studied corporate finance, why do not all companies use the method?

9 **Calculating Payback Period and NPV** Hideoshi Software has the following mutually exclusive projects.

| Year | Project A (¥) | Project B (¥) |
|------|---------------|---------------|
| 0 | −5,500 | −4,000 |
| 1 | 4,000 | 2,500 |
| 2 | 5,500 | 1,200 |
| 3 | 500 | 3,000 |

(a) Suppose Hideoshi's payback period cut-off is two years. Which of these two projects should be chosen?

(b) Suppose Hideoshi uses the NPV rule to rank these two projects. Which project should be chosen if the appropriate discount rate is 10 per cent?

10 **Calculating Payback** A project has a life of seven years and a payback period of seven years. What can you say about the project's NPV?

11 **Calculating Discounted Payback** An investment project has annual cash inflows of €7,000, €7,500, €8,000 and €8,500, and a discount rate of 10 per cent. What is the discounted payback period for these cash flows if the initial cost is €8,000? What if the initial cost is €13,000? What if it is €18,000?

12 **Average Accounting Return** Your firm is considering purchasing a machine with the following annual, end-of-year, book investment accounts. Depreciation is calculated using 25 per cent reducing balance (i.e. instead of depreciating the machine by the same amount each year, we depreciate the residual value of the investment by 25 per cent):

| | Purchase date | Year 1 | Year 2 | Year 3 | Year 4 |
|------|---------------|--------|--------|--------|--------|
| Gross investment | £16,000 | £16,000 | £16,000 | £16,000 | £16,000 |
| Less: depreciation for year | 0 | £4,000 | £3,000 | £2,250 | £1,687.50 |
| Net investment | £16,000 | £12,000 | £9,000 | £6,750 | £5,062.50 |

The machine generates, on average, £4,500 per year in additional net income.

(a) What is the average accounting return for this machine?

(b) What three flaws are inherent in this decision rule?

13 **Average Accounting Return** Bluerock Group has invested €8,000 in a high-tech project lasting three years. Depreciation is €4,000, €2,500 and €1,500 in years 1, 2 and 3, respectively. The project generates pre-tax income of €2,000 each year. The pre-tax income already includes the depreciation expense. If the tax rate is 25 per cent, what is the project's average accounting return (AAR)?

REGULAR
9–25

14  **Calculating IRR**  Calculate the NPV of the following project for discount rates of 0, 50 and 100 per cent. What is the IRR of the project?

| Year | 0 | 1 | 2 |
|---|---|---|---|
| Cash flow | −£7,000 | £5,000 | £20,000 |

15  **Calculating IRR**  Compute the internal rate of return for the cash flows of the following two projects:

| | Cash flows (dinar) | |
|---|---|---|
| Year | Project A | Project B |
| 0 | −5,000 | −3,000 |
| 1 | 2,000 | 2,500 |
| 2 | 2,500 | 1,000 |
| 3 | 3,000 | 500 |

16  **Calculating Profitability Index**  Bill plans to open a gym in a popular beach resort, Rothesay. The gym equipment will cost £160,000, to be paid immediately. Bill expects after-tax cash inflows of £40,000 annually for seven years, after which he plans to scrap the equipment and retire. The first cash inflow occurs at the end of the first year. Assume the required return is 14 per cent. What is the project's PI? Should it be accepted?

17  **Calculating Profitability Index**  Suppose the following two independent investment opportunities are available to Greenplain Ltd. The appropriate discount rate is 10 per cent.

| Year | Project Alpha (€) | Project Beta (€) |
|---|---|---|
| 0 | −500 | −2,000 |
| 1 | 300 | 300 |
| 2 | 700 | 1,800 |
| 3 | 600 | 1,700 |

(a)  Compute the profitability index for each of the two projects.

(b)  Which project(s) should Greenplain accept, based on the profitability index rule?

18  **Problems with IRR**  Suppose you are offered £5,000 today but must make the following payments:

| Year | Cash flows (£) |
|---|---|
| 0 | 5,000 |
| 1 | −2,500 |
| 2 | −2,000 |
| 3 | −1,000 |
| 4 | −1,000 |

(a)  What is the IRR of this offer?

(b)  If the appropriate discount rate is 10 per cent, should you accept this offer?

(c)  If the appropriate discount rate is 20 per cent, should you accept this offer?

(d)  What is the NPV of the offer if the appropriate discount rate is 10 per cent? 20 per cent?

(e)  Are the decisions under the NPV rule in part (d) consistent with those of the IRR rule?

19  **NPV versus IRR**   Consider the following cash flows on two mutually exclusive projects for Tomatina Recreation SA. Both projects require an annual return of 15 per cent.

| Year | Deepwater fishing (€) | New submarine ride (€) |
|---|---|---|
| 0 | −600,000 | −1,800,000 |
| 1 | 270,000 | 1,000,000 |
| 2 | 350,000 | 700,000 |
| 3 | 300,000 | 900,000 |

As a financial analyst for Tomatina, you are asked the following questions:

(a)  If your decision rule is to accept the project with the greater IRR, which project should you choose?

(b)  Because you are fully aware of the IRR rule's scale problem, you calculate the incremental IRR for the cash flows. Based on your computation, which project should you choose?

(c)  To be prudent, you compute the NPV for both projects. Which project should you choose? Is it consistent with the incremental IRR rule?

20  **Capital Budgeting Tools**   Consider the following cash flows:

| Year | 0 | 1 | 2 | 3 | 4 | 5 |
|---|---|---|---|---|---|---|
| Cash flow | −£15,000 | £4,000 | £5,000 | −£2,000 | £7,000 | £7,000 |

(a)  What is the payback period for the above project? Assume the cash flows are received continuously throughout each year.

(b)  If the discount rate is 10 per cent, what is the NPV of the project?

(c)  If the discount rate is 10 per cent, what is the IRR of the project? How many IRRs does the project have? Explain how you would deal with this problem.

(d)  If the discount rate is 10 per cent, what is the PI of the project?

21  **Comparing Investment Criteria**   Software games company Avalanche Entertainment is considering expanding its highly successful online game franchise to the board game or trading card environment. The company has decided that it will invest in one project but not both. Consider the following cash flows of the two mutually exclusive projects. Assume the discount rate for Avalanche Entertainment is 10 per cent.

| Year | Trading cards (€) | Board game (€) |
|---|---|---|
| 0 | −200 | −2,000 |
| 1 | 300 | 2,200 |
| 2 | 100 | 900 |
| 3 | 100 | 500 |

(a)  Based on the payback period rule, which project should be chosen?

(b)  Based on the NPV, which project should be chosen?

(c)  Based on the IRR, which project should be chosen?

(d)  Based on the incremental IRR, which project should be chosen?

22 **Capital Budgeting** Sandy Grey Ltd is in the process of deciding whether or not to revise its line of mobile phones that it manufactures and sells. Its sole market is large corporations, and it has not as yet focused on the retail sector. It has estimated that the revision will cost £220,000. Cash flows from increased sales will be £80,000 in the first year. These cash flows will increase by 5% per year. The firm estimates that the new line will be obsolete five years from now. Assume the initial cost is paid now, and all revenues are received at the end of each year. If the company requires a 10 per cent return for such an investment, should it undertake the revision? Use three investment evaluation techniques to arrive at your answer.

23 **Comparing Investment Criteria** The following problem is common in the automobile industry. You are required to assess the viability of two new car lines. Your company cannot afford to undertake both projects, and must choose one only. The appropriate discount rate is 12 per cent for this investment.

| Year | People carrier (€) | SUV (€) |
|------|--------------------|---------|
| 0 | −200,000 | −500,000 |
| 1 | 300,000 | 300,000 |
| 2 | 100,000 | 250,000 |
| 3 | 100,000 | 250,000 |

(a) Based on payback period, which project should be taken?

(b) Based on NPV, which project should be taken?

(c) Based on IRR, which project should be taken?

(d) Based on this analysis, is incremental IRR analysis necessary? If yes, please conduct the analysis.

24 **Comparing Investment Criteria** The treasurer of Amaro Canned Fruits has projected the cash flows of projects A, B and C as follows:

| Year | Project A (€) | Project B (€) | Project C (€) |
|------|---------------|---------------|---------------|
| 0 | −100,000 | −200,000 | −100,000 |
| 1 | 70,000 | 130,000 | 75,000 |
| 2 | 70,000 | 130,000 | 60,000 |

Suppose the relevant discount rate is 12 per cent a year.

(a) Compute the profitability index for each of the three projects.

(b) Compute the NPV for each of the three projects.

(c) Suppose these three projects are independent. Which project(s) should Amaro accept, based on the profitability index rule?

(d) Suppose these three projects are mutually exclusive. Which project(s) should Amaro accept, based on the profitability index rule?

(e) Suppose Amaro's budget for these projects is €300,000. The projects are not divisible. Which project(s) should Amaro accept?

25 **Comparing Investment Criteria** Consider the following cash flows of two mutually exclusive projects for Tadcaster Rubber Company. Assume the discount rate for Tadcaster Rubber Company is 10 per cent.

| Year | Dry prepreg (€) | Solvent prepreg (€) |
|------|-----------------|---------------------|
| 0    | −800,000        | −600,000            |
| 1    | 500,000         | 400,000             |
| 2    | 300,000         | 600,000             |
| 3    | 900,000         | 200,000             |

(a)  Based on the payback period, which project should be taken?

(b)  Based on the NPV, which project should be taken?

(c)  Based on the IRR, which project should be taken?

(d)  Based on this analysis, is incremental IRR analysis necessary? If yes, please conduct the analysis.

26  **Cash Flow Intuition**  A project has an initial cost of $I$, has a required return of $R$, and pays $C$ annually for $N$ years.

(a)  Find $C$ in terms of $I$ and $N$ such that the project has a payback period just equal to its life.

(b)  Find $C$ in terms of $I$, $N$ and $R$ such that this is a profitable project according to the NPV decision rule.

(c)  Find $C$ in terms of $I$, $N$ and $R$ such that the project has a benefit–cost ratio of 2.

27  **Comparing Investment Criteria**  You are a senior manager at Airbus and have been authorized to spend up to €200,000 for projects. The three projects you are considering have the following characteristics:

Project A:   Initial investment of €150,000. Cash flow of €50,000 at year 1 and €100,000 at year 2. This is a plant expansion project, where the required rate of return is 10 per cent.

Project B:   Initial investment of €200,000. Cash flow of €200,000 at year 1 and €111,000 at year 2. This is a new product development project, where the required rate of return is 20 per cent.

Project C:   Initial investment of €100,000. Cash flow of €100,000 at year 1 and €100,000 at year 2. This is a market expansion project, where the required rate of return is 20 per cent.

Assume the corporate discount rate is 10 per cent.

Please offer your recommendations, backed by your analysis:

|                  | A | B | C | Implications |
|------------------|---|---|---|--------------|
| Payback          |   |   |   |              |
| IRR              |   |   |   |              |
| Incremental IRR  |   |   |   |              |
| PI               |   |   |   |              |
| NPV              |   |   |   |              |

28  **Payback and NPV**  An investment under consideration has a payback of seven years and a cost of £483,000. If the required return is 12 per cent, what is the worst-case NPV? The best-case NPV? Explain. Assume the cash flows are conventional.

29  **Multiple IRRs**  This problem is useful for testing the ability of financial calculators and computer software. Consider the following cash flows. How many different IRRs are there? (*Hint*: Search between 20 per cent and 70 per cent.) When should we take this project?

CHALLENGE
26–34

| Year | Cash flow (£) |
|------|---------------|
| 0 | −504 |
| 1 | 2,862 |
| 2 | −6,070 |
| 3 | 5,700 |
| 4 | −2,000 |

30 **NPV Valuation**   Yuvhadit Ltd wants to set up a private cemetery business. According to the CFO, Barry M. Deep, business is 'looking up'. As a result, the cemetery project will provide a net cash inflow of €80,000 for the firm during the first year, and the cash flows are projected to grow at a rate of 6 per cent per year for ever. The project requires an initial investment of €800,000.

  (a)  If Yuvhadit requires a 12 per cent return on such undertakings, should the cemetery business be started?

  (b)  The company is somewhat unsure about the assumption of a 6 per cent growth rate in its cash flows. At what constant growth rate would the company just break even if it still required a 12 per cent return on investment?

31 **Calculating IRR**   Moshi Mining is set to open a gold mine in northern Tanzania. The mine will cost 6 million rand to open and will have an economic life of 12 years. It will generate a cash inflow of 1 million rand at the end of the first year, and the cash inflows are projected to grow at 10 per cent per year for the next 11 years. After 12 years, the mine will be abandoned. Abandonment costs will be 500,000 rand at the end of year 12.

  (a)  What is the IRR for the gold mine?

  (b)  Moshi Mining requires a 10 per cent return on such undertakings. Should the mine be opened?

32 **IRR and NPV**   You are out having dinner with your two colleagues, who are also studying finance. John, who loves the IRR method, tells you that ranking projects by IRR is fine as long as each project's cash flows can be reinvested at the project's IRR. Your other friend, Beverley, is confused, and asks whether NPV assumes that cash flows are always reinvested at the opportunity cost of capital. Take a deep breath and explain whether John and Beverley are correct.

33 **Calculating Incremental Cash Flows**   Darin Clay, the CFO of MakeMoney.com, has to decide between the following two projects:

| Year | Project Million (£) | Project Billion (£) |
|------|---------------------|---------------------|
| 0 | −1,500 | −$I_0$ |
| 1 | $I_0$ + 200 | $I_0$ + 500 |
| 2 | 1,200 | 1,500 |
| 3 | 1,500 | 2,000 |

The expected rate of return for either of the two projects is 12 per cent. What is the range of initial investment ($I_0$) for which Project Billion is more financially attractive than Project Million?

34 **Problems with IRR**   Kikmaheedin Ltd has a project with the following cash flows:

| Year | Cash flow (£) |
|------|---------------|
| 0 | 20,000 |
| 1 | −26,000 |
| 2 | 13,000 |

What is the IRR of the project? What is happening here?

# Davies Gold Mining

**MINI CASE**

Dick Davies, the owner of Davies Gold Mining, is evaluating a new gold mine in Tanzania. Barry Koch, the company's geologist, has just finished his analysis of the mine site. He has estimated that the mine would be productive for eight years, after which the gold would be completely mined. Barry has taken an estimate of the gold deposits to Andy Marshall, the company's financial officer. Andy has been asked by Dick to perform an analysis of the new mine and present his recommendation on whether the company should open the new mine.

Andy has used the estimates provided by Barry to determine the revenues that could be expected from the mine. He has also projected the expense of opening the mine and the annual operating expenses. If the company opens the mine, it will cost £500 million today, and it will have a cash outflow of £80 million nine years from today in costs associated with closing the mine and reclaiming the area surrounding it. The expected cash flows each year from the mine are shown in the following table. Davies Gold Mining has a 12 per cent required return on all of its gold mines.

| Year | Cash flow (£) |
|------|---------------|
| 0 | −500,000,000 |
| 1 | 60,000,000 |
| 2 | 90,000,000 |
| 3 | 170,000,000 |
| 4 | 230,000,000 |
| 5 | 205,000,000 |
| 6 | 140,000,000 |
| 7 | 110,000,000 |
| 8 | 70,000,000 |
| 9 | −80,000,000 |

1   Construct a spreadsheet to calculate the payback period, internal rate of return, modified internal rate of return, and net present value of the proposed mine.

2   Based on your analysis, should the company open the mine?

3   Bonus question: Most spreadsheets do not have a built-in formula to calculate the payback period. Write a VBA script that calculates the payback period for a project.

# Practical Case Study

At the end of 2008 the German-based pharmaceuticals group BASF announced major cutbacks in response to the ongoing recession facing European companies. Specifically, it announced that the working hours of 20,000 of its staff were to be reduced for two months. In addition, it planned to cut output by 20 per cent over the next year. The week before, Dow Chemical, a US-based rival to BASF, announced that it would be restructuring all of its operations in response to a cut in global demand. In the tourism sector, Tui Travel announced that it would simultaneously be reducing capacity and increasing prices in response to the recession.

1   Use NPV and other capital budgeting theories to explain the reasoning behind the decision of Tui Travel to reduce capacity and raise prices.

2   Is it possible for the value of these firms' shares to go up even though their sales revenues are extremely likely to fall as a result of their decisions? Explain your answer.

3   What do you think would be the effect of their business decisions on their risk? How would this factor into the value of each company's operations?

4   Can you think of any other business decisions these companies could have made to protect themselves against future economic conditions? Give some reasons why you think they did not choose these.

5   Look up the share price of the three firms and search Google News for information on each of the three companies between the end of 2008 and now. With hindsight, do you think these companies' strategies were successful? Explain.

# Endnotes

1   Depreciation will be treated in more detail in the next chapter.

2   Of course, we could have solved directly for $R$ in this example after setting NPV equal to zero. However, with long series of cash flows, one cannot generally solve directly for $R$. Instead, one is forced to use trial and error (or let a machine use trial and error).

3   One can derive the IRR directly for a problem with an initial outflow and up to four subsequent inflows. In the case of two subsequent inflows, for example, the quadratic formula is needed. In general, however, only trial and error will work for an outflow and five or more subsequent inflows.

4   This paragraph implicitly assumes that the cash flows of the project are risk-free. In this way we can treat the borrowing rate as the discount rate for a firm needing £100. With risky cash flows, another discount rate would be chosen. However, the intuition behind the decision to accept when the IRR is less than the discount rate would still apply.

5   The calculations are

$$-£100 + \frac{£230}{1.1} - \frac{£132}{(1.1)^2}$$
$$-£10 + 209.09 - 109.09 = 0$$

and

$$-£100 + \frac{£230}{1.2} - \frac{£132}{(1.2)^2}$$
$$-£100 + 191.67 - 91.67 = 0$$

Thus we have multiple rates of return.

6   We assume a zero rate of interest because his class lasted only 90 minutes. It just seemed like a lot longer.

7   Alternatively, we could have subtracted the larger project's cash flows from the smaller project's cash flows. This would have left an *inflow* at date 0, making it necessary to use the IRR rule for financing situations. This would work, but we find it more confusing.

8   In this example, we first showed that the NPVs of the two projects are equal when the discount rate is 10.55 per cent. We next showed that the incremental IRR is also 10.55 per cent. This is not a coincidence; this equality must *always* hold. The incremental IRR is the rate that causes the incremental cash flows to have zero NPV. The incremental cash flows have zero NPV when the two projects have the same NPV.

To help you grasp the key concepts of this chapter check out the extra resources posted on the Online Learning Centre at www.mcgraw-hill.co.uk/textbooks/hillier

Among other helpful resources there are PowerPoint presentations, chapter outlines and mini-cases.

# Chapter 7

# Making Capital Investment Decisions

In January 2006 Sharp Corporation, the world's leading producer of flat panel LCD TVs, announced that it would spend an additional 200 billion yen (£1/€1.2 billion) to build a new plant to produce LCD panels. This addition brought the total investment in the new plant to 350 billion yen (£1.7/€2.15 billion). The extra investment increased the production capacity of the new plant from 30,000 glass substrates per month to 90,000 glass substrates per month, and the new plant would have the capacity to produce the equivalent of 22 million 32-inch TV sets by 2008. Just several days earlier, Matsushita Electric Industrial Co., the world's leading plasma TV manufacturer, announced that it would invest 180 billion yen (£870 million/€1.1 billion) to build a new plant to produce plasma panels. The new plasma plant would more than double the company's production capacity to 11.1 million units per year.

This chapter follows up on our previous one by delving more deeply into capital budgeting and the evaluation of projects such as these flat panel manufacturing facilities. We identify the relevant cash flows of a project, including initial investment outlays, requirements for net working capital, and operating cash flows. Further, we look at the effects of depreciation and taxes. We also examine the impact of inflation, and show how to evaluate the NPV analysis of a project consistently.

## 7.1 Incremental Cash Flows

### Cash Flows – not Accounting Income

You may not have thought about it, but there is a big difference between corporate finance courses and financial accounting courses. Techniques in corporate finance generally use cash flows, whereas financial accounting generally stresses income or earnings numbers. Certainly our text follows this tradition: our net present value techniques discount cash flows, not earnings. When considering a single project, we discount the cash flows that the firm receives from the project. When valuing the firm as a whole, we discount dividends – not earnings – because dividends are the cash flows that an investor receives.

EXAMPLE
7.1
## Relevant Cash Flows

Weber-Decker GmbH just paid €1 million in cash for a building as part of a new capital budgeting project. This entire €1 million is an immediate cash outflow. However, assuming 20 per cent reducing balance depreciation, only €200,000 (= €1 million × 20 per cent) is considered an accounting expense in the current year. Current earnings are thereby reduced by only €200,000. The remaining €800,000 is expensed over the lifetime of the project. For capital budgeting purposes, the relevant cash outflow at date 0 is the full €1 million, not the reduction in earnings of only €200,000.

*Always* discount cash flows, not earnings, when performing a capital budgeting calculation. Earnings do not represent real money. You can't spend out of earnings, you can't eat out of earnings, and you can't pay dividends out of earnings. You can do these things only out of cash flow.

In addition, it is not enough to use cash flows. In calculating the NPV of a project, only cash flows that are *incremental* to the project should be used. These cash flows are the changes in the firm's cash flows that occur as a direct consequence of accepting the project. That is, we are interested in the difference between the cash flows of the firm with the project and the cash flows of the firm without the project.

The use of incremental cash flows sounds easy enough, but pitfalls abound in the real world. We now describe how to avoid some of the pitfalls of determining incremental cash flows.

## Sunk Costs

A sunk cost is a cost that has already occurred. Because sunk costs are in the past, they cannot be changed by the decision to accept or reject the project. Just as we 'let bygones be bygones', we should ignore such costs. Sunk costs are not incremental cash outflows.

EXAMPLE
7.2
## Sunk Costs

General Milk Ltd is currently evaluating the NPV of establishing a line of chocolate milk. As part of the evaluation, the company had paid a consulting firm £100,000 to perform a test marketing analysis. The expenditure was made last year. Is this cost relevant for the capital budgeting decision now confronting the management of General Milk Ltd?

The answer is no. The £100,000 is not recoverable, so the £100,000 expenditure is a sunk cost. Of course, the decision to spend £100,000 for a marketing analysis was a capital budgeting decision itself, and was perfectly relevant *before* it was sunk. Our point is that once the company had incurred the expense, the cost became irrelevant for any future decision.

## Opportunity Costs

Your firm may have an asset that it is considering selling, leasing, or employing elsewhere in the business. If the asset is used in a new project, potential revenues from alternative uses are lost. These lost revenues can meaningfully be viewed as costs. They are called opportunity costs because, by taking the project, the firm forgoes other opportunities for using the assets. Clearly, opportunity costs assume that another valuable opportunity will be forgone if the project is adopted. This, in itself, is a prediction of the future and is estimated with a degree of uncertainty.

## Opportunity Costs

Suppose Gonzales Trading has an empty warehouse in Salamanca that can be used to store a new line of electronic pinball machines. The company hopes to sell these machines to affluent European consumers. Should the warehouse be considered a cost in the decision to sell the machines?

The answer is yes. The company could sell the warehouse if the firm decides not to market the pinball machines. Thus the sales price of the warehouse is an opportunity cost in the pinball machine decision.

### Side Effects

Another difficulty in determining incremental cash flows comes from the side effects of the proposed project on other parts of the firm. A side effect is classified as either **erosion** or **synergy**. Erosion occurs when a new product reduces the sales, and hence the cash flows, of existing products. Synergy occurs when a new project increases the cash flows of existing projects. Because side effects predict the spending habits of customers, they are necessarily hypothetical and difficult to estimate.

## Synergies

Suppose Innovative Motors (IM) is determining the NPV of a new convertible sports car. Some of the customers who would purchase the car are owners of IM's SUVs. Are all sales and profits from the new convertible sports car incremental?

The answer is no, because some of the cash flow represents transfers from other elements of IM's product line. This is erosion, which must be included in the NPV calculation. Without taking erosion into account, IM might erroneously calculate the NPV of the sports car to be, say, £100 million. If half the customers are transfers from the SUV and lost SUV sales have an NPV of –£150 million, the true NPV is –£50 million (= £100 million – £150 million).

IM is also contemplating the formation of a racing team. The team is forecast to lose money for the foreseeable future, with perhaps the best projection showing an NPV of –£35 million for the operation. However, IM's managers are aware that the team will probably generate great publicity for all of IM's products. A consultant estimates that the increase in cash flows elsewhere in the firm has a present value of £65 million. Assuming that the consultant's estimates of synergy are trustworthy, the net present value of the team is £30 million (= £65 million – £35 million). The managers should form the team.

### Allocated Costs

Frequently a particular expenditure benefits a number of projects. Accountants allocate this cost across the different projects when determining income. However, for capital budgeting purposes, this **allocated cost** should be viewed as a cash outflow of a project only if it is an incremental cost of the project.

## Allocated Costs

Voetmann Consulting NV devotes one wing of its suite of offices to a library requiring a cash outflow of €100,000 a year in upkeep. A proposed capital budgeting project is expected to generate revenue equal to 5 per cent of the firm's overall sales. An executive at the firm, H. Sears, argues that €5,000 (= 5 per cent × €100,000) should be viewed as the proposed project's share of the library's costs. Is this appropriate for capital budgeting?

The answer is no. One must ask what the difference is between the cash flows of the entire firm with the project and the cash flows of the entire firm without the project. The firm will spend €100,000 on library upkeep whether or not the proposed project is accepted. Because acceptance of the proposed project does not affect this cash flow, the cash flow should be ignored when calculating the NPV of the project.

## 7.2 Whair Balls Ltd: An Example

We next consider the example of a proposed investment in machinery and related items. Our example involves Whair Balls Ltd and its multi-coloured bowling balls.

Whair Balls, originally established in 1965 to make footballs, is now a leading producer of tennis balls, baseballs, footballs and golf balls. In 1973 the company introduced 'High Flite', its first line of high-performance golf balls. Whair management has sought opportunities in whatever businesses seem to have some potential for cash flow. Recently Brian Honour, vice-president of Whair Balls, identified another segment of the sports ball market that looked promising and which he felt was not adequately served by larger manufacturers. That market was for brightly coloured bowling balls, and he believed many bowlers valued appearance and style above performance. He also believed that it would be difficult for competitors to take advantage of the opportunity because of both Whair's cost advantages and its highly developed marketing skills.

As a result, Whair Balls investigated the marketing potential of brightly coloured bowling balls. Whair sent a questionnaire to consumers in three markets: Glasgow, Newcastle and London. The results of the three questionnaires were much better than expected, and supported the conclusion that the brightly coloured bowling balls could achieve a 10 to 15 per cent share of the market. Of course, some people at Whair complained about the cost of the test marketing, which was £250,000. (As we shall see later, this is a sunk cost and should not be included in project evaluation.)

In any case, Whair Balls is now considering investing in a machine to produce bowling balls. The bowling balls would be manufactured in a building owned by the firm and located near Glasgow. This building, which is vacant, and the land can be sold for £150,000 after taxes.

Working with his staff, Brian Honour is preparing an analysis of the proposed new product. He summarizes his assumptions as follows. The cost of the bowling ball machine is £100,000. The machine has an estimated market value at the end of five years of £30,000. Production by year during the five-year life of the machine is expected to be as follows: 5,000 units, 8,000 units, 12,000 units, 10,000 units, and 6,000 units. The price of bowling balls in the first year will be £20. The bowling ball market is highly competitive, so Honour believes that the price of bowling balls will increase at only 2 per cent per year, as compared with the anticipated general inflation rate of 5 per cent. Conversely, the plastic used to produce bowling balls is rapidly becoming more expensive. Because of this, production cash outflows are expected to grow at 10 per cent per year. First-year production costs will be £10 per unit. Honour has determined, based on Whair's taxable income, that the appropriate incremental corporate tax rate in the bowling ball project is 28 per cent.

In Europe, assets are depreciated for tax purposes using a system called capital allowances or tax depreciation. This effectively entails assets being depreciated by a certain percentage each year. Assume the capital allowances rate on plant and machinery is 25 per cent per annum. That is, plant and machinery depreciate by 25 per cent per year. Depreciation of this kind is known as the reducing-balance method, in contrast to straight-line depreciation, by which asset values fall by the same amount each year.

Net working capital is defined as the difference between current assets and current liabilities. Like any other manufacturing firm, Whair finds that it must maintain an investment in working capital. It will purchase raw materials before production and sale, giving rise to an investment in inventory. It will maintain cash as a buffer against unforeseen expenditures. And its credit sales will generate trade receivables. Management determines that an immediate (year 0) investment in the different items of working capital of £10,000 is required. Working capital is forecast to rise in the early years of the project but to fall to £0 by the project's end. In other words, the investment in working capital is to be completely recovered by the end of the project's life.

Projections based on these assumptions and Honour's analysis appear in Tables 7.1 to 7.4. In these tables all cash flows are assumed to occur at the *end* of the year. Because of the large amount of information in these tables, it is important to see how they are related. Table 7.1 shows the basic data for both investment and income. Supplementary schedules on operations and depreciation, as presented in Tables 7.2 and 7.3, help explain where the numbers in Table 7.1 come from. Our goal is to obtain projections of cash flow. The data in Table 7.1 are all that are needed to calculate the relevant cash flows, as shown in Table 7.4.

## An Analysis of the Project

**Investments**    The investment outlays for the project are summarized in the top segment of Table 7.1. They consist of three parts:

1   *The bowling ball machine*: The purchase requires an immediate (year 0) cash outflow of £100,000. The firm realizes a cash inflow when the machine is sold in year 5. These cash

**TABLE 7.1**

| | Year 0 (£000) | Year 1 (£000) | Year 2 (£000) | Year 3 (£000) | Year 4 (£000) | Year 5 (£000) |
|---|---|---|---|---|---|---|
| Investments: | | | | | | |
| (1) Bowling ball machine | −100.00 | | | | | 30.00 |
| (2) Depreciation | | 25.00 | 18.75 | 14.06 | 10.55 | 7.91 |
| (3) Taxable profit on sale of bowling ball machine | | | | | | 6.27* |
| (4) Opportunity cost (warehouse) | −150.00 | | | | | 150.00 |
| (5) Net working capital (end of year) | 10.00 | 10.00 | 16.32 | 24.97 | 21.22 | 0 |
| (6) Change in net working capital | −10.00 | | −6.32 | −8.65 | 3.75 | 21.22 |
| (7) Total cash flow of investment [(1) + (4) + (6)] | −260.00 | | −6.32 | −8.65 | 3.75 | 201.22 |
| Income: | | | | | | |
| (8) Sales revenues | | 100.00 | 163.20 | 249.72 | 212.20 | 129.90 |
| (9) Operating costs | | −50.00 | −88.00 | −145.20 | −133.10 | −87.84 |
| (10) Depreciation | | −25.00 | −18.75 | −14.06 | −10.55 | −7.91 |
| (11) Profit on sale of machine | | | | | | 6.27 |
| (12) Income before taxes [(8) + (9) + (10) + (11)] | | 25.00 | 56.45 | 90.46 | 68.55 | 40.42 |
| (13) Tax at 28 per cent | | −7.00 | −15.81 | −25.33 | −19.19 | −11.32 |
| (14) Net income | | 18.00 | 40.64 | 65.13 | 49.36 | 29.10 |

(All cash flows occur at the *end* of the year.)
*We assume that the ending market value of the capital investment at year 5 is £30 (in thousands). The value of the investment for tax purposes is £23.73. The profit on sale of the machine is £30 − £23.73 = £6.27.

**Table 7.1** The worksheet for cash flows of Whair Balls

**TABLE 7.2**

| (1) Year | (2) Quantity produced | (3) Price (£) | (4) Sales revenues (£) | (5) Cost per unit (£) | (6) Operating costs (£) |
|---|---|---|---|---|---|
| 1 | 5,000 | 20.00 | 100,000 | 10.00 | 50,000 |
| 2 | 8,000 | 20.40 | 163,200 | 11.00 | 88,000 |
| 3 | 12,000 | 20.81 | 249,720 | 12.10 | 145,200 |
| 4 | 10,000 | 21.22 | 212,200 | 13.31 | 133,100 |
| 5 | 6,000 | 21.65 | 129,900 | 14.64 | 87,840 |

Prices rise at 2% a year.
Unit costs rise at 10% a year.

**Table 7.2** Operating revenues and costs of Whair Balls

**TABLE 7.3**

| | Year | | | | |
|---|---|---|---|---|---|
| | 1 | 2 | 3 | 4 | 5 |
| Starting value | £100 | £75 | £56.25 | £42.19 | £31.64 |
| Depreciation | 25% × £100 = £25 | 25% × £75 = £18.75 | 25% × £56.25 = £14.06 | 25% × £42.19 = £10.55 | 25% × £31.64 = £7.91 |
| Accumulated depreciation | £25 | £25 + £18.75 = £43.75 | £43.75 + £14.06 = £57.81 | £57.81 + £10.55 = £68.36 | £68.36 + £7.91 = £76.27 |
| Residual value | £75 | £56.25 | £42.19 | £31.64 | £23.73 |

**Table 7.3** Depreciation calculation using capital allowances (25 per cent reducing balance)

**TABLE 7.4**

| | Year 0 (£000) | Year 1 (£000) | Year 2 (£000) | Year 3 (£000) | Year 4 (£000) | Year 5 (£000) |
|---|---|---|---|---|---|---|
| (1) Sales revenue [line 8, Table 7.1] | | 100.00 | 163.20 | 249.72 | 212.20 | 129.90 |
| (2) Operating costs [line 9, Table 7.1] | | −50.00 | −88.00 | −145.20 | −133.10 | −87.84 |
| (3) Taxes [line 13, Table 7.1] | | −7.00 | −15.81 | −25.33 | −19.19 | −11.32 |
| (4) Cash flow from operations [(1) + (2) + (3)] | | 43.00 | 59.39 | 79.19 | 59.91 | 30.74 |
| (5) Total cash flow of investment [line 7, Table 7.1] | −260.00 | | −6.32 | −8.65 | 3.75 | 201.22 |
| (6) Total cash flow of project [(4) + (5)] | −260.00 | 43.00 | 53.07 | 70.54 | 63.66 | 231.96 |

**NPV** @ 4%:     £132.88
     10%:     £57.69
     15%:     £13.59
     16.91%:   £0
     20%:    −£18.81

**Table 7.4** Incremental cash flows for Whair Balls

flows are shown in line 1 of Table 7.1. As indicated in the footnote to the table, taxes are incurred when the asset is sold.

2   *The opportunity cost of not selling the warehouse*: If Whair accepts the bowling ball project, it will use a warehouse and land that could otherwise be sold. The estimated sales price of the warehouse and land is therefore included as an *opportunity cost* in year 0, as presented in line 4. Opportunity costs are treated as cash outflows for purposes of capital budgeting. However, note that if the project is accepted, management assumes that the warehouse will be sold for £150,000 (after taxes) in year 5.

   The test marketing cost of £250,000 is not included. The tests occurred in the past and should be viewed as a *sunk cost*.

3   *The investment in working capital*: Required working capital appears in line 5. Working capital rises over the early years of the project as expansion occurs. However, all working capital is assumed to be recovered at the end, a common assumption in capital budgeting. In other words, all inventory is sold by the end, the cash balance maintained as a buffer is liquidated, and all accounts receivable are collected. Increases in working capital in the early years must be funded by cash generated elsewhere in the firm. Hence these increases are viewed as cash *outflows*. To reiterate, it is the *increase* in working capital over a year that leads to a cash outflow in that year. Even if working capital is at a high level, there will be no cash outflow over a year if working capital stays constant over that year. Conversely, decreases in working capital in the later years are viewed as cash inflows. All of these cash flows are presented in line 6 of Table 7.1. A more complete discussion of working capital is provided later in this section.

To recap, there are three investments in this example: the bowling ball machine (line 1 in Table 7.1), the opportunity cost of the warehouse (line 4), and the changes in working capital (line 6). The total cash flow from these three investments is shown in line 7.

**Income and Taxes**   Next the determination of income is presented in the bottom segment of Table 7.1. While we are ultimately interested in cash flow – not income – we need the income calculation to determine taxes. Lines 8 and 9 of Table 7.1 show sales revenues and operating costs, respectively. The projections in these lines are based on the sales revenues and operating costs computed in columns 4 and 6 of Table 7.2. The estimates of revenues and costs follow from assumptions made by the corporate planning staff at Whair. In other words, the estimates critically depend on the fact that product prices are projected to increase at 2 per cent per year and costs per unit are projected to increase at 10 per cent per year.

Depreciation of the £100,000 capital investment is shown in line 10 of Table 7.1. Depreciation for tax purposes is based on the reducing-balance method. In the example, a 25 per cent rate is used.

Income before taxes is calculated in line 12 of Table 7.1. Taxes are provided in line 13 of this table, and net income is calculated in line 14.

**Salvage Value**   In calculating depreciation under current tax law, the expected economic life and future value of an asset are not issues. As a result, the book value of an asset can differ substantially from its actual market value. For example, consider the bowling machine Whair Balls is considering for its new project. The book value after the first year is £100,000 less the first year's depreciation of £25,000, or £75,000. Each year, the machine's value is written down by 25 per cent.

Suppose, at the end of the project, Whair sold the machine. At the end of the fifth year, the book value of the machine would be £23,730; but based on Whair's experience, it would probably be worth about £30,000. If the company actually sold it for this amount, then it would pay taxes at the ordinary income tax rate on the difference between the sale price of £30,000 and the book value of £23,730. Thus Whair would make an accounting profit on the machinery of £30,000 − £23,730 = £6,270.

Taxes must be paid on the profit because the difference between the market value and the book value is 'excess' depreciation, and it must be 'recaptured' when the asset is sold. In this case, Whair would have over-depreciated the asset by £6,270. Because the depreciation was too high, the company paid too little in taxes.

Notice this is not a tax on a long-term capital gain. Further, what is and what is not a capital gain is ultimately up to taxing authorities, and the specific rules can be very complex. We shall ignore capital gains taxes for the most part.

Finally, if the book value exceeds the market value, then the difference is treated as a loss for tax purposes. For example, if Whair sold the machine for £20,000, then the book value would exceed the market value by £270. In this case Whair would make a tax saving.

**Cash Flow**   Cash flow is finally determined in Table 7.4. We begin by reproducing lines 8, 9 and 13 in Table 7.1 as lines 1, 2 and 3 in Table 7.4. Cash flow from operations, which is sales minus both operating costs and taxes, is provided in line 4 of Table 7.4. Total investment cash flow, taken from line 7 of Table 7.1, appears as line 5 of Table 7.4. Cash flow from operations plus total cash flow of the investment equals total cash flow of the project, which is displayed as line 6 of Table 7.4.

**Net Present Value**   The NPV of the Whair bowling ball project can be calculated from the cash flows in line 6. As can be seen at the bottom of Table 7.4, the NPV is £57,600 if 10 per cent is the appropriate discount rate and –£18,810 if 20 per cent is the appropriate discount rate. If the discount rate is 16.91 per cent, the project will have a zero NPV. In other words, the project's internal rate of return is 16.91 per cent. If the discount rate of the Whair bowling ball project is above 16.91 per cent, it should not be accepted because its NPV would be negative.

## A Note about Net Working Capital

The investment in net working capital is an important part of any capital budgeting analysis. While we explicitly considered net working capital in lines 5 and 6 of Table 7.1, students may be wondering where the numbers in these lines came from. An investment in net working capital arises whenever (a) inventory is purchased, (b) cash is kept in the project as a buffer against unexpected expenditures, and (c) credit sales are made, generating trade receivables rather than cash. (The investment in net working capital is reduced by credit purchases, which generate trade payables.) This investment in net working capital represents a cash outflow because cash generated elsewhere in the firm is tied up in the project.

To see how the investment in net working capital is built from its component parts, we focus on year 1. We see in Table 7.1 that Whair's managers predict sales in year 1 to be £100,000 and operating costs to be £50,000. If both the sales and costs were cash transactions, the firm would receive £50,000 (= £100,000 – £50,000). As stated earlier, this cash flow would occur at the *end* of year 1.

Now let's give you more information. The managers:

1   Forecast that £9,000 of the sales will be on credit, implying that cash receipts at the end of year 1 will be only £91,000 (= £100,000 – £9,000). The accounts receivable of £9,000 will be collected at the end of year 2.

2   Believe that they can defer payment on £3,000 of the £50,000 of costs, implying that cash disbursements at the end of year 1 will be only £47,000 (= £50,000 – £3,000). Whair will pay off the £3,000 of trade payables at the end of year 2.

3   Decide that inventory of £2,500 should be left on hand at the end of year 1 to avoid *stockouts* (that is, running out of inventory).

4   Decide that cash of £1,500 should be earmarked for the project at the end of year 1 to avoid running out of cash.

Thus net working capital at the end of year 1 is

| £9,000 | – | £3,000 | + | £2,500 | + | £1,500 | = | £10,000 |
|---|---|---|---|---|---|---|---|---|
| Trade receivables | | Trade payables | | Inventory | | Cash | | Net working capital |

Because £10,000 of cash generated elsewhere in the firm must be used to offset this requirement for net working capital, Whair's managers correctly view the investment in net working capital as a cash outflow of the project. As the project grows over time, needs for net working capital increase. *Changes* in net working capital from year to year represent further cash flows, as indicated by the negative numbers for the first few years on line 6 of Table 7.1. However, in the declining years of the project, net working capital is reduced – ultimately to zero. That is, trade receivables are finally collected, the project's cash buffer is returned to the rest of the corporation, and all remaining inventory is sold off. This frees up cash in the later years, as indicated by positive numbers in years 4 and 5 on line 6.

Typically corporate worksheets (such as Table 7.1) treat net working capital as a whole. The individual components of working capital (receivables, inventory, and the like) do not generally appear in the worksheets. However, the reader should remember that the working capital numbers in the worksheets are not pulled out of thin air. Rather, they result from a meticulous forecast of the components, just as we illustrated for year 1.

## A Note about Depreciation

The Whair case made some assumptions about depreciation. Where did these assumptions come from? Assets are depreciated according to the tax rules that apply in each country. The UK system is very simple, with only two asset categories for depreciation: plant and machinery, and buildings. However, other countries may have more complex systems for estimating depreciation expenses, and these should be considered before carrying out a capital budgeting analysis.

Depreciation rates change regularly, and a financial manager must be up to date with the current applicable rates. For example, from 2010 the 25 per cent rate in the UK is reduced to 20 per cent reducing balance on plant and machinery. The 4 per cent straight-line depreciation on buildings will also be progressively reduced to zero over a number of years from 2010.

Currently, each country in the European Union has its own tax system, and this is seen as one of the major obstacles for full integration of the different European economies. However, a working group has been set up to develop a Common Consolidated Corporate Tax Base (CCCTB) for all countries. Although it will take several years for it to be enacted, the CCCTB is definitely a step in the right direction. The main recommendations of the working group are that all countries apply a 20 per cent reducing balance depreciation on plant and machinery, 2.5 per cent straight-line depreciation for buildings, and 4 per cent straight-line depreciation for long-term tangible assets (i.e. assets that will last for more than 25 years).

## Interest Expense

It may have bothered you that interest expense was ignored in the Whair example. After all, many projects are at least partially financed with debt, particularly a bowling ball machine that is likely to increase the debt capacity of the firm. As it turns out, our approach of assuming no debt financing is rather standard in the real world. Firms typically calculate a project's cash flows under the assumption that the project is financed only with equity. Any adjustments for debt financing are reflected in the discount rate, not the cash flows. The treatment of debt in capital budgeting will be covered in depth later in the text. Suffice it to say at this time that the full ramifications of debt financing are well beyond our current discussion.

# 7.3 Inflation and Capital Budgeting

Inflation is an important fact of economic life, and it must be considered in capital budgeting. We begin our examination of inflation by considering the relationship between interest rates and inflation.

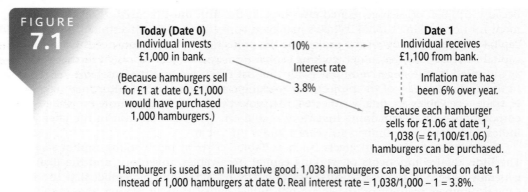

Hamburger is used as an illustrative good. 1,038 hamburgers can be purchased on date 1 instead of 1,000 hamburgers at date 0. Real interest rate = 1,038/1,000 – 1 = 3.8%.

**Figure 7.1** Calculation of real rate of interest

## Interest Rates and Inflation

Suppose a bank offers a one-year interest rate of 10 per cent. This means that an individual who deposits £1,000 will receive £1,100 (= £1,000 × 1.10) in one year. Although 10 per cent may seem like a handsome return, one can put it in perspective only after examining the rate of inflation.

Imagine that the rate of inflation is 6 per cent over the year, and it affects all goods equally. For example, a restaurant that charges £1.00 for a hamburger today will charge £1.06 for the same hamburger at the end of the year. You can use your £1,000 to buy 1,000 hamburgers today (date 0). Alternatively, if you put your money in the bank, you can buy 1,038 (= £1,100/£1.06) hamburgers at date 1. Thus lending increases your hamburger consumption by only 3.8 per cent.

Because the prices of all goods rise at this 6 per cent rate, lending lets you increase your consumption of any single good or any combination of goods by only 3.8 per cent. Thus 3.8 per cent is what you are *really* earning through your savings account, after adjusting for inflation. Economists refer to the 3.8 per cent number as the *real interest rate*. Economists refer to the 10 per cent rate as the *nominal interest rate* or simply the *interest rate*. This discussion is illustrated in Fig. 7.1.

We have used an example with a specific nominal interest rate and a specific inflation rate. In general, the formula between real and nominal interest rates can be written as follows:

$$1 + \text{Nominal interest rate} = (1 + \text{Real interest rate}) \times (1 + \text{Inflation rate})$$

Rearranging terms, we have

$$\text{Real interest rate} = \frac{1 + \text{Nominal interest rate}}{1 + \text{Inflation rate}} - 1 \qquad (7.1)$$

The formula indicates that the real interest rate in our example is 3.8 per cent (= 1.10/1.06 – 1).

Equation (7.1) determines the real interest rate precisely. The following formula is an approximation:

$$\text{Real interest rate} \cong \text{Nominal interest rate} - \text{Inflation rate} \qquad (7.2)$$

The symbol $\cong$ indicates that the equation is approximately true. This latter formula calculates the real rate in our example like this:

$$4\% = 10\% - 6\%$$

The student should be aware that, although Eq. (7.2) may seem more intuitive than Eq. (7.1), (7.2) is only an approximation, and should not be used in a formal analysis.

## Cash Flow and Inflation

The previous analysis defined two types of interest rate – nominal rates and real rates – and related them through Eq. (7.1). Capital budgeting requires data on cash flows as well as on interest rates. Like interest rates, cash flows can be expressed in either nominal or real terms.

A nominal cash flow refers to the actual money in cash to be received (or paid out). A real cash flow refers to the cash flow's purchasing power. These definitions are best explained by an example.

---

**EXAMPLE 7.6**

## Nominal versus Real Cash Flow

Burrows Publishing has just purchased the rights to the next book of famed romantic novelist Barbara Musk. Still unwritten, the book should be available to the public in four years. Currently, romantic novels sell for €10.00 in paperback. The publishers believe that inflation will be 6 per cent a year over the next four years. Because romantic novels are so popular, the publishers anticipate that their prices will rise by about 2 per cent per year more than the inflation rate over the next four years. Burrows Publishing plans to sell the novel at €13.60 [= $(1.08)^4 \times$ €10.00] four years from now, anticipating sales of 100,000 copies.

The expected cash flow in the fourth year of €1.36 million (= €13.60 × 100,000) is a *nominal cash flow*. That is, the firm expects to receive €1.36 million at that time. In other words, a nominal cash flow refers to the actual cash flow in euros to be received in the future.

The purchasing power of €1.36 million in four years is

$$€1.08 \text{ million} = \frac{€1.36 \text{ million}}{(1.06)^4}$$

The figure of €1.08 million is a *real cash flow* because it is expressed in terms of purchasing power. Extending our hamburger example, the €1.36 million to be received in four years will buy only 1.08 million hamburgers, because the price of a hamburger will rise from €1 to €1.26 [= €1 × $(1.06)^4$] over the period.

---

## Discounting: Nominal or Real?

Our previous discussion showed that interest rates can be expressed in either nominal or real terms. Similarly, cash flows can be expressed in either nominal or real terms. Given these choices, how should one express interest rates and cash flows when performing capital budgeting?

Financial practitioners correctly stress the need to maintain *consistency* between cash flows and discount rates. That is:

- *Nominal* cash flows must be discounted at the *nominal* rate.

- *Real* cash flows must be discounted at the *real* rate.

As long as one is consistent, either approach is correct. To minimize computational error, it is generally advisable in practice to choose the approach that is easiest. This idea is illustrated in the following two examples.

---

**EXAMPLE 7.7**

## Real and Nominal Discounting

Shields Electric forecasts the following nominal cash flows on a particular project:

|  | 0 | 1 | 2 |
|---|---|---|---|
| **Cash flow** | −£1,000 | £600 | £650 |

The nominal discount rate is 14 per cent, and the inflation rate is forecast to be 5 per cent. What is the value of the project?

**Using Nominal Quantities** The NPV can be calculated as

$$£26.47 = -£1,000 + \frac{£600}{1.14} + \frac{£650}{(1.14)^2}$$

The project should be accepted.

**Using Real Quantities** The real cash flows are these:

|  | 0 | 1 | 2 |
|---|---|---|---|
| **Cash flow** | −£1,000 | £571.43 $\left(\dfrac{£600}{1.05}\right)$ | £589.57 $\left(\dfrac{£650}{(1.05)^2}\right)$ |

As we have discussed, the real discount rate is 8.57143 per cent (= 1.14/1.05 − 1).
    The NPV can be calculated as

$$£26.47 = -£1,000 + \frac{£571.43}{1.0857143} + \frac{£589.57}{(1.0857143)^2}$$

The NPV is the same whether cash flows are expressed in nominal or in real quantities. It must always be the case that the NPV is the same under the two different approaches.
    Because both approaches always yield the same result, which one should be used? Use the approach that is simpler, because the simpler approach generally leads to fewer computational errors. The Shields Electric example begins with nominal cash flows, so nominal quantities produce a simpler calculation here.

EXAMPLE
**7.8**

## Real and Nominal NPV

Bella SpA generated the following forecast for a capital budgeting project:

|  | Year | | |
|---|---|---|---|
|  | 0 (€) | 1 (€) | 2 (€) |
| Capital expenditure | 1,210 | | |
| Revenues (in real terms) | | 1,900 | 2,000 |
| Cash expenses (in real terms) | | 950 | 1,000 |
| Depreciation (straight-line) | | 605 | 605 |

The president, Signora Bella, estimates inflation to be 10 per cent per year over the next two years. In addition, she believes that the cash flows of the project should be discounted at the nominal rate of 15.5 per cent. Her firm's tax rate is 40 per cent.

Signora Bella forecasts all cash flows in *nominal* terms, leading to the following spreadsheet:

| | Year | | |
|---|---|---|---|
| | **0**<br>**(€)** | **1**<br>**(€)** | **2**<br>**(€)** |
| Capital expenditure | −1,210 | | |
| Revenues | | 2,090 (= 1,900 × 1.10) | 2,420 [= 2,000 × (1.10)$^2$] |
| − Expenses | | −1,045 (= 950 × 1.10) | −1,210 [= 1,000 × (1.10)$^2$] |
| − Depreciation | | −605 (= 1,210/2) | −605 |
| Taxable income | | 440 | 605 |
| − Taxes (40%) | | −176 | −242 |
| Income after taxes | | 264 | 363 |
| + Depreciation | | +605 | +605 |
| Cash flow | | 869 | 968 |

$$\text{NPV} = -€1{,}210 + \frac{€869}{1.155} + \frac{€968}{(1.155)^2} = €268$$

Signora Bella's sidekick, Signor Barbi, prefers working in real terms. He first calculates the real rate to be 5 per cent (= 1.155/1.10 − 1). Next, he generates the following spreadsheet in *real* quantities:

| | Year | | |
|---|---|---|---|
| | **0**<br>**(€)** | **1**<br>**(€)** | **2**<br>**(€)** |
| Capital expenditure | −1,210 | | |
| Revenues | | 1,900 | 2,000 |
| − Expenses | | −950 | −1,000 |
| − Depreciation | | −550 (= 605/1.1) | −500 [= 605/(1.1)$^2$] |
| Taxable income | | 400 | 500 |
| − Taxes (40%) | | −160 | −200 |
| Income after taxes | | 240 | 300 |
| + Depreciation | | +550 | +500 |
| Cash flow | | 790 | 800 |

$$\text{NPV} = -€1{,}210 + \frac{€790}{1.05} + \frac{€800}{(1.05)^2} = €268$$

In explaining his calculations to Signora Bella, Signor Barbi points out these facts:

1  The capital expenditure occurs at date 0 (today), so its nominal value and its real value are equal.

2  Because yearly depreciation of €605 is a nominal quantity, one converts it to a real quantity by discounting at the inflation rate of 10 per cent.

It is no coincidence that both Signora Bella and Signor Barbi arrive at the same NPV number. Both methods must always generate the same NPV.

## 7.4  Alternative Definitions of Operating Cash Flow

The analysis we went through in the previous section is quite general, and can be adapted to just about any capital investment problem. In the next section we illustrate a particularly useful variation. Before we do so, we need to discuss the fact that different definitions of project operating cash flow are commonly used, both in practice and in finance texts.

As we shall see, the different approaches to operating cash flow all measure the same thing. If they are used correctly, they all produce the same answer, and one is not necessarily any better or more useful than another. Unfortunately, the fact that alternative definitions are used sometimes leads to confusion. For this reason, we examine several of these variations next to see how they are related.

In the discussion that follows, keep in mind that when we speak of cash flow, we literally mean *cash in less cash out*. This is all we are concerned with. Different definitions of operating cash flow simply amount to different ways of manipulating basic accounting information about sales, costs, depreciation and taxes to get at cash flow.

For a particular project and year under consideration, suppose we have the following estimates:

$$\text{Sales} = £1,500$$
$$\text{Costs} = £700$$
$$\text{Depreciation} = £600$$

With these estimates, notice that earnings before interest and taxes (EBIT) is

$$\begin{aligned} \text{EBIT} &= \text{Sales} - \text{Costs} - \text{Depreciation} \\ &= £1,500 - 700 - 600 \\ &= £200 \end{aligned}$$

Once again, we assume that no interest is paid, so the tax bill is

$$\begin{aligned} \text{Taxes} &= \text{EBIT} \times t_c \\ &= £200 \times 0.28 \\ &= £56 \end{aligned}$$

where $t_c$, the corporate tax rate, is 28 per cent.

When we put all of this together, we see that project operating cash flow, OCF, is

$$\begin{aligned} \text{OCF} &= \text{EBIT} + \text{Depreciation} - \text{Taxes} \\ &= £200 + 600 - 56 \\ &= £744 \end{aligned}$$

It turns out there are some other ways to determine OCF that could be (and are) used. We consider these next.

## The Bottom-Up Approach

Because we are ignoring any financing expenses, such as interest, in our calculations of project OCF, we can write project net income as

$$\begin{aligned} \text{Project net income} &= \text{EBIT} - \text{Taxes} \\ &= £200 - 56 \\ &= £144 \end{aligned}$$

If we simply add the depreciation to both sides, we arrive at a slightly different and very common expression for OCF:

$$\begin{aligned} \text{OCF} &= \text{Net income} + \text{Depreciation} \\ &= £144 + 600 \\ &= £744 \end{aligned} \tag{7.3}$$

This is the *bottom-up* approach. Here, we start with the accountant's bottom line (net income) and add back any non-cash deductions such as depreciation. It is crucial to remember that this definition of operating cash flow as net income plus depreciation is correct only if there is no interest expense subtracted in the calculation of net income.

## The Top-Down Approach

Perhaps the most obvious way to calculate OCF is this:

$$\begin{aligned} \text{OCF} &= \text{Sales} - \text{Costs} - \text{Taxes} \\ &= \pounds1{,}500 - 700 - 56 \\ &= \pounds744 \end{aligned} \qquad (7.4)$$

This is the *top-down* approach, the second variation on the basic OCF definition. Here we start at the top of the income statement with sales, and work our way down to net cash flow by subtracting costs, taxes and other expenses. Along the way, we simply leave out any strictly non-cash items such as depreciation.

## The Tax Shield Approach

The third variation on our basic definition of OCF is the *tax shield* approach. This approach will be very useful for some problems we consider in the next chapter. The tax shield definition of OCF is

$$\text{OCF} = (\text{Sales} - \text{Costs}) \times (1 - t_c) + \text{Depreciation} \times t_c \qquad (7.5)$$

where $t_c$ is again the corporate tax rate. Assuming that $t_c = 28$ per cent, the OCF works out to be

$$\begin{aligned} \text{OCF} &= (\pounds1{,}500 - 700) \times 0.72 + 600 \times 0.28 \\ &= \pounds576 + 168 \\ &= \pounds744 \end{aligned}$$

This is just as we had before.

This approach views OCF as having two components. The first part is what the project's cash flow would be if there were no depreciation expense. In this case, this would-have-been cash flow is £576.

The second part of OCF in this approach is the depreciation deduction multiplied by the tax rate. This is called the depreciation tax shield. We know that depreciation is a non-cash expense. The only cash flow effect of deducting depreciation is to reduce our taxes, a benefit to us. At the current 28 per cent corporate tax rate, every pound in depreciation expense saves us 28 pence in taxes. So, in our example, the £600 depreciation deduction saves us £600 × 0.28 = £168 in taxes.

## Conclusion

Now that we've seen that all of these approaches are the same, you're probably wondering why everybody doesn't just agree on one of them. One reason is that different approaches are useful in different circumstances. The best one to use is whichever happens to be the most convenient for the problem at hand.

## 7.5 Investments of Unequal Lives: The Equivalent Annual Cost Method

Suppose a firm must choose between two machines of unequal lives. Both machines can do the same job, but they have different operating costs and will last for different time periods. A simple application of the NPV rule suggests taking the machine whose costs have the lower present value. This choice might be a mistake, however, because the lower-cost machine may need to be replaced before the other one.

Let's consider an example. The Downtown Athletic Club must choose between two mechanical tennis ball throwers. Machine A costs less than machine B but will not last as long. The cash *outflows* from the two machines are shown here:

| | Date | | | | |
|---|---|---|---|---|---|
| | **0** | **1** | **2** | **3** | **4** |
| **Machine** | **(€)** | **(€)** | **(€)** | **(€)** | **(€)** |
| A | 500 | 120 | 120 | 120 | |
| B | 600 | 100 | 100 | 100 | 100 |

Machine A costs €500 and lasts three years. There will be maintenance expenses of €120 to be paid at the end of each of the three years. Machine B costs €600 and lasts four years. There will be maintenance expenses of €100 to be paid at the end of each of the four years. We place all costs in real terms, an assumption greatly simplifying the analysis. Revenues per year are assumed to be the same, regardless of machine, so they are ignored in the analysis. Note that all numbers in the previous chart are *outflows*.

To get a handle on the decision, let's take the present value of the costs of each of the two machines. Assuming a discount rate of 10 per cent, we have

$$\text{Machine A: } €798.42 = €500 + \frac{€120}{1.1} + \frac{€120}{(1.1)^2} + \frac{€120}{(1.1)^3}$$

$$\text{Machine B: } €916.99 = €600 + \frac{€100}{1.1} + \frac{€100}{(1.1)^2} + \frac{€100}{(1.1)^3} + \frac{€100}{(1.1)^4}$$

Machine B has a higher present value of outflows. A naive approach would be to select machine A because of its lower present value. However, machine B has a longer life, so perhaps its cost per year is actually lower.

How might one properly adjust for the difference in useful life when comparing the two machines? Perhaps the easiest approach involves calculating something called the *equivalent annual cost* of each machine. This approach puts costs on a per-year basis.

The previous equation showed that payments of (€500, €120, €120, €120) are equivalent to a single payment of €798.42 at date 0. We now wish to equate the single payment of €798.42 at date 0 with a three-year annuity. Using techniques of previous chapters, we have

$$€798.42 = C \times A^3_{0.10}$$

Here $A^3_{0.10}$ is an annuity of €1 a year for three years, discounted at 10 per cent. $C$ is the unknown – the annuity payment per year such that the present value of all payments equals €798.42. Because $A^3_{0.10}$ equals 2.4869, $C$ equals €321.05 (= €798.42/2.4869). Thus a payment stream of (€500, €120, €120, €120) is equivalent to annuity payments of €321.05 made at the *end* of each year for three years. We refer to €321.05 as the *equivalent annual cost* of machine A.

This idea is summarized in the following chart:

| | Date | | | |
|---|---|---|---|---|
| | **0** | **1** | **2** | **3** |
| | **(€)** | **(€)** | **(€)** | **(€)** |
| Cash outflows of machine A | 500 | 120 | 120 | 120 |
| Equivalent annual cost of machine A | | 321.05 | 321.05 | 321.05 |

The Downtown Athletic Club should be indifferent between cash outflows of (€500, €120, €120, €120) and cash outflows of (€0, €321.05, €321.05, €321.05). Alternatively, one can say that the purchase of the machine is financially equivalent to a rental agreement calling for annual lease payments of €321.05.

Now let's turn to machine B. We calculate its equivalent annual cost from

$$€916.99 = C \times A^4_{0.10}$$

Because $A^4_{0.10}$ equals 3.1699, $C$ equals €916.99/3.1699, or €289.28.

As we did for machine A, we can create the following chart for machine B:

| | Date | | | | |
|---|---|---|---|---|---|
| | **0** (€) | **1** (€) | **2** (€) | **3** (€) | **4** (€) |
| Cash outflows of machine B | €600 | €100 | €100 | €100 | €100 |
| Equivalent annual cost of machine B | | €289.28 | €289.28 | €289.28 | €289.28 |

The decision is easy once the charts of the two machines are compared. Would you rather make annual lease payments of €321.05 or €289.28? Put this way, the problem becomes a no-brainer: a rational person would rather pay the lower amount. Thus machine B is the preferred choice.

Two final remarks are in order. First, it is no accident that we specified the costs of the tennis ball machines in real terms. Although B would still have been the preferred machine had the costs been stated in nominal terms, the actual solution would have been much more difficult. As a general rule, always convert cash flows to real terms when working through problems of this type.

Second, such analysis applies only if one expects that both machines can be replaced. The analysis would differ if no replacement were possible. For example, imagine that the only company that manufactured tennis ball throwers just went out of business and no new producers are expected to enter the field. In this case, machine B would generate revenues in the fourth year whereas machine A would not. Here, simple net present value analysis for mutually exclusive projects including both revenues and costs would be appropriate.

## The General Decision to Replace

The previous analysis concerned the choice between machine A and machine B, both of which were new acquisitions. More typically firms must decide when to replace an existing machine with a new one. This decision is actually quite straightforward. One should replace if the annual cost of the new machine is less than the annual cost of the old machine. As with much else in finance, an example clarifies this approach better than further explanation.

---

**EXAMPLE 7.9**

## Replacement Decisions

Consider the situation of BIKE, which must decide whether to replace an existing machine. BIKE currently pays no taxes. The replacement machine costs £9,000 now and requires maintenance of £1,000 at the end of every year for eight years. At the end of eight years the machine would be sold for £2,000 after taxes.

The existing machine requires increasing amounts of maintenance each year, and its salvage value falls each year, as shown:

| Year | Maintenance (£) | After-tax salvage (£) |
|---|---|---|
| Present | 0 | 4,000 |
| 1 | 1,000 | 2,500 |
| 2 | 2,000 | 1,500 |
| 3 | 3,000 | 1,000 |
| 4 | 4,000 | 0 |

This chart tells us that the existing machine can be sold for £4,000 now after taxes. If it is sold one year from now, the resale price will be £2,500 after taxes, and £1,000 must be spent on maintenance during the year to keep it running. For ease of calculation, we assume that this maintenance fee is paid at the end of the year. The machine will last for four more years before it falls apart. In other words, salvage value will be zero at the end of year 4. If BIKE faces an opportunity cost of capital of 15 per cent, when should it replace the machine?

Our approach is to compare the annual cost of the replacement machine with the annual cost of the old machine. The annual cost of the replacement machine is simply its *equivalent annual cost* (EAC). Let's calculate that first.

**Equivalent Annual Cost of New Machine** The present value of the cost of the new replacement machine is as follows:

$$\begin{aligned} PV_{costs} &= £9,000 + £1,000 \times A_{0.15}^{8} - \frac{£2000}{(1.15)^8} \\ &= £9,000 + £1,000 \times (4.4873) - £2,000 \times (0.3269) \\ &= £12,833 \end{aligned}$$

Notice that the £2,000 salvage value is an inflow. It is treated as a *negative* number in this equation because it *offsets* the cost of the machine.

The EAC of a new replacement machine equals

$$\begin{aligned} PV/\text{8-year annuity factor at } 15\% &= \frac{PV}{A_{0.15}^{8}} \\ &= \frac{£12,833}{4.4873} \\ &= £2,860 \end{aligned}$$

This calculation implies that buying a replacement machine is financially equivalent to renting this machine for £2,860 per year.

**Cost of Old Machine** This calculation is a little trickier. If BIKE keeps the old machine for one year, the firm must pay maintenance costs of £1,000 a year from now. But this is not BIKE's only cost from keeping the machine for one year. BIKE will receive £2,500 at date 1 if the old machine is kept for one year, but would receive £4,000 today if the old machine were sold immediately. This reduction in sales proceeds is clearly a cost as well.

Thus the PV of the costs of keeping the machine for one more year before selling it equals

$$£4,000 + \frac{£1,000}{1.15} - \frac{£2,500}{1.15} = £2,696$$

That is, if BIKE holds the old machine for one year, BIKE does *not* receive the £4,000 today. This £4,000 can be thought of as an opportunity cost. In addition, the firm must pay £1,000 a year from now. Finally, BIKE does receive £2,500 a year from now. This last item is treated as a negative number because it offsets the other two costs.

Although we normally express cash flows in terms of present value, the analysis to come is easier if we express the cash flow in terms of its future value one year from now. This future value is

$$£2,696 \times 1.15 = £3,100$$

In other words, the cost of keeping the machine for one year is equivalent to paying £3,100 at the end of the year.

**Making the Comparison** Now let's review the cash flows. If we replace the machine immediately, we can view our annual expense as £2,860, beginning at the end of the year. This annual expense occurs for ever if we replace the new machine every eight years. This cash flow stream can be written as follows:

|  | Year 1 | Year 2 | Year 3 | Year 4 | ... |
|---|---|---|---|---|---|
| Expenses from replacing machine immediately | £2,860 | £2,860 | £2,860 | £2,860 | ... |

If we replace the old machine in one year, our expense from using the old machine for that final year can be viewed as £3,100, payable at the end of the year. After replacement, our annual expense is £2,860, beginning at the end of two years. This annual expense occurs for ever if we replace the new machine every eight years. This cash flow stream can be written like this:

|  | Year 1 | Year 2 | Year 3 | Year 4 | ... |
|---|---|---|---|---|---|
| Expenses from using old machine for one year and then replacing it | £3,100 | £2,860 | £2,860 | £2,860 | ... |

Put this way, the choice is a no-brainer. Anyone would rather pay £2,860 at the end of the year than £3,100 at the end of the year. Thus BIKE should replace the old machine immediately to minimize the expense at year 1.[1]

Two final points should be made about the decision to replace. First, we have examined a situation where both the old machine and the replacement machine generate the same revenues. Because revenues are unaffected by the choice of machine, revenues do not enter our analysis. This situation is common in business. For example, the decision to replace either the heating system or the air conditioning system in one's home office is unlikely to affect firm revenues. However, sometimes revenues will be greater with a new machine. The approach here can easily be amended to handle differential revenues.

Second, we want to stress the importance of the current approach. Applications of this approach are pervasive in business because *every* machine must be replaced at some point.

## Summary and Conclusions

This chapter discussed a number of practical applications of capital budgeting.

1   Capital budgeting must be placed on an incremental basis. This means that sunk costs must be ignored, whereas both opportunity costs and side effects must be considered.

2   In the Whair case we computed NPV using the following two steps:

   (a)   Calculate the net cash flow from all sources for each period.

   (b)   Calculate the NPV using these cash flows.

3   Inflation must be handled consistently. One approach is to express both cash flows and the discount rate in nominal terms. The other approach is to express both cash flows and the discount rate in real terms. Because either approach yields the same NPV calculation, the simpler method should be used. The simpler method will generally depend on the type of capital budgeting problem.

4   A firm should use the equivalent annual cost approach when choosing between two machines of unequal lives.

# Questions and Problems

CONCEPT

1 – 5

1 **Incremental Cash Flows** Which of the following should be treated as an incremental cash flow when computing the NPV of an investment?

(a) A reduction in the sales of a company's other products caused by the investment.

(b) An expenditure on plant and equipment that has not yet been made, and will be made only if the project is accepted.

(c) Costs of research and development undertaken in connection with the product during the past three years.

(d) Annual depreciation expense from the investment.

(e) Dividend payments by the firm.

(f) The resale value of plant and equipment at the end of the project's life.

(g) Salary and medical costs for production personnel who will be employed only if the project is accepted.

2 **Incremental Cash Flows** In the context of capital budgeting, what is an opportunity cost?

3 **Inflation and Capital Budgeting** In a hyperinflationary environment, how would you incorporate inflation into a capital budgeting analysis? Explain your methodology in words to a manager who is worried about the power of capital budgeting when inflation is very high.

4 **Operating Cash Flows** What is meant by operating cash flow? Review the different ways in which operating cash flow can be calculated.

5 **Equivalent Annual Cost** Explain what is meant by the equivalent annual cost method. When is EAC analysis appropriate for comparing two or more projects? Why is this method used? Are there any implicit assumptions required by this method that you find troubling? Explain.

REGULAR

6 – 24

6 **Calculating Project NPV** Your uncle has spent most of his retirement income on opening a new seafood restaurant. As part of the initial renovations he has ordered a wooden oven to cook squid in the style of the best Athenian restaurants he visited in his youth. The cost of the oven (£400,000) is staggering, but worth it, if it can make squid in the way he remembers. It is possible to buy this particular oven only from a local ovenmaker in Athens, and installation requires flying over two engineers at cost. The company tells your uncle that the total installation expense is £50,000. Feeling slightly sick, your uncle asks you how to deal with the installation cost in the company accounts. Is it a capital investment or is it an expense? The tax rate is 28 per cent and the relevant discount rate is 5 per cent. If the installation is treated as a capital investment cost, what is the present value of tax savings using a depreciation method of 20 per cent reducing balance? Assume that the oven will be scrapped for nothing in five years' time (you don't have much confidence in your uncle's business acumen). Which is better for your uncle: treating the installation cost as a capital investment or as an expense?

7 **Calculating Project NPV** Best Manufacturing Ltd is considering a new investment. Financial projections for the investment are tabulated here. The corporate tax rate is 28 per cent. Assume all sales revenue is received in cash, all operating costs and income taxes are paid in cash, and all cash flows occur at the end of the year. All net working capital is recovered at the end of the project, and the investment is sold at its residual value after depreciation.

| | Year 0 (£) | Year 1 (£) | Year 2 (£) | Year 3 (£) | Year 4 (£) |
|---|---|---|---|---|---|
| Investment | 10,000 | – | – | – | – |
| Sales revenue | – | 7,000 | 7,000 | 7,000 | 7,000 |
| Operating costs | – | 2,000 | 2,000 | 2,000 | 2,000 |
| Depreciation | – | 2,500 | 1,875 | 1,406 | 1,055 |
| Net working capital spending | 200 | 250 | 300 | 200 | ? |

(a)  Compute the incremental net income of the investment for each year.

(b)  Compute the incremental cash flows of the investment for each year.

(c)  Suppose the appropriate discount rate is 12 per cent. What is the NPV of the project?

8   **Calculating Project Cash Flow from Assets**   In the previous problem, suppose the project requires an initial investment in net working capital of £3,000 and the fixed asset will have a market value of £2,100 at the end of the project. What is the project's year 0 net cash flow? Year 1? Year 2? Year 3? What is the new NPV?

9   **NPV and Accelerated Depreciation**   In the previous problem, suppose the fixed asset is depreciated using the reducing-balance method at 20 per cent per annum. All the other facts are the same. What is the project's year 1 net cash flow now? Year 2? Year 3? What is the new NPV?

10  **Project Evaluation**   Your firm is contemplating the purchase of a new £925,000 computer-based order entry system. The system will be depreciated using reducing balance at 20 per cent per annum over its five-year life. It will be worth £90,000 at the end of that time. You will save £360,000 before taxes per year in order processing costs, and you will be able to reduce working capital by £125,000 (this is a one-time reduction). If the tax rate is 28 per cent, what is the IRR for this project?

11  **Project Evaluation**   Dog Up! Franks is looking at a new sausage system with an installed cost of €390,000. This cost will be depreciated straight-line to zero over the project's five-year life, at the end of which the sausage system can be scrapped for €60,000. The sausage system will save the firm €120,000 per year in pre-tax operating costs, and the system requires an initial investment in net working capital of €28,000. If the tax rate is 34 per cent and the discount rate is 10 per cent, what is the NPV of this project?

12  **Calculating Salvage Value**   An asset used in a four-year project is depreciated at 20 per cent reducing balance for tax purposes. The asset has an acquisition cost of £9,300,000 and will be sold for £3,100,000 at the end of the project. If the tax rate is 28 per cent, what is the after-tax salvage value of the asset?

13  **Calculating NPV**   Howell Petroleum is considering a new project that complements its existing business. The machine required for the project costs €2 million. The marketing department predicts that sales related to the project will be €1.2 million per year for the next four years, after which the market will cease to exist. The machine will be depreciated using a 20 per cent reducing-balance method. At the end of four years it will be sold at its residual value. Cost of goods sold and operating expenses related to the project are predicted to be 25 per cent of sales. Howell also needs to add net working capital of €100,000 immediately. The additional net working capital will be recovered in full at the end of the project's life. The corporate tax rate is 35 per cent. The required rate of return for Howell is 14 per cent. Should Howell proceed with the project?

14 **Calculating EAC** You are evaluating two different silicon wafer milling machines. The Techron I costs €210,000, has a three-year life, and has pre-tax operating costs of €34,000 per year. The Techron II costs €320,000, has a five-year life, and has pre-tax operating costs of €23,000 per year. For both milling machines, use 20 per cent reducing balance depreciation over the project's life and assume a salvage value of €20,000. If your tax rate is 35 per cent and your discount rate is 14 per cent, compute the EAC for both machines. Which do you prefer? Why?

15 **Comparing Mutually Exclusive Projects** Hagar Industrial Systems Company (HISC) is trying to decide between two different conveyor belt systems. System A costs 430,000 Norwegian kroner (NK), has a four-year life, and requires NK120,000 in pre-tax annual operating costs. System B costs NK540,000, has a six-year life, and requires NK80,000 in pre-tax annual operating costs. Both systems are to be depreciated using the reducing-balance method of 50 per cent per annum, and will have zero salvage value at the end of their life. Whichever system is chosen, it will *not* be replaced when it wears out. If the tax rate is 28 per cent and the discount rate is 20 per cent, which system should the firm choose?

16 **Comparing Mutually Exclusive Projects** Suppose in the previous problem that HISC always needs a conveyor belt system: when one wears out, it must be replaced. Which system should the firm choose now?

17 **Inflation and Company Value** Sparkling Water plc expects to sell 2 million bottles of drinking water each year in perpetuity. This year each bottle will sell for £1.25 in real terms and will cost £0.70 in real terms. Sales income and costs occur at year-end. Revenues will rise at a real rate of 7 per cent annually, while real costs will rise at a real rate of 5 per cent annually. The real discount rate is 10 per cent. The corporate tax rate is 28 per cent. What is Sparkling worth today?

18 **Calculating Nominal Cash Flow** Etonic SA is considering an investment of €250,000 in an asset with an economic life of five years. The firm estimates that the nominal annual cash revenues and expenses at the end of the first year will be €200,000 and €50,000, respectively. Both revenues and expenses will grow thereafter at the annual inflation rate of 3 per cent. Etonic will use the 20 per cent reducing-balance method to depreciate its asset over five years. The salvage value of the asset is estimated to be €30,000 in nominal terms at that time. The one-time net working capital investment of €10,000 is required immediately, and will be recovered at the end of the project. All corporate cash flows are subject to a 34 per cent tax rate. What is the project's total nominal cash flow from assets for each year?

19 **Equivalent Annual Cost** Bridgton Golf Academy is evaluating different golf practice equipment. The 'Dimple-Max' equipment costs £45,000, has a three-year life, and costs £5,000 per year to operate. The relevant discount rate is 12 per cent. Assume that the reducing balance (20 per cent) depreciation method is used. Furthermore, assume the equipment has a salvage value of £20,000 at the end of the project's life. The relevant tax rate is 28 per cent. All cash flows occur at the end of the year. What is the equivalent annual cost (EAC) of this equipment?

20 **Calculating NPV and IRR for a Replacement** A firm is considering an investment in a new machine with a price of £32 million to replace its existing machine. The current machine has a book value of £1 million and a market value of £9 million. The new machine is expected to have a four-year life, and the old machine has four years left in which it can be used. If the firm replaces the old machine with the new machine, it expects to save £8 million in operating costs each year over the next four years. Both machines will have no salvage value in four years. If the firm purchases the new machine, it will also need an investment of £500,000 in net working capital. The required return on the investment is 18 per cent, and the tax rate is 39 per cent.

(a)    What are the NPV and IRR of the decision to replace the old machine?

(b)    The new machine saves £32 million over the next four years and has a cost of £32 million. When you consider the time value of money, how is it possible that the decision to replace the old machine has a positive NPV?

21   **Calculating Project NPV**   With the growing popularity of casual surf print clothing, two recent MBA graduates decided to broaden this casual surf concept to encompass a 'surf lifestyle for the home'. With limited capital, they decided to focus on surf print table and floor lamps to accent people's homes. They projected unit sales of these lamps to be 5,000 in the first year, with growth of 15 per cent each year for the next five years. Production of these lamps will require £28,000 in net working capital to start. Total fixed costs are £75,000 per year, variable production costs are £20 per unit, and the units are priced at £45 each. The equipment needed to begin production will cost £60,000. The equipment will be depreciated using the reducing-balance method (20 per cent), and is not expected to have a salvage value. The effective tax rate is 28 per cent, and the required rate of return is 25 per cent. What is the NPV of this project?

22   **Calculating Project NPV**   Pilot Plus Pens is deciding when to replace its old machine. The machine's current salvage value is €2 million. Its current book value is €1 million. If not sold, the old machine will require maintenance costs of €400,000 at the end of the year for the next five years. Depreciation on the old machine is calculated using 20 per cent reducing balances. At the end of five years it will have a salvage value of €200,000. A replacement machine costs €3 million now and requires maintenance costs of €500,000 at the end of each year during its economic life of five years. At the end of the five years the new machine will have a salvage value of €500,000. It will be depreciated by the reducing-balance method (20 per cent). In five years a replacement machine will cost €3,500,000. Pilot will need to purchase this machine regardless of what choice it makes today. The corporate tax rate is 34 per cent and the appropriate discount rate is 12 per cent. The company is assumed to earn sufficient revenues to generate tax shields from depreciation. Should Pilot Plus Pens replace the old machine now or at the end of five years?

23   **Inflation**   Your company manufactures non-stick frying pans. However, it outsources the production of the glass covers for the pans. Until now, this has been a good option. However, your supplier has become unreliable and doubled his prices. As a result, you feel that now might be the time to start producing your own glass covers. At the moment, your company produces 200,000 non-stick pans per year. The producer charges you €2 per cover and you estimate the costs of producing your own cover to be €1.50. A new machine will be required to produce the covers, and this costs €150,000 in the market. The machine will last for 10 years, at which point it will have no value. The expansion will require an increase in working capital of €30,000. Your company pays 28 per cent tax, and the appropriate discount rate is 15 per cent. Inflation is expected to be 4 per cent per year for the next 10 years. Assume you use the 20 per cent reducing-balance method for depreciation. Should you undertake this investment? State clearly any additional assumptions you have made in your analysis.

24   **Project Analysis and Inflation**   Dickinson Brothers is considering investing in a machine to produce computer keyboards. The price of the machine will be £400,000, and its economic life is five years. The machine will be depreciated by the reducing-balance method (20 per cent), but will be worthless in five years. The machine will produce 10,000 keyboards each year. The price of each keyboard will be £40 in the first year and will increase by 5 per cent per year. The production cost per keyboard will be £20 in the first year and will increase by 10 per cent per year. The project will have an annual fixed cost of £50,000 and require an immediate investment of £25,000 in net working capital. The corporate tax rate for the company is 28 per cent. If the appropriate discount rate is 15 per cent, what is the NPV of the investment?

25 **Project Evaluation** Aguilera Acoustics (AA) projects unit sales for a new seven-octave voice emulation implant as follows:

| Year | Unit sales |
|------|------------|
| 1 | 85,000 |
| 2 | 98,000 |
| 3 | 106,000 |
| 4 | 114,000 |
| 5 | 93,000 |

Production of the implants will require €1,500,000 in net working capital to start, and additional net working capital investments each year equal to 15 per cent of the projected sales increase for the following year. Total fixed costs are €900,000 per year, variable production costs are €240 per unit, and the units are priced at €325 each. The equipment needed to begin production has an installed cost of €21,000,000. Because the implants are intended for professional singers, this equipment is considered industrial machinery and is thus depreciated by the reducing-balance method at 20 per cent per annum. In five years, this equipment can be sold for about 20 per cent of its acquisition cost. AA is in the 35 per cent marginal tax bracket and has a required return on all its projects of 18 per cent. Based on these preliminary project estimates, what is the NPV of the project? What is the IRR?

26 **Calculating Required Savings** A proposed cost-saving device has an installed cost of £480,000. The device will be used in a five-year project and be depreciated using the reducing-balance method at 20 per cent per annum. The required initial net working capital investment is £40,000, the marginal tax rate is 28 per cent, and the project discount rate is 12 per cent. The device has an estimated year 5 salvage value of £45,000. What level of pre-tax cost savings do we require for this project to be profitable?

27 **Calculating a Bid Price** Another utilization of cash flow analysis is setting the bid price on a project. To calculate the bid price, we set the project NPV equal to zero and find the required price. Thus the bid price represents a financial break-even level for the project. Guthrie Enterprises needs someone to supply it with 150,000 cartons of machine screws per year to support its manufacturing needs over the next five years, and you've decided to bid on the contract. It will cost you €780,000 to install the equipment necessary to start production: you'll depreciate this cost using 20 per cent reducing balances over the project's life. You estimate that in five years this equipment can be salvaged for €50,000. Your fixed production costs will be €240,000 per year, and your variable production costs should be €8.50 per carton. You also need an initial investment in net working capital of €75,000. If your tax rate is 35 per cent and you require a 16 per cent return on your investment, what bid price should you submit?

28 **Financial Break-Even Analysis** The technique for calculating a bid price can be extended to many other types of problem. Answer the following questions using the same technique as setting a bid price: that is, set the project NPV to zero and solve for the variable in question.

(a) In the previous problem, assume that the price per carton is €13 and find the project NPV. What does your answer tell you about your bid price? What do you know about the number of cartons you can sell and still break even? How about your level of costs?

(b) Solve the previous problem again with the price still at €13 – but find the quantity of cartons per year that you can supply and still break even. (*Hint*: It's less than 150,000.)

(c) Repeat (b) with a price of €13 and a quantity of 150,000 cartons per year, and find the highest level of fixed costs you could afford and still break even. (*Hint*: It's more than €240,000.)

29  **Calculating a Bid Price**   Your company has been approached to bid on a contract to sell 10,000 voice recognition (VR) computer keyboards a year for four years. Because of technological improvements, beyond that time they will be outdated and no sales will be possible. The equipment necessary for the production will cost £2.4 million and will be depreciated on a reducing balance basis (20 per cent). Production will require an investment in net working capital of £75,000, to be returned at the end of the project, and the equipment can be sold for £200,000 at the end of production. Fixed costs are £500,000 per year, and variable costs are £165 per unit. In addition to the contract, you feel your company can sell 3,000, 6,000, 8,000 and 5,000 additional units to companies in other countries over the next four years, respectively, at a price of £275. This price is fixed. The tax rate is 28 per cent, and the required return is 13 per cent. Additionally, the managing director of the company will undertake the project only if it has an NPV of £100,000. What bid price should you set for the contract?

30  **Project Analysis**   Benson Enterprises is evaluating alternative uses for a three-storey manufacturing and warehousing building that it has purchased for £225,000. The company can continue to rent the building to the present occupants for £12,000 per year. The present occupants have indicated an interest in staying in the building for at least another 15 years. Alternatively, the company could modify the existing structure to use for its own manufacturing and warehousing needs. Benson's production engineer feels the building could be adapted to handle one of two new product lines. The cost and revenue data for the two product alternatives are as follows:

|  | Product A (£) | Product B (£) |
|---|---|---|
| Initial cash outlay for building modifications | 36,000 | 54,000 |
| Initial cash outlay for equipment | 144,000 | 162,000 |
| Annual pre-tax cash revenues (generated for 15 years) | 105,000 | 127,500 |
| Annual pre-tax expenditures (generated for 15 years) | 60,000 | 75,000 |

The building will be used for only 15 years for either product A or product B. After 15 years the building will be too small for efficient production of either product line. At that time, Benson plans to rent the building to firms similar to the current occupants. To rent the building again, Benson will need to restore the building to its present layout. The estimated cash cost of restoring the building if product A has been undertaken is £3,750. If product B has been manufactured, the cash cost will be £28,125. These cash costs can be deducted for tax purposes in the year the expenditures occur.

Benson will depreciate the original building shell (purchased for £225,000) over a 30-year life to zero, regardless of which alternative it chooses. The building modifications and equipment purchases for either product are estimated to have a 15-year life. They will be depreciated by the 20 per cent reducing-balance method. At the end of the project's life the salvage value of the equipment will be equal to the residual value. The firm's tax rate is 28 per cent, and its required rate of return on such investments is 12 per cent.

For simplicity, assume all cash flows occur at the end of the year. The initial outlays for modifications and equipment will occur today (year 0), and the restoration outlays will occur at the end of year 15. Benson has other profitable ongoing operations that are sufficient to cover any losses. Which use of the building would you recommend to management?

31  **Project Analysis and Inflation**   Genetic Engineering Research Studies Ltd (GERS) has hired you as a consultant to evaluate the NPV of its proposed toad house. GERS plans to breed toads and sell them as ecologically desirable insect control mechanisms. They anticipate that the business will continue into perpetuity. Following the negligible start-up costs, GERS expects the following nominal cash flows at the end of the year:

| Revenues | £150,000 |
|---|---|
| Labour costs | £80,000 |
| Other costs | £40,000 |

The company will lease machinery for £20,000 per year. The lease payments start at the end of year 1 and are expressed in nominal terms. Revenues will increase by 5 per cent per year in real terms. Labour costs will increase by 3 per cent per year in real terms. Other costs will decrease by 1 per cent per year in real terms. The rate of inflation is expected to be 6 per cent per year. GERS's required rate of return is 10 per cent in real terms. The company has a 28 per cent tax rate. All cash flows occur at year-end. What is the NPV of GERS's proposed toad house today?

32  **Project Analysis and Inflation**  Sony International has an investment opportunity to produce a new 100-inch widescreen TV. The required investment on 1 January of this year is $32 million. The firm will depreciate the investment to zero using the straight-line method over four years. The investment has no resale value after completion of the project. The firm is in the 34 per cent tax bracket. The price of the product will be $400 per unit, in real terms, and will not change over the life of the project. Labour costs for year 1 will be $15.30 per hour, in real terms, and will increase at 2 per cent per year in real terms. Energy costs for year 1 will be $5.15 per physical unit, in real terms, and will increase at 3 per cent per year in real terms. The inflation rate is 5 per cent per year. Revenues are received and costs are paid at year-end. Refer to the following table for the production schedule:

|  | Year 1 | Year 2 | Year 3 | Year 4 |
|---|---|---|---|---|
| Physical production (units) | 100,000 | 200,000 | 200,000 | 150,000 |
| Labour input (hours) | 2,000,000 | 2,000,000 | 2,000,000 | 2,000,000 |
| Energy input (physical units) | 200,000 | 200,000 | 200,000 | 200,000 |

The real discount rate for Sony is 8 per cent. Calculate the NPV of this project.

33  **Project Analysis and Inflation**  After extensive medical and marketing research, Pill plc believes it can penetrate the pain reliever market. It is considering two alternative products. The first is a medication for headache pain. The second is a pill for headache and arthritis pain. Both products would be introduced at a price of £4 per package in real terms. The headache-only medication is projected to sell 5 million packages a year, whereas the headache and arthritis remedy would sell 10 million packages a year. Cash costs of production in the first year are expected to be £1.50 per package in real terms for the headache-only brand. Production costs are expected to be £1.70 in real terms for the headache and arthritis pill. All prices and costs are expected to rise at the general inflation rate of 5 per cent.

Either product requires further investment. The headache-only pill could be produced using equipment costing £10.2 million. That equipment would last three years and have no resale value. The machinery required to produce the broader remedy would cost £12 million and last three years. The firm expects that equipment to have a £1 million resale value (in real terms) at the end of year 3.

Pill plc uses reducing balance (20 per cent) depreciation. The firm faces a corporate tax rate of 28 per cent and believes that the appropriate real discount rate is 13 per cent. Which pain reliever should the firm produce?

34  **Calculating Project NPV**  Petracci SpA manufactures fine furniture. The company is deciding whether to introduce a new mahogany dining room table set. The set will sell for €5,600, including a set of eight chairs. The company feels that sales will be 1,300, 1,325, 1,375, 1,450 and 1,320 sets per year for the next five years, respectively. Variable costs will amount to 45 per cent of sales, and fixed costs are €1.7 million per year. The new tables will require inventory amounting to 10 per cent of sales, produced and stockpiled in the

year prior to sales. It is believed that the addition of the new table will cause a loss of 200 tables per year of the oak tables the company produces. These tables sell for €4,500 and have variable costs of 40 per cent of sales. The inventory for this oak table is also 10 per cent. Petracci currently has excess production capacity. If the company buys the necessary equipment today, it will cost €10.5 million. However, the excess production capacity means the company can produce the new table without buying the new equipment. The company controller has said that the current excess capacity will end in two years with current production. This means that if the company uses the current excess capacity for the new table, it will be forced to spend the €10.5 million in two years to accommodate the increased sales of its current products. In five years the new equipment will have a market value of €2.8 million if purchased today, and €6.1 million if purchased in two years. The equipment is depreciated using reducing balances at 20 per cent per annum. The company has a tax rate of 38 per cent, and the required return for the project is 14 per cent.

(a) Should Petracci undertake the new project?

(b) Can you perform an IRR analysis on this project? How many IRRs would you expect to find?

(c) How would you interpret the profitability index?

# Bethesda Mining Company

Bethesda Mining is a midsized coal mining company with 20 mines located in Wales and Scotland. The company operates deep mines as well as strip mines. Most of the coal mined is sold under contract, with excess production sold on the spot market.

The coal mining industry, especially high-sulphur coal operations such as Bethesda, has been hard-hit by environmental regulations. Recently, however, a combination of increased demand for coal and new pollution reduction technologies has led to an improved market demand for high-sulphur coal. Bethesda has just been approached by National Power plc with a request to supply coal for its electric generators for the next four years. Bethesda Mining does not have enough excess capacity at its existing mines to guarantee the contract. The company is considering opening a strip mine in Auchtermuchty on 5,000 acres of land purchased 10 years ago for £6 million. Based on a recent appraisal, the company feels it could receive £5 million on an after-tax basis if it sold the land today.

Strip mining is a process where the layers of topsoil above a coal vein are removed and the exposed coal is removed. Some time ago, the company would simply remove the coal and leave the land in an unusable condition. Changes in mining regulations now force a company to reclaim the land: that is, when mining is completed, the land must be restored to near its original condition. The land can then be used for other purposes. Because Bethesda is currently operating at full capacity, it will need to purchase additional necessary equipment, which will cost £30 million. The equipment will be depreciated using capital allowances (reducing balance) at 20 per cent per annum. The contract runs for only four years. At that time the coal from the site will be entirely mined. The company feels that the equipment can be sold for 60 per cent of its initial purchase price. However, Bethesda plans to open another strip mine at that time and will use the equipment at the new mine.

The contract calls for the delivery of 600,000 tons of coal per year at a price of £34 per ton. Bethesda Mining feels that coal production will be 650,000 tons, 725,000 tons, 810,000 tons and 740,000 tons, respectively, over the next four years. The excess production will be sold in the spot market at an average of £40 per ton. Variable costs amount to £13 per ton, and fixed costs are £2,500,000 per year. The mine will require a net working capital investment of 5 per cent of sales. The NWC will be built up in the year prior to the sales.

Bethesda will be responsible for reclaiming the land at termination of the mining. This will occur in year 5. The company uses an outside company for reclamation of all the company's strip mines. It is estimated the cost of reclamation will be £4 million. After the land is reclaimed, the company plans to donate the land to the National Trust for use as a public park and recreation area. This will occur in year 6 and result in a charitable expense deduction of £6 million. Bethesda faces a 28 per cent tax rate and has a 12 per cent required return on new strip mine projects. Assume that a loss in any year will result in a tax credit.

You have been approached by the chairman of the company with a request to analyse the project. Calculate the payback period, profitability index, average accounting return, net present value, internal rate of return, and modified internal rate of return for the new strip mine. Should Bethesda Mining take the contract and open the mine?

## Practical Case Study

In many emerging-market countries, concepts such as discount rates are significantly more cumbersome to estimate with any degree of accuracy. Furthermore, capital budgeting techniques can become significantly more difficult to use in practice. The following case is based on real experience, with identities and numbers changed for confidentiality.

As part of a consultancy assignment in Dar Es Salaam, Tanzania, you have been asked by a private cement manufacturing company to consider the viability of expanding its business operations into the north of the country.

The company has two main rivals in Tanzania. Tanga Cement Company Limited (SIMBA) (http://www.simbacement.co.tz/) and Tanzania Portland Cement Company Limited (TWIGA) (http://www.heidelbergcement.com/africa/en/twigacement/home.htm). Both SIMBA and TWIGA are listed on the Dar Es Salaam Stock Exchange (www.dse.co.tz). The company that has hired you as a consultant earns about one quarter the revenues of SIMBA.

The new expansion requires an investment of 5 billion Tanzanian shillings (TSh), and as a result of the investment you expect a permanent increase in total operating revenues for the firm of TSh800 million. While SIMBA is your closest rival in Dar Es Salaam, TWIGA has more extensive operations in the north of Tanzania, and so they are more likely to be your rivals in the new investment.

Growth in earnings is possible, but this depends on several factors. First, growth in the economy is uncertain. While Tanzania's economy has been fairly stable, analysts are uncertain as to how the country will fair in the future. This is largely because of uncertainty in international donor funding as a result of the recession affecting donor countries. Second, inflation appears to be higher on the street than the government statistics suggest. Your estimates are that a more appropriate inflation figure is 3 per cent higher than existing government statistics present. Third, the demand for industrial expansion (and consequently cement) has in the past been vibrant in Tanzania, but the future is less certain. Tanzanian economists are predicting that the country will continue to grow as in the past, less about 1.5 per cent. This is because they expect the global recession will largely bypass Tanzania, given that the country's economy is not tightly integrated into other developed country economies. However, you are not too sure. Table 31.1 in this textbook shows the main import and export partners for Tanzania, and the fortunes of these partners will naturally affect the Tanzanian economy.

Later chapters explore the estimate of discount rates in more detail, but for now we shall approach the issue in a more basic way. Given that the financial markets in Tanzania are not well developed, you have decided to survey experts in each sector on the appropriate discount rates to use for your closest rivals, TWIGA and SIMBA. The survey responses have been surprising:

| Dar Es Salaam Stock Exchange | Pension funds | Insurance companies | Brokers and dealers | Bank of Tanzania |
|---|---|---|---|---|
| 12 per cent | 16 per cent | 14 per cent | 22 per cent | 10 per cent |

A rule of thumb that you have been given is that you can approximate the growth rate in the economy as a whole by adding GDP growth to the rate of inflation. To then estimate the cost of capital for a private firm, you must add on a risk premium to reflect the increased risk.

The challenge facing you as a consultant is daunting, but it reflects reality in many parts of the world. The company has asked you to prepare a report on how you plan to carry out your analysis. Specifically, you must consider the following:

1  Cash flows: What factors will affect the estimated cash flows? Carry out your own analysis on Tanzania, its economy, the cement industry, and its rivals.

2  Growth rates: What factors will affect the growth rates of the firm? From your own analysis of the company and the project, report on the possible growth rates you may use.

3  Discount rates: Many of the models presented in later chapters do not work well in emerging markets, because good-quality price data are not available. Carry out your own investigations into possible discount rates for the project.

4  Funding: We cover financing in detail in later chapters. However, carry out your own analysis into the different sources of funding that are available in Tanzania for a project of this type and size.

5  Capital budgeting methods: There are many methods available that you can use. Which ones will you focus on? Explain.

## Relevant Accounting Standards

The main reason why accounting standards are important for capital budgeting is in the estimation of tax payments. Given that tax is derived from accounting statements, and reduces cash flow, all the accounting standards are relevant. However, depreciation is possibly the most important issue, and so IAS16 *Property, Plant and Equipment*, IFRS3 *Business Combinations* and IAS38 *Intangible Assets* are particularly relevant. The analyst should also be aware of current practice in depreciating assets. This can be quite complex, and more information will be found in each country's government tax site (for the UK, this is www.hmrc.gov.uk). Readers in the European Union should also be familiar with developments and harmonization towards a common tax base (http://ec.europa.eu).

Other important accounting standards include IAS2 *Inventories*, IAS17 *Leases*, IAS21 *The Effects of Changes in Foreign Exchange Rates* and IAS36 *Impairment of Assets*. Visit the IASPlus website (www.iasplus.com) for good summaries of each standard.

While it is easy to be overwhelmed by the number of accounting standards, everything that is needed to carry out a capital budgeting analysis is provided in this textbook, so don't worry. The accounting standards are for reference, and should be consulted only when a real capital budgeting analysis is undertaken.

## Additional Reading

A very interesting paper that links stock market efficiency and capital budgeting is Durnev, Morck and Yeung (2004). This has implications for capital budgeting when carried out in emerging and developed markets. Although the research uses US data, the authors do present a nice figure of stock market synchronicity (Fig. 1) for many countries and link this to market efficiency and capital budgeting.

Durnev, A., R. Morck and B. Yeung (2004) 'Value-enhancing capital budgeting and firm-specific stock return variation', *Journal of Finance*, vol. 59, no. 1, pp. 65–105.

# Endnote

1 One caveat is in order. Perhaps the old machine's maintenance is high in the first year but drops after that. A decision to replace immediately might be premature in that case. Therefore, we need to check the cost of the old machine in future years.

The cost of keeping the existing machine a second year is

$$\text{PV of costs at time } 1 = £2,500 + \frac{£2,000}{1.15} - \frac{£1,500}{1.15}$$
$$= £2,935$$

which has a future value of £3,375 (= £2,935 × 1.15).

The costs of keeping the existing machine for years 3 and 4 are also greater than the EAC of buying a new machine. Thus BIKE's decision to replace the old machine immediately is still valid.

Online **LearningCentre**

To help you grasp the key concepts of this chapter check out the extra resources posted on the Online Learning Centre at **www.mcgraw-hill.co.uk/textbooks/hillier**

Among other helpful resources there are PowerPoint presentations, chapter outlines and mini-cases.

# Chapter **8**

# Risk Analysis, Real Options, and Capital Budgeting

## KEY NOTATIONS

$A_R^T$    Present value of annuity of 1 unit per period for $T$ periods at interest rate per period of $R$

**NPV**    Net present value

**OCF**    Operating cash flow

$t_c$    Corporate tax rate

In 1836, defenders of the Alamo in San Antonio, Texas, held out for 13 days against great odds, and 'Remember the Alamo!' became a part of US history. In contrast, Disney's 2004 movie *The Alamo*, starring Billy Bob Thornton as Davy Crockett, lasted barely a weekend at the box office, and the last thing Disney's management wants to do is remember that particular bomb. Disney spent close to $100 million making the movie, plus millions more for marketing and distribution, but the film pulled in only about $22.5 million. In fact, about 4 out of 10 movies lose money at the box office, though DVD sales often help the final tally. Of course there are movies that do quite well. In 2005, the last of the *Star Wars* movies, *Revenge of the Sith*, pulled in about $849 million at a cost of $115 million.

Obviously, Disney didn't *plan* to lose $80 million on *The Alamo*, but it happened. As the short life and quick death of *The Alamo* show, projects don't always go as companies think they will. This chapter explores how this can happen, and what companies can do to analyse and possibly avoid these situations.

## 8.1 Sensitivity Analysis, Scenario Analysis, and Break-Even Analysis

One main point of this book is that NPV analysis is a superior capital budgeting technique. In fact, because the NPV approach uses cash flows rather than profits, uses all the cash flows, and discounts the cash flows properly, it is hard to find any theoretical fault with it. However, in our conversations with businesspeople we frequently hear the phrase 'a false sense of security'. These people point out that the documentation for capital budgeting proposals is often quite impressive. Cash flows are projected down to the last few pounds or euros for each year (or even each month). Opportunity costs and side effects are handled quite properly. Sunk costs are ignored – also quite properly. When a high net present value appears at the bottom, one's temptation is to say 'yes' immediately. Nevertheless, the projected cash flow often goes unmet in practice, and the firm ends up with a money loser.

### Sensitivity Analysis and Scenario Analysis

How can the firm get the net present value technique to live up to its potential? One approach is **sensitivity analysis**, which examines how sensitive a particular NPV calculation is to changes in

| TABLE 8.1 | | Year 1 (£m) | Years 2-6 (£m) |
|---|---|---|---|
| Revenues | | | 6,000 |
| Variable costs | | | 3,000 |
| Fixed costs | | | 1,791 |
| Depreciation | | | 300 |
| Pre-tax profit | | | 909 |
| Tax ($t_c = 0.28$) | | | 255 |
| Net profit | | | 654 |
| Cash flow | | | 954 |
| Initial investment costs | | 1,500 | |

Assumptions: (a) investment is depreciated in years 2 to 6 using the straight-line method for simplicity; (b) tax rate is 28 per cent; (c) the company receives no tax benefits for initial development costs.

**Table 8.1** Cash flow forecasts for Solar Electronics' jet engine: Base Case

underlying assumptions. Sensitivity analysis is also known as *what-if* analysis and *bop* (best, optimistic, and pessimistic) analysis.

Consider the following example. Solar Electronics (SE) has recently developed a solar-powered jet engine and wants to go ahead with full-scale production. The initial (year 1)[1] investment is £1,500 million, followed by production and sales over the next five years. The preliminary cash flow projection appears in Table 8.1. Should SE go ahead with investment in and production of the jet engine, the NPV at a discount rate of 15 per cent is (in millions)

$$\text{NPV} = -£1,500 + \sum_{t=1}^{5} \frac{£954}{(1.15)^t}$$
$$= -£1,500 + £954 \times A_{0.15}^{5}$$
$$= £1,700$$

Because the NPV is positive, basic financial theory implies that SE should accept the project. However, is this all there is to say about the venture? Before actual funding, we ought to check out the project's underlying assumptions about revenues and costs.

**Revenues**    Let's assume that the marketing department has projected annual sales to be

| Number of jet engines sold per year | = | Market share | × | Size of jet engine market per year |
|---|---|---|---|---|
| 3,000 | = | 0.30 | × | 10,000 |

| Annual sales revenues | = | Number of jet engines sold | × | Price per engine |
|---|---|---|---|---|
| £6,000 million | = | 3,000 | × | £2 million |

Thus it turns out that the revenue estimates depend on three assumptions:

1    Market share

2    Size of jet engine market

3    Price per engine

**Costs**    Financial analysts frequently divide costs into two types: variable costs and fixed costs. Variable costs change as the output changes, and they are zero when production is zero. Costs of direct labour and raw materials are usually variable. It is common to assume that a variable cost is constant per unit of output, implying that total variable costs are proportional to the level of production. For example, if direct labour is variable and one unit of final output requires £10 of direct labour, then 100 units of final output should require £1,000 of direct labour.

Fixed costs are not dependent on the amount of goods or services produced during the period. Fixed costs are usually measured as costs per unit of time, such as rent per month or salaries per year. Naturally, fixed costs are not fixed for ever. They are fixed only over a pre-determined time period.

The engineering department has estimated variable costs to be £1 million per engine. Fixed costs are £1,791 million per year. The cost breakdowns are

$$\begin{array}{ccccc}
\dfrac{\text{Variable cost}}{\text{per year}} & = & \dfrac{\text{Variable cost}}{\text{per unit}} & \times & \begin{array}{c}\text{Number of jet engines}\\\text{sold per year}\end{array}\\[1em]
\text{£3,000 million} & = & \text{£1 million} & \times & 3,000
\end{array}$$

$$\begin{array}{ccccc}
\dfrac{\text{Total cost before}}{\text{taxes per year}} & = & \dfrac{\text{Variable cost}}{\text{per unit}} & + & \dfrac{\text{Fixed cost}}{\text{per year}}\\[1em]
\text{£4,791 million} & = & \text{£3,000 million} & + & \text{£1,791}
\end{array}$$

These estimates for market size, market share, price, variable cost and fixed cost, as well as the estimate of initial investment, are presented in the middle column of Table 8.2. These figures represent the firm's expectations or best estimates of the different parameters. For comparison, the firm's analysts also prepared both optimistic and pessimistic forecasts for each of the different variables. These forecasts are provided in the table as well.

Standard sensitivity analysis calls for an NPV calculation for all three possibilities of a single variable, along with the expected forecast for all other variables. This procedure is illustrated in Table 8.3. For example, consider the NPV calculation of £8,940 million provided in the upper right corner of this table. This NPV occurs when the optimistic forecast of 20,000 units per year is used for market size while all other variables are set at their expected forecasts from Table 8.2. Note that each row of the middle column of Table 8.3 shows a value of £1,700 million. This occurs because the expected forecast is used for the variable that was singled out, as well as for all other variables.

Table 8.3 can be used for a number of purposes. First, taken as a whole, the table can indicate whether NPV analysis should be trusted. In other words, it reduces the false sense of security we spoke of earlier. Suppose that NPV is positive when the expected forecast for each variable is used. However, suppose further that every number in the pessimistic column is highly negative and every number in the optimistic column is highly positive. A change in a single forecast greatly alters the NPV estimate, making one wary of the net present value approach. A conservative manager might well scrap the entire NPV analysis in this situation. Fortunately, the solar plane engine does not exhibit this wide dispersion, because all but two of the numbers in Table 8.3 are positive. Managers viewing the table are likely to consider NPV analysis to be useful for the solar-powered jet engine.

| TABLE 8.2 Variable | Pessimistic | Expected or best | Optimistic |
|---|---|---|---|
| Market size (per year) | 5,000 | 10,000 | 20,000 |
| Market share | 20% | 30% | 50% |
| Price | £1.9 million | £2 million | £2.2 million |
| Variable cost (per engine) | £1.2 million | £1 million | £0.8 million |
| Fixed cost (per year) | £1,891 million | £1,791 million | £1,741 million |
| Investment | £1,900 million | £1,500 million | £1,000 million |

**Table 8.2** Different estimates for Solar Electronics' solar plane engine

TABLE
**8.3**

| | Pessimistic (£m) | Expected or best (£m) | Optimistic (£m) |
|---|---|---|---|
| Market size | − 1,921* | 1,700 | 8,940 |
| Market share | − 714* | 1,700 | 6,527 |
| Price | 975 | 1,700 | 3,148 |
| Variable cost | 251 | 1,700 | 3,148 |
| Fixed cost | 1,458 | 1,700 | 1,820 |
| Investment | 1,300 | 1,700 | 2,200 |

Under sensitivity analysis, one input is varied while all other inputs are assumed to meet their expectation. For example, an NPV of −£1,921 occurs when the pessimistic forecast of 5,000 is used for market size, while all other variables are set at their expected forecasts from Table 8.2.

*We assume that the other divisions of the firm are profitable, implying that a loss on this project can offset income elsewhere in the firm, thereby reducing the overall taxes of the firm.

**Table 8.3** NPV calculations for the solar plane engine using sensitivity analysis

Second, sensitivity analysis shows where more information is needed. For example, an error in the estimate of investment appears to be relatively unimportant because, even under the pessimistic scenario, the NPV of £1,300 million is still highly positive. By contrast, the pessimistic forecast for market share leads to a negative NPV of −£714 million, and a pessimistic forecast for market size leads to a substantially negative NPV of −£1,921 million. Because the effect of incorrect estimates on revenues is so much greater than the effect of incorrect estimates on costs, more information about the factors determining revenues might be needed.

Unfortunately, sensitivity analysis also suffers from some drawbacks. For example, sensitivity analysis may unwittingly *increase* the false sense of security among managers. Suppose all pessimistic forecasts yield positive NPVs. A manager might feel that there is no way the project can lose money. Of course, the forecasters may simply have an optimistic view of a pessimistic forecast. To combat this, some companies do not treat optimistic and pessimistic forecasts subjectively. Rather, their pessimistic forecasts are always, say, 20 per cent less than expected. Unfortunately, the cure in this case may be worse than the disease: a deviation of a fixed percentage ignores the fact that some variables are easier to forecast than others.

In addition, sensitivity analysis treats each variable in isolation when, in reality, the different variables are likely to be related. For example, if ineffective management allows costs to get out of control, it is likely that variable costs, fixed costs and investment will all rise above expectation at the same time. If the market is not receptive to a solar plane engine, both market share and price should decline together.

Managers frequently perform scenario analysis, a variant of sensitivity analysis, to minimize this problem. Simply put, this approach examines a number of different likely scenarios, where each scenario involves a confluence of factors. As a simple example, consider the effect of a few airline crashes. These crashes are likely to reduce flying in total, thereby limiting the demand for any new engines. Furthermore, even if the crashes do not involve solar-powered aircraft, the public could become more averse to any innovative and controversial technologies. Hence SE's market share might fall as well. Perhaps the cash flow calculations would look like those in Table 8.4 under the scenario of a plane crash. Given the calculations in the table, the NPV (in millions) would be

$$-£2,162 = -£1,500 - £198 \times A_{0.15}^5$$

A series of scenarios like this might illuminate issues concerning the project better than the standard application of sensitivity analysis would.

TABLE
8.4

| | Year 1 (£m) | Years 2–5 (£m) |
|---|---|---|
| Revenues | | 2,800 |
| Variable costs | | 1,400 |
| Fixed costs | | 1,791 |
| Depreciation[1] | | 300 |
| Pre-tax profit | | −691 |
| Tax ($t_c = 0.28$)* | | 193 |
| Net profit | | −498 |
| Cash flow | | −198 |
| Initial investment cost | −1,500 | |

Assumptions are: market size 7,000 (70 per cent of expectation); market share 20% (2/3 of expectation). Forecasts for all other variables are the expected forecasts as given in Table 8.2.

*Tax loss offsets income elsewhere in firm.

**Table 8.4** Cash flow forecast under the scenario of a plane crash

## Break-Even Analysis

Our discussion of sensitivity analysis and scenario analysis suggests that there are many ways to examine variability in forecasts. We now present another approach, break-even analysis. As its name implies, this approach determines the sales needed to break even. The approach is a useful complement to sensitivity analysis because it also sheds light on the severity of incorrect forecasts. We calculate the break-even point in terms of both accounting profit and present value.

**Accounting Profit**   Annual net profit under four different sales forecasts is as follows:

| Annual unit sales | Net profit (£m) |
|---|---|
| 0 | −1,506 |
| 1,000 | −786 |
| 3,000 | 654 |
| 10,000 | 5,694 |

A more complete presentation of costs and revenues appears in Table 8.5.

We plot the revenues, costs, and profits under the different assumptions about sales in Fig. 8.1. The revenue and cost curves cross at 2,091 jet engines. This is the break-even point – that is, the point where the project generates no profits or losses. As long as annual sales are above 2,091 jet engines, the project will make a profit.

This break-even point can be calculated very easily. Because the sales price is £2 million per engine and the variable cost is £1 million per engine,[2] the difference between sales price and variable cost per engine is

$$\text{Sales price} - \text{Variable cost} = £2 \text{ million} - £1 \text{ million}$$
$$= £1 \text{ million}$$

| Year 1 | | | | | Years 2–6 | | | | |
|---|---|---|---|---|---|---|---|---|---|
| Initial investment | Annual unit sales | Revenues | Variable costs | Fixed costs | Depreciation | Taxes* ($t_c$ = 0.28) | Net profit | Operating cash flows | NPV (evaluated date 1) |
| (£m) | | (£m) | (£m) | (£m) | (£m) | (£m) | (£m) | (£m) | (£m) |
| 1,500 | 0 | 0 | 0 | −1,791 | −300 | 585 | −1,506 | −1,206 | −5,541 |
| 1,500 | 1,000 | 2,000 | −1,000 | −1,791 | −300 | 305 | −786 | −486 | −3,128 |
| 1,500 | 3,000 | 6,000 | −3,000 | −1,791 | −300 | −255 | 654 | 954 | 1,700 |
| 1,500 | 10,000 | 20,000 | −10,000 | −1,791 | −300 | −2,215 | 5,694 | 5,994 | 18,594 |

*Loss is incurred in the first two rows. For tax purposes, this loss offsets income elsewhere in the firm.

**Table 8.5** Revenues and costs of project under different sales assumptions

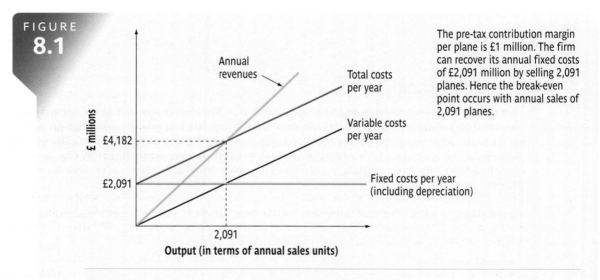

The pre-tax contribution margin per plane is £1 million. The firm can recover its annual fixed costs of £2,091 million by selling 2,091 planes. Hence the break-even point occurs with annual sales of 2,091 planes.

**Figure 8.1** Break-even point using accounting numbers

This difference is called the pre-tax contribution margin, because each additional engine contributes this amount to pre-tax profit. (Contribution margin can also be expressed on an after-tax basis.)

Fixed costs are £1,791 million and depreciation is £300 million, implying that the sum of these costs is

$$\text{Fixed costs} + \text{Depreciation} = £1,791 \text{ million} + £300 \text{ million}$$
$$= £2,091 \text{ million}$$

That is, the firm incurs costs of £2,091 million per year, regardless of the number of sales. Because each engine contributes £1 million, annual sales must reach the following level to offset the costs:

**Figure 8.2** Break-even point using net present value

Accounting profit break-even point:

$$\frac{\text{Fixed costs} + \text{Depreciation}}{\text{Sales price} - \text{Variable costs}} = \frac{£2,091 \text{ million}}{£1 \text{ million}}$$
$$= 2,091$$

Thus 2,091 engines is the break-even point required for an accounting profit.

The astute reader might be wondering why taxes have been ignored in the calculation of break-even accounting profit. The reason is that a firm with a pre-tax profit of £0 will also have an after-tax profit of £0 because no taxes are paid if no pre-tax profit is reported. Thus the number of units needed to break even on a pre-tax basis must be equal to the number of units needed to break even on an after-tax basis.

**Present Value**  As we have stated many times, we are more interested in present value than we are in profit. Therefore we should calculate break-even in terms of present value. Given a discount rate of 15 per cent, the solar plane engine has the following net present values for different levels of annual sales:

| Annual unit sales | NPV (£m) |
|---|---|
| 0 | −5,541 |
| 1,000 | −3,128 |
| 3,000 | 1,700 |
| 10,000 | 18,594 |

These NPV calculations are reproduced from the last column of Table 8.5.

Figure 8.2 relates the net present value of both the revenues and the costs to output. There are at least two differences between Fig. 8.2 and Fig. 8.1, one of which is quite important and the other is much less so. First the less important point: the monetary amounts on the vertical dimension of Fig. 8.2 are greater than those on the vertical dimension of Fig. 8.1 because the net present values are calculated over five years. More important, accounting break-even occurs when 2,091 units are sold annually, whereas NPV break-even occurs when 2,296 units are sold annually.

Of course, the NPV break-even point can be calculated directly. The firm originally invested £1,500 million. This initial investment can be expressed as a five-year equivalent annual cost (EAC), determined by dividing the initial investment by the appropriate five-year annuity factor:

$$EAC = \frac{\text{Initial investment}}{\text{5-year annuity factor at 15\%}}$$
$$= \frac{\text{Initial investment}}{A_{0.15}^5}$$
$$= \frac{£1{,}500 \text{ million}}{3.3522}$$
$$= £447.5 \text{ million}$$

Note that the EAC of £447.5 million is greater than the yearly depreciation of £300 million. This must occur, because the calculation of EAC implicitly assumes that the £1,500 million investment could have been invested at 15 per cent.

After-tax costs, regardless of output, can be viewed like this:

$$\underset{\text{million}}{£1{,}653} = \underset{\text{million}}{£447.5} + \underset{\text{million}}{£1{,}791} \times 0.72 - \underset{\text{million}}{£300} \times 0.28$$
$$= \text{EAC} + \text{Fixed costs} \times (1 - t_C) - \text{Depreciation} \times t_C$$

That is, in addition to the initial investment's equivalent annual cost of £447.5 million, the firm pays fixed costs each year and receives a depreciation tax shield each year. The depreciation tax shield is written as a negative number because it offsets the costs in the equation. Each plane contributes £0.72 million to after-tax profit, so it will take the following sales to offset the costs:

Present value break-even point:

$$\frac{\text{EAC} + \text{Fixed costs} \times (1 - t_C) - \text{Depreciation} \times t_C}{(\text{Sales price} - \text{Variable costs}) \times (1 - t_C)} = \frac{£1{,}653 \text{ million}}{£0.72 \text{ million}}$$
$$= 2{,}296$$

Thus 2,296 planes is the break-even point from the perspective of present value.

Why is the accounting break-even point different from the financial break-even point? When we use accounting profit as the basis for the break-even calculation, we subtract depreciation. Depreciation for the solar jet engines project is £300 million per year. If 2,091 solar jet engines are sold per year, SE will generate sufficient revenues to cover the £300 million depreciation expense plus other costs. Unfortunately, at this level of sales SE will not cover the economic opportunity costs of the £1,500 million laid out for the investment. If we take into account that the £1,500 million could have been invested at 15 per cent, the true annual cost of the investment is £447.5 million, not £300 million. Depreciation understates the true costs of recovering the initial investment. Thus companies that break even on an accounting basis are really losing money. They are losing the opportunity cost of the initial investment.

Is break-even analysis important? Very much so: all corporate executives fear losses. Break-even analysis determines how far down sales can fall before the project is losing money, either in an accounting sense or in an NPV sense.

## 8.2 Monte Carlo Simulation

Both sensitivity analysis and scenario analysis attempt to answer the question 'What if?' However, while both analyses are frequently used in the real world, each has its own limitations. Sensitivity analysis allows only one variable to change at a time. By contrast, many variables are likely to move at the same time in the real world. Scenario analysis follows specific scenarios, such as changes in inflation, government regulation, or the number of competitors. Although this methodology is often quite helpful, it cannot cover all sources of variability. In fact, projects are likely to exhibit a lot of variability under just one economic scenario.

Monte Carlo simulation is a further attempt to model real-world uncertainty. This approach takes its name from the famous European casino, because it analyses projects the way one might analyse gambling strategies. Imagine a serious blackjack player who wonders whether he should take a third card whenever his first two cards total 16. Most likely, a formal mathematical model would be too complex to be practical here. However, he could play thousands of hands in a casino, sometimes drawing a third card when his first two cards add to 16 and sometimes not drawing that third card. He could compare his winnings (or losses) under the two strategies to determine which were better. Of course he would probably lose a lot of money performing this test in a real casino, so simulating the results from the two strategies on a computer might be cheaper. Monte Carlo simulation of capital budgeting projects is in this spirit.

Imagine that Backyard Barbecues (BB), a manufacturer of both charcoal and gas grills, has a blueprint for a new grill that cooks with compressed hydrogen. The CFO, Edward H. Comiskey, being dissatisfied with simpler capital budgeting techniques, wants a Monte Carlo simulation for this new grill. A consultant specializing in the Monte Carlo approach, Lester Mauney, takes him through the five basic steps of the method.

## Step 1: Specify the Basic Model

Les Mauney breaks up cash flow into three components: annual revenue, annual costs, and initial investment. The revenue in any year is viewed as

$$\begin{array}{ccccc} \text{Number of grills sold} & & \text{Market share of BB's} & & \text{Price per} \\ \text{by entire industry} & \times & \text{hydrogen grill (in per cent)} & \times & \text{hydrogen grill} \end{array} \quad \textbf{(8.1)}$$

The cost in any year is viewed as

$$\begin{array}{c} \text{Fixed manufacturing costs} + \text{Variable manufacturing costs} + \text{Marketing costs} \\ + \text{Selling costs} \end{array}$$

Initial investment is viewed as

$$\text{Cost of patent} + \text{Test marketing costs} + \text{Cost of production facility}$$

## Step 2: Specify a Distribution for Each Variable in the Model

Here comes the hard part. Let's start with revenue, which has three components in Eq. 8.1. The consultant first models overall market size – that is, the number of grills sold by the entire industry. The trade publication *Outdoor Food (OF)* reported that 10 million grills of all types were sold in Europe last year, and it forecasts sales of 10.5 million next year. Mr Mauney, using *OF*'s forecast and his own intuition, creates the following distribution for next year's sales of grills by the entire industry:

| Probability | 20% | 60% | 20% |
|---|---|---|---|
| Next year's industry-wide unit sales | 10 million | 10.5 million | 11 million |

The tight distribution here reflects the slow but steady historical growth in the grill market. This probability distribution is graphed in Panel A of Fig. 8.3.

Lester Mauney realizes that estimating the market share of BB's hydrogen grill is more difficult. Nevertheless, after a great deal of analysis, he determines the distribution of next year's market share:

| Probability | 10% | 20% | 30% | 25% | 10% | 5% |
|---|---|---|---|---|---|---|
| Market share of BB's hydrogen grill next year | 1% | 2% | 3% | 4% | 5% | 8% |

Whereas the consultant assumed a symmetrical distribution for industry-wide unit sales, he believes a skewed distribution makes more sense for the project's market share. In his mind there is always the small possibility that sales of the hydrogen grill will really take off. This probability distribution is graphed in Panel B of Fig. 8.3.

FIGURE
**8.3**

For each of the three variables, a drawing is generated by computer simulation. In addition, price per grill is dependent on industry-wide unit sales.

**Figure 8.3** Probability distributions for industry-wide unit sales, market share of BB's hydrogen grill, and price of hydrogen grill

These forecasts assume that unit sales for the overall industry are unrelated to the project's market share. In other words, the two variables are *independent* of each other. Mr Mauney reasons that although an economic boom might increase industry-wide grill sales and a recession might decrease them, the project's market share is unlikely to be related to economic conditions.

Now Mr Mauney must determine the distribution of price per grill. Mr Comiskey, the CFO, informs him that the price will be in the area of €200 per grill, given what other competitors are charging. However, the consultant believes that the price per hydrogen grill will almost certainly depend on the size of the overall market for grills. As in any business, you can usually charge more if demand is high.

After rejecting a number of complex models for price, Mr Mauney settles on the following specification:

$$\text{Next year's price per hydrogen grill} = €190 + €1 \times \frac{\text{Industry-wide unit sales (in millions)} +/- €3}{} \qquad (8.2)$$

The grill price in Eq. (8.2) depends on the unit sales of the industry. In addition, random variation is modelled via the term '±€3', where a drawing of +€3 and a drawing of –€3 each occur 50 per cent of the time. For example, if industry-wide unit sales are 11 million, the price per share would be either of the following:

$$€190 + €11 + €3 = €204 \text{ (50\% probability)}$$
$$€190 + €11 - €3 = €198 \text{ (50\% probability)}$$

The relationship between the price of a hydrogen grill and industry-wide unit sales is graphed in Panel C of Fig. 8.3.

The consultant now has distributions for each of the three components of next year's revenue. However, he needs distributions for future years as well. Using forecasts from *Outdoor Food* and other publications, Mr Mauney forecasts the distribution of growth rates for the entire industry over the second year:

| Probability | 20% | 60% | 20% |
|---|---|---|---|
| Growth rate of industry-wide unit sales in second year | 1% | 3% | 5% |

Given both the distribution of next year's industry-wide unit sales and the distribution of growth rates for this variable over the second year, we can generate the distribution of industry-wide unit sales for the second year. A similar extension should give Mr Mauney a distribution for later years as well, though we won't go into the details here. And just as the consultant extended the first component of revenue (industry-wide unit sales) to later years, he would want to do the same thing for market share and unit price.

The preceding discussion shows how the three components of revenue can be modelled. Step 2 would be complete once the components of cost and investment are modelled in a similar way. Special attention must be paid to the interactions between variables here, because ineffective management is likely to allow the different cost components to rise together. However, you are probably getting the idea now, so we shall skip the rest of this step.

## Step 3: The Computer Draws One Outcome

As we said, next year's revenue in our model is the product of three components. Imagine that the computer randomly picks industry-wide unit sales of 10 million, a market share for BB's hydrogen grill of 2 per cent, and a +€3 random price variation. Given these drawings, next year's price per hydrogen grill will be

$$€190 + €10 + €3 = €203$$

and next year's revenue for BB's hydrogen grill will be

$$10 \text{ million} \times 0.02 \times €203 = €40.6 \text{ million}$$

Of course, we are not done with the entire *outcome* yet. We would have to perform drawings for revenue and costs in each future year. Finally, a drawing for initial investment would have to be made as well. In this way, a single outcome, made up of a drawing for each variable in the model, would generate a cash flow from the project in each future year.

How likely is it that the specific outcome discussed would be drawn? We can answer this because we know the probability of each component. Because industry sales of €10 million has a 20 per cent probability, a market share of 2 per cent also has a 20 per cent probability, and a random price variation of +€3 has a 50 per cent probability, the probability of these three drawings together in the same outcome is

$$0.02 = 0.20 \times 0.20 \times 0.50 \tag{8.3}$$

Of course the probability would get even smaller once drawings for future revenues, future costs, and the initial investment are included in the outcome.

This step generates the cash flow for each year from a single outcome. What we are ultimately interested in is the *distribution* of cash flow each year across many outcomes. We ask the computer to randomly draw over and over again to give us this distribution, which is just what is done in the next step.

## Step 4: Repeat the Procedure

The first three steps generate one outcome, but the essence of Monte Carlo simulation is repeated outcomes. Depending on the situation, the computer may be called on to generate thousands or even millions of outcomes. The result of all these drawings is a distribution of cash flow for each future year. This distribution is the basic output of Monte Carlo simulation.

Consider Fig. 8.4. Here, repeated drawings have produced the simulated distribution of the third year's cash flow. There would be, of course, a distribution like the one in this figure for each future year. This leaves us with just one more step.

## Step 5: Calculate NPV

Given the distribution of cash flow for the third year in Fig. 8.4, one can determine the expected cash flow for this year. In a similar manner, one can also determine the expected cash flow for each future year and then calculate the net present value of the project by discounting these expected cash flows at an appropriate rate.

Monte Carlo simulation is often viewed as a step beyond either sensitivity analysis or scenario analysis. Interactions between the variables are explicitly specified in Monte Carlo, so (at least in theory) this methodology provides a more complete analysis. And, as a byproduct, having to build a precise model deepens the forecaster's understanding of the project.

## 8.3 Real Options

In Chapter 6 we stressed the superiority of net present value (NPV) analysis over other approaches when valuing capital budgeting projects. However, both scholars and practitioners have pointed out problems with NPV. The basic idea here is that NPV analysis, as well as all the other approaches in Chapter 6, ignores the adjustments that a firm can make after a project is accepted. These adjustments are called real options. In this respect NPV underestimates the true value of a project. NPV's conservatism is best explained through a series of examples.

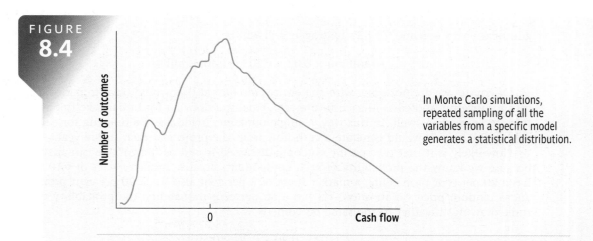

**FIGURE 8.4**

In Monte Carlo simulations, repeated sampling of all the variables from a specific model generates a statistical distribution.

**Figure 8.4** Simulated distribution of the third year's cash flow for BB's new hydrogen grill

The value of real option analysis comes from its ability to value managerial flexibility and corporate strategy. In almost all investments, managers continually assess and reassess ways in which costs can be reduced and revenues maximized. This activity requires identification of any possibility to expand, reduce, delay or even abandon production of an asset. Strategic flexibility provides an option to managers and, as with any option (see Chapters 22 and 23), it has value. Real option analysis is a methodology that allows you to value the strategic flexibility inherent in every project.

## The Option to Expand

Conrad Willig, an entrepreneur, recently learned of a chemical treatment causing water to freeze at 20 degrees Celsius rather than 0 degrees. Of all the many practical applications for this treatment, Mr Willig liked the idea of hotels made of ice more than anything else. Conrad estimated the annual cash flows from a single ice hotel to be £2 million, based on an initial investment of £12 million. He felt that 20 per cent was an appropriate discount rate, given the risk of this new venture. Believing that the cash flows would be perpetual, Mr Willig determined the NPV of the project to be

$$-£12,000,000 + £2,000,000/0.20 = -£2 \text{ million}$$

Most entrepreneurs would have rejected this venture, given its negative NPV. But Conrad was not your typical entrepreneur. He reasoned that NPV analysis missed a hidden source of value. While he was pretty sure that the initial investment would cost £12 million, there was some uncertainty concerning annual cash flows. His cash flow estimate of £2 million per year actually reflected his belief that there was a 50 per cent probability that annual cash flows would be £3 million and a 50 per cent probability that annual cash flows would be £1 million.

The NPV calculations for the two forecasts are given here:

Optimistic forecast:    −£12 million + £3 million/0.20 = £3 million
Pessimistic forecast:    −£12 million + £1 million/0.20 = − £7 million

On the surface, this new calculation doesn't seem to help Mr Willig much. An average of the two forecasts yields an NPV for the project of

$$50\% \times £3 \text{ million} + 50\% \times (-£7 \text{ million}) = -£2 \text{ million}$$

which is just the value he calculated in the first place.

However, if the optimistic forecast turns out to be correct, Mr Willig would want to *expand*. If he believes that there are, say, 10 locations in the country that can support an ice hotel, the true NPV of the venture would be

$$50\% \times 10 \times £3 \text{ million} + 50\% \times (-£7 \text{ million}) = £11.5 \text{ million}$$

Figure 8.5, which represents Mr Willig's decision, is often called a decision tree. The idea expressed in the figure is both basic and universal. The entrepreneur has the option to expand

**Figure 8.5** Decision tree for ice hotel

if the pilot location is successful. For example, think of all the people that start restaurants, most of them ultimately failing. These individuals are not necessarily overly optimistic. They may realize the likelihood of failure but go ahead anyway because of the small chance of starting the next McDonald's or Burger King.

## The Option to Abandon

Managers also have the option to abandon existing projects. Abandonment may seem cowardly, but it can often save companies a great deal of money. Because of this, the option to abandon increases the value of any potential project.

The example of ice hotels, which illustrated the option to expand, can also illustrate the option to abandon. To see this, imagine that Mr Willig now believes that there is a 50 per cent probability that annual cash flows will be £6 million and a 50 per cent probability that annual cash flows will be –£2 million. The NPV calculations under the two forecasts become

Optimistic forecast:  –£12 million + £6 million/0.2 = £18 million
Pessimistic forecast:  –£12 million – £2 million/0.2 = –£22 million

yielding an NPV for the project of

$$50\% \times £18 \text{ million} + 50\% \times (-£22 \text{ million}) = -£2 \text{ million} \qquad (8.4)$$

Furthermore, now imagine that Mr Willig wants to own, at most, just one ice hotel, implying that there is no option to expand. Because the NPV in Eq. (8.4) is negative, it looks as if he will not build the hotel.

But things change when we consider the abandonment option. As of date 1, the entrepreneur will know which forecast has come true. If cash flows equal those under the optimistic forecast, Conrad will keep the project alive. If, however, cash flows equal those under the pessimistic forecast, he will abandon the hotel. If Mr Willig knows these possibilities ahead of time, the NPV of the project becomes

$$50\% \times £18 \text{ million} + 50\% \times (-£12 \text{ million} - £2 \text{ million}/1.20) = £2.17 \text{ million}$$

Because Mr Willig abandons after experiencing the cash flow of –£2 million at date 1, he does not have to endure this outflow in any of the later years. The NPV is now positive, so Conrad will accept the project.

The example here is clearly a stylized one. Whereas many years may pass before a project is abandoned in the real world, our ice hotel was abandoned after just one year. And, while salvage values generally accompany abandonment, we assumed no salvage value for the ice hotel. Nevertheless, abandonment options are pervasive in the real world.

For example, consider the moviemaking industry. As shown in Fig. 8.6, movies begin with either the purchase or development of a script. A completed script might cost a movie studio a few million pounds and potentially lead to actual production. However, the great majority of scripts (perhaps well in excess of 80 per cent) are abandoned. Why would studios abandon scripts that they commissioned in the first place? The studios know ahead of time that only a few scripts will be promising, and they don't know which ones. Thus they cast a wide net, commissioning many scripts to get a few good ones. The studios must be ruthless with the bad scripts, because the expenditure here pales in comparison with the huge losses from producing a bad movie.

The few lucky scripts then move into production, where costs might be budgeted in the tens of millions of pounds, if not much more. At this stage, the dreaded phrase is that on-location production gets 'bogged down', creating cost overruns. But the studios are equally ruthless here. Should these overruns become excessive, production is likely to be abandoned midstream. Interestingly, abandonment almost always occurs because of high costs, not because of the fear that the movie won't be able to find an audience. Little information on that score will be obtained until the movie is actually released.

Movie studios have abandonment options throughout the production of a movie.

**Figure 8.6** The abandonment option in the movie industry

Release of the movie is accompanied by significant advertising expenditures, perhaps in the range of £5 to £10 million. Advertising will continue following strong ticket sales, but it is likely to be abandoned after a few weeks of poor box office performance.

Moviemaking is one of the riskiest businesses around, with studios receiving hundreds of millions of pounds or euros in a matter of weeks from a blockbuster while receiving practically nothing during this period from a flop. The abandonment options contain costs that might otherwise bankrupt the industry.

A recent example of companies actually exercising the option to abandon occurred in 2008, when economic conditions made the housing market collapse. In the UK, for example, major housebuilders were reporting sales of only one house per month throughout the whole country. Rather than continue to build new plots and estates, companies such as Barratt, Taylor Wimpey and Persimmon Homes abandoned many sites.

## Timing Options

One often finds urban land that has been vacant for many years. Yet this land is bought and sold from time to time. Why would anyone pay a positive price for land that has no source of revenue? Certainly, one could not arrive at a positive price through NPV analysis. However, the paradox can easily be explained in terms of real options.

Suppose that the land's highest and best use is as an office building. Total construction costs for the building are estimated to be €1 million. Currently, net rents (after all costs) are estimated to be €90,000 per year in perpetuity, and the discount rate is 10 per cent. The NPV of this proposed building would be

$$-€1 \text{ million} + €90,000/0.10 = -€100,000$$

Because this NPV is negative, one would not currently want to build. However, suppose that the government is planning various urban revitalization programmes for the city. Office rents are likely to increase if the programmes succeed. In this case the property's owner might want to erect the office building after all. Conversely, office rents will remain the same, or even fall, if the programmes fail. The owner will not build in this case.

We say that the property owner has a *timing option*. Although she does not currently want to build, she will want to build in the future should rents in the area rise substantially. This timing option explains why vacant land often has value. There are costs, such as taxes, from holding raw land, but the value of an office building after a substantial rise in rents may more than offset these holding costs. Of course, the exact value of the vacant land depends both on the probability of success in the revitalization programme and on the extent of the rent increase. Figure 8.7 illustrates this timing option.

FIGURE
**8.7**

Rents rise substantially → ● Erect office building

Do not build yet because
rents are too low ●

Rents either stay the same or fall → ● Do not build yet

Vacant land may have value today because the owner can erect a profitable office
building if rents rise.

**Figure 8.7** Decision tree for vacant land

Mining operations almost always provide timing options as well. Suppose you own a copper mine where the cost of mining each ton of copper exceeds the sales revenue. It's a no-brainer to say that you would not want to mine the copper currently. And because there are costs of ownership such as property taxes, insurance and security, you might actually want to pay someone to take the mine off your hands. However, we would caution you not to do so hastily. Copper prices in the future might increase enough so that production is profitable. Given that possibility, you could probably find someone to pay a positive price for the property today.

## 8.4 Decision Trees

As shown in the previous section, managers adjust their decisions on the basis of new information. For example, a project may be expanded if early experience is promising, whereas the same project might be abandoned in the wake of bad results. As we said earlier, the choices available to managers are called *real options*, and an individual project can often be viewed as a series of real options, leading to valuation approaches beyond the basic present value methodology of earlier chapters.

Earlier in this chapter we considered Solar Electronics' (SE's) solar-powered jet engine project, with cash flows as shown in Table 8.1. In that example SE planned to invest £1,500 million at year 1, and expected to receive £954 million per year in each of the next five years. Our calculations showed an NPV of £1,700 million, so the firm would presumably want to go ahead with the project.

To illustrate decision trees in more detail, let's move back one year to year 0, when SE's decision was more complicated. At that time, the engineering group had developed the technology for a solar-powered plane engine, but test marketing had not begun. The marketing department proposed that SE develop some prototypes and conduct test marketing of the engine. A corporate planning group, including representatives from production, marketing and engineering, estimated that this preliminary phase would take a year and cost £100 million. Furthermore, the group believed there was a 75 per cent chance that the marketing test would prove successful. After completion of the marketing tests, SE would decide whether to engage in full-scale production, necessitating the investment of £1,500 million.

The marketing tests add a layer of complexity to the analysis. Our previous work on the example assumed that the marketing tests had already proved successful. How do we analyse whether we want to go ahead with the marketing tests in the first place? This is where decision trees come in.

To recap, SE faces two decisions, both of which are represented in Fig. 8.8. First the firm must decide whether to go ahead with the marketing tests. And if the tests are performed, the firm must decide whether the results of the tests warrant full-scale production. The important point here, as we shall see, is that decision trees answer the two questions in *reverse* order. So let's work backward, first considering what to do with the results of the tests, which can be either successful or unsuccessful.

FIGURE
**8.8**

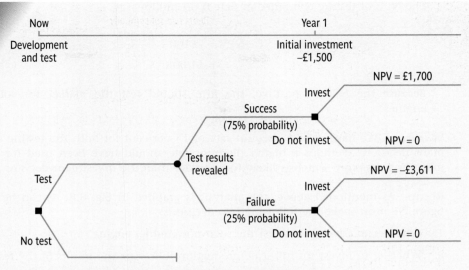

**Figure 8.8** Decision tree for SE (£ millions)

- *Assume tests have been successful (75 per cent probability).* Table 8.1 tells us that full-scale production will cost £1,500 million and will generate an annual cash flow of £954 million for five years, yielding an NPV of

$$-£1,500 + \sum_{t=1}^{5} \frac{£954}{(1.15)^t}$$
$$= -£1,500 + £954 \times A^5_{0.15}$$
$$= £1,700$$

Because the NPV is positive, successful marketing tests should lead to full-scale production. (Note that the NPV is calculated as of year 1, the time at which the investment of £1,500 million is made. Later we shall discount this number back to year 0, when the decision on test marketing is to be made.)

- *Assume tests have not been successful (25 per cent probability).* Here, SE's £1,500 million investment would produce an NPV of −£3,611 million, calculated as of year 1. (To save space, we shall not provide the raw numbers leading to this calculation.) Because the NPV here is negative, SE will not want full-scale production if the marketing tests are unsuccessful.

- *Decision on marketing tests.* Now we know what to do with the results of the marketing tests. Let's use these results to move back one year. That is, we now want to figure out whether SEC should invest £100 million for the test marketing costs in the first place. The expected pay-off evaluated at date 1 (in millions) is

$$\text{Expected payoff} = \begin{pmatrix} \text{Probability} \\ \text{of} \\ \text{success} \end{pmatrix} \times \begin{pmatrix} \text{Payoff} \\ \text{if} \\ \text{successful} \end{pmatrix} + \begin{pmatrix} \text{Probability} \\ \text{of} \\ \text{failure} \end{pmatrix} \times \begin{pmatrix} \text{Payoff} \\ \text{if} \\ \text{failure} \end{pmatrix}$$
$$= (0.75 \times £1,700) + (0.25 \times £0)$$
$$= £1,275$$

The NPV of testing computed at date 0 (in millions) is

$$NPV = -£100 + \frac{£1,275}{1.15}$$
$$= £1,008$$

Because the NPV is positive, the firm should test the market for solar-powered jet engines.

**Warning** We have used a discount rate of 15 per cent for both the testing and the investment decisions. Perhaps a higher discount rate should have been used for the initial test marketing decision, which is likely to be riskier than the investment decision.

**Recap** As mentioned above, the analysis is graphed in Fig. 8.8. As can be seen from the figure, SE must make the following two decisions:

1 Whether to develop and test the solar-powered jet engine.

2 Whether to invest for full-scale production following the results of the test.

Using a decision tree, we answered the second question before we answered the first one.

Decision trees represent the best approach to solving SE's problem, given the information presented so far in the text. However, we shall examine a more sophisticated approach to valuing options in a later chapter. Though this approach was first used to value financial options traded on organized option exchanges, it can be used to value real options as well.

# Summary and Conclusions

This chapter discussed a number of practical applications of capital budgeting.

1 Though NPV is the best capital budgeting approach conceptually, it has been criticized in practice for giving managers a false sense of security. Sensitivity analysis shows NPV under varying assumptions, giving managers a better feel for the project's risks. Unfortunately, sensitivity analysis modifies only one variable at a time, but many variables are likely to vary together in the real world. Scenario analysis examines a project's performance under different scenarios (such as war breaking out or oil prices skyrocketing). Finally, managers want to know how bad forecasts must be before a project loses money. Break-even analysis calculates the sales figure at which the project breaks even. Though break-even analysis is frequently performed on an accounting profit basis, we suggest that a net present value basis is more appropriate.

2 Monte Carlo simulation begins with a model of the firm's cash flows, based on both the interactions between different variables and the movement of each individual variable over time. Random sampling generates a distribution of these cash flows for each period, leading to a net present value calculation.

3 We analysed the hidden options in capital budgeting, such as the option to expand, the option to abandon, and timing options.

4 Decision trees represent an approach for valuing projects with these hidden, or real, options.

## Questions and Problems

CONCEPT
1–4

1 **NPV** 'NPV is just a tool, and as with any tool, it can be dangerous in the wrong hands.' Discuss this statement. In what way do sensitivity analysis, break-even analysis and scenario analysis improve things? Surely they are just tools as well?

2 **Monte Carlo Simulation** Explain the rationale underlying Monte Carlo simulation. How does it improve upon other forms of sensitivity analysis? Does it have any weaknesses? If so, what are they? How could you improve on the methodology?

3 **Real Options** Why does traditional NPV analysis tend to underestimate the true value of a capital budgeting project?

4 **Decision Trees** You are discussing a decision tree analysis with a co-worker. The project involves real options, such as expanding the project if successful, or abandoning the project if it fails. Your co-worker makes the following statement: 'This decision tree analysis is ridiculous. We looked at expanding or abandoning the project in two years, but there are many other options we should consider. For example, we could expand in one year, and expand further in two years. Or we could expand in one year, and abandon the project in two years. There are too many decisions for us to examine. Because of this, anything that decision tree analysis gives us is worthless.' How would you evaluate this statement? Considering that with any capital budgeting project there are an infinite number of decisions, when do you stop the decision tree analysis on an individual project?

REGULAR
5–23

5 **Sensitivity Analysis and Break-Even Point** We are evaluating a project that costs £896,000, has an eight-year life, and has no salvage value. Assume that depreciation is 20 per cent reducing-balance method. Sales are projected at 100,000 units per year. Price per unit is £38, variable cost per unit is £25, and fixed costs are £900,000 per year. The tax rate is 35 per cent, and we require a 15 per cent return on this project.

   (a) Calculate the accounting break-even point.

   (b) Calculate the base-case cash flow and NPV. What is the sensitivity of NPV to changes in the sales figure? Explain what your answer tells you about a 500-unit decrease in projected sales.

   (c) What is the sensitivity of OCF to changes in the variable cost figure? Explain what your answer tells you about a £1 decrease in estimated variable costs.

6 **Scenario Analysis** In the previous problem, suppose the projections given for price, quantity, variable costs and fixed costs are all accurate to within ±10 per cent. Calculate the best-case and worst-case NPV figures.

7 **Financial Break-Even** L.J.'s Toys just purchased a £200,000 machine to produce toy cars. The machine will be fully depreciated using 20 per cent reducing balances over its five-year economic life. Each toy sells for £25. The variable cost per toy is £5, and the firm incurs fixed costs of £350,000 each year. The corporate tax rate for the company is 25 per cent. The appropriate discount rate is 12 per cent. What is the financial break-even point for the project?

8 **Option to Wait** Your company is deciding whether to invest in a new machine. The new machine will increase cash flow by €280,000 per year. You believe the technology used in the machine has a 10-year life: in other words, no matter when you purchase the machine, it will be obsolete 10 years from today. The machine is currently priced at €1,500,000 and should be depreciated using 25 per cent reducing-balance method. If your required return is 12 per cent, should you purchase the machine? If so, when should you purchase it?

9 **Decision Trees** Ang Electronics has developed a new DVDR. If the DVDR is successful, the present value of the pay-off (when the product is brought to market) is £20 million. If the DVDR fails, the present value of the pay-off is £5 million. If the product goes

directly to market, there is a 50 per cent chance of success. Alternatively, Ang can delay the launch by one year and spend £2 million to test-market the DVDR. Test marketing would allow the firm to improve the product and increase the probability of success to 75 per cent. The appropriate discount rate is 15 per cent. Should the firm conduct test marketing?

10 **Decision Trees** The manager for a growing firm is considering the launch of a new product. If the product goes directly to market, there is a 50 per cent chance of success. For €120,000 the manager can conduct a focus group that will increase the product's chance of success to 70 per cent. Alternatively, the manager has the option to pay a consulting firm €400,000 to research the market and refine the product. The consulting firm successfully launches new products 90 per cent of the time. If the firm successfully launches the product, the pay-off will be €1.2 million. If the product is a failure, the NPV is zero. Which action will result in the highest expected pay-off to the firm?

11 **Decision Trees** B&B has a new baby powder ready to market. If the firm goes directly to the market with the product, there is only a 55 per cent chance of success. However, the firm can conduct customer segment research, which will take a year and cost €1 million. By going through research, B&B will be able to target potential customers better, and will increase the probability of success to 70 per cent. If successful, the baby powder will bring a present value profit (at time of initial selling) of €30 million. If unsuccessful, the present value pay-off is only €3 million. Should the firm conduct customer segment research or go directly to market? The appropriate discount rate is 15 per cent.

12 **Financial Break-Even Analysis** You are considering investing in a company that cultivates abalone for sale to local restaurants. Use the following information:

| | |
|---|---|
| Sales price per abalone | £2.00 |
| Variable costs per abalone | £0.72 |
| Fixed costs per year | £340,000 |
| Depreciation per year | £20,000 |
| Tax rate | 35% |

The discount rate for the company is 15 per cent, the initial investment in equipment is £140,000, and the project's economic life is seven years. Assume, for simplicity, that the equipment is depreciated on a straight-line basis over the project's life.

(a) What is the accounting break-even level for the project?

(b) What is the financial break-even level for the project?

13 **Scenario Analysis** You have been given the following figures to assess the viability of a new portable hospital scanner. It is expected that you will be able to capture 10 per cent of the total market of 1.1 million units. The market price will be €400,000 and the unit variable cost is 90 per cent of the market price. Fixed costs of running and manufacture amount to €2 billion per annum.

(a) What is the net income of the project?

(b) You have been approached by the management, who disagree on the figures that were originally used in the analysis. They want you to consider the following scenarios proposed by various directors in the company.

| | Director A | Director B | Director C |
|---|---|---|---|
| Market size | 0.8 million | 1 million | 1.2 million |
| Market share | 4% | 10% | 16% |
| Unit price | €300,000 | €375,000 | €400,000 |
| Variable cost % | 116% | 80% | 70% |
| Fixed cost | €5 billion | €3 billion | €1 billion |

Carry out a sensitivity analysis of the project. What are the main uncertainties in the project?

14 **Break-Even Intuition** Consider a project with a required return of $R$ per cent that costs £$I$ and will last for $N$ years. The project uses straight-line depreciation to zero over the $N$-year life; there are neither salvage value nor net working capital requirements.

(a) At the accounting break-even level of output, what is the IRR of this project? The payback period? The NPV?

(b) At the cash break-even level of output, what is the IRR of this project? The payback period? The NPV?

(c) At the financial break-even level of output, what is the IRR of this project? The payback period? The NPV?

15 **Project Analysis** You are considering a new product launch. The project will cost £720,000, have a four-year life, and have no salvage value; depreciation is 20 per cent reducing balance. Sales are projected at 190 units per year, price per unit will be £21,000, variable cost per unit will be £15,000, and fixed costs will be £225,000 per year. The required return on the project is 15 per cent, and the relevant tax rate is 28 per cent.

(a) Based on your experience, you think the unit sales, variable cost and fixed cost projections given here are probably accurate to within ±10 per cent. What are the upper and lower bounds for these projections? What is the base-case NPV? What are the best-case and worst-case scenarios?

(b) Evaluate the sensitivity of your base-case NPV to changes in fixed costs.

(c) What is the accounting break-even level of output for this project?

16 **Project Analysis** McGilla Golf has decided to sell a new line of golf clubs. The clubs will sell for £700 per set and have a variable cost of £320 per set. The company has spent £150,000 for a marketing study that determined the company will sell 55,000 sets per year for seven years. The marketing study also determined that the company will lose sales of 13,000 sets of its high-priced clubs. The high-priced clubs sell at £1,100 and have variable costs of £600. The company will also increase sales of its cheap clubs by 10,000 sets. The cheap clubs sell for £400 and have variable costs of £180 per set. The fixed costs each year will be £7,500,000. The company has also spent £1,000,000 on research and development for the new clubs. The plant and equipment required will cost £18,200,000 and will be depreciated on a 20 per cent reducing balance basis. At the end of the seven years, the salvage value of the plant and equipment will be equal to the written-down or residual value. The new clubs will also require an increase in net working capital of £950,000 that will be returned at the end of the project. The tax rate is 28 per cent, and the cost of capital is 14 per cent.

(a) Calculate the payback period, the NPV, and the IRR.

(b) You feel that the values are accurate to within only ±10 per cent. What are the best-case and worst-case NPVs? (*Hint:* The price and variable costs for the two existing sets of clubs are known with certainty; only the sales gained or lost are uncertain.)

(c) McGilla would like to know the sensitivity of NPV to changes in the price of the new clubs and the quantity of new clubs sold. What is the sensitivity of the NPV to each of these variables?

17 **Abandonment Value** We are examining a new project. We expect to sell 7,000 units per year at €60 net cash flow apiece for the next 10 years. In other words, the annual operating cash flow is projected to be €60 × 7,000 = €420,000. The relevant discount rate is 16 per cent, and the initial investment required is €1,800,000.

(a) What is the base-case NPV?

(b) After the first year, the project can be dismantled and sold for €1,400,000. If expected sales are revised based on the first year's performance, when would it make sense to abandon the investment? In other words, at what level of expected sales would it make sense to abandon the project?

(c) Explain how the €1,400,000 abandonment value can be viewed as the opportunity cost of keeping the project in one year.

(d) Suppose you think it is likely that expected sales will be revised upwards to 9,000 units if the first year is a success, and revised downwards to 4,000 units if the first year is not a success. If success and failure are equally likely, what is the NPV of the project? Consider the possibility of abandonment in answering. What is the value of the option to abandon?

18 **Abandonment and Expansion** In the previous problem, suppose the scale of the project can be doubled in one year in the sense that twice as many units can be produced and sold. Naturally, expansion would be desirable only if the project were a success. This implies that if the project is a success, projected sales after expansion will be 18,000. Again assuming that success and failure are equally likely, what is the NPV of the project? Note that abandonment is still an option if the project is a failure. What is the value of the option to expand?

19 **Decision Trees** Young screenwriter Carl Draper has just finished his first script. It has action, drama, and humour, and he thinks it will be a blockbuster. He takes the script to every motion picture studio in town and tries to sell it, but to no avail. Finally, ACME Studios offers to buy the script for either (a) $5,000 or (b) 1 per cent of the movie's profits. There are two decisions the studio will have to make. The first is to decide whether the script is good or bad, and the second is to decide whether the movie is good or bad. First, there is a 90 per cent chance that the script will be bad. If it is bad, the studio does nothing more and throws the script out. If the script is good, they will shoot the movie. After the movie is shot, the studio will review it, and there is a 70 per cent chance that the movie will be bad. If the movie is bad, it will not be promoted, and will not turn a profit. If the movie is good, the studio will promote it heavily; the average profit for this type of movie is $10 million. Carl rejects the $5,000 and says he wants the 1 per cent of profits. Was this a good decision by Carl?

20 **Accounting Break-Even** Samuelson GmbH has just purchased a €600,000 machine to produce calculators. The machine will be fully depreciated using the 20 per cent reducing-balance method over its economic life of five years, and will produce 20,000 calculators each year. The salvage value of the machine will be equal to its residual or written-down value. The variable production cost per calculator is €15, and total fixed costs are €900,000 per year. The corporate tax rate for the company is 30 per cent. For the firm to break even in terms of accounting profit, how much should it charge per calculator?

21 **Abandonment Decisions** Allied Products is considering a new product launch. The firm expects to have an annual operating cash flow of £25 million for the next 10 years. Allied Products uses a discount rate of 20 per cent for new product launches. The initial investment is £100 million. Assume that the project has no salvage value at the end of its economic life.

(a) What is the NPV of the new product?

(b) After the first year, the project can be dismantled and sold for £50 million. If the estimates of remaining cash flows are revised based on the first year's experience, at what level of expected cash flows does it make sense to abandon the project?

22 **Expansion Decisions** Applied Nanotech is thinking about introducing a new surface-cleaning machine. The marketing department has come up with the estimate that Applied Nanotech can sell 10 units per year at £0.3 million net cash flow per unit for the next five years. The engineering department has come up with the estimate that developing the machine will take a £10 million initial investment. The finance department has estimated that a 25 per cent discount rate should be used.

(a)   What is the base-case NPV?

(b)   If unsuccessful, after the first year the project can be dismantled and will have an after-tax salvage value of £5 million. Also, after the first year, expected cash flows will be revised up to 20 units per year or to 0 units, with equal probability. What is the revised NPV?

23   **Scenario Analysis**   You are the financial analyst for a tennis racket manufacturer. The company is considering using a graphite-like material in its tennis rackets. The company has estimated the information in the following table about the market for a racket with the new material. The company expects to sell the racket for five years. The equipment required for the project has no salvage value. The required return for projects of this type is 13 per cent, and the company has a 40 per cent tax rate. Should you recommend the project? Assume 20 per cent reducing balance depreciation.

|  | **Pessimistic** | **Expected** | **Optimistic** |
| --- | --- | --- | --- |
| Market size | 110,000 | 120,000 | 130,000 |
| Market share | 22% | 25% | 27% |
| Selling price | €115 | €120 | €125 |
| Variable costs per unit | €72 | €70 | €68 |
| Fixed costs per year | €850,000 | €800,000 | €750,000 |
| Initial investment | €1,500,000 | €1,500,000 | €1,500,000 |

24   **The Capital Budgeting Process**   This question takes a step back from the quantitative analysis and makes you think about how you would manage a capital budgeting project in a firm. You have just graduated from university and have taken up your first job in a local distribution firm. The firm stores alcoholic beverages for breweries, and distributes these to pubs and restaurants, depending on the specific orders placed with your customers. Your firm does not own any stock: it just holds it for others, and distributes it when needed. The directors are considering expanding their business by building two new warehouses to increase capacity, and hopefully revenues. As a corporate finance expert, you have been tasked with the job of managing the capital budgeting analysis from the initial idea to the start of operations.

Prepare a flow chart or mind map for presentation to the directors that will deal with the following issues:

(a)   Who will prepare the initial proposal?

(b)   What information will the proposal contain?

(c)   How will you evaluate it?

(d)   What approvals will be needed, and who will give them?

(e)   What happens if the expenditure is 25 per cent more than the original forecast?

(f)   What will happen when the warehouses have been built?

25   **Scenario Analysis**   Consider a project to supply Italy with 40,000 tonnes of machine screws annually for automobile production. You will need an initial €1,700,000 investment in threading equipment to get the project started; the project will last for five years. The accounting department estimates that annual fixed costs will be €450,000 and that variable costs should be €210 per tonne; accounting will depreciate the initial fixed asset investment using 20 per cent reducing-balance method over the five-year project life. It also estimates a salvage value of €500,000 after dismantling costs. The marketing department estimates that the automakers will let the contract at a selling price of €230 per tonne. The engineering department estimates you will need an initial net working capital investment of €450,000. You require a 13 per cent return and face a marginal tax rate of 38 per cent on this project.

(a) What is the estimated OCF for this project? The NPV? Should you pursue this project?

(b) Suppose you believe that the accounting department's initial cost and salvage value projections are accurate only to within ±15 per cent; the marketing department's price estimate is accurate only to within ±10 per cent; and the engineering department's net working capital estimate is accurate only to within ±5 per cent. What is your worst-case scenario for this project? Your best-case scenario? Do you still want to pursue the project?

26 **Sensitivity Analysis** In Problem 25, suppose you're confident about your own projections, but you're a little unsure about Italy's actual machine screw requirement. What is the sensitivity of the project OCF to changes in the quantity supplied? What about the sensitivity of NPV to changes in quantity supplied? Given the sensitivity number you calculated, is there some minimum level of output below which you wouldn't want to operate? Why?

27 **Abandonment Decisions** Consider the following project for Hand Clapper. The company is considering a four-year project to manufacture clap-command garage door openers. This project requires an initial investment of £8 million, which will be depreciated using the 20 per cent reducing-balance method over the project's life. An initial investment in net working capital of £2 million is required to support spare parts inventory: this cost is fully recoverable whenever the project ends. The company believes it can generate £7 million in pre-tax revenues with £3 million in total pre-tax operating costs. The tax rate is 28 per cent, and the discount rate is 16 per cent. The market value of the equipment over the life of the project is as follows:

| Year | Market value (£m) |
| --- | --- |
| 1 | 6.50 |
| 2 | 6.00 |
| 3 | 3.00 |
| 4 | 0.00 |

(a) Assuming Hand Clapper operates this project for four years, what is the NPV?

(b) Now compute the project NPVs assuming the project is abandoned after only one year, after two years, and after three years. What economic life for this project maximizes its value to the firm? What does this problem tell you about not considering abandonment possibilities when evaluating projects?

28 **Abandonment Decisions** M.V.P. Games has hired you to perform a feasibility study of a new video game that requires a £4 million initial investment. M.V.P. expects a total annual operating cash flow of £750,000 for the next 10 years. The relevant discount rate is 10 per cent. Cash flows occur at year-end.

(a) What is the NPV of the new video game?

(b) After one year, the estimate of remaining annual cash flows will be revised either upwards to £1.5 million or downwards to £120,000. Each revision has an equal probability of occurring. At that time, the video game project can be sold for £800,000. What is the revised NPV, given that the firm can abandon the project after one year?

29 **Financial Break-Even** The Wheatchopper Company is considering the purchase of a new harvester. Wheatchopper has hired you to determine the break-even purchase price in terms of present value of the harvester. This break-even purchase price is the price at which the project's NPV is zero. Base your analysis on the following facts:

• The new harvester is not expected to affect revenues, but pre-tax operating expenses will be reduced by €10,000 per year for 10 years.

- The old harvester is now 5 years old, with 10 years of its scheduled life remaining. It was originally purchased for €45,000, and has been depreciated using the 20 per cent reducing-balance method.

- The old harvester can be sold for €20,000 today.

- The new harvester will be depreciated by the 20 per cent reducing-balance method over its 10-year life.

- The corporate tax rate is 34 per cent.

- The firm's required rate of return is 15 per cent.

- The initial investment, the proceeds from selling the old harvester, and any resulting tax effects occur immediately.

- All other cash flows occur at year-end.

- The market value of each harvester at the end of its economic life is equal to its residual or written-down value.

30 **Sensitivity Analysis** Unmondo SpA is proposing to replace its old DVD stamping machinery with more modern equipment geared towards Blu-ray technology. The new machinery costs €9 million (the existing machinery has no value). The attraction of the Blu-ray stamper is that it is expected to cut manufacturing costs from their current level of €8 per DVD to €4 per Blu-ray disc. However, as the following table shows, there is some uncertainty about future sales and the performance of Blu-ray technology.

|  | Pessimistic | Expected | Optimistic |
| --- | --- | --- | --- |
| Sales (millions of units) | 0.4 | 0.5 | 0.6 |
| Manufacturing cost (€/unit) | 6 | 4 | 3 |
| Life of new machine (years) | 7 | 10 | 13 |

(a) Carry out a sensitivity analysis of the replacement decision, assuming a discount rate of 12 per cent. Unmondo does not pay taxes.

(b) Unmondo SpA could commission engineering tests to determine the actual improvement in manufacturing costs generated by the proposed new Blu-ray disc stamper. The study would cost €450,000. Would you advise Unmondo to go ahead with the study?

31 **Option to Abandon** You own an unused gold mine that will cost $300,000 to reopen. If you open the mine, you expect to be able to extract 1,000 ounces of gold a year for each of three years. After that, the deposit will be exhausted. The gold price is currently $1,000 an ounce, and each year the price is equally likely to rise or fall by $50 from its level at the start of the year. The extraction cost is $920 an ounce and the discount rate is 10%.

(a) Should you open the mine now, or delay one year in the hope of a rise in the gold price?

(b) What difference would it make to your decision if you could costlessly (but irreversibly) shut down the mine at any stage?

32 **Options to Abandon and Expand** Grace and Danger plc is introducing a new product this year. If its luminous golf balls (with integrated beeper) are a success, the firm expects to be able to sell 50,000 units a year at a price of £60 each (they won't go missing, so you will pay a lot for them!). If the new golf balls are not well received, only 30,000 units can be sold at a price of £55. The variable cost of each golf ball is £30 and the fixed costs are zero. The cost of the manufacturing equipment is £6 million, and the project life is estimated to be 10 years. The firm will use 20 per cent reducing balances as their method of depreciation, and at the end of the project's life the machine will be worth nothing. Grace and Danger's tax rate is 28 per cent, and the appropriate discount rate is 12 per cent.

(a) If each outcome is equally likely, what is the expected NPV? Will the firm accept the project?

(b) Suppose now that the firm can abandon the project and sell off the manufacturing equipment for £5.4 million if demand for the golf balls turns out to be weak. The firm will make the decision to continue or abandon after the first year of sales. Does the option to abandon change the firm's decision to accept the project?

(c) Now suppose Grace and Danger can expand production if the project is successful. By paying its workers overtime it can increase production by 25,000 golf balls; the variable cost of each ball will be higher, however, equal to £35 per golf ball. By how much does this option to expand production increase the NPV of the project?

## MINI CASE

# Bunyan Lumber Ltd

Bunyan Lumber Ltd harvests timber and delivers logs to timber mills for sale. The company was founded 70 years ago by Pete Bunyan. The current CEO is Paula Bunyan, the granddaughter of the founder. The company is currently evaluating a 5,000-acre forest it owns in the Scottish Highlands. Paula has asked Steve Boles, the company's finance officer, to evaluate the project. Paula's concern is when the company should harvest the timber.

Lumber is sold by the company for its 'pond value'. Pond value is the amount a mill will pay for a log delivered to the mill location. The price paid for logs delivered to a mill is quoted in pounds per thousands of board feet (MBF), and the price depends on the grade of the logs. The forest Bunyan Lumber is evaluating was planted by the company 20 years ago, and is made up entirely of Douglas fir trees. The table here shows the current price per MBF for the three grades of timber the company feels will come from the stand:

| Timber grade | Price per MBF (£) |
|---|---|
| 1P | 1,050 |
| 2P | 925 |
| 3P | 770 |

Steve believes that the pond value of lumber will increase at the inflation rate. The company is planning to thin the forest today, and it expects to realize a positive cash flow of £1,000 per acre from thinning. The thinning is done to increase the growth rate of the remaining trees, and it is always done 20 years following a planting.

The major decision the company faces is when to log the forest. When the company logs the forest, it will immediately replant saplings, which will allow for a future harvest. The longer the forest is allowed to grow, the larger the harvest becomes per acre. Additionally, an older forest has a higher grade of timber. Steve has compiled the following table with the expected harvest per acre in thousands of board feet, along with the breakdown of the timber grades:

| Years from today to begin harvest | Harvest (MBF) per acre | Timber grade (%) | | |
|---|---|---|---|---|
| | | 1P | 2P | 3P |
| 20 | 6 | 10 | 40 | 50 |
| 25 | 7.6 | 12 | 42 | 46 |
| 30 | 9 | 15 | 42 | 43 |
| 35 | 10 | 16 | 43 | 41 |

The company expects to lose 5 per cent of the timber it cuts, because of defects and breakage.

The forest will be clear-cut when the company harvests the timber. This method of harvesting allows for faster growth of replanted trees. All of the harvesting, processing, replanting and transportation are to be handled by subcontractors hired by Bunyan Lumber. The cost of the logging is expected to be £140 per MBF. A road system has to be constructed, and is expected to cost £50 per MBF on average. Sales preparation and administrative costs, excluding office overhead costs, are expected to be £18 per MBF.

As soon as the harvesting is complete, the company will reforest the land. Reforesting costs include the following:

| | Cost per acre (£) |
|---|---|
| Excavator piling | 150 |
| Broadcast burning | 300 |
| Site preparation | 145 |
| Planting costs | 225 |

All costs are expected to increase at the inflation rate.

Assume all cash flows occur at the year of harvest. For example, if the company begins harvesting the timber 20 years from today, the cash flow from the harvest will be received 20 years from today. When the company logs the land, it will immediately replant the land with new saplings. The harvest period chosen will be repeated for the foreseeable future. The company's nominal required return is 10 per cent, and the inflation rate is expected to be 3.7 per cent per year. Bunyan Lumber has a 35 per cent tax rate.

Clear-cutting is a controversial method of forest management. To obtain the necessary permits, Bunyan Lumber has agreed to contribute to a conservation fund every time it harvests the lumber. If the company harvested the forest today, the required contribution would be £100,000. The company has agreed that the required contribution will grow by 3.2 per cent per year. When should the company harvest the forest?

# Practical Case Study

Let's return to the practical cement case study from Chapter 7. The executives of the cement company have decided to go ahead with the investment appraisal, and have retained you for the more detailed analysis. In any capital budgeting investigation you need an estimate of future net cash flows, future growth rates, and appropriate discount rates. We shall leave a detailed discussion of discount rates until later in the text.

**Cash Flows**   In the first stage of the consultancy, you were informed that the investment will be TSh5 billion and operating revenues are expected to increase by TSh800 million per year. That was just an estimate, and after several interviews you have come up with a more detailed cash flow forecast. First, the TSh5 billion investment is made up of three components. The cement company will need to purchase the land for TSh2 billion and spend TSh2 billion on property, plant and machinery. The other TSh1 billion will be paid out in salaries, wages and other cash expenses every year.

You need to find out about taxation and depreciation in Tanzania. You know that the country follows International Accounting Standards, and so all the material in this textbook is appropriate. However, you need the actual depreciation rules, which differ in every country. The first place you should look is the Tanzanian Ministry of Finance website (http://www.mof.go.tz/mofdocs/revenue/incometax/start.htm). At this site you will find the appropriate corporate tax rate and all depreciation rates for your company.

Operating revenues are based on the expected total demand for cement and the current cement price of TSh90,000 per tonne. If the expansion goes ahead, the company expects to sell an additional 20,000 tonnes of cement at a constant gross profit margin of

44 per cent. However, these figures may change, depending on economic conditions and changing costs. The company expects to run the new operations indefinitely.

**Growth Rates**   In the previous chapter, you spent a lot of time thinking about the factors that drive growth rates. Now, with this information, you should consider several growth rate scenarios for your company. You should also be able to defend your assumptions.

**Discount Rates**   Similarly, you should consider the information you have been given by the experts, as well as all other information available in the markets, to come up with several discount rate scenarios. You should be able to defend your choices here as well.

1   Carry out a full capital budgeting analysis on the above problem, using one or more techniques you feel are appropriate here.

2   As with any real-life capital budgeting analysis, the leeway in assumptions can really make your analysis difficult. Carry out a full sensitivity analysis on the project, based on your own private analysis.

3   Clearly state and explain all assumptions in your analysis.

4   Discuss some factors, costs, inputs or assumptions that have not appeared in the analysis, and suggest ways in which you can gather this information for an extension of the analysis.

5   Write a consultancy report on the analysis.

Many students will be put off by the complexity of this analysis, but the practice of actually working with real, and often poor, data is one of the best skills you can develop. Corporate finance consultants get paid very handsomely for their work, and this is primarily because the investment decision is one of the most important facing a firm. If managers get it right, a good investment can add millions to firm value. Get it wrong and the firm can go bankrupt!

# Relevant Accounting Standards

This chapter is concerned with deepening the capital budgeting analysis, and does not require specific accounting standards. See Chapter 7 for those standards that are relevant for capital budgeting.

# Endnotes

1   Financial custom generally designates year 0 as 'today'. However, we use year 1 as today in this example because later in this chapter we shall consider another decision made a year earlier. That decision will have occurred at year 0.

2   Though the previous section considered both optimistic and pessimistic forecasts for sales price and variable cost, break-even analysis uses just the expected or best estimates of these variables.

To help you grasp the key concepts of this chapter check out the extra resources posted on the Online Learning Centre at www.mcgraw-hill.co.uk/textbooks/hillier

Among other helpful resources there are PowerPoint presentations, chapter outlines and mini-cases.

# Chapter 9

# Risk and Return: Lessons from Market History

## KEY NOTATIONS

| | |
|---|---|
| $Div_t$ | Dividend at time $t$ |
| $N$ | Number of assets; number of years |
| $n$ | Number of observations |
| $P_t$ | Price of an equity at time $t$ |
| $R_t$ | Return on investment at time $t$ |
| $r_t$ | Observed return at time $t$ |
| $\bar{R}$ | Mean return |
| SD | Standard deviation |
| $T$ | Number of years |
| Var | Variance |
| $\sigma$ | Standard deviation |
| $\sigma^2$ | Variance |

In any single day, the stock market will see winners and losers. Take, for example, one day in 2008 – Friday 1 August. The news was not particularly good to start off the month. In the US, the government announced that their economy was slowing down and the number of people in employment was falling. A report from the Royal Bank of Scotland showed that UK house prices fell by 4 per cent in the previous year (in Northern Ireland this figure was 19 per cent). In Australia, Morgan Stanley, an investment bank, predicted that house prices would fall a whopping 30 per cent by 2010. In Europe, share prices fell for the first time in three weeks after Ryanair (an Irish airline), BMW (a German automobile manufacturer), Michelin (a French tyre producer) and BT (a British telecoms company) all announced particularly bad trading results.

Could an investor have made money from buying shares in the morning and selling at night on 1 August 2008? The answer is yes. In the UK, Kingfisher plc, the home improvement group, increased by 4.9 per cent. In Sweden, Eniro AB (a postal and Internet search company) saw its shares grow by 2.05 per cent. Could an investor have lost money in these countries following the same strategy? The answer is also a definite yes. In the UK, prices in Centrica (an energy company) dropped by 5.64 per cent. In Europe, the electrical retailer Schneider dropped by 6.41 per cent, and in Sweden, the steel company SSAB fell by 4.46 per cent. These examples show that there are tremendous potential profits to be made, irrespective of whether markets are falling or growing. However, there is also the risk of losing money – lots of it. So what should you, as a stock market investor, expect when you invest your own money? In this chapter, we study decades of market history to find out.

## 9.1 Returns

### Monetary Returns

Suppose the Video Concept Company has several thousand shares of equity outstanding, and you are a shareholder. Further suppose that you purchased some of the shares in the company at the beginning of the year; it is now year-end and you want to figure out how well you have done on your investment. The return you get on an investment in shares, like that in bonds or any other investment, comes in two forms.

First, over the year most companies pay dividends to shareholders. As the owner of shares in the Video Concept Company, you are a part owner of the company. If the company is profitable, it will generally distribute some of its profits to the shareholders. Therefore, as the owner of shares, you will receive some cash, called a *dividend*, during the year. This cash is the *income component* of your return. In addition to the dividends, the other part of your return is the *capital gain* – or, if it is negative, the *capital loss* (negative capital gain) – on the investment.

For example, suppose we are considering the cash flows of the investment in Fig. 9.1, showing that you purchased 100 shares at the beginning of the year at a price of £37 per share. Your total investment, then, was

$$C_0 = £37 \times 100 = £3,700$$

Suppose that over the year the shares paid a dividend of £1.85 per share. During the year, then, you received income of

$$Div = £1.85 \times 100 = £185$$

Suppose, finally, that at the end of the year the market price of the equity is £40.33 per share. Because the shares increased in price, you had a capital gain of

$$Gain = (£40.33 - £37) \times 100 = £333$$

The capital gain, like the dividend, is part of the return that shareholders require to maintain their investment in the Video Concept Company. Of course, if the price of Video Concept shares had dropped in value to, say, £34.78, you would have recorded this capital loss:

$$Loss = (£34.78 - £37) \times 100 = -£222$$

The *total monetary return* on your investment is the sum of the dividend income and the capital gain or loss on the investment:

$$\text{Total monetary return} = \text{Dividend income} + \text{Capital gain (or loss)}$$

(From now on we shall refer to *capital losses* as *negative capital gains* and not distinguish them.) In our first example the total monetary return is given by

$$\text{Total monetary return} = £185 + £333 = £518$$

**Figure 9.1** Monetary returns

Notice that if you sold the shares at the end of the year, your total amount of cash would be the initial investment plus the total monetary return. In the preceding example you would have

$$\text{Total cash if equity is sold} = \text{Initial investment} + \text{Total monetary return}$$
$$= £3,700 + £518$$
$$= £4,218$$

As a check, notice that this is the same as the proceeds from the sale of shares plus the dividends:

$$\text{Proceeds from equity sale} + \text{Dividends}$$
$$= £40.33 \times 100 + £185$$
$$= £4,033 + £185$$
$$= £4,218$$

Suppose, however, that you hold your Video Concept shares and don't sell them at year-end. Should you still consider the capital gain as part of your return? Does this violate our previous present value rule that only cash matters?

The answer to the first question is a strong yes, and the answer to the second question is an equally strong no. The capital gain is every bit as much a part of your return as is the dividend, and you should certainly count it as part of your total return. That you have decided to hold on to the shares and not sell or *realize* the gain or the loss in no way changes the fact that, if you want to, you could get the cash value of the shares. After all, you could always sell the shares at year-end and immediately buy them back. The total amount of cash you would have at year-end would be the £518 gain plus your initial investment of £3,700. You would not lose this return when you bought back 100 shares. In fact, you would be in exactly the same position as if you had not sold the shares (assuming, of course, that there are no tax consequences and no brokerage commissions from selling the equity).

## Percentage Returns

It is more convenient to summarize the information about returns in percentage terms than in monetary terms, because the percentages apply to any amount invested. The question we want to answer is this: How much return do we get for each unit of currency invested? To find this out, let $t$ stand for the year we are looking at, let $P_t$ be the price of the equity at the beginning of the year, and let $Div_{t+1}$ be the dividend paid on the equity during the year. Consider the cash flows in Fig. 9.2.

**Figure 9.2** Percentage returns

In our example, the price at the beginning of the year was £37 per share and the dividend paid during the year on each share was £1.85. Hence the percentage income return, sometimes called the *dividend yield*, is

$$\text{Dividend yield} = \text{Div}_{t+1}/P_t$$
$$= £1.85/£37$$
$$= 0.05$$
$$= 5\%$$

The capital gain (or loss) is the change in the price of shares divided by the initial price. Letting $P_{t+1}$ be the price of the equity at year-end, we can compute the capital gain as follows:

$$\text{Capital gain} = (P_{t+1} - P_t)/P_t$$
$$= (£40.33 - £37)/£37$$
$$= £3.33/£37$$
$$= 0.09$$
$$= 9\%$$

Combining these two results, we find that the *total return* on the investment in Video Concept shares over the year, which we shall label $R_{t+1}$, was

$$R_{t+1} = \frac{\text{Div}_{t+1}}{P_t} + \frac{P_{t+1} - P_t}{P_t}$$
$$= 5\% + 9\%$$
$$= 14\%$$

From now on, we shall refer to returns in percentage terms.

To give a more concrete example, shares in Enel SpA, the Italian electricity supplier, began 2007 at €7.82 each. Enel paid dividends of €0.49 during 2007, and the share price at the end of the year was €8.14. What was the return on Enel for the year? For practice, see if you agree that the answer is 10.36 per cent. Of course, negative returns occur as well. For example, in the first six months of 2008 Enel's share price fell to €6.04 (price at 30 June), and no dividends were paid. Verify that the loss was 25.80 per cent for the six-month period.

## Calculating Returns

Suppose an equity begins the year with a price of €25 per share and ends with a price of €35 per share. During the year it paid a €2 dividend per share. What are its dividend yield, its capital gain, and its total return for the year? We can imagine the cash flows in Fig. 9.3.

**Figure 9.3** Cash flow: an investment example

$$R_1 = \frac{\text{Div}_1}{P_0} + \frac{P_1 - P_0}{P_0}$$

$$= \frac{€2}{€25} + \frac{€35 - 25}{€25}$$

$$= \frac{€12}{€25}$$

$$= 8\% + 40\%$$

$$= 48\%$$

Thus the equity's dividend yield, its capital gain yield and its total return are 8 per cent, 40 per cent and 48 per cent, respectively.

Suppose you had €5,000 invested. The total return you would have received on an investment in the shares is €5,000 × 0.48 = €2,400. If you know the total return on the equity, you do not need to know how many shares you would have had to purchase to figure out how much money you would have made on the €5,000 investment. You just use the total return.

**FIGURE 9.4**

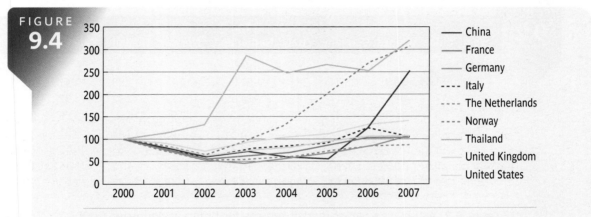

**Figure 9.4** Stock market index levels for a number of countries, 2000–2007

## 9.2 Holding Period Returns

In this section we shall discuss the rates of return on a number of different securities in different countries across Europe and the world. The countries we look at are China, France, Germany, Italy, the Netherlands, Norway, Thailand, the UK and the US. The large company share portfolios are based on indices representing the largest companies in each country. In turn, these are: Shanghai SE 50 Share Index (China), CAC40 (France), DAX30 (Germany), Milan MIB 30 (Italy), Amsterdam SE All Shares (Netherlands), Oslo SE OBX (Norway), Bangkok S.E.T. 50 (Thailand), FTSE 100 (UK), and S&P500 (US).

None of the returns are adjusted for taxes, transaction costs, or inflation. Figure 9.4 shows the relative performance of different stock markets over the period 2000–2007. During this time the trading of Internet and hi-tech companies became the vogue (2000), until the market collapsed in 2001. It took a number of years to recover, but this was a sustained growth period until 2007, when the subprime mortgage crisis erupted and caused the global credit crunch that markets faced in 2008.

Table 9.1 presents the index values for each stock market for every year between 2000 and 2001. Notice how most markets fell in 2001 and 2002. This was a result of the market for Internet and high-technology stocks collapsing. In addition, the terrorist attacks on the United States in 2001, together with the potential for conflict in the Gulf, dampened the performance of markets during this period. The turning point in countries' fortunes was mid-2002, and most markets saw sustained performance over the subsequent five years. China's growth has

**TABLE 9.1**

| Year | China | France | Germany | Italy | The Netherlands | Norway | Thailand | United Kingdom | United States |
|------|-------|--------|---------|-------|-----------------|--------|----------|----------------|---------------|
| 2000 | 100 | 100 | 100 | 100 | 100 | 100 | 100 | 100 | 100 |
| 2001 | 78.11 | 79.05 | 76.46 | 75.16 | 79.05 | 86.89 | 112.88 | 84.59 | 89.79 |
| 2002 | 64.73 | 54.45 | 55.69 | 61.14 | 51.66 | 64.98 | 132.43 | 63.47 | 71.99 |
| 2003 | 71.57 | 63.94 | 47.07 | 77.69 | 54.54 | 96.14 | 286.84 | 73.98 | 92.73 |
| 2004 | 60.67 | 69.85 | 56.16 | 87.50 | 57.74 | 133.68 | 248.19 | 80.79 | 104.38 |
| 2005 | 55.69 | 87.53 | 67.75 | 93.24 | 72.34 | 203.46 | 265.14 | 95.42 | 111.64 |
| 2006 | 128.41 | 104.48 | 84.28 | 123.43 | 84.23 | 271.28 | 252.55 | 107.96 | 131.58 |
| 2007 | 251.85 | 104.91 | 108.32 | 106.39 | 88.28 | 307.78 | 318.77 | 110.15 | 140.24 |

Table 9.1 Year-by-year stock market index levels for different countries, 2000–2007

**TABLE 9.2**

| Year | China | France | Germany | Italy | The Netherlands | Norway | Thailand | United Kingdom | United States |
|------|-------|--------|---------|-------|-----------------|--------|----------|----------------|---------------|
| 2000 | – | – | – | – | – | – | – | – | – |
| 2001 | −21.89 | −20.95 | −23.54 | −24.84 | −20.95 | −13.11 | 12.88 | −15.41 | −10.21 |
| 2002 | −17.13 | −31.13 | −27.17 | −18.65 | −34.65 | −25.22 | 17.32 | −24.97 | −19.83 |
| 2003 | 10.57 | 17.45 | −15.47 | 27.08 | 5.56 | 47.96 | 116.60 | 16.56 | 28.81 |
| 2004 | −15.23 | 9.23 | 19.31 | 12.62 | 5.88 | 39.05 | −13.48 | 9.21 | 12.57 |
| 2005 | −8.21 | 25.31 | 20.64 | 6.57 | 25.28 | 52.19 | 6.83 | 18.10 | 6.95 |
| 2006 | 130.57 | 19.37 | 24.40 | 32.37 | 16.44 | 33.34 | −4.75 | 13.15 | 17.86 |
| 2007 | 96.14 | 0.41 | 28.52 | −13.80 | 4.81 | 13.45 | 26.22 | 2.03 | 6.58 |

Table 9.2 Year-by-year stock market returns for different countries, 2000–2007

been astounding, as has that of Norway (probably because of oil). However, an assessment of the European countries shows quite stagnant performance between 2000 and 2007.

The figures in Table 9.1 clearly show that an investor must be careful when reading information on company or stock market performance. For example, if one was to look at the holding period return for the United Kingdom between 2000 and 2007, and compare this with the holding period return for the same country between 2002 and 2007, conflicting messages would be given. The average annual holding period return for the years 2000–2007 is 5.75 per cent, compared with the average annual holding period return for the period 2002–2007 of 18.97 per cent! Which is the correct performance measure? Unfortunately, both are correct from different perspectives.

Figure 9.4 gives the growth of an investment in various stock markets between 2000 and 2007. In other words, it shows what the worth of the investment would have been if the money that was initially invested had been left in the stock market, and if each year the dividends from the previous year had been reinvested in more shares. If $R_t$ is the return in year $t$ (expressed in decimals), the value you would have at the end of year $T$ is the product of 1 plus the return in each of the years:

$$(1 + R_1) \times (1 + R_2) \times \ldots \times (1 + R_t) \times \ldots \times (1 + R_T)$$

For example, in Table 9.2 the index values in Table 9.1 are presented as annual percentage returns.

Consider the returns for the Netherlands in 2005 (25.28 per cent), 2006 (16.44 per cent), and 2007 (4.81 per cent). An investment of €1 at the beginning of 2005 would have been worth

$$(1 + R_1) \times (1 + R_2) \times (1 + R_3) = (€1 + 0.2528) \times (€1 + 0.1644) \times (€1 + 0.0481)$$
$$= €1.2528 \times €1.1644 \times €1.0481$$
$$= €1.53$$

at the end of 2007. Notice that 0.53 – or 53 per cent – is the total return, and that it includes the return from reinvesting the first-year dividends in the stock market for two more years and reinvesting the second-year dividends for the final year. The 53 per cent is called a three-year holding period return.

## 9.3 Return Statistics

The history of capital market returns is too complicated to be handled in its undigested form. To use the history, we must first find some manageable ways of describing it, dramatically condensing the detailed data into a few simple statements.

This is where two important numbers summarizing the history come in. The first and most natural number is some single measure that best describes the past annual returns on the stock market. In other words, what is our best estimate of the return that an investor could have realized in a particular year over a period? This is the *average return*.

Figure 9.5 plots the histogram of the yearly stock market returns for the US between 1925 and 2005. This plot is the frequency distribution of the numbers. The height of the graph gives the number of sample observations in the range on the horizontal axis. We look at the US because it has the longest available period of stock market data.

Given a frequency distribution like that in Fig. 9.5, we can calculate the average or mean of the distribution. To compute the average of the distribution, we add up all the values and divide by the total ($T$) number (80 in our case because we have 80 years of data). The bar over the $R$ is used to represent the mean, and the formula is the ordinary formula for the average:

$$\text{Mean} = \bar{R} = \frac{R_1 + \ldots + R_T}{T}$$

The mean of the 80 annual large-company share price returns from 1926 to 2005 is 12.2 per cent.

EXAMPLE
9.2

## Calculating Average Returns

From Table 9.2, the returns on large French company shares between 2004 and 2007 are 0.0923, 0.2531, 0.1937 and 0.0041, respectively. The average, or arithmetic mean, return over these four years is

$$\bar{R} = \frac{0.0923 + 0.2531 + 0.1937 + 0.0041}{4}$$
$$= 0.1358 \text{ or } 13.58\%$$

## 9.4 Average Stock Returns and Risk-Free Returns

Now that we have computed the average return on the stock market, it seems sensible to compare it with the returns on other securities. The most obvious comparison is with the low-variability returns in the government bond market. These are free of most of the volatility we see in the stock market.

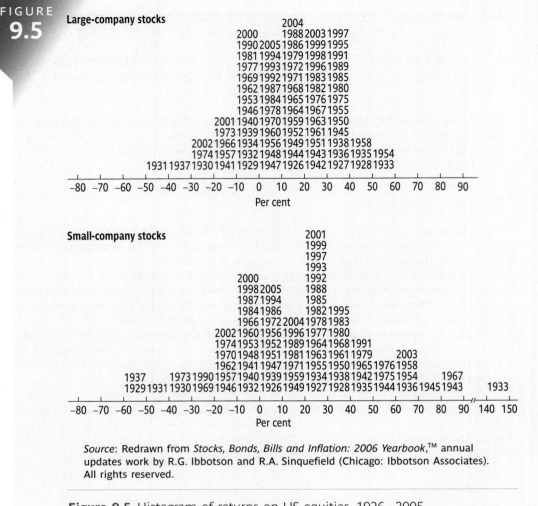

**Figure 9.5** Histogram of returns on US equities, 1926–2005

Governments borrow money by issuing bonds, which the investing public holds. As we discussed in an earlier chapter, these bonds come in many forms, and the ones we shall look at here are called *Treasury bills*, or *T-bills*. Once a week the government sells some bills at an auction. A typical bill is a pure discount bond that will mature in a year or less. Because governments can raise taxes to pay for the debt they incur – a trick that many of us would like to be able to perform – this debt is virtually free of the risk of default. Thus we shall call this the *risk-free return* over a short time (one year or less).

An interesting comparison, then, is between the virtually risk-free return on T-bills and the very risky return on equity. This difference between risky returns and risk-free returns is often called the *excess return on the risky asset*. It is called *excess* because it is the additional return resulting from the riskiness of equities, and is interpreted as an equity risk premium.

Table 9.3 shows the average share price return, bond return, T-bill return and inflation rate for the period from 1926 to 2005 for the United States. Given the length of period available for US data, it is a sensible choice for an analysis of returns and risk premiums over time.

One of the most significant observations of stock market data is this long-term excess of the share price return over the risk-free return. An investor for this period was rewarded for investment in the stock market with an extra or excess return over what would have been achieved by simply investing in T-bills.

TABLE
**9.3**

| Series | Arithmetic mean (%) | Risk premium (relative to US Treasury bills) (%) | Standard deviation (%) | Distribution |
|---|---|---|---|---|
| Large-company shares | 12.3 | 8.5 | 20.2 | |
| Small-company shares | 17.4 | 13.6 | 32.9 | |
| Long-term corporate bonds | 6.2 | 2.4 | 8.5 | |
| Long-term government | 5.8 | 2.0 | 9.2 | |
| Intermediate-term government | 5.5 | 1.7 | 5.7 | |
| US Treasury bills | 3.8 | | 3.1 | |
| Inflation | 3.1 | | 4.3 | |
| | | | | −90%  0%  90% |

The 1933 small-company total return was 142.9 per cent.
*Source*: Modified from *Stocks, Bonds, Bills and Inflation: 2006 Yearbook,*™ annual updates work by R.G. Ibbotson and R.A. Sinquefield (Chicago: Ibbotson Associates). All rights reserved.

**Table 9.3** Total US annual returns, 1926–2005

Why was there such a reward? Does it mean that it never pays to invest in T-bills, and that someone who invested in them instead of in the stock market needs a course in finance? A complete answer to these questions lies at the heart of modern finance, and Chapter 10 is devoted entirely to this. However, part of the answer can be found in the variability of the various types of investment. We see in Table 9.2 years when an investment in equities resulted in a loss of money (negative returns). The returns from an investment in equities are frequently negative across all countries, whereas an investment in T-bills never produces a negative return. So, we now turn our attention to measuring the variability of returns and an introductory discussion of risk.

We first look more closely at Table 9.3. We see that the standard deviation of T-bills is substantially less than that of equities, which suggests that the risk of T-bills is less than that of equities. Because the answer turns on the riskiness of investments in equities, we next turn our attention to measuring this risk.

## 9.5  Risk Statistics

The second number that we use to characterize the distribution of returns is a measure of the risk in returns. There is no universally agreed-upon definition of risk. One way to think about the risk of returns on company shares is in terms of the spread of frequency distributions in Table 9.3. The spread, or dispersion, of a distribution is a measure of how much a particular return can deviate from the mean return. If the distribution is very spread out, the returns that will occur are very uncertain. By contrast, a distribution whose returns are all within a few percentage points of each other is tight, and the returns are less uncertain. The measures of risk we shall discuss are variance and standard deviation.

### Variance

The variance and its square root, the standard deviation, are the most common measures of variability or dispersion. We shall use Var and $\sigma^2$ to denote the variance, and SD and $\sigma$ to represent the standard deviation. The letter $\sigma$ is, of course, the Greek sigma.

EXAMPLE
**9.3**

# Volatility

Consider the returns on China's stock market between 2004 and 2007. These are, respectively, −0.1523, −0.0821, 1.3057, and 0.9614. The variance of this sample is computed as follows:

$$\text{Var} = \frac{1}{T-1}[(R_1 - \bar{R})^2 + (R_2 - \bar{R})^2 + (R_3 - \bar{R})^2 + (R_4 - \bar{R})^2]$$

$$0.5420 = \frac{1}{3}\left[(-0.1523 - 0.5082)^2 + (-0.0821 - 0.5082)^2 + (1.3057 - 0.5082)^2 + (0.9614 - 0.5082)^2\right]$$

$$\text{SD} = \sqrt{0.5420}$$

$$= 0.7362 \text{ or } 73.62\%$$

This formula tells us just what to do: Take the $T$ individual returns ($R_1, R_2, \ldots$) and subtract the average return $\bar{R}$, square the result, and add them up. Finally, this total must be divided by the number of returns less one ($T − 1$). The standard deviation is always just the square root of the variance.

Using the US share price returns for the 80-year period from 1926 to 2005 in this formula, the resulting standard deviation is 20.2 per cent. The standard deviation is the standard statistical measure of the spread of a sample, and it will be the measure we use most of the time. Its interpretation is facilitated by a discussion of the normal distribution.

Standard deviations are widely reported for investment funds. For example, consider the Henderson All Stocks Credit A Investment Trust. How volatile is it? To find out, we went to www.morningstar.co.uk, searched on the fund's name, and hit the 'Risk/Measures' link. Here is what we found:

| **Henderson All Stocks Credit A Inc** | | | |
|---|---|---|---|
| **Morningstar Rating™** (Relative to Category) | | | 31/07/2008 |
| | **Morningstar Return** | **Morningstar Risk** | **Morningstar Rating™** |
| 3-Year | Average | Average | ★★★ |
| 5-Year | Average | Average | ★★★ |
| 10-Year | – | – | Not Rated |
| Overall | Average | Average | ★★★ |
| Category: Sterling Corporate Bond | | Click here to see our Methodology | |
| **Volatility Measurements** | | | 31/07/2008 |
| 3-Yr Std Dev | 3.51% | 3-Yr Sharpe Ratio | −1.54 |
| 3-Yr Mean Return | −0.12% | | |
| **Modern Portfolio Statistics** | | | 31/07/2008 |
| | | **Standard Index** IBOXX GBP Corp TR | **Best Fit Index** IBOXX GBP Corp TR |
| 3-Yr R-Squared | | 83.96 | 83.96 |
| 3-Yr Beta | | 0.89 | 0.89 |
| 3-Yr Alpha | | −1.27 | −1.27 |

Over the last three years, the standard deviation of the return on the fund was 3.51 per cent. When you consider the average share price has a standard deviation of about 50 per cent, this seems like a low number. But the All Stocks Credit A fund is a relatively well-diversified portfolio of low-risk corporate bonds, so this is an illustration of the power of diversification

FIGURE
9.6

In the case of a normal distribution there is a 68.26 per cent probability that a return will be within one standard deviation of the mean. In this example there is a 68.26 per cent probability that a yearly return will be between −7.9 per cent and 32.5 per cent.

There is a 95.44 per cent probability that a return will be within two standard deviations of the mean. In this example, there is a 95.44 per cent probability that a yearly return will be between −28.1 per cent and 52.7 per cent.

Finally, there is a 99.74 per cent probability that a return will be within three standard deviations of the mean. In this example, there is a 99.74 per cent probability that a yearly return will be between −48.3 per cent and 72.99 per cent.

**Figure 9.6** The normal distribution

and asset risk, a subject we shall discuss in detail later. The mean is the average return: so over the last three years, investors in the Henderson fund experienced poor performance with a negative return of −0.12 per cent per year. Also, under the Volatility Measurements section you will see the Sharpe ratio. The Sharpe ratio is defined as the risk premium of the asset divided by the standard deviation. It is a measure of return to the level of risk taken (as measured by standard deviation). The 'beta' for the All Stocks Credit A Fund is 0.89. We shall have more to say about this number – lots more – in the next chapter.

## Normal Distribution and Its Implications for Standard Deviation

A large enough sample drawn from a normal distribution looks like the bell-shaped curve drawn in Fig. 9.6. As you can see, this distribution is *symmetric* about its mean, not *skewed*, and has a much cleaner shape than the actual distribution of yearly returns drawn in Table 9.3. Of course, if we had been able to observe stock market returns for 1,000 years, we might have filled in a lot of the jumps and jerks in Fig. 9.5 and had a smoother curve.

In classical statistics the normal distribution plays a central role, and the standard deviation is the usual way to represent the spread of a normal distribution. For the normal distribution the probability of having a return that is above or below the mean by a certain amount depends only on the standard deviation. For example, the probability of having a return that is within one standard deviation of the mean of the distribution is approximately 0.68 or 2/3, and the probability of having a return that is within two standard deviations of the mean is approximately 0.95.

The 20.2 per cent standard deviation we found for US stock returns from 1926 to 2005 can now be interpreted in the following way. If stock returns are roughly normally distributed, the probability that a yearly return will fall within 20.2 per cent of the mean of 12.3 per cent will be approximately 2/3. That is, about 2/3 of the yearly returns will be between −7.9 per cent and 32.5 per cent. (Note that −7.9 = 12.3 − 20.2, and 32.5 = 12.3 + 20.2.) The probability that the return in any year will fall within two standard deviations is about 0.95. That is, about 95 per cent of yearly returns will be between −28.1 per cent and 52.7 per cent.

FIGURE
**9.7**

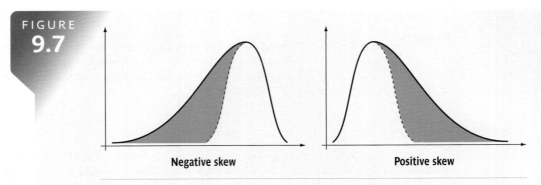

**Figure 9.7** Skewed distributions

## Other Measures of Risk

Although variance and standard deviation are the most common risk measures, there are other approaches to assessing risk that are sometimes utilized by investors. One of the major drawbacks of variance and standard deviation is that they implicitly assume that increases in share prices are just as risky as price falls. However, many investors perceive a decrease in the value of their investment to be significantly more risky than a growth in its value. This asymmetry in personal perspectives is seen to be the major weakness of the variance and standard deviation measures.

Asymmetric measures of risk use only the downside variation in returns from some target return, which could be the mean historical return or some benchmark return set by the investor. The semi-variance is calculated as follows:

$$\text{Semi-variance} = \frac{1}{n-1}\left[\sum_{r_t < \text{target}}^{n} (\text{target} - r_t)^2\right]$$

where $n$ is the number of observations below the target; $r_t$ is the observed return; and 'target' is the target return, which could be the historical mean return. The semi-variance has the advantage that only those deviations that are below the target or benchmark return are considered in the risk measure.

Another measure of risk that incorporates asymmetry in investment returns is that of skewness. Skewness refers to the extent to which a distribution is skewed to the left or right. In Fig. 9.6, the normal distribution is symmetric, which means that downside and upside observations are equally likely. However, many return series have an asymmetric distribution, and skewness measures the degree to which observations are likely to be on the downside or upside. Consider Fig. 9.7, which presents two skewed distributions. In the first diagram negative returns are more likely, whereas in the second diagram positive returns are more likely.

To measure the degree to which a return series is skewed, also known as skewness risk, simply divide the proportion of variation that is caused by upside deviations from the mean by the proportion of variation caused by downside deviations from the mean. Values of skewness risk above 1 correspond to positive skewness, whereas values of skewness risk below 1 correspond to negative skewness.

A second measure of risk that is related to the distribution of returns is kurtosis. Kurtosis is a measure of the frequency of very negative and very positive returns. The normal distribution predicts that approximately 4.56 per cent of all observed returns will be greater than two standard deviations away from the mean return. However, in many cases share price returns have a much greater prevalence of extreme values, and this is reflected in the size of the kurtosis measure. The formula for kurtosis is quite complex but, fortunately, all statistical packages and spreadsheets calculate this for you. For example, in Microsoft Excel® the formula for kurtosis is KURT. Similarly, the formula for skewness is SKEW.

## 9.6 More on Average Returns

Thus far in this chapter we have looked closely at simple average returns. But there is another way of computing an average return. The fact that average returns are calculated in two different ways leads to some confusion, so our goal in this section is to explain the two approaches, and also the circumstances under which each is appropriate.

### Arithmetic versus Geometric Averages

Let's start with a simple example. Suppose you buy a particular equity for £100. Unfortunately, the first year you own it, it falls to £50. The second year you own it, it rises back to £100, leaving you where you started (no dividends were paid).

What was your average return on this investment? Common sense seems to say that your average return must be exactly zero because you started with £100 and ended with £100. But if we calculate the returns year by year, we see that you lost 50 per cent in the first year (you lost half of your money). In the second year you made 100 per cent (you doubled your money). Your average return over the two years was thus (–50 per cent + 100 per cent)/2 = 25 per cent!

So which is correct, 0 per cent or 25 per cent? The answer is that both are correct; they just answer different questions. The 0 per cent is called the geometric average return. The 25 per cent is called the arithmetic average return. The geometric average return answers the question 'What was your average compound return per year over a particular period?' The arithmetic average return answers the question 'What was your return in an average year over a particular period?'

Notice that in previous sections the average returns we calculated were all arithmetic averages, so we already know how to calculate them. What we need to do now is (a) learn how to calculate geometric averages and (b) learn the circumstances under which one average is more meaningful than the other.

### Calculating Geometric Average Returns

First, to illustrate how we calculate a geometric average return, suppose a particular investment had annual returns of 10 per cent, 12 per cent, 3 per cent and –9 per cent over the last four years. The geometric average return over this four-year period is calculated as $(1.10 \times 1.12 \times 1.03 \times 0.91)^{1/4} - 1 = 3.66$ per cent. In contrast, the average arithmetic return we have been calculating is $(0.10 + 0.12 + 0.03 - 0.09)/4 = 4.0$ per cent.

In general, if we have $T$ years of returns, the geometric average return over these $T$ years is calculated using the formula

$$\text{Geometric average return} = [(1 + R_1) \times (1 + R_2) \times \cdots \times (1 + R_T)]^{1/T} - 1 \qquad (9.1)$$

This formula tells us that four steps are required:

1   Take each of the $T$ annual returns $R_1, R_2, \ldots, R_T$ and add 1 to each (after converting them to decimals).

2   Multiply all the numbers from step 1 together.

3   Take the result from step 2 and raise it to the power $1/T$.

4   Finally, subtract 1 from the result of step 3. The result is the geometric average return.

EXAMPLE 9.4

### Calculating the Geometric Average Return

Calculate the geometric average return for Italian stocks for 2003–2007 using the numbers given here.

First convert percentages to decimal returns, add 1, and then calculate their product:

| Milan index returns | Product |
|---|---|
| 27.08 | 1.2708 |
| 12.62 | × 1.1262 |
| 6.57 | × 1.0657 |
| 32.37 | × 1.3237 |
| −13.80 | × 0.8620 |
| | 1.7403 |

Notice that the number 1.7403 is what our investment is worth after five years if we started with a €1 investment. The geometric average return is then calculated as

$$\text{Geometric average return} = 1.7403^{1/5} - 1$$
$$= 0.1172 \text{ or } 11.72\%$$

Thus the geometric average return is about 11.72 per cent in this example. Here is a tip: if you are using a financial calculator, you can put €1 in as the present value, €1.7403 as the future value, and 5 as the number of periods. Then solve for the unknown rate. You should get the same answer we did.

You may have noticed in our examples thus far that the geometric average returns seem to be smaller. It turns out that this will always be true (as long as the returns are not all identical, in which case the two 'averages' will be the same). To illustrate, Table 9.4 shows the arithmetic averages and standard deviations from Table 9.3, along with the geometric average returns.

As shown in Table 9.4, the geometric averages are all smaller, but the magnitude of the difference varies quite a bit. The reason for this is that the difference is greater for more volatile investments. In fact, there is a useful approximation. Assuming all the numbers are expressed in decimals (as opposed to percentages), the geometric average return is approximately equal to the arithmetic average return minus half the variance. For example, looking at the large-company shares, the arithmetic average is 12.3 and the standard deviation is 20.2, implying that the variance is 0.0408. The approximate geometric average is thus 12.3% − 0.0408/2 = 10.26%, which is quite close to the actual value.

## Arithmetic Average Return or Geometric Average Return?

When we look at historical returns, the difference between the geometric and arithmetic average returns isn't too hard to understand. To put it slightly differently, the geometric average

**TABLE 9.4**

| Series | Geometric mean (%) | Arithmetic mean (%) | Standard deviation (%) |
|---|---|---|---|
| Large-company shares | 10.4 | 12.3 | 20.2 |
| Small-company shares | 12.6 | 17.4 | 32.9 |
| Long-term corporate bonds | 5.9 | 6.2 | 8.5 |
| Long-term government bonds | 5.5 | 5.8 | 9.2 |
| Intermediate-term government bonds | 5.3 | 5.5 | 5.7 |
| US Treasury bills | 3.7 | 3.8 | 3.1 |
| Inflation | 3.0 | 3.1 | 4.3 |

**Table 9.4** Geometric versus arithmetic average returns on US securities, 1926–2005

tells you what you actually earned per year on average, compounded annually. The arithmetic average tells you what you earned in a typical year. You should use whichever one answers the question you want answered.

A somewhat trickier question concerns forecasting the future, and there's a lot of confusion about this point among analysts and financial planners. The problem is this: if we have *estimates* of both the arithmetic and geometric average returns, then the arithmetic average is probably too high for longer periods and the geometric average is probably too low for shorter periods.

The good news is that there is a simple way of combining the two averages, which we shall call *Blume's formula*.[1] Suppose we calculated geometric and arithmetic return averages from $N$ years of data and we wish to use these averages to form a $T$-year average return forecast, $R(T)$, where $T$ is less than $N$. Here's how we do it:

$$R(T) = \left(\frac{T-1}{N-1} \times \text{Geometric average}\right) + \left(\frac{N-T}{N-1} \times \text{Arithmetic average}\right) \tag{9.2}$$

For example, suppose that from 25 years of annual returns data we calculate an arithmetic average return of 12 per cent and a geometric average return of 9 per cent. From these averages we wish to make one-year, five-year and ten-year average return forecasts. These three average return forecasts are calculated as follows:

$$R(1) = \left(\frac{1-1}{24} \times 9\%\right) + \left(\frac{25-1}{24} \times 12\%\right) = 12\%$$

$$R(5) = \left(\frac{5-1}{24} \times 9\%\right) + \left(\frac{25-5}{24} \times 12\%\right) = 11.5\%$$

$$R(10) = \left(\frac{10-1}{24} \times 9\%\right) + \left(\frac{25-10}{24} \times 12\%\right) = 10.875\%$$

Thus we see that one-year, five-year and ten-year forecasts are 12 per cent, 11.5 per cent and 10.875 per cent, respectively.

This concludes our discussion of geometric versus arithmetic averages. One last note: in the future, when we say 'average return' we mean arithmetic average unless we explicitly say otherwise.

## Summary and Conclusions

1   This chapter presented returns for a number of different asset classes. The general conclusion is that equities have outperformed bonds over most of the 20th century, though equities have also exhibited more risk.

2   The statistical measures in this chapter are necessary building blocks for the material of the next three chapters. In particular, standard deviation and variance measure the variability of the return on an individual security and on portfolios of securities. In the next chapter we shall argue that standard deviation and variance are appropriate measures of the risk of an individual security if an investor's portfolio is composed of that security only.

# onnect· Questions and Problems

1   **Returns**   What is meant by the term 'return'? What is the difference between monetary returns and percentage returns?

2   **Holding Period Returns**   In what situations would you use a holding period return or a percentage return? Are the two measures the same? Come up with an example where the holding period return gives a different figure from the percentage return.

3 **Return Statistics** Why would you wish to present return distributions? How do you think the distributions would change when you incorporated inflation into the return statistics?

4 **Risk Statistics** What do we mean by risk? In long-term investments, equities tend to give higher returns than bonds. Why then do all investors not invest in equities?

5 **Other Return Measures** What is the difference between arithmetic and geometric returns? Suppose you have invested in a company's shares for the last 10 years. Which number is more important to you, the arithmetic or geometric return?

6 **Investment Selection** Given that the Zimbabwe Industrials Index was up by over 12,000 per cent for 2007, why didn't all investors put their money in Zimbabwe?

7 **Investment Selection** Given that the Chinese stock markets were down by 46 per cent in the first six months of 2008, why did investors continue to hold shares in China? Why didn't they sell out before the market declined so sharply?

8 **Equities versus Gambling** Critically evaluate the following statement: 'Playing the stock market is like gambling; such speculative investing has no social value, other than the pleasure people get from this form of gambling.'

9 **Risk Premiums** Is it possible for the risk premium to be negative before an investment is undertaken? Can the risk premium be negative after the fact? Explain.

10 **Returns** Two years ago, General Materials' and Standard Fixtures' share prices were the same. During the first year, General Materials' share price increased by 10 per cent while Standard Fixtures' share price decreased by 10 per cent. During the second year, General Materials' share price decreased by 10 per cent and Standard Fixtures' share price increased by 10 per cent. Do these two equities have the same price today? Explain.

11 **Historical Returns** The historical returns presented in the chapter are not adjusted for inflation. What would happen to the estimated risk premium if we did account for inflation? The returns are also not adjusted for taxes. What would happen to the returns if we accounted for taxes? What would happen to the volatility?

12 **Calculating Returns** Suppose you bought an 8 per cent coupon bond one year ago for €1,200. The bond sells for €1,074 today.

(a) Assuming a €1,000 face value, what was your total euro return on this investment over the past year?

(b) What was your total nominal rate of return on this investment over the past year?

(c) If the inflation rate last year was 3 per cent, what was your total real rate of return on this investment?

13 **Calculating Returns and Variability** The returns of Diageo and GlaxoSmithKline are given below. Using these figures, calculate the average returns, the variances, and the standard deviations for Diageo and GlaxoSmithKline:

| | Returns (%) | |
| --- | --- | --- |
| **Year** | **Diageo** | **GSK** |
| 2008 | −6.7 | 3.2 |
| 2007 | 2.2 | −13.4 |
| 2006 | 18.4 | −5.1 |
| 2005 | 15.6 | 22.4 |
| 2004 | 0.5 | −0.4 |

14 **Calculating Returns and Variability** Refer to Table 9.1 in the text and look at the period from 2000 to 2007.

(a) Calculate the arithmetic average returns for each country's stock market over this period.

(b) Calculate the standard deviation of the returns for each country over this period.

15 **Calculating Returns and Variability** You have observed the following prices for Alcatel-Lucent, the French telecommunications firm, for a number of years: Jan 2003, €3.97; Jan 2004, €9.73; Jan 2005, €11.07; Jan 2006, €10.20; Jan 2007, €10.56; Jan 2008, €4.95; Jan 2009, €1.58. The company paid the following dividends: 2003–2005, nil; 2006, €0.16; 2007, €0.31; 2008, €0.09.

(a) What was the arithmetic average return on Alcatel-Lucent's shares over this period?

(b) What was the variance of Alcatel-Lucent's returns over this period? The standard deviation?

16 **Calculating Real Returns and Risk Premiums** In Problem 15, suppose the average inflation rate over this period was 4.2 per cent and the average T-bill rate over the period was 5.1 per cent.

(a) What was the average real return on Alcatel-Lucent's shares?

(b) What was the average nominal risk premium on Alcatel-Lucent's shares?

(c) What was the average real risk-free rate over this time period? What was the average real risk premium?

17 **Holding Period Return** G4S plc, the British security firm, had the following share prices: Jan 2004, £1.12; Jan 2005, £1.34; Jan 2006, £1.68; Jan 2007, £1.8825; Jan 2008, £2.18; Jan 2009, £2.07. The equity paid no dividends. What was the holding period return?

18 **Return Distributions** Refer back to Table 9.3. What range of returns would you expect to see 68 per cent of the time for large-company shares? What about 95 per cent of the time?

19 **Blume's Formula** Assume that the historical return on the stock market is a predictor of future returns. What return would you estimate for UK equities over the next year? The next 2 years? 3 years? 5 years?

20 **Arithmetic and Geometric Returns** An equity has had returns of 19 per cent, 17 per cent, 21 per cent, −8 per cent, 9 per cent, and −14 per cent over the last six years. What are its arithmetic and geometric returns?

21 **Arithmetic and Geometric Returns** An equity has had the following year-end prices and dividends:

| Year | Price (£) | Dividend (£) |
|------|-----------|--------------|
| 1 | 43.12 | – |
| 2 | 49.07 | 0.55 |
| 3 | 51.19 | 0.60 |
| 4 | 47.24 | 0.63 |
| 5 | 56.09 | 0.72 |
| 6 | 67.21 | 0.81 |

What are the arithmetic and geometric returns?

22 **Calculating Investment Returns** You bought one of Bergen Manufacturing's 8 per cent coupon bonds one year ago for NOK1,028.50. These bonds make annual payments and

mature six years from now. Suppose you decide to sell your bonds today, when the required return on the bonds is 7 per cent. If the inflation rate was 4.8 per cent over the past year, what would be your total real return on the investment?

23 **Using Return Distributions**   Suppose the returns on long-term government bonds are normally distributed. Based on the historical record for US securities, what is the approximate probability that your return on these bonds will be less than −3.5 per cent in a given year? What range of returns would you expect to see 95 per cent of the time? What range would you expect to see 99 per cent of the time?

24 **Using Return Distributions**   Assuming that the returns from holding small-company US shares are normally distributed, what is the approximate probability that your money will double in value in a single year? Triple in value?

25 **Distributions**   In the previous problem, what is the probability that the return will be less than −100 per cent? (Think.) What are the implications for the distribution of returns?

26 **Using Probability Distributions**   Suppose the returns on large-company US equities are normally distributed. Based on the historical record, use Table 22.3 (rounded to the nearest table value) in Chapter 22 to determine the probability that in any given year you will lose money by investing in US equities.

27 **Distributions**   Your investment portfolio has earned returns of 400 per cent once in the last ten years and zero per cent in eight years out of the last ten years, and has lost 90 per cent in one year. What were the average arithmetic return and standard deviation of returns for this portfolio?

28 **Inflation**   The inflation rates for the UK have been as follows: 2008, 4.0 per cent; 2007, 4.3 per cent; 2006, 3.2 per cent; 2005, 2.8 per cent; and 2004, 3.0 per cent. Calculate the average real return of Diageo and GlaxoSmithKline from question 13.

**CHALLENGE**

**29 – 30**

29 **Calculating Returns**   Go to the Yahoo! Finance website and look up the Belgian-French finance firm Dexia. Click on the *Historical Prices* link. Find the firm's closing price yesterday and its closing price exactly one year earlier. From the historical prices in Yahoo! Finance you will see the total dividend paid out in the last year. What has been the annual return on Dexia? What was the dividend yield? The capital gains yield?

30 **Using Probability Distributions**   Suppose the returns on long-term US corporate bonds and T-bills are normally distributed. Based on the historical record, use Table 22.3 (rounded to the nearest table value) in Chapter 22 to answer the following questions:

(a) What is the probability that in any given year the return on long-term corporate bonds will be greater than 10 per cent? Less than 0 per cent?

(b) What is the probability that in any given year the return on T-bills will be greater than 10 per cent? Less than 0 per cent?

(c) In 1979 the return on long-term corporate bonds was −4.18 per cent. How likely is it that this low of a return will recur at some point in the future? T-bills had a return of 10.32 per cent in this same year. How likely is it that this high of a return on T-bills will recur at some point in the future?

**MINI CASE**

# A Job at West Coast Yachts

You recently graduated from university, and your job search led you to West Coast Yachts at Kip Marina. Because you felt the company's business was seaworthy, you accepted a job offer. During your first day on the job, while you are finishing your employment paperwork, Dan Ervin, who works in Finance, stops by to inform you about the company's retirement plan.

Retirement plans are offered by many companies, and are tax-deferred savings vehicles, meaning that any deposits you make into the plan are deducted from your current pre-tax income, so no current taxes are paid on the money. For example, assume your salary will be £50,000 per year. If you contribute £3,000 to the plan, you will pay taxes on only £47,000 in income. There are also no taxes paid on any capital gains or income while you are invested in the plan, but you do pay taxes when you withdraw money at retirement. As is fairly common, the company also has a 5 per cent matched funding. This means that the company will match your contribution up to 5 per cent of your salary, but you must contribute to get the match.

The retirement plan has several options for investments, most of which are mutual funds. A mutual fund is a portfolio of assets. When you purchase shares in a mutual fund, you are actually purchasing partial ownership of the fund's assets. The return of the fund is the weighted average of the return of the assets owned by the fund, minus any expenses. The largest expense is typically the management fee, paid to the fund manager. The management fee is compensation for the manager, who makes all the investment decisions for the fund.

West Coast Yachts uses Skandla Life Assurance Company Ltd as its retirement plan administrator. Here are the investment options offered for employees:

- **Company Shares**   One option in the retirement plan is equity ownership of West Coast Yachts. The company is currently privately held. However, when you interviewed with the owner, Larissa Warren, she informed you that the company shares were expected to go public in the next three to four years. Until then, a company share price is simply set each year by the board of directors.

- **Skandla Market Index Fund**   This mutual fund tracks the FTSE 100 index. Equities in the fund are weighted exactly the same as the FTSE 100. This means that the fund return is approximately the return on the FTSE 100, minus expenses. Because an index fund purchases assets based on the compensation of the index it is following, the fund manager is not required to research stocks or make investment decisions. The result is that the fund expenses are usually low. The Skandla Index Fund charges expenses of 0.15 per cent of assets per year.

- **Skandla Small-Cap Fund**   This fund invests primarily in small-capitalization companies. The returns of the fund are therefore more volatile. The fund can also invest 10 per cent of its assets in companies based outside the United Kingdom. This fund charges 1.70 per cent in expenses.

- **Skandla Large-Company Equity Fund**   This fund invests primarily in large-capitalization companies based in the United Kingdom. The fund is managed by Evan Skandla, and has outperformed the market in six of the last eight years. The fund charges 1.50 per cent in expenses.

- **Skandla Bond Fund**   This fund invests in long-term corporate bonds issued by UK-domiciled companies. The fund is restricted to investments in bonds with an investment-grade credit rating. This fund charges 1.40 per cent in expenses.

- **Skandla Money Market Fund**   This fund invests in short-term, high-credit quality debt instruments, which include Treasury bills. The return on the money market fund is therefore only slightly higher than the return on Treasury bills. Because of the credit quality and short-term nature of the investments, there is only a very slight risk of negative return. The fund charges 0.60 per cent in expenses.

1   What advantages do the mutual funds offer compared with the company equity?

2   Assume that you invest 5 per cent of your salary and receive the full 5 per cent match from West Coast Yachts. What APR do you earn from the match? What conclusions do you draw about matching plans?

3    Assume you decide you should invest at least part of your money in large-capitalization companies based in the United Kingdom. What are the advantages and disadvantages of choosing the Skandla Large-Company Equity Fund compared with the Skandla Market Index Fund?

4    The returns on the Skandla Small-Cap Fund are the most volatile of all the mutual funds offered in the retirement plan. Why would you ever want to invest in this fund? When you examine the expenses of the mutual funds, you will notice that this fund also has the highest expenses. Does this affect your decision to invest in this fund?

5    A measure of risk-adjusted performance that is often used is the Sharpe ratio. The Sharpe ratio is calculated as the risk premium of an asset divided by its standard deviation. The standard deviation and return of the funds over the past 10 years are listed here. Calculate the Sharpe ratio for each of these funds. Assume that the expected return and standard deviation of the company equity will be 18 per cent and 70 per cent, respectively. Calculate the Sharpe ratio for the company shares. How appropriate is the Sharpe ratio for these assets? When would you use the Sharpe ratio?

|  | 10-Year annual return (%) | Standard deviation (%) |
|---|---|---|
| Skandla Market Index Fund | 11.48 | 15.82 |
| Skandla Small-Cap Fund | 16.68 | 19.64 |
| Skandla Large-Company Equity Fund | 11.85 | 15.41 |
| Skandla Bond Fund | 9.67 | 10.83 |

6    What portfolio allocation would you choose? Why? Explain your thinking carefully.

## Practical Case Study

1    **Calculating Yields**    Download the historical monthly share prices for Alcatel-Lucent from Yahoo! Finance. Find the closing share price for yesterday and for exactly two years ago. The dividends should also be listed in the monthly price series. What was the capital gains yield and dividend yield for Alcatel-Lucent equity for each of these years? Now calculate the capital gains yield and dividend yield for Alstom, the French design and infrastructure construction firm. How do the returns for these two companies compare?

2    **Calculating Average Returns**    Download the monthly adjusted prices for Deutsche Telekom AG. What is the return on the equity over the past 12 months? Now use the one-month total return and calculate the average monthly return. Is this one-twelfth of the annual return you calculated? Why or why not? What is the monthly standard deviation of Deutsche Telekom's shares over the past year?

## Relevant Accounting Standards

Now that we're moving into the realms of financial markets, accountancy standards take on less importance. However, one standard that has received a lot of attention in recent years is IAS39 *Financial Instruments: Recognition and Measurement*. This standard guides the accountant on how all financial instruments should be presented in a company's financial statements. In addition, you should also be aware of IFRS7 *Financial Instruments: Disclosure*. Visit the IASPlus website (www.iasplus.com) for more information.

# Additional Reading

The number of research papers about the financial markets would fill a whole book and more. As a result, we've had to be exceptionally selective in picking those papers that are most appropriate to the understanding and study of corporate finance. The first two papers study the US market, and look at broad relationships between returns and corporate characteristics. Fama and French (2006) show that share price returns are related to profitability and the market to book equity ratio. Lundblad (2007) reports a positive link between risk and return over a very long period.

Fama, E.F. and K.R. French (2006) 'Profitability, investment and average returns', *Journal of Financial Economics*, vol. 82, no. 3, pp. 491–518.

Lundblad, C. (2007) 'The risk return tradeoff in the long run: 1836–2003', *Journal of Financial Economics*, vol. 85, no. 1, pp. 123–150.

Another paper that the advanced reader may find interesting relates to stock market bubbles.

O'Hara, M. (2008) 'Bubbles: some perspectives (and loose talk) from history', *Review of Financial Studies*, vol. 21, no. 1, pp. 11–17.

# Endnote

1 This elegant result is due to Marshal Blume ('Unbiased estimates of long-run expected rates of return', *Journal of the American Statistical Association*, September 1974, pp. 634–638).

To help you grasp the key concepts of this chapter check out the extra resources posted on the Online Learning Centre at **www.mcgraw-hill.co.uk/textbooks/hillier**

Among other helpful resources there are PowerPoint presentations, chapter outlines, mini-cases and **Appendix 9A: The Historical Market Risk Premium: The Very Long Run.**

# Chapter 10

# Risk and Return: The Capital Asset Pricing Model

## KEY NOTATIONS

| | |
|---|---|
| $C$ | Cash flow |
| CAPM | Capital asset pricing model |
| CCAPM | Consumption capital asset pricing model |
| CML | Capital market line |
| Cov | Covariance |
| $\overline{\text{cov}}$ | Average covariance |
| $\text{Div}_t$ | Dividend at time $t$ |
| HCAPM | Human capital CAPM |
| M/B | Market-to-book ratio |
| $N$ | Number of assets; number of years |
| $n$ | Number of observations |
| P/E | Price – earnings ratio |
| $P_t$ | Price of an equity at time $t$ |
| $R$ | Return on investment |
| $\bar{R}$ | Expected or mean return |
| $R_F$ | Risk-free rate |
| $\bar{R}_F$ | Return on financial assets |
| $R_i$ | Return on an individual equity |
| $R_M$ | Return on the market |
| $\bar{R}_M$ | Expected return on the market |
| $\bar{R}_{NF}$ | Return on non-financial assets |
| $R_p$ | Expected return |
| $R_t$ | Return on investment at time $t$ |
| $r_t$ | Observed return at time $t$ |
| SD | Standard deviation |
| SML | Security market line |
| $T$ | Number of years |
| Var | Variation |
| $\overline{\text{var}}$ | Average variance |
| $X$ | Percentage of a portfolio in a particular security |
| $\beta$ | Beta |
| $\beta_c$ | Consumption beta |
| $\beta_F$ | Financial beta |
| $\beta_{NF}$ | Non-financial beta |
| $\delta$ | Fraction of total wealth invested in non-financial assets |
| $\rho$ | Correlation |
| $\sigma$ | Standard deviation |
| $\sigma^2$ | Variance |

Expected returns on equities can vary quite a bit. One important determinant is the industry in which a company operates. For example, in the UK, the FTSE-350 Construction and Materials index (representing construction and building firms such as Persimmon and Bovis) fell by 30 per cent in 2008, whereas the FTSE-350 Mining index (including firms such as Antofagasta and BHP Billiton) grew by 18 per cent.

These estimates raise some obvious questions. First, why do industry returns differ so much, and how are these specific numbers calculated? Also, does the higher return offered by mining companies mean that investors should prefer these to, say, the banking sector? As we shall see in this chapter, the answers to these questions form the basis of our modern understanding of risk and return.

## 10.1 Individual Securities

In the first part of Chapter 10 we shall examine the characteristics of individual securities. In particular, we shall discuss:

- *Expected return*: This is the return that an individual expects a security to earn over the next period. Of course, because this is only an expectation, the actual return may be either higher or lower. An individual's expectation may simply be the average return per period a security has earned in the past. Alternatively, it may be based on a detailed analysis of a firm's prospects, on some computer-based model, or on special (or inside) information.

- *Variance and standard deviation*: There are many ways to assess the volatility of a security's return. One of the most common is variance, which is a measure of the squared deviations of a security's return from its expected return. Standard deviation is the square root of the variance.

- *Covariance and correlation*: Returns on individual securities are related to one another. Covariance is a statistic measuring the interrelationship between two securities. Alternatively, this relationship can be restated in terms of the correlation between the two securities. Covariance and correlation are building blocks to an understanding of the beta coefficient.

## 10.2 Expected Return, Variance, and Covariance

### Expected Return and Variance

Suppose financial analysts believe that there are four equally likely states of the economy: depression, recession, normal, and boom. The returns on the Supertech Company are expected to follow the economy closely, whereas the returns on the Slowpoke Company are not. The return predictions are as follows:

|  | Supertech returns, $R_{At}$ (%) | Slowpoke returns, $R_{Bt}$ (%) |
|---|---|---|
| Depression | −20 | 5 |
| Recession | 10 | 20 |
| Normal | 30 | −12 |
| Boom | 50 | 9 |

Variance can be calculated in four steps. An additional step is needed to calculate standard deviation. (The calculations are presented in Table 10.1.) The steps are these:

1  Calculate the expected return:

**Supertech**

$$\frac{-0.20 + 0.10 + 0.30 + 0.50}{4} = 0.175 = 17.5\% = \bar{R}_A$$

**Slowpoke**

$$\frac{0.05 + 0.20 - 0.12 + 0.09}{4} = 0.055 = 5.5\% = \bar{R}_B$$

**TABLE 10.1**

| (1) State of economy | (2) Rate of return | (3) Deviation from expected return | (4) Squared value of deviation |
|---|---|---|---|
| **Supertech (Expected return = 0.175)** | | | |
| | $R_{At}$ | $(R_{At} - \bar{R}_A)$ | $(R_{At} - \bar{R}_A)^2$ |
| Depression | −0.20 | −0.375 $(= -0.20 - 0.175)$ | 0.140625 $[= (-0.375)^2]$ |
| Recession | 0.10 | −0.075 | 0.005625 |
| Normal | 0.30 | 0.125 | 0.015625 |
| Boom | 0.50 | 0.325 | 0.105625 |
| | | | 0.267500 |
| **Slowpoke (Expected return = 0.055)** | | | |
| | $R_{Bt}$ | $(R_{Bt} - \bar{R}_B)$ | $(R_{Bt} - \bar{R}_B)^2$ |
| Depression | 0.05 | −0.005 $(= 0.05 - 0.055)$ | 0.000025 $[= (-0.005)^2]$ |
| Recession | 0.20 | 0.145 | 0.021025 |
| Normal | −0.12 | −0.175 | 0.030625 |
| Boom | 0.09 | 0.035 | 0.001225 |
| | | | 0.052900 |

**Table 10.1** Calculating variance and standard deviation

2   For each company, calculate the deviation of each possible return from the company's expected return given previously. This is presented in the third column of Table 10.1.

3   The deviations we have calculated are indications of the dispersion of returns. However, because some are positive and some are negative, it is difficult to work with them in this form. For example, if we were to simply add up all the deviations for a single company, we would get zero as the sum.

   To make the deviations more meaningful, we multiply each one by itself. Now all the numbers are positive, implying that their sum must be positive as well. The squared deviations are presented in the last column of Table 10.1.

4   For each company, calculate the average squared deviation, which is the variance:[1]

**Supertech**

$$\frac{0.140625 + 0.005625 + 0.015625 + 0.105625}{4} = 0.066875$$

**Slowpoke**

$$\frac{0.000025 + 0.021025 + 0.030625 + 0.001225}{4} = 0.013225$$

Thus the variance of Supertech is 0.066875, and the variance of Slowpoke is 0.013225.

5   Calculate standard deviation by taking the square root of the variance:

**Supertech**

$$\sqrt{0.066875} = 0.2586 = 25.86\%$$

**Slowpoke**

$$\sqrt{0.013225} = 0.1150 = 11.50\%$$

Algebraically, the formula for variance can be expressed as

$$\text{Var}(R) = \text{Expected value of } (R - \bar{R})^2$$

where $\bar{R}$ is the security's expected return and $R$ is the actual return.

A look at the four-step calculation for variance makes it clear why it is a measure of the spread of the sample of returns. For each observation we square the difference between the actual return and the expected return. We then take an average of these squared differences. Squaring the differences makes them all positive. If we used the differences between each return and the expected return and then averaged these differences we would get zero, because the returns that were above the mean would cancel the ones below.

However, because the variance is still expressed in squared terms, it is difficult to interpret. Standard deviation has a much simpler interpretation, which was provided in Section 9.5. Standard deviation is simply the square root of the variance. The general formula for the standard deviation is

$$\text{SD}(R) = \sqrt{\text{Var}(R)}$$

## Covariance and Correlation

Variance and standard deviation measure the variability of individual securities. We now wish to measure the relationship between the return on one security and the return on another. Enter covariance and correlation.

   Covariance and correlation measure how two random variables are related. We explain these terms by extending the Supertech and Slowpoke example.

## Calculating Covariance and Correlation

EXAMPLE
10.1

We have already determined the expected returns and standard deviations for both Supertech and Slowpoke. (The expected returns are 0.175 and 0.055 for Supertech and Slowpoke, respectively. The standard deviations are 0.2586 and 0.1150, respectively.) In addition, we calculated the deviation of each possible return from the expected return for each firm. Using these data, we can calculate covariance in two steps. An extra step is needed to calculate correlation.

1   For each state of the economy, multiply Supertech's deviation from its expected return and Slowpoke's deviation from its expected return together. For example, Supertech's rate of return in a depression is −0.20, which is −0.375 (= −0.20 − 0.175) from its expected return. Slowpoke's rate of return in a depression is 0.05, which is −0.005 (= 0.05 − 0.055) from its expected return. Multiplying the two deviations together yields 0.001875 [= (−0.375) × (−0.005)]. The actual calculations are given in the last column of Table 10.2. This procedure can be written algebraically as

$$(R_{At} - \bar{R}_A) \times (R_{Bt} - \bar{R}_B) \tag{10.1}$$

where $R_{At}$ and $R_{Bt}$ are the returns on Supertech and Slowpoke in state $t$. $\bar{R}_A$ and $\bar{R}_B$ are the expected returns on the two securities.

$$\sigma_{AB} = \text{Cov}(R_A, R_B) = \frac{-0.0195}{4} = -0.004875$$

$$\rho_{AB} = \text{Corr}(R_A, R_B) = \frac{\text{Cov}(R_A, R_B)}{\text{SD}(R_A) \times \text{SD}(R_B)} = \frac{-0.004875}{0.2586 \times 0.1150} = -0.1639$$

| State of economy | Rate of return of Supertech, $R_{At}$ | Deviation from expected return, $(R_{At} - \bar{R}_A)$ (Expected return = 0.175) | Rate of return of Slowpoke, $R_{Bt}$ | Deviation from expected return, $(R_{Bt} - \bar{R}_B)$ (Expected return = 0.055) | Product of deviations, $(R_{At} - \bar{R}_A) \times (R_{Bt} - \bar{R}_B)$ |
|---|---|---|---|---|---|
| Depression | −0.20 | −0.375 (= −0.20 − 0.175) | 0.05 | −0.005 (= 0.05 − 0.055) | 0.001875 (= −0.375 × −0.005) |
| Recession | 0.10 | −0.075 | 0.20 | 0.145 | −0.010875 (= −0.075 × 0.145) |
| Normal | 0.30 | 0.125 | −0.12 | −0.175 | −0.021875 (= 0.125 × −0.175) |
| Boom | 0.50 | 0.325 | 0.09 | 0.035 | 0.011375 (= 0.325 × 0.035) |
|  | 0.70 |  | 0.22 |  | −0.0195 |

**Table 10.2** Calculating covariance and correlation

2   Calculate the average value of the four states in the last column. This average is the covariance. That is,[2]

$$\sigma_{AB} = \text{Cov}(R_A, R_B) = \frac{-0.0195}{4} = -0.004875$$

Note that we represent the covariance between Supertech and Slowpoke as either $\text{Cov}(R_A, R_B)$ or $\sigma_{AB}$. Equation (10.1) illustrates the intuition of covariance. Suppose Supertech's return is generally above its average when Slowpoke's return is above its average, and Supertech's return is generally below its average when Slowpoke's return is below its average. This shows a positive dependence or a positive relationship between the two returns. Note that the term in Eq. (10.1) will be *positive* in any state where both returns are *above* their averages. In addition, (10.1) will still be *positive* in any state where both terms are *below* their averages. Thus a positive relationship between the two returns will give rise to a positive value for covariance.

Conversely, suppose Supertech's return is generally above its average when Slowpoke's return is below its average, and Supertech's return is generally below its average when Slowpoke's return is above its average. This demonstrates a negative dependence or a negative relationship between the two returns. Note that the term in Eq. (10.1) will be *negative* in any state where one return is above its average and the other return is below its average. Thus a negative relationship between the two returns will give rise to a negative value for covariance.

Finally, suppose there is no relationship between the two returns. In this case, knowing whether the return on Supertech is above or below its expected return tells us nothing about the return on Slowpoke. In the covariance formula, then, there will be no tendency for the deviations to be positive or negative together. On average, they will tend to offset each other and cancel out, making the covariance zero.

Of course, even if the two returns are unrelated to each other, the covariance formula will not equal zero exactly in any actual history. This is due to sampling error; randomness alone will make the calculation positive or negative. But for a historical sample that is long enough, if the two returns are not related to each other, we should expect the covariance to come close to zero.

The covariance formula seems to capture what we are looking for. If the two returns are positively related to each other, they will have a positive covariance, and if they are negatively related to each other, the covariance will be negative. Last, and very important, if they are unrelated, the covariance should be zero.

The formula for covariance can be written algebraically as

$$\sigma_{AB} = \text{Cov}(R_A, R_B)$$
$$= \text{Expected value of } [(R_A - \bar{R}_A) \times (R_B - \bar{R}_B)]$$

where $\bar{R}_A$ and $\bar{R}_B$ are the expected returns for the two securities, and $R_A$ and $R_B$ are the actual returns. The ordering of the two variables is unimportant. That is, the covariance of $A$ with $B$ is equal to the covariance of $B$ with $A$. This can be stated more formally as $\text{Cov}(R_A, R_B) = \text{Cov}(R_B, R_A)$ or $\sigma_{AB} = \sigma_{BA}$.

The covariance we calculated is −0.004875. A negative number like this implies that the return on one security is likely to be above its average when the return on the other security is below its average, and vice versa. However, the size of the number is difficult to interpret. Like the variance figure, the covariance is in squared deviation units. Until we can put it in perspective, we don't know what to make of it.

We solve the problem by computing the correlation.

3   To calculate the correlation, divide the covariance by the standard deviations of both of the two securities. For our example, we have

$$\rho_{AB} = \text{Corr}(R_A, R_B) = \frac{\text{Cov}(R_A, R_B)}{\sigma_A \times \sigma_B}$$
$$= \frac{-0.004875}{0.2586 \times 0.1150} \tag{10.2}$$
$$= -0.1639$$

where $\sigma_A$ and $\sigma_B$ are the standard deviations of Supertech and Slowpoke, respectively. Note that we represent the correlation between Supertech and Slowpoke as either as $\text{Corr}(R_A, R_B)$ or $\rho_{AB}$. As with covariance, the ordering of the two variables is unimportant. That is, the correlation of $A$ with $B$ is equal to the correlation of $B$ with $A$. More formally, $\text{Corr}(R_A, R_B) = \text{Corr}(R_B, R_A)$ or $\rho_{AB} = \rho_{BA}$.

Because the standard deviation is always positive, the sign of the correlation between two variables must be the same as that of the covariance between the two variables. If the correlation is positive, we say that the variables are *positively correlated*; if it is negative, we say that they are *negatively correlated*; and if it is zero, we say that they are *uncorrelated*. Furthermore, it can be proved that the correlation is always between +1 and −1. This is due to the standardizing procedure of dividing by the two standard deviations.

We can compare the correlation between different *pairs* of securities. For example, it turns out that the correlation between Persimmon and Bovis (both construction companies) is much higher than the correlation between Persimmon and Antofagasta (a pharmaceutical firm). Hence we can state that the first pair of securities is more interrelated than the second pair.

Figure 10.1 shows the three benchmark cases for two assets, *A* and *B*. The figure shows two assets with return correlations of +1, −1 and 0. This implies perfect positive correlation, perfect negative correlation and no correlation, respectively. The graphs in the figure plot the separate returns on the two securities through time.

**Figure 10.1** Examples of different correlation coefficients: graphs plotting the separate returns on two securities through time

## 10.3 The Return and Risk for Portfolios

Suppose an investor has estimates of the expected returns and standard deviations on individual securities and the correlations between securities. How does the investor choose the best combination or **portfolio** of securities to hold? Obviously, the investor would like a portfolio with a high expected return and a low standard deviation of return. It is therefore worth while to consider:

1   The relationship between the expected return on individual securities and the expected return on a portfolio made up of these securities.

2   The relationship between the standard deviations of individual securities, the correlations between these securities, and the standard deviation of a portfolio made up of these securities.

To analyse these two relationships, we shall use the same example of Supertech and Slowpoke. The relevant calculations follow.

## The Expected Return on a Portfolio

The formula for expected return on a portfolio is very simple:

**The expected return on a portfolio is simply a weighted average of the expected returns on the individual securities.**

| Relevant data from example of Supertech and Slowpoke | | |
|---|---|---|
| **Item** | **Symbol** | **Value** |
| Expected return on Supertech | $\bar{R}_{\text{Super}}$ | 0.175 = 17.5% |
| Expected return on Slowpoke | $\bar{R}_{\text{Slow}}$ | 0.055 = 5.5% |
| Variance of Supertech | $\sigma^2_{\text{Super}}$ | 0.066875 |
| Variance of Slowpoke | $\sigma^2_{\text{Slow}}$ | 0.013225 |
| Standard deviation of Supertech | $\sigma_{\text{Super}}$ | 0.2586 = 25.86% |
| Standard deviation of Slowpoke | $\sigma_{\text{Slow}}$ | 0.1150 = 11.50% |
| Covariance between Supertech and Slowpoke | $\sigma_{\text{Super, Slow}}$ | −0.004875 |
| Correlation between Supertech and Slowpoke | $\rho_{\text{Super, Slow}}$ | −0.1639 |

## Portfolio Expected Returns

EXAMPLE
**10.2**

Consider Supertech and Slowpoke. From our earlier calculations, we find that the expected returns on these two securities are 17.5 per cent and 5.5 per cent, respectively.

The expected return on a portfolio of these two securities alone can be written as

$$\text{Expected return on portfolio} = X_{\text{Super}}\,(17.5\%) + X_{\text{Slow}}\,(5.5\%) = \bar{R}_{\text{p}}$$

where $X_{\text{Super}}$ is the percentage of the portfolio in Supertech, and $X_{\text{Slow}}$ is the percentage of the portfolio in Slowpoke. If the investor with £100 invests £60 in Supertech and £40 in Slowpoke, the expected return on the portfolio can be written as

$$\text{Expected return on portfolio} = (0.6 \times 17.5\%) + (0.4 \times 5.5\%) = 12.7\%$$

Algebraically, we can write

$$\text{Expected return on portfolio} = X_A\bar{R}_A + X_B\bar{R}_B = \bar{R}_{\text{p}} \tag{10.3}$$

where $X_A$ and $X_B$ are the proportions of the total portfolio in the assets $A$ and $B$, respectively. (Because our investor can invest in only two securities, $X_A + X_B$ must equal 1, or 100 per cent.) $\bar{R}_A$ and $\bar{R}_B$ are the expected returns on the two securities.

Now consider two securities, each with an expected return of 10 per cent. The expected return on a portfolio composed of these two securities must be 10 per cent, regardless of the proportions of the two securities held. This result may seem obvious at this point, but it will become important later. The result implies that you do not reduce or *dissipate* your expected return by investing in a number of securities. Rather, the expected return on your portfolio is simply a weighted average of the expected returns on the individual assets in the portfolio.

## Variance and Standard Deviation of a Portfolio

**The Variance**   The formula for the variance of a portfolio composed of two securities, $A$ and $B$, is

The variance of the portfolio:

$$\text{Var(portfolio)} = X_A^2 \sigma_A^2 + 2X_A X_B \sigma_{A,B} + X_B^2 \sigma_B^2$$

Note that there are three terms on the right-hand side of the equation. The first term involves the variance of $A$, $(\sigma_A^2)$, the second term involves the covariance between the two securities, $(\sigma_{A,B})$, and the third term involves the variance of $B$, $(\sigma_B^2)$. (As stated earlier in this chapter, $\sigma_{A,B} = \sigma_{B,A}$. That is, the ordering of the variables is not relevant when we are expressing the covariance between two securities.)

The formula indicates an important point. The variance of a portfolio depends on both the variances of the individual securities and the covariance between the two securities. The variance of a security measures the variability of an individual security's return. Covariance measures the relationship between the two securities. For given variances of the individual securities, a positive relationship or covariance between the two securities increases the variance of the entire portfolio. A negative relationship or covariance between the two securities decreases the variance of the entire portfolio. This important result seems to square with common sense. If one of your securities tends to go up when the other goes down, or vice versa, your two securities are offsetting each other. You are achieving what we call a *hedge* in finance, and the risk of your entire portfolio will be low. However, if both your securities rise and fall together, you are not hedging at all. Hence the risk of your entire portfolio will be higher.

The variance formula for our two securities, Super and Slow, is

$$\text{Var(portfolio)} = X_{\text{Super}}^2 \sigma_{\text{Super}}^2 + 2X_{\text{Super}} X_{\text{Slow}} \sigma_{\text{Super,Slow}} + X_{\text{Slow}}^2 \sigma_{\text{Slow}}^2 \qquad \textbf{(10.4)}$$

Given our earlier assumption that an individual with £100 invests £60 in Supertech and £40 in Slowpoke, $X_{\text{Super}} = 0.6$ and $X_{\text{Slow}} = 0.4$. Using this assumption and the relevant data from our previous calculations, the variance of the portfolio is

$$0.023851 = 0.36 \times 0.066875 + 2 \times [0.6 \times 0.4 \times (-0.004875)] + 0.16 \times 0.013225 \qquad \textbf{(10.4$'$)}$$

**The Matrix Approach**   Alternatively, Eq. (10.4) can be expressed in the following matrix format:

|  | **Supertech** | **Slowpoke** |
|---|---|---|
| **Supertech** | $X_{\text{Super}}^2 \sigma_{\text{Super}}^2$ <br> $0.024075 = 0.36 \times 0.066875$ | $X_{\text{Super}} X_{\text{Slow}} \sigma_{\text{Super,Slow}}$ <br> $-0.00117 = 0.6 \times 0.4 \times (-0.004875)$ |
| **Slowpoke** | $X_{\text{Super}} X_{\text{Slow}} \sigma_{\text{Super,Slow}}$ <br> $-0.00117 = 0.6 \times 0.4 \times (-0.004875)$ | $X_{\text{Slow}}^2 \sigma_{\text{Slow}}^2$ <br> $0.002116 = 0.16 \times 0.013225$ |

There are four boxes in the matrix. We can add the terms in the boxes to obtain Eq. (10.4), the variance of a portfolio composed of the two securities. The term in the upper left corner involves the variance of Supertech. The term in the lower right corner involves the variance of Slowpoke. The other two boxes contain the term involving the covariance. These two boxes are identical, indicating why the covariance term is multiplied by 2 in Eq. (10.4).

At this point, students often find the box approach to be more confusing than Eq. (10.4). However, the box approach is easily generalized to more than two securities, a task we perform later in this chapter.

**Standard Deviation of a Portfolio**   Given Eq. (10.4′), we can now determine the standard deviation of the portfolio's return. This is

$$\begin{aligned} \sigma_p &= \text{SD(portfolio)} \\ &= \sqrt{\text{Var(portfolio)}} = \sqrt{0.023851} \\ &= 0.1544 = 15.44\% \end{aligned} \tag{10.5}$$

The interpretation of the standard deviation of the portfolio is the same as the interpretation of the standard deviation of an individual security. The expected return on our portfolio is 12.7 per cent. A return of −2.74 per cent (= 12.7% − 15.44%) is one standard deviation below the mean, and a return of 28.14 per cent (= 12.7% + 15.44%) is one standard deviation above the mean. If the return on the portfolio is normally distributed, a return between −2.74 per cent and +28.14 per cent occurs about 68 per cent of the time.[3]

**The Diversification Effect**   It is instructive to compare the standard deviation of the portfolio with the standard deviation of the individual securities. The weighted average of the standard deviations of the individual securities is

$$\text{Weighted average of standard deviations} = X_{\text{Super}}\sigma_{\text{Super}} + X_{\text{Slow}}\sigma_{\text{Slow}} \tag{10.6}$$
$$0.2012 = 0.6 \times 0.2586 + 0.4 \times 0.115$$

One of the most important results in this chapter concerns the difference between Eqs (10.5) and (10.6). In our example, the standard deviation of the portfolio is *less* than a weighted average of the standard deviations of the individual securities.

We pointed out earlier that the expected return on the portfolio is a weighted average of the expected returns on the individual securities. Thus we get a different type of result for the standard deviation of a portfolio than we do for the expected return on a portfolio.

It is generally argued that our result for the standard deviation of a portfolio is due to diversification. For example, Supertech and Slowpoke are slightly negatively correlated ($\rho$ = −0.1639). Supertech's return is likely to be a little below average if Slowpoke's return is above average. Similarly, Supertech's return is likely to be a little above average if Slowpoke's return is below average. Thus the standard deviation of a portfolio composed of the two securities is less than a weighted average of the standard deviations of the two securities.

Our example has negative correlation. Clearly, there will be less benefit from diversification if the two securities exhibit positive correlation. How high must the positive correlation be before all diversification benefits vanish?

To answer this question, let us rewrite Eq. (10.4) in terms of correlation rather than covariance. The covariance can be rewritten as[4]

$$\sigma_{\text{Super,Slow}} = \rho_{\text{Super,Slow}}\sigma_{\text{Super}}\sigma_{\text{Slow}} \tag{10.7}$$

This formula states that the covariance between any two securities is simply the correlation between the two securities multiplied by the standard deviations of each. In other words, covariance incorporates both (1) the correlation between the two assets and (2) the variability of each of the two securities as measured by standard deviation.

From our calculations earlier in this chapter we know that the correlation between the two securities is −0.1639. Given the variances used in Eq. (10.4′), the standard deviations are 0.2586 and 0.115 for Supertech and Slowpoke, respectively. Thus the variance of a portfolio can be expressed as follows:

Variance of the portfolio's return:

$$= X_{\text{Super}}^2\sigma_{\text{Super}}^2 + 2X_{\text{Super}}X_{\text{Slow}}\rho_{\text{Super,Slow}}\sigma_{\text{Super}}\sigma_{\text{Slow}} + X_{\text{Slow}}^2\sigma_{\text{Slow}}^2$$
$$0.023851 = 0.36 \times 0.066875 + 2 \times 0.6 \times 0.4 \times (-0.1639) \times 0.2586 \times 0.115 \tag{10.8}$$
$$+ 0.16 \times 0.013225$$

The middle term on the right side is now written in terms of correlation, $\rho$, not covariance.

Suppose $\rho_{Super,\ Slow} = 1$, the highest possible value for correlation. Assume all the other parameters in the example are the same. The variance of the portfolio is

Variance of the portfolio's return:

$$
\begin{aligned}
&= 0.040466 \\
&= 0.36 \times 0.066875 + 2 \times (0.6 \times 0.4 \times 1 \times 0.2586 \times 0.115) \\
&\quad + 0.16 \times 0.013225
\end{aligned}
$$

The standard deviation is

$$
\text{Standard deviation of portfolio's return} = \sqrt{0.040466} = 0.2012 = 20.12\% \qquad (10.9)
$$

Note that Eqs (10.9) and (10.6) are equal. That is, the standard deviation of a portfolio's return is equal to the weighted average of the standard deviations of the individual returns when $\rho = 1$. Inspection of Eq. (10.8) indicates that the variance and hence the standard deviation of the portfolio must fall as the correlation drops below 1. This leads to the following result:

**As long as $\rho < 1$, the standard deviation of a portfolio of two securities is *less* than the weighted average of the standard deviations of the individual securities.**

In other words, the diversification effect applies as long as there is less than perfect correlation (as long as $\rho < 1$). Thus, our Supertech–Slowpoke example is a case of overkill. We illustrated diversification by an example with negative correlation. We could have illustrated diversification by an example with positive correlation – as long as it was not *perfect* positive correlation.

**An Extension to Many Assets**    The preceding insight can be extended to the case of many assets. That is, as long as correlations between pairs of securities are less than 1, the standard deviation of a portfolio of many assets is less than the weighted average of the standard deviations of the individual securities.

Now consider Table 10.3, which shows the standard deviation of the Dow Jones Euro Stoxx 50, (a portfolio of the 50 largest companies in the Eurozone) and the standard deviations of some of the individual securities listed in the index over a recent five-year period. Note that all of the individual securities in the table have higher standard deviations than that of the

**TABLE 10.3**

| Asset | Standard deviation (%) |
|---|---|
| DJ Euro Stoxx 50 Index | 13.10 |
| Carrefour SA | 41.08 |
| Fortis | 65.55 |
| Vinci SA | 35.17 |
| Intesa SanPaolo | 31.53 |
| Saint Gobain | 48.80 |
| Telecom Italia | 32.22 |
| Arcelormittal | 41.07 |
| Credit Agricole | 57.92 |
| Adidas | 29.47 |

*Source: Yahoo! Finance*, http://uk.finance.yahoo.com

**Table 10.3** Standard deviations for Dow Jones Euro Stoxx 50 Index and for selected equities in the Index

index. In general, the standard deviations of most of the individual securities in an index will be above the standard deviation of the index itself, though a few of the securities could have lower standard deviations than that of the index.

As long as the correlations between pairs of securities are less than 1, the standard deviation of an index is less than the weighted average of the standard deviations of the individual securities within the index.

## 10.4 The Efficient Set for Two Assets

Our results for expected returns and standard deviations are graphed in Fig. 10.2. The figure shows a dot labelled Slowpoke and a dot labelled Supertech. Each dot represents both the expected return and the standard deviation for an individual security. As can be seen, Supertech has both a higher expected return and a higher standard deviation.

The box or '□' in the graph represents a portfolio with 60 per cent invested in Supertech and 40 per cent invested in Slowpoke. You will recall that we previously calculated both the expected return and the standard deviation for this portfolio.

The choice of 60 per cent in Supertech and 40 per cent in Slowpoke is just one of an infinite number of portfolios that can be created. The set of portfolios is sketched by the curved line in Fig. 10.3.

Consider portfolio 1. This is a portfolio composed of 90 per cent Slowpoke and 10 per cent Supertech. Because it is weighted so heavily towards Slowpoke, it appears close to the Slowpoke point on the graph. Portfolio 2 is higher on the curve because it is composed of 50 per cent Slowpoke and 50 per cent Supertech. Portfolio 3 is close to the Supertech point on the graph because it is composed of 90 per cent Supertech and 10 per cent Slowpoke.

There are a few important points concerning this graph:

1 We argued that the diversification effect occurs whenever the correlation between the two securities is below 1. The correlation between Supertech and Slowpoke is −0.1639. The diversification effect can be illustrated by comparison with the straight line between the Supertech point and the Slowpoke point. The straight line represents points that would have been generated had the correlation coefficient between the two securities been 1. The diversification effect is illustrated in the figure because the curved line is always to the left of the straight line. Consider point 1'. This represents a portfolio composed of 90 per cent in Slowpoke and 10 per cent in Supertech *if* the correlation between the two were exactly 1. We argue that there is no diversification effect if $\rho = 1$. However, the diversification

**Figure 10.2** Expected returns and standard deviations for Supertech, Slowpoke, and a portfolio composed of 60 per cent in Supertech and 40 per cent in Slowpoke

effect applies to the curved line because point 1 has the same expected return as point 1' but has a lower standard deviation. (Points 2' and 3' are omitted to reduce the clutter of Fig. 10.3.)

Though the straight line and the curved line are both represented in Fig. 10.3, they do not simultaneously exist in the same world. *Either* $\rho = -0.1639$ and the curve exists *or* $\rho = 1$ and the straight line exists. In other words, though an investor can choose between different points on the curve if $\rho = -0.1639$, she cannot choose between points on the curve and points on the straight line.

2   The point MV represents the minimum variance portfolio. This is the portfolio with the lowest possible variance. By definition, this portfolio must also have the lowest possible standard deviation. (The term *minimum variance portfolio* is standard in the literature, and we shall use that term. Perhaps minimum standard deviation would actually be better because standard deviation, not variance, is measured on the horizontal axis of Fig. 10.3.)

3   An individual contemplating an investment in a portfolio of Slowpoke and Supertech faces an opportunity set or feasible set represented by the curved line in Fig. 10.3. That is, he can achieve any point on the curve by selecting the appropriate mix between the two securities. He cannot achieve any point above the curve because he cannot increase the return on the individual securities, decrease the standard deviations of the securities, or decrease the correlation between the two securities. Neither can he achieve points below the curve because he cannot lower the returns on the individual securities, increase the standard deviations of the securities, or increase the correlation. (Of course, he would not want to achieve points below the curve, even if he were able to do so.)

Were he relatively tolerant of risk, he might choose portfolio 3. (In fact, he could even choose the end point by investing all his money in Supertech.) An investor with less tolerance for risk might choose portfolio 2. An investor wanting as little risk as possible would choose MV, the portfolio with minimum variance or minimum standard deviation.

**FIGURE 10.3**

Portfolio 1 is composed of 90 per cent Slowpoke and 10 per cent Supertech ($\rho = -0.1639$).
Portfolio 2 is composed of 50 per cent Slowpoke and 50 per cent Supertech ($\rho = -0.1639$).
Portfolio 3 is composed of 10 per cent Slowpoke and 90 per cent Supertech ($\rho = -0.1639$).
Portfolio 1' is composed of 90 per cent Slowpoke and 10 per cent Supertech ($\rho = 1$).
Point MV denotes the minimum variance portfolio. This is the portfolio with the lowest possible variance. By definition, the same portfolio must also have the lowest possible standard deviation.

**Figure 10.3** Set of portfolios composed of holdings in Supertech and Slowpoke (correlation between the two securities is −0.1639)

FIGURE

**10.4**

Each curve represents a different correlation: the lower the correlation, the more bend in the curve.

**Figure 10.4** Opportunity sets composed of holdings in Supertech and Slowpoke

4   Note that the curve is backward bending between the Slowpoke point and MV. This indicates that, for a portion of the feasible set, standard deviation actually decreases as we increase expected return. Students frequently ask, 'How can an increase in the proportion of the risky security, Supertech, lead to a reduction in the risk of the portfolio?'

This surprising finding is due to the diversification effect. The returns on the two securities are negatively correlated with each other. One security tends to go up when the other goes down, and vice versa. Thus an addition of a small amount of Supertech acts as a hedge to a portfolio composed only of Slowpoke. The risk of the portfolio is reduced, implying backward bending. Actually, backward bending always occurs if $\rho > 0$. It may or may not occur when $\rho \le 0$. Of course, the curve bends backward only for a portion of its length. As we continue to increase the percentage of Supertech in the portfolio, the high standard deviation of this security eventually causes the standard deviation of the entire portfolio to rise.

5   No investor would want to hold a portfolio with an expected return below that of the minimum variance portfolio. For example, no investor would choose portfolio 1. This portfolio has less expected return but more standard deviation than the minimum variance portfolio has. We say that portfolios such as portfolio 1 are *dominated* by the minimum variance portfolio. Though the entire curve from Slowpoke to Supertech is called the *feasible set*, investors consider only the curve from MV to Supertech. Hence the curve from MV to Supertech is called the efficient set or the efficient frontier.

Figure 10.3 represents the opportunity set where $\rho = -0.1639$. It is worth while to examine Fig. 10.4, which shows different curves for different correlations. As can be seen, the lower the correlation, the more bend there is in the curve. This indicates that the diversification effect rises as $\rho$ declines. The greatest bend occurs in the limiting case where $\rho = -1$. This is perfect negative correlation. While this extreme case where $\rho = -1$ seems to fascinate students, it has little practical importance. Most pairs of securities exhibit positive correlation. Strong negative correlations, let alone perfect negative correlation, are unlikely occurrences indeed.[5]

Note that there is only one correlation between a pair of securities. We stated earlier that the correlation between Slowpoke and Supertech is $-0.1639$. Thus the curve in Fig. 10.4 representing this correlation is the correct one, and the other curves should be viewed as merely hypothetical.

The graphs we examined are not mere intellectual curiosities. Rather, efficient sets can easily be calculated in the real world. As mentioned earlier, data on returns, standard deviations and correlations are generally taken from past observations, though subjective notions can be used to determine the values of these parameters as well. Once the parameters have

FIGURE

10.5

**Figure 10.5** Return/risk trade-off for world stocks: portfolio of US and non-US stocks

been determined, any one of a whole host of software packages can be purchased to generate an efficient set. However, the choice of the preferred portfolio within the efficient set is up to you. As with other important decisions, such as what job to choose, what house or car to buy, and how much time to allocate to this book, there is no computer program to choose the preferred portfolio.

An efficient set can also be generated where the two individual assets are portfolios themselves. For example, the two assets in Fig. 10.5 are a diversified portfolio of US equities and a diversified portfolio of non-US equities. Expected returns, standard deviations and the correlation coefficient were calculated over the recent past. No subjectivity entered the analysis. The US equity portfolio with a standard deviation of about 0.173 is less risky than the non-US equity portfolio, which has a standard deviation of about 0.222. However, combining a small percentage of the non-US equity portfolio with the US portfolio actually reduces risk, as can be seen by the backward-bending nature of the curve. In other words, the diversification benefits from combining two different portfolios more than offset the introduction of a riskier set of equities into our holdings. The minimum variance portfolio occurs with about 80 per cent of our funds in US equities and about 20 per cent in non-US equities. Addition of non-US securities beyond this point increases the risk of the entire portfolio.

A point worth pondering concerns the potential pitfalls of using only past data to estimate future returns. The stock markets of many countries, especially China and India, have had phenomenal growth in the past few years. Thus a graph like Fig. 10.5 makes a large investment in these foreign markets seem attractive. However, because abnormally high returns cannot be sustained for ever, some subjectivity must be used in forecasting future expected returns. A good example concerns the Chinese and Indian stock markets. At the beginning of 2008, if you used historical returns as an estimate of future returns, both countries would have had a heavy weighting in your investment portfolio. However, as it turned out, China and India were two of the world's worst-performing stock markets in 2008!

## 10.5   The Efficient Set for Many Securities

The previous discussion concerned two securities. We found that a simple curve sketched out all the possible portfolios. Because investors generally hold more than two securities, we should look at the same graph when more than two securities are held. The shaded area in Fig. 10.6

FIGURE

**10.6**

**Figure 10.6** The feasible set of portfolios constructed from many securities

represents the opportunity set or feasible set when many securities are considered. The shaded area represents all the possible combinations of expected return and standard deviation for a portfolio. For example, in a universe of 100 securities, point 1 might represent a portfolio of, say, 40 securities. Point 2 might represent a portfolio of 80 securities. Point 3 might represent a different set of 80 securities, or the same 80 securities held in different proportions, or something else. Obviously, the combinations are virtually endless. However, note that all possible combinations fit into a confined region. No security or combination of securities can fall outside the shaded region. That is, no one can choose a portfolio with an expected return above that given by the shaded region. Furthermore, no one can choose a portfolio with a standard deviation below that given in the shaded area. Perhaps more surprisingly, no one can choose an expected return below that given in the curve. In other words, the capital markets actually prevent a self-destructive person from taking on a guaranteed loss.[6]

So far, Fig. 10.6 is different from the earlier graphs. When only two securities are involved, all the combinations lie on a single curve. Conversely, with many securities the combinations cover an entire area. However, notice that an individual will want to be somewhere on the upper edge between MV and *X*. The upper edge, which we indicate in Fig. 10.6 by a thick curve, is called the *efficient set*. Any point below the efficient set would receive less expected return and the same standard deviation as a point on the efficient set. For example, consider *R* on the efficient set and *W* directly below it. If *W* contains the risk level you desire, you should choose *R* instead to receive a higher expected return.

In the final analysis, Fig. 10.6 is quite similar to Fig. 10.3. The efficient set in Fig. 10.3 runs from MV to Supertech. It contains various combinations of the securities Supertech and Slowpoke. The efficient set in Fig. 10.6 runs from MV to *X*. It contains various combinations of many securities. The fact that a whole shaded area appears in Fig. 10.6 but not in Fig. 10.3 is just not an important difference; no investor would choose any point below the efficient set in Fig. 10.6 anyway.

We mentioned before that an efficient set for two securities can be traced out easily in the real world. The task becomes more difficult when additional securities are included, because the number of observations grows. For example, using subjective analysis to estimate expected returns and standard deviations for, say, 100 or 500 securities may very well become overwhelming, and the difficulties with correlations may be greater still. There are almost 5,000 correlations between pairs of securities from a universe of 100 securities.

Though much of the mathematics of efficient set computation had been derived in the 1950s,[7] the high cost of computer time restricted application of the principles. In recent years

TABLE
**10.4**

| Security | 1 | 2 | 3 | ... | N |
|---|---|---|---|---|---|
| 1 | $X_1^2\sigma_1^2$ | $X_1X_2\mathrm{Cov}(R_1, R_2)$ | $X_1X_3\mathrm{Cov}(R_1, R_3)$ | | $X_1X_N\mathrm{Cov}(R_1, R_N)$ |
| 2 | $X_2X_1\mathrm{Cov}(R_2, R_1)$ | $X_2^2\sigma_2^2$ | $X_2X_3\mathrm{Cov}(R_2, R_3)$ | | $X_2X_N\mathrm{Cov}(R_2, R_N)$ |
| 3 | $X_3X_1\mathrm{Cov}(R_3, R_1)$ | $X_3X_2\mathrm{Cov}(R_3, R_2)$ | $X_3^2\sigma_3^2$ | | $X_3X_N\mathrm{Cov}(R_3, R_N)$ |
| . | | | | | |
| . | | | | | |
| . | | | | | |
| N | $X_NX_1\mathrm{Cov}(R_N, R_1)$ | $X_NX_2\mathrm{Cov}(R_N, R_2)$ | $X_NX_3\mathrm{Cov}(R_N, R_3)$ | | $X_N^2\sigma_N^2$ |

The variance of the portfolio is the sum of the terms in all the boxes.

$\sigma_i$ is the standard deviation of security $i$.

$\mathrm{Cov}(R_i, R_j)$ is the covariance between security $i$ and security $j$.

Terms involving the standard deviation of a single security appear on the diagonal. Terms involving covariance between two securities appear off the diagonal.

**Table 10.4** Matrix used to calculate the variance of a portfolio

this cost has been almost eliminated. A number of software packages allow the calculation of an efficient set for portfolios of moderate size. By all accounts these packages sell quite briskly, so our discussion would appear to be important in practice.

## Variance and Standard Deviation in a Portfolio of Many Assets

We earlier calculated the formulae for variance and standard deviation in the two-asset case. Because we considered a portfolio of many assets in Fig. 10.6, it is worth while to calculate the formulae for variance and standard deviation in the many-asset case. The formula for the variance of a portfolio of many assets can be viewed as an extension of the formula for the variance of two assets.

To develop the formula, we employ the same type of matrix that we used in the two-asset case. This matrix is displayed in Table 10.4. Assuming that there are $N$ assets, we write the numbers 1 to $N$ on the horizontal axis and 1 to $N$ on the vertical axis. This creates a matrix of $N \times N = N^2$ boxes. The variance of the portfolio is the sum of the terms in all the boxes.

Consider, for example, the box in the second row and the third column. The term in the box is $X_2X_3 \mathrm{Cov}(R_2,R_3)$. $X_2$ and $X_3$ are the percentages of the entire portfolio that are invested in the second asset and the third asset, respectively. For example, if an individual with a portfolio of €1,000 invests €100 in the second asset, $X_2 = 10\%$ (= €100/€1,000). $\mathrm{Cov}(R_3, R_2)$ is the covariance between the returns on the third asset and the returns on the second asset. Next, note the box in the third row and the second column. The term in this box is $X_3X_2$ $\mathrm{Cov}(R_3, R_2)$. Because $\mathrm{Cov}(R_3, R_2) = \mathrm{Cov}(R_2, R_3)$, both boxes have the same value. The second security and the third security make up one pair. In fact, every pair of securities appears twice in the table: once in the lower left side and once in the upper right side.

Now consider boxes on the diagonal. For example, the term in the first box on the diagonal is $X_1^2\sigma_1^2$ Here, $\sigma_1^2$ is the variance of the return on the first security.

Thus the diagonal terms in the matrix contain the variances of the different securities. The off-diagonal terms contain the covariances. Table 10.5 relates the numbers of diagonal and off-diagonal elements to the size of the matrix. The number of diagonal terms (number of variance terms) is always the same as the number of securities in the portfolio. The number of off-diagonal terms (number of covariance terms) rises much faster than the number of diagonal terms. For example, a portfolio of 100 securities has 9,900 covariance terms. Because the variance of a portfolio's return is the sum of all the boxes, we have the following:

TABLE
**10.5**

| Number of securities in portfolio | Total number of terms | Number of variance terms (number of terms on diagonal) | Number of covariance terms (number of terms off diagonal) |
|---|---|---|---|
| 1 | 1 | 1 | 0 |
| 2 | 4 | 2 | 2 |
| 3 | 9 | 3 | 6 |
| 10 | 100 | 10 | 90 |
| 100 | 10,000 | 100 | 9,900 |
| . | . | . | . |
| . | . | . | . |
| . | . | . | . |
| $N$ | $N^2$ | $N$ | $N^2 - N$ |

In a large portfolio, the number of terms involving covariance between two securities is much greater than the number of terms involving variance of a single security.

**Table 10.5** Number of variance and covariance terms as a function of the number of securities in the portfolio

**The variance of the return on a portfolio with many securities is more dependent on the covariances between the individual securities than on the variances of the individual securities.**

To give a recent example of the impact of diversification, the FTSE 100 index, which contains 100 large, well-known UK equities, was down about 200 points in the first eight months of 2008, meaning a loss of about 3.5 per cent. As we saw in our previous chapter, this performance represents a fairly bad year for a portfolio of large-cap companies. However, as stated at the beginning of this chapter, mining companies were up 18 per cent. At the same time, banking stocks dropped by more than 30 per cent. So there were big winners and big losers, and these would have offset each other if you held a portfolio of mining and banking securities in 2008.

## 10.6 Diversification: An Example

The preceding point can be illustrated by altering the matrix in Table 10.4 slightly. Suppose we make the following three assumptions:

1   All securities possess the same variance, which we write as $\overline{var}$. In other words, $\sigma_i^2 = \overline{var}$ for every security.

2   All covariances in Table 10.4 are the same. We represent this uniform covariance as $\overline{cov}$. In other words. $Cov(R_i, R_j) = \overline{cov}$ for every pair of securities. It can easily be shown that $\overline{var} > \overline{cov}$.

3   All securities are equally weighted in the portfolio. Because there are $N$ assets, the weight of each asset in the portfolio is $1/N$. In other words, $X_i = 1/N$ for each security $i$.

Table 10.6 is the matrix of variances and covariances under these three simplifying assumptions. Note that all of the diagonal terms are identical. Similarly, all of the off-diagonal terms are identical. As with Table 10.4, the variance of the portfolio is the sum of the terms in the boxes in Table 10.6. We know that there are $N$ diagonal terms involving variance. Similarly, there are $N \times (N - 1)$ off-diagonal terms involving covariance. Summing across all the boxes in Table 10.6, we can express the variance of the portfolio as:

**TABLE 10.6**

| Security | 1 | 2 | 3 | ... | N |
|---|---|---|---|---|---|
| 1 | $(1/N^2)\,\overline{var}$ | $(1/N^2)\,\overline{cov}$ | $(1/N^2)\,\overline{cov}$ | | $(1/N^2)\,\overline{cov}$ |
| 2 | $(1/N^2)\,\overline{cov}$ | $(1/N^2)\,\overline{var}$ | $(1/N^2)\,\overline{cov}$ | | $(1/N^2)\,\overline{cov}$ |
| 3 | $(1/N^2)\,\overline{cov}$ | $(1/N^2)\,\overline{cov}$ | $(1/N^2)\,\overline{var}$ | | $(1/N^2)\,\overline{cov}$ |
| . | | | | | |
| . | | | | | |
| N | $(1/N^2)\,\overline{cov}$ | $(1/N^2)\,\overline{cov}$ | $(1/N^2)\,\overline{cov}$ | | $(1/N^2)\,\overline{var}$ |

**Table 10.6** Matrix used to calculate the variance of a portfolio when: (a) all securities possess the same variance, which we represent as $\overline{var}$; (b) all pairs of securities possess the same covariance, which we represent as $\overline{cov}$; (c) all securities are held in the same proportion, which is $1/N$

$$
\begin{array}{l}
\underset{\substack{\text{Variance of}\\ \text{portfolio}}}{} = \underset{\substack{\text{Number of}\\ \text{diagonal terms}}}{N} \times \underset{\substack{\text{Each diagonal}\\ \text{term}}}{\left[\dfrac{1}{N^2}\right]\overline{var}} + \underset{\substack{\text{Number of off-}\\ \text{diagonal terms}}}{N(N-1)} \times \underset{\substack{\text{Each off-}\\ \text{diagonal term}}}{\left[\dfrac{1}{N^2}\right]\overline{cov}} \qquad (10.10)
\end{array}
$$

$$
= \left[\frac{1}{N}\right]\overline{var} + \left[\frac{N^2-N}{N^2}\right]\overline{cov}
$$

$$
= \left[\frac{1}{N}\right]\overline{var} + \left[1-\frac{1}{N}\right]\overline{cov}
$$

Equation (10.10) expresses the variance of our special portfolio as a weighted sum of the average security variance and the average covariance.[8]

Now, let's increase the number of securities in the portfolio without limit. The variance of the portfolio becomes

$$
\text{Variance of portfolio (when } N \to \infty) = \overline{cov} \qquad (10.11)
$$

This occurs because (a) the weight on the variance term, $1/N$, goes to 0 as $N$ goes to infinity, and (b) the weight on the covariance term, $1 - 1/N$, goes to 1 as $N$ goes to infinity.

Equation (10.11) provides an interesting and important result. In our special portfolio, the variances of the individual securities completely vanish as the number of securities becomes large. However, the covariance terms remain. In fact, the variance of the portfolio becomes the average covariance, $\overline{cov}$. We often hear that we should diversify. In other words, we should not put all our eggs in one basket. The effect of diversification on the risk of a portfolio can be illustrated in this example. The variances of the individual securities are diversified away, but the covariance terms cannot be diversified away.

The fact that part, but not all, of our risk can be diversified away should be explored. Consider Mr Smith, who brings £1,000 to the roulette table at a casino. It would be very risky if he put all his money on one spin of the wheel. For example, imagine that he put the full £1,000 on red at the table. If the wheel showed red, he would get £2,000; but if the wheel showed black, he would lose everything. Suppose instead he divided his money over 1,000 different spins by betting £1 at a time on red. Probability theory tells us that he could count on winning about 50 per cent of the time. This means he could count on pretty nearly getting all his original £1,000 back.[9] In other words, risk is essentially eliminated with 1,000 different spins.

Now, let's contrast this with our stock market example, which we illustrate in Fig. 10.7. The variance of the portfolio with only one security is of course $\overline{var}$, because the variance of a portfolio with one security is the variance of the security. The variance of the portfolio drops as more securities are added, which is evidence of the diversification effect. However, unlike

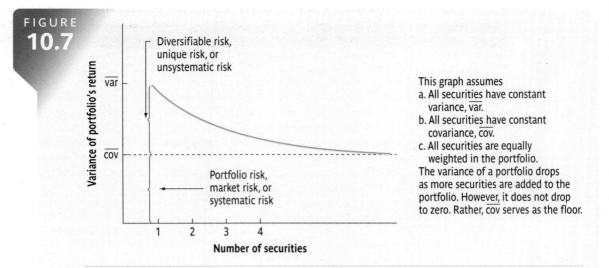

**Figure 10.7** Relationship between the variance of a portfolio's return and the number of securities in the portfolio

Mr Smith's roulette example, the portfolio's variance can never drop to zero. Rather, it reaches a floor of $\overline{\text{cov}}$, which is the covariance of each pair of securities.[10]

Because the variance of the portfolio asymptotically approaches $\overline{\text{cov}}$, each additional security continues to reduce risk. Thus, if there were neither commissions nor other transaction costs, it could be argued that we can never achieve too much diversification. However, there is a cost to diversification in the real world. Commissions per unit of money invested fall as we make larger purchases in a single security. Unfortunately, we must buy fewer shares of each security when buying more – and more different – securities. Comparing the costs and benefits of diversification, Meir Statman argues that a portfolio of about 30 equities is needed to achieve optimal diversification.[11]

We mentioned earlier that $\overline{\text{var}}$ must be greater than $\overline{\text{cov}}$. Thus the variance of a security's return can be broken down in the following way:

$$\begin{array}{ccc} \text{Total risk of} & & \text{Unsystematic or} \\ \text{individual security} & = \frac{\text{Portfolio risk}}{(\overline{\text{cov}})} + & \text{diversifiable risk} \\ (\overline{\text{var}}) & & (\overline{\text{var}} - \overline{\text{cov}}) \end{array}$$

*Total risk*, which is $\overline{\text{var}}$ in our example, is the risk we bear by holding onto one security only. *Portfolio risk* is the risk we still bear after achieving full diversification, which is $\overline{\text{cov}}$ in our example. Portfolio risk is often called systematic or market risk as well. Diversifiable, unique, or unsystematic risk is the risk that can be diversified away in a large portfolio, which must be $(\overline{\text{var}} - \overline{\text{cov}})$ by definition.

To an individual who selects a diversified portfolio, the total risk of a single security is not important. When considering adding a security to a diversified portfolio, the individual cares about only that portion of the risk of a security that cannot be diversified away. This risk can alternatively be viewed as the *contribution* of a security to the risk of an entire portfolio. We shall talk later about the case where securities make different contributions to the risk of the entire portfolio.

## Risk and the Sensible Investor

Having gone to all this trouble to show that unsystematic risk disappears in a well-diversified portfolio, how do we know that investors even want such portfolios? What if they like risk, and don't want it to disappear?

We must admit that, theoretically at least, this is possible, but we shall argue that it does not describe what we think of as the typical investor. Our typical investor is risk-averse. Risk-averse behaviour can be defined in many ways, but we prefer the following example: a fair gamble is one with zero expected return; a risk-averse investor would prefer to avoid fair gambles.

Why do investors choose well-diversified portfolios? Our answer is that they are risk-averse, and risk-averse people avoid unnecessary risk, such as the unsystematic risk on an equity. If you do not think this is much of an answer, consider whether you would take on such a risk. For example, suppose you had worked all summer and had saved €5,000, which you intended to use for your university expenses. Now, suppose someone came up to you and offered to flip a coin for the money: heads, you would double your money, and tails, you would lose it all.

Would you take such a bet? Perhaps you would, but most people would not. Leaving aside any moral question that might surround gambling, and recognizing that some people *would* take such a bet, it's our view that the average investor would not.

To induce the typical risk-averse investor to take a fair gamble, you must sweeten the pot. For example, you might need to raise the odds of winning from 50–50 to 70–30 or higher. The risk-averse investor can be induced to take fair gambles only if they are sweetened so that they become unfair to the investor's advantage.

## 10.7  Riskless Borrowing and Lending

Figure 10.6 assumes that all the securities in the efficient set are risky. Alternatively, an investor could combine a risky investment with an investment in a riskless or *risk-free* security, such as an investment in government treasury bills. This is illustrated in the following example.

---

**EXAMPLE 10.3**

### Riskless Lending and Portfolio Risk

Ms Bagwell is considering investing in the equity of Merville Enterprises. In addition, Ms Bagwell will either borrow or lend at the risk-free rate. The relevant parameters are these:

|  | Equity of Merville (%) | Risk-free asset (%) |
|---|---|---|
| Expected return | 14 | 10 |
| Standard deviation | 0.20 | 0 |

Suppose Ms Bagwell chooses to invest a total of £1,000, £350 of which is to be invested in Merville Enterprises and £650 placed in the risk-free asset. The expected return on her total investment is simply a weighted average of the two returns:

$$\text{Expected return on portfolio composed of one riskless and one risky asset} = 0.114 = (0.35 \times 0.14) + (0.65 \times 0.10) \qquad \textbf{(10.12)}$$

Because the expected return on the portfolio is a weighted average of the expected return on the risky asset (Merville Enterprises) and the risk-free return, the calculation is analogous to the way we treated two risky assets. In other words, Eq. (10.3) applies here.

Using Eq. (10.4), the formula for the variance of the portfolio can be written as

$$X_{\text{Merville}}^2 \sigma_{\text{Merville}}^2 + 2X_{\text{Merville}}X_{\text{Risk-free}}\sigma_{\text{Merville,Risk-free}} + X_{\text{Risk-free}}^2 \sigma_{\text{Risk-free}}^2$$

However, by definition, the risk-free asset has no variability. Thus both $\sigma_{\text{Merville,Risk-free}}$ and $\sigma_{\text{Risk-free}}^2$ are equal to zero, reducing the above expression to

$$\text{Variance of portfolio composed of one riskless and one risky asset} = X_{\text{Merville}}^2 \sigma_{\text{Merville}}^2 \qquad \textbf{(10.13)}$$
$$= (0.35)^2 \times (0.20)^2$$
$$= 0.0049$$

The standard deviation of the portfolio is

$$\text{Standard deviation of portfolio composed of one riskless and one risky asset} = X_{\text{Merville}}\sigma_{\text{Merville}} \tag{10.14}$$
$$= 0.35 \times 0.20$$
$$= 0.07$$

The relationship between risk and expected return for one risky and one riskless asset can be seen in Fig. 10.8. Ms Bagwell's split of 35–65 per cent between the two assets is represented on a *straight* line between the risk-free rate and a pure investment in Merville Enterprises. Note that, unlike the case of two risky assets, the opportunity set is straight, not curved.

**Figure 10.8** Relationship between expected return and risk for a portfolio of one risky asset and one riskless asset

Suppose that, alternatively, Ms Bagwell borrows £200 at the risk-free rate. Combining this with her original sum of £1,000, she invests a total of £1,200 in Merville. Her expected return would be

$$\text{Expected return on portfolio formed by borrowing to invest in risky asset} = 14.8\% = 1.20 \times 0.14 + (-0.2 \times 0.10)$$

Here, she invests 120 per cent of her original investment of £1,000 by borrowing 20 per cent of her original investment. Note that the return of 14.8 per cent is greater than the 14 per cent expected return on Merville Enterprises. This occurs because she is borrowing at 10 per cent to invest in a security with an expected return greater than 10 per cent.

The standard deviation is

$$\text{Standard deviation of portfolio formed by borrowing to invest in risky asset} = 0.24 = 1.20 \times 0.2$$

The standard deviation of 0.24 is greater than 0.20, the standard deviation of the Merville investment, because borrowing increases the variability of the investment. This investment also appears in Fig. 10.8.

So far, we have assumed that Ms Bagwell is able to borrow at the same rate at which she can lend.[12] Now let us consider the case where the borrowing rate is above the lending rate. The dotted line in Fig. 10.8 illustrates the opportunity set for borrowing opportunities in this case. The dotted line is below the solid line because a higher borrowing rate lowers the expected return on the investment.

## The Optimal Portfolio

The previous section concerned a portfolio formed between one riskless asset and one risky asset. In reality, an investor is likely to combine an investment in the riskless asset with a *portfolio* of risky assets. This is illustrated in Fig. 10.9.

Consider point $Q$, representing a portfolio of securities. Point $Q$ is in the interior of the feasible set of risky securities. Let us assume the point represents a portfolio of 30 per cent in Carrefour, the French supermarket chain, 45 per cent in LVMH, the luxury designer goods group, and 25 per cent in Vinci SA, the European road-builder. Individuals combining investments in $Q$ with investments in the riskless asset would achieve points along the straight line from $R_F$ to $Q$. We refer to this as line $I$. For example, point 1 on the line represents a portfolio of 70 per cent in the riskless asset and 30 per cent in equities represented by $Q$. An investor with €100 choosing point 1 as his portfolio would put €70 in the risk-free asset and €30 in $Q$. This can be restated as €70 in the riskless asset, €9 (= 0.3 × €30) in Carrefour, €13.50 (= 0.45 × €30) in LVMH, and €7.50 (= 0.25 × €30) in Vinci. Point 2 also represents a portfolio of the risk-free asset and $Q$, with more (65%) being invested in $Q$.

Point 3 is obtained by borrowing to invest in $Q$. For example, an investor with €100 of her own would borrow €40 from the bank or broker to invest €140 in $Q$. This can be stated as borrowing €40 and contributing €100 of her money to invest €42 (= 0.3 × €140) in Carrefour, €63 (= 0.45 × €140) in LVMH, and €35 (= 0.25 × €140) in Vinci.

These investments can be summarized as follows:

|                    | Point $Q$ (€) | Point 1 (Lending €70) (€) | Point 3 (Borrowing €40) (€) |
|--------------------|:-------------:|:-------------------------:|:---------------------------:|
| Carrefour          | 30            | 9                         | 42                          |
| LVMH               | 45            | 13.50                     | 63                          |
| Vinci              | 25            | 7.50                      | 35                          |
| Risk-free          | 0             | 70.00                     | −40                         |
| Total investment   | 100           | 100                       | 100                         |

Though any investor can obtain any point on line $I$, no point on the line is optimal. To see this, consider line $II$, a line running from $R_F$ through $A$. Point $A$ represents a portfolio of risky securities. Line $II$ represents portfolios formed by combinations of the risk-free asset and

FIGURE
**10.9**

Portfolio $Q$ is composed of 30 per cent Carrefour, 45 per cent LVMH, and 25 per cent Vinci.

**Figure 10.9** Relationship between expected return and standard deviation for an investment in a combination of risky securities and the riskless asset the securities in A. Points between $R_F$ and A are portfolios in which some money is invested in the riskless asset and the rest is placed in A. Points past A are achieved by borrowing at the riskless rate to buy more of A than we could with our original funds alone.

As drawn, line II is tangent to the efficient set of risky securities. Whatever point an individual can obtain on line I, he can obtain a point with the same standard deviation and a higher expected return on line II. In fact, because line II is tangent to the efficient set of risky assets, it provides the investor with the best possible opportunities. In other words, line II can be viewed as the efficient set of all assets, both risky and riskless. An investor with a fair degree of risk aversion might choose a point between $R_F$ and A, perhaps point 4. An individual with less risk aversion might choose a point closer to A or even beyond A. For example, point 5 corresponds to an individual borrowing money to increase investment in A.

The graph illustrates an important point. With riskless borrowing and lending, the portfolio of *risky* assets held by any investor would always be point A. Regardless of the investor's tolerance for risk, she would never choose any other point on the efficient set of risky assets (represented by curve XAY) nor any point in the interior of the feasible region. Rather, she would combine the securities of A with the riskless assets if she had high aversion to risk. She would borrow the riskless asset to invest more funds in A if she had low aversion to risk.

This result establishes what financial economists call the separation principle. That is, the investor's investment decision consists of two separate steps:

1  After estimating (a) the expected returns and variances of individual securities and (b) the covariances between pairs of securities, the investor calculates the efficient set of risky assets, represented by curve XAY in Fig. 10.9. He then determines point A, the tangency between the risk-free rate and the efficient set of risky assets (curve XAY). Point A represents the portfolio of risky assets that the investor will hold. This point is determined solely from his estimates of returns, variances and covariances. No personal characteristics, such as degree of risk aversion, are needed in this step.

2  The investor must now determine how he will combine point A, his portfolio of risky assets, with the riskless asset. He might invest some of his funds in the riskless asset and some in portfolio A. He would end up at a point on the line between $R_F$ and A in this case. Alternatively, he might borrow at the risk-free rate and contribute some of his own funds as well, investing the sum in portfolio A. He would end up at a point on line II beyond A. His position in the riskless asset – that is, his choice of where on the line he wants to be – is determined by his internal characteristics, such as his ability to tolerate risk.

## 10.8  Market Equilibrium

### Definition of the Market Equilibrium Portfolio

The preceding analysis concerns one investor. His estimates of the expected returns and variances for individual securities and the covariances between pairs of securities are his and his alone. Other investors would obviously have different estimates of these variables. However, the estimates might not vary much because everyone would be forming expectations from the same data about past price movements and other publicly available information.

Financial economists often imagine a world where all investors possess the *same* estimates of expected returns, variances and covariances. Though this can never be literally true, it can be thought of as a useful simplifying assumption in a world where investors have access to similar sources of information. This assumption is called homogeneous expectations.[13]

If all investors had homogeneous expectations, Fig. 10.9 would be the same for all individuals. That is, all investors would sketch out the same efficient set of risky assets, because they would be working with the same inputs. This efficient set of risky assets is represented by the curve XAY. Because the same risk-free rate would apply to everyone, all investors would view point A as the portfolio of risky assets to be held.

This point A takes on great importance, because all investors would purchase the risky securities that it represents. Investors with a high degree of risk aversion might combine A with an investment in the riskless asset, achieving point 4, for example. Others with low aversion to risk might borrow to achieve, say, point 5. Because this is a very important conclusion, we restate it:

**In a world with homogeneous expectations, all investors would hold the portfolio of risky assets represented by point *A*.**

If all investors choose the same portfolio of risky assets, it is possible to determine what that portfolio is. Common sense tells us that it is a market-value-weighted portfolio of all existing securities. It is the market portfolio.

In practice, economists use a broad-based index such as the FTSE 100, Dow Jones Euro Stoxx 50 or Standard & Poor's (S&P) 500 as a proxy for the market portfolio, depending on the country they analyse. Of course, in practice all investors do not hold the same portfolio. However, we know that many investors hold diversified portfolios, particularly when mutual funds or pension funds are included. A broad-based index is a good proxy for the highly diversified portfolios of many investors.

## Definition of Risk when Investors Hold the Market Portfolio

The previous section states that many investors hold diversified portfolios similar to broad-based indexes. This result allows us to be more precise about the risk of a security in the context of a diversified portfolio.

Researchers have shown that the best measure of the risk of a security in a large portfolio is the *beta* of the security. We illustrate beta by an example.

---

**EXAMPLE 10.4**

## Beta

Consider the following possible returns, both on the equity of Jelco plc and on the market:

| State | Type of economy | Return on market (%) | Return on Jelco plc (%) |
|-------|-----------------|----------------------|-------------------------|
| I | Bull | 15 | 25 |
| II | Bull | 15 | 15 |
| III | Bear | −5 | −5 |
| IV | Bear | −5 | −15 |

Though the return on the market has only two possible outcomes (15% and 5%), the return on Jelco has four possible outcomes. It is helpful to consider the expected return on a security for a given return on the market. Assuming each state is equally likely, we have

| Type of economy | Return on market (%) | Expected return on Jelco plc (%) |
|-----------------|----------------------|----------------------------------|
| Bull | 15 | $20 = 25 \times \frac{1}{2} + 15 \times \frac{1}{2}$ |
| Bear | −5 | $-10 = -5 \times \frac{1}{2} + (-15) \times \frac{1}{2}$ |

Jelco plc responds to market movements because its expected return is greater in bullish states than in bearish states. We now calculate exactly how responsive the security is to market movements. The market's return in a bullish economy is 20 per cent [= 15% − (−5%)] greater than the market's return in a bearish economy. However, the expected return on Jelco in a bullish economy is 30 per cent [= 20% − (−10%)] greater than its expected return in a bearish state. Thus Jelco plc has a responsiveness coefficient of 1.5 (= 30%/20%).

This relationship appears in Fig. 10.10. The returns for both Jelco and the market in each state are plotted as four points. In addition, we plot the expected return on the security for each of the two possible returns on the market. These two points, each of which we designate by an X, are joined by a line called the characteristic line of the security. The slope of the line is 1.5, the number calculated in the previous paragraph. This responsiveness coefficient of 1.5 is the beta of Jelco.

The interpretation of beta from Fig. 10.10 is intuitive. The graph tells us that the returns of Jelco are magnified 1.5 times over those of the market. When the market does well, Jelco's equity is expected to do even better. When the market does poorly, Jelco's equity is expected to do even worse. Now imagine an individual with a portfolio near that of the market who is considering the addition of Jelco to her portfolio. Because of Jelco's *magnification factor* of 1.5, she will view this security as contributing much to the risk of the portfolio. (We shall show shortly that the beta of the average security in the market is 1.) Jelco contributes more to the risk of a large, diversified portfolio than does an average security, because Jelco is more responsive to movements in the market.

**Figure 10.10** Performance of Jelco plc and the market portfolio

Further insight can be gleaned by examining securities with negative betas. One should view these securities as either hedges or insurance policies. The security is expected to do well when the market does poorly, and vice versa. Because of this, adding a negative-beta security to a large, diversified portfolio actually reduces the risk of the portfolio.[14]

Table 10.7 presents empirical estimates of betas for individual securities. As can be seen, some securities are more responsive to the market than others. For example, Siemens has a beta of 1.51. This means that for every 1 per cent movement in the market, Siemens is expected to move 1.51 per cent in the same direction. Conversely, SAP has a beta of only 0.56. This means that for every 1 per cent movement in the market, SAP is expected to move 0.56 per cent in the same direction.

We can summarize our discussion of beta by saying this:

**Beta measures the responsiveness of a security to movements in the market portfolio.**

## The Formula for Beta

Our discussion so far has stressed the intuition behind beta. The actual definition of beta is

$$\beta_i = \frac{\text{Cov}(R_i, R_M)}{\sigma^2(R_M)} \tag{10.15}$$

where $\text{Cov}(R_i, R_M)$ is the covariance between the return on asset $i$ and the return on the market portfolio, and $\sigma^2(R_M)$ is the variance of the market.

| TABLE 10.7 | Stock | Beta |
|---|---|---|
| | Alcatel-Lucent | 1.44 |
| | L'Oreal | 0.45 |
| | SAP | 0.56 |
| | Siemens | 1.51 |
| | Daimler | 1.25 |
| | Philips Electron | 0.92 |
| | Renault | 1.64 |
| | Volkswagen | 0.40 |

Source: Yahoo! Finance, http://uk.finance.yahoo.com

**Table 10.7** Estimates of beta for selected individual equities

One useful property is that the average beta across all securities, when weighted by the proportion of each security's market value to that of the market portfolio, is 1. That is,

$$\sum_{i=1}^{N} X_i \beta_i = 1 \qquad \qquad (10.16)$$

where $X_i$ is the proportion of security $i$'s market value to that of the entire market, and $N$ is the number of securities in the market.

Equation (10.16) is intuitive, once you think about it. If you weight all securities by their market values, the resulting portfolio is the market. By definition, the beta of the market portfolio is 1. That is, for every 1 per cent movement in the market, the market must move 1 per cent – *by definition*.

## A Test

We have put these questions on past corporate finance examinations:

1   What sort of investor rationally views the variance (or standard deviation) of an individual security's return as the security's proper measure of risk?

2   What sort of investor rationally views the beta of a security as the security's proper measure of risk?

A good answer might be something like the following:

A rational, risk-averse investor views the variance (or standard deviation) of her portfolio's return as the proper measure of the risk of her portfolio. If for some reason the investor can hold only one security, the variance of that security's return becomes the variance of the portfolio's return. Hence the variance of the security's return is the security's proper measure of risk.

If an individual holds a diversified portfolio, she still views the variance (or standard deviation) of her portfolio's return as the proper measure of the risk of her portfolio. However, she is no longer interested in the variance of each individual security's return. Rather, she is interested in the contribution of an individual security to the variance of the portfolio.

Under the assumption of homogeneous expectations, all individuals hold the market portfolio. Thus we measure risk as the contribution of an individual security to the variance of the market portfolio. This contribution, when standardized properly, is the beta of the security. Although few investors hold the market portfolio exactly, many hold reasonably diversified portfolios. These portfolios are close enough to the market portfolio that the beta of a security is likely to be a reasonable measure of its risk.

# 10.9 The Capital Asset Pricing Model

It is commonplace to argue that the expected return on an asset should be positively related to its risk. That is, individuals will hold a risky asset only if its expected return compensates for its risk. In this section we first estimate the expected return on the stock market as a whole. Next, we estimate expected returns on individual securities.

## Expected Return on Market

Economists frequently argue that the expected return on the market can be represented as

$$\bar{R}_M = R_F + \text{Risk premium}$$

In words, the expected return on the market is the sum of the risk-free rate plus some compensation for the risk inherent in the market portfolio. Note that the equation refers to the *expected* return on the market, not the actual return in a particular month or year. Because equities have risk, the actual return on the market over a particular period can, of course, be below $R_F$, or can even be negative.

Because investors want compensation for risk, the risk premium is presumably positive. But exactly how positive is it? It is generally argued that the place to start looking for the risk premium in the future is the average risk premium in the past. As reported in Chapter 9, Ibbotson and Sinquefield found that the average return on large US companies was 12.3 per cent over 1926–2005. The average risk-free rate over the same interval was 3.8 per cent. Thus the average difference between the two was 8.5 per cent (= 12.3% − 3.8%). Financial economists find this to be a useful estimate of the difference to occur in the future.

For example, if the risk-free rate, estimated by the current yield on a one-year Treasury bill, is 1 per cent, the expected return on the market is

$$9.5\% = 1\% + 8.5\%$$

Of course, the future equity risk premium could be higher or lower than the historical equity risk premium. This could be true if future risk is higher or lower than past risk, or if individual risk aversions are higher or lower than those of the past.

## Expected Return on an Individual Security

Now that we have estimated the expected return on the market as a whole, what is the expected return on an individual security? We have argued that the beta of a security is the appropriate measure of risk in a large, diversified portfolio. Because most investors are diversified, the expected return on a security should be positively related to its beta. This is illustrated in Fig. 10.11.

Actually, economists can be more precise about the relationship between expected return and beta. They posit that under plausible conditions the relationship between expected return and beta can be represented by the following equation:[15]

Capital asset pricing model

$$\underset{\substack{\text{Expected return} \\ \text{on a security}}}{\bar{R}} = \underset{\substack{\text{Risk-free} \\ \text{rate}}}{R_F} + \underset{\substack{\text{Beta of the} \\ \text{security}}}{\beta} \times \underset{\substack{\text{Difference between} \\ \text{expected return on} \\ \text{market and risk-free rate}}}{(\bar{R}_M - R_F)} \qquad (10.17)$$

This formula, called the **capital asset pricing model** (or CAPM for short), implies that the expected return on a security is linearly related to its beta. Because the average return on the market has been higher than the average risk-free rate over long periods of time, $\bar{R}_M - R_F$ is

FIGURE
**10.11**

**Figure 10.11** Relationship between expected return on an individual security and beta of the security

presumably positive. Thus the formula implies that the expected return on a security is *positively* related to its beta. The formula can be illustrated by assuming a few special cases:

- *Assume that $\beta = 0$.* Here $\bar{R} = R_F$ – that is, the expected return on the security is equal to the risk-free rate. Because a security with zero beta has no relevant risk, its expected return should equal the risk-free rate.

- *Assume that $\beta = 1$.* Equation (10.17) reduces to $\bar{R} = \bar{R}_M$. That is, the expected return on the security is equal to the expected return on the market. This makes sense, because the beta of the market portfolio is also 1.

Equation (10.17) can be represented graphically by the upward-sloping line in Fig. 10.11. Note that the line begins at $R_F$ and rises to $\bar{R}_M$ when beta is 1. This line is frequently called the security market line (SML).

As with any line, the SML has both a slope and an intercept. $R_F$, the risk-free rate, is the intercept. Because the beta of a security is the horizontal axis, $R_M - R_F$ is the slope. The line will be upward sloping as long as the expected return on the market is greater than the risk-free rate. Because the market portfolio is a risky asset, theory suggests that its expected return is above the risk-free rate. As mentioned, the empirical evidence of the previous chapter showed that the average return per year on the market portfolio (for large US companies as an example) over the past 80 years was 8.5 per cent above the risk-free rate.

## Capital Asset Pricing Model

EXAMPLE
**10.5**

The shares of Aardvark Enterprises have a beta of 1.5 and those of Zebra Enterprises have a beta of 0.7. The risk-free rate is assumed to be 3 per cent, and the difference between the expected return on the market and the risk-free rate is assumed to be 8.0 per cent. The expected returns on the two securities are

Expected return for Aardvark:

$$15.0\% = 3\% + 1.5 \times 8.0\% \tag{10.18}$$

Expected return for Zebra:

$$8.6\% = 3\% + 0.7 \times 8.0\%$$

Three additional points concerning the CAPM should be mentioned:

1 *Linearity*: The intuition behind an upwardly sloping curve is clear. Because beta is the appropriate measure of risk, high-beta securities should have an expected return above that of low-beta securities. However, both Fig. 10.11 and Eq. (10.17) show something more than an upward sloping curve: the relationship between expected return and beta corresponds to a *straight* line.

It is easy to show that the line of Fig. 10.11 is straight. To see this, consider security *S* with, say, a beta of 0.8. This security is represented by a point below the security market line in the figure. Any investor could duplicate the beta of security *S* by buying a portfolio with 20 per cent in the risk-free asset and 80 per cent in a security with a beta of 1. However, the home-made portfolio would itself lie on the SML. In other words, the portfolio dominates security *S* because the portfolio has a higher expected return and the same beta.

Now consider security *T* with, say, a beta greater than 1. This security is also below the SML in Fig. 10.11. Any investor could duplicate the beta of security *T* by borrowing to invest in a security with a beta of 1. This portfolio must also lie on the SML, thereby dominating security *T*.

Because no one would hold either *S* or *T*, their prices would drop. This price adjustment would raise the expected returns on the two securities. The price adjustment would continue until the two securities lay on the security market line. The preceding example considered two overpriced equities and a straight SML. Securities lying above the SML are *underpriced*. Their prices must rise until their expected returns lie on the line. If the SML is itself curved, many equities would be mispriced. In equilibrium, all securities would be held only when prices changed so that the SML became straight. In other words, linearity would be achieved.

2 *Portfolios as well as securities*: Our discussion of the CAPM considered individual securities. Does the relationship in Fig. 10.11 and Eq. (10.17) hold for portfolios as well?

Yes. To see this, consider a portfolio formed by investing equally in our two securities from Example 10.5, Aardvark and Zebra. The expected return on the portfolio is

Expected return on portfolio:

$$11.8\% = 0.5 \times 15.0\% + 0.5 \times 8.6\% \tag{10.19}$$

The beta of the portfolio is simply a weighted average of the betas of the two securities. Thus we have

Beta of portfolio:

$$1.1 = 0.5 \times 1.5 + 0.5 \times 0.7$$

Under the CAPM, the expected return on the portfolio is

$$11.8\% = 3\% + 1.1 \times 8.0\% \tag{10.20}$$

Because the expected return in Eq. (10.19) is the same as the expected return in Eq. (10.20), the example shows that the CAPM holds for portfolios as well as for individual securities.

3 *A potential confusion*: Students often confuse the SML in Fig. 10.11 with line *II* in Fig. 10.9. Actually, the lines are quite different. Line *II* traces the efficient set of portfolios formed from both risky assets and the riskless asset. Each point on the line represents an entire portfolio. Point *A* is a portfolio composed entirely of risky assets. Every other point on the line represents a portfolio of the securities in *A* combined with the riskless asset. The axes in Fig. 10.9 are the expected return on a *portfolio* and the standard deviation of a *portfolio*. Individual securities do not lie along line *II*.

The SML in Fig. 10.11 relates expected return to beta. Fig. 10.11 differs from Fig. 10.9 in at least two ways. First, beta appears in the horizontal axis of Fig. 10.11, but standard deviation appears in the horizontal axis of Fig. 10.9. Second, the SML in Fig. 10.11 holds both for all individual securities and for all possible portfolios, whereas line *II* in Fig. 10.9 holds only for efficient portfolios.

We stated earlier that, under homogeneous expectations, point *A* in Fig. 10.9 becomes the market portfolio. In this situation, line *II* is referred to as the capital market line (CML).

# 10.10 Criticisms of the CAPM

The capital asset pricing model represents one of the most important advances in financial economics. It is clearly useful for investment purposes because it shows how the expected return on an asset is related to its beta. In addition, we shall show in Chapter 12 that it is useful in corporate finance because the discount rate on a project is a function of the project's beta. However, never forget that, as with any other model, the CAPM is not revealed truth but, rather, a construct to be empirically tested and to give some insights into what is reality. Nobody who works in finance will ever say that they believe the CAPM fully explains the returns on securities, investments or financial portfolios. All the CAPM does, as with any other theoretical model, is give insights into the truth.

## Roll's (1977) Critique of the CAPM

Before we discuss empirical tests, it is important to understand whether CAPM can be tested at all. Richard Roll, in the *Journal of Financial Economics*, argued that, because it is practically impossible to construct a portfolio that contains every single security (i.e. the true market portfolio), any test of the CAPM that uses a market proxy (e.g. FTSE 100, DAX, CAC 40) will be testing that specific portfolio, and not the true market portfolio. This means that, for all intents and purposes, the CAPM is empirically untestable because the underlying market portfolio is unobservable. Any tests of the CAPM that use market proxies will be affected by this criticism.

Academics have spent a lot of time debating the merits of Roll's (1977) critique. However, use of the model in corporate finance and investment is widespread. Financial websites, such as Yahoo! Finance, Bloomberg and Morningstar, frequently provide estimates of the beta of listed firms. Given the CAPM's massive popularity, and taking into account the weaknesses associated with any empirical tests, it is important to know whether it is successful in explaining at least some of the variation in security returns.

## Empirical Tests of the CAPM

The first empirical tests of the CAPM occurred over 30 years ago and were quite supportive of the model. Using data from the 1930s to the 1960s on US stock markets, researchers showed that the average return on a portfolio of equities was positively related to the beta of the portfolio[16] – a finding consistent with the CAPM. Though some evidence in these studies was less consistent with the CAPM,[17] financial economists were quick to embrace the model, following these empirical papers.

Although a large body of empirical work developed in the following decades, often with varying results, the CAPM was not seriously called into question until the 1990s. Two papers by Fama and French[18] present evidence inconsistent with the model. Their work has received a great deal of attention, both in academic circles and in the popular press, with newspaper articles displaying headlines such as 'Beta Is Dead!' These papers make two related points. First, they conclude that, for US firms, the relationship between average return and beta is weak over the period from 1941 to 1990 and virtually nonexistent from 1963 to 1990. Second, they argue that the average return on a security is negatively related to both the firm's price–earnings (P/E) ratio and the firm's market-to-book (M/B) ratio. Other research has provided strong evidence against the CAPM by showing that securities that have performed well in the recent past tend to have higher returns in the near future (Carhart's (1997) momentum factor). In addition, Ang, Hodrick, Xing and Zhang (2009) found that equities with a greater sensitivity to volatility in market returns have lower returns than comparable firms with the same market beta. It is possible that these results are applicable only in the United States. However, the poor performance of beta has also been found in other countries by Fama and French (1998).

These contentions, if confirmed by other research, would be quite damaging to the CAPM. After all, the CAPM states that the expected returns on equities should be related only to beta, and not to other factors such as P/E, M/B, momentum, or market volatility.

A number of other researchers have also criticized the type of research carried out by Fama and French. We avoid an in-depth discussion of the fine points of the debate, but we mention a few issues. First, although Fama and French, Carhart, and Ang *et al.* cannot reject the hypothesis that average returns are unrelated to beta, we can also not reject the hypothesis that average returns are related to beta exactly as specified by the CAPM. In other words, although 50 years of data seem like a lot, they may simply not be enough to test the CAPM properly. Second, the results may be due to a statistical fallacy called a hindsight bias.[19] Third, P/E, M/B, momentum and market volatility are merely four of an infinite number of possible factors. Thus the relationship between average return and these variables may be spurious, being nothing more than the result of data mining. Fourth, average returns on US stocks are positively related to beta over the period from 1927 to the present. There appears to be no compelling reason for emphasizing a shorter period than this one. Fifth, average returns are actually positively related to beta over shorter periods when annual data, rather than monthly data, are used to estimate beta.[20] There appears to be no compelling reason for preferring either monthly data over annual data or vice versa. Thus we believe that, although the results of Fama and French, Carhart, Ang *et al.* and others are quite intriguing, they cannot be viewed as the final word.

## 10.11 Variations of the CAPM

The CAPM relates an individual security's return to the return on the market portfolio through its systematic risk, beta. Beta measures the sensitivity of an investor's wealth to movements in the underlying market portfolio. Many academics have argued that wealth, in itself, is not important in pricing securities. Instead, it is the effect of an investment on the consumption, or spending power, of an investor that is relevant. So, the more that an investment makes consumption riskier, the higher its expected returns should be.

This view has led to a variation of the CAPM, known as the consumption capital asset pricing model, or CCAPM. Systematic risk, or beta, in the CAPM measures the covariance of security returns with market returns. However, in the CCAPM beta is slightly more complex. The CCAPM is expressed as follows:

$$\underset{\substack{\text{Expected return} \\ \text{on a security}}}{\bar{R}} = \underset{\substack{\text{Risk-free} \\ \text{rate}}}{R_F} + \underset{\substack{\text{Consumption beta} \\ \text{of the security}}}{\beta_c} \times \underset{\substack{\text{Difference between} \\ \text{expected return on market} \\ \text{and risk-free rate}}}{(\bar{R}_M - R_F)} \qquad (10.21)$$

where the consumption beta, $\beta_c$, is equal to

$$\beta_c = \frac{\text{Cov}(\bar{R}, \text{consumption growth})}{\text{Cov}(\bar{R}_M, \text{consumption growth})}$$

In the CCAPM, if a security has a higher return when consumption growth is higher, its consumption beta will be high. Similarly, a low covariance between security returns and consumption growth will lead to a lower CCAPM beta.

Another variation in the CAPM recognizes that not all of an individual's wealth comes from financial assets. In recent years many people increased their wealth through investment in non-financial (human capital) assets such as housing and property. This has been particularly true in Europe (especially the UK and Spain), where property values (until 2008) had been growing at more than 10 per cent per annum. The Human Capital CAPM, or HCAPM, incorporates both sources of wealth creation. According to the HCAPM, the return on the market portfolio is a linear combination (weighted by the relative investment of assets) of the return on the underlying financial portfolio and the underlying non-financial portfolio. If $\delta$ represents the fraction of total wealth that is invested in non-financial assets (or human capital), and $\bar{R}_{NF}$ and $\bar{R}_F$ represent the returns on non-financial and financial assets respectively, the return on the market is equal to

$$\bar{R}_M = \delta\bar{R}_{NF} + (1 - \delta)\bar{R}_F$$

The return on financial assets is simply the market portfolio of the CAPM, whereas the return on non-financial assets is normally taken to be the growth in average earnings, or labour income. The HCAPM has the same form as the normal CAPM. However, if the return on the market portfolio is disaggregated into its two components, the return on a security can be expressed as a linear function of its financial and non-financial betas. In this form, the return on a security is expressed as follows:

$$\bar{R} = \beta_0 + \beta_F\bar{R}_F + \beta_{NF}\bar{R}_{NF}$$

Although both the CCAPM and HCAPM are theoretically sound, because of the difficulties in using the model with real data the models do not tend to be used in practice. The CCAPM requires reliable data on total consumption growth, and the HCAPM utilizes data on non-financial wealth, both of which are rarely available on a continuing basis. For this reason, the standard CAPM is the most commonly used theoretical model in corporate finance.

## Summary and Conclusions

This chapter set forth the fundamentals of modern portfolio theory. Our basic points are these:

1   This chapter showed us how to calculate the expected return and variance for individual securities, and the covariance and correlation for pairs of securities. Given these statistics, the expected return and variance for a portfolio of two securities $A$ and $B$ can be written as

$$\text{Expected return on portfolio} = X_A\bar{R}_A + X_B\bar{R}_B$$

$$\text{Var(portfolio)} = X_A^2\sigma_A^2 + 2X_AX_B\sigma_{AB} + X_B^2\sigma_B^2$$

2   In our notation, $X$ stands for the proportion of a security in a portfolio. By varying $X$ we can trace out the efficient set of portfolios. We graphed the efficient set for the two-asset case as a curve, pointing out that the degree of curvature or bend in the graph reflects the diversification effect: the lower the correlation between the two securities, the greater the bend. The same general shape of the efficient set holds in a world of many assets.

3   Just as the formula for variance in the two-asset case is computed from a $2 \times 2$ matrix, the variance formula is computed from an $N \times N$ matrix in the $N$-asset case. We showed that with a large number of assets, there are many more covariance terms than variance terms in the matrix. In fact the variance terms are effectively diversified away in a large portfolio, but the covariance terms are not. Thus a diversified portfolio can eliminate some, but not all, of the risk of the individual securities.

4   The efficient set of risky assets can be combined with riskless borrowing and lending. In this case a rational investor will always choose to hold the portfolio of risky securities represented by point $A$ in Fig. 10.9. Then he can either borrow or lend at the riskless rate to achieve any desired point on line $II$ in the figure.

5   The contribution of a security to the risk of a large, well-diversified portfolio is proportional to the covariance of the security's return with the market's return. This contribution, when standardized, is called beta. The beta of a security can also be interpreted as the responsiveness of a security's return to that of the market.

6   The CAPM states that

$$\bar{R} = R_F + \beta(\bar{R}_M - R_F)$$

In other words, the expected return on a security is positively (and linearly) related to the security's beta.

7   The CAPM is a theoretical construct and only gives an insight into reality. Other theoretical models exist that do just as good a job at explaining variation in expected security returns.

## connect Questions and Problems

CONCEPT
**1 – 11**

1   **Individual Securities**   What are the main characteristics of individual security returns? Provide a definition of each characteristic and state why it is important.

2   **Expected Return, Variance and Covariance**   Explain what is meant by correlation and how it is used to measure the relationship between the returns on two securities. How is correlation related to variance and covariance? Use mathematical formulae to illustrate your answer.

3   **Portfolio Risk and Return**   Explain in words that your grandfather would understand how diversification works. Use a non-finance example to clarify your explanation.

4   **The Efficient Set for Two Assets**   What is a minimum variance portfolio? In a world with only two assets, is it possible to have two portfolios with the same risk but different expected return? Explain your answer using a practical example.

5   **The Efficient Set for Many Securities**   In a portfolio of many securities, all having positive correlation with each other, is it possible for the minimum variance portfolio to have zero risk?

6   **Diversification**   Assume that every asset has the same expected return and variance. Furthermore, all assets have the same covariance with each other. As the number of assets in the portfolio grows, which becomes more important: variance or covariance? Clarify your answer using words, diagrams, formulae or a practical example.

7   **Riskless Borrowing and Lending**   Explain what is meant by an optimal portfolio. What are the conditions that must exist for there to be only one optimal portfolio? Do you think these conditions are likely to persist in the real world? Explain.

8   **Market Equilibrium**   A broker has advised you not to invest in oil industry shares because they have high standard deviations. Is the broker's advice sound for a risk-averse investor like yourself? Why or why not?

9   **Relationship between Risk and Expected Return**   Is it possible that a risky asset could have a beta of zero? Explain. Based on the CAPM, what is the expected return on such an asset? Is it possible that a risky asset could have a negative beta? What does the CAPM predict about the expected return on such an asset? Can you give an explanation for your answer?

10   **Criticisms of the CAPM**   Provide a brief overview of Roll's critique. Do you agree or disagree with it? Why?

11   **Variations of the CAPM**   Explain what is meant by the CCAPM and the HCAPM. Why do you think these models are not popular with practitioners?

REGULAR
12 – 39

**12  Diversifiable and Non-Diversifiable Risks**   In broad terms, why is some risk diversifiable? Why are some risks non-diversifiable? Does it follow that an investor can control the level of unsystematic risk in a portfolio, but not the level of systematic risk?

**13  Systematic versus Unsystematic Risk**   Classify the following events as mostly systematic or mostly unsystematic. Is the distinction clear in every case?

   **(a)**  Short-term interest rates increase unexpectedly.

   **(b)**  The interest rate a company pays on its short-term debt borrowing is increased by its bank.

   **(c)**  Oil prices unexpectedly decline.

   **(d)**  An oil tanker ruptures, creating a large oil spill.

   **(e)**  A manufacturer loses a multimillion-dollar product liability suit.

   **(f)**  A European Union decision substantially broadens producer liability for injuries suffered by product users.

**14  Expected Portfolio Returns**   If a portfolio has a positive investment in every asset, can the expected return on the portfolio be greater than that on every asset in the portfolio? Can it be less than that on every asset in the portfolio? If you answer yes to one or both of these questions, give an example to support your answer.

**15  Diversification**   The most important characteristic in determining the expected return of a well-diversified portfolio is the variances of the individual assets in the portfolio. True or false? Explain.

**16  Portfolio Risk**   If a portfolio has a positive investment in every asset, can the standard deviation on the portfolio be less than that on every asset in the portfolio? What about the portfolio beta?

**17  Covariance**   Briefly explain why the covariance of a security with the rest of a well-diversified portfolio is a more appropriate measure of the risk of the security than the security's variance.

**18  Beta**   Consider the following quotation from a leading investment manager: 'The shares of Southern plc have traded close to £12 for most of the past three years. Since Southern's equity has demonstrated very little price movement, it has a low beta. Jungle Instruments, on the other hand, has traded as high as £150 and as low as its current £75. Since JI's equity has demonstrated a large amount of price movement, the stock has a very high beta.' Do you agree with this analysis? Explain.

**19  Security Selection**   Is the following statement true or false? 'A risky security cannot have an expected return that is less than the risk-free rate, because no risk-averse investor would be willing to hold this asset in equilibrium.' Explain.

**20  Determining Portfolio Weights**   The Greek lottery provider, Greek Organization of Football Prognost SA, is traded on the Athens Stock Exchange. Its share price is €19. Another Greek firm, Halkor, has a share price of €0.81. What are the portfolio weights for a portfolio that has 70 shares of Greek Organization of Football Prognost and 11,000 shares of Halkor?

**21  Portfolio Expected Return**   You own a portfolio that is 40 per cent invested in Groupe Bruxelles Lambert, 30 per cent in Heidelberg Cement, and 30 per cent in Heineken. The expected returns on these three shares are 9 per cent, 14 per cent and 17 per cent, respectively. What is the expected return on the portfolio?

**22  Calculating Expected Return**   Based on the following information, calculate the expected return:

| State of economy | Probability of state of economy | Rate of return if state occurs |
|---|---|---|
| Recession | 0.30 | −0.10 |
| Normal | 0.40 | 0.12 |
| Boom | 0.30 | 0.25 |

23 **Calculating Returns and Standard Deviations** Based on the following information, calculate the expected return and standard deviation for the two equities:

| State of economy | Probability of state of economy | Rate of return if state occurs | |
|---|---|---|---|
| | | A | B |
| Recession | 0.10 | 0.06 | −0.20 |
| Normal | 0.60 | 0.07 | 0.13 |
| Boom | 0.30 | 0.11 | 0.33 |

24 **Returns and Standard Deviations** Consider the following information:

| State of economy | Probability of state of economy | Rate of return if state occurs | | |
|---|---|---|---|---|
| | | Equity A | Equity B | Equity C |
| Boom | 0.05 | 0.30 | 0.45 | 0.33 |
| Good | 0.30 | 0.12 | 0.10 | 0.15 |
| Poor | 0.50 | 0.01 | −0.15 | −0.05 |
| Bust | 0.15 | −0.06 | −0.30 | −0.09 |

(a) Your portfolio is invested 40 per cent each in A and C, and 20 per cent in B. What is the expected return of the portfolio?

(b) What is the variance of this portfolio? The standard deviation?

25 **Calculating Portfolio Betas** You own an equity portfolio invested 25 per cent in Q, 20 per cent in R, 15 per cent in S, and 40 per cent in T. The betas for these four equities are 0.6, 1.70, 1.15, and 1.34, respectively. What is the portfolio beta?

26 **Calculating Portfolio Betas** You own a portfolio invested equally in a risk-free asset and two equities. If one of the equities has a beta of 1.9 and the total portfolio is equally as risky as the market, what must the beta be for the other equity in your portfolio?

27 **Using CAPM** An equity has a beta of 1.2 and an expected return of 16 per cent. A risk-free asset currently earns 5 per cent.

(a) What is the expected return on a portfolio that is equally invested in the two assets?

(b) If a portfolio of the two assets has a beta of 0.75, what are the portfolio weights?

(c) If a portfolio of the two assets has an expected return of 8 per cent, what is its beta?

(d) If a portfolio of the two assets has a beta of 2.40, what are the portfolio weights? How do you interpret the weights for the two assets in this case? Explain.

28 **Using the SML** W has an expected return of 13 per cent and a beta of 1.1. If the risk-free rate is 4 per cent, complete the following table for portfolios of W and a risk-free asset. Illustrate the relationship between portfolio expected return and portfolio beta by

plotting the expected returns against the betas. What is the slope of the line that results?

| Percentage of portfolio in *W*, % | Portfolio expected return | Portfolio beta |
|---|---|---|
| 0 | | |
| 25 | | |
| 50 | | |
| 75 | | |
| 100 | | |
| 125 | | |
| 150 | | |

29 **Reward-to-Risk Ratios**   *Y* has a beta of 1.50 and an expected return of 17 per cent. *Z* has a beta of 0.80 and an expected return of 10.5 per cent. If the risk-free rate is 5.5 per cent and the market risk premium is 7.5 per cent, are these equities correctly priced? What would the risk-free rate have to be for the two equities to be correctly priced?

30 **Portfolio Returns and Deviations**   Shares in Hellenic Telecom have an expected return of 15%, and the standard deviation of these returns is 30%. National Bank of Greece's shares are expected to produce a return of 16% with a standard deviation of 40%. What would be the rate of return and risk of a portfolio made up of 40% of Hellenic Telecom's shares and 60% of National Bank of Greece's shares if the returns on these shares have a correlation of 0.6?

31 **Analysing a Portfolio**   You want to create a portfolio equally as risky as the market, and you have €1,000,000 to invest. Given this information, fill in the rest of the following table:

| Asset | Investment (€) | Beta |
|---|---|---|
| Equity *A* | 200,000 | 0.80 |
| Equity *B* | 250,000 | 1.30 |
| Equity *C* | | 1.50 |
| Risk-free asset | | |

32 **Analysing a Portfolio**   You have €100,000 to invest in a portfolio containing *X*, *Y* and a risk-free asset. You must invest all of your money. Your goal is to create a portfolio that has an expected return of 13.5 per cent and which has only 70 per cent of the risk of the overall market. If *X* has an expected return of 31 per cent and a beta of 1.8, *Y* has an expected return of 20 per cent and a beta of 1.3, and the risk-free rate is 7 per cent, how much money will you invest in *X*? How do you interpret your answer?

33 **Covariance and Correlation**   Based on the following information, calculate the expected return and standard deviation of each of the following equities. Assume each state of the economy is equally likely to happen. What are the covariance and correlation between the returns of the two equities?

| State of economy | Return on *A* | Return on *B* |
|---|---|---|
| Bear | 0.063 | −0.037 |
| Normal | 0.105 | 0.064 |
| Bull | 0.156 | 0.253 |

34 **Covariance and Correlation**   Based on the following information, calculate the expected return and standard deviation for each of the following equities. What are the covariance and correlation between the returns of the two equities?

| State of economy | Probability of state of economy | Return on *J* | Return on *K* |
|---|---|---|---|
| Bear | 0.25 | −0.020 | 0.050 |
| Normal | 0.60 | 0.092 | 0.062 |
| Bull | 0.15 | 0.154 | 0.074 |

35 **Portfolio Standard Deviation**   Suppose the expected returns and standard deviations of *A* and *B* are $E(R_A) = 0.15$, $E(R_B) = 0.25$, $\sigma_A = 0.40$, and $\sigma_B = 0.65$, respectively.

(a) Calculate the expected return and standard deviation of a portfolio that is composed of 40 per cent *A* and 60 per cent *B* when the correlation between the returns on *A* and *B* is 0.5.

(b) Calculate the standard deviation of a portfolio that is composed of 40 per cent *A* and 60 per cent *B* when the correlation coefficient between the returns on *A* and *B* is −0.5.

(c) How does the correlation between the returns on *A* and *B* affect the standard deviation of the portfolio?

36 **Correlation and Beta**   You have been provided with the following data about the equities of three firms, the market portfolio, and the risk-free asset:

| | Expected return | Standard deviation | Correlation* | Beta |
|---|---|---|---|---|
| Firm *A* | 0.13 | 0.38 | (i) | 0.9 |
| Firm *B* | 0.16 | (ii) | 0.40 | 1.1 |
| Firm *C* | 0.25 | 0.65 | 0.35 | (iii) |
| The market portfolio | 0.15 | 0.20 | (iv) | (v) |
| The risk-free asset | 0.05 | (vi) | (vii) | (viii) |

*With the market portfolio.

(a) Fill in the missing values in the table.

(b) Is the equity of Firm *A* correctly priced according to the capital asset pricing model (CAPM)? What about the equity of Firm *B*? Firm *C*? If these securities are not correctly priced, what is your investment recommendation for someone with a well-diversified portfolio?

37 **CML**   The market portfolio has an expected return of 12 per cent and a standard deviation of 10 per cent. The risk-free rate is 5 per cent.

(a) What is the expected return on a well-diversified portfolio with a standard deviation of 7 per cent?

(b) What is the standard deviation of a well-diversified portfolio with an expected return of 20 per cent?

38 **CAPM**   The expected rates of return on the French firms Publicis and Renault, the market portfolio (CAC 40) and the risk-free asset are given below, along with the standard deviations of these returns.

| Asset | Expected return (%) | Standard deviation (%) |
|---|---|---|
| Publicis | 17 | 40 |
| Renault | 10 | 20 |
| CAC 40 | 14 | 17 |
| Risk-free asset | 3 | 0 |

(a) Assuming that the returns are explained by the capital asset pricing model, specify the betas for Publicis and Renault, and the risk of a portfolio of Publicis and Renault with an expected return the same as the CAC 40.

(b) Specify the composition of a portfolio consisting of the CAC 40 and the risk-free asset that will produce an expected return of 10%. Contrast the risk on this portfolio with the risk of Renault.

39 **Portfolios** Below is given standard deviation and correlation information on three British companies: National Grid, Old Mutual, and Prudential.

| | National Grid | Old Mutual | Prudential | Standard deviation (%) |
|---|---|---|---|---|
| National Grid | 1 | 0.1 | −0.2 | 16 |
| Old Mutual | | 1 | 0.6 | 18 |
| Prudential | | | 1 | 24 |

(a) If a portfolio is made up of 20 per cent of National Grid, 30 per cent of Old Mutual and 50 per cent of Prudential, estimate the portfolio's standard deviation.

(b) If you were asked to design a portfolio using just National Grid and Prudential, what percentage investment in each share would produce a zero standard deviation?

40 **Systematic versus Unsystematic Risk** Consider the following information about *I* and *II*:

| | Probability of state | Rate of return if state occurs | |
|---|---|---|---|
| State of economy | of economy | *I* | *II* |
| Recession | 0.15 | 0.09 | −0.30 |
| Normal | 0.70 | 0.42 | 0.12 |
| Irrational exuberance | 0.15 | 0.26 | 0.44 |

The market risk premium is 10 per cent, and the risk-free rate is 4 per cent. Which security is the most systematic risk? Which one is the most unsystematic risk? Which stock is 'riskier'? Explain.

41 **CML and SML** Explain in detail, using diagrams to illustrate your answer, what is meant by the terms 'capital market line' and 'security market line'.

42 **SML** Suppose you observe the following situation:

| Security | Beta | Expected return |
|---|---|---|
| Renewable Energy Corp | 1.3 | 0.23 |
| STATOIL | 0.6 | 0.13 |

Assume these securities are correctly priced. Based on the CAPM, what is the expected return on the market? What is the risk-free rate?

43 **Portfolio Theory** This question is designed to test your understanding of the mean standard deviation diagram.

(a) Draw a mean standard deviation diagram to illustrate combinations of a risky asset and the risk-free asset.

(b) Extend this concept to a diagram of the risk-free asset and all possible risky portfolios.

(c)    Why does one line – the capital market line – dominate all other possible portfolio combinations?

(d)    Label the capital market line and that optimal portfolio.

(e)    What condition must hold at the optimal portfolio?

44    **Covariance and Portfolio Standard Deviation**    There are three securities in the market. The following table shows their possible pay-offs:

| State | Probability of outcome | Return on security 1 | Return on security 2 | Return on security 3 |
|-------|------------------------|----------------------|----------------------|----------------------|
| 1 | 0.10 | 0.25 | 0.25 | 0.10 |
| 2 | 0.40 | 0.20 | 0.15 | 0.15 |
| 3 | 0.40 | 0.15 | 0.20 | 0.20 |
| 4 | 0.10 | 0.10 | 0.10 | 0.25 |

(a)    What are the expected return and standard deviation of each security?

(b)    What are the covariances and correlations between the pairs of securities?

(c)    What are the expected return and standard deviation of a portfolio with half of its funds invested in security 1 and half in security 2?

(d)    What are the expected return and standard deviation of a portfolio with half of its funds invested in security 1 and half in security 3?

(e)    What are the expected return and standard deviation of a portfolio with half of its funds invested in security 2 and half in security 3?

(f)    What do your answers in parts (a), (c), (d) and (e) imply about diversification?

45    **SML**    Suppose you observe the following situation:

| | | Return if state occurs | |
|---|---|---|---|
| State of economy | Probability of state | A | B |
| Bust | 0.25 | −0.10 | −0.30 |
| Normal | 0.50 | 0.10 | 0.05 |
| Boom | 0.25 | 0.20 | 0.40 |

(a)    Calculate the expected return on each equity.

(b)    Assuming the capital asset pricing model holds and A's beta is greater than B's beta by 0.25, what is the expected market risk premium?

46    **Standard Deviation and Beta**    There are two securities in the market, A and B. The price of A today is €50. The price of A next year will be €40 if the economy is in a recession, €55 if the economy is normal, and €60 if the economy is expanding. The probabilities of recession, normal times and expansion are 0.1, 0.8 and 0.1, respectively. A pays no dividends and has a correlation of 0.8 with the market portfolio. B has an expected return of 9 per cent, a standard deviation of 12 per cent, a correlation with the market portfolio of 0.2, and a correlation with A of 0.6. The market portfolio has a standard deviation of 10 per cent. Assume the CAPM holds.

(a)    If you are a typical, risk-averse investor with a well-diversified portfolio, which security would you prefer? Why?

(b)    What are the expected return and standard deviation of a portfolio consisting of 70 per cent of A and 30 per cent of B?

(c)    What is the beta of the portfolio in part (b)?

**47 Minimum Variance Portfolio** Assume $A$ and $B$ have the following characteristics:

| Equity | Expected return (%) | Standard deviation (%) |
|--------|---------------------|------------------------|
| $A$ | 5 | 10 |
| $B$ | 10 | 20 |

The covariance between the returns on the two equities is 0.001.

(a) Suppose an investor holds a portfolio consisting only of $A$ and $B$. Find the portfolio weights, $X_A$ and $X_B$, such that the variance of her portfolio is minimized. (*Hint*: Remember that the sum of the two weights must equal 1.)

(b) What is the expected return on the minimum variance portfolio?

(c) If the covariance between the returns on the two equities is −0.02, what are the minimum variance weights?

(d) What is the variance of the portfolio in part (c)?

**48 Minimum Variance Portfolio** Consider the table below. Using either the historical return or expected return and Solver, compute the minimum variance portfolio for the universe of three Norwegian shares (Crew Gold, GGS and Marine Harvest) described below. Assume the risk-free return is 6 per cent. Which return measure did you use and why?

| | Correlation with | | | | | |
|--------|------------|------|-------------------|---------------------|---------------------|----------|
| Stock | Crew Gold | GGS | Marine Harvest | Expected return (%) | Historical return (%) | Variance |
| Crew Gold | 1 | 0.40 | 0.45 | 16 | 20.65 | 168 |
| GGS | 0.40 | 1 | −0.09 | 10 | −34.15 | 231 |
| Marine Harvest | 0.45 | −0.09 | 1 | 30 | 68.60 | 433 |

**49 Beta** The following returns are for the Swedish-Finnish paper manufacturer Stora Enso, and the Dow Jones Nordic 30.

| Month | Stora Enso (%) | N 30 index (%) | Month | Stora Enso (%) | N 30 index (%) |
|--------|----------------|----------------|--------|----------------|----------------|
| Mar 09 | −14.1 | −6.0 | Mar 08 | −15.3 | −4.5 |
| Feb 09 | −26.3 | −7.7 | Feb 08 | −6.7 | 4.0 |
| Jan 09 | −11.3 | −0.8 | Jan 08 | −9.5 | −13.0 |
| Dec 08 | −14.3 | −4.6 | Dec 07 | −3.7 | −1.4 |
| Nov 08 | −4.4 | −6.2 | Nov 07 | −10.5 | −6.1 |
| Oct 08 | −2.1 | −15.6 | Oct 07 | −11.4 | −1.7 |
| Sep 08 | −2.9 | −16.8 | Sep 07 | 4.8 | 4.2 |
| Aug 08 | 20.7 | 1.5 | Aug 07 | 2.0 | −1.8 |
| Jul 08 | −8.0 | −0.1 | Jul 07 | −9.7 | −1.0 |
| Jun 08 | −19.9 | −13.1 | Jun 07 | 1.0 | 0.0 |
| May 08 | −4.4 | 3.2 | May 07 | 4.6 | 1.2 |
| Apr 08 | 10.1 | 3.3 | Apr 07 | 1.5 | 5.5 |

Use a spreadsheet to calculate Stora Enso's beta for the full period. Now calculate the beta using data for April 2008 to March 2009. Calculate the beta for April 2007 to March 2008. What can you say about the different beta estimates? Is this evidence for or against CAPM? Explain your answer.

# A Job at West Coast Yachts, Part 2

You are discussing your retirement plan with Dan Ervin when he mentions that Sarah Brown, a representative from Skandla Financial Services, is visiting West Coast Yachts today. You decide that you should meet with Sarah, so Dan sets up an appointment for you later in the day.

When you sit down with Sarah, she discusses the various investment options available in the company's retirement account. You mention to Sarah that you researched West Coast Yachts before you accepted your new job. You are confident in management's ability to lead the company. Analysis of the company has led to your belief that the company is growing, and will achieve a greater market share in the future. Given these considerations, you are leaning towards investing 100 per cent of your retirement account in West Coast Yachts.

Assume the risk-free rate is the return on a 30-day T-bill. The correlation between the Skandla bond fund and large-cap equity fund is 0.27.

1   Considering the effects of diversification, how should Sarah respond to the suggestion that you invest 100 per cent of your retirement account in West Coast Yachts?

2   Sarah's response to investing your retirement account entirely in West Coast Yachts has convinced you that this may not be the best alternative. You now consider that a 100 per cent investment in the bond fund may be the best alternative. Is it?

3   Using the returns for the Skandla Large-Cap Equity Fund and the Skandla Bond Fund, graph the opportunity set of feasible portfolios.

4   After examining the opportunity set, you notice that you can invest in a portfolio consisting of the bond fund and the large-cap equity fund that will have exactly the same standard deviation as the bond fund. This portfolio will also have a greater expected return. What are the portfolio weights and expected return of this portfolio?

5   Examining the opportunity set, you notice there is a portfolio that has the lowest standard deviation. This is the minimum variance portfolio. What are the portfolio weights, expected return, and standard deviation of this portfolio? Why is the minimum variance portfolio important?

6   A measure of risk-adjusted performance that is often used is the Sharpe ratio. The Sharpe ratio is calculated as the risk premium of an asset divided by its standard deviation. The portfolio with the highest possible Sharpe ratio on the opportunity set is called the Sharpe optimal portfolio. What are the portfolio weights, expected return and standard deviation of the Sharpe optimal portfolio? How does the Sharpe ratio of this portfolio compare with the Sharpe ratios of the bond fund and the large-cap equity fund? Do you see a connection between the Sharpe optimal portfolio and the CAPM?

# Practical Case Study

**Using CAPM**   In Yahoo! Finance you can find estimates of beta for companies under the 'Detailed Data' link. Locate the beta for Associated British Foods (ABF.L) and Diageo (DGE.L). Using an estimate of the historical risk-free rate and market risk premium, calculate the expected return for each company based on the most recent beta. Is the expected return for each company what you would expect? Why or why not?

# Additional Reading

Capital asset pricing theory is probably the most tested theory in modern investment finance. Given this, it is important that the interested reader is directed to the most relevant recent research in the area. A number of papers listed below directly test the power of the CAPM or market model beta under a variety of environments and with a number of other control variables. While it is easy to say that the range of CAPM anomalies suggests that the model is inferior to other, more complex, models, it is still the most commonly used way to estimate the cost of equity (discount rate) of a listed firm. Most of the papers listed below study the US markets. The country or region of study is appended in bold to the end of each reference. The list does not follow any real theme, as is the case in other chapters. Moreover, the listing is a very small representation of recent research in the area. Those who wish to specialize should view the references as the tip of the iceberg, and use them to build up their own reading list.

Ang, A., R. Hodrick, Y. Xing and X. Zhang (2009) 'High idiosyncratic volatility and low returns: international and further evidence', *Journal of Financial Economics*, vol. 91, no. 1, pp. 1–23. **International**.

Bodnaruk, A. and P. Ostberg (2009) 'Does investor recognition predict returns?', *Journal of Financial Economics*, vol. 91, no. 2, pp. 208–226. **Sweden**.

Fama, E.F. and K.R. French (2006) 'The value premium and the CAPM', *Journal of Finance*, vol. 61, no. 5, pp. 2163–3185. **US**.

Fu, F. (2009) 'Idiosyncratic risk and the cross-section of expected stock returns', *Journal of Financial Economics*, vol. 91, no. 1, pp. 24–37. **US**.

Hong, H., T. Lim, and J. Stein (2000) 'Bad news travels slowly: size, analyst coverage, and the profitability of momentum strategies', *Journal of Finance*, vol. 55, no. 1, pp. 265–295. **US**.

Kearney, C. and V. Poti (2008) 'Have European stocks become more volatile? An empirical investigation of idiosyncratic and market risk in the euro area', *European Financial Management*, vol. 14, no. 3, pp. 419–444. **Europe**.

Kumar, P., S.M. Sorescu, R.D. Boehme and B.R. Danielsen (2008) 'Estimation risk, information, and the conditional CAPM: theory and evidence', *Review of Financial Studies*, vol. 21, no. 3, pp. 1037–1075. **US**.

Lewellen, J. and S. Nagel (2006) 'The conditional CAPM does not explain asset-pricing anomalies', *Journal of Financial Economics*, vol. 82, no. 2, pp. 289–314. **US**.

Pastor, L. (2000) 'Portfolio selection and asset pricing models', *Journal of Finance*, vol. 55, no. 1, pp. 179–223. **US**.

Piazzesi, M., M. Schneider and S. Tuzel (2007) 'Housing, consumption and asset pricing', *Journal of Financial Economics*, vol. 83, no. 3, pp. 531–569. **US**.

# Endnotes

1   In this example the four states give rise to four *possible* outcomes for each security. Had we used past data, the outcomes would have actually occurred. In that case, statisticians argue that the correct divisor is $N - 1$, where $N$ is the number of observations. Thus the denominator would be 3 [= (4 − 1)] in the case of past data, not 4. Note that the example in Section 9.5 involved past data and we used a divisor of $N - 1$. While this difference causes grief to both students and textbook writers, it is a minor point in practice. In the real world samples are generally so large that using $N$ or $N - 1$ in the denominator has virtually no effect on the calculation of variance.

2   As with variance, we divided by $N$ (4 in this example) because the four states give rise to four *possible* outcomes. However, had we used past data, the correct divisor would be $N - 1$ (3 in this example).

3   There are only four equally probable returns for Supertech and Slowpoke, so neither security possesses a normal distribution. Thus probabilities would be slightly different in our example.

4   As with covariance, the ordering of the two securities is not relevant when we express the correlation between the two securities: that is, $\rho_{Super, Slow} = \rho_{Slow, Super}$.

5   A major exception occurs with derivative securities. For example, the correlation between an equity share and a put on the equity is generally strongly negative. Puts will be treated later in the text.

6   Of course, someone dead set on parting with his money can do so. For example, he can trade frequently without purpose, so that commissions more than offset the positive expected returns on the portfolio.

7   The classic treatise is Harry Markowitz, *Portfolio Selection* (New York: John Wiley & Sons, 1959). Markowitz won the Nobel Prize in economics in 1990 for his work on modern portfolio theory.

8   Equation (10.10) is actually a weighted *average* of the variance and covariance terms because the weights, $1/N$ and $1 - 1/N$, sum to 1.

9   This example ignores the casino's cut.

10  Though it is harder to show, this risk reduction effect also applies to the general case where variances and covariances are *not* equal.

11  Meir Statman, 'How many stocks make a diversified portfolio?' *Journal of Financial and Quantitative Analysis* (September 1987).

12  Surprisingly, this appears to be a decent approximation because many investors can borrow from a stockbroker (called *going on margin*) when purchasing securities. The borrowing rate here is very near the riskless rate of interest, particularly for large investors. More will be said about this in a later chapter.

13  The assumption of homogeneous expectations states that all investors have the same beliefs concerning returns, variances and covariances. It does not say that all investors have the same aversion to risk.

14  Unfortunately, empirical evidence shows that virtually no equities have negative betas.

15  This relationship was first proposed independently by John Lintner and William F. Sharpe.

16  Perhaps the two best-known papers were F. Black, M.C. Jensen and M.S. Scholes, 'The capital asset pricing model: some empirical tests', in M. Jensen, ed., *Studies in the Theory of Capital Markets* (New York: Praeger, 1972), and E.F. Fama and J. MacBeth, 'Risk, return and equilibrium: some empirical tests', *Journal of Political Economy*, vol. 8, 1973, pp. 607–636.

17  For example, the studies suggest that the average return on a zero-beta portfolio is above the risk-free rate, a finding inconsistent with the CAPM.

18  E.F. Fama and K.R. French, 'The cross-section of expected stock returns', *Journal of Finance*, vol. 47, 1992, pp. 427–466, and E.F. Fama and K.R. French, 'Common risk factors in the returns on stocks and bonds,' *Journal of Financial Economics*, vol. 17, 1993, pp. 3–56.

19  For example, see W.J. Breen and R.A. Koraczyk, 'On selection biases in book-to-market based tests of asset pricing models', unpublished paper. Northwestern University, November 1993; and S.P. Kothari, J. Shanken and R.G. Sloan, 'Another look at the cross-section of expected stock returns', *Journal of Finance*, vol. 50, 1995, no. 1, pp. 185–224.

20  Points 4 and 5 are addressed in the Kothari, Shanken, and Sloan paper.

 Online **Learning Centre**

To help you grasp the key concepts of this chapter check out the extra resources posted on the Online Learning Centre at **www.mcgraw-hill.co.uk/textbooks/hillier**

Among other helpful resources there are PowerPoint presentations, chapter outlines and mini-cases.

# Chapter 11

# Factor Models and the Arbitrage Pricing Theory

PART THREE

In January 2006 Yahoo!, Apple Computer, and Dutch semiconductor company ASML joined a host of other companies in announcing operating results. As you might expect, news such as this tends to move share prices.

Yahoo!, for example, reported a profit increase of 83 per cent and a revenue increase of 39 per cent. But investors didn't say 'Yahoo!' Instead, the share price dropped by 12 per cent when the market opened. Apple announced revenues for the most recent quarter of $5.75 billion, an increase of 65 per cent over the same quarter in the previous year, and the company's net income nearly doubled to $565 million. So, did investors cheer? Not exactly: the share price fell by 2 per cent. Finally, ASML announced its earnings were less than half of the earnings from the same quarter in the previous year, on a sales decline of 30 per cent. Even with this apparently troubling news, the company's share value jumped over 6 per cent.

Two of these announcements seem positive, yet the share price fell. The third announcement seems negative, yet the share price jumped. So when is good news really good news? The answer is fundamental to understanding risk and return, and the good news is this chapter explores it in some detail.

## 11.1 Factor Models: Announcements, Surprises, and Expected Returns

We learned in the previous chapter how to construct portfolios and how to evaluate their returns. We now step back and examine the returns on individual securities more closely. By doing this we shall find that the portfolios inherit and alter the properties of the securities they comprise.

To be concrete, let us consider the return on the equity of a company called Flyers. What will determine this equity's return in, say, the coming month?

The return on any equity traded in a financial market consists of two parts. First, the *normal* or *expected return* from the equity is the part of the return that shareholders in the market predict or expect. It depends on all of the information shareholders have that bears on the company, and it uses all of our understanding of what will influence the share price in the next month.

The second part is the *uncertain* or *risky return* on the equity. This is the portion that comes from information that will be revealed within the month. The list of such information is endless, but here are some examples:

- News about Flyers' research
- Government figures released for the gross national product (GNP)
- Results of the latest arms control talks
- Discovery that a rival's product has been tampered with
- News that Flyers' sales figures are higher than expected
- A sudden drop in interest rates
- The unexpected retirement of Flyers' founder and chairman

A way to write the return on Flyers' shares in the coming month, then, is

$$R = \bar{R} + U$$

where $R$ is the actual total return in the month, $\bar{R}$ is the expected part of the return, and $U$ stands for the unexpected part of the return.

We must exercise some care in studying the effect of these or other news items on the return. For example, the government might give us GNP or unemployment figures for this month, but how much of that is new information for shareholders? Surely, at the beginning of the month, shareholders will have some idea or forecast of what the monthly GNP will be. The expectations of shareholders should be factored into the expected part of the return, $\bar{R}$, as of the beginning of the month. On the other hand, insofar as the announcement by the government is a surprise, and to the extent to which it influences the return on the shares, it will be part of $U$, the unanticipated part of the return.

As an example, suppose shareholders in the market had forecast that the GNP increase this month would be 0.5 per cent. If GNP influences our company's share price, this forecast will be part of the information shareholders use to form the expectation, $\bar{R}$, of the monthly return. If the actual announcement this month is exactly 0.5 per cent, the same as the forecast, then the shareholders learned nothing new, and the announcement is not news. It is like hearing a rumour about a friend when you knew it all along.

On the other hand, suppose the government announced that the actual GNP increase during the year was 1.5 per cent. Now shareholders have learned something – that the increase is one percentage point higher than they had forecast. This difference between the actual result and the forecast, one percentage point in this example, is sometimes called the *innovation* or *surprise*.

Any announcement can be broken into two parts, the anticipated or expected part and the surprise or innovation:

Announcement = Expected part + Surprise

The expected part of any announcement is part of the information the market uses to form the expectation, $\bar{R}$, of the return on the equity. The surprise is the news that influences the unanticipated return on the equity, $U$.

For example, to open the chapter, we compared Yahoo!, Apple Computer, and ASML. In Yahoo!'s case, even though the company's revenue and profits jumped substantially, neither number met investor expectations. In Apple's case, in addition to the good earnings, the company announced that sales in the next quarter would be lower than previously expected. And for ASML, even though sales and profits were below the previous year, both numbers exceeded expectations.

When we speak of news, then, we refer to the surprise part of any announcement and not the portion that the market has expected and therefore has already discounted.

## 11.2  Risk: Systematic and Unsystematic

The unanticipated part of the return – that portion resulting from surprises – is the true risk of any investment. After all, if we got what we had expected, there would be no risk and no uncertainty.

There are important differences, though, among various sources of risk. Look at our previous list of news stories. Some of these stories are directed specifically at Flyers, and some are more general. Which of the news items are of specific importance to Flyers?

Announcements about interest rates or GNP are clearly important for nearly all companies, whereas the news about Flyers' chairman, its research, its sales, or the affairs of a rival company are of specific interest to Flyers. We shall divide these two types of announcement and the resulting risk, then, into two components: a systematic portion, called *systematic risk*; and the remainder, which we call *specific* or *unsystematic risk*. The following definitions describe the difference:

- A *systematic risk* is any risk that affects a large number of assets, each to a greater or lesser degree.

- An *unsystematic risk* is a risk that specifically affects a single asset or a small group of assets.[1]

Uncertainty about general economic conditions, such as GNP, interest rates, or inflation, is an example of systematic risk. These conditions affect nearly all securities to some degree. An unanticipated or surprise increase in inflation affects wages and the costs of the supplies that companies buy, the value of the assets that companies own, and the prices at which companies sell their products. These forces to which all companies are susceptible are the essence of systematic risk.

In contrast, the announcement of a small oil strike by a company may affect that company alone or a few other companies. Certainly, it is unlikely to have an effect on the world oil market. To stress that such information is unsystematic and affects only some specific companies, we sometimes call it an *idiosyncratic risk*.

This permits us to break down the risk of Flyers' equity into its two components: the systematic and the unsystematic. As is traditional, we shall use the Greek epsilon, $\varepsilon$, to represent the unsystematic risk and write

$$R = \bar{R} + U$$
$$= \bar{R} + m + \varepsilon$$

where we have used the letter $m$ to stand for the systematic risk. Sometimes systematic risk is referred to as *market risk*. This emphasizes the fact that $m$ influences all assets in the market to some extent.

The important point about the way we have broken the total risk, $U$, into its two components, $m$ and $\varepsilon$, is that $\varepsilon$, because it is specific to the company, is unrelated to the specific risk of most other companies. For example, the unsystematic risk on Flyers' equity, $\varepsilon_F$, is unrelated to the unsystematic risk of a company, such as Vodafone, in another industry, $\varepsilon_V$. The risk that Flyers' equity will go up or down because of a discovery by its research team – or its failure to discover something – probably is unrelated to any of the specific uncertainties that affect Vodafone's equity.

Using the terms of the previous chapter, this means that the unsystematic risks of Flyers' equity and Vodafone's equity are unrelated to each other, or are uncorrelated. In the symbols of statistics:

$$\text{Corr}(\varepsilon_F, \varepsilon_V) = 0$$

## 11.3 Systematic Risk and Betas

The fact that the unsystematic parts of the returns on two companies are unrelated to each other does not mean that the systematic portions are unrelated. On the contrary, because both companies are influenced by the same systematic risks, their total returns will also be related.

For example, a surprise about inflation will influence almost all companies to some extent. How sensitive is Flyers' share price return to unanticipated changes in inflation? If Flyers' share price tends to go up on news that inflation is exceeding expectations, we would say that it is positively related to inflation. If the share price goes down when inflation exceeds expectations and up when inflation falls short of expectations, it is negatively related. In the unusual case where an equity's return is uncorrelated with inflation surprises, inflation has no effect on it.

We capture the influence of a systematic risk by using the beta coefficient. The beta coefficient, $\beta$, tells us the response of the equity's return to a systematic risk. In the previous chapter beta measured the responsiveness of a security's return to a specific risk factor, the return on the market portfolio. We used this type of responsiveness to develop the capital asset pricing model. Because we now consider many types of systematic risk, our current work can be viewed as a generalization of our work in the previous chapter.

If a company's share price return is positively related to the risk of inflation, it has a positive inflation beta; if it is negatively related to inflation, its inflation beta is negative; and if it is uncorrelated with inflation, its inflation beta is zero.

It's not hard to imagine some equities with positive inflation betas and others with negative inflation betas. The equity of a company owning gold mines will probably have a positive inflation beta, because an unanticipated rise in inflation is usually associated with an increase in gold prices. On the other hand, an automobile company facing stiff foreign competition might find that an increase in inflation means that the wages it pays are higher, but that it cannot raise its prices to cover the increase. This profit squeeze, as the company's expenses rise faster than its revenues, would give its equity a negative inflation beta.

Some structure is useful at this point. Suppose we have identified three systematic risks on which we want to focus. We may believe that these three are sufficient to describe the systematic risks that influence share price returns. Three likely candidates are inflation, GNP, and interest rates. Thus every equity will have a beta associated with each of these systematic risks: an inflation beta, a GNP beta, and an interest rate beta. We can write the return on the equity, then, in the following form:

$$
\begin{aligned}
R &= \bar{R} + U \\
&= \bar{R} + m + \varepsilon \\
&= \bar{R} + \beta_I F_I + \beta_{GNP} F_{GNP} + \beta_r F_r + \varepsilon
\end{aligned}
$$

where we have used the symbol $\beta_I$ to denote the stock's inflation beta, $\beta_{GNP}$ for its GNP beta, and $\beta_r$ to stand for its interest rate beta. In the equation, $F$ stands for a surprise, whether it be in inflation, GNP, or interest rates.

Let us go through an example to see how the surprises and the expected return add up to produce the total return, $R$, on a given security. To make it more familiar, suppose that the return is over a horizon of a year and not just a month. Suppose that at the beginning of the year inflation is forecast to be 5 per cent for the year, GNP is forecast to increase by 2 per cent, and interest rates are expected not to change. Suppose the security we are looking at has the following betas:

$$
\begin{aligned}
\beta_I &= 2 \\
\beta_{GNP} &= 1 \\
\beta_r &= -1.8
\end{aligned}
$$

The magnitude of the beta describes how great an impact a systematic risk has on a security's returns. A beta of +1 indicates that the security's return rises and falls one for one with the systematic factor. This means, in our example, that because the security has a GNP beta of 1, it experiences a 1 per cent increase in return for every 1 per cent surprise increase in GNP. If its GNP beta were −2, it would fall by 2 per cent when there was an unanticipated increase of 1 per cent in GNP, and it would rise by 2 per cent if GNP experienced a surprise 1 per cent decline.

Let us suppose that during the year the following events occur: inflation rises by 7 per cent, GNP rises by only 1 per cent, and interest rates fall by 2 per cent. Suppose we learn some good news about the company, perhaps that it is succeeding quickly with some new business strategy, and that this unanticipated development contributes 5 per cent to its return. In other words:

$$
\varepsilon = 5\%
$$

Let us assemble all of this information to find what return the security had during the year.

First we must determine what news or surprises took place in the systematic factors. From our information we know that

$$\text{Expected inflation} = 5\%$$
$$\text{Expected GNP change} = 2\%$$

and

$$\text{Expected change in interest rates} = 0\%$$

This means that the market had discounted these changes, and the surprises will be the difference between what actually takes place and these expectations:

$$
\begin{aligned}
F_I &= \text{Surprise in inflation} \\
&= \text{Actual inflation} - \text{Expected inflation} \\
&= 7\% - 5\% \\
&= 2\%
\end{aligned}
$$

Similarly,

$$
\begin{aligned}
F_{\text{GNP}} &= \text{Surprise in GNP} \\
&= \text{Actual GNP} - \text{Expected GNP} \\
&= 1\% - 2\% \\
&= -1\%
\end{aligned}
$$

and

$$
\begin{aligned}
F_r &= \text{Surprise in change in interest rates} \\
&= \text{Actual change} - \text{Expected change} \\
&= -2\% - 0\% \\
&= -2\%
\end{aligned}
$$

The total effect of the systematic risks on the security return, then, is

$$
\begin{aligned}
m &= \text{Systematic risk portion of return} \\
&= \beta_I F_I + \beta_{\text{GNP}} F_{\text{GNP}} + \beta_r F_r \\
&= [2 \times 2\%] + [1 \times (-1\%)] + [(-1.8) \times (-2\%)] \\
&= 6.6\%
\end{aligned}
$$

Combining this with the unsystematic risk portion, the total risky portion of the return on the security is

$$m + \varepsilon = 6.6\% + 5\% = 11.6\%$$

Last, if the expected return on the security for the year was, say, 4 per cent, the total return from all three components will be

$$
\begin{aligned}
R &= \bar{R} + m + \varepsilon \\
&= 4\% + 6.6\% + 5\% \\
&= 15.6\%
\end{aligned}
$$

The model we have been looking at is called a factor model, and the systematic sources of risk, designated $F$, are called the *factors*. To be perfectly formal, a *k-factor model* is a model where each security's return is generated by

$$R = \bar{R} + \beta_1 F_1 + \beta_2 F_2 + \cdots + \beta_\kappa F_\kappa + \varepsilon$$

where $\varepsilon$ is specific to a particular security, and is uncorrelated with the $\varepsilon$ term for other securities. In our preceding example we had a three-factor model. We used inflation, GNP, and the change in interest rates as examples of systematic sources of risk, or factors. Researchers have not settled on what is the correct set of factors. Like so many other questions, this might be one of those matters that is never laid to rest.

In practice, researchers frequently use different models for returns. They do not use all of the economic factors we used previously as examples; instead they use an index of stock market returns – such as the FTSE 100 or DAX – in addition to returns on arbitrage portfolios representing factors that have been identified as being important from earlier research. Using the single-factor model we can write returns like this:

$$R = \bar{R} + \beta(R_{\text{FTSE100}} - \bar{R}_{\text{FTSE100}}) + \varepsilon$$

Where there is only one factor (such as the returns on the FTSE 100 or DAX index), we do not need to put a subscript on the beta. In this form (with minor modifications) the factor model is called a **market model**. This term is employed because the index that is used for the factor is an index of returns on the whole market. The market model is written as

$$R = \bar{R} + \beta(R_{\text{M}} - \bar{R}_{\text{M}}) + \varepsilon$$

where $R_{\text{M}}$ is the return on the market portfolio.[2] The single $\beta$ is called the *beta coefficient*.

In the past 20 years practice has changed quite significantly in the area of factor models because of two seminal research articles, published by Eugene Fama and Kenneth French in 1993 and Mark Carhart in 1997. Both papers recognized that the market index alone cannot fully explain the variation in asset returns. Fama and French introduced the three-factor model using two new factors, HML and SMB. HML stands for 'High Minus Low Book to Market Equity' and represents the return on an arbitrage portfolio that is long (a positive investment) in high book to market equity companies and short (a negative investment or borrowing) in low book to market equity companies. An arbitrage portfolio has a zero net investment because the positive weights completely cancel out the negative weights on assets. Similarly, SML means 'Small Minus Big Companies', and corresponds to an arbitrage portfolio that is long in small companies and short in big companies. Carhart (1997) added another factor that represented a momentum effect that is measured by the return on an arbitrage portfolio that is long in the best-performing equities of the previous year and short in the worst-performing equities of the previous year. Algebraically, the four-factor model is expressed as

$$R - r_f = \bar{R} + \beta_1(R_{\text{M}} - r_f) + \beta_2\text{HML} + \beta_3\text{SMB} + \beta_4\text{MOM} + \varepsilon$$

where there are four factors representing the market risk premium, high minus low B/M, small minus big, and momentum arbitrage portfolios respectively. The Fama–French three-factor model is simply the four-factor model without the momentum factor.

## 11.4 Portfolios and Factor Models

Now let us see what happens to portfolios of equities when each follows a one-factor model. For purposes of discussion we shall take the coming one-month period and examine returns. We could have used a day, or a year, or any other period. If the period represents the time between decisions, however, we would rather it be short than long, and a month is a reasonable time frame to use.

We shall create portfolios from a list of $N$ securities, and use a one-factor model to capture the systematic risk. The $i$th security in the list will therefore have returns

$$R_i = \bar{R}_i + \beta_i F + \varepsilon_i \tag{11.1}$$

where we have subscripted the variables to indicate that they relate to the $i$th security. Notice that the factor $F$ is not subscripted. The factor that represents systematic risk could be a surprise in GNP, or we could use the market model and let the difference between the market return and what we expect that return to be, $R_{market} - \bar{R}_{market}$, be the factor. In either case, the factor applies to all of the securities in the portfolio.

The $\beta_i$ is subscripted because it represents the unique way the factor influences the $i$th security. To recapitulate our discussion of factor models, if $\beta_i$ is zero, the returns on the $i$th security are

$$R_i = \bar{R}_i + \varepsilon_i$$

In words, the $i$th security's returns are unaffected by the factor $F$ if $\beta_i$ is zero. If $\beta_i$ is positive, positive changes in the factor raise the $i$th security's returns, and negative changes lower them. Conversely, if $\beta_i$ is negative, its returns and the factor move in opposite directions.

Figure 11.1 illustrates the relationship between a security's excess returns, $R_i - \bar{R}_i$, and the factor $F$ for different betas, where $\beta_i > 0$. The lines in Fig. 11.1 plot Eq. (11.1) on the assumption that there has been no unsystematic risk: that is, $\varepsilon_i = 0$. Because we are assuming positive betas, the lines slope upwards, indicating that the return rises with $F$. Notice that if the factor is zero ($F = 0$), the line passes through zero on the $y$-axis.

Now let us see what happens when we create equity portfolios where each equity follows a one-factor model. Let $X_i$ be the proportion of equity $i$ in the portfolio. That is, if an individual with a portfolio of €100 wants €20 in Axa, we say $X_{AXA} = 20\%$. Because the $X$s represent the proportions of wealth we are investing in each of the equities, we know that they must add up to 100 per cent or 1:

$$X_1 + X_2 + X_3 + \cdots + X_N = 1$$

We know that the portfolio return is the weighted average of the returns on the individual assets in the portfolio. Algebraically, this can be written as follows:

$$R_P = X_1 R_1 + X_2 R_2 + X_3 R_3 + \cdots + X_N R_N \qquad (11.2)$$

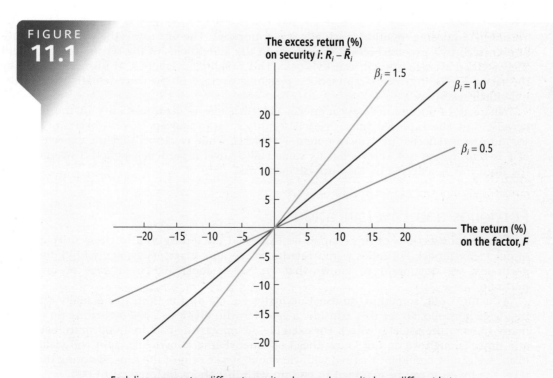

**FIGURE 11.1**

Each line represents a different security, where each security has a different beta.

**Figure 11.1** The one-factor model

We saw from Eq. (11.1) that each asset, in turn, is determined by both the factor $F$ and the unsystematic risk of $\varepsilon_i$. Thus by substituting Eq. (11.1) for each $R_i$ in Eq. (11.2), we have

$$
\begin{aligned}
R_P = \; & X_1(\underset{\text{(Return on equity 1)}}{\bar{R}_1 + \beta_1 F + \varepsilon_1}) + X_2(\underset{\text{(Return on equity 2)}}{\bar{R}_2 + \beta_2 F + \varepsilon_2}) \\
& + X_3(\underset{\text{(Return on equity 3)}}{\bar{R}_3 + \beta_3 F + \varepsilon_3}) + \cdots + X_N(\underset{\text{(Return on equity } N)}{\bar{R}_N + \beta_N F + \varepsilon_N})
\end{aligned}
\tag{11.3}
$$

Equation (11.3) shows us that the return on a portfolio is determined by three sets of parameters:

1   The expected return on each individual security, $\bar{R}_i$

2   The beta of each security multiplied by the factor $F$

3   The unsystematic risk of each individual security, $\varepsilon_i$

We express Eq. (11.3) in terms of these three sets of parameters like this:

Weighted average of expected returns:

$$
R_P = X_1\bar{R}_1 + X_2\bar{R}_2 + X_3\bar{R}_3 + \cdots + X_N\bar{R}_N
\tag{11.4}
$$

Weighted average of betas $\times$ F:

$$
+ (X_1\beta_1 + X_2\beta_2 + X_3\beta_3 + \cdots + X_N\beta_N)F
$$

Weighted average of unsystematic risks:

$$
+ X_1\varepsilon_1 + X_2\varepsilon_2 + X_3\varepsilon_3 + \cdots + X_N\varepsilon_N
$$

This rather imposing equation is actually straightforward. The first row is the weighted average of each security's expected return. The items in the parentheses of the second row represent the weighted average of each security's beta. This weighted average is, in turn, multiplied by the factor $F$. The third row represents a weighted average of the unsystematic risks of the individual securities.

Where does uncertainty appear in Eq. (11.4)? There is no uncertainty in the first row because only the expected value of each security's return appears there. Uncertainty in the second row is reflected by only one item, $F$. That is, while we know that the expected value of $F$ is zero, we do not know what its value will be over a particular period. Uncertainty in the third row is reflected by each unsystematic risk, $\varepsilon_i$.

## Portfolios and Diversification

In the previous sections of this chapter we expressed the return on a single security in terms of our factor model. Portfolios were treated next. Because investors generally hold diversified portfolios, we now want to know what Eq. (11.4) looks like in a *large* or diversified portfolio.[3]

As it turns out, something unusual occurs to Eq. (11.4): the third row actually *disappears* in a large portfolio. To see this, consider a gambler who divides £1,000 by betting on red over many spins of the roulette wheel. For example, he may participate in 1,000 spins, betting £1 at a time. Though we do not know ahead of time whether a particular spin will yield red or black, we can be confident that red will win about 50 per cent of the time. Ignoring the house take, the investor can be expected to end up with just about his original £1,000.

Though we are concerned with securities, not roulette wheels, the same principle applies. Each security has its own unsystematic risk, where the surprise for one security is unrelated to the surprise of another security. By investing a small amount in each security, we bring the weighted average of the unsystematic risks close to zero in a large portfolio.[4]

Although the third row completely vanishes in a large portfolio, nothing unusual occurs in either row 1 or row 2. Row 1 remains a weighted average of the expected returns on the individual securities as securities are added to the portfolio. Because there is no uncertainty at all in the first row, there is no way for diversification to cause this row to vanish. The terms inside the parentheses of the second row remain a weighted average of the betas. They do not vanish, either, when securities are added. Because the factor $F$ is unaffected when securities are added to the portfolios, the second row does not vanish.

Why does the third row vanish while the second row does not, though both rows reflect uncertainty? The key is that there are many unsystematic risks in row 3. Because these risks are independent of each other, the effect of diversification becomes stronger as we add more assets to the portfolio. The resulting portfolio becomes less and less risky, and the return becomes more certain. However, the systematic risk, $F$, affects all securities because it is outside the parentheses in row 2. Because we cannot avoid this factor by investing in many securities, diversification does not occur in this row.

## EXAMPLE 11.1

# Diversification and Unsystematic Risk

The preceding material can be further explained by the following example. We keep our one-factor model here but make three specific assumptions:

1 All securities have the same expected return of 10 per cent. This assumption implies that the first row of Eq. (11.4) must also equal 10 per cent because this row is a weighted average of the expected returns of the individual securities.

2 All securities have a beta of 1. The sum of the terms inside the parentheses in the second row of Eq. (11.4) must equal 1 because these terms are a weighted average of the individual betas. Because the terms inside the parentheses are multiplied by $F$, the value of the second row is $1 \times F = F$.

3 In this example, we focus on the behaviour of one individual, Walter V. Bagehot. Mr Bagehot decides to hold an equally weighted portfolio. That is, the proportion of each security in his portfolio is $1/N$.

We can express the return on Mr Bagehot's portfolio as follows:

Return on Walter V. Bagehot's portfolio:

$$R_P = \underbrace{10\%}_{\substack{\text{From}\\\text{row 1 of}\\\text{Eq. (11.4)}}} + \underbrace{F}_{\substack{\text{From}\\\text{row 2 of}\\\text{Eq. (11.4)}}} + \underbrace{\left(\frac{1}{N}\varepsilon_1 + \frac{1}{N}\varepsilon_2 + \frac{1}{N}\varepsilon_3 + \cdots + \frac{1}{N}\varepsilon_N\right)}_{\text{From row 3 of Eq. (11.4)}} \quad (11.4')$$

We mentioned before that as $N$ increases without limit, row 3 of Eq. (11.4) becomes equal to zero.[5] Thus the return to Walter Bagehot's portfolio when the number of securities is very large is

$$R_P = 10\% + F \quad (11.4'')$$

The key to diversification is exhibited in Eq. (11.4'). The unsystematic risk of row 3 vanishes while the systematic risk of row 2 remains.

This is illustrated in Fig. 11.2. Systematic risk, captured by variation in the factor $F$, is not reduced through diversification. Conversely, unsystematic risk diminishes as securities are added, vanishing as the number of securities becomes infinite. Our result is analogous to the diversification example of the previous chapter. In that chapter, we said that undiversifiable or systematic risk arises from positive covariances between securities. In this chapter, we say that systematic risk arises from a common factor $F$. Because a common factor causes positive covariances, the arguments of the two chapters are parallel.

**Figure 11.2** Diversification and portfolio risk for an equally weighted portfolio

## 11.5 Betas and Expected Returns

### The Linear Relationship

We have argued many times that the expected return on a security compensates for its risk. In the previous chapter we showed that market beta (the standardized covariance of the security's returns with those of the market) was the appropriate measure of risk under the assumptions of homogeneous expectations and riskless borrowing and lending. The capital asset pricing model, which posited these assumptions, implied that the expected return on a security was positively (and linearly) related to its beta. We shall find a similar relationship between risk and return in the one-factor model of this chapter.

We begin by noting that the relevant risk in large and well-diversified portfolios is all systematic, because unsystematic risk is diversified away. An implication is that when a well-diversified shareholder considers changing her holdings of a particular security, she can ignore its unsystematic risk.

Notice that we are not claiming that equities, like portfolios, have no unsystematic risk. Nor are we saying that the unsystematic risk of an equity will not affect its returns. Shares do have unsystematic risk, and their actual returns do depend on the unsystematic risk. Because this risk washes out in a well-diversified portfolio, however, shareholders can ignore this unsystematic risk when they consider whether to add an equity to their portfolio. Therefore, if shareholders are ignoring the unsystematic risk, only the systematic risk of a security can be related to its *expected* return.

This relationship is illustrated in the security market line of Fig. 11.3. Points *P*, *C*, *A*, and *L* all lie on the line emanating from the risk-free rate of 10 per cent. The points representing each of these four assets can be created by combinations of the risk-free rate and any of the other three assets. For example, because *A* has a beta of 2.0 and *P* has a beta of 1.0, a portfolio of 50 per cent in asset *A* and 50 per cent in the riskless rate has the same beta as asset *P*. The risk-free rate is 10 per cent and the expected return on security *A* is 35 per cent, implying that the combination's return of 22.5 per cent [(10% + 35%)/2] is identical to security *P*'s expected return. Because security *P* has both the same beta and the same expected return as a combination of the riskless asset and security *A*, an individual is equally inclined to add a small amount of security *P* and to add a small amount of this combination to her portfolio. However, the unsystematic risk of security *P* need not be equal to the unsystematic risk of the combination of security *A* and the risk-free rate, because unsystematic risk is diversified away in a large portfolio.

Of course, the potential combinations of points on the security market line are endless. We can duplicate *P* by combinations of the risk-free rate and either *C* or *L* (or both of them).

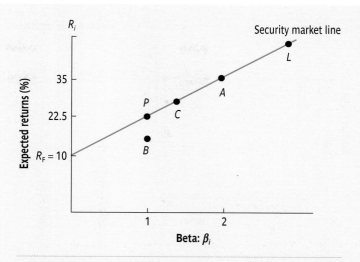

**FIGURE 11.3**

**Figure 11.3** A graph of beta and expected return for individual securities under the one-factor model

We can duplicate $C$ (or $A$ or $L$) by borrowing at the risk-free rate to invest in $P$. The infinite number of points on the security market line that are not labelled can be used as well.

Now consider security $B$. Because its expected return is below the line, no investor would hold it. Instead, the investor would prefer security $P$, a combination of security $A$ and the riskless asset, or some other combination. Thus security $B$'s price is too high. Its price will fall in a competitive market, forcing its expected return back up to the line in equilibrium.

The preceding discussion allows us to provide an equation for the security market line of Fig. 11.3. We know that a line can be described algebraically from two points. It is perhaps easiest to focus on the risk-free rate and asset $P$, because the risk-free rate has a beta of 0 and $P$ has a beta of 1.

Because we know that the return on any zero-beta asset is $R_F$ and the expected return on asset $P$ is $\bar{R}_P$, it can easily be shown that

$$\bar{R} = R_F + \beta(\bar{R}_P - R_F) \tag{11.5}$$

In Eq. (11.5), $\bar{R}$ can be thought of as the expected return on any security or portfolio lying on the security market line. $\beta$ is the beta of that security or portfolio.

## The Market Portfolio and the Single Factor

In the CAPM the beta of a security measures its responsiveness to movements in the market portfolio. In the one-factor model of the arbitrage pricing theory (APT) the beta of a security measures its responsiveness to the factor. We now relate the market portfolio to the single factor.

A large, diversified portfolio has no unsystematic risk, because the unsystematic risks of the individual securities are diversified away. Assuming enough securities so that the market portfolio is fully diversified, and assuming that no security has a disproportionate market share, this portfolio is fully diversified and contains no unsystematic risk.[6] In other words, the market portfolio is perfectly correlated with the single factor, implying that the market portfolio is really a scaled-up or scaled-down version of the factor. After scaling properly, we can treat the market portfolio as the factor itself.

The market portfolio, like every security or portfolio, lies on the security market line. When the market portfolio is the factor, the beta of the market portfolio is 1 by definition. This is shown in Fig. 11.4. (We deleted the securities and the specific expected returns from Fig. 11.3

FIGURE
**11.4**

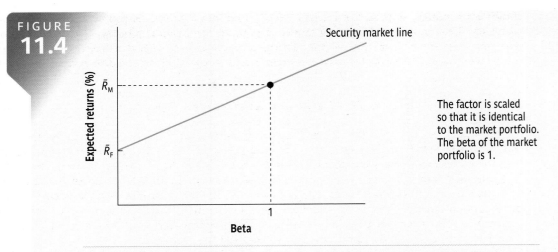

The factor is scaled so that it is identical to the market portfolio. The beta of the market portfolio is 1.

**Figure 11.4** A graph of beta and expected return for individual equities under the one-factor model

for clarity; the two graphs are otherwise identical.) With the market portfolio as the factor, Eq. (11.5) becomes

$$\bar{R} = R_F + \beta(\bar{R}_M - R_F)$$

where $\bar{R}_M$ is the expected return on the market. This equation shows that the expected return on any asset, $\bar{R}$, is linearly related to the security's beta. The equation is identical to that of the CAPM, which we developed in the previous chapter.

## 11.6 The Capital Asset Pricing Model and the Arbitrage Pricing Theory

The CAPM and the APT are alternative models of risk and return. It is worth while to consider the differences between the two models, both in terms of pedagogy and in terms of application.

### Differences in Pedagogy

We feel that the CAPM has at least one strong advantage from the student's point of view. The derivation of the CAPM necessarily brings the reader through a discussion of efficient sets. This treatment – beginning with the case of two risky assets, moving to the case of many risky assets, and finishing when a riskless asset is added to the many risky ones – is of great intuitive value. This sort of presentation is not as easily accomplished with the APT.

However, the APT has an offsetting advantage. The model adds factors until the unsystematic risk of any security is uncorrelated with the unsystematic risk of every other security. Under this formulation, it is easily shown that (a) unsystematic risk steadily falls (and ultimately vanishes) as the number of securities in the portfolio increases, but (b) the systematic risks do not decrease. This result was also shown in the CAPM, though the intuition was cloudier because the unsystematic risks could be correlated across securities.

### Differences in Application

One advantage of the APT is that it can handle multiple factors while the CAPM ignores them. Although the bulk of our presentation in this chapter focused on the one-factor model, a multifactor model, such as the Carhart (1997) four-factor model, is probably more reflective of reality. That is, we must abstract from many market-wide and industry-wide factors before the unsystematic risk of one security becomes uncorrelated with the unsystematic risks of other securities. Under the four-factor model, the relationship between risk and return can be expressed as

$$R - r_f = \bar{R} + \beta(R_M - r_f) + \gamma \text{HML} + \delta \text{SMB} + \eta \text{MOM} + \varepsilon \qquad (11.6)$$

In this equation, $\beta$ stands for the security's beta with respect to the first factor, $\gamma$ stands for the security's beta with respect to the second factor, and so on. The equation states that the security's expected return is related to the security's factor betas. The intuition in Eq. (11.6) is straightforward. Each factor represents risk that cannot be diversified away. The higher a security's beta with regard to a particular factor, the higher is the risk that the security bears. In a rational world, the expected return on the security should compensate for this risk. Equation (11.6) states that the expected return is a summation of the base expected return plus the compensation for each type of risk that the security bears.

As an example, consider the hypothetical coefficients for the four-factor model for British Land Company plc, the UK property developer. Assume that the expected monthly return on any equity, $\bar{R}_S$, can be described as

$$\bar{R}_S = 0.0041 + 0.0136\beta - 0.0001\gamma - 0.0006\delta + 0.0072\eta$$

Suppose British Land Company had the following betas: $\beta = 1.1$, $\gamma = 2$, $\delta = 3$, $\eta = 0.1$. The expected monthly return on that security would be

$$\begin{aligned} \bar{R}_{\text{BLC}} &= 0.0041 + 0.0136 \times 1.1 - 0.0001 \times 2 - 0.0006 \times 3 + 0.0072 \times 0.1 \\ &= 0.0041 + 0.01496 - 0.0002 - 0.0018 + 0.00072 \\ &= 0.01778 \end{aligned}$$

Assuming that British Land Company is unlevered, and that one of the firm's projects has risk equivalent to that of the firm, this value of 0.01778 (i.e. 1.78%) can be used as the monthly discount rate for the project. (Because annual data are often supplied for capital budgeting purposes, the annual rate of 0.2355 [$= (1.01778)^{12} - 1$] might be used instead.)

Because many factors appear on the right side of Eq. (11.6), the four-factor formulation has the potential to measure expected returns more accurately than does the CAPM. However, as we mentioned earlier, we cannot easily determine whether these factors are appropriate. The factors in the preceding study were included because they were found to explain a significant proportion of returns for US companies. They were not derived from theory, and they may not be particularly appropriate for European, Middle Eastern or African companies.

By contrast, the use of the market index in the CAPM formulation is implied by the theory of the previous chapter. We suggested in earlier chapters that market indices (such as the FTSE 100 and DJ Euro Stoxx 50) mirror stock market movements quite well.

## Summary and Conclusions

The previous chapter developed the capital asset pricing model (CAPM). As an alternative, this chapter developed the arbitrage pricing theory (APT) and introduced the Fama–French three-factor model and Carhart four-factor model.

1   The APT assumes that security returns are generated according to factor models. For example, we might describe a stock's return as

$$R = \bar{R} + \beta_I F_I + \beta_{\text{GNP}} F_{\text{GNP}} + \beta_r F_r + \varepsilon$$

where $I$, GNP and $r$ stand for inflation, gross national product and the interest rate, respectively. The three factors $F_I$, $F_{\text{GNP}}$ and $F_r$ represent systematic risk, because these factors affect many securities. The term $\varepsilon$ is considered unsystematic risk, because it is unique to each individual security.

2   For convenience, we frequently describe a security's return according to a one-factor model:

$$R = \bar{R} + \beta F + \varepsilon$$

3   The Fama–French and Carhart factor models are now frequently used by financial analysts. The Carhart four-factor model is expressed as follows:

$$R - r_f = \bar{R} + \beta(R_M - r_f) + \gamma \text{HML} + \delta \text{SMB} + \eta \text{MOM} + \varepsilon$$

where $(R_M - r_f)$ is the market risk premium, HML is the return on an arbitrage portfolio that is long in high B/M equities and short in low B/M stocks, SMB is the return on an arbitrage portfolio that is long in small market capitalization equities and short in large market capitalization equities, and MOM is the return on an arbitrage portfolio that is long in the best-performing equities and short in the worst-performing equities. The term $\varepsilon$ is considered unsystematic risk because it is unique to each individual security. The Fama–French three-factor model is simply the Carhart model without the momentum factor.

4   As securities are added to a portfolio, the unsystematic risks of the individual securities offset each other. A fully diversified portfolio has no unsystematic risk but still has systematic risk. This result indicates that diversification can eliminate some, but not all, of the risk of individual securities.

5   Because of this, the expected return on a security is positively related to its systematic risk. In a one-factor model the systematic risk is simply the beta of the CAPM. Thus the implications of the CAPM and the one-factor APT are identical. However, each security has many risks in a multifactor model such as the Carhart model. The expected return on a security is positively related to the beta of the security with each factor.

# connect **Questions and Problems**

**CONCEPT 1–6**

1   **Announcements, Surprises, and Expected Returns**   What is the difference between an expected return and observed return? Is it possible to predict the surprise component of an observed return?

2   **Systematic versus Unsystematic Risk**   You own equity in Lewis-Striden Drugs plc. Suppose you had expected the following events to occur last month:

(a)   The government would announce that real GNP had grown by 1.2 per cent during the previous quarter. The returns of Lewis-Striden are positively related to real GNP.

(b)   The government would announce that inflation over the previous quarter was 3.7 per cent. The returns of Lewis-Striden are negatively related to inflation.

(c)   Interest rates would rise 2.5 percentage points. The returns of Lewis-Striden are negatively related to interest rates.

(d)   The chairman of the firm would announce his retirement. The retirement would be effective six months from the announcement day. The chairman is well liked: in general, he is considered an asset to the firm.

(e)   Research data would conclusively prove the efficacy of an experimental drug. Completion of the efficacy testing means the drug will be on the market soon.

Suppose the following events actually occurred:

(a) The government announced that real GNP grew by 2.3 per cent during the previous quarter.

(b) The government announced that inflation over the previous quarter was 3.7 per cent.

(c) Interest rates rose 2.1 percentage points.

(d) The chairman of the firm died suddenly of a heart attack.

(e) Research results in the efficacy testing were not as strong as expected. The drug must be tested for another six months, and the efficacy results must be resubmitted to the FDA.

(f) Laboratory researchers had a breakthrough with another drug.

(g) A competitor announced that it will begin distribution and sale of a medicine that will compete directly with one of Lewis-Striden's top-selling products.

Discuss how each of the actual occurrences affects the returns on your Lewis-Striden shares. Which events represent systematic risk? Which events represent unsystematic risk?

3 **Systematic Risk and Betas** What is wrong with measuring the performance of an Irish growth fund portfolio manager against a benchmark composed of Greek equities?

4 **Portfolios and Factor Models** Explain, using formulae to illustrate your answer, how the risk of a portfolio falls as the number of securities in the portfolio grows. Why is the change in risk non-linear?

5 **Betas and Expected Returns** Why does the market portfolio lie on the security market line? What does it mean if a security lies below the security market line? What would happen to the returns of the security if traders exploit any possible arbitrage opportunities?

6 **CAPM versus APT** What is the relationship between the one-factor model and the CAPM?

7 **APT** Consider the following statement: 'For the APT to be useful, the number of systematic risk factors must be small.' Do you agree or disagree with this statement? Why?

8 **APT** David McClemore, the CFO of Ultra Bread, has decided to use an APT model to estimate the required return on the company's equity. The risk factors he plans to use are the risk premium on the stock market, the inflation rate, and the price of wheat. Because wheat is one of the biggest costs Ultra Bread faces, he feels this is a significant risk factor for Ultra Bread. How would you evaluate his choice of risk factors? Are there other risk factors you might suggest?

9 **Market Model versus the Carhart (1997) Model** What are the differences between the Carhart (1997) model and the market model?

10 **APT** In contrast to the CAPM, the APT does not indicate which factors are expected to determine the risk premium of an asset. How can we determine which factors should be included?

11 **Factor Models** How can the return on a portfolio be expressed in terms of a factor model?

12 **Factor Models** A researcher has determined that a two-factor model is appropriate to determine the return of an equity. The factors are the percentage change in GNP and an interest rate. GNP is expected to grow by 3 per cent, and the interest rate is expected to be 4.5 per cent. An equity has a beta of 1.2 on the percentage change in GNP and a beta of −0.8 on the interest rate. If the expected rate of return for the equity is 11 per cent, what is the revised expected return if GNP actually grows by 4.2 per cent and interest rates are 4.6 per cent?

REGULAR
7–18

13 **Factor Models** Suppose the Fama–French three-factor model is appropriate to describe the returns of an equity. Information about those three factors is presented in the following chart:

| Factor | $\beta$ | Expected value (%) | Actual value (%) |
|---|---|---|---|
| $(R_M - r_f)$ | 1.50 | 8.4 | 8.1 |
| HML | −1.40 | 3.1 | 3.8 |
| SMB | −0.67 | 9.5 | 10.3 |

(a) What is the systematic risk of the equity return?

(b) Suppose unexpected bad news about the firm was announced that causes the share price to drop by 2.6 per cent. If the expected return is 9.5 per cent, what is the total return on this equity?

14 **Factor Models** Suppose the Carhart (1997) factor model is appropriate to describe the returns on an equity. The current expected return on the equity is 10.5 per cent. Information about the factors is presented in the following chart:

| Factor | $\beta$ | Expected value (%) | Actual value (%) |
|---|---|---|---|
| $(R_M - r_f)$ | 1.04 | 3.5 | 4.8 |
| HML | −1.90 | 7.1 | 7.8 |
| SMB | 0.60 | 2.4 | 6.4 |
| Momentum | 0.44 | 0.23 | −3.2 |

(a) What is the systematic risk of the equity return?

(b) The firm announced that its market share had unexpectedly increased from 23 per cent to 27 per cent. Investors know from past experience that the share price return will increase by 0.36 per cent for every 1 per cent increase in its market share. What is the equity's unsystematic risk?

(c) What is the equity's total return?

15 **Factor Models** Suppose equity returns can be explained by the Fama–French three-factor model:

$$R = \bar{R} + \beta(R_M - r_f) + \gamma HML + \delta SMB + \varepsilon$$

Assume there is no firm-specific risk. The information for each equity is presented here:

| | $\beta$ | $\gamma$ | $\delta$ |
|---|---|---|---|
| Equity $A$ | 1.20 | 0.90 | 0.20 |
| Equity $B$ | 0.80 | 1.40 | −0.30 |
| Equity $C$ | 0.95 | −0.05 | 1.50 |

The risk premiums for the three factors are 5.5 per cent, 4.2 per cent and 4.9 per cent, respectively. If you create a portfolio with 20 per cent invested in $A$, 20 per cent invested in $B$, and the remainder in $C$, what is the expression for the return of your portfolio? Assuming that the risk free rate is 5 per cent, what is the expected return of your portfolio?

16 **Multifactor Models** Suppose equity returns can be explained by the Fama–French three-factor model. The firm-specific risks for all equities are independent. The following table shows the information for three diversified portfolios:

|  | $\beta$ | $\gamma$ | $\delta$ | E(R) (%) |
|---|---|---|---|---|
| Portfolio A | 0.75 | 1.20 | 0.04 | 18 |
| Portfolio B | 1.60 | −0.20 | 0.07 | 14 |
| Portfolio C | 0.85 | 1.20 | 0.65 | 22 |

Assuming that the base return on each portfolio is 6 per cent and the risk-free rate is 5 per cent, what are the risk premiums for each factor in this model?

17  **Market Model**   The following three equities are available in the market:

|  | E(R) (%) | $\beta$ |
|---|---|---|
| Equity A | 10.5 | 1.20 |
| Equity B | 13.0 | 0.98 |
| Equity C | 15.7 | 1.37 |
| Market | 14.2 | 1.00 |

Assume the market model is valid.

(a)  Write the market model equation for each equity.

(b)  What is the return on a portfolio with weights of 30 per cent equity A, 45 per cent equity B, and 25 per cent equity C?

(c)  Suppose the return on the market is 15 per cent and there are no unsystematic surprises in the returns. What is the return on each equity? What is the return on the portfolio?

18  **Portfolio Risk**   You are forming an equally weighted portfolio of equities. Many equities have the same beta of 0.84 for factor 1 and the same beta of 1.69 for factor 2. They also have the same expected return of 11 per cent. Assume a two-factor model describes the return on each of these equities.

(a)  Write the equation of the returns on your portfolio if you place only five equities in it.

(b)  Write the equation of the returns on your portfolio if you place in it a very large number of equities that all have the same expected returns and the same betas.

19  **APT**   There are two equity markets, each driven by the same common force $F$ with an expected value of zero and standard deviation of 10 per cent. There are many securities in each market: thus you can invest in as many securities as you wish. Because of restrictions, however, you can invest in only one of the two markets. The expected return on every security in both markets is 10 per cent.

The returns for each security $i$ in the first market are generated by the relationship

$$R_{1i} = 0.10 + 1.5F + \varepsilon_{1i}$$

where $\varepsilon_{1i}$ is the term that measures the surprises in the returns of security $i$ in the first market. These surprises are normally distributed; their mean is zero. The returns for security $j$ in the second market are generated by the relationship

$$R_{2j} = 0.10 + 0.5F + \varepsilon_{2j}$$

where $\varepsilon_{2j}$ is the term that measures the surprises in the returns of security $j$ in market 2. These surprises are normally distributed; their mean is zero. The standard deviation of $\varepsilon_{1i}$ and $\varepsilon_{2j}$ for any two securities, $i$ and $j$, is 20 per cent.

(a)  If the correlation between the surprises in the returns of any two securities in the first market is zero, and if the correlation between the surprises in the returns of any two securities in the second market is zero, in which market would a risk-averse

CHALLENGE
19–21

person prefer to invest? (*Note:* The correlation between $\varepsilon_{1i}$ and $\varepsilon_{1j}$ for any $i$ and $j$ is zero, and the correlation between $\varepsilon_{2i}$ and $\varepsilon_{2j}$ for any $i$ and $j$ is zero.)

(b) If the correlation between $\varepsilon_{1i}$ and $\varepsilon_{1j}$ in the first market is 0.9 and the correlation between $\varepsilon_{2i}$ and $\varepsilon_{2j}$ in the second market is zero, in which market would a risk-averse person prefer to invest?

(c) If the correlation between $\varepsilon_{1i}$ and $\varepsilon_{1j}$ in the first market is zero and the correlation between $\varepsilon_{2i}$ and $\varepsilon_{2j}$ in the second market is 0.5, in which market would a risk-averse person prefer to invest?

(d) In general, what is the relationship between the correlations of the disturbances in the two markets that would make a risk-averse person equally willing to invest in either of the two markets?

20 **APT** Assume that the following market model adequately describes the return-generating behaviour of risky assets:

$$R_{it} = \alpha_i + \beta_i R_{Mt} + \varepsilon_{it}$$

where $R_{it}$ is the return for the $i$th asset at time $t$, and $R_{Mt}$ is the return on a portfolio containing all risky assets in some proportion at time $t$. $R_{Mt}$ and $\varepsilon_{it}$ are statistically independent.

Short selling (i.e. negative positions) is allowed in the market. You are given the following information:

| Asset | $\beta_i$ | E($R_i$) (%) | Var($\varepsilon_i$) |
|-------|-----------|--------------|-----------------------|
| A | 0.7 | 8.41 | 0.0100 |
| B | 1.2 | 12.06 | 0.0144 |
| C | 1.5 | 13.95 | 0.0225 |

The variance of the market is 0.0121, and there are no transaction costs.

(a) Calculate the standard deviation of returns for each asset.

(b) Calculate the variance of return of three portfolios containing an infinite number of asset types $A$, $B$ or $C$, respectively.

(c) Assume the risk-free rate is 3.3 per cent and the expected return on the market is 10.6 per cent. Which asset will not be held by rational investors?

(d) What equilibrium state will emerge such that no arbitrage opportunities exist? Why?

21 **APT** Assume that the returns of individual securities are generated by the following two-factor model:

$$R_{it} = E(R_{it}) + \beta_{i1} F_{1t} + \beta_{i2} F_{2t}$$

where $R_{it}$ is the return for security $i$ at time $t$, and $F_{1t}$ and $F_{2t}$ are market factors with zero expectation and zero covariance.

In addition, assume that there is a capital market for four securities, and the capital market for these four assets is perfect in the sense that there are no transaction costs and short sales (i.e. negative positions) are permitted. The characteristics of the four securities follow:

| Security | $\beta_1$ | $\beta_2$ | E(R) (%) |
|----------|-----------|-----------|----------|
| 1 | 1.0 | 1.5 | 20 |
| 2 | 0.5 | 2.0 | 20 |
| 3 | 1.0 | 0.5 | 10 |
| 4 | 1.5 | 0.75 | 10 |

(a) Construct a portfolio containing (long or short) securities 1 and 2, with a return that does not depend on the market factor, $F_{1t}$, in any way. (*Hint*: Such a portfolio will have $\beta_1 = 0$.) Compute the expected return and $\beta_2$ coefficient for this portfolio.

(b) Following the procedure in (a), construct a portfolio containing securities 3 and 4 with a return that does not depend on the market factor $F_{1t}$. Compute the expected return and $\beta_2$ coefficient for this portfolio.

(c) There is a risk-free asset with expected return equal to 5 per cent, $\beta_1 = 0$, and $\beta_2 = 0$. Describe a possible arbitrage opportunity in such detail that an investor could implement it.

(d) What effect would the existence of these kinds of arbitrage opportunities have on the capital markets for these securities in the short and long run? Graph your analysis.

## MINI CASE
# The Fama–French Multifactor Model and Mutual Fund Returns

Dawn Browne, an investment broker, has been approached by client Jack Thomas about the risk of his investments. Dawn has recently read several articles concerning the risk factors that can potentially affect asset returns, and she has decided to examine Jack's mutual fund holdings. Jack is currently invested in the Fidelity Magellan Fund (FMAGX), the Fidelity Low-Priced Stock Fund (FLPSX), and the Baron Small Cap Fund (BSCFX).

Dawn would like to estimate the well-known multifactor model proposed by Mark Carhart in 1997 to determine the risk of each mutual fund:

$$R_{it} - R_{Ft} = \alpha_i + \beta_1(R_{Mt} - R_{Ft}) + \beta_2(SMB_t) + \beta_3(HML_t) + \beta_4(MOM) + \varepsilon_t$$

In models such as the one Dawn is considering, the alpha ($\alpha$) term is of particular interest. It is the regression intercept; but more important, it is also the excess return the asset earned. In other words, if the alpha is positive, the asset earned a return greater than it should have, given its level of risk; if the alpha is negative, the asset earned a return lower than it should have, given its level of risk. This measure is called 'Jensen's alpha', and it is a very widely used tool for mutual fund evaluation.

1 For a large-company equity mutual fund, would you expect the betas to be positive or negative for each of the factors in a Carhart multifactor model?

2 The SMB, HML, MOM factors, and risk-free rates for the US are available at Ken French's website: http://mba.tuck.dartmouth.edu/pages/faculty/ken.french/. Download the monthly factors and save the most recent 60 months for each factor. The historical prices for each of the mutual funds can be found on various Web sites, including finance.yahoo.com. Find the prices of each mutual fund for the same time as the Carhart factors, and calculate the returns for each month. Be sure to include dividends. For each mutual fund, estimate the multifactor regression equation using the Carhart factors. How well do the regression estimates explain the variation in the return of each mutual fund?

3 What do you observe about the beta coefficients for the different mutual funds? Comment on any similarities or differences.

4 If the market is efficient, what value would you expect for alpha? Do your estimates support market efficiency?

5 Which fund has performed best, considering its risk? Why?

## Additional Reading

Much of the research into asset pricing overlaps that of Chapter 10. The three papers that are listed below consider several factors that can influence share price returns. As with the previous chapter, the range of anomalies and factors that have been investigated is vast, and the listing is simply an example of research in this area.

Baker, M. and J. Wurgler (2006) 'Investor sentiment and the cross-section of stock returns', *Journal of Finance*, vol. 61, no. 4, pp. 1645–1680. **US**.

Davis, J.L., E.F. Fama and K.R. French (2000) 'Characteristics, covariances, and average returns: 1927 to 1997', *Journal of Finance*, vol. 55, no. 1, pp. 389–406. **US**.

Scowcroft, A. and J. Sefton (2005) 'Understanding momentum', *Financial Analysts Journal*, vol. 61, no. 2, pp. 64–82. **International**.

## Endnotes

1 In the previous chapter, we briefly mentioned that unsystematic risk is risk that can be diversified away in a large portfolio. This result will also follow from the present analysis.

2 Alternatively, the market model could be written as

$$R = \alpha + \beta R_M + \varepsilon$$

Here alpha ($\alpha$) is an intercept term equal to $\bar{R} - \beta \bar{R}_M$.

3 Technically, we can think of a large portfolio as one where an investor keeps increasing the number of securities without limit. In practice, *effective* diversification would occur if at least a few dozen securities were held.

4 More precisely, we say that the weighted average of the unsystematic risk approaches zero as the number of equally weighted securities in a portfolio approaches infinity.

5 Our presentation on this point has been non-rigorous. The student interested in more rigour should note that the variance of row 3 is

$$\frac{1}{N^2}\sigma_\varepsilon^2 + \frac{1}{N^2}\sigma_\varepsilon^2 + \frac{1}{N^2}\sigma_\varepsilon^2 + \cdots + \frac{1}{N^2}\sigma_\varepsilon^2 = \frac{1}{N^2}\sigma_\varepsilon^2$$

where $\sigma_\varepsilon^2$ is the variance of each $\varepsilon$. This can be rewritten as $\sigma_\varepsilon^2/N$, which tends to 0 as $N$ goes to infinity.

6 This assumption is plausible in the real world. For example, the market value of Royal Dutch Shell, which is the biggest company in the FTSE 100, is only 3–4 per cent of the market value of index.

 **Online** **Learning Centre**

To help you grasp the key concepts of this chapter check out the extra resources posted on the Online Learning Centre at **www.mcgraw-hill.co.uk/textbooks/hillier**

Among other helpful resources there are PowerPoint presentations, chapter outlines and mini-cases.

# Chapter 12

# Risk, Cost of Capital, and Capital Budgeting

In late 2005 Swiss Re, one of the world's leading reinsurers, published a report discussing how insurance companies create value for shareholders. One of the key components addressed in the report was the cost of capital. According to Swiss Re, the cost of capital for the US non-life insurance industry during the 1980s was about 15 per cent. By 2005 the cost of capital for the industry had dropped to 7 to 8 per cent. However, the cost of capital is important in more than just the insurance industry. One of the major reasons given for the sale and break-up of Lehman Brothers in 2008 was that the expected lowering of Lehman Brothers' debt rating would have increased the cost of capital for the company, thereby making business for the bank significantly more difficult.

In this chapter we learn how to compute a firm's cost of capital, and find out what it means to the firm and its investors. We shall also learn when to use cost of capital – and, perhaps more important, when not to use it.

## 12.1 The Cost of Equity Capital

Whenever a firm has extra cash, it can take one of two actions. It can pay out the cash immediately as a dividend. Alternatively, the firm can invest extra cash in a project, paying out the future cash flows of the project as dividends. Which procedure would shareholders prefer? If a shareholder can reinvest the dividend in a financial asset (an equity or bond) with the same risk as that of the project, the shareholders would desire the alternative with the higher expected return. In other words, the project should be undertaken only if its expected return is greater than that of a financial asset of comparable risk. This is illustrated in Fig. 12.1. This discussion implies a very simple capital budgeting rule:

**The discount rate of a project should be the expected return on a financial asset of comparable risk.**

From the firm's perspective, the expected return is the cost of equity capital. Under the CAPM, the expected return on equity can be written as

$$R_S = R_F + \beta \times (R_M - R_F) \qquad (12.1)$$

**Figure 12.1** Choices of a firm with extra cash

where $R_F$ is the risk-free rate and $R_M - R_F$ is the difference between the expected return on the market portfolio and the riskless rate. This difference is often called the expected *excess* market return or market risk premium. Note that we have dropped the overbar denoting expectations to simplify the notation, but remember that we are always thinking about expected returns with the CAPM.

We now have the tools to estimate a firm's cost of equity capital. To do this, we need to know three things:

1  The risk-free rate, $R_F$

2  The market risk premium, $R_M - R_F$

3  The company beta, $\beta$

EXAMPLE
12.1
## Cost of Equity

According to Yahoo! Finance, the beta of Repsol YPF SA, the Spanish oil and gas giant, is 1.04. Assume, for now, that the firm is 100 per cent equity financed: that is, it has no debt.

Repsol is considering a number of capital budgeting projects that will double its size. Because these new projects are similar to the firm's existing ones, the average beta on the new projects is assumed to be equal to Repsol's existing beta. Assume that the risk-free rate is 4.5 per cent. What is the appropriate discount rate for these new projects, assuming a market risk premium of 8.4 per cent?

We estimate the cost of equity, $R_S$, for Repsol as

$$R_S = 4.5\% + (8.4\% \times 1.04)$$
$$= 4.5\% + 8.74\%$$
$$= 13.24\%$$

Two key assumptions were made in this example: (a) the beta risk of the new projects is the same as the risk of the firm; and (b) the firm is all equity-financed. Given these assumptions, it follows that the cash flows of the new projects should be discounted at the 13.24 per cent rate.

EXAMPLE
12.2
## Project Evaluation and Beta

Kazakhmys plc is a metal producer listed on the London Stock Exchange. Suppose Kazakhmys is an all-equity firm. According to Yahoo! Finance, it has a beta of 1.57. Further, suppose the market risk premium is 9.5 per cent, and the risk-free rate is 5 per cent. We can determine the expected return on the equity of Kazakhmys by using the SML of Eq. 12.1. We find that the expected return is

$$5\% + (1.57 \times 9.5\%) = 19.92\%$$

Because this is the return that shareholders can expect in the financial markets on an equity with a $\beta$ of 1.57, it is also the return they expect on Kazakhmys plc.

Further suppose that Kazakhmys is evaluating the following non-mutually exclusive projects in Kazakhstan:

| Project | Project's beta, $\beta$ | Project's expected cash flows next year (£) | Project's internal rate of return (%) | Project's NPV when cash flows are discounted at 19.92% (£) | Accept or reject |
|---------|----------|----------|----------|----------|----------|
| A | 1.57 | 140 | 40 | 16.8 | Accept |
| B | 1.57 | 120 | 20 | 0.1 | Accept |
| C | 1.57 | 110 | 10 | –8.3 | Reject |

Each project initially costs £100. All projects are assumed to have the same risk as the firm as a whole. Because the cost of equity capital is 19.92 per cent, projects in an all-equity firm are discounted at this rate. Projects A and B have positive NPVs, and C has a negative NPV. Thus only A and B will be accepted. This is illustrated in Fig. 12.2.

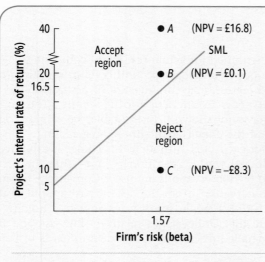

The diagonal line represents the relationship between the cost of equity capital and the firm's beta. An all-equity firm should accept a project whose internal rate of return is greater than the cost of equity capital, and should reject a project whose internal rate of return is less than the cost of equity capital. (This graph assumes that all projects are as risky as the firm.)

**Figure 12.2** Using the security market line to estimate the risk-adjusted discount rate for risky projects

## 12.2 Estimation of Beta

In the previous section we assumed that the beta of the company was known. Of course, beta must be estimated in the real world. We pointed out earlier that the beta of an equity is the standardized covariance of a security's return with the return on the market portfolio. As we have seen, the formula for security $i$ is

$$\text{Beta of security } i = \frac{\text{Cov}(R_i, R_M)}{\text{Var}(R_M)} = \frac{\sigma_{i,M}}{\sigma_M^2}$$

In words, the beta is the covariance of a security with the market, divided by the variance of the market return. Because we calculated both covariance and variance in earlier chapters, calculating beta involves no new material.

---

## Measuring Company Betas

The basic method of measuring company betas is to estimate

$$\frac{\text{Cov}(R_i, R_M)}{\text{Var}(R_M)}$$

using $t = 1, 2, \ldots, T$ observations

### Problems

1  Betas may vary over time.

2  The sample size may be inadequate.

3  Betas are influenced by changing financial leverage and business risk.

### Solutions

1  Problems 1 and 2 can be moderated by more sophisticated statistical techniques.

2  Problem 3 can be lessened by adjusting for changes in business and financial risk.

3  Look at average beta estimates of several comparable firms in the industry.

---

### Real-World Betas

It is instructive to see how betas are determined for actual real-world companies. Figure 12.3 plots monthly returns for two large European firms against monthly returns on the Dow Jones Euro Stoxx 50 index. Using a standard regression technique, we fit a straight line through the data points. The result is called the 'characteristic' line for the security. The slope of the characteristic line is beta. Though we have not shown it in the table, we can also determine the intercept (commonly called alpha) of the characteristic line by regression.

We use five years of monthly data for each plot. Although this choice is arbitrary, it is in line with calculations performed in the real world. Practitioners know that the accuracy of the beta coefficient is suspect when too few observations are used. Conversely, because firms may change their industry over time, observations from the distant past are out of date.

Because beta is a measure of the risk of a single security for someone holding a large, diversified portfolio, our results indicate that Unilever has relatively low risk and Deutsche Bank has relatively high risk. A more detailed discussion of the determinants of beta is presented in Section 12.3.

### Using an Industry Beta

Our approach to estimating the beta of a company from its own past data may seem sensible to you. However, it is frequently argued that people can better estimate a firm's beta by involving

**Figure 12.3** Plots of five years of monthly returns (2003–2008) on two individual securities against five years of monthly returns on the Dow Jones EuroStoxx 50 Index

the whole industry. Consider Table 12.1, which shows the betas of some prominent firms in the UK oil and gas industry. The average beta across all of the firms in the table is 0.99. Imagine a financial executive at Expro International trying to estimate the firm's beta. Because beta estimation is subject to large random variation in this volatile industry, the executive may be uncomfortable with the estimate of 0.82. However, the error in beta estimation on a single equity is much higher than the error for a portfolio of securities. Thus the executive of Expro International may use the industry beta of 0.99 as the estimate of its own firm's beta.

In contrast, consider BG Group. Assuming a risk-free rate of 5 per cent and a risk premium of 8.7 per cent, BG Group might estimate its cost of equity capital as

$$5\% + 0.81 \times 8.7\% = 12.04\%$$

| Company | Beta |
| --- | --- |
| Premier Oil | 1.07 |
| Burren Energy | 1.29 |
| Royal Dutch Shell | 0.76 |
| Expro International Group | 0.82 |
| Dana Petroleum | 1.50 |
| Hunting | 0.56 |
| JKX Oil and Gas | 1.17 |
| Abbot Group | 1.02 |
| Soco International | 0.70 |
| BP | 0.87 |
| Tullow Oil | 0.93 |
| Petrofac | 0.96 |
| Wood Group (John) | 0.81 |
| Cairn Energy | 1.53 |
| BG Group | 0.81 |
| Equally weighted portfolio | 0.99 |

*Source*: *Yahoo! Finance*, http://uk.finance.yahoo.com

**Table 12.1** Betas for firms in the British oil and gas industry, 2009

However, if BG Group believed the industry beta contained less estimation error, it could estimate its cost of equity capital as

$$5\% + 0.99 \times 8.7\% = 13.61\%$$

The difference is substantial here, presenting a difficult choice for a financial executive at BG Group.

While there is no formula for selecting the right beta, there is a very simple guideline. If you believe that the operations of a firm are similar to the operations of the rest of the industry, you should use the industry beta, simply to reduce estimation error.[1] However, if an executive believes that the operations of the firm are fundamentally different from those in the rest of the industry, the firm's beta should be used.

When we discussed financial statement analysis in Chapter 3, we noted that a problem frequently comes up in practice – namely, what *is* the industry? For example, Yahoo! Finance categorizes BG Group as an oil and gas company. However, the oil and gas industry encompasses exploration, drilling, production, transmission, and distribution of both commodities. The risk of these various business operations can be quite different.

## 12.3    Determinants of Beta

The regression analysis approach in the previous section doesn't tell us where beta comes from. Of course, the beta of a security does not come out of thin air. Rather, it is determined by the characteristics of the firm. We consider three factors: the cyclical nature of revenues, operating leverage, and financial leverage.

### Cyclicality of Revenues

The revenues of some firms are quite cyclical. That is, these firms do well in the expansion phase of the business cycle but do poorly in the contraction phase. Empirical evidence suggests that high-tech firms, retailers and automotive firms fluctuate with the business cycle. Firms in industries such as utilities, railroads, food and airlines are less dependent on the cycle. Because beta is the standardized covariance of a security's return with the market's return, it is not surprising that highly cyclical securities have high betas.

It is worth while to point out that cyclicality is not the same as variability. For example, a moviemaking firm has highly variable revenues, because hits and flops are not easily predicted. However, because the revenues of a studio are more dependent on the quality of its releases than on the phase of the business cycle, motion picture companies are not particularly cyclical. In other words, securities with high standard deviations need not have high betas, a point we have stressed before.

### Operating Leverage

We distinguished fixed costs from variable costs earlier in the text. At that time, we mentioned that fixed costs do not change as quantity changes. Conversely, variable costs increase as the quantity of output rises. This difference between variable and fixed costs allows us to define operating leverage.

EXAMPLE
**12.3**

## Operating Leverage Illustrated

Consider a typical problem faced by Carlsberg, the Danish alcoholic drinks firm. As part of the brewing process, Carlsberg often needs to choose between two production technologies. Assume that Carlsberg can choose either technology A or technology B when making a particular drink. The relevant differences between the two technologies are displayed here:

| Technology A | Technology B |
|---|---|
| Fixed cost: DKK1,000/year | Fixed cost: DKK2,000/year |
| Variable cost: DKK8/unit | Variable cost: DKK6/unit |
| Price: DKK10/unit | Price: DKK10/unit |
| Contribution margin: DKK2 (= DKK10 − 8) | Contribution margin: DKK4 (= DKK10 − 6) |

Technology A has lower fixed costs and higher variable costs than does technology B. Perhaps technology A involves less mechanization than does B. Or the equipment in A may be leased, whereas the equipment in B must be purchased. Alternatively, perhaps technology A involves few employees but many subcontractors, whereas B involves only highly skilled employees who must be retained in bad times. Because technology B has both lower variable costs and higher fixed costs, we say that it has higher operating leverage.

Figure 12.4 graphs the costs under both technologies. The slope of each total cost line represents variable costs under a single technology. The slope of A's line is steeper, indicating greater variable costs.

Because the two technologies are used to produce the same drinks, a unit price of DKK10 applies for both cases. An unexpected sale increases profit by DKK2 under A but increases profit by DKK4 under B. Similarly, an unexpected sale cancellation reduces profit by DKK2 under A but reduces profit by DKK4 under B. This is illustrated in Fig. 12.5. This figure shows the change in earnings before interest and taxes for a given change in volume. The slope of the right graph is greater, indicating that technology B is riskier.

Technology A has higher variable costs and lower fixed costs than does technology B. Technology B has higher operating leverage.

**Figure 12.4** Illustration of two different technologies

Technology B has lower variable costs than A, implying a higher contribution margin. The profits of the firm are more responsive to changes in volume under technology B than under A.

**Figure 12.5** Illustration of the effect of a change in volume on the change in earnings before interest and taxes (EBIT)

The cyclicality of a firm's revenues is a determinant of the firm's beta. Operating leverage magnifies the effect of cyclicality on beta. As mentioned earlier, business risk is generally defined as the risk of the firm without financial leverage. Business risk depends both on the responsiveness of the firm's revenues to the business cycle and on the firm's operating leverage.

Although the preceding discussion concerns firms, it applies to projects as well. If we cannot estimate a project's beta in another way, we can examine the project's revenues and operating leverage. Projects whose revenues appear strongly cyclical and whose operating leverage appears high are likely to have high betas. Conversely, weak cyclicality and low operating leverage imply low betas. As mentioned earlier, this approach is unfortunately qualitative in nature. Because start-up projects have little data, quantitative estimates of beta generally are not feasible.

## Financial Leverage and Beta

As suggested by their names, operating leverage and financial leverage are analogous concepts. Operating leverage refers to the firm's fixed costs of *production*. Financial leverage is the extent to which a firm relies on debt, and a levered firm is a firm with some debt in its capital structure. Because a *levered* firm must make interest payments regardless of the firm's sales, financial leverage refers to the firm's fixed costs of *finance*.

Consider our discussion in Chapter 10 concerning the beta of Jelco plc. In that example, we estimated beta from the returns on Jelco *equity*. Furthermore, the betas in Fig. 12.3 from real-world firms were estimated from returns on equity. Thus, in each case, we estimated the firm's equity beta. The beta of the assets of a levered firm is different from the beta of its equity. As the name suggests, the asset beta is the beta of the assets of the firm. The asset beta could also be thought of as the beta of the firm's shares had the firm been financed only with equity.

Imagine an individual who owns all the firm's debt and all its equity. In other words, this individual owns the entire firm. What is the beta of her portfolio of the firm's debt and equity?

As with any portfolio, the beta of this portfolio is a weighted average of the betas of the individual items in the portfolio. Let $B$ stand for the market value of the firm's debt and $S$ stand for the market value of the firm's equity. We have

$$\beta_{\text{Asset}} = \frac{S}{B+S} \times \beta_{\text{Equity}} + \frac{B}{B+S} \times \beta_{\text{Debt}} \qquad (12.2)$$

where $\beta_{\text{Equity}}$ is the beta of the equity of the *levered* firm. Notice that the beta of debt, $\beta_{\text{Debt}}$, is multiplied by $B/(B + S)$, the percentage of debt in the capital structure. Similarly, the beta of equity is multiplied by the percentage of equity in the capital structure. Because the portfolio contains both the debt of the firm and the equity of the firm, the beta of the portfolio is the *asset beta*. As we just said, the asset beta can also be viewed as the beta of the company's shares had the firm been all equity.

The beta of debt is very low in practice. If we make the common assumption that the beta of debt is zero, we have

$$\beta_{\text{Asset}} = \frac{S}{B+S} \times \beta_{\text{Equity}} \qquad (12.3)$$

Because $S/(B + S)$ must be below 1 for a levered firm, it follows that $\beta_{\text{Asset}} < \beta_{\text{Equity}}$. Rearranging this equation, we have

$$\beta_{\text{Equity}} = \beta_{\text{Asset}}\left(1 + \frac{B}{S}\right)$$

The equity beta will always be greater than the asset beta with financial leverage (assuming the asset beta is positive).[2]

## Asset versus Equity Betas

**EXAMPLE 12.4**

Consider a Swedish tree growing company, Rapid Firs, which is currently all equity and has a beta of 0.8. The firm has decided to move to a capital structure of one part debt to two parts equity. Because the firm is staying in the same industry, its asset beta should remain at 0.8. However, assuming a zero beta for its debt, its equity beta would become

$$\beta_{\text{Equity}} = \beta_{\text{Asset}}\left(1 + \frac{B}{S}\right)$$

$$1.2 = 0.8\left(1 + \frac{1}{2}\right)$$

If the firm had one part debt to one part equity in its capital structure, its equity beta would be

$$1.6 = 0.8(1 + 1)$$

However, as long as it stayed in the same industry, its asset beta would remain at 0.8. The effect of leverage, then, is to increase the equity beta.

## 12.4  Extensions of the Basic Model

### The Firm versus the Project

We now assume that the risk of a project differs from that of the firm, while going back to the all-equity assumption. We began the chapter by pointing out that each project should be paired with a financial asset of comparable risk. If a project's beta differs from that of the firm, the project should be discounted at the rate commensurate with its own beta. This is a very important point because firms frequently speak of a *corporate discount rate*. (*Hurdle rate, cut-off rate, benchmark* and *cost of capital* are frequently used synonymously.) Unless all projects in the corporation are of the same risk, choosing the same discount rate for all projects is incorrect.

The D.D. Ronnelley example assumes that the proposed project has identical risk to that of the software industry, allowing the industry beta to be used. However, the beta of a new project may be greater than the beta of existing firms in the same industry, because the very newness of the project is likely to increase its responsiveness to economy-wide movements. For example, a start-up computer venture may fail in a recession, whereas Dell or Apple will still be around. Conversely, in an economy-wide expansion, the venture may grow much faster than the old-line computer firms.

## Project Risk

**EXAMPLE 12.5**

D.D. Ronnelley, a publishing firm, may accept a project in computer software. Noting that computer software companies have high betas, the publishing firm views the software venture as more risky than the rest of its business. It should discount the project at a rate commensurate with the risk of software companies. For example, it might use the average beta of a portfolio of publicly traded software firms. Instead, if all projects in D.D. Ronnelley were discounted at the same rate, a bias would result. The firm would accept too many high-risk projects (software ventures) and reject too many low-risk projects (books and magazines). This point is illustrated in Fig. 12.6.

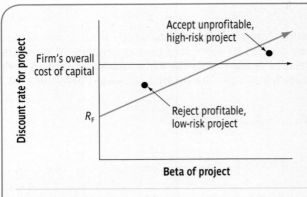

**Figure 12.6** Relationship between the firm's cost of capital and the security market line

Fortunately, a slight adjustment is all that is needed here. The new venture should be assigned a somewhat higher beta than that of the industry, to reflect added risk. The adjustment is necessarily ad hoc, so no formula can be given. Our experience indicates that this approach is widespread in practice today.

## The Cost of Capital with Debt

Section 12.1 showed how to choose the discount rate when a project is all equity-financed. In this section we discuss an adjustment when the project is financed with both debt and equity.

Suppose a firm uses both debt and equity to finance its investments. If the firm pays $R_B$ for its debt financing and $R_S$ for its equity, what is the overall or average cost of its capital? The cost of equity is $R_S$, as discussed in earlier sections. The cost of debt is the firm's borrowing rate, $R_B$, which we can often observe by looking at the yield to maturity on the firm's debt. If a firm uses both debt and equity, the cost of capital is a weighted average of each. This works out to be

$$\frac{S}{S + B} \times R_S + \frac{B}{S + B} \times R_B$$

The weights in the formula are, respectively, the proportion of total value represented by the equity,

$$\left(\frac{S}{S + B}\right)$$

and the proportion of total value represented by debt,

$$\left(\frac{B}{S + B}\right)$$

This is only natural. If the firm had issued no debt, and was therefore an all-equity firm, its average cost of capital would equal its cost of equity, $R_S$. At the other extreme, if the firm had issued so much debt that its equity was valueless, it would be an all-debt firm, and its average cost of capital would be its cost of debt, $R_B$.

Of course, interest is tax deductible at the corporate level, a point to be treated in more detail in a later chapter. The after-tax cost of debt is

$$\text{Cost of debt (after corporate tax)} = R_B \times (1 - t_C)$$

where $t_C$ is the corporation's tax rate.

Assembling these results, we get the average cost of capital (after tax) for the firm:

$$\text{Average cost of capital} = \left(\frac{S}{S+B}\right) \times R_S + \left(\frac{B}{S+B}\right) \times R_B \times (1 - t_C) \qquad (12.4)$$

Because the average cost of capital is a weighting of its cost of equity and its cost of debt, it is usually referred to as the **weighted average cost of capital**, $R_{\text{WACC}}$, and from now on we shall use this term.

## EXAMPLE 12.6

## WACC

According to the ArcelorMittal website, the European steelmaker has debt with a market value of €4.4 billion and equity with a market value of €71.4 billion. ArcelorMittal had eight different types of bond in issue as of September 2008, four of which were issued in Luxembourg (denominated in euros) and the other four were denominated in dollars. For the purposes of this question assume that the bonds are all the same, denominated in dollars, and pay interest of 6 per cent per annum. The company's shares have a beta of 1.81. Because of the range of countries and tax codes in regimes in which ArcelorMittal operated, the effective tax rate for the company was 13.1 per cent in 2008 (*Source*: ArcelorMittal financial accounts for 2008). Assume that the SML holds, that the risk premium on the market is 9.5 per cent (slightly higher than the historical equity risk premium), and that the current Treasury bill rate is 4.5 per cent. What is this firm's $R_{\text{WACC}}$?

To compute the $R_{\text{WACC}}$ using Eq. 12.4, we must know: (1) the after-tax cost of debt, $R_B \times (1 - t_C)$; (2) the cost of equity, $R_S$; and (3) the proportions of debt and equity used by the firm. These three values are computed next:

1   The pre-tax cost of debt is 6 per cent, implying an after-tax cost of 5.214 per cent [6% × (1 − 0.131)].

2   We compute the cost of equity capital by using the SML:

$$R_S = R_F + \beta(R_M - R_F)$$
$$= 4.5\% + 1.81 \times 9.5\%$$
$$= 21.695\%$$

3   We compute the proportions of debt and equity from the market values of debt and equity. Because the market value of the firm is €75.8 billion (= €4.4 billion + €71.4 billion), the proportions of debt and equity are 5.8 and 94.2 per cent, respectively.

The cost of equity, $R_S$, is 21.695 per cent, and the after-tax cost of debt, $R_B \times (1 - t_C)$, is 5.214 per cent. $B$ is €4.4 billion and $S$ is €71.4 billion. Therefore:

$$R_{\text{WACC}} = \frac{S}{B+S} \times R_S + \frac{B}{B+S} \times R_B \times (1 - t_C)$$
$$= \left(\frac{4.4}{75.8} \times 5.214\%\right) + \left(\frac{71.4}{75.8} \times 21.695\%\right)$$
$$= 20.738\%$$

This procedure is presented in table form next:

| (1) Financing components | (2) Market values (€) | (3) Weight | (4) Cost of capital (after corporate tax) (%) | (5) Weighted cost of capital (%) |
|---|---|---|---|---|
| Debt | 4.4 billion | 0.058 | 6 × (1 − 0.131) = 5.214 | 0.302 |
| Equity | 71.4 billion | 0.942 | 4.5 + 1.81 × 9.5 = 21.695 | 20.436 |
| Total | 75.8 billion | 1.00 | | 20.738 |

The weights we used in the previous example were market value weights. Market value weights are more appropriate than book value weights because the market values of the securities are closer to the actual money that would be received from their sale. Actually, it is usually useful to think in terms of 'target' market weights. These are the market weights expected to prevail over the life of the firm or project.

---

EXAMPLE
**12.7**

## Project Evaluation and the WACC

Suppose a firm has both a current and a target debt–equity ratio of 0.6, a cost of debt of 15.15 per cent, and a cost of equity of 20 per cent. The corporate tax rate is 34 per cent.

Our first step calls for transforming the debt–equity (B/S) ratio to a debt–value ratio. A B/S ratio of 0.6 implies 6 parts debt for 10 parts equity. Because value is equal to the sum of the debt plus the equity, the debt–value ratio is $6/(6 + 10) = 0.375$. Similarly, the equity–value ratio is $10/(6 + 10) = 0.625$. The $R_{WACC}$ will then be

$$R_{WACC} = \left(\frac{S}{S+B}\right) \times R_S + \left(\frac{S}{S+B}\right) \times R_B \times (1 - t_C)$$
$$= 0.625 \times 20\% + 0.375 \times 15.15\% \times 0.66$$
$$= 16.25\%$$

Suppose the firm is considering taking on a warehouse renovation costing £50 million that is expected to yield cost savings of £12 million a year for six years. Using the NPV equation and discounting the six years of expected cash flows from the renovation at the $R_{WACC}$, we have

$$NPV = -£50 + \frac{£12}{1 + R_{WACC}} + \cdots + \frac{£12}{(1 + R_{WACC})^6}$$
$$= -£50 + £12 \times A_{0.1625}^6$$
$$= -£50 + (12 \times 3.66)$$
$$= -£6.07$$

Should the firm take on the warehouse renovation? The project has a negative NPV using the firm's $R_{WACC}$. This means that the financial markets offer superior projects in the same risk class (namely, the firm's risk class). The answer is clear: the firm should reject the project.

---

## 12.5 Estimating Carrefour Group's Cost of Capital

In the previous section we calculated the cost of capital of ArcelorMittal and simplified a number of important inputs, such as the annual interest payment. We shall now calculate the cost of capital for Carrefour Group, the French supermarket chain, in the same way that a financial analyst would. Carrefour has stores in Europe, North and South America, as well as Asia operating under the names Carrefour, Pryca, Stoc, Marche Plus, Optique and Comod.

### Carrefour Group's Cost of Equity

Our first stop for Carrefour is www.reuters.com. Search for the company using its code (CARR.PA). As of September 2008 Carrefour has 693.96 million shares outstanding. The share price is €34.31 and the market value of the equity is 693.96 × €34.31 = €23,810 million.

To estimate Carrefour's cost of equity, we shall assume a market risk premium of 7 per cent. This is a subjective estimate based upon the sentiment of a number of analysts. Given that the rate on European T-bills is around 4.49 per cent (*Source*: Yahoo! Finance), a market risk premium of 7 per cent implies that the market is expected to go up by 11.49 per cent in the

FIGURE
12.7

| Stability | | |
| --- | --- | --- |
| 1 – 20 of 121 companies. | | |
| Ticker | Name | Beta |
| | **MktCap Weighted Average** | **0.17** |
| 0BNT.L | Kesko Oyj | 0.49 |
| 0EK1.L | Rallye SA | 1.41 |
| 0EXG.L | Jeronimo Martins SGPS SA | 0.39 |
| 0G1N.L | Sligro Food Group NV | 0.47 |
| 0G62.L | Schuitema NV | 0.27 |
| 0GWE.L | Axfood AB | 0.26 |
| 0H44.L | Metro AG | 0.54 |
| 0HAL.L | Carrefour SA | 0.67 |
| 0IG2.L | Delhaize Group | 1.48 |
| 0IZ3.L | Sonae SGPS SA | 1.78 |
| 0JEW.L | Etablissementen Franz Colruyt NV | 0.20 |
| 1352.T | HOHSUI CORP | 0.29 |
| 2211.T | Fujiya Co Ltd | 0.66 |
| 2655.T | MAXVALU TOHOKU CO LTD | 0.48 |
| 2683.T | UOKI CO LTD | 0.38 |
| 2687.T | CVS Bay Area Inc | 1.21 |
| 2692.T | ITOCHU-SHOKUHIN Co Ltd | 0.77 |
| 2791.T | DAIKOKUTENBUSSAN CO LTD | – |
| 3004.T | SHINYEI KAISHA | 0.91 |
| 3078.T | Universe Co Ltd | – |

Source: Reuters, http://uk.reuters.com

**Figure 12.7** Snapshot of betas for companies in the food distribution and convenience stores industry

next year. Carrefour's beta on Reuters is 0.67. Figure 12.7 shows the betas for other food distribution and convenience stores. As you can see, the industry average beta is 0.17, which is quite a bit lower than Carrefour's beta. Using Carrefour's own beta in the CAPM to estimate the cost of equity, we find

$$R_S = 0.0449 + 0.67(0.07) = 0.0918 \text{ or } 9.18\%$$

If we use the industry beta, we would find that the estimate for the cost of equity capital is

$$R_S = 0.0449 + 0.17(0.07) = 0.0568 \text{ or } 5.68\%$$

Notice that the estimates for the cost of equity are quite different, because Carrefour's beta is relatively far from the industry beta. The decision of which cost of equity estimate to use is up to the financial executive, based on knowledge and experience of both the company and the industry. In this case, we shall choose to use the cost of equity using Carrefour's estimated beta.

## Carrefour's Cost of Debt

We must now find out about the different bonds that Carrefour has issued. To do this, download the Carrefour financial accounts from the company's website and read the information on bonds. The information is reproduced below, and the figure in the last column is the value of each bond tranche in millions of euros:

| | Maturity date | Total |
|---|---|---|
| **Breakdown of Bonds** | | 8,149 |
| **Public issues** | | 7,601 |
| Bond Euro MTN, EUR, 7 years, 5.125% | 2014 | 1,250 |
| Bond Euro MTN, EUR, 5 years, E3M+15bp | 2012 | 200 |
| Bond Euro MTN, EUR, 10 years, 4.375% | 2016 | 600 |
| Bond Euro MTN, EUR, 10 years, 3.825% | 2015 | 50 |
| Bond Euro MTN, EUR, 10 years, 3.85% | 2015 | 50 |
| Bond Euro MTN, EUR, 8 years, 3.625% | 2013 | 750 |
| Bond Euros MTN,EUR, 4 years, 3.265% | 2008 | 500 |
| Bond Euro MTN, GBP, 10 years, 5.375% | 2012 | 796 |
| Bond Euro MTN, EUR, 8 years, 4.375% | 2011 | 1,100 |
| Bond Euro MTN, EUR, 2.5 years, 6.125% | 2010 | 1,000 |
| Bond, FRF, 10 years, 4.5% | 2009 | 1,000 |
| Bond, FRF, 10 years, 5.3% | 2008 | 305 |
| **Private issues** | | 547 |

Unlike the US, corporate bonds are not traded frequently in Europe and the rest of the world. This brings difficulties when calculating the weighted average cost of debt. If one does not have a current price, it is impossible to calculate the yield to maturity accurately. To find out the situation for Carrefour, we shall visit the stock exchange on which the bonds are listed, Euronext. A search for the company's bonds gives only two bonds:

**Results for "carrefour"**

Equities (6) | Futures/Options (3) | Bonds (2)

**Bonds (2)**

Download >>>> Prices      Prices & features

Powered by NYSE Euronext Data Solutions | Prices are delayed at least by 15 minutes

**NYSE Euronext**

| Name | Type | ISIN | Market | Last Trade | Volume | % Change | Time (CET) | Maturity |
|---|---|---|---|---|---|---|---|---|
| CARREFOUR 4,50%09 | COR | FR0000492282 | PAR | 98.92 % | 43 | 0.99 ⌃ | 11/09/08 09:50 | 18/03/09 |
| CARREFOUR 6 1/8%10 | COR | FR0000480691 | PAR | 100.75 % | 2 | −0.41 ⌄ | 05/08/08 09:00 | 26/05/10 |

Notice that the last transaction date for the Carrefour 6 1/8 per cent bond is one month earlier than that of the 4.5 per cent bond. The other bonds have no price data at all. We shall consequently need to use approximation techniques. One approach is to estimate the yield to maturity for the two available bonds, take a weighted average, and use this as the estimate of the cost of debt. This obviously isn't desirable, since we are ignoring the other bonds. However, in this situation it is possibly the best solution.

To make things slightly more simple, we shall calculate the yield to maturity on the short-term 4.5 per cent coupon bond, since it is similar to a zero-coupon bond and the most recently traded. The bond expires on 18 March 2009. If it is 11 September 2008 today, the bond effectively only has one coupon of 2.25 (= 4.5/2) per cent left to be paid on maturity of the bond. Given that we know the last trade was 98.92 per cent, we are able to calculate an approximate six-month return:

$$\left(\frac{102.25}{98.92}\right) - 1 = 0.0311 = 3.11\%$$

The effective yield to maturity or cost of debt is then calculated as

$$1.0311^2 - 1 = 0.0632 = 6.32\%$$

## Carrefour's WACC

We now have the various pieces necessary to calculate Carrefour's WACC. First, we need to calculate the capital structure weights. Carrefour's equity and debt are worth €23,810 million and €8,149 million, respectively. The capital structure weight for equity is €23,810 million/€31,959 billion = 0.745, and for debt it is €8,149 million/€31,959 million = 0.255, so the equity percentage is much higher. According to Carrefour's page on www.reuters.com (check the *Ratios* link), the effective tax rate for Carrefour is 30.12 per cent.

With these weights, Carrefour's $R_{WACC}$ is

$$R_{WACC} = 0.745 \times 9.18\% + 0.255 \times 6.32\% \times (1 - 0.3012)$$
$$= 7.97\%$$

Thus, using market value weights, we get 7.97 per cent for Carrefour's $R_{WACC}$.

So how does our estimate of the $R_{WACC}$ for Carrefour compare with others? A search of the Internet shows that Citigroup estimates that Carrefour has a WACC of 8 per cent, which is almost exactly the same as our own estimate.

## 12.6 Reducing the Cost of Capital

Chapters 9–12 develop the idea that both the expected return on an equity and the cost of capital of the firm are positively related to risk. Recently, a number of academics have argued that expected return and cost of capital are negatively related to liquidity as well.[3] In addition, these scholars make the interesting point that although it is quite difficult to lower the risk of a firm, it is much easier to increase the liquidity of the firm's equity. Therefore they suggest that a firm can actually lower its cost of capital through liquidity enhancement. We develop this idea next.

### What Is Liquidity?

Anyone who owns a home probably thinks of liquidity in terms of the time it takes to buy or sell the home. For example, apartments in city centre areas are generally quite liquid. Particularly in good times, an apartment may sell within days of being placed on the market. By contrast, single-family homes in suburban areas may take weeks or months to sell. Special properties such as multimillion-pound mansions may take even longer.

The concept of liquidity is similar, but not identical, in equities. Here, we speak of the *cost* of buying and selling instead. That is, equities that are expensive to trade are considered less liquid than those that trade cheaply. What do we mean by the cost to trade? We generally think of three costs here: brokerage fees, the bid–ask spread, and market impact costs.

Brokerage fees are the easiest to understand, because you must pay a broker to execute a trade. More difficult is the bid–ask spread. Consider the London Stock Exchange. If you want to trade 100 shares of XYZ plc, your broker will use a specialized trading terminal to get the best price at which you can buy and sell. Suppose the broker provides a quote of 100.00–100.07. This means that you can buy at £100.07 per share and sell at £100 per share. The spread of £0.07 is a cost to you, because you are losing £0.07 per share over a round-trip transaction (over a purchase and a subsequent sale).

Finally, we have *market impact costs*. Suppose a trader wants to sell 10,000 shares instead of just 100 shares. Here, someone has to take on extra risk when buying. First, she has to pay out £1,000,000 (= 10,000 × £100), cash that may not be easily available to her. Second, the trader may be selling this large amount because she has special information that the share price will fall imminently. The counterparty bears the risk of losing a lot of money on that

FIGURE
**12.8**

An increase in liquidity (i.e. a reduction in trading costs) lowers a firm's cost of capital.

**Figure 12.8** Liquidity and the cost of capital

trade. Consequently, to compensate for these risks, the transaction price may not be £100/share but a lower price. Similarly, a counterparty may be willing to sell a large block of equity only at a price above £100.07. The price drop associated with a large sale and the price rise associated with a large purchase are the market impact costs.

## Liquidity, Expected Returns, and the Cost of Capital

The cost of trading non-liquid shares reduces the total return that an investor receives. That is, if you buy a share for £100 and sell it later for £105, the gain before trading costs is £5. If you must pay £1 in commission when buying and another £1 when selling, the gain after trading costs is only £3. Both the bid–ask spread and market impact costs would reduce this gain still further.

As we shall see later, trading costs vary across securities. In the last four chapters we have stressed that investors demand a high expected return as compensation when investing in high-risk (e.g. high-beta) equities. Because the expected return to the investor is the cost of capital to the firm, the cost of capital is positively related to beta. Now we are saying the same thing for trading costs. Investors demand a high expected return when investing in equities with high trading costs – that is, with low liquidity. This high expected return implies a high cost of capital to the firm. This idea is illustrated in Fig. 12.8.

## Liquidity and Adverse Selection

Although there are a number of factors that influence liquidity, we focus on just one: *adverse selection*. As mentioned before, a counterparty will lose money on a trade if the trader has information that the counterparty does not have. If you have special information that the share is worth £110 in the preceding example, you will want to buy shares at £100.07. Conversely, if you know that the equity is worth only £90 and you currently own 100 shares, you will be happy to sell these shares at £100. In either of these cases, we say that the counterparty has been *picked off*, or has been subject to adverse selection.

Traders in the market must protect themselves in some way here. Of course, they cannot forbid informed individuals from trading with them, because they do not know ahead of time who these investors are. The next best alternative is to reduce the price at which you are willing to buy or increase the price at which you are willing to sell. The effect of this is that the bid–ask spread will widen, thereby increasing the costs of trading to *all* traders – both informed and uninformed. That is, if the spread is widened to, say, £99.98–£100.11, each trader pays a round-trip cost of £0.13 per share.

The key here is that the spread should be positively related to the ratio of informed to uninformed traders. That is, informed traders will pick off the market and uninformed traders will not. Thus informed traders in an equity raise the required return on equity, thereby increasing the cost of capital.

## What the Corporation Can Do

The corporation has an incentive to lower trading costs because (given the preceding discussion) a lower cost of capital should result. Amihud and Mendelson identify two general strategies for corporations. First, they argue that firms should try to bring in more uninformed investors. Stock splits may be a useful tool here. Imagine that a company has 1 million shares outstanding with a share price of £100. Because investors generally buy in round lots of 100 shares, these investors would need £10,000 (= £100 × 100 shares) for a purchase. A number of small investors might be 'priced out' of the equity, although large investors would not be. Thus the ratio of large investors to small investors would be high. Because large investors are generally more likely than small investors to be informed, the ratio of informed to uninformed investors is likely to be high.

A 2:1 stock split would give two shares of equity for every one that the investor previously held. Because every investor would still hold the same proportional interest in the firm, each investor would be no better off than before. Thus it is likely that the share price will fall to £50 from £100. Here, an individual with 100 shares worth £10,000 (= £100 × 100 shares) finds herself still worth £10,000 (= £50 × 200 shares) after the split.

However, a round lot becomes more affordable, thereby bringing more small and uninformed investors into the firm. Consequently, the adverse selection costs are reduced, leading to lower bid–ask spreads. In turn, it is hoped that the expected return on the equity, and the cost of equity capital, will fall as well. If this happens, the shares might actually trade at a price slightly above £50.

Another strategy to lower the cost of capital is to disclose more information. This narrows the gap between uninformed and informed investors, thereby lowering the cost of capital. Suggestions include providing more financial data about corporate segments, and more management forecasts. An interesting study by Coller and Yohn[4] concludes that the bid–ask spread is reduced after the release of these forecasts.

This section would not be complete without a discussion of security analysts. Analysts are employed by brokerage houses to follow companies in individual industries. For example, an analyst for a particular brokerage house might follow all the firms in, say, the auto industry. This analyst distributes reports and other information to the clients of the brokerage house. Virtually all brokerage houses have analysts following the major industries. Again, through dissemination of the information, analysts narrow the gap between the informed and the uninformed investors, thereby tending to reduce the bid–ask spread.

Although all major industries are covered, the smaller firms in industries are often ignored, implying a higher bid–ask spread and a higher cost of capital for these firms. Analysts frequently state that they avoid following companies that release little information, pointing out that they are more trouble than they are worth. Thus it behoves companies that are not followed to release as much information as possible to security analysts to attract their interest. Friendliness towards security analysts would be helpful as well. The argument here is not to get the analysts to make buy recommendations. Rather, it is simply to interest the analysts in following the company, thereby reducing the information asymmetry between informed and uninformed investors.

## International Considerations

Thirty years ago, most companies raised funds in their own country. However, in recent years there has been significantly greater choice on where firms raise capital. Naturally, the costs of capital across countries have become an important issue to financial managers who wish to minimize the cost of raising funds.

In 2006 the London Stock Exchange hired a financial consulting firm, Oxera, to compare the costs of capital in London with its regional competitors.[5] They decomposed the cost of raising capital into two main groups: the costs of going through an IPO (initial public

TABLE
**12.2**

| Costs | Evidence | Quantitative impact on cost of capital |
|---|---|---|
| **IPO costs** | | |
| Initial underwriting fees | Higher in US than in UK, Germany and France | 3–4% in Europe, 6.5–7% in US |
| IPO price discounts | Differs across countries | 10–15% |
| Initial listing fees | Deutsche Börse and LSE are lowest | < 0.1% |
| Professional fees | US highest, then UK. France and Germany are lowest | 3–6% |
| **Ongoing costs** | | |
| Trading costs and liquidity: fees | Lowest on LSE, then NYSE. Highest on Euronext, Deutsche Börse and Nasdaq | |
| Trading costs and liquidity: spreads | Lowest on NYSE. Higher in Europe | |
| Annual exchange fees | For smaller firms, European Exchanges are cheaper than the US. For larger firms, Deutsche Börse and Euronext are cheaper | < 0.1% |

*Source*: Partially reproduced from Oxera Consulting, *The Cost of Capital: International Comparisons* (2006).

**Table 12.2** Costs of raising capital across Europe and the US

offering), and the ongoing costs of maintaining a public listing. Note that these costs are in addition to the return required by investors. Thus, if investors required a 10 per cent return on an investment in a firm and the cost of raising the funds was 3 per cent, the cost of capital for the company would be 13 per cent.

Taking IPOs first, the costs can be decomposed into several components, including underwriting fees, professional fees, listing fees, and price discounts. The costs of maintaining a listing include regulatory, corporate governance and professional fees, annual listing fees, and trading costs. Table 12.2 presents an overview of the comparative costs of capital across Europe and the US.

## 12.7 How Do Corporations Estimate Cost of Capital in Practice?

The material in this chapter is quite complex, and the reader may be left wondering what firms actually do when they calculate the cost of capital in practice. Brounen, de Jong and Koedijk[6] surveyed executives in France, Germany, the Netherlands and the UK on the methods they used to estimate the cost of capital for their firm, and the responses are presented in Table 12.3.

There are notable differences across countries, but the most commonly used method is CAPM and beta. Historical returns on share prices are also commonly used, and in the Netherlands a surprisingly large number of companies use a cost of capital estimate that is set by investors. Regulators play an important role in the UK and France, whereas in Germany they are not considered at all.

TABLE
12.3

| | US | UK | The Netherlands | Germany | France |
|---|---|---|---|---|---|
| Capital asset pricing model | 73.49 | 47.06 | 55.56 | 33.96 | 45.16 |
| Historical returns | 39.41 | 31.25 | 30.77 | 18.00 | 27.27 |
| Multifactor models | 34.29 | 27.27 | 15.38 | 16.07 | 30.30 |
| Backed out from dividend growth model (i.e. $P = Div/r$) | 15.74 | 10.00 | 10.71 | 10.42 | 10.34 |
| Determined by investors | 13.93 | 18.75 | 44.83 | 39.22 | 34.38 |
| Determined by regulators | 7.04 | 16.13 | 3.70 | 0.00 | 16.13 |

*Source*: Table 3 from D. Brounen, A. de Jong and K. Koedijk, 'Corporate finance in Europe: confronting theory and practice', *Journal of Banking and Finance* (2006).

**Table 12.3** The percentage of firms estimating cost of capital that use specific methods

## 12.8   Economic Value Added and the Measurement of Financial Performance

This chapter shows how to calculate the appropriate discount rate for capital budgeting and other valuation problems. We now consider the concept of economic value added, which uses the same discount rate developed for capital budgeting. Consider the following simple example.

Many years ago, Henry Bodenheimer started Bodie's Blimps, one of the largest high-speed blimp manufacturers. Because growth was so rapid, Henry put most of his effort into capital budgeting. He forecast cash flows for various projects, and discounted them at the cost of capital appropriate to the beta of the blimp business. However, these projects have grown rapidly, in some cases becoming whole divisions. He now needs to evaluate the performance of these divisions to reward his division managers. How does he perform the appropriate analysis?

Henry is aware that capital budgeting and performance measurement are essentially mirror images of each other. Capital budgeting is forward-looking, because we must estimate future cash flows to value a project. By contrast, performance measurement is backward-looking. As Henry stated to a group of his executives, 'Capital budgeting is like looking through the windscreen while driving a car. You need to know what lies farther down the road to calculate a net present value. Performance measurement is like looking into the rear-view mirror. You find out where you have been.'

Henry first measured the performance of his various divisions by return on assets (ROA), an approach that we treated in Chapter 3. For example, if a division had earnings after tax of €1,000 and had assets of €10,000, the ROA would be

$$\frac{€1,000}{€10,000} = 10\%$$

He calculated the ROA ratio for each of his divisions, paying a bonus to each of his division managers based on the size of that division's ROA. However, while ROA was generally effective in motivating his managers, there were a number of situations where it appeared that ROA was counterproductive.

For example, Henry always believed that Sharon Smith, head of the supersonic division, was his best manager. The ROA of Smith's division was generally in the high double digits, but the best estimate of the weighted average cost of capital for the division was only 20 per cent.

Furthermore, the division had been growing rapidly. However, as soon as Henry paid bonuses based on ROA, the division stopped growing. At that time, Smith's division had after-tax earnings of €2,000,000 on an asset base of €2,000,000, for an ROA of 100 per cent (= €2 million/ €2 million).

Henry found out why the growth stopped when he suggested a project to Smith that would earn €1,000,000 per year on an investment of €2,000,000. This was clearly an attractive project with an ROA of 50 per cent (= €1 million/€2 million). He thought that Smith would jump at the chance to place his project into her division, because the ROA of the project was much higher than the cost of capital of 20 per cent. However, Smith did everything she could to kill the project. And, as Henry later figured out, Smith was rational to do so. Smith must have realized that if the project were accepted, the division's ROA would become

$$\frac{€2,000,000 + €1,000,000}{€2,000,000 + €2,000,000} = 75\%$$

Thus the ROA of Smith's division would fall from 100 per cent to 75 per cent if the project were accepted, with Smith's bonus falling in tandem.

Henry was later exposed to the economic value added (EVA) approach,[7] which seems to obviate this particular problem. The formula for EVA is

$$(ROA - Weighted\ average\ cost\ of\ capital) \times Total\ capital$$

Without the new project, the EVA of Smith's division would be

$$(100\% - 20\%) \times €2,000,000 = €1,600,000$$

This is an annual number. That is, the division would bring in €1.6 million above and beyond the cost of capital to the firm each year.

With the new project included, the EVA would jump to

$$(75\% - 20\%) \times €4,000,000 = €2,200,000$$

If Sharon Smith knew that her bonus was based on EVA, she would now have an incentive to accept, not reject, the project. Although ROA appears in the EVA formula, EVA differs substantially from ROA. The big difference is that ROA is a percentage number and EVA is a monetary value. In the preceding example EVA increased when the new project was added, even though the ROA actually decreased. In this situation, EVA correctly incorporates the fact that a high return on a large division may be better than a very high return on a smaller division. The situation here is quite similar to the scale problem in capital budgeting that we discussed in Section 6.6.

Further understanding of EVA can be achieved by rewriting the EVA formula. Because ROA × total capital is equal to earnings after tax, we can write the EVA formula as

$$Earnings\ after\ tax - Weighted\ average\ cost\ of\ capital \times Total\ capital$$

Thus EVA can simply be viewed as earnings after capital costs. Although accountants subtract many costs (including depreciation) to get the earnings number shown in financial reports, they do not subtract out capital costs. We can see the logic of accountants, because the cost of capital is very subjective. By contrast, costs such as COGS (cost of goods sold), SGA (sales, general, and administration), and even depreciation can be measured more objectively. However, even if the cost of capital is difficult to estimate, it is hard to justify ignoring it completely. After all, this textbook argues that the cost of capital is a necessary input to capital budgeting. Shouldn't it also be a necessary input to performance measurement?

This example argues that EVA can increase investment for firms that are currently underinvesting. However, there are many firms in the reverse situation: the managers are so focused on increasing earnings that they take on projects for which the profits do not justify the capital outlays. These managers either are unaware of capital costs or, knowing these costs, choose to ignore them. Because the cost of capital is right in the middle of the EVA formula, managers will not easily ignore these costs when evaluated on an EVA system.

One other advantage of EVA is that it is so stark: the number is either positive or it is negative. Plenty of divisions have negative EVAs for a number of years. Because these divisions are destroying more value than they are creating, a strong point can be made for liquidating these divisions. Although managers are, in general, emotionally opposed to this type of action, EVA analysis makes liquidation harder to ignore.

The preceding discussion puts EVA in a positive light. However, we can certainly find much to criticize with EVA as well. We now focus on two well-known problems with EVA. First, the preceding example uses EVA for performance measurement, where we believe it properly belongs. To us, EVA seems a clear improvement over ROA and other financial ratios. However, EVA has little to offer for capital budgeting, because it focuses only on current earnings. By contrast, net present value analysis uses projections of all future cash flows, where the cash flows will generally differ from year to year. Thus, as far as capital budgeting is concerned, NPV analysis has a richness that EVA does not have. Although supporters may argue that EVA correctly incorporates the weighted average cost of capital, remember that the discount rate in NPV analysis is the same weighted average cost of capital. That is, both approaches take the cost of equity capital based on beta and combine it with the cost of debt to get an estimate of this weighted average.

A second problem with EVA is that it may increase the short-sightedness of managers. Under EVA a manager will be well rewarded today if earnings are high today. Future losses may not harm the manager because there is a good chance that she will be promoted or have left the firm by then. Thus the manager has an incentive to run a division with more regard for short-term than long-term value. By raising prices or cutting quality the manager may increase current profits (and therefore current EVA). However, to the extent that customer satisfaction is reduced, future profits (and therefore future EVA) are likely to fall. But we should not be too harsh with EVA here, because the same problem occurs with ROA. A manager who raises prices or cuts quality will increase current ROA at the expense of future ROA. The problem, then, is not with EVA *per se* but with the use of accounting numbers in general. Because shareholders want the discounted present value of all cash flows to be maximized, managers with bonuses based on some function of current profits or current cash flows are likely to behave in a short-sighted way.

## Summary and Conclusions

Earlier chapters about capital budgeting assumed that projects generate riskless cash flows. The appropriate discount rate in that case is the riskless interest rate. Of course, most cash flows from real-world capital budgeting projects are risky. This chapter discussed the discount rate when cash flows are risky.

1   A firm with excess cash can either pay a dividend or make a capital expenditure. Because shareholders can reinvest the dividend in risky financial assets, the expected return on a capital budgeting project should be at least as great as the expected return on a financial asset of comparable risk.

2   The expected return on any asset is dependent on its beta. Thus we showed how to estimate the beta of an equity. The appropriate procedure employs regression analysis on historical returns.

3   We considered the case of a project whose beta risk was equal to that of the firm. If the firm is unlevered, the discount rate on the project is equal to

$$R_F + \beta \times (R_M - R_F)$$

where $R_M$ is the expected return on the market portfolio and $R_F$ is the risk-free rate. In words, the discount rate on the project is equal to the CAPM's estimate of the expected return on the security.

4   If the project's beta differs from that of the firm, the discount rate should be based on the project's beta. We can generally estimate the project's beta by determining the average beta of the project's industry.

5   The beta of a company is a function of a number of factors. Perhaps the three most important are:

(a)   Cyclicality of revenues;

(b)   Operating leverage;

(c)   Financial leverage.

6   Sometimes we cannot use the average beta of the project's industry as an estimate of the beta of the project. For example, a new project may not fall neatly into any existing industry. In this case we can estimate the project's beta by considering the project's cyclicality of revenues and its operating leverage. This approach is qualitative.

7   If a firm uses debt, the discount rate to use is the $R_{WACC}$. To calculate $R_{WACC}$, we must estimate the cost of equity and the cost of debt applicable to a project. If the project is similar to the firm, the cost of equity can be estimated using the SML for the firm's equity. Conceptually, a dividend growth model could be used as well, though it is likely to be far less accurate in practice.

8   Liquidity probably plays a role in determining a firm's cost of capital. A firm may be able to reduce its cost of capital by taking steps to improve liquidity.

# connect Questions and Problems

**CONCEPT 1–8**

1   **The Cost of Equity Capital**   Explain what is meant by the cost of equity capital. How is the cost of equity capital linked to the risk of the assets of a firm? How would you use cost of equity in a capital budget analysis?

2   **Estimation of Beta**   Explain why an equity's beta is important in capital budgeting. How do you calculate beta, and what are the pitfalls you may face in its calculation? Can you foresee any problems with using a historical beta for future capital budgeting projects? Explain.

3   **Determinants of Beta**   What factors determine the beta of an equity? Define and describe each.

4   **Extensions of the Basic Model**   How would you estimate the cost of capital for a project if its risk is different from the rest of the company? Similarly, how would you estimate the cost of capital for a project when the company has debt in its capital structure? Use an example to illustrate your answer.

5   **Practical Concerns**   What are the main issues you need to consider when estimating the cost of capital of a project in practice? State any potential problems or challenges you may face.

6   **Reducing the Cost of Capital**   Why would a firm wish to reduce its cost of capital? Review different ways in which this can be done. Which way do you think is the most effective? Explain.

7   **Estimating the Cost of Capital in Practice**   Corporations use many methods to estimate the cost of capital. Why do you think there is no consensus on the best method? If you were estimating the cost of capital in an emerging market, what method would you use? Explain.

REGULAR
9–31

8  **EVA**  Explain what is meant by economic value added, and show how it can be used to evaluate the performance of a firm.

9  **Project Risk**  If you can borrow all the money you need for a project at 6 per cent, doesn't it follow that 6 per cent is your cost of capital for the project?

10  **WACC and Taxes**  Why do we use an after-tax figure for cost of debt but not for cost of equity?

11  **SML Cost of Equity Estimation**  If you use the equity beta and the security market line to compute the discount rate for a project, what assumptions are you implicitly making? What are the advantages of using the SML approach to finding the cost of equity capital? What are the disadvantages? What are the specific pieces of information needed to use this method? Are all of these variables observable, or do they need to be estimated? What are some of the ways in which you could get these estimates?

12  **Cost of Debt Estimation**  How do you determine the appropriate cost of debt for a company? Does it make a difference if the company's debt is privately placed as opposed to being publicly traded? How would you estimate the cost of debt for a firm whose only debt issues are privately held by institutional investors?

13  **Cost of Capital**  Suppose Tom O'Bedlam, president of Bedlam Products, has hired you to determine the firm's cost of debt and cost of equity capital.

(a)  The shares currently sell for £50, and the dividend per share will probably be about £5. Tom argues, 'It will cost us £5 per share to use the shareholders' money this year, so the cost of equity is equal to 10 per cent (£5/£50).' What's wrong with this conclusion?

(b)  Based on the most recent financial statements, Bedlam Products' total liabilities are £8 million. Total interest expense for the coming year will be about £1 million. Tom therefore reasons, 'We owe £8 million, and we shall pay £1 million interest. Therefore, our cost of debt is obviously £1 million/£8 million = 12.5 per cent.' What's wrong with this conclusion?

(c)  Based on his own analysis, Tom is recommending that the company increase its use of equity financing, because 'Debt costs 12.5 per cent, but equity only costs 10 per cent: thus equity is cheaper.' Ignoring all the other issues, what do you think about the conclusion that the cost of equity is less than the cost of debt?

14  **Company Risk versus Project Risk**  Both Dow Chemical Company, a large natural gas user, and Superior Oil, a major natural gas producer, are thinking of investing in natural gas wells in Russia. Both are all-equity-financed companies. Dow and Superior are looking at identical projects. They've analysed their respective investments, which would involve a negative cash flow now and positive expected cash flows in the future. These cash flows would be the same for both firms. No debt would be used to finance the projects. Both companies estimate that their projects would have a net present value of €1 million at an 18 per cent discount rate and a –€1.1 million NPV at a 22 per cent discount rate. Dow has a beta of 1.25, whereas Superior has a beta of 0.75. The expected risk premium on the market is 8 per cent, and risk-free bonds are yielding 12 per cent. Should either company proceed? Should both? Explain.

15  **Divisional Cost of Capital**  Under what circumstances would it be appropriate for a firm to use different costs of capital for its different operating divisions? If the overall firm WACC were used as the hurdle rate for all divisions, would the riskier divisions or the more conservative divisions tend to get most of the investment projects? Why? If you were to try to estimate the appropriate cost of capital for different divisions, what problems might you encounter? What are two techniques you could use to develop a rough estimate for each division's cost of capital?

16  **Leverage**  Consider a levered firm's projects that have similar risks to the firm as a whole. Is the discount rate for the projects higher or lower than the rate computed using the security market line? Why?

17 **Calculating Cost of Equity** The Dybvig Corporation's equity has a beta of 1.3. If the risk-free rate is 4.5 per cent and the expected return on the market is 12 per cent, what is Dybvig's cost of equity capital?

18 **Calculating Cost of Debt** Advance plc is trying to determine its cost of debt. The firm has a debt issue outstanding with 12 years to maturity that is quoted at 105 per cent of face value. The issue makes semi-annual payments and has a coupon rate of 8 per cent annually. What is Advance's pre-tax cost of debt? If the tax rate is 28 per cent, what is the after-tax cost of debt?

19 **Calculating Cost of Debt** Shanken NV issued a 30-year, 10 per cent semi-annual bond seven years ago. The bond currently sells for 108 per cent of its face value. The company's tax rate is 35 per cent.

   (a) What is the pre-tax cost of debt?

   (b) What is the after-tax cost of debt?

   (c) Which is more relevant, the pre-tax or the after-tax cost of debt? Why?

20 **Calculating Cost of Debt** For the firm in the previous problem, suppose the book value of the debt issue is €20 million. In addition, the company has a second debt issue on the market, a zero coupon bond with seven years left to maturity: the book value of this issue is €80 million, and the bonds sell for 58 per cent of par. What is the company's total book value of debt? The total market value? What is your best estimate of the after-tax cost of debt now?

21 **Calculating WACC** Mullineaux Corporation has a target capital structure of 55 per cent equity and 45 per cent debt. Its cost of equity is 16 per cent, and the cost of debt is 9 per cent. The relevant tax rate is 35 per cent. What is Mullineaux's WACC?

22 **Taxes and WACC** Miller Manufacturing has a target debt–equity ratio of 0.60. Its cost of equity is 18 per cent, and its cost of debt is 10 per cent. If the tax rate is 35 per cent, what is Miller's WACC?

23 **Finding the Capital Structure** Fama's Llamas has a weighted average cost of capital of 11.5 per cent. The company's cost of equity is 16 per cent, and its cost of debt is 8.5 per cent. The tax rate is 35 per cent. What is Fama's debt–equity ratio?

24 **Book Value versus Market Value** Filer Manufacturing has 9.5 million shares of equity outstanding. The current share price is £53, and the book value per share is £5. Filer Manufacturing also has two bond issues outstanding. The first bond issue has a face value of £75 million and an 8 per cent coupon, and sells for 93 per cent of par. The second issue has a face value of £60 million and a 7.5 per cent coupon, and sells for 96.5 per cent of par. The first issue matures in 10 years, the second in 6 years.

   (a) What are Filer's capital structure weights on a book value basis?

   (b) What are Filer's capital structure weights on a market value basis?

   (c) Which are more relevant, the book or market value weights? Why?

25 **Calculating the WACC** In the previous problem, suppose the company's equity has a beta of 1.2. The risk-free rate is 5.2 per cent, and the market risk premium is 9 per cent. Assume that the overall cost of debt is the weighted average implied by the two outstanding debt issues. Both bonds make semi-annual payments. The tax rate is 35 per cent. What is the company's WACC?

26 **WACC** Kose SA has a target debt–equity ratio of 0.80. Its WACC is 10.5 per cent, and the tax rate is 35 per cent.

   (a) If Kose's cost of equity is 15 per cent, what is its pre-tax cost of debt?

   (b) If instead you know that the after-tax cost of debt is 6.4 per cent, what is the cost of equity?

**27  Finding the WACC**  Given the following information for Huntington Power, find the WACC. Assume the company's tax rate is 28 per cent.

*Debt*:    40,000 7 per cent coupon bonds outstanding, £100 par value, 20 years to maturity, selling for 103 per cent of par; the bonds make semi-annual payments.

*Equity*:   90,000 shares outstanding, selling for £57 per share; the beta is 1.10.

*Market*:  8 per cent market risk premium and 6 per cent risk-free rate.

**28  Finding the WACC**  Titan Mining Corporation has 9 million shares of equity outstanding and 1,200,000 8.5 per cent semi-annual bonds outstanding, par value £100 each. The equity currently sells for £34 per share and has a beta of 1.20, and the bonds have 15 years to maturity and sell for 93 per cent of par. The market risk premium is 10 per cent, T-bills are yielding 5 per cent, and Titan Mining's tax rate is 28 per cent.

(a)   What is the firm's market value capital structure?

(b)   If Titan Mining is evaluating a new investment project that has the same risk as the firm's typical project, what rate should the firm use to discount the project's cash flows?

**29  SML and WACC**  An all-equity firm is considering the following projects:

| Project | Beta | Expected return (%) |
|---------|------|---------------------|
| W | 0.60 | 11 |
| X | 0.90 | 13 |
| Y | 1.20 | 14 |
| Z | 1.70 | 16 |

The T-bill rate is 5 per cent, and the expected return on the market is 12 per cent.

(a)   Which projects have a higher expected return than the firm's 12 per cent cost of capital?

(b)   Which projects should be accepted?

(c)   Which projects would be incorrectly accepted or rejected if the firm's overall cost of capital were used as a hurdle rate?

**30  WACC and NPV**  Och SpA is considering a project that will result in initial after-tax cash savings of €3.5 million at the end of the first year, and these savings will grow at a rate of 5 per cent per year indefinitely. The firm has a target debt–equity ratio of 0.65, a cost of equity of 15 per cent, and an after-tax cost of debt of 5.5 per cent. The cost-saving proposal is somewhat riskier than the usual project the firm undertakes; management uses the subjective approach and applies an adjustment factor of +2 per cent to the cost of capital for such risky projects. Under what circumstances should Och take on the project?

**31  Preference Shares and WACC**  Saunders Investment Bank has the following financing outstanding. What is the WACC for the company?

*Debt*:               50,000 bonds with an 8 per cent coupon rate and a quoted price of 119.80; the bonds have 25 years to maturity. 150,000 zero coupon bonds with a quoted price of 13.85 and 30 years until maturity.

*Preference shares*:  120,000 shares of 6.5 per cent dividends with a current price of €112, and a par value = €100.

*Equity*:             2,000,000 shares; the current price is €65, and the beta is 1.1.

*Market*:             The corporate tax rate is 40 per cent, the market risk premium is 9 per cent, and the risk-free rate is 4 per cent.

**32 WACC and NPV** Photochronograph Corporation (PC) manufactures time series photographic equipment. It is currently at its target debt–equity ratio of 1.3. It's considering building a new £45 million manufacturing facility. This new plant is expected to generate after-tax cash flows of £5.7 million in perpetuity. There are three financing options:

(a) A new issue of equity. The required return on the company's equity is 17 per cent.

(b) A new issue of 20-year bonds. If the company issues these new bonds at an annual coupon rate of 9 per cent, they will sell at par.

(c) Increased use of trade payables financing. Because this financing is part of the company's ongoing daily business, the company assigns it a cost that is the same as the overall firm WACC. Management has a target ratio of accounts payable to long-term debt of 0.20. (Assume there is no difference between the pre-tax and after-tax accounts payable cost.)

What is the NPV of the new plant? Assume that PC has a 28 per cent tax rate.

**33 Project Evaluation** This is a comprehensive project evaluation problem bringing together much of what you have learned in this and previous chapters. Suppose you have been hired as a financial consultant to Defence Electronics International (DEI), a large, publicly traded firm that is the market share leader in radar detection systems (RDSs). The company is looking at setting up a manufacturing plant overseas to produce a new line of RDSs. This will be a five-year project. The company bought some land three years ago for £7 million in anticipation of using it as a toxic dump site for waste chemicals, but instead it built a piping system to discard the chemicals safely. If the company sold the land today it would receive £6.5 million after taxes. In five years the land can be sold for £4.5 million after taxes and reclamation costs. The company wants to build its new manufacturing plant on this land; the plant will cost £15 million to build. The following market data on DEI's securities are current:

| | |
|---|---|
| *Debt*: | 150,000 7 per cent coupon bonds outstanding, 15 years to maturity, selling for 92 per cent of par; the bonds have a £100 par value each and make semi-annual payments. |
| *Equity*: | 300,000 shares outstanding, selling for £75 per share; the beta is 1.3. |
| *Preference shares*: | 20,000 shares with 5 per cent dividends outstanding, selling for £72 per share. |
| *Market*: | 8 per cent expected market risk premium; 5 per cent risk-free rate. |

DEI's tax rate is 28 per cent. The project requires £900,000 in initial net working capital investment to become operational.

(a) Calculate the project's initial time 0 cash flow, taking into account all side effects.

(b) The new RDS project is somewhat riskier than a typical project for DEI, primarily because the plant is being located overseas. Management has told you to use an adjustment factor of +2 per cent to account for this increased riskiness. Calculate the appropriate discount rate to use when evaluating DEI's project.

(c) The manufacturing plant has an eight-year tax life, and DEI uses 20 per cent reducing balance depreciation for the plant. At the end of the project (i.e. the end of year 5), the plant can be scrapped for £5 million. What is the depreciation schedule for this manufacturing plant?

(d) The company will incur £400,000 in annual fixed costs. The plan is to manufacture 12,000 RDSs per year and sell them at £10,000 per machine; the variable production costs are £9,000 per RDS. What is the annual operating cash flow (OCF) from this project?

(e) DEI's financial controller is interested primarily in the impact of DEI's investments on the bottom line of reported accounting statements. What will you tell her is the accounting break-even quantity of RDSs sold for this project?

(f) Finally, DEI's president wants you to throw all your calculations, assumptions, and everything else into the report for the chief financial officer; all he wants to know is the RDS project's internal rate of return, IRR, and net present value, NPV. What will you report?

# The Cost of Capital for Goff Technological Printing

You have recently been hired by Goff Technological Printing, in the finance area. GTP was founded eight years ago by Chris Goff and currently operates 74 stores in the United Kingdom. GTP is privately owned by Chris and his family, and had sales of £97 million last year.

GTP sells primarily to in-store customers. Customers come to the store and talk with a sales representative. The sales representative assists the customer in determining the type of printing and labelling solutions that are necessary for the individual customer's computing needs. After the order is taken, the customer pays for the order immediately, and the printing technology is assembled to fill the order. Delivery of the printing technology averages 15 days but is guaranteed in 30 days.

GTP's growth to date has been financed from its profits. Whenever the company had sufficient capital, it would open a new store. Relatively little formal analysis has been used in the capital budgeting process. Chris has just read about capital budgeting techniques and has come to you for help. The company has never attempted to determine its cost of capital, and Chris would like you to perform the analysis. Because the company is privately owned, it is difficult to determine the cost of equity for the company. You have determined that, to estimate the cost of capital for GTP, you will use Domino Printing Sciences plc as a representative company. The following steps will allow you to calculate this estimate:

1 All publicly traded UK corporations are required to submit financial reports to Companies House detailing their financial operations over the previous six months or year, respectively. These corporate filings are always available on the company's website. Go to the Domino Printing Sciences website, follow the *Investor Relations* link and download the most recent set of financial accounts for Domino Printing Sciences. Look in the balance sheet to find the book value of debt and the book value of equity. If you look further down the report, you should find a section titled 'Borrowings' in the Notes to the Accounts that will list a breakdown of Domino Printing Sciences' long-term debt. For 2007, this was:

| Financial liabilities | | | | | | |
|---|---|---|---|---|---|---|
| Currency | Total £000 | Floating rate financial liabilities £000 | Fixed rate financial liabilities £000 | Weighted average fixed interest rate | Weighted average period for which the rate is fixed Years | Non-interest bearing financial liabilities £000 | Weighted average period until maturity Years |
| **At 31 October 2007** | | | | | | |
| Sterling | 1,464 | – | 540 | 4.7% | 4.1 | 924 | 1.9 |
| Euro | 4,750 | 18 | 4,665 | 4.7% | 4.4 | 67 | 1.0 |
| US dollar | 5,631 | 994 | 3,877 | 4.2% | 2.8 | 760 | 0.3 |
| Other | 2,634 | 519 | 2,115 | 4.6% | 4.2 | – | – |
| Gross financial liabilities | 14,479 | 1,531 | 11,197 | | | 1,751 | |
| **At 31 October 2006** | | | | | | |
| Sterling | 3,035 | – | 316 | 4.0% | 0.3 | 2,719 | 1.7 |
| Euro | 2,194 | 14 | 2,180 | 4.0% | 1.2 | – | – |
| US dollar | 9,001 | 1,738 | 6,523 | 4.3% | 3.3 | 740 | 0.3 |
| Other | 3,461 | 1,157 | 2,304 | 6.2% | 1.0 | – | – |
| Gross financial liabilities | 17,691 | 2,909 | 11,323 | | | 3,459 | |
| Short term receivables and payables have been excluded from interest rate profile disclosures. | | | | | | |

2   To estimate the cost of equity for Domino Printing Sciences, go to www.reuters.com and enter the ticker symbol 'DOPR' Follow the various links to find answers to the following questions: What is the most recent share price listed for Domino Printing Sciences? What is the market value of equity, or market capitalization? How many shares of equity does Domino Printing Sciences have outstanding? What is the beta for Domino Printing Sciences? Now go to www.ft.com, follow the *Markets Data* link and then the *Bonds and Rates* link. What is the yield on 3-month UK Treasury bills?

3   We now need to estimate the historical market risk premium. Go to Yahoo! Finance, and download the monthly historical prices for the FTSE 100 index for the last five years. Calculate the monthly returns, take the average, and multiply this by 12 to get the annualized historical return on the FTSE 100. What is the historical market risk premium for UK? Using the historical market risk premium, what is the cost of equity for Domino Printing Sciences using the CAPM?

4   Go to www.reuters.com and find the list of competitors in the industry. Find the beta for each of these competitors, and then calculate the industry average beta. Using the industry average beta, what is the cost of equity? Does it matter if you use the beta for Domino Printing Sciences or the beta for the industry in this case?

5   You now need to calculate the cost of debt for Domino Printing Sciences. Use the information on Domino Printing Sciences bonds to find the weighted average cost of debt for Domino using the book value weights. Try and find bond prices for Domino Printing Sciences debt. What should you do if no information is available? Does it make a difference in this case if you use book value weights or market value weights? Explain.

6   You now have all the necessary information to calculate the weighted average cost of capital for Domino Printing Sciences. Calculate the weighted average cost of capital for Domino Printing Sciences using book value weights and market value weights assuming Domino has a 30 per cent effective tax rate. Which cost of capital number is more relevant?

7   You used Domino Printing Sciences as a representative company to estimate the cost of capital for GTP. What are some of the potential problems with this approach in this situation? What improvements might you suggest?

# Additional Reading

The following papers consider the cost of capital for both debt and equity, and how it is affected by different factors, such as default risk, growth opportunities, and information quality. Brav (2009) considers the much wider issue of financing choices for private and public firms, and should also be read as additional reading for Chapters 14, 19 and 20.

Brav, O. (2009) 'Access to capital, capital structure, and the funding of the firm', *Journal of Finance*, vol. 64, no. 1, pp. 263–308. **UK**.

Driessen, J. (2005) 'Is default event risk priced in corporate bonds?', *Review of Financial Studies*, vol. 18, no. 1, pp. 165–195. **US**.

Easley, D. and M. O'Hara, 'Information and the cost of capital', *Journal of Finance*, vol. 59, no. 4, pp. 1553–1583. **US**.

Hirst, I., J. Danbolt and E. Jones (2008) 'Required rates of return for corporate investment appraisal in the presence of growth opportunities', *European Financial Management*, vol. 14, no. 5, pp. 989–1006. **UK**.

Sabal, J. (2004) 'The discount rate in emerging markets: a guide', *Journal of Applied Corporate Finance*, vol. 16. Nos. 2 and 3, pp. 155–166. **Discussion piece**.

Zou, H. and M.B. Adams (2008) 'Debt capacity, cost of debt, and corporate insurance', *Journal of Financial and Quantitative Analysis*, vol. 43, no. 2, pp. 433–466. **China**.

# Endnotes

1 As we shall see later, an adjustment must be made when the debt level in the industry is different from that of the firm. However, we ignore this adjustment here.

2 It can be shown that the relationship between a firm's asset beta and its equity beta with corporate taxes is

$$\beta_{Equity} = \beta_{Asset}\left[1 + (1 - t_c)\frac{B}{S}\right]$$

In this expression $t_c$ is the corporate tax rate. Tax effects are considered in more detail in a later chapter.

3 For example, see Y. Amihud and H. Mendelson, 'The liquidity route to a lower cost of capital', *Journal of Applied Corporate Finance* (Winter 2000), and M.J. Brennan and C. Tamarowski, 'Investor relations, liquidity, and stock prices', *Journal of Applied Corporate Finance* (Winter 2000).

4 M. Coller and T. Yohn, 'Management forecasts and information asymmetry: an examination of bid–ask spreads', *Journal of Accounting Research* (Fall 1997).

5 The full document, *The Cost of Capital: An International Comparison*, can be downloaded from Oxera's website, www.oxera.com.

6 Dirk Brounen, Abe de Jong, and Kees Koedijk, 'Corporate finance in Europe: confronting theory and practice', *Journal of Banking and Finance* (2006).

7 Stern Stewart & Company have a copyright on the terms *economic value added* and *EVA*.

Online **LearningCentre**

To help you grasp the key concepts of this chapter check out the extra resources posted on the Online Learning Centre at **www.mcgraw-hill.co.uk/textbooks/hillier**

Among other helpful resources there are PowerPoint presentations, chapter outlines and mini-cases.

# Chapter 13

# Corporate Financing Decisions and Efficient Capital Markets

The Chinese stock markets experienced explosive growth between 2005 and 2007, gaining 52 per cent and 216 per cent, September to September, 2006 and 2007, respectively. Of course, that spectacular run came to a jarring halt after the global credit crisis, when the Shanghai Composite lost over 60 per cent in 2008.

What caused the incredible growth in 2007, followed by the disastrous performance in 2008 for China? Even when the stock market was falling, the Chinese economy still grew at more than 10 per cent. Could prices have been inflated because investors were irrationally buying equities because of positive media attention about the Chinese economy? What made investors reverse their views so quickly? Did the Chinese stock markets experience a 'bubble' in prices, in which equity valuations were ridiculously high? Could other macroeconomic factors have been the root cause?

In this chapter we discuss the competing ideas, present some evidence on both sides, and then examine the implications for financial managers.

## 13.1 Can Financing Decisions Create Value?

Earlier parts of the book showed how to evaluate projects according to the net present value criterion. The real world is a competitive one, where projects with positive net present value are not always easy to come by. However, through hard work or through good fortune, a firm can identify winning projects. For example, to create value from capital budgeting decisions, the firm is likely to

1 locate an unsatisfied demand for a particular product or service;

2 create a barrier to make it more difficult for other firms to compete;

3 produce products or services at lower cost than the competition;

4 be the first to develop a new product.

The next five chapters concern *financing* decisions. Typical financing decisions include how much debt and equity to sell, what types of debt and equity to sell, and when to sell them. Just as the net present value criterion was used to evaluate capital budgeting projects, we now want to use the same criterion to evaluate financing decisions.

Though the procedure for evaluating financing decisions is identical to the procedure for evaluating projects, the results are different. It turns out that the typical firm has many more capital expenditure opportunities with positive net present values than financing opportunities with positive net present values. In fact, we later show that some plausible financial models imply that no valuable financial opportunities exist at all.

Though this dearth of profitable financing opportunities will be examined in detail later, a few remarks are in order now. We maintain that there are basically three ways to create valuable financing opportunities:

1   *Investors lack an understanding of the risk and valuation of complex securities.* Assume that a firm can raise capital either by issuing equity or by issuing a more complex security – say, a combination of shares and warrants. Suppose that, in truth, 100 shares are worth the same as 50 units of our complex security. If investors have a misguided, overly optimistic view of the complex security, perhaps the 50 units can be sold for more than the 100 shares of equity can be. Clearly, this complex security provides a valuable financing opportunity, because the firm is getting more than fair value for it.

Financial managers try to package securities to receive the greatest value. Many have argued that the global credit crisis in 2007 and 2008 was caused by investors (including financial institutions) not understanding how to quantify the risk and value of the complex securities that banks issued on the back of subprime mortgage loans.

However, the theory of efficient capital markets implies that investors cannot, in general, be easily fooled. It says that all securities are appropriately priced at all times, implying that the market as a whole is shrewd indeed. In our example, 50 units of the complex security would sell for the same price as 100 shares of equity. Thus corporate managers cannot attempt to create value by fooling investors. Instead, managers must create value in other ways.

2   *Reduce costs or increase subsidies.* We show later that certain forms of financing have greater tax advantages than other forms. Clearly, a firm packaging securities to minimize taxes can increase firm value. In addition, any financing technique involves other costs. For example, investment bankers, lawyers and accountants must be paid. A firm packaging securities to minimize these costs can also increase its value.

## EXAMPLE 13.1

# Valuing Financial Subsidies

Suppose Salamanca Electronics Company is thinking about relocating its plant to Mexico, where labour costs are lower. In the hope that it can stay in Salamanca, the company has submitted an application to the Castille y Leon region to issue €2 million in five-year, tax-exempt industrial bonds. The coupon rate on industrial revenue bonds in the Castille y Leon region is currently 5 per cent. This is an attractive rate, because the normal cost of debt capital for Salamanca Electronics Company is 10 per cent. What is the NPV of this potential financing transaction?

If the application is accepted and the industrial revenue bonds are issued by the Salamanca Electronics Company, the NPV (ignoring corporate taxes) is

$$\text{NPV} = €2,000,000 - \left[ \frac{€100,000}{1.1} + \frac{€100,000}{(1.1)^2} + \frac{€100,000}{(1.1)^3} + \frac{€100,000}{(1.1)^4} + \frac{€2,100,000}{(1.1)^5} \right]$$
$$= €2,000,000 - €1,620,921$$
$$= €379,079$$

This transaction has a positive NPV. The Salamanca Electronics Company obtains subsidized financing where the value of the subsidy is €379,079. Note that we used the normal cost of debt capital, 10 per cent, to discount the cash flows, because this is the rate that accurately reflects the cost of debt for securities of similar risk in the markets.

3  *Create a new security.* In recent decades there has been a massive surge in financial innovation. Though the advantage of each instrument is different, one general theme is that new complex securities cannot easily be duplicated by combinations of existing securities. Thus a previously unsatisfied clientele may pay extra for a specialized security catering to its needs. For example, puttable bonds let the purchaser sell the bond at a fixed price back to the firm. This innovation creates a price floor, allowing the investor to reduce his or her downside risk. Perhaps risk-averse investors or investors with little knowledge of the bond market would find this feature particularly attractive.

Corporations gain by issuing these unique securities at high prices. However, the value captured by the innovator may well be small in the long run, because the innovator usually cannot patent or copyright an idea. Soon many firms are issuing securities of the same kind, forcing prices down as a result.

It is now extremely likely that the era of complex securities has come to an end, at least for the foreseeable future. The collapse of banks such as Washington Mutual (WaMu), Lehman Brothers, Bear Stearns, Northern Rock, HBOS, Bradford & Bingley, and other casualties of 2008 was initially caused by the whole banking sector embracing complex securities to offset the risk of speculative lending policies. Post-global credit crunch will most likely see a return to the old days of basic equity and debt instruments as the financing securities of choice for most firms.

This brief introduction sets the stage for the next several chapters of the book. The rest of this chapter examines the efficient capital markets hypothesis. We show that if capital markets are efficient, corporate managers cannot create value by fooling investors. This is quite important, because managers must create value in other, perhaps more difficult, ways. The following chapters concern the costs and subsidies of various forms of financing.

## 13.2 A Description of Efficient Capital Markets

An efficient capital market is one in which share prices fully reflect available information. To illustrate how an efficient market works, suppose F-stop Camera Corporation (FCC) is attempting to develop a camera that will double the speed of the auto-focusing system now available. FCC believes this research has positive NPV.

Now consider a share of equity in FCC. What determines the willingness of investors to hold shares of FCC at a particular price? One important factor is the probability that FCC will be the first company to develop the new auto-focusing system. In an efficient market, we would expect the price of the shares of FCC to increase if this probability increases.

Suppose FCC hires a well-known engineer to develop the new auto-focusing system. In an efficient market, what will happen to FCC's share price when this is announced? If the well-known scientist is paid a salary that fully reflects his or her contribution to the firm, the share price will not necessarily change. Suppose instead that hiring the scientist is a positive NPV transaction. In this case, the share price of FCC will increase because the firm can pay the scientist a salary below his or her true value to the company.

When will the increase in the share price of FCC occur? Assume that the hiring announcement is made in a press release on Wednesday morning. In an efficient market, the FCC share price will *immediately* adjust to this new information. Investors should not be able to buy the shares on Wednesday afternoon and make a profit on Thursday. This would imply that it took the equity market a day to realize the implication of the FCC press release. The efficient market hypothesis predicts that the FCC share price on Wednesday afternoon will already reflect the information contained in the Wednesday morning press release.

The efficient market hypothesis (EMH) has implications for investors and for firms:

- Because information is reflected in prices immediately, investors should only expect to obtain a normal rate of return. Awareness of information when it is released does an investor no good. The price adjusts before the investor has time to trade on it.

- Firms should expect to receive fair value for securities that they sell. *Fair* means that the price they receive from issuing securities is the present value. Thus valuable financing opportunities that arise from fooling investors are unavailable in efficient capital markets.

**FIGURE 13.1**

*Efficient market response*: The price instantaneously adjusts to and fully reflects new information; there is no tendency for subsequent increases and decreases.

*Slow response*: The price adjusts slowly to the new information; 30 days elapse before the price completely reflects the new information.

*Overreaction*: The price overadjusts to the new information; there is a bubble in the price sequence.

**Figure 13.1** Reaction of share price to new information in efficient and inefficient markets

Figure 13.1 presents several possible adjustments in equity prices. The solid line represents the path taken by the security in an efficient market. In this case the price adjusts immediately to the new information, with no further price changes. The dotted line depicts a slow reaction. Here it takes the market 30 days to fully absorb the information. Finally, the broken line illustrates an overreaction and subsequent correction back to the true price. The broken line and the dotted line show the paths that the share price might take in an inefficient market. If the share price takes several days to adjust, trading profits would be available to investors who suitably timed their purchases and sales.

## Foundations of Market Efficiency

Figure 13.1 shows the consequences of market efficiency. But what are the conditions that *cause* market efficiency? Andrei Shleifer argues that there are three conditions, any one of which will lead to efficiency:[1] (a) rationality, (b) independent deviations from rationality, and (c) arbitrage. A discussion of these conditions follows.

**Rationality**    Imagine that all investors are rational. When new information is released in the marketplace, all investors will adjust their estimates of share prices in a rational way. In our example, investors will use the information in FCC's press release, in conjunction with existing information about the firm, to determine the NPV of FCC's new venture. If the information in the press release implies that the NPV of the venture is £10 million and there are 2 million shares, investors will calculate that the NPV is £5 per share. While FCC's old share price might be, say, £40, no one would now transact at that price. Anyone interested in selling would sell only at a price of at least £45 (= £40 + £5). Anyone interested in buying would now be willing to pay up to £45. In other words, the price would rise by £5. And the price would rise immediately, because rational investors would see no reason to wait before trading at the new price.

Of course, we all know times when family members, friends and, yes, even we seem to behave less than perfectly rationally. Thus perhaps it is too much to ask that *all* investors behave rationally. But the market will still be efficient if the following scenario holds.

**Independent Deviations from Rationality**    Suppose that FCC's press release is not all that clear. How many new cameras are likely to be sold? At what price? What is the likely cost per camera? Will other camera companies be able to develop competing products? How long is this likely to take? If these and other questions cannot be answered easily, it will be difficult to estimate NPV.

Now imagine that, with so many questions going unanswered, many investors do not think clearly. Some investors might get caught up in the romance of a new product, hoping for and ultimately believing in sales projections well above what is rational. They would overpay for new shares. And if they needed to sell shares (perhaps to finance current consumption), they would do so only at a high price. If these individuals dominate the market, the share price would probably rise beyond what market efficiency would predict.

However, because of emotional resistance, investors could just as easily react to new information in a pessimistic manner. After all, business historians tell us that investors were initially quite sceptical about the benefits of the telephone, the copier, the automobile, and the motion picture. Certainly, they could be overly sceptical about this new camera. If investors were primarily of this type, the share price would be likely to rise less than market efficiency would predict.

But suppose that about as many individuals were irrationally optimistic as were irrationally pessimistic. Prices would be likely to rise in a manner consistent with market efficiency, even though most investors would be classified as less than fully rational. Thus market efficiency does not require rational individuals – only countervailing irrationalities.

However, this assumption of offsetting irrationalities at *all* times may be unrealistic. Perhaps at certain times most investors are swept away by excessive optimism and at other times are caught in the throes of extreme pessimism. But even here there is an assumption that will produce efficiency.

**Arbitrage**    Imagine a world with two types of individual: the irrational amateur and the rational professional. The amateurs get caught up in their emotions, at times believing irrationally that an equity is undervalued and at other times believing the opposite. If the passions of the different amateurs do not cancel each other out, these amateurs, by themselves, would tend to carry shares either above or below their efficient prices.

Now let's bring in the professionals. Suppose professionals go about their business methodically and rationally. They study companies thoroughly, they evaluate the evidence objectively, they estimate share prices coldly and clearly, and they act accordingly. If an equity is underpriced, they would buy it. If it is overpriced, they would sell it. And their confidence would probably be greater than that of the amateurs. Whereas an amateur might risk only a small sum, these professionals might risk large ones, *knowing* as they do that the security is mispriced. Furthermore, they would be willing to rearrange their entire portfolio in search of a profit. *Arbitrage* is the word that comes to mind here, because arbitrage generates profit from the simultaneous purchase and sale of different, but substitute, securities. If the arbitrage of professionals dominates the speculation of amateurs, markets would still be efficient.

## 13.3  The Different Types of Efficiency

In our previous discussion we assumed that the market responds immediately to all available information. In actuality, certain information may affect share prices more quickly than other information. To handle differential response rates, researchers separate information into different types. The most common classification system identifies three types: information about past prices, publicly available information, and all information. The effect of these three information sets on prices is examined next.

### The Weak Form

Imagine a trading strategy that recommends buying a share after it has gone up three days in a row and recommends selling a share after it has gone down three days in a row. This strategy uses information based only on past prices. It does not use any other information, such as earnings, forecasts, merger announcements, or money supply figures. A capital market is said to be *weakly efficient* or to satisfy weak form efficiency if it fully incorporates the information

If an equity's price follows a cyclical pattern, the pattern will be quickly eliminated in an efficient market. A random pattern will emerge as investors buy at the trough and sell at the peak of a cycle.

**Figure 13.2** Investor behaviour tends to eliminate cyclical patterns

on past share prices. Thus the preceding strategy would not be able to generate profits if weak form efficiency holds.

Often weak form efficiency is represented mathematically as

$$P_t = P_{t-1} + \text{Expected return} + \text{Random error}_t \qquad (13.1)$$

Equation 13.1 states that the price today is equal to the sum of the last observed price plus the expected return on the equity (in pounds or euros) plus a random component occurring over the interval. The last observed price could have occurred yesterday, last week, or last month, depending on the sampling interval. The expected return is a function of a security's risk, and would be based on the models of risk and return in previous chapters. The random component is due to new information about the company. It could be either positive or negative, and has an expectation of zero. The random component in any period is unrelated to the random component in any past period. Hence this component is not predictable from past prices. If share prices follow Eq. 13.1 they are said to follow a **random walk**.[2]

Weak form efficiency is about the weakest type of efficiency that we would expect a financial market to display, because historical price information is the easiest kind of information about a company's equity to acquire. If it were possible to make extraordinary profits simply by finding patterns in share price movements, everyone would do it, and any profits would disappear in the scramble.

This effect of competition can be seen in Fig. 13.2. Suppose a company's share price displays a cyclical pattern, as indicated by the wavy curve. Shrewd investors would buy at the low points, forcing those prices up. Conversely, they would sell at the high points, forcing prices down. Via competition, cyclical regularities would be eliminated, leaving only random fluctuations.

## The Semi-Strong and Strong Forms

If weak form efficiency is controversial, even more contentious are the two stronger types of efficiency, **semi-strong form efficiency** and **strong form efficiency**. A market is semi-strong form efficient if prices reflect (incorporate) all publicly available information, including information such as published accounting statements for the firm as well as historical price information. A market is strong form efficient if prices reflect all information, public or private.

The information set of past prices is a subset of the information set of publicly available information, which in turn is a subset of all information. This is shown in Fig. 13.3. Thus strong form efficiency implies semi-strong form efficiency, and semi-strong form efficiency implies weak form efficiency. The distinction between semi-strong form efficiency and weak form efficiency is that semi-strong form efficiency requires not only that the market be efficient

FIGURE

**13.3**

All information relevant to a security

Information set of publicly available information

Information set of past prices

The information set of past prices is a subset of the set of all publicly available information, which in turn is a subset of all information. If today's price reflects only information about past prices, the market is weak form efficient. If today's price reflects all publicly available information, the market is semi-strong form efficient. If today's price reflects all information, both public and private, the market is strong form efficient.

Semi-strong form efficiency implies weak form efficiency, and strong form efficiency implies semi-strong form efficiency.

**Figure 13.3** Relationship among three different information sets

with respect to historical price information, but that *all* of the information available to the public be reflected in prices.

To illustrate the different forms of efficiency, imagine an investor who always sold a particular equity after its price had risen. A market that was only weak form efficient and not semi-strong form efficient would still prevent such a strategy from generating positive profits. According to weak form efficiency, a recent price rise does not imply that the equity is overvalued.

Now consider a firm reporting increased earnings. An individual might consider investing in the company's shares after reading the news release providing this information. However, if the market is semi-strong form efficient, the price should rise immediately upon the news release. Thus the investor would end up paying the higher price, eliminating all chance for profit.

At the furthest end of the spectrum is strong form efficiency. This form says that anything that is pertinent to the value of the security and that is known to at least one investor is, in fact, fully incorporated into the share price. A strict believer in strong form efficiency would deny that an insider who knew whether a company mining operation had struck gold could profit from that information. Such a devotee of the strong form efficient market hypothesis might argue that as soon as the insider tried to trade on his or her information, the market would recognize what was happening, and the price would shoot up before he or she could buy any shares. Alternatively, believers in strong form efficiency argue that there are no secrets, and as soon as the gold is discovered, the secret gets out.

One reason to expect that markets are weak form efficient is that it is so cheap and easy to find patterns in share prices. Anyone who can program a computer and knows a little bit of statistics can search for such patterns. It stands to reason that if there were such patterns, people would find and exploit them, in the process causing them to disappear.

Semi-strong form efficiency, though, implies more sophisticated investors than does weak form efficiency. An investor must be skilled in accounting, finance and statistics, and steeped in the idiosyncrasies of individual industries and companies. Furthermore, to acquire and use such skills requires talent, ability and time. In the jargon of the economist, such an effort is costly, and the ability to be successful at it is probably in scarce supply.

As for strong form efficiency, this is just further down the road than semi-strong form efficiency. It is difficult to believe that the market is so efficient that someone with valuable inside information cannot prosper from it. And empirical evidence tends to be unfavourable to this form of market efficiency.

## Some Common Misconceptions about the Efficient Market Hypothesis

No idea in finance has attracted as much attention as that of efficient markets, and not all of the attention has been flattering. To a certain extent this is because much of the criticism has been based on a misunderstanding of what the hypothesis does and does not say. We illustrate three misconceptions next.

**The Efficacy of Dart Throwing**   When the notion of market efficiency was first publicized and debated in the popular financial press, it was often characterized by the following quote: '. . . throwing darts at the financial page will produce a portfolio that can be expected to do as well as any managed by professional security analysts.'[3] This is almost, but not quite, true.

All the efficient market hypothesis really says is that, on average, the manager will not be able to achieve an abnormal or excess return. The excess return is defined with respect to some benchmark expected return, such as that from the security market line of Chapter 11 (SML). The investor must still decide how risky a portfolio he or she wants. In addition, a random dart thrower might wind up with all of the darts sticking into one or two high-risk equities that deal in genetic engineering. Would you really want all of your equity investments in two such equities?

The failure to understand this has often led to confusion about market efficiency. For example, sometimes it is wrongly argued that market efficiency means that it does not matter what you do, because the efficiency of the market will protect the unwary. However, someone once remarked, 'The efficient market protects the sheep from the wolves, but nothing can protect the sheep from themselves.'

What efficiency *does* say is that the price that a firm obtains when it sells a share of its equity is a fair price in the sense that it reflects the value of that equity given the information that is available about it. Shareholders need not worry that they are paying too much for an equity with a low dividend, or some other characteristic, because the market has already incorporated it into the price. However, investors still have to worry about such things as their level of risk exposure and their degree of diversification.

**Price Fluctuations**   Much of the public is sceptical of efficiency, because share prices fluctuate from day to day. However, daily price movement is in no way inconsistent with efficiency; an equity in an efficient market adjusts to new information by changing price. A great deal of new information comes into the stock market each day. In fact, the *absence* of daily price movements in a changing world might suggest an inefficiency.

**Shareholder Disinterest**   Many laypeople are sceptical that the market price can be efficient if only a fraction of the outstanding shares changes hands on any given day. However, the number of traders in a company's shares on a given day is generally far less than the number of people following the shares. This is true because an individual will trade only when his appraisal of the value of the equity differs enough from the market price to justify incurring brokerage commissions and other transaction costs. Furthermore, even if the number of traders following an equity is small relative to the number of outstanding shareholders, the company's shares can be expected to be efficiently priced as long as a number of interested traders use the publicly available information. That is, the share price can reflect the available information even if many shareholders never follow the company and are not considering trading in the near future.

## 13.4   The Evidence

The evidence on the efficient market hypothesis is extensive, with studies covering the broad categories of weak form, semi-strong form, and strong form efficiency. In the first category we investigate whether share price changes are random. We review both *event studies* and studies of the performance of mutual funds in the second category. In the third category we look at the performance of corporate insiders.

## The Weak Form

Weak form efficiency implies that a security's price movement in the past is unrelated to its price movement in the future. The work of Chapter 10 allows us to test this implication. In that chapter we discussed the concept of correlation between the returns on two different securities. For example, the correlation between the return on HSBC and the return on Lloyds Banking Group is likely to be relatively high, because both companies are in the same industry. Conversely, the correlation between the return on HSBC and the return on the shares of, say, an Australian fast-food chain is likely to be low.

Financial economists frequently speak of serial correlation, which involves only one security. This is the correlation between the current return on a security and the return on the same security over a later period. A positive coefficient of serial correlation for a particular share indicates a tendency towards *continuation*. That is, a higher-than-average return today is likely to be followed by higher-than-average returns in the future. Similarly, a lower-than-average return today is likely to be followed by lower-than-average returns in the future.

A negative coefficient of serial correlation for a particular security indicates a tendency towards *reversal*. A higher-than-average return today is likely to be followed by lower-than-average returns in the future. Similarly, a lower-than-average return today is likely to be followed by higher-than-average returns in the future. Both significantly positive and significantly negative serial correlation coefficients are indications of market inefficiencies; in either case, returns today can be used to predict future returns.

Serial correlation coefficients for share price returns near zero would be consistent with weak form efficiency. Thus a current share price return that is higher than average is as likely to be followed by lower-than-average returns as by higher-than-average returns. Similarly, a current return that is lower than average is as likely to be followed by higher-than-average returns as by lower-than-average returns.

Table 13.1 shows the serial correlation for daily share price changes for eight large UK companies. These coefficients indicate whether there are relationships between yesterday's return and today's return. As can be seen, the correlation coefficients are predominantly negative, implying that a higher-than-average return today makes a lower-than-average return tomorrow slightly more likely. Conversely, Imperial Tobacco's coefficient is slightly positive, implying that a higher-than-average return today makes a higher-than-average return tomorrow slightly more likely.

However, because correlation coefficients can, in principle, vary between −1 and 1, the reported coefficients are quite small. In fact, the coefficients are so small relative to both estimation errors and to transaction costs that the results are generally considered to be consistent with weak form efficiency.

| Company | Serial correlation coefficient |
|---|---|
| Hammerson Property | −0.0406 |
| Unilever plc | −0.0361 |
| International Power plc | −0.0608 |
| British Land plc | −0.0755 |
| Imperial Tobacco plc | 0.0185 |
| British American Tobacco plc | −0.0741 |
| Centrica plc* | −0.0732 |
| HSBC Holdings plc | −0.0403 |

*Centrica's time series starts on 23 October 2004.

**Table 13.1** Serial correlation coefficients for selected companies, January 2003 to September 2008

Although share price movements simulated from a random-walk process are random by definition, people often see patterns. People may also see patterns in The Gap's price movements. However, the price patterns of The Gap are quite similar to those of the randomly simulated series.

**Figure 13.4** Simulated and actual share price movements

The weak form of the efficient market hypothesis has been tested in many other ways as well. Our view of the literature is that the evidence, taken as a whole, is consistent with weak form efficiency.

This finding raises an interesting thought: if price changes are truly random, why do so many believe that prices follow patterns? The work of both psychologists and statisticians suggests that most people simply do not know what randomness looks like. For example, consider Fig. 13.4. The graph on the left was generated by a computer using random numbers and Eq. 13.1. Yet we have found that people examining the chart generally see patterns. Different people see different patterns and forecast different future price movements. However, in our experience, viewers are all quite confident of the patterns they see.

Next consider the graph on the right, which tracks actual movements in The Gap's share price. This graph may look quite non-random to some, suggesting weak form inefficiency. However, it also bears a close visual resemblance to the simulated series, and statistical tests indicate that it indeed behaves like a purely random series. Thus, in our opinion, people claiming to see patterns in historical share price data are probably seeing optical illusions.

## The Semi-Strong Form

The semi-strong form of the efficient market hypothesis implies that prices should reflect all publicly available information. We present two types of tests of this form.

**Event Studies** The *abnormal return* (AR) on a given security for a particular day can be calculated by subtracting the market's return on the same day ($R_m$) – as measured by a broad-based index such as the FTSE. All Share or Euro Stoxx 50 index – from the actual return ($R$) on the equity for that day.[4] We write this algebraically as

$$AR = R - R_m$$

The following system will help us understand tests of the semi-strong form:

$$\text{Information released at time } t - 1 \rightarrow AR_{t-1}$$
$$\text{Information released at time } t \quad \rightarrow AR_{t}$$
$$\text{Information released at time } t + 1 \rightarrow AR_{t+1}$$

The arrows indicate that the abnormal return in any time period is related only to the information released during that period.

According to the efficient market hypothesis, a company's abnormal return at time $t$, $AR_t$, should reflect the release of information at the same time, $t$. Any information released before then should have no effect on abnormal returns in this period because all of its influence should have been felt before. In other words, an efficient market would already have incorporated previous information into prices. Because a company's share price return today cannot depend on what the market does not yet know, information that will be known only in the future cannot influence the company's return either. Hence the arrows point in the direction that is shown, with information in any period affecting only that period's abnormal return. *Event studies* are statistical studies that examine whether the arrows are as shown or whether the release of information influences returns on other days.

These studies also speak of *cumulative abnormal returns* (CARs), as well as abnormal returns (ARs). As an example, consider a firm with ARs of 1 per cent, –3 per cent and 6 per cent for dates –1, 0 and 1, respectively, relative to a corporate announcement. The CARs for dates –1, 0 and 1 would be 1 per cent, –2 per cent [= 1 per cent + (–3 per cent)], and 4 per cent [= 1 per cent + (–3 per cent) + 6 per cent], respectively.

As an example, consider the study by Szewczyk, Tsetsekos and Zantout[5] on dividend omissions. Fig. 13.5 shows the plot of CARs for a sample of companies announcing dividend omissions. Because dividend omissions are generally considered to be bad events, we would expect abnormal returns to be negative around the time of the announcements. They are, as evidenced by a drop in the CAR on both the day before the announcement (day –1) and the day of the announcement (day 0). However, note that there is virtually no movement in the CARs in the days following the announcement. This implies that the bad news is fully incorporated into the stock price by the announcement day, a result consistent with market efficiency.

Over the years this type of methodology has been applied to many events. Announcements of dividends, earnings, mergers, capital expenditures, and new issues of equity are a few

**FIGURE 13.5**

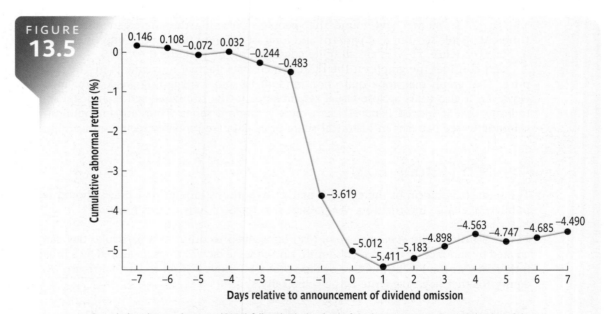

Cumulative abnormal returns (CARs) fall on both the day before the announcement and the day of the announcement of dividend omissions. CARs have little movement after the announcement date. This pattern is consistent with market efficiency.

*Source*: From Exhibit 2 in S.H. Szewczyk, G.P. Tsetsekos and Z.Z. Zantout, 'Do dividend omissions signal future earnings or past earnings?', *Journal of Investing* (Spring 1997).

**Figure 13.5** Cumulative abnormal returns for companies announcing dividend omissions examples of the vast literature in the area. The early event study tests generally supported the view that the market is semi-strong form (and therefore also weak form) efficient. However, a number of more recent studies present evidence that the market does not impound all relevant information immediately. Some conclude from this that the market is not efficient. Others argue that this conclusion is unwarranted, given statistical and methodological problems in the studies. This issue will be addressed in more detail later in the chapter.

**The Record of Mutual Funds**   If the market is efficient in the semi-strong form, then no matter what publicly available information mutual fund managers rely on to pick equities, their average returns should be the same as those of the average investor in the market as a whole. We can test efficiency, then, by comparing the performance of these professionals with that of a market index.

Consider Fig. 13.6, which presents the performance of various types of US mutual fund relative to the stock market as a whole. The far left of the figure shows that the universe of all funds covered in the study underperforms the market by 2.13 per cent per year after an appropriate adjustment for risk. Thus, rather than outperforming the market, the evidence shows underperformance. This underperformance holds for a number of types of fund as well. Returns in this study are net of fees, expenses and commissions, so fund returns would be higher if these costs were added back. However, the study shows no evidence that funds, as a whole, are *beating* the market.

European evidence is more positive regarding the investment decisions of fund managers. Otten and Bams (2002) examined the performance of funds in five European countries (UK, France, Italy, the Netherlands, and Germany) and found positive performance for some countries, before and after expenses are taken into account. Table 13.2 summarizes the main findings of the paper. In all cases, with the exception of Germany, mutual funds outperformed the market before fees were taken into account. Even once the returns have been calculated net of fees, the UK and Netherlands mutual funds return significantly positive performance.

By and large, mutual fund managers rely on publicly available information. Thus the finding that they do not outperform market indexes is consistent with semi-strong form and weak form efficiency. Obviously the European evidence casts some doubt on this finding but, in general, research has shown that mutual funds do not consistently outperform the market.

Does the evidence imply that, in general, mutual funds are bad investments for individuals? Not necessarily. Though many funds fail to achieve better returns than some indices of the market, they do permit the investor to buy a portfolio of many securities (the phrase

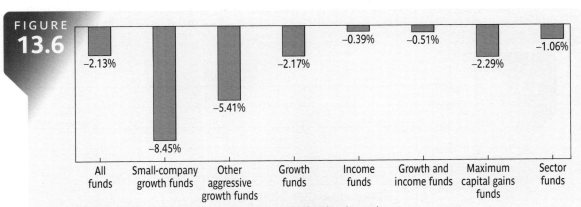

FIGURE
**13.6**

-2.13%    -2.17%    -0.39%    -0.51%    -2.29%    -1.06%

-5.41%

-8.45%

| All funds | Small-company growth funds | Other aggressive growth funds | Growth funds | Income funds | Growth and income funds | Maximum capital gains funds | Sector funds |

On average, mutual funds do not appear to be outperforming the market.

*Source*: Taken from Table 2 of L. Pastor and R.F. Stambaugh, 'Mutual fund performance and seemingly unrelated assets', *Journal of Financial Economics* 63 (2002).

**Figure 13.6** Annual return performance of different types of US mutual fund relative to a broad-based market index (1963–1998) (Performance is relative to the market model.)

| Country | After fees (%) | Before fees (%) |
|---|---|---|
| France | 0.80 | **2.04** |
| Germany | −2.17 | −1.32 |
| Italy | 0.43 | **2.32** |
| Netherlands | **3.08** | **3.59** |
| UK | **1.40** | **2.59** |

*Source*: Table 8, 'European mutual fund performance', by R. Otten and D. Bams, *European Financial Management Journal* (2002).

Figures are annualized alphas, and **bold** indicates that the figure is statistically significant from zero.

**Table 13.2** European fund performance after and before management fees 1991–1998

'a well-diversified portfolio' is often used). They might also provide a variety of services, such as keeping custody and records of all the company's shares.

## The Strong Form

Even the strongest adherents to the efficient market hypothesis would not be surprised to find that markets are inefficient in the strong form. After all, if an individual has information that no one else has, it is likely that she can profit from it.

One group of studies of strong form efficiency investigates insider trading. Insiders in firms have access to information that is not generally available. But if the strong form of the efficient market hypothesis holds, they should not be able to profit by trading on their information. Most government agencies require insiders in companies to reveal any trading they might do in their own company's securities. By examining the record of such trades, we can see whether they made abnormal returns.

Figure 13.7 shows the cumulative abnormal returns that UK directors earned from their trading between 1994 and 2005. It is clear that there is a strong market reaction in the days after insider trading, and that their trades were abnormally profitable. This view is supported

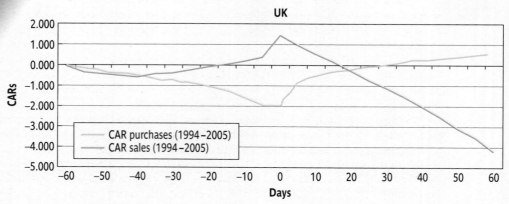

*Source*: The table is taken from the authors' own calculations using data from Hemscott plc.

**Figure 13.7** Cumulative abnormal returns from UK director trading using data in other countries. Given that it seems one can make abnormal profits from private information, strong form efficiency does not seem to be substantiated by the evidence.

## 13.5  The Behavioural Challenge to Market Efficiency

In Section 13.2 we presented Prof. Shleifer's three conditions, any one of which will lead to market efficiency. In that section we made a case that at least one of the conditions is likely to hold in the real world. However, there is definitely disagreement here. Many members of the academic community (including Prof. Shleifer) argue that none of the three conditions is likely to hold in reality. This point of view is based on what is called *behavioural finance*. Let us examine the behavioural view of each of these three conditions.

### Rationality

Are people really rational? Not always. Just travel to any casino to see people gambling, some-times with large sums of money. The casino's take implies a negative expected return for the gambler. Because gambling is risky and has a negative expected return, it can never be on the efficient frontier of our Chapter 10. In addition, gamblers will often bet on black at a roulette table after black has occurred a number of consecutive times, thinking that the run will con-tinue. This strategy is faulty, because roulette tables have no memory.

But, of course, gambling is only a sideshow as far as finance is concerned. Do we see irra-tionality in financial markets as well? The answer may well be yes. Many investors do not achieve the degree of diversification that they should. Others trade frequently, generating both commissions and taxes. In fact, taxes can be handled optimally by selling losers and holding onto winners. Although some individuals invest with tax minimization in mind, plenty of them do just the opposite. Many are more likely to sell their winners than their losers, a strategy leading to high tax payments.[6] The behavioural view is not that *all* investors are irrational. Rather, it is that some, perhaps many, investors are.

### Independent Deviations from Rationality

Are deviations from rationality generally random, and thereby likely to cancel out in a whole population of investors? On the contrary, psychologists have long argued that people deviate from rationality in accordance with a number of basic principles. Not all of these principles have an application to finance and market efficiency, but at least two seem to do so.

The first principle, called *representativeness*, can be explained with the gambling example just used. The gambler believing a run of black will continue is in error because the probability of a black spin is still only about 50 per cent. Gamblers behaving in this way exhibit the psychological trait of representativeness. That is, they draw conclusions from insufficient data. In other words, the gambler believes the small sample he observed is more representative of the population than it really is.

How is this related to finance? Perhaps a market dominated by representativeness leads to bubbles. People see a sector of the market – for example, subprime mortgages – having a short history of high revenue growth and extrapolate that it will continue for ever. When the growth inevitably stalls, prices have nowhere to go but down.

The second principle is *conservatism*, which means that people are too slow in adjusting their beliefs to new information. Suppose that your goal since childhood was to become a dentist. Perhaps you came from a family of dentists, perhaps you liked the security and rela-tively high income that comes with that profession, or perhaps teeth always fascinated you. As things stand now, you could probably look forward to a long and productive career in that occupation. However, suppose a new drug was developed that would prevent tooth decay. That drug would clearly reduce the demand for dentists. How quickly would you realize the implications as stated here? If you were emotionally attached to dentistry, you might adjust your beliefs slowly. Family and friends could tell you to switch out of dental courses at uni-versity, but you just might not be psychologically ready to do that. Instead, you might cling to your rosy view of dentistry's future.

Perhaps there is a relationship to finance here. For example, many studies report that prices seem to adjust slowly to the information contained in earnings announcements.[7] Could it be that, because of conservatism, investors are slow in adjusting their beliefs to new information? More will be said about this in the next section.

## Arbitrage

In Section 13.2 we suggested that professional investors, knowing that securities are mispriced, could buy the underpriced ones while selling correctly priced (or even overpriced) substitutes. This might undo any mispricing caused by emotional amateurs.

Trading of this sort is likely to be more risky than it appears at first glance. Suppose professionals generally believed that the shares of the copper mining firm Vedanta Resources plc were underpriced. They would buy them while selling their holdings in other mining firms – say, Anglo American and Rio Tinto plc. However, if amateurs were taking opposite positions, prices would adjust to correct levels only if the positions of amateurs were small relative to those of the professionals. In a world of many amateurs, a few professionals would have to take big positions to bring prices into line, perhaps even engaging heavily in short selling. Buying large amounts of one company's shares and short-selling large amounts of other company's shares is quite risky, even if the two shares are in the same industry. Here, unanticipated bad news about Vedanta Resources and unanticipated good news about the other two companies would cause the professionals to register large losses.

In addition, if amateurs mispriced Vedanta Resources today, what is to prevent Vedanta from being even *more* mispriced tomorrow? This risk of further mispricing, even in the presence of no new information, may also cause professionals to cut back their arbitrage positions. As an example, imagine a shrewd professional who believed banking stocks were overpriced in early 2007. Had he bet on a decline at that time, he would have lost in the near term: prices rose through the first six months of 2007. Yet he would have eventually made money, because prices later fell. However, near-term risk may reduce the size of arbitrage strategies.

In conclusion, the arguments presented here suggest that the theoretical underpinnings of the efficient capital markets hypothesis, presented in Section 13.2, might not hold in reality. That is, investors may be irrational, irrationality may be related across investors rather than cancelling out across investors, and arbitrage strategies may involve too much risk to eliminate market efficiencies.

## 13.6 Empirical Challenges to Market Efficiency

Section 13.4 presented empirical evidence supportive of market efficiency. We now present evidence challenging this hypothesis. (Adherents of market efficiency generally refer to results of this type as *anomalies*.)

## Limits to Arbitrage

Royal Dutch Petroleum and Shell Transport merged their interests in 1907, with all subsequent cash flows being split on a 60–40 per cent basis between the two companies. However, both companies continued to be publicly traded. You might imagine that the market value of Royal Dutch would always be 1.5 (= 60/40) times that of Shell. That is, if Royal Dutch ever became overpriced, rational investors would buy Shell instead of Royal Dutch. If Royal Dutch were underpriced, investors would buy Royal Dutch. In addition, arbitrageurs would go further by buying the underpriced security and selling the overpriced security short.

However, Fig. 13.8 shows that Royal Dutch and Shell have rarely traded at parity (i.e. 60/40) over the 1962 to 2004 period. Why would these deviations occur? As stated in the previous section, behavioural finance suggests that there are limits to arbitrage. That is, an investor buying the overpriced asset and selling the underpriced asset does not have a sure thing. Deviations from parity could actually *increase* in the short run, implying losses for the arbitrageur. The well-known statement 'Markets can stay irrational longer than you can stay solvent', attributed

FIGURE
13.8

Relative Royal Dutch and Shell prices, 1962–2004

Apparently arbitrage is unable to keep the ratio of the market value of Royal Dutch to the market value of Shell at parity.

*Source*: Author calculations.

**Figure 13.8** Deviations from parity of the ratio of the market value of Royal Dutch to the market value of Shell

to John Maynard Keynes, applies here. Thus risk considerations may force arbitrageurs to take positions that are too small to move prices back to parity.

Academics have documented a number of these deviations from parity. Froot and Dabora show similar results for both the twin companies of Unilever N.V. and Unilever plc, and for two classes of SmithKline Beecham shares.[8] Lamont and Thaler present similar findings for 3Com and its subsidiary Palm Inc.[9] Other researchers find price behaviour in closed-end mutual funds suggestive of parity deviations.

## Earnings Surprises

Common sense suggests that prices should rise when earnings are reported to be higher than expected, and should fall when the reverse occurs. However, market efficiency implies that prices will adjust immediately to the announcement, while behavioural finance would predict another pattern. Kolasinski and Li rank US companies by the extent of their *earnings surprise* – that is, the difference between current quarterly earnings and quarterly earnings four quarters ago, divided by the current share price.[10] They form a portfolio of companies with the most extreme positive surprises and another portfolio of companies with the most extreme negative surprises. Figure 13.9 shows returns from buying the two portfolios, net of the return on the overall market. As can be seen, prices adjust slowly to the earnings announcements, with the portfolio with the positive surprises outperforming the portfolio with the negative surprises over both the next month and the next six months. Many other researchers obtain similar results.

Why do prices adjust slowly? Behavioural finance suggests that investors exhibit conservatism because they are slow to adjust to the information contained in the announcements.

## Size

In 1981 two important papers presented evidence that, in the United States, the returns on equities with small market capitalizations were greater than the returns on equities with large market capitalizations over most of the 20th century.[11] The studies have since been replicated over different periods and in different countries. For example, Fig. 13.10 shows average returns

FIGURE
**13.9**

This figure shows returns net of the market return to a strategy of buying equities with extremely high positive earnings surprise (the difference between current quarterly earnings and quarterly earnings four quarters ago, divided by the current share price) and to a strategy of buying equities with extremely high negative earnings surprise. The graph shows a slow adjustment to the information in the earnings announcement.

*Source*: Adapted from Table 1 of A. Kolasinski and X. Li, 'Are corporate managers savvy about their stock price? Evidence from insider trading after earnings announcements', *Journal of Accounting and Public Policy* (2009).

**Figure 13.9** Returns to two investment strategies based on earnings surprise

over the period from 1963 to 1995 for five portfolios of US equities ranked by size. As can be seen, the average return on small stocks is quite a bit higher than the average return on large equities. Although much of the differential performance is merely compensation for the extra risk of small firms, researchers have generally argued that not all of it can be explained by risk differences. In addition, Donald Keim presented evidence that most of the difference in performance occurs in the month of January.[12]

## Value versus Growth

A number of papers have argued that equities with high book-value-to-share-price ratios and/ or high earnings-to-price ratios (generally called *value stocks*) outperform equities with low ratios (*growth stocks*). For example, Fama and French find that for 12 of 13 major international stock markets the average return on equities with high book-value-to-share-price ratios is above the average return on equities with low book-value-to-share-price ratios.[13] Figure 13.11 shows the returns for a number of European countries for the period 1997 to 2006. In every country, with the exception of Germany and Switzerland, value stocks outperformed growth stocks.

Because the return difference is so large, and because these ratios can be obtained so easily for individual companies, the results may constitute strong evidence against market efficiency. However, a number of papers suggest that the unusual returns are due to biases in commercial databases or to differences in risk, not to a true inefficiency.[14] Because the debate revolves around arcane statistical issues, we shall not pursue the issue further. However, it is safe to say that no conclusion is warranted at this time. As with so many other topics in finance and economics, further research is needed.

## Crashes and Bubbles

The US stock market crash of 19 October 1987 is extremely puzzling. The market dropped between 20 per cent and 25 per cent on a Monday following a weekend during which little surprising news was released. A drop of this magnitude for no apparent reason is not consistent with market efficiency. Because the US crash of 1929 is still an enigma, it is doubtful that the more recent 1987 debacle will be explained any time soon. The recent comments of an

FIGURE
**13.10**

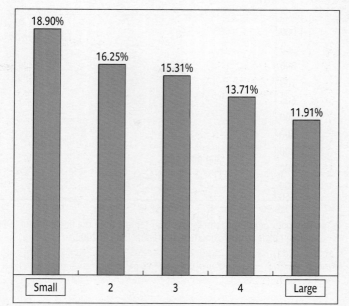

Portfolio | Small | 2 | 3 | 4 | Large

Historically, the average return on small stocks has been above the average return on large stocks.

*Source*: T. Loughran, 'Book-to-market across firm size, exchange and seasonality', *Journal of Financial and Quantitative Analysis* 32 (1997).

**Figure 13.10** Annual share price returns on portfolios sorted by size (market capitalization)

FIGURE
**13.11**

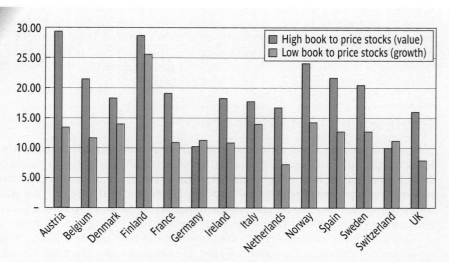

*Source*: The figures are the authors' own calculations based on data taken from Kenneth French's website (http://mba.tuck.dartmouth.edu/pages/faculty/ken.french/index.html)

**Figure 13.11** Annual percentage returns on low book-to-price firms and high book-to-price firms in selected countries for the period 1997–2006

FIGURE
**13.12**

The index of Internet stocks rose over tenfold from the beginning of 1996 to its high in March 2000 before falling to approximately its original level in 2002.

**Figure 13.12** Value of index of Internet stocks

eminent historian are apt here. When asked what, in his opinion, the effect of the French Revolution of 1789 was, he replied that it was too early to tell.

Perhaps the two US stock market crashes are evidence consistent with the bubble theory of speculative markets. That is, security prices sometimes move wildly above their true values. Eventually prices fall back to their original level, causing great losses for investors. Consider, for example, the behaviour of Internet stocks of the late 1990s. Figure 13.12 shows values of an index of Internet stocks from 1996 to 2002. The index rose over tenfold from January 1996 to its high in March 2000 before retreating to approximately its original level in 2002. For comparison, the figure also shows price movement for the Standard & Poor's 500 index. While this index rose and fell over the same period, the price movement was quite muted relative to that of Internet stocks.

Many commentators describe the rise and fall of Internet stocks as a *bubble*. Is it correct to do so? Unfortunately, there is no precise definition of the term. Some academics argue that the price movement in the figure is consistent with rationality. Prices rose initially, they say, because it appeared that the Internet would soon capture a large chunk of international commerce. Prices fell when later evidence suggested this would not occur quite so quickly. However, others argue that the initial rosy scenario was never supported by the facts. Rather, prices rose because of nothing more than 'irrational exuberance'.

## 13.7  Reviewing the Differences

It is fair to say that the controversy over efficient capital markets has not yet been resolved. Rather, academic financial economists have sorted themselves into three camps, with some adhering to market efficiency, some believing in behavioural finance, and others (perhaps the majority) not yet convinced that either side has won the argument. This state of affairs is certainly different from, say, 20 years ago, when market efficiency went unchallenged. In addition, the controversy here is perhaps the most contentious of any area of financial economics.

Because of the controversy, it does not appear that our textbook, or any textbook, can easily resolve the differing points of view. However, we can illustrate the differences between the camps by relating the two psychological principles mentioned earlier, representativeness and conservatism, to share price returns.

### Representativeness

This principle implies overweighting the results of small samples, as with the gambler who thinks a few consecutive spins of black on the roulette wheel make black a more likely outcome than red on the next spin. Financial economists have argued that representativeness leads to *overreaction* in share price returns. We mentioned earlier that financial bubbles are likely over-reactions to news. Internet companies showed great revenue growth for a short time in the late 1990s, causing many to believe that this growth would continue indefinitely. Share prices rose (too much) at this point. Similarly, most people in the banking sector thought that sub-prime mortgages would provide strong returns at little risk. It was only when these loans started to go bad in 2008, and banks such as Washington Mutual, Lehmann Brothers, Bear Stearns, Northern Rock, Royal Bank of Scotland and HBOS got into serious financial distress, that they realized how wrong they were. In both cases, when investors realized that they were wrong, prices plummeted.

## Conservatism

This principle states that individuals adjust their beliefs too slowly to new information. A market composed of this type of investor would probably lead to share prices that *underreact* in the presence of new information. The example concerning earnings surprises may illustrate this underreaction. Prices rose slowly following announcements of positive earnings surprises. Announcements of negative surprises had a similar, but opposite, reaction.

The global credit crisis of 2008 gives us another good example of conservatism in financial markets. When the British bank Northern Rock was nationalized in the early part of the year, investors thought or hoped that it would only be that bank which was affected. Then Bear Stearns, the US investment bank, had to be bought over by JP Morgan Chase in May 2008, and although investors were shaken they still clung to hopes that the credit crisis was nearly over. Fast forward to September 2008 and the banking sector had ground to a halt. In the space of one week, Lehmann Brothers went bankrupt in the world's largest-ever bankruptcy. HBOS, Britain's largest mortgage lender, had to be bought over by Lloyds TSB after its share price collapsed. The US and UK governments temporarily halted the practice of short selling, and the Russian stock markets had to close for a day because prices became too volatile. With hindsight, it is easy to see that the credit crisis had only really started when Northern Rock was nationalized. It could even be argued that if investors had acted rationally three years earlier, the disaster that hit the world's economies might have been averted.

## The Academic Viewpoints

The academic camps have different views of these results. The efficient market believers stress that representativeness and conservatism have opposite implications for share prices. Which principle, they ask, should dominate in any particular situation? In other words, why should investors overreact to news about Internet stocks but underreact to banking stocks? Proponents of market efficiency say that unless behaviourists can answer these two questions satisfactorily, we should not reject market efficiency in favour of behavioural finance. In addition, Eugene Fama[15] reviewed the academic studies on anomalies, finding that about half of them show overreaction and half show underreaction. He concluded that this evidence is consistent with the market efficiency hypothesis that anomalies are chance events.

Adherents of behavioural finance see things a little differently. First, they point out that, as discussed in Section 13.5, the three theoretical foundations of market efficiency appear to be violated in the real world. Second, there are simply too many anomalies, with a number of them being replicated in out-of-sample tests. This argues against anomalies being mere chance events. Finally, though the field has not yet determined why either overreaction or underreaction should dominate in a particular situation, much progress has already been made in a short time.[16]

# 13.8  Implications for Corporate Finance

So far this chapter has examined both theoretical arguments and empirical evidence concerning efficient markets. We now ask whether market efficiency has any relevance for corporate financial managers. The answer is that it does. Next we consider four implications of efficiency for managers.

## Accounting Choices, Financial Choices, and Market Efficiency

The accounting profession provides firms with a significant amount of leeway in their reporting practices. Managers clearly prefer high share prices to low share prices. Should managers use the leeway in accounting choices to report the highest possible income? Not necessarily. That is, accounting choice should not affect share price if two conditions hold. First, enough information must be provided in the annual report so that financial analysts can construct earnings under the alternative accounting methods. This appears to be the case for many, though not necessarily all, accounting choices. Second, the market must be efficient in the semi-strong form. In other words, the market must use all of this accounting information appropriately in determining the market price.

Of course, the issue of whether accounting choice affects share price is ultimately an empirical matter. A number of academic papers have addressed this issue. Kaplan and Roll found that the switch from accelerated to straight-line depreciation did not affect share prices.[17]

Several other accounting procedures have been studied. Hong, Kaplan and Mandelker found no evidence that the stock market was affected by the artificially higher earnings reported using the pooling method, compared with the purchase method, for reporting mergers and acquisitions.[18] In summary, empirical evidence suggests that accounting changes do not fool the market. Therefore the evidence does not suggest that managers can boost share price through accounting practices. In other words, the market appears efficient enough to see through different accounting choices.

One caveat is called for here. Our discussion specifically assumed that 'financial analysts can construct earnings under the alternative accounting methods'. However, companies such as Enron, WorldCom, Global Crossing, Parmalat and Xerox simply reported fraudulent numbers in recent years. There was no way for financial analysts to construct alternative earnings numbers, because these analysts were unaware how the reported numbers were determined. So it was not surprising that the share prices of these companies initially rose well above fair value. Yes, managers can boost prices in this way – as long as they are willing to serve time in prison once they are caught!

## The Timing Decision

Imagine a firm whose managers are contemplating the date to issue equity. This decision is frequently called the *timing* decision. If managers believe that their equity is overpriced, they are likely to issue shares immediately. Here, they are creating value for their current shareholders because they are selling shares for more than they are worth. Conversely, if the managers believe that their equity is underpriced, they are more likely to wait, hoping that the equity price will eventually rise to its true value.

However, if markets are efficient, securities are always correctly priced. Efficiency implies that equity is sold for its true worth, so the timing decision becomes unimportant. Figure 13.13 shows three possible share price adjustments to the issuance of new equity.

Ritter presents evidence that annual equity returns over the five years following an initial public offering (IPO) are about 2 per cent less for the issuing company than the returns on a non-issuing company of similar book-to-market ratio.[19] Annual share price returns over this period following a seasoned equity offering (SEO) are between 3 per cent and 4 per cent less for the issuing company than for a comparable non-issuing company. A company's first public offering is called an IPO and all subsequent offerings are termed SEOs. The upper half of Fig. 13.14 shows average annual returns of both IPOs and their control group, and the lower half of the figure shows average annual returns of both SEOs and their control group.

The evidence in Ritter's paper suggests that corporate managers issue SEOs when the company's equity is overpriced. In other words, managers appear to time the market successfully. The evidence that managers time their IPOs is less compelling: returns following IPOs are closer to those of their control group.

Does the ability of a corporate official to issue an SEO when the security is overpriced indicate that the market is inefficient in the semi-strong form or the strong form? The answer is actually somewhat more complex than it may first appear. On the one hand, officials are likely to have special information that the rest of us do not have, suggesting that the market

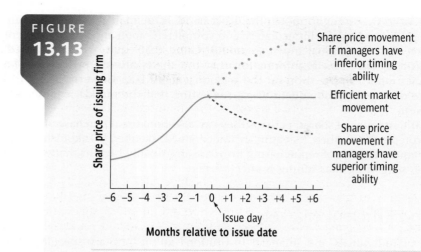

**FIGURE 13.13**

Share price movement if managers have inferior timing ability

Efficient market movement

Share price movement if managers have superior timing ability

Studies show that shares are more likely to be issued after equity prices have increased. No inferences about market efficiency can be drawn from this result. Rather, market efficiency implies that the share price of the issuing firm, on average, neither rises nor falls (relative to equity market indices) after issuance of equity.

**Figure 13.13** Three share price adjustments after issuing equity

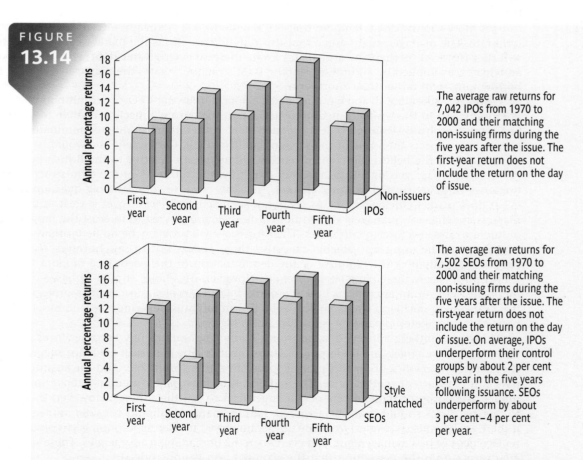

**FIGURE 13.14**

The average raw returns for 7,042 IPOs from 1970 to 2000 and their matching non-issuing firms during the five years after the issue. The first-year return does not include the return on the day of issue.

The average raw returns for 7,502 SEOs from 1970 to 2000 and their matching non-issuing firms during the five years after the issue. The first-year return does not include the return on the day of issue. On average, IPOs underperform their control groups by about 2 per cent per year in the five years following issuance. SEOs underperform by about 3 per cent–4 per cent per year.

*Source*: J. Ritter, 'Investment banking and security issuance', Chapter 9 of *Handbook of the Economics of Finance,* ed. G. Constantinides, M. Harris and R. Stulz (Amsterdam: North Holland, 2003).

**Figure 13.14** Returns on initial public offerings (IPOs) and seasoned equity offerings (SEOs) in years following issue need only be inefficient in the strong form. On the other hand, if the market were truly semi-strong efficient, the price would drop immediately and completely upon the announcement of an upcoming SEO. That is, rational investors would realize that equity is being issued, because corporate officials have special information that the shares are overpriced. Indeed, many empirical studies report a price drop on the announcement date. However, Fig. 13.13 shows a further price drop in the subsequent years, suggesting that the market is inefficient in the semi-strong form.

If firms can time the issuance of shares, perhaps they can also time the repurchase of shares. A firm would like to repurchase when its equity is undervalued. Ikenberry, Lakonishok and Vermaelen find that equity returns of repurchasing firms are abnormally high in the two years following repurchase, suggesting that timing is effective here.[20]

## Speculation and Efficient Markets

We normally think of individuals and financial institutions as the primary speculators in financial markets. However, industrial corporations speculate as well. For example, many companies make interest rate bets. If the managers of a firm believe that interest rates are likely to rise, they have an incentive to borrow, because the present value of the liability will fall with the rate increase. In addition, these managers will have an incentive to borrow long-term rather than short-term in order to lock in the low rates for a longer period. The thinking can get more sophisticated. Suppose that the long-term rate is already higher than the short-term rate. The manager might argue that this differential reflects the market's view that rates will rise. However, perhaps he anticipates a rate increase even greater than what the market anticipates, as implied by an upward-sloping term structure. Again, the manager will want to borrow long-term rather than short-term.

Firms also speculate in foreign currencies. Suppose that the CFO of a multinational corporation based in the United Kingdom believes that the euro will decline relative to sterling. She would probably issue euro-denominated debt rather than sterling-denominated debt, because she expects the value of the foreign liability to fall. Conversely, she would issue debt domestically if she believes foreign currencies will appreciate relative to the British pound.

We are perhaps getting a little ahead of our story: the subtleties of the term structure and exchange rates are treated in other chapters, not this one. However, the big question is this: What does market efficiency have to say about such activity? The answer is clear. If financial markets are efficient, managers should not waste their time trying to forecast the movements of interest rates and foreign currencies. Their forecasts will probably be no better than chance. And they will be using up valuable executive time. This is not to say, however, that firms should flippantly pick the maturity or the denomination of their debt in a random fashion. A firm must *choose* these parameters carefully. However, the choice should be based on other rationales, not on an attempt to beat the market. For example, a firm with a project lasting five years might decide to issue five-year debt. A firm might issue renminbi-denominated debt because it anticipates expanding into China in a big way.

The same thinking applies to acquisitions. Many corporations buy up other firms because they think these targets are underpriced. Unfortunately, the empirical evidence suggests that the market is too efficient for this type of speculation to be profitable. And the acquirer never pays just the current market price. The bidding firm must pay a premium above market to induce a majority of shareholders of the target firm to sell their shares. However, this is not to say that firms should never be acquired. Rather, managers should consider an acquisition if there are benefits (synergies) from the union. Improved marketing, economies in production, replacement of bad management, and even tax reduction are typical synergies. These synergies are distinct from the perception that the acquired firm is underpriced.

One final point should be mentioned. We talked earlier about empirical evidence suggesting that SEOs are timed to take advantage of overpriced equity. This makes sense – managers are likely to know more about their own firms than the market does. However, while managers may have special information about their own firms, it is unlikely that they have special information about interest rates, foreign currencies, or other firms. There are simply too many participants in these markets, many of whom are devoting all of their time to forecasting.

Managers typically spend most of their effort running their own firms, with only a small amount of time devoted to studying financial markets.

## Information in Market Prices

The previous section argued that it is quite difficult to forecast future market prices. However, the current and past prices of any asset are known – and of great use. Consider, for example, Becher's study of bank mergers.[21] The author finds that share prices of acquired banks rise about 23 per cent on average upon the first announcement of a merger. This is not surprising, because companies are generally bought out at a premium above current share price. However, the same study shows that prices of acquiring banks fall almost 5 per cent on average upon the same announcement. This is pretty strong evidence that bank mergers do not benefit, and may even hurt, acquiring companies. The reason for this result is unclear, though perhaps acquirers simply overpay for acquisitions. Regardless of the reason, the *implication* is clear. A bank should think deeply before acquiring another bank.

Furthermore, suppose you are the CFO of a company whose share price drops much more than 5 per cent upon announcement of an acquisition. The market is telling you that the merger is bad for your firm. Serious consideration should be given to cancelling the merger, even if, prior to the announcement, you thought the merger was a good idea.

Of course, mergers are only one type of corporate event. Managers should pay attention to the share price reaction to any of their announcements, whether it concerns a new venture, a divestiture, a restructuring, or something else.

This is not the only way in which corporations can use the information in market prices. Suppose you are on the board of directors of a company whose share price has declined precipitously since the current chief executive officer (CEO) was hired. In addition, the prices of competitors have risen over the same time. Though there may be extenuating circumstances, this can be viewed as evidence that the CEO is doing a poor job. Perhaps he should be fired. If this seems harsh, consider that Warner, Watts and Wruck find a strong negative correlation between managerial turnover and prior stock performance.[22] Figure 13.15 shows that share

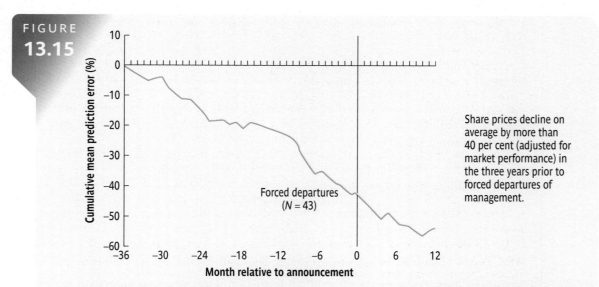

**FIGURE 13.15**

Share prices decline on average by more than 40 per cent (adjusted for market performance) in the three years prior to forced departures of management.

*Source*: Adapted from Figure 1 of Warner, Watts and Wruck, 'Stock prices and management changes', *Journal of Financial Economics* 20 (1988).

**Figure 13.15** Share price performance prior to forced departures of management prices fall on average about 40 per cent in price (relative to market movements) in the three years prior to the forced departure of a top manager.

Market efficiency implies that share prices reflect all available information. We recommend using this information as much as possible in corporate decisions as long as the manager feels that share prices accurately reflect the true value of company equity. In most emerging-market countries stock markets may not be very efficient, and you should be careful about using available share prices. In developed economies, at least with respect to executive firings and executive compensation, it looks as if real-world corporations do pay attention to market prices. The following box summarizes some key issues in the efficient markets debate:

# Efficient Market Hypothesis: A Summary

### Does not say:

1   Prices are uncaused.

2   Investors are foolish and too stupid to be in the market.

3   All shares of equity have the same expected returns.

4   Investors should throw darts to select shares.

5   There is no upward trend in share prices.

### Does say:

1   Prices reflect underlying value.

2   Financial managers cannot time equity and bond sales.

3   Managers cannot profitably speculate in foreign currencies.

4   Managers cannot boost share prices through creative accounting.

### Why doesn't everybody believe it?

1   There are optical illusions, mirages, and apparent patterns in charts of stock market returns.

2   The truth is less interesting.

3   There is evidence against efficiency:

   (a)   Two different, but financially identical, classes of shares of the same firm selling at different prices.

   (b)   Earnings surprises.

   (c)   Small versus large company share price returns.

   (d)   Value versus growth stocks.

   (e)   Crashes and bubbles.

### Three forms

*Weak form*: Current prices reflect past prices; chartism (technical analysis) is useless.

*Semi-strong form*: Prices reflect all public information; most financial analysis is useless.

*Strong form*: Prices reflect all that is knowable; nobody consistently makes superior profits.

## Summary and Conclusions

1   An efficient financial market processes the information available to investors, and incorporates it into the prices of securities. Market efficiency has two general implications. First, in any given time period, an equity's abnormal return depends on information or news received by the market in that period. Second, an investor who uses the same information as the market cannot expect to earn abnormal returns. In other words, systems for playing the market are doomed to fail.

2   What information does the market use to determine prices? The weak form of the efficient market hypothesis says that the market uses the history of prices, and is therefore efficient with respect to these past prices. This implies that security selection based on patterns of past share price movements is no better than random selection.

3   The semi-strong form states that the market uses all publicly available information in setting prices.

4   Strong form efficiency states that the market uses all of the information that anybody knows about equities, even inside information.

5   Much evidence from different financial markets supports weak form and semi-strong form efficiency but not strong form efficiency.

6   Behavioural finance states that the market is not efficient. Adherents argue that:

   (a)   investors are not rational;

   (b)   deviations from rationality are similar across investors;

   (c)   arbitrage, being costly, will not eliminate inefficiencies.

7   Behaviourists point to many studies, including those showing that small company shares outperform large company shares, value stocks outperform growth stocks, and share prices adjust slowly to earnings surprises, as empirical confirmation of their beliefs.

8   Four implications of market efficiency for corporate finance are:

   (a)   Managers cannot fool the market through creative accounting.

   (b)   Firms cannot successfully time issues of debt and equity.

   (c)   Managers cannot profitably speculate in foreign currencies and other instruments.

   (d)   Managers can reap many benefits by paying attention to market prices.

#  Questions and Problems

CONCEPT
1–8

1   **Financing Decisions and Firm Value**   What rule should a firm follow when making financing decisions? How can firms create valuable financing opportunities?

2   **Efficient Capital Markets**   What are the three conditions under which markets may be efficient? Describe these in detail, and provide a practical example illustrating each condition in practice.

3   **Efficient Market Hypothesis**   Explain what is meant by the efficient market hypothesis. Define the three forms of market efficiency, and explain why a characteristic of an efficient market is that investments in that market have zero NPVs.

4   **Efficient Market Hypothesis: The Evidence**   A stock market analyst is able to identify mispriced equities by comparing the average price for the last 10 days with the average price for the last 60 days. If this is true, what do you know about the market?

5 **Behavioural Finance** In recent years a new interpretation of market behaviour has emerged. Explain this theory, and review what it says about Shleifer's three conditions of market efficiency.

6 **Empirical Challenges to Market Efficiency** Discuss some of the anomalies to market efficiency that have been detected in academic research. Taken together, do these anomalies provide concrete evidence that the market is inefficient? Why or why not? Explain.

7 **Efficient Market Theory versus Behavioural Finance** Compare and contrast both theories. In your opinion, which is the most reflective of market behaviour? Explain.

8 **Implications for Corporate Finance** What do efficient market theory and behavioural finance imply for corporate decision-making? Provide three examples of how each theory may affect managerial behaviour.

REGULAR
9–27

9 **Efficient Market Hypothesis** Which of the following statements are true about the efficient market hypothesis?

(a) It implies perfect forecasting ability.

(b) It implies that prices reflect all available information.

(c) It implies an irrational market.

(d) It implies that prices do not fluctuate.

(e) It results from keen competition among investors.

10 **Efficient Market Hypothesis** What are the implications of the efficient market hypothesis for investors who buy and sell shares in an attempt to 'beat the market'?

11 **Efficient Market Hypothesis** Several celebrated investors have recorded huge returns on their investments over the past three decades. Does the success of these particular investors invalidate the EMH? Explain.

12 **Technical Analysis** What would a technical analyst say about market efficiency?

13 **Investor Sentiment** A technical analysis tool that is sometimes used to predict market movements is an investor sentiment index. Sentix, a German firm, publishes several investor sentiment indices. In the following table you will find the sentiment indices as at 8 September 2008, just prior to the weeks in which Lehman Brothers and Washington Mutual went bankrupt; HBOS was sold to Lloyds TSB; and AIG, Fortis Group and Bradford & Bingley were nationalized. The figures in parentheses are the previous month's sentiment index values.

| Region | Overall index | Headline index Current | Headline index Expected future | Index: private organizations Current | Index: private organizations Expected future | Index: financial institutions Current | Index: financial institutions Expected future |
|---|---|---|---|---|---|---|---|
| Asia ex Japan | 4.82 (7.19) | 23.75 (29.25) | −12.50 (−12.75) | 22.00 (29.50) | −8.00 (−5.50) | 25.50 (29.00) | −17.00 (−20.00) |
| Eastern Europe | 4.39 (6.42) | 22.50 (27.25) | −12.25 (−12.50) | 20.50 (28.50) | −8.50 (−5.50) | 24.50 (26.00) | −16.00 (−19.50) |
| Euro area | −20.18 (−15.34) | −12.00 (0.00) | −28.00 (−29.50) | −8.00 (2.50) | −22.00 (−25.50) | −16.00 (−2.50) | −34.00 (−33.50) |
| Japan | −19.76 (−12.79) | −21.75 (−8.75) | −17.75 (−16.75) | −19.50 (−6.50) | −14.50 (−13.50) | −24.00 (−11.00) | −21.00 (−20.00) |
| Latin America | 4.08 (6.90) | 21.25 (28.00) | −11.75 (−12.25) | 20.00 (28.00) | −8.00 (−5.50) | 22.50 (28.00) | −15.50 (−19.00) |
| USA | −25.68 (−32.96) | −33.50 (−38.25) | −17.50 (−27.50) | −28.00 (−35.00) | −14.00 (−25.50) | −39.00 (−41.50) | −21.00 (−29.50) |
| Global aggregate | −9.46 (−8.84) | −1.70 (2.87) | −16.91 (−19.88) | | | | |

What is the investor sentiment index intended to capture? How might it be useful in technical analysis?

14 **Efficient Markets** A hundred years ago or so, companies did not compile annual reports. Even if you owned equity in a particular company, you were unlikely to be allowed to see the balance sheet or income statement for the company. Assuming the market is semi-strong form efficient, what does this say about market efficiency then compared with now?

15 **Efficient Market Hypothesis** Aerotech, a Chinese aerospace technology research firm, announced this morning that it has hired the world's most knowledgeable and prolific space researchers. Before today, Aerotech's equity had been selling for RMB100. Assume that no other information is received over the next week, and the Chinese stock market as a whole does not move.

(a) What do you expect will happen to Aerotech's share price?

(b) Consider the following scenarios:

(i) The share price jumps to RMB118 on the day of the announcement. In subsequent days it floats up to RMB123, then falls back to RMB116.

(ii) The share price jumps to RMB116 and remains at that level.

(iii) The share price gradually climbs to RMB116 over the next week.

Which scenario(s) indicate market efficiency? Which do not? Why?

16 **Efficient Market Hypothesis** When the 56-year-old founder of the Turkish firm Gulf Oil and Minerals died of a heart attack, the share price immediately jumped from 18.00 lira a share to 20.25 lira, a 12.5 per cent increase. This is evidence of market inefficiency, because an efficient stock market would have anticipated his death and adjusted the price beforehand. Assume that no other information is received, and the stock market as a whole does not move. Is this statement about market efficiency true or false? Explain.

17 **Efficient Market Hypothesis** Newtech GmbH is going to adopt a new chip-testing device that can greatly improve its production efficiency. Do you think the lead engineer can profit from purchasing the firm's shares before the news release on the device? After reading the announcement in *Speigel*, should you be able to earn an abnormal return from purchasing the equity if the market is efficient?

18 **Efficient Market Hypothesis** In 2005 all companies in the European Union adopted IFRS (International Financial Reporting Standards). TransTrust NV changed how it accounts for inventory. Taxes are unaffected, although the resulting earnings report released once IFRS had been adopted is 20 per cent higher than what it would have been under the old accounting system. There is no other surprise in the earnings report, and the change in the accounting treatment was publicly announced. If the market is efficient, will the share price be higher when the market learns that the reported earnings are higher?

19 **Efficient Market Hypothesis** The Durkin Investing Agency has been the best stock picker in the country for the past two years. Before this rise to fame occurred, the Durkin newsletter had 200 subscribers. Those subscribers beat the market consistently, earning substantially higher returns after adjustment for risk and transaction costs. Subscriptions have skyrocketed to 10,000. Now, when the Durkin Investing Agency recommends an equity, the price instantly rises several points. The subscribers currently earn only a normal return when they buy recommended shares, because the price rises before anybody can act on the information. Briefly explain this phenomenon. Is Durkin's ability to pick winners consistent with market efficiency?

20 **Efficient Market Hypothesis** Your broker commented that well-managed firms are better investments than poorly managed firms. As evidence your broker cited a recent study examining 100 small manufacturing firms that eight years earlier had been listed in an industry magazine as the best-managed small manufacturers in the country. In the ensuing eight years the 100 firms listed have not earned more than the normal market return. Your broker continued to say that if the firms were well managed, they should have produced better-than-average returns. If the market is efficient, do you agree with your broker?

21 **Efficient Market Hypothesis** A famous economist just announced in the *Financial Times* his findings that the recession is over and the economy is again entering an expansion. Assume market efficiency. Can you profit from investing in the stock market after you read this announcement?

22 **Efficient Market Hypothesis** Suppose the market is semi-strong form efficient. Can you expect to earn excess returns if you make trades based on

(a) Your broker's information about record earnings for a company?

(b) Rumours about a merger of a firm?

(c) Yesterday's announcement of a successful new product test?

23 **Efficient Market Hypothesis** Imagine that a particular macroeconomic variable that influences your firm's net earnings is positively serially correlated. Assume market efficiency. Would you expect price changes in your shares to be serially correlated? Why or why not?

24 **Efficient Market Hypothesis** The efficient market hypothesis implies that all mutual funds should obtain the same expected risk-adjusted returns. Therefore, we can simply pick mutual funds at random. Is this statement true or false? Explain.

25 **Efficient Market Hypothesis** Assume that markets are efficient. During a trading day, British Golf plc announces that it has lost a contract for a large golfing project that, prior to the news, it was widely believed to have secured. If the market is efficient, how should the share price react to this information if no additional information is released?

26 **Efficient Market Hypothesis** Prospectors plc is a publicly traded gold prospecting company with operations in Northern Tanzania. Although the firm's searches for gold usually fail, the prospectors occasionally find a rich vein of ore. What pattern would you expect to observe for Prospectors' cumulative abnormal returns if the market is efficient?

27 **Evidence on Market Efficiency** Some people argue that the efficient market hypothesis cannot explain the 1987 market crash or the high price-to-earnings ratio of European shares in 2005 and 2006. What alternative hypothesis is currently used for these two phenomena?

**CHALLENGE**

**28–31**

28 **Cumulative Abnormal Returns** Iberia Airlines, Air France-KLM and Lufthansa announced purchases of planes on 18 July (18/7), 12 February (12/2) and 7 October (7/10), respectively. Given the following information, calculate the cumulative abnormal return (CAR) for these equities as a group. Graph the result and provide an explanation. All of the stocks have a beta of 1, and no other announcements are made.

| | Iberia | | | Air France-KLM | | | Lufthansa | |
|---|---|---|---|---|---|---|---|---|
| Date | Market return | Company return | Date | Market return | Company return | Date | Market return | Company return |
| 12/7 | −0.3 | −0.5 | 8/2 | −0.9 | −1.1 | 1/10 | 0.5 | 0.3 |
| 13/7 | 0.0 | 0.2 | 9/2 | −1.0 | −1.1 | 2/10 | 0.4 | 0.6 |
| 16/7 | 0.5 | 0.7 | 10/2 | 0.4 | 0.2 | 3/10 | 1.1 | 1.1 |
| 17/7 | −0.5 | −0.3 | 11/2 | 0.6 | 0.8 | 6/10 | 0.1 | −0.3 |
| 18/7 | −2.2 | 1.1 | 12/2 | −0.3 | −0.1 | 7/10 | −2.2 | −0.3 |
| 19/7 | −0.9 | −0.7 | 15/2 | 1.1 | 1.2 | 8/10 | 0.5 | 0.5 |
| 20/7 | −1.0 | −1.1 | 16/2 | 0.5 | 0.5 | 9/10 | −0.3 | −0.2 |
| 23/7 | 0.7 | 0.5 | 17/2 | −0.3 | −0.2 | 10/10 | 0.3 | 0.1 |
| 24/7 | 0.2 | 0.1 | 18/2 | 0.3 | 0.2 | 13/10 | 0.0 | −0.1 |

29 **Cumulative Abnormal Returns** The following diagram shows the cumulative abnormal returns (CAR) for 386 oil exploration companies announcing oil discoveries between 1950 and 1980. Month 0 in the diagram is the announcement month. Assume that no other information is received and the equity market as a whole does not move. Is the diagram consistent with market efficiency? Why or why not?

Time in months relative to event month

**30**  **Cumulative Abnormal Returns**   The following figures present the results of four cumulative abnormal returns (CAR) studies. Indicate whether the results of each study support, reject, or are inconclusive about the semi-strong form of the efficient market hypothesis. In each figure time 0 is the date of an event.

**31**  **Cumulative Abnormal Returns**   A study analysed the behaviour of the equity prices of firms that had lost monopoly cases. Included in the diagram are all firms that lost the initial court decision, even if the decision was later overturned on appeal. The event at time 0 is the initial, pre-appeal court decision. Assume no other information was released, aside from that disclosed in the initial trial. The stock prices all have a beta of 1. Is the diagram consistent with market efficiency? Why or why not?

Time in months relative to event month

# Your Retirement Account at West Coast Yachts

You have been at your job in West Coast Yachts for a week now and have decided you need to sign up for the company's retirement plan. Even after your discussion with Sarah Brown, the Skandla Financial Services representative, you are still unsure which investment option you should choose. Recall that the options available to you are owning shares of West Coast Yachts, the Skandla Market Index Fund, the Skandla Large Company Equity Fund, the Skandla Small-Cap Fund, the Skandla Bond Fund, and the Skandla Money Market Fund. You have decided that you should invest in a diversified portfolio, with 70 per cent of your investment in equity, 25 per cent in bonds, and 5 per cent in the money market fund. You have also decided to focus your equity investment on large-cap company shares, but you are debating whether to select the Market Index Fund or the Large-Company Equity Fund.

In thinking it over, you understand the basic difference between the two funds. One is a purely passive fund that replicates a widely followed large-cap index, the FTSE 100, and has low fees. The other is actively managed, with the intention that the skill of the portfolio manager will result in improved performance relative to an index. Fees are higher in the latter fund. You're just not certain which way to go, so you ask Dan Ervin, who works in the company's finance area, for advice.

After discussing your concerns, Dan gives you some information comparing the performance of equity mutual funds and the FTSE 100 Index Fund. The FTSE 100 Index Fund replicates the FTSE 100, and its return is only negligibly different from the Index itself. Fees are very low. As a result, the FTSE 100 Index Fund is essentially identical to the Skandla Market Index Fund offered in the retirement plan, but it has been in existence for much longer, so you can study its track record for over two decades. The graph below summarizes Dan's comments by showing the percentage of equity mutual funds that outperformed the FTSE 100 Index Fund over the previous 10 years. So, for example, from January 1991 to December 1991 about 70 per cent of equity mutual funds outperformed the FTSE 100 Index Fund. Dan suggests that you study the graph and answer the following questions:

1 What implications do you draw from the graph for mutual fund investors?

2 Is the graph consistent or inconsistent with market efficiency? Explain carefully.

3 What investment decision would you make for the equity portion of your retirement account? Why?

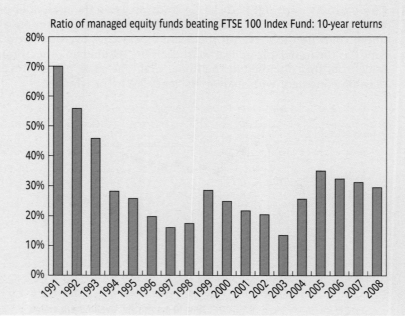

Ratio of managed equity funds beating FTSE 100 Index Fund: 10-year returns

## Practical Case Study

In many countries regulators have moved to ban an activity called equity short-selling. In order to sell equity short, a trader would open an account with a broker, borrow shares from existing shareholders for a fee, and promise to give them back at some point in the future. Short selling is normally used as an effective hedging tool. However, it can also be used to speculate against future falls in prices.

The practice of short selling came under intense scrutiny when it was blamed for the collapsing share prices of banks in 2008. Regulators argued that hedge funds were contributing to the collapse in share prices by irrationally forcing them down below their true level. As bank share prices imploded, there was clear evidence that many banks had very high levels of short selling. As a result, the British government imposed a short-selling ban on 18 September 2008 until 16 January 2009. Other countries imposed similar bans.

If share prices were forced down by a small number of hedge funds (and their short-selling followers) purely because of speculative activity, it would be clear evidence against the efficient market hypothesis.

1   Visit Yahoo! Finance and download the share prices of five British banks for the dates 1 August 2008 to 31 January 2009. Also download the FTSE 100 index for the same period.

2   Track each bank's share price before the ban, during the ban, and after the ban. Do the share price movements support the view that the market was irrationally depressed because of speculative activity?

3   Carry out your own investigation of short selling in Europe. How did other European governments deal with the short-selling controversy?

4   Write a report about the short-selling controversy in the context of the efficient market hypothesis and behavioural finance. What does it say about the validity (if at all) of either theory?

## Relevant Accounting Standards

If there is one area where International Financial Reporting Standards have faced a lot of criticism, it is with respect to their effect on market prices. Because financial assets and liabilities have to be reported at fair or market value, volatility in the stock markets inevitably leads to volatility in the accounting statements. The main standard is IAS39 *Financial Instruments: Recognition and Measurement*. IAS39 provides definitions for different types of financial securities and how to measure their value. Another is FRS7 *Financial Instruments: Disclosure*. Given their hypothesized impact on accounting statements and the corresponding reinforced share price revisions, it is very likely that both standards will change over the next few years. Keep updated by visiting the IASPlus website (www.iasplus.com).

## Additional Reading

In recent years the debate about market efficiency has exploded, with the arrival of a new and very intuitive portfolio of research findings in the behavioural finance paradigm. Subrahmanyam (2008) provides a very readable review of this research. The other papers in the list consider different aspects of market efficiency, such as predictability in returns and whether managers are more informed than the aggregate market about their own company. Conrad *et al.* (2003) is notable, because it criticizes extant research because of biases in research design. This is always a danger in finance research, because, unlike deterministic science experiments, the laboratory for financial markets and the economy is inherently random in nature. Keep this in mind when reading any empirical financial research.

Barberis, N. (2000) 'Investing for the long run when returns are predictable', *Journal of Finance*, vol. 55, no. 1, pp. 225–264. **US**.

Butler, A.W., G. Grullon and J.P. Weston (2005) 'Can managers forecast aggregate market returns?', *Journal of Finance*, vol. 60, no. 2, pp. 963–986. **US**.

Conrad, J., M. Cooper and G. Kaul (2003) 'Value versus glamour', *Journal of Finance*, vol. 58, no. 5, pp. 1969–1996. **US**.

Hill, P. and D. Hillier (2009) 'Market feedback, investment constraints and managerial behaviour', *European Financial Management* (forthcoming). **UK**.

Hwang, S., A. Keswani and M.B. Shackleton (2008) 'Surprise vs anticipated information announcements: are prices affected differently? An investigation in the context of stock splits', *Journal of Banking and Finance*, vol. 32, no. 5, pp. 643–653. **US**.

Subrahmanyam, A. (2008) 'Behavioural finance: a review and synthesis', *European Financial Management*, vol. 14, no. 1, pp. 12–29. **Review Article**.

# Endnotes

1   Andrei Shleifer, *Inefficient Markets: An Introduction to Behavioural Finance* (Oxford: Oxford University Press, 2000).

2   For purposes of this text the random walk can be considered synonymous with weak form efficiency. Technically, the random walk is a slightly more restrictive hypothesis, because it assumes that share price returns are identically distributed through time. The random walk model is normally used to predict price movements, not explain them (as the CAPM does). Two main assumptions of investor behaviour are required for it to hold. First, investors are rational, and their predictions of what will happen in the future are neither optimistic or pessimistic. That is, they are unbiased. The other assumption is that price changes are caused by the arrival of new information only. Given that new information arrives randomly, prices must evolve randomly: hence the term 'random walk'.

3   B.G. Malkiel, *A Random Walk Down Wall Street*, 8th ed. (New York: Norton, 2003).

4   We can also measure the abnormal return by using the market model. In this case the abnormal return is

$$AR = R - (\alpha + \beta R_{\mathrm{m}})$$

5   Samuel H. Szewczyk, George P. Tsetsekos and Zaher Z. Zantout, 'Do dividend omissions signal future earnings or past earnings?', *Journal of Investing* (Spring 1997).

6   For example see Brad Barber and Terrance Odean, 'The courage of misguided convictions', *Financial Analysts Journal* (November/December 1999).

7   For example see Vijay Singal, *Beyond the Random Walk* (New York: Oxford University Press, 2004), Chapter 4.

8   Kenneth A. Froot and Emil M. Dabora, 'How are stock prices affected by the location of trade?', *Journal of Financial Economics* 53 (August 1999).

9   Owen Lamont and Richard Thaler, 'Can the market add and subtract? Mispricing in tech stock carve-outs', *Journal of Political Economy* (April 2003).

10   Adam Kolasinski and Xu Li, 'Do managers detect mispricing? Evidence from insider trading and post-earnings-announcement drift' (Massachusetts Institute of Technology: unpublished paper, 2005).

11   See R.W. Banz, 'The relationship between return and market value of common stocks', *Journal of Financial Economics* (March 1981), and M.R. Reinganum, 'Misspecification of capital asset pricing: empirical anomalies based on earnings yields and market values', *Journal of Financial Economics* (March 1981).

12   D.B. Keim, 'Size-related anomalies and stock return seasonality: further empirical evidence', *Journal of Financial Economics* (June 1983). Also see Kathryn Easterday, 'The declining January effect? An

examination of monthly return for firms trading on NYSE, AMEX, and NASDAQ' (University of Cincinnati: unpublished paper, 2005) for similar conclusions with more recent data.

13  Taken from Table III of Eugene F. Fama and Kenneth R. French, 'Value versus growth: the international evidence', *Journal of Finance* 53 (December 1998).

14  For example see S.P. Kothari, J. Shanken and R.G. Sloan, 'Another look at the cross section of stock returns', *Journal of Finance* 50 (March 1995), and E.F. Fama and K.R. French, 'Multifactor explanations of asset pricing anomalies', *Journal of Finance* 51 (March 1996).

15  Eugene F. Fama, 'Market efficiency, long-term returns, and behavioural finance,' *Journal of Financial Economics* 49 (September 1998).

16  Excellent reviews of this progress can be found in Andrei Shleifer, *Inefficient Markets: An Introduction to Behavioural Finance*, op. cit., and in Nicholas Barberis and Richard Thaler, 'A survey of behavioural finance', in the *Handbook of the Economics of Finance*, eds. George Constantinides, Milton Harris, and Rene Stultz (Amsterdam: North Holland, 2003).

17  R.S. Kaplan and R. Roll, 'Investor evaluation of accounting information: some empirical evidence', *Journal of Business* 45 (April 1972).

18  H. Hong, R.S. Kaplan, and G. Mandelker, 'Pooling vs. purchase: the effects of accounting for mergers on stock prices', *Accounting Review* 53 (1978). The pooling method for mergers is no longer allowed under generally accepted accounting principles.

19  Jay Ritter, 'Investment banking and security issuance', Chapter 9 of *Handbook of the Economics of Finance*, ed. George Constantinides, Milton Harris, and Rene Stulz (Amsterdam: North Holland, 2003).

20  D. Ikenberry, J. Lakonishok and T. Vermaelen, 'Market underreaction to open market share repurchases', *Journal of Financial Economics* (October–November 1995).

21  David A. Becher, 'The valuation effects of bank mergers', *Journal of Corporate Finance* 6 (2000).

22  Jerold B. Warner, Ross L. Watts and Karen H. Wruck, 'Stock prices and top management changes', *Journal of Financial Economics* 20 (1988).

Online **LearningCentre**

To help you grasp the key concepts of this chapter check out the extra resources posted on the Online Learning Centre at **www.mcgraw-hill.co.uk/textbooks/hillier**

Among other helpful resources there are PowerPoint presentations, chapter outlines and mini-cases.

# Chapter 14

# Long-Term Financing: An Introduction

Recent years have been torrid for corporations throughout the world. As a result of the global recession, company after company announced plans to raise financing in the capital markets. What forms of long-term financing are available to companies? This chapter introduces the basic sources of long-term financing: ordinary shares, preference shares, and long-term debt. Subsequent chapters address the optimal mix of these sources. We shall also discuss how companies have financed themselves in recent years.

## 14.1 Ordinary Shares

Under International Financial Reporting Standards (IFRS) the term ordinary shares has no precise meaning. It is usually applied to equity that has no special preference either in dividends or in bankruptcy. Let us take a typical European firm as an example. Below is a description of the equity share capital of the Norwegian aluminium and renewable energy company Norsk Hydro ASA at the beginning of 2008.

| Norsk Hydro ASA Equity Share Capital 31 December 2007 (in millions Norwegian krone) | |
|---|---|
| Ordinary share capital | 1,370 |
| Additional paid-in capital | 360 |
| Other reserves | (1,348) |
| Retained earnings | 57,950 |
| Treasury stock | (4,283) |
| Total equity | 54,049 |

## Par and No-Par Shares

Owners of ordinary shares in a corporation are referred to as *shareholders* or *stockholders*. They receive share certificates for the *shares* they own. There is usually a stated value on each share certificate called the *par value*, which is similar in concept to the face value of a bond. Par value comes from a time when stock markets were not well regulated, but is now no longer needed. Many shares have no par value. The par value of each share of the equity of Norsk Hydro is NKr1.098.

The total par value is the number of shares issued multiplied by the par value of each share, and is sometimes referred to as the *dedicated capital* of a corporation.

## Authorized versus Outstanding Shares

Ordinary shares are the fundamental ownership units of the corporation. The articles of incorporation of a new company must state the number of ordinary shares the corporation is authorized to issue.

The board of directors of the corporation, after an agreement from the shareholders (in unitary board systems) or the supervisory board (in two-tier board systems) can amend the articles of incorporation to increase the number of shares authorized; there is no limit to the number of shares that can be authorized. In 2008 Norsk Hydro ASA had authorized 1,247,956,949 shares and had issued 1,209,304,379 outstanding shares. There is no requirement that all of the authorized shares actually be issued. Although there are no legal limits to authorizing shares of equity, some practical considerations may exist:

1  Some governments impose taxes based on the number of authorized shares.

2  Authorizing a large number of shares may create concern on the part of investors, because authorized shares can be issued later *with* the approval of the board of directors but *without* a vote of the shareholders or supervisory board.

Additional paid-in capital usually refers to amounts of directly contributed equity capital in excess of the par value.

## EXAMPLE 14.1 Par Value and Additional Paid-In Capital

Suppose 100 shares of equity have a par value of £2 each and are sold to shareholders for £10 per share. The additional paid-in capital would be (£10 − £2) × 100 = £8 × 100 = £800, and the total par value would be £2 × 100 = £200. What difference does it make if the total capital contribution is reported as par value or additional paid-in capital?

About the only difference is that the par value is locked in and cannot be distributed to shareholders except upon liquidation of the corporation.

The additional paid-in capital of Norsk Hydro is NKr360 million. This figure indicates that the price of new shares issued by Norsk Hydro has exceeded the par value, and the difference has been entered as *additional paid-in capital*.

## Retained Earnings

In 2007 Norsk Hydro paid out 69 per cent of its net income as dividends. This was unusual for the company, because historically this figure was nearer 40 per cent. The rest of the net income was retained in the business, and is called retained earnings. The cumulative amount of retained earnings (since original incorporation) at the beginning of 2008 was NKr57,950 million.

The sum of the equity components, or the total equity, can be referred to as the firm's book value. The book value represents the amount contributed directly and indirectly to the corporation by equity investors.

## EXAMPLE 14.2 Equity Accounting

Suppose Louest Rouge plc was formed in 1910 with 10,000 shares of equity issued, with each share valued at £1 par value. Because the shares were sold for £1, the first balance sheet showed a zero amount for capital surplus. By 2009 the company had become very profitable, and had retained profits of £100,000. The shareholders' equity of Louest Rouge in 2009 is as follows:

| Louest Rouge plc Equity Accounts 1 January 2009 | £ |
|---|---|
| Ordinary shares; par £1; 10,000 shares outstanding | 10,000 |
| Additional paid-in capital | 0 |
| Retained earnings | 100,000 |
| Total shareholders' equity | 110,000 |

$$\text{Book value per share} = \frac{£110,000}{10,000} = £11$$

Suppose the company has profitable investment opportunities and decides to sell 10,000 shares of new equity. The current market price is £20 per share. The effect of the sale of shares on the balance sheet at the end of the year will be:

| Louest Rouge plc Equity Accounts 31 December 2009 | £ |
|---|---|
| Ordinary shares, £1 par, 20,000 shares outstanding | 20,000 |
| Additional paid-in capital (£20 − £1) × 10,000 shares | 190,000 |
| Retained earnings | 100,000 |
| Total shareholders' equity | 310,000 |

$$\text{Book value per share} = \frac{£310,000}{20,000} = £15.5$$

What happened?

1   Because 10,000 shares of new equity were issued with par value of £1, the par value rose £10,000.

2   The total amount raised by the new issue was £20 × 10,000 = £200,000, and £190,000 was entered into additional paid-in capital.

3   The book value per share increased because the market price of the new equity was higher than the book value of the old equity.

## Market Value, Book Value, and Replacement Value

The book value of Norsk Hydro at the beginning of 2008 was NKr54,049 million. The company had bought back approximately NKr4,283 million worth of shares. The shares bought back are called *treasury stock*.

The book value per share was equal to:

$$\frac{\text{Total common shareholders' equity}}{\text{Shares outstanding}} = \frac{\text{NKr54,049 million}}{1,209 \text{ million}} = \text{NKr44.71}$$

Norsk Hydro is a publicly owned company. Its ordinary shares are traded on the Oslo Stock Exchange and a number of other stock exchanges across the world. Thousands of shares change hands every day. At the end of December 2008 the market price of Norsk Hydro equity was NKr27.8. Thus the market price was below the book value. However, market valuations were extremely volatile in 2008, and over the previous 52 weeks Norsk Hydro's share price fluctuated between NKr86.7 and NKr21.2.

## Shareholders' Rights

The value of a share of equity in a corporation is directly related to the general rights of shareholders. In addition to the right to vote for directors, shareholders usually have the following rights:

- The right to share proportionally in dividends paid.

- The right to share proportionally in assets remaining after liabilities have been paid in a liquidation.

- The right to vote on matters of great importance to shareholders, such as a merger, usually decided at the annual meeting or a special meeting.

- The right to share proportionally in any new equity sold. This is called the *pre-emptive right* and will be discussed in detail in later chapters.

## Dividends

A distinctive feature of corporations is that they issue shares of equity, and are authorized by law to pay dividends to the holders of those shares. Dividends paid to shareholders represent a return on the capital directly or indirectly contributed to the corporation by the shareholders. The payment of dividends occurs at the discretion of the board of directors.

Here are some important characteristics of dividends:

- Unless a dividend is declared by the board of directors of a corporation, it is not a liability of the corporation. A corporation cannot *default* on an undeclared dividend. As a consequence, corporations cannot become *bankrupt* because of non-payment of dividends. The amount of the dividend – and even whether or not it is paid – are decisions based on the business judgement of the board of directors.

- The payment of dividends by the corporation is not a business expense. Dividends are not deductible for corporate tax purposes. In short, dividends are paid out of after-tax profits of the corporation.

- Dividends received by individual shareholders are for the most part considered ordinary income by the tax authorities, and are fully or partially taxable depending on the specific tax rules of the country in which the dividends are paid. Corporations that own shares in other corporations are normally permitted to exclude some component of the amounts they receive as dividends. In other words, they are taxed only on a certain percentage of the dividends.

## Classes of Shares

Some firms issue more than one class of ordinary shares. The classes are usually created with unequal voting rights. All Chinese firms have two classes of equity, A and B class shares. A class shares can only be owned by Chinese nationals whereas B class shares can be owned by anyone. The number of A class shares is almost always more than the number of B class shares, ensuring that Chinese firms are ultimately controlled by Chinese nationals. A good example of an individual firm with dual class shares is Google, the Web search company. Google has two classes of equity, A and B. Class A shares are held by the public, and each share has one vote. Class B shares are held by company insiders, and each class B share has 10 votes. As a result, Google's founders and management control the company.

Many companies issue dual classes of equity. The reason has to do with control of the firm. Management of a firm can raise equity capital by issuing non-voting shares while maintaining voting control. Harry and Linda DeAngelo found that management's equity holdings are usually tilted towards the shares with the superior voting rights.[1] Moreover, Luigi Zingales found the premium associated with superior voting rights in Italian companies to be around 60 per cent.[2] Thus vote ownership is an important element of corporate control structure.

# 14.2 Corporate Long-Term Debt: The Basics

Securities issued by corporations may be classified roughly as *equity* securities and *debt* securities. The distinction between equity and debt is fundamental to much of the modern theory and practice of corporate finance.

At its crudest level, debt represents something that must be repaid; it is the result of borrowing money. When corporations borrow, they promise to make regularly scheduled interest payments and to repay the original amount borrowed (that is, the *principal*). The person or firm making the loan is called a *creditor* or *lender*.

## Interest versus Dividends

The corporation borrowing the money is called a *debtor* or *borrower*. The amount owed the creditor is a liability of the corporation; however, it is a liability of limited value. The corporation can legally default on its liability at any time. This can be a valuable option. The creditors benefit if the assets have a value greater than the value of the liability, but this would happen only if management were foolish. On the other hand, the corporation and the equity investors benefit if the value of the assets is less than the value of the liabilities, because equity investors can walk away from the liabilities and default on their payment.

From a financial point of view, the main differences between debt and equity are the following:

- Debt is not an ownership interest in the firm. Creditors do not usually have voting power. The device used by creditors to protect themselves is the loan contract (that is, the *indenture*).

- The corporation's payment of interest on debt is considered a cost of doing business and is fully tax-deductible. Thus interest expense is paid out to creditors before the corporate tax liability is computed. Dividends on ordinary and preference shares are paid to shareholders after the tax liability has been determined. Dividends are considered a return to shareholders on their contributed capital. Because interest expense can be used to reduce taxes, governments provide a direct tax subsidy on the use of debt when compared with equity. This point is discussed in detail in the next two chapters.

- Unpaid debt is a liability of the firm. If it is not paid, the creditors can legally claim the assets of the firm. This action may result in *liquidation* and *bankruptcy*. Thus one of the costs of issuing debt is the possibility of *financial failure*, which does not arise when equity is issued.

## Is it Debt or Equity?

Sometimes it is not clear whether a particular security is debt or equity. For example, suppose a 50-year bond is issued, with interest payable solely from corporate income if and only if earned, and repayment is subordinate to all other debts of the business. Corporations are very adept at creating hybrid or compound securities that look like equity but are called *debt*. Obviously the distinction between debt and equity is important for tax purposes. When corporations try to create a debt security that is really equity, they are trying to obtain the tax benefits of debt while eliminating its bankruptcy costs.

According to International Accounting Standard 32 (IAS32), a debt instrument has a contractual obligation to deliver cash or another financial asset, whereas equity is a security that has a residual cash flow after all other liabilities have been paid. When accounting for hybrid or compound securities, the instrument should be disaggregated into its equity and debt components and recorded accordingly. So, for example, a debt instrument that can be converted into equity would have its value arising from the debt and equity components valued and recorded separately in the company's accounts.

## Basic Features of Long-Term Debt

Long-term corporate debt usually is denominated in multiples of 100, (e.g. £100,000 or €1,000), called the *principal* or *face value*. Long-term debt is a promise by the borrowing firm to repay the principal amount by a certain date, called the *maturity date*. Debt price is often expressed as a percentage of the par or face value. For example, it might be said that Swedbank AB's debt is selling at 90, which means that a bond with a par value of SKr1,000 can be purchased for SKr900. In this case the debt is selling at a discount, because the market price is less than the par value. Debt can also sell at a premium with respect to par value. The borrower using long-term debt generally pays interest at a rate expressed as a fraction of par value. Thus, at SKr1,000 par value, Swedbank's 7 per cent debt means that SKr70 of interest is paid to holders of the debt, usually in semi-annual instalments (for example, SKr35 on 30 June and 31 December). These payments are referred to as 'coupons', and the 7 per cent is called the *coupon rate*.

## Different Types of Debt

Typical debt securities are called *bills, notes, debentures,* or *bonds*. A debenture is an unsecured corporate debt, whereas a bond is secured by a mortgage on the corporate property. However, in common parlance the word *bond* is used indiscriminately, and often refers to both secured and unsecured debt. A note usually refers to an unsecured debt with a maturity shorter than that of a debenture, perhaps under 10 years. A bill usually refers to a short-term debt instrument with a maturity less than a year. In the UK, government bonds are known as *gilts*.

Debentures and bonds are long-term debt or non-current liabilities. *Long-term debt* is any obligation that is payable more than one year from the date it was originally issued. Sometimes long-term debt is called *funded debt*. Debt that is due in less than one year is unfunded, and is accounted for as a current liability. Some debt is perpetual and has no specific maturity. This type of debt is referred to as a *consol*.

## Repayment

Long-term debt is typically repaid in regular amounts over the life of the debt. The payment of long-term debt by instalments is called *amortization*. At the end of the amortization the entire indebtedness is said to be *extinguished*. Amortization is typically arranged by a *sinking fund*. Each year the corporation places money into a sinking fund, and the money is used to buy back the bonds.

Debt may be extinguished before maturity by a call. Historically, almost all publicly issued corporate long-term debt has been *callable*. These are debentures or bonds for which the firm has the right to pay a specific amount, the *call price*, to retire (extinguish) the debt before the stated maturity date. The call price is always higher than the par value of the debt. Debt that is callable at 105 is debt that the firm can buy back from the holder at a price of £105 or €1,050 per debenture or bond, regardless of what the market value of the debt might be. Call prices are always specified when the debt is originally issued. As discussed in an earlier chapter, 'make-whole' call provisions have become the norm.

## Seniority

In general terms, *seniority* indicates preference in position over other lenders. Some debt is *subordinated*. In the event of default, holders of subordinated debt must give preference to other specified creditors. Usually, this means that the subordinated lenders will be paid off only after the specified creditors have been compensated. However, debt cannot be subordinated to equity. This is discussed in more detail in Section 14.5.

## Security

*Security* is a form of attachment to property: it provides that the property can be sold in the event of default, to satisfy the debt for which security is given. A mortgage is used for security in tangible property: for example, debt can be secured by mortgages on plant and equipment. Holders of such debt have prior claim on the mortgaged assets in case of default. Debentures are not secured by a mortgage. Thus, if mortgaged property is sold in the event of default, debenture holders will obtain something only if the mortgage bondholders have been fully satisfied.

## Indenture

The written agreement between the corporate debt issuer and the lender, setting forth maturity date, interest rate, and all other terms, is called an *indenture*. We treat this in detail in later chapters. For now, we note that:

1   The indenture completely describes the nature of the indebtedness.

2   It lists all restrictions placed on the firm by the lenders. These restrictions are placed in *restrictive covenants*.

Some typical restrictive covenants are the following:

1   Restrictions on further indebtedness

2   A maximum on the amount of dividends that can be paid

3   A minimum level of working capital

---

**EXAMPLE 14.3**

## Long-Term Debt

The following table shows some of the many debt securities of Siemens AG at the end of 2008 (in millions), listed in order of priority (highest first). Libor, Euribor and US$ Libor are the rates at which British, European and US banks lend to each other, respectively.

| Status | Currency | Amount outstanding | Issue date | Maturity date | Coupon | Coupon payment |
|---|---|---|---|---|---|---|
| Senior unsecured | € | 2,000 | 28 June 2001 | 4 July 2011 | Annually | 5.75% |
| Senior unsecured | $ | 500 | 16 March 2006 | 16 March 2012 | Quarterly | 3M US$ Libor + 0.15% |
| Senior unsecured | $ | 500 | 16 March 2006 | 16 March 2016 | Annually | 5.625% |
| Senior unsecured | $ | 750 | 16 August 2008 | 14 August 2009 | Quarterly | 3M US$ Libor + 0.05% |
| Senior unsecured | $ | 750 | 16 August 2008 | 16 February 2012 | Semi-Annually | 5.5% |
| Senior unsecured | $ | 1,750 | 16 August 2008 | 17 October 2016 | Semi-Annually | 5.75% |
| Senior unsecured | $ | 1,750 | 16 August 2006 | 17 August 2026 | Semi-annually | 6.125% |
| Senior unsecured | € | 1,200 | 11 June 2008 | 12 December 2011 | Annually | 5.25% |
| Senior unsecured | € | 1,000 | 11 June 2008 | 11 June 2014 | Annually | 5.375% |
| Senior unsecured | € | 1,200 | 11 June 2008 | 11 June 2018 | Annually | 5.625% |
| Junior subordinated unsecured | € | 900 | 14 September 2006 | 14 September 2066 but can be redeemed from 2016 | Annually until 2016, quarterly after | 3M Euribor + 1.25% + 1.00% step-up |
| Junior subordinated unsecured | £ | 750 | 14 September 2006 | 14 September 2066 but can be redeemed from 2016 | Annually until 2016, quarterly after | 3M Libor + 1.25% + 1.00% step-up |

Siemens AG has different notes and debentures that are demoninated in several currencies (dollars, euros and sterling). As can be seen, there are different maturities, coupon rates (fixed and floating) and the last two can be converted into equity after 2016.

## 14.3 Preference Shares

Preference shares represent equity of a corporation, but they are different from ordinary shares because they are preferred in the payment of dividends and in the assets of the corporation in the event of bankruptcy. *Preference* means only that the holder of the preference share must receive a dividend (in the case of an ongoing firm) before holders of ordinary shares are entitled to anything. Preference shares are the most common form of compound security, and can be viewed as equity or as debt, depending on the exact characteristics of the security.

In some companies a subsidiary will issue preference shares to raise funds and lend these funds to the parent company in order to minimize tax payments for the firm as a whole. The loan will be tax-deductible from the perspective of the parent company. From the subsidiary's perspective, the dividend paid to the preference share holders will be completely offset by the interest paid by the parent company. This type of complex transaction is more likely to occur when the parent and the subsidiary operate in different tax locales.

### Stated Value

Preference shares have a stated liquidating value, usually £100 or €100 per share. The dividend of preference shares is described in terms of pounds or euros per share. For example, '£5 preferred' translates into a dividend yield of 5 per cent of stated value.

### Cumulative and Non-Cumulative Dividends

A preference share dividend is not like interest on a bond. The board of directors may decide not to pay the dividends on preference shares, and their decision may not have anything to do with current net income of the corporation. Dividends payable on preference shares are either *cumulative* or *non-cumulative*. If preference share dividends are cumulative and are not paid in a particular year, they will be carried forward. Usually both the cumulated (past) preference share dividends plus the current preference share dividends must be paid before the ordinary shareholders can receive anything. Unpaid preference share dividends are *not* debts of the firm. Directors elected by the ordinary shareholders can defer preference share dividends indefinitely. However, if so,

(a)   ordinary shareholders must forgo dividends;

(b)   though holders of preference shares do not always have voting rights, they will typically be granted these rights if preference share dividends have not been paid for some time.

Because preference shareholders receive no interest on the cumulated dividends, some have argued that firms have an incentive to delay paying preferred dividends.

### Are Preference Shares really Debt?

A good case can be made that preference shares are really debt in disguise. Preference shareholders receive a stated dividend only, and if the corporation is liquidated, they get a stated value. In recent years, many new issues of preference shares have had obligatory sinking funds.

The yields on preference shares are typically very low. For example, BP plc has an 8% preference share with a stated £0.08 dividend. This dividend is perpetual – that is, it will be paid each year by BP plc for ever unless called. However, at a board meeting, holders of the

8% preference shares have two votes for every five shares held, compared with one vote for every ordinary share held.

The International Financial Reporting Standards, in their document IAS32 *Financial Instruments: Presentation*, discuss in detail how preference shares should be regarded. The fundamental issue is whether the preference share has predominantly debt characteristics or equity characteristics. For example, the preference share will be viewed as debt if it contractually pays a fixed dividend, and expires or is redeemed at a mandatory fixed future date. On the other hand, it will be regarded as equity if is not obligated to pay a dividend, or has a maturity date. When the preference share has clear debt and equity components, IFRS recommends that the equity and debt components be valued and reported separately in the financial accounts.

## Equity versus Debt

| Feature | Equity | Debt |
|---------|--------|------|
| Income | Dividends | Interest |
| Tax status | Dividends are taxed as personal income. Dividends are not a business expense. | Interest is taxed as personal income. Interest is a business expense, and corporations can deduct interest when computing corporate tax liability. |
| Control | Ordinary shares usually have voting rights. | Control is exercised with loan agreement. |
| Default | Firms cannot be forced into bankruptcy for non-payment of dividends. | Unpaid debt is a liability of the firm. Non-payment results in bankruptcy. |

Bottom line: Tax status favours debt, but default favours equity. Control features of debt and equity are different, but one is not better than the other.

## 14.4 Patterns of Financing

Firms receive funding from three main sources. First, they can reinvest their profits from existing operations; second, they can borrow from the banking sector; and finally, they can issue securities (debt and equity) to the public. Table 14.1 summarizes the patterns of funding for Germany, Japan, the United Kingdom and the United States between 1970 and 1994.

**TABLE 14.1**

| Source of capital | Germany | Japan | United Kingdom | United States |
|-------------------|---------|-------|----------------|---------------|
| Internal | 78.9% | 69.9% | 93.3% | 96.1% |
| Bank finance | 11.9% | 26.7% | 14.6% | 11.1% |
| New security issues and other | 9.2% | 3.4% | −7.9% | −7.2% |

*Source*: Jenny Corbett and Tim Jenkinson, 'How is investment financed? A study of Germany, Japan, the United Kingdom, and the United States', *The Manchester School*, vol. 65 (1997), pp. 69–93.

**Table 14.1** Financing patterns for Germany, Japan, the United Kingdom and the United States (1970–1994)

Corporations mostly rely on internal financing for their investment expenditure. However, bank financing is considerably more important for Japanese firms than it is for other countries. It may seem strange that the UK and US have a negative figure for the value of new security issues. This is because during the period of study many mergers and acquisitions took place, and these were paid by cash. In addition, many companies underwent share buybacks. As a result, the net value of securities actually decreased. Looking at the overall picture, it can be seen that there is a financial gap between the level of funds available from ongoing operations and the total investment expenditure. One of the challenges of the financial manager is to finance the gap.

Internal financing comes from internally generated cash flow, and is defined as net income plus depreciation minus dividends. External financing is net new debt and new shares of equity net of buybacks.

Several features of long-term financing seem clear from Table 14.1:

1   Internally generated cash flow has dominated as a source of financing. Typically, over 70 per cent of long-term financing comes from cash flows that corporations generate internally.

2   Typically, total firm spending is greater than internally generated cash flow. A financial deficit is created by the difference between total firm spending and internally generated cash flow. For example, in Germany, 78.9 per cent of financing came from internal cash flow, implying a financial deficit over the period of 21.1 per cent (= 100% − 78.9%). Bank loans constituted 11.9 per cent of total financing, and 9.2 per cent of investment capital was financed from new security issues.

## International Patterns in Capital Structure

Chapter 2 of this book established that there are many different corporate and ownership structures around the world. Firms that operate in China can look very different from similar firms doing business in the United Kingdom. State ownership is prevalent in many countries. There are even very large differences in the ownership levels and board structures of firms that are incorporated in Europe. These differences suggest the question: Are there differences in the capital structure of firms in different parts of the world?

Figure 14.1 presents the average leverage ratios (debt to market value of the firm) for many countries between 1990 and 2000. While countries such as Pakistan and Thailand have very high debt levels, most other countries use very little debt. The Pakistani example is surprising, given that it is largely a Muslim country, and Islamic financing forbids the use of debt. The figures are also in market value terms and not book value terms. Given that the value of debt does not change very much, countries with vibrant and strongly performing equity markets would tend to have lower leverage ratios. Likewise, in markets that are bearish and not performing well, leverage ratios will be higher.

## Which Are Best: Book or Market Values?

In general, financial economists prefer the use of market values when measuring debt ratios. This is true because market values reflect current rather than historical values. Most financial economists believe that current market values reflect true intrinsic values better than historically based values do. However, the use of market values contrasts with the perspective of many corporate practitioners.

Our conversations with corporate treasurers suggest to us that the use of book values is popular because of the volatility of the stock market, which has been a significant problem since the end of 2007. It is frequently claimed that the inherent volatility of the stock market makes market-based debt ratios move around too much. It is also true that restrictions of debt in bond covenants are usually expressed in book values rather than market values. Moreover, firms such as Standard & Poor's and Moody's use debt ratios expressed in book values to measure creditworthiness.

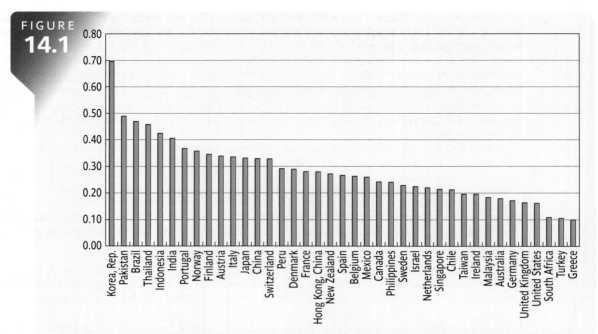

Source: J.P.H. Fan, S. Titman and G. Twite, 'An international comparison of capital structure and debt maturity choices', Working Paper (2006).

**Figure 14.1** International patterns of capital structure

A key fact is that, whether we use book or market values, debt ratios for most non-financial firms generally have been well below 100 per cent of total equity in recent years: that is, firms generally use less debt than equity.

## 14.5 Hierarchies in Long-Term Financing

In Example 14.3 it was shown that Siemens AG had many different types of debt. These were identified as senior and junior unsecured debt. If Siemens were to go bankrupt, the security holders would want as much of their initial investment back as possible. The hierarchy or priority of a company's securities determines who gets a claim on the assets of a bankrupt company first. In this section we shall review in more detail the different types of long-term financing and their priority in the list of corporate claims.

**Senior Secured Debt**   Senior secured debt is a debt instrument that is backed by a claim on the assets of the issuing company. This claim is known as *collateral*, and may comprise buildings, manufacturing facilities, airplanes, or any other fixed asset. Mortgaged debt is debt secured by property and buildings, and non-recourse debt is debt that is only partially secured by some assets in the company. Typically, the value of the collateral in non-recourse debt will be around 80 to 90 per cent of the total value of the debt. If the borrower defaults on the debt, the lender can only claim against the value of the collateral and no more. Senior secured debt has the first and highest claim on the assets of a defaulting company.

**Second Lien Loans**   Second lien loans are debt instruments that are normally secured to some form of collateral but are second in line for a claim of a company's assets behind senior secured debt.

**Senior Unsecured Debt**  The next financial security in the hierarchy is senior unsecured debt. Senior debt has a claim above other forms of debt, but in contrast to secured debt the issue is not supported by any collateral.

**Subordinated or Junior Debt**  The ranking of debt below senior debt is commonly known as either subordinated or junior debt. Subordinated debt has a claim below all other senior debt instruments. Subordinated debt is fairly risky, because in the event of a corporate default it is unlikely that the subordinated bondholders will receive any of their money back.

**Shareholder Loans**  Shareholder loans are very long-term low-interest loans given to a company by dominant shareholders. Because the loans are owned by the shareholders, they are commonly regarded as equity. For example, it wouldn't make sense for the shareholder who gave a loan to make their firm bankrupt, because this would directly hurt their shareholdings in the company. Given their unique nature, shareholder loans are the lowest ranking of all debt instruments.

**Preference Shares**  Preference shares have been discussed in Section 14.3. They fall below debt in the seniority of financial claims but sit above ordinary equity.

**Ordinary Equity**  Equity holders are at the very bottom of the financing hierarchy and are also known as residual claimants. This is because, in the event of a corporate bankruptcy, shareholders are the very last of all financial claimants to receive their money back. Normally, they would receive nothing at all.

# 14.6  Islamic Financing

In recent years many countries have developed financial instruments and business practices reflecting the religious values of Islam. This is known as *Islamic financing*, with the main characteristic being that interest of any kind is not allowed to be charged on financial securities. The United Kingdom is at the forefront of Islamic financing in Western Europe, with 23 banks having Islamic financing divisions. This is followed by Switzerland (5 banks), France (4 banks), and Luxembourg (4 banks). In the Middle East Bahrain is the Islamic financing centre, and Malaysia is the main country in South East Asia. Islamic financing need not be confined only to Muslims, and in Malaysia, for example, nearly a quarter of all users of Islamic products are non-Muslims.

Not having interest-bearing securities presents a number of challenges to firms wishing to raise financing for investment projects. In response, Islamic banks have created a number of innovative instruments and financing methods that are consistent with Islamic or Shariah principles and have debt-like characteristics. The most common of these involve elements of profit-sharing, known as *mudharabah*, joint ventures (*musharakah*), leasing (*ijarah*), and compensation for facilitating the financing activity (*murabahah*). Islamic securities that can be traded on exchanges are known as *sukuk*.

## Types of Islamic Financing Methods

**An Advanced Payment Sale**  A *bai salam* is a contract where two parties trade today in return for a good to be delivered at some specified date in the future. The transfer of cash must be made today, and the quality and quantity of the good must be specified at the time of the trade. One of the requirements of *bai salam* is that there can be no uncertainty in the quality or quantity of a good or commodity. Therefore raw agricultural produce is not allowed to be traded in this way, because flooding or an earthquake may result in loss of quality or quantity.

<table>
<tr><td>EXAMPLE<br>**14.4**</td><td>## Bai Salam</td></tr>
</table>

Shukran plc is undertaking a new warehouse expansion and has commissioned a company, Temsaah Ltd, to build it on the site of an existing warehouse. The warehouse with full facilities will take one year to build, and the price of the new warehouse will be £3,000,000 in one year. In a *bai salam* sale Shukran may pay £2.7 million today for the warehouse (fully specified at the time of the contract) to be ready for use exactly one year from the date of the trade.

**Stated Cost plus Profit**   *Murabahah* is one of the most common forms of Islamic financing contracts. In this transaction the seller of a commodity expressly states the cost that has been incurred in producing, manufacturing or buying a commodity or asset. A pre-agreed markup or profit margin is then applied to the cost in order to find the price of the trade. Clearly, a *murabahah* contract requires the seller to be honest about the base cost of the commodity. *Murabahah* is used for the financing of asset purchases and property investments. So that there is no doubt that it was the underlying asset that has been traded (to avoid accusations of interest payments in another form), the seller of the commodity or asset must be the owner before selling it. As in other Islamic financing contracts, a seller may consult the debt markets to ascertain competitive markup rates.

In a *murabahah* sale, the purchaser may pay the stated amount in fixed instalments. When only one payment in the future is made, this is known as a *bai' bithaman ajil* contract.

<table>
<tr><td>EXAMPLE<br>**14.5**</td><td>## Murabahah</td></tr>
</table>

Shukran plc is undertaking a new warehouse expansion and has commissioned a company, Temsaah Ltd, to build it on the site of an existing warehouse. Temsaah needs cash equalling the construction costs of £2.7 million today to finance the building of the warehouse. Unfortunately, Shukran does not have the funds in place. The CEO of Shukran goes to Bahrain Bank and enters into a *murabahah* transaction.

Bahrain Bank agrees to pay £2.7 million today to Temsaah, and notifies Shukran's CEO of the cost. Given market conditions, with comparable loans currently at 10 per cent, the manager of Bahrain Bank enters into an agreement with the CEO of Shukran to charge a markup of £270,000 on the building, to be paid in one year. This markup of 10 per cent makes the *murabahah* contract competitive with Western financing deals.

In this transaction, Bahrain Bank owns the warehouse until the date of the trade. In one year, Bahrain Bank sells the warehouse for £2,970,000 (£2,700,000 cost plus £270,000 markup), and the transfer of title deeds to Shukran takes place at that date. As you will have noticed, this transaction is actually a *bai' bithaman ajil* contract, which is a subtype of *murabahah* financing.

**Goodwill Loan**   Perhaps unique to the global financial markets, a *qard hassan* is a loan without any interest. The lender will provide the borrower with funds and, at some point in the future, these will be paid back to the bank. The borrower may, at his own discretion, repay an extra amount to compensate the lender for supplying the funds. A *qard hassan* is normally very small, say £2,000, and is given to pay for school education, medical fees or some other social improving purpose.

**Hire Purchase**   Hire purchase agreements originally came from the United Kingdom, and are most commonly used in the automobile industry. In a Western hire purchase agreement the buyer of an asset puts down an initial deposit on the price of an asset, and agrees to hire or rent it for a set period. When the sum of the rental payments reaches a certain amount the buyer may purchase outright the asset for a pre-agreed price, and take ownership.

With a little modification, hire purchase agreements are ideal instruments for Islamic financing. In an *ijarah thumma al bai'* contract the buyer agrees to first lease or rent the asset for a certain period. When this period has expired, the buyer may purchase the asset for a specific price that is agreed at the very beginning of the contract.

EXAMPLE
14.6

# Using Western Loans to Determine Payments in an Ijarah Thumma Al Bai'

Shufaa Al Beity wishes to purchase a car whose sale price is €25,000. Unfortunately, she is a student, and can't afford to part with that amount of money today. She decides to enter into an *ijarah thumma al bai'* contract to buy the car over five years in monthly instalments. How much would she pay?

To determine a set of monthly payments that is competitive with other Western lenders, an Islamic bank would study the range of Western loans that are on offer today. Assume that most banks are giving personal loans with an APR of 10 per cent. This is the effective interest rate on car loans for €25,000 over five years and equates to a rate of 0.7974 per cent per month (work it out yourself!). Using the standard annuity formula, the monthly payment on a loan of €25,000 paid over 60 monthly instalments at a rate of 0.7974 per cent per month is

$$C = \frac{€25,000}{A^{60}_{0.007974}} = \frac{€25,000}{47.5385} = €525.89$$

The total payment that Shufaa will need to make if she takes out a Western loan is $60 \times €525.89 = €31,553.37$. For an Islamic bank to be competitive with its Western counterpart, the total amount paid in an *ijarah thumma al bai'* must be equal to or less than €31,553.37.

Shufaa can only afford a monthly payment of €500, so she enters into an *ijarah thumma al bai'* contract where the Islamic bank buys the car from the car dealer for €25,000. It then leases the car to Shufaa for a monthly payment of €500 a month for 60 months. At the end of the term of the *ijarah thumma al bai'* she will have paid a total of €30,000. To be competitive with Western loans, the final payment must be less than or equal to €31,553.37 − €30,000 = €1,553.37.

**Joint Venture** A *musharakah* is a contract between two parties to invest in a joint venture and share in any profit and losses that may arise from the investment. Companies that require partial funding for an investment can go to an Islamic bank and enter into a *musharakah* agreement and raise the required funds.

This type of financing alternative is an important alternative to standard bank loans, and illustrates the co-operative nature of the Islamic approach to doing business. In each transaction the supplier and demander of funds directly bears the cash flow risk of the underlying investment.

**Leasing** Leasing or *ijarah* is a form of financing that is available to companies. With a lease, the lessee pays rent for an asset for a period of time from the lessor. In this type of contract the payments are for the use of the asset. Lease financing is covered in more detail later in the text.

**Profit Sharing** In a *mudharabah* contract a businessman uses the funds of a bank or lender to invest in a project. The two parties share the profits of the business according to predetermined ratios. In this transaction the lender bears the financial risk of the investment, but gains from the specialized skills of the entrepreneur. Both parties benefit financially from the joint investment through the contribution of different skills or assets.

**Safekeeping** Like Western banks, Islamic banks require deposits to fund their activities. A company or individual may lodge funds at an Islamic bank and be able to draw those funds at any time from the bank. In some situations the bank may give the depositor a *hibah*, which is a small sum of money to compensate the depositor for leaving the funds with the Islamic banks. This is known as *wadiah*. Although this could be seen as an interest payment in any other name, because the *hibah* payment is not contractual, it is not viewed as such under Shariah law.

**Sale and Buyback**    With a *bai' al-inah* agreement, a company buys an asset from a seller and agrees to pay for it at some point in the future. The seller immediately buys the asset back at a discount.

## Bai' Al-inah

**EXAMPLE**
**14.7**

Shukran plc needs £2,700,000 to undertake a new warehouse expansion. They approach an Islamic bank, which agrees to participate in a *bai' al-inah* agreement. In this transaction the bank sells a building today to Shukran for £3,000,000 to be paid in one year. Immediately, the bank buys the building back for £2,700,000 today. In this transaction Shukran now has £2,700,000 but must pay £3,000,000 to the bank in one year. This is very similar to a one-year loan, but the crucial thing is that a real asset and not money is driving the payments. This is acceptable under Islamic law.

---

## Summary and Conclusions

The basic sources of long-term financing are long-term debt, preference shares, and ordinary shares.

This chapter described the essential features of each.

1    We emphasized that ordinary shareholders have:

   (a)    residual risk and return in a corporation;

   (b)    voting rights;

   (c)    limited liability if the corporation elects to default on its debt and must transfer some or all of its assets to the creditors.

2    Long-term debt involves contractual obligations, set out in indentures. There are many kinds of debt, but the essential feature is that debt involves a stated amount that must be repaid. Interest payments on debt are considered a business expense and are tax-deductible.

3    Preference shares have some of the features of debt and some of the features of ordinary equity. Holders of preference shares have preference in liquidation and in dividend payments compared with holders of ordinary equity.

4    Firms need financing for capital expenditures, working capital, and other long-term uses. Most of the financing is provided from internally generated cash flow.

5    In many parts of the world, where the Muslim faith is common, standard investment instruments that involve interest payments are not acceptable. In response, Islamic financing has developed to counter the problems associated with raising capital for firms wishing to adhere to Islamic principles.

---

 **Questions and Problems**

**CONCEPT**
**1–6**

1    **Ordinary Shares**    What is the difference between voting rights and cash flow rights? Do you think this will have an impact on share values?

2    **Corporate Long-term Debt**    Why do you think companies have issued bonds in different currencies, maturities, and coupon rates? Shouldn't the coupon be the same on every bond? Explain.

3    **Preference Shares**    Preference shares don't offer a corporate tax shield on the dividends paid. Why do we still observe some firms issuing preference shares?

4    **Patterns of Financing**  Why do you think companies in certain countries prefer different forms of financing?

5    **Hierarchies**  What is meant by hierarchies in long-term financing, and why are bonds higher in priority than shares?

6    **Islamic Financing**  What are the principles underlying Islamic financing?

7    **Preference Shares and Bond Yields**  The yields on non-convertible preference shares are lower than the yields on corporate bonds. Why is there a difference? Which investors are the primary holders of preference shares? Why?

8    **Corporate Financing**  What are the main differences between corporate debt and equity? Why do some firms try to issue equity in the guise of debt?

9    **Corporate Financing**  The Cable Company has £1 million of positive NPV projects it would like to accept. If Cable's managers follow the historical pattern of long-term financing for UK industrial firms, what will their financing strategy be?

10   **Preference Shares**  Do you think preference shares are more like debt or equity? Why?

11   **Long-Term Financing**  New equity issues are generally only a small portion of all new issues. At the same time, companies continue to issue new debt. Why do companies tend to issue little new equity but continue to issue new debt?

12   **Internal versus External Financing**  What is the difference between internal financing and external financing?

13   **Internal versus External Financing**  What factors influence a firm's choices of external versus internal equity financing?

14   **Islamic Financing**  You plan to raise funds through following Islamic principles. You require funding today of 3 billion Bahraini dinars and would like to pay it back in equal amounts over 10 years in monthly instalments. How would you do this?

15   **Equity Accounts**  Following are the equity accounts for Kerch Manufacturing:

|  | SKr |
|---|---|
| Ordinary Shares, SKr0.50 par value | 165,320 |
| Additional paid-in capital | 2,876,145 |
| Retained earnings | 2,370,025 |
| Total | 5,411,490 |

(a)   How many shares are outstanding?

(b)   At what average price were the shares sold?

(c)   What is the book value per share?

16   **Equity Accounts**  The Eastern Pine equity accounts for last year are as follows:

| Ordinary shares, £2 par value | |
|---|---|
| 500 shares outstanding | ? |
| Additional paid-in capital | 250,000 |
| Retained earnings | 750,000 |
| Total | ? |

(a)   What are the ordinary share and total equity values for the equity account?

(b)   The company has decided to issue 5,000 shares of equity at a price of £30 per share. Show the effects of the new issue on the equity accounts.

17   **Equity Accounts**   Ulrich plc's articles of incorporation authorize the firm to issue 500,000 shares of £5 par value ordinary equity, of which 410,000 shares have been issued. Those shares were sold at an average of 30 per cent over par. In the quarter that ended last week, net income was £650,000; 30 per cent of that income was paid as a dividend. The previous balance sheet showed a retained earnings balance of £3,545,000.

(a)   Create the equity statement for the company.

(b)   Suppose the company sells 25,000 of the authorized but unissued shares at the price of £4 per share. What will the new equity statement look like?

18   **Corporate Voting**   The shareholders of Unicorn plc need to elect seven new directors. There are 500,000 shares outstanding, currently trading at £34 per share. You would like to serve on the board of directors; unfortunately no one else will be voting for you. How much will it cost you to be certain that you can be elected if the company uses straight voting? How much will it cost you if the company uses cumulative voting?

19   **Murabaha**   You manage an Islamic financing division and have been approached by a company for funding of 6 billion Bahrain dinars. The company wishes to pay the funding back in equal instalments over 10 years through Islamic principles. Western banks quote comparable interest-paying loans of 8 per cent. Construct a *murabahah* contract that makes you competitive with your Western counterparts.

20   **Ijarah Thumma Al Bai'**   You run an Islamic financing division and have been approached by a customer for a 40,000 Bahrain dinar *ijarah thumma al bai'* financing deal. The customer wishes to pay a maximum of 1,000 Bahrain dinars per month over five years. Comparable loans in Western banks are quoted at 12 per cent interest. Construct a financing deal for your customer.

21   **Bai' Al-Inah**   You run an Islamic financing bank and have been approached by a company to construct a sale and buyback financing deal. The firm requires financing of €20 billion and wishes to pay back the financing over 10 years. Comparable Western loans quote 8 per cent interest for financing of this type. Construct a *bai' al-inah* contract for your customer.

## Practical Case Study

Choose a company from your country. Download its financial accounts and find out how its long-term funding is structured. Does it have more debt than equity? Are there any securities that have debt and equity characteristics? Try and ascertain the funding hierarchy for the company.

## Relevant Accounting Standards

As with all the chapters dealing with financial instruments, the main accounting standard is IAS39 *Financial Instruments: Recognition and Measurement*. IAS39 provides definitions for different types of financial security, and how these should be treated in the financial accounts. This can sometimes be problematic, because many securities have equity and bond-like features. Visit the IASPlus website (www.iasplus.com) for more information.

# Additional Reading

The literature in this section investigates the factors that determine long-term financing decisions. Megginson *et al.* (2004), Iannotta and Navone (2008) and Mitton (2008) are particularly relevant, given their international focus. Dittmann and Ulbricht (2008) consider equity restructuring, and should also be read for Chapter 19.

Brophy, D., P. Ouimet and C. Sialm (2009) 'Hedge funds as investors of last resort?', *Review of Financial Studies*, vol. 22, no. 2, pp. 541–574. **US**.

Chang, X., S. Dasgupta and G. Hilary (2006) 'Analyst coverage and financing decisions', *Journal of Finance*, vol. 61, no. 6, pp. 3009–3048. **US**.

Dittmann, I. and N. Ulbricht (2008) 'Timing and wealth effects of German dual class stock unifications', *European Financial Management*, vol. 14, no. 1, pp. 163–196. **Germany**.

Dittmar, A.K. and R.F. Dittmar (2008) 'The timing of financing decisions: an examination of the correlation in financing waves', *Journal of Financial Economics*, vol. 90, no. 1, pp. 59–83. **US**.

Iannotta, G. and M. Navone (2008) 'Which factors affect bond underwriting fees? The role of banking relationships', *European Financial Management*, vol. 14, no. 5, pp. 944–961. **International**.

Megginson, W.L., R.C. Nash, J.M. Netter and A.B. Poulsen (2004) 'The choice of private versus public capital markets: evidence from privatizations', *Journal of Finance*, vol. 59, no. 6, pp. 2835–2870. **International**.

Mitton, T. (2008) 'Why have debt ratios increased for firms in emerging markets?', *European Financial Management*, vol. 14, no. 1, pp. 127–151. **International**.

# Endnotes

1  H. DeAngelo and L. DeAngelo, 'Managerial ownership of voting rights: a study of public corporations with dual classes of common stock', *Journal of Financial Economics*, vol. 14 (1985).

2  L. Zingales, 'The value of a voting right: a study of the Milan Stock Exchange experience', *Journal of Finance*, vol. 7 (1994).

**Online LearningCentre**

To help you grasp the key concepts of this chapter check out the extra resources posted on the Online Learning Centre at **www.mcgraw-hill.co.uk/textbooks/hillier**

Among other helpful resources there are PowerPoint presentations, chapter outlines and mini-cases.

# Chapter 15

# Capital Structure: Basic Concepts

In recent years, analysts of British soccer clubs have become seriously concerned about the level of indebtedness in their largest football institutions. Prior to 2007, British football had seen unparalleled injections of cash from worldwide television deals. This additional spending power led to massive transfer fees, which in turn required more funding. Several clubs, including Liverpool and Manchester United, were bought over by wealthy individuals backed by significant debt. In time, the debt that funds British football will expire and need to be renewed. Several questions arise: Is the level of debt in British football too high? Will we see a fallout in the football sector in the same way as in the banking sector? How should a company choose a capital structure for itself, and what are the important factors driving this? We shall explore this and other issues in the following chapters.

## 15.1 The Capital Structure Question and the Pie Theory

How should a firm choose its debt–equity ratio? We call our approach to the capital structure question the pie model. If you are wondering why we chose this name, just take a look at Fig. 15.1. The pie in question is the sum of the financial claims of the firm – debt and equity in this case. We *define* the value of the firm to be this sum. Hence the value of the firm, $V$, is

$$V = B + S \tag{15.1}$$

where $B$ is the market value of the debt and $S$ is the market value of the equity. Figure 15.1 presents two possible ways of slicing this pie between equity and debt: 40 per cent/60 per cent and 60 per cent/40 per cent. If the goal of a firm's management is to make the firm as valuable as possible, then the firm should pick the debt–equity ratio that makes the pie – the total value – as big as possible.

This discussion begs two important questions:

1 Why should the shareholders in the firm care about maximizing the value of the entire firm? After all, the value of the firm is, by definition, the sum of both the debt and the equity. Instead, why should the shareholders not prefer the strategy that maximizes their interests only?

2 What ratio of debt to equity maximizes the shareholders' interests?

Let us examine each of the two questions in turn.

**Figure 15.1** Two pie models of capital structure

## 15.2 Maximizing Firm Value versus Maximizing Shareholder Interests

The following example shows that the capital structure that maximizes the value of the firm is the one that financial managers should choose for the shareholders.

### EXAMPLE 15.1

## Debt and Firm Value

Suppose the market value of J.J. Sprint plc is £1,000. The company currently has no debt, and each of J.J. Sprint's 100 shares sells for £10. A company such as J.J. Sprint with no debt is called an *unlevered* company. Further suppose that J.J. Sprint plans to borrow £500 and pay the £500 proceeds to shareholders as an extra cash dividend of £5 per share. After the issuance of debt, the firm becomes *levered*. The investments of the firm will not change as a result of this transaction. What will the value of the firm be after the proposed restructuring?

Management recognizes that, by definition, only one of three outcomes can occur from restructuring. Firm value after restructuring can be: (a) greater than the original firm value of £1,000; (b) equal to £1,000; or (c) less than £1,000. After consulting with investment bankers, management believes that restructuring will not change firm value more than £250 in either direction. Thus it views firm values of £1,250, £1,000 and £750 as the relevant range. The original capital structure and these three possibilities under the new capital structure are presented next:

|  | No debt (original capital structure) £ | Value of debt plus equity after payment of dividend (three possibilities) | | |
|---|---|---|---|---|
|  |  | (a) £ | (b) £ | (c) £ |
| Debt | 0 | 500 | 500 | 500 |
| Equity | 1,000 | 750 | 500 | 250 |
| Firm value | 1,000 | 1,250 | 1,000 | 750 |

Note that the value of equity is below £1,000 under any of the three possibilities. This can be explained in one of two ways. First, the table shows the value of the equity *after* the extra cash dividend is paid. Because cash is paid out, a dividend represents a partial liquidation of the firm. Consequently there is less value in the firm for the equity-holders after the dividend payment. Second, in the event of a future liquidation, shareholders will be paid only after bondholders have been paid in full. Thus the debt is an encumbrance of the firm, reducing the value of the equity.

Of course, management recognizes that there are infinite possible outcomes. These three are to be viewed as *representative* outcomes only. We can now determine the pay-off to shareholders under the three possibilities:

| | **Pay-off to Shareholders after Restructuring** | | |
|---|:---:|:---:|:---:|
| | **(a)** **£** | **(b)** **£** | **(c)** **£** |
| Capital gains | −250 | −500 | −750 |
| Dividends | 500 | 500 | 500 |
| Net gain or loss to shareholders | 250 | 0 | −250 |

No one can be sure ahead of time which of the three outcomes will occur. However, imagine that managers believe that outcome (a) is most likely. They should definitely restructure the firm, because the shareholders would gain £250. That is, although the price of the shares declines by £250 to £750, they receive £500 in dividends. Their net gain is £250 = −£250 + £500. Also, notice that the value of the firm would rise by £250 = £1,250 − £1,000.

Alternatively, imagine that managers believe that outcome (c) is most likely. In this case they should not restructure the firm, because the shareholders would expect a £250 loss. That is, the equity falls by £750 to £250, and they receive £500 in dividends. Their net loss is −£250 = −£750 + £500. Also, notice that the value of the firm would change by −£250 = £750 − £1,000.

Finally, imagine that the managers believe that outcome (b) is most likely. Restructuring would not affect the shareholders' interest, because the net gain to shareholders in this case is zero. Also notice that the value of the firm is unchanged if outcome (b) occurs.

This example explains why managers should attempt to maximize the value of the firm. In other words, it answers question 1 in Section 15.1. We find in this example the following wisdom:

**Changes in capital structure benefit the shareholders *if and only if* the value of the firm increases.**

Conversely, these changes hurt the shareholders if and only if the value of the firm decreases. This result holds true for capital structure changes of many different types.[1] As a corollary, we can say the following:

**Managers should choose the capital structure that they believe will have the highest firm value because this capital structure will be most beneficial to the firm's shareholders.**

Note, however, that this example does not tell us which of the three outcomes is most likely to occur. Thus it does not tell us whether debt should be added to J.J. Sprint's capital structure. In other words, it does not answer question 2 in Section 15.1. This second question is treated in the next section.

## 15.3 Financial Leverage and Firm Value: An Example

### Leverage and Returns to Shareholders

The previous section shows that the capital structure producing the highest firm value is the one that maximizes shareholder wealth. In this section we wish to determine that optimal capital structure. We begin by illustrating the effect of capital structure on returns to shareholders. We shall use a detailed example, which we encourage students to study carefully. Once we fully understand this example, we shall be ready to determine the optimal capital structure.

Autoveloce SpA currently has no debt in its capital structure. The firm is considering issuing debt to buy back some of its equity. Both its current and proposed capital structures are presented in Table 15.1. The firm's assets are €8,000. There are 400 shares of the all-equity

TABLE 15.1

| | Current | Proposed |
|---|---|---|
| Assets | €8,000 | €8,000 |
| Debt | €0 | €4,000 |
| Equity (market and book) | €8,000 | €4,000 |
| Interest rate | 10% | 10% |
| Market value/share | €20 | €20 |
| Shares outstanding | 400 | 200 |

The proposed capital structure has leverage, whereas the current structure is all equity.

**Table 15.1** Financial structure of Autoveloce SpA

TABLE 15.2

| | Recession | Expected | Expansion |
|---|---|---|---|
| Return on assets (ROA) | 5% | 15% | 25% |
| Earnings | €400 | €1,200 | €2,000 |
| Return on equity (ROE) = Earnings/Equity | 5% | 15% | 25% |
| Earnings per share (EPS) | €1.00 | €3.00 | €5.00 |

**Table 15.2** Autoveloce's current capital structure: no debt

TABLE 15.3

| | Recession | Expected | Expansion |
|---|---|---|---|
| Return on assets (ROA) | 5% | 15% | 25% |
| Earnings before interest (EBI) | €400 | €1,200 | €2,000 |
| Interest | −400 | −400 | −400 |
| Earnings after interest | €0 | €800 | €1,600 |
| Return on equity (ROE) | | | |
| = Earnings after interest/Equity | 0 | 20% | 40% |
| Earnings per share (EPS) | 0 | €4.00 | €8.00 |

**Table 15.3** Autoveloce's proposed capital structure

firm, implying a market value per share of €20. The proposed debt issue is for €4,000, leaving €4,000 in equity. The interest rate is 10 per cent. Assume in all our examples that debt is issued at par.

The effect of economic conditions on earnings per share is shown in Table 15.2 for the current capital structure (all equity). Consider first the middle column, where earnings are expected to be €1,200. Because assets are €8,000, the return on assets (ROA) is 15 per cent (= €1,200/€8,000). Assets equal equity for this all-equity firm, so return on equity (ROE) is also 15 per cent. Earnings per share (EPS) is €3.00 (= €1,200/400). Similar calculations yield EPS of €1.00 and €5.00 in the cases of recession and expansion, respectively.

The case of leverage is presented in Table 15.3. ROA in the three economic states is identical in Tables 15.2 and 15.3, because this ratio is calculated before interest is considered. Debt

FIGURE
**15.2**

**Figure 15.2** Financial leverage: EPS and EBI for Autoveloce SpA

is €4,000 here, so interest is €400 (= 0.10 × €4,000). Thus earnings after interest are €800 (= €1,200 – €400) in the middle (expected) case. Because equity is €4,000, ROE is 20 per cent (= €800/€4,000). Earnings per share are €4.00 (= €800/200). Similar calculations yield earnings of €0 and €8.00 for recession and expansion, respectively.

Tables 15.2 and 15.3 show that the effect of financial leverage depends on the company's earnings before interest. If earnings before interest are equal to €1,200, the return on equity (ROE) is higher under the proposed structure. If earnings before interest are equal to €400, the ROE is higher under the current structure.

This idea is represented in Fig. 15.2. The solid line represents the case of no leverage. The line begins at the origin, indicating that earnings per share (EPS) would be zero if earnings before interest (EBI) were zero. The EPS rise in tandem with a rise in EBI.

The dotted line represents the case of €4,000 of debt. Here EPS are negative if EBI are zero. This follows because €400 of interest must be paid, regardless of the firm's profits.

Now consider the slopes of the two lines. The slope of the dotted line (the line with debt) is higher than the slope of the solid line. This occurs because the levered firm has *fewer* shares of equity outstanding than the unlevered firm. Therefore any increase in EBI leads to a greater rise in EPS for the levered firm, because the earnings increase is distributed over fewer shares of equity.

Because the dotted line has a lower intercept but a higher slope, the two lines must intersect. The *break-even* point occurs at €800 of EBI. Were earnings before interest to be €800, both firms would produce €2 of earnings per share (EPS). Because €800 is break-even, earnings above €800 lead to greater EPS for the levered firm. Earnings below €800 lead to greater EPS for the unlevered firm.

## The Choice between Debt and Equity

Tables 15.2 and 15.3 and Fig. 15.2 are important, because they show the effect of leverage on earnings per share. Students should study the tables and figure until they feel comfortable

| TABLE 15.4 | | Recession | Expected | Expansion |
|---|---|---|---|---|
| **Strategy A: Buy 100 shares of levered equity** | | | | |
| EPS of *levered* equity (taken from last line of Table 15.3) | | €0 | €4 | €8 |
| Earnings per 100 shares | | 0 | 400 | 800 |
| Initial cost = 100 shares @ €20/share = €2,000 | | | | |
| **Strategy B: Homemade leverage** | | | | |
| Earnings per 200 shares in current *unlevered* Autoveloce | | €1 × 200 = 200 | €3 × 200 = 600 | €5 × 200 = 1,000 |
| Interest at 10% on €2,000 | | − 200 | − 200 | − 200 |
| Net earnings | | €0 | €400 | €800 |
| Initial cost = Cost of equity − Amount borrowed = 200 shares @ €20/share − €2,000 = €2,000 | | | | |

Investor receives the same pay-off whether she (a) buys shares in a levered corporation or (b) buys shares in an unlevered firm and borrows on personal account. Her initial investment is the same in either case. Thus the firm neither helps nor hurts her by adding debt to capital structure.

**Table 15.4** Pay-off and cost to shareholders of Autoveloce SpA under the proposed structure and under the current structure with homemade leverage

with the calculation of each number in them. However, we have not yet presented the punch line. That is, we have not yet stated which capital structure is better for Autoveloce.

At this point many students believe that leverage is beneficial, because EPS are expected to be €4.00 with leverage and only €3.00 without leverage. However, leverage also creates *risk*. Note that in a recession EPS are higher (€1.00 versus €0) for the unlevered firm. Thus a risk-averse investor might prefer the all-equity firm, whereas a risk-neutral (or less risk-averse) investor might prefer leverage. Given this ambiguity, which capital structure *is* better?

Modigliani and Miller (MM or M & M) have a convincing argument that a firm cannot change the total value of its outstanding securities by changing the proportions of its capital structure. In other words, the value of the firm is always the same under different capital structures. In still other words, no capital structure is any better or worse than any other capital structure for the firm's shareholders. This rather pessimistic result is the famous MM Proposition I.[2]

Their argument compares a simple strategy, which we call strategy A, with a two-part strategy, which we call strategy B. Both of these strategies for shareholders of Autoveloce are illustrated in Table 15.4. Let us now examine the first strategy.

*Strategy A*: Buy 100 shares of the levered equity
The first line in the top panel of Table 15.4 shows EPS for the proposed levered equity in the three economic states. The second line shows the earnings in the three states for an individual buying 100 shares. The next line shows that the cost of these 100 shares is €2,000.

Let us now consider the second strategy, which has two parts to it.

*Strategy B*: Homemade leverage

1   Borrow €2,000 from either a bank or, more likely, a brokerage house. (If the brokerage house is the lender, we say that this activity is *going on margin*.)

2   Use the borrowed proceeds plus your own investment of €2,000 (a total of €4,000) to buy 200 shares of the current unlevered equity at €20 per share.

The bottom panel of Table 15.4 shows pay-offs under strategy B, which we call the *home-made leverage* strategy. First observe the middle column, which indicates that 200 shares of the unlevered equity are expected to generate €600 of earnings. Assuming that the €2,000 is borrowed at a 10 per cent interest rate, the interest expense is €200 (= 0.10 × €2,000). Thus the net earnings are expected to be €400. A similar calculation generates net earnings of either €0 or €800 in recession or expansion, respectively.

Now let us compare these two strategies, both in terms of earnings per year and in terms of initial cost. The top panel of the table shows that strategy A generates earnings of €0, €400 and €800 in the three states. The bottom panel of the table shows that strategy B generates the *same* net earnings in the three states.

The top panel of the table shows that strategy A involves an initial cost of €2,000. Similarly, the bottom panel shows an *identical* net cost of €2,000 for strategy B.

This shows a very important result. Both the cost and the pay-off from the two strategies are the same. Thus we must conclude that Autoveloce is neither helping nor hurting its shareholders by restructuring. In other words, an investor is not receiving anything from corporate leverage that she could not receive on her own.

Note that, as shown in Table 15.1, the equity of the unlevered firm is valued at €8,000. Because the equity of the levered firm is €4,000 and its debt is €4,000, the value of the levered firm is also €8,000. Now suppose that, for whatever reason, the value of the levered firm were actually greater than the value of the unlevered firm. Here strategy A would cost more than strategy B. In this case an investor would prefer to borrow on his own account and invest in the equity of the unlevered firm. He would get the same net earnings each year as if he had invested in the equity of the levered firm. However, his cost would be less. The strategy would not be unique to our investor. Given the higher value of the levered firm, no rational investor would invest in the shares of the levered firm. Anyone desiring shares in the levered firm would get the same euro return more cheaply by borrowing to finance a purchase of the unlevered firm's shares. The equilibrium result would be, of course, that the value of the levered firm would fall and the value of the unlevered firm would rise until they became equal. At this point individuals would be indifferent between strategy A and strategy B.

This example illustrates the basic result of Modigliani–Miller (MM) and is, as we have noted, commonly called their Proposition I. We restate this proposition as follows:

**MM Proposition I (no taxes): The value of the levered firm is the same as the value of the unlevered firm.**

This is perhaps the most important result in all of corporate finance. In fact, it is generally considered the beginning point of modern corporate finance. Before MM, the effect of leverage on the value of the firm was considered complex and convoluted. Modigliani and Miller showed a blindingly simple result: if levered firms are priced too high, rational investors will simply borrow on their personal accounts to buy shares in unlevered firms. This substitution is oftentimes called *homemade leverage*. As long as individuals borrow (and lend) on the same terms as the firms, they can duplicate the effects of corporate leverage on their own.

The example of Autoveloce SpA shows that leverage does not affect the value of the firm. Because we showed earlier that shareholders' welfare is directly related to the firm's value, the example also indicates that changes in capital structure cannot affect the shareholders' welfare.

## A Key Assumption

The MM result hinges on the assumption that individuals can borrow as cheaply as corporations. If, alternatively, individuals can borrow only at a higher rate, we can easily show that corporations can increase firm value by borrowing.

Is this assumption of equal borrowing costs a good one? Individuals who want to buy shares and borrow can do so by establishing a margin account with a broker. Under this arrangement the broker lends the individual a portion of the purchase price. For example, the individual might buy €10,000 of equity by investing €6,000 of her own funds and borrowing

€4,000 from the broker. Should the shares be worth €9,000 on the next day, the individual's net worth or equity in the account would be €5,000 = €9,000 – €4,000.[3]

The broker fears that a sudden price drop will cause the equity in the individual's account to be negative, implying that the broker may not get her loan repaid in full. To guard against this possibility, stock exchange rules require that the individual make additional cash contributions (replenish her margin account) as the share price falls. Because (a) the procedures for replenishing the account have developed over many years and (b) the broker holds the equity as collateral, there is little default risk to the broker. In particular, if margin contributions are not made on time, the broker can sell the shares to satisfy her loan. Therefore brokers generally charge low interest, with many rates being only slightly above the risk-free rate.

By contrast, corporations frequently borrow using illiquid assets (e.g. plant and equipment) as collateral. The costs to the lender of initial negotiation and ongoing supervision, as well as of working out arrangements in the event of financial distress, can be quite substantial. Thus it is difficult to argue that individuals must borrow at higher rates than corporations.

## 15.4  Modigliani and Miller: Proposition II (No Taxes)

### Risk to Equity-holders Rises with Leverage

At an Autoveloce board meeting a director said, 'Well, maybe it does not matter whether the corporation or the individual levers – as long as some leverage takes place. Leverage benefits investors. After all, an investor's expected return rises with the amount of the leverage present.' He then pointed out that, as shown in Tables 15.2 and 15.3, the expected return on unlevered equity is 15 per cent, whereas the expected return on levered equity is 20 per cent.

However, another director replied, 'Not necessarily. Though the expected return rises with leverage, the *risk* rises as well.' This point can be seen from an examination of Tables 15.2 and 15.3. With earnings before interest (EBI) varying between €400 and €2,000, earnings per share (EPS) for the shareholders of the unlevered firm vary between €1.00 and €5.00. EPS for the shareholders of the levered firm vary between €0 and €8.00. This greater range for the EPS of the levered firm implies greater risk for the levered firm's shareholders. In other words, levered shareholders have better returns in good times than do unlevered shareholders, but have worse returns in bad times. The two tables also show greater range for the ROE of the levered firm's shareholders. The earlier interpretation concerning risk applies here as well.

The same insight can be taken from Fig. 15.2. The slope of the line for the levered firm is greater than the slope of the line for the unlevered firm. This means that the levered shareholders have better returns in good times than do unlevered shareholders, but have worse returns in bad times, implying greater risk with leverage. In other words, the slope of the line measures the risk to shareholders, because the slope indicates the responsiveness of ROE to changes in firm performance (earnings before interest).

### Proposition II: Required Return to Equity-holders Rises with Leverage

Because levered equity has greater risk, it should have a greater expected return as compensation. In our example, the market *requires* only a 15 per cent expected return for the unlevered equity, but it requires a 20 per cent expected return for the levered equity.

This type of reasoning allows us to develop MM Proposition II. Here MM argue that the expected return on equity is positively related to leverage, because the risk to equity-holders increases with leverage.

To develop this position, recall that the firm's weighted average cost of capital, $R_{WACC}$, can be written as[4]

$$R_{WACC} = \frac{S}{B + S} \times R_S + \frac{B}{B + S} \times R_B \qquad (15.2)$$

where $R_B$ is the cost of debt; $R_S$ is the expected return on equity, also called the *cost of equity* or the *required return on equity*; $R_{WACC}$ is the firm's weighted average cost of capital; $B$ is the market value of the firm's debt or bonds; and $S$ is the market value of the firm's shares or equity.

Equation (15.2) is quite intuitive. It simply says that a firm's weighted average cost of capital is a weighted average of its cost of debt and its cost of equity. The weight applied to debt is the proportion of debt in the capital structure, and the weight applied to equity is the proportion of equity in the capital structure. Calculations of $R_{WACC}$ from Eq. (15.2) for both the unlevered and the levered firm are presented in Table 15.5.

An implication of MM Proposition I is that $R_{WACC}$ is a constant for a given firm, regardless of the capital structure.[5] For example, Table 15.5 shows that $R_{WACC}$ for Autoveloce is 15 per cent, with or without leverage.

Let us now define $R_0$ to be the *cost of capital for an all-equity firm*. For Autoveloce SpA, $R_0$ is calculated as

$$R_0 = \frac{\text{Expected earnings to unlevered firm}}{\text{Unlevered equity}} = \frac{€1,200}{€8,000} = 15\%$$

As can be seen from Table 15.5, $R_{WACC}$ is equal to $R_0$ for Autoveloce. In fact, $R_{WACC}$ must *always* equal $R_0$ in a world without corporate taxes.

Proposition II states the expected return on equity, $R_S$, in terms of leverage. The exact relationship, derived by setting $R_{WACC} = R_0$ and then rearranging Eq. (15.2), is[6]

MM Proposition II (no taxes):

$$R_S = R_0 + \frac{B}{S} \times (R_0 - R_B) \qquad (15.3)$$

---

**TABLE 15.5**

$$R_{WACC} = \frac{B}{B+S} \times R_B + \frac{S}{B+S} \times R_S$$

Unlevered firm:

$$15\% = \frac{0}{€8,000} \times 10\%^* + \frac{€8,000}{€8,000} \times 15\%^†$$

Levered firm:

$$15\% = \frac{€4,000}{€8,000} \times 10\%^* + \frac{€4,000}{€8,000} \times 20\%^‡$$

*10% is the cost of debt.
†From the 'Expected' column in Table 15.2 we learn that expected earnings after interest for the unlevered firm are €1,200. From Table 15.1 we learn that equity for the unlevered firm is

$$\frac{\text{Expected earnings after interest}}{\text{Equity}} = \frac{€1,200}{€8,000} = 15\%$$

‡From the 'Expected' column in Table 15.3 we learn that expected earnings after interest for the levered firm are €800. From Table 15.1 we learn that equity for the levered firm is €4,000. Thus $R_S$ for the levered firm is

$$\frac{\text{Expected earnings after interest}}{\text{Equity}} = \frac{€800}{€4,000} = 20\%$$

**Table 15.5** Cost of capital calculations for Autoveloce

FIGURE
15.3

$$R_S = R_0 + (R_0 - R_B)B/S$$

$R_S$ is the cost of equity.
$R_B$ is the cost of debt.
$R_0$ is the cost of capital for an all-equity firm.
$R_{WACC}$ is a firm's weighted average cost of capital. In a world with no taxes, $R_{WACC}$ for a levered firm is equal to $R_0$.
$R_0$ is a single point whereas $R_S$, $R_B$ and $R_{WACC}$ are all entire lines.

The cost of equity capital, $R_S$, is positively related to the firm's debt–equity ratio. The firm's weighted average cost of capital, $R_{WACC}$, is invariant to the firm's debt–equity ratio.

**Figure 15.3** The cost of equity, the cost of debt, and the weighted average cost of capital: MM Proposition II with no corporate taxes

Equation (15.3) implies that the required return on equity is a linear function of the firm's debt–equity ratio. Examining Eq. (15.3), we see that if $R_0$ exceeds the cost of debt, $R_B$, then the cost of equity rises with increases in the debt–equity ratio, $B/S$. Normally $R_0$ should exceed $R_B$. That is, because even unlevered equity is risky, it should have an expected return greater than that of riskless debt. Note that Eq. (15.3) holds for Autoveloce in its levered state:

$$0.20 = 0.15 + \frac{€4,000}{€4,000}(0.15 - 0.10)$$

Figure 15.3 graphs Eq. (15.3). As you can see, we have plotted the relation between the cost of equity, $R_S$, and the debt–equity ratio, $B/S$, as a straight line. What we witness in Eq. (15.3) and illustrate in Fig. 15.3 is the effect of leverage on the cost of equity. As the firm raises the debt–equity ratio, each euro of equity is levered with additional debt. This raises the risk of equity and therefore the required return, $R_S$, on the equity.

Figure 15.3 also shows that $R_{WACC}$ is unaffected by leverage, a point we have already made. (It is important for students to realize that $R_0$, the cost of capital for an all-equity firm, is represented by a single dot on the graph. By contrast, $R_{WACC}$ is an entire line.)

## MM Propositions I and II

EXAMPLE
15.2

Canary Motors, an all-equity firm, has expected earnings of £10 million per year in perpetuity. The firm pays all of its earnings out as dividends, so the £10 million may also be viewed as the shareholders' expected cash flow. There are 10 million shares outstanding, implying expected annual cash flow of £1 per share. The cost of capital for this unlevered firm is 10 per cent. In addition, the firm will soon build a new plant for £4 million. The plant is expected to generate additional cash flow of £1 million per year. These figures can be described as follows:

| Current company | New plant |
|---|---|
| Cash flow: £10 million | Initial outlay: £4 million |
| Number of outstanding shares: 10 million | Additional annual cash flow: £1 million |

The project's net present value is

$$-£4 \text{ million} + \frac{£1 \text{ million}}{0.1} = £6 \text{ million}$$

assuming that the project is discounted at the same rate as the firm as a whole. Before the market knows of the project, the *market value* balance sheet of the firm is this:

| CANARY MOTORS Market Value Balance Sheet (All Equity) | | |
|---|---|---|
| Old assets: $\dfrac{£10 \text{ million}}{0.1} = £100 \text{ million}$ | | Equity $\begin{array}{l}£100 \text{ million}\\(10 \text{ million shares})\end{array}$ |

The value of the firm is £100 million because the cash flow of £10 million per year is capitalized (discounted) at 10 per cent. A share of equity sells for £10 (= £100 million/10 million) because there are 10 million shares outstanding.

The firm will issue £4 million of either equity or debt. Let us consider the effect of equity and debt financing in turn.

**Equity Financing**  Imagine that the firm announces that in the near future it will raise £4 million in equity to build a new plant. The share price, and therefore the value of the firm, will rise to reflect the positive net present value of the plant. According to efficient markets, the increase occurs immediately. That is, the rise occurs on the day of the announcement, not on the date of either the onset of construction of the plant or the forthcoming equity offering. The market value balance sheet becomes this:

| CANARY MOTORS Market Value Balance Sheet (upon announcement of equity issue to construct plant) | | | |
|---|---|---|---|
| Old assets | £100 million | Equity | £106 million (10 million shares) |
| NPV of plant: $-£4 \text{ million} + \dfrac{£1 \text{ million}}{0.1}$ | £6 million | | |
| Total assets | £106 million | | |

Note that the NPV of the plant is included in the market value balance sheet. Because the new shares have not yet been issued, the number of outstanding shares remains 10 million. The price per share has now risen to £10.60 (= £106 million/10 million) to reflect news concerning the plant.

Shortly thereafter, £4 million of equity is issued, or *floated*. Because the shares are selling at £10.60 per share, 377,358 (= £4 million/£10.60) shares are issued. Imagine that funds are put in the bank *temporarily* before being used to build the plant. The market value balance sheet becomes this:

| CANARY MOTORS Market Value Balance Sheet (upon issuance of equity but before construction begins on plant) | | | |
|---|---|---|---|
| Old assets | £100 million | Equity | £110 million (10,377,358 shares) |
| NPV of plant | £6 million | | |
| Proceeds from new issue of equity (currently placed in bank) | £4 million | | |
| Total assets | £110 million | | |

The number of shares outstanding is now 10,377,358, because 377,358 new shares were issued. The share price is £10.60 (= £110,000,000/10,377,358). Note that the price has not changed. This is consistent with efficient capital markets, because the share price should move as a result of new information only.

Of course, the funds are placed in the bank only temporarily. Shortly after the new issue, the £4 million is given to a contractor, who builds the plant. To avoid problems in discounting, we assume that the plant is built immediately. The market value balance sheet then looks like this:

**CANARY MOTORS**
**Market Value Balance Sheet**
**(upon completion of the plant)**

| | | | |
|---|---|---|---|
| Old assets | £100 million | Equity | £110 million (10,377,358 shares) |
| PV of plant: $\dfrac{£1 \text{ million}}{0.1} =$ | £10 million | | |
| Total assets | £110 million | | |

Though total assets do not change, the composition of the assets does change. The bank account has been emptied to pay the contractor. The present value of cash flows of £1 million a year from the plant is reflected as an asset worth £10 million. Because the building expenditures of £4 million have already been paid, they no longer represent a future cost. Hence they no longer reduce the value of the plant. According to efficient capital markets, the share price remains £10.60.

Expected yearly cash flow from the firm is £11 million, £10 million of which comes from the old assets and £1 million from the new. The expected return to shareholders is

$$R_S = \frac{£11 \text{ million}}{£110 \text{ million}} = 0.10$$

Because the firm is all equity, $R_S = R_0 = 0.10$.

**Debt Financing**    Alternatively, imagine the firm announces that in the near future it will borrow £4 million at 6 per cent to build a new plant. This implies yearly interest payments of £240,000 (= £4,000,000 × 6%). Again, the share price rises immediately to reflect the positive net present value of the plant. Thus we have the following:

**CANARY MOTORS**
**Market Value Balance Sheet**
**(upon announcement of debt issue to construct plant)**

| | | | |
|---|---|---|---|
| Old assets | £100 million | Equity | £106 million (10 million shares) |
| NPV of plant: $-£4 \text{ million} + \dfrac{£1 \text{ million}}{0.1}$ | £6 million | | |
| Total assets | £106 million | | |

The value of the firm is the same as in the equity financing case, because (a) the same plant is to be built, and (b) MM proved that debt financing is neither better nor worse than equity financing.

At some point £4 million of debt is issued. As before, the funds are placed in the bank temporarily. The market value balance sheet becomes this:

**CANARY MOTORS**
**Market Value Balance Sheet**
**(upon debt issuance but before construction begins on plant)**

| | | | |
|---|---|---|---|
| Old assets | £100 million | Debt | £4 million |
| NPV of plant | £6 million | Equity | £106 million (10 million shares) |
| Proceeds from debt issue (currently invested in bank) | £4 million | | |
| Total assets | £110 million | Debt plus equity | £110 million |

Note that debt appears on the right side of the market value balance sheet. The share price is still £10.60, in accordance with our discussion of efficient capital markets.

Finally the contractor receives £4 million and builds the plant. The market value balance sheet turns into this:

| CANARY MOTORS<br>Market Value Balance Sheet<br>(upon completion of the plant) | | | |
|---|---|---|---|
| Old assets | £100 million | Debt | £4 million |
| PV of plant | £10 million | Equity | £106 million<br>(10 million shares) |
| Total assets | £110 million | Debt plus equity | £110 million |

The only change here is that the bank account has been depleted to pay the contractor. The shareholders expect yearly cash flow after interest of

$$\underset{\substack{\text{Cash flow on}\\\text{old assets}}}{£10,000,000} + \underset{\substack{\text{Cash flow on}\\\text{new assets}}}{£1,000,000} - \underset{\substack{\text{Interest:}\\\text{£4 million} \times 6\%}}{£240,000} = £10,760,000$$

The shareholders expect to earn a return of

$$\frac{£10,760,000}{£106,000,000} = 10.15\%$$

This return of 10.15 per cent for levered shareholders is higher than the 10 per cent return for the unlevered shareholders. This result is sensible because, as we argued earlier, levered equity is riskier. In fact, the return of 10.15 per cent should be exactly what MM Proposition II predicts. This prediction can be verified by plugging values into

$$R_S = R_0 + \frac{B}{S} \times (R_0 - R_B)$$

We obtain

$$10.15\% = 10\% + \frac{£4,000,000}{£106,000,000} \times (10\% - 6\%)$$

This example was useful for two reasons. First, we wanted to introduce the concept of market value balance sheets, a tool that will prove useful elsewhere in the text. Among other things, this technique allows us to calculate the share price of a new issue of shares. Second, the example illustrates three aspects of Modigliani and Miller:

1   The example is consistent with MM Proposition I, because the value of the firm is £110 million after either equity or debt financing.

2   Students are often more interested in share price than in firm value. We show that the share price is always £10.60, regardless of whether debt or equity financing is used.

3   The example is consistent with MM Proposition II. The expected return to shareholders rises from 10 to 10.15 per cent, just as Eq. (15.3) states. This rise occurs because the shareholders of a levered firm face more risk than do the shareholders of an unlevered firm.

## MM: An Interpretation

The Modigliani–Miller results indicate that managers cannot change the value of a firm by repackaging the firm's securities. Though this idea was considered revolutionary when it was originally proposed in the late 1950s, the MM approach and proof have since met with wide acclaim.[7]

MM argue that the firm's overall cost of capital cannot be reduced as debt is substituted for equity, even though debt appears to be cheaper than equity. The reason for this is that, as the firm adds debt, the remaining equity becomes more risky. As this risk rises, the cost of equity capital rises as a result. The increase in the cost of the remaining equity capital offsets the higher proportion of the firm financed by low-cost debt. In fact, MM prove that the two effects exactly offset each other, so that both the value of the firm and the firm's overall cost of capital are invariant to leverage.

## In Their Own Words

### In Professor Miller's Words . . .

The Modigliani–Miller results are not easy to understand fully. This point is related in a story told by Merton Miller.*

How difficult it is to summarize briefly the contribution of the [Modigliani–Miller] papers was brought home to me very clearly last October after Franco Modigliani was awarded the Nobel Prize in Economics in part – but, of course, only in part – for the work in finance. The television camera crews from our local stations in Chicago immediately descended upon me. 'We understand,' they said, 'that you worked with Modigliani some years back in developing these M and M theorems and we wonder if you could explain them briefly to our television viewers.'

'How briefly?' I asked.

'Oh, take ten seconds,' was the reply.

Ten seconds to explain the work of a lifetime! Ten seconds to describe two carefully reasoned articles, each running to more than thirty printed pages and each with sixty or so long footnotes! When they saw the look of dismay on my face, they said, 'You don't have to go into details. Just give us the main points in simple, commonsense terms.'

The main point of the first or cost-of-capital article was, in principle at least, simple enough to make. It said that in an economist's ideal world of complete and perfect capital markets and with full and symmetric information among all market participants, the total market value of all the securities issued by a firm was governed by the earning power and risk of its underlying real assets and was independent of how the mix of securities issued to finance it was divided between debt instruments and equity capital . . .

Such a summary, however, uses too many shorthanded terms and concepts, like perfect capital markets, that are rich in connotations to economists but hardly so to the general public. So I thought, instead, of an analogy that we ourselves had invoked in the original paper . . .

'Think of the firm,' I said, 'as a gigantic tub of whole milk. The farmer can sell the whole milk as is. Or he can separate out the cream and sell it at a considerably higher price than the whole milk would bring. (That's the analogy of a firm selling low-yield and hence high-priced debt securities.) But, of course, what the farmer would have left would be skim milk with low butterfat content and that would sell for much less than whole milk. That corresponds to the levered equity. The M and M proposition says that if there were no costs of separation (and, of course, no government dairy support programmes), the cream plus the skim milk would bring the same price as the whole milk.'

The television people conferred among themselves and came back to inform me that it was too long, too complicated, and too academic.

'Don't you have anything simpler?' they asked. I thought of another way that the M and M proposition is presented these days, which emphasizes the notion of market completeness and stresses the role of securities as devices for 'partitioning' a firm's pay-offs in each possible state of the world among the group of its capital suppliers.

'Think of the firm,' I said, 'as a gigantic pizza, divided into quarters. If now you cut each quarter in half into eighths, the M and M proposition says that you will have more pieces but not more pizza.'

Again there was a whispered conference among the camera crew, and the director came back and said:

'Professor, we understand from the press releases that there were two M and M propositions. Can we try the other one?'

[Professor Miller tried valiantly to explain the second proposition, though this was apparently even more difficult to get across. After his attempt:]

Once again there was a whispered conversation. They shut the lights off. They folded up their equipment. They thanked me for giving them the time. They said that they'd get back to me. But I knew that I had somehow lost my chance to start a new career as a packager of economic wisdom for TV viewers in convenient ten-second bites. Some have the talent for it . . . and some just don't.

*Taken from *GSB Chicago*, University of Chicago (Autumn 1986).

Food found its way into this chapter earlier when we viewed the firm as a pie. MM argue that the size of the pie does not change, no matter how shareholders and bondholders divide it. MM say that a firm's capital structure is irrelevant; it is what it is by some historical accident. The theory implies that firms' debt–equity ratios could be anything. They are what they are because of whimsical and random managerial decisions about how much to borrow and how much equity to issue.

## Summary of Modigliani–Miller Propositions without Taxes

**Assumptions**

- No taxes.

- No transaction costs.

- Individuals and corporations borrow at same rate.

**Results**

Proposition I: $V_L = V_U$ (Value of levered firm equals value of unlevered firm)

Proposition II: $R_S = R_0 + \dfrac{B}{S}(R_0 - R_B)$

**Intuition**

Proposition I: Through homemade leverage individuals can either duplicate or undo the effects of corporate leverage.

Proposition II: The cost of equity rises with leverage because the risk to equity rises with leverage.

Although scholars are always fascinated with far-reaching theories, students are perhaps more concerned with real-world applications. Do real-world managers follow MM by treating capital structure decisions with indifference? Unfortunately for the theory, virtually all companies in certain industries, such as banking, choose high debt–equity ratios. Conversely, companies in other industries, such as pharmaceuticals, choose low debt–equity ratios. In fact, almost any industry has a debt–equity ratio to which companies in that industry tend to adhere. Thus companies do not appear to be selecting their degree of leverage in a frivolous or random manner. Because of this, financial economists (including MM themselves) have argued that real-world factors may have been left out of the theory.

Though many of our students have argued that individuals can borrow only at rates above the corporate borrowing rate, we disagreed with this argument earlier in the chapter. But when we look elsewhere for unrealistic assumptions in the theory, we find two:[8]

1    Taxes were ignored.

2    Bankruptcy costs and other agency costs were not considered.

We turn to taxes in the next section. Bankruptcy costs and other agency costs will be treated in the next chapter. A summary of the main Modigliani–Miller results without taxes is presented in the nearby boxed section.

## 15.5  Corporate Taxes

### The Basic Insight

The previous part of this chapter showed that firm value is unrelated to debt in a world without taxes. We now show that in the presence of corporate taxes the firm's value is positively related to its debt. The basic intuition can be seen from a pie chart, such as the one in Fig. 15.4. Consider the all-equity firm on the left. Here both shareholders and tax authorities have claims on the firm. The value of the all-equity firm is, of course, that part of the pie owned by the shareholders. The proportion going to taxes is simply a cost.

The pie on the right for the levered firm shows three claims: shareholders, debtholders, and taxes. The value of the levered firm is the sum of the value of the debt and the value of the equity. In selecting between the two capital structures in the picture, a financial manager should select the one with the higher value. Assuming that the total area is the same for both pies,[9] value is maximized for the capital structure paying the least in taxes. In other words, the manager should choose the capital structure that the government hates the most.

We shall show that, because of a quirk in corporate tax law, the proportion of the pie allocated to taxes is less for the levered firm than it is for the unlevered firm. Thus managers should select high leverage.

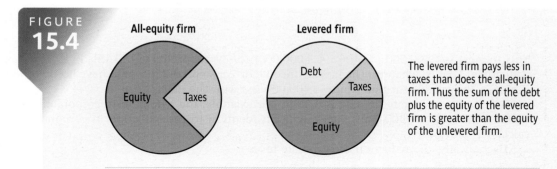

**Figure 15.4**  Two pie models of capital structure under corporate taxes

EXAMPLE
15.3

# Taxes and Cash Flow

Wasserprodukte GmbH has a corporate tax rate, $t_C$, of 35 per cent and expected earnings before interest and taxes (EBIT) of €1 million each year. Its entire earnings after taxes are paid out as dividends.

The firm is considering two alternative capital structures. Under Plan I Wasserprodukte would have no debt in its capital structure. Under Plan II the company would have €4,000,000 of debt, $B$. The cost of debt, $R_B$, is 10 per cent.

The chief financial officer for Wasserprodukte makes the following calculations:

|  | Plan I (€) | Plan II (€) |
|---|---|---|
| Earnings before interest and corporate taxes (EBIT) | 1,000,000 | 1,000,000 |
| Interest ($R_B B$) | 0 | 400,000 |
| Earnings before taxes (EBT) = (EBIT − $R_B B$) | 1,000,000 | 600,000 |
| Taxes ($t_C = 0.35$) | 350,000 | 210,000 |
| Earnings after corporate taxes (EAT) = [(EBIT − $R_B B$) × (1 − $t_C$)] | 650,000 | 390,000 |
| Total cash flow to both shareholders and bondholders [EBIT × (1 − $t_C$) + $t_C R_B B$] | 650,000 | 790,000 |

The most relevant numbers for our purposes are the two on the bottom line. Dividends, which are equal to earnings after taxes in this example, are the cash flow to shareholders, and interest is the cash flow to bondholders. Here we see that more cash flow reaches the owners of the firm (both shareholders and bondholders) under Plan II. The difference is €140,000 = €790,000 − €650,000. It does not take us long to realize the source of this difference. The government receives less tax under Plan II (€210,000) than it does under Plan I (€350,000). The difference here is €140,000 = €350,000 − €210,000.

This difference occurs because the way governments treat interest is different from the way they treat earnings going to shareholders.[10] Interest totally escapes corporate taxation, whereas earnings after interest but before corporate taxes (EBT) are taxed at the corporate tax rate.

## Present Value of the Tax Shield

The previous discussion shows a tax advantage to debt or, equivalently, a tax disadvantage to equity. We now want to value this advantage. The interest in monetary terms is

$$\text{Interest} = \underbrace{R_B}_{\text{Interest rate}} \times \underbrace{R}_{\substack{\text{Amount} \\ \text{borrowed}}}$$

This interest is €400,000 (= 10% × €4,000,000) for Wasserprodukte. All this interest is tax-deductible. That is, whatever the taxable income of Wasserprodukte would have been without the debt, the taxable income is now €400,000 *less* with the debt.

Because the corporate tax rate is 0.35 in our example, the reduction in corporate taxes is €140,000 (= 0.35 × €400,000). This number is identical to the reduction in corporate taxes calculated previously.

Algebraically, the reduction in corporate taxes is

$$\underbrace{t_C}_{\substack{\text{Corporate} \\ \text{tax rate}}} \times \underbrace{R_B \times B}_{\text{interest paid}} \tag{15.4}$$

That is, whatever the taxes that a firm would pay each year without debt, the firm will pay $t_C R_B B$ less with the debt of $B$. Expression (15.4) is often called the *tax shield from debt*. Note that it is an *annual* amount.

As long as the firm expects to be paying tax, we can assume that the cash flow in Expression (15.4) has the same risk as the interest on the debt. Thus its value can be determined by discounting at the cost of debt, $R_B$. Assuming that the cash flows are perpetual, the present value of the tax shield is

$$\frac{t_C R_B B}{R_B} = t_C B$$

## Value of the Levered Firm

We have just calculated the present value of the tax shield from debt. Our next step is to calculate the value of the levered firm. The annual after-tax cash flow of an unlevered firm is

$$\text{EBIT} \times (1 - t_C)$$

where EBIT is earnings before interest and taxes. The value of an unlevered firm (that is, a firm with no debt) is the present value of $\text{EBIT} \times (1 - t_C)$:

$$V_U = \frac{\text{EBIT} \times (1 - t_C)}{R_0}$$

Here $V_U$ is the present value of an unlevered firm; $\text{EBIT} \times (1 - t_C)$ represents firm cash flows after corporate taxes; $t_C$ is the corporate tax rate; and $R_0$ is the cost of capital to an all-equity firm. As can be seen from the formula, $R_0$ now discounts *after-tax* cash flows.

As shown previously, leverage increases the value of the firm by the tax shield, which is $t_C B$ for perpetual debt. Thus we merely add this tax shield to the value of the unlevered firm to get the value of the levered firm.

We can write this algebraically as follows:[11]

**MM Proposition I (corporate taxes):**

$$V_L = \frac{\text{EBIT} \times (1 - t_C)}{R_0} + \frac{t_C R_B B}{R_B} = V_U + t_C B \qquad (15.5)$$

Equation (15.5) is MM Proposition I under corporate taxes. The first term in Eq. (15.5) is the value of the cash flows of the firm with no debt tax shield. In other words, this term is equal to $V_U$, the value of the all-equity firm. The value of the levered firm is the value of an all-equity firm plus $t_C B$, the tax rate times the value of the debt. $t_C B$ is the present value of the tax shield in the case of perpetual cash flows.[12] Because the tax shield increases with the amount of debt, the firm can raise its total cash flow and its value by substituting debt for equity.

## MM with Corporate Taxes

EXAMPLE
**15.4**

Divided Airlines is currently an unlevered firm. The company expects to generate €153.85 in earnings before interest and taxes (EBIT) in perpetuity. The corporate tax rate is 35 per cent, implying after-tax earnings of €100. All earnings after tax are paid out as dividends.

The firm is considering a capital restructuring to allow €200 of debt. Its cost of debt capital is 10 per cent. Unlevered firms in the same industry have a cost of equity capital of 20 per cent. What will the new value of Divided Airlines be?

The value of Divided Airlines will be equal to

$$V_L = \frac{\text{EBIT} \times (1 - t_C)}{R_0} + t_C B$$

$$= \frac{€100}{0.20} + (0.35 \times €200)$$

$$= €500 + €70$$

$$= €570$$

The value of the levered firm is €570, which is greater than the unlevered value of €500. Because $V_L = B + S$, the value of levered equity, $S$, is equal to €570 − €200 = €370. The value of Divided Airlines as a function of leverage is illustrated in Fig. 15.5.

**Figure 15.5** The effect of financial leverage on firm value: MM with corporate taxes in the case of Divided Airlines

## Expected Return and Leverage under Corporate Taxes

MM Proposition II under no taxes proposes a positive relationship between the expected return on equity and leverage. This result occurs because the risk of equity increases with leverage. The same intuition also holds in a world of corporate taxes. The exact formula in a world of corporate taxes is this:[13]

MM Proposition II (corporate taxes):

$$R_S = R_0 + \frac{B}{S} \times (1 - t_C) \times (R_0 - R_B) \tag{15.6}$$

Applying the formula to Divided Airlines, we get

$$R_S = 0.2351 = 0.20 + \frac{200}{370} \times (1 - 0.35) \times (0.20 - 0.10)$$

This calculation is illustrated in Fig. 15.6.

Whenever $R_0 > R_B$, $R_S$ increases with leverage, a result that we also found in the no-tax case. As stated earlier in this chapter, $R_0$ should exceed $R_B$. That is, because equity (even unlevered equity) is risky, it should have an expected return greater than that on the less risky debt.

FIGURE
**15.6**

$$R_S = R_0 + (1 - t_C)(R_0 - R_B)B/S$$
$$= 0.20 + \left(0.65 \times 0.10 \times \frac{200}{370}\right)$$
$$= 0.2351$$

Financial leverage adds risk to the firm's equity. As compensation, the cost of equity rises with the firm's risk. Note that $R_0$ is a single point whereas $R_S$, $R_B$ and $R_{WACC}$ are all entire lines.

**Figure 15.6** The effect of financial leverage on the cost of debt and equity capital

Let's check our calculations by determining the value of the levered equity in another way. The algebraic formula for the value of levered equity is

$$S = \frac{(EBIT - R_B B) \times (1 - t_C)}{R_S}$$

The numerator is the expected cash flow to levered equity after interest and taxes. The denominator is the rate at which the cash flow to equity is discounted.

For Divided Airlines we get

$$\frac{(€153.85 - 0.10 \times €200)(1 - 0.35)}{0.2351} = €370$$

which is the same result we obtained earlier (ignoring a small rounding error).

## The Weighted Average Cost of Capital, $R_{WACC}$, and Corporate Taxes

In Chapter 12 we defined the weighted average cost of capital (with corporate taxes) as follows (note that $V_L = S + B$):

$$R_{WACC} = \frac{S}{V_L} R_S + \frac{B}{V_L} R_B (1 - t_C)$$

Note that the cost of debt capital, $R_B$, is multiplied by $(1 - t_C)$, because interest is tax-deductible at the corporate level. However, the cost of equity, $R_S$, is not multiplied by this factor, because dividends are not deductible. In the no-tax case $R_{WACC}$ is not affected by leverage. This result is reflected in Fig. 15.3, which we discussed earlier. However, because debt is tax-advantaged relative to equity, it can be shown that $R_{WACC}$ declines with leverage in a world with corporate taxes. This result can be seen in Fig. 15.6.

For Divided Airlines, $R_{WACC}$ is equal to

$$R_{WACC} = \left(\frac{370}{570} \times 0.2351\right) + \left(\frac{200}{570} \times 0.10 \times 0.65\right)$$
$$= 0.1754$$

Divided Airlines has reduced its $R_{WACC}$ from 0.20 (with no debt) to 0.1754 with reliance on debt. This result is intuitively pleasing, because it suggests that when a firm lowers its $R_{WACC}$, the firm's value will increase. Using the $R_{WACC}$ approach, we can confirm that the value of Divided Airlines is €570:

$$V_L = \frac{\text{EBIT} \times (1 - t_C)}{R_{WACC}}$$

$$= \frac{€100}{0.1754}$$

$$= €570$$

## Share Prices and Leverage under Corporate Taxes

At this point students often believe the numbers – or at least are too intimidated to dispute them. However, they sometimes think we have asked the wrong question. 'Why are we choosing to maximize the value of the firm?' they will say. 'If managers are looking out for the shareholders' interests, why aren't they trying to maximize share price?' If this question occurred to you, you have come to the right section.

Our response is twofold. First, we showed in the first section of this chapter that the capital structure that maximizes firm value is also the one that most benefits the interests of the shareholders.

However, that general explanation is not always convincing to students. As a second procedure, we calculate the share price of Divided Airlines both before and after the exchange of debt for equity. We do this by presenting a set of market value balance sheets. The market value balance sheet for the company in its all-equity form can be represented as follows:

| DIVIDED AIRLINES Market Value Balance Sheet (all-equity firm) | | | |
|---|---|---|---|
| Physical assets | | Equity | €500 |
| $\dfrac{€153.85}{0.20} \times (1 - 0.35) =$ €500 | | | (100 shares) |

Assuming that there are 100 shares outstanding, each share is worth €5 = €500/100.

Next imagine the company announces that in the near future it will issue €200 of debt to buy back €200 of equity. We know from our previous discussion that the value of the firm will rise to reflect the tax shield of debt. If we assume that capital markets price securities efficiently, the increase occurs immediately. That is, the rise occurs on the day of the announcement, not on the date of the debt-for-equity exchange. The market value balance sheet now becomes this:

| DIVIDED AIRLINES Market Value Balance Sheet (upon announcement of debt issue) | | | |
|---|---|---|---|
| Physical assets | €500 | Equity | €570 |
| | | | (100 shares) |
| Present value of tax shield: $t_C B = 35\% \times €200 =$ | 70 | | |
| Total assets | €570 | | |

Note that the debt has not yet been issued. Therefore only equity appears on the right side of the balance sheet. Each share is now worth €570/100 = €5.70, implying that the shareholders have benefited by €70. The shareholders gain because they are the owners of a firm that has improved its financial policy.

The introduction of the tax shield to the balance sheet is perplexing to many students. Although physical assets are tangible, the ethereal nature of the tax shield bothers these students. However, remember that an asset is any item with value. The tax shield has value because it reduces the stream of future taxes. The fact that one cannot touch the shield in the way that one can touch a physical asset is a philosophical, not a financial, consideration.

At some point the exchange of debt for equity occurs. Debt of €200 is issued, and the proceeds are used to buy back shares. How many shares are repurchased? Because shares are now selling at €5.70 each, the number of shares that the firm acquires is €200/€5.70 = 35.09. This leaves 64.91 (= 100 – 35.09) shares outstanding. The market value balance sheet is now this:

| DIVIDED AIRLINES Market Value Balance Sheet (after exchange has taken place) | | | |
|---|---|---|---|
| Physical assets | €500 | Equity (100 – 35.09 = 64.91 shares) | €370 |
| Present value of tax shield | 70 | Debt | 200 |
| Total assets | €570 | Debt plus equity | €570 |

Each share is worth €370/64.91 = €5.70 after the exchange. Notice that the share price does not change on the exchange date. As we mentioned, the share price moves on the date of the announcement only. Because the shareholders participating in the exchange receive a price equal to the market price per share after the exchange, they do not care whether they exchange their equity.

This example was provided for two reasons. First, it shows that an increase in the value of the firm from debt financing leads to an increase in the price of the shares. In fact, the shareholders capture the entire €70 tax shield. Second, we wanted to provide more work with market value balance sheets.

A summary of the main results of Modigliani–Miller with corporate taxes is presented in the following boxed section:

## Summary of Modigliani–Miller Propositions with Corporate Taxes

### Assumptions

- Corporations are taxed at the rate $t_C$, on earnings after interest.

- No transaction costs.

- Individuals and corporations borrow at same rate.

### Results

Proposition I: $V_L = V_U + t_C B$ (for a firm with perpetual debt)

Proposition II: $R_S = R_0 + \dfrac{B}{S}(1 - t_C)(R_0 - R_B)$

### Intuition

Proposition I: Because corporations can deduct interest payments but not dividend payments, corporate leverage lowers tax payments.

Proposition II: The cost of equity rises with leverage because the risk to equity rises with leverage.

# 15.6 Personal Taxes

So far in this chapter we have considered corporate taxes only. Because interest on debt is tax-deductible, whereas dividends on equity are not deductible, we argued that the tax system gives firms an incentive to issue debt. But corporations are not the only ones paying taxes; individuals must pay taxes on both the dividends and the interest that they receive. We cannot fully understand the effect of taxes on capital structure until all taxes, both corporate and personal, are considered.

## The Basics of Personal Taxes

Let's begin by examining an all-equity firm that receives €1 of pre-tax earnings. If the corporate tax rate is $t_c$, the firm pays taxes $t_c$, leaving itself with earnings after taxes of $1 - t_C$. Let's assume that this entire amount is distributed to the shareholders as dividends. If the personal tax rate on share dividends is $t_S$, the shareholders pay taxes of $(1 - t_C) \times t_S$, leaving them with $(1 - t_C) \times (1 - t_S)$ after taxes.

Alternatively, imagine that the firm is financed with debt. Here, the entire €1 of earnings will be paid out as interest, because interest is deductible at the corporate level. If the personal tax rate on interest is $t_B$, the bondholders pay taxes of $t_B$, leaving them with $1 - t_B$ after taxes.

## The Effect of Personal Taxes on Capital Structure

To explore the effect of personal taxes on capital structure, let's consider three questions:

1   Ignoring costs of financial distress, what is the firm's optimal capital structure if dividends and interest are taxed at the same personal rate: that is, $t_S = t_B$?

   The firm should select the capital structure that gets the most cash into the hands of its investors. This is tantamount to selecting a capital structure that minimizes the total amount of taxes at both the corporate and personal levels.

   As we have said, beginning with €1 of pre-tax corporate earnings, shareholders receive $(1 - t_C) \times (1 - t_S)$, and bondholders receive $1 - t_B$. We can see that if $t_S = t_B$, bondholders receive more than shareholders. Thus the firm should issue debt, not equity, in this situation. Intuitively, income is taxed twice – once at the corporate level and once at the personal level – if it is paid to shareholders. Conversely, income is taxed only at the personal level if it is paid to bondholders.

   Note that the assumption of no personal taxes, which we used in the previous chapter, is a special case of the assumption that both interest and dividends are taxed at the same rate. Without personal taxes, the shareholders receive $1 - t_C$ while the bondholders receive €1. Thus, as we stated in a previous section, firms should issue debt in a world without personal taxes.

2   Under what conditions will the firm be indifferent between issuing equity or debt?

   The firm will be indifferent if the cash flow to shareholders equals the cash flow to bondholders. That is, the firm is indifferent when

$$(1 - t_C) \times (1 - t_S) = 1 - t_B \tag{15.7}$$

3   What should companies do in the real world?

   Although this is clearly an important question, it is, unfortunately, a hard one – perhaps too hard to answer definitively. Nevertheless, let's begin by working with the highest tax rates for a specific country, the UK. As of 2009, the corporate tax rate was 28 per cent. For investors in the highest tax bracket, interest income was taxed at 40 per cent. Investors in this highest bracket faced an effective 25 per cent tax rate on dividends.

   At these rates, the left side of Eq. (15.7) becomes $(1 - 0.28) \times (1 - 0.25)$, which equals 0.54. The right side of the equation becomes $1 - 0.28$, which equals 0.72. Because any rational firm would rather get £0.72 instead of £0.54 into its investors' hands, it appears at first glance that firms should prefer debt over equity, just as we argued earlier.

Does anything else in the real world alter this conclusion? Perhaps: our discussion on equity income is not yet complete. Firms can repurchase shares with excess cash instead of paying a dividend. Although capital gains in the UK are taxed at 18 per cent, the shareholder pays a capital gains tax only on the gain from sale, not on the entire proceeds from the repurchase. Thus the *effective* tax rate on capital gains is actually lower than 18 per cent. Because firms both pay dividends and repurchase shares, the effective personal tax rate on *share distributions* must be below 18 per cent.

This lower effective tax rate makes equity issuance less burdensome, but the lower rate will not induce any firm to choose shares over bonds. For example, suppose that the effective tax rate on share distributions is 10 per cent. From every pound of pre-tax corporate

| TABLE 15.6 | | | |
|---|---|---|---|
| Country | Corporation tax | Income tax | Capital gains tax |
| Australia | 30% | 17–47% | Income tax rate (halved if asset is held for 1 year) |
| Austria | 25% | 21–50% | 25% |
| Belgium | 33.99% | 25–50% | 0% |
| China | 25% | 5–45% | 20% (0% for equities) |
| Denmark | 28% | 38–59% | Treated as income with special levies |
| Finland | 26% | 25–53% | 26–28% |
| France | 33.33% | 5.5–40% | 26% |
| Germany | 38.36% | 15–42% | Individual, 0%; company, 25% |
| Greece | 25% | 0–40% | Treated as income |
| India | 30% | 0–30% | Treated as income tax if asset is held for less than 3 years; 20% if held for more |
| Ireland | 12.5% | 20–41% | 20% |
| Italy | 37.25% | 23–45% | 12.5% |
| Netherlands | 20%/23.5%/25.5% | 34.15–52% | 0% |
| Norway | 28% | 28–54.3% | 28% |
| Poland | 19% | 19–40% | 19% |
| Portugal | 25% | 10.5–42% | 10% if shares are held for less than one year; 0% otherwise |
| Russia | 24% | 13% | 13% |
| South Africa | 36.89% | 18–40% | Individuals, 0–10%; companies, 14.5% |
| Spain | 32.5% | 15–45% | 35%; 15% for long-term holdings |
| Sweden | 28% | 0–55% | 30% |
| Switzerland | 21.3% | 0–45.5% | 0% |
| Tanzania | 35% | 0–35% | 0% |
| Thailand | 30% | 5–37% | Treated as income |
| Turkey | 20% | 15–35% | Treated as income |
| United Kingdom | 28% | 0–40% | 18% |
| United States | 40% | 0–44.3% | Treated as income if asset is held for less than 1 year; otherwise 15% |

*Source*: Federation of International Trade Associations, KPMG.

**Table 15.6** Tax rates around the world, 2009

income, shareholders in the UK receive $(1 - 0.28) \times (1 - 0.10)$, which equals £0.648. This amount is less than the £0.72 that bondholders receive. In fact, as long as the effective tax rate on equity income is positive, bondholders will still receive more than shareholders from a pound of pre-tax corporate income. And we have assumed that all bondholders face a tax rate of 40 per cent on interest income. In reality, plenty of bondholders are in lower tax brackets, further tipping the scales towards bond financing.

Given that bonds appear to have the tax advantage in the UK, is there anything that might cause British firms to issue equity rather than bonds? Yes – the same costs of financial distress we discussed earlier in the chapter. We previously said that these costs are an offset to debt's tax advantage, causing firms to employ less than 100 per cent leverage. The same point applies in the presence of personal taxes. And as long as the personal tax rate on equity income is below the personal tax rate on interest, the tax advantage to debt is smaller in a world with personal taxes than in a world without personal taxes. Thus the optimal amount of debt will be lower in a world with personal taxes than in a world without them.

## International Comparison of Tax Rates

Tax systems across the world are extremely varied, and the various combinations of corporation tax, income tax and capital gains tax make a lot of the discussion on tax and capital structure very country specific. The previous section considered the UK's tax system in detail. However, this has little relevance to an Italian financial manager whose shareholders are all from Italy. A sample of country tax rates is presented in Table 15.6. However, the reader should be mindful of these figures for several reasons. First, every country's tax system is a complex set of rules that include credits, discounts and exemptions for various taxpayer groups. The figures are effective tax rates for listed firms that won't correspond exactly to every individual's situation. Second, tax systems and tax rates change regularly. This means that some of the figures may become out of date over time (the figures are correct at January 2009). In fact, the authors fully expect these rates to change as the full implications of the 2008 global financial crisis are impounded into each country's economy and its government finances.

## Summary and Conclusions

1   We began our discussion of the capital structure decision by arguing that the particular capital structure that maximizes the value of the firm is also the one that provides the most benefit to the shareholders.

2   In a world of no taxes, the famous Proposition I of Modigliani and Miller proves that the value of the firm is unaffected by the debt–equity ratio. In other words, a firm's capital structure is a matter of indifference in that world. The authors obtain their results by showing that either a high or a low corporate ratio of debt to equity can be offset by homemade leverage. The result hinges on the assumption that individuals can borrow at the same rate as corporations, an assumption we believe to be quite plausible.

3   MM's Proposition II in a world without taxes states that

$$R_S = R_0 + \frac{B}{S}(R_0 - R_B)$$

This implies that the expected rate of return on equity (also called the *cost of equity* or the *required return on equity*) is positively related to the firm's leverage. This makes intuitive sense, because the risk of equity rises with leverage, a point illustrated by Fig. 15.2.

4   Although the above work of MM is quite elegant, it does not explain the empirical findings on capital structure very well. MM imply that the capital structure decision is a matter of

indifference, whereas the decision appears to be a weighty one in the real world. To achieve real-world applicability, we next considered corporate taxes.

5   In a world with corporate taxes but no bankruptcy costs, firm value is an increasing function of leverage. The formula for the value of the firm is

$$V_L = V_U + t_C B$$

Expected return on levered equity can be expressed as

$$R_S = R_0 + (1 - t_C) \times (R_0 - R_B) \times \frac{B}{S}$$

Here, value is positively related to leverage. This result implies that firms should have a capital structure composed almost entirely of debt. Because real-world firms select more moderate levels of debt, the next chapter considers modifications to the results of this chapter.

6   If distributions to shareholders are taxed at a lower effective personal tax rate than are interest payments, the tax advantage to debt at the corporate level is partially offset.

## connect  Questions and Problems

**CONCEPT**
**1 – 6**

1   **Capital Structure and the Pie Theory**  Use a pizza analogy to explain why capital structure should not influence firm value in a world with no taxes, transaction costs or financial distress costs.

2   **Maximizing Firm Value versus Maximizing Shareholder Interests**  Explain why, in a world with no taxes, transaction costs or financial distress costs, maximizing firm value is the same as maximizing share value.

3   **Financial Leverage and Firm Value**  In a world with no taxes, no transaction costs and no costs of financial distress, is the following statement true, false, or uncertain? 'If a firm issues equity to repurchase some of its debt, the share price of the firm's equity will rise because the shares are less risky.' Explain.

4   **Financial Leverage and Firm Value: An Example**  In a world with no taxes, no transaction costs and no costs of financial distress, is the following statement true, false, or uncertain? 'Moderate borrowing will not increase the required return on a firm's equity.' Explain.

5   **Corporate Taxes**  How do corporate taxes affect the Modigliani–Miller theory of capital structure? Illustrate your answer with a practical example.

6   **Personal Taxes**  When would a firm be indifferent between issuing debt or equity? Illustrate your answer with a practical example.

**REGULAR**
**7 – 39**

7   **MM Propositions**  List the three assumptions that lie behind the Modigliani–Miller theory in a world without taxes. Are these assumptions reasonable in the real world? Explain.

8   **MM Propositions**  What is the quirk in the tax code that makes a levered firm more valuable than an otherwise identical unlevered firm?

9   **Business Risk versus Financial Risk**  Explain what is meant by business and financial risk. Suppose firm A has greater business risk than firm B. Is it true that firm A also has a higher cost of equity capital? Explain.

10  **MM Propositions**   How would you answer in the following debate?

Q:  Isn't it true that the riskiness of a firm's equity will rise if the firm increases its use of debt financing?

A:  Yes, that's the essence of MM Proposition II.

Q:  And isn't it true that, as a firm increases its use of borrowing, the likelihood of default increases, thereby increasing the risk of the firm's debt?

A:  Yes.

Q:  In other words, increased borrowing increases the risk of the equity *and* the debt?

A:  That's right.

Q:  Well, given that the firm uses only debt and equity financing, and given that the risks of both are increased by increased borrowing, does it not follow that increasing debt increases the overall risk of the firm and therefore decreases the value of the firm?

A:  ??

11  **Optimal Capital Structure**   Is there an easily identifiable debt–equity ratio that will maximize the value of a firm? Why or why not?

12  **Financial Leverage**   Why is the use of debt financing referred to as financial 'leverage'?

13  **Homemade Leverage**   What is homemade leverage?

14  **Capital Structure Goal**   What is the basic goal of financial management with regard to capital structure?

15  **EBIT and Leverage**   Geld NV has no debt outstanding and a total market value of €150,000. Earnings before interest and taxes, EBIT, are projected to be €14,000 if economic conditions are normal. If there is strong expansion in the economy, then EBIT will be 30 per cent higher. If there is a recession, then EBIT will be 60 per cent lower. Geld is considering a €60,000 debt issue with a 5 per cent interest rate. The proceeds will be used to repurchase shares of equity. There are currently 2,500 shares outstanding. Ignore taxes for this problem.

(a)  Calculate earnings per share, EPS, under each of the three economic scenarios before any debt is issued. Also calculate the percentage changes in EPS when the economy expands or enters a recession.

(b)  Repeat part (a) assuming that Geld goes through with recapitalization. What do you observe?

16  **EBIT, Taxes, and Leverage**   Repeat parts (a) and (b) in Problem 15 assuming Geld has a tax rate of 20 per cent.

17  **ROE and Leverage**   Suppose the company in Problem 15 has a market-to-book ratio of 1.0.

(a)  Calculate return on equity, ROE, under each of the three economic scenarios before any debt is issued. Also calculate the percentage changes in ROE for economic expansion and recession, assuming no taxes.

(b)  Repeat part (a) assuming the firm goes through with the proposed recapitalization.

(c)  Repeat parts (a) and (b) of this problem assuming the firm has a tax rate of 20 per cent.

18  **Break-Even EBIT**   Rolston plc is comparing two different capital structures: an all-equity plan (Plan I) and a levered plan (Plan II). Under Plan I Rolston would have 150,000 shares of equity outstanding. Under Plan II there would be 60,000 shares of equity outstanding and £1.5 million in debt outstanding. The interest rate on the debt is 10 per cent and there are no taxes.

(a)  If EBIT is £200,000, which plan will result in the higher EPS?

(b)  If EBIT is £700,000, which plan will result in the higher EPS?

(c)  What are the break-even EBIT?

19  **MM and Share Value**  In Problem 18, use MM Proposition I to find the share price under each of the two proposed plans. What is the value of the firm?

20  **Break-Even EBIT and Leverage**  Kolby SpA is comparing two different capital structures. Plan I would result in 1,100 shares of equity and €16,500 in debt. Plan II would result in 900 shares of equity and €27,500 in debt. The interest rate on the debt is 10 per cent.

(a)  Ignoring taxes, compare both of these plans with an all-equity plan, assuming that EBIT will be €10,000. The all-equity plan would result in 1,400 shares of equity outstanding. Which of the three plans has the highest EPS? The lowest?

(b)  In part (a) what are the break-even levels of EBIT for each plan as compared with that for an all-equity plan? Is one higher than the other? Why?

(c)  Ignoring taxes, when will EPS be identical for Plans I and II?

(d)  Repeat parts (a), (b) and (c) assuming that the corporate tax rate is 31.4 per cent. Are the break-even levels of EBIT different from before? Why or why not?

21  **Leverage and Share Value**  Ignoring taxes in Problem 20, what is the price per share of equity under Plan I? Plan II? What principle is illustrated by your answers?

22  **Homemade Leverage**  Star plc, a prominent consumer products firm, is debating whether or not to convert its all-equity capital structure to one that is 40 per cent debt. Currently there are 2,000 shares outstanding, and the share price is £70. EBIT are expected to remain at £16,000 per year for ever. The interest rate on new debt is 8 per cent, and there are no taxes.

(a)  Ms Brown, a shareholder of the firm, owns 100 shares of equity. What is her cash flow under the current capital structure, assuming the firm has a dividend payout rate of 100 per cent?

(b)  What will Ms Brown's cash flow be under the proposed capital structure of the firm? Assume that she keeps all 100 of her shares.

(c)  Suppose Star does convert, but Ms Brown prefers the current all-equity capital structure. Show how she could unlever her shares to re-create the original capital structure.

(d)  Using your answer to part (c), explain why Star's choice of capital structure is irrelevant.

23  **Homemade Leverage and WACC**  ABC AG and XYZ AG are identical firms in all respects except for their capital structure. ABC is all equity financed with NKr600,000 in equity shares. XYZ uses both shares and perpetual debt; its equity is worth NKr300,000 and the interest rate on its debt is 10 per cent. Both firms expect EBIT to be NKr73,000. Ignore taxes.

(a)  Knut owns NKr30,000 worth of XYZ's shares. What rate of return is he expecting?

(b)  Show how Knut could generate exactly the same cash flows and rate of return by investing in ABC and using homemade leverage.

(c)  What is the cost of equity for ABC? What is it for XYZ?

(d)  What is the WACC for ABC? For XYZ? What principle have you illustrated?

24  **MM**  Nina plc uses no debt. The weighted average cost of capital is 13 per cent. If the current market value of the equity is £35 million and there are no taxes, what is EBIT?

25  **MM and Taxes**  In the previous question, suppose the corporate tax rate is 28 per cent. What is EBIT in this case? What is the WACC? Explain.

26  **Calculating WACC**  Weston Industries has a debt–equity ratio of 1.5. Its WACC is 12 per cent, and its cost of debt is 12 per cent. The corporate tax rate is 35 per cent.

(a)  What is Weston's cost of equity capital?

(b)  What is Weston's unlevered cost of equity capital?

(c) What would the cost of equity be if the debt–equity ratio were 2? What if it were 1.0? What if it were zero?

27 **Calculating WACC** Shadow plc has no debt but can borrow at 8 per cent. The firm's WACC is currently 12 per cent, and the tax rate is 28 per cent.

(a) What is Shadow's cost of equity?

(b) If the firm converts to 25 per cent debt, what will its cost of equity be?

(c) If the firm converts to 50 per cent debt, what will its cost of equity be?

(d) What is Shadow's WACC in part (b)? In part (c)?

28 **MM and Taxes** Bruce & Co. expects its EBIT to be £95,000 every year for ever. The firm can borrow at 11 per cent. Bruce currently has no debt, and its cost of equity is 22 per cent. If the tax rate is 28 per cent, what is the value of the firm? What will the value be if Bruce borrows £60,000 and uses the proceeds to repurchase shares?

29 **MM and Taxes** In Problem 28, what is the cost of equity after recapitalization? What is the WACC? What are the implications for the firm's capital structure decision?

30 **MM Proposition I** Levered plc and Unlevered plc are identical in every way except their capital structures. Each company expects to earn £96 million before interest per year in perpetuity, with each company distributing all its earnings as dividends. Levered's perpetual debt has a market value of £275 million and costs 8 per cent per year. Levered has 4.5 million shares outstanding, currently worth £100 per share. Unlevered has no debt and 10 million shares outstanding, currently worth £80 per share. Neither firm pays taxes. Is Levered's equity a better buy than Unlevered's equity?

31 **MM** Tool Manufacturing has an expected EBIT of £35,000 in perpetuity and a tax rate of 28 per cent. The firm has £70,000 in outstanding debt at an interest rate of 9 per cent, and its unlevered cost of capital is 14 per cent. What is the value of the firm according to MM Proposition I with taxes? Should Tool change its debt–equity ratio if the goal is to maximize the value of the firm? Explain.

32 **Firm Value** Old School Corporation expects an EBIT of £9,000 every year for ever. Old School currently has no debt, and its cost of equity is 17 per cent. The firm can borrow at 10 per cent. If the corporate tax rate is 28 per cent, what is the value of the firm? What will the value be if Old School converts to 50 per cent debt? To 100 per cent debt?

33 **MM Proposition I with Taxes** Bigelli SpA is financed entirely with equity. The company is considering a loan of €1 million. The loan will be repaid in equal instalments over the next two years, and it has an 8 per cent interest rate. The company's tax rate is 35 per cent. According to MM Proposition I with taxes, what would be the increase in the value of the company after the loan?

34 **MM Proposition I without Taxes** Alpha NV and Beta NV are identical in every way except their capital structures. Alpha NV, an all-equity firm, has 5,000 shares of equity outstanding, currently worth €20 per share. Beta NV uses leverage in its capital structure. The market value of Beta's debt is €25,000, and its cost of debt is 12 per cent. Each firm is expected to have earnings before interest of €35,000 in perpetuity. Neither firm pays taxes. Assume that every investor can borrow at 12 per cent per year.

(a) What is the value of Alpha NV?

(b) What is the value of Beta NV?

(c) What is the market value of Beta NV's equity?

(d) How much will it cost to purchase 20 per cent of each firm's equity?

(e) Assuming each firm meets its earnings estimates, what will be the euro return to each position in part (d) over the next year?

(f) Construct an investment strategy in which an investor purchases 20 per cent of Alpha's equity and replicates both the cost and euro return of purchasing 20 per cent of Beta's equity.

(g) Is Alpha's equity more or less risky than Beta's equity? Explain.

35 **Cost of Capital** Acetate SA has equity with a market value of €20 million and debt with a market value of €10 million. Treasury bills that mature in one year yield 8 per cent per year, and the expected return on the market portfolio over the next year is 18 per cent. The beta of Acetate's equity is 0.90. The firm pays no taxes.

(a) What is Acetate's debt–equity ratio?

(b) What is the firm's weighted average cost of capital?

(c) What is the cost of capital for an otherwise identical all-equity firm?

36 **Homemade Leverage** The Veblen Company and the Knight Company are identical in every respect except that Veblen is not levered. The market value of Knight Company's 6 per cent bonds is SKr1 million. Financial information for the two firms appears here. All earnings streams are perpetuities. Neither firm pays taxes. Both firms distribute all earnings available to ordinary shareholders immediately.

|  | Veblen (SKr) | Knight (SKr) |
|---|---|---|
| Projected operating income | 300,000 | 300,000 |
| Year-end interest on debt | – | 60,000 |
| Market value of equity | 2,400,000 | 1,714,000 |
| Market value of debt | – | 1,000,000 |

(a) An investor who can borrow at 6 per cent per year wishes to purchase 5 per cent of Knight's equity. Can he increase his Krona return by purchasing 5 per cent of Veblen's equity if he borrows so that the initial net costs of the two strategies are the same?

(b) Given the two investment strategies in (a), which will investors choose? When will this process cease?

37 **MM Propositions** Locomotive plc is planning to repurchase part of its ordinary share equity by issuing corporate debt. As a result, the firm's debt–equity ratio is expected to rise from 40 per cent to 50 per cent. The firm currently has £7.5 million worth of debt outstanding. The cost of this debt is 10 per cent per year. Locomotive expects to have an EBIT of £3.75 million per year in perpetuity. Locomotive pays no taxes.

(a) What is the market value of Locomotive plc before and after the repurchase announcement?

(b) What is the expected return on the firm's equity before the announcement of the share repurchase plan?

(c) What is the expected return on the equity of an otherwise identical all-equity firm?

(d) What is the expected return on the firm's equity after the announcement of the share repurchase plan?

38 **Share Value and Leverage** Green Manufacturing plc plans to announce that it will issue £2 million of perpetual debt and use the proceeds to repurchase equity. The bonds will sell at par with a 6 per cent annual coupon rate. Green is currently an all-equity firm worth £10 million with 500,000 shares of equity outstanding. After the sale of the bonds, Green will maintain the new capital structure indefinitely. Green currently generates annual pre-tax earnings of £1.5 million. This level of earnings is expected to remain constant in perpetuity. Green is subject to a corporate tax rate of 28 per cent.

(a) What is the expected return on Green's equity before the announcement of the debt issue?

(b) Construct Green's market value balance sheet before the announcement of the debt issue. What is the price per share of the firm's equity?

(c) Construct Green's market value balance sheet immediately after the announcement of the debt issue.

(d) What is Green's share price immediately after the repurchase announcement?

(e) How many shares will Green repurchase as a result of the debt issue? How many shares of equity will remain after the repurchase?

(f) Construct the market value balance sheet after the restructuring.

(g) What is the required return on Green's equity after the restructuring?

39 **MM with Taxes** Williamsen GmbH, has a debt–equity ratio of 2.5. The firm's weighted average cost of capital is 15 per cent, and its pre-tax cost of debt is 10 per cent. Williamsen is subject to a corporate tax rate of 35 per cent.

(a) What is Williamsen's cost of equity capital?

(b) What is Williamsen's unlevered cost of equity capital?

(c) What would Williamson's weighted average cost of capital be if the firm's debt–equity ratio were 0.75? What if it were 1.5?

40 **Weighted Average Cost of Capital** In a world of corporate taxes only, show that the $R_{\text{WACC}}$ can be written as $R_{\text{WACC}} = R_0 \times [1 - t_C(B/V)]$.

41 **Cost of Equity and Leverage** Assuming a world of corporate taxes only, show that the cost of equity, $R_S$, is as given in the chapter by MM Proposition II with corporate taxes.

42 **Business and Financial Risk** Assume a firm's debt is risk-free, so that the cost of debt equals the risk-free rate, $R_f$. Define $\beta_A$ as the firm's *asset* beta – that is, the systematic risk of the firm's assets. Define $\beta_S$ to be the beta of the firm's equity. Use the capital asset pricing model, CAPM, along with MM Proposition II to show that $\beta_S = \beta_A \times (1 + B/S)$, where $B/S$ is the debt–equity ratio. Assume the tax rate is zero.

43 **Shareholder Risk** Suppose a firm's business operations mirror movements in the economy as a whole very closely – that is, the firm's asset beta is 1.0. Use the result of Problem 42 to find the equity beta for this firm for debt–equity ratios of 0, 1, 5 and 20. What does this tell you about the relationship between capital structure and shareholder risk? How is the shareholders' required return on equity affected? Explain.

44 **Unlevered Cost of Equity** Beginning with the cost of capital equation – that is,

$$R_{\text{WACC}} = \frac{S}{B + S} R_S + \frac{B}{B + S} R_B$$

show that the cost of equity capital for a levered firm can be written as follows:

$$R_S = R_0 + \frac{B}{S}(R_0 - R_B)$$

# Stephenson Real Estate Recapitalization

**MINI CASE**

Stephenson Real Estate was founded 25 years ago by the current CEO, Robert Stephenson. The company purchases real estate, including land and buildings, and rents the property to tenants. The company has shown a profit every year for the past 18 years, and the shareholders are satisfied with the company's management. Prior to founding Stephenson Real Estate, Robert was the founder and CEO of a failed sheep-farming operation. The resulting bankruptcy made him extremely averse to debt financing. As a result, the company is entirely equity financed, with 15 million shares outstanding. The shares currently trade at £32.50 per share.

Stephenson is evaluating a plan to purchase a huge tract of land in south-eastern England for £100 million. The land will subsequently be leased to tenant farmers. This purchase is expected to increase Stephenson's annual pre-tax earnings by £25 million in perpetuity. Kim Weyand, the company's new CFO, has been put in charge of the project. Kim has determined that the company's current cost of capital is 12.5 per cent. She feels that the company would be more valuable if it included debt in its capital structure, so she is evaluating whether the company should issue debt to entirely finance the project. Based on some conversations with investment banks, she thinks that the company can issue bonds at par value with an 8 per cent coupon rate. Based on her analysis, she also believes that a capital structure in the range of 70 per cent equity/30 per cent debt would be optimal. If the company goes beyond 30 per cent debt, its bonds would carry a lower rating and a much higher coupon, because the possibility of financial distress and the associated costs would rise sharply. Stephenson has a 28 per cent corporate tax rate.

1   If Stephenson wishes to maximize its total market value, would you recommend that it issue debt or equity to finance the land purchase? Explain.

2   Construct Stephenson's market value balance sheet before it announces the purchase.

3   Suppose Stephenson decides to issue equity to finance the purchase.

   (a)   What is the net present value of the project?

   (b)   Construct Stephenson's market value balance sheet after it announces that the firm will finance the purchase using equity. What would be the new price per share of the firm's equity? How many shares will Stephenson need to issue to finance the purchase?

   (c)   Construct Stephenson's market value balance sheet after the equity issue but before the purchase has been made. How many shares of equity does Stephenson have outstanding? What is the price per share of the firm's equity?

   (d)   Construct Stephenson's market value balance sheet after the purchase has been made.

4   Suppose Stephenson decides to issue debt to finance the purchase.

   (a)   What will the market value of the Stephenson company be if the purchase is financed with debt?

   (b)   Construct Stephenson's market value balance sheet after both the debt issue and the land purchase. What is the price per share of the firm's equity?

5   Which method of financing maximizes the per-share price of Stephenson's equity?

## Practical Case Study

1   Locate the annual balance sheets for the British firms Thomson Reuters plc, Capita Group plc and Next plc. For each company calculate the long-term debt–equity ratio for the prior two years. Why would these companies use such different capital structures?

2   Download the annual income statements for Marks and Spencer plc. For the most recent year, calculate the average tax rate and EBIT, and find the total interest expense. From the annual balance sheets calculate the total long-term debt (including the portion due within one year). Using the interest expense and total long-term debt, calculate the average cost of debt. Next, find the estimated beta for Marks and Spencer on the Yahoo! Finance website. Use this reported beta, a current T-bill rate for the UK, and the historical average market risk premium found in a previous chapter to calculate the levered cost of equity. Now calculate the unlevered cost of equity, then the unlevered EBIT. What is the unlevered value of Marks and Spencer? What is the value of the interest tax shield and the value of the levered Marks and Spencer?

## Additional Reading

If you wish to delve deeper into the theory of capital structure and how it affects corporate strategy, you should read:

Hillier, D., M. Grinblatt and S. Titman (2008) *Financial Markets and Corporate Strategy: European Edition*, 1st edn, McGraw-Hill.

An excellent paper that looks at the determinants of capital structure in a number of different countries is given below. The paper should also be read as part of your reading for Chapter 2 on macro governance and Chapter 16.

Antoniou, A., Y. Guney and K. Paudyal (2008) 'The determinants of capital structure: capital market-oriented versus bank-oriented institutions', *Journal of Financial and Quantitative Analysis*, vol. 43, no. 1, pp. 59–92. **International**.

## Endnotes

1   This result may not hold exactly in a more complex case where debt has a significant possibility of default. Issues of default are treated in the next chapter.

2   The original paper is F. Modigliani and M. Miller, 'The cost of capital, corporation finance and the theory of investment', *American Economic Review* (June 1958).

3   We are ignoring the one-day interest charge on the loan.

4   Because we do not have taxes here, the cost of debt is $R_B$, not $R_B (1 - t_C)$ as it was in Chapter 12.

5   This statement holds in a world of no taxes. It does not hold in a world with taxes, a point to be brought out later in this chapter (see Fig. 15.6).

6   This can be derived from Eq. (15.2) by setting $R_{WACC} = R_0$, yielding

$$\frac{B}{B+S}R_B + \frac{S}{B+S}R_S = R_0$$

Multiplying both sides by $(B + S)/S$ yields

$$\frac{B}{S}R_B + R_S = \frac{B+S}{S}R_0$$

We can rewrite the right side as

$$\frac{B}{S}R_B + R_S = \frac{B}{S}R_0 + R_0$$

Moving $(B/S)R_B$ to the right side and rearranging yields

$$R_S = R_0 + \frac{B}{S}(R_0 - R_B)$$

7  Both Merton Miller and Franco Modigliani were awarded separate Nobel Prizes, in part for their work on capital structure.

8  MM were aware of both of these issues, as can be seen in their original paper.

9  Under the MM propositions developed earlier, the two pies should be of the same size.

10  Note that shareholders actually receive more under Plan I (€650,000) than under Plan II (€390,000). Students are often bothered by this, because it seems to imply that they are better off without leverage. However, remember that there are more shares outstanding in Plan I than in Plan II. A full-blown model would show that earnings *per share* are higher with leverage.

11  This relationship holds when the debt level is assumed to be constant through time. A different formula would apply if the debt–equity ratio was assumed to be a non-constant over time. For a deeper treatment of this point, see J.A. Miles and J.R. Ezzel, 'The weighted average cost of capital, perfect capital markets and project life', *Journal of Financial and Quantitative Analysis* (September 1980).

12  The following example calculates the present value if we assume the debt has a finite life. Suppose Maxwell plc has £1 million in debt with an 8 per cent coupon rate. If the debt matures in two years and the cost of debt capital, $R_B$, is 10 per cent, what is the present value of the tax shields if the corporate tax rate is 28 per cent? The debt is amortized in equal instalments over two years.

| Year | Loan balance (£) | Interest (£) | Tax shield (£) | Present value of tax shield (£) |
|---|---|---|---|---|
| 0 | 1,000,000 | | | |
| 1 | 500,000 | 80,000 | 0.28 × 80,000 | 22,400 |
| 2 | 0 | 40,000 | 0.28 × 40,000 | 11,200 |
| | | | | 33,600 |

The present value of the tax saving is

$$PV = \frac{0.28 \times £80,000}{1.10} + \frac{0.28 \times £80,000}{(1.10)^2} = £33,600$$

Maxwell plc's value is higher than that of a comparable unlevered firm by £33,600.

13  This relationship can be shown as follows. Given MM Proposition I under taxes, a levered firm's market value balance sheet can be written as

| | |
|---|---|
| $V_U$ = Value of unlevered firm | $B$ = Debt |
| $t_C B$ = Tax shield | $S$ = Equity |

The value of the unlevered firm is simply the value of the assets without benefit of leverage. The balance sheet indicates that the firm's value increases by $t_C B$ when debt of $B$ is added. The expected cash flow *from* the left side of the balance sheet can be written as

$$V_U R_0 + t_C B R_B \qquad \text{(a)}$$

Because assets are risky, their expected rate of return is $R_0$. The tax shield has the same risk as the debt, so its expected rate of return is $R_B$.

The expected cash *to* bondholders and shareholders together is

$$S R_S + B R_B \qquad \text{(b)}$$

Expression (b) reflects the fact that equity earns an expected return of $R_S$ and debt earns the interest rate $R_B$.

Because all cash flows are paid out as dividends in our no-growth perpetuity model, the cash flows going into the firm equal those going to shareholders. Hence (a) and (b) are equal:

$$SR_S + BR_B = V_U R_0 + t_C B R_B \tag{c}$$

Dividing both sides of (c) by $S$, subtracting $BR_B$ from both sides, and rearranging yields

$$R_S = \frac{V_U}{S} \times R_0 - (1 - t_C) \times \frac{B}{S} R_B \tag{d}$$

Because the value of the levered firm, $V_L$, equals $V_U + t_C B = B + S$, it follows that $V_U = S + (1 - t_C) \times B$. Thus (d) can be rewritten as

$$R_S = \frac{S + (1 - t_C) \times B}{S} \times R_0 - (1 - t_C) \times \frac{B}{S} R_B \tag{e}$$

Bringing the terms involving $(1 - t_C) \times (B/S)$ together produces Eq. (15.6).

To help you grasp the key concepts of this chapter check out the extra resources posted on the Online Learning Centre at **www.mcgraw-hill.co.uk/textbooks/hillier**

Among other helpful resources there are PowerPoint presentations, chapter outlines and mini-cases.

# Capital Structure: Limits to the Use of Debt

## KEY NOTATIONS

| | |
|---|---|
| B | Market value of a firm's debt or bonds |
| CF | Cash flow |
| EBIT | Earnings before interest and taxes |
| G | Value of government's claim on a firm from taxes |
| L | Value that lawyers and others receive when a firm is under financial distress |
| LBO | Leveraged buyout |
| $R_{WACC}$ | Weighted average cost of capital |
| S | Market value of a firm's shares or equity |
| V | Value of a firm |
| $V_M$ | Value of marketable claims on a firm |
| $V_N$ | Value of non-marketable claims on a firm |
| $V_T$ | Total value of a firm |

Although the use of debt brings benefits in the form of tax shields, there are dangers from having too much debt. Take Italy's flagship airline, Alitalia, which despite having government support has made an annual profit only once since 1999. According to Alitalia, in 2008 it had €1.172bn in debt and made a loss of €495 million in 2007. The debt and interest payments had effectively crippled the airline.

As the Alitalia situation suggests, financial leverage has a number of drawbacks, and there is a limit to the financial leverage a company can bear. The risk of too much leverage is bankruptcy. Chapter 30 covers bankruptcy law and the turnaround strategies that firms follow once they are in financial distress. In this chapter we discuss the costs associated with bankruptcies, and how companies attempt to avoid this process.

## 16.1 Costs of Financial Distress

### Bankruptcy Risk or Bankruptcy Cost?

Debt puts pressure on the firm, because interest and principal payments are obligations. If these obligations are not met, the firm may risk some sort of financial distress. The ultimate distress is *bankruptcy*, where ownership of the firm's assets is legally transferred from the shareholders to the bondholders. These debt obligations are fundamentally different from equity obligations. Although shareholders like and expect dividends, they are not legally entitled to them in the way bondholders are legally entitled to interest and principal payments.

We show next that bankruptcy costs, or more generally financial distress costs, tend to offset the advantages to debt. We begin by positing a simple example of bankruptcy. All taxes are ignored to focus only on the costs of debt.

EXAMPLE
## 16.1

## Bankruptcy Costs

Knight NV plans to be in business for one more year. It forecasts a cash flow of either €100 or €50 in the coming year, each occurring with 50 per cent probability. The firm has no other assets. Previously issued debt requires payments of €49 of interest and principal. Day NV has identical cash flow prospects, but has €60 of interest and principal obligations. The cash flows of these two firms can be represented as follows:

| | Knight NV | | Day NV | |
|---|---|---|---|---|
| | **Boom times (prob. 50%) (€)** | **Recession (prob. 50%) (€)** | **Boom times (prob. 50%) (€)** | **Recession (prob. 50%) (€)** |
| Cash flow | 100 | 50 | 100 | 50 |
| Payment of interest and principal on debt | 49 | 49 | 60 | 50 |
| Distribution to shareholders | 51 | 1 | 40 | 0 |

For Knight NV in both boom times and recession, and for Day NV in boom times, cash flow exceeds interest and principal payments. In these situations the bondholders are paid in full, and the shareholders receive any residual. However, the most interesting of the four columns involves Day NV in a recession. Here the bondholders are owed €60, but the firm has only €50 in cash. Because we assumed that the firm has no other assets, the bondholders cannot be satisfied in full. If bankruptcy occurs, the bondholders will receive all of the firm's cash, and the shareholders will receive nothing. Importantly, the shareholders do not have to come up with the additional €10 (= €60 − €50). Corporations have limited liability in Europe and most other countries, implying that bondholders cannot sue the shareholders for the extra €10.[1]

We assume that (a) both bondholders and shareholders are risk-neutral and (b) the interest rate is 10 per cent. Because of this risk-neutrality, cash flows to both shareholders and bondholders are to be discounted at the 10 per cent rate.[2] We can evaluate the debt, the equity, and the entire firm for both Knight and Day as follows:

$$S_{\text{KNIGHT}} = €23.64 = \frac{€51 \times \frac{1}{2} + €1 \times \frac{1}{2}}{1.10} \qquad S_{\text{DAY}} = €18.18 = \frac{€40 \times \frac{1}{2} + 0 \times \frac{1}{2}}{1.10}$$

$$B_{\text{KNIGHT}} = €44.54 = \frac{€49 \times \frac{1}{2} + €49 \times \frac{1}{2}}{1.10} \qquad B_{\text{DAY}} = €50 = \frac{€60 \times \frac{1}{2} + €50 \times \frac{1}{2}}{1.10}$$

$$V_{\text{KNIGHT}} = €68.18 \qquad V_{\text{DAY}} = €68.18$$

Note that the two firms have the same value, even though Day runs the risk of bankruptcy. Furthermore, notice that Day's bondholders are valuing the bonds with 'their eyes open'. Though the promised payment of principal and interest is €60, the bondholders are willing to pay only €50. Hence their *promised* return or yield is

$$\frac{€60}{€50} - 1 = 20\%$$

Day's debt can be viewed as a *junk bond* because the probability of default is so high. As with all junk bonds, Day's bondholders demand a high promised yield.

Day's example is not realistic, because it ignores an important cash flow to be discussed next. A more realistic set of numbers might be these:

| | Day NV | | | |
|---|---|---|---|---|
| | **Boom times (prob. 50%) (€)** | **Recession (prob. 50%) (€)** | | |
| Earnings | 100 | 50 | $S_{\text{DAY}} = €18.18 =$ | $\dfrac{€40 \times \frac{1}{2} + 0 \times \frac{1}{2}}{1.10}$ |
| Debt repayment | 60 | 35 | $B_{\text{DAY}} = €43.18 =$ | $\dfrac{€60 \times \frac{1}{2} + €35 \times \frac{1}{2}}{1.10}$ |
| Distribution to shareholders | 40 | 0 | $V_{\text{DAY}} = €61.36$ | |

Why do the bondholders receive only €35 in a recession? If cash flow is only €50, bondholders will be informed that they will not be paid in full. These bondholders are likely to hire lawyers to negotiate, or even to sue the company. Similarly, the firm is likely to hire lawyers to defend itself. Further costs will be incurred if the case gets to a bankruptcy court. These fees are always paid before the bondholders get paid. In this example we are assuming that bankruptcy costs total €15 (= €50 − 35).

The value of the firm is now €61.36, an amount below the €68.18 figure calculated earlier. By comparing Day's value in a world with no bankruptcy costs with Day's value in a world with these costs, we conclude the following:

**The possibility of bankruptcy has a negative effect on the value of the firm. However, it is not the *risk* of bankruptcy itself that lowers value; rather, it is the costs associated with bankruptcy that lower value.**

The explanation follows from our pie example. In a world without bankruptcy costs, the bondholders and the shareholders share the entire pie. However, bankruptcy costs eat up some of the pie in the real world, leaving less for the shareholders and bondholders.

Because the bondholders are aware that they would receive little in a recession, they pay the low price of €43.18. In this case, their promised return is

$$\frac{€60}{€43.18} - 1 = 39.0\%$$

The bondholders are paying a fair price if they are realistic about both the probability and the cost of bankruptcy. It is the *shareholders* who bear these future bankruptcy costs. To see this, imagine that Day NV was originally all equity. The shareholders want the firm to issue debt with a promised payment of €60 and use the proceeds to pay a dividend. If there had been no bankruptcy costs, our results show that bondholders would pay €50 to purchase debt with a promised payment of €60. Hence a dividend of €50 could be paid to the shareholders. However, if bankruptcy costs exist, bondholders would pay only €43.18 for the debt. In that case, only a dividend of €43.18 could be paid to the shareholders. Because the dividend is smaller with bankruptcy costs, the shareholders are hurt by these costs.

## 16.2 Description of Financial Distress Costs

The preceding example showed that bankruptcy costs can lower the value of the firm. In fact, the same general result holds even if a legal bankruptcy is prevented. Thus *financial distress costs* may be a better phrase than *bankruptcy costs*. It is worth while to describe these costs in more detail.

### Direct Costs of Financial Distress: Legal and Administrative Costs of Liquidation or Reorganization

As mentioned earlier, lawyers are involved throughout all the stages before and during bankruptcy. With fees often in the hundreds of pounds or euros an hour, these costs can add up quickly. Someone once remarked that bankruptcies are to lawyers what blood is to sharks. In addition, administrative and accounting fees can substantially add to the total bill. If a trial takes place, we must not forget expert witnesses. Each side may hire a number of these witnesses to testify about the fairness of a proposed settlement, and their fees can easily rival those of lawyers or accountants.

One of the most well-publicized bankruptcies in recent years concerned Lehman Brothers, at the time one of the biggest banks in the world. This bankruptcy followed large write-downs on subprime mortgage assets and a general collapse in interbank credit in September 2008. *Business Week* stated:

The Lehman Brothers bankruptcy is quickly becoming one giant mess.

Scores of hedge funds that had hundreds of millions in cash and other securities parked with Lehman's prime brokerage operation in London have had their accounts frozen. A number of these hedge funds have filed formal objections with the bankruptcy court and at least one fund, New York-based Bay Harbour Management, is mounting a legal challenge to the court's hastily-approved sale of Lehman's brokerage arm to Barclays Capital.

Now a new and even more troubling scenario is arising: legal disputes stemming from the estimated $1 trillion in derivatives transactions that Lehman had entered into on behalf of itself and some of its customers. Already, at least three lawsuits have been filed, alleging that nearly $600 million in collateral posted by some of Lehman's trading partners in derivatives transactions hasn't been returned and is in jeopardy of disappearing as the bankruptcy process unfolds.

To date, the most aggrieved of Lehman's trading partners is Bank of America, which at one time was considering buying Lehman as the investment firm was lurching towards bankruptcy. The Charlotte, NC based lender is seeking to recover nearly $500 million the bank 'posted as collateral to 'support derivative transactions between BofA and the respective Lehman Entities'', according to a lawsuit filed in New York State Supreme Court.[3]

Bankruptcy costs can be absolutely massive with large companies like Lehman Brothers. For example, as of 2008, the direct costs of Enron's bankruptcy (in 2001) included thousands of jobs, more than $60 billion in market value, $2 billion in pension plans, $7.3 billion in compensation, and at least $30 billion of claims still in courts. Think of the legal fees resulting from all of this . . .

A number of academic studies have measured the direct costs of financial distress. Although large in absolute amount, these costs are actually small as a percentage of firm value. White, Altman and Weiss estimate the direct costs of financial distress to be about 3 per cent of the market value of the firm.[4] Bris, Welch and Zhu find that direct costs are about 8 per cent of pre-bankruptcy assets. However, since the costs are fixed, irrespective of the size of the firm, the proportional costs can be between 20 and 25 per cent for smaller firms.[5]

Of course, few firms end up in bankruptcy. Thus the preceding cost estimates must be multiplied by the probability of bankruptcy to yield the *expected* cost of bankruptcy. For example, consider a firm that has a 5 per cent probability of going into bankruptcy each year. If the firm declares bankruptcy, the direct costs it incurs amount to 8 per cent of the total value of the firm. The *expected* bankruptcy cost must be then 0.4 per cent (= 0.05 × 0.08).

## Indirect Costs of Financial Distress

**Impaired Ability to Conduct Business**    Bankruptcy hampers conduct with customers and suppliers. Sales are frequently lost because of both fear of impaired service and loss of trust. For example, in 2008 many loyal HBOS and Royal Bank of Scotland customers switched to other banks when rumours of the banks' funding situation spread. These buyers questioned whether they would be able to get access to their money were the banks to fail. Sometimes the taint of impending bankruptcy is enough to drive customers away.

Though these costs clearly exist, it is quite difficult to measure them. Altman estimates that both direct and indirect costs of financial distress are frequently greater than 20 per cent of firm value.[6] Andrade and Kaplan estimate total distress costs to be between 10 per cent and 20 per cent of firm value.[7] Bar-Or estimates expected future distress costs for firms that are currently healthy to be 8 to 10 per cent of operating value, a number below the estimates of either Altman or Andrade and Kaplan.[8] However, unlike Bar-Or, these authors consider distress costs for firms already in distress, not expected distress costs for currently healthy firms.

Cutler and Summers examine the costs of the well-publicized Texaco bankruptcy.[9] In January 1984 Pennzoil reached what it believed to be a binding agreement to acquire three-sevenths of Getty Oil. However, less than a week later Texaco acquired all of Getty at a higher per-share price. Pennzoil then sued Getty for breach of contract. Because Texaco had previously indemnified Getty against litigation, Texaco became liable for damages.

In November 1985 the Texas State Court awarded damages of $12 billion to Pennzoil, although this amount was later reduced. As a result, Texaco filed for bankruptcy. Cutler and Summers identify nine important events over the course of the litigation. They find that Texaco's market value (share price times number of shares outstanding) fell a cumulative $4.1 billion over these events, whereas Pennzoil rose only $682 million. Thus Pennzoil gained about one-sixth of what Texaco lost, resulting in a net loss to the two firms of almost $3.5 billion.

What could explain this net loss? Cutler and Summers suggest that it is probably due to costs that Texaco and Pennzoil incurred from the litigation and subsequent bankruptcy. The authors argue that direct bankruptcy fees represent only a small part of these costs, estimating Texaco's after-tax legal expenses to be about $165 million. Legal costs to Pennzoil were more difficult to assess, because Pennzoil's lead lawyer, Joe Jamail, stated publicly that he had no set fee. However, using a clever statistical analysis, the authors estimate his fee to be about $200 million. Thus we must search elsewhere for the bulk of the costs.

Indirect costs of financial distress may be the culprit. An affidavit by Texaco stated that, following the lawsuit, some of its suppliers were demanding cash payment. Other suppliers halted or cancelled shipments of crude oil. Certain banks restricted Texaco's use of futures contracts on foreign exchange. The affidavit stressed that these constraints were reducing Texaco's ability to run its business, leading to deterioration of its financial condition. Could these sorts of indirect costs explain the $3.5 billion disparity between Texaco's drop and Pennzoil's rise in market value? Unfortunately, although it is quite likely that indirect costs play a role here, there is simply no way to obtain a decent quantitative estimate for them.

## Agency Costs

When a firm has debt, conflicts of interest arise between shareholders and bondholders. Because of this, shareholders are tempted to pursue selfish strategies. These conflicts of interest, which are magnified when financial distress is incurred, impose agency costs on the firm. We describe three kinds of selfish strategy that shareholders use to hurt the bondholders and help themselves. These strategies are costly, because they will lower the market value of the whole firm.

**Selfish Investment Strategy 1: Incentive to Take Large Risks**   Firms near bankruptcy often take great chances, because they believe that they are playing with someone else's money. To see this, imagine a levered firm considering two *mutually exclusive* projects, a low-risk one and a high-risk one. There are two equally likely outcomes, recession and boom. The firm is in such dire straits that should a recession hit, it will come near to bankruptcy with one project and actually fall into bankruptcy with the other. The cash flows for the entire firm if the low-risk project is taken can be described as follows:

| Value of entire firm if low-risk project is chosen | | | | | | |
|---|---|---|---|---|---|---|
| | Probability | Value of firm (£) | = | Shares (£) | + | Bonds (£) |
| Recession | 0.5 | 100 | = | 0 | + | 100 |
| Boom | 0.5 | 200 | = | 100 | + | 100 |

If recession occurs, the value of the firm will be £100; if a boom occurs, the value of the firm will be £200. The expected value of the firm is £150 (= 0.5 × £100 + 0.5 × £200).

The firm has promised to pay bondholders £100. Shareholders will obtain the difference between the total pay-off and the amount paid to the bondholders. In other words, the bondholders have the prior claim on the pay-offs, and the shareholders have the residual claim.

Now suppose that the riskier project can be substituted for the low-risk project. The pay-offs and probabilities are as follows:

| Value of entire firm if high-risk project is chosen | | | | | | |
|---|---|---|---|---|---|---|
| | **Probability** | **Value of firm (£)** | **=** | **Shares (£)** | **+** | **Bonds (£)** |
| Recession | 0.5 | 50 | = | 0 | + | 50 |
| Boom | 0.5 | 240 | = | 140 | + | 100 |

The expected value of the *firm* is £145 (= 0.5 × £50 + 0.5 × £240), which is lower than the expected value of the firm with the low-risk project. Thus the low-risk project would be accepted if the firm were all equity. However, note that the expected value of the *equity* is £70 (= 0.5 × 0 + 0.5 × £140) with the high-risk project, but only £50 (= 0.5 × 0 + 0.5 × £100) with the low-risk project. Given the firm's present levered state, shareholders will select the high-risk project, even though the high-risk project has a *lower* NPV.

The key is that, relative to the low-risk project, the high-risk project increases firm value in a boom and decreases firm value in a recession. The increase in value in a boom is captured by the shareholders because the bondholders are paid in full (they receive £100) regardless of which project is accepted. Conversely, the drop in value in a recession is lost by the bondholders because they are paid in full with the low-risk project but receive only £50 with the high-risk one. The shareholders will receive nothing in a recession anyway, whether the high-risk or low-risk project is selected. Thus financial economists argue that shareholders expropriate value from the bondholders by selecting high-risk projects.

**Selfish Investment Strategy 2: Incentive towards Underinvestment** Shareholders of a firm with a significant probability of bankruptcy often find that new investment helps the bondholders at the shareholders' expense. The simplest case might be a property owner facing imminent bankruptcy. If he took €100,000 out of his own pocket to refurbish the building, he could increase the building's value by, say, €150,000. Though this investment has a positive net present value, he will turn it down if the increase in value cannot prevent bankruptcy. 'Why,' he asks, 'should I use my own funds to improve the value of a building that the bank will soon repossess?'

This idea is formalized by the following simple example. Consider the firm in Table 16.1, which must decide whether to accept or reject a new project. The first two columns in the table show cash flows without the project. The firm receives cash inflows of £5,000 and £2,400 under a boom and a recession, respectively. Because the firm must pay principal and interest of £4,000, the firm will default in a recession.

Alternatively, as indicated in the next two columns of the table, the firm could raise equity to invest in a new project. The project brings in £1,700 in either state, which is enough to prevent bankruptcy even in a recession. Because £1,700 is much greater than the project's cost

**TABLE 16.1**

| | Firm without project | | Firm with project costing £1,000 | |
|---|---|---|---|---|
| | **Boom (£)** | **Recession (£)** | **Boom (£)** | **Recession (£)** |
| Firm cash flows | 5,000 | 2,400 | 6,700 | 4,100 |
| Bondholders' claim | 4,000 | 2,400 | 4,000 | 4,000 |
| Shareholders' claim | 1,000 | 0 | 2,700 | 100 |

The project has positive NPV. However, much of its value is captured by bondholders. Rational managers, acting in the shareholders' interest, will reject the project.

**Table 16.1** Example illustrating incentive to underinvest of £1,000, the project has a positive NPV at any plausible interest rate. Clearly, an all-equity firm would accept the project.

However, the project hurts the shareholders of the levered firm. To see this, imagine that the old shareholders contribute the £1,000 *themselves*.[10] Assuming that a boom and a recession are equally likely, the expected value of the shareholders' interest without the project is £500 (= 0.5 × £1,000 + 0.5 × 0). The expected value with the project is £1,400 (= 0.5 × £2,700 + 0.5 × £100). The shareholders' interest rises by only £900 (= £1,400 – £500) while costing £1,000.

Why does a project with a positive NPV hurt the shareholders? The key is that the shareholders contribute the full £1,000 investment, but the shareholders and bondholders *share* the benefits. The shareholders take the entire gain if boom times occur. Conversely, the bondholders reap most of the cash flow from the project in a recession.

The discussion of selfish strategy 1 is quite similar to the discussion of selfish strategy 2. In both cases an investment strategy for the levered firm is different from the one for the unlevered firm. Thus leverage results in distorted investment policy. Whereas the unlevered corporation always chooses projects with positive net present value, the levered firm may deviate from this policy.

**Selfish Investment Strategy 3: Milking the Property**  Another strategy is to pay out extra dividends or other distributions in times of financial distress, leaving less in the firm for the bondholders. This is known as *milking the property*, a phrase taken from real estate. Strategies 2 and 3 are very similar. In strategy 2, the firm chooses not to raise new equity. Strategy 3 goes one step further because equity is actually withdrawn through the dividend.

**Summary of Selfish Strategies**  The distortions just discussed occur only when there is a probability of bankruptcy or financial distress. Thus these distortions *should not* affect, say, Vodafone because bankruptcy is not a realistic possibility for a diversified blue-chip firm such as this. In other words, Vodafone's debt will be virtually risk-free, regardless of the projects it accepts. The same argument could be made for nationalized banks, such as the Royal Bank of Scotland, that are protected by the government. By contrast, small firms in risky industries, such as computers, are more likely to experience financial distress and, in turn, to be affected by such distortions.

Who pays for the cost of selfish investment strategies? We argue that it is ultimately the shareholders. Rational bondholders know that when financial distress is imminent, they cannot expect help from shareholders. Rather, shareholders are likely to choose investment strategies that reduce the value of the bonds. Bondholders protect themselves accordingly by raising the interest rate that they require on the bonds. Because the shareholders must pay these high rates, they ultimately bear the costs of selfish strategies. For firms that face these distortions, debt will be difficult and costly to obtain. These firms will have low leverage ratios.

The relationship between shareholders and bondholders is very similar to the relationship between Erroll Flynn and David Niven, good friends and movie stars in the 1930s. Niven reportedly said that the good thing about Flynn was that you knew exactly where you stood with him. When you needed his help, you could always count on him to let you down.

# 16.3 Can Costs of Debt Be Reduced?

Each of the costs of financial distress we have mentioned is substantial in its own right. The sum of them may well affect debt financing severely. Thus managers have an incentive to reduce these costs. We now turn to some of their methods. However, it should be mentioned at the outset that the methods here can, at most, reduce the costs of debt. They cannot *eliminate* them entirely.

## Protective Covenants

Because shareholders must pay higher interest rates as insurance against their own selfish strategies, they frequently make agreements with bondholders in the hopes of lower rates. These agreements, called **protective covenants**, are incorporated as part of the loan document (or *indenture*) between shareholders and bondholders. The covenants must be taken seriously, because a broken covenant can lead to default. Protective covenants can be classified into two types: negative covenants and positive covenants.

A negative covenant limits or prohibits actions that the company may take. Here are some typical negative covenants:

- Limitations are placed on the amount of dividends a company may pay.
- The firm may not pledge any of its assets to other lenders.
- The firm may not merge with another firm.
- The firm may not sell or lease its major assets without approval by the lender.
- The firm may not issue additional long-term debt.

A positive covenant specifies an action that the company agrees to take or a condition the company must abide by. Here are some examples:

- The company agrees to maintain its working capital at a minimum level.
- The company must furnish periodic financial statements to the lender.

These lists of covenants are not exhaustive. The authors have seen loan agreements with more than 30 covenants.

Smith and Warner examined public issues of debt and found that 91 per cent of the bond indentures included covenants that restricted the issuance of additional debt, 23 per cent restricted dividends, 39 per cent restricted mergers, and 36 per cent limited the sale of assets.[11]

Protective covenants should reduce the costs of bankruptcy, ultimately increasing the value of the firm. Thus shareholders are likely to favour all reasonable covenants. To see this, consider three choices by shareholders to reduce bankruptcy costs:

1  *Issue no debt.* Because of the tax advantages to debt, this is a very costly way of avoiding conflicts.

2  *Issue debt with no restrictive and protective covenants.* In this case, bondholders will demand high interest rates to compensate for the unprotected status of their debt.

3  *Write protective and restrictive covenants into the loan contracts.* If the covenants are clearly written, the creditors may receive protection without large costs being imposed on the shareholders. The creditors will gladly accept a lower interest rate.

Thus bond covenants, even if they reduce flexibility, can increase the value of the firm. They can be the lowest-cost solution to the shareholder–bondholder conflict. A list of typical bond covenants and their uses appears in Table 16.2.

## Consolidation of Debt

One reason why bankruptcy costs are so high is that different creditors (and their lawyers) contend with each other. This problem can be alleviated by proper arrangement of bondholders and shareholders. For example, perhaps one, or at most a few, lenders can shoulder the entire debt. Should financial distress occur, negotiating costs are minimized under this arrangement. In addition, bondholders can purchase equity as well. In this way, shareholders and debtholders are not pitted against each other, because they are not separate entities. This appears to be the approach in Japan, where large banks generally take significant equity positions in the firms to which they lend money.[12]

# 16.4 Integration of Tax Effects and Financial Distress Costs

Modigliani and Miller argue that the firm's value rises with leverage in the presence of corporate taxes. Because this relationship implies that all firms should choose maximum debt, the theory does not predict the behaviour of firms in the real world. Other authors have suggested that bankruptcy and related costs reduce the value of the levered firm.

**TABLE 16.2**

| Shareholder action or firm circumstances | Covenant type | Reason for covenant |
|---|---|---|
| As firm approaches financial distress, shareholders may want firm to make high-risk investments. | Financial statement restrictions<br>**1** Minimum working capital<br>**2** Minimum interest coverage<br>**3** Minimum net worth | High-risk investments transfer value from bondholders to shareholders when financial distress is a realistic possibility. Covenants reduce probability of financial distress. |
| Shareholders may attempt to transfer corporate assets to themselves. | Restrictions on asset disposition<br>**1** Limit on dividends<br>**2** Limit on sale of assets<br>**3** Collateral and mortgages | Covenants limit the ability of shareholders to transfer assets to themselves and to *underinvest*. |
| Shareholders may attempt to increase risk of firm. | Restrictions on switching assets | Increased firm risk helps shareholders and hurts bondholders. |
| Shareholders may attempt to issue new debt of equal or greater priority. | Dilution restrictions<br>**1** Limit on leasing<br>**2** Limit on further borrowing | Covenants restrict *dilution of the claim of existing bondholders.* |

**Table 16.2** Loan covenants

The integration of tax effects and distress costs appears in Fig. 16.1. In the top graph of the figure the diagonal straight line represents the value of the firm in a world without bankruptcy costs. The hump-shaped curve represents the value of the firm with these costs. This curve rises as the firm moves from all equity to a small amount of debt. Here the present value of the distress costs is minimal, because the probability of distress is so small. However, as more and more debt is added, the present value of these costs rises at an *increasing* rate. At some point the increase in the present value of these costs from an additional unit of debt equals the increase in the present value of the tax shield. This is the debt level maximizing the value of the firm and is represented by $B^*$ in Fig. 16.1. In other words, $B^*$ is the optimal amount of debt. Bankruptcy costs increase faster than the tax shield beyond this point, implying a reduction in firm value from further leverage.

In the bottom graph of Fig. 16.1 the weighted average cost of capital ($R_{WACC}$) falls as debt is added to the capital structure. After reaching $B^*$ the weighted average cost of capital rises. The optimal amount of debt produces the lowest weighted average cost of capital.

Our discussion implies that a firm's capital structure decision involves a trade-off between the tax benefits of debt and the costs of financial distress. In fact, this approach is frequently called the *trade-off* or the *static trade-off* theory of capital structure. The implication is that there is an optimal amount of debt for any individual firm. This amount of debt becomes the firm's target debt level. Because financial distress costs cannot be expressed in a precise way, no formula has yet been developed to determine a firm's optimal debt level exactly. However, the last section of this chapter offers some rules of thumb for selecting a debt–equity ratio in the real world.

## Pie Again

Now that we have considered bankruptcy costs, let's return to the pie approach of the previous chapter. The cash flows of the firm go to four different claimants: shareholders, bondholders,

FIGURE
**16.1**

The tax shield increases the value of the levered firm. Financial distress costs lower the value of the levered firm. The two offsetting factors produce an optimal amount of debt at B*.

According to the static theory, the $R_{WACC}$ falls initially, because of the tax advantage of debt. Beyond point B* it begins to rise, because of financial distress costs.

**Figure 16.1** The optimal amount of debt and the value of the firm

the government (in the form of taxes) and, during the bankruptcy process, lawyers (and others). Algebraically, we must have

$$CF = \text{Payments to shareholders}$$
$$+$$
$$\text{Payments to bondholders}$$
$$+$$
$$\text{Payments to the government}$$
$$+$$
$$\text{Payments to lawyers (and others)}$$

It follows that the total value of the firm, $V_T$, equals the sum of the following four components:

$$V_T = S + B + G + L$$

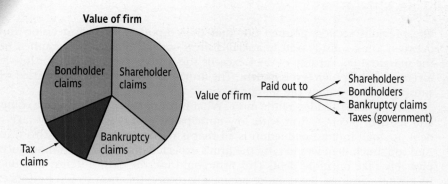

**Figure 16.2** The pie model with real-world factors

where $S$ is the value of the equity, $B$ is the value of the bonds, $G$ is the value of the government claims from taxes, and $L$ stands for the value that lawyers and others receive when the firm is under financial distress. This relationship is illustrated in Fig. 16.2.

Nor have we even begun to exhaust the list of financial claims to the firm's cash flows. To give an unusual example, everyone reading this book has an economic claim to the cash flows of Mercedes-Benz. After all, if you are injured in an accident, you might sue Mercedes-Benz. Win or lose, Mercedes-Benz will expend resources dealing with the matter. If you think this is far-fetched and unimportant, ask yourself what Mercedes-Benz might be willing to pay every man, woman and child in the world to have them promise that they would never sue Mercedes-Benz, no matter what happened. The law does not permit such payments, but that does not mean that a value to all of those potential claims does not exist. We guess that it would run into the billions of euros, and, for Mercedes-Benz or any other company, there should be a slice of the pie labelled $LS$ for 'potential lawsuits.'

Figure 16.2 illustrates the essence of MM's intuition. While $V_T$ is determined by the firm's cash flows, the firm's capital structure merely cuts $V_T$ into slices. Capital structure does *not* affect the total value, $V_T$.

There is, however, a difference between claims such as those of shareholders and bondholders on the one hand and those of government and potential litigants in lawsuits on the other. The first set of claims are marketable claims, and the second set are non-marketable claims. Marketable claims can be bought and sold in financial markets, but the non-marketable claims cannot. This distinction between marketable and non-marketable claims is important. When equity is issued, shareholders pay cash to the firm for the privilege of later receiving dividends. Similarly, bondholders pay cash to the firm for the privilege of receiving interest in the future. However, the government pays nothing to the firm for the privilege of receiving taxes in the future. Similarly, lawyers pay nothing to the firm for the privilege of receiving fees from the firm in the future.

When we speak of the *value of the firm*, we are referring just to the value of the marketable claims, $V_M$, and not the value of non-marketable claims, $V_N$. What we have shown is that capital structure does not affect the total value:

$$V_T = S + B + G + L$$
$$= V_M - V_N$$

But as we saw, the value of the marketable claims, $V_M$, can change with changes in the capital structure.

By the pie theory, any increase in $V_M$ must imply an identical decrease in $V_N$. Rational financial managers will choose a capital structure to maximize the value of the marketable claims, $V_M$. Equivalently, rational managers will work to minimize the value of the non-marketable claims, $V_N$. These are taxes and bankruptcy costs in the previous example, but they also include all the other non-marketable claims such as the potential lawsuits, $LS$, claim.

## 16.5 Signalling

The previous section pointed out that the corporate leverage decision involves a trade-off between a tax subsidy and financial distress costs. This idea was graphed in Fig. 16.1, where the marginal tax subsidy of debt exceeds the distress costs of debt for low levels of debt. The reverse holds for high levels of debt. The firm's capital structure is optimized where the marginal subsidy to debt equals the marginal cost.

Let's explore this idea a little more. What is the relationship between a company's profitability and its debt level? A firm with low anticipated profits will probably take on a low level of debt. A small interest deduction is all that is needed to offset all of this firm's pre-tax profits. And too much debt would raise the firm's expected distress costs. A more successful firm would probably take on more debt. This firm could use the extra interest to reduce the taxes from its greater earnings. Being more financially secure, this firm would find its extra debt increasing the risk of bankruptcy only slightly. In other words, rational firms raise debt levels (and the concomitant interest payments) when profits are expected to increase.

How do investors react to an increase in debt? Rational investors are likely to infer a higher firm value from a higher debt level. Thus these investors are likely to bid up a firm's share price after the firm has, say, issued debt in order to buy back equity. We say that investors view debt as a *signal* of firm value.

Now we get to the incentives of managers to fool the public. Consider a firm whose level of debt is optimal. That is, the marginal tax benefit of debt exactly equals the marginal distress costs of debt. However, imagine that the firm's manager desires to increase the firm's current share price, perhaps because he knows that many of his shareholders want to sell their equity soon. This manager might want to increase the level of debt just to make investors *think* that the firm is more valuable than it really is. If the strategy works, investors will push up the price of the shares.

This implies that firms can fool investors by taking on *some* additional leverage. Now let's ask the big question. Are there benefits to extra debt but no costs, implying that all firms will take on as much debt as possible? The answer, fortunately, is that there are costs as well. Imagine that a firm has issued extra debt just to fool the public. At some point, the market will learn that the company is not that valuable after all. At this time the share price should actually fall *below* what it would have been had the debt never been increased. Why? Because the firm's debt level is now above the optimal level. That is, the marginal tax benefit of debt is below the marginal cost of debt. Thus if the current shareholders plan to sell, say, half of their shares now and retain the other half, an increase in debt will help them on immediate sales but probably hurt them on later ones.

Now here is the important point. We said that in a world where managers do not attempt to fool investors, valuable firms issue more debt than less valuable ones do. It turns out that even when managers attempt to fool investors, the more valuable firms will still want to issue more debt than the less valuable firms. That is, while all firms will increase debt levels somewhat to fool investors, the costs of extra debt prevent the less valuable firms from issuing more debt than the more valuable firms do. Thus investors can still treat debt level as a signal of firm value. In other words, investors can still view an announcement of debt as a positive sign for the firm.

The foregoing is a simplified example of debt signalling, and you might argue that it is too simplified. For example, perhaps the shareholders of some firms want to sell most of their equity immediately, whereas the shareholders of other firms want to sell only a little of theirs now. It is impossible to tell here whether the firms with the most debt are the most valuable, or merely the ones with the most impatient shareholders. Because other objections can be brought up as well, signalling theory is best validated by empirical evidence. And, fortunately, the empirical evidence tends to support the theory.

For example, consider the evidence concerning exchange offers. Firms often change their debt levels through exchange offers, of which there are two types. The first type of offer allows shareholders to exchange some of their equity for debt, thereby increasing leverage. The second type allows bondholders to exchange some of their debt for equity, decreasing leverage. Figure 16.3 shows the share price behaviour of firms that change their proportions of debt and equity via exchange offers. The solid line in the figure indicates that share prices rise substantially on

Exchange offers change the debt–equity ratios of firms. The graph shows that share prices increase for firms whose exchange offers increase leverage. Conversely, share prices decrease for firms whose offers decrease leverage.

*Source*: K. Shah, 'The nature of information conveyed by pure capital structure changes', *Journal of Financial Economics* 36 (August 1994).

**Figure 16.3** Equity returns at the time of announcements of exchange offers

the date when an exchange offering increasing leverage is announced. (This date is referred to as date 0 in the figure.) Conversely, the dotted line in the figure indicates that the share price falls substantially when an offer decreasing leverage is announced.

The market infers from an increase in debt that the firm is better off, leading to a share price rise. Conversely, the market infers the reverse from a decrease in debt, implying a share price fall. Thus, we say that managers signal information when they change leverage.

## 16.6  Shirking, Perquisites, and Bad Investments: A Note on Agency Cost of Equity

A previous section introduced the static trade-off model, where a rise in debt increases both the tax shield and the costs of distress. We now extend the trade-off model by considering an important agency cost of equity. A discussion of this cost of equity is contained in a well-known quote from Adam Smith:[13]

> The directors of such [joint-stock] companies, however, being the managers of other people's money than of their own, it cannot well be expected that they should watch over it with the same anxious vigilance with which the partners in a private copartnery frequently watch over their own. Like the stewards of a rich man, they are apt to consider attention to small matters as not for their master's honour, and very easily give themselves a dispensation from having it. Negligence and profusion, therefore, must always prevail, more or less, in the management of the affairs of such a company.

This elegant prose can be restated in modern vocabulary. An individual will work harder for a firm if she is one of its owners than if she is just an employee. In addition, the individual will work harder if she owns a large percentage of the company than if she owns a small percentage. This idea has an important implication for capital structure, which we illustrate with the following example.

EXAMPLE
**16.2**

# Agency Costs

Ms Pagell is an owner-entrepreneur running a computer services firm worth £1 million. She currently owns 100 per cent of the firm. Because of the need to expand, she must raise another £2 million. She can either issue £2 million of debt at 12 per cent interest or issue £2 million in equity. The cash flows under the two alternatives are presented here:

| | Debt issue | | | | Equity issue | | | |
|---|---|---|---|---|---|---|---|---|
| **Work intensity** | **Cash flow (£)** | **Interest (£)** | **Cash flow to equity (£)** | **Cash flow to Ms Pagell (100% of equity) (£)** | **Cash flow (£)** | **Interest (£)** | **Cash flow to equity (£)** | **Cash flow to Ms Pagell (33⅓% of equity) (£)** |
| 6-hour days | 300,000 | 240,000 | 60,000 | 60,000 | 300,000 | 0 | 300,000 | 100,000 |
| 10-hour days | 400,000 | 240,000 | 160,000 | 160,000 | 400,000 | 0 | 400,000 | 133,333 |

Like any entrepreneur, Ms Pagell can choose the degree of intensity with which she works. In our example she can work either a 6- or a 10-hour day. With the debt issue, the extra work brings her £100,000 (= £160,000 − £60,000) more income. However, let's assume that with an equity issue she retains only a one-third interest in the equity. Here, the extra work brings her merely £33,333 (= £133,333 − £100,000). Being human, she is likely to work harder if she issues debt. In other words, she has more incentive to *shirk* if she issues equity.

In addition, she is likely to obtain more *perquisites* (a big office, a company car, more expense account meals) if she issues equity. If she is a one-third shareholder, two-thirds of these costs are paid for by the other shareholders. If she is the sole owner, any additional perquisites reduce her equity stake alone.

Finally, she is more likely to take on capital budgeting projects with negative net present values. It might seem surprising that a manager with any equity interest at all would take on negative NPV projects: the share price would clearly fall here. However, managerial salaries generally rise with firm size, providing managers with an incentive to accept some unprofitable projects after all the profitable ones have been taken on. That is, when an unprofitable project is accepted, the loss in share value to a manager with only a small equity interest may be less than the increase in salary. In fact, it is our opinion that losses from accepting bad projects are far greater than losses from either shirking or excessive perquisites. Hugely unprofitable projects have bankrupted whole firms, something that even the largest expense account is unlikely to do.

Thus, as the firm issues more equity, our entrepreneur will probably increase leisure time, work-related perquisites, and unprofitable investments. These three items are called *agency costs*, because managers of the firm are agents of the shareholders.[14]

This example is quite applicable to a small company considering a large equity offering. Because a manager-owner will greatly dilute his or her share of the total equity in this case, a significant drop in work intensity or a significant increase in fringe benefits is possible. However, the example may be less applicable for a large corporation with many shareholders. For example, consider a large company such as ICI issuing shares for the umpteenth time. The typical manager there already has such a small percentage stake in the firm that any temptation for negligence has probably been experienced before. An additional offering cannot be expected to increase this temptation.

Who bears the burden of these agency costs? Shareholders do not bear these costs as long as they invest with their eyes open. Knowing that Ms Pagell may work shorter hours, they will pay only a low price for the equity. Thus it is the owner who is hurt by agency costs. However, Ms Pagell can protect herself to some extent. Just as shareholders reduce bankruptcy costs through protective covenants, an owner may allow monitoring by new shareholders. However, though proper reporting and surveillance may reduce the agency costs of equity, these techniques are unlikely to eliminate them.

It is commonly suggested that leveraged buyouts (LBOs) significantly reduce these costs of equity. In an LBO, a purchaser (usually a team of existing management) buys out the shareholders at a price above the current market. In other words, the company goes private: the equity is placed in the hands of only a few people. Because the managers now own a substantial chunk of the business, they are likely to work harder than when they were simply hired hands.

## Effect of Agency Costs of Equity on Debt–Equity Financing

The preceding discussion of the agency costs of equity should be viewed as an extension of the static trade-off model. That is, we stated in Section 16.4 that the change in the value of the firm when debt is substituted for equity is the difference between (a) the tax shield on debt and (b) the increase in the costs of financial distress (including the agency costs of debt). Now the change in the value of the firm is (a) the tax shield on debt plus (b) the reduction in the agency costs of equity minus (c) the increase in the costs of financial distress (including the agency costs of debt). The optimal debt–equity ratio would be higher in a world with agency costs of equity than in a world without these costs. However, because costs of financial distress are so significant, the costs of equity do not imply 100 per cent debt financing.

## Free Cash Flow

Any reader of murder mysteries knows that a criminal must have both motive and opportunity. The discussion thus far has been about motive. Managers with only a small ownership interest have an incentive for wasteful behaviour. For example, they bear only a small portion of the costs of, say, excessive expense accounts, and they reap all of the benefits.

Now let's talk about opportunity. A manager can pad his expense account only if the firm has the cash flow to cover it. Thus we might expect to see more wasteful activity in a firm with a capacity to generate large cash flows than in one with a capacity to generate only small cash flows. This simple idea, which is formally called the *free cash flow hypothesis*,[15] is backed by a fair amount of empirical research. For example, a frequently cited paper found that firms with high free cash flow are more likely to make bad acquisitions than firms with low free cash flow.[16]

The hypothesis has important implications for capital structure. Since dividends leave the firm, they reduce free cash flow. Thus, according to the free cash flow hypothesis, an increase in dividends should benefit the shareholders by reducing the ability of managers to pursue wasteful activities. Furthermore, since interest and principal also leave the firm, debt reduces free cash flow as well. In fact, interest and principal should have a greater effect than dividends have on the free-spending ways of managers, because bankruptcy will occur if the firm is unable to make future debt payments. By contrast, a future dividend reduction will cause fewer problems to the managers, since the firm has no legal obligation to pay dividends. Because of this, the free cash flow hypothesis argues that a shift from equity to debt will boost firm value.

In summary, the free cash flow hypothesis provides still another reason for firms to issue debt. We previously discussed the cost of equity: new equity dilutes the holdings of managers with equity interests, increasing their *motive* to waste corporate resources. We now state that debt reduces free cash flow, because the firm must make interest and principal payments. The free cash flow hypothesis implies that debt reduces the *opportunity* for managers to waste resources.

## 16.7   The Pecking-Order Theory

Although the trade-off theory has dominated corporate finance circles for a long time, attention has also been paid to the *pecking-order theory*.[17] To understand this view of the world, let's put ourselves in the position of a corporate financial manager whose firm needs new capital. The manager faces a choice between issuing debt and issuing equity. Previously, we evaluated the choice in terms of tax benefits, distress costs, and agency costs. However, there is one consideration that we have so far neglected: timing.

Imagine the manager saying:

> I want to issue equity in one situation only – when it is overvalued. If the equity of my firm is selling at £50 per share, but I think that it is actually worth £60, I will not issue equity. I would actually be giving new shareholders a gift because they would receive equity worth £60 but would only have to pay £50 for it. More important, my current shareholders would be upset because the firm would be receiving £50 in cash but giving away something worth £60. So if I believe that my equity is undervalued, I would issue bonds. Bonds, particularly those with little or no risk of default, are likely to be priced correctly. Their value is determined primarily by the market-wide interest rate, a variable that is publicly known.
>
> But suppose our equity is selling at £70. Now I'd like to issue equity. If I can get some fool to buy our shares for £70 while the equity is really worth only £60, I will be making £10 for our current shareholders.

Although this may strike you as a cynical view, it seems to square well with reality. Before the United States adopted insider trading and disclosure laws, many managers were alleged to have unfairly trumpeted their firm's prospects prior to equity issuance. And even today, managers seem more willing to issue equity after the price of their shares has risen than after their shares have fallen in price. Thus timing might be an important motive in equity issuance, perhaps even more important than the motives in the trade-off model. After all, the firm in the preceding example *immediately* makes £10 by properly timing the issuance of equity. £10 worth of agency costs and bankruptcy cost reduction might take many years to realize.

The key that makes the example work is *asymmetric information*: the manager must know more about his firm's prospects than the typical investor does. If the manager's estimate of the true worth of the company is no better than the estimate of a typical investor, any attempts by the manager at timing will fail. This assumption of asymmetry is quite plausible. Managers should know more about their company than outsiders do because managers work at the company every day. (One caveat is that some managers are perpetually optimistic about their firm, blurring good judgement.)

But we are not done with this example yet; we must consider the investor. Imagine an investor saying:

> I make investments carefully because they involve my hard-earned money. However, even with all the time I put into studying shares, I can't possibly know what the managers themselves know. After all, I've got a day job to be concerned with. So I watch what the managers do. If a firm issues equity, the firm was probably overvalued beforehand. If a firm issues debt, it was probably undervalued.

When we look at both issuers and investors, we see a kind of poker game, with each side trying to outwit the other. What should the issuing firm do in this poker game? Clearly, the firm should issue debt if the equity is undervalued. But what if the equity is overvalued? Here it gets tricky, because a first thought is that the firm should issue equity. However, if a firm issues equity, investors will infer that the shares are overvalued. They will not buy them until the share price has fallen enough to eliminate any advantage from equity issuance. In fact, it can be shown that only the most overvalued firms have any incentive to issue equity. Should even a moderately overpriced firm issue equity, investors will infer that this firm is among the *most* overpriced, causing the shares to fall more than is deserved. Thus the end result is that virtually no one will issue equity.[18]

This result, that essentially all firms should issue debt, is clearly an extreme one. It is as extreme as (a) the Modigliani–Miller (MM) result that, in a world without taxes, firms are indifferent to capital structure, and (b) the MM result that, in a world of corporate taxes but no financial distress costs, all firms should be 100 per cent debt-financed. Perhaps we in finance have a penchant for extreme models!

But just as we can temper MM's conclusions by combining financial distress costs with corporate taxes, we can temper those of the pure pecking-order theory. This pure version assumes that timing is the financial manager's only consideration. In reality, a manager must consider taxes, financial distress costs and agency costs as well. Thus a firm may issue debt only up to a point. If financial distress becomes a real possibility beyond that point, the firm may issue equity instead.

## Rules of the Pecking Order

The previous discussion presented the basic ideas behind the pecking-order theory. What are the practical implications of the theory for financial managers? The theory provides the following two rules for the real world.

**Rule 1: Use Internal Financing**   For expository purposes, we have oversimplified by comparing equity to *riskless* debt. Managers cannot use special knowledge of their firm to determine whether this type of debt is mispriced, because the price of riskless debt is determined solely by the market-wide interest rate. However, in reality, corporate debt has the possibility of default. Thus, just as managers tend to issue equity when they think it is overvalued, managers also tend to issue debt when they think it is overvalued.

When would managers view their debt as overvalued? Probably in the same situations when they think their equity is overvalued. For example, if the public thinks that the firm's prospects are rosy but the managers see trouble ahead, these managers would view their debt – as well as their equity – as being overvalued. That is, the public might see the debt as nearly risk-free, whereas the managers see a strong possibility of default.

Thus investors are likely to price a debt issue with the same scepticism that they have when pricing an equity issue. The way managers get out of this box is to finance projects out of retained earnings. You don't have to worry about investor scepticism if you can avoid going to investors in the first place. So the first rule of the pecking order is this:

**Use internal financing.**

**Rule 2: Issue Safe Securities First**   Although investors fear mispricing of both debt and equity, the fear is much greater for equity. Corporate debt still has relatively little risk compared with equity, because if financial distress is avoided, investors receive a fixed return. Thus the pecking-order theory implies that if outside financing is required, debt should be issued before equity. Only when the firm's debt capacity is reached should the firm consider equity.

Of course, there are many types of debt. For example, because convertible debt is more risky than straight debt, the pecking-order theory implies that managers should issue straight debt before issuing convertibles. So, the second rule of pecking-order theory is this:

**Issue the safest securities first.**

## Implications

A number of implications associated with the pecking-order theory are at odds with those of the trade-off theory.

1   *There is no target amount of leverage.* According to the trade-off model, each firm balances the benefits of debt, such as the tax shield, with the costs of debt, such as distress costs. The optimal amount of leverage occurs where the marginal benefit of debt equals the marginal cost of debt.

   By contrast, the pecking-order theory does not imply a target amount of leverage. Rather, each firm chooses its leverage ratio based on financing needs. Firms first fund projects out of retained earnings. This should lower the percentage of debt in the capital structure, because profitable, internally funded projects raise both the book value and the market value of equity. Additional projects are funded with debt, clearly raising the debt level. However, at some point the debt capacity of the firm may be exhausted, giving way to equity issuance. Thus the amount of leverage is determined by the happenstance of available projects. Firms do not pursue a target ratio of debt to equity.

2 *Profitable firms use less debt.* Profitable firms generate cash internally, implying less need for outside financing. Because firms desiring outside capital turn to debt first, profitable firms end up relying on less debt. The trade-off model does not have this implication. Here the greater cash flow of more profitable firms creates greater debt capacity. These firms will use that debt capacity to capture the tax shield and the other benefits of leverage.

3 *Companies like financial slack.* The pecking-order theory is based on the difficulties of obtaining financing at a reasonable cost. A sceptical investing public thinks an equity is overvalued if the managers try to issue more of it, thereby leading to a share price decline. Because this happens with bonds, only to a lesser extent, managers rely first on bond financing. However, firms can issue only so much debt before encountering the potential costs of financial distress.

Wouldn't it be easier to have the cash ahead of time? This is the idea behind *financial slack*. Because firms know that they will have to fund profitable projects at various times in the future, they accumulate cash today. They are then not forced to go to the capital markets when a project comes up. However, there is a limit to the amount of cash a firm will want to accumulate. As mentioned earlier in this chapter, too much free cash may tempt managers to pursue wasteful activities.

## 16.8 Growth and the Debt–Equity Ratio

Although the trade-off between the tax shield and bankruptcy costs (as illustrated in Fig. 16.1) is often viewed as the 'standard model' of capital structure, it has its critics. For example, some point out that bankruptcy costs in the real world appear to be much smaller than the tax subsidy. Thus the model implies that the optimal debt/value ratio should be near 100 per cent, an implication at odds with reality.[19]

Perhaps the pecking-order theory is more consistent with the real world here. That is, firms are likely to have more equity in their capital structure than implied by the static trade-off theory, because internal financing is preferred to external financing.

There is another approach that implies significant equity financing, even in a world with low bankruptcy costs. This idea, developed by Berens and Cuny,[20] argues that equity financing follows from growth. To explain the idea, we first consider an example of a no-growth firm. Next, we examine the effect of growth on firm leverage.

### No Growth

Imagine a world of perfect certainty[21] where a firm has annual earnings before interest and taxes (EBIT) of €100. In addition, the firm has issued €1,000 of debt at an interest rate of 10 per cent, implying interest payments of €100 per year. Here are the cash flows to the firm:

| | Date | | | |
|---|---|---|---|---|
| | **1**<br>(€) | **2**<br>(€) | **3**<br>(€) | **4 . . .**<br>(€) |
| Earnings before interest and taxes (EBIT) | 100 | 100 | 100 | 100 . . . |
| Interest | −100 | −100 | −100 | −100 . . . |
| Taxable income | 0 | 0 | 0 | 0 |

The firm has issued just enough debt so that all EBIT are paid out as interest. Because interest is tax-deductible, the firm pays no taxes. In this example the equity is worthless, because shareholders receive no cash flows. Since debt is worth €1,000, the firm is also valued at €1,000. Therefore the debt-to-value ratio is 100 per cent (= €1,000/€1,000).

Had the firm issued less than €1,000 of debt, the corporation would have positive taxable income and, consequently, would have ended up paying some taxes. Had the firm issued more than €1,000 of debt, interest would have exceeded EBIT, causing default. Consequently, the optimal debt-to-value ratio is 100 per cent.

## Growth

Now imagine another firm where EBIT are also €100 at date 1 but are growing at 5 per cent per year.[22] To eliminate taxes, this firm also wants to issue enough debt so that interest equals EBIT. Because EBIT are growing at 5 per cent per year, interest must also grow at this rate. This is achieved by increasing debt by 5 per cent per year.[23] The debt, EBIT, interest and taxable income levels are these:

| | Date | | | | |
|---|---|---|---|---|---|
| | **0** (€) | **1** (€) | **2** (€) | **3** (€) | **4 . . .** (€) |
| Debt | 1,000 | 1,050 | 1,102.50 | 1,157.63 . . . | |
| New debt issued | | 50 | 52.50 | 55.13 . . . | |
| EBIT | | 100 | 105 | 110.25 | 115.76 . . . |
| Interest | | −100 | −105 | −110.25 | −115.76 . . . |
| Taxable income | | 0 | 0 | 0 | 0 |

Note that interest on a particular date is always 10 per cent of the debt on the previous date. Debt is set so that interest is exactly equal to EBIT. As in the no-growth case, the levered firm has the maximum amount of debt at each date. Default would occur if interest payments were increased.

Because growth is 5 per cent per year, the value of the firm is[24]

$$V_{\text{Firm}} = \frac{€100}{0.10 - 0.05} = €2,000$$

The equity at date 0 is the difference between the value of the firm at that time, €2,000, and the debt of €1,000. Hence equity must be equal to €1,000,[25] implying a debt-to-value ratio of 50 per cent (= €1,000/€2,000). Note the important difference between the no-growth and the growth example. The no-growth example has no equity; the value of the firm is simply the value of the debt. With growth, there is equity as well as debt.

We can also value the equity in another way. It may appear at first glance that the shareholders receive nothing, because the EBIT are paid out as interest each year. However, the new debt issued each year can be paid as a dividend to the shareholders. Because the new debt is €50 at date 1 and grows at 5 per cent per year, the value of the shareholders' interest is

$$\frac{€50}{0.10 - 0.05} = €1,000$$

the same number that we obtained in the previous paragraph.

As we mentioned earlier, any further increase in debt above €1,000 at date 0 would lower the value of the firm in a world with bankruptcy costs. Thus, with growth, the optimal amount of debt is less than 100 per cent. Note, however, that bankruptcy costs need not be as large as the tax subsidy. In fact, even with infinitesimally small bankruptcy costs, firm value would decline if promised interest rose above €100 in the first year. The key to this example is that *today's* interest is set equal to *today's* income. Although the introduction of future growth opportunities increases firm value, it does not increase the current level of debt needed to shield today's income from today's taxes. Because equity is the difference between firm value and debt, growth increases the value of equity.

The preceding example captures an essential feature of the real world: growth. The same conclusion is reached in a world of inflation but with no growth opportunities. Thus the result of this section, that 100 per cent debt financing is suboptimal, holds whether inflation or growth opportunities are present. Furthermore, high-growth firms should have lower debt ratios than low-growth firms. Most firms have growth opportunities, and inflation has been with us for most of this and the previous centuries, so this section's example is based on realistic assumptions.[26]

## 16.9 Market Timing Theory

In recent years a new view of capital structure has emerged that believes leverage ratios have nothing to do with a pecking order or optimal capital structure. The view, which was originally put forward by Baker and Wurgler,[27] suggests that differentials between market and book valuations drive capital structure levels in firms. For example, if a firm requires funding during a period when its market value to book value ratio is high, it is more likely to raise equity. Similarly, in low market to book value periods, debt is likely to be the funding vehicle of choice. This has a permanent effect on capital structures that has nothing to do with bankruptcy costs or pecking orders.

The pecking-order theory also puts forward a timing motivation for funding choices. However, this theory argues that asymmetric information between managers and outside shareholders drives managers to always issue debt before equity, whenever it is possible to do so. Market timing theory disagrees, and states that asymmetric information is irrelevant. Managers simply take advantage of market conditions when they decide to raise capital.

Capital structure is one area (of the many!) in which finance academics are divided, and there are supporters in each of the three camps (trade-off, pecking order and market timing). So how does the empirical evidence stack up? Fama and French[28] showed that leverage ratios took too long to move back to mean levels after markets received a shock. This would indicate that, over the short term at least, there is no target capital structure. Similarly, Welch[29] finds that companies tend to issue shares when market valuations are high. In contrast, Kayhan and Titman[30] show that, over the longer term, capital structures do move towards a target level!

Finally, almost all research has examined only US securities, and very little work comparing the validity of the three theories has focused on Europe or the rest of the world. Given the institutional and ownership differences between the US and the rest of the world, it is possible that the relationship between financing decisions and managerial behaviour will be different.

## 16.10 How Firms Establish Capital Structure

The theories of capital structure are among the most elegant and sophisticated in the field of finance. Financial economists should (and do!) pat themselves on the back for contributions in this area. However, the practical applications of the theories are less than fully satisfying. Consider that our work on net present value produced an *exact* formula for evaluating projects. Prescriptions for capital structure under either the trade-off model, the pecking-order theory, or market timing are vague by comparison. No exact formula is available for evaluating the optimal debt–equity ratio. Because of this, we turn to evidence from the real world.

The following empirical regularities are worth while to consider when formulating capital structure policy.

**Most corporations have low debt–asset ratios**   How much debt is used in the real world? The average debt ratio is never greater than 100 per cent. Figure 16.4 shows the debt-to-equity ratios of firms in different European countries in recent years. The main thing to notice is that there is quite a lot of variation in the debt ratios.

Should we view these ratios as being high or low? Because academics generally see corporate tax reduction as the chief motivation for debt, we might wonder whether real-world companies issue enough debt to greatly reduce, if not downright eliminate, corporate taxes. The empirical evidence suggests that this is not the case. For example, corporate taxes in the United Kingdom for 2008 were just under £50 billion. Thus it is clear that corporations do not issue debt up to the point where tax shelters are completely used up. There are clearly limits to the amount of debt corporations can issue, perhaps because of the financial distress costs discussed earlier in this chapter.

**A number of firms use no debt**   In a fascinating study, Agrawal and Nagarajan examined approximately 100 firms on the New York Stock Exchange without long-term debt.[31] They found that these firms are averse to leverage of any kind, with little short-term debt as well.

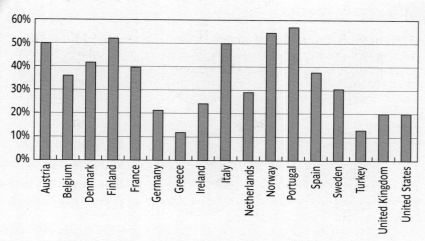

Source: J.P.H. Fan, S. Titman and G. Twite, 'An international comparison of capital structure and debt maturity choices', Working Paper (2006).

**Figure 16.4** Estimated ratios of debt to equity, various countries

In addition, they have levels of cash and marketable securities well above their levered counterparts. Typically, the managers of these firms have high equity ownership. Furthermore, there is significantly greater family involvement in all-equity firms than in levered firms.

Thus a story emerges. Managers of all-equity firms are less diversified than the managers of similar, but levered, firms. Because of this, significant leverage represents an added risk that the managers of all-equity firms are loath to accept.

**There are differences in the capital structures of different industries**    There are significant inter-industry differences in debt ratios, which persist over time. As can be seen in Table 16.3, debt/asset ratios tend to be quite low in high-growth industries with ample future investment

| Debt to asset ratios | Germany | The Netherlands | United Kingdom |
|---|---|---|---|
| Consumer goods | 22.10 | 25.18 | 20.52 |
| Consumer services | 22.34 | 22.98 | 26.83 |
| Financials | 43.30 | 31.80 | 25.13 |
| Healthcare | 20.94 | 20.20 | 13.00 |
| Industrial | 22.32 | 23.42 | 20.65 |
| Materials | 20.04 | 26.08 | 20.18 |
| Oil and gas | 13.19 | 24.74 | 15.90 |
| Technology | 11.88 | 18.55 | 10.74 |
| Telecommunication | 16.50 | 32.84 | 26.49 |
| Utility | 13.39 | 29.71 | 34.09 |

Source: Thomson Financial, www.thomsonreuters.com

**Table 16.3** Average capital structure ratios for various industries in Germany, the Netherlands and the United Kingdom, 1998–2007

FIGURE
**16.5**

Source: Figure 1 of D. Brounen, A. de Jong and K. Koedijk, 'Capital structure policies in Europe: survey evidence', *Journal of Banking and Finance* (2006).

**Figure 16.5**   Survey results on the use of target debt–equity ratios

opportunities, such as the healthcare and technology industries. This is true even when the need for external financing is great. Industries with large investments in tangible assets, such as real estate, tend to have high leverage. Consistent with Fig. 16.4, there are also differences in average industry capital structures across countries.

**Most corporations employ target debt–equity ratios**   Brounen, de Jong and Koedijk asked 313 chief financial officers (CFOs) of European firms whether they use target debt–equity ratios, with the results being presented in Fig. 16.5.[32] As can be seen, a great majority of firms across countries use targets, although the strictness of the targets varies across companies. A notable exception to this is in France, where most firms do not pursue a target debt ratio. Even in the UK, nearly half of all firms do not consider a target debt ratio to be important.

How should companies establish target debt–equity ratios? While there is no mathematical formula for establishing a target ratio, we present three important factors affecting the ratio:

1   *Taxes*: As we pointed out earlier, firms can deduct interest for tax purposes only to the extent of their profits before interest. Thus highly profitable firms are more likely to have larger target ratios than less profitable firms.[33]

2   *Types of assets*: Financial distress is costly with or without formal bankruptcy proceedings. The costs of financial distress depend on the types of assets that the firm has. For example, if a firm has a large investment in land, buildings, and other tangible assets, it will have smaller costs of financial distress than a firm with a large investment in research and development. Research and development typically has less resale value than land: thus most of its value disappears in financial distress. Therefore firms with large investments in tangible assets are likely to have higher target debt–equity ratios than firms with large investments in research and development.

3   *Uncertainty of operating income*: Firms with uncertain operating income have a high probability of experiencing financial distress, even without debt. Thus these firms must finance mostly with equity. For example, pharmaceutical firms have uncertain operating income because no one can predict whether today's research will generate new, profitable drugs. Consequently, these firms issue little debt. By contrast, the operating income of firms in regulated industries, such as utilities, generally has low volatility. Relative to other industries, utilities use a great deal of debt.

One final note is in order. Because no formula supports them, the preceding points may seem too nebulous to assist financial decision-making. Instead, many real-world firms simply base their capital structure decisions on industry averages. This may strike some as a cowardly approach, but it at least keeps firms from deviating far from accepted practice. After all, the existing firms in any industry are the survivors. Therefore we should pay at least some attention to their decisions.

## Summary and Conclusions

1   We mentioned in the last chapter that, according to theory, firms should create all-debt capital structures under corporate taxation. Because firms generally employ moderate amounts of debt in the real world, the theory must have been missing something at that point. We stated in this chapter that costs of financial distress cause firms to restrain their issuance of debt. These costs are of two types: direct and indirect. Lawyers' and account-ants' fees during the bankruptcy process are examples of direct costs. We mentioned four examples of indirect costs:

   (a)   Impaired ability to conduct business

   (b)   Incentive to take on risky projects

   (c)   Incentive towards underinvestment

   (d)   Distribution of funds to shareholders prior to bankruptcy

2   Because financial distress costs are substantial, and the shareholders ultimately bear them, firms have an incentive to reduce costs. Protective covenants and debt consolidation are two common cost reduction techniques.

3   Because costs of financial distress can be reduced but not eliminated, firms will not finance entirely with debt. Figure 16.1 illustrates the relationship between firm value and debt. In the figure, firms select the debt–equity ratio at which firm value is maximized.

4   Signalling theory argues that profitable firms are likely to increase their leverage, because the extra interest payments will offset some of the pre-tax profits. Rational shareholders will infer higher firm value from a higher debt level. Thus investors view debt as a signal of firm value.

5   Managers owning a small proportion of a firm's equity can be expected to work less, maintain more lavish expense accounts, and accept more pet projects with negative NPVs than managers owning a large proportion of equity. Because new issues of equity dilute a manager's percentage interest in the firm, such agency costs are likely to increase when a firm's growth is financed through new equity rather than through new debt.

6   The pecking-order theory implies that managers prefer internal to external financing. If external financing is required, managers tend to choose the safest securities, such as debt. Firms may accumulate slack to avoid external equity.

7   The market timing theory suggests that there is no pecking order or trade-off of capital structure choices. Observed debt ratios are simply a function of past market to book valu-ations and the timing of funding requirements. Firms will have more equity if they needed funding when market to book valuations were high. Conversely, if financing was required during low market to book periods, debt will tend to dominate.

8   Berens and Cuny argue that significant equity financing can be explained by real growth and inflation, even in a world of low bankruptcy costs.

9   Debt–equity ratios vary across industries. We present three factors determining the target debt–equity ratio:

   (a)   *Taxes*: Firms with high taxable income should rely more on debt than firms with low taxable income.

(b)  *Types of assets*: Firms with a high percentage of intangible assets such as research and development should have low debt. Firms with primarily tangible assets should have higher debt.

(c)  *Uncertainty of operating income*: Firms with high uncertainty of operating income should rely mostly on equity.

## connect  Questions and Problems

CONCEPT
1 – 10

1  **Costs of Financial Distress**   What are the direct and indirect costs of bankruptcy? Briefly explain each.

2  **Description of Financial Distress Costs**   Are managers liable to act differently when their firm is in financial distress? Explain your answer using practical examples.

3  **Costs of Debt**   What steps can shareholders take to reduce the costs of debt?

4  **Trade-Off Theory**   How does the existence of financial distress costs and agency costs affect Modigliani and Miller's theory in a world where corporations pay taxes?

5  **Signalling**   Explain how managers can signal to the market the value of their firm through their capital structure decisions. Do you think this is an effective strategy? Explain.

6  **Agency Costs of Equity**   What are the sources of agency costs of equity?

7  **Pecking-Order Theory**   Explain what is meant by the pecking-order theory and how it relates to observed capital structures of companies. Where does a deeply discounted equity rights issue fit into the pecking order of financing choices? Explain your answer.

8  **Growth and the Debt–Equity Ratio**   How does growth affect the desired debt to equity ratio of a company? Explain the impact of growth opportunities in the context of the static trade-off theory and pecking-order theory of capital structure.

9  **Market Timing Theory**   Is the market timing theory of financing choices consistent with the pecking-order theory or trade-off theory? Explain your answer.

10  **Observed Capital Structures**   In all countries, it appears that some firms have a target debt ratio while others do not have one. What does this say about the validity of the trade-off theory, pecking-order theory, and market timing theory? Explain.

REGULAR
11 – 22

11  **Shareholder Incentives**   Do you agree or disagree with the following statement? 'A firm's shareholders will never want the firm to invest in projects with negative net present values.' Why?

12  **Capital Structure Decisions**   Because of large losses incurred in the past several years, a firm has €2 billion in tax loss carry-forwards. This means that the next €2 billion of the firm's income will be free from corporate income taxes. Security analysts estimate that it will take many years for the firm to generate €2 billion in earnings. The firm has a moderate amount of debt in its capital structure. The firm's CEO is deciding whether to issue debt or equity to raise the funds needed to finance an upcoming project. Which method of financing would you recommend? Why?

13  **Observed Capital Structures**   Refer to the observed capital structures given in Table 16.3 of the text. What do you notice about the types of industry with respect to their average debt–asset ratios? Are certain types of industry more likely to be highly leveraged than others? What are some possible reasons for this observed segmentation? Do the operating results and tax history of the firms play a role? How about their future earnings prospects? What about the different institutional characteristics of each country? Explain.

14  **Bankruptcy and Corporate Ethics**  Firms sometimes use the threat of a bankruptcy filing to force creditors to renegotiate terms. Critics argue that in such cases the firm is using bankruptcy laws 'as a sword rather than a shield'. Is this an ethical tactic?

15  **Bankruptcy and Corporate Ethics**  If a company files for bankruptcy as a means of reducing labour costs, is this move ethical? Justify your argument.

16  **Firm Value**  Janetta plc has a profit before interest and taxes of £750,000 per year that is expected to continue in perpetuity. The unlevered cost of equity for the company is 15 per cent, and the corporate tax rate is 28 per cent. The company also has a perpetual bond issue outstanding, with a market value of £1.5 million.

(a)  What is the value of the company?

(b)  The CFO of the company informs the company chairman that the value of the company is £3.2 million. Is the CFO correct?

17  **Agency Costs**  Tom Scott is the owner, chairman and primary salesperson for Scott Manufacturing. Because of this, the company's profits are driven by the amount of work Tom does. If he works 40 hours each week, the company's profit before interest and taxes will be £500,000 per year; if he works a 50-hour week, the company's profit before interest and taxes will be £600,000 per year. The company is currently worth £3 million. The company needs a cash infusion of £2 million, and it can issue equity or issue debt with an interest rate of 9 per cent. Assume there are no corporate taxes.

(a)  What are the cash flows to Tom under each scenario?

(b)  Under which form of financing is Tom likely to work harder?

(c)  What specific new costs will occur with each form of financing?

18  **Capital Structure and Growth**  Knut Construction currently has debt outstanding with a market value of NKr80,000 and a cost of 12 per cent. The company has an EBIT rate of NKr9,600 that is expected to continue in perpetuity. Assume there are no taxes.

(a)  What is the value of the company's equity? What is the debt-to-value ratio?

(b)  What are the equity value and debt-to-value ratio if the company's growth rate is 5 per cent?

(c)  What are the equity value and debt-to-value ratio if the company's growth rate is 10 per cent?

19  **Capital Structure and Non-Marketed Claims**  Suppose the chief executive of the company in the previous problem stated that the company should increase the amount of debt in its capital structure because of the tax-advantaged status of its interest payments. His argument is that this action would increase the value of the company. How would you respond?

20  **Costs of Financial Distress**  Steinberg plc and Dietrich plc are identical firms except that Dietrich is more levered. Both companies will remain in business for one more year. The companies' economists agree that the probability of the continuation of the current expansion is 80 per cent for the next year, and the probability of a recession is 20 per cent. If the expansion continues, each firm will generate profit before interest and taxes of £2 million. If a recession occurs, each firm will generate profit before interest and taxes of £800,000. Steinberg's debt obligation requires the firm to pay £750,000 at the end of the year. Dietrich's debt obligation requires the firm to pay £1 million at the end of the year. Neither firm pays taxes. Assume a discount rate of 15 per cent.

(a)  What are the potential pay-offs in one year to Steinberg's shareholders and bondholders? What about those for Dietrich's?

(b)  Steinberg's CEO recently stated that Steinberg's value should be higher than Dietrich's because the firm has less debt and therefore less bankruptcy risk. Do you agree or disagree with this statement?'

21 **Agency Costs** Kašna Corporation's economists estimate that a good business environment and a bad business environment are equally likely for the coming year. The managers of Kašna must choose between two mutually exclusive projects. Assume that the project Kašna chooses will be the firm's only activity, and that the firm will close one year from today. Kašna is obligated to make a Kc50,000 payment to bondholders at the end of the year. The projects have the same systematic risk but different volatilities. Consider the following information pertaining to the two projects:

| Economy | Probability | Low-volatility project pay-off | High-volatility project pay-off |
|---|---|---|---|
| Bad | 0.50 | Kc50,000 | Kc10,000 |
| Good | 0.50 | Kc70,000 | Kc80,000 |

(a) What is the expected value of the firm if the low-volatility project is undertaken? What if the high-volatility project is undertaken? Which of the two strategies maximizes the expected value of the firm?

(b) What is the expected value of the firm's equity if the low-volatility project is undertaken? What is it if the high-volatility project is undertaken?

(c) Which project would Kašna's shareholders prefer? Explain.

(d) Suppose bondholders are fully aware that shareholders might choose to maximize equity value rather than total firm value and opt for the high-volatility project. To minimize this agency cost, the firm's bondholders decide to use a bond covenant to stipulate that the bondholders can demand a higher payment if Kašna chooses to take on the high-volatility project. What payment to bondholders would make shareholders indifferent between the two projects?

22 **Financial Distress** Good Time plc is a regional chain department store. It will remain in business for one more year. The probability of a boom year is 60 per cent and the probability of a recession is 40 per cent. It is projected that the company will generate a total cash flow of £250 million in a boom year and £100 million in a recession. The company's required debt payment at the end of the year is £150 million. The market value of the company's outstanding debt is £108.93 million. The company pays no taxes. Assume a discount rate of 12 per cent.

(a) What pay-off do bondholders expect to receive in the event of a recession?

(b) What is the promised return on the company's debt?

(c) What is the expected return on the company's debt?

23 **Personal Taxes, Bankruptcy Costs, and Firm Value** When personal taxes on interest income and bankruptcy costs are considered, the general expression for the value of a levered firm in a world in which the tax rate on equity distributions equals zero is

$$V_L = V_U + \{1 - [(1 - t_C)/(1 - t_B)]\} \times B - C(B)$$

where $V_L$ is the value of a levered firm, $V_U$ is the value of an unlevered firm, $B$ is the value of the firm's debt, $t_C$ is the tax rate on corporate income, $t_B$ is the personal tax rate on interest income, and $C(B)$ is the present value of the costs of financial distress.

(a) In their no-tax model, what do Modigliani and Miller assume about $t_C$, $t_B$ and $C(B)$? What do these assumptions imply about a firm's optimal debt–equity ratio?

(b) In their model with corporate taxes, what do Modigliani and Miller assume about $t_C$, $t_B$ and $C(B)$? What do these assumptions imply about a firm's optimal debt–equity ratio?

(c) Consider an all-equity Belgian firm that is certain to be able to use interest deductions to reduce its corporate tax bill. If the corporate tax rate is 33.99 per cent, the personal tax rate on interest income is 50 per cent, and there are no costs of financial distress, by how much will the value of the firm change if it issues €1 million in debt and uses the proceeds to repurchase equity?

(d)   Consider another all-equity Belgian firm that does not pay taxes owing to large tax loss carry-forwards from previous years. The personal tax rate on interest income is 50 per cent, and there are no costs of financial distress. What would be the change in the value of this firm from adding €1 of perpetual debt rather than €1 of equity?

24   **Personal Taxes, Bankruptcy Costs, and Firm Value**   Overnight Publishing SA (OP) has €2 million in excess cash. The firm plans to use this cash either to retire all of its outstanding debt or to repurchase equity. The firm's debt is held by one institution that is willing to sell it back to OP for €2 million. The institution will not charge OP any transaction costs. Once OP becomes an all-equity firm, it will remain unlevered for ever. If OP does not retire the debt, the company will use the €2 million in cash to buy back some of its equity on the open market. Repurchasing equity also has no transaction costs. The company will generate €1,100,000 of annual earnings before interest and taxes in perpetuity, regardless of its capital structure. The firm immediately pays out all earnings as dividends at the end of each year. OP is subject to a corporate tax rate of 33.33 per cent, and the required rate of return on the firm's unlevered equity is 20 per cent. The personal tax rate on interest income is 40 per cent, and there are no taxes on equity distribution. Assume there are no bankruptcy costs.

(a)   What is the value of OP if it chooses to retire all of its debt and become an unlevered firm?

(b)   What is the value of OP if it decides to repurchase equity instead of retiring its debt?
(Hint: Use the equation for the value of a levered firm with personal tax on interest income from the previous problem.)

(c)   Assume that expected bankruptcy costs have a present value of €300,000. How does this influence OP's decision?

## MINI CASE — McKenzie Corporation's Capital Budgeting

Sam McKenzie is the founder and CEO of McKenzie Restaurants plc, a British company. Sam is considering opening several new restaurants. Sally Thornton, the company's CFO, has been put in charge of the capital budgeting analysis. She has examined the potential for the company's expansion and determined that the success of the new restaurants will depend critically on the state of the economy over the next few years.

McKenzie currently has a bond issue outstanding with a face value of £25 million that is due in one year. Covenants associated with this bond issue prohibit the issuance of any additional debt. This restriction means that the expansion will be entirely financed with equity at a cost of £9 million. Sally has summarized her analysis in the following table, which shows the value of the company in each state of the economy next year, both with and without expansion:

| Economic growth | Probability | Without expansion | With expansion |
| --- | --- | --- | --- |
| Low | 0.30 | £20,000,000 | £24,000,000 |
| Normal | 0.50 | £34,000,000 | £45,000,000 |
| High | 0.20 | £41,000,000 | £53,000,000 |

1   What is the expected value of the company in one year, with and without expansion? Would the company's shareholders be better off with or without expansion? Why?

2   What is the expected value of the company's debt in one year, with and without the expansion?

3    One year from now, how much value creation is expected from the expansion? How much value is expected for shareholders? For bondholders?

4    If the company announces that it is not expanding, what do you think will happen to the price of its bonds? What will happen to the price of the bonds if the company does expand?

5    If the company opts not to expand, what are the implications for the company's future borrowing needs? What are the implications if the company does expand?

6    Because of the bond covenant, the expansion would have to be financed with equity. How would it affect your answer if the expansion were financed with cash on hand instead of new equity?

## Practical Case Study

For this case study, you will need to access Yahoo! Finance. For your own country, choose an industry and find the debt to equity ratio of each company in the industry. Now choose another country and find the debt to equity ratios of all the companies in the same industry. Is the median leverage different between countries? If so, explain why you think this might be the case. If not, what does this tell you about the three theories (trade-off, pecking order, market timing) of capital structure? Write a brief report on your findings.

## Additional Reading

Since Baker and Wurgler's (2002) paper on market timing, the capital structure literature has taken on a completely new lease of life. For many years researchers believed that pecking orders and static trade-offs were the only intuitive reasons why managers chose capital structures in practice. Now we have market timing and dynamic trade-offs to consider, and things are uncertain again. The references to papers discussed in the main text are provided in the endnotes. The following papers will add to your reading pleasure.

**Trade-Offs, Pecking Orders and Market Timing**

Alti, A. (2006) 'How persistent is the impact of market timing on capital structure?', *Journal of Finance*, vol. 61, no. 4, pp. 1681–1710. **US.**

Byoun, S. (2008) 'How and when do firms adjust their capital structures toward targets?', *Journal of Finance*, vol. 63, no. 6, pp. 3069–3096. **US.**

Chang, X. and S. Dasgupta (2009) 'Target behavior and financing: how conclusive is the evidence?', *Journal of Finance* (forthcoming). **US.**

Elliott, W.B., J. Koeter-Kant and R.S. Warr (2007) 'A valuation-based test of market timing', *Journal of Corporate Finance*, vol. 13, no. 1, pp. 112–128. **US.**

Elliott, W.B., J. Koeter-Kant and R.S. Warr (2008) 'Market timing and the debt-equity choice', *Journal of Financial Intermediation*, vol. 17, no. 2, pp. 175–197. **US.**

Graham, J.R. (2003) 'Taxes and corporate finance: a review', *Review of Financial Studies*, vol. 16, no. 4, pp. 1075–1129. **Review paper.**

Graham, J.R. and A.L. Tucker (2006) 'Tax shelters and corporate debt policy', *Journal of Financial Economics*, vol. 81, no. 3, pp. 563–594. **US.**

Hennessy, C. and T.M. Whited (2005) 'Debt dynamics', *Journal of Finance*, vol. 60, no. 3, pp. 1129–1165. **US.**

Hovakimian, A. (2006) 'Are observed capital structures determined by equity market timing?', *Journal of Financial and Quantitative Analysis*, vol. 41, no. 1, pp. 221–243. **US.**

Kayhan, A. and S. Titman (2007) 'Firm's histories and their capital structures', *Journal of Financial Economics*, vol. 83, no. 1, pp. 1–32. **US**.

Leary, M.T. and M.R. Roberts (2005) 'Do firms rebalance their capital structures?', *Journal of Finance*, vol. 60, no. 6, pp. 2575–2619. **US**.

Lemmon, M., M.R. Roberts and J.F. Zender (2008) 'Back to the beginning: persistence and the cross-section of corporate capital structure', *Journal of Finance*, vol. 63, no. 4, pp. 1575–1608. **US**.

Mahajan, A. and S. Tartaroglu (2008) 'Equity market timing and capital structure: international evidence', *Journal of Banking and Finance*, vol. 32, no. 5, pp. 754–766. **International**.

### Other Papers on Capital Structure Choice

Almeida, H. and T. Philippon (2007) 'The risk-adjusted cost of financial distress', *Journal of Finance*, vol. 62, no. 6, pp. 2557–2586. **US**.

Booth, L., V. Aivazian, A. Demirguc-Kunt and V. Maksimovic (2001) 'Capital structures in developing countries', *Journal of Finance*, vol. 56, no. 1, pp. 87–130. **International**.

Desai, M.A., C.F. Foley and J.R. Hines (2004) 'A multinational perspective on capital structure choice and internal capital markets', *Journal of Finance*, vol. 59, no. 6, pp. 2451–2487. **International**.

Dittmar, A. and A. Thakor (2007) 'Why do firms issue equity?', *Journal of Finance*, vol. 62, no. 1, pp. 1–54. **US**.

Fama, E.F. and K.R. French (2005) 'Financing decisions: who issues stock?', *Journal of Financial Economics*, vol. 76, no. 3, pp. 549–582. **US**.

Faulkender, M. and M.A. Petersen (2006) 'Does the source of capital affect capital structure?', *Review of Financial Studies*, vol. 19, no. 1, pp. 45–79. **US**.

Gonzalez, V.M. and F. Gonzalez (2008) 'Influence of bank concentration and institutions on capital structure: new international evidence', *Journal of Corporate Finance*, vol. 14, no. 4, pp. 363–375. **International**.

Kisgen, D.J. (2006) 'Credit ratings and capital structure', *Journal of Finance*, vol. 61, no. 3, pp. 1035–1072. **US**.

Molina, C.A. (2005) 'Are firms underleveraged? An examination of the effect of leverage on default probabilities', *Journal of Finance*, vol. 60, no. 3, pp. 1427–1459. **US**.

# Endnotes

1  There are situations where the limited liability of corporations can be 'pierced'. Typically, fraud or misrepresentation must be present.

2  Normally, we assume that investors are *averse* to risk. In that case, the cost of debt capital, $R_B$, is less than the cost of equity capital, $R_S$, which rises with leverage as shown in the previous chapter. In addition, $R_B$ may rise when the increase in leverage allows the possibility of default.

   For simplicity, we assume *risk neutrality* in this example. This means that investors are indifferent to the level of risk. Here, $R_S = R_B$ because risk-neutral investors do not demand compensation for bearing risk. In addition, neither $R_S$ nor $R_B$ rises with leverage. Because the interest rate is 10 per cent, our assumption of risk neutrality implies that $R_S = 10$ per cent as well.

   Though financial economists believe that investors are risk-averse, they frequently develop examples based on risk neutrality to isolate a point unrelated to risk. This is our approach because we want to focus on bankruptcy costs – not bankruptcy risk. The same qualitative conclusions from this example can be drawn in a world of risk aversion, albeit with *much* more difficulty for the reader.

3  'Lehman bankruptcy gets ugly', *Business Week*, 2 October 2008.

4  M.J. White, 'Bankruptcy costs and the new bankruptcy code', *Journal of Finance* (May 1983); E.I. Altman, 'A further empirical investigation of the bankruptcy cost question', *Journal of Finance* (September 1984); and L.A. Weiss, 'Bankruptcy resolution: direct costs and violation of priority of claims', *Journal of Financial Economics*, vol. 27 (1990).

5  Arturo Bris, Ivo Welch and Ning Zhu, 'The costs of bankruptcy: Chapter 7 liquidation versus Chapter 11 reorganization', *Journal of Finance*, vol. 61, no. 3 (2006), pp. 1253–1303; James Ang, Jess Chua and John McConnell, 'The administrative costs of bankruptcy: a note', *Journal of Finance*, vol. 37, no. 1 (1982), pp. 219–226.

6   E.I. Altman, *op. cit.*

7   Gregor Andrade and Steven N. Kaplan, 'How costly is financial (not economic) distress? Evidence from highly leveraged transactions that became distressed', *Journal of Finance* (October 1998).

8   Yuval Bar-Or, 'An investigation of expected financial distress costs', unpublished paper, Wharton School, University of Pennsylvania (March 2000).

9   David M. Cutler and Lawrence H. Summers, 'The costs of conflict resolution and financial distress: Evidence from the Texaco–Pennzoil litigation', *Rand Journal of Economics* (Summer 1988).

10  The same qualitative results will obtain if the £1,000 is raised from new shareholders. However, the arithmetic becomes much more difficult, because we must determine how many new shares are issued.

11  C.W. Smith and J.B. Warner, 'On financial contracting: an analysis of bond covenants', *Journal of Financial Economics*, vol. 7 (1979).

12  Legal limitations may prevent this practice in other countries.

13  Adam Smith, *The Wealth of Nations* [1776], Cannon edition (New York: Modern Library, 1937), p. 700, as quoted in M.C. Jensen and W. Meckling, 'Theory of the firm: managerial behavior, agency costs, and ownership structure', *Journal of Financial Economics*, vol. 3 (1978).

14  As previously discussed, *agency costs* are generally defined as the costs from the conflicts of interest among shareholders, bondholders, and managers.

15  The seminal theoretical article is Michael C. Jensen, 'The agency costs of free cash flow: corporate finance and takeovers', *American Economic Review* (May 1986), pp. 323–339.

16  L. Lang, R. Stulz and R. Walkling, 'Managerial performance, Tobin's Q and the gains in tender offers', *Journal of Financial Economics* (1989).

17  The pecking-order theory is generally attributed to S.C. Myers, 'The capital structure puzzle', *Journal of Finance*, vol. 39 (July 1984).

18  In the interest of simplicity, we have not presented our results in the form of a rigorous model. To the extent that a reader wants a deeper explanation, we refer him or her to S.C. Myers, *op. cit.*

19  See Merton Miller's Presidential Address to the American Finance Association, reprinted as 'Debt and taxes', *Journal of Finance* (May 1977).

20  J.L. Berens and C.L. Cuny, 'Inflation, growth and capital structure', *Review of Financial Studies*, vol. 8 (Winter 1995).

21  The same qualitative results occur under uncertainty, though the mathematics is more troublesome.

22  For simplicity, assume that growth is achieved without earnings retention. The same conclusions would be reached with retained earnings, though the arithmetic would become more involved. Of course, growth without earnings retention is less realistic than growth with retention.

23  Because the firm makes no real investment, the new debt is used to buy back shares of equity.

24  The firm can also be valued by a variant of Eq. 15.5:

$$V_L = V_U + \text{PVTS}$$
$$= \frac{€100(1 - t_C)}{0.10 - 0.05} + \frac{t_C \times €100}{0.10 - 0.05} = €2{,}000$$

where PVTS is present value of tax shield. Because of firm growth, both *VU* and PVTS are growing perpetuities.

25  Students are often surprised that equity has value when taxable income is zero. Actually, the equity-holders are receiving cash flow each period. The proceeds from the new debt can be used either to pay dividends or to buy back shares.

26  Our example assumes a single perpetual bond with level coupon payments. Berens and Cuny (BC) point out (p. 1201) that, with a number of different bonds, a firm might be able to construct an equally optimal capital structure with a greater debt-to-value (D/V) ratio. Because both capital structures are equally optimal, a firm might choose either one.

    Although the analysis with many financing instruments is more complex, a firm can still choose a low D/V with no ill effect. Thus BC's conclusion that firms *can* employ a significant amount of equity in a world with a low level of bankruptcy costs still holds.

27  M. Baker and J. Wurgler, 'Market timing and capital structure', *Journal of Finance* (2002).

28  E. Fama and K. French, 'Testing trade-off and pecking order predictions about dividends and debt', *Review of Financial Studies* (2002).

29  I. Welch, 'Capital structure and stock returns', *Journal of Political Economy* (2003).

30  A. Kayhan and S. Titman, 'Firms' histories and their capital structures', *Journal of Financial Economics* (2007).

31  Anup Agrawal and Nandu Nagarajan, 'Corporate capital structure, agency costs, and ownership control: the case of all-equity firms', *Journal of Finance*, vol. 45 (September 1990).

32  D. Brounen, A. de Jong and K. Koedijk, 'Capital structure policies in Europe: survey evidence', *Journal of Banking and Finance* (2006).

33  By contrast, the pecking-order theory argues that profitable firms will employ less debt because they can invest out of retained earnings. However, the pecking-order theory argues against the use of target ratios in the first place.

Online **LearningCentre**

To help you grasp the key concepts of this chapter check out the extra resources posted on the Online Learning Centre at **www.mcgraw-hill.co.uk/textbooks/hillier**

Among other helpful resources there are PowerPoint presentations, chapter outlines, mini-cases, and two appendices:

- Appendix 16A: Some Useful Formulas of Financial Structure
- Appendix 16B: The Miller Model and the Graduated Income Tax.

# Chapter 17

# Valuation and Capital Budgeting for the Levered Firm

The Private Finance Initiative (PFI) is a scheme that brings together the private and public sectors in big social infrastructure projects. Under PFI, a private consortium of firms will design, build, finance and operate an asset or service according to specifications imposed by the public sector. In return, the government will pay the private consortium periodic payments for this collaboration. The rationale underlying PFI is that private organizations are more efficient at running big investment projects, and this brings cost savings in addition to improved service and quality.

An example of the PFI is the building of the British Embassy in Berlin in 2000. Under this scheme, Arteos (a subsidiary of Bilfinger Berger, the German construction firm) financed and built the building. In addition, they were contracted to operate it for 30 years, after which ownership reverts to the British government. Why did Bilfinger Berger enter into the contract? One of the reasons was the attractive financial package offered to the company by the British government to undertake the collaboration.

Similarly, when a corporation opens a major plant or considers relocation, municipalities or regions often create a package loaded with subsidies, including tax credits, subsidized debt, educational training, road and infrastructure creation, and other incentives.

With subsidized debt, the government or region guarantees the debt, which allows the company to borrow at a much lower interest rate. If the interest rate on the debt is lower than the company's normal cost of debt, how does a company evaluate the financial benefits of this and other such subsidies? In this chapter, we illustrate how to evaluate projects using the adjusted present value method and some flow to equity approaches in capital budgeting that allow us to answer this question.

## 17.1 Adjusted Present Value Approach

When financing issues are an important part of an investment proposal, a good methodology to use is the adjusted present value method. The approach separates project cash flows from financing cash flows and values these separately. If the combined present values are positive, the project should be taken. The adjusted present value (APV) method is described by the following formula:

$$APV = NPV + NPVF$$

In words, the value of a project to a levered firm (APV) is equal to the value of the project to an unlevered firm (NPV) plus the net present value of the financing side effects (NPVF). We can generally think of four side effects:

1 *The tax subsidy to debt*: This was discussed in Chapter 15, where we pointed out that for perpetual debt the value of the tax subsidy is $t_c B$. ($t_c$ is the corporate tax rate, and $B$ is the value of the debt.) The material about valuation under corporate taxes in Chapter 15 is actually an application of the APV approach.

2 *The costs of issuing new securities*: As we shall discuss in detail in Chapter 20, bankers participate in the public issuance of corporate debt. These bankers must be compensated for their time and effort, a cost that lowers the value of the project.

3 *The costs of financial distress*: The possibility of financial distress, and bankruptcy in particular, arises with debt financing. As stated in the previous chapter, financial distress imposes costs, thereby lowering value.

4 *Subsidies to debt financing*: The interest on debt issued by state and local governments may not be taxable to the investor, or the tax may be discounted. Because of this, the yield on government debt can be substantially below the yield on taxable debt. Frequently corporations can obtain financing from a municipality at the tax-exempt rate because the municipality can borrow at that rate as well. As with any subsidy, this subsidy adds value.

Although each of the preceding four side effects is important, the tax deduction to debt almost certainly has the highest value in most actual situations. For this reason, the following example considers the tax subsidy but not the other three side effects. A later example will deal with all three.

Consider a project of P.B. Singer plc with the following characteristics:

- Cash inflows: £500,000 per year for the indefinite future.
- Cash costs: 72 per cent of sales.
- Initial investment: £520,000.
- $t_C = 28\%$
- $R_0 = 20$ per cent, where $R_0$ is the cost of capital for a project of an all-equity firm.

If both the project and the firm are financed with only equity, the project's cash flows are as follows:

|  | (£) |
|---|---|
| Cash inflows | 500,000 |
| Cash costs | −360,000 |
| Profit before tax | 140,000 |
| Corporate tax (28% tax rate) | −39,200 |
| Unlevered cash flow (UCF) | £100,800 |

The distinction between present value and net present value is important for this example. The *present value* of a project is determined before the initial investment at date 0 is subtracted. The initial investment is subtracted for the calculation of *net* present value.

Given a discount rate of 20 per cent, the present value of the project is

$$\frac{£100,800}{0.20} = £504,000$$

The net present value (NPV) of the project – that is, the value of the project to an all-equity firm – is

$$£504,000 - £520,000 = -£16,000$$

Because the NPV is negative, the project would be rejected by an all-equity firm.

Now imagine that the firm finances the project with exactly £135,483.90 in debt, so that the remaining investment of £384,516.10 (= £520,000 − £135,483.90) is financed with equity. The net present value of the project under leverage, which we call the adjusted present value, or the APV, is

$$
\begin{aligned}
\text{APV} &= \text{NPV} + t_C \times B \\
&= -\pounds16{,}000 + 0.28 \times \pounds135{,}483.90 \\
&= \pounds21{,}935
\end{aligned}
$$

That is, the value of the project when financed with some leverage is equal to the value of the project when financed with all equity plus the tax shield from the debt. Because this number is positive, the project should be accepted.

You may be wondering why we chose such a precise amount of debt. Actually, we chose it so that the ratio of debt to the present value of the project under leverage is 0.25.[1]

In this example, debt is a fixed proportion of the present value of the project, not a fixed proportion of the initial investment of £520,000. This is consistent with the goal of a target debt-to-*market*-value ratio, which we find is followed by companies in many countries. For example, banks typically lend to property developers a fixed percentage of the appraised market value of a project, not a fixed percentage of the initial investment.

## 17.2 Flow to Equity Approach

The **flow to equity (FTE)** approach is an alternative capital budgeting approach. The formula simply calls for discounting the cash flow from the project to the shareholders of the levered firm at the cost of equity capital, $R_S$. For a perpetuity this becomes

$$
\frac{\text{Cash flow from project to equity-holders of the levered firm}}{R_S}
$$

There are three steps to the FTE approach.

### Step 1: Calculating Levered Cash Flow (LCF)[2]

Assuming an interest rate of 10 per cent, the perpetual cash flow to shareholders in our P.B. Singer plc example is

|  | (£) |
| --- | --- |
| Cash inflows | 500,000 |
| Cash costs | −360,000 |
| Interest (10% × £135,483.90) | −13,548 |
| Income after interest | 126,452 |
| Corporate tax (28% tax rate) | −35,407 |
| Levered cash flow (LCF) | 91,045 |

Alternatively, we can calculate levered cash flow (LCF) directly from unlevered cash flow (UCF). The key here is that the difference between the cash flow that shareholders receive in an unlevered firm and the cash flow that shareholders receive in a levered firm is the after-tax interest payment. (Repayment of principal does not appear in this example because the debt is perpetual.) We write this algebraically as

$$
\text{UCF} - \text{LCF} = (1 - t_C)R_B B
$$

The term on the right side of this expression is the after-tax interest payment. Thus because cash flow to the unlevered shareholders (UCF) is £100,800 and the after-tax interest payment is £9,754.84 (= 0.72 × 0.10 × £135,483.90), cash flow to the levered shareholders (LCF) is

$$£100,800 - £9,755 = £91,045$$

which is exactly the number we calculated earlier.

## Step 2: Calculating $\bar{R}_S$

The next step is to calculate the discount rate, $R_S$. Note that we assumed that the discount rate on unlevered equity, $R_0$, is 0.20. As we saw in an earlier chapter, the formula for $R_S$ is

$$R_S = R_0 + \frac{B}{S}(1 - t_C)(R_0 - R_B)$$

Note that our target debt-to-value ratio of 1/4 implies a target debt-to-equity ratio of 1/3. Applying the preceding formula to this example, we have

$$R_S = 0.20 + \frac{1}{3}(0.72)(0.20 - 0.10)$$
$$= 0.224$$

## Step 3: Valuation

The present value of the project's LCF is

$$\frac{\text{LCF}}{R_S} = \frac{£91,045}{0.224} = £406,451$$

Because the initial investment is £520,000 and £135,483.90 is borrowed, the firm must advance the project £384,516.10 (= £520,000 − £135,483.90) out of its own cash reserves. The *net present value* of the project is simply the difference between the present value of the project's LCF and the investment not borrowed. Thus the NPV is

$$£406,451 - £384,516.10 = £21,935$$

which is identical to the result found with the APV approach.

## 17.3 Weighted Average Cost of Capital Method

Finally, we can value a project using the **weighted average cost of capital** (WACC) method. Although this method was discussed in earlier chapters, it is worth while to review it here. The WACC approach begins with the insight that projects of levered firms are simultaneously financed with both debt and equity. The cost of capital is a weighted average of the cost of debt and cost of equity. The cost of equity is $R_S$. Ignoring taxes, the cost of debt is simply the borrowing rate, $R_B$. However, with corporate taxes, the appropriate cost of debt is $(1 - t_C)R_B$, the after-tax cost of debt.

The formula for determining the weighted average cost of capital, $R_{\text{WACC}}$, is

$$R_{\text{WACC}} = \frac{S}{S + B}R_S + \frac{B}{S + B}R_B(1 - t_C)$$

The weight for equity, $S/(S + B)$, and the weight for debt, $B/(S + B)$, are target ratios. Target ratios are generally expressed in terms of market values, not accounting values. (Recall that another phrase for accounting value is *book value*.)

The formula calls for discounting the *unlevered* cash flow of the project (UCF) at the weighted average cost of capital, $R_{\text{WACC}}$. The net present value of the project can be written algebraically as

$$\sum_{t=1}^{\infty} \frac{\text{UCF}_t}{(1 + R_{\text{WACC}})^t} - \text{Initial investment}$$

If the project is a perpetuity, the net present value is

$$\frac{\text{UCF}}{R_{\text{WACC}}} - \text{Initial investment}$$

We previously stated that the target debt-to-value ratio of our project is 1/4 and the corporate tax rate is 0.28, implying that the weighted average cost of capital is

$$R_{WACC} = \frac{3}{4} \times 0.224 + \frac{1}{4} \times 0.10 \times 0.72$$
$$= 0.186$$

Note that $R_{WACC}$, 0.186, is lower than the cost of equity capital for an all-equity firm, 0.20. This must always be the case, because debt financing provides a tax subsidy that lowers the average cost of capital.

We previously determined the UCF of the project to be £100,800, implying that the present value of the project is

$$\frac{£100,800}{0.186} = £541,935$$

This initial investment is £520,000, so the NPV of the project is:

$$£541,935 - £520,000 = £21,935$$

Note that all three approaches yield the same value.

## 17.4 A Comparison of the APV, FTE and WACC Approaches

Capital budgeting techniques in the early chapters of this text applied to all-equity firms. Capital budgeting for the levered firm could not be handled earlier in the book, because the effects of debt on firm value were deferred until the previous two chapters. We learned there that debt increases firm value through tax benefits, but decreases value through bankruptcy and related costs.

In this chapter, we provide three approaches to capital budgeting for the levered firm. The adjusted present value (APV) approach first values the project on an all-equity basis. That is, the project's after-tax cash flows under all-equity financing (called unlevered cash flows, or UCF) are placed in the numerator of the capital budgeting equation. The discount rate, assuming all-equity financing, appears in the denominator. At this point, the calculation is identical to that performed in the early chapters of this book. We then add the net present value of the debt. We point out that the net present value of the debt is likely to be the sum of four parameters: tax effects, flotation costs, bankruptcy costs, and interest subsidies.

The flow to equity (FTE) approach discounts the after-tax cash flow from a project going to the shareholders of a levered firm (LCF). LCF, which stands for levered cash flow, is the residual to shareholders after interest has been deducted. The discount rate is $R_S$, the cost of capital to the shareholders of a levered firm. For a firm with leverage, $R_S$ must be greater than $R_0$, the cost of capital for an unlevered firm. This follows from our material in Chapter 15 showing that leverage raises the risk to the shareholders.

The last approach is the weighted average cost of capital (WACC) method. This technique calculates the project's after-tax cash flows assuming all-equity financing (UCF). The UCF is placed in the numerator of the capital budgeting equation. The denominator, $R_{WACC}$, is a weighted average of the cost of equity capital and the cost of debt capital. The tax advantage of debt is reflected in the denominator, because the cost of debt capital is determined net of corporate tax. The numerator does not reflect debt at all.

### Which Method Is Best?

The net present value of our project is exactly the same under each of the three methods. In theory, this should always be the case.[3] However, one method usually provides an easier computation than another, and in many cases one or more of the methods are virtually impossible computationally. We first consider when it is best to use the WACC and FTE approaches.

If the risk of a project stays constant throughout its life, it is plausible to assume that $R_0$ remains constant throughout the project's life. This assumption of constant risk appears to be reasonable for most real-world projects. In addition, if the debt-to-value ratio remains constant over the life of the project, both $R_S$ and $R_{WACC}$ will remain constant as well. Under this latter assumption, either the FTE or the WACC approach is easy to apply. However, if the debt-to-value ratio varies from year to year, both $R_S$ and $R_{WACC}$ vary from year to year as well. Using the FTE or the WACC approach when the denominator changes every year is computationally quite complex, and when computations become complex, the error rate rises. Thus both the FTE and WACC approaches present difficulties when the debt-to-value *ratio* changes over time.

The APV approach is based on the *level* of debt in each future period. Consequently, when the debt level can be specified precisely for future periods, the APV approach is quite easy to use. However, when the debt level is uncertain, the APV approach becomes more problematic. For example, when the debt-to-value ratio is constant, the debt level varies with the value of the project. Because the value of the project in a future year cannot be easily forecast, the level of debt cannot be easily forecast either.

Thus we suggest the following guideline:

**Use WACC or FTE if the firm's target debt-to-value *ratio* applies to the project over its life. Use APV if the project's *level* of debt is known over the life of the project.**

There are a number of situations where the APV approach is preferred. For example, in a leveraged buyout (LBO) the firm begins with a large amount of debt but rapidly pays down the debt over a number of years. Because the schedule of debt reduction in the future is known when the LBO is arranged, tax shields in every future year can be easily forecast. Thus the APV approach is easy to use here. (An illustration of the APV approach applied to LBOs is provided in the appendix to this chapter.) By contrast, the WACC and FTE approaches are virtually impossible to apply here, because the debt-to-equity value cannot be expected to be constant over time. In addition, situations involving interest subsidies and flotation costs are much easier to handle with the APV approach. Finally, the APV approach handles the lease-versus-buy decision much more easily than does either the FTE or the WACC approach.

The preceding examples are special cases. Typical capital budgeting situations are more amenable to either the WACC or the FTE approach than to the APV approach. In many countries, financial managers think in terms of target debt-to-value *ratios*. If a project does better than expected, both its value and its debt capacity are likely to rise. The manager will increase debt correspondingly here. Conversely, the manager would be likely to reduce debt if the value of the project were to decline unexpectedly. Of course, because financing is a time-consuming task, the ratio cannot be adjusted daily or monthly. Rather, the adjustment can be expected to occur over the long run. As mentioned before, the WACC and FTE approaches are more appropriate than the APV approach when a firm focuses on a target debt-to-value ratio.

Because of this, we recommend that the WACC and the FTE approaches, rather than the APV approach, be used in most real-world situations. In addition, frequent discussions with business executives have convinced us that the WACC is by far the most widely used method in the real world. Thus practitioners seem to agree with us that, outside the special situations mentioned, the APV approach is a less important method of capital budgeting.[4]

## The Three Methods of Capital Budgeting with Leverage

1   Adjusted present value (APV) method:

$$\sum_{t=1}^{\infty} \frac{UCF_t}{(1 + R_0)^t} + \text{Additional effects of debt} - \text{Initial investment}$$

where $UCF_t$ is the project's cash flow at date $t$ to the equity-holders of an unlevered firm, and $R_0$ is the cost of capital for project in an unlevered firm.

2   Flow to equity (FTE) method:

$$\sum_{t=1}^{\infty} \frac{LCF_t}{(1 + R_S)^t} - (\text{Initial investment} - \text{Amount borrowed})$$

where $LCF_t$ is the project's cash flow at date $t$ to the equity-holders of a levered firm, and $R_S$ is the cost of equity capital with leverage.

3   Weighted average cost of capital (WACC) method:

$$\sum_{t=1}^{\infty} \frac{UCF_t}{(1 + R_{WACC})^t} - \text{Initial investment}$$

where $R_{WACC}$ is the weighted average cost of capital.

### Notes

1   The middle term in the APV formula implies that the value of a project with leverage is greater than the value of the project without leverage. Because $R_{WACC} < R_0$, the WACC formula implies that the value of a project with leverage is greater than the value of the project without leverage.

2   In the FTE method, cash flow *after interest* (LCF) is used. Initial investment is reduced by *amount borrowed* as well.

### Guidelines

1   Use WACC or FTE if the firm's target debt-to-value *ratio* applies to the project over its life.

2   Use APV if the project's *level* of debt is known over the life of the project.

## 17.5 Capital Budgeting when the Discount Rate Must Be Estimated

The previous sections of this chapter introduced APV, FTE and WACC – the three basic approaches to valuing a levered firm. However, one important detail remains. The example in Sections 17.1 to 17.3 *assumed* a discount rate. We now want to show how this rate is determined for real-world firms with leverage, with an application to the three preceding approaches. The example in this section brings together the work in Chapters 9–12 on the discount rate for unlevered firms with that in Chapter 15 on the effect of leverage on the cost of capital.

EXAMPLE
**17.1**

## Cost of Capital

World-Wide Enterprises (WWE) is a large conglomerate thinking of entering the widget business, where it plans to finance projects with a debt-to-value ratio of 25 per cent (or, alternatively, a debt-to-equity ratio of 1/3). There is currently one firm in the widget industry, Asian Widgets (AW). This firm is financed with 40 per cent debt and 60 per cent equity. The beta of AW's equity is 1.5. AW has a borrowing rate of 12 per cent, and WWE expects to borrow for its widget venture at 10 per cent. The corporate tax rate for both firms is 0.40, the market risk premium is 8.5 per cent, and the riskless interest rate is 8 per cent. What is the appropriate discount rate for WWE to use for its widget venture?

As shown in Sections 17.1–17.3, a corporation may use one of three capital budgeting approaches: APV, FTE or WACC. The appropriate discount rates for these three approaches are $R_0$, $R_S$ and $R_{WACC}$, respectively. Because AW is WWE's only competitor in widgets, we look at AW's cost of capital to calculate $R_0$, $R_S$ and $R_{WACC}$ for WWE's widget venture. The following four-step procedure will allow us to calculate all three discount rates:

1  *Determining AW's cost of equity capital*: First, we determine AW's cost of equity capital using the security market line (SML):

AW's cost of equity capital:

$$R_S = R_F + \beta \times (\bar{R}_M - R_F)$$
$$= 8\% + 1.5 \times 8.5\%$$
$$= 20.75\%$$

where $\bar{R}_M$ is the expected return on the market portfolio and $R_F$ is the risk-free rate.

2  *Determining AW's hypothetical all-equity cost of capital*: We must standardize the preceding number in some way, because AW and WWE's widget ventures have different target debt-to-value ratios. The easiest approach is to calculate the hypothetical cost of equity capital for AW, assuming all-equity financing. This can be determined from MM's Proposition II under taxes:

AW's cost of capital if all equity:

$$R_S = R_0 + \frac{B}{S}(1 - t_C)(R_0 - R_B)$$
$$20.75\% = R_0 + \frac{0.4}{0.6}(0.60)(R_0 - 12\%)$$

By solving the equation, we find that $R_0 = 0.1825$. Of course, $R_0$ is less than $R_S$ because the cost of equity capital would be less when the firm employs no leverage.

At this point, firms in the real world generally make the assumption that the business risk of their venture is about equal to the business risk of the firms already in the business. Applying this assumption to our problem, we assert that the hypothetical discount rate of WWE's widget venture if all equity financed is also 0.1825.[5] This discount rate would be employed if WWE uses the APV approach because the APV approach calls for $R_0$, the project's cost of capital in a firm with no leverage.

3  *Determining $R_S$ for WWE's widget venture*: Alternatively, WWE might use the FTE approach, where the discount rate for levered equity is determined like this:

Cost of equity capital for WWE's widget venture:

$$R_S = R_0 + \frac{B}{S}(1 - t_C)(R_0 - R_B)$$
$$= 18.25\% + \frac{1}{3}(0.60)(18.25\% - 10\%)$$
$$= 19.9\%$$

Note that the cost of equity capital for WWE's widget venture, 0.199, is less than the cost of equity capital for AW, 0.2075. This occurs because AW has a higher debt-to-equity ratio. (As mentioned, both firms are assumed to have the same business risk.)

4  *Determining $R_{WACC}$ for WWE's widget venture*: Finally, WWE might use the WACC approach. Here is the appropriate calculation:

$R_{WACC}$ for WWE's widget venture:

$$R_{WACC} = \frac{B}{S + B}R_B(1 - t_C) + \frac{S}{S + B}R_S$$
$$= \frac{1}{4} \times 10\%(0.60) + \frac{3}{4} \times 19.9\%$$
$$= 16.425\%$$

The preceding example shows how the three discount rates, $R_0$, $R_S$ and $R_{WACC}$, are determined in the real world. These are the appropriate rates for the APV, FTE and WACC approaches, respectively. Note that $R_S$ for Asian Widgets is determined first, because the cost of equity capital can be determined from the beta of the firm's equity. As discussed in an earlier chapter, beta can easily be estimated for any publicly traded firm such as AW.

## 17.6 APV Example

As mentioned earlier in this chapter, firms generally set a target debt-to-equity ratio, allowing the use of WACC and FTE for capital budgeting. APV does not work as well here. However, as we also mentioned earlier, APV is the preferred approach when there are side benefits and side costs to debt. Because the analysis can be tricky, we now devote an entire section to an example where, in addition to the tax subsidy to debt, both flotation costs and interest subsidies come into play.

**EXAMPLE 17.2**

### APV

Bicksler Enterprises is considering a £10 million project that will last five years. The investment will be depreciated at 25 per cent reducing balance for tax purposes. At the end of the five years, the investment will be sold for its residual book value. The cash revenues less cash expenses per year are £3,500,000. The corporate tax bracket is 28 per cent. The risk-free rate is 10 per cent, and the cost of unlevered equity is 20 per cent.

First we shall calculate the depreciation in each year.

| | $C_0$ | $C_1$ | $C_2$ | $C_3$ | $C_4$ | $C_5$ |
|---|---|---|---|---|---|---|
| Initial outlay | −£10,000,000 | | | | | |
| Depreciation | | 0.25 × (£10,000,000) = £2,500,000 | 0.25 × (£7,500,000) = £1,875,000 | 0.25 × (£5,625,000) = £1,406,250 | 0.25 × (£4,218,750) = £1,054,688 | 0.25 × (£3,164,063) = £791,016 |
| Residual value | | £7,500,000 | £5,625,000 | £4,218,750 | £3,164,063 | £2,373,047 |

The cash flow projections each year are below. Because the investment is sold at its residual value, there are no tax implications for the final cash flow of £2,373,047. If, for example, Bicksler sold the investment for £3,000,000 it would be liable to pay tax on the profit of £626,953 (£3,000,000 − £2,373,047):

| | $C_0$ | $C_1$ | $C_2$ | $C_3$ | $C_4$ | $C_5$ | $C_6$ |
|---|---|---|---|---|---|---|---|
| Initial outlay | −£10,000,000 | | | | | | £2,373,047 |
| Depreciation tax shield | | 0.28 × £2,500,000 = £700,000 | 0.28 × £1,875,000 = £525,000 | 0.28 × £1,406,250 = £393,750 | 0.28 × £1,054,688 = £295,313 | 0.28 × £791,016 = £197,754 | |
| Revenue less expenses | | (1 − 0.28) × £3,500,000 = £2,520,000 | £2,520,000 | £2,520,000 | £2,520,000 | £2,520,000 | |

We stated before that the APV of a project is the sum of its all-equity value plus the additional effects of debt. We examine each in turn.

**All-Equity Value**    Assuming the project is financed with all equity, we shall discount the revenues and initial outlay cash flows by the cost of unlevered equity. The depreciation tax shield should be discounted at the risk-free rate. The present value of each cash flow is given below:

| | $C_0$ | $C_1$ | $C_2$ | $C_3$ | $C_4$ | $C_5$ | $C_6$ |
|---|---|---|---|---|---|---|---|
| Initial outlay | −£10,000,000 | | | | | | £794,729 |
| Depreciation tax shield | | £636,364 | £433,884 | £295,830 | £201,703 | £122,790 | |
| Revenue less expenses | | £2,100,000 | £1,750,000 | £1,458,333 | £1,215,278 | £1,012,731 | |
| Present value | −£10,000,000 | £2,736,364 | £2,183,884 | £1,754,164 | £1,416,981 | £1,135,521 | £794,729 |

The net present value is thus

$$-£10,000,000 + £2,736,364 + £2,183,884 + £1,754,164 + £1,416,981 + £1,135,521 + £794,729 = £21,642$$

This calculation uses the techniques presented in the early chapters of this book. Notice again that the depreciation tax shield is discounted at the riskless rate of 10 per cent. The revenues and expenses are discounted at the higher rate of 20 per cent.

An all-equity firm would accept the project, because the NPV is £21,642. However, equity flotation costs and economic volatility (not mentioned yet) would more than likely make the NPV negative. However, debt financing may add enough value to the project to justify acceptance. We consider the effects of debt next.

**Additional Effects of Debt** Bicksler Enterprises can obtain a five-year, non-amortizing loan for £7,500,000 after flotation costs at the risk-free rate of 10 per cent. Flotation costs are fees paid when equity or debt is issued. These fees may go to printers, lawyers, and bankers, among others. Bicksler Enterprises is informed that flotation costs will be 1 per cent of the gross proceeds of its loan. The previous chapter indicates that debt financing alters the NPV of a typical project. We look at the effects of debt next.

**Flotation Costs** Given that flotation costs are 1 per cent of the gross proceeds, we have

$$£7,500,000 = (1 − 0.01) \times \text{Gross proceeds}$$
$$= 0.99 \times \text{Gross proceeds}$$

Thus the gross proceeds are

$$\frac{£7,500,000}{1 − 0.01} = \frac{£7,500,000}{0.99}$$
$$= £7,575,758$$

This implies flotation costs of £75,758 (= 1% × £7,575,758). To check the calculation, note that net proceeds are £7,500,000 (= £7,575,758 − £75,758). In other words, Bicksler Enterprises receives only £7,500,000. The flotation costs of £75,758 are received by intermediaries such as bankers.

Under International Financial Reporting Standards, flotation costs directly attributable to an investment in a particular asset should be depreciated using the same method as the asset itself. In our case, depreciation would be charged on the flotation costs using 25 per cent reducing balance. The tax shield can then be calculated accordingly. Flotation costs are paid immediately, but are deducted from taxes by amortizing on a 25 per cent reducing-balance basis over the life of the loan. The depreciation schedule on the flotation costs is presented below:

| | $C_0$ | $C_1$ | $C_2$ | $C_3$ | $C_4$ | $C_5$ |
|---|---|---|---|---|---|---|
| Flotation costs | −£75,758 | | | | | |
| Depreciation | | 0.25 × (£75,758) = £18,940 | 0.25 × (£56,818) = £14,205 | 0.25 × (£42,613) = £10,653 | 0.25 × (£31,960) = £7,990 | 0.25 × (£23,970) = £5,993 |
| Residual value | | £56,818 | £42,613 | £31,960 | £23,970 | £17,977 |

The cash flows from flotation costs are as follows:

| | Date 0 | Date 1 | Date 2 | Date 3 | Date 4 | Date 5 | Date 6 |
|---|---|---|---|---|---|---|---|
| Flotation costs | −£75,758 | | | | | | |
| Deduction | | £18,940 | £14,205 | £10,653 | £7,990 | £5,993 | £17,977 |
| Tax shield from flotation costs | | 0.28(£18,940) = £5,303 | 0.28(£14,205) = £3,977 | 0.28(£10,653) = £2,983 | 0.28(£7,990) = £2,237 | 0.28(£5,993) = £1,678 | 0.28(£17,977) = £5,034 |
| PV(Costs) | −£75,758 | £4,821 | £3,287 | £2,241 | £1,528 | £1,042 | £2,841 |

When we discount at 10 per cent, the net cost of flotation is

$$-£75,758 + £4,821 + £3,287 + £2,241 + £1,528 + £1,042 + £2,841 = -£59,998$$

The net present value of the project after the flotation costs of debt but before the benefits of debt is

$$£21,642 - £59,998 = -£38,356$$

**Tax Subsidy**  Interest must be paid on the gross proceeds of the loan, even though intermediaries receive the flotation costs. Because the gross proceeds of the loan are £7,575,578, annual interest is £757,576 (= £7,575,758 × 0.10). The interest cost after taxes is £545,455 [= £757,576 × (1 − 0.28)]. Because the loan is non-amortizing, the entire debt of £7,575,758 is repaid at date 5. These terms are indicated here:

| | Date 0 | Date 1 | Date 2 | Date 3 | Date 4 | Date 5 |
|---|---|---|---|---|---|---|
| Loan (gross proceeds) | **£7,575,758** | | | | | |
| Interest paid | | 10% × £7,575,758 = £757,576 | £757,576 | £757,576 | £757,576 | £757,576 |
| Interest cost after taxes | | (1 − 0.28) × £757,576 = **£545,455** | **£545,455** | **£545,455** | **£545,455** | **£545,455** |
| Repayment of debt | | | | | | **£7,575,758** |

The relevant cash flows are listed in boldface in the preceding table. They are: (a) loan received, (b) annual interest cost after taxes, and (c) repayment of debt. Note that we include the *gross* proceeds of the loan as an inflow, because the flotation costs have previously been subtracted.

In Chapter 15 we mentioned that the financing decision can be evaluated in terms of net present value. The net present value of the loan is simply the sum of the net present values of each of the three cash flows. This can be represented as follows:

$$\text{NPV (loan)} = +\text{Amount borrowed} - \begin{matrix}\text{Present value} \\ \text{of after-tax} \\ \text{interest payments}\end{matrix} - \begin{matrix}\text{Present value} \\ \text{of loan} \\ \text{repayments}\end{matrix} \tag{17.1}$$

The calculations for this example are:

$$£804,105 = +£7,575,758 - \frac{£545,455}{0.10} \times \left[1 - \left(\frac{1}{1.10}\right)^5\right] - \frac{£7,575,758}{(1.10)^5} \tag{17.1'}$$

The NPV (loan) is positive, reflecting the interest tax shield.[6]

The adjusted present value of the project with this financing is

$$\text{APV} = \text{All-equity value} - \text{Flotation cost of debt} + \text{NPV (loan)} \tag{17.2}$$

$$\pounds768,749 = \pounds21,642 - \pounds59,998 + \pounds804,105 \tag{17.2'}$$

Though we previously saw that an all-equity firm would probably not accept the project (once equity flotation costs were taken into account), a firm would *accept* the project if a £7,500,000 (net) loan could be obtained.

Because the loan just discussed was at the market rate of 10 per cent, we have considered only two of the three additional effects of debt (flotation costs and tax subsidy) so far. We now examine another loan, where the third effect arises.

**Non–Market-Rate Financing**   A number of companies are fortunate enough to obtain subsidized financing from a governmental authority. Suppose that the project of Bicksler Enterprises is deemed socially beneficial, and the British government grants the firm a £7,500,000 loan at 8 per cent interest. In addition, all flotation costs are absorbed by the state. Clearly, the company will choose this loan over the one we previously calculated. Here are the cash flows from the loan:

| | Date 0 | Date 1 | Date 2 | Date 3 | Date 4 | Date 5 |
|---|---|---|---|---|---|---|
| Loan received | **£7,500,000** | | | | | |
| Interest paid | | 8% × £7,500,000 = £600,000 | £600,000 | £600,000 | £600,000 | £600,000 |
| After-tax interest | | (1 − 0.28) × £600,000 = **£432,000** | **£432,000** | **£432,000** | **£432,000** | **£432,000** |
| Repayment of debt | | | | | | **£7,500,000** |

The relevant cash flows are listed in boldface in the preceding table. Using Eq. (17.1), the NPV (loan) is

$$\pounds1,205,470 = +\pounds7,500,000 - \frac{\pounds432,000}{0.10} \times \left[1 - \left(\frac{1}{1.10}\right)^5\right] - \frac{\pounds7,500,000}{(1.10)^5} \tag{17.1''}$$

Why do we discount the cash flows in Eq. (17.1″) at 10 per cent when the firm is borrowing at 8 per cent? We discount at 10 per cent because that is the fair or market-wide rate. That is, 10 per cent is the rate at which the firm could borrow *without* benefit of subsidization. The net present value of the subsidized loan is larger than the net present value of the earlier loan, because the firm is now borrowing at the below-market rate of 8 per cent. Note that the NPV (loan) calculation in Eq. (17.1″) captures both the tax effect *and* the non–market-rate effect.

The net present value of the project with subsidized debt financing is

$$\text{APV} = \text{All-equity value} - \text{Flotation costs of debt} + \text{NPV (loan)}$$

$$\pounds1,227,112 = \pounds21,642 - \pounds0 + \pounds1,205,470 \tag{17.2''}$$

The preceding example illustrates the adjusted present value (APV) approach. The approach begins with the present value of a project for the all-equity firm. Next, the effects of debt are added in. The approach has much to recommend it. It is intuitively appealing, because individual components are calculated separately and added together in a simple way. And, if the debt from the project can be specified precisely, the present value of the debt can be calculated precisely.

## 17.7 Beta and Leverage

A previous chapter provides the formula for the relationship between the beta of the equity and leverage of the firm in a world without taxes. We reproduce this formula here:

The no-tax case:

$$\beta_{\text{Equity}} = \beta_{\text{Asset}}\left(1 + \frac{\text{Debt}}{\text{Equity}}\right) \tag{17.3}$$

As pointed out earlier, this relationship holds under the assumption that the beta of debt is zero.

Because firms must pay corporate taxes in practice, it is worth while to provide the relationship in a world with corporate taxes. It can be shown that the relationship between the beta of the unlevered firm and the beta of the levered equity is the following:[7]

The corporate tax case:

$$\beta_{\text{Equity}} = \left[1 + \frac{(1 - t_C)\text{Debt}}{\text{Equity}}\right]\beta_{\text{Unlevered firm}} \tag{17.4}$$

when (a) the corporation is taxed at the rate of $t_C$ and (b) the debt has a zero beta.

Because $[1 + (1 - t_C)\text{Debt/Equity}]$ must be more than 1 for a levered firm, it follows that $\beta_{\text{Unlevered firm}} < \beta_{\text{Equity}}$. The corporate tax case of Eq. (17.4) is quite similar to the no-tax case of Eq. (17.3), because the beta of levered equity must be greater than the beta of the unlevered firm in either case. The intuition that leverage increases the risk of equity applies in both cases.

However, notice that the two equations are not equal. It can be shown that leverage increases the equity beta less rapidly under corporate taxes. This occurs because, under taxes, leverage creates a *riskless* tax shield, thereby lowering the risk of the entire firm.

EXAMPLE
17.3

## Unlevered Betas

Ross McDermott plc is considering a scale-enhancing project. The market value of the firm's debt is £100 million, and the market value of the firm's equity is £200 million. The debt is considered riskless. The corporate tax rate is 28 per cent. Regression analysis indicates that the beta of the firm's equity is 2. The risk-free rate is 10 per cent, and the expected market premium is 8.5 per cent. What would the project's discount rate be in the hypothetical case that Ross McDermott plc is all-equity?

We can answer this question in two steps.

1 *Determining beta of hypothetical all-equity firm*: Rearranging Eq. (17.4), we have this:

Unlevered beta:

$$\frac{\text{Equity}}{\text{Equity} + (1 - t_C) \times \text{Debt}} \times \beta_{\text{Equity}} = \beta_{\text{Unlevered firm}}$$

$$\frac{\text{£200 million}}{\text{£200 million} + (1 - 0.28) \times \text{£100 million}} \times 2 = 1.47 \tag{17.5}$$

2 *Determining discount rate*: We calculate the discount rate from the security market line (SML) as follows:

Discount rate:

$$R_S = R_F + \beta \times (R_M - R_F)$$
$$= 10\% + 1.47 \times 8.5\%$$
$$= 22.5\%$$

## The Project Is not Scale Enhancing

Because the previous example assumed that the project is scale enhancing, we began with the beta of the firm's equity. If the project is not scale enhancing, we could begin with the equity betas of firms in the industry of the project. For each firm, we could calculate the hypothetical beta of the unlevered equity by Eq. (17.5). The SML could then be used to determine the project's discount rate from the average of these betas.

---

**EXAMPLE 17.4**

## More Unlevered Betas

The Irish firm J. Lowes plc, which currently manufactures staples, is considering a €1 million investment in a project in the aircraft adhesives industry. The corporation estimates unlevered after-tax cash flows (UCF) of €300,000 per year into perpetuity from the project. The firm will finance the project with a debt-to-value ratio of 0.5 (or, equivalently, a debt-to-equity ratio of 1:1).

The three competitors in this new industry are currently unlevered, with betas of 1.2, 1.3 and 1.4. Assuming a risk-free rate of 5 per cent, a market risk premium of 9 per cent, and a corporate tax rate of 12.5 per cent, what is the net present value of the project?

We can answer this question in five steps.

1  *Calculating the average unlevered beta in the industry*: The average unlevered beta across all three existing competitors in the aircraft adhesives industry is

$$\frac{1.2 + 1.3 + 1.4}{3} = 1.3$$

2  *Calculating the levered beta for J. Lowes's new project*: Assuming the same unlevered beta for this new project as for the existing competitors, we have, from Eq. (17.4),

Levered beta:

$$\beta_{\text{Equity}} = \left[1 + \frac{(1 - t_C)\text{Debt}}{\text{Equity}}\right]\beta_{\text{Unlevered firm}}$$
$$= \left(1 + \frac{0.875 \times 1}{1}\right) \times 1.3$$
$$= 2.4375$$

3  *Calculating the cost of levered equity for the new project*: We calculate the discount rate from the security market line (SML) as follows:

Discount rate:

$$R_S = R_F + \beta \times (R_M - R_F)$$
$$= 0.05 + 2.4375 \times 0.09$$
$$= 0.269$$

4  *Calculating the WACC for the new project*: The formula for determining the weighted average cost of capital, $R_{\text{WACC}}$, is

$$R_{\text{WACC}} = \frac{B}{V} R_B(1 - t_C) + \frac{S}{V} R_S$$
$$= \frac{1}{2} \times 0.05 \times 0.875 + \frac{1}{2} \times 0.269$$
$$= 0.156$$

5  *Determining the project's value*: Because the cash flows are perpetual, the NPV of the project is

$$\frac{\text{Unlevered cash flows (UCF)}}{R_{\text{WACC}}} - \text{Initial investment}$$
$$\frac{\text{€300,000}}{0.156} - \text{€1 million} = \text{€923,077}$$

## Summary and Conclusions

Earlier chapters of this text showed how to calculate net present value for projects of all-equity firms. We pointed out in the last two chapters that the introduction of taxes and bankruptcy costs changes a firm's financing decisions. Rational corporations should employ some debt in a world of this type. Because of the benefits and costs associated with debt, the capital budgeting decision for levered firms is different from that for unlevered firms. The present chapter has discussed three methods for capital budgeting by levered firms: the adjusted present value (APV), flows to equity (FTE), and weighted average cost of capital (WACC) approaches.

1  The APV formula can be written as

$$\sum_{t=1}^{\infty} \frac{UCF_t}{(1 + R_0)^t} + \text{Additional effects of debt} - \text{Initial investment}$$

There are four additional effects of debt:

(a)  Tax shield from debt financing

(b)  Flotation costs

(c)  Bankruptcy costs

(d)  Benefit of non–market-rate financing

2  The FTE formula can be written as

$$\sum_{t=1}^{\infty} \frac{LCF_t}{(1 + R_S)^t} - (\text{Initial investment} - \text{Amount borrowed})$$

3  The WACC formula can be written as

$$\sum_{t=1}^{\infty} \frac{UCF_t}{(1 + R_{WACC})^t} - \text{Initial investment}$$

4  Corporations frequently follow this guideline:

(a)  Use WACC or FTE if the firm's target debt-to-value *ratio* applies to the project over its life.

(b)  Use APV if the project's *level* of debt is known over the life of the project.

5  The APV method is used frequently for special situations such as interest subsidies, LBOs, and leases. The WACC and FTE methods are commonly used for more typical capital budgeting situations. The APV approach is a rather unimportant method for typical capital budgeting situations.

6  The beta of the equity of the firm is positively related to the leverage of the firm.

---

## connect Questions and Problems

CONCEPT
1–6

1  **Adjusted Present Value**   How is the APV of a project calculated?

2  **Flow to Equity**   What is the main difference between the FTE approach and APV and WACC?

3  **Weighted Average Cost of Capital**   Is WACC consistent with a target debt–equity ratio? Explain.

4   **APV, FTE and WACC**   Compare and contrast the three methods of capital budgeting. What are their strengths and weaknesses? When and why should you use each method instead of the other two? Are the three methods consistent when a firm does not have a target debt-to-equity ratio? Explain.

5   **Discount Rate in Capital Budgeting**   Review the steps required in calculating the correct discount rate for capital budgeting when a firm has a high level of debt in its capital structure.

6   **Beta and Leverage**   What are the two types of risk that are measured by a levered beta?

7   **Capital Budgeting**   You are determining whether your company should undertake a new project, and have calculated the NPV of the project using the WACC method when the CFO, a former accountant, notices that you did not use the interest payments in calculating the cash flows of the project. What should you tell him? If he insists that you include the interest payments in calculating the cash flows, what method can you use?

8   **NPV and APV**   Zoso is a rental car company that is considering whether to add 25 cars to its fleet. The company depreciates all its rental cars using 20 per cent reducing balance, and at the end of five years assumes that the cars will be sold at residual value. The new cars are expected to generate £120,000 per year in earnings before taxes and depreciation for five years. The company is entirely financed by equity and has a 28 per cent tax rate. The required return on the company's unlevered equity is 10 per cent, and the new fleet will not change the risk of the company.

(a)   What is the maximum price that the company should be willing to pay for the new fleet of cars if it remains an all-equity company?

(b)   Suppose the company can purchase the fleet of cars for £375,000. Additionally assume the company can issue £250,000 of five-year, 8 per cent debt to finance the project. All principal will be repaid in one balloon payment at the end of the fifth year. What is the adjusted present value (APV) of the project?

9   **APV**   Gemini plc, an all-equity firm, is considering a €2.4 million investment that will be depreciated according to 25 per cent reducing balances. At the end of its four-year life the investment will be sold for its residual value. The project is expected to generate earnings before taxes and depreciation of €850,000 per year for four years. The investment will not change the risk level of the firm. The company can obtain a four-year, 9.5 per cent loan to finance the project from a local bank. All principal will be repaid in one balloon payment at the end of the fourth year. The bank will charge the firm €24,000 in flotation fees, which will be amortized over the four-year life of the loan. If the company financed the project entirely with equity, the firm's cost of capital would be 13 per cent. The corporate tax rate is 12.5 per cent. Using the adjusted present value method, determine whether the company should undertake the project.

10   **Flow to Equity**   Milano Pizza owns three identical restaurants, popular for their speciality pizzas. Each restaurant has a debt–equity ratio of 40 per cent and makes interest payments of €29,500 at the end of each year. The cost of the firm's levered equity is 19 per cent. Each store estimates that annual sales will be €1 million; annual cost of goods sold will be €450,000; and annual general and administrative costs will be €325,000. These cash flows are expected to remain the same for ever. The corporate tax rate is 37.2 per cent.

(a)   Use the flow to equity approach to determine the value of the company's equity.

(b)   What is the total value of the company?

11   **WACC**   If Wild Widgets were an all-equity company, it would have a beta of 1.1. The company has a target debt–equity ratio of 0.40. The expected return on the market portfolio is 13 per cent, and Treasury bills currently yield 7 per cent. The company has one bond issue outstanding that matures in 20 years and has a 9 per cent coupon rate, compounded semi-annually. The bond currently sells for £97.50. The corporate tax rate is 28 per cent.

(a)   What is the company's cost of debt?

(b)   What is the company's cost of equity?

(c)   What is the company's weighted average cost of capital?

12 **Beta and Leverage** North Pole Fishing Equipment plc and South Pole Fishing Equipment plc would have identical equity betas of 1.25 if both were all-equity financed. The market value information for each company is shown here:

| | North Pole | South Pole |
|---|---|---|
| Debt | £1,400,000 | £2,600,000 |
| Equity | £2,600,000 | £1,400,000 |

The expected return on the market portfolio is 12.40 per cent, and the risk-free rate is 5.30 per cent. Both companies are subject to a corporate tax rate of 28 per cent. Assume the beta of debt is zero.

(a) What is the equity beta of each of the two companies?

(b) What is the required rate of return on each of the two companies' equity?

13 **NPV of Loans** Daniel Kaffe, CFO of Kendrick Enterprises, is evaluating a 10-year, 9 per cent loan with gross proceeds of €4,250,000. The interest payments on the loan will be made annually. Flotation costs are estimated to be 1.25 per cent of gross proceeds, and will be amortized using a 25 per cent reducing-balance method over the 10-year life of the loan. The company has a tax rate of 40 per cent, and the loan will not increase the risk of financial distress for the company.

(a) Calculate the net present value of the loan excluding flotation costs.

(b) Calculate the net present value of the loan including flotation costs.

14 **NPV for an All-Equity Company** Shattered Glass plc is an all-equity firm. The cost of the company's equity is currently 16 per cent, and the risk-free rate is 6 per cent. The company is currently considering a project that will cost £12.6 million and last six years. Assume 20 per cent reducing balance depreciation and the asset will be sold in six years at its residual value. The project will generate revenues minus expenses each year in the amount of £4.4 million. If the company has a tax rate of 28 per cent, should it accept the project?

15 **WACC** National Electric (NEC) is considering a €50 million project in its power systems division. Tom Edison, the company's chief financial officer, has evaluated the project and determined that the project's unlevered cash flows will be €3.5 million per year in perpetuity. Mr Edison has devised two possibilities for raising the initial investment: issuing 10-year bonds or issuing equity. NEC's pre-tax cost of debt is 7.2 per cent, and its cost of equity is 10.9 per cent. The company's target debt-to-value ratio is 80 per cent. The project has the same risk as NEC's existing businesses, and it will support the same amount of debt. NEC is in the 34 per cent tax bracket. Should NEC accept the project?

16 **WACC** Bolero plc has compiled the following information on its financing costs:

| Type of financing | Book value (£) | Market value (£) | Cost (%) |
|---|---|---|---|
| Long-term debt | 2,000,000 | 2,000,000 | 3.5 |
| Short-term debt | 9,000,000 | 8,000,000 | 6.8 |
| Ordinary shares | 6,000,000 | 22,000,000 | 14.5 |
| Total | 17,000,000 | 32,000,000 | |

The company is in the 28 per cent tax bracket, and has a target debt–equity ratio of 60 per cent. The target short-term debt/long-term debt ratio is 20 per cent.

(a) What is the company's weighted average cost of capital using book value weights?

(b) What is the company's weighted average cost of capital using market value weights?

(c)  What is the company's weighted average cost of capital using target capital structure weights?

(d)  What is the difference between WACCs? Which is the correct WACC to use for project evaluation?

17  **APV**   Triad SA has established a joint venture with Tobacco Road Construction SA to build a toll road in Normandy. The initial investment in paving equipment is €25 million. The equipment will be depreciated using the 20 per cent reducing-balance method over its economic life of five years, at the end of which it will be sold for its residual value. Earnings before interest, taxes and depreciation collected from the toll road are projected to be €3.4 million per annum for 20 years, starting from the end of the first year. The corporate tax rate is 33 per cent. The required rate of return for the project under all-equity financing is 13 per cent. The pre-tax cost of debt for the joint partnership is 8.5 per cent. To encourage investment in the country's infrastructure, the French government will subsidize the project with a €15 million, 15-year loan at an interest rate of 5 per cent per year. All principal will be repaid in one balloon payment at the end of year 15. What is the adjusted present value of this project?

18  **APV**   For the company in the previous problem, what is the value of being able to issue subsidized debt instead of having to issue debt at the terms it would normally receive? Assume the face amount and maturity of the debt issue are the same.

19  **APV**   MVP GmbH has produced football supplies for over 20 years. The company currently has a debt–equity ratio of 50 per cent and is in the 29.8 per cent tax bracket. The required return on the firm's levered equity is 16 per cent. MVP is planning to expand its production capacity. The equipment to be purchased is expected to generate the following unlevered cash flows:

| Year | Cash flow (€) |
|------|---------------|
| 0 | −24,000,000 |
| 1 | 8,000,000 |
| 2 | 13,000,000 |
| 3 | 10,000,000 |

The company has arranged a €12 million debt issue to partially finance the expansion. Under the loan the company would pay interest of 9 per cent at the end of each year on the outstanding balance at the beginning of the year. The company would also make year-end principal payments of €4 million per year, completely retiring the issue by the end of the third year. Using the adjusted present value method, should the company proceed with the expansion?

20  **WACC**   Neon Corporation's share price returns have a covariance with the market portfolio of 0.048. The standard deviation of the returns on the market portfolio is 20 per cent, and the expected market risk premium is 7.5 per cent. The company has bonds outstanding with a total market value of £30 million and a yield to maturity of 8 per cent. The company also has 5 million ordinary shares outstanding, each selling for £20. The company's CEO considers the firm's current debt–equity ratio optimal. The corporate tax rate is 28 per cent, and Treasury bills currently yield 6 per cent. The company is considering the purchase of additional equipment that would cost £40 million. The expected unlevered cash flows from the equipment are £13 million per year for five years. Purchasing the equipment will not change the risk level of the firm.

(a)  Use the weighted average cost of capital approach to determine whether Neon should purchase the equipment.

(b)  Suppose the company decides to fund the purchase of the equipment entirely with debt. What is the cost of capital for the project now? Explain.

CHALLENGE
21 – 24

21 **APV, FTE and WACC** Seger plc is an unlevered firm with expected annual earnings before taxes of £35 million in perpetuity. The current required return on the firm's equity is 20 per cent, and the firm distributes all of its earnings as dividends at the end of each year. The company has 1.5 million ordinary shares outstanding, and is subject to a corporate tax rate of 28 per cent. The firm is planning a recapitalization under which it will issue £40 million of perpetual 9 per cent debt and use the proceeds to buy back shares.

(a) Calculate the value of the company before the recapitalization plan is announced. What is the value of equity before the announcement? What is the price per share?

(b) Use the APV method to calculate the company value after the recapitalization plan is announced. What is the value of equity after the announcement? What is the price per share?

(c) How many shares will be repurchased? What is the value of equity after the repurchase has been completed? What is the price per share?

(d) Use the flow to equity method to calculate the value of the company's equity after the recapitalization.

22 **APV, FTE and WACC** Mojito Mint Company has a debt–equity ratio of 0.45. The required return on the company's unlevered equity is 17 per cent, and the pre-tax cost of the firm's debt is 9 per cent. Sales revenue for the company is expected to remain stable indefinitely at last year's level of £23,500,000. Variable costs amount to 60 per cent of sales. The tax rate is 28 per cent, and the company distributes all its earnings as dividends at the end of each year.

(a) If the company were financed entirely by equity, how much would it be worth?

(b) What is the required return on the firm's levered equity?

(c) Use the weighted average cost of capital method to calculate the value of the company. What is the value of the company's equity? What is the value of the company's debt?

(d) Use the flow to equity method to calculate the value of the company's equity.

23 **APV, FTE and WACC** Lone Star Industries just issued £160,000 of perpetual 10 per cent debt and used the proceeds to repurchase equity. The company expects to generate £75,000 of earnings before interest and taxes in perpetuity. The company distributes all its earnings as dividends at the end of each year. The firm's unlevered cost of capital is 18 per cent, and the corporate tax rate is 28 per cent.

(a) What is the value of the company as an unlevered firm?

(b) Use the adjusted present value method to calculate the value of the company with leverage.

(c) What is the required return on the firm's levered equity?

(d) Use the flow to equity method to calculate the value of the company's equity.

24 **Projects that Are not Scale Enhancing** Blue Angel Ltd, a private firm in the holiday gift industry, is considering a new project. The company currently has a target debt–equity ratio of 0.40, but the industry target debt–equity ratio is 0.35. The industry average beta is 1.2. The market risk premium is 8 per cent, and the risk-free rate is 7 per cent. Assume all companies in this industry can issue debt at the risk-free rate. The corporate tax rate is 28 per cent. The project requires an initial outlay of £450,000 and is expected to result in a £75,000 cash inflow at the end of the first year. The project will be financed at Blue Angel's target debt–equity ratio. Annual cash flows from the project will grow at a constant rate of 5 per cent until the end of the fifth year, and remain constant for ever thereafter. Should Blue Angel invest in the project?

# The Leveraged Buyout of Cheek Products Ltd

Cheek Products Ltd was founded 53 years ago by Joe Cheek, and originally sold snack foods such as crisps and biscuits. Through acquisitions, the company has grown into a conglomerate with major divisions in the snack food industry, home security systems, cosmetics and plastics. Additionally, the company has several smaller divisions. In recent years the company has been underperforming, but the company's management doesn't seem to be aggressively pursuing opportunities to improve operations (or the share price).

Meg Whalen is a financial analyst specializing in identifying potential buyout targets. She believes that two major changes are needed at Cheek. First, she thinks that the company would be better off if it sold several divisions and concentrated on its core competencies in snack foods and home security systems. Second, the company is financed entirely with equity. Because the cash flows of the company are relatively steady, Meg thinks the company's debt–equity ratio should be at least 0.25. She believes these changes would significantly enhance shareholder wealth, but she also believes that the existing board and company management are unlikely to take the necessary actions. As a result, Meg thinks the company is a good candidate for a leveraged buyout.

A leveraged buyout (LBO) is the acquisition by a small group of equity investors of a public or private company. Generally, an LBO is financed primarily with debt. The new shareholders service the heavy interest and principal payments with cash from operations and/or asset sales. Shareholders generally hope to reverse the LBO within three to seven years by way of a public offering or sale of the company to another firm. A buyout is therefore likely to be successful only if the firm generates enough cash to serve the debt in the early years, and if the company is attractive to other buyers a few years down the road.

Meg has suggested the potential LBO to her partners, Ben Feller and Brenton Flynn. Ben and Brenton have asked Meg to provide projections of the cash flows for the company. Meg has provided the following estimates (in millions):

|  | 2011 (£) | 2012 (£) | 2013 (£) | 2014 (£) | 2015 (£) |
|---|---|---|---|---|---|
| Sales | 1,627 | 1,824 | 1,965 | 2,012 | 2,106 |
| Costs | 432 | 568 | 597 | 645 | 680 |
| Depreciation | 287 | 305 | 318 | 334 | 340 |
| EBT | 908 | 951 | 1,050 | 1,033 | 1,086 |
| Capital expenditures | 165 | 143 | 180 | 182 | 195 |
| Change in NWC | (72) | (110) | 60 | 56 | 64 |
| Asset sales | 840 | 610 |  |  |  |

Meg estimates that at the end of five years the growth rate in cash flows will be 3.5 per cent per year. The capital expenditures are for new projects and the replacement of equipment that wears out. Additionally, the company would realize cash flow from the sale of several divisions. Even though the company will sell these divisions, overall sales should increase because of a more concentrated effort on the remaining divisions.

After ploughing through the company's financials and various pro forma scenarios, Ben and Brenton feel that in five years they will be able to sell the company to another party or take it public again. They are also aware that they will have to borrow a considerable amount of the purchase price. The interest payments on the debt for each of the next five years if the LBO is undertaken will be these (in millions):

|  | 2011 (£m) | 2012 (£m) | 2013 (£m) | 2014 (£m) | 2015 (£m) |
|---|---|---|---|---|---|
| Interest payments | 1,140 | 1,100 | 1,180 | 1,150 | 1,190 |

The company currently has a required return on assets of 14 per cent. Because of the high debt level, the debt will carry a yield to maturity of 12.5 per cent for the next five years. When the debt is refinanced in five years, they believe the new yield to maturity will be 8 per cent.

Cheek currently has 104 million shares of equity outstanding that sell for £53 per share. The corporate tax rate is 28 per cent. If Meg, Ben and Brenton decide to undertake the LBO, what is the most they should offer per share?

## Practical Case Study

We now return to our cement example in Chapters 7 and 8. So far, we have gone with a consensus discount rate and assumed away any complications from leverage. The cement company for which you are carrying out consultancy has no debt funding. However, it wishes to borrow from a multinational bank in Tanzania the total amount required for the loan. If it does this, its debt–equity ratio will increase to 50 per cent. Assuming that the surveyed discount rates (see Chapter 7 case study) are for the firm prior to any debt increase, how would you now alter the analysis to take into account the increased debt? Use all information available to you, including the financial statements of other relevant companies.

## Endnotes

1 That is, the present value of the project after the initial investment has been made is £541,935.49 (= £21,935.49 + £520,000). Thus the debt-to-value ratio of the project is 0.25 (£135,483.90/£541,935.49). This level of debt can be calculated directly. Note that

$$\text{Present value of levered project} = \text{Present value of unlevered project} + t_C \times B$$
$$V_{\text{With debt}} = £504,000 + 0.28 \times 0.25 \times V_{\text{With debt}}$$

Rearranging the last line, we have

$$V_{\text{With debt}} \times (1 - 0.28 \times 0.25) = £504,000$$
$$V_{\text{With debt}} = £541,935.5$$

Debt is 0.25 of value: £135,483.90 (= 0.25 × £541,935.5).

2 We use the term *levered cash flow* (LCF) for simplicity. A more complete term would be *cash flow from the project to the shareholders of a levered firm*. Similarly, a more complete term for *unlevered cash flow* (UCF) would be *cash flow from the project to the shareholders of an unlevered firm*.

3 See I. Inselbag and H. Kaufold, 'Two DCF approaches for valuing companies under alternative financial strategies (and how to choose between them)', *Journal of Applied Corporate Finance* (Spring 1997).

4 There is a lot of debate in the academic literature as to the best method in practice. For recent developments, see L. Booth, 'Finding value where none exists: the adjusted present value method', *Journal of Applied Corporate Finance* (Spring 2002); L. Booth, 'Capital cash flows, APV and valuation', *European Financial Management* (2007); M. Massari, F. Roncaglio and L. Zanetti, 'On the equivalence between the APV and WACC approach in a growing leveraged firm', *European Financial Management* (2008).

5 Alternatively, a firm might assume that its venture would be somewhat riskier because it is a new entrant. Thus the firm might select a discount rate slightly higher than 0.1825. Of course, no exact formula exists for adjusting the discount rate upwards.

6 The NPV (loan) must be zero in a no-tax world, because interest provides no tax shield there. To check this intuition, we calculate

$$\text{No-tax case: } 0 = +£7,575,758 - \frac{£757,576}{0.10} \times \left[1 - \left(\frac{1}{1.10}\right)^5\right] - \frac{£7,575,758}{(1.10)^5}$$

7 This result holds only if the beta of debt equals zero. To see this, note that:

$$V_U + t_C B = V_L = B + S \tag{a}$$

where $V_U$ is the value of an unlevered firm, $V_L$ is the value of a levered firm, $B$ is the market value of debt in a levered firm, and $S$ is the market value of equity in a levered firm.

As we stated in the text, the beta of the levered firm is a weighted average of the debt beta and the equity beta:

$$\frac{B}{B+S} \times \beta_B + \frac{S}{B+S} \times \beta_S$$

where $\beta_B$ and $\beta_S$ are the betas of the debt and the equity of the levered firm, respectively. Because $V_L = B + S$, we have

$$\frac{B}{V_L} \times \beta_B + \frac{S}{V_L} \times \beta_S \tag{b}$$

The beta of the levered firm can *also* be expressed as a weighted average of the beta of the unlevered firm and the beta of the tax shield:

$$\frac{V_U}{V_U + t_C B} \times \beta_U + \frac{t_C B}{V_U + t_C B} \times \beta_B$$

where $\beta_U$ is the beta of the unlevered firm. This follows from Eq. (a). Because $V_L = V_U + t_C B$, we have

$$\frac{V_U}{V_L} \times \beta_U + \frac{t_C B}{V_L} \times \beta_B \tag{c}$$

We can equate (b) and (c) because both represent the beta of a levered firm. Eq. (a) tells us that $V_U = S + (1 - t_C) \times B$. Under the assumption that $\beta_B = 0$, equating (b) and (c) and using Eq. (a) yields Eq. (17.4).

The generalized formula for the levered beta (where $\beta_B$ is not zero) is

$$\beta_S = \beta_U + (1 - t_C)(\beta_U - \beta_B)\frac{B}{S}$$

and

$$\beta_U = \frac{S}{B(1 - t_C) + S}\beta_S + \frac{B(1 - t_C)}{B(1 - t_C) + S}\beta_B$$

# Chapter 18

# Dividends and Other Payouts

## KEY NOTATIONS

| | |
|---|---|
| Div | Dividends |
| EPS | Earnings per share |
| NPV | Net present value |
| $R_s$ | Discount rate |
| s | Speed of adjustment of current dividends to target |
| t | Target payout ratio |
| V | Value of firm |

On 27 February 2009 dividends featured heavily in the news. With cash in scarce supply, on this day many firms announced a drop or non-payment of dividends for 2008. For example, William Hill plc announced that it wouldn't be able to pay its promised dividend (its share price dropped over 3 per cent as a result). Liberty plc also stated it would scrap its dividend (its share price fell 2.54 per cent on the announcement). Elsewhere, Trinity Mirror plc's share price dropped 4.84 per cent when it announced no dividends, and Berkeley Group's price fell by 2.13 per cent on its dividend omission.

Why are dividends so important? This chapter explores the importance of dividends to corporate managers, and the reasons why firms like to pay them.

## 18.1 Different Types of Dividend

The term *dividend* usually refers to a cash distribution of earnings. If a distribution is made from sources other than current or accumulated retained earnings, the term *distribution* rather than dividend is used. However, it is acceptable to refer to a distribution from earnings as a *dividend* and a distribution from capital as a *liquidating dividend*. More generally, any direct payment by the corporation to shareholders may be considered part of dividend policy.

The most common type of dividend is in the form of cash. Public companies usually pay regular cash dividends twice or four times a year. Sometimes firms will pay a regular cash dividend and an *extra cash dividend*. Paying a cash dividend reduces corporate cash and retained earnings – except in the case of a liquidating dividend (where paid-in capital may be reduced).

Another type of dividend is paid out in shares of equity. This dividend is referred to as a stock dividend. It is not a true dividend, because no cash leaves the firm. Rather, a stock dividend increases the number of shares outstanding, thereby reducing the value of each share. A stock dividend is commonly expressed as a ratio: for example, with a 2 per cent stock dividend a shareholder receives 1 new share for every 50 currently owned.

When a firm declares a stock split, it increases the number of shares outstanding. Because each share is now entitled to a smaller percentage of the firm's cash flow, the share price should fall. For example, if the managers of a firm whose equity is selling at 90 rand declare a 3:1 stock split, the price of a share of equity should fall to about 30 rand. A stock split strongly resembles a stock dividend except that it is usually much larger.

## 18.2 Standard Method of Cash Dividend Payment

The decision to pay a dividend rests in the hands of the board of directors of the corporation. A dividend is distributable to shareholders of record on a specific date. When a dividend has been declared, it becomes a liability of the firm and cannot be easily rescinded by the corporation. The amount of dividend is expressed as pounds/euros/currency per share (*dividend per share*), as a percentage of the market price (*dividend yield*), or as a percentage of earnings per share (*dividend payout*).

The mechanics of a dividend payment can be illustrated by the example in Fig. 18.1 and the following chronology:

1 *Declaration date*: On 15 January (the declaration date) the board of directors passes a resolution to pay a dividend of £1 per share on 16 February to all holders of record on 30 January.

2 *Date of record*: The corporation prepares a list on 30 January of all individuals believed to be shareholders as of this date. The word *believed* is important here: the dividend will not be paid to individuals whose notification of purchase is received by the company after 30 January.

3 *Ex-dividend date*: The procedure for the date of record would be unfair if efficient brokerage houses could notify the corporation by 30 January of a trade occurring on 29 January, whereas the same trade might not reach the corporation until 2 February if executed by a less efficient house. To eliminate this problem, all brokerage firms entitle shareholders to receive the dividend if they purchased the equity three business days before the date of record. The second day before the date of record, which is Wednesday 28 January in our example, is called the *ex-dividend date*. Before this date the shares are said to trade *cum dividend*.

4 *Date of payment*: The dividend cheques are mailed to the shareholders on 16 February.

Obviously, the ex-dividend date is important, because an individual purchasing the security before the ex-dividend date will receive the current dividend, whereas another individual purchasing the security on or after this date will not receive the dividend. The share price will therefore fall on the ex-dividend date (assuming no other events occur). It is worth while to note that this drop is an indication of efficiency, not inefficiency, because the market rationally attaches value to a cash dividend. In a world with neither taxes nor transaction costs, the share price would be expected to fall by the amount of the dividend:

$$
\begin{array}{ll}
\text{Before ex-dividend date} & \text{Price} = £(P + 1) \\
\text{On or after ex-dividend date} & \text{Price} = £P
\end{array}
$$

FIGURE 18.1

| Thursday, 15 January | Wednesday, 28 January | Friday, 30 January | Monday, 16 February | Days |
|---|---|---|---|---|
| Declaration date | Ex-dividend date | Record date | Payment date | |

1 *Declaration date*: The board of directors declares a payment of dividends.
2 *Record date*: The declared dividends are distributable to shareholders of record on a specific date.
3 *Ex-dividend date*: A share of equity becomes ex dividend on the date the seller is entitled to keep the dividend; under stock exchange rules, shares are traded ex dividend on and after the second business day before the record date.
4 *Payment date*: The dividend cheques are mailed to shareholders of record.

**Figure 18.1** Example of procedure for dividend payment

**Perfect world case**

**Ex-date**

$$\text{Price} = \pounds(P+1) \quad \underset{-t \quad \cdots \quad -2 \quad -1 \quad 0 \quad +1 \quad +2 \quad \cdots \quad t}{\rule{6cm}{0.4pt}}$$

£1 is the ex-dividend price drop

Price = £*P*

In a world without taxes, the share price will fall by the amount of the dividend on the ex-date (time 0). If the dividend is £1 per share, the price will be equal to *P* on the ex-date.

| Before ex-date (–1) | Price = £(*P* + 1) |
| Ex-date (0) | Price = £*P* |

**Figure 18.2** Price behaviour around the ex-dividend date for a £1 cash dividend

This is illustrated in Fig. 18.2.

The amount of the price drop may depend on tax rates. For example, consider the case with no capital gains taxes. On the day before an equity goes ex-dividend, a purchaser must decide either (a) to buy the shares immediately and pay tax on the forthcoming dividend, or (b) to buy the shares tomorrow, thereby missing the dividend. If all investors are in the 25 per cent bracket and the dividend is £1, the share price should fall by £0.75 on the ex-dividend date. That is, if the share price falls by this amount on the ex-dividend date, purchasers will receive the same return from either strategy.

As an example of the price drop on the ex-dividend date, consider an extraordinary dividend paid by Microsoft in 2004. The shares went ex dividend on 15 November 2004 with a total dividend of $3.08 per share, consisting of a $3 special dividend and a $0.08 regular dividend. The following share price chart shows the price of Microsoft shares on each of the four days prior to the ex-dividend date and on the ex-dividend date:

The shares closed at $29.97 on 12 November (a Friday) and opened at $27.34 on 15 November, a drop of $2.63. With a 15 per cent tax rate on dividends we would have expected a drop of $2.62, and the actual price drop was almost exactly that amount.

## 18.3  The Benchmark Case: An Illustration of the Irrelevance of Dividend Policy

A powerful argument can be made that dividend policy does not matter. This will be illustrated with the Bristol Corporation. Bristol is an all-equity firm started 10 years ago. The current financial managers know at the present time (date 0) that the firm will dissolve in one year (date 1). At date 0 the managers are able to forecast cash flows with perfect certainty. The managers know that the firm will receive a cash flow of £10,000 immediately and another £10,000 next year. Bristol has no additional positive NPV projects.

### Current Policy: Dividends Set Equal to Cash Flow

At the present time, dividends (Div) at each date are set equal to the cash flow of £10,000. The value of the firm can be calculated by discounting these dividends. This value is expressed as

$$V_0 = \text{Div}_0 + \frac{\text{Div}_1}{1 + R_S}$$

where $\text{Div}_0$ and $\text{Div}_1$ are the cash flows paid out in dividends, and $R_S$ is the discount rate. The first dividend is not discounted because it will be paid immediately.

Assuming $R_S = 10$ per cent, the value of the firm is

$$£10,000 + \frac{£10,000}{1.1} = £19,090.91$$

If 1,000 shares are outstanding, the value of each share is

$$£10 + \frac{£10}{1.1} = £19.09 \tag{18.1}$$

To simplify the example, we assume that the ex-dividend date is the same as the date of payment. After the imminent dividend is paid, the share price will immediately fall to £9.09 (= £19.09 − £10). Several members of Bristol's board have expressed dissatisfaction with the current dividend policy and have asked you to analyse an alternative policy.

### Alternative Policy: Initial Dividend Is Greater than Cash Flow

Another policy is for the firm to pay a dividend of £11 per share immediately, which is, of course, a total dividend payout of £11,000. Because the cash runoff is only £10,000, the extra £1,000 must be raised in one of a few ways. Perhaps the simplest would be to issue £1,000 of bonds or equity now (at date 0). Assume that equity is issued, and the new shareholders will desire enough cash flow at date 1 to let them earn the required 10 per cent return on their date 0 investment. The new shareholders will demand £1,100 of the date 1 cash flow, leaving only £8,900 to the old shareholders. The dividends to the old shareholders will be these:

|                                        | Date 0 (£) | Date 1 (£) |
|----------------------------------------|------------|------------|
| Aggregate dividends to old shareholders | 11,000     | 8,900      |
| Dividends per share                     | 11.00      | 8.90       |

The present value of the dividends per share is therefore

$$£11 + \frac{£8.90}{1.1} = £19.09 \tag{18.2}$$

Students often find it instructive to determine the price at which the new equity is issued. Because the new shareholders are not entitled to the immediate dividend, they would pay £8.09 (= £8.90/1.1) per share. Thus 123.61 (= £1,000/£8.09) new shares are issued.

**Figure 18.3** Current and alternative dividend policies

## The Indifference Proposition

Note that the values in Eqs (18.1) and (18.2) are equal. This leads to the initially surprising conclusion that the change in dividend policy did not affect the value of a share of equity. However, on reflection, the result seems sensible. The new shareholders are parting with their money at date 0 and receiving it back with the appropriate return at date 1. In other words, they are taking on a zero NPV investment. As illustrated in Fig. 18.3, old shareholders are receiving additional funds at date 0 but must pay the new shareholders their money with the appropriate return at date 1. Because the old shareholders must pay back principal plus the appropriate return, the act of issuing new equity at date 0 will not increase or decrease the value of the old shareholders' holdings. That is, they are giving up a zero NPV investment to the new shareholders. An increase in dividends at date 0 leads to the necessary reduction of dividends at date 1, so the value of the old shareholders' holdings remains unchanged.

This illustration is based on the pioneering work of Miller and Modigliani (MM). Although our presentation is in the form of a numerical example, the MM paper proves that investors are indifferent to dividend policy in a more general setting.

## Homemade Dividends

To illustrate the indifference investors have towards dividend policy in our example, we used present value equations. An alternative and perhaps more intuitively appealing explanation avoids the mathematics of discounted cash flows.

FIGURE
18.4

The graph illustrates both (a) how managers can vary dividend policy and (b) how individuals can undo the firm's dividend policy.

*Managers varying dividend policy*: A firm paying out all cash flows immediately is at point A on the graph. The firm could achieve point B by issuing equity to pay extra dividends or achieve point C by buying back old equity with some of its cash.

*Individuals undoing the firm's dividend policy*: Suppose the firm adopts the dividend policy represented by point B: dividends per share of £11 at date 0 and £8.90 at date 1. An investor can reinvest £1 of the dividends at 10 per cent, which will place her at point A. Suppose, alternatively, the firm adopts the dividend policy represented by point A. An investor can sell off £1 of equity at date 0, placing him at point B. No matter what dividend policy the firm establishes, a shareholder can undo it.

**Figure 18.4** Homemade dividends: a trade-off between dividends per share at date 0 and dividends per share at date 1

Suppose individual investor $X$ prefers dividends per share of £10 at both dates 0 and 1. Would she be disappointed when informed that the firm's management is adopting the alternative dividend policy (dividends of £11 and £8.90 on the two dates, respectively)? Not necessarily: she could easily reinvest the £1 of unneeded funds received on date 0, yielding an incremental return of £1.10 at date 1. Thus she would receive her desired net cash flow of £11 − £1 = £10 at date 0 and £8.90 + £1.10 = £10 at date 1.

Conversely, imagine investor $Z$ preferring £11 of cash flow at date 0 and £8.90 of cash flow at date 1, who finds that management will pay dividends of £10 at both dates 0 and 1. He can sell off shares of equity at date 0 to receive the desired amount of cash flow. That is, if he sells off shares (or fractions of shares) at date 0 totalling £1, his cash flow at date 0 becomes £10 + £1 = £11. Because a £1 sale of shares at date 0 will reduce his dividends by £1.10 at date 1, his net cash flow at date 1 would be £10 − £1.10 = £8.90.

The example illustrates how investors can make homemade dividends. In this instance, corporate dividend policy is being undone by a potentially dissatisfied shareholder. This homemade dividend is illustrated by Fig. 18.4. Here the firm's cash flows of £10 per share at both dates 0 and 1 are represented by point A. This point also represents the initial dividend payout. However, as we just saw, the firm could alternatively pay out £11 per share at date 0 and £8.90 per share at date 1, a strategy represented by point B. Similarly, by either issuing new equity or buying back old equity, the firm could achieve a dividend payout represented by any point on the diagonal line.

The previous paragraph describes the choices available to the managers of the firm. The same diagonal line also represents the choices available to the shareholder. For example, if the shareholder receives a per-share dividend distribution of (£11, £8.90), he or she can either reinvest some of the dividends to move down and to the right on the graph, or sell off shares of equity and move up and to the left.

The implications of the graph can be summarized in two sentences:

1   By varying dividend policy, managers can achieve any payout along the diagonal line in Fig. 18.4.

2   Either by reinvesting excess dividends at date 0 or by selling off shares of equity at this date, an individual investor can achieve any net cash payout along the diagonal line.

Thus because both the corporation and the individual investor can move only along the diagonal line, dividend policy in this model is irrelevant. The changes the managers make in dividend policy can be undone by an individual who, by either reinvesting dividends or selling off equity, can move to a desired point on the diagonal line.

## A Test

You can test your knowledge of this material by examining these true statements:

1 Dividends are relevant.

2 Dividend policy is irrelevant.

The first statement follows from common sense. Clearly, investors prefer higher dividends to lower dividends at any single date if the dividend level is held constant at every other date. In other words, if the dividend per share at a given date is raised while the dividend per share for each other date is held constant, the share price will rise. This act can be accomplished by management decisions that improve productivity, increase tax savings, or strengthen product marketing. In fact, you may recall that in Chapter 5 we argued that the value of a firm's equity is equal to the discounted present value of all its future dividends.

The second statement is understandable once we realize that dividend policy cannot raise the dividend per share at one date while holding the dividend level per share constant at all other dates. Rather, dividend policy merely establishes the trade-off between dividends at one date and dividends at another date. As we saw in Fig. 18.4, an increase in date 0 dividends can be accomplished only by a decrease in date 1 dividends. The extent of the decrease is such that the present value of all dividends is not affected.

Thus, in this simple world, dividend policy does not matter. That is, managers choosing either to raise or to lower the current dividend do not affect the current value of their firm. This theory is powerful, and the work of MM is generally considered a classic in modern finance. With relatively few assumptions, a rather surprising result is shown to be perfectly true. Nevertheless, because we want to examine many real-world factors ignored by MM, their work is only a starting point in this chapter's discussion of dividends. Later parts of this chapter investigate these real-world considerations.

## Dividends and Investment Policy

The preceding argument shows that an increase in dividends through issuance of new shares neither helps nor hurts the shareholders. Similarly, a reduction in dividends through share repurchases neither helps nor hurts shareholders.

What about reducing capital expenditures to increase dividends? Earlier chapters show that a firm should accept all positive net present value projects. To do otherwise would reduce the value of the firm. Thus we have an important point:

**Firms should never give up a positive NPV project to increase a dividend (or to pay a dividend for the first time).**

This idea was implicitly considered by Miller and Modigliani. One of the assumptions underlying their dividend irrelevance proposition was this: 'The investment policy of the firm is set ahead of time and is not altered by changes in dividend policy.'

As later sections will show, there is always more to real life than theory predicts.

## 18.4 Share Repurchases

Instead of paying dividends, a firm may use cash to repurchase shares of its own equity. Share repurchases have taken on increased importance in recent years. Consider Fig. 18.5, which shows the average ratios of dividends to earnings, repurchases to earnings, and total payout (both dividends and repurchases) to earnings for US industrial firms over the years from 1984 to 2004. As can be seen, the ratio of repurchases to earnings was far less than the ratio of dividends to earnings in the early years. However, the ratio of repurchases to earnings exceeded the ratio of dividends to earnings by 1998. This trend reversed after 1999, with the ratio of repurchases to earnings falling slightly below the ratio of dividends to earnings by 2004.

FIGURE
**18.5**

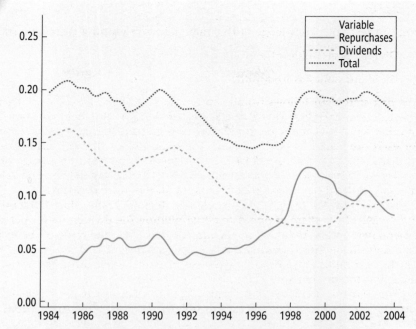

The graph shows the average ratios of repurchases, dividends and total payout (both repurchases and dividends) to earnings for US industrial companies over the years from 1984 to 2004. The graph indicates growth in repurchases over much of the sample period.

*Source*: Figure 3 of Brandon Julio and David Ikenberry, 'Reappearing dividends', *Journal of Applied Corporate Finance* (2004).

**Figure 18.5** Ratios of various payouts to earnings

Across Europe the pattern is historically quite different, most notably because share repurchases were not common, and in several cases were illegal, on the continent and the UK. For example, Ferris, Sen and Yui[1] show that, in 2002, less than 1 per cent of all British firms repurchased shares. Similarly, Rau and Vermaelen[2] report that although the level of British repurchases is low, the activity was significantly more common in the UK than in the rest of Europe combined. However, in recent years the pattern has shifted significantly, and by 2005 share repurchases were over half the value of all cash dividends in the European Union.[3] Table 18.1 shows the trend in share repurchases over the period 1989 to 2005. It is clear that, in all countries, share repurchases have become a much more important part of payout policy since 1999.

Share repurchases are typically accomplished in one of three ways. First, companies may simply purchase their own equity, just as anyone would buy shares of a particular company. In these *open market purchases* the firm does not reveal itself as the buyer. Thus the seller does not know whether the shares were sold back to the firm or to just another investor.

Second, the firm could institute a *tender offer*. Here, the firm announces to all of its shareholders that it is willing to buy a fixed number of shares at a specific price. For example, suppose Arts and Crafts (A&C) NV has 1 million shares outstanding, with a share price of €50. The firm makes a tender offer to buy back 300,000 shares at €60 per share. A&C chooses a price above €50 to induce shareholders to sell – that is, tender – their shares. In fact, if the tender price is set high enough, shareholders may want to sell more than the 300,000 shares. In the extreme case where all outstanding shares are tendered, A&C will buy back 3 out of every 10 shares that a shareholder has.

Finally, firms may repurchase shares from specific individual shareholders, a procedure called a *targeted repurchase*. For example, suppose International Biotechnology AB purchased

**TABLE 18.1**

| Year | Austria (€m) | Belgium (€m) | Denmark (€m) | Finland (€m) | France (€m) | Germany (€m) | Greece (€m) | Ireland (€m) | Italy (€m) | Luxembourg (€m) | Netherlands (€m) | Portugal (€m) | Spain (€m) | Sweden (€m) | United Kingdom (€m) | All countries (€m) |
|---|---|---|---|---|---|---|---|---|---|---|---|---|---|---|---|---|
| 1989 | 0 | 0 | 8 | 129 | 577 | 0 | 0 | 0 | 260 | 0 | 114 | 6 | 46 | 40 | 4,965 | 6,146 |
| 1990 | 0 | 0 | 27 | 134 | 278 | 54 | 0 | 0 | 366 | 0 | 19 | 0 | 37 | 3 | 1,543 | 2,461 |
| 1991 | 0 | 0 | 0 | 22 | 99 | 0 | 0 | 0 | 99 | 0 | 19 | 0 | 2 | 17 | 316 | 575 |
| 1992 | 0 | 0 | 0 | 83 | −11 | 210 | 0 | 5 | 202 | 0 | 18 | 3 | 6 | 35 | 462 | 1,013 |
| 1993 | 0 | 5 | 1 | 9 | 91 | 45 | 0 | 58 | 1 | 0 | 1 | −14 | 33 | 14 | 1,049 | 1,293 |
| 1994 | 0 | 0 | 16 | 5 | 151 | 70 | 0 | 6 | 0 | 0 | 432 | 11 | 23 | 0 | 1,100 | 1,813 |
| 1995 | 0 | 0 | 2 | 40 | 252 | 2 | 0 | 71 | 0 | 5 | 5 | 7 | 59 | 2 | 898 | 1,344 |
| 1996 | 0 | 0 | 0 | 104 | 86 | 1 | 0 | 1 | 0 | 3 | 140 | 16 | 82 | 363 | 1,152 | 1,946 |
| 1997 | 1 | 0 | 16 | 20 | 472 | 71 | 0 | 13 | 27 | 2 | 540 | 17 | 67 | 1,743 | 6,726 | 9,717 |
| 1998 | 0 | 0 | 331 | 388 | 888 | 4 | 0 | 66 | 182 | 3 | 1,405 | 60 | 218 | 610 | 13,569 | 17,723 |
| 1999 | 24 | 0 | 463 | 247 | 5,019 | 1,601 | 0 | 29 | 153 | 1 | 1,464 | 36 | 177 | 408 | 6,706 | 16,329 |
| 2000 | 105 | 107 | 665 | 542 | 4,291 | 4,583 | 4 | 16 | 697 | 0 | 1,443 | 38 | 173 | 2,874 | 10,518 | 26,056 |
| 2001 | 160 | 190 | 176 | 689 | 11,875 | 2,289 | 162 | 43 | 1,797 | 6 | 1,639 | 39 | 168 | 1,685 | 9,695 | 30,611 |
| 2002 | 19 | 341 | 449 | 351 | 5,883 | 1,164 | 0 | 65 | 824 | 2 | 1,176 | 28 | 257 | 415 | 13,409 | 2,4382 |
| 2003 | 4 | 57 | 492 | 1,595 | 5,917 | 1,424 | 4 | 13 | 658 | 35 | 837 | 54 | 189 | 477 | 10,123 | 21,880 |
| 2004 | 0 | 363 | 704 | 2,727 | 8,419 | 2,234 | 43 | 34 | 182 | 265 | 1,091 | 32 | 382 | 1,001 | 13,335 | 30,814 |
| 2005 | 35 | 1,076 | 984 | 4,428 | 6,184 | 3,508 | 256 | 349 | 1,355 | 48 | 7,383 | 31 | 1,126 | 2,733 | 29,344 | 58,841 |
| Total | 349 | 2,138 | 4,336 | 11,515 | 50,473 | 17,259 | 468 | 767 | 6,804 | 370 | 17,726 | 363 | 3,047 | 12,420 | 124,909 | 252,943 |

*Source:* Henk von Eije and William Megginson, 'Dividends and share repurchases in the European Union', *Journal of Financial Economics* (2008).

**Table 18.1** Share repurchases in Europe between 1989 and 2005 approximately 10 per cent of the outstanding shares of Prime Robotics Ltd (P-R Ltd) in April at around SKr38 per share. At that time, International Biotechnology announced to the Stockholm Stock Exchange that it might eventually try to take control of P-R Ltd. In May, P-R Ltd repurchased International Biotechnology holdings at SKr48 per share, well above the market price at that time. This offer was not extended to other shareholders.

Companies engage in targeted repurchases for a variety of reasons. In some rare cases a single large shareholder can be bought out at a price lower than that in a tender offer. The legal fees in a targeted repurchase may also be lower than those in a more typical buyback. In addition, the shares of large shareholders are often repurchased to avoid a takeover unfavourable to management.

We now consider an example of a repurchase presented in the theoretical world of a perfect capital market. We next discuss real-world factors involved in the repurchase decision.

## Dividend versus Repurchase: Conceptual Example

Imagine that Telephonic Industries has excess cash of £300,000 (or £3 per share) and is considering an immediate payment of this amount as an extra dividend. The firm forecasts that, after the dividend, earnings will be £450,000 per year, or £4.50 for each of the 100,000 shares outstanding. Because the price–earnings ratio is 6 for comparable companies, the shares of the firm should sell for £27 (= £4.50 × 6) after the dividend is paid. These figures are presented in the top half of Table 18.2. Because the dividend is £3 per share, the equity would have sold for £30 a share *before* payment of the dividend.

Alternatively, the firm could use the excess cash to repurchase some of its own equity. Imagine that a tender offer of £30 a share is made. Here, 10,000 shares are repurchased so that the total number of shares remaining is 90,000. With fewer shares outstanding, the earnings per share will rise to £5 (= £450,000/90,000). The price–earnings ratio remains at 6 because both the business and financial risks of the firm are the same in the repurchase case as they were in the dividend case. Thus the price of a share after the repurchase is £30 (= £5 × 6). These results are presented in the bottom half of Table 18.2.

If commissions, taxes and other imperfections are ignored in our example, the shareholders are indifferent between a dividend and a repurchase. With dividends each shareholder owns a share worth £27 and receives £3 in dividends, so that the total value is £30. This figure is the same as both the amount received by the selling shareholders and the value of the equity for the remaining shareholders in the repurchase case.

This example illustrates the important point that, in a perfect market, the firm is indifferent between a dividend payment and a share repurchase. This result is quite similar to the

| TABLE 18.2 | | For entire firm (£) | Per share (£) |
|---|---|---|---|
| **Extra dividend** | | | **(100,000 shares outstanding)** |
| Proposed dividend | | 300,000 | 3.00 |
| Forecast annual earnings after dividend | | 450,000 | 4.50 |
| Market value of equity after dividend | | 2,700,000 | 27.00 |
| **Repurchase** | | | **(90,000 shares outstanding)** |
| Forecast annual earnings after repurchase | | 450,000 | 5.00 |
| Market value of equity after repurchase | | 2,700,000 | 30.00 |

**Table 18.2** Dividend versus repurchase example for Telephonic Industries

indifference propositions established by MM for debt versus equity financing and for dividends versus capital gains.

You may often read in the popular financial press that a repurchase agreement is beneficial because earnings per share increase. Earnings per share do rise for Telephonic Industries if a repurchase is substituted for a cash dividend: the EPS is £4.50 after a dividend and £5 after the repurchase. This result holds because the drop in shares after a repurchase implies a reduction in the denominator of the EPS ratio.

However, the financial press frequently places undue emphasis on EPS figures in a repurchase agreement. Given the irrelevance propositions we have discussed, the increase in EPS here is not beneficial. Table 18.2 shows that, in a perfect capital market, the total value to the shareholder is the same under the dividend payment strategy as under the repurchase strategy.

## Dividends versus Repurchases: Real-World Considerations

We previously referred to Fig. 18.5, which showed growth in share repurchases relative to dividends. Why do some firms choose repurchases over dividends? Here are perhaps five of the most common reasons.

**1. Flexibility** Firms often view dividends as a commitment to their shareholders, and are quite hesitant to reduce an existing dividend. Repurchases do not represent a similar commitment. Thus a firm with a permanent increase in cash flow is likely to increase its dividend. Conversely, a firm whose cash flow increase is only temporary is likely to repurchase shares of equity.

**2. Executive Compensation** Executives are frequently given share options as part of their overall compensation. Let's revisit the Telephonic Industries example of Table 18.2, where the firm's equity was selling at £30 when the firm was considering either a dividend or a repurchase. Further imagine that Telephonic had granted 1,000 share options to its CEO, Ralph Taylor, two years earlier. At that time the share price was, say, only £20. This means that Mr Taylor can buy 1,000 shares for £20 a share at any time between the grant of the options and their expiration, a procedure called *exercising* the options. His gain from exercising is directly proportional to the rise in the share price above £20. As we saw in the example, the price of the equity would fall to £27 following a dividend, but would remain at £30 following a repurchase. The CEO would clearly prefer a repurchase to a dividend, because the difference between the share price and the exercise price of £20 would be £10 (= £30 – £20) following the repurchase but only £7 (= £27 – £20) following the dividend. Existing share options will always have greater value when the firm repurchases shares instead of paying a dividend, because the share price will be greater after a repurchase than after a dividend.

**3. Offset to Dilution** In addition, the exercise of share options increases the number of shares outstanding. In other words, exercise causes dilution of the shares. Firms frequently buy back shares of equity to offset this dilution. However, it is hard to argue that this is a valid reason for repurchase. As we showed in Table 18.2, repurchase is neither better nor worse for the shareholders than a dividend. Our argument holds whether or not share options have been exercised previously.

**4. Undervaluation** Many companies buy back shares because they believe that a repurchase is their best investment. This occurs more frequently when managers believe that the share price is temporarily depressed.

The fact that some companies repurchase their equity when they believe it is undervalued does not imply that the management of the company must be correct; only empirical studies can make this determination. The immediate market reaction to the announcement of a share repurchase is usually quite favourable. In addition, some empirical work has shown that the long-term share price performance of securities after a buyback is better than the share price performance of comparable companies that do not repurchase.

**5. Taxes** Because taxes for both dividends and share repurchases are treated in depth in the next section, suffice it to say at this point that repurchases provide a tax advantage over dividends.

## 18.5 Personal Taxes and Dividends

Section 18.3 asserted that in a world without taxes and other frictions, dividend policy is irrelevant. Similarly, Section 18.4 concluded that the choice between a share repurchase and a dividend is irrelevant in a world of this type. This section examines the effect of taxes on both dividends and repurchases. Our discussion is facilitated by classifying firms into two types: those without sufficient cash to pay a dividend, and those with sufficient cash to do so.

### Firms without Sufficient Cash to Pay a Dividend

It is simplest to begin with a firm without cash and owned by a single entrepreneur. If this firm should decide to pay a dividend of £100, it must raise capital. The firm might choose among a number of different equity and bond issues to pay the dividend. However, for simplicity, we assume that the entrepreneur contributes cash to the firm by issuing shares to himself. This transaction, diagrammed in the left side of Fig. 18.6, would clearly be a *wash* in a world of no taxes. £100 cash goes into the firm when equity is issued, and is immediately paid out as a dividend. Thus the entrepreneur neither benefits nor loses when the dividend is paid, a result consistent with Miller–Modigliani.

Now assume that dividends are taxed at the owner's personal tax rate of 25 per cent (in the UK, this is the effective tax rate on dividend income for individuals earning over £34,800[4]). The firm still receives £100 upon issuance of equity. However, the entrepreneur does not get to keep the full £100 dividend. Instead the dividend payment is taxed, implying that the owner receives only £75 net after tax. Thus the entrepreneur loses £25.

Though the example is clearly contrived and unrealistic, similar results can be reached for more plausible situations. Thus financial economists generally agree that, in a world of personal taxes, firms should not issue equity to pay dividends.

The direct costs of issuance will add to this effect. Bankers must be paid when new capital is raised. Thus the net receipts due to the firm from a new issue are less than 100 per cent of total capital raised. Because the size of new issues can be lowered by a reduction in dividends, we have another argument in favour of a low-dividend policy.

Of course, our advice not to finance dividends through new equity issues might need to be modified somewhat in the real world. A company with a large and steady cash flow for many years in the past might be paying a regular dividend. If the cash flow unexpectedly dried up for a single year, should new equity be issued so that dividends could be continued? Although our previous discussion would imply that new equity should not be issued, many

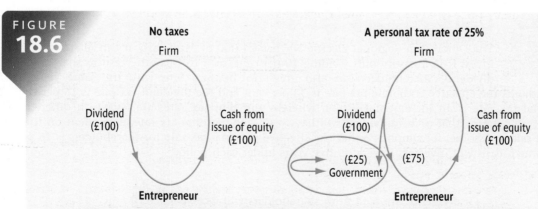

**FIGURE 18.6**

No taxes

A personal tax rate of 25%

In the no-tax case, the entrepreneur receives the £100 in dividends that he gave to the firm when purchasing equity. The entire operation is called a *wash*; in other words, it has no economic effect. With taxes, the entrepreneur still receives £100 in dividends. However, he must pay £25 in taxes to the government. The entrepreneur loses and the government wins when a firm issues equity to pay a dividend.

**Figure 18.6** Firm issues equity to pay a dividend

managers might issue the equity anyway, for practical reasons. In particular, shareholders appear to prefer dividend stability. Thus managers might be forced to issue equity to achieve this stability, knowing full well the adverse tax consequences.

## Firms with Sufficient Cash to Pay a Dividend

The previous discussion argued that in a world with personal taxes, a firm should not issue equity to pay a dividend. Does the tax disadvantage of dividends imply the stronger policy, 'Never, under any circumstances, pay dividends in a world with personal taxes'?

We argue next that this prescription does not necessarily apply to firms with excess cash. To see this, imagine a firm with £1 million in extra cash after selecting all positive NPV projects and determining the level of prudent cash balances. The firm might consider the following alternatives to a dividend:

1 *Select additional capital budgeting projects.* Because the firm has taken all the available positive NPV projects already, it must invest its excess cash in negative NPV projects. This is clearly a policy at variance with the principles of corporate finance.

   In spite of our distaste for this policy, researchers have suggested that many managers purposely take on negative NPV projects in lieu of paying dividends.[5] The idea here is that managers would rather keep the funds in the firm because their prestige, pay and perquisites are often tied to the firm's size. Although managers may help themselves here, they are hurting shareholders. We broached this subject in the section titled 'Free Cash Flow' in Chapter 16, and we shall have more to say about it later in this chapter.

2 *Acquire other companies.* To avoid the payment of dividends, a firm might use excess cash to acquire another company. This strategy has the advantage of acquiring profitable assets. However, a firm often incurs heavy costs when it embarks upon an acquisition programme. In addition, acquisitions are invariably made above the market price. Premiums of 20 to 80 per cent are not uncommon. Because of this, a number of researchers have argued that mergers are not generally profitable to the acquiring company, even when firms are merged for a valid business purpose. Therefore a company making an acquisition merely to avoid a dividend is unlikely to succeed.

3 *Purchase financial assets.* The strategy of purchasing financial assets in lieu of a dividend payment can be illustrated with the following example.

EXAMPLE
**18.1**

## Dividends and Taxes

The Dutch firm Regional Electric NV has €1,000 of extra cash. It can retain the cash and invest it in Treasury bills yielding 10 per cent, or it can pay the cash to shareholders as a dividend. Shareholders can also invest in Treasury bills with the same yield. In the Netherlands the effective corporate tax rate is 30 per cent and the dividend tax rate is 15 per cent. The personal tax rate is an incremental system whereby different tax rates are levied on different salary bands. This means that each individual will have a unique personal tax rate, dependent on their individual salary. Assume, for simplicity, that the effective personal tax rate for shareholders is 28 per cent. How much cash will investors have after five years under each policy?

If dividends are paid now, shareholders will receive

$$€1,000 \times (1 - 0.15) = €850$$

today after taxes. Because their return after personal tax on Treasury bills is 7.2 [$= 10 \times (1 - 0.28)$] per cent, shareholders will have

$$€850 \times (1.072)^5 = €1,203.35 \tag{18.3}$$

in five years. Note that interest income is taxed at the personal tax rate (28 per cent in this example), but dividends are taxed at the lower rate of 15 per cent.

If Regional Electric NV retains the cash to invest in Treasury bills, its after-tax interest rate will be 0.07 [= $0.10 \times (1 - 0.3)$]. At the end of five years, the firm will have

$$€1,000 \times (1.07)^5 = €1,402.55$$

If these proceeds are then paid as a dividend, the shareholders will receive

$$€1,402.55 \times (1 - 0.15) = €1,192.17 \tag{18.4}$$

after personal taxes at date 5. The value in Eq. (18.3) is greater than that in Eq. (18.4), implying that cash to shareholders will be greater if the firm pays the dividend now.

This example shows that for a firm with extra cash the dividend payout decision will depend on personal and corporate tax rates. If personal tax rates are higher than corporate tax rates, a firm will have an incentive to reduce dividend payouts. However, if personal tax rates are lower than corporate tax rates, a firm will have an incentive to pay out any excess cash as dividends.

Table 16.2 shows quite clearly that tax systems differ considerably across countries. In some countries many investors face marginal tax rates that are above the corporate tax rate. However, at the same time, many investors face marginal tax rates well below the maximum. The interaction between personal and corporate tax rates within a country will mean that the environment faced by investors will be unique and a function of where they stay. As a result, firms may or may not have an incentive not to hoard cash. This is an important point, because many US textbooks (which consider only the US environment) would argue that firms will pay dividends because of tax reasons. However, from a European or Asian perspective, this may not necessarily be a valid assertion.

4 *Repurchase shares.* The example we described in the previous section showed that investors are indifferent between share repurchase and dividends in a world without taxes and transaction costs. However, under current international tax laws, shareholders will generally prefer a repurchase to a dividend.

As an example, consider an individual receiving a dividend of €1 on each of 100 shares of an equity. With a 15 per cent tax rate, that individual would pay taxes of €15 on the dividend. Selling shareholders would pay lower taxes if the firm repurchased €100 of existing shares. This occurs because taxes are paid only on the *profit* from a sale. The individual's gain on a sale would be only €40 if the shares sold for €100 were originally purchased for, say, €60. The capital gains tax would be €6 (= $0.15 \times €40$), a number below the tax on dividends of €15. Note that the tax from a repurchase is less than the tax on a dividend, even though the same 15 per cent tax rate applies to both the repurchase and the dividend.

Of all the alternatives to dividends mentioned in this section, the strongest case can be made for repurchases. In fact, academics have long wondered why firms *ever* pay a dividend instead of repurchasing shares. There have been at least two possible reasons for avoiding repurchases. First, in many countries, including the UK, there is the fear that share repurchase programmes can lead to illegal price manipulation. Second, tax authorities can penalize firms repurchasing their own shares if the only reason is to avoid the taxes that would be levied on dividends. However, this threat has not materialized with the growth in corporate repurchases.

## Summary of Personal Taxes

This section suggests that, because of personal taxes, firms have an incentive to reduce dividends. For example, they might increase capital expenditures, acquire other companies, or purchase financial assets. However, because of financial considerations and legal constraints, rational firms with large cash flows will probably exhaust these activities with plenty of cash left over for dividends.

It is harder to explain why firms pay dividends instead of repurchasing shares. The tax savings from buybacks are significant, and fear of either the stock exchange or tax authorities seems overblown. Academics are of two minds here. Some argue that corporations were simply slow to grasp the benefits from repurchases. However, since the idea has now firmly caught on, the trend towards replacement of dividends with buybacks will continue. We might even conjecture that dividends will be as unimportant in the future as repurchases were in the past. Conversely, others argue that companies have paid dividends all along for good reason. Perhaps the legal hassles, particularly from tax authorities, are significant after all. Or there may be other, more subtle benefits from dividends. We consider potential benefits of dividends in the next section.

## 18.6 Real-World Factors Favouring a High-Dividend Policy

The previous section pointed out that because individuals pay taxes on dividends, financial managers might seek ways to reduce dividends. While we discussed the problems with taking on more capital budgeting projects, acquiring other firms, and hoarding cash, we stated that a share repurchase has many of the benefits of a dividend, with less of a tax disadvantage. This section considers reasons why a firm might pay its shareholders high dividends even in the presence of personal taxes on these dividends.

### Desire for Current Income

It has been argued that many individuals desire current income. The classic example is the group of retired people and others living on a fixed income. The argument further states that these individuals would bid up the share price should dividends rise, and bid down the share price should dividends fall.

This argument does not hold in Miller and Modigliani's theoretical model. An individual preferring high current cash flow but holding low-dividend securities could easily sell off shares to provide the necessary funds. Thus in a world of no transactions costs a high-current-dividend policy would be of no value to the shareholder.

However, the current income argument is relevant in the real world. Equity sales involve brokerage fees and other transaction costs – direct cash expenses that could be avoided by an investment in high-dividend securities. In addition, equity sales are time-consuming, further leading investors to buy high-dividend securities.

To put this argument in perspective, remember that financial intermediaries such as mutual funds can perform repackaging transactions at low cost. Such intermediaries could buy low-dividend equities and, by a controlled policy of realizing gains, pay their investors at a higher rate.

### Behavioural Finance

Suppose it turned out that the transaction costs in selling no-dividend securities could not account for the preference of investors for dividends. Would there still be a reason for high dividends? We introduced the topic of behavioural finance in Chapter 13, pointing out that the ideas of behaviourists represent a strong challenge to the theory of efficient capital markets. It turns out that behavioural finance also has an argument for high dividends.

The basic idea here concerns *self-control*, a concept that, though quite important in psychology, has received virtually no emphasis in finance. Although we cannot review all that psychology has to say about self-control, let's focus on one example – losing weight. Suppose Alfred Martin, a university student, just got back from the Christmas break more than a few pounds heavier than he would like. Alfred wishes to lose weight through doing yoga. Each day Alfred would balance the costs and the benefits of doing yoga. Perhaps he would choose to exercise on most days, because losing the weight is important to him. However, when he is too busy with exams, he might rationally choose not to exercise, because he cannot afford the time. So he may rationally choose to avoid doing yoga on days when other social commitments become too time-consuming.

Unfortunately, Alfred must make a proactive choice to do yoga every day, and there may be too many days when his lack of self-control gets the better of him. He may tell himself that he doesn't have the time to exercise on a particular day, simply because he is starting to find yoga boring, not because he really doesn't have the time. Before long, he is avoiding yoga on most days – and overeating in reaction to the guilt from not exercising!

Is there an alternative? One way would be to set rigid rules. Perhaps Alfred may decide to do yoga every day *no matter what*. This is not necessarily the best approach for everyone, but there is no question that many of us (perhaps most of us) live by a set of rules.

What does this have to do with dividends? Investors must also deal with self-control. Suppose a retiree wants to consume £20,000 a year from savings, in addition to her pension. On the one hand, she could buy shares with a dividend yield high enough to generate £20,000 in dividends. On the other hand, she could place her savings in no-dividend shares, selling off £20,000 each year for consumption. Though these two approaches seem equivalent financially, the second one may allow for too much leeway. If lack of self-control gets the better of her, she might sell off too much, leaving little for her later years. Better, perhaps, to short-circuit this possibility by investing in dividend-paying equities with a firm personal rule of *never* 'dipping into principal'. Although behaviourists do not claim that this approach is for everyone, they argue that enough people think this way to explain why firms pay dividends – even though, as we said earlier, dividends are tax-disadvantaged.

Does behavioural finance argue for increased share repurchases as well as increased dividends? The answer is no, because investors will sell the shares that firms repurchase. As we have said, selling shares involves too much leeway. Investors might sell too many shares, leaving little for later years. Thus the behaviourist argument may explain why companies pay dividends in a world with personal taxes.

## Agency Costs

Although shareholders, bondholders and management form firms for mutually beneficial reasons, one party may later gain at the other's expense. For example, take the potential conflict between bondholders and shareholders. Bondholders would like shareholders to leave as much cash as possible in the firm so that this cash would be available to pay the bondholders during times of financial distress. Conversely, shareholders would like to keep this extra cash for themselves. That's where dividends come in. Managers, acting on behalf of the shareholders, may pay dividends simply to keep the cash away from the bondholders. In other words, a dividend can be viewed as a wealth transfer from bondholders to shareholders. There is empirical evidence for this view of things. For example, DeAngelo and DeAngelo find that firms in financial distress are reluctant to cut dividends.[6] Of course, bondholders know about the propensity of shareholders to transfer money out of the firm. To protect themselves, bondholders frequently create loan agreements stating that dividends can be paid only if the firm has earnings, cash flow and working capital above specified levels.

Although managers may be looking out for shareholders in any conflict with bondholders, managers may pursue selfish goals at the expense of shareholders in other situations. For example, as discussed in a previous chapter, managers might pad expense accounts, take on pet projects with negative NPVs, or simply not work hard. Managers find it easier to pursue these selfish goals when the firm has plenty of free cash flow. After all, one cannot squander funds if the funds are not available in the first place. And that is where dividends come in. Several scholars have suggested that the board of directors can use dividends to reduce agency costs.[7] By paying dividends equal to the amount of 'surplus' cash flow, a firm can reduce management's ability to squander the firm's resources.

This discussion suggests a reason for increased dividends, but the same argument applies to share repurchases as well. Managers, acting on behalf of shareholders, can just as easily keep cash from bondholders through repurchases as through dividends. And the board of directors, also acting on behalf of shareholders, can reduce the cash available to spendthrift managers just as easily through repurchases as through dividends. Thus the presence of agency costs is not an argument for dividends over repurchases. Rather, agency costs imply that firms may increase either dividends or share repurchases rather than hoard large amounts of cash.

## Information Content of Dividends, and Dividend Signalling

**Information Content**   While there are many things researchers do not know about dividends, we know one thing for sure: the share price of a firm generally rises when the firm announces a dividend increase, and generally falls when a dividend reduction is announced. For example, Asquith and Mullins estimate that share prices rise about 3 per cent following announcements of dividend initiations.[8] Michaely, Thaler and Womack find that share prices fall about 7 per cent following announcements of dividend omissions.[9]

The question is how we should *interpret* this empirical evidence. Consider the following three positions on dividends:

1   From the homemade dividend argument of MM, dividend policy is irrelevant, given that future earnings (and cash flows) are held constant.

2   Because of tax effects, a firm's share price is negatively related to the current dividend when future earnings (or cash flows) are held constant.

3   Because of shareholders' desire for current income, a firm's share price is positively related to its current dividend, even when future earnings (or cash flows) are held constant.

At first glance, the empirical evidence that share prices rise when dividend increases are announced may seem consistent with position 3 and inconsistent with positions 1 and 2. In fact, many writers have said this. However, other authors have countered that the observation itself is consistent with all three positions. They point out that companies do not like to cut a dividend. Thus firms will raise the dividend only when future earnings, cash flow and so on are expected to rise enough so that the dividend is not likely to be reduced later to its original level. A dividend increase is management's *signal* to the market that the firm is expected to do well.

It is the expectation of good times, and not only the shareholders' affinity for current income, that raises share price. The rise in the share price following the dividend signal is called the information content effect of the dividend. To recapitulate, imagine that the share price is unaffected or even negatively affected by the level of dividends, given that future earnings (or cash flows) are held constant. Nevertheless, the information content effect implies that share prices may rise when dividends are raised – if dividends simultaneously cause shareholders to *increase* their expectations of future earnings and cash flows.

**Dividend Signalling**   We just argued that the market infers a rise in earnings and cash flows from a dividend increase, leading to a higher share price. Conversely, the market infers a decrease in cash flows from a dividend reduction, leading to a drop in share price. This raises an interesting corporate strategy: could management increase dividends just to make the market *think* that cash flows will be higher, even when management knows that cash flows will not rise?

While this strategy may seem dishonest, academics take the position that managers frequently attempt the strategy. Academics begin with the following accounting identity for an all-equity firm:

$$\text{Cash flow}^{10} = \text{Capital expenditures} + \text{Dividends} \qquad (18.5)$$

Equation (18.5) must hold if a firm is neither issuing nor repurchasing equity. That is, the cash flow from the firm must go somewhere. If it is not paid out in dividends, it must be used in some expenditure. Whether the expenditure involves a capital budgeting project or a purchase of Treasury bills, it is still an expenditure.

Imagine that we are in the middle of the year, and investors are trying to make some forecast of cash flow over the entire year. These investors may use Eq. (18.5) to estimate cash flow. For example, suppose the firm announces that current dividends will be £50 million and the market believes that capital expenditures are £80 million. The market would then determine cash flow to be £130 million (= £50 million + £80 million).

Now, suppose that the firm had, alternatively, announced a dividend of £70 million. The market might assume that cash flow remains at £130 million, implying capital expenditures of £60 million (= £130 million – £70 million). Here, the increase in dividends would hurt the share price, because the market anticipates that valuable capital expenditures will be crowded out. Alternatively, the market might assume that capital expenditures remain at £80 million, implying the estimate of cash flow to be £150 million (= £70 million + £80 million). The share price would probably rise here, because share prices usually increase with cash flow. In general, academics believe that models where investors assume capital expenditures remain the same are more realistic. Thus an increase in dividends raises the share price.

Now we come to the incentives of managers to fool the public. Suppose you are a manager who wants to boost the share price, perhaps because you are planning to sell some of your personal holdings of the company's equity immediately. You might increase dividends so that the market would raise its estimate of the firm's cash flow, thereby also boosting the current share price.

If this strategy is appealing, would anything prevent you from raising dividends without limit? The answer is yes, because there is also a _cost_ to raising dividends. That is, the firm will have to forgo some of its profitable projects. Remember that cash flow in Eq. (18.5) is a constant, so an increase in dividends is obtained only by a reduction in capital expenditures. At some point the market will learn that cash flow has not increased, but instead profitable capital expenditures have been cut. Once the market absorbs this information, share prices should fall below what they would have been had dividends never been raised. Thus if you plan to sell, say, half of your shares and retain the other half, an increase in dividends should help you on the immediate sale but hurt you when you sell your remaining shares years later. So your decision on the level of dividends will be based, among other things, on the timing of your personal equity sales.

This is a simplified example of dividend signalling, where the manager sets dividend policy based on maximum benefit for himself.[11] Alternatively, a given manager may have no desire to sell his shares immediately but knows that, at any one time, plenty of ordinary shareholders will want to do so. Thus for the benefit of shareholders in general, a manager will always be aware of the trade-off between current and future share price. And this, then, is the essence of signalling with dividends. It is not enough for a manager to set dividend policy to maximize the true (or intrinsic) value of the firm. He must also consider the effect of dividend policy on the current share price, even if the current share price does not reflect true value.

Does a motive to signal imply that managers will increase dividends rather than share repurchases? The answer is probably no: most academic models imply that dividends and share repurchases are perfect substitutes.[12] Rather, these models indicate that managers will consider reducing capital spending (even on projects with positive NPVs) to increase either dividends or share repurchases.

## 18.7  The Clientele Effect

In the previous two sections we pointed out that the existence of personal taxes favours a low-dividend policy, whereas other factors favour high dividends. The finance profession had hoped that it would be easy to determine which of these sets of factors dominates. Unfortunately, after years of research, no one has been able to conclude which of the two is more important. This is surprising: we might be sceptical that the two sets of factors would cancel each other out so perfectly.

However, one particular idea, known as the _clientele effect_, implies that the two sets of factors are likely to cancel each other out after all. To understand this idea, let's separate investors in high tax brackets from those in low tax brackets. Individuals in high tax brackets are likely to prefer either no or low dividends. Low tax bracket investors generally fall into two categories. First, there are individual investors in low brackets. They are likely to prefer some dividends if they desire current income. Second, in many countries, pension funds pay no taxes on either dividends or capital gains. Because they face no tax consequences, pension funds will also prefer dividends if they have a preference for current income. Suppose that 40 per cent of all investors prefer high dividends and 60 per cent prefer low dividends, yet only 20 per cent of firms pay high dividends while 80 per cent pay low dividends. Here, the high-dividend firms will be in short supply, implying that their equity should be bid up while the shares of low-dividend firms should be bid down.

However, the dividend policies of all firms need not be fixed in the long run. In this example, we would expect enough low-dividend firms to increase their payout so that 40 per cent of the firms pay high dividends and 60 per cent of the firms pay low dividends. After this adjustment, no firm will gain from changing its dividend policy. Once payouts of corporations conform to the desires of shareholders, no single firm can affect its market value by switching from one dividend strategy to another.

Clienteles are likely to form in the following way:

| Group | Equities |
| --- | --- |
| Individuals in high tax brackets | Zero- to low-payout shares |
| Individuals in low tax brackets | Low- to medium-payout shares |
| Tax-free institutions | Medium- to high-payout shares |

To see if you understand the clientele effect, consider the following statement: 'In a world where many investors like high dividends, a firm can boost its share price by increasing its dividend payout ratio.' True or false?

The statement is likely to be false. As long as there are already enough high-dividend firms to satisfy dividend-loving investors, a firm will not be able to boost its share price by paying high dividends. A firm can boost its share price only if an *unsatisfied* clientele exists.

Our discussion of clienteles followed from the fact that tax brackets vary across investors. If shareholders care about taxes, equities should attract clienteles based on dividend yield. Is there any evidence that this is the case?

Consider Fig. 18.7. Here, John Graham and Alok Kumar[13] rank equities by their dividend yields (the ratio of dividend to share price) and place them into five portfolios, called quintiles. The bottom quintile contains the 20 per cent of shares with the lowest dividend yields; the next quintile contains the 20 per cent of shares with the next lowest dividend yields; and so on. The figure shows the weight of each quintile in the portfolios of low-, medium- and high-income investors. As can be seen, relative to low-income investors, high-income investors put a greater percentage of their assets into low-dividend securities. Conversely, again relative to low-income investors, high-income investors put a smaller percentage of their assets into high-dividend securities.

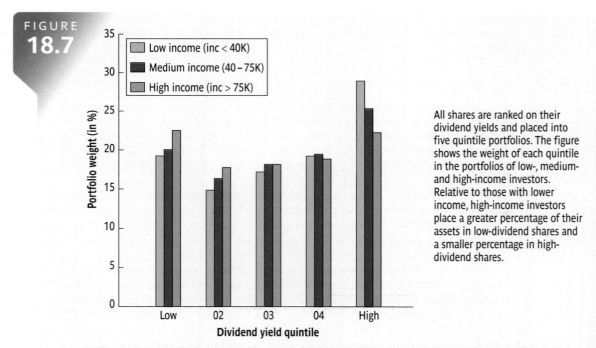

**FIGURE 18.7**

All shares are ranked on their dividend yields and placed into five quintile portfolios. The figure shows the weight of each quintile in the portfolios of low-, medium- and high-income investors. Relative to those with lower income, high-income investors place a greater percentage of their assets in low-dividend shares and a smaller percentage in high-dividend shares.

*Source*: Adapted from Fig. 2 of John Graham and Alok Kumar, 'Do dividend clienteles exist? Evidence on dividend preferences of retail investors', *Journal of Finance* (2006).

**Figure 18.7** Preferences of investors for dividend yield

## 18.8  A Catering Theory of Dividends

A very recent perspective on why companies pay dividends has been proposed by Malcom Baker and Jeffrey Wurgler. The basic premise is that there are times when companies are mispriced in the stock market, or when there are changes in the demand for dividend-paying equities. This may be because of the clientele effect, which predicts that if the proportion of dividend-paying companies in a market increases or decreases, the demand for dividend-paying shares will shift to a new equilibrium, temporarily imparting a premium or discount on shares of companies that pay dividends.

Instead of focusing on investor decisions, the *catering theory of dividends* predicts that managers will rationally respond to time variation in investor demand for dividends by modifying their company's dividend policy. In effect, the theory makes less of a statement about market efficiency or behavioural finance than it does about the logical business decisions by corporate management. Baker and Wurgler[14] show that management behaviour in the US is consistent with this theory. They consider dividend initiation and omission decisions and relate them to share price premiums for dividend-paying shares. For initiations in particular, the relationship with a price premium for dividends is exceptionally strong. This is clearly shown by Fig. 18.8, where the link between dividend premium (market to book value) and dividend initiation is presented.

So, according to the catering theory, will dividend increases lead to a positive price reaction? Not necessarily. If the time-varying demand for dividend-paying shares is low, an announcement by a company that it is increasing its dividend is not likely to be met with a positive reaction. In this situation, a dividend omission may elicit a more positive market response.

**FIGURE 18.8**

The log difference in the market-to-book ratio of dividend payers and non-payers (the dividend premium, dashed line – left axis) and one-year-ahead rate of dividend initiations (solid line – right axis). A firm is defined as a dividend payer at time *t* if it has positive dividends per share by the ex date. The initiation rate Initiate in *t* + 1 is defined as the percentage rate of new dividend payers at time *t* + 1 among surviving non-payers from *t*.

*Source*: Figure 2 of Malcolm Baker and Jeffrey Wurgler, 'A catering theory of dividends', *Journal of Finance*, vol. 59, no. 3, pp. 1125–1165.

**Figure 18.8** The dividend premium and the rate of dividend initiation, 1962 to 2000

*Source*: Figure 4 of Henk von Eije and William Megginson, 'Dividends and share repurchases in the European Union', *Journal of Financial Economics* (2008).

**Figure 18.9** Dividends and share repurchases in the European Union

## 18.9 What We Know and Do Not Know about Dividend Policy

### Corporate Dividends Are Substantial

We pointed out earlier in the chapter that dividends are tax-disadvantaged relative to capital gains, because dividends are taxed upon payment whereas taxes on capital gains are deferred until sale. Nevertheless, the total monetary value of dividends paid by companies is substantial. In Europe, the total real dividends (share repurchases and cash dividends) have increased significantly since 2000. For example, consider Fig. 18.9, which shows the total real cash dividends and share repurchases by the EU15 companies between 1989 and 2005. Share repurchases increase from virtually zero in 1996 to €60 billion (2000 prices) in 2005. Similarly, cash dividends grow from approximately €40 billion in 1993 to over €100 billion in 2005.

We could argue that the taxation on dividends is actually minimal, perhaps because dividends are paid primarily to individuals in low tax brackets, or because institutions such as pension funds, which normally pay no taxes, are the primary recipients. However, Peterson, Peterson and Ang conducted an in-depth study of dividends for one representative year, 1979.[15] They found that about two-thirds of dividends went to individuals, and that the average marginal tax bracket for these individuals was about 40 per cent. Thus we must conclude that large amounts of dividends are paid, even in the presence of substantial taxation.

### Fewer Companies Pay Dividends

Although dividends are substantial, von Eije and Megginson point out that the percentage of European companies paying cash dividends has fallen over the last few decades. They show that these have largely been replaced by share repurchases. Fama and French[16] argue that the decline was caused primarily by an explosion of small, currently unprofitable companies that have recently listed on various stock exchanges. For the most part, firms of this type do not pay dividends. Figure 18.10 shows that the proportion of cash dividend payers among European industrial firms dropped substantially between 1989 and 2005.

This figure also shows an *increase* in the proportion of dividend payers across the whole of Europe from 2002 to 2005. Interestingly, this is the same pattern as seen in the US.[17] One reason given for the US was the cut in the maximum tax rate on dividends to 15 per cent, signed into law in May 2003. However, clearly this can't be the reason for Europe. Furthermore,

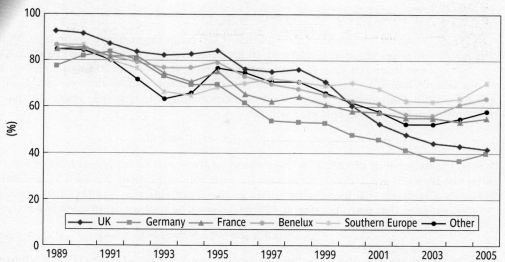

*Source*: Figure 3 of Henk von Eije and William Megginson, 'Dividends and share repurchases in the European Union', *Journal of Financial Economics* (2008).

**Figure 18.10** Proportion of cash dividend payers among European industrial firms

the resurgence in dividend payers has been observed only over the two- and three-year period from 2002 to 2005. Perhaps this trend is just a statistical aberration.

Figure 18.10 does not imply that dividends across *all* firms declined from 1989 to 2005. DeAngelo, DeAngelo and Skinner[18] point out that while small firms have shied away from dividends, the largest firms have substantially increased their dividends over recent decades. This increase has created such concentration in dividends that the 25 top dividend-paying firms accounted for more than 50 per cent of aggregate dividends in the United States in 2000. DeAngelo and colleagues conclude (p. 425):

> Industrial firms exhibit a two-tier structure in which a small number of firms with very high earnings collectively generates the majority of earnings and dominates the dividend supply, while the vast majority of firms has at best a modest collective impact on aggregate earnings and dividends.

## Corporations Smooth Dividends

In 1956 John Lintner made two important observations concerning dividend policy.[19] First, real-world companies typically set long-term target ratios of dividends to earnings. A firm is likely to set a low target ratio if it has many positive NPV projects relative to available cash flow, and a high ratio if it has few positive NPV projects. Second, managers know that only part of any change in earnings is likely to be permanent. Because managers need time to assess the permanence of any earnings rise, dividend changes appear to lag earnings changes by a number of periods.

Taken together, Lintner's observations suggest that two parameters describe dividend policy: the target payout ratio, *t*, and the speed of adjustment of current dividends to the target, *s*. Dividend changes will tend to conform to the following model:

$$\text{Dividend change} \equiv \text{Div}_1 - \text{Div}_0 = s \times (t\text{EPS}_1 - \text{Div}_0) \tag{18.6}$$

where $\text{Div}_1$ and $\text{Div}_0$ are dividends in the next year and dividends in the current year, respectively. $\text{EPS}_1$ is earnings per share in the next year.

<table>
<tr><td>EXAMPLE<br>**18.2**</td><td></td></tr>
</table>

## Dividend Smoothing

Calculator Graphics International (CGI) has a target payout ratio of 0.30. Last year's earnings per share were £10 and, in accordance with the target, CGI paid cash dividends of £3 per share last year. However, earnings have jumped to £20 this year. Because the managers do not believe that this increase is permanent, they do *not* plan to raise dividends all the way to £6 (= 0.30 × £20). Rather, their speed of adjustment coefficient, $s$, is 0.5, implying that the *increase* in dividends from last year to this year will be

$$0.5 \times (£6 - £3) = £1.50$$

That is, the increase in dividends is the product of the speed of adjustment coefficient, 0.50, times the difference between what dividends would be with full adjustment [£6 (= 0.30 × £20)] and last year's dividends. Dividends will increase by £1.50, so dividends this year will be £4.50 (= £3 + £1.50).

Now, suppose that earnings stay at £20 next year. The increase in dividends next year will be

$$0.5 \times (£6 - £4.50) = £0.75$$

In words, the increase in dividends from this year to next year will be the speed of adjustment coefficient (0.50) times the difference between what dividends would have been next year with full adjustment (£6) and this year's dividends (£4.50). Because dividends will increase by £0.75, dividends next year will be £5.25 (= £4.50 + £0.75). In this way, dividends will slowly rise every year if earnings in all future years remain at £20. However, dividends will reach £6 only at infinity.

The limiting cases in Eq. (18.6) occur when $s = 1$ and $s = 0$. If $s = 1$, the actual change in dividends will be equal to the target change in dividends. Here, full adjustment occurs immediately. If $s = 0$, $Div_1 = Div_0$. In other words, there is no change in dividends at all. Real-world companies can be expected to set $s$ between 0 and 1.

An implication of Lintner's model is that the dividends-to-earnings ratio rises when a company begins a period of bad times, and the ratio falls when a company starts a period of good times. Thus dividends display less variability than do earnings. In other words, firms *smooth* dividends.

## Payouts Provide Information to the Market

We previously observed that the price of a firm's shares frequently rises when either its current dividend is increased or a share repurchase is announced. Conversely, the price of a firm's shares can fall significantly when its dividend is cut. In other words, there is information content in payouts. For example, consider the number of dividend cuts presented in the opening vignette. This was a very strong signal that companies have less cash to pay out to shareholders, and the accompanying price falls may suggest that investors are looking at current dividends for clues concerning the level of future earnings and dividends.

## A Sensible Payout Policy

The knowledge of the finance profession varies across topic areas. For example, capital budgeting techniques are both powerful and precise. A single net present value equation can accurately determine whether a multimillion-pound or -euro project should be accepted or rejected. The capital asset pricing model and the arbitrage pricing model provide empirically validated relationships between expected return and risk.

However, the profession has less knowledge of capital structure policy. Though a number of elegant theories relate firm value to the level of debt, no formula can be used to calculate the firm's optimal debt–equity ratio. Academics and practitioners are forced too frequently to employ rules of thumb, such as treating the industry's average ratio as the optimal one for the firm. The field's knowledge of dividend policy is, perhaps, similar to its knowledge of capital structure policy.

We do know the following:

- The intrinsic value of a firm is reduced when positive NPV projects are rejected to pay a dividend.

- Firms should avoid issuing shares to pay a dividend in a world with personal taxes.

- Share repurchases represent a sensible alternative to dividends.

However, there is no formula for calculating the optimal dividend-to-earnings ratio. In addition, there is no formula for determining the optimal mix between share repurchases and dividends. It can be argued that, for tax reasons, firms should always substitute share repurchases for dividends. But while the volume of repurchases has greatly increased over time, Fig. 18.8 does not suggest that dividends are on the way out.

## The Pros and Cons of Paying Dividends

| | Pros | | Cons |
|---|---|---|---|
| 1 | Dividends may appeal to investors who desire stable cash flow but do not want to incur the transaction costs from periodically selling shares of equity. | 1 | Dividends are taxed as ordinary income. |
| 2 | Behavioural finance argues that investors with limited self-control can meet current consumption needs with high-dividend shares while adhering to the policy of never dipping into principal. | 2 | Dividends can reduce internal sources of financing. Dividends may force the firm to forgo positive NPV projects or to rely on costly external equity financing. |
| 3 | Managers, acting on behalf of shareholders, can pay dividends in order to keep cash from bondholders. | 3 | Once established, dividend cuts are hard to make without adversely affecting a firm's share price. |
| 4 | The board of directors, acting on behalf of shareholders, can use dividends to reduce the cash available to spendthrift managers. | | |
| 5 | Managers may increase dividends to signal their optimism concerning future cash flow. | | |

## Some Survey Evidence about Dividends

A recent study surveyed a large number of financial executives regarding dividend policy. One of the questions asked was this: 'Do these statements describe factors that affect your company's dividend decisions?' Table 18.3 shows some of the results.

As shown in Table 18.3, financial managers are very disinclined to cut dividends. Moreover, they are very conscious of their previous dividends, and desire to maintain a relatively steady dividend. In contrast, the cost of external capital and the desire to attract 'prudent man' investors (those with fiduciary duties) are less important.

Table 18.4 is drawn from the same survey, but here the responses are to the question 'How important are the following factors to your company's dividend decisions?' Not surprisingly, given the responses in Table 18.3 and our earlier discussion, the highest priority is maintaining a consistent dividend policy. The next several items are also consistent with our previous analysis. Financial managers are very concerned about earnings stability and future earnings levels in making dividend decisions, and they consider the availability of good investment opportunities. Survey respondents also believed that attracting both institutional and individual (retail) investors was relatively important.

In contrast to our discussion in the earlier part of this chapter of taxes and flotation costs, the financial managers in this survey did not think that personal taxes paid on dividends

TABLE 18.3

| Policy statements | Percentage who agree or strongly agree |
|---|---|
| **1** We try to avoid reducing dividends per share. | 93.8 |
| **2** We try to maintain a smooth dividend from year to year. | 89.6 |
| **3** We consider the level of dividends per share that we have paid in recent quarters. | 88.2 |
| **4** We are reluctant to make dividend changes that might have to be reversed in the future. | 77.9 |
| **5** We consider the change or growth in dividends per share. | 66.7 |
| **6** We consider the cost of raising external capital to be smaller than the cost of cutting dividends. | 42.8 |
| **7** We pay dividends to attract investors subject to 'prudent man' investment restrictions. | 41.7 |

Survey respondents were asked the question, 'Do these statements describe factors that affect your company's dividend decisions?'

*Source*: Adapted from Table 4 of A. Brav, J.R. Graham, C.R. Harvey and R. Michaely, 'Payout policy in the 21st century', *Journal of Financial Economics* (2005).

**Table 18.3** Survey responses on dividend decisions

TABLE 18.4

| Policy statements | Percentage who think this is important or very important |
|---|---|
| **1** Maintaining consistency with our historic dividend policy. | 84.1 |
| **2** Stability of future earnings. | 71.9 |
| **3** A sustainable change in earnings. | 67.1 |
| **4** Attracting institutional investors to purchase our stock. | 52.5 |
| **5** The availability of good investment opportunities for our firm to pursue. | 47.6 |
| **6** Attracting retail investors to purchase our stock. | 44.5 |
| **7** Personal taxes our stockholders pay when receiving dividends. | 21.1 |
| **8** Flotation costs to issuing new equity. | 9.3 |

Survey respondents were asked the question, 'How important are the following factors to your company's dividend decisions?'

*Source*: Adapted from Table 5 of A. Brav, J.R. Graham, C.R. Harvey and R. Michaely, 'Payout policy in the 21st century', *Journal of Financial Economics* (2005).

**Table 18.4** Survey responses on dividend decisions

by shareholders are very important. And even fewer think that equity flotation costs are relevant.

# 18.10  Stock Dividends and Stock Splits

Another type of dividend is paid out in shares of equity. This type of dividend is called a stock or share dividend. A stock dividend is not a true dividend, because it is not paid in cash. The effect of a stock dividend is to increase the number of shares that each owner holds. Because there are more shares outstanding, each is worth less.

A stock dividend is commonly expressed as a percentage: for example, a 20 per cent stock dividend means that a shareholder receives one new share for every five currently owned (a 20 per cent increase). Because every shareholder receives 20 per cent more shares, the total number of shares outstanding rises by 20 per cent. As we shall see in a moment, the result is that each share of equity is worth about 20 per cent less.

A stock split is essentially the same thing as a stock dividend, except that a split is expressed as a ratio instead of a percentage. When a split is declared, each share is split up to create additional shares. For example, in a three-for-one stock split, each old share is split into three new shares.

## Some Details about Stock Splits and Stock Dividends

Stock splits and stock dividends have essentially the same impacts on the corporation and the shareholder: they increase the number of shares outstanding and reduce the value per share. Unlike US accounting standards, IFRS makes no distinction between a cash dividend and a stock dividend. IFRS considers a stock dividend as being a cash dividend to shareholders with a simultaneous purchase of shares by the same shareholders.

## Value of Stock Splits and Stock Dividends

The laws of logic tell us that stock splits and stock dividends can (a) leave the value of the firm unaffected, (b) increase its value, or (c) decrease its value. Unfortunately, the issues are complex enough that we cannot easily determine which of the three relationships holds.

**The Benchmark Case**  A strong case can be made that stock dividends and splits do not change either the wealth of any shareholder or the wealth of the firm as a whole. Consider an all-equity firm with a total market value of €660,000 and 10,000 shares. With the 10 per cent stock dividend, the number of shares increases to 11,000, so it seems that each would be worth €660,000/11,000 = €60.

For example, a shareholder who had 100 shares worth €66 each before the dividend would have 110 shares worth €60 each afterwards. The total value of the equity is €6,600 either way: so the stock dividend doesn't really have any economic effect.

Now consider a two-for-one stock split. After the stock split there are 20,000 shares outstanding, so each should be worth €660,000/20,000 = €33. In other words, the number of shares doubles and the price halves. From these calculations it appears that stock dividends and splits are just paper transactions. This is the view taken by the International Accounting Standards Board in their International Financial Reporting Standards (IFRS).

Although these results are relatively obvious, there are reasons that are often given to suggest that there may be some benefits to these actions. The typical financial manager is aware of many real-world complexities, and for that reason the stock split or stock dividend decision is not treated lightly in practice.

**Popular Trading Range**  Proponents of stock dividends and stock splits frequently argue that a security has a proper trading range. When the security is priced above this level, many investors do not have the funds to buy the common trading unit of 100 shares, called a *round lot*. Although securities can be purchased in *odd-lot* form (fewer than 100 shares), the commissions are greater. Thus firms will split the shares to keep the price in this trading range.

For example, in early 2003 Microsoft announced a two-for-one stock split. This was the ninth split for Microsoft since the company went public in 1986. The stock had split three-for-two on two occasions and two-for-one a total of seven times. So for every share of Microsoft you owned in 1986 when the company first went public, you would own 288 shares as of the most recent stock split in 2003. Similarly, since Wal-Mart went public in 1970, it has split its stock two-for-one 11 times, and Dell Computer has split three-for-two once and two-for-one six times since going public in 1988.

Although this argument of a trading range is a popular one, its validity is questionable for a number of reasons. Mutual funds, pension funds and other institutions have steadily increased their trading activity since World War II, and now handle a sizeable percentage of total trading volume. Because these institutions buy and sell in huge amounts, the individual share price is of little concern.

Furthermore, we sometimes observe share prices that are quite large that do not appear to cause problems. To take an extreme case, consider the Swiss chocolatier Lindt. On 20 February 2006 Lindt shares were selling for around SwFr24,595 each, or about £13,878 (€16,288). This is fairly expensive, but also consider Berkshire-Hathaway, the company run by legendary investor Warren Buffet. In November 2008 each share in the company sold for about $101,000!

Finally, there is evidence that stock splits may actually decrease the liquidity of the company's shares. Following a two-for-one split, the number of shares traded should more than double if liquidity is increased by the split. This doesn't appear to happen, and the reverse is sometimes observed.

## Reverse Splits

A less frequently encountered financial manoeuvre is the reverse split. In 2008 Ericsson, the multinational telecommunications firm, underwent a one-for-five reverse stock split. In a one-for-five reverse split each investor exchanges five old shares for one new share. The par value is quintupled in the process. As with stock splits and stock dividends, a case can be made that a reverse split has no real effect.

Given real-world imperfections, three related reasons are cited for reverse splits. First, transaction costs to shareholders may be less after the reverse split. Second, the liquidity and marketability of a company's equity might be improved when its price is raised to the popular trading range. Third, shares selling at prices below a certain level are not considered respectable, meaning that investors underestimate these firms' earnings, cash flow, growth and stability. Some financial analysts argue that a reverse split can achieve instant respectability. As was the case with stock splits, none of these reasons is particularly compelling, especially not the third one.

There are two other reasons for reverse splits. First, stock exchanges have minimum price-per-share requirements. A reverse split may bring the share price up to such a minimum. In 2001–2002, in the wake of a bear market, this motive became an increasingly important one in the US. In 2001 106 companies asked their shareholders to approve reverse splits. There were 111 reverse splits in 2002 and 75 in 2003, but only 14 by mid-year 2004. It is likely that this will happen again in 2010 and 2011. The most common reason for these reverse splits is that some exchanges can delist companies whose share price drops below an acceptable value per share. In 2002 and 2003 many US companies, particularly Internet-related technology companies, found themselves in danger of being delisted, and used reverse splits to boost their share prices. Second, companies sometimes perform reverse splits and, at the same time, buy out any shareholders who end up with fewer than a certain number of shares.

In October 2005 Sagient Research Systems, a publisher of independent financial research, announced a 1-for-101 reverse stock split. At the same time the company would repurchase all shares held by shareholders with fewer than 100 shares. The purpose of the reverse split was to allow the company to go dark. The reverse split and share repurchase meant the company would have fewer than 300 shareholders, so it would no longer be required to file periodic reports with the SEC. What made the proposal especially imaginative was that, immediately after the reverse stock split, the company underwent a 101-for-1 split to restore the equity to its original cost!

## Summary and Conclusions

1   The dividend policy of a firm is irrelevant in a perfect capital market, because the share-holder can effectively undo the firm's dividend strategy. If a shareholder receives a greater dividend than desired, he or she can reinvest the excess. Conversely, if the shareholder receives a smaller dividend than desired, he or she can sell off extra shares of equity. This argument is due to MM, and is similar to their homemade leverage concept, discussed in a previous chapter.

2   Shareholders will be indifferent between dividends and share repurchases in a perfect capital market.

3   Because dividends are taxed, companies should not issue equity to pay out a dividend.

4   Also because of taxes, firms have an incentive to reduce dividends. For example, they might consider increasing capital expenditures, acquiring other companies, or purchasing financial assets. However, because of financial considerations and legal constraints, rational firms with large cash flows will probably exhaust these activities with plenty of cash left over for dividends.

5   In a world with personal taxes, a strong case can be made for repurchasing shares instead of paying dividends.

6   Nevertheless, there are a number of justifications for dividends, even in a world with personal taxes:

   (a)   Investors in no-dividend equities incur transaction costs when selling off shares for current consumption.

   (b)   Behavioural finance argues that investors with limited self-control can meet current consumption needs via high-dividend equities while adhering to a policy of 'never dipping into principal'.

   (c)   Managers, acting on behalf of shareholders, can pay dividends to keep cash from bondholders. The board of directors, also acting on behalf of shareholders, can use dividends to reduce the cash available to spendthrift managers.

7   The stock market reacts positively to increases in dividends (or an initial payment) and negatively to decreases in dividends. This suggests that there is information content in dividend payments.

8   High (low) dividend firms should arise to meet the demands of dividend-preferring (capital-gains-preferring) investors. Because of these clienteles, it is not clear that a firm can create value by changing its dividend policy.

9   Time-varying demand for dividends means that in some periods companies that pay dividends are traded at a premium and in other cases they are not. Managers will time their dividend policies to take advantage of this premium.

##  Questions and Problems

**CONCEPT 1–10**

1   **Different Types of Dividend**   Explain the difference between a cash dividend and a stock dividend.

2   **The Dividend Payment Process**   When a dividend is paid, give some reasons why the share price decline may not be the same as the actual dividend payment.

3   **Dividend Policy Irrelevance**   How is it possible that dividends are so important, but at the same time dividend policy is irrelevant?

4  **Share Repurchases**   What is the impact of a share repurchase on a company's debt ratio? Does this suggest another use for excess cash?

5  **Dividends and Taxes**   Explain the importance of taxes in dividend policy. In a world with taxes, would dividend policy be relevant to you even if you are a tax-exempt financial institution? Explain.

6  **Real-World Factors**   What are the real-world factors that would encourage firms to follow a high dividend policy? Review these factors and comment on their appropriateness for corporate financial decision-making.

7  **Clienteles**   What is meant by dividend clienteles? If dividend clienteles exist, what does that imply for firms that adopt a new dividend policy in order to increase firm value?

8  **Catering Theory**   What is the catering theory of dividends, and how would it influence a manager looking to improve the value of her firm through dividend policy?

9  **Dividend Policy in Practice**   Do you think dividend policy is important in practice? Justify your answer using information you have read in this chapter.

10  **Stock Dividends and Stock Splits**   Why would firms have a reverse split? Should these have any impact on the value of the firm?

REGULAR

11 – 46

11  **Dividend Policy**   It is sometimes suggested that firms should follow a 'residual' dividend policy. With such a policy, the main idea is that a firm should focus on meeting its investment needs and maintaining its desired debt–equity ratio. Having done so, the firm pays out any leftover, or residual, income as dividends. What do you think would be the chief drawback to a residual dividend policy?

12  **Dividend Chronology**   On Tuesday 8 December Home Potere SpA's board of directors declares a dividend of 75 cents per share payable on Wednesday 17 January to shareholders of record as of Wednesday 3 January. When is the ex-dividend date? If a shareholder buys equity before that date, who gets the dividends on those shares – the buyer or the seller?

13  **Alternative Dividends**   Some corporations, like one British company that offers its large shareholders free crematorium use, pay dividends in kind (that is, offer their services to shareholders at below-market cost). Should mutual funds invest in equities that pay these dividends in kind? (The fundholders do not receive these services.)

14  **Dividends and Share Price**   If increases in dividends tend to be followed by (immediate) increases in share prices, how can it be said that dividend policy is irrelevant?

15  **Dividends and Stock Price**   Last month, Central Virginia Power Company, which had been having trouble with cost overruns on a nuclear power plant that it had been building, announced that it was 'temporarily suspending payments due to the cash flow crunch associated with its investment programme'. The company's share price dropped from $28.50 to $25 when this announcement was made. How would you interpret this change in the share price? (That is, what would you say caused it?)

16  **Dividend Reinvestment Plans**   DRK plc has recently developed a dividend reinvestment plan, or DRIP. The plan allows investors to reinvest cash dividends automatically in DRK in exchange for new shares of equity. Over time, investors in DRK will be able to build their holdings by reinvesting dividends to purchase additional shares of the company.

Many companies offer dividend reinvestment plans. Most companies with DRIPs charge no brokerage or service fees. In fact, the shares of DRK will be purchased at a 10 per cent discount from the market price. A consultant for DRK estimates that about 75 per cent of DRK's shareholders will take part in this plan. This is somewhat higher than the average.

Evaluate DRK's dividend reinvestment plan. Will it increase shareholder wealth? Discuss the advantages and disadvantages involved here.

17   **Dividend Policy**   Quarter 2 of 2008 was a dreadful period for initial public offerings in Europe, with only about €114 million raised and down about 50 per cent from the previous year. Relatively few of the 133 firms involved paid cash dividends. Why do you think that most chose not to pay cash dividends?

18   **Investment and Dividends**   The Phew Charitable Trust pays no taxes on its capital gains, or on its dividend income or interest income. Would it be irrational for it to have low-dividend, high-growth equities in its portfolio? Would it be irrational for it to have government bonds in its portfolio? Explain.

19   **Dividends and Share Value**   The growing perpetuity model expresses the value of a share of equity as the present value of the expected dividends from that equity. How can you conclude that dividend policy is irrelevant when this model is valid?

20   **Bird-in-the-Hand Argument**   The bird-in-the-hand argument, which states that a dividend today is safer than the uncertain prospect of a capital gain tomorrow, is often used to justify high dividend payout ratios. Explain the fallacy behind this argument.

21   **Dividends and Income Preference**   'The desire for current income is not a valid explanation of preference for high current dividend policy, because investors can always create home-made dividends by selling a portion of their shares.' Is this statement true or false? Why?

22   **Dividends and Clientele**   Cap Henderson owns Neotech equity, because its price has been steadily rising over the past few years, and he expects this performance to continue. Cap is trying to convince Sarah Jones to purchase some Neotech equity, but she is reluctant, because Neotech has never paid a dividend. She depends on steady dividends to provide her with income.

(a)   What preferences are these two investors demonstrating?

(b)   What argument should Cap use to convince Sarah that Neotech equity is the investment for her?

(c)   Why might Cap's argument not convince Sarah?

23   **Dividends and Taxes**   Your aunt is in a high tax bracket and would like to minimize the tax burden of her investment portfolio. She is willing to buy and sell to maximize her after-tax returns, and she has asked for your advice. What would you suggest she do?

24   **Dividends versus Capital Gains**   If the market places the same value on €1 of dividends as on €1 of capital gains, then firms with different payout ratios will appeal to different clienteles of investors. One clientele is as good as another: therefore a firm cannot increase its value by changing its dividend policy. Yet empirical investigations reveal a strong correlation between dividend payout ratios and other firm characteristics. For example, small, rapidly growing firms that have recently gone public almost always have payout ratios that are zero: all earnings are reinvested in the business. Explain this phenomenon if dividend policy is irrelevant.

25   **Dividend Irrelevance**   In spite of the theoretical argument that dividend policy should be irrelevant, the fact remains that many investors like high dividends. If this preference exists, a firm can boost its share price by increasing its dividend payout ratio. Explain the fallacy in this argument.

26   **Dividends and Share Prices**   Empirical research has found that there have been significant increases in share price on the day an initial dividend (i.e. the first time a firm pays a cash dividend) is announced. What does this finding imply about the information content of initial dividends?

27   **Dividends and Taxes**   Lea SpA has declared a €6-per-share dividend. Italy has a gradual tax system, where higher tax rates are charged at higher salary bands. Capital gains are taxed, dependent on how long you hold the shares of the company, and the amount recorded for tax purposes is deflated by the inflation rate between the date of purchase and the date of sale. We're going to make things simple. Suppose the tax rate on capital

gains and dividends is zero. Lea sells for €80 per share, and the equity is about to go ex dividend. What do you think the ex-dividend price will be?

28 **Stock Dividends** The owners' equity accounts for Hexagon International are shown here:

|  | **(£)** |
| --- | --- |
| Ordinary shares (£1 par value) | 10,000 |
| Additional Paid in Capital | 180,000 |
| Retained earnings | 586,500 |
| Total owners' equity | 776,500 |

(a) If Hexagon shares currently sell for £25 per share, and a 10 per cent stock dividend is declared, how many new shares will be distributed? Show how the equity accounts would change.

(b) If Hexagon declared a 25 per cent stock dividend, how would the accounts change?

29 **Stock Splits** For the company in Problem 28, show how the equity accounts will change if:

(a) Hexagon declares a four-for-one stock split. How many shares are outstanding now? What is the new par value per share?

(b) Hexagon declares a one-for-five reverse stock split. How many shares are outstanding now? What is the new par value per share?

30 **Stock Splits and Stock Dividends** Roll AB currently has 150,000 shares outstanding that sell for SKr65 per share. Assuming no market imperfections or tax effects exist, what will the share price be after:

(a) a five-for-three stock split?

(b) a 15 per cent stock dividend?

(c) a 42.5 per cent stock dividend?

(d) a four-for-seven reverse stock split?

Determine the new number of shares outstanding in parts (a) to (d).

31 **Regular Dividends** The balance sheet for Levy AG is shown here in market value terms. There are 5,000 shares outstanding.

| **Market Value Balance Sheet** | | | |
| --- | --- | --- | --- |
| | **(€)** | | **(€)** |
| Cash | 20,000 | Equity | 175,000 |
| Fixed assets | 155,000 | | |
| Total | 175,000 | Total | 175,000 |

The company has declared a dividend of €1.50 per share. The equity goes ex dividend tomorrow. Ignoring any tax effects, what are the shares selling for today? What will they sell for tomorrow? What will the market value balance sheet look like after the dividends are paid?

32 **Share Repurchase** In the previous problem, suppose Levy has announced it is going to repurchase €4,025 worth of stock. What effect will this transaction have on the equity of the firm? How many shares will be outstanding? What will the price per share be after the repurchase? Ignoring tax effects, show how the share repurchase is effectively the same as a cash dividend.

**33  Stock Dividends**  The market value balance sheet for Outbox Manufacturing is shown here. Outbox has declared a 25 per cent stock dividend. The stock goes ex dividend tomorrow (the chronology for a stock dividend is similar to that for a cash dividend). There are 15,000 shares of equity outstanding. What will the ex-dividend price be?

| Market Value Balance Sheet | | | |
|---|---|---|---|
| | **(£)** | | **(£)** |
| Cash | 190,000 | Debt | 160,000 |
| Fixed assets | 330,000 | Equity | 360,000 |
| Total | 520,000 | Total | 520,000 |

**34  Stock Dividends**  The company with the equity accounts shown here has declared a 12 per cent stock dividend when the market value of its equity is €20 per share. What effects on the equity accounts will the distribution of the stock dividend have?

| | **(€)** |
|---|---|
| Ordinary shares (€1 par value) | 350,000 |
| Additional Paid in Capital | 1,650,000 |
| Retained earnings | 3,000,000 |
| Total owners' equity | 5,000,000 |

**35  Stock Splits**  In the previous problem, suppose the company instead decides on a five-for-one stock split. The firm's 70 cent per share cash dividend on the new (post-split) shares represents an increase of 10 per cent over last year's dividend on the pre-split equity. What effect does this have on the equity accounts? What was last year's dividend per share?

**36  Residual Dividend Policy**  Soprano SpA, a litter-recycling company, uses a residual dividend policy. (See Question 11.) A debt–equity ratio of 0.80 is considered optimal. Earnings for the period just ended were €1,200, and a dividend of €480 was declared. How much in new debt was borrowed? What were total capital outlays?

**37  Residual Dividend Policy**  Worthington AG has declared an annual dividend of 0.80 Swiss francs (SwFr) per share. For the year just ended, earnings were SwFr7 per share.

(a)  What is Worthington's payout ratio?

(b)  Suppose Worthington has 7 million shares outstanding. Borrowing for the coming year is planned at SwFr18 million. What are planned investment outlays assuming a residual dividend policy? (See Question 11) What target capital structure is implicit in these calculations?

**38  Residual Dividend Policy**  Red Zeppelin plc follows a strict residual dividend policy. (See Question 11.) Its debt–equity ratio is 3.

(a)  If earnings for the year are £180,000, what is the maximum amount of capital spending possible with no new equity?

(b)  If planned investment outlays for the coming year are £760,000, will Red Zeppelin pay a dividend? If so, how much?

(c)  Does Red Zeppelin maintain a constant dividend payout? Why or why not?

**39  Residual Dividend Policy**  Preti Rock SA predicts that earnings in the coming year will be €56 million. There are 12 million shares, and PR maintains a debt–equity ratio of 2.

(a)  Calculate the maximum investment funds available without issuing new equity, and the increase in borrowing that goes along with it.

(b)   Suppose the firm uses a residual dividend policy. (See Question 11) Planned capital expenditures total €72 million. Based on this information, what will the dividend per share be?

(c)   In part (b), how much borrowing will take place? What is the addition to retained earnings?

(d)   Suppose PR plans no capital outlays for the coming year. What will the dividend be under a residual policy? What will new borrowing be?

40   **Dividends and Share Price**   Mann Company belongs to a risk class for which the appropriate discount rate is 10 per cent. Mann currently has 100,000 outstanding shares, selling at £100 each. The firm is contemplating the declaration of a £5 dividend at the end of the fiscal year that just began. Assume there are no taxes on dividends. Answer the following questions based on the Miller and Modigliani model, which is discussed in the text.

(a)   What will be the price of the shares on the ex-dividend date if the dividend is declared?

(b)   What will be the price of the shares at the end of the year if the dividend is not declared?

(c)   If Mann makes £2 million of new investments at the beginning of the period, earns net income of £1 million, and pays the dividend at the end of the year, how many shares of new equity must the firm issue to meet its funding needs?

(d)   Is it realistic to use the MM model in the real world to value equity? Why or why not?

41   **Homemade Dividends**   You own 1,000 shares of equity in Avondale Property ASA. You will receive a 0.70 krone (NKr) per share dividend in one year. In two years, Avondale will pay a liquidating dividend of NKr40 per share. The required return on Avondale shares is 15 per cent. What is the current share price of your equity (ignoring taxes)? If you would rather have equal dividends in each of the next two years, show how you can accomplish this by creating homemade dividends. (*Hint*: Dividends will be in the form of an annuity.)

42   **Homemade Dividends**   In the previous problem, suppose you want only NKr200 total in dividends in the first year. What will your homemade dividend be in two years?

43   **Share Repurchase**   Flychucker SA is evaluating an extra dividend versus a share repurchase. In either case €5,000 would be spent. Current earnings are €0.95 per share, and the equity currently sells for €40 per share. There are 200 shares outstanding. Ignore taxes and other imperfections in answering parts (a) and (b).

(a)   Evaluate the two alternatives in terms of the effect on the price per share of the equity and shareholder wealth.

(b)   What will be the effect on Flychucker's EPS and P/E ratio under the two different scenarios?

(c)   In the real world, which of these actions would you recommend? Why?

44   **Dividends and Firm Value**   The net income of Novis AS is 32,000 kroner (DKr). The company has 10,000 outstanding shares and a 100 per cent payout policy. The expected value of the firm one year from now is DKr1,545,600. The appropriate discount rate for Novis is 12 per cent, and the dividend tax rate is zero.

(a)   What is the current value of the firm, assuming the current dividend has not yet been paid?

(b)   What is the ex-dividend price of Novis's equity if the board follows its current policy?

(c) At the dividend declaration meeting, several board members claimed that the dividend is too meagre and is probably depressing Novis's price. They proposed that Novis sell enough new shares to finance a DKr4.25 dividend.

  (i) Comment on the claim that the low dividend is depressing the share price. Support your argument with calculations.

  (ii) If the proposal is adopted, at what price will the new shares sell? How many will be sold?

45 **Dividend Policy**  Gibson AG has a current period cash flow of €1.2 million and pays no dividends. The present value of the company's future cash flows is €15 million. The company is entirely financed with equity, and has 1 million shares outstanding. Assume the dividend tax rate is zero.

  (a) What is the share price of the Gibson equity?

  (b) Suppose the board of directors of Gibson AG announces its plan to pay out 50 per cent of its current cash flow as cash dividends to its shareholders. How can Jens Hagendorff, who owns 1,000 shares of Gibson equity, achieve a zero payout policy on his own?

46 **Dividend Smoothing**  Sharpe SA just paid a dividend of €1.25 per share of equity. Its target payout ratio is 40 per cent. The company expects to have an earnings per share of €4.50 one year from now.

  (a) If the adjustment rate is 0.3 as defined in the Lintner model, what is the dividend one year from now?

  (b) If the adjustment rate is 0.6 instead, what is the dividend one year from now?

  (c) Which adjustment rate is more conservative? Why?

47 **Expected Return, Dividends, and Taxes**  Gecko Company and Gordon Company are two firms whose business risk is the same but which have different dividend policies. Gecko pays no dividend, whereas Gordon has an expected dividend yield of 6 per cent. Suppose the capital gains tax rate is zero, whereas the dividend tax rate is 12.5 per cent. Gecko has an expected earnings growth rate of 15 per cent annually, and its share price is expected to grow at this same rate. If the after-tax expected returns on the two equities are equal (because they are in the same risk class), what is the pre-tax required return on Gordon's shares?

48 **Dividends and Taxes**  As discussed in the text, in the absence of market imperfections and tax effects, we would expect the share price to decline by the amount of the dividend payment when the equity goes ex dividend. Once we consider the role of taxes, however, this is not necessarily true. One model has been proposed that incorporates tax effects into determining the ex-dividend price:[20]

$$\frac{P_0 - P_X}{D} = \frac{1 - t_P}{1 - t_G}$$

Here $P_0$ is the price just before the share goes ex, $P_X$ is the ex-dividend share price, $D$ is the amount of the dividend per share, $t_P$ is the relevant marginal personal tax rate on dividends, and $t_G$ is the effective marginal tax rate on capital gains.

  (a) If $t_P = t_G = 0$, how much will the share price fall when the equity goes ex?

  (b) If $t_P = 15$ per cent and $t_G = 0$, how much will the share price fall?

  (c) If $t_P = 15$ per cent and $t_G = 20$ per cent, how much will the share price fall?

  (d) What does this problem tell you about real-world tax considerations and the dividend policy of the firm?

49 **Dividends versus Reinvestment**   National Business Machine plc (NBM) has £2 million of extra cash after taxes have been paid. NBM has two choices to make use of this cash. One alternative is to invest the cash in financial assets. The resulting investment income will be paid out as a special dividend at the end of three years. In this case, the firm can invest in either Treasury bills yielding 7 per cent or an 11 per cent preferred stock. Another alternative is to pay out the cash now as dividends. This would allow the shareholders to invest on their own in Treasury bills, with the same yield, or in preferred stock. The corporate tax rate is 28 per cent. Assume the investor has a 40 per cent personal income tax rate, which is applied to interest income and preferred stock dividends. The personal dividend tax rate is 12.5 per cent on cash dividends. Should the cash be paid today or in three years? Which of the two options generates the highest after-tax income for the shareholders?

50 **Dividends versus Reinvestment**   After completing its capital spending for the year, Carlson Manufacturing has £1,000 extra cash. Carlson's managers must choose between investing the cash in Treasury bonds that yield 8 per cent or paying the cash out to investors, who would invest in the bonds themselves.

(a)   If the corporate tax rate is 28 per cent, what personal tax rate would make the investors equally willing to receive the dividend or to let Carlson invest the money?

(b)   Is the answer to (a) reasonable? Why or why not?

# Electronic Calendrier SA

Electronic Calendrier (EC) is a small company founded 15 years ago by electronics engineers Georges Thiébald and Louis-Lucien Klotz. EC manufactures integrated circuits to capitalize on the complex mixed-signal design technology, and has recently entered the market for frequency timing generators, or silicon timing devices, which provide the timing signals or 'clocks' necessary to synchronize electronic systems. Its clock products originally were used in PC video graphics applications, but the market subsequently expanded to include motherboards, PC peripheral devices, and other digital consumer electronics, such as digital television boxes and games consoles. EC also designs and markets custom application-specific integrated circuits (ASICs) for industrial customers. The ASIC's design combines analogue and digital, or mixed-signal, technology. In addition to Georges and Louis-Lucien, Katherine Pancol, who provided capital for the company, is the third primary owner. Each owns 25 per cent of the 1 million shares outstanding. Several other individuals, including current employees, own the remaining company shares.

Recently, the company designed a new computer motherboard. The company's design is both more efficient and less expensive to manufacture, and the EC design is expected to become standard in many personal computers. After investigating the possibility of manufacturing the new motherboard, EC determined that the costs involved in building a new plant would be prohibitive. The owners also decided that they were unwilling to bring in another large outside owner. Instead, EC sold the design to an outside firm. The sale of the motherboard design was completed for an after-tax payment of €30 million.

1   Georges believes the company should use the extra cash to pay a special one-time dividend. How will this proposal affect the share price? How will it affect the value of the company?

2   Louis-Lucent believes that the company should use the extra cash to pay off debt and upgrade and expand its existing manufacturing capability. How would Louis-Lucent's proposals affect the company?

3   Katherine is in favour of a share repurchase. She argues that a repurchase will increase the company's P/E ratio, return on assets, and return on equity. Are her arguments correct? How will a share repurchase affect the value of the company?

4   Another option discussed by Georges, Louis-Lucent and Katherine would be to begin a regular dividend payment to shareholders. How would you evaluate this proposal?

5   One way to value a share of equity is the dividend growth, or growing perpetuity, model. Consider the following. The dividend payout ratio is 1 minus $b$, where $b$ is the 'retention' or 'ploughback' ratio. So the dividend next year will be the earnings next year, $E_1$, times 1 minus the retention ratio. The most commonly used equation to calculate the sustainable growth rate is the return on equity times the retention ratio. Substituting these relationships into the dividend growth model, we get the following equation to calculate the price of a share of equity today:

$$P_0 = \frac{E_1(1-b)}{R_S - \text{ROE} \times b}$$

What are the implications of this result in terms of whether the company should pay a dividend or upgrade and expand its manufacturing capability? Explain.

6   Does the question of whether the company should pay a dividend depend on whether the company is organized as a corporation or partnership?

## Practical Case Study

Use the annual financial statements for Man Group plc, Cairn Energy plc, and Tui Travel plc to find the dividend payout ratio for each company for the last three years. Why would these companies pay out a different percentage of income as dividends?

## Relevant Accounting Standards

Dividend policy in itself is not affected by accounting standards. However, the presentation of dividends is affected by IAS1 *Presentation of Financial Statements*, IAS27 *Consolidated and Separate Financial Statements*, and IAS33 *Earnings per Share*. Visit the IASPlus website (www.iasplus.com) for more information.

## Additional Reading

Dividend policy, the reasons why firms issue dividends, the factors affecting dividend policy, and their importance to investors are issues that have been bothering academics since Modigliani and Miller published their original dividend irrelevance theorem. The papers that are referenced below consider dividends in detail.

### Theoretical Developments

Allen, F., A.E. Bernardo and I. Welch (2000) 'A theory of dividends based on tax clienteles', *Journal of Finance*, vol. 55, no. 6, pp. 2499–2536.

DeAngelo, H. and L. DeAngelo (2006) 'The irrelevance of the MM dividend irrelevance theorem', *Journal of Financial Economics*, vol. 80, no. 2, pp. 299–315.

**Dividend Policy, Share Repurchases, and Stock Splits**

Bell, L. and T. Jenkinson (2002) 'New evidence of the impact of dividend taxation and on the identity of the marginal investor', *Journal of Finance*, vol. 57, no. 3, pp. 1321–1346. **UK**.

Brav, A., J.R. Graham, C.R. Harvey and R. Michaely (2005) 'Payout policy in the 21st century', *Journal of Financial Economics*, vol. 77, no. 3, pp. 483–527. **US**.

Brockman, P. and E. Unlu (2009) 'Dividend policy, creditor rights, and the agency costs of debt', *Journal of Financial Economics* (forthcoming). **International**.

DeAngelo, H., L. DeAngelo and R.M. Stulz (2006) 'Dividend policy and the earned/contributed capital mix: a test of the life-cycle theory', *Journal of Financial Economics*, vol. 81, no. 1, pp. 227–254. **US**.

Graham, J.R. and A. Kumar (2006) 'Do dividend clienteles exist? Evidence on dividend preferences of retail investors', *Journal of Finance*, vol. 61, no. 3, pp. 1305–1336. **US**.

Grinstein, Y. and R. Michaely (2005) 'Institutional holdings and payout policy', *Journal of Finance*, vol. 60, no. 3, pp. 1389–1426. **US**.

Henock, L. and H. White (2007) 'Do managers intentionally use repurchase tender offers to signal private information? Evidence from firm financial reporting behaviour', *Journal of Financial Economics*, vol. 85, no. 1, pp. 205–233. **US**.

Hoberg, G. and N. Prabhala (2009) 'Disappearing dividends, catering, and risk', *Review of Financial Studies*, vol. 22, no. 1, pp. 79–116. **US**.

Holmen, M., J.D. Knopf and S. Peterson (2008) 'Inside shareholders' effective tax rates and dividends', *Journal of Banking and Finance*, vol. 32, no. 9, pp. 1860–1869. **Sweden**.

Kinkki, S. (2008) 'Minority protection and dividend policy in Finland', *European Financial Management*, vol. 14, no. 3, pp. 470–502. **Finland**.

Kunz, R.M. and S. Rosa-Majhensek (2008) 'Stock splits in Switzerland: to signal or not to signal', *Financial Management*, vol. 37, no. 2, pp. 193–226. **Switzerland**.

La Porta, L., F. Lopez-de-Silanes, A. Shliefer and R. Vishney (2000) 'Agency problems and dividend policy around the world', *Journal of Finance*, vol. 55, no. 1, pp. 1–33. **International**.

Li, W. and E. Lie (2006) 'Dividend changes and catering incentives', *Journal of Financial Economics*, vol. 80, no. 2, pp. 293–308. **US**.

Massa, M., Z. Rehman and T. Vermaelen (2007) 'Mimicking repurchases', *Journal of Financial Economics*, vol. 84, no. 3, pp. 591–884. **US**.

Moder, W.J. (2007) 'The effect of shareholder taxes on corporate payout choice', *Journal of Financial and Quantitative Analysis*, vol. 42, no. 4, pp. 991–1019. **US**.

Oswald, D. and S. Young (2008) 'Share reacquisitions, surplus cash, and agency problems', *Journal of Banking and Finance*, vol. 32, no. 5, pp. 795–806. **UK**.

Schultz, P. (2000) 'Stock splits, tick size, and sponsorship', *Journal of Finance*, vol. 55, no. 1, pp. 429–450. **US**.

**Other Relevant Research**

Del Brio, E.B. and A. De Miguel (2009) 'Dividends and market signalling: an analysis of corporate insider trading', *European Financial Management* (forthcoming). **Spain**.

Dong, M., C. Robinson and C. Veld (2005) 'Why individual investors want dividends', *Journal of Corporate Finance*, vol. 12, no. 1, pp. 121–158. **The Netherlands**.

Liu, Y., S.H. Szewczyck and Z. Zantout (2008) 'Underreaction to dividend reductions and omissions?', *Journal of Finance*, vol. 62, no. 2, pp. 987–1020. **US**.

Pinkowitz, L., R. Stulz and R. Williamson (2006) 'Does the contribution of corporate cash holdings and dividends to firm value depend on governance? A cross-country analysis', *Journal of Finance*, vol. 61, no. 6, pp. 2725–2751. **International**.

# Endnotes

1   Stephen Ferris, Nilanjan Sen and Ho Pei Yui, 'God save the Queen and her dividends: corporate payouts in the United Kingdom', *Journal of Business* 79 (2006).

2   Raghavendra Rau and Theo Vermaelen, 'Regulation, taxes, and share repurchases in the United Kingdom', *Journal of Business* 75 (2002).

**3** Henk von Eije and William Megginson, 'Dividends and share repurchases in the European Union', *Journal of Financial Economics* (2008).

**4** Like all countries' tax systems, the British approach to taxation is highly complex. In the UK, individuals earning under £34,800 pay 10 per cent tax on dividends, and if your pay is above £34,800 you pay 32.5 per cent taxation. To partially avoid double taxation, the British government awards a 10 per cent tax credit on an individual's *total* dividend income, which is equal to the dividend you receive from the company plus the 10 per cent dividend tax credit. Although it seems as if a higher rate taxpayer will pay 22.5 per cent on dividend income, they actually pay 25 per cent on dividend income. This will baffle even the most intelligent of us, so it is better to illustrate the tax situation in the form of an example.

Consider a company that reports net income of £100, and the corporation tax rate is 28 per cent. What is the effective dividend tax rate of a higher tax rate individual and a lower tax rate individual?

|  | Low | High |
|---|---|---|
| Rate of personal dividend tax | 10% | 32.5% |
| Operating income | £100 | £100 |
| Corporate tax @ 28% | £28 | £28 |
| Net dividend | £72 | £72 |
| Total dividend income [= Net dividend × 1/(1 − 10%)] | £80.00 | £80.00 |
| Income tax | £8.00 | £26.00 |
| Tax credit | £8.00 | £8.00 |
| Tax due from shareholder | – | £18.00 |
| Received by shareholder | £72 | £54.00 |
| Effective tax rate (Tax paid/Net dividend) | 0% | 25% |
| Reported tax rate (Tax paid/Total dividend income) | 0% | 22.5% |

**5** See, for example, M.C. Jensen, 'Agency costs of free cash flows, corporate finance, and takeovers', *American Economic Review* (May 1986).

**6** H. DeAngelo and L. DeAngelo, 'Dividend policy and financial distress: an empirical investigation of troubled NYSE firms', *Journal of Finance*, vol. 45 (1990).

**7** Michael Rozeff, 'How companies set their dividend payout ratios', in *The Revolution in Corporate Finance*, edited by Joel M. Stern and Donald H. Chew (New York: Basil Blackwell, 1986). See also Robert S. Hansen, Raman Kumar and Dilip K. Shome, 'Dividend policy and corporate monitoring: evidence from the regulated electric utility industry', *Financial Management* (Spring 1994).

**8** P. Asquith and D. Mullins Jr, 'The impact of initiating dividend payments on shareholder wealth', *Journal of Business* (19 January 1983).

**9** R. Michaely, R.H. Thaler and K. Womack, 'Price reactions to dividend initiations and omissions: overreactions or drift', *Journal of Finance*, vol. 50 (1995).

**10** The correct representation of Eq. (18.5) involves cash flow, not earnings. However, with little loss of understanding, we could discuss dividend signalling in terms of earnings, not cash flow.

**11** Papers examining fully developed models of signalling include: S. Bhattacharya, 'Imperfect information, dividend policy, and the "bird in the hand" fallacy', *Bell Journal of Economics*, vol. 10 (1979); S. Bhattacharya, 'Non-dissipative signaling structure and dividend policy', *Quarterly Journal of Economics*, vol. 95 (1980), p. 1; S. Ross, 'The determination of financial structure: the incentive signaling approach', *Bell Journal of Economics*, vol. 8 (1977), p. 1; M. Miller and K. Rock, 'Dividend policy under asymmetric information', *Journal of Finance* (1985).

**12** Signalling models where dividends and repurchases are not perfect substitutes are contained in Franklin Allen, Antonio Bernardo and Ivo Welch, 'A theory of dividends based on tax clienteles', *Journal of Finance* (2002); and John Kose and Joseph Williams, 'Dividends, dilution and taxes: a signaling equilibrium', *Journal of Finance* (1985).

13  John Graham and Alok Kumar, 'Do dividend clienteles exist? Evidence on dividend preferences of retail investors', *Journal of Finance* (forthcoming).

14  Malcolm Baker and Jeffrey Wurgler, 'A catering theory of dividends', *Journal of Finance*, vol. 59 (2004).

15  P. Peterson, D. Peterson and J. Ang, 'Direct evidence on the marginal rate of taxation on dividend income', *Journal of Financial Economics*, vol. 14 (1985).

16  E.F. Fama and K.R. French, 'Disappearing dividends: changing firm characteristics or lower propensity to pay?', *Journal of Financial Economics* (April 2001).

17  Brandon Julio and David Ikenberry, 'Reappearing dividends', *Journal of Applied Corporate Finance* (2004).

18  Harry DeAngelo, Linda DeAngelo and Douglas Skinner, 'Are dividends disappearing? Dividend concentration and the consolidation of earnings', *Journal of Financial Economics* (2004).

19  J. Lintner, 'Distribution and incomes of corporations among dividends, retained earnings, and taxes', *American Economic Review* (May 1956).

20  N. Elton and M. Gruber, 'Marginal stockholder tax rates and the clientele effect', *Review of Economics and Statistics*, vol. 52 (19 February 1970).

To help you grasp the key concepts of this chapter check out the extra resources posted on the Online Learning Centre at **www.mcgraw-hill.co.uk/textbooks/hillier**

Among other helpful resources there are PowerPoint presentations, chapter outlines and mini-cases.

# Chapter 19

# Equity Financing

When a firm wishes to raise capital for new investment, it has two real choices. One option is to issue new equity. Another option is to borrow funds from financial institutions or through the public issue of debt. Every day in the financial press you will read about companies that have gone to the markets to raise new equity.

Take the Royal Bank of Scotland Group (RBSG) as an example. In 2007 it had undertaken a very expensive takeover of the Dutch bank ABN AMRO. Then, in the wake of the 2008 financial crisis, it reported total bad debts amounting to £5.9 billion. With a sharply deteriorating economic outlook, the bank sought equity financing of £12 billion. Unfortunately, the capital injection was not enough to save the bank, and in October 2008 the British government effectively nationalized RBSG by investing £5 billion in preference shares and underwriting a further £15 billion equity issue.

In this chapter we examine the process by which companies such as Royal Bank of Scotland Group plc sell equity to the public, the costs of doing so, and the role of intermediaries in the process. We pay particular attention to what is probably the most important stage in a company's financial life cycle – the initial public offering. Such offerings are the process by which companies convert from being privately owned to being publicly owned. For many people, starting a company, growing it, and taking it public is the ultimate entrepreneurial dream.

## 19.1 The Public Issue

When considering the steps involved in a public issue of equity, it is important to remember that each country has its own specific regulations and traditions, although the European Union has a comprehensive directive that covers all member countries. Table 19.1 illustrates the process for the UK, which is very similar to that of most other European countries.

## 19.2 Alternative Issue Methods

When a company decides to issue a new security, it can sell it as a public issue or a private issue. In a public issue the shares will be traded on a stock exchange, and the firm is required to register the issue with the stock exchange on which it is listed. If the issue is sold to only a few institutions it is called a *private placement* or *placing*, and can be treated as a private issue. A registration statement is normally not required in this case.[1]

There are two kinds of public issue: the *general cash offer* and the *rights issue.* Cash offers are sold to all interested investors, and rights offers are sold to existing shareholders. Equity is sold by both the cash offer and the rights offer, though almost all debt is sold by cash offer.

The first public equity issue that is made by a company is referred to as an **initial public offering (IPO)** or an **unseasoned new issue**. All initial public offerings are cash offers because, if the firm's existing shareholders wanted to buy the shares, the firm would not need to sell them publicly. IPO activity is positively related to the performance of stock markets, and this was reflected in the dearth of new issues in 2009. A **seasoned new issue** refers to a new offering where the company's securities have been previously issued. A seasoned new issue of ordinary shares will normally be through a rights issue.

Methods of issuing new securities are shown in Table 19.2, and are discussed in the next few sections.

TABLE
**19.1**

| Steps in public offering | Time | Activities |
|---|---|---|
| **1** Pathfinder prospectus | Several months before issue | An initial indicative prospectus is released that presents the proposed offering. |
| **2** Pre-underwriting conferences | About four weeks before the full prospectus is issued | The amount of money to be raised and the type of security to be issued are discussed. Initial expressions of interest are collected, and an issue price is set. An underwriter and approved adviser will be appointed. |
| **3** Full prospectus | Several weeks before the offering takes place | The prospectus contains all relevant financial and business information. |
| **4** Public offering and sale | Shortly after the last day of the registration period | In a typical firm-commitment contract, the underwriter buys a stipulated amount of equity from the firm and sells it at a higher price. The selling group assists in the sale. |
| **5** Market stabilization | Usually within 30 days of the offering | The underwriter stands ready to place orders to buy at a specified price on the market. |

**Table 19.1** The process of raising capital

## 19.3 The Cash Offer

As just mentioned, equity is sold to all interested investors in a cash offer. If the cash offer is a public one, banks are usually involved. Banks are financial intermediaries that perform a wide variety of services. In addition to taking deposits and making loans, they also aid in the sale of securities, facilitate mergers and other corporate reorganizations, act as brokers to both individual and institutional clients, and trade for their own accounts. Until late 2008 much of this activity was undertaken by investment banks. However, the financial crisis at the time resulted in investment banks either disappearing entirely (for example, Lehman Brothers), being bought over by another bank (Merrill Lynch by Bank of America), or changing into normal banks (Goldman Sachs and Morgan Stanley). While investment banks, *per se*, no longer exist in the traditional sense, the investment banking function still exists in banks.

For corporate issuers, the investment banking function includes the following:

- Formulating the method used to issue new securities.

- Pricing the new securities.

- Selling the new securities.

There are three basic methods of issuing securities for cash:

1. *Firm commitment:* Under this method, the bank (or a group of banks) buys the securities for less than the offering price and accepts the risk of not being able to sell them. Because this function involves risk, we say that the banker *underwrites* the securities in a firm commitment. In other words, when participating in a firm commitment offering, the banker acts as an *underwriter*. (Because firm commitments are so prevalent, we shall use *banker* and *underwriter* interchangeably in this chapter.)

**TABLE 19.2**

| Method | Type | Definition |
|---|---|---|
| **Public** | | |
| Traditional negotiated cash offer | Firm commitment cash offer | Company negotiates an agreement with a bank to underwrite and distribute the new shares. A specified number of shares are bought by underwriters and sold at a higher price. |
| | Best-efforts cash offer | Company has underwriters sell as many of the new shares as possible at the agreed-upon price. There is no guarantee concerning how much cash will be raised. Some best-efforts offerings do not use an underwriter. |
| | Dutch auction cash offer | Company has underwriters auction shares to determine the highest offer price obtainable for a given number of shares to be sold. |
| Privileged | Pre-emptive rights issue | Company offers the new equity directly to its existing shareholders. |
| Subscription | Standby rights issue | Like the pre-emptive rights issue, this contains a privileged subscription arrangement with existing shareholders. The net proceeds are guaranteed by the underwriters. |
| Non-traditional cash offer | Shelf cash offer | Qualifying companies can authorize all the shares they expect to sell over a specified period and sell them when needed. |
| | Competitive firm cash offer | Company can elect to award the underwriting contract through a public auction instead of negotiation. |
| **Private** | Direct placement | Securities are sold directly to the purchaser. |

**Table 19.2** The methods of issuing new securities

To minimize the risks here, bankers combine to form an underwriting group (syndicate) to share the risk and to help sell the issue. In such a group, one or more managers arrange or co-manage the deal. The manager is designated as the lead manager or principal manager. The lead manager typically has responsibility for all aspects of the issue. The other investment bankers in the syndicate serve primarily to sell the issue to their clients.

The difference between the underwriter's buying price and the offering price is called the *spread* or *discount*. It is the basic compensation received by the underwriter. Sometimes the underwriter will get non-cash compensation in the form of warrants or equity in addition to the spread.

Firm commitment underwriting is really just a purchase–sale arrangement, and the syndicate's fee is the spread. The issuer receives the full amount of the proceeds less the spread, and all the risk is transferred to the underwriter. If the underwriter cannot sell all of the issue at the agreed-upon offering price, it may need to lower the price on the unsold shares. However, because the offering price usually is not set until the underwriters have investigated how receptive the market is to the issue, this risk is usually minimal. This is particularly true with seasoned new issues, because the price of the new issue can be based on prior trades in the security.

2   *Best efforts*: The underwriter bears risk with a firm commitment, because it buys the entire issue. Conversely, the syndicate avoids this risk under a best-efforts offering, because it does not purchase the shares. Instead it merely acts as an agent, receiving a commission for each share sold. The syndicate is legally bound to use its best efforts to sell the securities at the agreed-upon offering price. If the issue cannot be sold at the offering price, it is usually withdrawn. This form of underwriting has become relatively rare.

3   *Dutch auction underwriting*: With Dutch auction underwriting the underwriter does not set a fixed price for the shares to be sold. Instead the underwriter conducts an auction in which investors bid for shares. The offer price is determined based on the submitted bids. A Dutch auction is also known by the more descriptive name *uniform price auction*. This approach to selling securities to the public is relatively rare in the IPO market, and has not been widely used there, but it is very common in the bond markets. For example, it is the sole procedure used by the government to sell enormous quantities of notes, bonds and bills to the public.

   Dutch auction underwriting was much in the news in 2004, because the web search company Google elected to use this approach. The best way to understand a Dutch or uniform price auction is to consider a simple example. Suppose the Rial Company wants to sell 400 shares to the public. The company receives five bids as follows:

| Bidder | Quantity | Price |
|--------|----------|-------|
| A | 100 shares | £16 |
| B | 100 shares | £14 |
| C | 100 shares | £12 |
| D | 200 shares | £12 |
| E | 200 shares | £10 |

Thus bidder A is willing to buy 100 shares at £16 each, bidder B is willing to buy 100 shares at £14, and so on. The Rial Company examines the bids to determine the highest price that will result in all 400 shares being sold. For example, at £14 A and B would buy only 200 shares, so that price is too high. Working our way down, all 400 shares won't be sold until we hit a price of £12, so £12 will be the offer price in the IPO. Bidders A to D will receive shares; bidder E will not.

   There are two additional important points to observe in our example. First, all the winning bidders will pay £12 – even bidders A and B, who actually bid a higher price. The fact that all successful bidders pay the same price is the reason for the name 'uniform price auction'. The idea in such an auction is to encourage bidders to bid aggressively by providing some protection against bidding a price that is too high.

   Second, notice that at the £12 offer price there are actually bids for 500 shares, which exceeds the 400 shares Rial wants to sell. Thus there has to be some sort of allocation. How this is done varies a bit, but in the IPO market the approach has been simply to compute the ratio of shares offered to shares bid at the offer price or better, which in our example is 400/500 = 0.8, and allocate bidders that percentage of their bids. In other words, bidders A to D would each receive 80 per cent of the shares they bid at a price of £12 per share.

   In most offerings the principal underwriter is permitted to buy shares if the market price falls below the offering price. The purpose is to *support* the market and *stabilize* the price from temporary downward pressure. If the issue remains unsold after a time (for example, 30 days), members may leave the group and sell their shares at whatever price the market will allow.

   Many underwriting contracts contain a Green Shoe provision, which gives the members of the underwriting group the option to purchase additional shares at the offering price.[2] The stated reason for the Green Shoe option is to cover excess demand and oversubscription. Green Shoe options usually last for about 30 days and involve no more than a percentage (usually less than 15 per cent) of the newly issued shares. The Green Shoe option is a benefit to the underwriting syndicate and a cost to the issuer. If the market price of the new issue goes above the offering price within 30 days, the underwriters can buy shares from the issuer and immediately resell the shares to the public.

The period after a new issue is initially sold to the public is called the *aftermarket*. During this period the members of the underwriting syndicate generally do not sell shares of the new issue for less than the offer price.

Almost all underwriting agreements contain *lock-ups*. Such arrangements specify how long insiders must wait after an IPO before they can sell some of their shares. Typically, lock-up periods are set at 180 days, but they can last for several years. Lock-ups are important, because it is not unusual for the number of locked-up insider shares to be larger than the number of shares held by the public. Thus there is the possibility that, when the lock-up period ends, a large number of shares will be sold by insiders, thereby depressing share prices.

Beginning well before an offering and extending for a period following an IPO, many countries require that a firm and its managing underwriters observe a 'quiet period'. This means that all communications with the public must be limited to ordinary announcements and other purely factual matters. The logic is that all relevant information should be contained in the prospectus. An important result of this requirement is that the underwriter's analysts are prohibited from making recommendations to investors. As soon as the quiet period ends, however, the managing underwriters typically publish research reports, usually accompanied by a favourable 'buy' recommendation.

Firms that don't stay quiet can have their IPOs delayed. For example, just before Google's IPO, an interview with cofounders Sergy Brin and Larry Page appeared in *Playboy*. The interview almost caused a postponement of the IPO, but Google was able to amend its prospectus in time (by including the article!).

## Investment Banking

Investment banking is at the heart of new security issues. The investment banking arm of big banks provide advice, market the securities (after investigating the market's receptiveness to the issue), and underwrite the proceeds. They accept the risk that the market price may fall between the date the offering price is set and the time the issue is sold.

In addition, banks have the responsibility of pricing fairly. When a firm goes public, particularly for the first time, the buyers know relatively little about the firm's operations. After all, it is not rational for a buyer of, say, only 1,000 shares of equity to study the company at length. Instead, the buyer must rely on the judgement of the bank, which has presumably examined the firm in detail. Given this asymmetry of information, what prevents the banker from pricing the issued securities too high? Although the underwriter has a short-term incentive to price high, it has a long-term incentive to make sure its customers do not pay too much; they might desert the underwriter in future deals if they lose money on this one. Thus, as long as banks plan to stay in business over time, it is in their self-interest to price fairly.

In other words, financial economists argue that each bank has a reservoir of 'reputation capital'.[3] Mispricing of new issues or unethical dealings are likely to reduce this reputation capital.

---

## In Their Own Words

### Robert S. Hansen on the Economic Rationale for the Firm Commitment Offer

Underwriters provide four main functions: certification, monitoring, marketing, and risk bearing.

Certification assures investors that the offer price is fair. Investors have concerns about whether the offer price is unfairly above the equity's intrinsic value. Certification increases issuer value by reducing investor doubt about fairness, making a better offer price possible.

Monitoring of issuing firm management and performance builds value because it adds to shareholders' ordinary monitoring. Underwriters provide collective monitoring on behalf of both capital suppliers and current shareholders. Individual shareholder monitoring is limited because the shareholder bears the entire cost, whereas all owners collectively share the benefit, pro rata. By contrast, in underwriter monitoring all shareholders share both the costs and benefits, pro rata.

Due diligence and legal liability for the proceeds give investors assurance. However, what makes certification and monitoring credible is lead bank reputation in competitive capital markets, where they are disciplined over time. Evidence that irreputable behavior is damaging to a bank's future abounds. Capital market participants punish poorly performing banks by refusing to hire them. The participants pay banks for certification and meaningful monitoring in 'quasi-rents' in the spread, which represent the fair cost of 'renting' the reputations.

Marketing is finding long-term investors who can be persuaded to buy the securities at the offer price. This would not be needed if demand for new shares were 'horizontal'. There is much evidence that issuers and syndicates repeatedly invest in costly marketing practices, such as expensive road shows to identify and expand investor interest. Another is organizing members to avoid redundant pursuit of the same customers. Lead banks provide trading support in the issuer's equity for several weeks after the offer.

Underwriting risk is like the risk of selling a put option. The syndicate agrees to buy all new shares at the offer price and resell them at that price or at the market price, whichever is lower. Thus, once the offer begins, the syndicate is exposed to potential losses on unsold inventory should the market price fall below the offer price. The risk is likely to be small, because offerings are typically well prepared for quick sale.

*Robert S. Hansen is the Freeman Senior Research Professor of Finance at Tulane University.*

Banks put great importance on their relative rankings, and view downward movement in their placement with much distaste. While this jockeying for position may seem as unimportant as the currying of royal favour in the court of Louis XVI, it is explained by the preceding discussion. In any industry where reputation is so important, the firms in the industry must guard theirs with great vigilance.

There are two basic methods for selecting the syndicate. In a **competitive offer** the issuing firm can offer its securities to the underwriter bidding highest. In a **negotiated offer** the issuing firm works with one underwriter. Because the firm generally does not negotiate with many underwriters concurrently, negotiated deals may suffer from lack of competition.

Whereas competitive bidding occurs frequently in other areas of commerce, it may surprise you that negotiated deals in banking occur with all but the largest issuing firms. Investment bankers argue that they must expend much time and effort learning about the issuer before setting an issue price and a fee schedule. Except in the case of large issues, these underwriters could not expend the time and effort without the near certainty of receiving the contract.

Studies generally show that issuing costs are higher in negotiated deals than in competitive ones. However, many financial economists argue that issuing firms are not necessarily hurt by negotiated deals. They point out that the underwriter gains much information about the issuing firm through negotiation – information likely to increase the probability of a successful offering.[4]

## The Offering Price

Determining the correct offering price is the most difficult thing the lead underwriter must do for an initial public offering. The issuing firm faces a potential cost if the offering price is set too high or too low. If the issue is priced too high, it may be unsuccessful and be withdrawn. If the issue is priced below the true market price, the issuer's existing shareholders will experience an opportunity loss.

Ljunqvist has found that unseasoned new equity issues are generally offered below their true market price in the vast majority of countries.[5] Underpricing helps new shareholders earn a higher return on the shares they buy. However, the existing shareholders of the issuing firm are not necessarily helped by underpricing. To them it is an indirect cost of issuing new securities. Figure 19.1 shows the issue date average return on new IPOs for a variety of European countries.

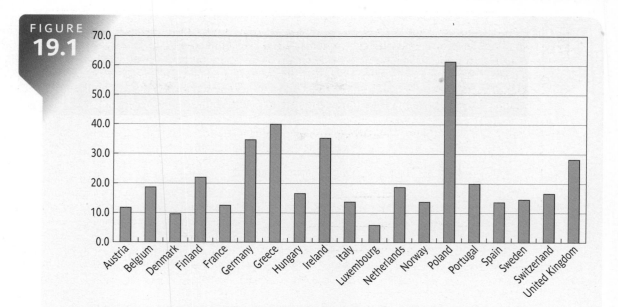

*Source*: A. Ljunqvist, 'IPO underpricing', Chapter 7 of *Handbook of Corporate Finance: Empirical Corporate Finance*, Volume A (Handbooks in Finance Series, Elsevier/North Holland), B. Espen Eckbo (ed.) (2006).

**Figure 19.1** Equal weighted average initial IPO returns in per cent for 19 European countries between 1990 and 2003

## Underpricing: A Possible Explanation

There are several possible explanations for underpricing, but so far there is no agreement among scholars as to which explanation is correct. In our opinion there are two important facts associated with the underpricing puzzle that are key elements to a unifying theory. First, much of the apparent underpricing is concentrated in smaller issues. This point is documented in Table 19.3, which shows that underpricing tends to be attributable to firms with few or no sales in the prior year. These firms tend to be young firms with uncertain future prospects. The increased uncertainty in some way probably attracts risk-averse investors only if underpricing exists. Second, when the price of a new issue is too low, the issue is often *oversubscribed*. This means investors will not be able to buy all of the shares they want, and the underwriters will allocate the shares among investors. The average investor will find it difficult to get shares in an oversubscribed offering, because there will not be enough shares to go around. Although initial public offerings have positive initial returns on average, a significant fraction of them have price drops. An investor submitting an order for all new issues may find that he or she will be allocated more shares in issues that go down in price.

Consider this tale of two investors. Ms Smarts knows precisely what companies are worth when their shares are offered. Mr Average knows only that prices usually rise one month after the IPO. Armed with this information, Mr Average decides to buy 1,000 shares of every IPO. Does Mr Average actually earn an abnormally high average return across all initial offerings?

The answer is no, and at least one reason is Ms Smarts. For example, because Ms Smarts knows that company XYZ is underpriced, she invests all her money in its IPO. When the issue is oversubscribed, the underwriters must allocate the shares between Ms Smarts and Mr Average. If they do this on a pro rata basis, and if Ms Smarts has bid for twice as many shares as Mr Average, she will get two shares for each one Mr Average receives. The net result is that when an issue is underpriced, Mr Average cannot buy as much of it as he wants.

TABLE
19.3

| Annual sales of issuing firms | 1980–1989 | | 1990–1998 | | 1999–2000 | | 2001–2005 | |
|---|---|---|---|---|---|---|---|---|
| | Number of firms | First-day average return (%) | Number of firms | First-day average return (%) | Number of firms | First-day average return (%) | Number of firms | First-day average return (%) |
| 0 ≤ Sales < $10m | 393 | 10.1 | 671 | 17.2 | 328 | 69.8 | 77 | 6.1 |
| $10m ≤ Sales < $20m | 253 | 8.7 | 377 | 18.7 | 139 | 79.9 | 27 | 10.5 |
| $20m ≤ Sales < $50m | 492 | 7.6 | 777 | 18.7 | 152 | 74.5 | 70 | 9.7 |
| $50m ≤ Sales < $100m | 345 | 6.5 | 574 | 13.0 | 89 | 60.4 | 72 | 16.1 |
| $100m ≤ Sales < $200m | 241 | 4.6 | 444 | 11.9 | 54 | 35.5 | 79 | 14.7 |
| $200m ≤ Sales | 278 | 3.5 | 628 | 8.7 | 87 | 26.0 | 209 | 10.9 |
| All | 2,002 | 7.1 | 3,471 | 14.8 | 849 | 64.6 | 534 | 11.3 |

Data are from Securities Data Co., with corrections by the authors. Sales, measured in millions, are for the last 12 months prior to going public. All sales have been converted into dollars of 2003 purchasing power, using the Consumer Price Index. There are 6,854 IPOs, after excluding IPOs with an offer price of less than $5.00 per share, units, REITs, ADRs, closed-end funds, banks and S&Ls, firms not listed on CRSP within six months of the offer date, and 140 firms with missing sales. The average first-day return is 18.5 per cent.

*Source*: Professor Jay R. Ritter, University of Florida.

**Table 19.3** Average first-day returns, categorized by sales, for IPOs: 1980–2005

Ms Smarts also knows that company ABC is overpriced. In this case, she avoids its IPO altogether, and Mr Average ends up with a full 1,000 shares. To summarize, Mr Average receives fewer shares when more knowledgeable investors swarm to buy an underpriced issue, but he gets all he wants when the smart money avoids the issue.

## In Their Own Words

### Jay Ritter on IPO Underpricing around the World

The United States is not the only country in which initial public offerings (IPOs) are underpriced. The phenomenon exists in every country with a stock market, although the extent of underpricing varies from country to country.

In general, countries with developed capital markets have more moderate underpricing than those with emerging markets. During the Internet bubble of 1999–2000, however, underpricing in the developed capital markets increased dramatically. In the United States, for example, the average first-day return during 1999–2000 was 65 per cent. At the same time that underpricing in the developed capital markets increased, the underpricing of IPOs sold to residents of China moderated. The Chinese average has come down to a mere 267 per cent, which is lower than it had been in the early 1990s. After the bursting of the Internet bubble in mid-2000, the level of underpricing in the United States, Germany, and other developed capital markets returned to more traditional levels.

The table opposite gives a summary of the average first-day returns on IPOs for 39 countries around the world, with the figures collected from a number of studies by various authors. In countries where the first-day price change is limited by regulations, the return is measured until price limits are no longer binding.

| TABLE 19.4 | | | | | | | |
|---|---|---|---|---|---|---|---|
| Country | Sample size | Time period | Average first-day return (%) | Country | Sample size | Time period | Average first-day return (%) |
| Australia | 381 | 1976–1995 | 12.1 | Malaysia | 401 | 1980–1998 | 104.1 |
| Austria | 76 | 1984–1999 | 6.5 | Mexico | 37 | 1987–1990 | 33.0 |
| Belgium | 86 | 1984–1999 | 14.6 | Netherlands | 143 | 1982–1999 | 10.2 |
| Brazil | 62 | 1979–1990 | 78.5 | New Zealand | 201 | 1979–1999 | 23.0 |
| Canada | 500 | 1971–1999 | 6.3 | Nigeria | 63 | 1989–1993 | 19.1 |
| Chile | 55 | 1982–1997 | 8.8 | Norway | 68 | 1984–1996 | 12.5 |
| China | 1,124 | 1992–2000 | 267.0 | Philippines | 104 | 1987–1997 | 22.7 |
| Denmark | 117 | 1984–1998 | 5.4 | Poland | 149 | 1991–1998 | 35.6 |
| Finland | 99 | 1984–1997 | 10.1 | Portugal | 21 | 1992–1998 | 10.6 |
| France | 571 | 1983–2000 | 11.6 | Singapore | 128 | 1973–1992 | 31.4 |
| Germany | 407 | 1978–1999 | 27.7 | South Africa | 118 | 1980–1991 | 32.7 |
| Greece | 129 | 1987–1994 | 51.7 | Spain | 99 | 1986–1998 | 10.7 |
| Hong Kong | 334 | 1980–1996 | 15.9 | Sweden | 251 | 1980–1994 | 34.1 |
| India | 98 | 1992–1993 | 35.3 | Switzerland | 120 | 1983–2000 | 34.9 |
| Indonesia | 106 | 1989–1994 | 15.1 | Taiwan | 293 | 1986–1998 | 31.1 |
| Iran | 279 | 1991–2004 | 22.4 | Thailand | 292 | 1987–1997 | 46.7 |
| Israel | 285 | 1990–1994 | 12.1 | Turkey | 138 | 1990–1996 | 13.6 |
| Italy | 164 | 1985–2000 | 23.9 | United Kingdom | 3,122 | 1959–2001 | 17.4 |
| Japan | 1,689 | 1970–2001 | 28.4 | United States | 14,840 | 1960–2001 | 18.4 |
| Korea | 477 | 1980–1996 | 74.3 | | | | |

*Source*: Jay R. Ritter is Cordell Professor of Finance at the University of Florida. An outstanding scholar, he is well respected for his insightful analyses of new issues and companies going public.

**Table 19.4** IPO underpricing around the world

This is called the *winner's curse*, and it explains much of the reason why IPOs have such a large average return. When the average investor wins and gets his allocation, it is because those who knew better avoided the issue. To counteract the winner's curse and attract the average investor, underwriters underprice issues.[6]

## 19.4 The Announcement of New Equity and the Value of the Firm

It seems reasonable to believe that new long-term financing is arranged by firms after positive net present value projects are put together. As a consequence, when the announcement of external financing is made, the firm's market value should go up. As we mentioned in an earlier chapter, this is precisely the opposite of what actually happens in the case of new equity financing. Asquith and Mullins, Masulis and Korwar, and Mikkelson and Partch for the US, Gajewski and Ginglinger for France, Martin-Ugedo for Spain, and Barnes and Walker for the UK, have all found that the market value of existing equity drops on the announcement of a new public issue of equity.[7] Plausible reasons for this strange result include the following:

- *Managerial information:* If managers have superior information about the market value of the firm, they may know when the firm is overvalued. If they do, they might attempt to issue new shares when the market value exceeds the correct value. This will benefit existing shareholders. However, the potential new shareholders are not stupid. They will infer overvaluation from the new issue, thereby bidding down the share price on the announcement date of the issue.

- *Debt capacity*: The stereotypical firm chooses a debt–equity ratio that balances the tax shield from the debt with the cost of financial distress. When the managers of a firm have special information that the probability of financial distress has risen, the firm is more likely to raise capital through equity than through debt. If the market infers this chain of events, the share price should fall on the announcement date of an equity issue.

- *Falling earnings*:[8] When managers raise capital in amounts that are unexpectedly large (as most unanticipated financings will be), and if investors have a reasonable fix on the firm's upcoming investments and dividend payouts (as they do because capital expenditure announcements are often well known, as are future dividends), the unanticipated financings are roughly equal to unanticipated shortfalls in earnings (this follows directly from the firm's sources and uses of funds identity). Therefore an announcement of a new equity issue will also reveal a future earnings shortfall.

## 19.5 The Cost of New Issues

Issuing securities to the public is not free, and the costs of different issuing methods are important determinants of which will be used. The costs fall into six categories:

1 *Spread or underwriting discount*: The spread is the difference between the price the issuer receives and the price offered to the public.

2 *Other direct expenses*: These are costs incurred by the issuer that are not part of the compensation to underwriters. They include filing fees, legal fees, and taxes – all reported in the prospectus.

3 *Indirect expenses*: These costs are not reported in the prospectus, and include management time spent on the new issue.

4 *Abnormal returns*: In a seasoned issue of equity, the price drops upon announcement of the issue. The drop protects new shareholders against the firm's selling overpriced equity to new shareholders.

5 *Underpricing*: For initial public offerings, the equity typically rises substantially after the issue date. This is a cost to the firm, because the shares are sold for less than their efficient price in the aftermarket.[9]

6 *Green Shoe option*: The Green Shoe option gives the underwriters the right to buy additional shares at the offer price to cover over-allotments. This is a cost to the firm, because the underwriter will buy additional shares only when the offer price is below the price in the aftermarket.

An interesting study by Seth Armitage reports two of these six costs – underwriting discount and other non-underwriting direct expenses.[10] Table 19.5, which is reproduced from Table 1 of the paper, provides three main insights:

1 The total issue costs decline as the gross proceeds of the offering increase for both US and UK companies. Thus it appears that issuance costs are subject to substantial economies of scale.[11]

2 Issue costs in the US are higher than in the UK for most levels of gross proceeds.

3 Last, and perhaps most important, the costs of issuing securities to the public are quite large. For example, total direct expenses are approximately 6 per cent in the UK, and this rises to nearly 15 per cent for small issues. This implies that issuing equity is a weighty decision, especially for smaller companies. Although there are many benefits, such as raising needed capital and spreading ownership, the costs cannot be ignored.

**TABLE 19.5**

| UK rights issues and open offers, purged sample | | | | | US SEOs | | |
|---|---|---|---|---|---|---|---|
| Gross proceeds (£m) | N | Non-underwriting costs (%) | Underwriting costs (%) | Total costs (%) | Gross proceeds ($m) | N | Total costs (%) |
| 312.5+ | 19 | 0.72 | 1.44 | 2.17 | 500+ | 9 | 3.15 |
| 125.0–312.4 | 32 | 0.88 | 1.77 | 2.65 | 200–499.9 | 55 | 3.47 |
| 62.5–124.9 | 48 | 1.07 | 1 71 | 2.79 | 100–199.9 | 152 | 4.22 |
| 50.0–62.4 | 21 | 1.60 | 1.94 | 3.54 | 80–99.9 | 71 | 4.73 |
| 37.5–49.9 | 31 | 1.35 | 1.71 | 3.07 | 60–79.9 | 143 | 5.18 |
| 25.0–37.4 | 44 | 1.87 | 1.83 | 3.70 | 40–59.9 | 261 | 5.87 |
| 12.5–24.9 | 85 | 2.03 | 1.67 | 3.68 | 20–39.9 | 425 | 6.93 |
| 6.25–12.4 | 86 | 3.72 | 1.41 | 5.16 | 10–19.9 | 310 | 8.72 |
| 1.25–6.24 | 180 | 6.90 | 1.39 | 8.27 | 2–9.9 | 167 | 13.28 |
| 0.1–1.24 | 37 | 13.48 | 0.99 | 14.36 | | | |
| Total | 583 | 4.18 | 1.53 | 5.78 | | 1,593 | 7.11 |
| Median | | 2.55 | 1.75 | 4.28 | | | |

*Source*: Table 1 from Seth Armitage, 'The direct costs of UK rights issues and open offers', *European Financial Management*, vol. 6 (2000).

**Table 19.5** Cost of issue by issue size

# 19.6 Rights

When new shares of equity are offered to the general public, the proportionate ownership of existing shareholders is likely to be reduced. However, if a pre-emptive right is contained in the firm's articles of incorporation, the firm must first offer any new issue of equity to existing shareholders. This assures each owner his or her proportionate owner's share.

An issue of equity to existing shareholders is called a *rights issue* or *rights offering*. Here each shareholder is issued an *option* to buy a specified number of new shares from the firm at a specified price within a specified time, after which the rights expire. For example, consider the £12.246 billion rights issue undertaken by the Royal Bank of Scotland in April 2008. The firm's equity was selling at £3.58 on the announcement date, and current shareholders were able to buy a fixed number of shares at £2.00 per share within two months. The terms of the option are evidenced by certificates known as *share warrants* or *rights*. Such rights are often traded on securities exchanges or over the counter.

## The Mechanics of a Rights Issue

The various considerations confronting a financial manager in a rights offering are illustrated by the situation of the Royal Bank of Scotland, whose initial financial statements are given in Table 19.6.

The Royal Bank of Scotland earned £7.712 billion after taxes and had approximately 10 billion shares outstanding. Earnings per share were £0.764, and the equity sold at 4.68 times earnings (that is, its price–earnings ratio was 4.68). The market price of each share was therefore £3.58. The company planned to raise just over £12 billion of new equity funds by a rights offering.

The process of issuing rights differs from the process of issuing shares of equity for cash. Existing shareholders are notified that they have been given one right for each share of equity they own. Exercise occurs when a shareholder sends payment to the firm's subscription agent (usually a bank) and turns in the required number of rights. Shareholders of the Royal Bank

**ROYAL BANK OF SCOTLAND GROUP PLC**
**Statement of Financial Position and Income Statement for 2007**

**Statement of Financial Position (£millions)**

| Assets | | Shareholder equity | |
|---|---|---|---|
| | | Ordinary shares | 53,038 |
| | | Retained earnings | 1,847,481 |
| Total | 1,900,519 | Total | 1,900,519 |

**Income Statement (£millions)**

| | |
|---|---|
| Earnings before taxes | 9,908 |
| Taxes | 2,188 |
| Net income | 7,712 |
| Earnings per share | 0.764 |
| Shares outstanding (millions) | 10,094.24 |
| Market price per share | 3.58 |
| Total market value (£millions) | 36,137 |

**Table 19.6** Financial statement before rights offering

of Scotland had several choices: (a) subscribe for the full number of entitled shares; (b) order all the rights sold; or (b) do nothing and let the rights expire.

The financial management of Royal Bank of Scotland had to answer the following questions:

1    What price should the existing shareholders be allowed to pay for a share of new equity?

2    How many rights will be required to purchase one share of equity?

3    What effect will the rights offering have on the existing share price of the company?

## Subscription Price

In a rights issue the subscription price is the price that existing shareholders are allowed to pay for a share of equity. A rational shareholder will subscribe to the rights offering only if the subscription price is below the market price of the equity on the offer's expiration date. For example, if the share price at expiration is £1.50 and the subscription price is £2.00, no rational shareholder will subscribe. Why pay £2.00 for something worth £1.50? The Royal Bank of Scotland chose a price of £2.00, which was well below the existing market price of £3.58. As long as the market price did not fall below the subscription price of £2.00 before expiration, the rights offering would succeed.

## Number of Rights Needed to Purchase a Share

Royal Bank of Scotland wanted to raise £12,246,020,924 in new equity. With a subscription price of £2.00, it needed to issue 6,123,010,462 new shares. This can be determined by dividing the total amount to be raised by the subscription price:

$$\text{Number of new shares} = \frac{\text{Funds to be raised}}{\text{Subscription price}}$$

$$= \frac{£12,246,020,924}{£2.00}$$

$$= 6,123,010,462 \text{ shares}$$

Because shareholders typically get one right for each share of equity they own, just over 6 billion rights were issued by Royal Bank of Scotland. To determine how many rights must be exercised to get one share of equity, we can divide the number of existing outstanding shares of equity by the number of new shares:

$$\frac{\text{Number of rights needed}}{\text{to buy a share of equity}} = \frac{\text{'Old' shares}}{\text{'New' shares}} = \frac{10{,}094{,}241{,}000}{6{,}123{,}010{,}462} = 1.648 \text{ rights}$$

Clearly, it is impossible to own exactly 1.648 shares, and so in a rights issue one must construct terms so that the number of rights and shares are integers. In the Royal Bank of Scotland's case the correct terms were 18 'old' shares for 11 'new' shares (18/11 = 1.64). In markets parlance this would be called an '11 for 18 rights issue of 6,123,010,462 shares at £2.00 per share'. Thus each shareholder had to give up 18 rights plus £2.00 to receive 11 shares of new equity. If all the shareholders do this, the Royal Bank of Scotland will raise the required £12.246 billion.

It should be clear that the subscription price, the number of new shares, and the number of rights needed to buy a new share of equity are interrelated. If the Royal Bank of Scotland lowered the subscription price it would have had to issue more new shares to raise £12.246 billion in new equity. Several alternatives appear here:

| Subscription price | Number of new shares | Number of rights needed to buy a share of equity |
|---|---|---|
| £3.00 | 4,082,006,974 | 2.47 |
| £2.00 | 6,123,010,462 | 1.648 |
| £1.00 | 12,246,020,924 | 1 |

## Effect of Rights Offering on the Share Price

Rights clearly have value. In the case of the Royal Bank of Scotland the right to be able to buy a share of equity worth £3.58 for £2.00 was valuable.

Suppose a shareholder of the Royal Bank of Scotland owns 18 shares of equity just before the rights offering. This situation is depicted in Table 19.7. Initially the price of the Royal Bank of Scotland was £3.58 per share, so the shareholder's total holding is worth 18 × £3.58 = £64.44. The shareholder who has 18 shares will receive 18 rights. The Royal Bank of Scotland rights issue gave shareholders with 18 rights the opportunity to purchase 11 additional shares for £2.00. The holding of the shareholder who exercises these rights and buys the new shares would increase to 29 shares. The value of the new holding would be £64.44 + £22 = £86.44 (the £64.44 initial value plus the £22 paid to the company). Because the shareholder now holds 29 shares, the price per share would drop to £86.44/29 = £2.98 (rounded to two decimal places).

The difference between the old share price of £3.58 and the new share price of £2.98 reflects the fact that the old shares carried rights to subscribe to the new issue. The difference must be equal to the value of one right: that is, £3.58 − £2.98 = £0.60.

Just as we learned of an ex-dividend date in the previous chapter, there is an ex-rights date here. An individual buying the equity prior to the ex-rights date will receive the rights when they are distributed. An individual buying the equity on or after the ex-rights date will not receive the rights. In our example the price of the equity prior to the ex-rights date was £3.58. An individual buying on or after the ex-rights date is not entitled to the rights. The price on or after the ex-rights date will be £2.98.

Table 19.8 shows what happens to the Royal Bank of Scotland. If all shareholders exercise their rights the number of shares will increase to 16,217,251,462, and the value of the firm will increase to £48,327,409,357. After the rights offering the value of each share will drop to £2.98 (= £48,327,409,357/16,217,251,462).

TABLE
**19.7**

| | The shareholder |
|---|---|
| Initial position | |
| Number of shares | 18 |
| Share price | £3.58 |
| Value of holding | £64.44 |
| Terms of offer | |
| Subscription price | £2.00 |
| Number of rights issued | 18 |
| Number of rights for a share | 11 |
| After offer | |
| Number of shares | 29 |
| Value of holding | £86.44 |
| Share price | £2.98 |
| Value of a right | |
| Old price − New price | £3.58 − £2.98 = £0.60 |
| New price − Subscription price / Number of rights for a share | (£2.98 − £2.00)/1.648 = £0.60 |

**Table 19.7** The value to the individual shareholder of the Royal Bank of Scotland's rights

TABLE
**19.8**

| | |
|---|---|
| Initial position | |
| Number of 'old' shares | 10,094,241,000 |
| Share price | £3.58 |
| Value of firm | £36,137,382,780 |
| Terms of offer | |
| Subscription price | £2.00 |
| Number of rights issued | 10,094,241,000 |
| Number of 'new' shares | 6,123,010,462 |
| After offer | |
| Number of shares | 16,217,251,462 |
| Share price | £2.98 |
| Value of firm | £48,327,409,357 |
| Value of one right | £3.58 − £2.98 = £0.60 |
| | or (£2.98 − £2.00)/1.648 = £0.60 |

**Table 19.8** The Royal Bank of Scotland rights offering

An investor holding no shares of Royal Bank of Scotland equity who wants to subscribe to the new issue can do so by buying rights. An outside investor buying 18 rights will pay £0.60 × 18 = £10.78 (to account for previous rounding). If the investor exercises the rights at a subscription cost of £2.00 to purchase 11 new shares, the total cost would be £22 + £10.78 = £32.78. In return for this expenditure the investor will receive 11 shares of the new equity (worth £2.98 per share), totalling £32.78.

Of course, outside investors can also buy Royal Bank of Scotland shares directly at £2.98 per share. In an efficient stock market it will make no difference whether new equity is obtained via rights or via direct purchase.

## Effects on Shareholders

Shareholders can exercise their rights or sell them. In either case the shareholder will neither win nor lose by the rights offering. The hypothetical holder of 18 shares of the Royal Bank of Scotland has a portfolio worth £64.44. On the one hand, if the shareholder exercises the rights, he or she ends up with 11 shares worth a total of £32.78. In other words, by spending £32.78, the investor increases the value of the holding by £32.78, which means that he or she is neither better nor worse off.

On the other hand, a shareholder who sells the 18 rights for £0.60 each obtains £0.60 × 18 = £10.78 in cash. Because the 18 shares are each worth £2.98, the holdings are valued at

$$
\begin{aligned}
\text{Shares} &= 18 \times £2.98 = £53.64 \\
\text{Sold rights} &= 18 \times £0.60 = \underline{£10.80} \\
\text{Total} &\phantom{= 18 \times £0.60 } = £64.44
\end{aligned}
$$

The new £53.64 market value plus £10.80 in cash is exactly the same as the original holding of £64.44. Thus shareholders can neither lose nor gain from exercising or selling rights.

It is obvious that the new market price of the firm's equity will be lower after the rights offering than it was before the rights issue. The lower the subscription price, the greater the price decline of a rights issue. However, our analysis shows that the shareholders have suffered no loss because of the rights issue.

## The Underwriting Arrangements

Undersubscription can occur if investors throw away rights, or if bad news causes the market price of the equity to fall below the subscription price. To ensure against these possibilities, rights offerings are typically arranged by standby underwriting. Here the underwriter makes a firm commitment to purchase the unsubscribed portion of the issue at the subscription price less a take-up fee. The underwriter usually receives a standby fee as compensation for this risk-bearing function.

In practice the subscription price is usually set well below the current market price, making the probability of a rights failure quite small. Though a small percentage (less than 10 per cent) of shareholders fail to exercise valuable rights, shareholders are usually allowed to purchase unsubscribed shares at the subscription price. This oversubscription privilege makes it unlikely that the corporate issuer would need to turn to its underwriter for help.

## 19.7 Shelf Registration

To simplify the procedures for issuing securities, many stock exchanges allow shelf registration. Shelf registration permits a corporation to register an offering that it reasonably expects to sell within a specified number of years. A master registration statement is filed at the time of registration. The company is permitted to sell the issue whenever it wants over the shelf registration period as long as it distributes a short-form statement.

Hershman reports on the use of the *dribble* method of new equity issuance.[12] With dribbling, a company registers the issue and hires an underwriter to be its selling agent. The company sells shares in small amounts from time to time via a stock exchange. For example, in June 2006 Internet search provider Ask Jeeves filed a $400 million shelf registration to sell a combination of equity, debt securities, and other instruments.

The rule has been very controversial. Several arguments have been made against shelf registration:

1 The timeliness of disclosure is reduced with shelf registration, because the master registration statement may have been prepared up to two years before the actual issue occurs.

2 Some bankers have argued that shelf registration will cause a market overhang, because registration informs the market of future issues. It has been suggested that this overhang will depress market prices. However, an empirical analysis by Bhagat, Marr and Thompson found that shelf registration is less costly than conventional underwriting, and found no evidence to suggest a market overhang effect.[13]

## 19.8 The Private Equity Market

The previous sections of this chapter assumed that a company is big enough, successful enough, and old enough to raise capital in the public equity market. Of course, many firms have not reached this stage, and cannot use the public equity market. For start-up firms, or firms in financial trouble, the public equity market is often not available. For these companies the private equity market may be the best option.

### Private Placement

Private placements avoid the costly procedures associated with the registration requirements that are part of public issues. Stock exchanges tend to restrict private placement issues to no more than a couple of dozen knowledgeable investors, including institutions such as insurance companies and pension funds. The biggest drawback of privately placed securities is that the securities cannot be easily resold. Most private placements involve debt securities, but equity securities can also be privately placed.

### The Private Equity Firm

A large amount of private equity investment is undertaken by professional private equity managers representing large institutional investors such as mutual funds and pension funds. The limited partnership is the dominant form of intermediation in this market. Typically, the institutional investors act as the limited partners, and the professional managers act as general partners. The general partners are firms that specialize in funding and managing equity investments in closely held private firms. The private equity market has been important for both traditional start-up companies and established public firms. Thus the private equity market can be divided into venture equity and non-venture equity markets. A large part of the non-venture market is made up of firms in financial distress. Firms in financial distress are not likely to be able to issue public equity, and typically cannot use traditional forms of debt such as bank loans or public debt. For these firms the best alternative is to find a private equity market firm.

Outside the United States the UK is the leading centre for private equity, and most private equity firms are based there. Table 19.9 lists the main European private equity firms in 2007, and their country of management.

### Suppliers of Venture Capital

As we have pointed out, venture capital is an important part of the private equity market. There are at least four types of supplier of venture capital. First, a few old-line, wealthy families have traditionally provided start-up capital to promising businesses. For example, over the years, the Rockefeller family has made the initial capital contribution to a number of successful businesses. These families have been involved in venture capital for at least a century.

Second, a number of private partnerships and corporations have been formed to provide investment funds. The organizer behind the partnership might raise capital from institutional investors, such as insurance companies and pension funds. Alternatively, a group of individuals might provide the funds to be ultimately invested with budding entrepreneurs.

| TABLE 19.9 | Firm name | Country of management |
|---|---|---|
| | AAC Capital | Netherlands |
| | Apax Partners | United Kingdom |
| | Axa Private Equity | France |
| | Barclays Private Equity Partners | United Kingdom |
| | Carlyle Group | United Kingdom |
| | CVC Capital Partners | United Kingdom |
| | Doughty Hanson | United Kingdom |
| | Duke Street Capital | United Kingdom |
| | Industri Kapital | Sweden |
| | Intermediate Capital Group | United Kingdom |
| | Pamplona Capital Management | United Kingdom |
| | Terra Firma Capital Partners | United Kingdom |
| | Marfin Investment Group | Greece |
| | MidEuropa Partners | United Kingdom |

*Source*: PEREP Analytics.

**Table 19.9** Major European private equity fundraisers in 2007

Of the early partnerships, the most well-known is clearly American Research and Development (ARD), which was formed in 1946. Though ARD invested in many companies, its success was due largely to its investment in Digital Equipment Corporation (DEC). When Textron acquired ARD in 1972, over 85 per cent of the shareholders' distribution was due to the investment in DEC.[14] Among the more recent venture capitalists, Arthur Rock & Co. of San Francisco may be the best known. Because of its huge success with Apple Computer and other high-tech firms, it has achieved near mythic stature in the venture capital industry.

Venture capital is a sub-activity of all private equity financing. The most common form of private equity financing in recent years is through buy-outs. Examples of private equity buy-out activity include EMI, Boots and Chrysler. Table 19.10 provides a breakdown of European private equity funding between 2002 and 2007.[15] The majority of venture capital funds are in the high-tech industry. Because of the global financial crisis in 2008, buy-out and venture capital activity dropped significantly on 2007 and 2006 levels. This was due to a general lack of financing opportunities, an inability to exit from private equity investments, and falling valuations.

Stories used to abound about how easily an individual could obtain venture capital. Though that might have been the case in an earlier era, it is certainly not the case today. Venture capital firms employ various screening procedures to prevent inappropriate funding. For example, because of the large demand for funds, many venture capitalists have at least one employee whose full-time job consists of reading business plans. Only the very best plans can expect to attract funds. Maier and Walker indicate that only about 2 per cent of requests actually receive financing.[16]

Third, large industrial or financial corporations have established venture capital subsidiaries. Manufacturers Hanover Venture Capital Corp., Citicorp Venture Capital and Chemical Venture Capital Corporation of Chemical Bank are examples. However, subsidiaries of this type appear to make up only a small portion of the venture capital market.

Fourth, there are also participants in an informal venture capital market.[17] Rather than belonging to any venture capital firm, these investors (often referred to as *angels*) act as individuals when providing financing. However, they should not, by any means, be viewed as isolated. Wetzel and others indicate that there is a rich network of angels, continually relying on each other for advice. A number of researchers have stressed that in any informal network there is likely to be one knowledgeable and trustworthy individual who, when backing a venture, brings a few less experienced investors in with him.

| TABLE 19.10 | | 2002 (€bn) | 2003 (€bn) | 2004 (€bn) | 2005 (€bn) | 2006 (€bn) | 2007 (€bn) |
|---|---|---|---|---|---|---|---|
| | Venture high-tech | 4.2 | 2.3 | 2.5 | 5.1 | 5.0 | 7.3 |
| | Venture non-high-tech | 4.3 | 3.4 | 6.3 | 5.8 | 12.5 | 3.1 |
| | **Total venture** | **8.5** | **5.7** | **8.8** | **10.9** | **17.5** | **10.4** |
| | Buyout | 18.3 | 21.0 | 17.8 | 57.7 | 84.3 | 60.0 |
| | Not available | 0.7 | 0.3 | 0.9 | 3.2 | 10.5 | 8.6 |
| | **Funds raised** | **27.5** | **27.0** | **27.5** | **71.8** | **112.3** | **79.0** |

*Source*: European Private Equity and Venture Capital Association (EVCA).

**Table 19.10** Breakdown of private equity funding, 2002–2007

The venture capital community has unfortunately chosen to refer to these individuals as 'dumb dentists'. Although a number indeed may be dentists, their intelligence should not be called into question. Wetzel asserts that the prototypical angel has income over $100,000, net worth over $1,000,000, and substantial business experience and knowledge. As we might expect, the informal venture capitalist is able to tolerate high risks.

Though this informal market may seem small and unimportant, it is perhaps the largest of all sources of venture capital. Wetzel says that aggregate investments from this source in the US total around $50 billion, about twice the amount invested by more professional venture capitalists. The size of each contribution is smaller here. Perhaps, on average, only $250,000 per venture is raised when the informal market is tapped.

## Stages of Financing

Bruno and Tyebjee identify six stages in venture capital financing:[18]

1. *Seed money stage*: A small amount of financing needed to prove a concept or develop a product. Marketing is not included in this stage.

2. *Start-up*: Financing for firms that started within the past year. Funds are likely to pay for marketing and product development expenditures.

3. *First-round financing*: Additional money to begin sales and manufacturing after a firm has spent its start-up funds.

4. *Second-round financing*: Funds earmarked for working capital for a firm that is currently selling its product but still losing money.

5. *Third-round financing*: Financing for a company that is at least breaking even and is contemplating an expansion. This is also known as *mezzanine financing*.

6. *Fourth-round financing*: Money provided for firms that are likely to go public within half a year. This round is also known as *bridge financing*.

Although these categories may seem vague to the reader, we have found that the terms are well accepted within the industry. For example, the venture capital firms listed in Pratt's *Guide to Venture Capital* indicate which of these stages they are interested in financing. Table 19.11 presents a breakdown of where private equity funding was made in Europe in 2007. The majority of investments were in small firms and those that needed to expand. Start-ups (companies that require capital to start commercial operations) were the other target for funding.

The penultimate stage in venture capital finance is the initial public offering.[19] Venture capitalists are very important participants in initial public offerings. Venture capitalists rarely sell all of the shares they own at the time of the initial public offering. Instead they usually

| TABLE 19.11 | Amount of investment (%) | Number of investments (%) | Number of companies (%) |
|---|---|---|---|
| Small | 7.6 | 16.4 | 16.0 |
| Mid-market | 34.1 | 6.7 | 8.6 |
| Large | 20.0 | 0.8 | 1.0 |
| Mega | 17.1 | 0.3 | 0.4 |
| **All buyouts** | **78.8** | **24.2** | **24.2** |
| Replacement capital | 4.2 | 2.3 | 3.0 |
| Rescue/Turnaround | 0.2 | 1.0 | 1.0 |
| Expansion | 13.4 | 33.8 | 33.9 |
| Start-up | 3.2 | 30.3 | 29.5 |
| Seed | 0.2 | 8.4 | 8.3 |
| **Total** | **100.0** | **100.0** | **100.0** |
| **Total in numbers (€bn)** | **72.2** | **8,166** | **5,207** |

*Source*: The European Private Equity and Venture Capital Association (EVCA).

**Table 19.11** Breakdown of private equity funding by funding stage, 2007

FIGURE 19.2

*Source*: Joshua Lerner, ' Venture capitalists and the decision to go public', *Journal of Financial Economics*, vol. 35 ( June 1994).

**Figure 19.2** Initial public offerings by venture-capital-backed biotechnology firms, January 1978 to January 1992

sell out in subsequent public offerings. However, there is considerable evidence that venture capitalists can successfully time IPOs by taking firms public when the market values are at the highest. Figure 19.2 shows the number of IPOs of privately held US venture-capital-backed biotechnology companies in each month from 1978 to 1992. The venture-capital-backed IPOs clearly coincide with the ups and downs in the biotech market index in the top panel.

## Summary and Conclusions

This chapter looked closely at how equity is issued. The main points follow:

1 Large issues have proportionately much lower costs of issuing equity than small ones.

2 Firm-commitment underwriting is far more prevalent for large issues than is best-efforts underwriting. Smaller issues probably primarily use best efforts because of the greater uncertainty of these issues. For an offering of a given size, the direct expenses of best-efforts underwriting and firm-commitment underwriting are of the same magnitude.

3 Rights issues are cheaper than general cash offers, and eliminate the problem of under-pricing. Yet most new equity issues are underwritten general cash offers.

4 Shelf registration is a new method of issuing new debt and equity. The direct costs of shelf issues seem to be substantially lower than those of traditional issues.

5 Private equity is an increasingly important influence in start-up firms and subsequent financing.

## connect‌ Questions and Problems

**CONCEPT 1–7**

1 **The Public Issue** Review the steps involved in the public issue of equity. Do a search on Google for a public equity issue in your country, download all relevant news stories, and track the issue process for the company. Is it similar to the one presented in this chapter?

2 **Alternative Issue Methods** Review the other ways in which equity can be issued. In what situations would a firm opt to go for these alternative methods?

3 **The Cash Offer** Why are most equity issues underpriced? Is this is a sign of market inefficiency? Explain.

4 **Announcement Effects** Why do you think the share price tends to go down when an equity issue is announced?

5 **The Costs of New Issues** Review the various costs that are involved in a new equity issue. Are these likely to be different in a seasoned issue than an initial public offering? Explain.

6 **Shelf Registration** Why would shareholders not be keen on shelf registration? What steps could they take to avoid shelf registration?

7 **The Private Equity Market** Provide an overview of the private equity market. Why would firms wish to go private once they have listed on a stock exchange?

Use the following information to answer the next three questions. Eyetech Pharmaceuticals, Inc., a company that develops treatments for eye problems, went public in January 2004. Assisted by the investment bank Merrill Lynch, Eyetech sold 6.5 million shares at $21 each, thereby raising a total of $136.5 million. At the end of the first day of trading the shares sold for $32.40 per share, down slightly from a high of $33.00. Based on the end-of-day numbers, Eyetech shares were apparently underpriced by about $11 each, meaning that the company missed out on an additional $67 million.

**REGULAR 8–25**

8 **IPO Pricing** The Eyetech IPO was underpriced by about 54 per cent. Should Eyetech be upset at Merrill Lynch over the underpricing?

9 **IPO Pricing** In the previous question, would it affect your thinking to know that the company was incorporated less than four years earlier, had only $30 million in revenues for the first nine months of 2003, and had never earned a profit? Additionally, the company had only one product, Macugen, which had won fast-track status from the FDA but still did not have approval to be sold.

**10 IPO Pricing** In the previous two questions, how would it affect your thinking to know that in addition to the 6.5 million shares offered in the IPO, Eyetech had an additional 32 million shares outstanding? Of the 32 million shares, 10 million shares were owned by pharmaceutical giant Pfizer, and 12 million shares were owned by the 13 directors and executive officers.

**11 Cash Offer versus Rights Offer** Rhubarb International is planning to raise capital by selling a large new issue of equity. Rhubarb is currently a publicly traded corporation, and it is trying to choose between an underwritten cash offer and a rights issue (not underwritten) to current shareholders. Rhubarb management is interested in minimizing the selling costs, and has asked you for advice on the choice of issue methods. What is your recommendation, and why?

**12 IPO Underpricing** In 1980 a certain assistant professor of finance bought 12 initial public offerings of equity. He held each of these for approximately one month and then sold. The investment rule he followed was to submit a purchase order for every firm-commitment initial public offering of oil and gas exploration companies. There were 22 of these offerings, and he submitted a purchase order for approximately $1,000 in equity for each of the companies. With 10 of these, no shares were allocated to this assistant professor. With 5 of the 12 offerings that were purchased, fewer than the requested number of shares were allocated.

The year 1980 was very good for oil and gas exploration company owners: on average, for the 22 companies that went public, the shares were selling for 80 per cent above the offering price a month after the initial offering date. The assistant professor looked at his performance record and found that the $8,400 invested in the 12 companies had grown to $10,000, representing a return of only about 20 per cent (commissions were negligible). Did he have bad luck, or should he have expected to do worse than the average initial public offering investor? Explain.

**13 IPO Pricing** The following material represents the cover page and summary of the prospectus for the initial public offering of the Pest Investigation Control Corporation SA (PICC), which is going public tomorrow with a firm-commitment initial public offering managed by the investment banking firm of Bigelli and Pindado.

Answer the following questions:

(a) Assume that you know nothing about PICC other than the information contained in the prospectus. Based on your knowledge of finance, what is your prediction for the price of PICC tomorrow? Provide a short explanation of why you think this will occur.

(b) Assume that you have several thousand euros to invest. When you get home from class tonight you find that your stockbroker, whom you have not talked to for weeks, has called. She has left a message that PICC is going public tomorrow, and that she can get you several hundred shares at the offering price if you call her back first thing in the morning. Discuss the merits of this opportunity.

---

**PROSPECTUS**                                                                 **PICC**

**200,000 shares**
**PEST INVESTIGATION CONTROL CORPORATION**

Of the shares being offered hereby, all 200,000 are being sold by the Pest Investigation Control Corporation SA ('the Company'). Before the offering there has been no public market for the shares of PICC, and no guarantee can be given that any such market will develop.

*These securities have not been approved or disapproved by the Autorité des Marchés Financiers, nor has the Authority passed judgement upon the accuracy or adequacy of this prospectus. Any representation to the contrary is a criminal offence.*

| | Price to public | Underwriting discount | Proceeds to company* |
|---|---|---|---|
| Per share | €11.00 | €1.10 | €9.90 |
| Total | €2,200,000 | €220,000 | €1,980,000 |

*Before deducting expenses estimated at €27,000 and payable by the company.

*This is an initial public offering. The ordinary shares are being offered, subject to prior sale, when, as, and if delivered to and accepted by the Underwriters and subject to approval of certain legal matters by their Counsel and by Counsel for the Company. The Underwriters reserve the right to withdraw, cancel, or modify such offer and to reject offers in whole or in part.*

**Bigelli and Pindado, Bankers**
**12 July 2009**
**Prospectus Summary**

| | |
|---|---|
| The Company | The Pest Investigation Control Corporation (PICC) breeds and markets toads and tree frogs as ecologically safe insect-control mechanisms. |
| The Offering | 200,000 ordinary shares of equity, no par value. |
| Listing | The Company will seek listing on Euronext. |
| Shares Outstanding | As of 30 June 2009, 400,000 ordinary shares of equity were outstanding. After the offering, 600,000 ordinary shares of equity will be outstanding. |
| Use of Proceeds | To finance expansion of inventory and receivables and general working capital, and to pay for country club memberships for certain finance professors. |

**Selected Financial Information**
**(amounts in thousands of euros except per-share data)**

| | Fiscal Year Ended 30 June | | | | As of 30 June 2009 | |
|---|---|---|---|---|---|---|
| | 2007 | 2008 | 2009 | | Actual | As adjusted for this offering |
| Revenues | 60.00 | 120.00 | 240.00 | Working capital | 0.8 | 1,961 |
| Net earnings | 3.80 | 15.90 | 36.10 | Total assets | 511 | 2,464 |
| Earnings per share | 0.01 | 0.04 | 0.09 | Shareholders' equity | 423 | 2,376 |

**14 Competitive and Negotiated Offers** What are the comparative advantages of a competitive offer and a negotiated offer, respectively?

**15 Seasoned Equity Offers** What are the possible reasons why the share price typically drops on the announcement of a seasoned new equity issue?

**16 Raising Capital** Megabucks Industries is planning to raise fresh equity capital by selling a large new issue of equity. Megabucks, a publicly traded corporation, is trying to choose between an underwritten cash offer and a rights issue (not underwritten) to current shareholders. Megabucks' management is interested in maximizing the wealth of current shareholders, and has asked you for advice on the choice of issue methods. What is your recommendation? Why?

**17 Shelf Registration** Explain why shelf registration has been used by many firms instead of syndication.

18  **IPOs**  Every IPO is unique, but what are the basic empirical regularities in IPOs?

19  **Rights Offerings**  Again plc is proposing a rights offering. Currently there are 350,000 shares outstanding at £85 each. There will be 70,000 new shares offered at £70 each.

    (a)  What is the new market value of the company?

    (b)  How many rights are associated with one of the new shares?

    (c)  What is the ex-rights price?

    (d)  What is the value of a right?

    (e)  Ignoring regulations, why might a company have a rights offering rather than a general cash offer?

20  **Rights Offering**  Faff plc has announced a rights issue to raise £50 million for a new journal, the *Journal of Financial Excess*. This journal will review potential articles after the author pays a non-refundable reviewing fee of £5,000 per page. The equity currently sells for £40 per share, and there are 5.2 million shares outstanding.

    (a)  What is the maximum possible subscription price? What is the minimum?

    (b)  If the subscription price is set at £35 per share, how many shares must be sold? How many rights will it take to buy one share?

    (c)  What is the ex-rights price? What is the value of a right?

    (d)  Show how a shareholder with 1,000 shares before the offering and no desire (or money) to buy additional shares is not harmed by the rights offer.

21  **Rights**  Stone Shoe plc has concluded that additional equity financing will be needed to expand operations, and that the needed funds will be best obtained through a rights issue. It has correctly determined that, as a result of the rights issue, the share price will fall from £80 to £74.50 (£80 is the 'rights-on' price; £74.50 is the ex-rights price, also known as the *when-issued* price). The company is seeking £15 million in additional funds with a per-share subscription price equal to £40. How many shares are there currently, before the offering? (Assume that the increment to the market value of the equity equals the gross proceeds from the offering.)

22  **IPO Underpricing**  Carlyle Ltd and Mullan Ltd have both announced IPOs at £40 per share. One of these is undervalued by £11, and the other is overvalued by £6, but you have no way of knowing which is which. You plan on buying 1,000 shares of each issue. If an issue is underpriced, it will be rationed, and only half your order will be filled. If you *could* get 1,000 shares in Carlyle and 1,000 shares in Mullan, what would your profit be? What profit do you actually expect? What principle have you illustrated?

23  **Calculating Flotation Costs**  Groene Heuvels has just gone public. Under a firm-commitment agreement Groene Heuvels received €19.75 for each of the 5 million shares sold. The initial offering price was €21 per share, and the equity rose to €26 per share in the first few minutes of trading. Groene Heuvels paid €800,000 in direct legal and other costs, and €250,000 in indirect costs. What was the flotation cost as a percentage of funds raised?

24  **Price Dilution**  Raggio SpA has 100,000 shares of equity outstanding. Each share is worth €90, so the company's market value of equity is €9,000,000. Suppose the firm issues 20,000 new shares at the following prices: €90, €85 and €70. What will the effect be of each of these alternative offering prices on the existing price per share?

25  **Equity Offerings**  The Newton Company has 10,000 shares of equity that each sell for £40. Suppose the company issues 5,000 shares of the new equity at the following prices: £40, £20 and £10. What is the effect of each of the alternative offering prices on the existing price per share?

26  **Dilution**  Larme SA wishes to expand its facilities. The company currently has 10 million shares outstanding and no debt. The equity sells for €50 per share, but the book value per share is €40. Net income for Larme is currently €15 million. The new facility will cost €35 million, and it will increase net income by €500,000.

**CHALLENGE**

**26–34**

(a) Assuming a constant price–earnings ratio, what will the effect be of issuing new equity to finance the investment? To answer, calculate the new book value per share, the new total earnings, the new EPS, the new share price, and the new market-to-book ratio. What is going on here?

(b) What would the new net income for Larme have to be for the share price to remain unchanged?

27 **Dilution** Elvis Heavy Metal Mining (EHMM) plc wants to diversify its operations. Some recent financial information for the company is shown here:

| | |
|---|---|
| Share price | £98 |
| Number of shares | 14,000 |
| Total assets | £6,000,000 |
| Total liabilities | £2,400,000 |
| Net income | £630,000 |

EHMM is considering an investment that has the same P/E ratio as the firm. The cost of the investment is £1,100,000, and it will be financed with a new equity issue. The return on the investment will equal EHMM's current ROE. What will happen to the book value per share, the market value per share, and the EPS? What is the NPV of this investment? Does dilution take place?

28 **Dilution** In the previous problem, what would the ROE on the investment have to be if we wanted the price after the offering to be £98 per share? (Assume the P/E ratio remains constant.) What is the NPV of this investment? Does any dilution take place?

29 **Rights** A company's equity currently sells for £45 per share. Last week the firm issued rights to raise new equity. To purchase a new share, a shareholder must remit £10 and three rights.

(a) What is the ex-rights share price?

(b) What is the price of one right?

(c) When will the price drop occur? Why will it occur then?

30 **Rights** Gipfel equity is currently selling at €13 per share. There are 1 million shares outstanding. The firm is planning to raise €2 million to finance a new project. What are the ex-rights share price, the value of a right, and the appropriate subscription prices under the following scenarios?

(a) Two shares of outstanding equity are entitled to purchase one additional share of the new issue.

(b) Four shares of outstanding equity are entitled to purchase one additional share of the new issue.

(c) How does the shareholders' wealth change from part (a) to part (b)?

31 **Rights** Hoobastink Mfg. is considering a rights offer. The company has determined that the ex-rights price would be €52. The current price is €55 per share, and there are 5 million shares outstanding. The rights issue would raise a total of €60 million. What is the subscription price?

32 **Value of Right** Show that the value of a right can be written as

$$\text{Value of a right} = P_{RO} - P_X = \frac{P_{RO} - P_S}{N + 1}$$

where $P_{RO}$, $P_S$ and $P_X$ stand for the 'rights-on' price, the subscription price and the ex-rights price, respectively, and $N$ is the number of rights needed to buy one new share at the subscription price.

33 **Selling Rights** Wuttke plc wants to raise £3.65 million via a rights issue. The company currently has 490,000 ordinary shares outstanding that sell for £30 per share. Its underwriter has set a subscription price of £22 per share and will charge Wuttke a 6 per cent

spread. If you currently own 6,000 shares of equity in the company and decide not to participate in the rights issue, how much money can you get by selling your rights?

34　**Valuing a Right**　Mitsi Inventory Systems has announced a rights offer. The company has announced that it will take four rights to buy a new share in the offering at a subscription price of €40. At the close of business the day before the ex-rights day, the company's shares sell for €80 per share. The next morning you notice that the equity sells for €72 per share and the rights sell for €6 each. Are the equity and/or the rights correctly priced on the ex-rights day? Describe a transaction in which you could use these prices to create an immediate profit.

# West Coast Yachts Goes Public

Larissa Warren and Dan Ervin have been discussing the future of West Coast Yachts. The company has been experiencing fast growth, and the future looks like clear sailing. However, the fast growth means that the company's growth can no longer be funded by internal sources, so Larissa and Dan have decided the time is right to take the company public. To this end, they have entered into discussions with the bank of Crowe & Mallard. The company has a working relationship with Robin Perry, the underwriter who assisted with the company's previous bond offering. Crowe & Mallard have helped numerous small companies in the IPO process, so Larissa and Dan feel confident with this choice.

Robin begins by telling Larissa and Dan about the process. Although Crowe & Mallard charged an underwriter fee of 4 per cent on the bond offering, the underwriter fee is 7 per cent on all initial equity offerings of the size of West Coast Yachts' initial offering. Robin tells Larissa and Dan that the company can expect to pay about £1,200,000 in legal fees and expenses, £12,000 in registration fees, and £15,000 in other filing fees. Additionally, to be listed on the London Stock Exchange, the company must pay £100,000. There are also transfer agent fees of £6,500 and engraving expenses of £450,000. The company should also expect to pay £75,000 for other expenses associated with the IPO.

Finally, Robin tells Larissa and Dan that to file with the London Stock Exchange, the company must provide three years' worth of audited financial statements. She is unsure of the costs of the audit. Dan tells Robin that the company provides audited financial statements as part of its bond indenture, and the company pays £300,000 per year for the outside auditor.

1　At the end of the discussion Dan asks Robin about the Dutch auction IPO process. What are the differences in the expenses to West Coast Yachts if it uses a Dutch auction IPO versus a traditional IPO? Should the company go public with a Dutch auction or use a traditional underwritten offering?

2　During the discussion of the potential IPO and West Coast Yachts' future, Dan states that he feels the company should raise £50 million. However, Larissa points out that if the company needs more cash soon, a secondary offering close to the IPO would be potentially problematic. Instead she suggests that the company should raise £80 million in the IPO. How can we calculate the optimal size of the IPO? What are the advantages and disadvantage of increasing the size of the IPO to £80 million?

3　After deliberation, Larissa and Dan have decided that the company should use a firm-commitment offering with Crowe & Mallard as the lead underwriter. The IPO will be for £60 million. Ignoring underpricing, how much will the IPO cost the company as a percentage of the funds received?

4　Many of the employees of West Coast Yachts have shares of equity in the company because of an existing employee stock purchase plan. To sell the equity, the employees can tender their shares to be sold in the IPO at the offering price, or the employees can retain their equity and sell it in the secondary market after West Coast Yachts goes public (once the 180-day lock-up expires). Larissa asks you to advise the employees about which option is best. What would you suggest to the employees?

# Practical Case Study

Do a search on Google news for ten announcements of new funding for companies in the last year. Look at the share price between the announcement date and five days later. Can you see any pattern between share price reaction and funding type? In what ways could you improve this very simplistic analysis?

# Relevant Accounting Standards

The most important accounting standard for equities is IAS39 *Financial Instruments: Recognition and Measurement*. Visit the IASPlus website (www.iasplus.com) for more information.

# Additional Reading

Research in equity financing covers many areas, and this is reflected in the number of recent papers published in the area. To aid understanding and targeted reading, the reference list below will be categorized into separate but overlapping topics. As with every good academic paper, its implications can span several different areas. Equity financing research is no different in this regard.

**Initial Public Offerings**

Binay, M.M., V.A. Gatchev and C.A. Pirinsky (2007) 'The role of underwriter-investor relationships in the IPO process', *Journal of Financial & Quantitative Analysis*, vol. 42, no. 3, pp. 785–810. **US**.

Bodnaruk, A., E. Kandel and M. Massa (2008) 'Shareholder diversification and the decision to go public', *Review of Financial Studies*, vol. 21, no. 6, pp. 2779–2824. **Sweden**.

Brau, J.C. and S.E. Fawcett (2006) 'Initial public offerings: an analysis of theory and practice', *Journal of Finance*, vol. 61, no. 1, pp. 399–436. **US**.

Chemmanur, T.J. and I. Paeglis (2005) 'Management quality, certification, and initial public offerings', *Journal of Financial Economics*, vol. 76, no. 2, pp. 331–368. **US**.

Cook, D.O., R. Kieschnick and R.A. Van Ness (2006) 'On the marketing of IPOs', *Journal of Financial Economics*, vol. 82, no. 1, pp. 35–61. **US**.

Corwin, S.A. and P. Schultz (2005) 'The pole of IPO underpricing syndicates: pricing, information production, and underwriter competition', *Journal of Finance*, vol. 60, no. 1, pp. 443–486. **US**.

Deloof, M., W. De Maeseneire and K. Inghelbrecht (2009) 'How do investment banks value initial public offerings (IPOs)?', *Journal of Business Finance and Accounting*, vol. 36, nos. 1–2, pp. 130–160. **Belgium**.

Derrien, F. and A. Kecskes (2007) 'The initial public offering of listed firms', *Journal of Finance*, vol. 62, no. 1, pp. 447–479. **UK**.

Ellul, A. and M. Pagano (2006) 'IPO underpricing and after-market liquidity', *Review of Financial Studies*, vol. 19, no. 2, pp. 381–421. **UK**.

Holmen, M. and P. Hogfeldt (2004) 'A law and finance analysis of initial public offerings', *Journal of Financial Intermediation*, vol. 13, no. 3, pp. 324–358. **Sweden**.

Jenkinson, T. and H. Jones (2009) 'IPO pricing and allocation: a survey of the views of institutional investors', *Review of Financial Studies* (forthcoming). **International**.

Kaustia, M. and S. Knupfer (2008) 'Do investors overweight personal experience? Evidence from IPO subscriptions', *Journal of Finance*, vol. 63, no. 6, pp. 2679–2702. **Finland**.

Kerins, F., K. Kutsuna and R. Smith (2007) 'Why are IPOs underpriced? Evidence from Japan's hybrid auction-method offerings', *Journal of Financial Economics*, vol. 85, no. 3, pp. 637–666. **Japan**.

Kutsuna, K., J. Kiholm Smith and R. Smith (2009) 'Public information, IPO price formation, and long-run returns: Japanese evidence', *Journal of Finance*, vol. 64, no. 1, pp. 505–546. **Japan**.

Ljungqvist, A. and W.J. Wilhelm (2005) 'Does prospect theory explain IPO market behavior?', *Journal of Finance*, vol. 60, no. 4, pp. 1759–1790. **US**.

Pastor, L. and P. Veronesi (2005) 'Rational IPO waves', *Journal of Finance*, vol. 60, no. 4, pp. 1713–1757. **US**.

Roosenboom, P. and W. Schramade, 'The price of power: valuing the controlling position of owner-managers in French IPO firms', *Journal of Corporate Finance* (2006), vol. 12, no. 2, pp. 270–295. **France**.

## Private Equity and Venture Capital

Botazzi, L., M. Da Rin and T. Hellmann (2008) 'Who are the active investors? Evidence from venture capital', *Journal of Financial Economics*, vol. 89, no. 3, pp. 488–512, **Europe**.

Cochrane, J.H. 'The risk and return of venture capital', *Journal of Financial Economics*, vol. 75, no. 1, pp. 3–52. **US**.

Cronqvist, H. and M. Nilsson (2005) 'The choice between rights offerings and private equity placements', *Journal of Financial Economics*, vol. 78, no. 2, pp. 375–407. **Sweden**.

Cumming, D. (2008) 'Contracts and exits in venture capital finance', *Review of Financial Studies*, vol. 21, no. 5, pp. 1947–1982. **Europe**.

Hochberg, Y.V., A. Ljungqvist and Y. Lu (2007) 'Whom you know matters: venture capital networks and investment performance', *Journal of Finance*, vol. 62, no. 1, pp. 251–301. **US**.

Kaplan, S. and A. Schoar (2005) 'Private equity performance: returns, persistence, and capital flows', *Journal of Finance*, vol. 60, no. 4, pp. 1791–1823. **US**.

Kaplan, S., S. Berk and P. Stromberg (2009) 'Should investors bet on the jockey or the horse? Evidence from the evolution of firms from early business plans to public companies', *Journal of Finance*, vol. 64, no. 1, pp. 75–115. **US**.

Nahata, R. (2008) 'Venture capital reputation and investment performance', *Journal of Financial Economics*, vol. 90, no. 2, pp. 127–151. **US**.

Phalippou, L. and O. Gottschalg (2009) 'The performance of private equity funds', *Review of Financial Studies* (forthcoming). **US**.

Renneboog, L., T. Simons and M. Wright (2007) 'Why do public firms go private in the UK? The impact of private equity investors, incentive realignment and undervaluation', *Journal of Corporate Finance*, vol. 13, no. 4, pp. 591–628. **UK**.

## Seasoned Equity Offerings, Rights Issues, and Reverse LBOs

Cao, J. and J. Lerner (2009) 'The performance of reverse leveraged buyouts', *Journal of Financial Economics*, vol. 91, no. 2, pp. 139–157. **US**.

Iqbal, A. (2008) 'The importance of the sequence in UK rights issues', *Journal of Business Finance and Accounting*, vol. 35, nos. 1–2, 150–176. **UK**.

Lee, G. and R.W. Masulis (2009) 'Seasoned equity offerings: quality of accounting information and expected flotation costs', *Journal of Financial Economics* (forthcoming). **US**.

## Other Relevant Research

Boubakri, N., J.-C. Cosset and O. Guedhami (2005) 'Postprivatization corporate governance: the role of ownership structure and investor protection', *Journal of Financial Economics*, vol. 76, no. 2, pp. 369–399. **International**.

Hoberg, G. (2007) 'The underwriter persistence phenomenon', *Journal of Finance*, vol. 62, no. 3, pp. 1169–1206. **US**.

Sarkissian, S. and M. Schill (2009) 'Are there permanent valuation gains to overseas listing?', *Review of Financial Studies*, vol. 22, no. 1, pp. 371–412. **International**.

# Endnotes

1   As with the majority of the material covered in this chapter, the specific approach to placings is different in each country. Information on country regulations can usually be found in the listing rules of each stock exchange. These are normally downloadable from the exchange's website.

2   The Green Shoe Corporation was the first firm to allow this provision.

3   For example see: L. Krigman, W. Shaw and K. Womack, 'Why do firms switch underwriters?', *Journal of Financial Economics* (2001); R. Carter and S. Manaster, 'Initial public offerings and underwriter reputation', *Journal of Finance* (1990): and R. Beatty and J. Ritter, 'Investment banking, reputation, and the underpricing of initial public offerings', *Journal of Financial Economics* (1986).

4   This choice has been studied by: D. Logue and S. Tiniç, 'Optimal choice of contracting methods: negotiated versus competitive underwritings revisited', *Journal of Financial Economics* (1999); Robert S. Hansen and Naveen Khanna, 'Why negotiation with a single syndicate may be preferred to making syndicates compete: the problem of trapped bidders', *Journal of Business*, vol. 67 (1994); S. Bhagat, 'The effect of management's choice between negotiated and competitive equity offerings on shareholder wealth', *Journal of Financial and Quantitative Analysis* (1986); and D. Logue and R. Jarrow, 'Negotiation vs. competitive bidding in the sales of securities by public utilities', *Financial Management*, vol. 7 (1978).

5   A. Ljunqvist, 'IPO underpricing', Chapter 7 of *Handbook of Corporate Finance: Empirical Corporate Finance*, Volume A, (Handbooks in Finance Series, Elsevier/North Holland), B. Espen Eckbo (Ed.) (2006).

6   This explanation was first suggested in K. Rock, 'Why new issues are underpriced', *Journal of Financial Economics*, vol. 15 (1986).

7   P. Asquith and D. Mullins, 'Equity issues and offering dilution', *Journal of Financial Economics*, vol. 15 (1986); R. Masulis and A.N. Korwar, 'Seasoned equity offerings: an empirical investigation', *Journal of Financial Economics*, vol. 15 (1986); W.H. Mikkelson and M.M. Partch, 'The valuation effects of security offerings and the issuance process', *Journal of Financial Economics*, vol. 15 (1986); J.-F. Gajewski and E. Ginglinger, 'Seasoned equity issues in a closely held market: evidence from France', *European Finance Review*, vol. 6 (2002); and J. Martin-Ugedo, 'Equity rights issues in Spain: flotation costs and wealth effects', *Journal of Business Finance and Accounting*, vol. 30 (2003). E. Barnes and M. Walker, 'The seasoned-equity issues of UK firms: market reaction and issuance method', *Journal of Business Finance and Accounting*, vol. 33 (2006), actually find that private placings elicit a positive response in contrast to a public listing, which is associated with significant negative returns.

8   Robert S. Haugen and Claire Crutchley, 'Corporate earnings and financings: an empirical analysis', *Journal of Business*, vol. 20 (1990).

9   Some people have argued that the price in the aftermarket is not efficient after all. However, R. Ibbotson, 'Price performance of common stock new issues', *Journal of Financial Economics*, vol. 2 (1975), shows that, on average, new issues exhibit no abnormal price performance over the first five years following issuance. This result is generally viewed as being consistent with market efficiency. That is, the equity obtains an efficient price immediately following issuance, and remains at an efficient price.

10  Seth Armitage, 'The direct costs of UK rights issues and open offers', *European Financial Management*, vol. 6 (2000).

11  The notion of economies of scale has been contested by Oya Altinkilic and Robert S. Hansen, 'Are there scale economies in underwriting spreads? Evidence of rising external financing costs', *Review of Financial Studies*, vol. 13 (2000). They provide data and analysis showing that underwriter cost will be U-shaped.

12  A. Hershman, 'New strategies in equity financing', *Dunn's Business Monthly* (June 1983).

13  S. Bhagat, M.W. Marr and G.R. Thompson, 'The Rule 415 experiment: equity markets', *Journal of Finance*, vol. 19 (December 1985).

14  S.E. Pratt, 'Overview and introduction to the venture capital industry', *Guide to Venture Capital Sources*, 10th edn, 1987 (Venture Economics. Laurel Avenue, Box 348, Wellesley Hills, MA 02181, USA).

15  The majority of information in this section comes from the European Private Equity and Venture Capital Association, a non-profit trade association of around 1,300 private equity firms (www.evca.eu).

16  J.B. Maier and D. Walker, 'The role of venture capital in financing small business', *Journal of Business Venturing* (Summer 1987).

17  See W.E. Wetzel, 'The informal venture capital market: aspects of scale and market efficiency', *Journal of Business Venturing* (Fall 1987).

18  A.V. Bruno and T.T. Tyebjee, 'The entrepreneur's search for capital', *Journal of Business Venturing* (Winter 1985).

19  A very influential paper by Christopher Barry, Chris J. Muscarella, John W. Peavey III and Michael R. Vetsuypens, 'The role of venture capital in the creation of public companies: Evidence from the going public process', *Journal of Financial Economics*, vol. 27 (1990), shows that venture capitalists do not usually sell shares at the time of the initial public offering, but they usually have board seats and act as advisers to managers.

To help you grasp the key concepts of this chapter check out the extra resources posted on the Online Learning Centre at **www.mcgraw-hill.co.uk/textbooks/hillier**

Among other helpful resources there are PowerPoint presentations, chapter outlines and mini-cases.

# Chapter

# 20

# Debt Financing

In its basic form, a bond is a simple financial instrument. You lend a company some amount, say £10,000. The company pays you interest on a regular basis, and it repays the original loan amount of £10,000 at some point in the future. Bonds can have unusual characteristics. For example, in 2002 Berkshire Hathaway, the company run by legendary US investment guru Warren Buffett, issued some bonds with a surprising feature. Bond buyers were required to *make* interest payments to Berkshire Hathaway for the privilege of owning the bonds, and the interest payments had to be made up front! Furthermore, if you paid $10,663.63 for one of these bonds, Berkshire Hathaway promised to pay you $10,000 in five years. Does this sound like a good deal? Investors must have thought it did; they bought $400 million of the bonds.

## 20.1 Debt Financing: A Review

Long-term debt securities are promises by the issuing firm to pay interest and principal on the unpaid balance. The *maturity* of a long-term debt instrument refers to the length of time the debt remains outstanding with some unpaid balance. Debt securities can be *short-term* (maturities of one year or less) or *long-term* (maturities of more than one year). Short-term debt is sometimes referred to as *unfunded debt* and long-term debt as *funded debt*.

The two major forms of long-term debt are publicly issued and privately placed debt. We discuss public-issue bonds first, and most of what we say about them holds true for privately placed long-term debt as well. The main difference between publicly issued and privately placed debt is that private debt is directly placed with a lending institution.

There are many other attributes to long-term debt, including security, call features, sinking funds, ratings, and protective covenants. The following table illustrates the features for a floating rate bond recently issued by Standard Life Bank plc

## Features of Standard Life Bank plc Bond

|  | Term | Explanation |
|---|---|---|
| Amount of issue | £1.5 billion | The company issued £1.5 billion worth of bonds. |
| Date of issue | 9 July 2008 | The bonds were sold on 9 July 2008. |
| Maturity | 26 May 2011 | The bonds mature on 26 May 2011. |
| Face value | £100,000 | The denomination of the bonds is £100,000. |
| Annual coupon | LIBOR + 0.60% | Each bondholder will receive 3 month LIBOR plus 0.60 per cent per quarter |

| | Term | Explanation |
|---|---|---|
| Offer price | £100,000 | The offer price is the face value of the bond. |
| Coupon payment dates | 26/2, 26/5, 26/8, 26/11 | Coupons of 3 month LIBOR plus 0.60 per cent will be paid on these dates until maturity. |
| Security | Senior | The bonds are the first claim for all bondholders on all property owned by the company. |
| Sinking fund | None | The bonds have no sinking fund. |
| Call provision | At any time | The bonds do not have a deferred call. |
| Call price | Not applicable | The bonds cannot be called. |
| Rating | Moody's Aaa S&P AAA | The bonds are of investment grade rating. |

## 20.2  The Public Issue of Bonds

The general procedures followed for a public issue of bonds are the same as those for equities, as described in the previous chapter. First, the offering must be approved by the board of directors. Sometimes a vote of shareholders (or supervisory board if the company operates in a country with a two-tier board system) is also required. Second, a registration statement is prepared for review by the relevant regulatory authority. Third, if accepted, the registration statement becomes *effective* at some point in the near future, and the securities are sold.

However, the registration statement for a public issue of bonds must include an indenture, a document not relevant for the issue of equities. An indenture is a written agreement between the corporation (the borrower) and a trust company. It is sometimes referred to as the *deed of trust*.[1] The trust company is appointed by the corporation to represent the bondholders. The trust company must (a) make sure the terms of the indenture are obeyed, (b) manage the sinking fund (if appropriate), and (c) represent bondholders if the company defaults on its payments.

The typical bond indenture can be a document of several hundred pages, and it generally includes the following provisions:

1  The basic terms of the bonds

2  A description of property used as security

3  Details of the protective covenants

4  The sinking fund arrangements

5  The call provision

Each of these is discussed next.

### The Basic Terms

Bonds usually have a denomination (also known as *face value* or *principal value*) denominated in multiples of 100. For example, in the UK, government bonds have a face value of £100 and corporate bonds tend to have a face value of £100,000. In Europe the denomination is often €1,000 or €10,000. In the US the denomination is normally $1,000. The denomination of the bond is always stated on the bond certificate. In addition, the *par value* (i.e. initial accounting value) of a bond is almost always the same as the face value.

Transactions between bond buyers and bond sellers determine the market value of the bond. Actual bond market values depend on the general level of interest rates, among other factors, and need not equal the face value. Bond prices are quoted as a percentage of the denomination. This is illustrated in the following example.

## Bond Prices

EXAMPLE
**20.1**

Suppose Nero SpA has issued 100 bonds. The amount stated on each bond certificate is €1,000. The total denomination, face value or principal value of the bonds is €100,000. Further suppose the bonds are currently *priced* at 100, which means 100 per cent of €1,000. This means that buyers and sellers are holding bonds at a price per bond of €1,000. If interest rates rise, the price of the bond might fall to, say, 97, which means 97 per cent of €1,000, or €970.

Suppose the bonds have a stated interest rate of 12 per cent due on 1 January 2050. The bond indenture might read as follows:

The bond will mature on 1 January 2050, and will be limited in aggregate denomination to €100,000. Each bond will bear interest at the rate of 12.0% per annum from 1 January 2010, or from the most recent interest payment date to which interest has been paid or provided for. Interest is payable semi-annually on 1 July and 1 January of each year.

As is typical of industrial bonds, the Nero bonds are registered. The indenture might read as follows:

Interest is payable semi-annually on 1 July and 1 January of each year to the person in whose name the bond is registered at the close of business on 15 June or 15 December, respectively.

This means that the company has a registrar who will record the ownership of each bond. The company will pay the interest and principal by cheque, mailed directly to the address of the owner of record.

When a bond is registered with attached coupons, the bondholder must separate a coupon from the bond certificate and send it to the company registrar (paying agent). Some bonds are in bearer form. This means that ownership is not recorded in the company books. As with a registered bond with attached coupons, the holder of the bond certificate separates the coupons and sends them to the company to receive payment.

There are two drawbacks to bearer bonds. First, they can easily be lost or stolen. Second, because the company does not know who owns its bonds, it cannot notify bondholders of important events. Consider, for example, Mr and Mrs De Loof, who go to their safe deposit box and clip the coupon on their 12 per cent, €1,000 bond issued by Nero SpA. They send the coupon to the paying agent and feel richer. A few days later a notice comes from the paying agent that the bond was retired and its principal paid off one year earlier. In other words, the bond no longer exists. Mr and Mrs De Loof must forfeit one year of interest. (Of course, they can turn their bond in for €1,000.)

However, bearer bonds have the advantage of secrecy, because even the issuing company does not know who the bond's owners are. This secrecy is particularly vexing to tax authorities, because tax collection on interest is difficult if the holder is unknown.

## A Note on Bond Price Quotes

If you buy a bond between coupon payment dates, the price you pay is usually more than the price you are quoted. The reason is that standard convention in the bond market is to quote prices net of 'accrued interest', meaning that accrued interest is deducted to arrive at the quoted price. This quoted price is called the clean price. The price you actually pay, however, includes the accrued interest. This price is the dirty price, also known as the 'full' or 'invoice' price.

An example is the easiest way to understand these issues. Suppose you buy a UK government bond with a 12 per cent annual coupon, payable semi-annually. You actually pay £108 for this bond, so £108 is the dirty, or invoice, price. Further, on the day you buy it, the next coupon is due in four months, so you are between coupon dates. Notice that the next coupon will be £6.

The accrued interest on a bond is calculated by taking the fraction of the coupon period that has passed, in this case two months out of six, and multiplying this fraction by the next coupon, £6. So the accrued interest in this example is $2/6 \times £6 = £2$. The bond's quoted price (i.e. its clean price) would be £108 − £2 = £106.

## Security

Debt securities are also classified according to the *collateral* protecting the bondholder. Collateral is a general term for the assets that are pledged as security for payment of debt. For example, *collateral trust bonds* involve a pledge of equity held by the corporation.

### EXAMPLE 20.2

### Collateral Trust Bonds

Suppose Railroad Holdings plc owns all of the ordinary shares of Track plc: that is, Track plc is a wholly owned subsidiary of Railroad Holdings plc. Railroad issues debt securities that pledge the equity of Track plc as collateral. The debts are collateral trust bonds; UK Sur Bank will hold them. If Railroad Holdings plc defaults on the debt, UK Sur Bank will be able to sell the equity of Track plc to satisfy Railroad's obligation.

*Mortgage securities* are secured by a mortgage on real estate or other long-term assets of the borrower. The legal document that describes the mortgage is called a *mortgage trust indenture* or *trust deed*. The mortgage can be *closed-end*, so that there is a limit on the amount of bonds that can be issued. More frequently it is *open-end*, without limit to the amount of bonds that may be issued.

### EXAMPLE 20.3

### Mortgage Securities

Suppose London Bond Company has buildings and land worth £10 million, and a £4 million mortgage on these properties. If the mortgage is closed-end, London Bond Company cannot issue more bonds on this property.

If the bond indenture contains no clause limiting the amount of additional bonds that can be issued, it is an open-end mortgage. In this case London Bond Company can issue additional bonds on its property, making the existing bonds riskier. For example, if additional mortgage bonds of £2 million are issued, the property has been pledged for a total of £6 million of bonds. If London Bond Company must liquidate its property for £4 million, the original bondholders will receive 4/6, or 67 per cent, of their investment. If the mortgage had been closed-end, they would have received 100 per cent of the stated value.

The value of a mortgage depends on the market value of the underlying property. Because of this, mortgage bonds sometimes require that the property be properly maintained and insured. Of course, a building and equipment bought in 1914 for manufacturing slide rules might not have much value no matter how well the company maintains it. The value of any property ultimately depends on its next best economic use. Bond indentures cannot easily insure against losses in economic value.

Sometimes mortgages are on specific property – for example, a single building. More often, blanket mortgages are used. A blanket mortgage pledges many assets owned by the company.

Some bonds represent unsecured obligations of the company. A debenture is an unsecured bond, where no specific pledge of property is made. Debenture holders have a claim on property not otherwise pledged – the property that remains after mortgages and collateral trusts are taken into account.

## Protective Covenants

A protective covenant is that part of the indenture or loan agreement that limits certain actions of the borrowing company. Protective covenants can be classified into two types: negative covenants and positive covenants. A negative covenant limits or prohibits actions that the company may take. Here are some typical examples:

- Limitations are placed on the amount of dividends a company may pay.
- The firm cannot pledge any of its assets to other lenders.
- The firm cannot merge with another firm.
- The firm may not sell or lease its major assets without approval by the lender.
- The firm cannot issue additional long-term debt.

A positive covenant specifies an action that the company agrees to take or a condition the company must abide by. Here are some examples:

- The company agrees to maintain its working capital at a minimum level.
- The company must furnish periodic financial statements to the lender.

The financial implications of protective covenants were treated in detail in the chapters about capital structure. In that discussion we argued that protective covenants can benefit shareholders, because if bondholders are assured that they will be protected in times of financial stress, they will accept a lower interest rate.

## The Sinking Fund

Bonds can be entirely repaid at maturity, at which time the bondholder will receive the stated value of the bond; or they can be repaid before maturity. Early repayment is more typical.

In a direct placement of debt, the repayment schedule is specified in the loan contract. For public issues, the repayment takes place through the use of a sinking fund and a call provision.

A *sinking fund* is an account managed by the bond trustee for the purpose of repaying the bonds. Typically, the company makes yearly payments to the trustee. The trustee can purchase bonds in the market or can select bonds randomly using a lottery and purchase them, generally at face value. There are many different kinds of sinking fund arrangements:

- Most sinking funds start between 5 and 10 years after the initial issuance.
- Some sinking funds establish equal payments over the life of the bond.
- Most high-quality bond issues establish payments to the sinking fund that are not sufficient to redeem the entire issue. As a consequence, there is the possibility of a large *balloon* payment at maturity.

Sinking funds have two opposing effects on bondholders:

1 *Sinking funds provide extra protection to bondholders.* A firm experiencing financial difficulties would have trouble making sinking fund payments. Thus sinking fund payments provide an early warning system to bondholders.

2 *Sinking funds give the firm an attractive option.* If bond prices fall below the face value, the firm will satisfy the sinking fund by buying bonds at the lower market prices. If bond prices rise above the face value, the firm will buy the bonds back at the lower face value (or other fixed price, depending on the specific terms).

## The Call Provision

A *call provision* lets the company repurchase or *call* the entire bond issue at a predetermined price over a specified period.

Generally the call price is above the bond's face value. The difference between the call price and the face value is the call premium. For example, if the call price is 105 – that is, 105 per cent of, say, €1,000 – the call premium is €50. The amount of the call premium usually becomes smaller over time. One typical arrangement is to set the call premium initially equal to the annual coupon payment, and then make it decline to zero over the life of the bond.

Call provisions are not usually operative during the first few years of a bond's life. For example, a company may be prohibited from calling its bonds for the first 10 years. This is referred to as a deferred call. During this period the bond is said to be call-protected.

In just the last few years a new type of call provision, a 'make-whole' call, has become widespread in the corporate bond market. With such a feature, bondholders receive approximately what the bonds are worth if they are called. Because bondholders don't suffer a loss in the event of a call, they are 'made whole'.

To determine the make-whole call price, we calculate the present value of the remaining interest and principal payments at a rate specified in the indenture. For example, assume that the Standard Life Bank plc issue was callable, and that the discount rate is 'Treasury rate plus 0.20%.' What this means is that we determine the discount rate by first finding a UK Treasury issue with the same maturity. We calculate the yield to maturity on the Treasury issue and then add on an additional 0.20 per cent to get the discount rate we use.

## 20.3 Bond Refunding

Replacing all or part of an issue of outstanding bonds is called bond refunding. Usually, the first step in a typical bond refunding is to call the entire issue of bonds at the call price. Bond refunding raises two questions:

1  Should firms issue callable bonds?

2  Given that callable bonds have been issued, when should the bonds be called?

We attempt to answer these questions in this section, focusing on traditional fixed-price call features.

### Should Firms Issue Callable Bonds?

Common sense tells us that call provisions have value. First, many publicly issued bonds have call provisions. Second, it is obvious that a call works to the advantage of the issuer. If interest rates fall and bond prices go up, the option to buy back the bonds at the call price is valuable. In bond refunding, firms will typically replace the called bonds with a new bond issue. The new bonds will have a lower coupon rate than the called bonds.

However, bondholders will take the call provision into account when they buy the bond. For this reason we can expect that bondholders will demand higher interest rates on callable bonds than on non-callable bonds. In fact, financial economists view call provisions as being zero-sum in efficient capital markets.[2] Any expected gains to the issuer from being allowed to refund the bond at lower rates will be offset by higher initial interest rates. We illustrate the zero-sum aspect to callable bonds in the following example.

EXAMPLE
20.4

Suppose Scandanavian Intercable ASA intends to issue perpetual bonds of 1,000 Norwegian kroner (NKr) face value at a 10 per cent interest rate. Annual coupons have been set at NKr100. There is an equal chance that by the end of the year interest rates will do one of the following:

1  Fall to $6\frac{2}{3}$ per cent. If so, the bond price will increase to NKr1,500.

2  Increase to 20 per cent. If so, the bond price will fall to NKr500.

▶ **Non-Callable Bond** Suppose the market price of the non-callable bond is the expected price it will have next year plus the coupon, all discounted at the current 10 per cent interest rate.[3] The value of the non-callable bond is this:

Value of non-callable bond:

$$\frac{\text{First-year coupon} + \text{Expected price at end of year}}{1 + r}$$

$$= \frac{\text{NKr}100 + (0.5 \times \text{NKr}1,500) + (0.5 \times \text{NKr}500)}{1.10}$$

$$= \text{NKr}1,000$$

**Callable Bond** Now suppose Scandinavian Intercable ASA decides to issue callable bonds. The call premium is set at NKr100 over par value, and the bonds can be called *only* at the end of the first year.[4] In this case the call provision will allow the company to buy back its bonds at NKr1,100 (NKr1,000 par value plus the NKr100 call premium). Should interest rates fall, the company will buy a bond for NKr1,100 that would be worth NKr1,500 in the absence of a call provision. Of course, if interest rates rise, Scandinavian Intercable would not want to call the bonds for NKr1,100 because they are worth only NKr500 on the market.

Suppose rates fall and Scandinavian Intercable calls the bonds by paying NKr1,100. If the firm simultaneously issues new bonds with a coupon of NKr100, it will bring in NKr1,500 (NKr100/0.0667) at the $6\frac{2}{3}$ per cent interest rate. This will allow Scandinavian Intercable to pay an extra dividend to shareholders of NKr400 (NKr1,500 − NKr1,100). In other words, if rates fall from 10 per cent to $6\frac{2}{3}$ per cent, exercise of the call will transfer NKr400 of potential bondholder gains to the shareholders.

When investors purchase callable bonds, they realize that they will forfeit their anticipated gains to shareholders if the bonds are called. As a consequence, they will not pay NKr1,000 for a callable bond with a coupon of NKr100.

How high must the coupon on the callable bond be so that it can be issued at the par value of NKr1,000? We can answer this in three steps.

**Step 1: Determining End-of-Year Value If Interest Rates Drop** If the interest rate drops to $6\frac{2}{3}$ per cent by the end of the year, the bond will be called for NKr1,100. The bondholder will receive both this and the annual coupon payment. If we let $C$ represent the coupon on the callable bond, the bondholder gets the following at the end of the year:

$$\text{NKr}1,100 + C$$

**Step 2: Determining End-of-Year Value If Interest Rates Rise** If interest rates rise to 20 per cent, the value of the bondholder's position at the end of the year is

$$\frac{C}{0.20} + C$$

That is, the perpetuity formula tells us that the bond will sell at $C/0.20$. In addition, the bondholder receives the coupon payment at the end of the year.

**Step 3: Solving for $C$** Because interest rates are equally likely to rise or to fall, the expected value of the bondholder's end-of-year position is

$$(\text{NKr}1,000 + C) \times 0.5 + \left(\frac{C}{0.20} + C\right) \times 0.5$$

Using the current interest rate of 10 per cent, we set the present value of these payments equal to par:

$$\text{NKr}1,000 = \frac{(\text{NKr}1,000 + C) \times 0.5 + \left(\dfrac{C}{0.20} + C\right) \times 0.5}{1.10}$$

$C$ is the unknown in the equation. The equation holds if $C$ = NKr157.14. In other words, callable bonds can sell at par only if their coupon rate is 15.714 per cent.

**The Paradox Restated**   If Scandinavian Intercable issues a non-callable bond, it will need to pay only a 10 per cent interest rate. By contrast, Scandinavian Intercable must pay an interest rate of 15.7 per cent on a callable bond. The interest rate differential makes an investor indifferent to either bond in our example. Because the return to the investor is the same with either bond, the cost of debt capital is the same to Scandinavian Intercable with either bond. Thus our example suggests that there is neither an advantage nor a disadvantage to issuing callable bonds.

Why, therefore, are callable bonds issued in the real world? This question has vexed financial economists for a long time. We now consider four specific reasons why a company might use a call provision:

1   Superior interest rate predictions

2   Taxes

3   Financial flexibility for future investment opportunities

4   Less interest rate risk

**Superior Interest Rate Forecasting**   Company insiders may know more about interest rate changes on the company's bonds than does the investing public. For example, managers may be better informed about potential changes in the firm's credit rating. Thus a company may prefer the call provision at a particular time because it believes that the expected fall in interest rates (the probability of a fall multiplied by the amount of the fall) is greater than the bondholders believe.

Although this is possible, there is reason to doubt that inside information is the rationale for call provisions. Suppose firms really had superior ability to predict changes that would affect them. Bondholders would infer that a company expected an improvement in its credit rating whenever it issued callable bonds. Bondholders would require an increase in the coupon rate to protect them against a call if this occurred. As a result, we would expect that there would be no financial advantage to the firm from callable bonds over non-callable bonds.

Of course, there are many non-company-specific reasons why interest rates can fall. For example, the interest rate level is connected to the anticipated inflation rate. But it is difficult to see how companies could have more information about the general level of interest rates than other participants in the bond markets.

**Taxes**   Call provisions may have tax advantages if the bondholder is taxed at a lower rate than the company. We have seen that callable bonds have higher coupon rates than non-callable bonds. Because the coupons provide a deductible interest expense to the corporation and are taxable income to the bondholder, the corporation will gain more than a bondholder in a low tax bracket will lose. Presumably, some of the tax savings can be passed on to the bondholders in the form of a high coupon.

**Future Investment Opportunities**   As we have explained, bond indentures contain protective covenants that restrict a company's investment opportunities. For example, protective covenants may limit the company's ability to acquire another firm or to sell certain assets (for example, a division of the company). If the covenants are sufficiently restrictive, the cost to the shareholders in lost net present value can be large. However, if bonds are callable, the company can buy back the bonds at the call price and take advantage of a superior investment opportunity.[5]

**Less Interest Rate Risk**   The call provision will reduce the sensitivity of a bond's value to changes in the level of interest rates. As interest rates increase, the value of a non-callable bond will fall. Because the callable bond has a higher coupon rate, the value of a callable bond will fall less than the value of a non-callable bond. Kraus has argued that by reducing the sensitivity of a bond's value to changes in interest rates, the call provision may reduce the risk of shareholders as well as bondholders.[6] He argues that because the bond is a liability of the corporation, the shareholders bear risk as the bond changes value over time. Thus it can be shown that, under certain conditions, reducing the risk of bonds through a call provision will also reduce the risk of equity.

## Calling Bonds: When Does it Make Sense?

The value of the company is the value of the equity plus the value of the bonds. From the Modigliani–Miller theory and the pie model in earlier chapters we know that firm value is unchanged by how it is divided between these two instruments. Therefore maximizing shareholder wealth means minimizing the value of the callable bond. In a world with no transaction costs it can be shown that the company should call its bonds whenever the callable bond value exceeds the call price. This policy minimizes the value of the callable bonds.

The preceding analysis is modified slightly by including the costs from issuing new bonds. These extra costs change the refunding rule to allow bonds to trade at prices above the call price. The objective of the company is to minimize the sum of the value of the callable bonds plus new issue costs. It has been observed that many real-world firms do not call their bonds when the market value of the bonds reaches the call price. Instead, they wait until the market value of the bonds exceeds the call price. Perhaps these issue costs are an explanation. Also, when a bond is called, the holder has about 30 days to surrender the bond and receive the call price in cash. In 30 days the market value of the bonds could fall below the call price. If so, the firm is giving away money. To forestall this possibility, it can be argued that firms should wait until the market value of the bond exceeds the call price before calling bonds.

# 20.4 Bond Ratings

Firms frequently pay to have their debt rated. The two leading bond-rating firms are Moody's Investors Service and Standard & Poor's. The debt ratings depend on (a) the likelihood that the firm will default and (b) the protection afforded by the loan contract in the event of default. The ratings are constructed from information supplied by the corporation, primarily the financial statements of the firm. The rating classes are shown in the accompanying box.

The highest rating debt can have is AAA or Aaa. Debt rated AAA or Aaa is judged to be the best quality and to have the lowest degree of risk. The lowest rating is D, which indicates that the firm is in default. Since the 1980s a growing part of corporate borrowing has taken the form of *low-grade bonds*. These bonds are also known as either *high-yield bonds* or *junk bonds*. Low-grade bonds are corporate bonds that are rated below *investment grade* by the major rating agencies (that is, below BBB for Standard & Poor's or Baa for Moody's).

Bond ratings are important, because bonds with lower ratings tend to have higher interest costs. However, the most recent evidence is that bond ratings merely reflect bond risk. There is no conclusive evidence that bond ratings affect risk.[7] It is not surprising that the share prices and bond prices of firms do not show any unusual behaviour on the days around a rating change. Because the ratings are based on publicly available information, they probably do not, in themselves, supply new information to the market.[8]

## Bond Ratings

|  | Very high quality | High quality | Speculative | Very poor |
|---|---|---|---|---|
| Standard & Poor's | AAA AA | A BBB | BB B | CCC CC C D |
| Moody's | Aaa Aa | A Baa | Ba B | Caa Ca C D |

At times both Moody's and Standard & Poor's adjust these ratings. S&P uses plus and minus signs: A+ is the strongest A rating and A– the weakest. Moody's uses a 1, 2, or 3 designation, with 1 indicating the strongest. These increments are called notches.

| Moody's | S&P | |
|---------|-----|---|
| Aaa | AAA | Debt rated Aaa and AAA has the highest rating. Capacity to pay interest and principal is extremely strong. |
| Aa | AA | Debt rated Aa and AA has a very strong capacity to pay interest and repay principal. Together with the highest rating, this group constitutes the high-grade bond class. |
| A | A | Debt rated A has a strong capacity to pay interest and repay principal. However, it is somewhat more susceptible to adverse changes in circumstances and economic conditions. |
| Baa | BBB | Debt rated Baa and BBB is regarded as having an adequate capacity to pay interest and repay principal. Whereas it normally exhibits adequate protection parameters, adverse economic conditions or changing circumstances are more likely to lead to a weakened capacity to pay interest and repay principal for debt in this category than in higher-rated categories. These bonds are medium-grade obligations. |
| BaB | BBB | Debt rated in these categories is regarded, on balance, as predominantly speculative. Ba and BB indicate the lowest degree of speculation, and Ca and CC the highest. |
| Caa Ca | CCC CC | Although such debt is likely to have some quality and protective characteristics, these are outweighed by large uncertainties or major risk exposure to adverse conditions. |
| C | C | This rating is reserved for income bonds on which no interest is being paid. |
| D | D | Debt rated D is in default, and payment of interest and/or repayment of principal is in arrears. |

*Source*: Data from various editions of *Standard & Poor's Bond Guide* and *Moody's Bond Guide*.

Rating agencies don't always agree. For example, some bonds are known as 'crossover' or '5B' bonds. The reason is that they are rated triple-B (or Baa) by one rating agency and double-B (or Ba) by another: a 'split rating'.

## Junk Bonds

The investment community has labelled bonds with a Standard & Poor's rating of BB and below or a Moody's rating of Ba and below as junk bonds. These bonds are also called *high-yield*, *speculative* or *low-grade*; we shall use all three terms interchangeably. Issuance of junk bonds has grown greatly in recent years, leading to increased public interest in this form of financing. However, since the middle of 2008 the junk bond market has closed down completely. With the arrival of the global financial crisis and the credit crunch faced by banks, speculative-grade debt is no longer available in Europe and the rest of the world. In the whole of 2008 there were no issues of junk bonds in Europe. This change in sentiment is striking. In 2007, €26 billion of speculative-grade debt was issued in Europe.

During economic downturns, junk bonds are most likely to default because of their speculative nature. Figure 20.1 presents data by Standard & Poor's on junk bond defaults in the recent past. As can be seen, the default rate on junk bonds in 2009 reached levels last seen during the bursting of the Internet bubble in 2001 and 2002. Moreover, expectations are that the default rate in 2010 will reach record levels. Table 20.1 presents data on default rates by Standard & Poor's on cumulative bases for 10 years. It shows that junk bonds can have a 10-year cumulative (if rated CCC) rate as high as 58.3 per cent.

The market for junk bonds took on increased importance when they were used to finance mergers and other corporate restructurings. Whereas a firm can issue only a small amount of

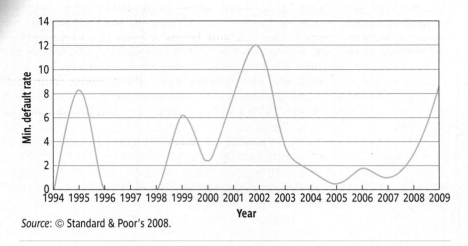

Figure 20.1 Historical default rates, junk bonds only: 1994–2009

| | | Years after issuance | | | | | | | | | |
|---|---|---|---|---|---|---|---|---|---|---|---|
| | | **1** | **2** | **3** | **4** | **5** | **6** | **7** | **8** | **9** | **10** |
| AAA | Marginal | 0.00 | 0.00 | 0.00 | 0.00 | 0.03 | 0.00 | 0.00 | 0.00 | 0.00 | 0.00 |
| | Cumulative | 0.00 | 0.00 | 0.00 | 0.00 | 0.03 | 0.03 | 0.03 | 0.03 | 0.03 | 0.03 |
| AA | Marginal | 0.00 | 0.00 | 0.32 | 0.16 | 0.03 | 0.03 | 0.00 | 0.00 | 0.03 | 0.02 |
| | Cumulative | 0.00 | 0.00 | 0.32 | 0.48 | 0.51 | 0.54 | 0.54 | 0.59 | 0.57 | 0.59 |
| A | Marginal | 0.01 | 0.10 | 0.02 | 0.09 | 0.06 | 0.11 | 0.06 | 0.21 | 0.11 | 0.06 |
| | Cumulative | 0.01 | 0.11 | 0.13 | 0.22 | 0.28 | 0.39 | 0.45 | 0.65 | 0.76 | 0.82 |
| BBB | Marginal | 0.36 | 3.22 | 1.43 | 1.28 | 0.77 | 0.45 | 0.20 | 0.20 | 0.14 | 0.40 |
| | Cumulative | 0.36 | 3.56 | 4.49 | 6.16 | 6.89 | 7.31 | 7.50 | 7.68 | 7.87 | 8.18 |
| BB | Marginal | 1.19 | 2.48 | 4.40 | 2.01 | 2.51 | 1.16 | 1.60 | 0.88 | 1.70 | 3.60 |
| | Cumulative | 1.19 | 3.64 | 7.88 | 9.74 | 12.00 | 12.93 | 14.36 | 15.07 | 16.52 | 19.60 |
| B | Marginal | 2.85 | 6.85 | 7.40 | 8.55 | 6.00 | 4.16 | 3.72 | 2.28 | 1.96 | 0.86 |
| | Cumulative | 2.85 | 9.51 | 16.20 | 23.37 | 27.94 | 30.96 | 33.46 | 34.97 | 36.25 | 36.80 |
| CCC | Marginal | 7.98 | 15.57 | 19.55 | 12.10 | 4.26 | 9.45 | 5.60 | 3.15 | 0.00 | 4.28 |
| | Cumulative | 7.98 | 22.31 | 37.50 | 45.06 | 47.37 | 52.35 | 55.01 | 56.43 | 56.43 | 58.30 |

Rated by S&P at issuance.
Based on 1,719 issues.

*Source*: Edward I. Altman, NYU Salomon Center.

Table 20.1 Mortality rates (per cent) by original rating, 1971–2004: all rated corporate bonds

high-grade debt, the same firm can issue much more debt if low-grade financing is allowed as well. Therefore the use of junk bonds lets acquirers effect takeovers that they could not do with only traditional bond financing techniques.

At this time it is not clear how the great growth in junk bond financing between 2000 and 2007 altered the returns on these instruments. Financial theory indicates that the expected returns on an asset should be negatively related to its marketability.[9] Because trading volume in junk bonds has greatly increased in recent years, the marketability has risen as well. This should lower the expected return on junk bonds, thereby benefiting corporate issuers. With the collapse in the junk bond market in 2008, yields on junk bonds have rocketed.[10]

We discussed the costs of issuing securities in a previous chapter and established that the costs of issuing debt are substantially less than the costs of issuing equity. Table 20.2 clarifies several questions regarding the costs of issuing debt securities. It contains a breakdown of direct costs for bond issues after the investment and non-investment grades have been separated.

First, there are substantial economies of scale here as well. Second, investment-grade issues have much lower direct costs, particularly for straight bonds. Finally, there are relatively few non-investment-grade issues in the smaller size categories, reflecting the fact that such issues are more commonly handled as private placements, which we discuss in a later section.

## 20.5  Some Different Types of Bond

Until now we have considered 'plain vanilla' bonds in our discussions. In this section we look at some more unusual types: floating-rate bonds, deep-discount bonds, and income bonds.

### Floating-Rate Bonds

The conventional bonds we have discussed in this chapter have *fixed monetary obligations*. That is, the coupon rate is set as a fixed percentage of the par value. However, the Standard Life Bank plc bond presented in Section 20.1 is an example of a floating-rate bond. With floating-rate bonds, the coupon payments are adjustable. The adjustments are tied to an *interest rate index* such as the Treasury bill interest rate, the London Interbank Offered Rate (LIBOR) or the European Interbank Offered Rate (EURIBOR).

In most cases the coupon adjusts with a lag to some base rate. For example, suppose a coupon rate adjustment is made on 1 June. The adjustment may be from a simple average of yields on six-month Treasury bills issued during March, April and May. In addition, the majority of these *floaters* have put provisions, and floor and ceiling provisions:

1   With a *put provision* the holder has the right to redeem his or her note at par on the coupon payment date. Frequently, the investor is prohibited from redeeming at par during the first few years of the bond's life.

2   With floor and ceiling provisions the coupon rate is subject to a minimum and maximum. For example, the minimum coupon rate might be 8 per cent and the maximum rate might be 14 per cent.

The popularity of floating-rate bonds is connected to *inflation risk*. When inflation is higher than expected, issuers of fixed-rate bonds tend to make gains at the expense of lenders; and when inflation is less than expected, lenders make gains at the expense of borrowers. Because the inflation risk of long-term bonds is borne by both issuers and bondholders, it is in their interests to devise loan agreements that minimize inflation risk.[11]

Floaters reduce inflation risk because the coupon rate is tied to the current interest rate, which, in turn, is influenced by the rate of inflation. We can see this most clearly by considering the formula for the present value of a bond. As inflation increases the interest rate (the denominator of the formula), inflation increases a floater's coupon rate (the numerator of the formula). Hence bond value is hardly affected by inflation. Conversely, the coupon rate of fixed-rate bonds cannot change, implying that the prices of these bonds are at the mercy of inflation.

As an alternative, an individual who is concerned with inflation risk can invest in short-term notes, such as Treasury bills, and *roll them over*.[12] The investor can accomplish essentially the same objective by buying a floater that is adjusted to the Treasury bill rate. However, the purchaser of a floater can reduce transactions costs relative to rolling over short-term Treasury bills, because floaters are long-term bonds. The same type of reduction in transaction costs

TABLE 20.2

| Proceeds ($m) | Convertible bonds | | | | | | Straight bonds | | | | | |
| | Investment grade | | | Non-investment grade | | | Investment grade | | | Non-investment grade | | |
| | Number of issues | Gross spread (%) | Total direct cost (%) | Number of issues | Gross spread (%) | Total direct cost (%) | Number of issues | Gross spread (%) | Total direct cost (%) | Number of issues | Gross spread (%) | Total direct cost (%) |
|---|---|---|---|---|---|---|---|---|---|---|---|---|
| 2–9.99 | 0 | – | – | 0 | – | – | 40 | 0.62 | 1.90 | 0 | – | – |
| 10–19.99 | 0 | – | – | 1 | 4.00 | 5.67 | 68 | 0.50 | 1.35 | 2 | 2.74 | 4.80 |
| 20–39.99 | 0 | – | – | 11 | 3.47 | 5.02 | 119 | 0.58 | 1.21 | 13 | 3.06 | 4.36 |
| 40–59.99 | 3 | 1.92 | 2.43 | 21 | 3.33 | 4.48 | 132 | 0.39 | 0.86 | 12 | 3.01 | 3.93 |
| 60–79.99 | 4 | 1.65 | 2.09 | 47 | 2.78 | 3.40 | 68 | 0.57 | 0.97 | 43 | 2.99 | 4.07 |
| 80–99.99 | 3 | 0.89 | 1.16 | 9 | 2.54 | 3.19 | 100 | 0.66 | 0.94 | 56 | 2.74 | 3.66 |
| 100–199.99 | 28 | 2.22 | 2.55 | 50 | 2.57 | 3.00 | 341 | 0.55 | 0.80 | 321 | 2.71 | 3.39 |
| 200–499.99 | 26 | 1.99 | 2.18 | 17 | 2.62 | 2.85 | 173 | 0.50 | 0.81 | 156 | 2.49 | 2.90 |
| 500 and up | 12 | 1.96 | 2.09 | 1 | 2.50 | 2.57 | 97 | 0.28 | 0.38 | 20 | 2.45 | 2.71 |
| Total | 76 | 1.99 | 2.26 | 157 | 2.81 | 3.47 | 1,138 | 0.51 | 0.85 | 623 | 2.68 | 3.35 |

*Source:* Inmoo Lee, Scott Lockhead, Jay Ritter and Quanshui Zhao, 'The costs of raising capital', *Journal of Financial Research*, vol. 19 (Spring 1996); updated by the authors.

**Table 20.2** Average gross spreads and total direct costs for domestic debt issues: 1990–2003 makes floaters attractive to some corporations.[13] They benefit from issuing a floater instead of issuing a series of short-term notes.

In an earlier section we discussed callable bonds. Because the coupon on floaters varies with market-wide interest rates, floaters always sell at or near par. Therefore it is not surprising that floaters do not generally have call features.

A particularly interesting type of floating-rate bond is an *inflation-linked* bond. Such bonds have coupons that are adjusted according to the rate of inflation (the principal amount may be adjusted as well). Many countries, such as the UK, US, Canada and Israel, began issuing such bonds in the late 1990s. The issues are sometimes called 'TIPS', or treasury inflation protection securities.

## Deep-Discount Bonds

A bond that pays no coupon must be offered at a price that is much lower than its face value. Such bonds are known as original-issue discount bonds, deep-discount bonds, pure discount bonds, or zero coupon bonds. They are frequently called *zeros* for short.

Suppose DDB AG issues 1,000 Swiss Francs (SwFr) of five-year deep-discount bonds when the market-wide interest rate is 10 per cent. These bonds do not pay any coupons. The initial price is set at SwFr621 because $SwFr621 = SwFr1,000/(1.10)^5$.

Because these bonds have no intermediate coupon payments, they are attractive to certain investors and unattractive to others. For example, consider an insurance company forecasting death benefit payments of SwFr1,000,000 five years from today. The company would like to be sure that it will have the funds to pay off the liability in five years' time. The company could buy five-year zero coupon bonds with a face value of SwFr1,000,000. The company is matching assets with liabilities here, a procedure that eliminates interest rate risk. That is, regardless of the movement of interest rates, the firm's set of zeros will always be able to pay off the SwFr1,000,000 liability.

Conversely, the firm would be at risk if it bought coupon bonds instead. For example, if it bought five-year coupon bonds, it would need to reinvest the coupon payments through to the fifth year. Because interest rates in the future are not known with certainty today, we cannot be sure whether these bonds will be worth more or less than SwFr1,000,000 by the fifth year.

Now, consider a couple saving for their child's university education in 15 years. They *expect* that, with inflation, four years of university should cost SwFr150,000 in 15 years. Thus they buy 15-year zero coupon bonds with a face value of SwFr150,000.[14] If they have forecast inflation perfectly (and if university costs keep pace with inflation), their child's tuition will be fully funded. However, if inflation rises more than expected, the tuition will be more than SwFr150,000. Because the zero coupon bonds produce a shortfall, the child might end up working his way through university. As an alternative, the parents might have considered rolling over Treasury bills. Because the yields on Treasury bills rise and fall with the inflation rate, this simple strategy is likely to cause less risk than the strategy with zeros.

The key to these examples concerns the distinction between nominal and real quantities. The insurance company's liability is SwFr1,000,000 in *nominal* Swiss francs. Because the face value of a zero coupon bond is a nominal quantity, the purchase of zeros eliminates risk. However, it is easier to forecast university costs in real terms than in nominal terms. Thus a zero coupon bond is a poor choice to reduce the financial risk of a child's university education.

## Income Bonds

Income bonds are similar to conventional bonds, except that coupon payments depend on company income. Specifically, coupons are paid to bondholders only if the firm's income is sufficient.

Income bonds are a financial puzzle because, from the firm's standpoint, they appear to be a cheaper form of debt than conventional bonds. Income bonds provide the same tax advantage to corporations from interest deductions that conventional bonds do. However, a company that issues income bonds is less likely to experience financial distress. When a coupon payment is omitted because of insufficient corporate income, an income bond is not in default.

Why don't firms issue more income bonds? Two explanations have been offered:

1 *The 'smell of death' explanation*: Firms that issue income bonds signal the capital markets of their increased prospect of financial distress.

2 *The 'deadweight costs' explanation*: The calculation of corporate income is crucial to determining the status of bondholders' income, and shareholders and bondholders will not necessarily agree on how to calculate the income. This creates agency costs associated with the firm's accounting methods.

Although these are possibilities, the work of McConnell and Schlarbaum suggests that no truly satisfactory reason exists for the lack of more investor interest in income bonds.[15]

## Other Types of Bond

Many bonds have unusual or exotic features. One such feature explains why the Berkshire Hathaway bond we described at the beginning of the chapter actually had what amounts to a negative coupon rate. The buyers of these bonds also received the right to purchase shares of equity in Berkshire at a fixed price per share over the subsequent five years. Such a right, which is called a *warrant*, would be very valuable if the share price climbed substantially (a later chapter discusses this subject in greater depth).

Bond features are really limited only by the imaginations of the parties involved. Unfortunately, there are far too many variations for us to cover in detail here. We therefore mention only a few of the more common types.

A *convertible bond* can be swapped for a fixed number of shares of equity any time before maturity at the holder's option. Convertibles are relatively common, but the number has been decreasing in recent years.

A *put bond* allows the *holder* to force the issuer to buy the bond back at a stated price. For example, Skyepharma plc, a UK speciality drug company, has bonds outstanding that allow the holder to force Skyepharma to buy the bonds back at 100 per cent of face value. The put feature is therefore just the reverse of the call provision.

A given bond may have many unusual features. Two of the most recent exotic bonds are CoCo bonds, which have a coupon payment, and NoNo bonds, which are zero coupon bonds. CoCo and NoNo bonds are contingent convertible, putable, callable, subordinated bonds. The contingent convertible clause is similar to the normal conversion feature, except that the contingent feature must be met. For example, a contingent feature may require that the company equity trade at 110 per cent of the conversion price for 20 out of the most recent 30 days. Valuing a bond of this sort can be quite complex, and the yield to maturity calculation is often meaningless. For example, in 2006 a NoNo issued by Merrill Lynch was selling at a price of $939.99, with a yield to maturity of negative 1.63 per cent. At the same time a NoNo issued by Countrywide Financial was selling for $1,640, which implied a yield to maturity of negative 59 per cent!

## Islamic Bonds

Having read Section 14.6 on Islamic financing, you may think it would be impossible for any type of bond to be acceptable to Islamic law. This is because any interest payment or attempt to make money from money is forbidden. With the massive increase in the price of oil over the last few years, many Islamic investment funds and banks have been seeking ways to diversify their investment portfolios in ways that are consistent with their religious beliefs. One such instrument is a *sukuk*, otherwise known as an Islamic bond.

A *sukuk* isn't a simple certificate like a bond that promises set periodic payments over the period of the bond. It is more akin to a financing company that is involved in profit sharing (*musharakah*), stated cost plus profit (*murabahah*) or sale and leasebacks (*ijarah*). Taking an *ijarah*

| Step | Company | SPV | Sukuk holders |
|---|---|---|---|
| **1** Create SPV | | | |
| **2** Company sells assets | + Asset value | − Asset value | |
| **3** SPV issues securities to market | | + Asset value | − Asset value |
| **4** Company leases asset from SPV | − Periodic payment | + Periodic payment − Periodic payment | + Periodic payment |
| **5** Company buys assets back from SPV. SPV pays back *sukuk* holders | − Asset value | + Asset value − Asset value | + Asset value |

**Table 20.3** Cash flows from a *sukuk* or Islamic bond

*sukuk* as an example, a company wishes to raise funds just now in return for a set periodic payment in the future. To be compliant with Islamic law, the financing instrument cannot have any interest, or make money from money. An *ijarah sukuk* is structured as follows:

1    The company that wishes to raise funds creates a subsidiary specifically for the *ijarah sukuk*. This is generally known as a special purpose vehicle (SPV) or special investment vehicle (SIV).

2    The company sells its own assets (for example, a manufacturing plant, technical machinery, or property) to the SPV with a value equal to the amount of financing required.

3    The SPV issues securities or *sukuk* to the market. The *sukuk* pays periodic payments (fixed or floating depending on the underlying asset) from the cash flows generated by the assets. The money raised by the *sukuk* issue is used to pay for the assets in step 2.

4    The company immediately leases the assets back from the SPV, making periodic payments (fixed or floating depending on the asset) to the SPV. The payments are passed on to the *sukuk* holders.

5    At the end of the financing period the company buys the assets back from the SPV, and the SPV passes these on to the holders of the *sukuk*.

The cash flows from the *sukuk* to different parties are presented in Table 20.3. Notice how the cash flows from the *sukuk* are exactly the same as that of a bond, except that money is being generated from the underlying asset and not money in itself.

## 20.6  Private Placement Compared with Public Issues

Earlier in this chapter we described the mechanics of issuing debt to the public. However, more than 50 per cent of all debt is privately placed. There are two basic forms of direct private long-term financing: term loans and private placement.

Term loans are direct business loans with maturities of 1–15 years. The typical term loan is amortized over the life of the loan. That is, the loan is repaid by equal annual payments of interest and principal. The lenders are banks and insurance companies. A private placement, which also involves the sale of a bond or loan directly to a limited number of investors, is similar to a term loan except that the maturity is longer.

Here are some important differences between direct long-term financing and public issues:

• A direct long-term loan avoids the cost of registration with stock exchange authorities.

• Direct placement is likely to have more restrictive covenants.

- It is easier to renegotiate a term loan and a private placement in the event of a default. It is harder to renegotiate a public issue, because hundreds of holders are usually involved.

- Life insurance companies and pension funds dominate the private placement segment of the bond market. Banks are significant participants in the term loan market.

- The costs of distributing bonds are lower in the private market.

The interest rates on term loans and private placements are usually higher than those on an equivalent public issue. Hayes, Joehnk and Melicher found that the yield to maturity on private placements was 0.46 per cent higher than on similar public issues.[16] This finding reflects the trade-off between a higher interest rate and more flexible arrangements in the event of financial distress, as well as the lower transaction costs associated with private placements.

## 20.7  Long-Term Syndicated Bank Loans

Most bank loans are for less than a year. They serve as a short-term 'bridge' for the acquisition of inventory, and are typically self-liquidating: that is, when the firm sells the inventory, the cash is used to repay the bank loan. We talk about the need for short-term bank loans in Part Seven. Now we focus on long-term bank loans.

First, we introduce the concept of *commitment*. Most bank loans are made with a commitment to a firm. That commitment establishes a line of credit and allows the firm to borrow up to a predetermined limit. Most commitments are in the form of a revolving credit commitment (i.e. a revolver) with a fixed term of up to three years or more. Revolving credit commitments are drawn or undrawn, depending on whether the firm has a current need for the funds.

Now we turn to the concept of *syndication*. Very large banks such as Citigroup typically have a larger demand for loans than they can supply, and small regional banks frequently have more funds on hand than they can profitably lend to existing customers. Basically, they cannot generate enough good loans with the funds they have available. As a result, a very large bank may arrange a loan with a firm or country and then sell portions of it to a syndicate of other banks. With a syndicated loan, each bank has a separate loan agreement with the borrowers.

A syndicated loan is a corporate loan made by a group (or syndicate) of banks and other institutional investors. A syndicated loan may be publicly traded. It may be a line of credit and be 'undrawn', or it may be drawn and be used by a firm. Syndicated loans are always rated investment grade. However, a *leveraged* syndicated loan is rated speculative grade (i.e. it is 'junk'). In addition, syndicated loan prices are reported for a group of publicly traded loans. Altman and Suggitt report slightly higher default rates for syndicated loans than for comparable corporate bonds.[17]

## Summary and Conclusions

This chapter described some important aspects of long-term debt financing:

1   The written agreement describing the details of the long-term debt contract is called an *indenture*. Some of the main provisions are security, repayment, protective covenants, and call provisions.

2   There are many ways in which shareholders can take advantage of bondholders. Protective covenants are designed to protect bondholders from management decisions that favour equity-holders at bondholders' expense.

3   Unsecured bonds are called *debentures* or *notes*. They are general claims on the company's value. Most public industrial bonds are unsecured. In contrast, utility bonds are usually

secured. Mortgage bonds are secured by tangible property, and collateral trust bonds are secured by financial securities such as equities and bonds. If the company defaults on secured bonds, the trustee can repossess the assets. This makes secured bonds more valuable.

4  Long-term bonds usually provide for repayment of principal before maturity. This is accomplished by a sinking fund. With a sinking fund, the company retires a certain number of bonds each year. A sinking fund protects bondholders because it reduces the average maturity of the bond, and its payment signals the financial condition of the company.

5  Most publicly issued bonds are callable. A callable bond is less attractive to bondholders than a non-callable bond. A callable bond can be bought back by the company at a call price that is less than the true value of the bond. As a consequence, callable bonds are priced to obtain higher stated interest rates for bondholders than non-callable bonds.

   Generally, companies should exercise the call provision whenever the bond's value is greater than the call price.

   There is no single reason for call provisions. Some sensible reasons include taxes, greater flexibility, management's ability to predict interest rates, and the fact that callable bonds are less sensitive to interest rate changes.

6  There are many different types of bond, including floating-rate bonds, deep-discount bonds, and income bonds. This chapter also compared private placement with public issuance.

7  Islamic businesses can invest in special types of bond, known as *sukuk*, that are designed to be consistent with Shariah law.

## onnect  Questions and Problems

**CONCEPT**
**1 – 7**

1  **Debt Financing**  Review the characteristics of a bond. Why do you think short-term debt is known as unfunded debt and long-term debt as funded debt?

2  **The Public Issue of Bonds**  Explain what is meant by a bond covenant, and provide examples of the different forms of covenant you might see in a bond indenture.

3  **Bond Refunding**  Why would a firm choose to issue callable bonds?

4  **Bond Ratings**  If bond rating agencies, such as S&P and Moody's, use public information to provide a credit rating for companies, why does a rating downgrade affect prices? Is this evidence of market inefficiency?

5  **Different Types of Bond**  Explain what is meant by a *sukuk*. Why do you think it is called a bond?

6  **Private Placement versus Public Issue**  What are the benefits of a private placement over a public issue of bonds?

7  **Long-Term Syndicated Bank Loans**  What are the main agency issues involved in a syndicated loan? Do you think syndicated loans should be priced differently from public debt issues? Explain.

**REGULAR**
**8 – 30**

8  **Call Provisions**  A company is contemplating a long-term bond issue. It is debating whether to include a call provision. What are the benefits to the company from including a call provision? What are the costs? How do these answers change for a put provision?

9  **Coupon Rate**  How does a bond issuer decide on the appropriate coupon rate to set on its bonds? Explain the difference between the coupon rate and the required return on a bond.

10 **Bond Ratings** Companies pay rating agencies such as Moody's and S&P to rate their bonds, and the costs can be substantial. However, companies are not required to have their bonds rated in the first place; doing so is strictly voluntary. Why do you think they do it?

11 **Bond Ratings** Most European government treasury bonds are not rated. Why? Often, junk bonds are not rated. Why?

12 **Crossover Bonds** Looking back at the crossover bonds we discussed in the chapter, why do you think split ratings such as these occur?

13 **Bond Market** What are the implications for bond investors of the lack of transparency in the bond market?

14 **Rating Agencies** A controversy erupted regarding bond-rating agencies when some agencies began to provide unsolicited bond ratings. Why do you think this is controversial?

15 **Bonds as Equity** Recently several companies have issued bonds with 100-year maturities. Critics charge that the issuers are really selling equity in disguise. What are the issues here? Why would a company want to sell 'equity in disguise'?

16 **Callable Bonds** Do you agree or disagree with the following statement? 'In an efficient market, callable and non-callable bonds will be priced in such a way that there will be no advantage or disadvantage to the call provision.' Why?

17 **Bond Prices** If interest rates fall, will the price of non-callable bonds move up higher than that of callable bonds? Why or why not?

18 **Junk Bonds** What is a 'junk bond'? What are some of the controversies created by junk bond financing?

19 **Sinking Funds** Sinking funds have both positive and negative characteristics for bondholders. Why?

20 **Mortgage Bonds** Which is riskier to a prospective creditor – an open-end mortgage or a closed-end mortgage? Why?

21 **Public Issues versus Direct Financing** Which of the following are characteristics of public issues, and which are characteristics of direct financing?

(a) Stock exchange registration required

(b) Higher interest cost

(c) Higher fixed cost

(d) Quicker access to funds

(e) Active secondary market

(f) Easily renegotiated

(g) Lower flotation costs

(h) Regular amortization required

(i) Ease of repurchase at favourable prices

(j) High total cost to small borrowers

(k) Flexible terms

(l) Less intensive investigation required

22 **Bond Ratings** In general, why don't bond prices change when bond ratings change?

23 **Accrued Interest** You purchase a UK government bond with an invoice price of £114. The bond has a coupon rate of 7.2 per cent, and there are five months to the next semi-annual coupon date. What is the clean price of the bond?

24  **Accrued Interest**  You purchase a bond with a coupon rate of 6.5 per cent and a clean price of 8,650 Danish kroner. If the next semi-annual coupon payment is due in three months, what is the invoice price?

25  **Bond Refunding**  KIC plc plans to issue £5 million of bonds with a coupon rate of 12 per cent and 30 years to maturity. The current market interest rate on these bonds is 11 per cent. In one year, the interest rate on the bonds will be either 14 per cent or 7 per cent with equal probability. Assume investors are risk-neutral.

(a)  If the bonds are non-callable, what is the price of the bonds today?

(b)  If the bonds are callable one year from today at £145,000, will their price be greater than or less than the price you computed in (a)? Why?

26  **Bond Refunding**  Impresse Nuovo Affari SpA has an outstanding perpetual bond with a 10 per cent coupon rate that can be called in one year. The bonds make annual coupon payments. The call premium is set at €150 over par value. There is a 40 per cent chance that the interest rate in one year will be 12 per cent, and a 60 per cent chance that the interest rate will be 7 per cent. If the current interest rate is 10 per cent, what is the current market price of the bond?

27  **Bond Refunding**  Bowdeen Manufacturing intends to issue callable, perpetual bonds with annual coupon payments. The bonds are callable at £125,000. One-year interest rates are 11 per cent. There is a 60 per cent probability that long-term interest rates one year from today will be 13 per cent, and a 40 per cent probability that long-term interest rates will be 9 per cent. Assume that if interest rates fall the bonds will be called. What coupon rate should the bonds have in order to sell at par value?

28  **Bond Refunding**  Istanbul Industries has decided to borrow money by issuing perpetual bonds with a coupon rate of 8 per cent, payable annually. The one-year interest rate is 8 per cent. Next year, there is a 35 per cent probability that interest rates will increase to 9 per cent, and there is a 65 per cent probability that they will fall to 6 per cent.

(a)  What will the market value of these bonds be if they are non-callable?

(b)  If the company instead decides to make the bonds callable in one year, what coupon will be demanded by the bondholders for the bonds to sell at par? Assume that the bonds will be called if interest rates rise and that the call premium is equal to the annual coupon.

(c)  What will be the value of the call provision to the company?

29  **Bond Refunding**  An outstanding issue of Public Express Airlines debentures has a call provision attached. The total principal value of the bonds is $250 million, and the bonds have an annual coupon rate of 8 per cent. The total cost of refunding would be 12 per cent of the principal amount raised. The appropriate tax rate for the company is 30 per cent. How low does the borrowing cost need to drop to justify refunding with a new bond issue?

30  **Bond Refunding**  Charles River Associates is considering whether to refinance either of the two perpetual bond issues the company currently has outstanding. Here is information about the two bond issues:

|                               | Bond A       | Bond B       |
|-------------------------------|--------------|--------------|
| Coupon rate                   | 8%           | 9%           |
| Value outstanding             | €75,000,000  | €87,500,000  |
| Call premium                  | 8.5%         | 9.5%         |
| Transaction cost of refunding | €10,000,000  | €12,000,000  |
| Current interest rate         | 7%           | 7.25%        |

The corporate tax rate is 12.5 per cent. What is the NPV of the refunding for each bond? Which bond should the company refinance?

**31** **Valuing the Call Feature** Consider the prices in the following three Treasury issues as of 24 February 2009:

| | | | | | |
|---|---|---|---|---|---|
| 6.500 | 12 May | 106:10 | 106:12 | –13 | 5.28 |
| 8.250 | 12 May | 103:14 | 103:16 | –3 | 5.24 |
| 12.000 | 12 May | 134:25 | 134:31 | –15 | 5.32 |

The bond in the middle is callable in February 2010. What is the implied value of the call feature? (*Hint*: Is there a way to combine the two non-callable issues to create an issue that has the same coupon as the callable bond?)

**32** **Treasury Bonds** The following Treasury bond quote appeared in the *Wall Street Journal* on 11 May 2004:

| | | | | | |
|---|---|---|---|---|---|
| 9.125 | 9 May | 100:03 | 100:04 | . . . | –2.15 |

Why would anyone buy this Treasury bond with a negative yield to maturity? How is this possible?

**33** **Sukuk** Medhat International is a manufacturing firm operated along Islamic principles. They wish to raise 20 billion Bahrain dinars and pay this back in equal instalments over six years. Comparable Western bonds have eight per cent coupons. Construct a *sukuk* that is competitive with Western bonds.

# Financing West Coast Yachts' Expansion Plans with a Bond Issue

Larissa Warren, the owner of West Coast Yachts, has decided to expand her operations. She asked her newly hired financial analyst, Dan Ervin, to enlist an underwriter to help sell £30 million in new 20-year bonds to finance new construction. Dan has entered into discussions with Robin Perry, an underwriter from the firm of Crowe & Mallard, about which bond features West Coast Yachts should consider, and also what coupon rate the issue is likely to have. Although Dan is aware of bond features, he is uncertain of the costs and benefits of some features, so he isn't sure how each feature would affect the coupon rate of the bond issue.

1 You are Robin's assistant, and she has asked you to prepare a memo to Dan describing the effect of each of the following bond features on the coupon rate of the bond. She would also like you to list any advantages or disadvantages of each feature.

(a) The security of the bond – that is, whether the bond has collateral.

(b) The seniority of the bond.

(c) The presence of a sinking fund.

(d) A call provision with specified call dates and call prices.

(e) A deferred call accompanying the call provision in (d).

(f) A make-whole call provision.

(g) Any positive covenants. Also, discuss several possible positive covenants West Coast Yachts might consider.

(h) Any negative covenants. Also, discuss several possible negative covenants West Coast Yachts might consider.

(i) A conversion feature (note that West Coast Yachts is not a publicly traded company).

(j) A floating-rate coupon.

Dan is also considering whether to issue coupon-bearing bonds or zero coupon bonds. The YTM on either bond issue will be 8 per cent. The coupon bond would have an 8 per cent coupon rate. The company's tax rate is 28 per cent.

2 How many of the coupon bonds must West Coast Yachts issue to raise the £30 million? How many of the zeros must it issue?

3 In 20 years, what will be the principal repayment due if West Coast Yachts issues the coupon bonds? What if it issues the zeros?

4 What are the company's considerations in issuing a coupon bond compared with a zero coupon bond?

5 Suppose West Coast Yachts issues the coupon bonds with a make-whole call provision. The make-whole call rate is the Treasury rate plus 0.40 per cent. If West Coast calls the bonds in seven years when the Treasury rate is 5.6 per cent, what is the call price of the bond? What if it is 9.1 per cent?

6 Are investors really made whole with a make-whole call provision?

7 After considering all the relevant factors, would you recommend a zero coupon issue or a regular coupon issue? Why? Would you recommend an ordinary call feature or a make-whole call feature? Why?

## Practical Case Study

Look up the websites and financial reports for Société Générale, Crédit Agricole, Enel SpA and ING Groep, and find the credit rating for each firm. For some of these companies you will need to search closely for the information. While it may seem a bit of a bore to do this, searching for data and reading through corporate financial websites gives fantastic experience in understanding corporate finance. Which companies (if any?) have an investment-grade rating? Which companies are rated below investment grade? Are any unrated? Compare the change in share price over the last year, and the rating for each company. Is there a relationship? What do credit ratings say about a firm's share price performance?

## Relevant Accounting Standards

The most important accounting standard for bonds is IAS39 *Financial Instruments: Recognition and Measurement*. However, you should also know IAS23 *Borrowing Costs*, which deals with the way interest payments and other charges are presented in the financial accounts. Visit the IASPlus website (www.iasplus.com) for more information.

# Additional Reading

The literature on debt financing can be conveniently separated into three areas: pricing, risk, and structure. This is the approach we take in listing the relevant papers in the area.

**Bond Pricing**

Cai, N., J. Helwege and A. Warga (2007) 'Underpricing in the corporate bond market', *Review of Financial Studies*, vol. 20, no. 6, pp. 2021–2046. **US.**

Cremers, K.J.M., V.B. Nair and C. Wei (2007) 'Governance mechanisms and bond prices', *Review of Financial Studies*, vol. 20, no. 5, pp. 1359–1388. **US.**

**Bond Risk and Credit Ratings**

Avramov, D., T. Chordia, G. Jostova and A. Philipov (2009) 'Dispersion in analysts' earnings forecasts and credit rating', *Journal of Financial Economics*, vol. 91, no. 1, pp. 83–101. **US.**

Behr, P. and A. Guttler (2008) 'The informational content of unsolicited ratings', *Journal of Banking and Finance*, vol. 32, no. 5, pp. 587–599. **US.**

Berger, A.N., M.A. Espinosa-Vega, W. Scott Frame and N.H. Miller (2005) 'Debt maturity, risk, and asymmetric information', *Journal of Finance*, vol. 60, no. 6, pp. 2895–2923. **US.**

Brooks, R., R. Faff, D. Hillier and J. Hillier (2004) 'The national market impact of sovereign rating changes', *Journal of Banking and Finance*, vol. 28, no. 1, pp. 233–250. **International.**

**Bond Covenants and Structures**

Billett, M.T., T. Dolly King and D.C. Mauer (2007) 'Growth opportunities and the choice of leverage, debt maturity, and covenants', *Journal of Finance*, vol. 62, no. 2, pp. 697–730. **US.**

Chava, S. and M.R. Roberts (2008) 'How does financing impact investment? The role of debt covenants', *Journal of Finance*, vol. 63, no. 5, pp. 2085–2121. **US.**

Datta, S., M. Iskandar-Datta and K. Raman (2005) 'Managerial stock ownership and the maturity structure of corporate debt', *Journal of Finance*, vol. 60, no. 5, pp. 2333–2350. **US.**

Jimenez, G., V. Salas and J. Saurina (2006) 'Determinants of collateral', *Journal of Financial Economics*, vol. 81, no. 1, pp. 255–281. **Spain.**

Qian, J. and P.E. Strahan (2007) 'How laws and institutions shape financial contracts: the case of bank loans', *Journal of Finance*, vol. 62, no. 6, pp. 2803–2834. **International.**

Sufi, A. (2007) 'Information asymmetry and financing arrangements: evidence from syndicated loans', *Journal of Finance*, vol. 62, no. 2, pp. 629–668. **US.**

**Other Relevant Research**

Carey, M. and G. Nini (2007) 'Is the corporate loan market globally integrated? A pricing puzzle', *Journal of Finance*, vol. 62, no. 6, pp. 2969–3007. **International.**

Roberts, M.R. and A. Sufi (2009) 'Control rights and capital structure: an empirical investigation', *Journal of Finance* (forthcoming). **US.**

# Endnotes

1 The term *loan agreement* or *loan contract* is usually used for privately placed debt and term loans.

2 See A. Kraus, 'An analysis of call provisions and the corporate refunding decision', *Midland Corporate Finance Journal*, vol. 1 (Spring 1983), p. 1.

3 We are assuming that the current price of the non-callable bonds is the expected value discounted at the risk-free rate of 10 per cent. This is equivalent to assuming that the risk is unsystematic and carries no risk premium.

4 Normally, bonds can be called over a period of many years. Our assumption that the bond can be called only at the end of the first year was introduced for simplicity.

5 This argument is from Z. Bodie and R.A. Taggart, 'Future investment opportunities and the value of the call provision on a bond', *Journal of Finance*, vol. 33 (1978), p. 4.

6 A. Kraus, 'An analysis of call provisions and the corporate refunding decision', *Midland Corporate Finance Journal*, vol. 1 (Spring 1983). Kraus points out that the call provision will not always reduce the equity's interest rate risk. If the firm as a whole bears interest rate risk, more of this risk may be shifted from shareholders to bondholders with non-callable debt. In this case, shareholders may actually bear more risk with callable debt.

7 M. Weinstein, 'The systematic risk of corporate bonds', *Journal of Financial and Quantitative Analysis* (September 1981); J. P. Ogden, 'Determinants of relative interest rate sensitivity of corporate bonds', *Financial Management* (Spring 1987); and F. Reilly and M. Joehnk, 'The association between market-based risk measures for bonds and bond ratings', *Journal of Finance* (December 1976).

8 M. Weinstein, 'The effect of a ratings change announcement on bond price', *Journal of Financial Economics*, vol. 5 (1977). However, Robert W. Holthausen and Richard W. Leftwich, 'The effect of bond rating changes on common stock prices', *Journal of Financial Economics*, vol. 17 (September 1986), find that bond rating downgrades are associated with abnormal negative returns on the equity of the issuing firm. In addition, R. Brooks, R. Faff, D. Hillier and J. Hillier, 'The national market impact of sovereign rating changes', *Journal of Banking and Finance* (2004), vol. 28, no. 1, pp. 233–250, show that stock market indices react negatively to downgrades of government credit ratings.

9 For example, see Y. Amihud and H. Mendelson, 'Asset pricing and the bid–ask spread', *Journal of Financial Economics* (December 1986).

10 The actual risk of junk bonds is not known with certainty, because it is not easy to measure default rate. Paul Asquith, David W. Mullins Jr and Eric D. Wolff, 'Original-issue high-yield bonds: aging analysis of defaults, exchanges, and calls', *Journal of Finance* (September 1989), show that the default rate on junk bonds can be greater than 30 per cent over the life of the bond. They look at cumulative default rates and find that of all junk bonds issued in 1977 and 1978, 34 per cent had defaulted by 31 December 1988. Table 20.1 shows yearly default rates. Edward I. Altman, 'Setting the record straight on junk bonds: a review of the research on default rates and returns', *Journal of Applied Corporate Finance* (Summer 1990), shows that yearly default rates of 5 per cent are consistent with cumulative default rates of over 30 per cent.

11 See B. Cornell, 'The future of floating-rate bonds', in *The Revolution in Corporate Finance*, ed. by J.M. Stern and D.H. Chew Jr. (New York: Basil Blackwell, 1986).

12 That is, the investor could buy a bill, receive the face value at maturity, use these proceeds to buy a second bill, receive the face value from the second bill at maturity, and so on. This was the principal funding strategy followed by the banking sector between 2000 and 2007. Unfortunately, with the global credit crunch the supply of these short-term funds dried up, and the banking sector needed to be bailed out by the world's governments.

13 Cox, Ingersoll and Ross developed a framework for pricing floating-rate notes: see J. Cox, J. Ingersoll and S.A. Ross, 'An analysis of variable rate loan contracts', *Journal of Finance*, vol. 35 (May 1980).

14 A more precise strategy would be to buy zeros maturing in years 15, 16, 17 and 18, respectively. In this way the bonds might mature just in time to meet tuition payments.

15 J. McConnell and G. Schlarbaum, 'The income bond puzzle', in *The Revolution in Corporate Finance*, ed. by J.M. Stern and D.H. Chew Jr. (New York: Basil Blackwell, 1986).

16 P.A. Hayes, M.D. Joehnk and R.W. Melicher, 'Determinants of risk premiums in the public and private bond market', *Journal of Financial Research* (Fall 1979).

17 Edward I. Altman and Heather J. Suggitt, 'Default rates in the syndicated bank loan market: a longitudinal analysis', *Journal of Banking and Finance*, vol. 24 (2000).

Online **LearningCentre**

To help you grasp the key concepts of this chapter check out the extra resources posted on the Online Learning Centre at **www.mcgraw-hill.co.uk/textbooks/hillier**

Among other helpful resources there are PowerPoint presentations, chapter outlines and mini-cases.

# Chapter **21**

# Leasing and Off-Balance-Sheet Financing

Instead of incurring major capital expenditure through purchasing fixed assets, leasing allows a company to dispense with the need to raise capital for investment. For example, many airlines lease planes instead of owning them. The International Lease Finance Corporation (ILFC), which is the world's largest airplane leasing company by fleet value, leases airplanes to airlines such as Air France-KLM, British Midland, Iberia, Tui Travel and Aer Lingus. The company currently owns around 1,000 jets. So why is ILFC in the business of buying airplanes, only to lease them out? And why don't companies that lease from ILFC simply purchase the airplanes themselves? This chapter provides answers to these and other questions associated with leasing.

## 21.1 Types of Lease Financing

Quite simply, off-balance-sheet items are any assets or liabilities that do not appear in a company's balance sheet. Examples include leases, subsidiaries, loan commitments and derivative contracts. The banking sector has many more off-balance-sheet items, but we shall not discuss these in detail here. As a result of the events of the global financial crisis in 2008, the International Accounting Standards Board (IASB) identified the treatment of off-balance-sheet items as a major priority. Specifically, accounting regulations will change so that off-balance-sheet financing will come back onto the balance sheet, and financial statements will be more representative. It is very likely that, as a consequence of these changes, many off-balance-sheet strategies will become less popular. We may even see this chapter disappear in future editions of the textbook!

The most popular form of off-balance-sheet financing in corporate finance is leasing, and we shall focus most of our discussion in this chapter on the activity.

## Leasing Basics

A *lease* is a contractual agreement between a lessee and lessor. The agreement establishes that the lessee has the right to use an asset and in return must make periodic payments to the lessor, the owner of the asset. The lessor is either the asset's manufacturer or an independent leasing company. If the lessor is an independent leasing company, it must buy the asset from a manufacturer. Then the lessor delivers the asset to the lessee, and the lease goes into effect.

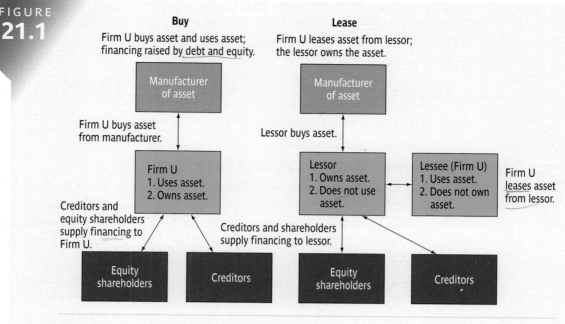

**FIGURE 21.1**

**Buy**
Firm U buys asset and uses asset; financing raised by debt and equity.

**Lease**
Firm U leases asset from lessor; the lessor owns the asset.

**Figure 21.1** Buying versus leasing

As far as the lessee is concerned, it is the use of the asset that is most important, not who owns the asset. The use of an asset can be obtained by a lease contract. Because the user can also buy the asset, leasing and buying involve alternative financing arrangements for the use of an asset. This is illustrated in Fig. 21.1.

The specific example in Fig. 21.1 happens often in the computer industry. Firm U, the lessee, might be a hospital, a law firm, or any other firm that uses computers. The lessor is an independent leasing company that purchased the equipment from a manufacturer such as Dell, Sony, HP or Apple. Leases of this type are called direct leases. In the figure, the lessor issued both debt and equity to finance the purchase.

Of course, a manufacturer such as Apple could lease its *own* computers, though we do not show this situation in the example. Leases of this type are called sales-type leasing. In this case, Apple would compete with the independent computer leasing company.

## Operating Leases

Years ago, a lease where the lessee received an operator along with the equipment was called an operating lease. Though the operating lease defies an exact definition today, this form of leasing has several important characteristics:

- Operating leases are usually not fully amortized. This means that the payments required under the terms of the lease are not enough to recover the full cost of the asset for the lessor. This occurs because the term or life of the operating lease is usually less than the economic life of the asset. Thus the lessor must expect to recover the costs of the asset by renewing the lease or by selling the asset for its residual value.

- Operating leases usually require the lessor to maintain and insure the leased assets.

- Perhaps the most interesting feature of an operating lease is the cancellation option. This option gives the lessee the right to cancel the lease contract before the expiration date. If the option to cancel is exercised, the lessee must return the equipment to the lessor. The value of a cancellation clause depends on whether future technological or economic conditions are likely to make the value of the asset to the lessee less than the value of the future lease payments under the lease.

To leasing practitioners, the preceding characteristics constitute an operating lease. However, accountants use the term in a slightly different way, as we shall see shortly.

## Financial Leases

Financial leases are the exact opposite of operating leases, as seen from their important characteristics:

- Financial leases do not provide for maintenance or service by the lessor.
- Financial leases are fully amortized.
- The lessee usually has a right to renew the lease on expiration.
- Generally, financial leases cannot be cancelled. In other words, the lessee must make all payments or face the risk of bankruptcy.

Because of these characteristics, particularly (2), this lease provides an alternative method of financing to purchase. Hence its name is a sensible one. Two special types of financial lease are the sale and leaseback arrangement and the leveraged lease.

**Sale and Leaseback**    A sale and leaseback occurs when a company sells an asset it owns to another firm and immediately leases it back. In a sale and leaseback two things happen:

1   The lessee receives cash from the sale of the asset.
2   The lessee makes periodic lease payments, thereby retaining use of the asset.

For example, in December 2008 Tesco plc, Britain's largest retailer, made two sale and leaseback deals for seven of its stores. The company sold the stores for £308 million, and at the same time agreed to lease the stores back with periodic payments.

**Leveraged Leases**    A leveraged lease is a three-sided arrangement between the lessee, the lessor, and the lenders:

1   The lessee uses the assets and makes periodic lease payments.
2   The lessor purchases the assets, delivers them to the lessee, and collects the lease payments. However, the lessor puts up no more than 40 to 50 per cent of the purchase price.
3   The lenders supply the remaining financing and receive interest payments from the lessor. Thus the arrangement on the right side of Fig. 21.1 would be a leveraged lease if the bulk of the financing was supplied by creditors.

The lenders in a leveraged lease typically use a non-recourse loan. This means that the lessor is not obligated to the lender in case of a default. However, the lender is protected in two ways:

1   The lender has a first lien on the asset.
2   In the event of loan default, the lease payments are made directly to the lender.

The lessor puts up only part of the funds but gets the lease payments and all the tax benefits of ownership. These lease payments are used to pay the debt service of the non-recourse loan. The lessee benefits because, in a competitive market, the lease payment is lowered when the lessor saves taxes.

## 21.2  Accounting and Leasing

Twenty years ago a firm could arrange to use an asset through a lease and not disclose the asset or the lease contract on the balance sheet. Lessees needed to report information on leasing activity only in the footnotes of their financial statements. Thus leasing led to off-balance-sheet financing. Things have changed significantly in recent years, and leasing now has an accounting standard all to itself: IAS 17 *Leases*.

The International Accounting Standards Board (IASB) recognizes that leases have different characteristics, and this affects how they should be recorded in the financial statements of a firm. The major issue relates to the effective ownership of an asset, the risks and rewards of ownership, and to whom this should be attributed. Specifically, a lease is considered a finance lease if the lessee bears the majority of risks and reward of the asset, whereas it is viewed as an operating lease if the lessor bears the risk.

The accounting treatments of operating and finance leases are very different. In an operating lease, lease payments are treated as expenses and appear in a firm's income statement. In contrast, with a finance lease, the leased asset appears on the balance sheet and is depreciated in the same way as other assets. The value to be recorded in the balance sheet must be the fair or realizable value of the asset or, if lower, the present value of the lease payments. This means that, for all intents and purposes, assets that are funded by a finance lease are regarded in exactly the same way as normal assets in a company, without the need to undertake a substantial capital expenditure to purchase the asset.

Under IAS 17 lessors follow the opposite rule to lessees. This means that if a firm leases out an asset as an operating lease, the lessor has effective ownership of the asset, and it must be recorded in the balance sheet and depreciated accordingly. Similarly, a lessor treats the income from a finance lease as revenue, and it appears in the firm's income statement.

## 21.3 The Cash Flows of Leasing

In this section we identify the basic cash flows used in evaluating a lease. Consider the decision confronting Xomox Ltd, which manufactures long-distance gas pipes. Business has been expanding, and Xomox currently has a five-year backlog of gas pipe orders for a trans-Scandinavian pipeline.

The International Boring Machine Corporation (IBMC) makes a pipe-boring machine that can be purchased for £10,000. Xomox has determined that it needs a new machine, and the IBMC model will save Xomox £6,000 per year in reduced electricity bills for the next five years. These savings are known with certainty, because Xomox has a long-term electricity purchase agreement with UK Electric Utilities plc.

Xomox has an effective corporate tax rate of 28 per cent. We assume that 20 per cent reducing-balance method depreciation is used for the pipe-boring machine, and the machine has no value after five years.[1]

However, Friendly Leasing Corporation has offered to lease the same pipe-boring machine to Xomox for £2,500 per year for five years. With the lease, Xomox would remain responsible for maintenance, insurance and operating expenses.

Simon Smart, a recently hired Masters graduate, has been asked to calculate the incremental cash flows from leasing the IBMC machine in lieu of buying it. He has prepared Table 21.1, which shows the direct cash flow consequences of buying the pipe-boring machine and also signing the lease agreement with Friendly Leasing.

Depreciation is 20 per cent reducing balance. Because the depreciable base is £10,000, depreciation expense and tax benefit (tax rate = 28 per cent) from depreciation per year are calculated as given in Table 21.2. Because the asset has no value at the end of five years, the tax benefit from depreciation is 28 per cent of £4,096 = £1,147.

To simplify matters, Simon Smart has prepared Table 21.3, which subtracts the direct cash flows of buying the pipe-boring machine from those of leasing it. Noting that only the net advantage of leasing is relevant to Xomox, he concludes the following from his analysis:

1   Operating costs are not directly affected by leasing. Xomox will save £3,960 (after taxes) from use of the IBMC boring machine, regardless of whether the machine is owned or leased. Thus this cash flow stream does not appear in Table 21.3.

2   If the machine is leased, Xomox will save the £10,000 it would have used to purchase the machine. This saving shows up as an initial cash *inflow* of £10,000 in year 0.

3   If Xomox leases the pipe-boring machine, it will no longer own this machine, and must give up the depreciation tax benefits. These lost tax benefits show up as an *outflow*.

TABLE
21.1

| | Year 0 (£) | Year 1 (£) | Year 2 (£) | Year 3 (£) | Year 4 (£) | Year 5 (£) |
|---|---|---|---|---|---|---|
| **Buy** | | | | | | |
| Cost of machine | −10,000 | | | | | |
| After-tax operating savings | | 4,320 | 4,320 | 4,320 | 4,320 | 4,320 |
| [£4,320 = £6,000 × (1 − 0.28)] | | | | | | |
| Depreciation tax benefit | | 560 | 448 | 358 | 287 | 1,147 |
| | −10,000 | 4,880 | 4,768 | 4,678 | 4,607 | 5,467 |
| **Lease** | | | | | | |
| Lease payments | | −2,500 | −2,500 | −2,500 | −2,500 | −2,500 |
| Tax benefits of lease payments | | 700 | 700 | 700 | 700 | 700 |
| (£700 = £2,500 × 0.28) | | | | | | |
| After-tax operating savings | | 3,960 | 3,960 | 3,960 | 3,960 | 3,960 |
| **Total** | | 2,160 | 2,160 | 2,160 | 2,160 | 2,160 |

**Table 21.1** Cash flows to Xomox from using the IBMC pipe-boring machine: buy versus lease

TABLE
21.2

| Initial cost (£) | Depreciation (£) | Balance (£) | Tax benefit (£) |
|---|---|---|---|
| 10,000 | 2,000 | 8,000 | 560 |
| | 1,600 | 6,400 | 448 |
| | 1,280 | 5,120 | 358 |
| | 1,024 | 4,096 | 287 |
| | | | 1,147 |

**Table 21.2** Depreciation schedule for asset

4  If Xomox chooses to lease the machine, it must pay £2,500 per year for five years. The first payment is due at the end of the first year. (This is a break: Sometimes the first payment is due immediately.) The lease payments are tax-deductible and, as a consequence, generate tax benefits of £700 (= 0.28 × £2,500).

The net cash flows have been placed in the bottom line of Table 21.3. These numbers represent the cash flows from *leasing* relative to the cash flows from the purchase. It is arbitrary that we express the flows in this way. We could have expressed the cash flows from the *purchase* relative to the cash flows from leasing. These cash flows would look like this:

| | Year 0 | Year 1 | Year 2 | Year 3 | Year 4 | Year 5 |
|---|---|---|---|---|---|---|
| Net cash flows from purchase alternative relative to lease alternative | −£10,000 | £2,360 | £2,248 | £2,158 | £2,087 | £2,947 |

Of course, the cash flows here are the opposite of those in the bottom line of Table 21.3. Depending on our purpose, we may look at either the purchase relative to the lease or vice versa. Thus the student should become comfortable with either viewpoint.

| TABLE 21.3 | | | | | | | |
|---|---|---|---|---|---|---|---|
| **Lease minus buy** | **Year 0 (£)** | **Year 1 (£)** | **Year 2 (£)** | **Year 3 (£)** | **Year 4 (£)** | **Year 5 (£)** |
| **Lease** | | | | | | |
| Lease payment | | −2,500 | −2,500 | −2,500 | −2,500 | −2,500 |
| Tax benefit of lease payment | | 700 | 700 | 700 | 700 | 700 |
| **Buy (minus)** | | | | | | |
| Cost of machine | −(−10,000) | | | | | |
| Lost depreciation tax benefit | | −560 | −448 | −358 | −287 | −1,147 |
| **Total** | 10,000 | −2,360 | −2,248 | −2,158 | −2,087 | −2,947 |

The bottom line presents the cash flows from leasing relative to the cash flows from purchase. The cash flows would be exactly the *opposite* if we considered the purchase relative to the lease.

**Table 21.3** Incremental cash flow consequences for Xomox from leasing instead of purchasing

Now that we have the cash flows, we can make our decision by discounting the flows properly. However, because the discount rate is tricky, we take a detour in the next section before moving back to the Xomox case. In this next section we show that cash flows in the lease-versus-buy decision should be discounted at the *after-tax* interest rate (i.e. the after-tax cost of debt capital).

## 21.4 A Detour for Discounting and Debt Capacity with Corporate Taxes

The analysis of leases is difficult, and both financial practitioners and academics have made conceptual errors. These errors revolve around taxes. We hope to avoid their mistakes by beginning with the simplest type of example: a loan for one year. Though this example is unrelated to our lease-versus-buy situation, principles developed here will apply directly to lease–buy analysis.

### Present Value of Riskless Cash Flows

Consider a corporation that lends €100 for a year. If the interest rate is 10 per cent, the firm will receive €110 at the end of the year. Of this amount, €10 is interest and the remaining €100 is the original principal. A corporate tax rate of 34 per cent implies taxes on the interest of €3.40 (0.34 × €10). Thus the firm ends up with €106.60 (= €110 − €3.40) after taxes on a €100 investment.

Now, consider a company that borrows €100 for a year. With a 10 per cent interest rate, the firm must pay €110 to the bank at the end of the year. However, the borrowing firm can take the €10 of interest as a tax deduction. The corporation pays €3.40 (= 0.34 × €10) less in taxes than it would have paid had it not borrowed the money at all. Thus, considering this reduction in taxes, the firm must pay €106.60 (= €110 − €3.40) on a €100 loan. The cash flows from both lending and borrowing are displayed in Table 21.4.

The previous two paragraphs show a very important result: The firm could not care less whether it receives €100 today or €106.60 next year.[2] If it received €100 today, it could lend it out, thereby receiving €106.60 after corporate taxes at the end of the year. Conversely, if it knows today that it will receive €106.60 at the end of the year, it could borrow €100 today. The after-tax interest and principal payments on the loan would be paid with the €106.60 that the firm will receive at the end of the year. Because of this interchangeability, we say that

**TABLE 21.4**

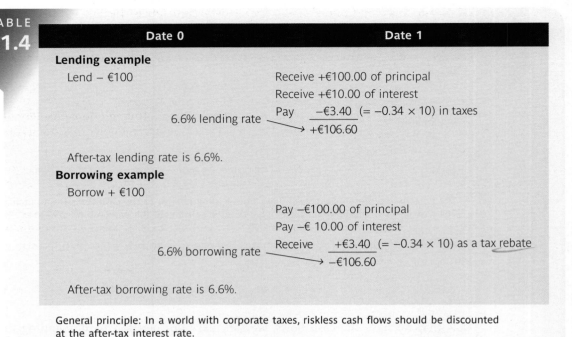

| Date 0 | Date 1 |
|---|---|
| **Lending example** | |
| Lend − €100 | Receive +€100.00 of principal |
| | Receive +€10.00 of interest |
| 6.6% lending rate | Pay     −€3.40  (= −0.34 × 10) in taxes |
| | +€106.60 |
| After-tax lending rate is 6.6%. | |
| **Borrowing example** | |
| Borrow + €100 | |
| | Pay −€100.00 of principal |
| | Pay −€ 10.00 of interest |
| 6.6% borrowing rate | Receive    +€3.40  (= −0.34 × 10) as a tax rebate |
| | −€106.60 |
| After-tax borrowing rate is 6.6%. | |

General principle: In a world with corporate taxes, riskless cash flows should be discounted at the after-tax interest rate.

**Table 21.4** Lending and borrowing in a world with corporate taxes (interest rate is 10 per cent and corporate tax rate is 34 per cent)

a payment of €106.60 next year has a present value of €100. Because €100 = €106.60/1.066, a riskless cash flow should be discounted at the after-tax interest rate of 0.066 [= 0.10 × (1 − 0.34)].

Of course, the preceding discussion considered a specific example. The general principle is this:

**In a world with corporate taxes, the firm should discount riskless cash flows at the after-tax riskless rate of interest.**

## Optimal Debt Level and Riskless Cash Flows

In addition, our simple example can illustrate a related point concerning optimal debt level. Consider a firm that has just determined that the current level of debt in its capital structure is optimal. Immediately following that determination, it is surprised to learn that it will receive a guaranteed payment of €106.60 in one year from, say, a tax-exempt government lottery. This future windfall is an asset that, like any asset, should raise the firm's optimal debt level. How much does this payment raise the firm's optimal level?

Our analysis implies that the firm's optimal debt level must be €100 more than it previously was. That is, the firm could borrow €100 today, perhaps paying the entire amount out as a dividend. It would owe the bank €110 at the end of the year. However, because it receives a tax rebate of €3.40 (= 0.34 × €10), its net repayment will be €106.60. Thus its borrowing of €100 today is fully offset by next year's government lottery proceeds of €106.60. In other words, the lottery proceeds act as an irrevocable trust that can service the increased debt. Note that we need not know the optimal debt level before the lottery was announced. We are merely saying that whatever this pre-lottery optimal level was, the optimal debt level is €100 more after the lottery announcement.

Of course, this is just one example. The general principle is this:[3]

**In a world with corporate taxes, we determine the increase in the firm's optimal debt level by discounting a future guaranteed after-tax inflow at the after-tax riskless interest rate.**

Conversely, suppose that a second, unrelated firm is surprised to learn that it must pay €106.60 next year to the government for back taxes. Clearly, this additional liability impinges on the second firm's debt capacity. By the previous reasoning, it follows that the second firm's optimal debt level must be lowered by exactly €100.

## 21.5 NPV Analysis of the Lease-versus-Buy Decision

Our detour leads to a simple method for evaluating leases: discount all cash flows at the after-tax interest rate. From the bottom line of Table 21.3, Xomox's incremental cash flows from leasing versus purchasing are these:

| | Year 0 | Year 1 | Year 2 | Year 3 | Year 4 | Year 5 |
|---|---|---|---|---|---|---|
| Net cash flows from lease alternative relative to purchase alternative | £10,000 | −£2,360 | −£2,248 | −£2,158 | −£2,087 | −£2,947 |

Let us assume that Xomox can either borrow or lend at the interest rate of 7.8472 per cent. If the corporate tax rate is 28 per cent, the correct discount rate is the after-tax rate of 5.65 per cent [= 7.8472% × (1 − 0.28)]. When 5.65 per cent is used to compute the NPV of the lease, we have

| | Year 0 | Year 1 | Year 2 | Year 3 | Year 4 | Year 5 |
|---|---|---|---|---|---|---|
| Present value of net cash flows from lease alternative relative to purchase alternative | £10000 | −£2,233.79 | −£2,013.99 | −£1,830.30 | −£1,674.89 | −£2,238.80 |

$$\text{NPV} = £10{,}000 - £2{,}233.79 - £2{,}013.99 - £1{,}830.30 - £1{,}674.89 - £2{,}238.80$$
$$= £8.23 \tag{21.1}$$

Because the net present value of the incremental cash flows from leasing relative to purchasing is positive, Xomox prefers to lease the assets.

Equation (21.1) is the correct approach to lease-versus-buy analysis. However, students are often bothered by two things. First, they question whether the cash flows in Table 21.3 are truly riskless. We examine this issue next. Second, they feel that this approach lacks intuition. We address this concern a little later.

### The Discount Rate

Because we discounted at the after-tax riskless rate of interest, we have implicitly assumed that the cash flows in the Xomox example are riskless. Is this appropriate?

A lease payment is like the debt service on a secured bond issued by the lessee, and the discount rate should be approximately the same as the interest rate on such debt. In general, this rate will be slightly higher than the riskless rate considered in the previous section. The various tax shields could be somewhat riskier than the lease payments, for two reasons. First, the value of the depreciation tax benefits depends on the ability of Xomox to generate enough taxable income to use them. Second, the corporate tax rate may change in the future. For these two reasons, a firm might be justified in discounting the depreciation tax benefits at a rate higher than that used for the lease payments. However, our experience is that real-world companies discount both the depreciation shield and lease payments at the same rate. This implies that financial practitioners view these two risks as minor. We adopt the real-world convention of discounting the two flows at the same rate. This rate is the after-tax interest rate on secured debt issued by the lessee.

At this point some students still ask, Why not use $R_{WACC}$ as the discount rate in lease-versus-buy analysis? Of course, $R_{WACC}$ should not be used for lease analysis, because the cash flows are more like debt service cash flows than operating cash flows, and therefore the risk is much less. The discount rate should reflect the risk of the incremental cash flows.

## 21.6 Does Leasing ever Pay? The Base Case

We previously looked at the lease–buy decision from the point of view of the potential lessee, Xomox. Let's now look at the decision from the point of view of the lessor, Friendly Leasing. This firm faces three cash flows, all of which are displayed in Table 21.5. First, Friendly purchases the machine for £10,000 at year 0. Second, because the asset is depreciated reducing balance over five years, the depreciation expense and depreciation tax shield at the end of each of the five years are as follows:

| Initial cost (£) | Depreciation (£) | Balance (£) | Tax benefit (£) |
|---|---|---|---|
| 10,000 | 2,000 | 8,000 | 560 |
| | 1,600 | 6,400 | 448 |
| | 1,280 | 5,120 | 358 |
| | 1,024 | 4,096 | 287 |
| | | | 1,147 |

Third, because the yearly lease payment is £2,500, the after-tax lease payment is £1,800 [= £2,500 × (1 − 0.28)].

Now examine the total cash flows to Friendly Leasing, displayed in the bottom line of Table 21.5. These cash flows are exactly the *opposite* of those of Xomox, displayed in the bottom line of Table 21.3. Those of you with a healthy sense of scepticism may be thinking something interesting: 'If the cash flows of the lessor are exactly the opposite of those of the lessee, the combined cash flow of the two parties must be zero each year. Thus there does not seem to be any joint benefit to this lease. Because the net present value to the lessee was £8.23, the NPV to the lessor must be −£8.23. The joint NPV is £0 (= £8.23 − £8.23). There does not appear to be any way for the NPV of both the lessor and the lessee to be positive at the same time. Because one party would inevitably lose money, the leasing deal could never fly.'

This is one of the most important results of leasing. Though Table 21.5 concerns one particular leasing deal, the principle can be generalized. As long as (a) both parties are subject to the same interest and tax rates and (b) transaction costs are ignored, there can be no leasing deal that benefits both parties. However, there is a lease payment for which both parties would

| TABLE 21.5 | Year 0 (£) | Year 1 (£) | Year 2 (£) | Year 3 (£) | Year 4 (£) | Year 5 (£) |
|---|---|---|---|---|---|---|
| Cash for machine | −10,000 | | | | | |
| Depreciation tax benefit | | 560 | 448 | 358 | 287 | 1,147 |
| After-tax lease payment [£1,800 = £2,500 × (1 − 0.28)] | | 1,800 | 1,800 | 1,800 | 1,800 | 1,800 |
| Total | −10,000 | 2,360 | 2,248 | 2,158 | 2,087 | 2,947 |

**Table 21.5** Cash flows to Friendly Leasing as lessor of IBMC pipe-boring machine

calculate an NPV of zero. Given that fee, Xomox would be indifferent to whether it leased or bought, and Friendly Leasing would be indifferent to whether it leased or not.[4]

A student with an even healthier sense of scepticism might be thinking, 'This textbook appears to be arguing that leasing is not beneficial. Yet we know that leasing occurs frequently in the real world. Maybe, just maybe, the textbook is wrong.' Although we shall not admit to being wrong (what authors would?!), we freely admit that our explanation is incomplete at this point. The next section considers factors that give benefits to leasing.

## 21.7  Reasons for Leasing

Proponents of leasing make many claims about why firms should lease assets rather than buy them. Some of the reasons given to support leasing are good, and some are not. We discuss here the reasons for leasing we think are good, and some of the ones we think are not.

### Good Reasons for Leasing

Leasing is a good choice if at least one of the following is true:

- Taxes may be reduced by leasing.

- The lease contract may reduce certain types of uncertainty.

- Transaction costs can be higher for buying an asset and financing it with debt or equity than for leasing the asset.

**Tax Advantages**  The most important reason for long-term leasing is tax reduction. If the corporate income tax were repealed, long-term leasing would probably disappear. The tax advantages of leasing exist because firms are in different tax brackets.

Should a user be in a low tax bracket purchase, he will receive little tax benefit from depreciation and interest deductions. Should the user lease, the lessor will receive the depreciation shield and the interest deductions. In a competitive market, the lessor must charge a low lease payment to reflect these tax shields. Thus the user is likely to lease rather than purchase.

In our example with Xomox and Friendly Leasing, the value of the lease to Xomox was £8.23. However, the value of the lease to Friendly was exactly the opposite (–£8.23). Because the lessee's gains came at the expense of the lessor, no deal could be arranged.

However, if Friendly Leasing pays no taxes, both Friendly and Xomox will find positive NPV in leasing. The value of the lease to Xomox is still £8.23.

Given a lease payment of £2,500, the cash flows to Friendly Leasing look like this:

|  | Year 0 | Year 1 | Year 2 | Year 3 | Year 4 | Year 5 |
|---|---|---|---|---|---|---|
| Cost of machine | −£10,000 |  |  |  |  |  |
| Lease payment |  | £2,500 | £2,500 | £2,500 | £2,500 | £2,500 |
| Total | −£10,000 | £2,500 | £2,500 | £2,500 | £2,500 | £2,500 |

The value of the lease to Friendly is

$$\text{Value of lease} = -£10,000 - £2,500 \times A^5_{0.0784722}$$
$$= -£10,000 + £10,022.10$$
$$= £22.10$$

Notice that the discount rate is the interest rate of 7.84722 per cent because tax rates are zero. In addition, the full lease payment of £2,500 – and not some lower after-tax number – is used because there are no taxes. Finally, note that depreciation is ignored, also because no taxes apply.

As a consequence of different tax rates, the lessee (Xomox) gains £8.23 and the lessor (Friendly) gains £22.10. Both the lessor and the lessee can gain if their tax rates are different, because the lessee uses the depreciation and interest tax shields that cannot be used by the lessor. The government loses tax revenue, and some of the tax gains to the lessee may be (if so desired) passed on to the lessor in the form of lower lease payments.

Because both parties can gain when tax rates differ, the lease payment is agreed upon through negotiation. Before negotiation begins, each party needs to know the *reservation payment* of both parties. This is the payment that will make one party indifferent to whether it enters the lease deal. In other words, this is the payment that makes the value of the lease zero. These payments are calculated next.

**Reservation Payment of Lessee**  We now solve for $L_{MAX}$, the payment that makes the value of the lease to the lessee zero. When the lessee is in the 28 per cent bracket his cash flows, in terms of $L_{MAX}$, are as follows:

| Lease minus buy | Year 0 (£) | Year 1 (£) | Year 2 (£) | Year 3 (£) | Year 4 (£) | Year 5 (£) |
|---|---|---|---|---|---|---|
| **Lease** | | | | | | |
| Lease payment | | $-L_{MAX}$ | $-L_{MAX}$ | $-L_{MAX}$ | $-L_{MAX}$ | $-L_{MAX}$ |
| Tax benefit of lease payment | | $L_{MAX} \times 0.28$ | $L_{MAX} \times 0.28$ | $L_{MAX} \times 0.28$ | $L_{MAX} \times 0.28$ | $L_{MAX} \times 0.28$ |
| **Buy (minus)** | | | | | | |
| Cost of machine | $-(-10,000)$ | | | | | |
| Lost depreciation tax benefit | | $-560$ | $-448$ | $-358$ | $-287$ | $-1,147$ |
| **Total** | 10,000 | $-L_{MAX}(1-0.28) - 560$ | $-L_{MAX}(1-0.28) - 448$ | $-L_{MAX}(1-0.28) - 358$ | $-L_{MAX}(1-0.28) - 287$ | $-L_{MAX}(1-0.28) - 1,147$ |

The only way to solve for $L_{MAX}$ is through trial and error in a spreadsheet. A solution is presented below:

| Lease minus buy | Year 0 (£) | Year 1 (£) | Year 2 (£) | Year 3 (£) | Year 4 (£) | Year 5 (£) |
|---|---|---|---|---|---|---|
| **Lease** | | | | | | |
| Lease payment | | $-2,503$ | $-2,503$ | $-2,503$ | $-2,503$ | $-2,503$ |
| Tax benefit of lease payment | | 700.84 | 700.84 | 700.84 | 700.84 | 700.84 |
| **Buy (minus)** | | | | | | |
| Cost of machine | 10,000 | | | | | |
| Lost depreciation tax benefit | | $-560$ | $-448$ | $-358.4$ | $-286.72$ | $-1,146.88$ |
| **Total** | 10,000 | $-2,362.16$ | $-2,250.16$ | $-2,160.56$ | $-2,088.88$ | $-2,949.04$ |
| PV(CF) | 10,000 | $-2,235.84$ | $-2,015.93$ | $-1,832.14$ | $-1,676.62$ | $-2,240.44$ |
| NPV(CF) | $-0.96$ | | | | | |

The value of the lease approximately equals zero when $L_{MAX}$ is £2,503.

After performing this calculation, the lessor knows that he will never be able to charge a payment above £2,503.

**Reservation Payment of Lessor**  We now solve for $L_{MIN}$, the payment that makes the value of the lease to the lessor zero. The cash flows to the lessor, in terms of $L_{MIN}$, are these:

| | Year 0 | Year 1 | Year 2 | Year 3 | Year 4 | Year 5 |
|---|---|---|---|---|---|---|
| Cost of machine | $-£10,000$ | | | | | |
| Lease payment | | $L_{MIN}$ | $L_{MIN}$ | $L_{MIN}$ | $L_{MIN}$ | $L_{MIN}$ |

This chart implies that

$$\text{Value of lease} = -£10,000 + L_{MIN} \times A^5_{0.0784722}$$

The value of the lease equals zero when

$$L_{MIN} = \frac{£10,000}{A^5_{0.0784722}}$$
$$= £2,494.49$$

After performing this calculation, the lessee knows that the lessor will never agree to a lease payment below £2,494.49.

**A Reduction of Uncertainty**   We have noted that the lessee does not own the property when an operating lease expires. The value of the property at this time is called the *residual value*, and the lessor has a firm claim to it. When the lease contract is signed, there may be substantial uncertainty about what the residual value of the asset will be. Thus, under a lease contract, this residual risk is borne by the lessor. Conversely, the user bears this risk when purchasing.

It is common sense that the party best able to bear a particular risk should do so. If the user has little risk aversion, she will not suffer by purchasing. However, if the user is highly averse to risk, she should find a third-party lessor more capable of assuming this burden.

This latter situation frequently arises when the user is a small or newly formed firm. Because the risk of the entire firm is likely to be quite high, and because the principal shareholders are likely to be undiversified, the firm desires to minimize risk wherever possible. A potential lessor, such as a large, publicly held financial institution, is far more capable of bearing the risk. Conversely, this situation is not expected to happen when the user is a blue chip corporation. That potential lessee is more able to bear risk.

**Transaction Costs**   The costs of changing an asset's ownership are generally greater than the costs of writing a lease agreement. Consider the choice that confronts a person who lives in Oslo but must do business in London for two days. It will clearly be cheaper to rent a hotel room for two nights than it would be to buy an apartment for two days and then to sell it.

Unfortunately, leases generate agency costs as well. For example, the lessee might misuse or overuse the asset because she has no interest in the asset's residual value. This cost will be implicitly paid by the lessee through a high lease payment. Although the lessor can reduce these agency costs through monitoring, monitoring itself is costly.

Thus leasing is most beneficial when the transaction costs of purchase and resale outweigh the agency and monitoring costs of a lease. Flath argues that this occurs in short-term leases but not in long-term leases.[5]

# Bad Reasons for Leasing

**Leasing and Accounting Income**   In our discussion of accounting and leasing we pointed out that a firm's statement of financial position shows fewer liabilities with an operating lease than with either a finance lease or a purchase financed with debt. We indicated that a firm desiring to project a strong balance sheet might select an operating lease. In addition, the firm's return on assets (ROA) is generally higher with an operating lease than with either a finance lease or a purchase. To see this, we look at the numerator and denominator of the ROA formula in turn.

With an operating lease, lease payments are treated as an expense. If the asset is purchased, both depreciation and interest charges are expenses. At least in the early part of the asset's life, the yearly lease payment is generally less than the sum of yearly depreciation and yearly interest. Thus accounting income, the numerator of the ROA formula, is higher with an operating lease than with a purchase. Because accounting expenses with a finance lease are analogous to depreciation and interest with a purchase, the increase in accounting income does not occur with a finance lease.

In addition, leased assets do not appear on the statement of financial position with an operating lease. Thus the total asset value of a firm, the denominator of the ROA formula, is less with an operating lease than it is with either a purchase or a capitalized lease. The two preceding effects imply that the firm's ROA should be higher with an operating lease than with either a purchase or a finance lease.

| TABLE 21.6 | Assets (€) | | Liabilities (€) | |
|---|---|---|---|---|
| **Initial situation** | | | | |
| Current | 50,000 | | Debt | 60,000 |
| Non-current | 50,000 | | Equity | 40,000 |
| Total | 100,000 | | Total | 100,000 |
| **Buy with secured loan** | | | | |
| Current | 50,000 | | Debt | 66,000 |
| Non-current | 50,000 | | Equity | 44,000 |
| Machine | 10,000 | | Total | 110,000 |
| Total | 110,000 | | | |
| **Lease** | | | | |
| Current | 50,000 | | Lease | 10,000 |
| Non-current | 50,000 | | Debt | 56,000 |
| Machine | 10,000 | | Equity | 44,000 |
| Total | 110,000 | | Total | 110,000 |

This example shows that leases reduce the level of debt elsewhere in the firm. Though the example illustrates a point, it is not meant to show a precise method for calculating debt displacement.

**Table 21.6** Debt displacement elsewhere in the firm when a lease is instituted

Of course, in an efficient capital market, accounting information cannot be used to fool investors. It is unlikely, then, that leasing's impact on accounting numbers should create value for the firm. Savvy investors should be able to see through attempts by management to improve the firm's financial statements.

**One Hundred Per Cent Financing**    It is often claimed that leasing provides 100 per cent financing, whereas secured equipment loans require an initial down payment. However, if a firm has a target debt–equity ratio and follows International Accounting Standards, financial leases will displace debt elsewhere in the firm.

For example, a firm that purchases equipment will generally issue debt to finance the purchase. The debt becomes a liability of the firm. A lessee incurs a liability equal to the present value of all future lease payments. Because of this, we argue that leases displace debt. The statements of financial position in Table 21.6 illustrate how leasing might affect debt.

Suppose a firm initially has €100,000 of assets and a 150 per cent target debt–equity ratio. The firm's debt is €60,000, and its equity is €40,000. As in the Xomox case, suppose the firm must use a new €10,000 machine. The firm has two alternatives:

1   *The firm can purchase the machine.* If it does, it will finance the purchase with a secured loan and with equity. The debt capacity of the machine is assumed to be the same as for the firm as a whole.

2   *The firm can lease the asset and get 100 per cent financing.* That is, the present value of the future lease payments will be €10,000.

If the firm finances the machine with both secured debt and new equity, its debt will increase by €6,000 and its equity by €4,000. Its target debt–equity ratio of 150 per cent will be maintained.

Conversely, consider the lease alternative. Under International Accounting Standards, a finance lease must appear in the statement of financial position. As just mentioned, the present value of the lease liability is €10,000. If the leasing firm is to maintain a debt–equity ratio of 150 per cent, debt elsewhere in the firm must fall by €4,000 when the lease is instituted. Because debt must be repurchased, net liabilities rise by only €6,000 (= €10,000 – €4,000) when €10,000 of assets are placed under lease.

Debt displacement is a hidden cost of leasing. If a firm leases, it will not use as much regular debt as it would otherwise. The benefits of debt capacity will be lost – particularly the lower taxes associated with interest expense.

**Other Reasons**   There are, of course, many special reasons why some companies find advantages in leasing. In one celebrated case, the US Navy leased a fleet of tankers instead of asking Congress for appropriations. Thus leasing may be used to circumvent capital expenditure control systems set up by bureaucratic firms.

## 21.8  Some Unanswered Questions about Leasing

Our analysis suggests that the primary advantage of long-term leasing results from the differential tax rates of the lessor and the lessee. Other valid reasons for leasing are lower contracting costs and risk reduction. There are several questions our analysis has not specifically answered.

### Are the Uses of Leases and Debt Complementary?

Ang and Peterson find that firms with high debt tend to lease frequently as well.[6] This result should not be puzzling. The corporate attributes that provide high debt capacity may also make leasing advantageous. Thus, even though leasing displaces debt (that is, leasing and borrowing are substitutes) for an individual firm, high debt and high leasing can be positively associated when we look at a number of firms.

### Why Are Leases Offered by both Manufacturers and Third-Party Lessors?

The offsetting effects of taxes can explain why both manufacturers (for example, computer firms) and third-party lessors offer leases.

- For manufacturer lessors, the basis for determining depreciation is the manufacturer's cost. For third-party lessors, the basis is the sales price that the lessor paid to the manufacturer. Because the sales price is generally greater than the manufacturer's cost, this is an advantage to third-party lessors.

- However, the manufacturer must recognize a profit for tax purposes when selling the asset to the third-party lessor. The manufacturer's profit for some equipment can be deferred if the manufacturer becomes the lessor. This provides an incentive for manufacturers to lease.

**Why Are some Assets Leased more than Others?**   Certain assets appear to be leased more frequently than others. Smith and Wakeman have looked at non-tax incentives that affect leasing.[7] Their analysis suggests many asset and firm characteristics that are important in the lease-or-buy decision. The following are among the things they mention:

- The more sensitive the value of an asset is to usage and maintenance decisions, the more likely it is that the asset will be purchased instead of leased. They argue that ownership provides a better incentive to minimize maintenance costs than does leasing.

- Price discrimination opportunities may be important. Leasing may be a way of circumventing laws against charging too *low* a price.

## Are the Reasons for Leasing Different across Firms?

At different stages in a company's life cycle, there are changing pressures and opportunities facing management. For example, small firms that are growing quickly find it difficult to regularly source new debt financing. In contrast, large established firms find it significantly easier to go to the debt markets or banks to arrange debt. Lasfer and Levis show that smaller firms use leases because they are unable to get other forms of debt, whereas larger firms use debt and leasing interchangeably.[8] They also find that large lessee firms are significantly more profitable than small lessee firms, suggesting that leases are used as a complement to debt in large firms, whereas they are a substitute for debt in small firms.

Lasfer and Levis's findings are supported by the recent work of Eisfeldt and Rampini,[9] who argue that leasing enhances debt capacity more than secured lending or debt. Because smaller firms are financially constrained, they value the debt capacity provided by leases, and hence lease more than larger firms.

## 21.9 Special-Purpose Vehicles

One of the biggest growth sectors in corporate finance in the 21st century has been the use of special-purpose vehicles (SPVs). An SPV is a company that is specifically formed to undertake a particular objective. The major benefit of SPVs is that they allow firms to transfer significant risks off their own balance sheet onto that of the newly created SPV.

To avoid accounting regulations regarding the consolidation of financial accounts, most SPVs are not owned by the parent or sponsoring firm. This is achieved by the sponsoring firm setting up another offshore firm whose shares are held by a trustee or charitable trust and, in effect, not owned by anyone. To ensure that the SPV firm is not connected in any legal way to the sponsoring firm, an administration company is hired to manage the SPV's assets.

Special-purpose vehicles are not just used to undertake off-balance-sheet financing. However, a strong reason for them is that they allow firms to increase the effective level of debt capacity without it showing up on the balance sheet. When a firm (the sponsor) creates an SPV, it transfers risky assets and liabilities to the new company. Given that the assets are no longer in the sponsoring firm, they do not appear on its balance sheet.

Moreover, because SPVs are separate legal entities and operate without the assistance of the parent, they do not use the same credit facilities or financing channels as the sponsoring firm. An SPV is able to issue its own debt and, if the new firm has been given enough cash from the sponsor, it can achieve a higher credit rating than the sponsor, reducing the overall cost of capital.

Until 2007, SPVs were very active in the securitization industry. Securitization involves packaging assets, such as car loans, mortgages and credit card loans, and selling these on to investors. So, for example, a bank could transfer its subprime mortgage portfolio to an SPV; the SPV would repackage the portfolio, and issue a security to investors with the repackaged subprime mortgage portfolio as collateral for the loan. The SPV is secure because the assets are perfectly aligned with liabilities. This perfect form of off-balance-sheet financing allowed banks to transfer risky mortgage assets off their balance sheets and make more loans because they had less risk. The use of SPVs therefore allowed banks to avoid regulatory scrutiny of their capital adequacy ratios, and under-represented the level of debt the bank actually bore.

Special-purpose vehicles have been correctly identified as one of the contributors to the global credit crunch of 2007, and the resulting worldwide recession that followed it. As a result, accounting standard-setters such as the International Accounting Standards Board (IASB) have made accounting for SPVs a priority. In late 2008 they issued a consultative document on consolidated financial accounts, the basis for which will form a new revised standard in 2009 or 2010. The new accounting standard will require the following disclosures:

1   Information on who actually controls the SPV, and the accounting consequences that arise from it.

2   Information on the financial interest that the sponsor has in the SPV's activities.

3    Information about restrictions on assets and liabilities held in subsidiaries, including the claims of non-controlling interests.

4    Information about any unconsolidated structured entities (SPVs) that the reporting entity does not control, but with which the reporting entity has involvement.

With these new accounting regulations, it is highly likely that SPVs will become less popular with banks and other industrial companies, especially if the reason for setting them up was to do with off-balance-sheet financing.

Another reason for setting up SPVs is because of Islamic financing (Chapter 20). Specifically, this is known as *sukuk*, and allows a firm that is being run on Islamic principles to avoid the use of interest payments and receipts.

## Summary and Conclusions

Off-balance-sheet financing has become a major issue for most of the world's corporations. While many may see off-balance-sheet financing as a bad thing, it has many positive characteristics. In particular, leasing can help firms increase debt capacity when they would otherwise be financially constrained. A large fraction of the corporate world's equipment is leased rather than purchased. This chapter both described the institutional arrangements surrounding leases and showed how to evaluate leases financially. It also examined special-purpose vehicles and how they can be used to shift risk off a company's balance sheet.

1    Leases can be separated into two polar types. Though operating leases allow the lessee to use the equipment, ownership remains with the lessor. Although the lessor in a financial lease legally owns the equipment, the lessee maintains effective ownership, because financial leases are fully amortized.

2    When a firm purchases an asset with debt, both the asset and the liability appear on the firm's balance sheet. If a lease meets at least one of a number of criteria, it must be capitalized. This means that the present value of the lease appears as both an asset and a liability. A lease escapes capitalization if it does not meet any of these criteria. Leases not meeting the criteria are called *operating leases*, though the accountant's definition differs somewhat from the practitioner's definition. Operating leases do not appear on the statement of financial position (balance sheet). For cosmetic reasons, many firms prefer that a lease be called *operating*.

3    Firms generally lease for tax purposes. To protect their interests, tax authorities allow financial arrangements to be classified as leases only if a number of criteria are met.

4    We showed that risk-free cash flows should be discounted at the after-tax risk-free rate. Because both lease payments and depreciation tax shields are nearly riskless, all relevant cash flows in the lease–buy decision should be discounted at a rate near this after-tax rate. We use the real-world convention of discounting at the after-tax interest rate on the lessee's secured debt.

5    If the lessor is in the same tax bracket as the lessee, the cash flows to the lessor are exactly the opposite of the cash flows to the lessee. Thus the sum of the value of the lease to the lessee plus the value of the lease to the lessor must be zero. Although this suggests that leases can never fly, there are actually at least three good reasons for leasing:

    (a)    Differences in tax brackets between lessor and lessee

    (b)    Shift of risk bearing to the lessor

    (c)    Minimization of transaction costs.

We also documented a number of bad reasons for leasing.

# Questions and Problems

**CONCEPT**
**1 – 9**

1   **Types of Lease Financing**   Review the different types of lease financing that are available to firms.

2   **Accounting and Leasing**   Why has leasing been viewed as off-balance-sheet funding when it appears in the financial statements? Is this term now a misnomer? Explain.

3   **The Cash Flows of Leasing**   If you did not have the financing to purchase an asset, would you compare it with the buy decision in your leasing analysis? Explain.

4   **Discounting and Taxes**   In a world with taxes, what is the appropriate discount rate when evaluating a lease? Explain.

5   **NPV Analysis of the Lease-versus-Buy Decision**   Why is WACC not appropriate for discounting cash flows in a lease-versus-buy decision?

6   **Does Leasing ever Pay?**   If the cash flows to the lessee are exactly the opposite of the cash flows to the lessor, why does leasing exist in practice? Explain, using an example.

7   **Reasons for Leasing**   Review the reasons why firms undertake leasing. Explain why some of these reasons are not beneficial for shareholders.

8   **Unanswered Questions**   Why do some firms lease and others do not? What are some of the reasons why firms may or may not lease?

9   **Special-Purpose Vehicles**   Explain what is meant by an SPV and how it is structured. What are the main criticisms of SPVs?

**REGULAR**
**10 – 24**

10   **Accounting for Leases**   Discuss the accounting criteria for determining whether a lease must be reported in the statement of financial position. In each case, give a rationale for the criterion.

11   **Accounting for Off-Balance-Sheet Items**   Discuss the IASB proposals for consolidating SPV accounts with sponsor accounts. Give a rationale for why this is required and why it has not been addressed until recently.

12   **Sale and Leaseback**   Why might a firm choose to engage in a sale and leaseback transaction? Give two reasons.

Use the following information to solve Problems 13–17. You work for a nuclear research laboratory that is contemplating leasing a diagnostic scanner (leasing is a common practice with expensive, high-tech equipment). The scanner costs £3,000,000, and it would be depreciated 20 per cent reducing balance. At the end of four years, the scanner will have zero value. You can lease it for £895,000 per year for four years.

13   **Lease or Buy**   Assume that the tax rate is 28 per cent. You can borrow at 8 per cent before taxes. Should you lease or buy?

14   **Leasing Cash Flows**   What are the cash flows from the lease from the lessor's viewpoint? Assume a 28 per cent tax bracket.

15   **Finding the Break-Even Payment**   What would the lease payment have to be for both lessor and lessee to be indifferent about the lease?

16   **Taxes and Leasing Cash Flows**   Assume that your company does not contemplate paying taxes for the next several years. What are the cash flows from leasing in this case?

17   **Setting the Lease Payment**   In the previous question, over what range of lease payments will the lease be profitable for both parties?

18   **Lease or Buy**   Super Sonics Entertainment is considering buying a machine that costs NKr3,500,000. The machine will be depreciated using the 20 per cent reducing-balance method. At the end of five years it will be sold at its accounting residual value. The company can lease the machine with year-end payments of NKr942,000. The company can issue bonds at a 9 per cent interest rate. If the corporate tax rate is 28 per cent, should the company buy or lease?

Use the following information to solve Problems 19–21. The Wildcat Oil Company is trying to decide whether to lease or buy a new computer-assisted drilling system for its oil exploration business. Management has decided that it must use the system to stay competitive; it will provide £700,000 in annual pre-tax cost savings. The system costs £6 million and will be depreciated at 20 per cent reducing-balance method. At the end of five years, it will have no value. Wildcat's tax rate is 28 per cent, and the firm can borrow at 9 per cent. Lambert Leasing Company has offered to lease the drilling equipment to Wildcat for payments of £1,400,000 per year. Lambert's policy is to require its lessees to make payments at the start of the year.

19 **Lease or Buy**   What is the NPV of the lease to Wildcat? (This is also known as the Net Advantage to Leasing, NAL.) What is the maximum lease payment that would be acceptable to the company?

20 **Leasing and Salvage Value**   Suppose it is estimated that the equipment will have an after-tax residual value of £500,000 at the end of the lease. What is the maximum lease payment acceptable to Wildcat now?

21 **Deposits in Leasing**   Many lessors require a security deposit in the form of a cash payment or other pledged collateral. Suppose Lambert requires Wildcat to pay a £200,000 security deposit at the inception of the lease. If the lease payment is still £1,400,000, is it advantageous for Wildcat to lease the equipment now?

22 **Setting the Lease Price**   Raymond Rayon Corporation wants to expand its manufacturing facilities. Liberty Leasing Corporation has offered Raymond Rayon the opportunity to lease a machine for $1,500,000 for six years. The machine will be fully depreciated by the straight-line method. The corporate tax rate for Raymond Rayon is 25 per cent, whereas Liberty Leasing has a corporate tax rate of 40 per cent. Both companies can borrow at 8 per cent. Assume lease payments occur at year-end. What is Raymond's reservation price? What is Liberty's reservation price?

23 **Setting the Lease Price**   An asset costs £360,000 and will be depreciated in a straight-line manner over its three-year life. It will have no salvage value. The corporate tax rate is 34 per cent, and the appropriate interest rate is 10 per cent.

(a)   What set of lease payments will make the lessee and the lessor equally well off?

(b)   Show the general condition that will make the value of a lease to the lessor the negative of the value to the lessee.

(c)   Assume that the lessee pays no taxes and the lessor is in the 34 per cent tax bracket. For what range of lease payments does the lease have a positive NPV for both parties?

24 **Lease or Buy**   Wolfson plc has decided to purchase a new machine that costs £4.2 million. The machine will be depreciated on a 20 per cent reducing balance basis and will be worth nothing at the end of four years. The corporate tax rate is 28 per cent. The Sur Bank has offered Wolfson a four-year loan for £4.2 million. The repayment schedule is four yearly principal repayments of £1.05 million and an interest charge of 9 per cent on the outstanding balance of the loan at the beginning of each year. Both principal repayments and interest are due at the end of each year. Cal Leasing Corporation offers to lease the same machine to Wolfson. Lease payments of £1.2 million per year are due at the beginning of each of the four years of the lease.

(a)   Should Wolfson lease the machine or buy it with bank financing?

(b)   What is the annual lease payment that will make Wolfson indifferent to whether it leases the machine or purchases it?

25 **Lease versus Borrow**   Return to the case of the diagnostic scanner discussed in Problems 13–17. Suppose the entire £3,000,000 purchase price of the scanner is borrowed. The rate on the loan is 8 per cent, and the loan will be repaid in equal instalments. Create a lease-versus-buy analysis that explicitly incorporates the loan payments. Show that the NPV of leasing instead of buying is not changed from what it was in Problem 13. Why is this so?

26 **Lease or Buy** High electricity costs have made Farmer Corporation's chicken-plucking machine economically worthless. Only two machines are available to replace it. The International Plucking Machine (IPM) model is available only on a lease basis. The lease payments will be £2,100 for five years, due at the beginning of the year. This machine will save Farmer £6,000 per year through reductions in electricity costs in every year. As an alternative, Farmer can purchase a more energy-efficient machine from Basic Machine Corporation (BMC) for £15,000. This machine will save £9,000 per year in electricity costs. A local bank has offered to finance the machine with a £15,000 loan. The interest rate on the loan will be 10 per cent on the remaining balance, and five annual principal payments of £3,000. Farmer has a target debt-to-asset ratio of 67 per cent. Farmer has a corporation tax rate of 28 per cent. After five years, both machines will be worth nothing. The depreciation method is 20 per cent reducing-balance method and the asset will be worthless after 5 years.

(a) Should Farmer lease the IPM machine or purchase the more efficient BMC machine?

(b) Does your answer depend on the form of financing for direct purchase?

(c) How much debt is displaced by this lease?

---

| MINI CASE | # The Decision to Lease or Buy at Warf Computers |
|---|---|

Warf Computers has decided to proceed with the manufacture and distribution of the virtual keyboard (VK) the company has developed. To undertake this venture, the company needs to obtain equipment for the production of the microphone for the keyboard. Because of the required sensitivity of the microphone and its small size, the company needs specialized equipment for production.

Nick Warf, the company president, has found a vendor for the equipment. Clapton Acoustical Equipment has offered to sell Warf Computers the necessary equipment at a price of £5 million. The equipment will be depreciated using the 20 per cent reducing-balance method. At the end of four years the market value of the equipment is expected to be £600,000.

Alternatively, the company can lease the equipment from Hendrix Leasing. The lease contract calls for four annual payments of £1.3 million, due at the beginning of each year. Additionally, Warf Computers must make a security deposit of £300,000 that will be returned when the lease expires. Warf Computers can issue bonds with a yield of 11 per cent, and the company has a marginal tax rate of 28 per cent.

1 Should Warf buy or lease the equipment?

2 Nick mentions to James Hendrix, the president of Hendrix Leasing, that although the company will need the equipment for four years, he would like a lease contract for two years instead. At the end of the two years, the lease could be renewed. Nick would also like to eliminate the security deposit, but he would be willing to increase the lease payments to £2.3 million for each of the two years. When the lease is renewed in two years, Hendrix would consider the increased lease payments in the first two years when calculating the terms of the renewal. The equipment is expected to have a market value of £2 million in two years. What is the NAL of the lease contract under these terms? Why might Nick prefer this lease? What are the potential ethical issues concerning the new lease terms?

3 In the leasing discussion, James informs Nick that the contract could include a purchase option for the equipment at the end of the lease. Hendrix Leasing offers three purchase options:

(a) An option to purchase the equipment at the fair market value.

(b) An option to purchase the equipment at a fixed price. The price will be negotiated before the lease is signed.

(c) An option to purchase the equipment at a price of £250,000.

How would the inclusion of a purchase option affect the value of the lease?

4   James also informs Nick that the lease contract can include a cancellation option. The cancellation option would allow Warf Computers to cancel the lease on any anniversary date of the contract. In order to cancel the lease, Warf Computers would be required to give 30 days' notice prior to the anniversary date. How would the inclusion of a cancellation option affect the value of the lease?

## Practical Case Study

Download the financial accounts of five companies in your country. Look for information on special-purpose vehicles, operating leases, financial leases, and sale and leasebacks. In each case, decide whether the financing is long-term or short-term and how it affects the debt to equity ratio of each firm. Do you see evidence that leasing is used as a substitute for debt? Alternatively, is it used as a complement to debt? A reading of Yan (2006) may help for this case study. Write a brief report on your findings.

## Relevant Accounting Standards

Because of its importance, leasing has an accounting standard all to itself, titled IAS17 *Leasing*. Off-balance-sheet financing has received a lot of attention because of the role of SPVs in the global banking crisis in 2008, and accounting standards pertaining to off-balance-sheet financing are being actively considered by the International Accounting Standards Board. The relevant standard is IAS27 *Consolidated and Separate Financial Statements*. However, expect to see major changes in this standard, or even a complete replacement, in the next few years. Another standard that is important for special-purpose vehicles is IAS24 *Related Party Disclosures*. IAS23 *Borrowing Costs* is of interest because it deals with financial leases.

## Additional Reading

The following papers are of interest:

Gronlund, T., A. Louko and M. Vaihekoski (2008) 'Corporate real estate sale and leaseback effect: empirical evidence from Europe', *European Financial Management*, vol. 14, no. 4, pp. 820–843. **Europe**.

Yan, A. (2006) 'Leasing and debt financing: substitutes or complements?', *Journal of Financial and Quantitative Analysis*, vol. 41, no. 3, pp. 709–731. **US**.

## Endnotes

1   For simplicity, we have assumed that lease payments are made at the end of each year. Actually, most leases require lease payments to be made at the beginning of the year.

2   For simplicity, assume that the firm received €100 or €106.60 *after* corporate taxes. Because $0.66 = 1 - 0.34$, the pre-tax inflows would be €151.52 (€100/0.66) and €161.52 (€106.60/0.66), respectively.

3   This principle holds for riskless or guaranteed cash flows only. Unfortunately, there is no easy formula for determining the increase in optimal debt level from a *risky* cash flow.

4   The last line of Table 21.3 presents the cash flows from the lease alternative relative to the purchase alternative. As pointed out earlier, our cash flows are now reversed, because we are now presenting the cash flows from the purchase alternative relative to the lease alternative.

5   D. Flath, 'The economics of short-term leasing', *Economic Inquiry*, vol. 18 (April 1980).

6   J. Ang and P.P. Peterson, 'The leasing puzzle', *Journal of Finance*, vol. 39 (September 1984).

7   C.W. Smith Jr and L.M. Wakeman, 'Determinants of corporate leasing policy', *Journal of Finance* (July 1985).

8   M. Lasfer and M. Levis (1998) 'The determinants of the leasing decision of small and large companies', *European Financial Management*, vol. 4, no. 2, pp. 159–184.

9   A.L. Eisfeldt and A.A. Rampini (2009) 'Leasing, ability to repossess, and debt capacity', *Review of Financial Studies* (forthcoming).

To help you grasp the key concepts of this chapter check out the extra resources posted on the Online Learning Centre at **www.mcgraw-hill.co.uk/textbooks/hillier**

Among other helpful resources there are PowerPoint presentations, chapter outlines and mini-cases.

# Chapter 22

# Options and Corporate Finance: Concepts

On 31 December 2008 the closing share prices for the British companies Experian and Smith & Nephew were £4.32 and £4.385, respectively. Each company had a call option trading on Euronext Liffe with a £4.40 strike price and an expiration date of 31 March 2009. You might expect that the prices on these call options would be similar, but they weren't. The Experian options sold for £0.5349 and Smith & Nephew options traded at £0.4253. Why did these options, which for all intents and purposes had exactly the same terms, have an £0.11 price difference when the share prices differed by £0.06? A big reason is that the volatility of the underlying shares is an important determinant of an option's underlying value; and, in fact, these two equities had very different volatilities. In this chapter we explore this issue – and many others – in much greater depth using the Nobel-Prize-winning Black–Scholes option pricing model.

## 22.1 Options

An **option** is a contract giving its owner the right to buy or sell an asset at a fixed price on or before a given date. For example, an option on a building might give the buyer the right to buy the building for €1 million on or any time before the Saturday prior to the third Wednesday in January 2014. Options are a unique type of financial contract, because they give the buyer the right, but not the *obligation*, to do something. The buyer uses the option only if it is advantageous to do so; otherwise the option can be thrown away.

There is a special vocabulary associated with options. Here are some important definitions:

- *Exercising the option*: The act of buying or selling the underlying asset via the option contract.

- *Strike or exercise price*: The fixed price in the option contract at which the holder can buy or sell the underlying asset.

- *Expiration date*: The maturity date of the option; after this date, the option is dead.

- *American and European options*: An American option may be exercised any time up to the expiration date. A European option differs from an American option in that it can be exercised only on the expiration date.

## 22.2 Call Options

The most common type of option is a **call option**. A call option gives the owner the right to buy an asset at a fixed price during a particular period. There is no restriction on the kind of asset, but the most common ones traded on exchanges are options on shares and bonds.

For example, call options on Associated British Foods plc shares can be purchased on Euronext Liffe. Associated British Foods does not issue (that is, sell) call options on its equity. Instead, individual investors are the original buyers and sellers of call options on Associated British Foods equity. A representative call option on Associated British Foods equity enables an investor to buy 100 shares of Associated British Foods on or before 15 July at an exercise price of £7.00. This is a valuable option if there is some probability that the share price of Associated British Foods will exceed £7.00 on or before 15 July.

## The Value of a Call Option at Expiration

What is the value of a call option contract on equity at expiration? The answer depends on the value of the underlying shares at expiration.

Let's continue with the Associated British Foods example. Suppose the share price is £8.00 at expiration. The buyer[1] of the call option has the right to buy the underlying shares at the exercise price of £7.00. In other words, he has the right to exercise the call. Having the right to buy something for £7.00 when it is worth £8.00 is obviously a good thing. The value of this right is £1.00 (= £8.00 − £7.00) on the expiration day.[2]

The call would be worth even more if the share price were higher on expiration day. For example, if Associated British Foods were selling for £8.50 on the date of expiration, the call would be worth £1.50 (= £8.50 − £7.00) at that time. In fact, the call's value increases by £1 for every £1 rise in the share price.

If the share price is greater than the exercise price, we say that the call is *in the money*. Of course, it is also possible that the value of the equity will turn out to be less than the exercise price, in which case we say that the call is *out of the money*. The holder will not exercise in this case. For example, if the share price at the expiration date is £6.00, no rational investor would exercise. Why pay £7.00 for shares worth only £6.00? Because the option holder has no obligation to exercise the call, she can *walk away* from the option. As a consequence, if Associated British Food's share price is less than £7.00 on the expiration date, the value of the call option will be £0. In this case, the value of the call option is not the difference between Associated British Food's share price and £7.00, as it would be if the holder of the call option had the *obligation* to exercise the call.

Here is the pay-off of this call option at expiration:

| | Pay-off on the expiration date | |
|---|---|---|
| | **If share price is less than £7.00** | **If share price is greater than £7.00** |
| Call option value | £0 | Share price − £7.00 |

Figure 22.1 plots the value of the call at expiration against the value of Associated British Foods' equity. This is referred to as the *hockey stick diagram* of call option values. If the share

**Figure 22.1** The value of a call option on the expiration date

price is less than £7.00, the call is out of the money and worthless. If the share price is greater than £7.00, the call is in the money and its value rises one-for-one with increases in the share price. Notice that the call can never have a negative value. It is *a limited liability instrument*, which means that all the holder can lose is the initial amount she paid for it.

### EXAMPLE 22.1

## Call Option Pay-Offs

Suppose Mr Optimist holds a one-year call option on equity of the Belgian imaging and IT company Agfa-Gevaert. It is a European call option and can be exercised at €1.80.

Assume that the expiration date has arrived. What is the value of the Agfa-Gevaert call option on the expiration date? If Agfa-Gevaert is selling for €2.00 per share, Mr Optimist can exercise the option – purchase Agfa-Gevaert at £1.80 – and then immediately sell the share at €2.00. Mr Optimist will have made €0.20 (= €2.00 – €1.80). Thus the price of this call option must be €0.20 at expiration.

Instead, assume that Agfa-Gevaert is selling for €1.00 per share on the expiration date. If Mr Optimist still holds the call option, he will throw it out. The value of the Agfa-Gevaert call on the expiration date will be zero in this case.

## 22.3 Put Options

A **put option** can be viewed as the opposite of a call option. Just as a call gives the holder the right to buy the share at a fixed price, a put gives the holder the right to *sell* the share for a fixed exercise price.

### The Value of a Put Option at Expiration

The circumstances that determine the value of the put are the opposite of those for a call option, because a put option gives the holder the right to sell shares. Let us assume that the exercise price of the put is £50 and the share price at expiration is £40. The owner of this put option has the right to sell the share for *more* than it is worth, something that is clearly profitable. That is, he can buy the share at the market price of £40 and immediately sell it at the exercise price of £50, generating a profit of £10 (= £50 – £40). Thus the value of the option at expiration must be £10.

The profit would be greater still if the share price were lower. For example, if the share price were only £30, the value of the option would be £20 (= £50 – £30). In fact, for every £1 by which the share price declines at expiration, the value of the put rises by £1.

However, suppose that the equity at expiration is trading at £60 – or any price above the exercise price of £50. The owner of the put would not want to exercise here. It is a losing proposition to sell shares for £50 when they trade in the open market at £60. Instead, the owner of the put will walk away from the option. That is, he will let the put option expire.

Here is the pay-off of this put option:

|  | Pay-off on the expiration date | |
| --- | --- | --- |
|  | If share price is less than £50 | If share price is greater than £50 |
| Put option value | £50 − Share price | £0 |

Figure 22.2 plots the values of a put option for all possible values of the underlying equity. It is instructive to compare Fig. 22.2 with Fig. 22.1 for the call option. The call option is valuable when the share price is above the exercise price, and the put is valuable when the share price is below the exercise price.

A put option gives the owner the right to sell an asset at a fixed price during a particular period. If the share price is greater than the exercise price of £50, the put value is zero. If the share price is less than £50, the put value is:

£50 − Share price

**Figure 22.2** The value of a put option on the expiration date

## EXAMPLE 22.2

### Put Option Pay-Offs

Ms Pessimist believes that the German healthcare firm Bayer AG will fall from its current €42.00 share price. She buys a put. Her put option contract gives the right to sell a share of Bayer equity at €42.00 one year from now. If the price of Bayer is €44.00 on the expiration date, she will tear up the put option contract, because it is worthless. That is, she will not want to sell shares worth €44.00 for the exercise price of €42.00.

On the other hand, if Bayer is selling for €40.00 on the expiration date, she will exercise the option. In this case she can buy a share of Bayer in the market for €40.00 and turn around and sell the share at the exercise price of €42.00. Her profit will be €2.00 (= €42.00 − €40.00). The value of the put option on the expiration date therefore will be €2.00.

## 22.4 Writing Options

An investor who sells (or writes) a call on equity must deliver shares of the equity if required to do so by the call option holder. Notice that the seller is obligated to do so.

If, at expiration date, the price of the equity is greater than the exercise price, the holder will exercise the call, and the seller must give the holder shares of equity in exchange for the exercise price. The seller loses the difference between the share price and the exercise price. For example, assume that the share price is £60 and the exercise price is £50. Knowing that exercise is imminent, the option seller buys equity in the open market at £60. Because she is obligated to sell at £50, she loses £10 (= £50 − £60). Conversely, if at the expiration date the price of the equity is below the exercise price, the call option will not be exercised and the seller's liability is zero.

Why would the seller of a call place herself in such a precarious position? After all, the seller loses money if the share price ends up above the exercise price, and she merely avoids losing money if the share price ends up below the exercise price. The answer is that the seller is paid to take this risk. On the day that the option transaction takes place, the seller receives the price that the buyer pays.

Now let's look at the seller of puts. An investor who sells a put on equity agrees to purchase shares of equity if the put holder should so request. The seller loses on this deal if the share price falls below the exercise price. For example, assume that the share price is £40 and the exercise price is £50. The holder of the put will exercise in this case. In other words, she will sell the underlying share at the exercise price of £50. This means that the seller of the put must buy the underlying equity at the exercise price of £50. Because each share is worth only £40, the loss here is £10 (= £40 − £50).

**Figure 22.3** The payoffs to sellers of calls and puts and to buyers of equity

The values of the 'sell-a-call' and 'sell-a-put' positions are depicted in Fig. 22.3. The graph on the left side of the figure shows that the seller of a call loses nothing when the share price at expiration date is below £50. However, the seller loses a pound for every pound that the share price rises above £50. The graph in the centre of the figure shows that the seller of a put loses nothing when the share price at expiration date is above £50. However, the seller loses a pound for every pound that the share price falls below £50.

It is worth while to spend a few minutes comparing the graphs in Fig. 22.3 with those in Figs 22.1 and 22.2. The graph of selling a call (the graph in the left side of Fig. 22.3) is the mirror image of the graph of buying a call (Fig. 22.1).[3] This occurs because options are a zero-sum game. The seller of a call loses what the buyer makes. Similarly, the graph of selling a put (the middle graph in Fig. 22.3) is the mirror image of the graph of buying a put (Fig. 22.2). Again, the seller of a put loses what the buyer makes.

Figure 22.3 also shows the value at expiration of simply buying equity. Notice that buying the share is the same as buying a call option on the share with an exercise price of zero. This is not surprising. If the exercise price is zero, the call holder can buy the share for nothing, which is really the same as owning it.

## 22.5 Option Quotes

Now that we understand the definitions for calls and puts, let's see how these options are quoted. Table 22.1 presents information, obtained from the NYSE Euronext website (www.euronext.com), about Air France-KLM options expiring in March 2009. At the time of these quotes, Air France-KLM was selling for €9.19.

There are three boxes in Table 22.1. The first relates to the option contract, and it can be seen that Air France-KLM's option ticker is AFA, is denominated in euros, and is of American type (that is, it can be exercised before the expiration date). Each option contract relates to purchasing 100 shares. On 31 December 2008 the last transaction involved 24 contracts, and the total number of contracts outstanding on 30 December 2008 was 9,182.

The second box relates to the underlying asset, which is Air France-KLM equity. This is traded on Euronext Amsterdam and is denominated in euros. There were 4,301 shares traded in the equity on 31 December 2008, and the closing price was €9.19. Other price information, such as high and low price, is also presented.

The final box provides information on individual call and put contracts. Only the March 2009, €8.00 put contract was traded on 31 December 2008. Fast-forward three months and the share price of Air France-KLM was just over €6 – a profit of nearly €2 per contract for the €8 March put holder!

TABLE
**22.1**

| Codes and classification | | | | | | | |
|---|---|---|---|---|---|---|---|
| **Code** | AFA | **Market** | Liffe Amsterdam | **Vol.** | | 24 | 31/12/08 |
| **Exercise type** | American | **Currency** | € | **O.I.** | | 9,182 | 30/12/08 |

| Underlying | | | | | | |
|---|---|---|---|---|---|---|
| **Name** | AIR FRANCE-KLM | **ISIN** | FR0000031122 | **Market** | Euronext Amsterdam | |
| **Currency** | € | **Best bid** | 9.01   31/12/08 14:00 | **Best ask** | 9.59 | 31/12/08 14:00 |
| **Time** | CET | **Last** | 9.19   31/12/08 14:00 | **Last change** | −1.61 | |
| **Volume** | 4,301 | **High** | 9.55 | **Low** | 9.19 | |

**March 2009 prices – 31/12/08**

| | Calls | | | | | | | | Puts | | | | | |
|---|---|---|---|---|---|---|---|---|---|---|---|---|---|---|
| Settl. | Day volume | Vol | Time (CET) | Last | Bid | Ask | C | Strike | P | Bid | Ask | Last | Time (CET) | Vol | Day volume | Settl. |
| 1.75 | – | – | – | – | 1.70 | 1.85 | **C** | **8** | **P** | 0.40 | 0.50 | 0.45 | 12:07 | 10 | 20 | 0.45 |
| 1.25 | – | – | – | – | 1.20 | 1.30 | **C** | **8.8** | **P** | 0.70 | 0.80 | – | – | – | – | 0.75 |
| 1.00 | – | – | – | – | 0.95 | 1.05 | **C** | **9.2** | **P** | 0.85 | 0.95 | – | – | – | – | 0.90 |
| 0.80 | – | – | – | – | 0.75 | 0.85 | **C** | **9.6** | **P** | 1.05 | 1.15 | – | – | – | – | 1.10 |
| 0.65 | – | – | – | – | 0.60 | 0.70 | **C** | **10** | **P** | 1.30 | 1.40 | – | – | – | – | 1.35 |

*Note*: Settlement price is for the trading day 31/12/2008.

**Table 22.1** Information about the options of Air France-KLM Corporation

## 22.6 Option Combinations

Puts and calls can serve as building blocks for more complex option contracts. For example, Fig. 22.4 illustrates the pay-off from buying a put option on a share and simultaneously buying the share.

If the share price is greater than the exercise price, the put option is worthless, and the value of the combined position is equal to the value of the equity. If instead the exercise price is greater than the share price, the decline in the value of the shares will be exactly offset by the rise in the value of the put.

The strategy of buying a put and buying the underlying share is called a *protective put.* It is as if we are buying insurance for the equity, which can always be sold at the exercise price, regardless of how far the market price of the share falls.

Note that the combination of buying a put and buying the underlying equity has the same *shape* in Fig. 22.4 as the call purchase in Fig. 22.1. To pursue this point, let's consider the graph for buying a call, which is shown at the far left of Fig. 22.5. This graph is the same as Fig. 22.1, except that the exercise price is £50 here. Now, let's try the strategy of:

- (Leg A) Buying a call.

- (Leg B) Buying a risk-free, zero coupon bond (i.e., a T-bill) with a face value of £50 that matures on the same day that the option expires.

We have drawn the graph of leg A of this strategy at the far left of Fig. 22.5, but what does the graph of leg B look like? It looks like the middle graph of the figure. That is, anyone buying this zero coupon bond will be guaranteed to receive £50, regardless of the price of the share at expiration.

**Figure 22.4** Pay-off to the combination of buying a put and buying the underlying equity

The graph of buying a call and buying a zero coupon bond is the same as the graph of buying a put and buying the share in Figure 22.4

**Figure 22.5** Pay-off to the combination of buying a call and buying a zero coupon bond

What does the graph of *simultaneously* buying both leg A and leg B of this strategy look like? It looks like the far right graph of Fig. 22.5. That is, the investor receives a guaranteed £50 from the bond, regardless of what happens to the share price. In addition, the investor receives a pay-off from the call of £1 for every £1 that the share price rises above the exercise price of £50.

The far right graph of Fig. 22.5 looks *exactly* like the far right graph of Fig. 22.4. Thus an investor gets the same pay-off from the strategy of Fig. 22.4 and the strategy of Fig. 22.5, regardless of what happens to the price of the underlying equity. In other words, the investor gets the same pay-off from:

1   Buying a put and buying the underlying equity.

2   Buying a call and buying a risk-free, zero coupon bond.

If investors have the same pay-offs from the two strategies, the two strategies must have the same cost. Otherwise, all investors will choose the strategy with the lower cost and avoid the strategy with the higher cost. This leads to the following interesting result:

$$\begin{array}{l}\text{Price of underlying} \\ \text{equity}\end{array} + \begin{array}{l}\text{Price of} \\ \text{put}\end{array} = \begin{array}{l}\text{Price of} \\ \text{call}\end{array} + \begin{array}{l}\text{Present value of} \\ \text{exercise price}\end{array} \qquad (22.1)$$

Cost of first strategy = Cost of second strategy

This relationship is known as <u>put–call parity</u> and is one of the most fundamental relationships concerning options. It says that there are two ways of buying a protective put. You can buy a put and buy the underlying equity simultaneously. Here, your total cost is the share price of the underlying equity plus the price of the put. Or you can buy the call and buy a zero coupon bond. Here, your total cost is the price of the call plus the price of the zero coupon bond. The price of the zero coupon bond is equal to the present value of the exercise price – that is, the present value of £50 in our example.

Equation (22.1) is a very precise relationship. It holds only if the put and the call have both the same exercise price and the same expiration date. In addition, the maturity date of the zero coupon bond must be the same as the expiration date of the options.

To see how fundamental put–call parity is, let's rearrange the formula, yielding

$$\begin{array}{l}\text{Price of underlying} \\ \text{equity}\end{array} = \begin{array}{l}\text{Price of} \\ \text{call}\end{array} - \begin{array}{l}\text{Price of} \\ \text{put}\end{array} + \begin{array}{l}\text{Present value of} \\ \text{exercise price}\end{array}$$

This relationship now states that you can replicate the purchase of a share of equity by buying a call, selling a put, and buying a zero coupon bond. (Note that because a minus sign comes before 'Price of put', the put is sold, not bought.) Investors in this three-legged strategy are said to have purchased a *synthetic* share.

Let's do one more transformation:

**Covered call strategy:**

$$\begin{array}{l}\text{Price of underlying} \\ \text{equity}\end{array} - \begin{array}{l}\text{Price of} \\ \text{call}\end{array} = - \begin{array}{l}\text{Price of} \\ \text{put}\end{array} + \begin{array}{l}\text{Present value of} \\ \text{exercise price}\end{array}$$

Many investors like to buy a share and write the call on the share simultaneously. This is a conservative strategy known as <u>selling a covered call.</u> The preceding put–call parity relationship tells us that this strategy is equivalent to selling a put and buying a zero coupon bond. Figure 22.6 develops the graph for the covered call. You can verify that the covered call can be replicated by selling a put and simultaneously buying a zero coupon bond.

**Figure 22.6** Pay-off to the combination of buying a share and selling a call

Of course, there are other ways of rearranging the basic put–call relationship. For each rearrangement, the strategy on the left side is equivalent to the strategy on the right side. The beauty of put–call parity is that it shows how any strategy in options can be achieved in two different ways.

To test your understanding of put–call parity, suppose Nokia Oyj shares are selling for €10.95. A three-month call option with a €10.95 strike price goes for €0.35. The risk-free rate is 0.5 per cent per month. What's the value of a three-month put option with a €10.95 strike price?

We can rearrange the put–call parity relationship to solve for the price of the put as follows:

$$\text{Price of put} = -\text{Price of underlying equity} + \text{Price of call} + \text{Present value of strike price}$$

$$= -€10.95 + €0.35 + €10.95 / 1.005^3$$
$$= €0.1873$$

As shown, the value of the put is €0.1873.

## A Synthetic T-Bill

**EXAMPLE 22.3**

Suppose shares of Smolira plc are selling for £110. A call option on Smolira with one year to maturity and a £110 strike price sells for £15. A put with the same terms sells for £5. What's the risk-free rate?

To answer, we need to use put–call parity to determine the price of a risk-free, zero coupon bond:

Price of underlying share + Price of put − Price of call = Present value of exercise price

Plugging in the numbers, we get

$$£110 + £5 - £15 = £100$$

Because the present value of the £110 strike price is £100, the implied risk-free rate is 10 per cent.

## 22.7 Valuing Options

In the last section we determined what options are worth on the expiration date. Now we wish to determine the value of options when you buy them well before expiration.[4] We begin by considering the lower and upper bounds on the value of a call.

### Bounding the Value of a Call

**Lower Bound**    Consider an American call that is in the money prior to expiration. For example, assume that the share price is £60 and the exercise price is £50. In this case, the option cannot sell below £10. To see this, note the following simple strategy if the option sells at, say, £9:

| Date | Transaction | (£) |
|------|-------------|-----|
| Today | (1) Buy call. | −9 |
| Today | (2) Exercise call – that is, buy underlying share at exercise price. | −50 |
| Today | (3) Sell share at current market price. | +60 |
| Arbitrage profit | | +1 |

FIGURE
**22.7**

Figure 22.7 The upper and lower boundaries of call option values

The type of profit that is described in this transaction is an *arbitrage* profit. Arbitrage profits come from transactions that have no risk or cost, and cannot occur regularly in normal, well-functioning financial markets. The excess demand for these options would quickly force the option price up to at least £10 (= £60 − £50).

Of course, the price of the option is likely to be above £10. Investors will rationally pay more than £10, because of the possibility that the share will rise above £60 before expiration. For example, suppose the call actually sells for £12. In this case we say that the *intrinsic value* of the option is £10, meaning it must always be worth at least this much. The remaining £12 − £10 = £2 is sometimes called the *time premium,* and it represents the extra amount that investors are willing to pay because of the possibility that the share price will rise before the option expires.

**Upper Bound**   Is there an upper boundary for the option price as well? It turns out that the upper boundary is the price of the underlying share. That is, an option to buy equity cannot have a greater value than the equity itself. A call option can be used to buy equity with a payment of the exercise price. It would be foolish to buy equity this way if the shares could be purchased directly at a lower price. The upper and lower bounds are represented in Fig. 22.7.

## The Factors Determining Call Option Values

The previous discussion indicated that the price of a call option must fall somewhere in the shaded region of Fig. 22.7. We shall now determine more precisely where in the shaded region it should be. The factors that determine a call's value can be broken into two sets. The first set contains the features of the option contract. The two basic contractual features are the exercise price and the expiration date. The second set of factors affecting the call price concerns characteristics of the equity and the market.

**Exercise Price**   An increase in the exercise price reduces the value of the call. For example, imagine that there are two calls on a share selling at £60. The first call has an exercise price of £50 and the second one has an exercise price of £40. Which call would you rather have? Clearly, you would rather have the call with an exercise price of £40, because that one is £20 (= £60 − £40) in the money. In other words, the call with an exercise price of £40 should sell for more than an otherwise identical call with an exercise price of £50.

**Expiration Date**   The value of an American call option must be at least as great as the value of an otherwise identical option with a shorter term to expiration. Consider two American calls: one has a maturity of nine months, and the other expires in six months. Obviously, the nine-month call has the same rights as the six-month call, and it also has an additional three

FIGURE
**22.8**

The call price is positively related to the share price. In addition, the change in the call price for a given change in the share price is greater when the share price is high than when it is low.

**Figure 22.8** Value of an American call as a function of share price

months within which these rights can be exercised. It cannot be worth less, and will generally be more valuable.[5]

Share Price    Other things being equal, the higher the share price, the more valuable the call option will be. For example, if a share is worth £80, a call with an exercise price of £100 isn't worth very much. If the share soars to £120, the call becomes much more valuable.

Now consider Fig. 22.8, which shows the relationship between the call price and the share price prior to expiration. The curve indicates that the call price increases as the share price increases. Furthermore, it can be shown that the relationship is represented not by a straight line, but by a *convex* curve. That is, the increase in the call price for a given change in the share price is greater when the share price is high than when the share price is low.

There are two special points on the curve in Fig. 22.8:

1    *The equity is worthless.* The call must be worthless if the underlying equity is worthless. That is, if the equity has no chance of attaining any value, it is not worth while to pay the exercise price to obtain the share.

2    *The share price is very high relative to the exercise price.* In this situation, the owner of the call knows that she will end up exercising the call. She can view herself as the owner of the share now, with one difference: she must pay the exercise price at expiration.

Thus the value of her position – that is, the value of the call – is

$$\text{Share price} - \text{Present value of exercise price}$$

These two points on the curve are summarized in the bottom half of Table 22.2.

The Key Factor: The Variability of the Underlying Asset    The greater the variability of the underlying asset, the more valuable the call option will be. Consider the following example. Suppose that just before the call expires, the share price will be either £100 with probability 0.5 or £80 with probability 0.5. What will be the value of a call with an exercise price of £110? Clearly, it will be worthless, because no matter what happens to the equity, the share price will always be below the exercise price.

What happens if the share price is more variable? Suppose we add £20 to the best case and take £20 away from the worst case. Now the equity has a one-half chance of being worth £60 and a one-half chance of being worth £120. We have spread the share returns, but of course the expected value of the share has stayed the same:

$$(1/2 \times £80) + (1/2 \times £100) = £90 = (1/2 \times £60) + (1/2 \times £120)$$

Notice that the call option has value now, because there is a one-half chance that the share price will be £120, or £10 above the exercise price of £110. This illustrates an important point.

TABLE
22.2

| Increase in | Call option* | Put option* |
| --- | :---: | :---: |
| Value of underlying asset (share price) | + | − |
| Exercise price | − | + |
| Share price volatility | + | + |
| Interest rate | + | − |
| Time to expiration | + | + |

In addition to the preceding, we have presented the following four relationships for American calls:

1 The call price can never be greater than the share price (*upper bound*).

2 The call price can never be less than either zero or the difference between the share price and the exercise price (*lower bound*).

3 The call is worth zero if the underlying equity is worth zero.

4 When the share price is much greater than the exercise price, the call price tends towards the difference between the share price and the present value of the exercise price.

*The signs (+, −) indicate the effect of the variables on the value of the option. For example, the two +s for share volatility indicate that an increase in volatility will increase both the value of a call and the value of a put.

**Table 22.2** Factors affecting American option values

There is a fundamental distinction between holding an option on an underlying asset and holding the underlying asset. If investors in the marketplace are risk-averse, a rise in the variability of the equity will decrease its market value. However, the holder of a call receives pay-offs from the positive tail of the probability distribution. As a consequence, a rise in the variability in the underlying equity increases the market value of the call.

This result can also be seen from Fig. 22.9. Consider two shares, A and B, each of which is normally distributed. For each security, the figure illustrates the probability of different share prices on the expiration date. As can be seen from the figures, share B has more volatility than does share A. This means that share B has a higher probability of both abnormally high returns and abnormally low returns. Let us assume that options on each of the two securities have the same exercise price. To option holders, a return much below average on share B is no worse than a return only moderately below average on share A. In either situation, the option expires out of the money. However, to option holders, a return much above average on share B is better than a return only moderately above average on share A. Because a call's price at the expiration date is the difference between the share price and the exercise price, the value of the call on B at expiration will be higher in this case.

**The Interest Rate**  Call prices are also a function of the level of interest rates. Buyers of calls do not pay the exercise price until they exercise the option, if they do so at all. The ability to delay payment is more valuable when interest rates are high and less valuable when interest rates are low. Thus the value of a call is positively related to interest rates.

## A Quick Discussion of Factors Determining Put Option Values

Given our extended discussion of the factors influencing a call's value, we can examine the effect of these factors on puts very easily. Table 22.2 summarizes the five factors influencing the prices of both American calls and American puts. The effect of three factors on puts are the opposite of the effect of these three factors on calls:

1 The put's market value *decreases* as the share price increases, because puts are in the money when the equity sells below the exercise price.

FIGURE
22.9

The call on share B is worth more
than the call on share A because
share B is more volatile.
At expiration, a call that is deep in
the money is more valuable than
a call that is only slightly in the
money. However, at expiration,
a call way out of the money is
worth zero, just as is a call only
slightly out of the money.

**Figure 22.9** Distribution of equity price at expiration for both security A and
security B. Options on the two securities have the same exercise price

2    The value of a put with a high exercise price is *greater* than the value of an otherwise
identical put with a low exercise price, for the reason given in (1).

3    A high interest rate *adversely* affects the value of a put. The ability to sell a share at a fixed
exercise price sometime in the future is worth less if the present value of the exercise price
is reduced by a high interest rate.

The effect of the other two factors on puts is the same as the effect of these factors on calls:

4    The value of an American put with a distant expiration date is greater than an otherwise
identical put with an earlier expiration.[6] The longer time to maturity gives the put holder
more flexibility, just as it did in the case of a call.

5    Volatility of the underlying share price increases the value of the put. The reasoning is
analogous to that for a call. At expiration, a put that is way in the money is more valuable
than a put only slightly in the money. However, at expiration, a put way out of the money
is worth zero, just as is a put only slightly out of the money.

## 22.8  An Option Pricing Formula

We have explained *qualitatively* that the value of a call option is a function of five variables:

1    The current price of the underlying asset, which for equity options is the share price

2    The exercise price

3    The time to expiration date

4    The variance of the underlying asset

5    The risk-free interest rate

It is time to replace the qualitative model with a precise option valuation model. The model
we choose is the famous Black–Scholes option pricing model. You can put numbers into the
Black–Scholes model and get values back.

The Black–Scholes model is represented by a rather imposing formula. A derivation of the
formula is simply not possible in this textbook, as many students will be happy to learn. However,
some appreciation for the achievement as well as some intuitive understanding is in order.

In the early chapters of this book we showed how to discount capital budgeting projects using
the net present value formula. We also used this approach to value shares and bonds. Why,
students sometimes ask, can't the same NPV formula be used to value puts and calls? This is
a good question: the earliest attempts at valuing options used NPV. Unfortunately, the attempts
were not successful, because no one could determine the appropriate discount rate. An option
is generally riskier than the underlying share, but no one knew exactly how much riskier.

Black and Scholes attacked the problem by pointing out that a strategy of borrowing to finance an equity purchase duplicates the risk of a call. Then, knowing the price of an equity already, we can determine the price of a call such that its return is identical to that of the share-with-borrowing alternative.

We illustrate the intuition behind the Black–Scholes approach by considering a simple example where a combination of a call and an equity eliminates all risk. This example works because we let the future share price be one of only *two* values. Hence the example is called a *two-state* or *binomial option pricing model*. By eliminating the possibility that the share price can take on other values, we are able to duplicate the call exactly.

## A Two-State Option Model

Consider the following example. Suppose the current market price of a share is £50 and the share price will either be £60 or £40 at the end of the year. Further, imagine a call option on this share with a one-year expiration date and a £50 exercise price. Investors can borrow at 10 per cent. Our goal is to determine the value of the call.

To value the call correctly, we need to examine two strategies. The first is to simply buy the call. The second is to:

1    Buy one-half of a share of equity.

2    Borrow £18.18, implying a payment of principal and interest at the end of the year of £20 (= £18.18 × 1.10).

As you will see shortly, the cash flows from the second strategy match the cash flows from buying a call. (A little later, we shall show how we came up with the exact fraction of a share of equity to buy and the exact borrowing amount.) Because the cash flows match, we say that we are *duplicating* the call with the second strategy.

At the end of the year, the future pay-offs are set out as follows:

|  | Future pay-offs | |
| --- | :---: | :---: |
| **Initial transactions** | **If share price is £60** | **If share price is £40** |
| 1. Buy a call | £60 − £50 =  £10 | £0 |
| 2. Buy ½ share of equity | ½ × £60 =  £30 | ½ × £40 = £20 |
| Borrow £18.18 at 10% | −(£18.18 × 1.10) = −£20 | −£20 |
| Total from equity and borrowing strategy | £10 | £0 |

Note that the future pay-off structure of the 'buy-a-call' strategy is duplicated by the strategy of 'buy share and borrow.' That is, under either strategy an investor would end up with £10 if the share price rose and £0 if the share price fell. Thus these two strategies are equivalent as far as traders are concerned.

If two strategies always have the same cash flows at the end of the year, how must their initial costs be related? The two strategies must have the *same* initial cost. Otherwise, there will be an arbitrage possibility. We can easily calculate this cost for our strategy of buying shares and borrowing:

| Buy ½ share of equity | ½ × £50 =  £25.00 |
| --- | --- |
| Borrow £18.18 | −£18.18 |
|  | £6.82 |

Because the call option provides the same pay-offs at expiration as does the strategy of buying equity and borrowing, the call must be priced at £6.82. This is the value of the call option in a market without arbitrage profits.

We left two issues unexplained in the preceding example.

**Determining the Delta**    How did we know to buy one-half share of equity in the duplicating strategy? Actually, the answer is easier than it might at first appear. The call price at the end of the year will be either £10 or £0, whereas the share price will be either £60 or £40. Thus the call price has a potential swing of £10 (= £10 – £0) next period, whereas the share price has a potential swing of £20 (= £60 – £40). We can write this in terms of the following ratio:

$$\text{Delta} = \frac{\text{Swing of call}}{\text{Swing of equity}}$$
$$= \frac{£10 - £0}{£60 - £40}$$
$$= \frac{1}{2}$$

As indicated, this ratio is called the *delta* of the call. In words, a £1 swing in the share price gives rise to a £1/2 swing in the price of the call. Because we are trying to duplicate the call with the equity, it seems sensible to buy one-half share of equity instead of buying one call. In other words, the risk of buying one-half share of equity should be the same as the risk of buying one call.

**Determining the Amount of Borrowing**   How did we know how much to borrow? Buying one-half share of equity brings us either £30 or £20 at expiration, which is exactly £20 more than the pay-offs of £10 and £0, respectively, from the call. To duplicate the call through a purchase of equity, we should also borrow enough money so that we have to pay back exactly £20 of interest and principal. This amount of borrowing is merely the present value of £20, which is £18.18 (= £20/1.10).

Now that we know how to determine both the delta and the borrowing, we can write the value of the call as follows:

$$\text{Value of call} = \text{Share price} \times \text{Delta} - \text{Amount borrowed} \tag{22.2}$$
$$£6.82 = £50 \times \frac{1}{2} - £18.18$$

We shall find this intuition useful in explaining the Black–Scholes model.

**Risk-Neutral Valuation**   Before leaving this simple example, we should comment on a remarkable feature. We found the exact value of the option without even knowing the probability that the equity would go up or down! If an optimist thought the probability of an up move was high and a pessimist thought it was low, they would still agree on the option value. How can that be? The answer is that the current £50 share price already balances the views of the optimists and the pessimists. The option reflects that balance, because its value depends on the share price.

This insight provides us with another approach to valuing the call. If we don't need the probabilities of the two states to value the call, perhaps we can select *any* probabilities we want and still come up with the right answer. Suppose we select probabilities such that the return on the equity is equal to the risk-free rate of 10 per cent. We know that the equity return, given a rise, is 20 per cent (= £60/£50 – 1), and the equity return, given a fall, is –20 per cent (= £40/£50 – 1). Thus we can solve for the probability of a rise necessary to achieve an expected return of 10 per cent as follows:

$$10\% = \text{Probability of a rise} \times 20\% + (1 - \text{Probability of rise}) \times -20\%$$

Solving this formula, we find that the probability of a rise is 3/4 and the probability of a fall is 1/4. If we apply these probabilities to the call, we can value it as

$$\text{Value of call} = \frac{\frac{3}{4} \times £10 + \frac{1}{4} \times £0}{1.10}$$
$$= £6.82$$

the same value we got from the duplicating approach.

Why did we select probabilities such that the expected return on the equity is 10 per cent? We wanted to work with the special case where investors are *risk-neutral*. This case occurs when the expected return on *any* asset (including both the share and the call) is equal to the risk-free rate. In other words, this case occurs when investors demand no additional compensation beyond the risk-free rate, regardless of the risk of the asset in question.

What would have happened if we had assumed that the expected return on a share of equity was greater than the risk-free rate? The value of the call would still be £6.82. However, the calculations would be difficult. For example, if we assumed that the expected return on the equity was, say, 11 per cent, we would have had to derive the expected return on the call. Although the expected return on the call would be higher than 11 per cent, it would take a lot of work to determine the expected return precisely. Why do any more work than you have to? Because we can't think of any good reason, we (and most other financial economists) choose to assume risk neutrality.

Thus the preceding material allows us to value a call in the following two ways:

1   Determine the cost of a strategy duplicating the call. This strategy involves an investment in a fractional share of equity financed by partial borrowing.

2   Calculate the probabilities of a rise and a fall under the assumption of risk neutrality. Use these probabilities, in conjunction with the risk-free rate, to discount the pay-offs of the call at expiration.

## The Black–Scholes Model

The preceding example illustrates the duplicating strategy. Unfortunately, a strategy such as this will not work in the real world over, say, a one-year time frame, because there are many more than two possibilities for next year's share price. However, the number of possibilities is reduced as the period is shortened. Is there a time period over which the share price can have only two outcomes? Academics argue that the assumption that there are only two possibilities for the share price over the next infinitesimal instant is quite plausible.[7]

In our opinion, the fundamental insight of Black and Scholes is to shorten the time period. They show that a specific combination of equity and borrowing can indeed duplicate a call over an infinitesimal time horizon. Because the share price will change over the first instant, another combination of equity and borrowing is needed to duplicate the call over the second instant, and so on. By adjusting the combination from moment to moment, they can continually duplicate the call. It may boggle the mind that a formula can (a) determine the duplicating combination at any moment and (b) value the option based on this duplicating strategy. Suffice it to say that their dynamic strategy allows them to value a call in the real world, just as we showed how to value the call in the two-state model.

This is the basic intuition behind the Black–Scholes (BS) model. Because the actual derivation of their formula is, alas, far beyond the scope of this text, we simply present the formula itself:

Black–Scholes model:

$$C = SN(d_1) - Ee^{-Rt}N(d_2)$$

where

$$d_1 = \frac{\ln(S/E) + (R + \sigma^2/2)t}{\sqrt{\sigma^2 t}}$$
$$d_2 = d_1 - \sqrt{\sigma^2 t}$$

This formula for the value of a call, $C$, is one of the most complex in finance. However, it involves only five parameters: $S$, the current share price; $E$, the exercise price of the call; $R$, the annual risk-free rate of return, continuously compounded; $\sigma^2$, the variance (per year) of the continuous share price return; and $t$, the time (in years) to expiration date.

In addition, there is this statistical concept:

$$N(d) = \text{Probability that a standardized, normally distributed,}$$
$$\text{random variable will be less than or equal to } d.$$

Rather than discuss the formula in its algebraic state, we illustrate the formula with an example.

## Black–Scholes

Consider Private Equipment Company (PEC). On 4 October of year 0, the PEC 21 April call option (exercise price = £49) had a closing value of £4. The equity itself was selling at £50. On 4 October the option had 199 days to expiration (maturity date = 21 April, year 1). The annual risk-free interest rate, continuously compounded, was 7 per cent.

This information determines three variables directly:

1   The share price, $S$, is £50.

2   The exercise price, $E$, is £49.

3   The risk-free rate, $R$, is 0.07.

In addition, the time to maturity, $t$, can be calculated quickly: the formula calls for $t$ to be expressed in *years*.

4   We express the 199-day interval in years as $t = 199/365$.

In the real world, an option trader would know $S$ and $E$ exactly. Traders generally view government Treasury bills as riskless, so a current quote from newspapers, such as the *Financial Times* or a similar source, would be obtained for the interest rate. The trader would also know (or could count) the number of days to expiration exactly. Thus the fraction of a year to expiration, $t$, could be calculated quickly.

The problem comes in determining the variance of the underlying equity's return. The formula calls for the variance between the purchase date of 4 October and the expiration date. Unfortunately, this represents the future, so the correct value for variance is not available. Instead, traders frequently estimate variance from past data, just as we calculated variance in an earlier chapter. In addition, some traders may use intuition to adjust their estimate. For example, if anticipation of an upcoming event is likely to increase the volatility of the share price, the trader might adjust her estimate of variance upwards to reflect this.

The preceding discussion was intended merely to mention the difficulties in variance estimation, not to present a solution. For our purposes, we assume that a trader has come up with an estimate of variance:

5   The variance of Private Equipment Corporation has been estimated to be 0.09 per year.

Using these five parameters, we calculate the Black–Scholes value of the PEC option in three steps:

Step 1: *Calculate $d_1$ and $d_2$.* These values can be determined by a straightforward, albeit tedious, insertion of our parameters into the basic formula. We have

$$d_1 = \left[ \ln\left(\frac{S}{E}\right) + \left(R + \frac{\sigma^2}{2}\right)t \right] \bigg/ \sqrt{\sigma^2 t}$$

$$= \left[ \ln\left(\frac{50}{49}\right) + \left(0.07 + \frac{0.09}{2}\right) \times \frac{199}{365} \right] \bigg/ \sqrt{0.09 \times \frac{199}{365}}$$

$$= \frac{0.0202 + 0.0627}{0.2215}$$

$$= 0.3742$$

$$d_2 = d_1 - \sqrt{\sigma^2 t}$$

$$= 0.1527$$

Step 2: *Calculate* $N(d_1)$ and $N(d_2)$. We can best understand the values $N(d_1)$ and $N(d_2)$ by examining Fig. 22.10. The figure shows the normal distribution with an expected value of 0 and a standard deviation of 1. This is frequently called the **standardized normal distribution**. We mentioned in an earlier chapter that the probability that a drawing from this distribution will be between –1 and +1 (within one standard deviation of its mean, in other words) is 68.26 per cent.

Shaded area represents cumulative probability. Because the probability is 0.6459 that a drawing from the standard normal distribution will be below 0.3742, we say that N(0.3742) = 0.6459. That is, the cumulative probability of 0.3742 is 0.6459.

**Figure 22.10** Graph of cumulative probability

Now let us ask a different question: What is the probability that a drawing from the standardized normal distribution will be *below* a particular value? For example, the probability that a drawing will be below 0 is clearly 50 per cent because the normal distribution is symmetric. Using statistical terminology, we say that the **cumulative probability** of 0 is 50 per cent. Statisticians also say that $N(0) = 50\%$. It turns out that

$$N(d_1) = N(0.3742) = 0.6459$$
$$N(d_2) = N(0.1527) = 0.5607$$

The first value means that there is a 64.59 per cent probability that a drawing from the standardized normal distribution will be below 0.3742. The second value means that there is a 56.07 per cent probability that a drawing from the standardized normal distribution will be below 0.1527. More generally, $N(d)$ is the probability that a drawing from the standardized normal distribution will be below $d$. In other words, $N(d)$ is the cumulative probability of $d$. Note that $d_1$ and $d_2$ in our example are slightly above zero, so $N(d_1)$ and $N(d_2)$ are slightly greater than 0.50.

Perhaps the easiest way to determine $N(d_1)$ and $N(d_2)$ is from the Microsoft Excel® function NORMSDIST. In our example, NORMSDIST(0.3742) and NORMSDIST(0.1527) are 0.6459 and 0.5607, respectively.

We can also determine the cumulative probability from Table 22.3. For example, consider $d = 0.37$. This can be found in the table as 0.3 on the vertical and 0.07 on the horizontal. The value in the table for $d = 0.37$ is 0.1443. This value is *not* the cumulative probability of 0.37. We must first make an adjustment to determine cumulative probability. That is:

$$N(0.37) = 0.50 + 0.1443 = 0.6443$$
$$N(-0.37) = 0.50 - 0.1443 = 0.3557$$

Unfortunately, our table handles only two significant digits, whereas our value of 0.3742 has four significant digits. Hence we must interpolate to find N(0.3742). Because $N(0.37) = 0.6443$ and $N(0.38) = 0.6480$, the difference between the two values is 0.0037 (= 0.6480 − 0.6443). Since 0.3742 is 42 per cent of the way between 0.37 and 0.38, we interpolate as[8]

$$N(0.3742) = 0.6443 + 0.42 \times 0.0037 = 0.6459$$

| d | 0.00 | 0.01 | 0.02 | 0.03 | 0.04 | 0.05 | 0.06 | 0.07 | 0.08 | 0.09 |
|-----|--------|--------|--------|--------|--------|--------|--------|--------|--------|--------|
| 0.0 | 0.0000 | 0.0040 | 0.0080 | 0.0120 | 0.0160 | 0.0199 | 0.0239 | 0.0279 | 0.0319 | 0.0359 |
| 0.1 | 0.0398 | 0.0438 | 0.0478 | 0.0517 | 0.0557 | 0.0596 | 0.0636 | 0.0675 | 0.0714 | 0.0753 |
| 0.2 | 0.0793 | 0.0832 | 0.0871 | 0.0910 | 0.0948 | 0.0987 | 0.1026 | 0.1064 | 0.1103 | 0.1141 |
| 0.3 | 0.1179 | 0.1217 | 0.1255 | 0.1293 | 0.1331 | 0.1368 | 0.1406 | 0.1443 | 0.1480 | 0.1517 |
| 0.4 | 0.1554 | 0.1591 | 0.1628 | 0.1664 | 0.1700 | 0.1736 | 0.1772 | 0.1808 | 0.1844 | 0.1879 |
| 0.5 | 0.1915 | 0.1950 | 0.1985 | 0.2019 | 0.2054 | 0.2088 | 0.2123 | 0.2157 | 0.2190 | 0.2224 |

$N(d)$ represents areas under the standard normal distribution function. Suppose that $d_1 = 0.24$. The table implies a cumulative probability of $0.5000 + 0.0948 = 0.5948$. If $d_1$ is equal to 0.2452, we must estimate the probability by interpolating between $N(0.25)$ and $N(0.24)$.

**Table 22.3** Cumulative probabilities of the standard normal distribution function

Step 3: *Calculate C.* We have

$$
\begin{aligned}
C &= S \times N(d_1) - Ee^{-Rt} \times N(d_2) \\
&= [£50 \times N(d_1)] - [£49 \times e^{-0.07 \times (199/365)} \times N(d_2)] \\
&= (£50 \times 0.6459) - (£49 \times 0.9626 \times 0.5607) \\
&= £32.295 - £26.447 \\
&= £5.85
\end{aligned}
$$

The estimated price of £5.85 is greater than the £4 actual price, implying that the call option is underpriced. A trader believing in the Black–Scholes model would buy a call. Of course, the Black–Scholes model is fallible. Perhaps the disparity between the model's estimate and the market price reflects error in the trader's estimate of variance.

The previous example stressed the calculations involved in using the Black–Scholes formula. Is there any intuition behind the formula? Yes, and that intuition follows from the share purchase and borrowing strategy in our binomial example. The first line of the Black–Scholes equation is

$$
C = S \times N(d_1) - Ee^{-Rt}N(d_2)
$$

which is exactly analogous to Eq. (22.2):

$$
\text{Value of call} = \text{Share price} \times \text{Delta} - \text{Amount borrowed}
$$

We presented this equation in the binomial example. It turns out that $N(d_1)$ is the delta in the Black–Scholes model. $N(d_1)$ is 0.6459 in the previous example. In addition, $Ee^{-Rt} N(d_2)$ is the amount that an investor must borrow to duplicate a call. In the previous example, this value is £26.45 (= £49 × 0.9626 × 0.5607). Thus the model tells us that we can duplicate the call of the preceding example by both:

1   buying 0.6459 share of equity;

2   borrowing £26.45.

It is no exaggeration to say that the Black–Scholes formula is among the most important contributions in finance. It allows anyone to calculate the value of an option, given a few parameters. The attraction of the formula is that four of the parameters are observable: the current share price, $S$; the exercise price, $E$; the interest rate, $R$; and the time to expiration date, $t$. Only one of the parameters must be estimated: the variance of return, $\sigma^2$.

To see how truly attractive this formula is, note what parameters are not needed. First, the investor's risk aversion does not affect value. The formula can be used by anyone, regardless of willingness to bear risk. Second, it does not depend on the expected return on the equity! Investors with different assessments of the equity's expected return will nevertheless agree on the call price. As in the two-state example, this is because the call depends on the share price, and that price already balances investors' divergent views.

## 22.9 The 'Greeks'

In the previous section, you were introduced to the ratio delta, which is the change in the option price with respect to a change in the value of the underlying asset. This measure of risk is one of four measures in option pricing that are important to corporate finance practitioners.

Table 22.2 presented the main factors that influence the price of an option. These are the value of the underlying asset (the share price), the exercise price, volatility in the value of the underlying asset, the interest rate, and time to expiry. While we know that the exercise price will not change during the lifetime of the option, it is certain that the other factors will vary to some extent.

The 'Greeks' measure the rate of change in the value of a call or put with respect to these major factors. Fortunately for you, their derivation and calculation (with the exception of delta) are beyond the scope of this book. However, it is important that the reader is aware of the 'Greeks' and what they represent.

Delta measures the rate of change in the value of an option with respect to a change in the underlying equity's share price. The delta for call options will always be between 0 and 1, and for put options it will always be between 0 and –1. Thus, if a delta is 0.8, this means that the call will increase in value by €0.80 for every €1.00 increase in the underlying share price. Clearly, since put option values fall when the value of the underlying equity goes up, the delta of put options will be negative.

Gamma measures the rate of change in delta with respect to a change in the value of the underlying share price. Since delta is central to the valuation of options, it is also important to understand how delta behaves during the lifetime of an option. Consider a call option that has a gamma of 0.05 and a delta of 0.8. If the underlying share price increases in value by €1.00, the delta of the option will grow by 0.05 to 0.85. Similarly, if the underlying share price falls by €1.00, the delta of the option will fall by 0.05 to 0.75.

Gamma has several important characteristics:

1 Gamma is very small when options are deep out of the money (that is, when the share price is low relative to the exercise price for call options, or when the share price is high relative to the exercise price for put options).

2 Gamma is very small when options are deep in the money (that is, when the share price is high relative to the exercise price for call options, or when the share price is low relative to the exercise price for put options).

3 Gamma is at its highest when options are at the money (that is, when the share price is equal to the exercise price of the option).

4 Gamma is positive when you hold the option (that is, you are long in the option) and negative when you have written the option (that is, you are short in the option).

Theta measures the rate of change in the value of an option with respect to the change in time to maturity of the option. An option will necessarily lose value as the exercise date gets closer and, as a result, theta is always negative. Options lose value faster the closer they are to expiry.

Finally, vega measures the rate of change in an option's value with respect to a change in its implied volatility. Implied volatility can be calculated using the Black–Scholes option-pricing model when both the underlying share price and option value are available. It is useful as a measure of expected volatility during the remaining life of an option. Many traders take the market's estimate of an option value to be the correct estimate, and use this to calculate the volatility of the asset. Call and put options increase in value when volatility increases, and, as a result, vega will always be positive.

## 22.10 Shares and Bonds as Options

The previous material in this chapter described, explained and valued publicly traded options. This is important material to any finance student, because much trading occurs in these listed options. However, the study of options has another purpose for the student of corporate finance.

You may have heard the one-liner about the elderly gentleman who was surprised to learn that he had been speaking prose all of his life. The same can be said about the corporate finance student and options. Although options were formally defined for the first time in this chapter, many corporate policies discussed earlier in the text were actually options in disguise. Though it is beyond the scope of this chapter to recast all of corporate finance in terms of options, the rest of the chapter considers three examples of implicit options:

1   Shares and bonds as options

2   Capital structure decisions as options

3   Capital budgeting decisions as options

We begin by illustrating the implicit options in shares and bonds.

---

EXAMPLE
**22.5**

## Shares and Bonds as Options

The Popov Company has been awarded the contract for athletics-related ice cream packaging at the 2012 Olympic Games in London. Because it is unlikely that there will be much need for athletics-related ice cream after the Olympics, their enterprise will disband after the games. The firm has issued debt to help finance this venture. Interest and principal due on the debt next year will be £800, at which time the debt will be paid off in full. The firm's cash flows next year are forecast as follows:

| | Popov's Cash Flow Schedule | | | |
|---|---|---|---|---|
| | **Very successful games (£)** | **Moderately successful games (£)** | **Moderately unsuccessful games (£)** | **Outright failure (£)** |
| Cash flow before interest and principal | 1,000 | 850 | 700 | 550 |
| Interest and principal | −800 | −800 | −700 | −550 |
| Cash flow to shareholders | 200 | 50 | 0 | 0 |

As can be seen, there are four equally likely scenarios. If either of the first two scenarios occurs, the bondholders will be paid in full. The extra cash flow goes to the shareholders. However, if either of the last two scenarios occurs, the bondholders will not be paid in full. Instead they will receive the firm's entire cash flow, leaving the shareholders with nothing.

---

This example is similar to the bankruptcy examples presented in our chapters about capital structure. Our new insight is that the relationship between the equity and the firm can be expressed in terms of options. We consider call options first, because the intuition is easier. The put option scenario is treated next.

## The Firm Expressed in Terms of Call Options

**The Shareholders**   We now show that equity can be viewed as a call option on the firm. To illustrate this, Fig. 22.11 graphs the cash flow to the shareholders as a function of the cash

FIGURE
**22.11**

The shareholders can be viewed as having a call option on the firm. If the cash flows of the firm exceed £800, the shareholders pay £800 in order to receive the firm's cash flows. If the cash flows of the firm are less than £800, the shareholders do not exercise their option. They walk away from the firm, receiving nothing.

**Figure 22.11** Cash flow to shareholders of Popov Company as a function of cash flow of firm

FIGURE
**22.12**

The bondholders can be viewed as owning the firm but writing a call option on the firm to the shareholders as well. If the cash flows of the firm exceed £800, the call is exercised against the bondholders. The bondholders give up the firm and receive £800. If the cash flows are less than £800, the call expires. The bondholders receive the cash flows of the firm in this case.

**Figure 22.12** Cash flow to bondholders of Popov Company as a function of cash flow of firm

flow to the firm. The shareholders receive nothing if the firm's cash flows are less than £800: here all of the cash flows go to the bondholders. However, the shareholders earn a pound for every pound that the firm receives above £800. The graph looks exactly like the call option graphs that we considered earlier in this chapter.

But what is the underlying asset upon which the equity is a call option? The underlying asset is the firm itself. That is, we can view the *bondholders* as owning the firm. However, the shareholders have a call option on the firm, with an exercise price of £800.

If the firm's cash flow is above £800, the shareholders would choose to exercise this option. In other words, they would buy the firm from the bondholders for £800. Their net cash flow is the difference between the firm's cash flow and their £800 payment. This would be £200 (= £1,000 – £800) if the games are very successful and £50 (= £850 – £800) if the games are moderately successful.

Should the value of the firm's cash flows be less than £800, the shareholders would not choose to exercise their option. Instead, they would walk away from the firm, as any call option holder would do. The bondholders would then receive the firm's entire cash flow.

This view of the firm is a novel one, and students are frequently bothered by it on first exposure. However, we encourage students to keep looking at the firm in this way until the view becomes second nature to them.

**The Bondholders**    What about the bondholders? Our earlier cash flow schedule showed that they would get the entire cash flow of the firm if the firm generated less cash than £800. Should the firm earn more than £800, the bondholders would receive only £800. That is, they are entitled only to interest and principal. This schedule is graphed in Fig. 22.12.

In keeping with our view that the shareholders have a call option on the firm, what does the bondholders' position consist of? The bondholders' position can be described by two claims:

1    They own the firm.

2    They have written a call on the firm with an exercise price of £800.

As we mentioned before, the shareholders walk away from the firm if cash flows are less than £800. Thus the bondholders retain ownership in this case. However, if the cash flows are greater than £800, the shareholders exercise their option. They call the equity away from the bondholders for £800.

## The Firm Expressed in Terms of Put Options

The preceding analysis expresses the positions of the shareholders and the bondholders in terms of call options. We can now express the situation in terms of put options.

**The Shareholders**   The shareholders' position can be expressed by three claims:

1    They own the firm.

2    They owe £800 in interest and principal to the bondholders.

If the debt were risk-free, these two claims would fully describe the shareholders' situation. However, because of the possibility of default, we have a third claim as well:

3    The shareholders own a put option on the firm, with an exercise price of £800. The group of bondholders is the seller of the put.

**Now consider two possibilities.**

1    *Cash flow is less than £800*:   Because the put has an exercise price of £800, the put is in the money. The shareholders 'put' – that is, sell – the firm to the bondholders. Normally, the holder of a put receives the exercise price when the asset is sold. However, the share-holders already owe £800 to the bondholders. Thus the debt of £800 is simply cancelled – and no money changes hands – when the equity is delivered to the bondholders. Because the shareholders give up the equity in exchange for extinguishing the debt, the shareholders end up with nothing if the cash flow is below £800.

2    *Cash flow is greater than £800*:   Because the put is out of the money here, the shareholders do not exercise. Thus the shareholders retain ownership of the firm, but pay £800 to the bondholders as interest and principal.

**The Bondholders**   The bondholders' position can be described by two claims:

1    The bondholders are owed £800.

2    They have sold a put option on the firm to the shareholders, with an exercise price of £800.

**Again, consider two possibilities.**

1    *Cash flow is less than £800*:   As mentioned before, the shareholders will exercise the put in this case. This means that the bondholders are obligated to pay £800 for the firm. Because they are owed £800, the two obligations offset each other. Thus the bondholders simply end up with the firm in this case.

2    *Cash flow is greater than £800*:   Here, the shareholders do not exercise the put. Thus the bondholders merely receive the £800 that is due them.

Expressing the bondholders' position in this way is illuminating. With a riskless default-free bond, the bondholders are owed £800. Thus we can express the risky bond in terms of a riskless bond and a put:

$$\text{Value of risky bond} = \text{Value of default-free bond} - \text{Value of put option}$$

That is, the value of the risky bond is the value of the default-free bond less the value of the shareholders' option to sell the company for £800.

TABLE
**22.4**

| Shareholders | Bondholders |
|---|---|
| **Positions viewed in terms of call options** | |
| **1** Shareholders own a call on the firm with an exercise price of £800. | **1** Bondholders own the firm. |
| | **2** Bondholders have sold a call on the firm to the shareholders. |
| **Positions viewed in terms of put options** | |
| **1** Shareholders own the firm. | **1** Bondholders are owed £800 in interest and principal. |
| **2** Shareholders owe £800 in interest and principal to bondholders. | **2** Bondholders have sold a put on the firm to the shareholders. |
| **3** Shareholders own a put option on the firm with an exercise price of £800. | |

**Table 22.4** Positions of shareholders and bondholders in Popov Company in terms of calls and puts

## A Resolution of the Two Views

We have argued that the positions of the shareholders and the bondholders can be viewed either in terms of calls or in terms of puts. These two viewpoints are summarized in Table 22.4.

We have found from experience that it is generally harder for students to think of the firm in terms of puts than in terms of calls. Thus it would be helpful if there were a way to show that the two viewpoints are equivalent. Fortunately there is *put–call parity*. In an earlier section, we presented the put–call parity relationship as Eq. (22.1), which we now repeat:

$$\underset{\text{equity}}{\text{Price of underlying}} + \underset{\text{of put}}{\text{Price}} = \underset{\text{of call}}{\text{Price}} + \underset{\text{of exercise price}}{\text{Present value}}$$

Using the results of this section, Eq. (22.1) can be rewritten like this:

$$\underset{\text{on firm}}{\text{Value of call}} = \underset{\text{firm}}{\text{Value of}} + \underset{\text{on firm}}{\text{Value of put}} - \underset{\text{default-free bond}}{\text{Value of}} \qquad (22.3)$$

$$\underset{\substack{\text{position in terms} \\ \text{of call options}}}{\text{Shareholders'}} = \underset{\substack{\text{in terms of put options}}}{\text{Shareholders' position}}$$

Going from Eq. (22.1) to Eq. (22.3) involves a few steps. First, we treat the firm, not the equity, as the underlying asset in this section. (In keeping with common convention, we refer to the *value* of the firm and the *price* of the equity.) Second, the exercise price is now £800, the principal and interest on the firm's debt. Taking the present value of this amount at the riskless rate yields the value of a default-free bond. Third, the order of the terms in Eq. (22.1) is rearranged in Eq. (22.3).

Note that the left side of Eq. (22.3) is the shareholders' position in terms of call options, as shown in Table 22.4. The right side of Eq. (22.3) is the shareholders' position in terms of put options, as shown in the same table. Thus put–call parity shows that viewing the shareholders' position in terms of call options is equivalent to viewing the shareholders' position in terms of put options.

Now let's rearrange the terms in Eq. (22.3) to yield the following:

$$\text{Value of firm} - \text{Value of call on firm} = \text{Value of default-free bond} - \text{Value of put on firm} \qquad \textbf{(22.4)}$$

$$\underbrace{\phantom{xxxxx}}_{\substack{\text{Bondholders' position in} \\ \text{terms of call options}}} = \underbrace{\phantom{xxxxx}}_{\substack{\text{Bondholders' position in} \\ \text{terms of put options}}}$$

The left side of Eq. (22.4) is the bondholders' position in terms of call options, as shown in Table 22.4. (The minus sign on this side of the equation indicates that the bondholders are *writing* a call.) The right side of the equation is the bondholders' position in terms of put options, as shown in Table 22.4. Thus put–call parity shows that viewing the bondholders' position in terms of call options is equivalent to viewing the bondholders' position in terms of put options.

## A Note about Loan Guarantees

In the Popov example given earlier, the bondholders bore the risk of default. Of course, bondholders generally ask for an interest rate that is high enough to compensate them for bearing risk. When firms experience financial distress, they can no longer attract new debt at moderate interest rates. Thus firms experiencing distress have frequently sought loan guarantees from the government. Our framework can be used to understand these guarantees.

If the firm defaults on a guaranteed loan, the government must make up the difference. In other words, a government guarantee converts a risky bond into a riskless bond. What is the value of this guarantee?

Recall that with option pricing:

$$\text{Value of default-free bond} = \text{Value of risky bond} + \text{Value of put option}$$

This equation shows that the government is assuming an obligation that has a cost equal to the value of a put option.

This analysis differs from that of either politicians or company spokespeople. They generally say that the guarantee will cost the taxpayers nothing, because the guarantee enables the firm to attract debt, thereby staying solvent. However, it should be pointed out that although solvency may be a strong possibility, it is never a certainty. Thus, when the guarantee is made, the government's obligation has a cost in terms of present value. To say that a government guarantee costs the government nothing is like saying a put on the equity of Apple has no value because the equity is *likely* to rise in price.

Several governments (such as those of Britain, France, Germany and the US) used loan guarantees to help firms get through the major recession that began in 2008. Under the guarantees, if a company defaulted on new loans, the lenders could obtain the full value of their claims from the company's government. From the lender's point of view, the loans became as risk-free as Treasury bonds. Loan guarantees enable firms to borrow cash to get through a difficult time.

Who benefits from a typical loan guarantee?

1    If existing risky bonds are guaranteed, all gains accrue to the existing bondholders. The shareholders gain nothing, because the limited liability of corporations absolves the shareholders of any obligation in bankruptcy.

2    If new debt is issued and guaranteed, the new debtholders do not gain. Rather, in a competitive market, they must accept a low interest rate because of the debt's low risk. The shareholders gain here, because they are able to issue debt at a low interest rate. In addition, some of the gains accrue to the old bondholders, because the firm's value is greater than would otherwise be true. Therefore, if shareholders want all the gains from

loan guarantees, they should renegotiate or retire existing bonds before the guarantee is in place.

3 Obviously, employees of distressed firms benefit, because otherwise the firm may go into bankruptcy if new funding is not provided from lenders. In addition, employees of firms that are suppliers and customers of distressed firms would also benefit. This was the main rationale underlying the government rescue packages of 2008 and 2009.

## 22.11 Options and Corporate Decisions: Some Applications

In this section we explore the implications of options analysis in two key areas: capital budgeting and mergers. We start with mergers, and show a very surprising result. We then go on to show that the net present value rule has some important wrinkles in a leveraged firm.

### Mergers and Diversification

Elsewhere in this book, we discuss mergers and acquisitions. There we mention that diversification is frequently cited as a reason for two firms to merge. Is diversification a good reason to merge? It might seem so. After all, in an earlier chapter we spent a lot of time explaining why diversification is valuable for investors in their own portfolios, because of the elimination of unsystematic risk.

To investigate this issue, let's consider two companies, Sunshine Swimwear (SS) and Polar Winterwear (PW). For obvious reasons, both companies have highly seasonal cash flows; and, in their respective off-seasons, both companies worry about cash flow. If the two companies were to merge, the combined company would have a much more stable cash flow. In other words, a merger would diversify away some of the seasonal variation and, in fact, would make bankruptcy much less likely.

Notice that the operations of the two firms are very different, so the proposed merger is a purely 'financial' merger. This means that there are no 'synergies' or other value-creating possibilities except, possibly, gains from risk reduction. Here is some pre-merger information:

|  | Sunshine Swimwear | Polar Winterwear |
| --- | --- | --- |
| Market value of assets | €30 million | €10 million |
| Face value of pure discount debt | €12 million | €4 million |
| Debt maturity | 3 years | 3 years |
| Asset return standard deviation | 50% | 60% |

The risk-free rate, continuously compounded, is 5 per cent. Given this, we can view the equity in each firm as a call option, and calculate the following using Black–Scholes to determine equity values (check these for practice):

|  | Sunshine Swimwear | Polar Winterwear |
| --- | --- | --- |
| Market value of equity | €20.394 million | €6.992 million |
| Market value of debt | €9.606 million | €3.008 million |

If you check these, you may get slightly different answers if you use Table 22.3 (we used a spreadsheet). Notice that we calculated the market value of debt using the market value balance sheet identity.

After the merger, the combined firm's assets will simply be the sum of the pre-merger values, €30 + €10 = €40, because no value was created or destroyed. Similarly, the total face value of the debt is now €16 million. However, we shall assume that the combined firm's asset return standard deviation is 40 per cent. This is lower than for either of the two individual firms, because of the diversification effect.

So, what is the impact of this merger? To find out, we compute the post-merger value of the equity. Based on our discussion, here is the relevant information:

| | Combined firm |
|---|---|
| Market value of assets | €40 million |
| Face value of pure discount debt | €16 million |
| Debt maturity | 3 years |
| Asset return standard deviation | 40% |

Once again, we can calculate equity and debt values:

| | Combined firm |
|---|---|
| Market value of equity | €26.602 million |
| Market value of debt | €13.398 million |

What we notice is that this merger is a terrible idea, at least for the shareholders! Before the merger, the equity in the two separate firms was worth a total of €20.394 + €6.992 = €27.386 million compared with only €26.602 million post-merger; so the merger vaporized €27.386 − €26.602 = €0.784 million.

Where did €0.784 million in equity go? It went to the bondholders. Their bonds were worth €9.606 + €3.008 = €12.614 million before the merger and €13.398 million after, a gain of exactly €0.784 million. Thus this merger neither created nor destroyed value, but it shifted it from the shareholders to the bondholders.

Our example shows that pure financial mergers are a bad idea, and it also shows why. The diversification works in the sense that it reduces the volatility of the firm's return on assets. This risk reduction benefits the bondholders by making default less likely. This is sometimes called the 'co-insurance' effect. Essentially, by merging, the firms insure each other's bonds. The bonds are thus less risky, and they rise in value. If the bonds increase in value, and there is no net increase in asset values, then the equity must decrease in value. Thus pure financial mergers are good for creditors but not for shareholders.

Another way to see this is that because the equity is a call option, a reduction in return variance on the underlying asset has to reduce its value. The reduction in value in the case of a purely financial merger has an interesting interpretation. The merger makes default (and thus bankruptcy) *less* likely to happen. That is obviously a good thing from a bondholder's perspective, but why is it a bad thing from a shareholder's perspective? The answer is simple: The right to go bankrupt is a valuable shareholder option. A purely financial merger reduces the value of that option.

## Options and Capital Budgeting

We now consider two issues regarding capital budgeting. What we shall show is that, for a levered firm, the shareholders might prefer a lower NPV project to a higher one. We then show that they might even prefer a *negative* NPV project to a positive NPV project.

As usual, we shall illustrate these points first with an example. Here is the basic background information for the firm:

| | |
|---|---|
| Market value of assets | £20 million |
| Face value of pure discount debt | £40 million |
| Debt maturity | 5 years |
| Asset return standard deviation | 50% |

The risk-free rate is 4 per cent. As we have now done several times, we can calculate equity and debt values:

| | |
|---|---|
| Market value of equity | £5.724 million |
| Market value of debt | £14.276 million |

This firm has a fairly high degree of leverage: the debt–equity ratio based on market values is £14.276/£5.724 = 2.5, or 250 per cent. This is high, but not unheard of. Notice also that the option here is out of the money: as a result, the delta is 0.546.

The firm has two mutually exclusive investments under consideration. The projects affect both the market value of the firm's assets and the firm's asset return standard deviation as follows:

|  | Project A | Project B |
|---|---|---|
| NPV | £4 | £2 |
| Market value of firm's assets (£20 + NPV) | £24 | £22 |
| Firm's asset return standard deviation | 40% | 60% |

Which project is better? It is obvious that project A has the higher NPV, but by now you are wary of the change in the firm's asset return standard deviation. One project reduces it; the other increases it. To see which project the shareholders like better, we have to go through our by now familiar calculations:

|  | Project A | Project B |
|---|---|---|
| Market value of equity | £5.938 | £ 8.730 |
| Market value of debt | £18.062 | £13.270 |

There is a dramatic difference between the two projects. Project A benefits both the shareholders and the bondholders, but most of the gain goes to the bondholders. Project B has a huge impact on the value of the equity, plus it reduces the value of the debt. Clearly the shareholders prefer B.

What are the implications of our analysis? Basically, we have discovered two things. First, when the equity has a delta significantly smaller than 1.0, any value created will go partially to bondholders. Second, shareholders have a strong incentive to increase the variance of the return on the firm's assets. More specifically, shareholders will have a strong preference for variance-increasing projects as opposed to variance-decreasing ones, even if that means a lower NPV.

Let's do one final example. Here is a different set of numbers:

| Market value of assets | £20 million |
|---|---|
| Face value of pure discount debt | £100 million |
| Debt maturity | 5 years |
| Asset return standard deviation | 50% |

The risk-free rate is 4 per cent, so the equity and debt values are these:

| Market value of equity | £2 million |
|---|---|
| Market value of debt | £18 million |

Notice that the change from our previous example is that the face value of the debt is now £100 million, so the option is far out of the money. The delta is only 0.24, so most of any value created will go to the bondholders.

The firm has an investment under consideration that must be taken now or never. The project affects both the market value of the firm's assets and the firm's asset return standard deviation as follows:

| Project NPV | –£1 million |
|---|---|
| Market value of firm's assets (£20 million + NPV) | £19 million |
| Firm's asset return standard deviation | 70% |

Thus the project has a negative NPV, but it increases the standard deviation of the firm's return on assets. If the firm takes the project, here is the result:

| Market value of equity | £4.821 million |
|---|---|
| Market value of debt | £14.179 million |

This project more than doubles the value of the equity! Once again, what we are seeing is that shareholders have a strong incentive to increase volatility, particularly when the option is far out of the money. What is happening is that the shareholders have relatively little to lose, because bankruptcy is the likely outcome. As a result, there is a strong incentive to go for a long shot, even if that long shot has a negative NPV. It's a bit like using your very last euro on a lottery ticket. It's a bad investment, but there aren't a lot of other options!

## Summary and Conclusions

This chapter serves as an introduction to options.

1   The most familiar options are puts and calls. These options give the holder the right to sell or buy shares of equity at a given exercise price. American options can be exercised any time up to and including the expiration date. European options can be exercised only on the expiration date.

2   We showed that a strategy of buying a share and buying a put is equivalent to a strategy of buying a call and buying a zero coupon bond. From this, the put–call parity relationship was established:

$$\begin{matrix} \text{Value of} \\ \text{stock} \end{matrix} + \begin{matrix} \text{Value of} \\ \text{put} \end{matrix} - \begin{matrix} \text{Value of} \\ \text{call} \end{matrix} = \begin{matrix} \text{Present value of} \\ \text{exercise price} \end{matrix}$$

3   The value of an option depends on five factors:

(a) The price of the underlying asset

(b) The exercise price

(c) The expiration date

(d) The variability of the underlying asset

(e) The interest rate on risk-free bonds

The Black–Scholes model can determine the intrinsic price of an option from these five factors.

4   The 'Greeks' (delta, gamma, theta, and vega) measure different aspects of the risk of options.

5   Much of corporate financial theory can be presented in terms of options. In this chapter, we pointed out that:

(a) Equity can be represented as a call option on the firm.

(b) Shareholders enhance the value of their call by increasing the risk of their firm.

## Questions and Problems

CONCEPT
1–11

1   **Options**   Many laypeople find the whole concept of options difficult to understand. Use a non-financial example to explain how options work, and why they're so important for flexible decision-making.

2   **Call Options**   Explain what is meant by a call option. What are the main reasons why a corporation would consider buying a call option?

3   **Put Options**   Are put options the same as writing a call option? Explain.

4 **Writing Options** Why would a corporation wish to write a put option on an asset?

5 **Option Quotes** Look at Table 22.1. Why does the settlement price fall as the strike price increases for call options? Conversely, why does the settlement price increase as the strike price gets higher for put options? Can you think of a situation where, for call options, the settlement price would increase as the strike price gets higher? Explain.

6 **Option Combinations** Why would a corporation wish to combine put and call options on a commodity? Provide an example of a case where this might happen.

7 **Valuing Options** Review the factors that affect the value of call and put options.

8 **Option Pricing** Why can't you just value an option using discounted cash flows, as in net present value?

9 **The Greeks** Why are the Greeks important to a corporation?

10 **Shares and Bonds as Options** Show how a share of equity can be viewed as an option. Why is this perspective helpful?

11 **Options and Corporate Decisions** In many countries, governments have encouraged bank mergers to reduce their risk. Use option analysis to show why this may be bad news for the bank's shareholders. Does this mean that you shouldn't buy the shares of a newly merged bank? Explain.

12 **Options** Complete the following sentence for each of these investors:

(a) A buyer of call options.

(b) A buyer of put options.

(c) A seller (writer) of call options.

(d) A seller (writer) of put options.

'The (buyer/seller) of a (put/call) option (pays/receives) money for the (right/obligation) to (buy/sell) a specified asset at a fixed price for a fixed length of time.'

13 **American and European Options** What is the difference between an American option and a European option?

14 **Option Pricing** You notice that the share price of Patel Corporation is £50 per share. Call options with an exercise price of £35 per share are selling for £10. What's wrong here? Describe how you can take advantage of this mispricing if the option expires today.

15 **Option Risk** True or false: 'Unsystematic risk is irrelevant in valuing shares because it can be diversified away; therefore it is also irrelevant for valuing a call option on the share.' Explain.

16 **Option Pricing** Suppose a certain share currently sells for £30. If a put option and a call option are available with £30 exercise prices, which do you think will sell for more, the put or the call? Explain.

17 **Option Price and Interest Rates** Suppose the interest rate on T-bills suddenly and unexpectedly rises. All other things being the same, what is the impact on call option values? On put option values?

18 **Contingent Liabilities** When you take out an ordinary student loan, it is usually the case that whoever holds that loan is given a guarantee by the government, meaning that the government will make up any payments you skip. This is just one example of the many loan guarantees made by governments. Such guarantees don't show up in calculations of government spending or in official deficit figures. Why not? Should they show up?

19 **Options and Expiration Dates** What is the impact of lengthening the time to expiration on an option's value? Explain.

20  **Options and Share Price Volatility**   What is the impact of an increase in the volatility of the underlying equity's return on an option's value? Explain.

21  **Insurance as an Option**   An insurance policy is considered analogous to an option. From the policyholder's point of view, what type of option is an insurance policy? Why?

22  **Equity as a Call Option**   It is said that the shareholders of a levered firm can be thought of as holding a call option on the firm's assets. Explain what is meant by this statement.

23  **Option Valuation and NPV**   You are CEO of Titan Industries and have just been awarded a large number of employee share options. The company has two mutually exclusive projects available. The first project has a large NPV and will reduce the total risk of the company. The second project has a small NPV and will increase the total risk of the company. You have decided to accept the first project when you remember your employee share options. How might this affect your decision?

24  **Put–Call Parity**   One thing put–call parity tells us is that, given any three of a share, a call, a put and a T-bill, the fourth can be synthesized or replicated using the other three. For example, how can we replicate a share of equity using a call, a put and a T-bill?

25  **Two-State Option Pricing Model**   T-bills currently yield 5.5 per cent. Equity in Nina Manufacturing is currently selling for 55 Swedish krona (SKr) per share. There is no possibility that the equity will be worth less than SKr50 per share in one year.

(a)  What is the value of a call option with a SKr45 exercise price? What is the intrinsic value?

(b)  What is the value of a call option with a SKr35 exercise price? What is the intrinsic value?

(c)  What is the value of a put option with a SKr45 exercise price? What is the intrinsic value?

26  **Understanding Option Quotes**   Use the option quote information from Euronext Liffe shown here for Xstrata plc to answer the questions that follow. The equity is currently selling for £7.47.

March 2009 Prices – 02/01/09

| | Calls | | | | | | | | | | Puts | | | | | | | |
|---|---|---|---|---|---|---|---|---|---|---|---|---|---|---|---|---|---|---|
| Settl. | Day volume | Vol | Time (CET) | Last | Bid | Ask | AQ Bid | AQ Ask | C | Strike | P | AQ Bid | AQ Ask | Bid | Ask | Last | Time (CET) | Vol | Day volume | Settl. |
| 346.75 | – | – | – | – | – | – | 329.00 | 359.00 | C | 440 | P | 27.25 | 39.25 | – | – | – | – | – | – | 36.75 |
| 318.25 | – | – | – | – | – | – | 300.25 | 330.25 | C | 480 | P | 38.25 | 50.25 | – | 50.00 | 50.00 | 15:34 | 2 | 2 | 47.75 |
| 288.50 | – | – | – | – | – | – | 270.50 | 300.50 | C | 520 | P | 46.75 | 61.75 | 58.00 | 65.00 | 74.00 | 10:27 | 10 | 10 | 58.00 |
| 265.25 | – | – | – | – | 235.00 | 245.00 | 248.25 | 273.25 | C | 560 | P | 62.00 | 77.00 | 72.00 | 77.00 | 91.00 | 10:27 | 10 | 10 | 74.25 |
| 239.75 | – | – | – | – | 220.00 | 235.00 | 222.75 | 247.75 | C | 600 | P | 76.00 | 91.00 | 84.00 | 90.00 | 109.00 | 10:27 | 10 | 10 | 88.75 |
| 214.50 | – | – | – | – | 210.00 | 225.00 | 197.25 | 222.25 | C | 640 | P | 90.50 | 105.50 | 101.00 | 106.00 | – | – | – | – | 103.25 |
| 193.00 | 8 | 3 | 12:47 | 158.00 | 193.00 | 199.00 | 175.00 | 200.00 | C | 680 | P | 108.00 | 123.00 | 119.00 | 124.00 | 134.00 | 14:10 | 5 | 5 | 121.50 |
| 175.00 | 10 | 10 | 11:50 | 136.00 | 172.00 | 178.00 | 159.50 | 179.50 | C | 720 | P | 128.75 | 145.75 | 138.00 | 143.00 | – | – | – | – | 143.50 |
| 154.25 | 20 | 10 | 11:50 | 120.00 | 153.00 | 159.00 | 138.50 | 158.50 | C | 760 | P | 147.50 | 164.50 | 159.00 | 164.00 | – | – | – | – | 162.50 |
| 137.25 | 11 | 1 | 14:44 | 114.00 | 135.00 | 141.00 | 121.50 | 141.50 | C | 800 | P | 170.25 | 187.25 | 181.00 | 186.00 | 195.00 | 16:26 | 3 | 3 | 185.25 |
| 121.25 | – | – | – | – | 119.00 | 125.00 | 105.50 | 125.50 | C | 840 | P | 194.25 | 211.25 | 205.00 | 210.00 | – | – | – | – | 209.00 |
| 110.25 | – | – | – | – | 105.00 | 110.00 | 96.00 | 113.00 | C | 880 | P | 221.75 | 241.75 | – | – | – | – | – | – | 238.00 |
| 99.50 | 14 | 2 | 17:05 | 88.00 | 88.00 | 88.00 | 85.00 | 102.00 | C | 920 | P | 250.50 | 270.50 | – | – | – | – | – | – | 267.00 |
| 87.50 | – | – | – | – | – | – | 72.75 | 89.75 | C | 960 | P | 278.25 | 298.25 | – | – | – | – | – | – | 294.75 |
| 77.00 | – | – | – | – | – | – | 62.00 | 79.00 | C | 1,000 | P | 307.50 | 327.50 | – | – | – | – | – | – | 324.25 |
| 59.75 | – | – | – | – | – | – | 47.00 | 62.00 | C | 1,100 | P | 388.50 | 413.50 | – | – | – | – | – | – | 406.75 |
| 44.25 | – | – | – | – | – | – | 31.25 | 46.25 | C | 1,200 | P | 472.75 | 497.75 | – | – | – | – | – | – | 491.25 |
| 34.00 | – | – | – | – | – | 300.00 | 22.50 | 37.50 | C | 1,300 | P | 561.50 | 591.50 | – | – | – | – | – | – | 580.75 |
| 25.25 | – | – | – | – | – | – | 15.25 | 27.25 | C | 1,400 | P | 652.75 | 682.75 | – | – | – | – | – | – | 672.00 |
| 18.25 | – | – | – | – | – | – | 9.75 | 21.75 | C | 1,500 | P | 747.50 | 777.50 | – | – | – | – | – | – | 765.25 |
| 14.50 | – | – | – | – | – | – | 6.25 | 18.25 | C | 1,600 | P | 844.00 | 874.00 | – | – | – | – | – | – | 861.75 |
| 12.00 | – | – | – | – | – | – | 3.50 | 15.50 | C | 1,700 | P | 941.50 | 971.50 | – | – | – | – | – | – | 959.00 |
| 8.25 | – | – | – | – | – | – | 0.50 | 12.50 | C | 1,800 | P | 1,039.25 | 1,069.25 | – | – | – | – | – | – | 1,056.00 |
| 5.50 | – | – | – | – | – | – | 0.25 | 10.25 | C | 1,900 | P | 1,137.50 | 1,167.50 | – | – | – | – | – | – | 1,153.75 |
| 4.50 | – | – | – | – | – | – | – | 9.25 | C | 2,000 | P | 1,237.00 | 1,267.00 | – | – | – | – | – | – | 1,253.25 |

(a) Are the call options in the money? What is the intrinsic value of an Xstrata plc call option?

(b) Are the put options in the money? What is the intrinsic value of an Xstrata plc put option?

(c) Looking at the quotes on their own, do you think that the market expects the price of Xstrata to increase or decrease during the period of the option? What range of prices are anticipated? Look at the share price history for Xstrata on Yahoo! Finance and find out what actually happened. Who made a profit from their trading – the call or put holders?

27 **Calculating Pay-Offs** Use the option quote information on Fortis from Euronext Liffe shown here to answer the questions that follow.

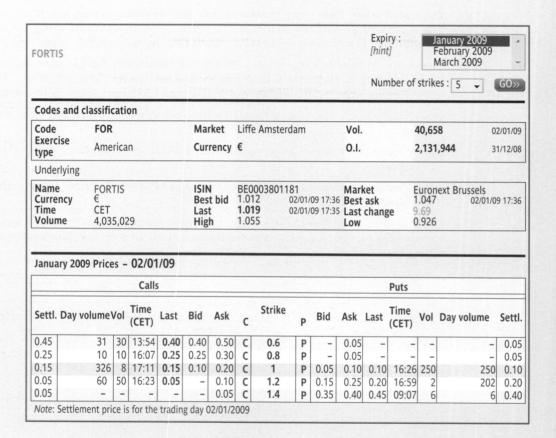

(a) Suppose you buy 10 contracts of the January €1.20 call option. How much will you pay, ignoring commissions?

(b) In part (a), suppose that Fortis equity is selling for €1.40 per share on the expiration date. How much is your options investment worth? What if the terminal share price is €1.05? Explain.

(c) Suppose you buy 10 contracts of the January €0.80 put option. What is your maximum gain? On the expiration date, Fortis is selling for €0.64 per share. How much is your options investment worth? What is your net gain?

(d) In part (c), suppose you *sell* 10 of the January €0.80 put contracts. What is your net gain or loss if Fortis is selling for €0.64 at expiration? For €1.32? What is the break-even price -- that is, the terminal share price that results in a zero profit?

28 **Two-State Option Pricing Model** The price of Ervin plc share will be either £75 or £95 at the end of the year. Call options are available with one year to expiration. T-bills currently yield 6 per cent.

    (a) Suppose the current price of Ervin equity is £80. What is the value of the call option if the exercise price is £70 per share?

    (b) Suppose the exercise price is £90 in part (a). What is the value of the call option now?

29 **Two-State Option Pricing Model** The price of Norwegian Property ASA shares will be either NKr6.00 or NKr8.00 at the end of the year. Call options are available with one year to expiration. T-bills currently yield 5 per cent.

    (a) Suppose the current price of Norwegian Property shares is NKr7.00. What is the value of the call option if the exercise price is NKr4.50 per share?

    (b) Suppose the exercise price is NKr7.00 in part (a). What is the value of the call option now?

30 **Put–Call Parity** An equity is currently selling for €61 per share. A call option with an exercise price of €65 sells for €4.12 and expires in three months. If the risk-free rate of interest is 2.6 per cent per year, compounded continuously, what is the price of a put option with the same exercise price?

31 **Put–Call Parity** A put option that expires in six months with an exercise price of €50 sells for €4.89. The equity is currently priced at €53, and the risk-free rate is 3.6 per cent per year, compounded continuously. What is the price of a call option with the same exercise price?

32 **Put–Call Parity** A put option and a call option with an exercise price of €70 and three months to expiration sell for €2.87 and €4.68, respectively. If the risk-free rate is 4.8 per cent per year, compounded continuously, what is the current share price?

33 **Put–Call Parity** A put option and a call option with an exercise price of £65 expire in two months and sell for £2.86 and £4.08, respectively. If the equity is currently priced at £65.80, what is the annual continuously compounded rate of interest?

34 **Black–Scholes** What are the prices of a call option and a put option with the following characteristics?

> Share price = £38
> Exercise price = £35
> Risk-free rate = 6% per year, compounded continuously
> Maturity = 3 months
> Standard deviation = 54% per year

35 **Black–Scholes** What are the prices of a call option and a put option with the following characteristics?

> Share price = £86
> Exercise price = £90
> Risk-free rate = 4% per year, compounded continuously
> Maturity = 8 months
> Standard deviation = 62% per year

36 **Delta** What are the deltas of a call option and a put option with the following characteristics? What does the delta of the option tell you?

> Share price = £87
> Exercise price = £85
> Risk-free rate = 5% per year, compounded continuously
> Maturity = 9 months
> Standard deviation = 56% per year

37  **Black–Scholes and Asset Value**  You own a plot of land in Ardnamurchin, Scotland, that is currently unused. Similar plots have recently sold for £1.6 million. Over the past five years the price of land in the area has increased 12 per cent per year, with an annual standard deviation of 20 per cent. A buyer has recently approached you and wants an option to buy the land in the next 12 months for £1.75 million. The risk-free rate of interest is 5 per cent per year, compounded continuously. How much should you charge for the option?

38  **Black–Scholes and Asset Value**  In the previous problem, suppose you wanted the option to sell the land to the buyer in one year. Assuming all the facts are the same, describe the transaction that would occur today. What is the price of the transaction today?

39  **Time Value of Options**  You are given the following information concerning options on a particular equity:

> Share price = £86
> Exercise price = £90
> Risk-free rate = 6% per year, compounded continuously
> Maturity = 6 months
> Standard deviation = 53% per year

(a)  What is the intrinsic value of the call option? Of the put option?

(b)  What is the time value of the call option? Of the put option?

(c)  Does the call or the put have the larger time value component? Would you expect this to be true in general?

40  **Risk-Neutral Valuation**  An equity is currently priced at £75. The equity will either increase or decrease by 15 per cent over the next year. There is a call option on the equity with a strike price of £70 and one year until expiration. If the risk-free rate is 12 per cent, what is the risk-neutral value of the call option?

41  **Risk-Neutral Valuation**  In the previous problem, assume the risk-free rate is only 8 per cent. What is the risk-neutral value of the option now? What happens to the risk-neutral probabilities of a share price increase and a share price decrease?

42  **Black–Scholes**  A call option matures in six months. The underlying share price is £85, and the share's return has a standard deviation of 20 per cent per year. The risk-free rate is 4 per cent per year, compounded continuously. If the exercise price is £0, what is the price of the call option?

43  **Black–Scholes**  A call option has an exercise price of £80 and matures in six months. The current share price is £84, and the risk-free rate is 5 per cent per year, compounded continuously. What is the price of the call if the standard deviation of the share is 0 per cent per year?

44  **Black–Scholes**  An equity is currently priced at £35. A call option with an expiration of one year has an exercise price of £50. The risk-free rate is 12 per cent per year, compounded continuously, and the standard deviation of the equity's return is infinitely large. What is the price of the call option?

45  **Equity as an Option**  Sunburn Sunscreen has a zero coupon bond issue outstanding with a €10,000 face value that matures in one year. The current market value of the

firm's assets is €10,500. The standard deviation of the return on the firm's assets is 38 per cent per year, and the annual risk-free rate is 5 per cent per year, compounded continuously. Based on the Black–Scholes model, what is the market value of the firm's equity and debt?

46 **Equity as an Option and NPV**   Suppose the firm in the previous problem is considering two mutually exclusive investments. Project A has an NPV of €700, and project B has an NPV of €1,000. As the result of taking project A, the standard deviation of the return on the firm's assets will increase to 55 per cent per year. If project B is taken, the standard deviation will fall to 34 per cent per year.

(a) What is the value of the firm's equity and debt if project A is undertaken? If project B is undertaken?

(b) Which project would the shareholders prefer? Can you reconcile your answer with the NPV rule?

(c) Suppose the shareholders and bondholders are in fact the same group of investors. Would this affect your answer to (b)?

(d) What does this problem suggest to you about shareholder incentives?

47 **Equity as an Option**   Frostbite Thermalwear has a zero coupon bond issue outstanding with a face value of €20,000 that matures in one year. The current market value of the firm's assets is €22,000. The standard deviation of the return on the firm's assets is 53 per cent per year, and the annual risk-free rate is 5 per cent per year, compounded continuously. Based on the Black–Scholes model, what is the market value of the firm's equity and debt? What is the firm's continuously compounded cost of debt?

48 **Mergers and Equity as an Option**   Suppose Sunburn Sunscreen and Frostbite Thermalwear in the previous problems have decided to merge. Because the two companies have seasonal sales, the combined firm's return on assets will have a standard deviation of 31 per cent per year.

(a) What is the combined value of equity in the two existing companies? The value of debt?

(b) What is the value of the new firm's equity? The value of debt?

(c) What was the gain or loss for shareholders? For bondholders?

(d) What happened to shareholder value here?

49 **Equity as an Option and NPV**   A company has a single zero coupon bond outstanding that matures in 10 years with a face value of £30 million. The current value of the company's assets is £22 million, and the standard deviation of the return on the firm's assets is 39 per cent per year. The risk-free rate is 6 per cent per year, compounded continuously.

(a) What is the current market value of the company's equity?

(b) What is the current market value of the company's debt?

(c) What is the company's continuously compounded cost of debt?

(d) The company has a new project available. The project has an NPV of £750,000. If the company undertakes the project, what will be the new market value of equity? Assume volatility is unchanged.

(e) Assuming the company undertakes the new project and does not borrow any additional funds, what is the new continuously compounded cost of debt? What is happening here?

50 **Two-State Option Pricing Model**   Ken is interested in buying a European call option written on Southeastern Airlines plc, a non-dividend-paying equity, with a strike price of £110 and one year until expiration. Currently, Southeastern's equity sells for £100 per share. In one year Ken knows that Southeastern's share will be trading at either £125 per share or £80 per share. Ken is able to borrow and lend at the risk-free EAR of 2.5 per cent.

(a) What should the call option sell for today?

(b) If no options currently trade on the equity, is there a way to create a synthetic call option with identical pay-offs to the call option just described? If there is, how would you do it?

(c) How much does the synthetic call option cost? Is this greater than, less than, or equal to what the actual call option costs? Does this make sense?

51 **Two-State Option Pricing Model** Rob wishes to buy a European put option on BioLabs plc, a non-dividend-paying equity, with a strike price of £40 and six months until expiration. BioLab's equity is currently selling for £30 per share, and Rob expects that the share price will either rise to £60 or fall to £15 in six months. Rob can borrow and lend at the risk-free EAR of 21 per cent.

(a) What should the put option sell for today?

(b) If no options currently trade on the equity, is there a way to create a synthetic put option with identical pay-offs to the put option just described? If there is, how would you do it?

(c) How much does the synthetic put option cost? Is this greater than, less than, or equal to what the actual put option costs? Does this make sense?

52 **Two-State Option Pricing Model** Maverick Manufacturing plc must purchase gold in three months for use in its operations. Maverick's management has estimated that if the price of gold were to rise above $875 per ounce, the firm would go bankrupt. The current price of gold is $850 per ounce. The firm's chief financial officer believes that the price of gold will either rise to $900 per ounce or fall to $825 per ounce over the next three months. Management wishes to eliminate any risk of the firm going bankrupt. Maverick can borrow and lend at the risk-free APR of 16.99 per cent.

(a) Should the company buy a call option or a put option on gold? To avoid bankruptcy, what strike price and time to expiration would the company like this option to have?

(b) How much should such an option sell for in the open market?

(c) If no options currently trade on gold, is there a way for the company to create a synthetic option with identical pay-offs to the option just described? If there is, how would the firm do it?

(d) How much does the synthetic option cost? Is this greater than, less than, or equal to what the actual option costs? Does this make sense?

53 **Black–Scholes and Collar Cost** An investor is said to take a position in a 'collar' if she buys the asset, buys an out-of-the-money put option on the asset, and sells an out-of-the-money call option on the asset. The two options should have the same time to expiration. Suppose Marie wishes to purchase a collar on Zurich Re, a non-dividend-paying equity, with six months until expiration. She would like the put to have a strike price of 50 Swiss Francs (SwFr) and the call to have a strike price of SwFr120. The current price of Zurich Re's equity is SwFr80 per share. Marie can borrow and lend at the continuously compounded risk-free rate of 10 per cent per annum, and the annual standard deviation of the equity's return is 50 per cent. Use the Black–Scholes model to calculate the total cost of the collar that Marie is interested in buying. What is the effect of the collar?

54 **Debt Valuation and Time to Maturity** McLemore Industries has a zero coupon bond issue that matures in two years with a face value of £30,000. The current value of the company's assets is £13,000, and the standard deviation of the return on assets is 60 per cent per year.

**CHALLENGE**

**54–62**

(a) Assume the risk-free rate is 5 per cent per year, compounded continuously. What is the value of a risk-free bond with the same face value and maturity as the company's bond?

(b) What price would the bondholders have to pay for a put option on the firm's assets with a strike price equal to the face value of the debt?

(c) Using the answers from (a) and (b), what is the value of the firm's debt? What is the continuously compounded yield on the company's debt?

(d) From an examination of the value of the assets of McLemore Industries, and the fact that the debt must be repaid in two years, it seems likely that the company will default on its debt. Management has approached bondholders and proposed a plan whereby the company would repay the same face value of debt, but the repayment would not occur for five years. What is the value of the debt under the proposed plan? What is the new continuously compounded yield on the debt? Explain why this occurs.

**55  Debt Valuation and Asset Variance**  Brozik plc has a zero coupon bond that matures in five years with a face value of £60,000. The current value of the company's assets is £57,000, and the standard deviation of its return on assets is 50 per cent per year. The risk-free rate is 6 per cent per year, compounded continuously.

(a) What is the value of a risk-free bond with the same face value and maturity as the current bond?

(b) What is the value of a put option on the firm's assets with a strike price equal to the face value of the debt?

(c) Using the answers from (a) and (b), what is the value of the firm's debt? What is the continuously compounded yield on the company's debt?

(d) Assume the company can restructure its assets so that the standard deviation of its return on assets increases to 60 per cent per year. What happens to the value of the debt? What is the new continuously compounded yield on the debt? Reconcile your answers in (c) and (d).

(e) What happens to bondholders if the company restructures its assets? What happens to shareholders? How does this create an agency problem?

**56  Two-State Option Pricing and Corporate Valuation**  Strudler Property plc, a construction firm financed by both debt and equity, is undertaking a new project. If the project is successful the value of the firm in one year will be £500 million, but if the project is a failure the firm will be worth only £320 million. The current value of Strudler is £400 million, a figure that includes the prospects for the new project. Strudler has outstanding zero coupon bonds due in one year with a face value of £380 million. Treasury bills that mature in one year yield 7 per cent EAR. Strudler pays no dividends.

(a) Use the two-state option pricing model to find the current value of Strudler's debt and equity.

(b) Suppose Strudler has 500,000 shares of equity outstanding. What is the price per share of the firm's equity?

(c) Compare the market value of Strudler's debt with the present value of an equal amount of debt that is riskless with one year until maturity. Is the firm's debt worth more than, less than, or the same as the riskless debt? Does this make sense? What factors might cause these two values to be different?

(d) Suppose that in place of the preceding project Strudler's management decides to undertake a project that is even more risky. The value of the firm will either increase to £800 million or decrease to £200 million by the end of the year. Surprisingly, management concludes that the value of the firm today will remain at exactly £400 million if this risky project is substituted for the less risky one. Use the two-state option pricing model to determine the value of the firm's debt and equity if the firm plans on undertaking this new project. Which project do bondholders prefer?

**57  Black–Scholes and Dividends**  In addition to the five factors discussed in the chapter, dividends also affect the price of an option. The Black–Scholes option pricing model with dividends is

$$C = S \times e^{-dt} \times N(d_1) - E \times e^{-Rt} \times N(d_2)$$
$$d_1 = [\ln(S/E) + (R - d + \sigma^2/2) \times t]/(\sigma \times \sqrt{t})$$
$$d_2 = d_1 - \sigma \times \sqrt{t}$$

All of the variables are the same as the Black–Scholes model without dividends except for the variable $d$, which is the continuously compounded dividend yield on the share.

(a) What effect do you think the dividend yield will have on the price of a call option? Explain.

(b) Genmab A/S is currently priced at 2.26 Danish kroner (DKr) per share, the standard deviation of its return is 50 per cent per year, and the risk-free rate is 5 per cent per year compounded continuously. What is the price of a call option with a strike price of DKr2.00 and a maturity of six months if the share has a dividend yield of 2 per cent per year?

58 **Put–Call Parity and Dividends** The put–call parity condition is altered when dividends are paid. The dividend adjusted put–call parity formula is

$$S \times e^{-dt} + P = E \times e^{-Rt} + C$$

where $d$ is again the continuously compounded dividend yield.

(a) What effect do you think the dividend yield will have on the price of a put option? Explain.

(b) From the previous question, what is the price of a put option with the same strike price and time to expiration as the call option?

59 **Put Delta** In the chapter, we noted that the delta for a put option is $N(d_1) - 1$. Is this the same thing as $-N(-d_1)$? (*Hint*: Yes, but why?)

60 **Black–Scholes Put Pricing Model** Use the Black–Scholes model for pricing a call, put–call parity, and the previous question to show that the Black–Scholes model for directly pricing a put can be written as follows:

$$P = E \times e^{-Rt} \times N(-d_2) - S \times N(-d_1)$$

61 **Black–Scholes** An equity is currently priced at £50. The share will never pay a dividend. The risk-free rate is 12 per cent per year, compounded continuously, and the standard deviation of the share's return is 60 per cent. A European call option on the share has a strike price of £100 and no expiration date, meaning that it has an infinite life. Based on Black–Scholes, what is the value of the call option? Do you see a paradox here? Do you see a way out of the paradox?

62 **Delta** You purchase one call and sell one put with the same strike price and expiration date. What is the delta of your portfolio? Why?

MINI CASE

# Clissold Industries Options

You are currently working for Clissold Industries. The company, which went public five years ago, engages in the design, production and distribution of lighting equipment and speciality products worldwide. Because of recent events, Mal Clissold, the company president, is concerned about the company's risk, so he asks for your input.

In your discussion with Mal, you explain that the CAPM proposes that the market risk of the company's equity is the determinant of its expected return. Even though Mal agrees with this, he argues that his portfolio consists entirely of Clissold Industry shares and options, so he is concerned with the total risk, or standard deviation, of the company's equity. Furthermore, even though he has calculated the standard deviation of the company's equity for the past five years, he would like an estimate of the share's volatility moving forward.

Mal states that you can find the estimated volatility of the share for future periods by calculating the implied standard deviation of option contracts on the company equity. When you examine the factors that affect the price of an option, all of the factors except the standard deviation of the shares are directly observable in the market. You can also observe the option price as well. Mal states that because you can observe all of the option factors except the standard deviation, you can simply solve the Black–Scholes model and find the implied standard deviation.

To help you find the implied standard deviation of the company's equity, Mal has provided you with the following option prices on four call options that expire in six months. The risk-free rate is 6 per cent, and the current share price is £50.

| Strike price (£) | Option price (£) |
|---|---|
| 30 | 23.00 |
| 40 | 16.05 |
| 50 | 9.75 |
| 55 | 7.95 |

1   How many different volatilities would you expect to see for the equity?

2   Unfortunately, solving for the implied standard deviation is not as easy as Mal suggests. In fact, there is no direct solution for the standard deviation of the equity even if we have all other variables for the Black–Scholes model. Mal would still like you to estimate the implied standard deviation of the share. To do this, set up a spreadsheet using the Solver function in Microsoft Excel® to calculate the implied volatilities for each of the options.

3   Are all of the implied volatilities for the options the same? (*Hint*: No.) What are the possible reasons that can cause different volatilities for these options?

4   After you discuss the importance of volatility for option prices, your boss mentions that he has heard of the FTSE 100 Volatility Index (VFTSE) on Euronext. What is the VFTSE, and what does it represent?

5   Look for current option quotes for the FTSE 100 Volatility on Euronext. To find these, search on the Euronext website for the ISIN: QS0011052162. What does the implied volatility of a VFTSE option represent?

## Relevant Accounting Standards

IAS39 *Financial Instruments: Recognition and Measurement* and IFRS7 *Financial Instruments: Disclosure* are exceptionally important for options. Since the potential exposure to losses from options can be significant, it is important that their impact is reflected in a firm's accounting statements. Visit the IASPlus website (www.iasplus.com) for more information.

## Additional Reading

A very rich empirical and theoretical research field considers option pricing dynamics. The reference list below focuses on options as they relate to corporate finance.

Amram, M., F. Li and C.A. Perkins (2006) 'How Kimberly-Clark uses real options', *Journal of Applied Corporate Finance*, vol. 18, no. 2, pp. 40–47. **US**.

Giaccotto, C., G.M. Goldberg and S.P. Hegde (2007) 'The value of embedded real options: evidence from consumer automobile lease contracts', *Journal of Finance*, vol. 62, no. 1, pp. 411–445. **US**.

McDonald, R.L. (2006) 'The role of real options in capital budgeting: theory and practice', *Journal of Applied Corporate Finance*, vol. 18, no. 2, pp. 28–39. **Theoretical paper**.

## Endnotes

1  We use *buyer*, *owner* and *holder* interchangeably.

2  This example assumes that the call lets the holder purchase one share at £7.00. In reality, one call option contract would let the holder purchase 100 shares. The profit would then equal £100 [= (£8.00 − £7.00) × 100].

3  Actually, because of differing exercise prices, the two graphs are not quite mirror images of each other.

4  Our discussion in this section is of American options, because they are more commonly traded in the real world. As necessary, we shall indicate differences for European options. American options are differentiated from European options through their ability to be exercised at any time before the expiration date. The terminology has nothing to do with where the options are traded.

5  This relationship need not hold for a European call option. Consider a firm with two otherwise identical European call options, one expiring at the end of May and the other expiring a few months later. Further assume that a *huge* dividend is paid in early June. If the first call is exercised at the end of May, its holder will receive the underlying share. If he does not sell the share, he will receive the large dividend shortly thereafter. However, the holder of the second call will receive the share through exercise after the dividend is paid. Because the market knows that the holder of this option will miss the dividend, the value of the second call option could be less than the value of the first.

6  Though this result must hold in the case of an American put, it need not hold for a European put.

7  A full treatment of this assumption can be found in John C. Hull, *Options, Futures and Other Derivatives*, 7th ed. (Upper Saddle River, NJ: Prentice Hall, 2008).

8  This method is called *linear interpolation*. It is only one of a number of possible methods of interpolation.

To help you grasp the key concepts of this chapter check out the extra resources posted on the Online Learning Centre at **www.mcgraw-hill.co.uk/textbooks/hillier**

Among other helpful resources there are PowerPoint presentations, chapter outlines and mini-cases.

# Chapter 23

# Options and Corporate Finance: Extensions and Applications

**KEY NOTATIONS**

| | |
|---|---|
| E | Exercise price |
| NPV | Net present value |
| R | Continuously compounded risk-free rate |
| RSU | Restricted stock unit |
| S | Share price |
| t | Time to maturity |
| $\sigma$ | Standard deviation |

In 2009 many companies announced that they would exchange their employee share options for restricted stock units (RSUs). An RSU is a share of equity that can't be sold or exchanged until it is vested. The vesting period can vary, but is usually between three and five years. When an RSU vests, the employee receives a full share of equity. The biggest advantage of RSUs for employees is that they receive the equity no matter what the share price. In comparison, with employee share options, the employee may receive nothing.

The reason for this change in policy was that most executive share options were worthless as a result of the major market falls in 2008. For example, the Dow Jones Euro STOXX 50, an index of the 50 largest continental European companies, fell by more than 40 per cent. The main purpose for executive share options is that they reward employees for good performance and loyalty to their company. If the options are worth nothing, there is no financial reason why the best executives should stay in a company if their services are demanded elsewhere. Restricted stock units are therefore better in a down market because executives always receive something for their efforts.

## 23.1 Executive Share Options

### Why Options?

Executive compensation is usually made up of base salary plus some or all of the following elements:

1 Long-term compensation

2 Annual bonuses

3 Retirement contributions

4 Options

TABLE
**23.1**

| Country | Ratio of CEO to factory worker pay |
|---------|-----------------------------------|
| Belgium | 18 to 1 |
| France | 23 to 1 |
| Germany | 20 to 1 |
| Italy | 26 to 1 |
| Netherlands | 18 to 1 |
| Spain | 17 to 1 |
| Sweden | 19 to 1 |
| Switzerland | 19 to 1 |
| UK | 32 to 1 |
| USA | 39 to 1 |

*Source*: Economic Policy Institute.

**Table 23.1** Salaries of CEOs relative to those of factory workers, 2005

When stock markets are on an upward trajectory, the final component of compensation, options, is by far the biggest part of total compensation for many top executives. In many parts of Europe full disclosure of executive pay is not yet normal practice. However, this hasn't stopped politicians and the media from decrying the total pay of executives, whose share options are a major component of their total remuneration. Table 23.1 lists the ratio of CEO to factory worker pay for various countries in 2005.

Factory workers very rarely receive executive share options and, as a result, in years when share prices are rising, the differential can be striking. Obviously, executives did not receive anything like near their 2005 remuneration levels a few years later when stock markets around the world tumbled, but the table is significant nonetheless.

Executive share options were extremely popular in the late 1990s and early 2000s as an alternative to increases in base pay. Some of the reasons given for using options were these:

- Options align executives' interests with those of the shareholders. By aligning interests, executives are more likely to make decisions for the benefit of the shareholders.

- Options allow the company to lower the executive's base pay. This removes pressures on morale caused by disparities between the salaries of executives and those of other employees.

- Options put an executive's pay at risk, rather than guaranteeing it regardless of the performance of the firm.

At the same time, there are a number of significant criticisms of executive share options. The most notable criticism is that share options encourage managers to take on more risky projects so as to increase the size of their personal remuneration. Given the role of executive compensation in the banking sector, and the perverse incentives to maximize bank share price at the expense of bank risk, regulators across the world have moved to limit top executive pay. For the foreseeable future, the days of extremely high remuneration deals for executives seem to be over.

## Valuing Executive Compensation

In this section we value executive share options. Not surprisingly, the complexity of the total compensation package often makes valuation a difficult task. The economic value of the options depends on factors such as the volatility of the underlying equity and the exact terms of the option grant.

Only a few countries fully disclose the details of executive pay, and in Example 23.1 we shall estimate the economic value of the options held by the chief executive of a hypothetical company. Example 23.1 is necessarily simplistic, but it serves to illustrate the way we can value executive share options. Simple matters such as requiring the executive to hold the option for a fixed period – the freeze-out period – before exercising can significantly diminish the value of a standard option.

Equally important, the Black–Scholes formula has to be modified if the equity pays dividends, and is no longer applicable if the volatility of the equity is changing randomly over time. Intuitively, a call option on a dividend-paying equity is worth less than a call on a equity that pays no dividends: all other things being equal, the dividends will lower the share price. Nevertheless, let us see what we can do.

| EXAMPLE 23.1 | ## Options at Kinky Kinks |

Consider Ray Davies, the chief executive officer (CEO) of Kinky Kinks, who has been granted 2 million executive share options. The average share price at the time of the options grant was €39.71. We shall assume that his options are at the money. The risk-free rate is 5 per cent and the options expire in five years. The preceding information implies that:

- The share price ($S$) of €39.71 equals the exercise price ($E$).

- The risk-free rate $R = 0.05$.

- The time interval $t = 5$.

In addition, the variance of Kinky Kinks is estimated to be $(0.2168)^2 = 0.0470$

This information allows us to value Ray Davies's options using the Black–Scholes model:

$$C = SN(d_1) - Ee^{-Rt}N(d_2)$$
$$d_1 = [(R + 1/2\sigma^2)t]/\sqrt{\sigma^2 t} = 0.758$$
$$d_2 = d_1 - \sqrt{\sigma^2 t} = 0.273$$
$$N(d_1) = 0.776$$
$$N(d_2) = 0.608$$
$$e^{-0.05 \times 5} = 0.7788$$
$$C = €39.71 \times 0.776 - €39.71 \times (0.778 \times 0.608)$$
$$= €12.03$$

Thus the value of a call option on one share of Kinky Kinks equity is €12.03. Because Mr Davies was granted options on 2 million shares, the market value of his options, as estimated by the Black–Scholes formula, is about €24 million (= 2 million × €12.03).

The value of the options we computed in Example 23.1 is the economic value of the options if they were to trade in the market. The real question is this: Whose value are we talking about? Are these the costs of the options to the company? Are they the values of the options to the executives?

The total value of €24 million for Ray Davies's options in Example 23.1 is the amount that the options would trade at in the financial markets, and which traders and investors would be willing to pay for them.[1] If Kinky Kinks was very large, it would not be unreasonable to view this as the cost of granting the options to the CEO, Ray Davies. Of course, in return, the company would expect Mr Davies to improve the value of the company to its shareholders by more than this amount. As we have seen, perhaps the main purpose of options is to align the interests of management with those of the shareholders of the firm. Under no circumstances, though, is the €24 million necessarily a fair measure of what the options are worth to Mr Davies.

As an illustration, suppose that the CEO of London Conversation plc has options on 1 million shares with an exercise price of €30 per share, and the current share price of London Conversation is €50. If the options were exercised today, they would be worth €20 million (an underestimation of their market value). Suppose, in addition, that the CEO owns €5 million in company equity and has €5 million in other assets. The CEO clearly has a very undiversified personal portfolio. By the standards of modern portfolio theory, having 25/30 or about 83 per cent of your personal wealth in one equity and its options is unnecessarily risky.

Although the CEO is wealthy by most standards, shifts in share price impact on the CEO's economic well-being. If the price drops from €50 per share to €30 per share, the current exercise value of the options on 1 million shares drops from €20 million down to zero. Ignoring the fact that if the options had more time to mature they might not lose all of this value, we nevertheless have a rather startling decline in the CEO's net worth from about €30 million to €8 million (€5 million in other assets plus equity that is now worth €3 million). But that is the purpose of giving the options and the equity holdings to the CEO – namely, to make the CEO's fortunes rise and fall with those of the company. It is why the company requires the executive to hold the options for at least a freeze-out period rather than letting the executive sell them to realize their value.

The implication is that when options are a large portion of an executive's net worth, the total value of the position to the executive is less than market value. As a purely financial matter, an executive might be happier with €5 million in cash rather than €20 million in options. At least the executive could then diversify his personal portfolio. The shift in 2009 from executive share options to restricted stock units suggests that, in practice, the effective minimum value of executive share options is not zero. If companies systematically respond to deep out-of-the-money options by converting them to RSUs, the firms are exercising another option to exchange the share option for an RSU. As with any option, this has value to the holder, in this case the senior executive.

## 23.2 Investment in Real Projects and Options

Earlier in the text we considered projects where forecasts for future cash flows were made at date 0. The expected cash flow in each future period was discounted at an appropriate risky rate, yielding an NPV calculation. For independent projects a positive NPV meant acceptance, and a negative NPV meant rejection. This approach treated risk through the discount rate.

We later considered decision tree analysis, an approach that handles risk in a more sophisticated way. We pointed out that the firm will make investment and operating decisions on a project over its entire life. We value a project today, assuming that future decisions will be optimal. However, we do not yet know what these decisions will be, because much information remains to be discovered. The firm's ability to delay its investment and operating decisions until the release of information is an option. We now illustrate this option through an example.

### EXAMPLE 23.2

## Options and Capital Budgeting

Consider a hypothetical issue that could face BP plc, the British energy company. BP is considering the purchase of an oil field in the Hammerfest-Varanger Basin, to the north of Norway. The seller has listed the property for £10,000 (Norwegian kroner equivalent) and is eager to sell immediately. Initial drilling costs are £500,000. BP anticipates that 10,000 barrels of oil can be extracted each year for many decades. Because the termination date is so far in the future, and is so hard to estimate, the firm views the cash flow stream from the oil as a perpetuity. With oil prices at £50 per barrel and extraction costs at £46 a barrel, the firm anticipates a net margin of £4 per barrel. Because oil prices are expected to rise at the inflation rate, the firm assumes that its cash flow per barrel will always be £4 in real terms. The appropriate real discount rate is 10 per cent. Assume that BP has enough tax credits from bad years in the past that it will not need to pay taxes on any profits from the oil field. Should BP buy the property?

The NPV of the oil field to BP is

$$-£110,000 = -£10,000 - £500,000 + \frac{£4 \times 10,000}{0.10}$$

According to this analysis, BP should not purchase the land.

Though this approach uses the standard capital budgeting techniques of this and other textbooks, it is actually inappropriate for this situation. To see this, consider the analysis of Professor I.M. Jolly, a consultant to BP. He agrees that the price of oil is *expected* to rise at the rate of inflation. However, he points out that the next year is quite perilous for oil prices. On the one hand, OPEC is considering a long-term agreement that would raise oil prices to £65 per barrel in real terms for many years in the future. On the other hand, the economic recession may last a lot longer than analysts and politicians predict. Professor Jolly argues that oil will be priced at £35 in real terms for many years should this scenario play out. Full information about both these developments will be known in exactly one year.

Should oil prices rise to £65 a barrel, the NPV of the project would be

$$£1,390,000 = -£10,000 - £500,000 + \frac{(£65 - £46) \times 10,000}{0.10}$$

However, should oil prices fall to £35 a barrel, the NPV of the oil field will be even more negative than it is today.

Professor Jolly makes two recommendations to BP's board. He argues that:

1   The land should be purchased.

2   The drilling decision should be delayed until information about both OPEC's new agreement and the extent of the global recession is known.

Professor Jolly explains his recommendations to the board by first assuming that the land has already been purchased. He argues that, under this assumption, the drilling decision should be delayed. Second, he investigates his assumption that the land should have been purchased in the first place. This approach of examining the second decision (whether to drill) after assuming that the first decision (to buy the land) has been made was also used in our earlier presentation on decision trees. Let us now work through Professor Jolly's analysis.

*Assume the land has already been purchased*. If the land has already been purchased, should drilling begin immediately? If drilling begins immediately, the NPV is –£110,000; if the drilling decision is delayed until new information is released in a year, the optimal choice can be made at that time. If oil prices drop to £35 a barrel, BP should not drill. Instead the firm should walk away from the project, losing nothing beyond its £10,000 purchase price for the land. If oil prices rise to £65, drilling should begin.

Professor Jolly points out that, by delaying, the firm will invest the £500,000 of drilling costs only if oil prices rise. Thus, by delaying, the firm saves £500,000 in the case where oil prices drop. Jolly concludes that, once the land is purchased, the drilling decision should be delayed.

*Should the land have been purchased in the first place?* We now know that if the land has been purchased, it is optimal to defer the drilling decision until the release of information. Given that we know this optimal decision concerning drilling, should the land be purchased in the first place? Without knowing the exact probability that oil prices will rise, Professor Jolly is nevertheless confident that the land should be purchased. The NPV of the project at £65 oil prices is £1,390,000, whereas the cost of the land is only £10,000. Professor Jolly believes that an oil price rise is possible, though by no means probable. Even so, he argues that the high potential return is clearly worth the risk.

This example presents an approach that is similar to our decision tree analysis in a previous chapter. Our purpose in this section is to discuss this type of decision in an option framework. When BP purchases the land, it is actually purchasing a call option. That is, once the land has been purchased, the firm has an option to buy an active oil field at an exercise price of £500,000. As it turns out, one should generally not exercise a call option immediately. In this case, the firm should delay exercise until relevant information concerning future oil prices is released.

This section points out a serious deficiency in classical capital budgeting: Net present value calculations typically ignore the flexibility that real-world firms have. In our example the standard techniques generated a negative NPV for the land purchase. Yet, by allowing the firm the option to change its investment policy according to new information, the land purchase can easily be justified.

We encourage the reader to look for hidden options in projects. Because options are beneficial, managers are short-changing their firm's projects if capital budgeting calculations ignore flexibility.

## 23.3 Valuing a Start-Up

Ralph Simmons was not your typical Masters student. Since childhood he had one ambition: to open a restaurant that sold wild boar meat. He went to business school because he realized that, although he knew 101 ways to cook wild boar, he didn't have the business skills necessary to run a restaurant. He was extremely focused, with each course at university being important to him only to the extent that it could further his dream.

While taking his business school's course in entrepreneurship, he began to develop a business plan for his restaurant, which he now called Wild Boar For Everyone. He thought about marketing; he thought about raising capital; he thought about dealing with future employees. He even devoted a great deal of time to designing the physical layout of the restaurant. Against the professor's advice in his entrepreneurship class, he designed the restaurant in the shape of a wild boar, where the front door went through the animal's mouth. Of course his business plan would not be complete without financial projections. After much thought he came up with the projections shown in Table 23.2.

The table starts with sales projections, which rise from £300,000 in the first year to a steady state of £1 million a year. Cash flows from operations are shown in the next line, although we leave out the intermediate calculations needed to move from line 1 to line 2. After subtracting working capital, the table shows net cash flows in line 4. Net cash flows are negative initially, which is quite common in start-ups, but they become positive by year 3. However, the rest of the table presents the unfortunate truth. The cash flows from the restaurant yield a present value of £582,561, assuming a discount rate of 20 per cent. Unfortunately, the cost of the building is greater, at £700,000, implying a negative net present value of −£117,439.

The projections indicate that Ralph's lifelong dream may not come to pass. He cannot expect to raise the capital needed to open his restaurant; and if he did obtain the funding, the restaurant would probably go under anyway. Ralph checked and rechecked the numbers, hoping vainly to discover either a numerical error or a cost-saving omission that would move his venture from the red to the black. In fact, Ralph saw that, if anything, his forecasts are generous: a 20 per cent discount rate and an infinitely lived building are on the optimistic side.

It wasn't until Ralph took a course in corporate strategy that he saw the hidden value in his venture. In that course his instructor repeatedly stated the importance of positioning a firm to take advantage of new opportunities. Although Ralph didn't see the connection at first, he finally realized the implications for Wild Boar for Everyone. His financial projections were based on expectations. There was a 50 per cent probability that wild boar meat would be more popular than he thought, in which case actual cash flows would exceed projections.

**TABLE 23.2**

| | Year 1 (£) | Year 2 (£) | Year 3 (£) | Year 4 (£) | All future years (£) |
|---|---|---|---|---|---|
| (1) Sales | 300,000 | 600,000 | 900,000 | 1,000,000 | 1,000,000 |
| (2) Cash flows from operations | −100,000 | −50,000 | +75,000 | +250,000 | +250,000 |
| (3) Increase in working capital | 50,000 | 20,000 | 10,000 | 10,000 | 0 |
| (4) Net cash flows [(2) − (3)] | −150,000 | −70,000 | 65,000 | 240,000 | 250,000 |
| Present value of net cash flows in years 1–4 (discounted at 20%) | | | −£20,255 | | |
| Present value of terminal value | | | $\dfrac{£250,000}{0.20} \times \dfrac{1}{(1.20)^4} = £602,816$ | | |
| Present value of restaurant | | | £602,816 − £20,255 = £582,561 | | |
| − Cost of building | | | −£700,000 | | |
| Net present value of restaurant | | | −£117,439 | | |

**Table 23.2** Financial projections for Wild Boar for Everyone

And there was a 50 per cent probability that the meat would be less popular, in which case the actual flows would fall short of projections.

If the restaurant did poorly it would probably fold in a few years, because he would not want to keep losing money for ever. However, if the restaurant did well he would be in a position to expand. With wild boar meat being popular in one locale, it would probably prove popular in other locales as well. Thus he recognized two options: the option to abandon under bad conditions and the option to expand under good conditions. Although both options can be valued according to the principles of the previous chapter, we focus on the option to expand, because it is probably much more valuable.

Ralph reasoned that, as much as he personally liked wild boar meat, consumer resistance in some regions of the United Kingdom would doom Wild Boar for Everyone. So he developed a strategy of catering only to those regions where wild boar meat is somewhat popular already. He forecast that although he could expand quickly if the first restaurant proved successful, the market would limit him to 30 additional restaurants.

Ralph believes that this expansion will occur about four years from now. He believes that he will need three years of operating the first restaurant to (a) get the initial restaurant running smoothly and (b) have enough information to place an accurate value on the restaurant. If the first restaurant is successful enough, he will need another year to obtain outside capital. Thus he will be ready to build the 30 additional units around the fourth year.

Ralph will value his enterprise, including the option to expand, according to the Black–Scholes model. From Table 23.2 we see that each unit costs £700,000, implying a total cost over the 30 additional units of £21,000,000 (= 30 × £700,000). The present value of the cash inflows from these 30 units is £17,476,830 (= 30 × £582,561), according to the table. However, because the expansion will occur around the fourth year, this present value calculation is provided from the point of view of four years in the future. The present value as of today is £8,428,255 [= £17,476,830/(1.20)$^4$], assuming a discount rate of 20 per cent per year. Thus Ralph views his potential restaurant business as an option, where the exercise price is £21,000,000 and the value of the underlying asset is £8,428,255. The option is currently out of the money, a result that follows from the negative value of a typical restaurant, as calculated in Table 23.2. Of course, Ralph is hoping that the option will move into the money within four years.

Ralph needs three additional parameters to use the Black–Scholes model: $R$, the continuously compounded interest rate; $t$, the time to maturity; and $\sigma$, the standard deviation of the underlying asset. Ralph uses the yield on a four-year zero coupon bond, which is 3.5 per cent, as the estimate of the interest rate. The time to maturity is four years. The estimate of standard deviation is a little trickier because there are no historical data on wild boar restaurants. Ralph finds that the average annual standard deviation of the returns on publicly traded restaurants is 0.35. Because Wild Boar for Everyone is a new venture, he reasons that the risk here would be somewhat greater. He finds that the average annual standard deviation for restaurants that have gone public in the last few years is 0.45. Ralph's restaurant is newer still, so he uses a standard deviation of 0.50.

There are now enough data to value Ralph's venture. The value according to the Black–Scholes model is £1,455,196. The actual calculations are shown in Example 23.3. Of course, Ralph must start his pilot restaurant before he can take advantage of this option. Thus the net value of the call option plus the negative present value of the pilot restaurant is £1,337,757 (= £1,455,196 − £117,439). Because this value is large and positive, Ralph decides to stay with his dream of Wild Boar for Everyone. He knows that the probability that the restaurant will fail is greater than 50 per cent. Nevertheless, the option to expand is important enough that his restaurant business has value. And if he needs outside capital, he probably can attract the necessary investors.

This finding leads to the appearance of a paradox. If Ralph approaches investors to invest in a single restaurant with no possibility of expansion, he will probably not be able to attract capital. After all, Table 23.2 shows a net present value of −£117,439. However, if Ralph thinks bigger, he will probably be able to attract all the capital he needs. But this is really not a paradox at all. By thinking bigger, Ralph is offering investors the option – not the obligation – to expand.

The example we have chosen may seem frivolous, and certainly we added offbeat characteristics for interest. However, if you think that business situations involving options are unusual or unimportant, let us state emphatically that nothing is further from the truth.

The notion of embedded options is at the heart of business. There are two possible outcomes for virtually every business idea. On the one hand the business may fail, in which case the managers will probably try to shut it down in the most cost-efficient way. On the other hand the business may prosper, in which case the managers will try to expand. Thus virtually every business has both the option to abandon and the option to expand. You may have read pundits claiming that the net present value approach to capital budgeting is wrong or incomplete. Although criticism of this type frequently irritates the finance establishment, the pundits definitely have a point. If virtually all projects have embedded options, only an approach such as the one we have outlined can be appropriate. Ignoring the options is likely to lead to serious undervaluation.

## EXAMPLE 23.3 Valuing a Start-Up Firm (Wild Boar for Everyone) as an Option

1   The value of a single restaurant is negative, as indicated by the net present value calculation in Table 23.2 of –£117,439. Thus the restaurant would not be funded if there was no possibility of expansion.

2   If the pilot restaurant is successful, Ralph Simmons plans to create 30 additional restaurants around year 4. This leads to the following observations:

(a)   The total cost of 30 units is £21,000,000 (= 30 × £700,000).

(b)   The present value of future cash flows as of year 4 is £17,476,830 (= 30 × £582,561).

(c)   The present value of these cash flows today is £8,428,255 [= £17,476,830/(1.20)$^4$].

Here we assume that cash flows from the project are discounted at 20% per annum.
Thus the business is essentially a call option, where the exercise price is £21,000,000 and the underlying asset is worth £8,428,255.

3   Ralph Simmons estimates the standard deviation of the annual return on Wild Boar for Everyone's equity to be 0.50.

Parameters of the Black–Scholes model:

$$S \text{ (share price)} = £8,428,255$$
$$E \text{ (exercise price)} = £21,000,000$$
$$t \text{ (time to maturity)} = 4 \text{ years}$$
$$\sigma \text{ (standard deviation)} = 0.50$$
$$R \text{ (continuously compounded interest rate)} = 3.5\%$$

Calculation from the Black–Scholes model:

$$C = SN(d_1) - Ee^{-Rt}N(d_2)$$
$$d_1 = [\ln(S/E) + (R + 1/2\sigma^2)t]/\sqrt{\sigma^2 t}$$
$$d_2 = d_1 - \sqrt{\sigma^2 t}$$
$$d_1 = \left\{\ln\frac{8,428,255}{21,000,000} + \left[0.035 + \frac{1}{2}(0.50)^2\right]4\right\}\Big/\sqrt{(0.50)^2\,4} = -0.27293$$
$$d_2 = -0.27293 - \sqrt{(0.50)^2\,4} = -1.27293$$
$$N(d_1) = N(-0.27293) = 0.3936$$
$$N(d_2) = N(-1.27293) = 0.1020$$
$$C = £8,428,255 \times 0.3936 - £21,000,000 \times e^{-0.035\times4} \times 0.1020$$
$$= £1,455,196$$

The value of the business including the cost of the pilot restaurant is £1,337,757 (= £1,455,196 – £117,439).

## 23.4 More about the Binomial Model

Earlier in this chapter we examined three applications of options: executive compensation, options to abandon or expand, and the start-up decision. In two cases we valued the option using the Black–Scholes model. Although this model is justifiably well known, it is not the only approach to option valuation. As mentioned in the previous chapter, the two-state or binomial model is an alternative and – in some situations – a superior approach to valuation. The rest of this chapter examines two applications of the binomial model.

### Heating Oil

**Two-Date Example**  Consider Anthony Meyer, a typical heating oil distributor, whose business consists of buying heating oil at the wholesale level and reselling the oil to homeowners at a somewhat higher price. Most of his revenue comes from sales during the winter. Today, 1 September, heating oil sells for €2.00 per litre. Of course, this price is not fixed. Rather, oil prices will vary from 1 September until 1 December, the time when his customers will probably make their big winter purchases of heating oil. Let's simplify the situation by assuming that Mr Meyer believes that oil prices will be at either €2.74 or €1.46 on 11 December. Figure 23.1 portrays this possible price movement, which represents a great deal of uncertainty, because Mr Meyer has no idea which of the two possible prices will actually occur. However, this price variability does not translate into that much risk, because he can pass price changes on to his customers. That is, he will charge his customers more if he ends up paying €2.74 per litre than if he ends up paying €1.46 per litre.

Of course, Mr Meyer is avoiding risk by passing on that risk to his customers. His customers accept the risk, perhaps because they are each too small to negotiate a better deal. This is not the case with CECO, a large electric utility in his area. CECO approaches Mr Meyer with the following proposition. The utility would like to be able to buy *up to* 6 million litres of oil from him at €2.10 per litre on 1 December.

Although this arrangement represents a lot of oil, both Mr Meyer and CECO know that Mr Meyer can expect to lose money on it. If prices rise to €2.74 per litre the utility will happily buy all 6 million litres at only €2.10 per litre, clearly creating a loss for the distributor. However, if oil prices decline to €1.46 per litre the utility will not buy any oil. After all, why should CECO pay €2.10 per litre to Mr Meyer when the utility can buy all the oil it wants at €1.46 per litre in the open market? In other words, CECO is asking for a *call option* on heating oil. To compensate Mr Meyer for the risk of loss, the two parties agree that CECO will pay him €1,000,000 up front for the right to buy up to 6 million litres of oil at €2.10 per litre.

**FIGURE 23.1**

€2.00

€2.74
(€0.64 = €2.74 – 2.10)

€1.46
(€0)

1 September          1 December

The price of heating oil on 1 December will be either €2.74 or €1.46. Because the price on 1 September is €2.00, we say that $u = 1.37 (= €2.74/€2.00)$ and $d = 0.73 (= €1.46/€2.00)$. The loss per litre to Mr Meyer (or, equivalently, the gain per litre to CECO) of €0.64 in the up state or €0 in the down state is shown in parentheses.

**Figure 23.1** Movement of heating oil prices from 1 September to 1 December in a two-date example

Is this a fair deal? Although small distributors may evaluate a deal like this by gut feel, we can evaluate it more quantitatively by using the binomial model described in the previous chapter. In that chapter we pointed out that option problems can be handled most easily by assuming *risk-neutral pricing*. In this approach we first note that oil will either rise 37 per cent (= €2.74/€2.00 − 1) or fall −27 per cent (= €1.46/€2.00 − 1) from 1 September to 1 December. We can think of these two numbers as the possible returns on heating oil. In addition, we introduce two new terms, $u$ and $d$. We define $u$ as $1 + 0.37 = 1.37$ and $d$ as $1 − 0.27 = 0.73$.[2] Using the methodology of the previous chapter, we value the contract in the following two steps.

**Step 1: Determining the Risk-Neutral Probabilities** We determine the probability of a price rise such that the expected return on oil exactly equals the risk-free rate. Assuming an 8 per cent annual interest rate, which implies a 2 per cent rate over the next three months, we can solve for the probability of a rise as follows:[3]

$$2\% = \text{Probability of rise} \times 0.37 + (1 − \text{Probability of rise}) \times (−0.27)$$

Solving this equation, we find that the probability of a rise is approximately 45 per cent, implying that the probability of a fall is 55 per cent. In other words, if the probability of a price rise is 45 per cent, the expected return on heating oil is 2 per cent. In accordance with what we said in the previous chapter, these are the probabilities that are consistent with a world of risk neutrality. That is, under risk neutrality, the expected return on any asset would equal the riskless rate of interest. No one would demand an expected return above this riskless rate, because risk-neutral individuals do not need to be compensated for bearing risk.

**Step 2: Valuing the Contract** If the price of oil rises to €2.74 on 11 December, CECO will want to buy oil from Mr Meyer at €2.10 per litre. Mr Meyer will lose €0.64 per litre, because he buys oil in the open market at €2.74 per litre, only to resell it to CECO at €2.10 per litre. This loss of €0.64 is shown in parentheses in Fig. 23.1. Conversely, if the market price of heating oil falls to €1.46 per litre, CECO will not buy any oil from Mr Meyer. That is, CECO would not want to pay €2.10 per litre to him when the utility could buy heating oil in the open market at €1.46 per litre. Thus we can say that Mr Meyer neither gains nor loses if the price drops to €1.46. The gain or loss of zero is placed in parentheses under the price of €1.46 in Fig. 23.1. In addition, as mentioned earlier, Mr Meyer receives €1,000,000 up front.

Given these numbers, the value of the contract to Mr Meyer can be calculated as

$$\underbrace{[0.45 \times (€2.10 − €2.74) \times 6{,}000{,}000 + 0.55 \times 0]/1.02}_{\text{Value of the call option}} + €1{,}000{,}000 = −€694{,}118 \qquad (23.1)$$

As in the previous chapter, we are valuing an option using risk-neutral pricing. The cash flows of −€0.64 (= €2.10 − €2.74) and €0 per litre are multiplied by their risk-neutral probabilities. The entire first term in Eq. (23.1) is then discounted at €1.02, because the cash flows in that term occur on 1 December. The €1,000,000 is not discounted because Mr Meyer receives it today, 1 September. Because the present value of the contract is negative, Mr Meyer would be wise to reject the contract.

As stated before, the distributor has sold a call option to CECO. The first term in the preceding equation, which equals −€1,694,118, can be viewed as the value of this call option. It is a negative number because the equation looks at the option from Mr Meyer's point of view. Therefore the value of the call option would be +€1,694,118 to CECO. On a per-litre basis, the value of the option to CECO is

$$[0.45(€2.74 − €2.10) + 0.55 \times 0]/1.02 = €0.282 \qquad (23.2)$$

Equation (23.2) shows that CECO will gain €0.64 (= €2.74 − €2.10) per litre in the up state, because CECO can buy heating oil worth €2.74 for only €2.10 under the contract. By contrast, the contract is worth nothing to CECO in the down state, because the utility will not pay €2.10 for oil selling for only €1.46 in the open market. Using risk-neutral pricing, the formula tells us that the value of the call option on one litre of heating oil is €0.282.

FIGURE
**23.2**

The figure shows the prices of a litre of heating oil on three dates, given $u = 1.25$ and $d = 0.80$. There are three possible prices for heating oil on 1 December. For each one of these three prices, we calculate the price on 1 December of a call option on a litre of heating oil with an exercise price of €2.10. These numbers are in parentheses. Call prices at earlier dates are determined by the binomial model and are also shown in parentheses.

**Figure 23.2** Movement of heating oil prices in a three-date model

**Three-Date Example** Although the preceding example captures a number of aspects of the real world, it has one deficiency. It assumes that the price of heating oil can take on only two values on 1 December. This is clearly not plausible: oil can take on essentially any value in reality. Although this deficiency seems glaring at first glance, it is easily correctable. All we have to do is to introduce more intervals over the three-month period of our example.

For example, consider Fig. 23.2, which shows the price movement of heating oil over two intervals of 1½ months each.[4] As shown in the figure, the price will be either €2.50 or €1.60 on 15 October. We refer to €2.50 as the price in the *up state* and €1.60 as the price in the *down state*. Thus heating oil has returns of 25 per cent (= €2.50/€2.00) and −20 per cent (= €1.60/€2) in the two states.

We assume the same variability as we move forward from 15 October to 1 December. That is, given a price of €2.50 on 15 October, the price on 1 December will be either €3.12 (= €2.50 × 1.25) or €2 (= €2.50 × 0.80). Similarly, given a price of €1.60 on 15 October, the price on 1 December will be either €2 (= €1.60 × 1.25) or €1.28 (= €1.60 × 0.80). This assumption of constant variability is quite plausible, because the rate of new information impacting on heating oil (or most commodities or assets) is likely to be similar from month to month.

Note that there are three possible prices on 1 December, but there are two possible prices on 15 October. Also note that there are two paths to a price of €2 on 1 December. The price could rise to €2.50 on 15 October before falling back down to €2 on 1 December. Alternatively, the price could fall to €1.60 on 15 October before going back up to €2 on 1 December. In other words the model has symmetry, where an up movement followed by a down movement yields the same price on 1 December as a down movement followed by an up movement.

How do we value CECO's option in this three-date example? We employ the same procedure that we used in the two-date example, although we now need an extra step because of the extra date.

**Step 1: Determining the Risk-Neutral Probabilities** As we did in the two-date example, we determine what the probability of a price rise would be such that the expected return on heating oil exactly equals the riskless rate. However, in this case we work with an interval of 1½ months. Assuming an 8 per cent annual rate of interest, which implies a 1 per cent rate over a 1½ month interval,[5] we can solve for the probability of a rise like this:

$$1\% = \text{Probability of rise} \times 0.25 + (1 - \text{Probability of rise}) \times (-0.20)$$

Solving the equation, we find that the probability of a rise here is 47 per cent, implying that the probability of a fall is 53 per cent. In other words, if the probability of a rise is 47 per cent, the expected return on heating oil is 1 per cent per each 1½-month interval. Again, these probabilities are determined under the assumption of risk-neutral pricing.

Note that the probabilities of 47 per cent and 53 per cent hold for both the interval from 1 September to 15 October and the interval from 15 October to 1 December. This is the case because the return in the up state is 25 per cent and the return in the down state is −20 per cent for each of the two intervals. Thus the preceding equation must apply to each of the intervals separately.

**Step 2: Valuing the Option as of 15 October** As indicated in Fig. 23.2, the option to CECO will be worth €1.02 per litre on 1 December if the price of heating oil has risen to €3.12 on that date. That is, CECO can buy oil from Mr Meyer at €2.10 when it would otherwise have to pay €3.12 in the open market. However, the option will be worthless on 1 December if the price of a litre of heating oil is either €2 or €1.28 on that date. Here the option is out of the money, because the exercise price of €2.10 is above either €2 or €1.28.

Using these option prices on 1 December, we can calculate the value of the call option on 15 October. If the price of a litre of heating oil is €2.50 on 15 October, Fig. 23.2 shows us that the call option will be worth either €1.02 or €0 on 1 December. Thus if the price of heating oil is €2.50 on 15 October, the value of the option on one litre of heating oil at that time is

$$[0.47 \times €1.02 + 0.53 \times 0]/1.01 = €0.474$$

Here we are valuing an option using the same risk-neutral pricing approach that we used in the earlier two-date example. This value of €0.474 is shown in parentheses in Fig. 23.2.

We also want to value the option on 15 October if the price at that time is €1.60. However, the value here is clearly zero, as indicated by this calculation:

$$[0.47 \times €0 + 0.53 \times €0]/1.01 = 0$$

This is obvious once we look at Fig. 23.2. We see from the figure that the call must end up out of the money on 1 December if the price of heating oil is €1.60 on 15 October. Thus the call must have zero value on 15 October if the price of heating oil is €1.60 on that date.

**Step 3: Valuing the Option on 1 September** In the previous step we saw that the price of the call on 15 October would be €0.474 if the price of a litre of heating oil was €2.50 on that date. Similarly, the price of the option on 15 October would be €0 if oil was selling at €1.60 on that date. From these values, we can calculate the call option value on 1 September:

$$[0.47 \times €0.474 + 0.53 \times €0]/1.01 = €0.220$$

Notice that this calculation is completely analogous to the calculation of the option value in the previous step, as well as the calculation of the option value in the two-date example that we presented earlier. In other words the same approach applies, regardless of the number of intervals used. As we shall see later, we can move to many intervals, which produces greater realism, yet still maintain the same basic methodology.

The previous calculation has given us the value to CECO of its option on one litre of heating oil. Now we are ready to calculate the value of the contract to Mr Meyer. Given the calculations from the previous equation, the contract's value can be written as

$$-€0.220 \times 6,000,000 + €1,000,000 = -€320,000$$

| TABLE 23.3 | Number of intervals* | Call value (€) |
|---|---|---|
| | 1 | 0.282 |
| | 2 | 0.220 |
| | 3 | 0.244 |
| | 4 | 0.232 |
| | 6 | 0.228 |
| | 10 | 0.228 |
| | 20 | 0.228 |
| | 30 | 0.228 |
| | 40 | 0.228 |
| | 50 | 0.226 |
| | 99 | 0.226 |
| | Black–Scholes infinity | 0.226 |

In this example the value of the call according to the binomial model varies as the number of intervals increases. However, the value of the call converges rapidly to the Black–Scholes value. Thus the binomial model, even with only a few intervals, appears to be a good approximation to Black–Scholes.

*The number of intervals is always one less than the number of dates.

**Table 23.3** Value of a call on one litre of heating oil

That is, Mr Meyer is giving away an option worth €0.220 for each of the 6 million litres of heating oil. In return, he is receiving only €1,000,000 up front. On balance, he is losing €320,000. Of course, the value of the contract to CECO is the opposite, so the value to this utility is €320,000.

**Extension to Many Dates**  We have looked at the contract between CECO and Mr Meyer using both a two-date example and a three-date example. The three-date case is more realistic, because more possibilities for price movements are allowed here. However, why stop at just three dates? Moving to four dates, five dates, 50 dates, 500 dates, and so on should give us ever more realism. Note that as we move to more dates we are merely shortening the interval between dates without increasing the overall time period of three months (1 September to 1 December).

For example, imagine a model with 90 dates over the three months. Here each interval is approximately one day long, because there are about 90 days in a three-month period. The assumption of two possible outcomes in the binomial model is more plausible over a one-day interval than it is over a 1½-month interval, let alone a three-month interval. Of course, we could probably achieve greater realism still by going to an interval of, say, one hour or one minute.

How do we adjust the binomial model to accommodate increases in the number of intervals? It turns out that two simple formulae relate $u$ and $d$ to the standard deviation of the return of the underlying asset:[6]

$$u = e^{\sigma/\sqrt{n}}$$
and
$$d = 1/u$$

where $\sigma$ is the standard deviation of the annualized return on the underlying asset (heating oil, in this case) and $n$ is the number of intervals over a year.

When we created the heating oil example we assumed that the annualized standard deviation of the return on heating oil was 0.63 (or, equivalently, 63 per cent). Because there are four quarters in a year, $u = e^{0.63/\sqrt{4}} = 1.37$ and $d = 1/1.37 = 0.73$, as shown in the two-date example of Fig. 23.1. In the three-date example of Fig. 23.2, where each interval is 1½ months long, $u = e^{0.63/\sqrt{8}} = 1.25$ and $d = 1/1.25 = 0.80$. Thus the binomial model can be applied in practice if the standard deviation of the return of the underlying asset can be estimated.

We stated earlier that the value of the call option on a litre of heating oil was estimated to be €0.282 in the two-date model and €0.220 in the three-date model. How does the value of the option change as we increase the number of intervals while keeping the time period constant at three months (from 1 September to 1 December)? We have calculated the value of the call for various time intervals in Table 23.3.[7] The realism increases with the number of intervals, because the restriction of only two possible outcomes is more plausible over a short interval than over a long one. Thus the value of the call when the number of intervals is 99 or infinity is likely to be more realistic than this value when the number of intervals is, say, one or two.

However, a very interesting phenomenon can be observed from the table. Although the value of the call changes as the number of intervals increases, convergence occurs quite rapidly. The call's value with six intervals is almost identical to the value with 99 intervals. Thus a small number of intervals appears serviceable for the binomial model. Six intervals in a three-month period implies that each interval is two weeks long. Of course, the assumption that heating oil can take on only one of two prices in two weeks is simply not realistic. The paradox is that this unrealistic assumption still produces a realistic call price.

What happens when the number of intervals goes to infinity, implying that the length of the interval goes to zero? It can be proved mathematically that we end up with the value of the Black–Scholes model. This value is also presented in Table 23.3. Thus we can argue that the Black–Scholes model is the best approach to value the heating oil option. It is also quite easy to apply. We can use a calculator to value options with Black–Scholes, whereas we must generally use a computer program for the binomial model. However, as shown in Table 23.3, the values from the binomial model, even with relatively few intervals, are quite close to the Black–Scholes value. Thus, although Black–Scholes may save us time, it does not materially affect our estimate of value.

At this point it seems as if the Black–Scholes model is preferable to the binomial model. Who wouldn't want to save time and still get a slightly more accurate value? However, such is not always the case. There are plenty of situations where the binomial model is preferred to the Black–Scholes model. One such situation is presented in the next section.

## 23.5 Shutdown and Reopening Decisions

Some of the earliest and most important examples of special options have occurred in the natural resources and mining industries.

### Valuing a Palladium Mine

The Woborov palladium mine was founded in 1878 on one of the richest veins of palladium in Russia. Palladium is a platinum-like metal that is used for industrial purposes across the world. Thirty years later, by 1908, the mine had been played out; but occasionally, depending on the price of palladium, it is reopened. Currently, palladium is not actively mined at Woborov, but its equity is still traded on the Russian Stock Exchange and Euronext under the ticker symbol WOB. WOB has no debt and, with about 20 million outstanding shares, its market value (share price times number of shares outstanding) exceeds €1 billion. WOB owns about 160 acres of land surrounding the mine, and has a 100-year government lease to mine palladium there. However, land in the Russian tundra has a market value of only a few thousand euros (rouble equivalent). WOB holds cash securities, and other assets worth about €30 million. What could possibly explain why a company with €30 million in assets and a closed palladium mine with no cash flow has the market value that WOB has?

The answer lies in the options that WOB implicitly owns in the form of a palladium mine. Assume that the current price of palladium is about €320 per ounce, and the cost of extraction and processing at the mine is about €350 per ounce. It is no wonder that the mine is closed. Every ounce of palladium extracted costs €350 and can be sold for only €320, for a loss of €30 per ounce. Presumably, if the price of palladium were to rise, the mine could be opened. It costs €2 million to open the mine; when it is opened, production is 50,000 ounces per year. Geologists believe that the amount of palladium in the mine is essentially unlimited, and WOB has the right to mine it for the next 100 years. Under the terms of its lease WOB cannot stockpile palladium, and must sell each year all the palladium it mines that year. Closing the mine, which costs €1 million, requires equipment to be mothballed and some environmental precautions to be put in place. We shall refer to the €2 million required to open the mine as the entry fee or investment and the €1 million to close it as the closing or abandonment cost. (We cannot avoid the abandonment cost by simply keeping the mine open and not operating.)

From a financial perspective WOB is really just a package of options on the price of palladium disguised as a company and a mine. The basic option is a call on the price of palladium, where the exercise price is the €350 extraction cost. The option is complicated by having an exercise fee of €2 million – the opening cost – whenever it is exercised and a closing fee of €1 million when it is abandoned. It is also complicated by the fact that it is a perpetual option with no final maturity.

## The Abandonment and Opening Decisions

Before valuing the option implicit in WOB, it is useful to see what we can say by just applying common sense. To begin with, the mine should be opened only when the price of palladium is sufficiently above the extraction cost of €350 per ounce. Because it costs €2 million to open the mine, the mine should not be opened whenever the price of palladium is only slightly above €350. At a palladium price of, say, €350.10 the mine wouldn't be opened, because the ten-cent profit per ounce translates into €5,000 per year (= 50,000 ounces × €0.10/ounce). This would not begin to cover the €2 million opening costs. More significantly, though, the mine probably would not be opened if the price rose to €360 per ounce, even though a €10 profit per ounce – €500,000 per year – would pay the €2 million opening costs at any reasonable discount rate. The reason is that here, as in all option problems, volatility (in this case the volatility of palladium) plays a significant role. Because the palladium price is volatile, the price has to rise sufficiently above €350 per ounce to make it worth opening the mine. If the price at which the mine is opened is too close to the extraction price of €350 per ounce, say at €360 per ounce, we would open the mine every time the price jogged above €360. Unfortunately, we would then find ourselves operating at a loss or facing a closing decision whenever palladium jogged back down €10 per ounce (or only 3 per cent) to €350.

The estimated volatility of the return on palladium is about 15 per cent per year. This means that a single annual standard deviation movement in the palladium price is 15 per cent of €320, or €48 per year. Surely, with this amount of random movement in the palladium price, a threshold of, for example, €352 is much too low at which to open the mine. A similar logic applies to the closing decision. If the mine is open, we shall clearly keep it open as long as the palladium price is above the extraction cost of €350 per ounce, because we are profiting on every ounce of palladium mined. But we also won't close the mine down simply because the palladium price drops below €350 per ounce. We shall tolerate a running loss, because palladium may later rise back above €350. If, alternatively, we closed the mine, we would pay the €1 million abandonment cost, only to pay another €2 million to reopen the mine if the price rose again.

To summarize, if the mine is currently closed, then it will be opened – at a cost of €2 million – whenever the price of palladium rises *sufficiently* above the extraction cost of €350 per ounce. If the mine is currently operating, then it will be closed down – at a cost of €1 million – whenever the price of palladium falls *sufficiently* below the extraction cost of €350 per ounce. WOB's problem is to find these two threshold prices at which it opens a closed mine and closes an open mine. We call these prices $p_{open}$ and $p_{close}$, respectively, where

$$p_{open} > €350/\text{ounce} > p_{close}$$

In other words, WOB will open the mine if the palladium price option is sufficiently in the money, and will close it when the option is sufficiently out of the money.

We know that the more volatile the palladium price, the further away $p_{open}$ and $p_{close}$ will be from €350 per ounce. We also know that the greater the cost of opening the mine, the higher $p_{open}$ will be; and the greater the cost of abandoning the mine, the lower $p_{close}$ will be. Interestingly, we should also expect that $p_{open}$ will be higher if the abandonment cost is increased. After all, if it costs more to abandon the mine, WOB will need to be more assured that the price will stay above the extraction cost when it decides to open the mine. Otherwise WOB will face the costly choice between abandonment and operating at a loss if the price falls below €350 per ounce. Similarly, raising the cost of opening the mine will make WOB more reluctant to close an open mine. As a result, $p_{close}$ will be lower.

The preceding arguments have enabled us to reduce the problem of valuing WOB to two stages. First, we have to determine the threshold prices, $p_{open}$ and $p_{close}$. Second, given the best choices for these thresholds, we must determine the value of a palladium option that is exercised for a cost of €2 million when the palladium price rises above $p_{open}$ and is shut down for a cost of €1 million whenever the palladium price is below $p_{close}$.

When the mine is open – that is, when the option is exercised – the annual cash flow is equal to the difference between the palladium price and the extraction cost of €350 per ounce times 50,000 ounces. When the mine is shut down, it generates no cash flow.

The following diagram describes the decisions available at each point in time:

How do we determine the critical values for $p_{open}$ and $p_{close}$ and then the value of the mine? It is possible to get a good approximation by using the tools we have currently developed.

## Valuing the Simple Palladium Mine

Here is what has to be done both to determine $p_{open}$ and $p_{close}$ and to value the mine.

**Step 1**   Find the risk-free interest rate and the volatility. We assume a semi-annual interest rate of 3.4 per cent and a volatility of 15 per cent per year for palladium.

**Step 2**   Construct a binomial tree and fill it in with palladium prices. Suppose, for example, that we set the steps of the tree six months apart. If the annual volatility is 15 per cent, $u$ is equal to $e^{0.15/\sqrt{2}}$, which is approximately equal to 1.11. The other parameter, $d$, is 0.90 ($= 1/1.11$). Figure 23.3 illustrates the tree. Starting at the current price of €320, the first 11 per cent increase takes the price to €355 in six months. The first 10 per cent decrease takes the price to €288. Subsequent steps are up 11 per cent or down 10 per cent from the previous price. The tree extends for the 100-year life of the lease or 200 six-month steps.

Using our analysis from the previous section, we now compute the risk-adjusted probabilities for each step. Given a semi-annual interest rate of 3.4 per cent, we have

$$3.4\% = \text{Probability of a rise} \times 0.11 + (1 - \text{Probability of a rise}) \times -0.10$$

Solving this equation gives us 0.64 for the probability of a rise, implying that the probability of a fall is 0.36. These probabilities are the same for each six-month interval. In other words,

FIGURE
**23.3**

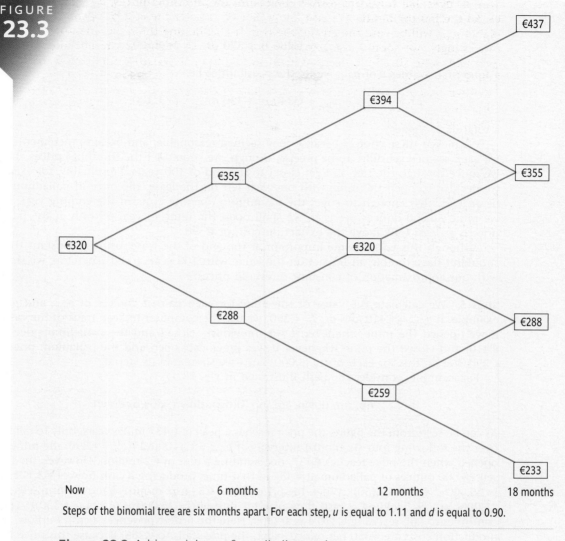

Steps of the binomial tree are six months apart. For each step, *u* is equal to 1.11 and *d* is equal to 0.90.

**Figure 23.3** A binomial tree for palladium prices

if the probability of a rise is 0.64, the expected return on palladium is 3.4 per cent per each six-month interval. These probabilities are determined under the assumption of risk-neutral pricing. In other words, if investors are risk-neutral, they will be satisfied with an expected return equal to the risk-free rate, because the extra risk of palladium will not concern them.

**Step 3**  Now we turn the computer on and let it simulate, say, 5,000 possible paths through the tree. At each node the computer has a 0.64 probability of picking an 'up' movement in the price and a corresponding 0.36 probability of picking a 'down' movement in the price. A typical path might be represented by whether the price rose or fell each six-month period over the next 100 years: it would be a list like

up, up, down, up, down, down, . . . , down

where the first 'up' means the price rose from €320 to €355 in the first six months, the next 'up' means it again went up in the second half of the year from €355 to €394, and so on, ending with a down move in the last half of year 100.

With 5,000 such paths we shall have a good sample of all the future possibilities for movement in the palladium price.

**Step 4** Next we consider possible choices for the threshold prices, $p_{open}$ and $p_{close}$. For $p_{open}$, we let the possibilities be

$$p_{open} = €360 \text{ or } €370 \text{ or } \ldots \text{ or } €500,$$

a total of 15 values. For $p_{close}$ we let the possibilities be

$$p_{close} = €340 \text{ or } €330 \text{ or } \ldots \text{ or } €100,$$

a total of 25 values.

We picked these choices because they seemed reasonable, and because increments of €10 for each seemed sensible. To be precise, though, we should let the threshold prices change as we move through the tree and get closer to the end of 100 years. Presumably, for example, if we decided to open the mine with one year left on the lease, the price of palladium should be at least high enough to cover the €2 million opening costs in the coming year. Because we mine 50,000 ounces per year, we shall open the mine in year 99 only if the palladium price is at least €40 above the extraction cost, or €390.

Although this will become important at the end of the lease, using a constant threshold shouldn't have too big an impact on the value with 100 years to go. Therefore we shall stick with our approximation of constant threshold prices.

**Step 5** We calculate the value of the mine for each pair of choices of $p_{open}$ and $p_{close}$. For example, if $p_{open} = €410$ and $p_{close} = €290$, we use the computer to keep track of the cash flows if we opened the mine whenever it was previously closed and the palladium price rose to €410, and closed the mine whenever it was previously open and the palladium price fell to €290. We do this for each of the 5,000 paths we simulated in Step 4.

For example, consider the path illustrated in Fig. 23.4:

up, up, down, up, up, down, down, down, down

As can be seen from the figure, the price reaches a peak of €437 in 2½ years, only to fall to €288 over the following four six-month intervals. If $p_{open} = €410$ and $p_{close} = €290$, the mine will be opened when the price reaches €437, necessitating a cost of €2 million. However, the firm can sell 25,000 ounces of palladium at €437 at that time, producing a cash flow of €2.175 million [= 25,000 × (€437 – €350)]. When the price falls to €394 six months later, the firm sells another 25,000 ounces, yielding a cash flow of €1.1 million [= 25,000 × (€394 – €350)]. The price continues to fall, reaching €320 a year later. Here the firm experiences a cash outflow, because production costs are €350 per ounce. Next, the price falls to €288. Because this price is below $p_{close}$ of €290, the mine is closed at a cost of €1 million. Of course, the price of palladium will fluctuate in further years, leading to the possibility of future mine openings and closings.

This path is just a possibility. It may or may not occur in any simulation of 5,000 paths. For each of the 5,000 paths that the computer simulated, we have a sequence of semi-annual cash flows using a $p_{open}$ of €410 and a $p_{close}$ of €290. We calculate the present value of each of these cash flows, discounting at the interest rate of 3.4 per cent. Summing across all the cash flows, we have the present value of the palladium mine for one path.

We then take the average present value of the palladium mine across all the 5,000 simulated paths. This number is the expected value of the mine from following a policy of opening the mine whenever the palladium price hits €410 and closing it at a price of €290.

**Step 6** The final step is to compare the different expected discounted cash flows from Step 5 for the range of possible choices for $p_{open}$ and $p_{close}$, and to pick the highest one. This is the best estimate of the expected value of the mine. The values for $p_{close}$ and $p_{open}$ corresponding to this estimate are the points at which to open a closed mine and to shut an open one.

As mentioned in Step 3, there are 15 different values for $p_{open}$ and 25 different values for $p_{close}$, implying 375 (= 15 × 25) different pairs. Consider Table 23.4, which shows the present values associated with the 20 best pairs. The table indicates that the best pair is $p_{open} = €400$ and $p_{close} = €140$, with a present value of €1.467 billion. This number represents the average present value across 5,000 simulations, all assuming the preceding values of $p_{open}$ and $p_{close}$.

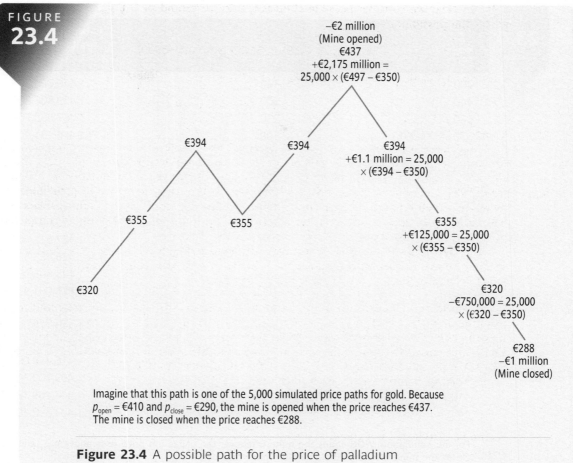

**Figure 23.4** A possible path for the price of palladium

The next best pair is $p_{open} = €460$ and $p_{close} = €300$, with a present value of €1.459 billion. The third best pair has a somewhat lower present value, and so on.

Of course, our estimate of the value of the mine is €1.467 billion, the present value of the best pair of choices. The market capitalization (price × number of shares outstanding) of WOB should reach this value if the market makes the same assumptions that we did. Note that the value of the firm is quite high using an option framework. However, as stated earlier, WOB would appear worthless if a regular discounted cash flow approach were used. This occurs because the initial palladium price of €320 is below the extraction cost of €350.

This example is not easy, either in concepts or in implementation. However, the extra work involved in mastering this example is worth it, because the example illustrates the type of modelling that actually occurs in corporate finance departments in the real world.

Furthermore, the example illustrates the benefits of the binomial approach. We merely calculate the cash flows associated with each of a number of simulations, discount the cash flows from each simulation, and average present values across the simulations. Because the Black–Scholes model is not amenable to simulations, it cannot be used for this type of problem. In addition, there are a number of other situations where the binomial model is more appropriate than the Black–Scholes model. For example, it is well known that the Black–Scholes model cannot properly handle options with dividend payments prior to the expiration date. This model also does not adequately handle the valuation of an American put. By contrast, the binomial model can easily handle both of these situations.

Thus any student of corporate finance should be well versed in both models. The Black–Scholes model should be used whenever appropriate, because it is simpler to use than the binomial model. However, for the more complex situations where the Black–Scholes model breaks down, the binomial model becomes a necessary tool.

TABLE
**23.4**

| $p_{open}$ (€) | $p_{close}$ (€) | Estimated value of palladium mine (€) |
|---|---|---|
| 400 | 140 | 1,466,720,900 |
| 460 | 300 | 1,459,406,200 |
| 380 | 290 | 1,457,838,700 |
| 370 | 100 | 1,455,131,900 |
| 360 | 190 | 1,449,708,200 |
| 420 | 150 | 1,448,711,400 |
| 430 | 340 | 1,448,450,200 |
| 430 | 110 | 1,445,396,500 |
| 470 | 200 | 1,435,687,400 |
| 500 | 320 | 1,427,512,000 |
| 410 | 290 | 1,426,483,500 |
| 420 | 290 | 1,423,865,300 |
| 400 | 160 | 1,423,061,900 |
| 360 | 320 | 1,420,748,700 |
| 360 | 180 | 1,419,112,000 |
| 380 | 280 | 1,417,405,400 |
| 450 | 310 | 1,416,238,000 |
| 450 | 280 | 1,409,709,800 |
| 440 | 220 | 1,408,269,100 |
| 440 | 240 | 1,403,398,100 |

For our simulation, WOB opens the mine whenever the palladium price rises above $p_{open}$ and closes the mine whenever the palladium price falls below $p_{close}$.

**Table 23.4** Valuation of Woborov (WOB) palladium mine for the 20 best choices of $p_{open}$ and $p_{close}$

# Summary and Conclusions

Real options, which are pervasive in business, are not captured by net present value analysis. Chapter 8 valued real options via decision trees. Given the work on options in the previous chapter, we are now able to value real options according to the Black–Scholes model and the binomial model.

In this chapter, we described and valued five different types of options:

1 Executive share options, which are technically not real options

2 The option to expand and abandon operations

3 The embedded option in a start-up company

4 The option in simple business contracts

5 The option to shut down and reopen a project

We tried to keep the presentation simple and straightforward from a mathematical point of view. The binomial approach to option pricing in Chapter 22 was extended to many periods. This adjustment brings us closer to the real world, because the assumption of only two prices at the end of an interval is more plausible when the interval is short.

**Questions and Problems**

1  **Executive Share Options**  Why do companies issue options to executives if they cost the company more than they are worth to the executive? Why not just give cash and split the difference? Wouldn't that make both the company and the executive better off?

2  **Real Options**  What are the two options that many businesses have?

3  **Valuing a Start-Up**  Given that anything is possible in the future, why can't an entrepreneur who is seeking funding choose assumptions that make a start-up look good when it isn't? Is this more a danger with real option analysis than with normal capital budgeting analysis?

4  **The Binomial Model**  Why is the binomial model more appropriate for real option analysis than Black–Scholes?

5  **Shutdown and Reopening Decisions**  Given that every corporate investment has an abandonment and reopening option, why isn't real option analysis used for every capital budgeting decision?

6  **Project Analysis**  Why does a strict NPV calculation typically understate the value of a company or project?

7  **Real Options**  Utility companies often face a decision to build new plants that burn coal, oil, or both. If the prices of both coal and oil are highly volatile, how valuable is the decision to build a plant that can burn either coal or oil? What happens to the value of this option as the correlation between coal and oil prices increases?

8  **Real Options**  Your company owns a vacant plot in a suburban area. What is the advantage of waiting to develop the plot?

9  **Real Options**  Star Mining buys a gold mine, but the cost of extraction is currently too high to make the mine profitable. In option terminology, what type of option(s) does the company have on this mine?

10  **Real Options and Capital Budgeting**  Your company currently uses traditional capital budgeting techniques, including net present value. After hearing about the use of real option analysis, your boss decides that your company should use real option analysis in place of net present value. How would you evaluate this decision?

11  **Insurance as an Option**  Insurance, whether purchased by a corporation or by an individual, is in essence an option. What type of option is an insurance policy?

12  **Real Options**  How would the analysis of real options change if a company has competitors?

13  **Employee Share Options**  Gary Levin is the chief executive officer of Mountainbrook Trading plc. The board of directors has just granted Mr Levin 20,000 at-the-money European call options on the company's equity, which is currently trading at £50 per share. The equity pays no dividends. The options will expire in four years, and the standard deviation of the returns on the shares is 55 per cent. Treasury bills that mature in four years currently yield a continuously compounded interest rate of 6 per cent.

(a)  Use the Black–Scholes model to calculate the value of the share options.

(b)  You are Mr Levin's financial adviser. He must choose between the previously mentioned share option package and an immediate £450,000 bonus. If he is risk-neutral, which would you recommend?

(c)  How would your answer to (b) change if Mr Levin were risk-averse and he could not sell the options prior to expiration?

14  **Employee Share Options**  Joseph-Benoit Suvee has just been named the new chief executive officer of BluBell Fitness NV. In addition to an annual salary of €400,000, his three-year contract states that his compensation will include 10,000 at-the-money European call options on the company's shares that expire in three years. The current share price is €40 per share, and the standard deviation of the returns on the firm's equity is 68 per cent. The company does not pay a dividend. Treasury bills that mature in three years yield a continuously compounded interest rate of 5 per cent. Assume that Mr Suvee's annual salary payments

occur at the end of the year, and that these cash flows should be discounted at a rate of 9 per cent. Using the Black–Scholes model to calculate the value of the share options, determine the total value of the compensation package on the date the contract is signed.

15 **Binomial Model**   Gasworks AG has been approached to sell up to 5 million litres of gasoline in three months at a price of €1.85 per litre. Gasoline is currently selling on the wholesale market at €1.65 per litre and has a standard deviation of 46 per cent. If the risk-free rate is 6 per cent per year, what is the value of this option?

16 **Real Options**   Webber plc is an international conglomerate with a real estate division that owns the right to erect an office building on a parcel of land in the outskirts of Leeds over the next year. This building would cost £10.5 million to construct. Because of low demand for office space in the area, such a building is worth approximately £10 million today. If demand increases, the building would be worth £12.5 million a year from today. If demand decreases, the same office building would be worth only £8 million in a year. The company can borrow and lend at the risk-free rate of 2.5 per cent effective annual rate. A local competitor in the real estate business has recently offered £750,000 for the right to build an office building on the land. Should the company accept this offer? Use a two-state model to value the real option.

17 **Real Options**   Jet Black is an international conglomerate with a petroleum division, and is currently competing in an auction to win the right to drill for crude oil on a large piece of land in one year. The current market price of crude oil is $55 per barrel, and the land is believed to contain 125,000 barrels of oil. If found, the oil would cost $10 million to extract. Treasury bills that mature in one year yield a continuously compounded interest rate of 6.5 per cent, and the standard deviation of the returns on the price of crude oil is 50 per cent. Use the Black–Scholes model to calculate the maximum bid that the company should be willing to make at the auction.

18 **Real Options**   Sardano and Sons is a large, publicly held company that is considering leasing a warehouse. One of the company's divisions specializes in manufacturing steel, and this particular warehouse is the only facility in the area that suits the firm's operations. The current price of steel is £3,600 per ton. If the price of steel falls over the next six months, the company will purchase 400 tons of steel and produce 4,800 steel rods. Each steel rod will cost £120 to manufacture, and the company plans to sell the rods for £360 each. It will take only a matter of days to produce and sell the steel rods. If the price of steel rises or remains the same, it will not be profitable to undertake the project, and the company will allow the lease to expire without producing any steel rods. Treasury bills that mature in six months yield a continuously compounded interest rate of 4.5 per cent, and the standard deviation of the returns on steel is 45 per cent. Use the Black–Scholes model to determine the maximum amount that the company should be willing to pay for the lease.

19 **Real Options**   Mouillez Pour L'Été SA (MPLE) manufactures filters for swimming pools. The company is deciding whether to implement a new technology in its pool filters. One year from now the company will know whether the new technology is accepted in the market. If the demand for the new filters is high, the present value of the cash flows in one year will be €10 million. Conversely, if the demand is low, the value of the cash flows in one year will be €6 million. The value of the project today under these assumptions is €9.1 million, and the risk-free rate is 6 per cent. Suppose that in one year, if the demand for the new technology is low, the company can sell the technology for €7 million. What is the value of the option to abandon?

20 **Binomial Model**   There is an American put option on an equity that expires in two months. The share price is £63, and the standard deviation of the share returns is 65 per cent. The option has a strike price of £70, and the monthly risk-free interest rate is a 0.42 per cent annual percentage rate. What is the price of the put option today using one-month steps? (*Hint*: How will you find the value of the option if it can be exercised early? When would you exercise the option early?)

21 **Real Options**   You are in discussions to purchase an option on an office building with a strike price of £47 million. The building is currently valued at £45 million. The option

**CHALLENGE**

**20–21**

will allow you to purchase the building either six months from today or one year from today. Six months from today, accrued rent payments from the building in the amount of £500,000 will be made to the owners. If you exercise the option in six months, you will receive the accrued rent payments; otherwise the payment will be made to the current owners. A second accrued rent payment of £500,000 will be paid one year from today with the same payment terms. The standard deviation of the value of the building is 25 per cent, and the risk-free rate is an 8.16 per cent annual percentage rate. What is the price of the option today using six-month steps? (*Hint*: The value of the building in six months will be reduced by the accrued rent payment if you do not exercise the option at that time.)

## MINI CASE

# Exotic Cuisines Employee Share Options

As a new university graduate, you've taken a management position with Exotic Cuisines plc, a restaurant chain that just went public last year. The company's restaurants specialize in exotic main dishes, using ingredients such as roe deer, crocodile and pheasant. A concern you had going in was that the restaurant business is very risky. However, after some due diligence, you discovered a common misperception about the restaurant industry. It is widely thought that 90 per cent of new restaurants close within three years; however, recent evidence suggests the failure rate is closer to 60 per cent over three years. So it is a risky business, although not as risky as you originally thought.

During your interview process, one of the benefits mentioned was employee share options. Upon signing your employment contract you received options with a strike price of £50 for 10,000 shares of company equity. As is fairly common, your share options have a three-year vesting period and a 10-year expiration, meaning that you cannot exercise the options for three years, and you lose them if you leave before they vest. After the three-year vesting period you can exercise the options at any time. Thus the employee share options are European (and subject to forfeit) for the first three years and American afterwards. Of course, you cannot sell the options, nor can you enter into any sort of hedging agreement. If you leave the company after the options vest, you must exercise within 90 days or forfeit.

Exotic Cuisines equity is currently trading at £24.38 per share, a slight increase from the initial offering price last year. There are no market-traded options on the company's equity. Because the company has been traded for only about a year, you are reluctant to use the historical returns to estimate the standard deviation of the equity's return. However, you have estimated that the average annual standard deviation for restaurant company shares is about 55 per cent. Because Exotic Cuisines is a newer restaurant chain, you decide to use a 60 per cent standard deviation in your calculations. The company is relatively young, and you expect that all earnings will be reinvested back into the company for the near future. Therefore you expect no dividends will be paid for at least the next 10 years. A three-year Treasury note currently has a yield of 3.8 per cent, and a 10-year Treasury note has a yield of 4.4 per cent.

1   You're trying to value your options. What minimum value would you assign? What is the maximum value you would assign?

2   Suppose that in three years the company's equity is trading at £60. At that time should you keep the options or exercise them immediately? What are some of the important determinants in making such a decision?

3   Your options, like most employee share options, are not transferable or tradable. Does this have a significant effect on the value of the options? Why?

4   Why do you suppose employee share options usually have a vesting provision? Why must they be exercised shortly after you depart the company even after they vest?

5   As we have seen, much of the volatility in a company's share price is due to systematic or market-wide risks. Such risks are beyond the control of a company and its employees. What are the implications for employee share options? In light of your answer, can you recommend an improvement over traditional employee share options?

## Practical Case Study

Consider the cement example from Chapter 7. What are the real options that exist for the project? How would you incorporate these into your consultancy work? What would be the process you would follow to arrive at future decisions, and what would be the main inputs into your analysis?

## Relevant Accounting Standards

The important standard for executive share options is IFRS2 *Share-Based Payment*. Also, although not directly linked to real option analysis, there is an accounting standard for exploration and mining activities. This is IFRS6 *Exploration for and Evaluation of Mineral Resources*. Visit the IASPlus website (www.iasplus.com) for more information.

## Additional Reading

This chapter focuses on practical applications of real option analysis, and consequently the reading list reflects this. The references are categorized into executive compensation research (which should also be read in conjunction with material in Chapter 2) and other research related to the application of real option analysis.

**Executive Compensation**

Babenko, L. (2009) 'Share repurchases and pay-performance sensitivity of employee compensation contracts', *Journal of Finance*, vol. 64, no. 1, pp. 117–150. **US**.

Burns, N. and S. Kedia (2006) 'The impact of performance-based compensation on misreporting', *Journal of Financial Economics*, vol. 79, no. 1, pp. 35–57. **US**.

Chhaochharia, V. and Y. Grinstein (2009) 'CEO compensation and board structure', *Journal of Finance*, vol. 64, no. 1, pp. 231–261. **US**.

Coles, J.L., N.D. Daniel and L. Naveen (2006) 'Managerial incentives and risk taking', *Journal of Financial Economics*, vol. 80, no. 2, pp. 431–468. **US**.

Cvitanic, J., Z. Wiener and F. Zapatero (2008) 'Analytic pricing of employee stock options', *Review of Financial Studies*, vol. 21, no. 2, pp. 683–724. **US**.

Efendi, J., A. Srivastava and E.P. Swanson (2007) 'Why do corporate managers misstate financial statements? The role of option compensation and other factors', *Journal of Financial Economics*, vol. 85, no. 3, pp. 667–708. **US**.

Kato, H.K., M. Lemmon, M. Luo and J. Schalheim (2005) 'An empirical examination of the costs and benefits of executive stock options: evidence from Japan', *Journal of Financial Economics*, vol. 78, no. 2, pp. 435–461. **Japan**.

Narayanan, M.P. and H.N. Seyhun (2008) 'The dating game: do managers designate option grant dates to increase the compensation?', *Review of Financial Studies*, vol. 21, no. 5, pp. 1907–1945. **US**.

**Other Relevant Research**

Hackbarth, D. and E. Morellec (2008) 'Stock returns in mergers and acquisitions', *Journal of Finance*, vol. 63, no. 3, pp. 1213–1252. **US**.

Hillier, D. and A. Marshall (1998) 'A model of complex equity funding for contingent acquisitions: a case study of non-interest bearing convertible unsecured loan stock', *Journal of Corporate Finance*, vol. 4, no. 2, pp. 133–152. **UK**.

# Endnotes

1   We ignore warrant dilution in this example. See Chapter 24 for a discussion of warrant dilution.

2   As we shall see later, here $u$ and $d$ are consistent with a standard deviation of the annual return on heating oil of 0.63.

3   For simplicity, we ignore both storage costs and a convenience yield.

4   Though it is not apparent at first glance, we shall see later that the price movement in Fig. 23.2 is consistent with the price movement in Fig. 23.1.

5   For simplicity, we ignore interest compounding.

6   See John C. Hull, *Options, Futures, and Other Derivatives*, 7th ed. (Prentice Hall, 2008), for a derivation of these formulae.

7   In this discussion we have used both *intervals* and *dates*. To keep the terminology straight, remember that the number of intervals is always one less than the number of dates. For example, if a model has two dates, it has only one interval.

**Online LearningCentre**

To help you grasp the key concepts of this chapter check out the extra resources posted on the Online Learning Centre at **www.mcgraw-hill.co.uk/textbooks/hillier**

Among other helpful resources there are PowerPoint presentations, chapter outlines and mini-cases.

# Chapter 24

# Warrants and Convertibles

In the last few years there has been a major paradigm shift in the way in which corporate finance is practised. We have come through a sustained period of deregulation and globalization in the world's markets. Financial innovation and the introduction of new securities have been commonplace as a result of the free markets that have spread throughout the world. However, things are very much different going into the second decade of the 21st century.

The financial world has seen a glut of corporate insolvencies. Governments of the major developed economies have all reduced interest rates to near zero and pumped cash into their ailing firms. Whole industries have effectively been nationalized and bought over by governments. Corporate strategies that were successful because of the availability of cheap debt are no longer possible. Finally, financial instruments that may have been viable and popular in a vibrant economy have become obsolete.

Convertible bonds are part of many companies' capital structure. They allow bondholders to convert the debt instruments into equity during a specified window in the future. The conversion feature is an embedded option that holders will exercise if the convertible is in the money. At the turn of the century these became exceptionally popular investment targets of hedge funds that looked for a quick return from conversion. However, by 2009 the market for new corporate convertible bonds was moribund. Because of the massive share price declines in 2008, the embedded options in convertible bonds were so far out of the money that they were worthless. Growth prospects for the equity markets were also uncertain. Finally, the funds that used to buy the newly issued bonds had ceased to exist with the lack of available credit.

Does this mean that convertible bonds should not be given a chapter in a corporate finance textbook? We disagree. Given their importance in firms' capital structure, which will continue to be the case for at least the next 10 years, it is necessary to understand and value these instruments. Moreover, convertibles have become a major concern to corporate managers, who are facing conversions in the next few years of bonds that were issued 10 or 20 years ago.

Warrants are similar to standard call options, except that the company must issue new shares if the holder chooses to exercise them. Again, because of changes in the global financial environment, they have become less popular. However, they are present in the financial structure of many companies, and tend to be issued in conjunction with standard bond issues.

This chapter is concerned with valuing the option embedded in these financial instruments.

## 24.1 Warrants

Warrants are securities that give holders the right, but not the obligation, to buy shares of equity directly from a company at a fixed price for a given period. Each warrant specifies the number of shares of equity that the holder can buy, the exercise price, and the expiration date.

From the preceding description of warrants, it is clear that they are similar to call options. The differences in contractual features between warrants and the call options that trade on Euronext Liffe are small. For example, warrants have longer maturity periods. Some warrants are actually perpetual, meaning that they never expire.

Warrants are referred to as *equity kickers*, because they are usually issued in combination with privately placed bonds.[1] In most cases warrants are attached to the bonds when issued. The loan agreement will state whether the warrants are detachable from the bond – that is, whether they can be sold separately. Usually, the warrant can be detached immediately.

In the last few years only a very few corporations have issued warrants, and these have largely been in the United States. More recently, governments have purchased warrants from banks as part of the financial rescue plans put in place to combat the global credit crunch in 2008.[2]

To illustrate warrants, we shall focus on the famed banana company Chiquita Brands International, which issued warrants in the United States in 2006. Each warrant gave the holder the right to purchase one share of equity at an exercise price of $19.32. The warrants expired on 19 March 2009. On 1 March 2006 Chiquita Brands shares closed at $17.57, and the price of a warrant was $4.05.

The relationship between the value of Chiquita's warrants and its share price can be viewed as similar to the relationship between a call option and the share price, described in a previous chapter. Figure 24.1 depicts the relationship for Chiquita's warrants. The lower limit on the value of the warrants is zero if Chiquita's share price is below $19.32 per share. If the price of Chiquita's equity rises above $19.32 per share, the lower limit is the share price minus $19.32. The upper limit is the share price of Chiquita. A warrant to buy one share of equity cannot sell at a price above the price of the underlying shares.

The price of Chiquita's warrants on 1 March 2006 was higher than the lower limit. The height of the warrant price above the lower limit will depend on the following:

1    The variance of Chiquita's share price returns

2    The time to expiration date

3    The risk-free rate of interest

4    The share price of Chiquita

5    The exercise price

6    Cash dividends

With the exception of cash dividends, these are the same factors that determine the value of a call option.[3]

**Figure 24.1** Chiquita warrants on 1 March 2006

Warrants can also have unusual features. For example, when the French specialist metals group Carbone Lorraine was unable to raise financing for solar power acquisitions in 2008, it entered into a financing deal with Société Générale. Under the deal, Carbone Lorraine issued convertible warrants to SocGen that allowed the French bank to buy up to 17.5 per cent of Carbone Lorraine's equity at a 10 per cent discount whenever the metals company needed funds. This innovative financing deal was a warrant, where the decision to exercise was with the issuer, not the holder. In effect, it mimicked an equity-linked credit line that bypassed the credit squeeze in the markets at the time.

## 24.2 The Difference between Warrants and Call Options

From the holder's point of view, warrants are similar to call options on equity. A warrant, like a call option, gives its holder the right to buy shares at a specified price. Warrants usually have an expiration date, though in most cases they are issued with longer lives than call options. From the firm's point of view, however, a warrant is very different from a call option on the company's equity.

The most important difference between call options and warrants is that call options are issued by individuals and warrants are issued by firms. When a warrant is exercised, a firm must issue new shares of equity. Each time a warrant is exercised, then, the number of shares outstanding increases.

To illustrate, suppose Endrun Ltd issues a warrant giving holders the right to buy one share of equity at €25. Further, suppose the warrant is exercised. Endrun must print one new share certificate. In exchange for the share certificate, it receives €25 from the holder.

In contrast, when a call option is exercised, there is no change in the number of shares outstanding. Suppose Ms Eager holds a call option on the equity of Endrun. The call option gives Ms Eager the right to buy one share of the equity of Endrun for €25. If Ms Eager chooses to exercise the call option, a seller, say Mr Swift, is obligated to give her one share of Endrun's equity in exchange for €25. If Mr Swift does not already own a share, he must enter the stock market and buy one. The call option is a side bet between buyers and sellers on the value of Endrun shares. When a call option is exercised, one investor gains and the other loses. The total number of shares outstanding of the Endrun Company remains constant, and no new funds are made available to the company.

Warrants also affect accounting numbers. Warrants and (as we shall see) convertible bonds cause the number of shares to increase. This causes the firm's net income to be spread over more shares, thereby decreasing earnings per share. Firms with significant amounts of warrants and convertible issues must report earnings on a primary basis and a fully diluted basis.

## 24.3 Warrant Pricing and the Black–Scholes Model

We now wish to express the gains from exercising a call and a warrant in more general terms. The gain on a call can be written like this:

Gain from exercising a single call:

$$\underbrace{\frac{\text{Firm's value net of debt}}{\#}}_{\text{(Value of a share of equity)}} - \text{Exercise price} \tag{24.1}$$

We define the *firm's value net of debt* to be the total firm value less the value of the debt. The # stands for the number of shares outstanding. The ratio on the left is the value of a share of equity. The gain on a warrant can be written as follows:

Gain from exercising a single warrant:

$$\underbrace{\frac{\text{Firm's value net of debt} + \text{Exercise price} \times \#_w}{\# + \#_w}}_{\text{(Value of a share of equity after warrant is exercised)}} - \text{Exercise price} \tag{24.2}$$

The numerator of the left term is the firm's value net of debt *after* the warrant is exercised. It is the sum of the firm's value net of debt *prior* to the warrant's exercise plus the proceeds the firm receives from the exercise. The proceeds equal the product of the exercise price multiplied by the number of warrants. The number of warrants appears as $\#_w$. (Our analysis uses the plausible assumption that all warrants in the money will be exercised.) The denominator, $\# + \#_w$, is the number of shares outstanding *after* the exercise of the warrants. The ratio on the left is the value of a share of equity after exercise. By rearranging terms, we can rewrite Eq. (24.2) as[4]

Gain from exercising a single warrant:

$$\frac{\#_w}{\# + \#_w} \times \underbrace{\left( \frac{\text{Firm's value net of debt}}{\#} - \text{Exercise price} \right)}_{\text{(Gain from a call on a firm with no warrants)}}$$

(24.3)

Equation (24.3) relates the gain on a warrant to the gain on a call. Note that the term within parentheses is Eq. (24.1). Thus the gain from exercising a warrant is a proportion of the gain from exercising a call in a firm without warrants. The proportion $\#/(\# + \#_w)$ is the ratio of the number of shares in the firm without warrants to the number of shares after all the warrants have been exercised. This ratio must always be less than 1. Thus the gain on a warrant must be less than the gain on an identical call in a firm without warrants.

The preceding implies that we can value a warrant using the Black–Scholes model, adjusted for the dilution effect:

$$w = \frac{1}{\left( 1 + \dfrac{\#_w}{\#} \right)} c_w$$

(24.4)

where $c_w$ is the value of a call option written on the equity of a firm *without* warrants.[5]

## Warrant Valuation

EXAMPLE
**24.1**

Veld NV is planning to issue 10,000 warrants that, when exercised, can be converted on a one-for-one basis. The proceeds of the warrant issuance will be distributed to the existing shareholders. Besides this dividend, the company is not planning to pay out any other cash dividend during the lifetime of the warrants. The company currently has 50,000 shares outstanding. If the share price of Veld NV is €2.50 and the exercise price of the warrants is €2.30, what is the value of the warrant today? The continuously compounded annual risk-free rate of interest is 7 per cent, the variance of returns of Veld NV is 0.09, and the time to expiry is 1 year.

**Step 1.** First we need to calculate the value of a comparable call option on the firm's equity. This is done by simply plugging the relevant values into the Black–Scholes option pricing formula (see Chapter 22).

**Step 1(a).** Calculate $d_1$ and $d_2$:

$$\begin{aligned}
d_1 &= \left[ \ln\left( \frac{S}{E} \right) + (R + \sigma^2/2)t \right] \Big/ \sqrt{\sigma^2 t} \\
&= \left[ \ln\left( \frac{€2.50}{€2.30} \right) + (0.07 + 0.09/2)1 \right] \Big/ \sqrt{0.09} \\
&= (0.0834 + 0.115)/0.3 \\
&= 0.6613 \\
d_2 &= d_1 - \sqrt{\sigma^2 t} \\
&= 0.3613
\end{aligned}$$

**Step 1(b).** Calculate $N(d_1)$ and $N(d_2)$ using a spreadsheet or tables:

$$N(d_1) = N(0.6613) = 0.7458$$
$$N(d_2) = N(0.3613) = 0.6411$$

**Step 1(c).** Calculate $c_w$:

$$
\begin{aligned}
c_w &= S \times [N(d_1)] - Ee^{-Rt} \times [N(d_2)] \\
&= €2.50 \times [N(d_1)] - €2.30 \times e^{-0.07} \times N(d_2) \\
&= (€2.50 \times 0.7458) - (€2.30 \times 0.9324 \times 0.6411) \\
&= €1.8645 - €1.3749 \\
&= €0.49
\end{aligned}
$$

**Step 2.** The value of the Veld NV warrant is thus

$$
w = \frac{1}{\left(1 + \dfrac{\#_w}{\#}\right)} c_w = \frac{1}{\left(1 + \dfrac{10{,}000}{50{,}000}\right)} €0.49
$$
$$= 0.8333(€0.49)$$
$$= €0.4083$$

## 24.4 Convertible Bonds

A convertible bond is similar to a bond with warrants. The most important difference is that a bond with warrants can be separated into distinct securities whereas a convertible bond cannot. A convertible bond gives the holder the right to exchange it for a given number of shares any time up to and including the maturity date of the bond.

Preference shares can frequently be converted into equity. A convertible preference share is the same as a convertible bond except that it has an infinite maturity date.

EXAMPLE
**24.2**

## Convertibles

At the end of 2008 AIG sold its Swiss bank, AIG Private Bank, to an Abu Dhabi investment group, Aabar Investments PJSC, for 307 million Swiss francs (€205 million). Aabar Investments was primarily an oil and gas investment company, and this acquisition diversified its operations into the financial sector.

Aabar Investments was able to purchase AIG Private Bank because it had raised €1.3 billion by issuing a convertible bond to the International Petroleum Investment Company (IPIC), which is itself wholly owned by the Abu Dhabi Investment Company. The Abu Dhabi Investment Company is Abu Dhabi's sovereign wealth fund, which invests overseas on behalf of the Abu Dhabi government.

On 24 September Aabar Investments issued one convertible bond, which was convertible into 2.228 billion new shares. The number of shares received for each bond (2.228 billion in this example) is called the conversion ratio.

Bond traders also speak of the conversion price of the bond. This is calculated as the ratio of the face value of the bond to the conversion ratio. The conversion price of the bond was 3 Emirati dirhams (Dh), which meant that the face value of the Aabar convertible bond was Dh6.684 billion (= 3 × 2.228 billion) or €1.3 billion.

When Aabar Investments issued its convertible bonds, its equity was valued at Dh2.52 per share. The conversion price of Dh3.00 was 19 per cent higher than the actual equity value. This 19 per cent is referred to as the conversion premium. It reflects the fact that the conversion option in Aabar convertible bonds was *out of the money*. This conversion premium is typical.

Convertibles are almost always protected against stock splits and share dividends. If Aabar's equity had been split two for one, the conversion ratio would have been increased from 2.228 billion to 4.456 billion.

Conversion ratio, conversion price and conversion premium are well-known terms in the real world. For that reason alone, the student should master the concepts. However, conversion price and conversion premium implicitly assume that the bond is selling at par. If the bond is selling at another price, the terms have little meaning. By contrast, conversion ratio can have a meaningful interpretation regardless of the price of the bond.

## 24.5 The Value of Convertible Bonds

The value of a convertible bond can be described in terms of three components: straight bond value, conversion value, and option value. We examine these three components next.

### Straight Bond Value

The straight bond value is what the convertible bonds would sell for if they could not be converted into equity. It will depend on the general level of interest rates and on the default risk. Consider a convertible bond issued by a hypothetical firm, Cold Dawn plc. On 1 November 2009 Cold Dawn plc raised £300 million by issuing 6.75 per cent convertible subordinated debentures due in 2025. It planned to use the proceeds to invest in new plant and equipment. Like typical debentures, they had a sinking fund and were callable. Cold Dawn's bonds differed from other debentures in their convertible feature: each bond was convertible into 2,353 shares of Cold Dawn equity any time before maturity. When Cold Dawn issued its convertible bonds, its share price was £22.625. The conversion price of £42.50 (= £100,000/2,353) was 88 per cent higher than the actual equity price. Suppose that straight debentures issued by Cold Dawn plc had been rated A, and A-rated bonds were priced to yield 4 per cent per six months on 1 November 2009. The straight bond value of Cold Dawn convertible bonds can be determined by discounting the £3,375 semi-annual coupon payment and principal amount at 4 per cent:

$$\text{Straight bond} = \sum_{t=1}^{32} \frac{£3,375}{1.04^t} + \frac{£100,000}{(1.04)^{32}}$$

$$= £3,375 \times A_{0.04}^{32} + \frac{£100,000}{(1.04)^{32}}$$

$$= £60,323 + £28,506$$

$$= £88,829$$

The straight bond value of a convertible bond is a minimum value. The price of Cold Dawn's convertible could not have gone lower than the straight bond value.

Figure 24.2 illustrates the relationship between straight bond value and share price. In Fig. 24.2 we have been somewhat dramatic, and implicitly assumed that the convertible bond is default free. In this case the straight bond value does not depend on the share price, so it is graphed as a straight line.

### Conversion Value

The value of convertible bonds depends on conversion value. Conversion value is what the bonds would be worth if they were immediately converted into equity at current prices. Typically, we compute conversion value by multiplying the number of shares of equity that will be received when the bond is converted by the current price of the equity.

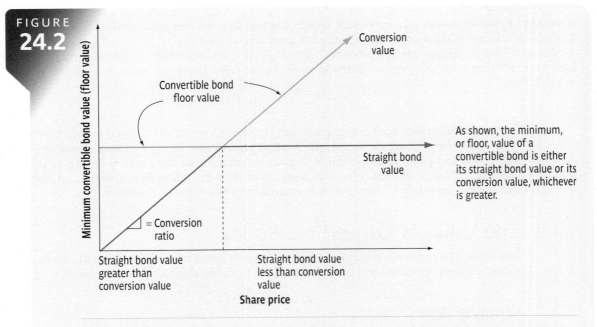

**Figure 24.2** Minimum value of a convertible bond versus the value of the equity for a given interest rate

On 1 November 2009 each Cold Dawn convertible bond could have been converted into 2,353 shares of Cold Dawn equity. Cold Dawn shares were selling for £22.625. Thus the conversion value was 2,353 × £22.625 = £53,237. A convertible cannot sell for less than its conversion value. Arbitrage prevents this from happening. If Cold Dawn's convertible sold for less than £53,237, investors would have bought the bonds and converted them into equity and sold the shares. The profit would have been the difference between the value of the shares sold and the bond's conversion value.

Thus convertible bonds have two minimum values: the straight bond value and the conversion value. The conversion value is determined by the value of the firm's underlying equity. This is illustrated in Fig. 24.2. As the value of equity rises and falls, the conversion price rises and falls with it. When the value of Cold Dawn's equity increases by £1, the conversion value of its convertible bonds increases by £2,353.

## Option Value

The value of a convertible bond will generally exceed both the straight bond value and the conversion value.[6] This occurs because holders of convertibles need not convert immediately. Instead, by waiting, they can take advantage of whichever is greater in the future: the straight bond value or the conversion value. This option to wait has value, and it raises the value over both the straight bond value and the conversion value.

When the value of the firm is low, the value of convertible bonds is most significantly influenced by their underlying value as straight debt. However, when the value of the firm is very high, the value of convertible bonds is mostly determined by their underlying conversion value. This is illustrated in Fig. 24.3.

The bottom portion of the figure implies that the value of a convertible bond is the maximum of its straight bond value and its conversion value, plus its option value:

$$\text{Value of convertible bond} = \frac{\text{The greater of}}{\text{(Straight bond value, Conversion value)}} + \text{Option value}$$

FIGURE
24.3

As shown, the value of a convertible bond is the sum of its floor value and its option value.

**Figure 24.3** Value of a convertible bond versus the value of the equity for a given interest rate

EXAMPLE
24.3

## Conversion

Suppose Moulton plc has outstanding 1,000 shares of equity and 100 bonds. Each bond has a face value of £100,000 at maturity. They are discount bonds, and pay no coupons. At maturity each bond can be converted into 10 shares of newly issued equity.

What circumstances will make it advantageous for the holders of Moulton convertible bonds to convert to equity at maturity?

If the holders of the convertible bonds convert, they will receive $100 \times 10 = 1,000$ shares of equity. Because there were already 1,000 shares, the total number of shares outstanding becomes 2,000 upon conversion. Thus converting bondholders own 50 per cent of the value of the firm, $V$. If they do not convert, they will receive £10,000,000 or $V$, whichever is less. The choice for the holders of the Moulton bonds is obvious. They should convert if 50 per cent of $V$ is greater than £10,000,000. This will be true whenever $V$ is greater than £20,000,000. This is illustrated as follows:

| Pay-off to convertible bondholders and shareholders of the Moulton Company | | |
|---|---|---|
| (1)<br>$V \leq £10,000,000$ | (2)<br>$£10,000,000 < V \leq £20,000,000$ | (3)<br>$V > £20,000,000$ |
| Decision: Bondholders will not convert | Bondholders will not convert | Bondholders will convert |
| Convertible bondholders  $V$ | £10,000,000 | $0.5V$ |
| Shareholders  0 | $V - £10,000,000$ | $0.5V$ |

# 24.6 Reasons for Issuing Warrants and Convertibles

Probably there is no other area of corporate finance where real-world practitioners get as confused as they do on the reasons for issuing convertible debt. To separate fact from fantasy, we present a rather structured argument. We first compare convertible debt with straight debt. Then we compare convertible debt with equity. For each comparison, we ask in what situations the firm is better off with convertible debt and in what situations it is worse off.

## Convertible Debt versus Straight Debt

Convertible debt pays a lower interest rate than does otherwise identical straight debt. For example, if the interest rate is 10 per cent on straight debt, the interest rate on convertible debt might be 9 per cent. Investors will accept a lower interest rate on a convertible because of the potential gain from conversion.

Imagine a firm that seriously considers both convertible debt and straight debt, finally deciding to issue convertibles. When would this decision have benefited the firm and when would it have hurt the firm? We consider two situations.

**The Share Price later Rises so that Conversion Is Indicated**  The firm clearly likes to see the share price rise. However, it would have benefited even more had it previously issued straight debt instead of a convertible. Although the firm paid out a lower interest rate than it would have with straight debt, it was obligated to sell the convertible holders a chunk of the equity at a below-market price.

**The Share Price later Falls or Does not Rise enough to Justify Conversion**  The firm hates to see the share price fall. However, as long as the share price does fall, the firm is glad that it had previously issued convertible debt instead of straight debt. This is because the interest rate on convertible debt is lower. Because conversion does not take place, our comparison of interest rates is all that is needed.

**Summary**  Compared with straight debt, the firm is worse off having issued convertible debt if the underlying equity subsequently does well. The firm is better off having issued convertible debt if the underlying equity subsequently does poorly. In an efficient market we cannot predict future share prices. Thus we cannot argue that convertibles either dominate or are dominated by straight debt.

## Convertible Debt versus Equity

Next, imagine a firm that seriously considers both convertible debt and equity but finally decides to issue convertibles. When would this decision benefit the firm and when would it hurt the firm? We consider our two situations.

**The Share Price later Rises so that Conversion Is Indicated**  The firm is better off having previously issued a convertible instead of equity. To see this, consider the Cold Dawn case. The firm could have issued equity for £22. Instead, by issuing a convertible, the firm effectively received £42.50 for a share upon conversion.

**The Share Price later Falls or Does not Rise enough to Justify Conversion**  No firm wants to see its share price fall. However, given that the price did fall, the firm would have been better off if it had previously issued equity instead of a convertible. The firm would have benefited by issuing equity above its later market price. That is, the firm would have received more than the subsequent worth of the equity. However, the drop in share price did not affect the value of the convertible much because the straight bond value serves as a floor.

**Summary**  Compared with equity, the firm is better off having issued convertible debt if the underlying equity subsequently does well. The firm is worse off having issued convertible debt if the underlying equity subsequently does poorly. We cannot predict future share prices in an efficient market. Thus we cannot argue that issuing convertibles is better or worse than issuing equity. The preceding analysis is summarized in Table 24.1.

Modigliani–Miller (MM) pointed out that, abstracting from taxes and bankruptcy costs, the firm is indifferent to whether it issues equity or issues debt. The MM relationship is a quite general one. Their pedagogy could be adjusted to show that the firm is indifferent to whether it issues convertibles or issues other instruments. To save space (and the patience of students) we have omitted a full-blown proof of MM in a world with convertibles. However, our results are perfectly consistent with MM. Now we turn to the real-world view of convertibles.

## The 'Free Lunch' Story

The preceding discussion suggests that issuing a convertible bond is no better and no worse than issuing other instruments. Unfortunately, many corporate executives fall into the trap of arguing that issuing convertible debt is actually better than issuing alternative instruments. This is a free lunch type of explanation, of which we are quite critical.

---

**EXAMPLE 24.4**

## Are Convertibles always Better?

The share price of RW SE is €20. Suppose this company can issue subordinated debentures at 10 per cent. It can also issue convertible bonds at 6 per cent with a conversion value of €800. The conversion value means that the holders can convert a convertible bond into 40 (= €800/€20) shares of equity.

A company treasurer who believes in free lunches might argue that convertible bonds should be issued because they represent a cheaper source of financing than either subordinated bonds or equity. The treasurer will point out that if the company does poorly and the price does not rise above €20, the convertible bondholders will not convert the bonds into equity. In this case the company will have obtained debt financing at below-market rates by attaching worthless equity kickers. On the other hand, if the firm does well and the price of its equity rises to €25 or above, convertible holders will convert. The company will issue 40 shares. The company will receive a bond with face value of €1,000 in exchange for issuing 40 shares of equity, implying a conversion price of €25. The company will have issued equity at €25 per share, or 20 per cent above the €20 equity price prevailing when the convertible bonds were issued. This enables it to lower its cost of equity capital. Thus, the treasurer happily points out, regardless of whether the company does well or poorly, convertible bonds are the cheapest form of financing.

Although this argument may sound quite plausible at first, there is a flaw. The treasurer is comparing convertible financing *with straight debt* when the share price subsequently falls. However, the treasurer compares convertible financing *with equity* when the share price subsequently rises. This is an unfair mixing of comparisons. By contrast, our analysis of Table 24.1 was fair, because we examined both share price increases and decreases when comparing a convertible with each alternative instrument. We found that no single alternative dominated convertible bonds in *both* up and down markets.

## The 'Expensive Lunch' Story

Suppose we stand the treasurer's argument on its head by comparing (a) convertible financing with straight debt when share prices rise and (b) convertible financing with equity when share prices fall.

From Table 24.1, we see that convertible debt is more expensive than straight debt when share prices subsequently rise. The firm's obligation to sell convertible holders a chunk of equity at a below-market price more than offsets the lower interest rate on a convertible.

Also from Table 24.1, we see that convertible debt is more expensive than equity when share prices subsequently fall. Had the firm issued equity, it would have received a price higher than its subsequent worth. Therefore the expensive lunch story implies that convertible debt

| TABLE 24.1 | If firm subsequently does poorly | If firm subsequently prospers |
|---|---|---|
| Convertible bonds (CBs) | No conversion because of low share price. | Conversion because of high share price. |
| Compared with: | | |
| Straight bonds | CBs provide cheap financing, because coupon rate is lower. | CBs provide expensive financing, because bonds are converted, which dilutes existing equity. |
| Equity | CBs provide expensive financing, because firm could have issued equity at high prices. | CBs provide cheap financing, because firm issues equity at high prices when bonds are converted. |

**Table 24.1** The case for and against convertible bonds (CBs)

is an inferior form of financing. Of course, we dismiss both the free lunch and the expensive lunch arguments.

## A Reconciliation

In an efficient financial market there is neither a free lunch nor an expensive lunch. Convertible bonds can be neither cheaper nor more expensive than other instruments. A convertible bond is a package of straight debt and an option to buy equity. The difference between the market value of a convertible bond and the value of a straight bond is the price investors pay for the call option feature. In an efficient market, this is a fair price.

In general, if a company prospers, issuing convertible bonds will turn out to be worse than issuing straight bonds and better than issuing equity. In contrast, if a company does poorly, convertible bonds will turn out to be better than issuing straight bonds and worse than issuing equity.

## 24.7 Why Are Warrants and Convertibles Issued?

From studies it is known that firms that issue convertible bonds are different from other firms. Here are some of the differences:

- The bond ratings of firms using convertibles are lower than those of other firms.[7]

- Convertibles tend to be used by smaller firms with high growth rates and more financial leverage.[8]

- Convertibles are usually subordinated and unsecured.

The kind of company that uses convertibles provides clues to why they are issued. Here are some explanations that make sense.

### Matching Cash Flows

If financing is costly, it makes sense to issue securities whose cash flows match those of the firm. A young, risky and (it hopes) growing firm might prefer to issue convertibles or bonds with warrants, because these will have lower initial interest costs. When the firm is successful, the convertibles (or warrants) will be converted. This causes expensive dilution, but it occurs when the firm can most afford it.

| | Firm risk | |
|---|:---:|:---:|
| | **Low** | **High** |
| Straight bond yield (%) | 10 | 15 |
| Convertible bond yield (%) | 6 | 7 |

The yields on straight bonds reflect the risk of default. The yields on convertibles are not sensitive to default risk.

**Table 24.2** A hypothetical case of the yields on convertible bonds

## Risk Synergy

Another argument for convertible bonds and bonds with warrants is that they are useful when it is very costly to assess the risk of the issuing company. Suppose you are evaluating a new product by a start-up company. The new product is a genetically engineered virus that may increase the yields of corn crops in northern climates. It may also cause cancer. This type of product is difficult to value properly. Thus the risk of the company is very hard to determine: it may be high, or it may be low. If you could be sure the risk of the company was high, you would price the bonds for a high yield, say 15 per cent. If it was low, you would price them at a lower yield, say 10 per cent.

Convertible bonds and bonds with warrants can protect somewhat against mistakes of risk evaluation. Convertible bonds and bonds with warrants have two components: straight bonds and call options on the company's underlying equity. If the company turns out to be a low-risk company, the straight bond component will have high value and the call option will have low value. However, if the company turns out to be a high-risk company, the straight bond component will have low value and the call option will have high value. This is illustrated in Table 24.2.

However, although risk has effects on value that cancel each other out in convertibles and bonds with warrants, the market and the buyer nevertheless must make an assessment of the firm's potential to value securities, and it is not clear that the effort involved is that much less than is required for a straight bond.

## Agency Costs

Convertible bonds can resolve agency problems associated with raising money. In a previous chapter we showed that straight bonds are like risk-free bonds minus a put option on the assets of the firm. This creates an incentive for creditors to force the firm into low-risk activities. By contrast, holders of equity have incentives to adopt high-risk projects. High-risk projects with negative NPV transfer wealth from bondholders to shareholders. If these conflicts cannot be resolved, the firm may be forced to pass up profitable investment opportunities. However, because convertible bonds have an equity component, less expropriation of wealth can occur when convertible debt is issued instead of straight debt.[9] In other words, convertible bonds mitigate agency costs. One implication is that convertible bonds have less restrictive debt covenants than do straight bonds in the real world. Casual empirical evidence seems to bear this out.

## Backdoor Equity

A popular theory of convertibles views them as backdoor equity.[10] The basic story is that young, small, high-growth firms cannot usually issue debt on reasonable terms because of high financial distress costs. However, the owners may be unwilling to issue equity if current share prices are too low.

Lewis, Rogalski and Seward examine the risk shifting and backdoor equity theories of convertible bond debt. They find evidence for both theories.

## The European Puzzle

Until very recently, there has been no research on convertible bond issuance in Europe. However, two recent papers that have explored this issue provide additional insights into why European managers issue convertibles. Bancel and Mittoo (2004) and Dutordoir and Van de Gucht (2009) both ask the question 'Why do European firms issue convertible debt instead of straight debt or equity?'[11] Surprisingly, their findings differ somewhat from the established view of convertible issuance that has been propagated by US researchers.

Bancel and Mittoo surveyed 229 firms in 16 European companies that issued convertible bonds. This sample represented 295 convertible bond issues, amounting to a total of €97,933 million. Only 29 firms responded to the sample, and most of these were French. Normally, such a small sample would be problematic, but given that this was the first study of its type, we can be forgiving. They found that there was no one reason why firms opt for convertibles over other forms of financing. French respondents argued that the liquidity of the convertibles market was a strong motivator for issuing convertibles. Clearly, this appears to be consistent with the situation in financial markets as we move into the second decade of the 21st century. In addition, firms whose equity appears to be overvalued opt for convertibles to avoid the share price falling because of equity dilution.

Dutordoir and Van de Gucht act as an interesting counterpoint to the work of Bancel and Mittoo and earlier US research. Using a much larger sample of security issues, they find that European issuers of convertible bonds are actually large companies with low financing costs. This is the opposite to US convertible issuers, who tend to be small and highly levered. Again, unlike the US, convertible bonds in Europe are rarely callable, and only 27 per cent have been converted into equity. In Europe, it appears that convertible bonds are not used as backdoor equity but instead as 'sweetened debt', to reduce financing costs of raising debt.

The findings of Dutordoir and Van de Gucht raise important questions about the motivation for European firms that issue convertible bonds. Given that issuers tend to be large, financially healthy and mature, the explanations relating to financing costs that have been proposed do not appear to explain the reality in Europe. A possible reason may simply be market timing, as argued by Baker and Wurgler and discussed in an earlier chapter. The contrast in findings between the US and Europe highlights the need to recognize differences in environment, culture and motivations of corporate managers in these two very heterogeneous regions. As the situation with convertible bonds shows, students who blindly take US research findings and apply them fully to the environment in other parts of the world may make very big and expensive mistakes.

## 24.8 Conversion Policy

There is one aspect of convertible bonds that we have omitted so far. Firms are sometimes granted a call option on the bond. It should be noted that, in the US, call features are significantly more common than in Europe. The typical arrangements for calling a convertible bond are simple. When the bond is called, the holder has about 30 days to choose between the following:

1   Converting the bond to equity at the conversion ratio

2   Surrendering the bond and receiving the call price in cash

What should bondholders do? It should be obvious that if the conversion value of the bond is greater than the call price, conversion is better than surrender; and if the conversion value is less than the call price, surrender is better than conversion. If the conversion value is greater than the call price, the call is said to force conversion.

What should financial managers do? Calling the bonds does not change the value of the firm as a whole. However, an optimal call policy can benefit the shareholders at the expense of the bondholders. Because we are speaking about dividing a pie of fixed size, the optimal call policy is simple: do whatever the bondholders do not want you to do.

Bondholders would love the shareholders to call the bonds when the bonds' market value is below the call price. Shareholders would be giving bondholders extra value. Alternatively, should the value of the bonds rise above the call price, the bondholders would love the shareholders not to call the bonds, because bondholders would be allowed to hold onto a valuable asset.

There is only one policy left. This is the policy that maximizes shareholder value and minimizes bondholder value:

**Call the bond when its value is equal to the call price.**

It is a puzzle that firms do not always call convertible bonds when the conversion value reaches the call price. Ingersoll examined the call policies of 124 firms between 1968 and 1975.[12] In most cases he found that the company waited to call the bonds until the conversion value was much higher than the call price. The median company waited until the conversion value of its bonds was 44 per cent higher than the call price. This is not even close to our optimal strategy. Why?

One reason is that if firms attempt to implement the optimal strategy, it may not be truly optimal. Recall that bondholders have 30 days to decide whether to convert bonds to equity or to surrender bonds for the call price in cash. In 30 days the share price could drop, forcing the conversion value below the call price. If so, the convertible is 'out of the money' and the firm is giving away money. The firm would be giving up cash for equity worth much less. Because of this possibility, firms in the real world usually wait until the conversion value is substantially above the call price before they trigger the call.[13] This is sensible.

## Summary and Conclusions

1   A warrant gives the holder the right to buy shares of equity at an exercise price for a given period. Typically, warrants are issued in a package with privately placed bonds. Afterwards they may become detached and trade separately.

2   A convertible bond is a combination of a straight bond and a call option. The holder can give up the bond in exchange for shares.

3   Convertible bonds and warrants are like call options. However, there are some important differences:

   (a)   Warrants and convertible securities are issued by corporations. Call options are traded between individual investors.

      (i)   Warrants are usually issued privately and are combined with a bond. In most cases the warrants can be detached immediately after the issue. In some cases, warrants are issued with preference shares, with equity, or in executive compensation programmes.

      (ii)   Convertibles are usually bonds that can be converted into equity.

      (iii)   Call options are sold separately by individual investors (called *writers* of call options).

   (b)   Warrants and call options are exercised for cash. The holder of a warrant gives the company cash and receives new shares of the company's equity. The holder of a call option gives another individual cash in exchange for shares. When someone converts a bond, it is exchanged for equity. As a consequence, bonds with warrants and convertible bonds have different effects on corporate cash flow and capital structure.

▶ (c) Warrants and convertibles cause dilution to the existing shareholders. When warrants are exercised and convertible bonds converted, the company must issue new shares of equity. The percentage ownership of the existing shareholders will decline. New shares are not issued when call options are exercised.

4 Many arguments, both plausible and implausible, are given for issuing convertible bonds and bonds with warrants. One plausible rationale for such bonds has to do with risk. Convertibles and bonds with warrants are associated with risky companies. Lenders can do several things to protect themselves from high-risk companies:

(a) They can require high yields.

(b) They can lend less or not at all to firms whose risk is difficult to assess.

(c) They can impose severe restrictions on such debt.

Another useful way to protect against risk is to issue bonds with equity kickers. This gives the lenders the chance to benefit from risks, and reduces the conflicts between bondholders and shareholders concerning risk.

5 A puzzle particularly vexes financial researchers: convertible bonds may have call provisions. Companies appear to delay calling convertibles until the conversion value greatly exceeds the call price. From the shareholders' standpoint, the optimal call policy would be to call the convertibles when the conversion value equals the call price.

# connect Questions and Problems

**CONCEPT**

**1–7**

1 **Warrants** Why are warrants sometime referred to as equity kickers? What does this mean?

2 **Warrants and Options** What is the primary difference between a warrant and a traded call option?

3 **Warrant Pricing** Why is the dilution factor important in warrant pricing?

4 **Convertible Bonds** What are the main advantages of convertible bonds to issuing firms? To convertible bondholders?

5 **Reasons for Issuing Warrants and Convertibles** Why do firms issue convertibles? What impact do convertibles have on firms with target debt to equity ratios? Discuss convertible bonds in the context of the trade-off, pecking order and market timing theories of capital structure.

6 **Why Are Warrants and Convertibles Issued?** Why are convertible bonds viewed as backdoor equity?

7 **Conversion Policy** When should a firm force conversion of convertibles? Why?

**REGULAR**

**8–29**

8 **Warrants** Explain the following limits on the prices of warrants:

(a) If the share price is below the exercise price of the warrant, the lower bound on the price of a warrant is zero.

(b) If the share price is above the exercise price of the warrant, the lower bound on the price of a warrant is the difference between the share price and the exercise price.

(c) An upper bound on the price of any warrant is the current value of the firm's equity.

9 **Convertible Bonds and Equity Volatility** Suppose you are evaluating a callable, convertible bond. If the share price volatility increases, how will this affect the price of the bond?

10  **Convertible Bond Value**  What happens to the price of a convertible bond if interest rates increase?

11  **Dilution**  What is dilution, and why does it occur when warrants are exercised?

12  **Warrants and Convertibles**  What is wrong with the simple view that it is cheaper to issue a bond with a warrant or a convertible feature because the required coupon is lower?

13  **Warrants and Convertibles**  Why do firms issue convertible bonds and bonds with warrants?

14  **Convertible Bonds**  Why will convertible bonds not be voluntarily converted to equity before expiration?

15  **Warrant Valuation**  A warrant with six months until expiration entitles its owner to buy 10 shares of the issuing firm's equity for an exercise price of €31 per share. If the current market price of the equity is €15 per share, will the warrant be worthless?

16  **Conversion Price**  A convertible bond has a conversion ratio of 22.4. What is the conversion price?

17  **Conversion Ratio**  A convertible bond has a conversion price of €64.85. What is the conversion ratio of the bond?

18  **Conversion Value**  A convertible bond has a conversion ratio of 15. If the shares are currently priced at €62, what is the conversion value of the bond?

19  **Conversion Premium**  Eckely plc recently issued bonds with a conversion ratio of 14.5. If the share price at the bond issue was £46.24, what was the conversion premium?

20  **Convertible Bonds**  Hannon Home Products recently issued £43,000,000 worth of 8 per cent convertible debentures. Each convertible bond has a face value of £100,000. Each convertible bond can be converted into 2,425 shares of equity any time before maturity. The share price is £31.25, and the market value of each bond is £118,000.

  (a)  What is the conversion ratio?

  (b)  What is the conversion price?

  (c)  What is the conversion premium?

  (d)  What is the conversion value?

  (e)  If the share price increases by £2, what is the new conversion value?

21  **Warrant Value**  A warrant gives its owner the right to purchase three shares of equity at an exercise price of 32 Swedish krona (SKr) per share. The current market price of the equity is SKr39. What is the minimum value of the warrant?

22  **Convertible Bond Value**  An analyst has recently informed you that at the issuance of a company's convertible bonds, one of the two following sets of relationships existed:

|  | Scenario A | Scenario B |
|---|---|---|
| Face value of bond (£) | 1,000 | 1,000 |
| Straight value of convertible bond (£) | 900 | 950 |
| Market value of convertible bond (£) | 1,000 | 900 |

Assume the bonds are available for immediate conversion. Which of the two scenarios do you believe is more likely? Why?

23  **Convertible Bond Value**  Sportime Fitness Centre AB issued convertible bonds with a conversion price of 25 Norwegian kroner (NKr). The bonds are available for immediate conversion. The current price of the company's equity is NKr22 per share. The current

market price of the convertible bonds is NKr990. The convertible bonds' straight value is not known.

(a) What is the minimum price for the convertible bonds?

(b) Explain the difference between the current market price of each convertible bond and the value of the equity into which it can be immediately converted.

24 **Convertible Bonds** You own a callable, convertible bond with a conversion ratio of 3,500. The equity is currently selling for £40 per share. The issuer of the bond has announced a call at a call price of 110. What are your options here? What should you do?

25 **Warrant Value** General Modems has five-year warrants that currently trade in the open market. Each warrant gives its owner the right to purchase one share of equity for an exercise price of £35.

(a) Suppose the equity is currently trading for £33 per share. What is the lower limit on the price of the warrant? What is the upper limit?

(b) Suppose the equity is currently trading for £39 per share. What is the lower limit on the price of the warrant? What is the upper limit?

26 **Convertible Bonds** Trichet SA has just issued a 30-year callable, convertible bond with a coupon rate of 7 per cent annual coupon payments. The bond has a conversion price of €125. The company's equity is selling for €32 per share. The owner of the bond will be forced to convert if the bond's conversion value is ever greater than or equal to €1,100. The required return on an otherwise identical non-convertible bond is 12 per cent.

(a) What is the minimum value of the bond?

(b) If the share price were to grow by 15 per cent per year for ever, how long would it take for the bond's conversion value to exceed €1,100?

27 **Convertible Bonds** Rob Stevens is the chief executive officer of Isner Construction plc and owns 500,000 shares. The company currently has 4 million shares and convertible bonds with a face value of £20 million outstanding. The convertible bonds have a conversion price of £20, and the equity is currently selling for £25.

(a) What percentage of the firm's equity does Mr Stevens own?

(b) If the company decides to call the convertible bonds and force conversion, what percentage of the firm's equity will Mr Stevens own? He does not own any convertible bonds.

28 **Warrants** Survivor NV, an all-equity firm, has three shares outstanding. Yesterday, the firm's assets consisted of five ounces of platinum, currently worth €1,000 per ounce. Today, the company issued Ms Wu a warrant for its fair value of €1,000. The warrant gives Ms Wu the right to buy a single share of the firm's equity for €2,100, and can be exercised only on its expiration date one year from today. The firm used the proceeds from the issuance to immediately purchase an additional ounce of platinum.

(a) What was the price of a single share of equity *before* the warrant was issued?

(b) What was the price of a single share of equity immediately *after* the warrant was issued?

(c) Suppose platinum is selling for €1,100 per ounce on the warrant's expiration date in one year. What will be the value of a single share of equity on the warrant's expiration date?

29 **Warrants** The capital structure of Ricketti Enterprises plc consists of 10 million shares of equity and 1 million warrants. Each warrant gives its owner the right to purchase one share of equity for an exercise price of £15. The current share price is £17, and each warrant is worth £3. What is the new share price if all warrant holders decide to exercise today?

**CHALLENGE 30–32**

30 **Convertible Calculations** You have been hired to value a new 25-year callable, convertible bond. The bond has a 6.80 per cent coupon rate, payable annually. The conversion price is £150, and the equity currently sells for £44.75. The stock price is expected to grow at 12 per cent per year. The bond is callable at £1,200, but based on prior experience it won't be called unless the conversion value is £1,300. The required return on this bond is 10 per cent. What value would you assign to this bond?

31 **Warrant Value** Superior Clamps AB has a capital structure consisting of 4 million shares of equity and 500,000 warrants. Each warrant gives its owner the right to purchase one share of newly issued equity for an exercise price of €20. The warrants are European, and will expire one year from today. The market value of the company's assets is €88 million, and the annual variance of the returns on the firm's assets is 0.04. Treasury bills that mature in one year yield a continuously compounded interest rate of 7 per cent. The company does not pay a dividend. Use the Black–Scholes model to determine the value of a single warrant.

32 **Warrant Value** Omega Airline's capital structure consists of 1.5 million shares of equity and zero coupon bonds with a face value of $10 million that mature in six months. The firm just announced that it will issue warrants with an exercise price of $95 and six months until expiration to raise the funds to pay off its maturing debt. Each warrant can be exercised only at expiration and gives its owner the right to buy a single newly issued share of equity. The firm will place the proceeds from the warrant issue immediately into Treasury bills.

The market value balance sheet shows that the firm will have assets worth $160 million after the announcement. The company does not pay dividends. The standard deviation of the returns on the firm's assets is 65 per cent, and Treasury bills with a six-month maturity yield 6 per cent. How many warrants must the company issue today to be able to use the proceeds from the sale to pay off the firm's debt obligation in six months?

## MINI CASE
## S&S Air's Convertible Bond

Kartner Meister was recently hired by S&S Air AB to assist the company with its short-term financial planning, and to evaluate the company's performance. Kartner graduated from university five years ago with a finance degree. He has been employed in the finance department of a major German company since then.

S&S Air was founded 10 years ago by two friends, Stephan Lochner and Hans Multscher. The company has manufactured and sold light airplanes over this period, and the company's products have received high reviews for safety and reliability. The company has a niche market in that it sells primarily to individuals who own and fly their own airplanes. The company has two models: the Birdie, which sells for €53,000; and the Eagle, which sells for €78,000.

S&S Air is not publicly traded, but the company needs new funds for investment opportunities. In consultation with Conrad Witz of underwriter Koerbecke and Pleydenwurff, Kartner decided that a convertible bond issue with a 20-year maturity is the way to go. He met with the owners, Stephan and Hans, and presented his analysis of the convertible bond issue. Because the company is not publicly traded, Kartner looked at comparable publicly traded companies and determined that the average P/E ratio for the industry is 12.5. Earnings per share for the company are €1.60. With this in mind, Kartner concluded that the conversion price should be €25 per share.

Several days later Stephan, Hans and Kartner met again to discuss the potential bond issue. Both Hans and Stephan have researched convertible bonds, and have questions for Kartner. Hans begins by asking Kartner whether the convertible bond issue will have a lower coupon rate than a comparable bond without a conversion feature. Kartner replies that to sell the bond at par value, the convertible bond issue would require a 6 per cent coupon rate with a conversion value of €800, while a plain vanilla bond would have a 7 per cent coupon rate.

Hans nods in agreement, and he explains that the convertible bonds are a win–win form of financing. He states that if the value of the company equity does not rise above the conversion price, the company has issued debt at a cost below the market rate (6 per cent instead of 7 per cent). If the company's equity does rise to the conversion value, the company has effectively issued shares at above the current value.

Stephan immediately disagrees, arguing that convertible bonds are a no-win form of financing. He argues that if the value of the company equity rises to €25, the company is forced to sell shares at the conversion price. This means the new shareholders (those who bought the convertible bonds) benefit from a bargain price. Put another way, if the company prospers, it would have been better to have issued straight debt so that the gains would not be shared.

Kartner has gone back to Conrad for help. As Conrad's assistant, you've been asked to prepare another memo answering the following questions:

1  Why do you think Kartner is suggesting a conversion price of €25? Given that the company is not publicly traded, does it even make sense to talk about a conversion price?

2  What is the floor value of the S&S Air convertible bond?

3  What is the conversion ratio of the bond?

4  What is the conversion premium of the bond?

5  What is the value of the option?

6  Is there anything wrong with Hans' argument that it is cheaper to issue a bond with a convertible feature because the required coupon is lower?

7  Is there anything wrong with Stephan's argument that a convertible bond is a bad idea because it allows new shareholders to participate in gains made by the company?

8  How can you reconcile the arguments made by Hans and Stephan?

9  During the debate, a question comes up concerning whether the bonds should have an ordinary (not make-whole) call feature. Kartner confuses everybody by stating: 'The call feature lets S&S Air force conversion, thereby minimizing the problem Stephan has identified.' What is he talking about? Is he making sense?

## Practical Case Study

Download the financial accounts of 10 companies and look for any issues of warrants or convertibles. You may find examples of bonds that have conversion options or warrant-like properties. Are convertibles an important part of your firms' capital structures? Write a brief report on the use of convertibles and warrants for your sample of firms.

## Relevant Accounting Standards

The most important accounting standard for warrants and convertibles is IAS39 *Financial Instruments: Recognition and Measurement*. IAS39 provides definitions for different types of financial security, and states how the different components of a security should be valued and presented in a firm's financial accounts. Visit the IASPlus website (www.iasplus.com) for more information.

# Additional Reading

Much of the recent research in this area has already been discussed in the main text. The following papers will add to your understanding.

Choi, D., M. Germansky and H. Tookes (2009) 'Convertible bond arbitrage, liquidity externalities, and stock prices', *Journal of Financial Economics*, vol. 91, no. 2, pp. 227–251. **US**.

Gajewski, J.-F., E. Ginglinger and M. Lasfer (2007) 'Why do companies include warrants in seasoned equity offerings?', *Journal of Corporate Finance*, vol. 13, no. 1, pp. 25–42. **France**.

Gillet, R. and H. De La Bruslerie (2009) 'The consequences of issuing convertible bonds: dilution and/or financial restructuring', *European Financial Management* (forthcoming). **France**.

# Endnotes

1   Warrants are also issued with publicly distributed bonds and new issues of equity.

2   At the turn of the 21st century many banks began issuing options on other companies under the name 'call warrants'. These are not warrants in the real sense, because the companies on which the call warrants are written do not issue new equity in response to an exercise of the call warrants. Call warrants have become quite common, and in 2001, 830 call warrants were listed on Euronext Brussels, 1,047 on Euronext Amsterdam, and 4,952 on Euronext Paris. Call warrants have also been issued elsewhere in Europe, Asia and Australia. In this chapter we shall not consider the valuation of these call warrants. See Jenke Ter Horst and Chris Veld, 'An empirical analysis of the pricing of bank issued options versus options exchange options', *European Financial Management* (2008) for more information on call warrants.

3   Just like call options, warrants are protected against stock splits and stock dividends, but not against cash dividends. The latter generally does not cause a problem for the valuation of call options, since these only have short maturities, and therefore a relatively small amount of dividends are paid during their lifetime. Given that warrants generally have maturities of several years, the effect of cash dividends can be significant.

4   To derive Eq. (24.3), we separate 'Exercise price' in Eq. (24.2). This yields

$$\frac{\text{Firm's value net of debt}}{\# + \#_w} - \frac{\#}{\# + \#_w} \times \text{Exercise price}$$

By rearranging terms, we can obtain Eq. (24.3).

5   Equation 24.4 is not exactly correct. After a warrant is issued, the share price and volatility of returns will change to reflect the warrant's existence. However, Schulz and Trautmann (G.U. Schulz and S. Trautmann, 'Robustness of option-like warrant valuation', *Journal of Banking and Finance* (1994), pp. 841–859) report that Eq. (24.4) performs just as well as more complex valuation models, except when the warrant is deep out of the money.

6   The most plausible exception is when conversion would provide the investor with a dividend much greater than the interest available prior to conversion. The optimal strategy here could very well be to convert immediately, implying that the market value of the bond would exactly equal the conversion value. Other exceptions occur when the firm is in default or the bondholders are forced to convert.

7   E.F. Brigham, 'An analysis of convertible debentures', *Journal of Finance*, vol. 21 (1966).

8   W.H. Mikkelson, 'Convertible calls and security returns', *Journal of Financial Economics*, vol. 9 (September 1981), p. 3.

9   A. Barnea, R.A. Haugen, and L. Senbet, *Agency Problems and Financial Contracting*, Prentice Hall Foundations of Science Series (New York: Prentice Hall, 1985), Chapter VI.

10  J. Stein, 'Convertible bonds as backdoor equity financing', *Journal of Financial Economics*, vol. 32 (1992). See also C.M. Lewis, R.J. Rogalski and J.K. Seward, 'Understanding the design of convertible debt', *The Journal of Applied Corporate Finance* (Spring 1998).

11 F. Bancel and U.R. Mittoo, 'Why do European firms issue corporate debt?', *European Financial Management*, vol. 10 (2004); M. Dutordoir and L. Van de Gucht, 'Why do Western European firms issue convertibles instead of straight debt or equity?', *European Financial Management* (forthcoming, 2009).

12 J. Ingersoll, 'An examination of corporate call policies on convertible bonds', *Journal of Finance* (May 1977). See also M. Harris and A. Raviv, 'A sequential signalling model of convertible debt policy', *Journal of Finance* (December 1985). Harris and Raviv describe a signal equilibrium that is consistent with Ingersoll's result. They show that managers with favourable information will delay calls to avoid depressing stock prices.

13 See Z.A. Altintig and A.W. Butler, 'Are they still called late? The effect of notice period on calls of convertible bonds', *Journal of Corporate Finance* (March 2005); and P. Asquith, 'Convertible bonds are not called late', *Journal of Finance* (September 1995). On the other hand, the stock market usually reacts negatively to the announcement of a call. For example, see A.K. Singh, A.R. Cowan and N. Nayar, 'Underwritten calls of convertible bonds', *Journal of Financial Economics* (March 1991), and M.A. Mazzeo and W.T. Moore, 'Liquidity costs and stock price response to convertible security calls', *Journal of Business* (July 1992). Ederington, Caton and Campbell tested various theories about when it is optimal to call convertibles. They found evidence consistent for the preceding 30-day 'safety margin' theory. They also found that calls of in-the-money convertibles are highly unlikely if dividends to be received (after conversion) exceed the company's interest payment. See L.H. Ederington, G.L. Caton and C.J. Campbell, 'To call or not to call convertible debt', *Financial Management* (Spring 1997).

To help you grasp the key concepts of this chapter check out the extra resources posted on the Online Learning Centre at www.mcgraw-hill.co.uk/textbooks/hillier

Among other helpful resources there are PowerPoint presentations, chapter outlines and mini-cases.

# Chapter 25

# Financial Risk Management with Derivatives

Anyone studying corporate finance must be familiar with the principles of financial risk management. Many students think that only financial institutions use derivatives such as futures and swaps. However, every company that does business overseas, sources raw materials from other countries, borrows or lends money, or buys commodities today for delivery in the future will use risk management techniques to manage risk and optimize their business.

For example, in 2008 BMW was faced with a very challenging problem. Its biggest growth area for 'X series' cars was the United States. However, because the cars are made in Germany, the euro's strength against the dollar was making them too expensive in the US. Moreover, at the time, the euro was expected to strengthen further over the coming months. What could BMW do to ensure that its cars did not become too expensive in the United States? This chapter will review some of the methods open to BMW's management.

## 25.1 Derivatives, Hedging and Risk

The name *derivatives* is self-explanatory. A derivative is a financial instrument whose pay-offs and values are derived from, or depend on, something else. Often, we speak of the thing that the derivative depends on as the *primitive* or the *underlying*. For example, in Chapter 22 we studied how options work. An option is a derivative. The value of a call option depends on the value of the underlying equity on which it is written. Actually, call options are quite complicated examples of derivatives. The vast majority of derivatives are simpler than call options. Most derivatives are forward or futures agreements, or what are called *swaps*, and we shall study each of these in some detail.

Why do firms use derivatives? The answer is that derivatives are tools for changing the firm's risk exposure. Someone once said that derivatives are to finance what scalpels are to surgery. By using derivatives the firm can cut away unwanted portions of risk exposure, and even transform the exposures into quite different forms. A central point in finance is that risk is undesirable. In our chapters about risk and return we pointed out that individuals would choose risky securities only if the expected return compensated for the risk. Similarly, a firm will accept a project with high risk only if the return on the project compensates for this risk. Not surprisingly, then, firms are usually looking for ways to reduce their risk. When the firm reduces its risk exposure with the use of derivatives, it is said to be hedging. Hedging offsets the firm's risk, such as the risk in a project, by one or more transactions in the financial markets.

Derivatives can also be used merely to change or even increase the firm's risk exposure. When this occurs, the firm is speculating on the movement of some economic variables – those that underlie the derivative. For example, if a derivative is purchased that will rise in value if interest rates rise, and if the firm has no offsetting exposure to interest rate changes, then the firm is speculating that interest rates will rise and give it a profit on its derivatives position. Using derivatives to translate an opinion about whether interest rates or some other economic variable will rise or fall is the opposite of hedging – it is risk enhancing. Speculating on your views on the economy and using derivatives to profit if that view turns out to be correct is not necessarily wrong, but the speculator should always remember that sharp tools cut deep: if the opinions on which the derivatives position is based turn out to be incorrect, then the consequences can prove costly. Efficient market theory teaches how difficult it is to predict what markets will do. Most of the sad experiences with derivatives have occurred not from their use as instruments for hedging and offsetting risk, but rather from speculation.

## 25.2 Forward Contracts

We can begin our discussion of hedging by considering forward contracts. You have probably been dealing in forward contracts your whole life without knowing it. Suppose you walk into a bookshop on, say, 1 February to buy the best-seller *Learn to Play Silky Football: The Bobo Philosophy*. The cashier tells you that the book is currently sold out, but he takes your phone number, saying that he will reorder it for you. He says the book will cost £10.00. If you agree on 1 February to pick up and pay £10.00 for the book when called, you and the cashier have engaged in a **forward contract**. That is, you have agreed both to pay for the book and to pick it up when the bookshop notifies you. Because you are agreeing to buy the book at a later date, you are *buying* a forward contract on 1 February. In commodity parlance you will be taking delivery when you pick up the book. The book is called the **deliverable instrument**.

The cashier, acting on behalf of the bookshop, is selling a forward contract. (Alternatively, we say that he is writing a forward contract.) The bookshop has agreed to turn the book over to you at the predetermined price of £10.00 as soon as the book arrives. The act of turning the book over to you is called **making delivery**. Table 25.1 illustrates the book purchase. Note that the agreement takes place on 1 February. The price is set and the conditions for sale are set at that time. In this case, the sale will occur when the book arrives. In other cases, an exact date of sale would be given. However, *no* cash changes hands on 1 February; cash changes hands only when the book arrives.

Though forward contracts may have seemed exotic to you before you began this chapter, you can see that they are quite commonplace. Dealings in your personal life probably have involved forward contracts. Similarly, forward contracts occur all the time in business. Every time a firm orders an item that cannot be delivered immediately, a forward contract takes place. Sometimes, particularly when the order is small, an oral agreement will suffice. At other times, particularly when the order is larger, a written agreement is necessary.

Note that a forward contract is not an option. Both the buyer and the seller are obligated to perform under the terms of the contract. By contrast, the buyer of an option *chooses* whether to exercise the option.

| TABLE 25.1 | 1 February | Date when book arrives |
|---|---|---|
| | **Buyer:** | **Buyer:** |
| | 1 Agrees to pay the purchase price of £10.00. | 1 Pays purchase price of £10.00. |
| | 2 Agrees to receive book when book arrives. | 2 Receives book. |
| | **Seller:** | **Seller:** |
| | 1 Agrees to give up book when book arrives. | 1 Gives up book. |
| | 2 Agrees to accept payment of £10.00 when book arrives. | 2 Accepts payment of £10.00. |

Note that cash does not change hands on 1 February. Cash changes hands when the book arrives.

**Table 25.1** Illustration of book purchase as a forward contract

A forward contract should be contrasted with a cash transaction – that is, a transaction where exchange is immediate. Had the book been on the bookshop's shelf, your purchase of it would constitute a cash transaction.

In Islamic financing the equivalent hedge transaction is called a *bai salam*. The difference between a *bai salam* and a forward contract is that money is transferred today in a *bai salam*, but is transferred at a future date with a forward. See Chapter 14 for more information on the *bai salam*.

## 25.3 Futures Contracts

A variant of the forward contract takes place on financial exchanges. Contracts on exchanges are usually called futures contracts. There are a number of futures exchanges around the world, and more are being established. The big three futures exchanges are Euronext Liffe, Eurex, and the Chicago Mercantile Exchange. While trading on the exchanges spans whole geographic regions, there are many smaller exchanges, such as OMX (Nordic and Baltic markets), BELFOX (Belgium), IDEM (Italy), MEFF (Spain), and LME (London).

Figure 25.1 gives a partial *Financial Times* listing for selected futures contracts. Taking a look at the Liffe cocoa contracts, note that the contracts traded on Liffe are for delivery of 10 tonnes of cocoa, and are quoted in pounds sterling per tonne. The price of cocoa for delivery in the future is expected to fall over 2009. For example, the price of a 2 March 2009 cocoa futures contract is £1,808, falling to £1,751 for a July contract and £1,649 for a December 2009 contract.

For the Liffe cocoa contract with a March maturity, the first number in the row is the *settlement price* (£1,808), and it is essentially the closing price for the day. For purposes of marking to market, this is the figure used. The change, listed next, is the movement in the settlement price since the previous trading session (–£28). The highest price (£1,855) and lowest price (£1,802) over the life of the contract are shown next. Finally, there were 5,890 contracts traded, and *open interest* (72,860), the number of contracts outstanding at the end of the day, is shown.

Though we are discussing a futures contract, let us work with a forward contract first. Suppose you wrote a *forward* contract for September cocoa at £1,735. From our discussion of forward contracts, this would mean that you would agree to turn over an agreed-upon weight of cocoa beans for £1,735 per 10 tonnes on some specified date in the month of September.

A futures contract differs somewhat from a forward contract. First, the seller can choose to deliver the cocoa on any day during the delivery month – that is, the month of September. This gives the seller leeway that he would not have with a forward contract. When the seller decides to deliver, he notifies the exchange clearing house that he wants to do so. The clearing house then notifies an individual who bought a September cocoa contract that she must stand ready to accept delivery within the next few days. Though each exchange selects the buyer in a different way, the buyer is generally chosen in a random fashion. Because there are so many buyers at any one time, the buyer selected by the clearing house to take delivery almost certainly did not originally buy the contract from the seller now making delivery.

Second, futures contracts are traded on an exchange, whereas forward contracts are generally traded off an exchange. Because of this, there is generally a liquid market in futures contracts. A buyer can net out her futures position with a sale. A seller can net out his futures position with a purchase. If a buyer of a futures contract does not subsequently sell her contract, she must take delivery.

Third, and most important, the prices of futures contracts are marked to the market daily. That is, suppose the price falls to £1,705 on Monday's close. Because all buyers lost £30 per contract on that day, they each must turn over the £30 per contract to their brokers within 24 hours, who subsequently remit the proceeds to the clearing house. All sellers gained £30 per contract on that day, so they each receive £30 per contract from their brokers. Their brokers are subsequently compensated by the clearing house. Because there is a buyer for every seller, the clearing house must break even every day.

Now suppose that the price rises to £1,750 on the close of the following Tuesday. Each buyer receives £45 (£1,750 – £1,705) per contract, and each seller must pay £45 per contract.

FIGURE 25.1

# FT COMMODITIES & AGRICULTURE

09/01/2009

## BASIC METALS — LONDON METAL EXCHANGE

| $/tonne | Cash Official | 3 Mth Official | Kerb PM 3 Mth close | Day's High/Low (3 Mth) | Open Interest (Lots) | Turnover (Lots) |
|---|---|---|---|---|---|---|
| Aluminium | 1520-20.5 | 1555-56 | 1569-70 | 1590/1542 | 668,730 | 150,978 |
| Alum Alloy | 1100-10 | 1135-45 | 1190-1200 | 1190/1170 | 6,646 | 6,609 |
| Amer Alloy | 1020-21 | 1050-60 | 1095-1100 | 1100/1090 | 22,628 | 3,036 |
| Copper | 3279.5-80 | 3329-30 | 3400-3405 | 3450/3244 | 243,694 | 100,517 |
| Lead | 1180-85 | 1199-200 | 1200-1205 | 1208/1150 | 66,123 | 43,768 |
| Nickel | 11370-75 | 11425-50 | 12150-12175 | 12175/11250 | 84,083 | 31,512 |
| Tin | 11300-50 | 11275-300 | 11800-11850 | 12000/11250 | 19,463 | 10,616 |
| Zinc | 1219.5-20 | 1245-45.5 | 1290-1295 | 1300/1230 | 221,852 | 59,032 |

Spot: 1.5248 3 mths: 1.5222 6 mths: 1.5211 9 mths: 1.5201 AM Official £/$ rate: 1.5318.
LME Closing £/$ rate: – . Kerb close 17:00.
Source: Amalgamated Metal Trading www.amt.co.uk

### HIGH GRADE COPPER COMEX

| | Sett price | Day's chge | High | Low | Vol | Open int |
|---|---|---|---|---|---|---|
| Jan | 154.55 | +8.25 | 154.50 | 146.00 | 0.23 | 0.92 |
| Feb | 155.30 | +8.10 | 155.60 | 148.65 | 0.15 | 1.96 |
| Mar | 155.95 | +8.05 | 156.50 | 147.40 | 16.17 | 51.40 |
| Apr | 156.65 | +7.95 | 156.50 | 150.65 | 0.23 | 2.15 |
| Total | | | | | 15.9 | 77.0 |

### LME WAREHOUSE STOCKS (tonnes)

| Aluminium | +12,050 | to | 2,406,225 |
|---|---|---|---|
| Aluminium Alloy | +1,260 | to | 105,200 |
| Copper | +5,875 | to | 363,575 |
| Lead | +425 | to | 45,025 |
| Nickel | -210 | to | 78,594 |
| Zinc | +25 | to | 259,775 |
| Tin | +50 | to | 7,975 |

For further trading information see www.lme.co.uk

## PRECIOUS METALS

### GOLD COMEX (100 Troy oz: $/troy oz)

| | Sett price | Day's chge | High | Low | Vol 000s | 0 int 000s |
|---|---|---|---|---|---|---|
| Feb | 855.0 | +0.5 | 869.3 | 845.0 | 111.9 | 190.2 |
| Apr | 856.5 | +0.6 | 870.5 | 847.1 | 11.02 | 50.34 |
| Total | | | | | 139.2 | 328.3 |

### LONDON BULLION MARKET

| Gold (Troy oz) | $ price | £ equiv | € equiv |
|---|---|---|---|
| Close | 854.35-856.35 | | |
| Opening | 855.90-857.30 | | |
| Morning fix | 854.00 | 560.26 | 622.72 |
| Afternoon fix | 847.25 | 559.17 | 626.48 |
| Day's High | 860.05 | | |
| Day's Low | 845.60 | | |
| Previous Close | 857.00-858.60 | | |

## SOFTS

### COCOA LIFFE (10 tonnes: £/tonne)

| | Sett price | Day's change | High | Low | Vol 000s | 0 int 000s |
|---|---|---|---|---|---|---|
| Mar | 1808 | -28 | 1855 | 1802 | 5.89 | 72.86 |
| May | 1764 | -24 | 1805 | 1757 | 1.56 | 38.61 |
| Jul | 1751 | -18 | 1780 | 1748 | 0.24 | 30.99 |
| Sep | 1735 | -13 | 1755 | 1733 | 1.02 | 11.42 |
| Dec | 1681 | -13 | 1705 | 1679 | 0.66 | 14.31 |
| Mar | 1649 | -20 | 1677 | 1649 | 0.68 | 1.40 |
| Total | | | | | 10.1 | 169.6 |

### COCOA NYBOT (10 tonnes: $/tonne)

| Mar | 2585 | -31 | 2674 | 2569 | 0.46 | 60.22 |
|---|---|---|---|---|---|---|
| May | 2579 | -28 | 2663 | 2569 | 0.19 | 24.86 |
| Jul | 2570 | -19 | 2635 | 2555 | 0.19 | 12.45 |
| Sep | 2546 | -13 | 2611 | 2529 | 0.19 | 7.46 |
| Dec | 2511 | -11 | 2568 | 2494 | 0.08 | 10.59 |
| Mar | 2487 | -4 | 2533 | 2502 | 0.12 | 2.83 |
| Total | | | | | 9.39 | 120.2 |

### COCOA ICCO (SDR's/tonne)

| | Price | Prevday |
|---|---|---|
| Jan 8 | 1758.23 | 1728.53 |
| Daily | . . . . . . . . . | |

### COFFEE LIFFE (5 tonnes: £/tonne)

| Jan | 2012 | +60 | 2030 | 1960 | 0.29 | 14.43 |
|---|---|---|---|---|---|---|
| Jul | 1969 | -46 | 2035 | 1967 | 5.35 | 67.30 |
| Total | | | | | 11.5 | 125.3 |

### COFFEE 'C' NYBOT (37,500lbs: cents/lbs)

| Mar | 116.90 | +3.45 | 119.50 | 113.75 | 0.53 | 72.37 |
|---|---|---|---|---|---|---|
| May | 118.95 | +3.40 | 121.60 | 116.00 | 0.15 | 27.54 |
| Jul | 121.05 | +3.40 | 123.55 | 118.50 | 0.01 | 8.59 |

## MEAT & LIVESTOCK

### LIVE CATTLE CME (40,000lbs: cents/lbs)

| | Sett price | Day's change | High | Low | Vol 000s | 0 int 000s |
|---|---|---|---|---|---|---|
| Feb | 83.100 | -0.050 | 83.900 | 82.850 | 27.75 | 82.84 |
| Apr | 86.825 | -0.125 | 87.550 | 86.550 | 23.25 | 65.74 |
| Jun | 85.700 | +0.325 | 86.150 | 84.850 | 9.60 | 35.06 |
| Aug | 86.700 | +0.600 | 86.900 | 85.725 | 2.67 | 17.21 |
| Total | | | | | 64.5 | 210.0 |

### LEAN HOGS CME (40,000lbs: cents/lbs)

| Feb | 62.450 | +0.025 | 63.150 | 62.350 | 21.52 | 56.73 |
|---|---|---|---|---|---|---|
| Apr | 68.600 | -0.450 | 69.850 | 68.475 | 18.74 | 43.84 |
| May | 80.425 | -0.550 | 80.500 | 79.825 | 0.08 | 1.78 |
| Jun | 80.750 | -0.800 | 81.750 | 80.325 | 7.57 | 32.80 |
| Total | | | | | 50.4 | 150.2 |

### PORK BELLIES CME (40,000lbs: cents/lbs)

| Feb | 83.575 | -1.075 | 84.950 | 83.400 | 0.06 | 0.66 |
|---|---|---|---|---|---|---|
| Mar | 83.550 | -0.100 | 85.600 | 83.550 | - | 0.15 |
| May | 85.300 | -0.050 | 85.400 | 85.100 | - | 0.23 |
| Jul | 84.150 | -0.850 | 84.250 | 83.250 | | 0.14 |
| Total | | | | | 0.07 | 1.19 |

### FEEDER CATTLE CME (40,000lbs: cents/lbs)

| Jan | 94.100 | -0.600 | 94.475 | 93.450 | 0.81 | 2.73 |
|---|---|---|---|---|---|---|
| Mar | 92.675 | -0.425 | 93.400 | 92.250 | 2.60 | 11.87 |
| Apr | 94.000 | -0.500 | 94.550 | 93.650 | 0.30 | 2.58 |
| May | 95.600 | -0.675 | 96.100 | 95.100 | 0.61 | 2.13 |
| Total | | | | | 0.48 | 20.6 |

## SPOT MARKETS

### CRUDE OIL FOB (per barrel) + or –

| Duhai | $39.29-39.31 | -0.9 |
|---|---|---|

Source: Financial Times, www.ft.com

**Figure 25.1** Data on futures contracts, Friday 9 January 2009

Finally, suppose that on Tuesday a seller notifies his broker of his intention to deliver.[1] The delivery price will be £1,750, which is Tuesday's close.

There are clearly many cash flows in futures contracts. However, after all the dust settles, the *net price* to the buyer must be the price at which she bought originally. That is, an individual buying at Friday's closing price of £1,735 and being called to take delivery on Tuesday pays £30 per contract on Monday, receives £45 per contract on Tuesday, and takes delivery at £1,750. Her net outflow per 10 tonnes is –£1,735 (= –£30 + £45 – £1,750), which is the price at which she contracted on Friday. (Our analysis ignores the time value of money.) Conversely, an individual selling at Friday's closing price of £1,735 and notifying his broker concerning delivery the following Tuesday receives £30 per contract on Monday, pays £45 per contract on Tuesday, and makes delivery at £1,735. His net inflow per contract is £1,735 (= £30 – £45 + £1,750), which is the price at which he contracted on Friday. These details are presented in the box below.

## Illustration of Example Involving Marking to Market in Futures Contracts

Both buyer and seller originally transact at Friday's closing price. Delivery takes place at Tuesday's closing price.*

|  | **Friday 9 January** | **Monday 12 January** | **Tuesday 13 January** | **Delivery (notification given by seller on Tuesday)** |
|---|---|---|---|---|
| Closing price | £1,735 | £1,705 | £1,750 | |
| Buyer | Buyer purchases futures contract at closing price of £1,735/10 tonnes. | Buyer must pay £30 per contract to clearing house within one business day. | Buyer receives £45 per contract from clearing house within one business day. | Buyer pays £1,750 per contract and receives cocoa within one business day. |

Buyer's net payment of –£1,735 (= –£30 + £45 – £1,750) is the same as if buyer purchased a forward contract for £1,735.

| | | | | |
|---|---|---|---|---|
| Seller | Seller sells futures contract at closing price of £1,735/contract. | Seller receives £30/contract from clearing house within one business day. | Seller pays £45/contract to clearing house within one business day. | Seller receives £1,750 per contract and delivers cocoa within one business day. |

Seller's net receipts of £1,735 (= £30 – £45 + £1,750) are the same as if seller sold a forward contract for £1,735.

*For simplicity, we assume that buyer and seller both (a) initially transact at the same time and (b) meet in the delivery process. This is actually very unlikely to occur in the real world, because the clearing house assigns the buyer to take delivery in a random manner.

For simplicity, we assumed that the buyer and seller who initially transact on Friday's close meet in the delivery process. The point in the example is that the buyer's net payment of £1,735 per contract is the same as if she purchased a forward contract for £1,735. Similarly, the seller's net receipt of £1,735 per contract is the same as if he sold a forward contract for £1,735. The only difference is the timing of the cash flows. The buyer of a forward contract knows that he will make a single payment of £1,735 on the expiration date. He will not need to worry about any other cash flows in the interim. Conversely, though the cash flows to the buyer of a futures contract will net to exactly £1,735 as well, the pattern of cash flows is not known ahead of time.

The mark-to-the-market provision on futures contracts has two related effects. The first concerns differences in net present value. For example, a large price drop immediately following purchase means an immediate out-payment for the buyer of a futures contract. Though the net outflow of £1,735 is still the same as under a forward contract, the present value of the cash outflows is greater to the buyer of a futures contract. Of course, the present value of the cash outflows is less to the buyer of a futures contract if a price rise follows purchase.[2] Though this effect could be substantial in certain theoretical circumstances, it appears to be of quite limited importance in the real world.[3]

Second, the firm must have extra liquidity to handle a sudden outflow prior to expiration. This added risk may make the futures contract less attractive.

Students frequently ask, 'Why in the world would managers of the commodity exchanges ruin perfectly good contracts with these bizarre mark-to-the-market provisions?' Actually, the reason is a very good one. Consider the forward contract concerning the bookshop. Suppose the public quickly loses interest in *Learn to Play Silky Football: The Bobo Philosophy*. By the time the bookshop calls the buyer, other shops may have dropped the price of the book to £6.00. Because the forward contract was for £10.00, the buyer has an incentive not to take delivery on the forward contract. Conversely, should the book become a hot item selling at £15.00, the bookshop may simply not call the buyer.

Mark-to-the-market provisions minimize the chance of default on a futures contract. If the price rises, the seller has an incentive to default on a forward contract. However, after paying the clearing house, the seller of a futures contract has little reason to default. If the price falls, the same argument can be made for the buyer. Because changes in the value of the underlying asset are recognized daily, there is no accumulation of loss, and the incentive to default is reduced.

Because of this default issue, forward contracts generally involve individuals and institutions who know and can trust each other. However, lawyers earn a handsome living writing supposedly airtight forward contracts, even among friends. The genius of the mark-to-the-market system is that it can prevent default where it is most likely to occur – among investors who do not know each other.

## 25.4 Hedging

Now that we have determined how futures contracts work, let us talk about hedging. There are two types of hedges, long and short. We discuss the short hedge first.

**EXAMPLE 25.1**

## Futures Hedging

In January, Simon Agyei-Ampomah, a Ghanaian farmer, anticipates a harvest of 5,000 tonnes of cocoa at the end of September. He has two alternatives.

1 *Write futures contracts against his anticipated harvest.* The September cocoa contract on Euronext Liffe is trading at £1,735 per 10 tonnes on 9 January. He executes the following transaction:

| Date of transaction | Transaction | Price per 10 tonnes |
|---|---|---|
| 9 January | Write 500 September futures contracts | £1,735 |

He notes that transportation costs to the designated delivery point in London are £10 per 10 tonnes. Thus his net price per contract is £1,725 = £1,735 – £10.

2 *Harvest the cocoa without writing a futures contract.* Alternatively, Mr Agyei-Ampomah could harvest the cocoa without the benefit of a futures contract. The risk would be quite great here, because no one knows what the cash price in September will be. If prices rise, he will profit. Conversely, he will lose if prices fall.

We say that strategy 2 is an unhedged position because there is no attempt to use the futures markets to reduce risk. Conversely, strategy 1 involves a hedge. That is, a position in the futures market offsets the risk of a position in the physical – that is, in the actual – commodity.

Though hedging may seem quite sensible to you, it should be mentioned that not everyone hedges. Mr Agyei-Ampomah might reject hedging for at least two reasons.

First, he may simply be uninformed about hedging. We have found that not everyone in business understands the hedging concept. Many executives have told us that they do not want to use futures markets for hedging their inventories because the risks are too great. However, we disagree. While there are large price fluctuations in these markets, hedging actually reduces the risk that an individual holding inventories bears.

Second, Mr Agyei-Ampomah may have a special insight or some special information that commodity prices will rise. He would not be wise to lock in a price of £1,735 if he expects the cash price in September to be well above this price.

The hedge of strategy 1 is called a **short hedge** because Mr Agyei-Ampomah reduces his risk by *selling* a futures contract. The short hedge is very common in business. It occurs whenever someone either anticipates receiving inventory or is holding inventory. Mr Agyei-Ampomah is anticipating the harvest of cocoa. A manufacturer of soya bean meal and oil may hold large quantities of raw soya beans that are already paid for. However, the prices to be received for meal and oil are not known, because no one knows what the market prices will be when the meal and oil are produced. The manufacturer may write futures contracts in meal and oil to lock in sales prices. An oil company may hold large inventories of petroleum to be processed into heating oil. The firm could sell futures contracts in heating oil to lock in the sales price. A mortgage banker may assemble mortgages slowly before selling them in bulk to a financial institution. Movements of interest rates affect the value of the mortgages while they are in inventory. The mortgage banker could sell Treasury bond futures contracts to offset this interest rate risk. (This last example is treated later in this chapter.)

## EXAMPLE 25.2 — More Hedging

On 1 April, Maan Chemical agreed to sell petrochemicals (in US dollars) to the Dutch government in the future. The delivery dates and prices have been determined. Because oil is a basic ingredient of the production process, Maan Chemical will need to have large quantities of oil on hand. The firm can get the oil in one of two ways:

1  *Buy the oil as the firm needs it.* This is an unhedged position because, as of 1 April, the firm does not know the prices it will later have to pay for the oil. Oil is quite a volatile commodity, so Maan Chemical is bearing a good bit of risk. The key to this risk bearing is that the sales price to the Dutch government has already been fixed. Thus Maan Chemical cannot pass on increased costs to the consumer.

2  *Buy futures contracts.*[4] The firm can buy futures contracts with expiration months corresponding to the dates when the firm needs inventory. The futures contracts lock in the purchase price to Maan Chemical. Because there is a crude oil futures contract for every month, selecting the correct futures contract is not difficult. Many other commodities have only five contracts per year, frequently necessitating buying contracts one month away from the month of production.

As mentioned earlier, Maan Chemical is interested in hedging the risk of fluctuating oil prices because it cannot pass any cost increases on to the consumer. Suppose, alternatively, that Maan Chemical was not selling petrochemicals on fixed contract to the Dutch government. Instead, imagine that the petrochemicals were to be sold to private industry at currently prevailing prices. The price of petrochemicals should move directly with oil prices, because oil is a major component of petrochemicals. Because cost increases are likely to be passed on to the consumer, Maan Chemical would probably not want to hedge in this case. Instead, the firm is likely to choose strategy 1, buying the oil as it is needed. If oil prices increase between 1 April and 1 September, Maan Chemical will, of course, find that its inputs have become quite costly. However, in a competitive market, its revenues are likely to rise as well.

Strategy 2 is called a long hedge because one *purchases* a futures contract to reduce risk. In other words, one takes a long position in the futures market. In general, a firm institutes a long hedge when it is committed to a fixed sales price. One class of situations involves actual written contracts with customers, such as Maan Chemical had with the Dutch government. Alternatively, a firm may find that it cannot easily pass on costs to consumers, or does not want to pass on these costs.

## 25.5 Interest Rate Futures Contracts

In this section we consider interest rate futures contracts. Our examples deal with futures contracts on Treasury bonds because of their high popularity. We first price Treasury bonds and Treasury bond forward contracts. Differences between futures and forward contracts are explored. Hedging examples are provided next.

### Pricing of Treasury Bonds

As mentioned earlier in the text, a Treasury bond pays semi-annual interest over its life. In addition, the face value of the bond is paid at maturity. Consider a 20-year, 8 per cent coupon bond that was issued on 1 March. The first payment is to occur in six months – that is, on 1 September. The value of the bond can be determined as follows:

Pricing of Treasury bond:

$$P_{\text{TB}} = \frac{€40}{1 + R_1} + \frac{€40}{(1 + R_2)^2} + \frac{€40}{(1 + R_3)^3} + \cdots + \frac{€40}{(1 + R_{39})^{39}} + \frac{€1,040}{(1 + R_{40})^{40}} \tag{25.1}$$

Because an 8 per cent coupon bond pays interest of €80 a year, the semi-annual coupon is €40. The principal and semi-annual coupons are both paid at maturity. As we mentioned in a previous chapter, the price of the Treasury bond, $P_{\text{TB}}$, is determined by discounting each payment on a bond at the appropriate spot rate. Because the payments are semi-annual, each spot rate is expressed in semi-annual terms. That is, imagine a horizontal term structure where the effective annual yield is 12 per cent for all maturities. Because each spot rate, $R$, is expressed in semi-annual terms, each spot rate is $\sqrt{1.12} - 1 = 5.83\%$. Coupon payments occur every six months, so there are 40 spot rates over the 20-year period.

### Pricing of Forward Contracts

Now imagine a *forward* contract where, on 1 March, you agree to buy a new 20-year, 8 per cent coupon Treasury bond in six months (on 1 September). As with typical forward contracts, you will pay for the bond on 1 September, not 1 March. The cash flows from both the Treasury bond issued on 1 March and the forward contract that you purchase on 1 March are presented in Fig. 25.2. The cash flows on the Treasury bond begin exactly six months earlier than do the cash flows on the forward contract. The Treasury bond is purchased with cash on 1 March (date 0). The first coupon payment occurs on 1 September (date 1). The last coupon payment occurs at date 40, along with the face value of €1,000. The forward contract compels you to pay $P_{\text{FORW.CONT.}}$, the price of the forward contract, on 1 September (date 1). You receive a new Treasury bond at that time. The first coupon payment you receive from the bond occurs on 1 March of the following year (date 2). The last coupon payment occurs at date 41, along with the face value of €1,000.

Given the 40 spot rates, Eq. (25.1) showed how to price a Treasury bond. How do we price the forward contract on a Treasury bond? Just as we saw earlier in the text that net present value analysis can be used to price bonds, we shall now show that net present value analysis can be used to price forward contracts. Given the cash flows for the forward contract in Fig. 25.2, the price of the forward contract must satisfy the following equation:

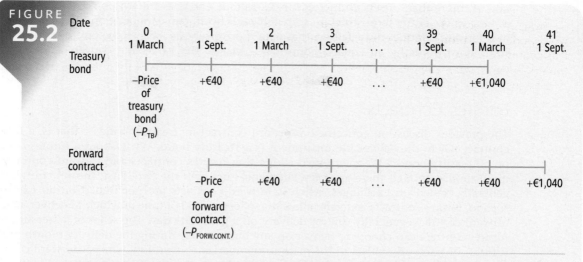

FIGURE
**25.2**

**Figure 25.2** Cash flows for both a Treasury bond and a forward contract on a Treasury bond

$$\frac{P_{\text{FORW.CONT.}}}{1 + R_1} = \frac{€40}{(1 + R_2)^2} + \frac{€40}{(1 + R_3)^3} + \frac{€40}{(1 + R_4)^4} + \cdots + \frac{€40}{(1 + R_{40})^{40}} + \frac{€1,040}{(1 + R_{41})^{41}} \qquad (25.2)$$

The right side of Eq. (25.2) discounts all the cash flows from the delivery instrument (the Treasury bond issued on 1 September) back to date 0 (1 March). Because the first cash flow occurs at date 2 (1 March of the subsequent year), it is discounted by $1/(1 + R_2)^2$. The last cash flow of €1,040 occurs at date 41, so it is discounted by $1/(1 + R_{41})^{41}$. The left side represents the cost of the forward contract as of date 0. Because the actual out-payment occurs at date 1, it is discounted by $1/(1 + R_1)$.

Students often ask, 'Why are we discounting everything back to date 0, when we are actually paying for the forward contract on 1 September?' The answer is simply that we apply the same techniques to Eq. (25.2) that we apply to all capital budgeting problems: We want to put everything in today's (date 0's) euros. Given that the spot rates are known in the marketplace, traders should have no more trouble pricing a forward contract by Eq. (25.2) than they would have pricing a Treasury bond by Eq. (25.1).

Forward contracts are similar to the underlying bonds themselves. If the entire term structure of interest rates unexpectedly shifts upwards on 2 March, the Treasury bond issued the previous day should fall in value. This can be seen from Eq. (25.1). A rise in each of the spot rates lowers the present value of each of the coupon payments. Hence the value of the bond must fall. Conversely, a fall in the term structure of interest rates increases the value of the bond.

The same relationship holds with forward contracts, as we can see by rewriting Eq. (25.2) like this:

$$\begin{aligned}
P_{\text{FORW.CONT.}} = &\frac{€40 \times (1 + R_1)}{(1 + R_2)^2} + \frac{€40 \times (1 + R_1)}{(1 + R_3)^3} + \frac{€40 \times (1 + R_1)}{(1 + R_4)^4} \\
&+ \cdots + \frac{€40 \times (1 + R_1)}{(1 + R_{40})^{40}} + \frac{€1,040 \times (1 + R_1)}{(1 + R_{41})^{41}}
\end{aligned} \qquad (25.3)$$

We went from Eq. (25.2) to Eq. (25.3) by multiplying both the left and the right sides by $(1 + R_1)$. If the entire term structure of interest rates unexpectedly shifts upwards on 2 March, the *first* term on the right side of Eq. (25.3) should fall in value.[5] That is, both $R_1$ and $R_2$ will rise by an equal amount. However, $R_2$ enters as a *squared* term, $1/(1 + R_2)^2$, so an increase in $R_2$ more than offsets the increase in $R_1$. As we move further to the right, an increase in any spot rate, $R_i$, more than offsets an increase in $R_1$. Here $R_i$ enters as the $i$th power, $1/(1 + R_i)^i$. Thus, as long as the entire term structure shifts upwards by an equal amount on 2 March, the value of a forward contract must fall on that date. Conversely, as long as the entire term structure shifts downwards by an equal amount on 2 March, the value of a forward contract must rise.

## Futures Contracts

The previous discussion concerned a forward contract in Treasury bonds – that is, a forward contract where the deliverable instrument is a Treasury bond. What about a futures contract on a Treasury bond?[6] We mentioned earlier that futures contracts and forward contracts are quite similar, though there are a few differences between the two. First, futures contracts are generally traded on exchanges, whereas forward contracts are not traded on an exchange. Second, futures contracts generally allow the seller a period of time in which to deliver, whereas forward contracts generally call for delivery on a particular day. The seller of a Treasury bond futures contract can choose to deliver on any business day during the delivery month.[7] Third, futures contracts are subject to the mark-to-the-market convention, whereas forward contracts are not. Traders in Treasury bill futures contracts must adhere to this convention. Fourth, there is generally a liquid market for futures contracts allowing contracts to be quickly netted out. That is, a buyer can sell his futures contract at any time, and a seller can buy back her futures contract at any time. Conversely, because forward markets are generally quite illiquid, traders cannot easily net out their positions. The popularity of the Treasury bond futures contract has produced liquidity even higher than that on other futures contracts and positions in this contract can be netted out quite easily.

This discussion is not intended to be an exhaustive list of differences between Treasury bond forward and futures contracts. Rather, it is intended to show that both contracts share fundamental characteristics. Though there are differences, the two instruments should be viewed as variations of the same species, not different species. Thus the pricing Eq. (25.3), which is exact for the forward contract, should be a decent approximation for the futures contract.

## Hedging in Interest Rate Futures

Now that we have the basic institutional details under our belts, we are ready for examples of hedging using either futures contracts or forward contracts on Treasury bonds. Because the T-bond futures contract is extremely popular whereas the forward contract is traded sporadically, our examples use the futures contract.

---

**EXAMPLE 25.3**

## Interest Rate Hedging

Erik Werenskiold owns a mortgage banking company. On 1 March he made a commitment to lend a total of €1 million to various homeowners on 1 May. The loans are 20-year mortgages carrying a 12 per cent coupon, the going interest rate on mortgages at the time. Thus the mortgages are made at par. Though homeowners would not use the term, we could say that he is buying a *forward contract* on a mortgage. That is, he agrees on 1 March to give €1 million to his borrowers on 1 May in exchange for principal and interest from them every month for the next 20 years.

Like many mortgage bankers, he has no intention of paying the €1 million out of his own pocket. Rather, he intends to sell the mortgages to an insurance company. Thus the insurance company will actually lend the funds, and will receive principal and interest over the next 20 years. Mr Werenskiold does not currently have an insurance company in mind. He plans to visit the mortgage departments of insurance companies over the next 60 days to sell the mortgages to one or many of them. He sets 30 April as a deadline for making the sale, because the borrowers expect the funds on the following day.

Suppose Mr Werenskiold sells the mortgages to Superbe Insurance on 15 April. What price will Superbe pay for the bonds?

You may think the insurance company will obviously pay €1 million for the loans. However, suppose interest rates have risen above 12 per cent by 15 April. The insurance company will buy the mortgage at a discount. For example, suppose the insurance company agrees to pay only €940,000 for the mortgages. Because the mortgage banker agreed to lend a full €1 million to the borrowers, the mortgage banker must come up with the additional €60,000 (= €1 million − €940,000) out of his own pocket.

Alternatively, suppose interest rates fall below 12 per cent by 15 April. The mortgages can be sold at a premium under this scenario. If the insurance company buys the mortgages at €1.05 million, the mortgage banker will have made an unexpected profit of €50,000 (= €1.05 million − €1 million).

Because Erik Werenskiold is unable to forecast interest rates, this risk is something that he would like to avoid. The risk is summarized in Table 25.2.

| | Mortgage interest rate on 15 April | |
| | Above 12% | Below 12% |
|---|---|---|
| Sale price to Superbe Insurance | Below €1 million (we assume €940,000). | Above €1 million (we assume €1.05 million). |
| Effect on mortgage banker | He loses, because he must lend the full €1 million to borrowers. | He gains because he lends only €1 million to borrowers. |
| Euro gain or loss | Loss of €60,000 (= €1 million − 940,000). | Gain of €50,000 (= €1.05 million − €1 million). |

The interest rate on 1 March, the date when the loan agreement was made with the borrowers, was 12 per cent. 15 April is the date the mortgages were sold to Superbe Insurance.

**Table 25.2** Effects of changing interest rates on Erik Werenskiold, mortgage banker

Seeing the interest rate risk, students at this point may ask, 'What does the mortgage banker get out of this loan to offset his risk bearing?' Mr Werenskiold wants to sell the mortgages to the insurance company so that he can get two fees. The first is an *origination fee*, which is paid to the mortgage banker by the insurance company on 15 April – that is, on the date the loan is sold. An industry standard in certain locales is 1 per cent of the value of the loan, which is €10,000 (= 1% × €1 million). In addition, Mr Werenskiold will act as a collection agent for the insurance company. For this service he will receive a small portion of the outstanding balance of the loan each month. For example, if he is paid 0.03 per cent of the loan each month, he will receive €300 (= 0.03% × €1 million) in the first month. As the outstanding balance of the loan declines, he will receive less.

Though Mr Werenskiold will earn profitable fees on the loan, he bears interest rate risk. He loses money if interest rates rise after 1 March, and he profits if interest rates fall after 1 March. To hedge this risk, he writes June Treasury bond futures contracts on 1 March. As with mortgages, Treasury bond futures contracts fall in value if interest rates rise. Because he *writes* the contract, he makes money on these contracts if they fall in value. Therefore, with an interest rate rise, the loss he endures in the mortgages is offset by the gain he earns in the futures market. Conversely, Treasury bond futures contracts rise in value if interest rates fall. Because he writes the contracts, he suffers losses on them when rates fall. With an interest rate fall, the profit he makes on the mortgages is offset by the loss he suffers in the futures markets.

The details of this hedging transaction are presented in Table 25.3. The column on the left is labelled 'cash markets' because the deal in the mortgage market is transacted off an exchange. The column on the right shows the offsetting transactions in the futures market. Consider the first row. The mortgage banker enters into a forward contract on 1 March. He simultaneously writes Treasury bond futures contracts. Ten contracts are written because the deliverable instrument on each contract is

| | **Cash markets** | **Futures markets** |
|---|---|---|
| 1 March | Mortgage banker makes forward contracts to lend €1 million at 12 per cent for 20 years. The loans are to be funded on 1 May. No cash changes hands on 1 March. | Mortgage banker writes 10 June Treasury bond futures contracts. |
| 15 April | Loans are sold to Superbe Insurance. Mortgage banker will receive sale price from Superbe on the 1 May funding date. | Mortgage banker buys back all the futures contracts. |
| If interest rates rise: | Loans are sold at a price below €1 million. Mortgage banker loses because he receives less than the €1 million he must give to borrowers. | Each futures contract is bought back at a price below the sales price, resulting in *profit*. Mortgage banker's profit in futures market offsets loss in cash market. |
| If interest rates fall: | Loans are sold at a price above €1 million. Mortgage banker *gains* because he receives more than the €1 million he must give to borrowers. | Each futures contract is bought back at a price above the sales price, resulting in *loss*. Mortgage banker's loss in futures market offsets gain in cash market. |

**Table 25.3** Illustration of hedging strategy for Erik Werenskiold, mortgage banker

€100,000 of Treasury bonds. The total is €1 million (= 10 × €100,000), which is equal to the value of the mortgages. Mr Werenskiold would prefer to write May Treasury bond futures contracts. Here, Treasury bonds would be delivered on the futures contract during the same month that the loan is funded. Because there is no May T-bond futures contract, Mr Werenskiold achieves the closest match through a June contract.

If held to maturity, the June contract would obligate the mortgage banker to deliver Treasury bonds in June. Interest rate risk ends in the cash market when the loans are sold. Interest rate risk must be terminated in the futures market at that time. Thus Mr Werenskiold nets out his position in the futures contract as soon as the loan is sold to Superbe Insurance.

As our example shows, risk is clearly reduced via an offsetting transaction in the futures market. However, is risk totally eliminated? Risk would be totally eliminated if losses in the cash markets were *exactly* offset by gains in the futures markets, and vice versa. This is unlikely to happen, because mortgages and Treasury bonds are not identical instruments. First, mortgages may have different maturities from Treasury bonds. Second, Treasury bonds have a different payment stream than do mortgages. Principal is paid only at maturity on T-bonds, whereas principal is paid every month on mortgages. Because mortgages pay principal continuously, these instruments have a shorter *effective* time to maturity than do Treasury bonds of equal maturity.[8] Third, mortgages have default risk whereas Treasury bonds do not. The term structure applicable to instruments with default risk may change even when the term structure for risk-free assets remains constant. Fourth, mortgages may be paid off early and hence have a shorter *expected maturity* than Treasury bonds of equal maturity.

Because mortgages and Treasury bonds are not identical instruments, they are not identically affected by interest rates. If Treasury bonds are less volatile than mortgages, financial consultants may advise Mr Werenskiold to write more than 10 T-bond futures contracts. Conversely, if these bonds are more volatile, the consultant may state that fewer than 10 futures contracts are indicated. An optimal ratio of futures to mortgages will reduce risk as much as possible. However, because the price movements of mortgages and Treasury bonds are not *perfectly correlated*, Mr Werenskiold's hedging strategy cannot eliminate all risk.

The preceding strategy is called a *short hedge*, because Mr Werenskiold sells futures contracts to reduce risk. Though it involves an interest rate futures contract, this short hedge is analogous to short hedges in agricultural and metallurgical futures contracts. We argued at the beginning of this chapter that individuals and firms institute short hedges to offset inventory price fluctuation. Once Mr Werenskiold makes a contract to lend money to borrowers, the mortgages effectively become his inventory. He writes a futures contract to offset the price fluctuation of his inventory.

We now consider an example where a mortgage banker institutes a long hedge.

## EXAMPLE 25.4

## Short versus Long Hedging

Margareth Boswell is another mortgage banker. Her firm faces problems similar to those facing Mr Werenskiold's firm. However, she tackles the problems through the use of **advance commitments**, a strategy the opposite of Mr Werenskiold's. That is, she promises to deliver loans to a financial institution *before* she lines up borrowers. On 1 March her firm agreed to sell mortgages to No-State Insurance. The agreement specifies that she must turn over 12 per cent coupon mortgages with a face value of €1 million to No-State by 1 May. No-State is buying the mortgages at par, implying that they will pay Ms Boswell €1 million on 1 May. As of 1 March, Ms Boswell had not signed up any borrowers. Over the next two months, she will seek out individuals who want mortgages beginning on 1 May.

| | Cash markets | Futures markets |
|---|---|---|
| 1 March | Mortgage banker makes a forward contract (advance commitment) to deliver €1 million of mortgages to No-State Insurance. The insurance company will pay par to Ms Boswell for the loans on 1 May. The borrowers are to receive their funding from the mortgage banker on 1 May. The mortgages are to be 12 per cent coupon loans for 20 years. | Mortgage banker buys 10 June Treasury bond futures contracts. |
| 15 April | Mortgage banker signs up borrowers to 12 per cent coupon, 20-year mortgages. She promises that the borrowers will receive funds on 1 May. | Mortgage banker sells all futures contracts. |
| If interest rates rise: | Mortgage banker issues mortgages to borrowers at a discount. Mortgage banker gains because she receives par from the insurance company. | Futures contracts are sold at a price below purchase price, resulting in loss. Mortgage banker's loss in futures market offsets gain in cash market. |
| If interest rates fall: | Loans to borrowers are issued at a premium. Mortgage banker loses because she receives only par from insurance company. | Futures contracts are sold at a price above purchase price, resulting in gain. Mortgage banker's gain in futures market offsets loss in cash market. |

**Table 25.4** Illustration of advance commitment for Margareth Boswell, mortgage banker

As with Mr Werenskiold, changing interest rates will affect Ms Boswell. If interest rates fall before she signs up a borrower, the borrower will demand a premium on a 12 per cent coupon loan. That is, the borrower will receive more than par on 1 May.[9] Because Ms Boswell receives par from the insurance company, she must make up the difference.

Conversely, if interest rates rise, a 12 per cent coupon loan will be made at a discount. That is, the borrower will receive less than par on 1 May. Because Ms Boswell receives par from the insurance company, the difference is pure profit to her.

The details are provided in Table 25.4. As did Mr Werenskiold, Ms Boswell finds the risk burdensome. Therefore she offsets her advance commitment with a transaction in the futures markets. Because she *loses* in the cash market when interest rates fall, she *buys* futures contracts to reduce the risk. When interest rates fall, the value of her futures contracts increases. The gain in the futures market offsets the loss in the cash market. Conversely, she gains in the cash markets when interest rates rise. The value of her futures contracts decreases when interest rates rise, offsetting her gain.

We call this a *long hedge* because Ms Boswell offsets risk in the cash markets by buying a futures contract. Though it involves an interest rate futures contract, this long hedge is analogous to long hedges in agricultural and metallurgical futures contracts. We argued at the beginning of this chapter that individuals and firms institute long hedges when their finished goods are to be sold at a fixed price. Once Ms Boswell makes the advance commitment with No-State Insurance, she has fixed her sales price. She buys a futures contract to offset the price fluctuation of her raw materials – that is, her mortgages.

## 25.6 Duration Hedging

The last section concerned the risk of interest rate changes. We now want to explore this risk in a more precise manner. In particular, we want to show that the concept of duration is a prime determinant of interest rate risk. We begin by considering the effect of interest rate movements on bond prices.

### The Case of Zero Coupon Bonds

Imagine a world where the interest rate is 10 per cent across all maturities. A one-year pure discount bond pays €110 at maturity. A five-year pure discount bond pays €161.05 at maturity. Both of these bonds are worth €100, as given by the following:

Value of one-year pure discount bond:

$$€100 = \frac{€110}{1.10}$$

Value of five-year pure discount bond:

$$€100 = \frac{€161.05}{(1.10)^5}$$

Which bond will change more when interest rates move? To find out, we calculate the value of these bonds when interest rates are either 8 or 12 per cent. The results are presented in Table 25.5. As can be seen, the five-year bond has greater price swings than the one-year bond. That is, both bonds are worth €100 when interest rates are 10 per cent. The five-year bond is worth more than the one-year bond when interest rates are 8 per cent and worth less than the one-year bond when interest rates are 12 per cent. We state that the five-year bond is subject to more price volatility. This point, which was mentioned in passing in an earlier section of the chapter, is not difficult to understand. The interest rate term in the denominator,

| TABLE 25.5 | Interest rate (%) | One-year pure discount bond | Five-year pure discount bond |
|---|---|---|---|
| | 8 | $€101.85 = \dfrac{€110}{1.08}$ | $€109.61 = \dfrac{€161.05}{(1.08)^5}$ |
| | 10 | $€100.00 = \dfrac{€110}{1.10}$ | $€100.00 = \dfrac{€161.05}{(1.10)^5}$ |
| | 12 | $€98.21 = \dfrac{€110}{1.12}$ | $€91.38 = \dfrac{€161.05}{(1.12)^5}$ |

For a given interest rate change, a five-year pure discount bond fluctuates more in price than a one-year pure discount bond does.

**Table 25.5** Value of a pure discount bond as a function of interest rate

$1 + R$, is taken to the fifth power for a five-year bond and only to the first power for the one-year bond. Thus the effect of a changing interest rate is magnified for the five-year bond. The general rule is this:

**The percentage price changes in long-term pure discount bonds are greater than the percentage price changes in short-term pure discount bonds.**

## The Case of Two Bonds with the Same Maturity but with Different Coupons

The previous example concerned pure discount bonds of different maturities. We now want to see the effect of different coupons on price volatility. To abstract from the effect of differing maturities, we consider two bonds with the same maturity but with different coupons.

Consider a five-year, 10 per cent coupon bond and a five-year, 1 per cent coupon bond. When interest rates are 10 per cent, the bonds are priced like this:

Value of five-year, 10 per cent coupon bond:

$$€100 = \frac{€10}{1.10} + \frac{€10}{(1.10)^2} + \frac{€10}{(1.10)^3} + \frac{€10}{(1.10)^4} + \frac{€110}{(1.10)^5}$$

Value of five-year, 1 per cent coupon bond:

$$€65.88 = \frac{€1}{1.10} + \frac{€1}{(1.10)^2} + \frac{€1}{(1.10)^3} + \frac{€1}{(1.10)^4} + \frac{€101}{(1.10)^5}$$

Which bond will change more in *percentage terms* if interest rates change?[10] To find out, we first calculate the value of these bonds when interest rates are either 8 or 12 per cent. The results are presented in Table 25.6. As we would expect, the 10 per cent coupon bond always sells for more than the 1 per cent coupon bond. Also as we would expect, each bond is worth more when the interest rate is 8 per cent than when the interest rate is 12 per cent.

We calculate percentage price changes for both bonds as the interest rate changes from 10 to 8 per cent and from 10 to 12 per cent:

TABLE
**25.6**

| Interest rate | Value |
|---|---|
| Five-year, 10% coupon bond | |
| 8% | $€107.99 = \dfrac{€10}{1.08} + \dfrac{€10}{(1.08)^2} + \dfrac{€10}{(1.08)^3} + \dfrac{€10}{(1.08)^4} + \dfrac{€110}{(1.08)^5}$ |
| 10% | $€100.00 = \dfrac{€10}{1.10} + \dfrac{€10}{(1.10)^2} + \dfrac{€10}{(1.10)^3} + \dfrac{€10}{(1.10)^4} + \dfrac{€110}{(1.10)^5}$ |
| 12% | $€92.79 = \dfrac{€10}{1.12} + \dfrac{€10}{(1.12)^2} + \dfrac{€10}{(1.12)^3} + \dfrac{€10}{(1.12)^4} + \dfrac{€110}{(1.12)^5}$ |
| Five-year, 1% coupon bond | |
| 8% | $€72.05 = \dfrac{€1}{1.08} + \dfrac{€1}{(1.08)^2} + \dfrac{€1}{(1.08)^3} + \dfrac{€1}{(1.08)^4} + \dfrac{€101}{(1.08)^5}$ |
| 10% | $€65.88 = \dfrac{€1}{1.10} + \dfrac{€1}{(1.10)^2} + \dfrac{€1}{(1.10)^3} + \dfrac{€1}{(1.10)^4} + \dfrac{€101}{(1.10)^5}$ |
| 12% | $€60.35 = \dfrac{€1}{1.12} + \dfrac{€1}{(1.12)^2} + \dfrac{€1}{(1.12)^3} + \dfrac{€1}{(1.12)^4} + \dfrac{€101}{(1.12)^5}$ |

**Table 25.6** Value of coupon bonds at different interest rates

| | 10% Coupon bond | 1% Coupon bond |
|---|---|---|
| Interest rate changes from 10% to 8%: | $7.99\% = \dfrac{€107.99}{€100} - 1$ | $9.37\% = \dfrac{€72.05}{€65.88} - 1$ |
| Interest rate changes from 10% to 12%: | $-7.21\% = \dfrac{€92.79}{€100} - 1$ | $-8.39\% = \dfrac{€60.35}{€65.88} - 1$ |

As we can see, the 1 per cent coupon bond has a greater percentage price increase than the 10 per cent coupon bond when the interest rate falls. Similarly, the 1 per cent coupon bond has a greater percentage price decrease than the 10 per cent coupon bond when the interest rate rises. Thus we say that the percentage price changes on the 1 per cent coupon bond are greater than the percentage price changes on the 10 per cent coupon bond.

## Duration

The question, of course, is 'Why?' We can answer this question only after we have explored a concept called **duration**. We begin by noticing that any coupon bond is actually a combination of pure discount bonds. For example, the five-year, 10 per cent coupon bond is made up of five pure discount bonds:

1   A pure discount bond paying €10 at the end of year 1
2   A pure discount bond paying €10 at the end of year 2
3   A pure discount bond paying €10 at the end of year 3
4   A pure discount bond paying €10 at the end of year 4
5   A pure discount bond paying €110 at the end of year 5

Similarly, the five-year, 1 per cent coupon bond is made up of five pure discount bonds. Because the price volatility of a pure discount bond is determined by its maturity, we would like to determine the average maturity of the five pure discount bonds that make up a five-year coupon bond. This leads us to the concept of duration.

We calculate average maturity in three steps. For the 10 per cent coupon bond, we have these:

Step 1: *Calculate present value of each payment.* We do this as follows:

| Year | Payment (€) | Present value of payment by discounting at 10% (€) |
|------|-------------|----------------------------------------------------|
| 1 | 10 | 9.091 |
| 2 | 10 | 8.264 |
| 3 | 10 | 7.513 |
| 4 | 10 | 6.830 |
| 5 | 110 | 68.302 |
| | | 100.00 |

Step 2: *Express the present value of each payment in relative terms.* We calculate the relative value of a single payment as the ratio of the present value of the payment to the value of the bond. The value of the bond is €100. We obtain these values:

| Year | Payment (€) | Present value of payment (€) | Relative value (€) = $\dfrac{\text{Present value of Payment}}{\text{Value of bond}}$ |
|------|-------------|------------------------------|-------------------------------------------------------------------------------------|
| 1 | 10 | 9.091 | 9.091/100 = 0.09091 |
| 2 | 10 | 8.264 | 0.08264 |
| 3 | 10 | 7.513 | 0.07513 |
| 4 | 10 | 6.830 | 0.06830 |
| 5 | 110 | 68.302 | 0.68302 |
| | | 100.00 | 1.0 |

The bulk of the relative value, 68.302 per cent, occurs at year 5 because the principal is paid back at that time.

Step 3: *Weight the maturity of each payment by its relative value*:

$$4.1699 \text{ years} = 1 \text{ year} \times 0.09091 + 2 \text{ years} \times 0.08264 + 3 \text{ years} \times 0.07513$$
$$+ 4 \text{ years} \times 0.06830 + 5 \text{ years} \times 0.68302$$

There are many ways to calculate the average maturity of a bond. We have calculated it by weighting the maturity of each payment by the payment's present value. We find that the *effective* maturity of the bond is 4.1699 years. *Duration* is a commonly used word for effective maturity. Thus the bond's duration is 4.1699 years. Note that duration is expressed in units of time.[11]

Because the five-year, 10 per cent coupon bond has a duration of 4.1699 years, its percentage price fluctuations should be the same as those of a zero coupon bond with a duration of 4.1699 years.[12] It turns out that the five-year, 1 per cent coupon bond has a duration of 4.8742 years. Because the 1 per cent coupon bond has a higher duration than the 10 per cent bond, the 1 per cent coupon bond should be subject to greater price fluctuations. This is exactly what we found earlier. In general we say the following:

**The percentage price changes of a bond with high duration are greater than the percentage price changes of a bond with low duration.**

A final question: Why *does* the 1 per cent bond have a greater duration than the 10 per cent bond, even though they both have the same five-year maturity? As mentioned earlier, duration is an average of the maturity of the bond's cash flows, weighted by the present value of each cash flow. The 1 per cent coupon bond receives only €1 in each of the first four years. Thus the weights applied to years 1 to 4 in the duration formula will be low. Conversely, the 10 per cent coupon bond receives €10 in each of the first four years. The weights applied to years 1 to 4 in the duration formula will be higher.

## Matching Liabilities with Assets

Earlier in this chapter we argued that firms can hedge risk by trading in futures. Because some firms are subject to interest rate risk, we showed how they can hedge with interest rate futures contracts. Firms may also hedge interest rate risk by matching liabilities with assets. This ability to hedge follows from our discussion of duration.

## Using Duration

The Bank of Amsterdam has the following market value balance sheet:

| BANK OF AMSTERDAM Market Value Balance Sheet | | |
|---|---|---|
| | **Market value (€)** | **Duration** |
| **Assets** | | |
| Overnight money | 35 million | 0 |
| Accounts receivable–backed loans | 500 million | 3 months |
| Inventory loans | 275 million | 6 months |
| Industrial loans | 40 million | 2 years |
| Mortgages | 150 million | 14.8 years |
| | 1,000 million | |
| **Liabilities and owners' equity** | | |
| Chequing and savings accounts | 400 million | 0 |
| Certificates of deposit | 300 million | 1 year |
| Long-term financing | 200 million | 10 years |
| Equity | 100 million | |
| | 1,000 million | |

The bank has €1,000 million of assets and €900 million of liabilities. Its equity is the difference between the two: €100 million (= €1,000 million – €900 million). Both the market value and the duration of each individual item are provided in the balance sheet. Both overnight money and chequing and savings accounts have a duration of zero. This is because the interest paid on these instruments adjusts immediately to changing interest rates in the economy.

The bank's managers think that interest rates are likely to move quickly in the coming months. Because they do not know the direction of the movement, they are worried that their bank is vulnerable to changing rates. They call in a consultant, Jan Mandyn, to determine a hedging strategy.

Mr Mandyn first calculates the duration of the assets and the duration of the liabilities:[13]

Duration of assets:

$$2.56 \text{ years} = 0 \text{ years} \times \frac{€35 \text{ million}}{€1,000 \text{ million}} + \frac{1}{4} \text{year} \times \frac{€500 \text{ million}}{€1,000 \text{ million}}$$

$$+ \frac{1}{2} \text{year} \times \frac{€275 \text{ million}}{€1,000 \text{ million}} + 2 \text{ years} \times \frac{€40 \text{ million}}{€1,000 \text{ million}} \tag{25.4}$$

$$+ 14.8 \text{ years} \times \frac{€150 \text{ million}}{€1,000 \text{ million}}$$

Duration of liabilities:

$$2.56 = 0 \text{ years} \times \frac{\text{€400 million}}{\text{€900 million}} + 1 \text{ year} \times \frac{\text{€300 million}}{\text{€900 million}} + 10 \text{ years} \times \frac{\text{€200 million}}{\text{€900 million}} \qquad (25.5)$$

The duration of the assets, 2.56 years, equals the duration of the liabilities. Because of this, Mr Mandyn argues that the firm is immune to interest rate risk.

Just to be on the safe side, the bank calls in a second consultant, Gabrielle Aertsen. Ms Aertsen argues that it is incorrect to simply match durations, because assets total €1,000 million and liabilities total only €900 million. If both assets and liabilities have the same duration, the price change on a *euro* of assets should be equal to the price change on a euro of liabilities. However, the *total* price change will be greater for assets than for liabilities, because there are more assets than liabilities in this bank. The firm will be immune from interest rate risk only when the duration of the liabilities is greater than the duration of the assets. Ms Aertsen states that the following relationship must hold if the bank is to be immunized – that is, immune to interest rate risk:

$$\begin{array}{c} \text{Duration of} \\ \text{assets} \end{array} \times \begin{array}{c} \text{Market value of} \\ \text{assets} \end{array} = \begin{array}{c} \text{Duration of} \\ \text{liabilities} \end{array} \times \begin{array}{c} \text{Market value} \\ \text{of liabilities} \end{array} \qquad (25.6)$$

She says that the bank should not *equate* the duration of the liabilities with the duration of the assets. Rather, using Eq. (25.6), the bank should match the duration of the liabilities to the duration of the assets. She suggests two ways to achieve this match.

1   *Increase the duration of the liabilities without changing the duration of the assets.* Ms Aertsen argues that the duration of the liabilities could be increased to

$$\text{Duration of assets} \times \frac{\text{Market value of assets}}{\text{Market value of liabilities}} = 2.56 \text{ years} \times \frac{\text{€1,000 million}}{\text{€900 million}}$$
$$= 2.84 \text{ years}$$

Equation (25.5) then becomes

$$2.56 \times \text{€1 billion} = 2.84 \times \text{€900 million}$$

2   *Decrease the duration of the assets without changing the duration of the liabilities.* Alternatively, Ms Aertsen points out that the duration of the assets could be decreased to

$$\text{Duration of liabilities} \times \frac{\text{Market value of liabilities}}{\text{Market value of assets}} = 2.56 \text{ years} \times \frac{\text{€900 million}}{\text{€1,000 million}}$$
$$= 2.30 \text{ years}$$

Equation (25.6) then becomes

$$2.30 \times \text{€1 billion} = 2.56 \times \text{€900 million}$$

Duration and the accompanying immunization strategies are useful in other areas of finance. For example, many firms establish pension funds to meet obligations to retirees. If the assets of a pension fund are invested in bonds and other fixed-income securities, the duration of the assets can be computed. Similarly, the firm views the obligations to retirees as analogous to interest payments on debt. The duration of these liabilities can be calculated as well. The manager of a pension fund would commonly choose pension assets so that the duration of the assets is matched with the duration of the liabilities. In this way, changing interest rates would not affect the net worth of the pension fund.

Life insurance companies receiving premiums today are legally obligated to provide death benefits in the future. Actuaries view these future benefits as analogous to interest and principal payments of fixed-income securities. The duration of these expected benefits can be calculated. Insurance firms frequently invest in bonds where the duration of the bonds is matched to the duration of the future death benefits.

The business of a leasing company is quite simple. The firm issues debt to purchase assets, which are then leased. The lease payments have a duration, as does the debt. Leasing companies frequently structure debt financing so that the duration of the debt matches the duration of the lease. If a firm did not do this, the market value of its equity could be eliminated by a quick change in interest rates.

# 25.7 Swaps Contracts

Swaps are close cousins to forward and futures contracts. Swaps are arrangements between two counterparties to exchange cash flows over time. There is enormous flexibility in the forms that swaps can take, but the two basic types are interest rate swaps and currency swaps. Often these are combined when interest received in one currency is swapped for interest in another currency.

## Interest Rate Swaps

Like other derivatives, swaps are tools that firms can use to easily change their risk exposures and their balance sheets. Consider a firm that has borrowed and carried on its books an obligation to repay a 10-year loan for €100 million of principal with a 9 per cent coupon rate paid annually. Ignoring the possibility of calling the loan, the firm expects to have to pay coupons of €9 million every year for 10 years and a balloon payment of €100 million at the end of the 10 years. Suppose, though, that the firm is uncomfortable with having this large fixed obligation on its books. Perhaps the firm is in a cyclical business where its revenues vary and could conceivably fall to a point where it would be difficult to make the debt payment.

Suppose, too, that the firm earns a lot of its revenue from financing the purchase of its products. Typically, for example, a manufacturer might help its customers finance their purchase of its products through a leasing or credit subsidiary. Usually these loans are for relatively short periods and are financed at some premium over the prevailing short-term rate of interest. This puts the firm in the position of having revenues that move up and down with interest rates while its costs are relatively fixed.

What the firm would really prefer is to have a floating-rate loan rather than a fixed-rate loan. That way, when interest rates rise, the firm would have to pay more on the loan, but it would be making more on its product financing. An interest rate swap is ideal in this situation.

Of course, the firm could also just go into the capital markets and borrow €100 million at a variable interest rate and then use the proceeds to retire its outstanding fixed-rate loan. Although this is possible, it is generally quite expensive, requiring underwriting a new loan and the repurchase of the existing loan. The ease of entering a swap is its inherent advantage.

The particular swap would be one that exchanged its fixed obligation for an agreement to pay a floating rate. Every year it would agree to pay a coupon based on whatever the prevailing interest rate was at the time in exchange for an agreement from a counterparty to pay the firm's fixed coupon.

A common reference point for floating-rate commitments is called LIBOR. LIBOR stands for the London Interbank Offered Rate, and it is the rate that most international banks charge one another for sterling and US dollar loans in the London market. LIBOR is commonly used as the reference rate for a floating-rate commitment, and, depending on the creditworthiness of the borrower, the rate can vary from LIBOR to LIBOR plus one point or more over LIBOR. For euro-denominated loans the applicable rate is EURIBOR.

If we assume that our firm has a credit rating that requires it to pay EURIBOR plus 50 basis points, then in a swap it would be exchanging its fixed 9 per cent obligation for the obligation to pay whatever the prevailing EURIBOR rate is plus 50 basis points. Table 25.7 displays how the cash flows on this swap would work. In the table, we have assumed that EURIBOR starts at 8 per cent and rises for three years to 11 per cent and then drops to 7 per cent. As the table shows, the firm would owe a coupon of 8.5% × €100 million = €8.5 million in year 1, €9.5 million in year 2, €10.5 million in year 3, and €11.5 million in year 4. The precipitous drop to 7 per cent lowers the annual payments to €7.5 million thereafter. In return, the firm

TABLE
25.7

| Year | Coupons | | | | | | | | | |
|------|---|---|---|---|---|---|---|---|---|----|
| | 1 | 2 | 3 | 4 | 5 | 6 | 7 | 8 | 9 | 10 |
| **A. Swap** | | | | | | | | | | |
| Fixed obligation | 9 | 9 | 9 | 9 | 9 | 9 | 9 | 9 | 9 | 9 |
| EURIBOR floating | −8.5 | −9.5 | −10.5 | −11.5 | −7.5 | −7.5 | −7.5 | −7.5 | −7.5 | −7.5 |
| **B. Original loan** | | | | | | | | | | |
| Fixed obligation | −9 | −9 | −9 | −9 | −9 | −9 | −9 | −9 | −9 | 109 |
| Net effect | −8.5 | −9.5 | 10.5 | 11.5 | 7.5 | 7.5 | 7.5 | 7.5 | 7.5 | −107.5 |

Table 25.7 Fixed for floating swap: cash flows (€ million)

receives the fixed payment of €9 million each year. Actually, rather than swapping the full payments, the cash flows would be netted. Because the firm is paying variable and receiving fixed – which it uses to pay its lender – in the first year, for example, the firm owes €8.5 million and is owed by its counterparty, who is paying fixed, €9 million. Hence, net, the firm would receive a payment of €.5 million. Because the firm has to pay its lender €9 million but gets a net payment from the swap of €.5 million, it really pays out only the difference, or €8.5 million. In each year, then, the firm would effectively pay only EURIBOR plus 50 basis points.

Notice, too, that the entire transaction can be carried out without any need to change the terms of the original loan. In effect, by swapping, the firm has found a counterparty that is willing to pay its fixed obligation in return for the firm paying a floating obligation.

## Currency Swaps

FX stands for foreign exchange, and currency swaps are sometimes called FX swaps. Currency swaps are swaps of obligations to pay cash flows in one currency for obligations to pay in another currency.

Currency swaps arise as a natural vehicle for hedging the risk in international trade. For example, consider the problem of BMW, which sells a broad range of its product line in the United States market. Every year the firm can count on receiving revenue from the United States in dollars. We shall study international finance later in this book, but for now we can just observe that because exchange rates fluctuate, this subjects the firm to considerable risk.

If BMW manufactures its products in Germany and exports them to the US, then the firm has to pay its workers and its suppliers in euros but it is receiving some of its revenues in dollars. The €/$ exchange rate changes over time. As the dollar rises in value, the US revenues are worth more euros, but as it falls they decline. Suppose the firm can count on selling $100 million of automobiles each year in the United States. If the exchange rate is $2 for each €, then the firm will receive €50 million. But if the exchange rate were to rise to $3 for each €, the firm would receive only €33.333 million for its $100 million. Naturally the firm would like to protect itself against these currency swings.

To do so, BMW can enter a currency swap. We shall learn more about exactly what the terms of such a swap might be, but for now we can assume that the swap is for five years at a fixed term of $100 million for €50 million each year. Now, no matter what happens to the exchange rate between dollars and the euro over the next five years, as long as BMW makes $100 million each year from the sale of its automobiles, it will swap this for €50 million each year.

We have not addressed the question of how the market sets prices for swaps – either interest rate swaps or currency swaps. In the fixed for floating example, and in the currency swap, we just quoted some terms. We won't go into great detail on exactly how it is done, but we can stress the most important points.

Swaps, like forwards and futures, are essentially zero-sum transactions, which is to say that in both cases the market sets prices at a fair level, and neither party has any substantial bargain or loss at the moment the deal is struck. For example, in the currency swap, the swap rate is some average of the market expectation of what the exchange rate will be over the life of the swap. In the interest rate swap, the rates are set as the fair floating and fixed rates for the creditor, taking into account the creditworthiness of the counterparties. We can actually price swaps fairly once we know how to price forward contracts. In our interest rate swap example the firm swapped EURIBOR plus 50 basis points for a 9 per cent fixed rate, all on a principal amount of €100 million. This is equivalent to a series of forward contracts extending over the life of the swap. In year 1, for example, having made the swap, the firm is in the same position that it would be if it had sold a forward contract entitling the buyer to receive EURIBOR plus 50 basis points on €100 million in return for a fixed payment of €9 million (9 per cent of €100 million). Similarly, the currency swap can also be viewed as a series of forward contracts.

## Exotics

Up to now we have dealt with the meat and potatoes of the derivatives markets: swaps, options, forwards, and futures. Exotics are the complicated blends of these that often produce surprising results for buyers.

One of the more interesting types of exotic is called an *inverse floater*. In our fixed for floating swap the floating payments fluctuated with EURIBOR. An inverse floater is one that fluctuates inversely with some rate such as EURIBOR or LIBOR. For example, the floater might pay an interest rate of 20 per cent minus EURIBOR. If EURIBOR is 9 per cent, then the inverse pays 11 per cent, and if EURIBOR rises to 12 per cent, the payments on the inverse would fall to 8 per cent. Clearly, the purchaser of an inverse profits from the inverse if interest rates fall.

Both floaters and inverse floaters have a supercharged version called *superfloaters* and *super-inverses* that fluctuate more than one for one with movements in interest rates. As an example of a superinverse floater, consider a floater that pays an interest rate of 30 per cent minus *twice* LIBOR. When LIBOR is 10 per cent, the inverse pays

$$30\% - 2 \times 10\% = 30\% - 20\% = 10\%$$

And if LIBOR falls by 3 per cent to 7 per cent, then the return on the inverse rises by 6 per cent from 10 per cent to 16 per cent:

$$30\% - 2 \times 7\% = 30\% - 14\% = 16\%$$

Sometimes derivatives are combined with options to bound the impact of interest rates. The most important of these instruments are called *caps* and *floors*. A cap is so named because it puts an upper limit or a cap on the impact of a rise in interest rates. A floor, conversely, provides a floor below which the interest rate impact is insulated.

To illustrate the impact of these, consider a firm that is borrowing short-term and is concerned that interest rates might rise. For example, using LIBOR as the reference interest rate, the firm might purchase a 7 per cent cap. The cap pays the firm the difference between LIBOR and 7 per cent on some principal amount, provided that LIBOR is greater than 7 per cent. As long as LIBOR is below 7 per cent, the holder of the cap receives no payments.

By purchasing the cap the firm has assured itself that even if interest rates rise above 7 per cent, it will not have to pay more than a 7 per cent rate. Suppose that interest rates rise to 9 per cent. While the firm is borrowing short-term and paying 9 per cent rates, this is offset by the cap, which is paying the firm the difference between 9 per cent and the 7 per cent limit. For any LIBOR rate above 7 per cent the firm receives the difference between LIBOR and 7 per cent, and as a consequence it has capped its cost of borrowing at 7 per cent.

On the other side, consider a financial firm that is in the business of lending short-term and is concerned that interest rates – and consequently its revenues – might fall. The firm could purchase a floor to protect itself from such declines. If the limit on the floor is 7 per cent, then the floor pays the difference between 7 per cent and LIBOR whenever LIBOR is below 7 per cent, and nothing if LIBOR is above 7 per cent. Thus, if interest rates were to fall to, say, 5 per cent while the firm is receiving only 5 per cent from its lending activities, the floor is paying it the difference between 7 per cent and 5 per cent, or an additional 2 per cent. By purchasing the floor the firm has assured itself of receiving no less than 7 per cent from the combination of the floor and its lending activities.

We have only scratched the surface of what is available in the world of derivatives. Derivatives are designed to meet marketplace needs, and the only binding limitation is the human imagination. Nowhere should the buyer's warning *caveat emptor* be taken more seriously than in the derivatives markets, and this is especially true for the exotics. If swaps are the meat and potatoes of the derivatives markets, then caps and floors are the meat and potatoes of the exotics. As we have seen, they have obvious value as hedging instruments. But much attention has been focused on truly exotic derivatives, some of which appear to have arisen more as the residuals that were left over from more straightforward deals. We won't examine these in any detail, but suffice it to say that some of these are so volatile and unpredictable that market participants have dubbed them 'toxic waste'.

## 25.8 Financial Risk Management in Practice

Because the true extent of derivatives does not usually appear in financial statements, it is much more difficult to observe the use of derivatives by firms compared with, say, bank debt. Much of our knowledge of corporate derivative use comes from academic surveys. Most surveys report that the use of derivatives appears to vary widely among large publicly traded firms. Large firms are far more likely to use derivatives than are small firms. Table 25.8 shows that for firms that use derivatives, foreign currency and interest rate derivatives are the most frequently used.

The prevailing view is that derivatives can be very helpful in reducing the variability of firm cash flows, which in turn reduces the various costs associated with financial distress. Therefore it is somewhat puzzling that large firms use derivatives more often than small firms – because large firms tend to have less cash flow variability than small firms. Also, some surveys report that firms occasionally use derivatives when they want to speculate about future prices, and not just to hedge risks. However, most of the evidence is consistent with the theory that derivatives are most frequently used by firms where financial distress costs are high and access to the capital markets is constrained.

Research on the financial risk management practices of European firms is less common. Capstaff, Marshall and Hutton examined whether French firms changed the way they hedged currency risk after the introduction of the euro. They found that the level of hedging fell in firms with high levels of eurozone sales, whereas those companies that imported goods from outside the eurozone maintained their level of hedging.[14]

Lee, Marshall, Szto and Tang[15] examined the financial risk management practices of companies in the UK, the US and the Asia Pacific region by carrying out a survey of risk managers. The vast majority of firms have a centralized risk management department that co-ordinates the activities of corporate risk divisions of regional operations. The risk management function of US firms faces less stringent controls than comparable risk departments in British and Asian corporations. The reporting schedule of British and Asian firms is also more frequent than in the US, which is possibly a consequence of different accounting standards in the US and the rest of the world.

By far the most common tool used by firms to manage risk is the forward contract, customized to the specific requirements of the business. Table 25.9 presents the main concerns of risk managers in using derivatives to manage risk. The most important issue is their effectiveness in managing risk, followed by the additional risks associated with derivative use. Transaction costs are also regarded as important.

TABLE
**25.8**

| Companies that use derivatives | | |
| --- | --- | --- |
| | Overall (%) | Under $1 billion (%) | Over $1 billion (%) |
| December 2005 | 68 | 53 | 83 |
| December 2004 | 74 | 67 | 83 |

| Do you use derivatives to manage . . .? | | |
| --- | --- | --- |
| | Overall (%) | Under $1 billion (%) | Over $1 billion (%) |
| Short-term assets | 55 | 35 | 68 |
| Long-term assets | 29 | 17 | 37 |
| Short-term liabilities | 59 | 54 | 63 |
| Long-term liabilities | 61 | 67 | 57 |

| In which asset classes do you use derivatives? | | | | |
| --- | --- | --- | --- | --- |
| | Overall (%) | | Over $1 billion (%) | |
| | 2005 | 2004 | 2005 | 2004 |
| Interest rates | 70 | 73 | 77 | 76 |
| Currencies | 67 | 54 | 80 | 68 |
| Credit | 9 | 7 | 12 | 13 |
| Energy | 17 | 10 | 21 | 11 |
| Commodities | 20 | 11 | 30 | 13 |
| Equities | 7 | 12 | 10 | 16 |

*Source*: Adapted from *Treasury and Risk Management* (December/January 2006). Results are based on a survey of 190 financial executives. In the sample, 30 per cent of the companies had revenues under $500 million, 18 per cent were between $500 million and $1 billion, 33 per cent were between $1 billion and $5 billion, and 19 per cent had revenues over $5 billion.

**Table 25.8** Derivative usage: survey results

TABLE
**25.9**

| Issues of concern to risk managers | UK (%) | US (%) | Asia (%) |
| --- | --- | --- | --- |
| Board approval | 16 | 9 | 18 |
| Compliance with accounting and disclosure requirements | 17 | 21 | 10 |
| Associated risks of derivative use | 17 | 15 | 17 |
| Effectiveness in managing risk | 24 | 26 | 22 |
| Ease of use | 10 | 11 | 13 |
| Transaction costs | 14 | 17 | 18 |
| Other issues | 2 | 1 | 2 |
| | 100 | 100 | 100 |

*Source*: F.M. Lee, A. Marshall, Y.K. Szto and J. Tang, 'The practice of financial risk management: an international comparison', *Thunderbird International Business Review*, vol. 43 (May–June 2001).

**Table 25.9** Main concerns in using derivatives to manage risk

# Summary and Conclusions

1  Firms hedge to reduce risk. This chapter showed a number of hedging strategies.

2  A forward contract is an agreement by two parties to sell an item for cash at a later date. The price is set at the time the agreement is signed. However, cash changes hands on the date of delivery. Forward contracts are generally not traded on organized exchanges.

3  Futures contracts are also agreements for future delivery. They have certain advantages, such as liquidity, that forward contracts do not. An unusual feature of futures contracts is the mark-to-the-market convention. If the price of a futures contract falls on a particular day, every buyer of the contract must pay money to the clearing house. Every seller of the contract receives money from the clearing house. Everything is reversed if the price rises. The mark-to-the-market convention prevents defaults on futures contracts.

4  We divided hedges into two types: short hedges and long hedges. An individual or firm that sells a futures contract to reduce risk is instituting a short hedge. Short hedges are generally appropriate for holders of inventory. An individual or firm that buys a futures contract to reduce risk is instituting a long hedge. Long hedges are typically used by firms with contracts to sell finished goods at a fixed price.

5  An interest rate futures contract employs a bond as the deliverable instrument. Because of their popularity, we worked with Treasury bond futures contracts. We showed that Treasury bond futures contracts can be priced using the same type of net present value analysis as is used to price Treasury bonds themselves.

6  Many firms face interest rate risk. They can reduce this risk by hedging with interest rate futures contracts. As with other commodities, a short hedge involves the sale of a futures contract. Firms that are committed to buying mortgages or other bonds are likely to institute short hedges. A long hedge involves the purchase of a futures contract. Firms that have agreed to sell mortgages or other bonds at a fixed price are likely to institute long hedges.

7  Duration measures the average maturity of all the cash flows in a bond. Bonds with high duration have high price variability. Firms frequently try to match the duration of their assets with the duration of their liabilities.

8  Swaps are agreements to exchange cash flows over time. The first major type is an interest rate swap, in which one pattern of coupon payments – say, fixed payments – is exchanged for another – say, coupons that float with LIBOR. The second major type is a currency swap, in which an agreement is struck to swap payments denominated in one currency for payments in another currency over time.

# ɔnnect‍ Questions and Problems

CONCEPT
1 – 8

1  **Derivatives: Hedging and Risk**  Discuss the differences between hedging and speculation with derivatives. Many corporations' risk management divisions earn significant profits each year. What does this say about derivative use in large corporations?

2  **Forward Contracts**  Explain what is meant by a forward contract. Use a non-financial example to illustrate how a forward contract works.

3  **Futures Contracts**  What is the difference between a forward contract and a futures contract? Why do you think that futures contracts are much more common? Are there any circumstances under which you might prefer to use forwards instead of futures? Explain.

4   **Hedging**   In what situations would a firm wish to hedge? Create three different examples of hedging activity by corporations, and discuss their effect on the cash flows of the firm.

5   **Interest Rate Futures Contracts**   Explain how interest rates can be hedged by futures contracts. Provide an example of how you could use one to hedge against an increase in interest rates.

6   **Duration Hedging**   What is duration, and how can it be used to hedge against interest rate changes? Use an example to illustrate your answer.

7   **Swaps**   Explain why a swap is effectively a series of forward contracts. Suppose a firm enters a swap agreement with a swap dealer. Describe the nature of the default risk faced by both parties.

8   **Financial Risk Management**   Using Table 25.8, discuss the main concerns of corporations when using derivatives to manage risk.

REGULAR
9 – 37

9   **Hedging Strategies**   If a firm is selling futures contracts on lumber as a hedging strategy, what must be true about the firm's exposure to lumber prices?

10   **Hedging Strategies**   If a firm is buying call options on pork belly futures as a hedging strategy, what must be true about the firm's exposure to pork belly prices?

11   **Hedging Commodities**   Bubbling Crude plc, a large oil producer based in Aberdeen, would like to hedge against adverse movements in the price of oil, because this is the firm's primary source of revenue. What should the firm do? Provide at least two reasons why it probably will not be possible to achieve a completely flat risk profile with respect to oil prices.

12   **Sources of Risk**   A company produces an energy-intensive product and uses natural gas as the energy source. The competition uses primarily oil. Explain why this company is exposed to fluctuations in both oil and natural gas prices.

13   **Hedging Commodities**   If a textile manufacturer wanted to hedge against adverse movements in cotton prices, it could buy cotton futures contracts or buy call options on cotton futures contracts. What would be the pros and cons of the two approaches?

14   **Option**   Explain why a put option on a bond is conceptually the same as a call option on interest rates.

15   **Hedging Interest Rates**   A company has a large bond issue maturing in one year. When it matures, the company will float a new issue. Current interest rates are attractive, and the company is concerned that rates next year will be higher. What are some hedging strategies that the company might use in this case?

16   **Swaps**   Suppose a firm enters a fixed for floating interest rate swap with a swap dealer. Describe the cash flows that will occur as a result of the swap.

17   **Transaction versus Economic Exposure**   What is the difference between transactions and economic exposure? Which can be hedged more easily? Why?

18   **Hedging Exchange Rate Risk**   If a Dutch company exports its goods to the UK, how would it use a futures contract on sterling to hedge its exchange rate risk? Would it buy or sell sterling futures? Does the way the exchange rate is quoted in the futures contract matter?

19   **Hedging Strategies**   For the following scenarios, describe a hedging strategy using futures contracts that might be considered. If you think that a cross-hedge would be appropriate, discuss the reasons for your choice of contract.

   (a)   A public utility is concerned about rising costs.

   (b)   A chocolate manufacturer is concerned about rising costs.

   (c)   A corn farmer fears that this year's harvest will be at record high levels across the country.

(d) A manufacturer of photographic film is concerned about rising costs.

(e) A natural gas producer believes there will be excess supply in the market this year.

(f) A bank derives all its income from long-term, fixed-rate residential mortgages.

(g) An equity mutual fund invests in large, blue-chip equities and is concerned about a decline in the stock market.

(h) A Spanish importer of Swiss army knives will pay for its order in six months in Swiss francs.

(i) A Norwegian exporter of construction equipment has agreed to sell some cranes to a German construction firm. The Norwegian firm will be paid in euros in three months.

20 **Swaps** Syco SA, a distributor of food and food-related products, has announced it has signed an interest rate swap. The interest rate swap effectively converts the company's €100 million, 4.6 per cent interest rate bonds for a variable-rate payment, which is the six-month EURIBOR minus 0.52 per cent. Why would Syco use a swap agreement? In other words, why didn't Syco just go ahead and issue floating-rate bonds, because the net effect of issuing fixed-rate bonds and then doing a swap is to create a variable rate bond?

21 **Hedging Strategies** Allan Hodgson is interested in entering the import/export business. During a recent visit to his financial advisers, he said, 'If we play the game right, this is the safest business in the world. By hedging all of our transactions in the foreign exchange futures market, we can eliminate all of our risk.' Do you agree with Mr Hodgson's assessment of hedging? Why or why not?

22 **Hedging Strategies** Suntharee Lhaopadchan is a Thai student who is planning a one-year stay in the United Kingdom. She expects to arrive in the United Kingdom in eight months. She is worried about depreciation in the Thai baht relative to the British pound over the next eight months, and wishes to take a position in foreign exchange futures to hedge this risk. What should Miss Lhaopadchan's hedging position be? Assume the exchange rate between the baht and sterling is quoted as baht/pound.

23 **Futures Quotes** Refer to Figure 25.1 in the text to answer this question. Suppose you purchase a June 2009 live cattle futures contract on 9 January 2009 at the last price of the day. What will your profit or loss be if live cattle prices turn out to be $.80 per lb at expiration?

24 **Futures Quotes** Refer to Figure 25.1 in the text to answer this question. Suppose you sell five April 2009 gold futures contracts on 9 January 2009 at the last price of the day. What will your profit or loss be if gold prices turn out to be $911.15 per ounce at expiration? What if gold prices are $809.05 per ounce at expiration?

25 **Put and Call Pay-Offs** Suppose a financial manager buys call options on 50,000 barrels of oil with an exercise price of $75 per barrel. She simultaneously sells a put option on 50,000 barrels of oil with the same exercise price of $75 per barrel. Consider her gains and losses if oil prices are $70, $72, $75, $78 and $80. What do you notice about the pay-off profile?

26 **Marking to Market** You are long 10 gold futures contracts, established at an initial settle price of $880 per ounce, where each contract represents 100 ounces. Over the subsequent four trading days gold settles at $873, $879, $882 and $886, respectively. Compute the cash flows at the end of each trading day, and compute your total profit or loss at the end of the trading period.

27 **Marking to Market** You are short 25 gasoline futures contracts, established at an initial settle price of €1.52 per gallon, where each contract represents 42,000 litres. Over the subsequent four trading days gasoline settles at €1.46, €1.55, €1.59 and €1.62, respectively. Compute the cash flows at the end of each trading day, and compute your total profit or loss at the end of the trading period.

28 **Duration** What is the duration of a bond with three years to maturity and a coupon of 9 per cent paid annually, if the bond sells at par?

29 **Duration** What is the duration of a bond with four years to maturity and a coupon of 9 per cent paid annually if the bond sells at par?

30 **Duration** Blåkopi Private Bank has the following market value balance sheet:

| Asset or liability | Market value (Nkr billions) | Duration (in years) |
|---|---|---|
| Government deposits | 28 | 0 |
| Trade receivables | 580 | 0.20 |
| Short-term loans | 390 | 0.65 |
| Long-term loans | 84 | 5.25 |
| Mortgages | 315 | 14.25 |
| Chequing and savings deposits | 520 | 0 |
| Certificates of deposit | 340 | 1.60 |
| Long-term financing | 260 | 9.80 |
| Equity | 277 | N/A |

(a) What is the duration of the assets?

(b) What is the duration of the liabilities?

(c) Is the bank immune from interest rate risk?

31 **Hedging with Futures** Refer to Figure 25.1 in the text to answer this question. Suppose today is 9 January 2009, and your firm produces chocolate and needs 75,000 tonnes of cocoa in March 2009 for an upcoming promotion. You would like to lock in your costs today, because you are concerned that cocoa prices might go up between now and May.

(a) How could you use cocoa futures contracts to hedge your risk exposure? What price would you effectively be locking in, based on the closing price of the day?

(b) Suppose cocoa prices are £1,764 per contract in March. What is the profit or loss on your futures position? Explain how your futures position has eliminated your exposure to price risk in the cocoa market.

32 **Interest Rate Swaps** ABC Company and XYZ Company need to raise funds to pay for capital improvements at their manufacturing plants. ABC Company is a well-established firm with an excellent credit rating in the debt market; it can borrow funds either at 11 per cent fixed rate or at EURIBOR + 1 per cent floating rate. XYZ Company is a fledgling start-up firm without a strong credit history. It can borrow funds either at 10 per cent fixed rate or at EURIBOR + 3 per cent floating rate.

(a) Is there an opportunity here for ABC and XYZ to benefit by means of an interest rate swap?

(b) Suppose you've just been hired at a bank that acts as a dealer in the swaps market, and your boss has shown you the borrowing rate information for your clients ABC and XYZ. Describe how you could bring these two companies together in an interest rate swap that would make both firms better off while netting your bank a 2.0 per cent profit.

33 **Duration** Per and Birthe Clausen have a son who will begin university three years from today. Expenses of €30,000 will need to be paid at the beginning of each of the four years that their son plans to attend university. What is the duration of this liability to the couple if they can borrow and lend at the market interest rate of 10 per cent?

34 **Duration** What is the duration of a bond with two years to maturity if the bond has a coupon rate of 8 per cent paid semi-annually, and the market interest rate is 7 per cent?

35 **Forward Pricing** The forward price ($F$) of a contract on an asset with neither carrying costs nor convenience yield is the current spot price of the asset ($S_0$) multiplied by 1 plus the appropriate interest rate between the initiation of the contract and the delivery date of the asset. Derive this relationship by comparing the cash flows that result from the following two strategies:

Strategy 1: Buy silver on the spot market today and hold it for one year. (*Hint*: Do not use any of your own money to purchase the silver.)

Strategy 2: Take on a long position in a silver forward contract for delivery in one year. Assume that silver is an asset with neither carrying costs nor convenience yield.

36 **Forward Pricing** You enter into a forward contract to buy a 10-year, zero coupon bond that will be issued in one year. The face value of the bond is £100,000, and the one-year and 11-year spot interest rates are 5 per cent and 9 per cent, respectively.

(a) What is the forward price of your contract?

(b) Suppose both the one-year and 11-year spot rates unexpectedly shift downwards by 2 per cent. What is the new price of the forward contract?

37 **Forward Pricing** This morning you agreed to buy a one-year Treasury bond in six months. The bond has a face value of £100,000. Use the spot interest rates listed here to answer the following questions:

| Time (months) | EAR (%) |
|---|---|
| 6 | 7.42 |
| 12 | 8.02 |
| 18 | 8.79 |
| 24 | 9.43 |

(a) What is the forward price of this contract?

(b) Suppose shortly after you purchased the forward contract, all rates increased by 30 basis points. For example, the six-month rate increased from 7.42 per cent to 7.72 per cent. What is the price of a forward contract otherwise identical to yours, given these changes?

38 **Financial Engineering** Suppose there were call options and forward contracts available on coal, but no put options. Show how a financial engineer could synthesize a put option using the available contracts. What does your answer tell you about the general relationship between puts, calls, and forwards?

## McAfee Mortgages Ltd

Jennifer McAfee recently received her university Masters degree and has decided to enter the mortgage brokerage business. Rather than work for someone else, she has decided to open her own shop. Her cousin Finn has approached her about a mortgage for a house he is building. The house will be completed in three months, and he will need the mortgage at that time. Finn wants a 25-year, fixed-rate mortgage for the amount of £500,000 with monthly payments.

Jennifer has agreed to lend Finn the money in three months at the current market rate of 8 per cent. Because Jennifer is just starting out, she does not have £500,000 available for the loan, so she approaches Ian MacDuff, the president of IM Insurance, about purchasing the mortgage from her in three months. Ian has agreed to purchase the mortgage in three months, but he is unwilling to set a price on the mortgage. Instead, he has agreed in writing to purchase the mortgage at the market rate in three months. There are Treasury bond futures contracts available for delivery in three months. A Treasury bond contract is for £100,000 in face value of Treasury bonds.

1   What is the monthly mortgage payment on Finn's mortgage?

2   What is the most significant risk Jennifer faces in this deal?

3   How can Jennifer hedge this risk?

4   Suppose that in the next three months the market rate of interest rises to 9 per cent.

    (a)   How much will Ian be willing to pay for the mortgage?

    (b)   What will happen to the value of Treasury bond futures contracts? Will the long or short position increase in value?

5   Suppose that in the next three months the market rate of interest falls to 7 per cent.

    (a)   How much will Ian be willing to pay for the mortgage?

    (b)   What will happen to the value of T-bond futures contracts? Will the long or short position increase in value?

6   Are there any possible risks Jennifer faces in using Treasury bond futures contracts to hedge her interest rate risk?

## Practical Case Study

Every company that uses international accounting standards must have a statement on its hedging activity. Download the financial accounts of a company from your country. Read through the risk section and write a report on their hedging activity, if any.

## Relevant Accounting Standards

The derivative positions held by all companies that follow IFRS must be reported at fair value. Guidance is contained in IAS39 *Financial Instruments: Recognition and Measurement*. You should also be familiar with IFRS7 *Financial Instruments: Disclosures*. Visit the IASPlus website for more information (www.iasplus.com).

## Additional Reading

With the exception of Nocco and Stulz (2006) and Gates and Nantes (2006), the papers listed below relate to corporate hedging activity. Nocco and Stulz (2006) and Gates and Nantes (2006) provide interesting reviews of enterprise risk management, which integrates all the disparate risks a company faces into one cohesive policy.

**Corporate Hedging**

Clark, E. and A. Judge (2009) 'Foreign currency derivatives versus foreign currency debt and the hedging premium', *European Financial Management* (forthcoming). **UK.**

Faulkender, M. (2005) 'Hedging or market timing? Selecting the interest rate exposure of corporate debt', *Journal of Finance*, vol. 60, no. 2, pp. 931–962. **US**.

Graham, J.R. and D.A. Rogers (2002) 'Do firms hedge in response to tax incentives?', *Journal of Finance*, vol. 57, no. 2, pp. 815–839. **US**.

Guay, W. and S.P. Kothari (2003) 'How much do firms hedge with derivatives?', *Journal of Financial Economics*, vol. 70, no. 3, pp. 423–461. **US**.

Haushalter, G.D. (2000) 'Financing policy, basis risk, and corporate hedging: evidence from oil and gas producers', *Journal of Finance*, vol. 55, no. 1, pp. 107–152. **US**.

Jin, Y. and P. Jorion (2006) 'Firm value and hedging: evidence from US oil and gas producers', *Journal of Finance*, vol. 61, no. 2, pp. 893–929. **US**.

Marshall, A. (2000) 'Foreign exchange risk management in UK, USA, and Asia Pacific multinational companies', *Journal of Multinational Financial Management*, vol. 10, no. 2, pp. 185–211. **International**.

Enterprise Risk Management

Gates, S. and A. Nantes (2006) 'Incorporating strategic risk into enterprise risk management: a survey of current corporate practice', *Journal of Applied Corporate Finance*, vol. 18, no. 4, pp. 81–90. **US**.

Nocco, B.W. and R.M. Stulz (2006) 'Enterprise risk management: theory and practice', *Journal of Applied Corporate Finance*, vol. 18, no. 4, pp. 8–20. **Theoretical paper**.

# Endnotes

1   He will deliver on Thursday, two days later.

2   The direction is reversed for the seller of a futures contract. However, the general point that the net present value of cash flows may differ between forward and futures contracts holds for sellers as well.

3   See J.C. Cox, J.E. Ingersoll and S.A. Ross, 'The relationship between forward and future prices', *Journal of Financial Economics* (1981).

4   Alternatively, the firm could buy the oil on 1 April and store it. This would eliminate the risk of price movements, because the firm's oil costs would be fixed upon the immediate purchase. However, this strategy would be inferior to strategy 2 in the common case where the difference between the futures contract quoted on 1 April and the 1 April cash price is less than the storage costs.

5   We are assuming that each spot rate shifts by the same amount. For example, suppose that on 1 March $R_1 = 5\%$, $R_2 = 5.4\%$ and $R_3 = 5.8\%$. Assuming that all rates increase by 0.5 per cent on 2 March, $R_1$ becomes 5.5 per cent (5% + 0.5%), $R_2$ becomes 5.9 per cent, and $R_3$ becomes 6.3 per cent.

6   Futures contracts on bonds are also called *interest rate futures contracts*.

7   Delivery occurs two days after the seller notifies the clearing house of her intention to deliver.

8   Alternatively, we can say that mortgages have shorter duration than do Treasury bonds of equal maturity. A precise definition of duration is provided later in this chapter.

9   Alternatively, the mortgage would still be at par if a coupon rate below 12 per cent were used. However, this is not done, because the insurance company wants to buy only 12 per cent mortgages.

10   The bonds are at different prices initially. Thus we are concerned with percentage price changes, not absolute price changes.

11   The mathematical formula for duration is

$$\text{Duration} = \frac{PV(C_1)1 + PV(C_2)2 + \cdots + PV(C_T)T}{PV}$$

and

$$PV = PV(C_1) + PV(C_2) + \cdots + PV(C_T)$$
$$PV(C_T) = \frac{C_T}{(1+R)^T}$$

where $C_T$ is the cash to be received in time $T$ and $R$ is the current discount rate.

Also note that in our numerical example we discounted each payment by the interest rate of 10 per cent. This was done because we wanted to calculate the duration of the bond before a change in the interest rate occurred. After a change in the rate to, say, 8 or 12 per cent all three of our steps would need to reflect the new interest rate. In other words, the duration of a bond is a function of the current interest rate.

12  Actually, this relationship holds exactly only in the case of a one-time shift in a flat yield curve, where the change in the spot rate is identical for all maturities.

13  Note that the duration of a group of items is an average of the duration of the individual items, weighted by the market value of each item. This is a simplifying step that greatly increases duration's practicality.

14  J. Capstaff, A. Marshall and J. Hutton, 'The introduction of the euro and derivatives use in French firms', *Journal of International Financial Management and Accounting*, vol. 18 (2007).

15  F.M. Lee, A. Marshall, Y.K. Szto and J. Tang, 'The practice of financial risk management: an international comparison', *Thunderbird International Business Review*, vol. 43 (May–June 2001).

To help you grasp the key concepts of this chapter check out the extra resources posted on the Online Learning Centre at **www.mcgraw-hill.co.uk/textbooks/hillier**

Among other helpful resources there are PowerPoint presentations, chapter outlines and mini-cases.

# Chapter 26

## PART SEVEN

## Short-Term Finance and Planning

On 1 January 2005 retailing giant Wal-Mart began requiring its 100 largest suppliers to put radio frequency identification (RFID) tags on cases and pallets shipped to three of its distribution centres and 100 of its stores. By October 2005 the company had expanded the requirement to three additional distribution centres and 900 more stores. The next 200 largest suppliers also had to begin adding the RFID tags.

RFID tags are essentially high-tech replacements for bar codes. The advantage is that they can be read from a distance, so an entire warehouse can be scanned in seconds. RFID tag sales are expected to grow from about £700 million (€760 million) in 2003 to about £1.98 billion (€2.2 billion) in 2009.

So why the rapid growth in high-tech bar codes? Look no further than Wal-Mart for the answer. Specifically, the company thought it would save $6.7 billion in labour costs by eliminating individual scans, $600 million by reducing out-of-stock items, $575 million by reducing theft, $300 million with better tracking, and $180 million by reducing inventory. The total cost savings for Wal-Mart are estimated at $8.35 billion per year! As this example suggests, proper management of short-term assets such as inventory can have a significant impact on the profitability of a company, and the value investors place on it.

Short-term financial planning is one activity that concerns everyone in business. As this chapter illustrates, such planning demands, among other things, sales projections from marketing, cost numbers from accounting, and inventory requirements from operations.

## 26.1  Tracing Cash and Net Working Capital

In this section we trace the components of cash and net working capital as they change from one year to the next. Our goal is to describe the short-term operating activities of the firm, and their impact on cash and working capital.

*Current assets* are cash and other assets that are expected to be converted to cash within the year. Current assets are presented in the balance sheet in order of their accounting liquidity – the ease with which they can be converted to cash at a fair price, and the time it takes to do so. Table 26.1 gives the balance sheet and income statement of the global pharmaceutical firm Sanofi-Aventis SA for 2005, 2006 and 2007. The items found in the current asset section of the Sanofi-Aventis balance sheet are cash and cash equivalents, financial assets to be sold or expire within one year, other current assets, accounts receivable, inventories, and assets held for sale.

Analogous to their investment in current assets, firms use several kinds of short-term debt, called *current liabilities*. Current liabilities are obligations that are expected to require cash payment within one year or within the operating cycle, whichever is shorter.[1] The items found as current liabilities are accounts payable, other current liabilities (such as accrued wages, taxes, and other expenses payable), and short-term debt and long-term debt to be paid off within one year.

| TABLE 26.1 | Consolidated statement of financial position | | |
|---|---|---|---|
| (€ million) | 31 December 2007 | 31 December 2006 | 31 December 2005 |
| **ASSETS** | | | |
| Property, plant and equipment | 6,538 | 6,219 | 6,184 |
| Goodwill | 27,199 | 28,472 | 30,234 |
| Intangible assets | 19,182 | 23,738 | 30,229 |
| Investments in associates | 2,493 | 2,637 | 2,477 |
| Financial assets – non-current | 1,037 | 1,045 | 1,318 |
| Deferred tax assets | 2,912 | 3,492 | 3,382 |
| **Non-current assets** | **59,361** | **65,603** | **73,824** |
| Assets held for sale | – | – | 676 |
| Inventories | 3,729 | 3,659 | 3,430 |
| Accounts receivable | 4,904 | 5,032 | 5,021 |
| Other current assets | 2,126 | 2,208 | 2,434 |
| Financial assets – current | 83 | 108 | 311 |
| Cash and cash equivalents | 1,711 | 1,153 | 1,249 |
| **Current assets** | **12,553** | **12,160** | **13,121** |
| **TOTAL ASSETS** | **71,914** | **77,763** | **86,945** |

| (€ million) | 31 December 2007 | 31 December 2006 | 31 December 2005 |
|---|---|---|---|
| **LIABILITIES AND EQUITY** | | | |
| Equity attributable to equity holders of the company | 44,542 | 45,600 | 46,128 |
| Minority interests | 177 | 220 | 189 |
| **Total equity** | **44,719** | **45,820** | **46,317** |
| Long-term debt | 3,734 | 4,499 | 4,750 |
| Provisions and other non-current liabilities | 6,857 | 7,920 | 8,250 |
| Deferred tax liabilities | 6,935 | 9,246 | 12,208 |
| **Non-current liabilities** | **17,526** | **21,665** | **25,208** |
| Liabilities related to assets held for sale | – | – | 259 |
| Accounts payable | 2,749 | 3,008 | 3,193 |
| Other current liabilities | 4,713 | 4,825 | 5,543 |
| Short-term debt and current portion of long-term debt | 2,207 | 2,445 | 6,425 |
| **Current liabilities** | **9,669** | **10,278** | **15,420** |
| **TOTAL LIABILITIES AND EQUITY** | **71,914** | **77,763** | **86,945** |

**Table 26.1** Financial statements of Sanofi-Aventis SA

## 26.2 Defining Cash in Terms of Other Elements

Now we shall define cash in terms of the other elements of the *statement of financial position* or *balance sheet*. The balance sheet equation is

$$\text{Net working capital} + \text{Non-current assets} = \text{Non-current Liabilities} + \text{Equity} \qquad (26.1)$$

TABLE
26.1

| Consolidated income statement | | | |
|---|---|---|---|
| (€ million) | Year ended 31 December 2007 | Year ended 31 December 2006 | Year ended 31 December 2005 |
| **Net sales** | **28,052** | **28,373** | **27,311** |
| Other revenues | 1,155 | 1,116 | 1,202 |
| Cost of sales | (7,571) | (7,587) | (7,566) |
| **Gross profit** | **21,636** | **21,902** | **20,947** |
| Research and development expenses | (4,537) | (4,430) | (4,044) |
| Selling and general expenses | (7,554) | (8,020) | (8,250) |
| Other operating income | 522 | 391 | 261 |
| Other operating expenses | (307) | (116) | (124) |
| Amortization of intangibles | (3,654) | (3,998) | (4,037) |
| **Operating income before restructuring, impairment of property, plant and equipment and intangibles, gains and losses on disposals, and litigation** | **6,106** | **5,729** | **4,753** |
| Restructuring costs | (137) | (274) | (972) |
| Impairment of property, plant and equipment and intangibles | (58) | (1,163) | (972) |
| Gains and losses on disposals, and litigation | – | 536 | 79 |
| **Operating income** | **5,911** | **4,828** | **2,888** |
| Financial expenses | (329) | (455) | (532) |
| Financial income | 190 | 375 | 287 |
| **Income before tax and associates** | **5,772** | **4,748** | **2,643** |
| Income tax expense | (687) | (800) | (477) |
| Share of profit/loss of associates | 597 | 451 | 427 |
| **Net income** | **5,682** | **4,399** | **2,593** |
| Net income attributable to minority interests | 419 | 393 | 335 |
| **Net income attributable to equity holders of the Company** | **5,263** | **4,006** | **2,258** |
| Average number of shares outstanding (million) | 1,346.9 | 1,346.8 | 1,336.5 |
| Average number of shares outstanding after dilution (million) | 1,353.9 | 1,358.8 | 1,346.5 |
| – Basic earnings per share (in euros) | 3.91 | 2.97 | 1.69 |
| – Diluted earnings per share (in euros) | 3.89 | 2.95 | 1.68 |

Table 26.1 *Continued*

Net working capital is cash plus the other elements of net working capital:

$$\text{Net working capital} = \text{Cash} + \text{Other current assets} - \text{Current liabilities} \qquad (26.2)$$

Substituting Eq. (26.2) into Eq. (26.1) yields

$$\text{Cash} + \frac{\text{Other current}}{\text{assets}} - \text{Current liabilities} = \frac{\text{Non-current}}{\text{liabilities}} + \text{Equity} - \frac{\text{Non-current}}{\text{assets}} \qquad (26.3)$$

and rearranging, we find that

$$\text{Cash} = \frac{\text{Non-current}}{\text{liabilities}} + \text{Equity} - \frac{\text{Net working capital}}{\text{(excluding cash)}} - \frac{\text{Non-current}}{\text{assets}} \quad (26.4)$$

The natural interpretation of Eq. (26.4) is that increasing non-current liabilities and equity and decreasing non-current assets and net working capital (excluding cash) will increase cash to the firm.

## The Sources and Uses of Cash

We first introduced the statement of cash flows in Chapter 3. This is the accounting statement that describes the sources and uses of cash. In this section we look at where cash comes from, and how it is used. From the right side of Eq. (26.4) we can see that an increase in non-current liabilities or equity leads to an increase in cash. Moreover, a decrease in net working capital or non-current assets leads to an increase in cash. In addition, the sum of net income and depreciation increases cash, whereas dividend payments decrease cash. This reasoning allows an accountant to create a statement of cash flows, which shows all the transactions that affect a firm's cash position.

Let us trace the changes in cash for Sanofi-Aventis during 2007. From the firm's statement of cash flows (Table 26.2), we find that Sanofi-Aventis generated cash as follows:

1   Generated cash flow of €7,917 million from operations.

2   Made €329 million on selling property, plant and equipment and intangible assets.

3   Issued new shares, raising €271 million.

4   Took out new long-term debt of €1,639 million.

| TABLE 26.2 | Consolidated statements of cash flows | | |
|---|---|---|---|
| (€ million) | Year ended 31 December 2007 | Year ended 31 December 2006 | Year ended 31 December 2005 |
| **Net income attributable to equity holders of the company** | **5,263** | **4,006** | **2,258** |
| Minority interests, excluding BMS | 16 | 18 | 36 |
| Share of undistributed earnings of associates | 133 | 96 | 170 |
| Depreciation, amortization and impairment of property, plant and equipment and intangible assets | 4,664 | 6,113 | 5,951 |
| Gains and losses on disposals of non-current assets, net of tax | (64) | (558) | (125) |
| Net change in deferred taxes | (1,476) | (2,463) | (2,100) |
| Net change in provisions | (247) | 284 | 27 |
| Cost of employee benefits (stock options and capital increase) | 134 | 149 | 231 |
| Impact of work down of Aventis inventories remeasured at fair value, net of tax | – | 21 | 249 |
| Unrealized gains and losses recognized in income | (506) | (56) | (60) |
| **Operating cash flow before changes in working capital** | **7,917** | **7,610** | **6,637** |

**Table 26.2** Sources and uses of cash in Sanofi-Aventis SA

## TABLE 26.2

| Consolidated statements of cash flows | | | |
|---|---|---|---|
| (€ million) | Year ended 31 December 2007 | Year ended 31 December 2006 | Year ended 31 December 2005 |
| (Increase)/decrease in inventories | (89) | (372) | (586) |
| (Increase)/decrease in accounts receivable | (60) | (241) | (738) |
| Increase/(decrease) in accounts payable and accrued expenses | (156) | (77) | 474 |
| Net change in other current assets, financial assets - current and other current liabilities | (506) | (316) | 611 |
| **Net cash provided by operating activities** | **7,106** | **6,604** | **6,398** |
| Acquisitions of property, plant and equipment and intangible assets | (1,610) | (1,454) | (1,143) |
| Acquisitions of investments in consolidated undertakings, net of cash acquired | (214) | (509) | (692) |
| Acquisitions of available-for-sale financial assets | (221) | (4) | (4) |
| Proceeds from disposals of property, plant and equipment, intangible assets and other non-current assets, net of tax | 329 | 1,174 | 733 |
| Net change in loans and other non-current financial assets | – | 3 | 5 |
| **Net cash used in investing activities** | **(1,716)** | **(790)** | **(1,101)** |
| Issuance of Sanofi-Aventis shares | 271 | 307 | 314 |
| Dividends paid: | | | |
| • to Sanofi-Aventis shareholders | (2,364) | (2,042) | (1,604) |
| • to minority shareholders, excluding BMS | (9) | (8) | (10) |
| Additional long-term borrowings | 1,639 | 864 | 5,268 |
| Repayments of long-term borrowings | (2,065) | (1,351) | (7,959) |
| Net change in short-term borrowings | (509) | (3,674) | (2,099) |
| Acquisition of treasury shares | (1,806) | – | – |
| Disposals of treasury shares, net of tax | 23 | 50 | 105 |
| **Net cash provided by/(used in) financing activities** | **(4,820)** | **(5,854)** | **(5,985)** |
| **Impact of exchange rates on cash and cash equivalents** | **(12)** | **(56)** | **97** |
| **Net change in cash and cash equivalents** | **558** | **(96)** | **(591)** |
| **Cash and cash equivalents, beginning of period** | **1,153** | **1,249** | **1,840** |
| **Cash and cash equivalents, end of period** | **1,711** | **1,153** | **1,249** |

**Table 26.2** *Continued*

Sanofi-Aventis used cash for the following reasons:
- Paid off taxes of €1,476 million.
- Increased inventories by €89 million.
- Increased accounts receivable by €60 million.
- Decreased accounts payable and accrued expenses by €156 million.
- Purchased €1,610 of new property, plant and equipment and intangible assets.
- Purchased €221 million of financial assets.
- Paid dividends of €2,373 (= €2,364 + €9) million.
- Repaid €2,065 million of long-term debt.

- Reduced short-term debt by €509 million.
- Purchased €1,806 million of treasury shares.

This example illustrates the difference between a firm's cash position on the balance sheet and its cash flows from operations.

## 26.3 The Operating Cycle and the Cash Cycle

Short-term finance is concerned with the firm's short-term operating activities. A typical manufacturing firm's short-term operating activities consist of a sequence of events and decisions:

| Events | Decisions |
|--------|-----------|
| **1** Buying raw materials. | **1** How much inventory to order? |
| **2** Paying cash for purchases. | **2** To borrow or draw down cash balance? |
| **3** Manufacturing the product. | **3** What choice of production technology? |
| **4** Selling the product. | **4** To offer cash terms or credit terms to customers? |
| **5** Collecting cash. | **5** How to collect cash? |

These activities create patterns of cash inflows and cash outflows that are both unsynchronized and uncertain. They are unsynchronized because the payment of cash for raw materials does not happen at the same time as the receipt of cash from selling the product. They are uncertain because future sales and costs are not known with certainty.

Figure 26.1 depicts the short-term operating activities and cash flows for a typical manufacturing firm along the cash flow time line. The operating cycle is the interval between the arrival of inventory stock and the date when cash is collected from receivables.

The cash cycle begins when cash is paid for materials, and ends when cash is collected from receivables. The cash flow time line consists of an operating cycle and a cash cycle. The need for short-term financial decision-making is suggested by the gap between the cash inflows

**FIGURE 26.1**

The *operating cycle* is the period from the arrival of stock until the receipt of cash. (Sometimes the operating cycle is defined to include the time from placement of the order until arrival of the stock.) The *cash cycle* begins when cash is paid for materials, and ends when cash is collected from receivables.

**Figure 26.1** Cash flow time line and the short-term operating activities of a typical manufacturing firm and cash outflows. This is related to the lengths of the operating cycle and the accounts or trades payable period. This gap can be filled either by borrowing or by holding a liquidity reserve for marketable securities. The gap can be shortened by changing the inventory, receivable and payable periods. Now we take a closer look at the operating cycle.

The length of the operating cycle is equal to the sum of the lengths of the inventory and accounts receivable periods. The inventory period is the length of time required to order raw materials, produce and sell a product. The accounts receivable period is the length of time required to collect cash receipts.

The cash cycle is the time between cash disbursement and cash collection. It can be thought of as the operating cycle less the accounts payable period:

$$\text{Cash cycle} = \text{Operating cycle} - \text{Accounts payable period}$$

The accounts payable period is the length of time for which the firm is able to delay payment on the purchase of various resources, such as labour and raw materials.

In practice, the inventory period, the accounts receivable period and the accounts payable period are measured by days in inventory, days in receivables, and days in payables, respectively. We illustrate how the operating cycle and the cash cycle can be measured in the following example.

---

**EXAMPLE 26.1**

## Cash Cycle

Sanofi-Aventis SA is a global pharmaceutical firm with the statement of financial position and income statement shown in Table 26.1 for 2005, 2006 and 2007. We can determine the operating cycle and the cash cycle for Sanofi-Aventis after calculating the appropriate ratios for inventory, receivables and payables. Consider inventory first. The average inventory is

$$\text{Average inventory} = \frac{\text{€3,729 million} + \text{€3,659 million}}{2}$$
$$= \text{€3,694 million}$$

The terms in the numerator are the ending inventory in 2007 and 2006, respectively.

We next calculate the inventory turnover ratio:

$$\text{Inventory turnover ratio} = \frac{\text{Cost of goods sold}}{\text{Average inventory}}$$
$$= \frac{\text{€7,571 million}}{\text{€3,694 million}}$$
$$= 2.05$$

This implies that the inventory cycle occurs 2.05 times a year. Finally, we calculate days in inventory:

$$\text{Days in inventory} = \frac{365 \text{ days}}{2.05}$$
$$= 178.05 \text{ days}$$

Our calculation implies that the inventory cycle is slightly more than 178 days.

We perform analogous calculations for receivables and payables:[2]

$$\frac{\text{Average}}{\text{accounts receivable}} = \frac{\text{€4,903 million} + \text{€5,032 million}}{2}$$
$$= \text{€4,967.5 million}$$

$$\text{Average} \atop \text{receivable turnover}} = \frac{\text{Credit sales}}{\text{Average accounts receivable}}$$

$$= \frac{€28,052 \text{ million}}{€4,967.5 \text{ million}}$$

$$= 5.65$$

$$\text{Days in} \atop \text{receivables}} = \frac{365}{5.65}$$

$$= 64.60 \text{ days}$$

$$\text{Average} \atop \text{payables}} = \frac{€2,749 \text{ million} + €3,008 \text{ million}}{2}$$

$$= €2,878.5 \text{ million}$$

$$\text{Accounts payable} \atop \text{deferral period}} = \frac{\text{Cost of goods sold}}{\text{Average payables}}$$

$$= \frac{€7,571 \text{ million}}{€2,878.5 \text{ million}}$$

$$= 2.63$$

$$\text{Days in} \atop \text{payables}} = \frac{365}{2.63}$$

$$= 138.78 \text{ days}$$

The preceding calculations allow us to determine both the operating cycle and the cash cycle:

$$\text{Operating} \atop \text{cycle}} = \text{Days in} \atop \text{inventory}} + \text{Days in} \atop \text{receivables}}$$

$$= 178.05 \text{ days} + 64.60 \text{ days}$$

$$= 242.65 \text{ days}$$

$$\text{Cash cycle} = \text{Operating cycle} - \text{Days in payables}$$

$$= 242.65 \text{ days} - 138.78 \text{ days}$$

$$= 103.87 \text{ days}$$

The cash cycle is longer in some industries than in others because of different products and industry practices. Table 26.3 illustrates this point by comparing the current assets and current liabilities for four different companies. Of the four, Wal-Mart has the highest level of inventories. Does this mean Wal-Mart is less efficient? Probably not; instead, it is likely that the relatively high inventory levels are consistent with the industry. Wal-Mart needs a higher level of inventory to satisfy customers who walk into its stores. In contrast, Dell makes products to order, so its inventory levels are lower. What might seem surprising is Boeing's relatively low level of inventory, especially given that much of its inventory consists of aircraft under construction. However, notice that the current assets for Boeing are only 37 per cent of total assets, implying that fixed assets are large, as you would expect from such a capital-intensive company – plus Boeing has been aggressive in recent years in reducing its inventory. In contrast, Amazon's fixed assets are small relative to its current assets, which again is what we would expect given the nature of its business.

## 26.4 Some Aspects of Short-Term Financial Policy

The policy that a firm adopts for short-term finance will be composed of at least two elements:

| TABLE 26.3 | Amazon.com (%) | Boeing (%) | Dell (%) | Wal-Mart (%) |
|---|---|---|---|---|
| Cash and near cash | 27.41 | 11.04 | 30.47 | 4.56 |
| Marketable securities | 26.70 | 0.94 | 8.72 | 0.00 |
| Accounts receivable | 9.82 | 8.17 | 17.69 | 1.43 |
| Inventories | 15.31 | 12.42 | 2.49 | 24.49 |
| Other current assets | 0.00 | 4.49 | 17.24 | 1.53 |
| Total current assets | 79.25 | 37.07 | 76.62 | 32.02 |
| Accounts payable | 52.19 | 27.23 | 42.58 | 29.20 |
| Short-term borrowings | 0.00 | 3.20 | 26.34 | 6.47 |
| Other short-term liabilities | 0.00 | 4.32 | 0.00 | 0.00 |
| Current liabilities | 52.19 | 34.75 | 68.92 | 35.67 |

Table 26.3 Current assets and current liabilities as a percentage of total assets for selected companies

1  *The size of the firm's investment in current assets*: This is usually measured relative to the firm's level of total operating revenues. A flexible or accommodative short-term financial policy would maintain a high ratio of current assets to sales. A restrictive short-term financial policy would entail a low ratio of current assets to sales.

2  *The financing of current assets*: This is measured as the proportion of short-term debt to long-term debt. A restrictive short-term financial policy means a high proportion of short-term debt relative to long-term financing, and a flexible policy means less short-term debt and more long-term debt.

## The Size of the Firm's Investment in Current Assets

Flexible short-term financial policies include:

- Keeping large balances of cash and marketable securities
- Making large investments in inventory
- Granting liberal credit terms, which results in a high level of accounts receivable

Restrictive short-term financial policies are:

- Keeping low cash balances and no investment in marketable securities
- Making small investments in inventory
- Allowing no credit sales and no accounts receivable

Determining the optimal investment level in short-term assets requires an identification of the different costs of alternative short-term financing policies. The objective is to trade off the cost of restrictive policies against those of the flexible ones to arrive at the best compromise.

Current asset holdings are highest with a flexible short-term financial policy and lowest with a restrictive policy. Thus flexible short-term financial policies are costly in that they require higher cash outflows to finance cash and marketable securities, inventory, and accounts receivable. However, future cash inflows are highest with a flexible policy. Sales are stimulated by the use of a credit policy that provides liberal financing to customers. A large amount of inventory on hand ('on the shelf') provides a quick delivery service to customers and increases in sales.[3] In addition, the firm can probably charge higher prices for the quick delivery service and the liberal credit terms of flexible policies. A flexible policy may also result in fewer production stoppages because of inventory shortages.[4]

Managing current assets can be thought of as involving a trade-off between costs that rise with the level of investment and costs that fall with the level of investment. Costs that rise with the level of investment in current assets are called carrying costs. Costs that fall with increases in the level of investment in current assets are called shortage costs.

Carrying costs are generally of two types. First, because the rate of return on current assets is low compared with that of other assets, there is an opportunity cost. Second, there is the cost of maintaining the economic value of the item. For example, the cost of warehousing inventory belongs here.

## Determinants of Corporate Liquid Asset Holdings

| Firms with high holdings of liquid assets will have | Firms with low holdings of liquid assets will have |
|---|---|
| High-growth opportunities | Low-growth opportunities |
| High-risk investments | Low-risk investments |
| Small firms | Large firms |
| Low-credit firms | High-credit firms |

Firms will hold more liquid assets (i.e. cash and marketable securities) to ensure that they can continue investing when cash flow is low relative to positive NPV investment opportunities. Firms that have good access to capital markets will hold less liquid assets.

*Source*: Tim Opler, Lee Pinkowitz, René Stulz and Rohan Williamson, 'The determinants and implication of corporate cash holdings', *Journal of Financial Economics*, vol. 52 (1999).

Shortage costs are incurred when the investment in current assets is low. If a firm runs out of cash, it will be forced to sell marketable securities. If a firm runs out of cash and cannot readily sell marketable securities, it may need to borrow, or default on an obligation. (This general situation is called *cash-out*.) If a firm has no inventory (a *stockout*) or if it cannot extend credit to its customers, it will lose customers.

There are two kinds of shortage costs:

1  *Trading or order costs*: Order costs are the costs of placing an order for more cash (*brokerage costs*) or more inventory (*production set-up costs*).

2  *Costs related to safety reserves*: These are costs of lost sales, lost customer goodwill, and disruption of production schedules.

Figure 26.2 illustrates the basic nature of carrying costs. The total costs of investing in current assets are determined by adding the carrying costs and the shortage costs. The minimum point on the total cost curve (CA*) reflects the optimal balance of current assets. The curve is generally quite flat at the optimum, and it is difficult, if not impossible, to find the precise optimal balance of shortage and carrying costs. Usually, we are content with a choice near the optimum.

If carrying costs are low, or shortage costs are high, the optimal policy calls for substantial current assets. In other words, the optimal policy is a flexible one. This is illustrated in the middle graph of Fig. 26.2.

If carrying costs are high, or shortage costs are low, the optimal policy is a restrictive one. That is, the optimal policy calls for modest current assets. This is illustrated in the bottom graph of the figure.

Opler, Pinkowitz, Stulz and Williamson examine the determinants of holdings of cash and marketable securities by publicly traded firms.[5] They find evidence that firms behave according to the static trade-off model described earlier. Their study focuses only on liquid assets (i.e.

FIGURE
26.2

Flexible policy

Restrictive policy

*Carrying costs* increase with the level of investment in current assets. They include both opportunity costs and the costs of maintaining the asset's economic value. *Shortage costs* decrease with increases in the level of investment in current assets. They include trading costs and the costs of running out of the current asset (for example, being short of cash).

**Figure 26.2** Carrying costs and shortage costs

**Figure 26.3** Financing policy for an idealized economy

cash and market securities), so that carrying costs are the opportunity costs of holding liquid assets and shortage costs are the risks of not having cash when investment opportunities are good.

## Alternative Financing Policies for Current Assets

In the previous section we examined the level of investment in current assets. Now we turn to the level of current liabilities, assuming the investment in current assets is optimal.

**An Ideal Model**   In an ideal economy short-term assets can always be financed with short-term debt, and long-term assets can be financed with long-term debt and equity. In this utopian economy, net working capital is always zero.

Imagine the simple case of a grain elevator operator. Grain elevator operators buy crops after harvest, store them, and sell them during the year. They have high inventories of grain after the harvest, and end with low inventories just before the next harvest.

Bank loans with maturities of less than one year are used to finance the purchase of grain. These loans are paid with the proceeds from the sale of grain.

The situation is shown in Fig. 26.3. Long-term assets are assumed to grow over time, whereas current assets increase at the end of the harvest and then decline during the year. Short-term assets end at zero just before the next harvest. These assets are financed by short-term debt, and long-term assets are financed with long-term debt and equity. Net working capital – current assets minus current liabilities – is always zero.

**Different Strategies in Financing Current Assets**   Current assets cannot be expected to drop to zero in the real world, because a long-term rising level of sales will result in some permanent investment in current assets. A growing firm can be thought of as having a permanent requirement for both current assets and long-term assets. This total asset requirement will exhibit balances over time reflecting (a) a secular growth trend, (b) a seasonal variation around the trend, and (b) unpredictable day-to-day and month-to-month fluctuations. This is depicted in Figure 26.4. (We have not tried to show the unpredictable day-to-day and month-to-month variations in the total asset requirement.)

Now let us look at how this asset requirement is financed. First, consider the strategy (strategy F in Fig. 26.5) where long-term financing covers more than the total asset requirement, even at seasonal peaks. The firm will have excess cash available for investment in marketable securities when the total asset requirement falls from peaks. Because this approach implies chronic short-term cash surpluses and a large investment in net working capital, it is considered a flexible strategy.

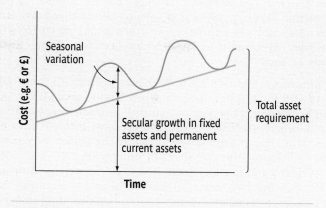

**Figure 26.4** The total asset requirement over time

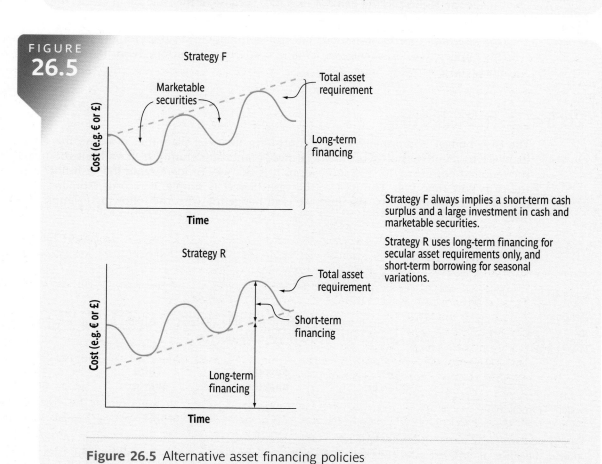

**Figure 26.5** Alternative asset financing policies

When long-term financing does not cover the total asset requirement, the firm must borrow short-term to make up the deficit. This restrictive strategy is labelled strategy R in Fig. 26.5.

## Which Is Best?

What is the most appropriate amount of short-term borrowing? There is no definitive answer. Several considerations must be included in a proper analysis:

1 *Cash reserves*: The flexible financing strategy implies surplus cash and little short-term borrowing. This strategy reduces the probability that a firm will experience financial distress. Firms may not need to worry as much about meeting recurring short-term obligations. However, investments in cash and marketable securities are zero net present value investments at best.

2 *Maturity hedging*: Most firms finance inventories with short-term bank loans and non-current assets with long-term financing. Firms tend to avoid financing long-lived assets with short-term borrowing. This type of maturity mismatching would necessitate frequent financing and is inherently risky, because short-term interest rates are more volatile than longer rates. This type of activity was precisely the reason why many banks found themselves in difficulty during the global credit crunch of 2007 and 2008. Banks financed long-term assets (loans and mortgages granted to borrowers) by short-term borrowing. In some cases this borrowing had just a 30-day maturity. For example, Northern Rock plc, the British bank that requested emergency central bank funding in September 2007, funded its loans and mortgages by 61 per cent short-term borrowing and 39 per cent deposits just before it made the request to the Bank of England. Because of the collapse in credit, the funding base of Northern Rock collapsed.

3 *Term structure*: Short-term interest rates are normally lower than long-term interest rates. This implies that, on average, it is more costly to rely on long-term borrowing than on short-term borrowing.

## 26.5 Cash Budgeting

The cash budget is a primary tool of short-term financial planning. It allows the financial manager to identify short-term financial needs (and opportunities). It will tell the manager the required borrowing for the short term. It is the way of identifying the cash flow gap on the cash flow time line. The idea of the cash budget is simple: it records estimates of cash receipts and disbursements. We illustrate cash budgeting with the following example of Fun Toys.

EXAMPLE
26.2

## Cash Collections

All of Fun Toys' cash inflows come from the sale of toys. Cash budgeting for Fun Toys starts with a sales forecast for the next year, by quarter:

|  | First quarter | Second quarter | Third quarter | Fourth quarter |
|---|---|---|---|---|
| Sales (€ millions) | 100 | 200 | 150 | 100 |

Fun Toys' fiscal year starts on 1 July. Fun Toys' sales are seasonal, and are usually very high in the second quarter because of holiday sales. But Fun Toys sells to department stores on credit, and sales do not generate cash immediately. Instead, cash comes later from collections on accounts receivable. Fun Toys has a 90-day collection period, and 100 per cent of sales are collected the following quarter. In other words

$$\text{Collections} = \text{Last quarter's sales}$$

This relationship implies that

$$\text{Accounts receivable at end of last quarter} = \text{Last quarter's sales} \qquad (26.5)$$

We assume that sales in the fourth quarter of the previous fiscal year were €100 million. From Eq. (26.5) we know that accounts receivable at the end of the fourth quarter of the previous fiscal year were €100 million, and collections in the first quarter of the current fiscal year are €100 million.

The first quarter sales of the current fiscal year of €100 million are added to the accounts receivable, but €100 million of collections are subtracted. Therefore Fun Toys ended the first quarter with accounts receivable of €100 million. The basic relation is

$$\text{Ending accounts receivable} = \text{Starting accounts receivable} + \text{Sales} - \text{Collections}$$

Table 26.4 shows cash collections for Fun Toys for the next four quarters. Though collections are the only source of cash here, this need not always be the case. Other sources of cash could include sales of assets, investment income, and long-term financing.

| | First quarter | Second quarter | Third quarter | Fourth quarter |
|---|---|---|---|---|
| Sales | 100 | 200 | 150 | 100 |
| Cash collections | 100 | 100 | 200 | 150 |
| Starting receivables | 100 | 100 | 200 | 150 |
| Ending receivables | 100 | 200 | 150 | 100 |

**Table 26.4** Sources of cash (in € millions)

## Cash Outflow

Next, we consider cash disbursements. They can be put into four basic categories, as shown in Table 26.5.

1 *Payments of accounts payable*: These are payments for goods or services, such as raw materials. These payments will generally be made after purchases. Purchases will depend on the sales forecast. In the case of Fun Toys, assume that:

> Payments = Last quarter's purchases
> Purchases = 1/2 next quarter's sales forecast

2 *Wages, taxes, and other expenses*: This category includes all other normal costs of doing business that require actual expenditures. Depreciation, for example, is often thought of as a normal cost of business, but it requires no cash outflow.

3 *Capital expenditures*: These are payments of cash for long-lived assets. Fun Toys plans a major capital expenditure in the fourth quarter.

4 *Long-term financing*: This category includes interest and principal payments on long-term outstanding debt and dividend payments to shareholders.

The total forecast outflow appears in the last line of Table 26.5.

## The Cash Balance

The net cash balance appears in Table 26.6, and a large net cash outflow is forecast in the second quarter. This large outflow is not caused by an inability to earn a profit. Rather, it results from delayed collections on sales. This results in a cumulative cash shortfall of €30 million in the second quarter.

TABLE
**26.5**

| | First quarter | Second quarter | Third quarter | Fourth quarter |
|---|---|---|---|---|
| Sales | 100 | 200 | 150 | 100 |
| Purchases | 100 | 75 | 50 | 50 |
| Uses of cash | | | | |
| Payments of accounts payable | 50 | 100 | 75 | 50 |
| Wages, taxes, and other expenses | 20 | 40 | 30 | 20 |
| Capital expenditures | 0 | 0 | 0 | 100 |
| Long-term financing expenses: | | | | |
| interest and dividends | 10 | 10 | 10 | 10 |
| Total uses of cash | 80 | 150 | 115 | 180 |

**Table 26.5** Disbursement of cash (in € millions)

TABLE
**26.6**

| | First quarter | Second quarter | Third quarter | Fourth quarter |
|---|---|---|---|---|
| Total cash receipts | 100 | 100 | 200 | 150 |
| Total cash disbursements | 80 | 150 | 115 | 180 |
| Net cash flow | 20 | (50) | 85 | (30) |
| Cumulative excess cash balance | 20 | (30) | 55 | 25 |
| Minimum cash balance | 5 | 5 | 5 | 5 |
| Cumulative finance surplus (deficit) | | | | |
| Requirement | 15 | (35) | 50 | 20 |

**Table 26.6** The cash balance (in € millions)

Fun Toys had established a minimum operating cash balance equal to €5 million to facilitate transactions, protect against unexpected contingencies, and maintain compensating balances at its banks. This means that it has a cash shortfall in the second quarter equal to €35 million.

## 26.6 The Short-Term Financial Plan

Fun Toys has a short-term financing problem. It cannot meet the forecast cash outflows in the second quarter from internal sources. Its financing options include: (a) unsecured bank borrowing; (b) secured borrowing; and (c) other sources.

### Unsecured Loans

The most common way to finance a temporary cash deficit is to arrange a short-term unsecured bank loan. Firms that use short-term bank loans usually ask their bank for either a non-committed or a committed *line of credit*. A *non-committed* line is an informal arrangement that allows firms to borrow up to a previously specified limit without going through the normal paperwork. The interest rate on the line of credit is usually set equal to the bank's prime lending rate plus an additional percentage.

*Committed* lines of credit are formal legal arrangements, and usually involve a commitment fee paid by the firm to the bank (usually the fee is approximately 0.25 per cent of the total committed funds per year). For larger firms the interest rate is often tied to the Interbank

Offered Rate (LIBOR or EURIBOR) or to the bank's cost of funds, rather than the benchmark rate. Mid-sized and smaller firms often are required to keep compensating balances in the bank.

**Compensating balances** are deposits the firm keeps with the bank in low-interest or non-interest-bearing accounts. Compensating balances are commonly of the order of 2 to 5 per cent of the amount used. By leaving these funds with the bank without receiving interest, the firm increases the effective interest earned by the bank on the line of credit. For example, if a firm borrowing £100,000 must keep £5,000 as a compensating balance, the firm effectively receives only £95,000. A stated interest rate of 10 per cent implies yearly interest payments of £10,000 (= £100,000 × 0.10). The effective interest rate is 10.53 per cent (= £10,000/£95,000).

## Secured Loans

Banks and other finance companies often require *security* for a loan. Security for short-term loans usually consists of accounts receivable or inventories.

Under **accounts receivable financing**, receivables are either *assigned* or *factored*. Under assignment, the lender not only has a lien on the receivables but also has recourse to the borrower. Factoring involves the sale of accounts receivable. The purchaser, who is called a *factor*, must then collect on the receivables. The factor assumes the full risk of default on bad accounts.

As the name implies, an **inventory loan** uses inventory as collateral. Some common types of inventory loans are:

- *Blanket inventory lien*: The blanket inventory lien gives the lender a lien against all the borrower's inventories.

- *Trust receipt*: Under this arrangement the borrower holds the inventory in trust for the lender. The document acknowledging the loan is called the trust receipt. Proceeds from the sale of inventory are remitted immediately to the lender.

- *Field warehouse financing*: In field warehouse financing, a public warehouse company supervises the inventory for the lender.

## Other Sources

A variety of other sources of short-term funds are employed by corporations. The most important of these are the issuance of **commercial paper** and financing through **banker's acceptances**. Commercial paper consists of short-term notes issued by large, highly rated firms. Typically these notes are of short maturity, ranging up to 270 days (beyond that limit the firm will normally be required to file a registration statement with the appropriate stock exchange). Because the firm issues these directly, and because it usually backs the issue with a special bank line of credit, the rate the firm obtains is often significantly below the rate the bank would charge it for a direct loan.

A banker's acceptance is an agreement by a bank to pay a sum of money. These agreements typically arise when a seller sends a bill or draft to a customer. The customer's bank *accepts* this bill and notes the acceptance on it, which makes it an obligation of the bank. In this way a firm that is buying something from a supplier can effectively arrange for the bank to pay the outstanding bill. Of course, the bank charges the customer a fee for this service.

## Summary and Conclusions

1   This chapter introduced the management of short-term finance. Short-term finance involves short-lived assets and liabilities. We traced and examined the short-term sources and uses of cash as they appear on the firm's financial statements. We saw how current assets and current liabilities arise in the short-term operating activities and the cash cycle of the firm. From an accounting perspective, short-term finance involves net working capital.

2 Managing short-term cash flows involves the minimization of costs. The two major costs are carrying costs (the interest and related costs incurred by overinvesting in short-term assets such as cash) and shortage costs (the cost of running out of short-term assets). The objective of managing short-term finance and short-term financial planning is to find the optimal trade-off between these costs.

3 In an ideal economy a firm could perfectly predict its short-term uses and sources of cash, and net working capital could be kept at zero. In the real world net working capital provides a buffer that lets the firm meet its ongoing obligations. The financial manager seeks the optimal level of each of the current assets.

4 The financial manager can use the cash budget to identify short-term financial needs. The cash budget tells the manager what borrowing is required or what lending will be possible in the short term. The firm has a number of possible ways of acquiring funds to meet short-term shortfalls, including unsecured and secured loans.

# connect Questions and Problems

**CONCEPT 1–6**

1 **Net Working Capital** Why is short-term financial planning crucial to a company?

2 **Cash** Review the different ways in which cash can increase or decrease in a firm. Use the accounting equation to support your answer.

3 **The Operating Cycle and Cash Cycle** What are some of the characteristics of a firm with a long operating cycle? Similarly, what are some of the characteristics of a firm with a long cash cycle?

4 **Short-term Financial Policy** Review the various financing policies to manage current assets.

5 **Cash Budgeting** Explain what is meant by cash budgeting.

6 **The Short-term Financial Plan** Review the various ways a firm can finance a short-term cash deficit.

**REGULAR 7–25**

7 **Sources and Uses** For the year just ended, you have gathered the following information about the Mia plc:

(a) A £200 dividend was paid.

(b) Trade payables increased by £500.

(c) Fixed asset purchases were £900.

(d) Inventories increased by £625.

(e) Long-term debt decreased by £1,200.

Label each as a source or use of cash and describe its effect on the firm's cash balance.

8 **Cost of Current Assets** Loftis Manufacturing NV has recently installed a just-in-time (JIT) inventory system. Describe the effect this is likely to have on the company's carrying costs, shortage costs, and operating cycle.

9 **Operating and Cash Cycles** Is it possible for a firm's cash cycle to be longer than its operating cycle? Explain why or why not.

10 **Shortage Costs** What are the costs of shortages? Describe them.

11 **Reasons for Net Working Capital** In an ideal economy, net working capital is always zero. Why might net working capital be positive in a real economy?

Use the following information to answer Questions 12–16. Last month, BlueSky Airlines announced that it would stretch out its bill payments to 45 days from 30 days. The reason given was that the company wanted to 'control costs and optimize cash flow'. The increased payable period will be in effect for all of the company's 4,000 suppliers.

12 **Operating and Cash Cycles** What impact did this change in payables policy have on BlueSky's operating cycle? Its cash cycle?

13 **Operating and Cash Cycles** What impact did the announcement have on BlueSky's suppliers?

14 **Corporate Ethics** Is it ethical for large firms to unilaterally lengthen their payable periods, particularly when dealing with smaller suppliers?

15 **Payables Period** Why don't all firms simply increase their payables periods to shorten their cash cycles?

16 **Payables Period** BlueSky lengthened its payables period to 'control costs and optimize cash flow'. Exactly what is the cash benefit to BlueSky from this change?

17 **Changes in the Cash Account** Indicate the impact of the following corporate actions on cash, using the letter I for an increase, D for a decrease, or N when no change occurs.

(a) A dividend is paid with funds received from a sale of debt.

(b) Property is purchased and paid for with short-term debt.

(c) Inventory is bought on credit.

(d) A short-term bank loan is repaid.

(e) Next year's taxes are prepaid.

(f) Preference shares are redeemed.

(g) Sales are made on credit.

(h) Interest on long-term debt is paid.

(i) Payments for previous sales are collected.

(j) The trade payables balance is reduced.

(k) A dividend is paid.

(l) Production supplies are purchased and paid with a short-term note.

(m) Utility bills are paid.

(n) Cash is paid for raw materials purchased for inventory.

(o) Marketable securities are sold.

18 **Cash Equation** Eurasian Natural Resources plc, a Kazakhstani firm listed on the London Stock Exchange, has total non-current assets of $4,938 million. Non-current liabilities are $1,038 million. Current assets, other than cash, are $2,098 million. Current liabilities are $1,161 million. Total equity is worth $7,176 million. How much cash does the company have?

19 **Changes in the Operating Cycle** Indicate the effect that the following will have on the operating cycle. Use the letter I to indicate an increase, D for a decrease, and N for no change.

(a) Receivables average goes up.

(b) Credit repayment times for customers are increased.

(c) Inventory turnover goes from 3 times to 6 times.

(d) Payables turnover goes from 6 times to 11 times.

(e) Receivables turnover goes from 7 times to 9 times.

(f) Payments to suppliers are accelerated.

20 **Changes in Cycles** Indicate the impact of the following on the cash and operating cycles, respectively. Use the letter I to indicate an increase, D for a decrease, and N for no change.

(a) The terms of cash discounts offered to customers are made less favourable.

(b) The cash discounts offered by suppliers are increased: thus payments are made earlier.

(c) An increased number of customers begin to pay in cash instead of with credit.

(d) Fewer raw materials than usual are purchased.

(e) A greater percentage of raw material purchases are paid for with credit.

(f) More finished goods are produced for inventory instead of for order.

21 **Calculating Cash Collections** Pindado SA has projected the following quarterly sales amounts for the coming year:

|       | Q1    | Q2    | Q3    | Q4    |
|-------|-------|-------|-------|-------|
| Sales | €800  | €760  | €940  | €870  |

(a) Trade receivables at the beginning of the year are €300. Pindado has a 45-day collection period. Calculate cash collections in each of the four quarters by completing the following:

|                      | Q1 | Q2 | Q3 | Q4 |
|----------------------|----|----|----|----|
| Beginning receivables |    |    |    |    |
| Sales                |    |    |    |    |
| Cash collections     |    |    |    |    |
| Ending receivables   |    |    |    |    |

(b) Rework (a) assuming a collection period of 60 days.

(c) Rework (a) assuming a collection period of 30 days.

22 **Calculating Cycles** Consider the following financial statement information for Bulldog Ice plc: calculate the operating and cash cycles. How do you interpret your answer?

| Item                | Beginning (£) | | Ending (£) |
|---------------------|---------------|--------|------------|
| Inventory           | 8,413         |        | 10,158     |
| Accounts receivable | 5,108         |        | 5,439      |
| Accounts payable    | 6,927         |        | 7,625      |
| Net sales           |               | 67,312 |            |
| Cost of goods sold  |               | 52,827 |            |

**23  Calculating Payments**  Lewellen Products has projected the following sales for the coming year:

|           | **Q1** | **Q2** | **Q3** | **Q4** |
|-----------|--------|--------|--------|--------|
| Sales (£) | 540    | 630    | 710    | 785    |

Sales in the year following this one are projected to be 15 per cent greater in each quarter.

(a)  Calculate payments to suppliers, assuming that Lewellen places orders during each quarter equal to 30 per cent of projected sales for the next quarter. Assume that the company pays immediately. What is the payables period in this case?

|                          | **Q1** | **Q2** | **Q3** | **Q4** |
|--------------------------|--------|--------|--------|--------|
| Payment of accounts (£)  |        |        |        |        |

(b)  Rework (a) assuming a 90-day payables period.

|                          | **Q1** | **Q2** | **Q3** | **Q4** |
|--------------------------|--------|--------|--------|--------|
| Payment of accounts (£)  |        |        |        |        |

(c)  Rework (a) assuming a 60-day payables period.

|                          | **Q1** | **Q2** | **Q3** | **Q4** |
|--------------------------|--------|--------|--------|--------|
| Payment of accounts (£)  |        |        |        |        |

**24  Calculating Payments**  Marshall plc's purchases from suppliers in a quarter are equal to 75 per cent of the next quarter's forecast sales. The payables period is 60 days. Wages, taxes and other expenses are 20 per cent of sales, and interest and dividends are £60 per quarter. No capital expenditures are planned.
   Here are the projected quarterly sales:

|           | **Q1** | **Q2** | **Q3** | **Q4** |
|-----------|--------|--------|--------|--------|
| Sales (£) | 750    | 920    | 890    | 790    |

Sales for the first quarter of the following year are projected at £970. Calculate the company's cash outlays by completing the following:

|                                                     | **Q1** | **Q2** | **Q3** | **Q4** |
|-----------------------------------------------------|--------|--------|--------|--------|
| Payment of accounts                                 |        |        |        |        |
| Wages, taxes, other expenses                        |        |        |        |        |
| Long-term financing expenses (interest and dividends) |        |        |        |        |
| Total                                               |        |        |        |        |

**25  Calculating Cash Collections**  The following is the sales budget for Freezing Snow plc for the first quarter of 2010:

| | January | February | March |
|---|---|---|---|
| Sales budget (£) | 150,000 | 173,000 | 194,000 |

Credit sales are collected as follows:

65 per cent in the month of the sale.
20 per cent in the month after the sale.
15 per cent in the second month after the sale.

The accounts receivable balance at the end of the previous quarter was £57,000 (£41,000 of which was uncollected December sales).

(a) Compute the sales for November.

(b) Compute the sales for December.

(c) Compute the cash collections from sales for each month from January to March.

**CHALLENGE**

**26 – 31**

26 **Calculating the Cash Budget** Here are some important figures from the budget of Sagmo AB for the second quarter of 2010:

| | April (NKr) | May (NKr) | June (NKr) |
|---|---|---|---|
| Credit sales | 380,000 | 396,000 | 438,000 |
| Credit purchases | 147,000 | 175,500 | 200,500 |
| Cash disbursements | | | |
| Wages, taxes, and expenses | 39,750 | 48,210 | 50,300 |
| Interest | 11,400 | 11,400 | 11,400 |
| Equipment purchases | 83,000 | 91,000 | 0 |

The company predicts that 5 per cent of its credit sales will never be collected, 35 per cent of its sales will be collected in the month of the sale, and the remaining 60 per cent will be collected in the following month. Credit purchases will be paid in the month following the purchase.

In March 2010 credit sales were NKr210,000, and credit purchases were NKr156,000. Using this information, complete the following cash budget:

| | April (NKr) | May (NKr) | June (NKr) |
|---|---|---|---|
| Beginning cash balance | 280,000 | | |
| Cash receipts | | | |
| Cash collections from credit sales | | | |
| Total cash available | | | |
| Cash disbursements | | | |
| Purchases | | | |
| Wages, taxes, and expenses | | | |
| Interest | | | |
| Equipment purchases | | | |
| Total cash disbursements | | | |
| Ending cash balance | | | |

**27 Sources and Uses** Here are the most recent balance sheets for the Danish Transport and Logistics firm DSV A/S. Excluding accumulated depreciation, determine whether each item is a source or a use of cash, and the amount:

| CONDENSED BALANCE SHEET | | |
|---|---|---|
| (DKKm) | 31.12.07 | 30.09.08 |
| Goodwill and customer relationships | 2,456 | 2,460 |
| Other intangibles, property, plant and equipment | 2,784 | 2,089 |
| Other non-current assets | 608 | 773 |
| **Total non-current assets** | **5,848** | **5,322** |
| Receivables | 4,333 | 4,038 |
| Cash and intercompany balances | 2,849 | 1,930 |
| **Total current assets** | **7,182** | **5,968** |
| **Total assets** | **13,030** | **11,290** |
| **Equity** | **1,614** | **2,805** |
| Interest-bearing long-term debt | 260 | 191 |
| Other non-current liabilities, including provisions | 617 | 590 |
| **Non-current liabilities** | **877** | **781** |
| Interest-bearing short-term debt, including intercompany debt | 6,358 | 3,967 |
| Other short-term debt | 4,181 | 3,737 |
| **Total current liabilities** | **10,539** | **7,704** |
| **Total equity and liabilities** | **13,030** | **11,290** |

ROIC came to 20.2%. The calculation of ROIC included DKK 2,237 million relating to goodwill and customer relationships. The item consists of the Division's goodwill, customer relationships and goodwill allocated from DSV. Number of employees: 10,314.

**28 Cash Budgeting** The sales budget for your company in the coming year is based on a 20 per cent quarterly growth rate with the first-quarter sales projection at £100 million. In addition to this basic trend, the seasonal adjustments for the four quarters are 0, −£10, −£5 and £15 million, respectively. Generally, 50 per cent of the sales can be collected within the quarter and 45 per cent in the following quarter; the rest of sales are bad debt. The bad debts are written off in the second quarter after the sales are made. The beginning accounts payable balance is £81 million. Assuming all sales are on credit, compute the cash collections from sales for each quarter.

**29 Calculating the Cash Budget** Wildcat SA has estimated sales (in millions) for the next four quarters as follows:

| | Q1 | Q2 | Q3 | Q4 |
|---|---|---|---|---|
| Sales (€m) | 230 | 195 | 270 | 290 |

Sales for the first quarter of the year after this one are projected at €250 million. Accounts receivable at the beginning of the year were €79 million. Wildcat has a 45-day collection period.

Wildcat's purchases from suppliers in a quarter are equal to 45 per cent of the next quarter's forecast sales, and suppliers are normally paid in 36 days. Wages, taxes and other expenses run at about 30 per cent of sales. Interest and dividends are €15 million per quarter.

Wildcat plans a major capital outlay in the second quarter of €90 million. Finally, the company started the year with a €73 million cash balance and wishes to maintain a €30 million minimum balance.

(a) Complete a cash budget for Wildcat by filling in the following:

| WILDCAT SA Cash Budget (€ millions) | | | | |
|---|---|---|---|---|
| | Q1 | Q2 | Q3 | Q4 |
| Beginning cash balance | 73 | | | |
| Net cash inflow | | | | |
| Ending cash balance | | | | |
| Minimum cash balance | 30 | | | |
| Cumulative surplus (deficit) | | | | |

(b) Assume that Wildcat can borrow any needed funds on a short-term basis at a rate of 3 per cent per quarter, and can invest any excess funds in short-term marketable securities at a rate of 2 per cent per quarter. Prepare a short-term financial plan by filling in the following schedule. What is the net cash cost (total interest paid minus total investment income earned) for the year?

| WILDCAT SA Short-Term Financial Plan (€ millions) | | | | |
|---|---|---|---|---|
| | Q1 | Q2 | Q3 | Q4 |
| Beginning cash balance | 73 | | | |
| Net cash inflow | | | | |
| New short-term investments | | | | |
| Income from short-term investments | | | | |
| Short-term investments sold | | | | |
| New short-term borrowing | | | | |
| Interest on short-term borrowing | | | | |
| Short-term borrowing repaid | | | | |
| Ending cash balance | | | | |
| Minimum cash balance | 30 | | | |
| Cumulative surplus (deficit) | | | | |
| Beginning short-term investments | | | | |
| Ending short-term investments | | | | |
| Beginning short-term debt | | | | |
| Ending short-term debt | | | | |

30 **Cash Management Policy** Rework Problem 29 assuming the following:

(a) Wildcat maintains a minimum cash balance of €45 million.

(b) Wildcat maintains a minimum cash balance of €15 million.

Based on your answers in (a) and (b), do you think the firm can boost its profit by changing its cash management policy? Should other factors be considered as well? Explain.

31 **Short-Term Finance Policy** Renault SA and Peugeot SA are competing automobile manufacturing firms. Download their annual financial accounts for the most recent period from each company's website.

(a) How are the current assets of each firm financed?

(b) Which firm has the larger investment in current assets? Why?

(c) Which firm is more likely to incur carrying costs, and which is more likely to incur shortage costs? Why?

# Wolgemut Manufacturing Working Capital Management

You have recently been hired by Wolgemut Manufacturing to work in its established treasury department. Wolgemut Manufacturing is a small company that produces highly customized cardboard boxes in a variety of sizes for different purchasers. Adam Wolgemut, the owner of the company, works primarily in the sales and production areas of the company. Currently, the company basically puts all receivables in one pile and all payables in another, and a part-time accountant periodically comes in and attacks the piles. Because of this disorganized system, the finance area needs work, and that's what you've been brought in to do.

The company currently has a cash balance of €115,000, and it plans to purchase new machinery in the third quarter at a cost of €200,000. The purchase of the machinery will be made with cash because of the discount offered for a cash purchase. Adam wants to maintain a minimum cash balance of €90,000 to guard against unforeseen contingencies. All of Wolgemut's sales to customers and purchases from suppliers are made with credit, and no discounts are offered or taken.

The company had the following sales each quarter of the year just ended:

|  | Q1 | Q2 | Q3 | Q4 |
|---|---|---|---|---|
| Gross sales (€) | 565,000 | 585,000 | 628,000 | 545,000 |

After some research and discussions with customers, you're projecting that sales will be 8 per cent higher in each quarter next year. Sales for the first quarter of the following year are also expected to grow at 8 per cent. You calculate that Wolgemut currently has an accounts receivable period of 57 days and an accounts receivable balance of €426,000. However, 10 per cent of the accounts receivable balance is from a company that has just entered bankruptcy, and it is likely that this portion will never be collected.

You've also calculated that Wolgemut typically orders supplies each quarter to the amount of 50 per cent of the next quarter's projected gross sales, and suppliers are paid in 53 days on average. Wages, taxes and other costs run at about 25 per cent of gross sales. The company has a quarterly interest payment of €120,000 on its long-term debt. Finally, the company uses a local bank for its short-term financial needs. It currently pays 1.2 per cent per quarter on all short-term borrowing, and maintains a money market account that pays 0.5 per cent per quarter on all short-term deposits.

Adam has asked you to prepare a cash budget and short-term financial plan for the company under the current policies. He has also asked you to prepare additional plans based on changes in several inputs.

1  Use the numbers given to complete the cash budget and short-term financial plan.

2  Rework the cash budget and short-term financial plan assuming Wolgemut changes to a minimum cash balance of €70,000.

3  Rework the sales budget assuming an 11 per cent growth rate in sales and a 5 per cent growth rate in sales. Assume a €90,000 target cash balance.

4  Assuming the company maintains its target cash balance at €90,000, what sales growth rate would result in a zero need for short-term financing? To answer this question, you may need to set up a spreadsheet and use the 'Solver' function.

## Practical Case Study

1 **Cash and Operating Cycles** Find the most recent financial statements for ArcelorMittal and Nokia. Calculate the cash and operating cycle for each company for the most recent year. Are the numbers similar for these companies? Why or why not?

2 **Cash and Operating Cycles** Download the most recent quarterly financial statements for Rio Tinto plc. Calculate the operating and cash cycle for Rio Tinto over each of the last four quarters. Comment on any changes in the operating or cash cycle over this period.

## Relevant Accounting Standards

The relevant accounting standards are those that apply to the presentation of financial statements and cash flow. These are IAS1 *Presentation of Financial Statements* and IAS7 *Statement of Cash Flows*.

## Additional Reading

Working capital management does not receive much empirical attention in the finance literature. The following paper, however, links corporate governance to the choice between credit or cash use in a firm.

Yun, H. (2009) 'The choice of corporate liquidity and corporate governance', *Review of Financial Studies* (forthcoming). **US.**

## Endnotes

1 As we shall learn in this chapter, the operating cycle begins when inventory is received and ends when cash is collected from the sale of inventory.

2 We assume that Sanofi-Aventis makes no cash sales.

3 This is true of some types of finished goods.

4 This is true of inventory of raw material but not of finished goods.

5 Tim Opler, Lee Pinkowitz, René Stulz and Rohan Williamson, 'The determinants and implication of corporate cash holdings', *Journal of Financial Economics*, vol. 52 (1999).

**Online LearningCentre**

To help you grasp the key concepts of this chapter check out the extra resources posted on the Online Learning Centre at **www.mcgraw-hill.co.uk/textbooks/hillier**

Among other helpful resources there are PowerPoint presentations, chapter outlines and mini-cases.

# Chapter 27

# Cash Management

## KEY NOTATIONS

| | |
|---|---|
| $F$ | Fixed cost of selling securities to replenish cash |
| $L$ | Lower control limit |
| $R$ | Opportunity cost of holding cash |
| $R_B$ | Cost of debt capital |
| $T$ | Total amount of new cash needed for transaction purposes |
| $U$ | Upper control limit |
| $Z$ | Target cash balance |

As most people know, many banks ran out of cash in 2008 and 2009 as bad debts and lack of short-term financing and profitable opportunities combined to cause the most severe crisis in the financial sector for decades. Governments stepped into the breach and used taxpayers' money to shore up their institutions. The non-financial sector was also seriously affected. All across Europe construction companies and other firms, such as estate agents, found they had no cash, because the housing market was almost non-existent. The automobile industry suffered deeply, and many firms changed their manufacturing strategy, made workers redundant, and cut production to save cash. Cash is one of the most important issues a firm needs to consider. Even if a firm is growing and has excellent performance, if it runs out of cash it cannot survive. In this chapter we examine cash management and the various issues a firm must consider.

## 27.1 Reasons for Holding Cash

The term *cash* is a surprisingly imprecise concept. The economic definition of cash includes currency, savings account deposits at banks, and undeposited cheques. However, financial managers often use the term *cash* to include short-term marketable securities. Short-term marketable securities are frequently referred to as *cash equivalents* and include Treasury bills, certificates of deposit, and repurchase agreements. (Several different types of short-term marketable security are described at the end of this chapter.) The balance sheet item 'cash' usually includes cash equivalents.

The previous chapter discussed the management of net working capital. Net working capital includes both cash and cash equivalents. This chapter is concerned with cash, not net working capital, and it focuses on the narrow economic definition of cash.

The basic elements of net working capital management, such as carrying costs, shortage costs and opportunity costs, are relevant for cash management. However, cash management is concerned more with how to minimize cash balances by collecting and disbursing cash effectively.

There are two primary reasons for holding cash. First, cash is needed to satisfy the **transactions motive**. Transaction-related needs come from normal disbursement and collection activities of the firm. The disbursement of cash includes the payment of wages and salaries, trade debts, taxes and dividends. Cash is collected from sales from operations, sales of assets, and new financing. The cash inflows (*collections*) and outflows (*disbursements*) are not perfectly synchronized, and some level of cash holdings is necessary as a buffer. If the firm maintains too small a cash balance it may run out of cash. If so, it must sell marketable securities or borrow. Selling marketable securities and borrowing involve *trading costs*.

FIGURE
**27.1**

Trading costs are increased when the firm must sell securities to establish a cash balance. Opportunity costs are increased when there is a cash balance, because there is no return to cash.

**Figure 27.1** Costs of holding cash

Another reason to hold cash is for compensating balances. Cash balances are kept at banks to compensate for banking services rendered to the firm. The cash balance for most firms can be thought of as consisting of transaction balances and compensating balances. However, it would not be correct for a firm to add the amount of cash required to satisfy its transaction needs to the amount of cash needed to satisfy its compensatory balances to produce a target cash balance. The same cash can be used to satisfy both requirements.

The cost of holding cash is, of course, the opportunity cost of lost interest. To determine the target cash balance, the firm must weigh the benefits of holding cash against the costs. It is generally a good idea for firms to figure out first how much cash to hold to satisfy transaction needs. Next, the firm must consider compensating balance requirements, which will impose a lower limit on the level of the firm's cash holdings. Because compensating balances merely provide a lower limit, we ignore compensating balances for the following discussion of the target cash balance.

## 27.2 Determining the Target Cash Balance

The target cash balance involves a trade-off between the opportunity costs of holding too much cash and the trading costs of holding too little. Figure 27.1 presents the problem graphically. If a firm tries to keep its cash holdings too low, it will find itself selling marketable securities (and perhaps later buying marketable securities to replace those sold) more frequently than if the cash balance was higher. Thus trading costs will tend to fall as the cash balance becomes larger. In contrast, the opportunity costs of holding cash rise as the cash holdings rise. At point $C^*$ in Fig. 27.1, the sum of both costs, depicted as the total cost curve, is at a minimum. This is the target or optimal cash balance.

### The Baumol Model

William Baumol was the first to provide a formal model of cash management incorporating opportunity costs and trading costs.[1] His model can be used to establish the target cash balance.

Suppose Golden Socks plc began week 0 with a cash balance of $C = £1.2$ million, and outflows exceed inflows by £600,000 per week. Its cash balance will drop to zero at the end of week 2, and its average cash balance will be $C/2 = £1.2$ million$/2 = £600,000$ over the two-week period. At the end of week 2 Golden Socks must replace its cash either by selling marketable securities or by borrowing. Figure 27.2 shows this situation.

**FIGURE 27.2**

Starting cash: $C = £1,200,000$

$£600,000 = C/2$ — Average cash

Ending cash: 0

0   1   2   3   4   Weeks

Golden Socks plc begins week 0 with cash of £1,200,000. The balance drops to zero by the second week. The average cash balance is $C/2 = £1,200,000/2 = £600,000$ over the period.

**Figure 27.2** Cash balances for Golden Socks plc

If $C$ were set higher, say at £2.4 million, cash would last four weeks before the firm would need to sell marketable securities, but the firm's average cash balance would increase to £1.2 million (from £600,000). If $C$ were set at £600,000, cash would run out in one week, and the firm would need to replenish cash more frequently, but its average cash balance would fall from £600,000 to £300,000.

Because transaction costs must be incurred whenever cash is replenished (for example, the brokerage costs of selling marketable securities), establishing large initial cash balances will lower the trading costs connected with cash management. However, the larger the average cash balance, the greater the opportunity cost (the return that could have been earned on marketable securities).

To solve this problem, Golden Socks needs to know the following three things:

1   $F$ = The fixed cost of selling securities to replenish cash.

2   $T$ = The total amount of new cash needed for transaction purposes over the relevant planning period – say, one year.

and

3   $R$ = The opportunity cost of holding cash: this is the interest rate on marketable securities.

With this information, Golden Socks can determine the total costs of any particular cash-balance policy. It can then determine the optimal cash-balance policy.

**The Opportunity Costs**   The total opportunity costs of cash balances, in monetary terms, must be equal to the average cash balance multiplied by the interest rate:

$$\text{Opportunity costs } (£) = (C/2) \times R$$

The opportunity costs of various alternatives are given here:

| Initial cash balance, $C$ (£) | Average cash balance, $C/2$ (£) | Opportunity costs, $(C/2) \times R$ $(R = 0.10)$ (£) |
|---|---|---|
| 4,800,000 | 2,400,000 | 240,000 |
| 2,400,000 | 1,200,000 | 120,000 |
| 1,200,000 | 600,000 | 60,000 |
| 600,000 | 300,000 | 30,000 |
| 300,000 | 150,000 | 15,000 |

**The Trading Costs**   We can determine total trading costs by calculating the number of times that Golden Socks must sell marketable securities during the year. The total amount of cash disbursement during the year is £600,000 × 52 weeks = £31.2 million. If the initial cash balance is set at £1.2 million, Golden Socks will sell £1.2 million of marketable securities every two weeks. Thus trading costs are given by

$$\frac{£31.2 \text{ million}}{£1.2 \text{ million}} \times F = 26F$$

The general formula is

$$\text{Trading costs } (£) = (T/C) \times F$$

A schedule of alternative trading costs follows:

| Total disbursements during relevant period, T (£) | Initial cash balance, C (£) | Trading costs, (T/C) × F (F = £1,000) (£) |
|---|---|---|
| 31,200,000 | 4,800,000 | 6,500 |
| 31,200,000 | 2,400,000 | 13,000 |
| 31,200,000 | 1,200,000 | 26,000 |
| 31,200,000 | 600,000 | 52,000 |
| 31,200,000 | 300,000 | 104,000 |

**The Total Cost**   The total cost of cash balances consists of the opportunity costs plus the trading costs:

$$\text{Total cost} = \text{Opportunity costs} + \text{Trading costs}$$
$$= (C/2) \times R + (T/C) \times F$$

| Cash balance (£) | Total cost (£) | = | Opportunity costs (£) | + | Trading costs (£) |
|---|---|---|---|---|---|
| 4,800,000 | 246,500 | | 240,000 | | 6,500 |
| 2,400,000 | 133,000 | | 120,000 | | 13,000 |
| 1,200,000 | 86,000 | | 60,000 | | 26,000 |
| 600,000 | 82,000 | | 30,000 | | 52,000 |
| 300,000 | 119,000 | | 15,000 | | 104,000 |

**The Solution**   We can see from the preceding schedule that a £600,000 cash balance results in the lowest total cost of the possibilities presented: £82,000. But what about £700,000, or £500,000, or other possibilities? To determine minimum total costs precisely, Golden Socks must equate the marginal reduction in trading costs as balances rise with the marginal increase in opportunity costs associated with cash balance increases. The target cash balance should be the point where the two offset each other. This can be calculated with either numerical iteration or calculus. We shall use calculus; but if you are unfamiliar with such an analysis, you can skip to the solution.

Recall that the total cost equation is

$$\text{Total cost (TC)} = (C/2) \times R + (T/C) \times F$$

If we differentiate the TC equation with respect to the cash balance and set the derivative equal to zero, we shall find

$$\frac{d\text{TC}}{dC} = \frac{R}{2} - \frac{TF}{C^2} = 0$$

We obtain the solution for the general cash balance, $C^*$, by solving this equation for $C$:

$$\frac{R}{2} = \frac{TF}{C^2}$$
$$C^* = \sqrt{2TF/R}$$

If $F = £1,000$, $T = £31,200,000$, and $R = 0.10$, then $C^* = £789,936.71$. Given the value of $C^*$, opportunity costs are

$$(C^*/2) \times R = \frac{£789,936.71}{2} \times 0.10$$
$$= £39,496.84$$

Trading costs are

$$(TC^*) \times F = \frac{£31,200,000}{£789,936.71} \times 1,000$$
$$= £39,496.84$$

Hence total costs are

$$£39,496.84 + £39,496.84 = £78,993.68$$

**Limitations** The Baumol model represents an important contribution to cash management. The limitations of the model include the following:

1 *The model assumes the firm has a constant disbursement rate.* In practice, disbursements can be only partially managed, because due dates differ, and costs cannot be predicted with certainty.

2 *The model assumes there are no cash receipts during the projected period.* In fact, most firms experience both cash inflows and outflows daily.

3 *No safety stock is allowed.* Firms will probably want to hold a safety stock of cash designed to reduce the possibility of a cash shortage or *cash-out*. However, to the extent that firms can sell marketable securities or borrow in a few hours, the need for a safety stock is minimal.

The Baumol model is possibly the simplest and most stripped-down, sensible model for determining the optimal cash position. Its chief weakness is that it assumes discrete, certain cash flows. We next discuss a model designed to deal with uncertainty.

## The Miller–Orr Model

Merton Miller and Daniel Orr developed a cash balance model to deal with cash inflows and outflows that fluctuate randomly from day to day.[2] In the Miller–Orr model both cash inflows and cash outflows are included. The model assumes that the distribution of daily net cash flows (cash inflow minus cash outflow) is normally distributed. On each day the net cash flow could be the expected value or some higher or lower value. We shall assume that the expected net cash flow is zero.

Figure 27.3 shows how the Miller–Orr model works. The model operates in terms of upper ($U$) and lower ($L$) control limits and a target cash balance ($Z$). The firm allows its cash balance to wander randomly within the lower and upper limits. As long as the cash balance is between $U$ and $L$, the firm makes no transaction. When the cash balance reaches $U$, such as at point $X$, the firm buys $U - Z$ units (e.g. euros or pounds) of marketable securities.

This action will decrease the cash balance to $Z$. In the same way, when cash balances fall to $L$, such as at point $Y$ (the lower limit), the firm should sell $Z - L$ securities and increase the cash balance to $Z$. In both situations cash balances return to $Z$. Management sets the lower limit, $L$, depending on how much risk of a cash shortfall the firm is willing to tolerate.

Like the Baumol model, the Miller–Orr model depends on trading costs and opportunity costs. The cost per transaction of buying and selling marketable securities, $F$, is assumed to be fixed. The percentage opportunity cost per period of holding cash, $R$, is the daily interest rate on marketable securities. Unlike in the Baumol model, the number of transactions per period is a random variable that varies from period to period, depending on the pattern of cash inflows and outflows.

As a consequence, trading costs per period depend on the expected number of transactions in marketable securities during the period. Similarly, the opportunity costs of holding cash are a function of the expected cash balance per period.

Given $L$, which is set by the firm, the Miller–Orr model solves for the target cash balance, $Z$, and the upper limit, $U$. Expected total costs of the cash balance return policy ($Z$, $U$) are

**Figure 27.3** The Miller–Orr model

*U* is the upper control limit.
*L* is the lower control limit.
The target cash balance is *Z*.
As long as cash is between *L* and *U*, no transaction is made.

equal to the sum of expected transaction costs and expected opportunity costs. The values of $Z$ (the return cash point) and $U$ (the upper limit) that minimize the expected total cost have been determined by Miller and Orr:

$$Z^* = \sqrt[3]{3F\sigma^2/(4R)} + L$$

$$U^* = 3Z^* - 2L$$

Here * denotes optimal values, and $\sigma^2$ is the variance of net daily cash flows.

The average cash balance in the Miller–Orr model is

$$\text{Average cash balance} = \frac{4Z - L}{3}$$

EXAMPLE
27.1

## Miller–Orr

To clarify the Miller–Orr model, suppose $F = £1,000$, the interest rate is 10 per cent annually, and the standard deviation of daily net cash flows is £2,000. The daily opportunity cost, $R$, is

$$(1 + R)^{365} - 1 = 0.10$$
$$1 + R = \sqrt[365]{1.10} = 1.000261$$
$$R = 0.000261$$

The variance of daily net cash flows is

$$\sigma^2 = (2,000)^2 = 4,000,000$$

Let us assume that $L = 0$:

$$Z^* = \sqrt[3]{(3 \times £1,000 \times 4,000,000)/(4 \times 0.000261) + 0}$$
$$= \sqrt[3]{£11,493,900,000,000}$$
$$= £22,568$$
$$U^* = 3 \times £22,568$$
$$= £67,704$$

$$\text{Average cash balance} = \frac{4 \times £22,568}{3}$$
$$= £30,091$$

**Implications of the Miller–Orr Model**   To use the Miller–Orr model, the manager must do four things:

1   Set the lower control limit for the cash balance. This lower limit can be related to a minimum safety margin decided on by management.

2   Estimate the standard deviation of daily cash flows.

3   Determine the interest rate.

4   Estimate the trading costs of buying and selling marketable securities.

These four steps allow the upper limit and return point to be computed. Miller and Orr tested their model using nine months of data for cash balances for a large industrial firm. The model was able to produce average daily cash balances much lower than the averages actually obtained by the firm.[3]

The Miller–Orr model clarifies the issues of cash management. First, the model shows that the best return point, $Z^*$, is positively related to trading costs, $F$, and negatively related to $R$. This finding is consistent with and analogous to the Baumol model. Second, the Miller–Orr model shows that the best return point and the average cash balance are positively related to the variability of cash flows. That is, firms whose cash flows are subject to greater uncertainty should maintain a larger average cash balance.

## Other Factors Influencing the Target Cash Balance

**Borrowing**   In our previous examples the firm obtained cash by selling marketable securities. Another alternative is to borrow cash. Borrowing introduces additional considerations to cash management:

- Borrowing is likely to be more expensive than selling marketable securities, because the interest rate is likely to be higher.

- The need to borrow will depend on management's desire to hold low cash balances. A firm is more likely to need to borrow to cover an unexpected cash outflow with greater cash flow variability and lower investment in marketable securities.

**Compensating Balance**   The costs of trading securities are well below the lost income from holding cash for large firms. Consider a firm faced with either selling £2 million of Treasury bills to replenish cash or leaving the money idle overnight. The daily opportunity cost of £2 million at a 10 per cent annual interest rate is $0.10/365 = 0.027$ per cent per day. The daily return earned on £2 million is $0.00027 \times £2$ million = £540. The cost of selling £2 million of Treasury bills is much less than £540. As a consequence, a large firm will buy and sell securities many times a day before it will leave substantial amounts idle overnight.

However, most large firms hold more cash than cash balance models imply, suggesting that managers disagree with this logic. Here are some possible reasons:

- Firms have cash in the bank as a compensating balance in payment for banking services.

- Large corporations have thousands of accounts with several dozen banks. Sometimes it makes more sense to leave cash alone than to manage each account daily.

## 27.3 Managing the Collection and Disbursement of Cash

A firm's cash balance as reported in its financial statements (*book cash* or *ledger cash*) is not the same thing as the balance shown in its bank account (*bank cash* or *collected bank cash*). The difference between bank cash and book cash is called float and represents the net effect of cheques in the process of collection.

EXAMPLE
**27.2**

# Float

Imagine that Great Mechanics International plc (GMI) currently has £100,000 on deposit with its bank. It purchases some raw materials, paying its vendors with a cheque written on 8 July for £100,000. The company's books (that is, ledger balances) are changed to show the £100,000 reduction in the cash balance. But the firm's bank will not find out about this cheque until it has been deposited at the vendor's bank and has been presented to the firm's bank for payment on, say, 15 July. Until the cheque's presentation, the firm's bank cash is greater than its book cash, and it has *positive float*.

Position prior to 8 July:

$$\text{Float} = \text{Firm's bank cash} - \text{Firm's book cash}$$
$$= £100{,}000 - £100{,}000$$
$$= 0$$

Position from 8 July to 14 July:

$$\text{Disbursement float} = \text{Firm's bank cash} - \text{Firm's book cash}$$
$$= £100{,}000 - 0$$
$$= £100{,}000 \qquad \textit{positive}$$

While the cheque is *clearing*, GMI has a balance with the bank of £100,000 and can obtain the benefit of this cash. For example, the bank cash could be invested in marketable securities. Cheques written by the firm generate *disbursement float*, causing an immediate decrease in book cash but no immediate change in bank cash.

EXAMPLE
**27.3**

# More Float

Imagine that GMI receives a cheque from a customer for £100,000. Assume, as before, that the company has £100,000 deposited at its bank and has a *neutral float position*. It deposits the cheque and increases its book cash by £100,000 on 8 November. However, the cash is not available to GMI until its bank has presented the cheque to the customer's bank and received £100,000 on, say, 15 November. In the meantime, the cash position at GMI will reflect a collection float of £100,000.

Position prior to 8 November:

$$\text{Float} = \text{Firm's bank cash} - \text{Firm's book cash}$$
$$= £100{,}000 - £100{,}000$$
$$= 0$$

Position from 8 November to 14 November:

$$\text{Collection float} = \text{Firm's bank cash} - \text{Firm's book cash}$$
$$= £100{,}000 - £200{,}000$$
$$= -£100{,}000$$

Cheques received by the firm represent *collection float*, which increases book cash immediately but does not immediately change bank cash. The firm is helped by disbursement float and is hurt by collection float. The sum of disbursement float and collection float is *net float*.

A firm should be concerned more with net float and bank cash than with book cash. If a financial manager knows that a cheque will not clear for several days, he or she will be able to keep a lower cash balance at the bank than might be true otherwise. Good float management can generate a great deal of money. For example, suppose the average daily sales of the power distribution firm Schneider Electric SA are about €400 million. If Schneider Electric speeds up the collection process or slows down the disbursement process by one day, it frees up €400 million, which can be invested in marketable securities. With an interest rate of 4 per cent, this represents overnight interest of approximately €44,000 [= (€400 million/365) × 0.04].

Float management involves controlling the collection and disbursement of cash. The objective in cash collection is to reduce the lag between the time customers pay their bills and the time the cheques are collected. The objective in cash disbursement is to slow down payments, thereby increasing the time between when cheques are written and when cheques are presented. In other words, collect early and pay late. Of course, to the extent that the firm succeeds in doing this, the customers and suppliers lose money, and the trade-off is the effect on the firm's relationship with them.

Collection float can be broken down into three parts: mail float, in-house processing float, and availability float:

1 *Mail float* is the part of the collection and disbursement process where cheques are trapped in the postal system.

2 *In-house processing float* is the time it takes the receiver of a cheque to process the payment and deposit it in a bank for collection.

3 *Availability float* refers to the time required to clear a cheque through the banking system. The clearing process takes place using the central clearing system of the country in which the bank operates (e.g. the Central Exchange in the UK), clearing banks, or local clearing houses.

## Float

**EXAMPLE 27.4**

A cheque for £1,000 is mailed from a customer on Monday 1 September. Because of mail, processing and clearing delays it is not credited as available cash in the firm's bank until the following Monday, seven days later. The float for this cheque is

$$\text{Float} = £1,000 \times 7 \text{ days} = £7,000$$

Another cheque for £7,000 is mailed on 1 September. It is available on the next day. The float for this cheque is

$$\text{Float} = £7,000 \times 1 \text{ day} = £7,000$$

The measurement of float depends on the time lag and the amount of money involved. The cost of float is an opportunity cost: the cash is unavailable for use while cheques are tied up in the collection process. The cost of float can be determined by: (a) estimating the average daily receipts; (b) calculating the average delay in obtaining the receipts; and (c) discounting the average daily receipts by the *delay-adjusted cost of capital*.

## Average Float

**EXAMPLE 27.5**

Suppose that Concepts Ltd has two receipts each month:

| | Amount (£) | Number of days' delay | Float (£) |
|---|---|---|---|
| Item 1 | 5,000,000 | × 3 = | 15,000,000 |
| Item 2 | 3,000,000 | × 5 = | 15,000,000 |
| Total | 8,000,000 | | 30,000,000 |

Here is the average daily float over the month:

Average daily float:

$$\frac{\text{Total float}}{\text{Total days}} = \frac{£30,000,000}{30}$$
$$= £1,000,000$$

Another procedure we can use to calculate average daily float is to determine average daily receipts and multiply by the average daily delay:

Average daily receipts:

$$\frac{\text{Total receipts}}{\text{Total days}} = \frac{£8,000,000}{30}$$
$$= £266,666.67$$

$$\text{Weighted average delay} = (5/8) \times 3 + (3/8) \times 5$$
$$= 1.875 + 1.875 = 3.75 \text{ days}$$

$$\text{Average daily float} = \text{Average daily receipts} \times \text{Weighted average delay}$$
$$= £266,666.67 \times 3.75 = £1,000,000$$

## Cost of Float

EXAMPLE **27.6**

Suppose Concepts Ltd has average daily receipts of £266,667. The float results in this amount being delayed 3.75 days. The present value of the delayed cash flow is

$$V = \frac{£266,667}{1 + R_B}$$

where $R_B$ is the cost of debt capital for Concepts, adjusted to the relevant time frame. Suppose the annual cost of debt capital is 10 per cent. Then:

$$R_B = 0.1 \times (3.75/365) = 0.00103$$

and

$$V = \frac{£266,667}{1 + 0.00103}$$
$$= £266,392.62$$

Thus the net present value of the delay float is £266,392.62 − £266,667 = −£274.38 per day. For a year, this is −£274.38 × 365 = −£100,148.70.

## Accelerating Collections

The following is a depiction of the basic parts of the cash collection process:

The total time in this process is made up of mailing time, cheque processing time, and cheque clearing time. The amount of time cash spends in each part of the cash collection process depends on where the firm's customers and banks are located, and how efficient the firm is at collecting cash. Some of the techniques used to accelerate collections and reduce collection time are lockboxes, concentration banking, and wire transfers.

**Lockboxes**   The lockbox is the most widely used device in the US to speed up collections of cash. It is a special post office box set up to intercept trade receivables payments. In Europe it is generally not used, and other methods are substantially more commonplace.

The collection process is started by customers mailing their cheques to a post office box instead of sending them to the firm. The lockbox is maintained by a local bank, and is typically located no more than several hundred miles away. In the typical lockbox system the local bank collects the lockbox cheques from the post office several times a day. The bank deposits the cheques directly to the firm's account. Details of the operation are recorded (in some computer-usable form) and sent to the firm.

A lockbox system reduces mailing time, because cheques are received at a nearby post office instead of at corporate headquarters. Lockboxes also reduce the firm's processing time, because they reduce the time required for a corporation to physically handle receivables and to deposit cheques for collection. A bank lockbox should enable a firm to get its receipts processed, deposited and cleared faster than if it were to receive cheques at its headquarters and deliver them itself to the bank for deposit and clearing.

**Concentration Banking**   Another way to speed up collection is to get the cash from the bank branches to the firm's main bank more quickly. This is done by a method called concentration banking.

With a concentration banking system the firm's sales offices are usually responsible for collecting and processing customer cheques. The sales office deposits the cheques into a local deposit bank account. Surplus funds are transferred from the deposit bank to the concentration bank. The purpose of concentration banking is to obtain customer cheques from nearby receiving locations. Concentration banking reduces mailing time, because the firm's sales office is usually nearer than corporate headquarters to the customer. Furthermore, bank clearing time will be reduced because the customer's cheque is usually drawn on a local bank. Figure 27.4 illustrates this process, where concentration banks are combined with lockboxes in a total cash management system.

The corporate cash manager uses the pools of cash at the concentration bank for short-term investing or for some other purpose. The concentration banks usually serve as the source of short-term investments. They also serve as the focal point for transferring funds to disbursement banks.

**Wire Transfers**   Wire transfers are the most common method of transferring cash in Europe. After the customers' cheques get into the local banking network, the objective is to transfer the surplus funds (funds in excess of required compensating balances) from the local branch to the concentration bank. The fastest and most expensive way is by wire transfer. Wire transfers take only a few minutes, and the cash becomes available to the firm upon receipt of a wire notice at the concentration bank. Wire transfers take place electronically, from one computer to another, and eliminate the mailing and cheque clearing times associated with other cash transfer methods.

The main wire service is SWIFT, operated by the Society for Worldwide Interbank Financial Telecommunication.

## Delaying Disbursements

Accelerating collections is one method of cash management; paying more slowly is another. The cash disbursement process is illustrated in Fig. 27.5. Techniques to slow down disbursement will attempt to increase mail time and cheque clearing time.

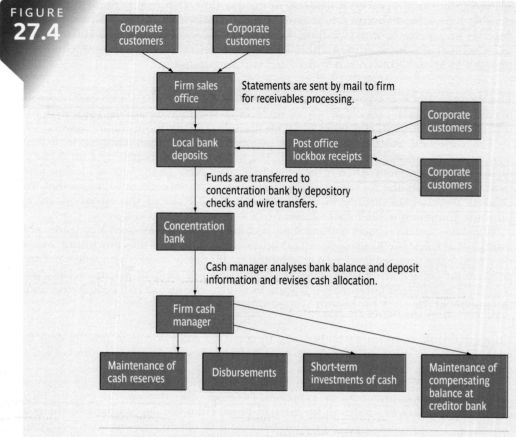

FIGURE
**27.4**

**Figure 27.4** Lockboxes and concentration banks in a cash management system

**Disbursement Float ('Playing the Float Game')**   Even though the cash balance at the bank may be €1 million, a firm's books may show only €500,000 because it has written €500,000 in payment cheques. The disbursement float of €500,000 is available for the corporation to use until the cheques are presented for payment. Float in terms of slowing down payment cheques comes from mail delivery, cheque processing time, and collection of funds. This is illustrated in Fig. 27.5. Disbursement float can be increased by writing a cheque on a geographically distant bank. For example, a British supplier might be paid with cheques drawn on an Italian bank. This will increase the time required for the cheques to clear through the banking system.

## Zero-Balance Accounts

Some firms set up a zero-balance account (ZBA) to handle disbursement activity. The account has a zero balance as cheques are written. As cheques are presented to the zero-balance account for payment (causing a negative balance), funds are automatically transferred in from a central control account. The master account and the ZBA are located in the same bank. Thus the transfer is automatic and involves only an accounting entry in the bank.

## Drafts

Firms sometimes use drafts instead of cheques. Drafts differ from cheques because they are drawn not on a bank but on the issuer (the firm) and are payable by the issuer. The bank acts only as an agent, presenting the draft to the issuer for payment. When a draft is transmitted to a firm's bank for collection, the bank must present the draft to the issuing firm for

**Figure 27.5** Cash disbursement

acceptance before making payment. After the draft has been accepted, the firm must deposit the necessary cash to cover the payment. The use of drafts rather than cheques allows a firm to keep lower cash balances in its disbursement accounts, because cash does not need to be deposited until the drafts are presented for payment.

## Ethical and Legal Questions

The cash manager must work with cash balances collected by the bank and not the firm's book balance, which reflects cheques that have been deposited but not collected. If not, a cash manager could be drawing on uncollected cash as a source for making short-term investments. Most banks charge a penalty for use of uncollected funds. However, banks may not have good enough accounting and control procedures to be fully aware of the use of uncollected funds. This raises some ethical and legal questions for the firm.

## Electronic Data Interchange and the Single Euro Payments Area: The End of Float?

*Electronic data interchange* (EDI) is a general term that refers to the growing practice of direct electronic information exchange between all types of business. One important use of EDI, often called financial EDI, or FEDI, is to transfer financial information and funds electronically between parties, thereby eliminating paper invoices, paper cheques, mailing and handling. For example, it is possible to arrange to have your cheque account directly debited each month to pay many types of bill, and corporations now routinely directly deposit pay cheques into employee accounts. More generally, EDI allows a seller to send a bill electronically to a buyer, thereby avoiding the mail. The buyer can then authorize payment, which also occurs electronically. Its bank then transfers the funds to the seller's account at a different bank. The net effect is that the length of time required to initiate and complete a business transaction is shortened considerably, and much of what we normally think of as float is sharply reduced or eliminated. As the use of FEDI increases (which it will), float management will evolve to focus much more on issues surrounding computerized information exchange and fund transfers.

The Single Euro Payments Area (SEPA) is an attempt to reduce payment times across most countries in Europe. The initiative aims to harmonize payments across Europe by treating the different countries within the region as a single area. As a result, the payment system in Europe will be akin to a domestic market, and clearing times will be improved accordingly. The process towards full SEPA adoption began in January 2007, when all banks in Europe agreed to use an IBAN (International Bank Account Number) to identify transactions. The forms of payment affected by SEPA are credit transfers, direct debits, and credit and debit card payments. Full adoption of SEPA is expected by the end of 2010.

## 27.4 Investing Idle Cash

If a firm has a temporary cash surplus, it can invest in short-term marketable securities. The market for short-term financial assets is called the *money market*. The maturity of short-term financial assets that trade in the money market is one year or less.

Most large firms manage their own short-term financial assets, transacting through banks and dealers. Some large firms and many small firms use money market funds. These are funds that invest in short-term financial assets for a management fee. The management fee is compensation for the professional expertise and diversification provided by the fund manager. Among the many money market mutual funds, some specialize in corporate customers. Banks also offer *sweep accounts*, where the bank takes all excess available funds at the close of each business day and invests them for the firm.

Firms have temporary cash surpluses for these reasons: to help finance seasonal or cyclical activities of the firm, to help finance planned expenditures of the firm, and to provide for unanticipated contingencies.

### Seasonal or Cyclical Activities

Some firms have a predictable cash flow pattern. They have surplus cash flows during part of the year and deficit cash flows the rest of the year. For example, Toys 'R' Us, a retail toy firm, has a seasonal cash flow pattern influenced by holiday sales. Such a firm may buy marketable securities when surplus cash flows occur and sell marketable securities when deficits occur. Of course, bank loans are another short-term financing device. Figure 27.6 illustrates the use of bank loans and marketable securities to meet temporary financing needs.

### Planned Expenditures

Firms frequently accumulate temporary investments in marketable securities to provide the cash for a plant construction programme, dividend payment, and other large expenditures. Thus firms may issue bonds and shares before the cash is needed, investing the proceeds in short-term marketable securities, and then selling the securities to finance the expenditures.

The important characteristics of short-term marketable securities are their maturity, default risk, marketability and taxability.

**Maturity** *Maturity* refers to the time period over which interest and principal payments are made. For a given change in the level of interest rates, the prices of longer-maturity securities

**FIGURE 27.6**

Time 1: A surplus cash flow exists. Seasonal demand for investing is low. The surplus cash flow is invested in short-term marketable securities.

Time 2: A deficit cash flow exists. Seasonal demand for investing is high. The financial deficit is financed by selling marketable securities, and by bank borrowing.

**Figure 27.6** Seasonal cash demands

will change more than those of shorter-maturity securities. As a consequence, firms that invest in long-maturity securities are accepting greater risk than firms that invest in securities with short-term maturities. This type of risk is usually called *interest rate risk*. Most firms limit their investments in marketable securities to those maturing in less than 90 days. Of course, the expected return on securities with short-term maturities is usually less than the expected return on securities with longer maturities.

**Default Risk**   *Default risk* refers to the probability that interest or principal will not be paid on the due date or in the promised amount. In previous chapters we observed that various financial reporting agencies, such as Moody's and Standard & Poor's, compile and publish ratings of various corporate and public securities. These ratings are connected to default risk. Of course, some securities have negligible default risk, such as Treasury bills. Given the purposes of investing idle corporate cash, firms typically avoid investing in marketable securities with significant default risk.

**Marketability**   *Marketability* refers to how easy it is to convert an asset to cash. Sometimes marketability is referred to as *liquidity*. It has two characteristics:

1  *No price pressure effect*: If an asset can be sold in large amounts without changing the market price, it is marketable. Price pressure effects are those that come about when the price of an asset must be lowered to facilitate the sale.

2  *Time*: If an asset can be sold quickly at the existing market price, it is marketable. In contrast, a Renoir painting or antique desk appraised at €1 million will probably sell for much less if the owner must sell on short notice.

In general, marketability is the ability to sell an asset for its face market value quickly and in large amounts. The most marketable of all securities are Treasury bills of developed countries.

**Taxability**   Several kinds of security have varying degrees of tax exemption.

The interest on government bonds tends to be exempt from taxes. Pre-tax expected returns on government bonds must be lower than on similar taxable investments, and therefore are more attractive to corporations in high marginal tax brackets.

The market price of securities will reflect the total demand and supply of tax influences. The position of the firm may be different from that of the market.

## Different Types of Money Market Security

Money market securities are generally highly marketable and short-term. They usually have low risk of default. They are issued by governments (Treasury bills, for example), domestic and foreign banks (certificates of deposit, for example), and business corporations (commercial paper, for example).

*Treasury bills* are obligations of the government that mature in 90, 180, 270 or 360 days. They are pure discount securities. The 90-day and 180-day bills will be sold by auction every week, and 270-day and 360-day bills will be sold at longer intervals, such as every month.

*Treasury notes and bonds* have original maturities of more than one year. They are interest-bearing securities. The interest may be exempt from state and local taxes.

*Commercial paper* refers to short-term securities issued by finance companies, banks and corporations. Commercial paper typically is unsecured. Maturities range from a few weeks to 270 days. There is no active secondary market in commercial paper. As a consequence, their marketability is low. (However, firms that issue commercial paper will directly repurchase before maturity.) The default risk of commercial paper depends on the financial strength of the issuer. Moody's and Standard & Poor's publish quality ratings for commercial paper.

*Certificates of deposit (CDs)* are short-term loans to commercial banks. There are active markets in CDs of 3-month, 6-month, 9-month and 12-month maturities.

*Repurchase agreements* are sales of government securities (for example, Treasury bills) by a bank or securities dealer with an agreement to repurchase. An investor typically buys some Treasury securities from a bond dealer and simultaneously agrees to sell them back at a later date at a specified higher price. Repurchase agreements are usually very short-term – overnight to a few days.

*Eurodollar CDs* are deposits of cash with foreign banks.

*Banker's acceptances* are time drafts (orders to pay) issued by a business firm (usually an importer) that have been accepted by a bank that guarantees payment.

## Summary and Conclusions

The chapter discussed how firms manage cash.

1   A firm holds cash to conduct transactions and to compensate banks for the various services they render.

2   The optimal amount of cash for a firm to hold depends on the opportunity cost of holding cash and the uncertainty of future cash inflows and outflows. The Baumol model and the Miller–Orr model are two transaction models that provide rough guidelines for determining the optimal cash position.

3   The firm can use a variety of procedures to manage the collection and disbursement of cash to speed up the collection of cash and slow down payments. Some methods to speed collection are lockboxes, concentration banking and wire transfers. The financial manager must always work with collected company cash balances and not with the company's book balance. To do otherwise is to use the bank's cash without the bank knowing it, raising ethical and legal questions.

4   Because of seasonal and cyclical activities, to help finance planned expenditures, or as a reserve for unanticipated needs, firms temporarily find themselves with cash surpluses. The money market offers a variety of possible vehicles for parking this idle cash.

## connect  Questions and Problems

**CONCEPT**
**1 – 4**

1   **Reasons for Holding Cash**   Is it possible for a firm to have too much cash? Why would shareholders care if a firm accumulates large amounts of cash?

2   **Determining the Target Cash Balance**   Show, using both the Baumol model and the Miller–Orr model, how a firm can determine its optimal cash balance.

3   **Collection and Disbursement of Cash**   Which would a firm prefer: a net collection float or a net disbursement float? Why?

4   **Investing Idle Cash**   What options are available to a firm if it believes it has too much cash? How about too little?

**REGULAR**
**5 – 32**

5   **Agency Issues**   Are shareholders and creditors likely to agree on how much cash a firm should keep on hand?

6   **Cash Management versus Liquidity Management**   What is the difference between cash management and liquidity management?

7   **Short-Term Investments**   Why are preference shares with a dividend tied to short-term interest rates an attractive short-term investment for corporations with excess cash?

8   **Float**   Suppose a firm has a book balance of €2 million. At the automatic teller machine (ATM) the cash manager finds out that the bank balance is €2.5 million. What is the situation here? If this is an ongoing situation, what ethical dilemma arises?

9   **Short-Term Investments**   For each of the short-term marketable securities given here, provide an example of the potential disadvantages the investment has for meeting a corporation's cash management goals:

(a) Treasury bills.

(b) Preference shares.

(c) Negotiable certificates of deposit (NCDs).

(d) Commercial paper.

(e) Revenue anticipation notes.

(f) Repurchase agreements.

10 **Agency Issues** It is sometimes argued that excess cash held by a firm can aggravate agency problems (discussed in Chapter 1) and, more generally, reduce incentives for shareholder wealth maximization. How would you frame the issue here?

11 **Use of Excess Cash** One option a firm usually has with any excess cash is to pay its suppliers more quickly. What are the advantages and disadvantages of this use of excess cash?

12 **Use of Excess Cash** Another option usually available is to reduce the firm's outstanding debt. What are the advantages and disadvantages of this use of excess cash?

13 **Float** An unfortunately common practice goes like this (warning – don't try this at home). Suppose you are out of money in your bank current account; however, your local grocery store will, as a convenience to you as a customer, cash a cheque for you. So you cash a cheque for £200. Of course, this cheque will bounce unless you do something. To prevent this, you go to the grocery the next day and cash another cheque for £200. You take this £200 and deposit it. You repeat this process every day, and in doing so you make sure that no cheques bounce. Eventually, manna from heaven arrives (perhaps in the form of money from home), and you are able to cover your outstanding cheques.

To make it interesting, suppose you are absolutely certain that no cheques will bounce along the way. Assuming this is true, and ignoring any question of legality (what we have described is probably illegal cheque-kiting), is there anything unethical about this? If you say yes, then why? In particular, who is harmed?

14 **Interpreting Miller–Orr** Based on the Miller–Orr model, describe what will happen to the lower limit, the upper limit, and the spread (the distance between the two) if the variation in net cash flow grows. Give an intuitive explanation for why this happens. What happens if the variance drops to zero?

15 **Changes in Target Cash Balances** Indicate the likely impact of each of the following on a company's target cash balance. Use the letter I to denote an increase and D to denote a decrease. Briefly explain your reasoning in each case.

(a) Commissions charged by brokers decrease.

(b) Interest rates paid on money market securities rise.

(c) The compensating balance requirement of a bank is raised.

(d) The firm's credit rating improves.

(e) The cost of borrowing increases.

(f) Direct fees for banking services are established.

16 **Using the Baumol Model** Given the following information, calculate the target cash balance using the Baumol model:

Annual interest rate: 7%
Fixed order cost: €10
Total cash needed: €5,000

How do you interpret your answer?

17 **Opportunity versus Trading Costs** White Whale NV has an average daily cash balance of €400. Total cash needed for the year is €25,000. The interest rate is 5 per cent, and replenishing the cash costs €6 each time. What are the opportunity cost of holding cash, the trading cost, and the total cost? What do you think of White Whale's strategy?

18  **Costs and the Baumol Model**  D&C Accountants needs a total of £4,000 in cash during the year for transactions and other purposes. Whenever cash runs low, the firm sells off £300 in securities and transfers the cash in. The interest rate is 6 per cent per year, and selling off securities costs £25 per sale.

(a)  What is the opportunity cost under the current policy? The trading cost? With no additional calculations, would you say that D&C keeps too much or too little cash? Explain.

(b)  What is the target cash balance derived using the Baumol model?

19  **Calculating Net Float**  Each business day, on average, a company writes cheques totalling €25,000 to pay its suppliers. The usual clearing time for the cheques is four days. Meanwhile, the company is receiving payments from its customers each day, in the form of cheques, totalling €40,000. The cash from the payments is available to the firm after two days.

(a)  Calculate the company's disbursement float, collection float, and net float.

(b)  How would your answer to part (a) change if the collected funds were available in one day instead of two?

20  **Costs of Float**  Purple Feet Wine Ltd receives an average of £9,000 in cheques per day. The delay in clearing is typically four days. The current interest rate is 0.025 per cent per day.

(a)  What is the company's float?

(b)  What is the most Purple Feet should be willing to pay today to eliminate its float entirely?

(c)  What is the highest daily fee the company should be willing to pay to eliminate its float entirely?

21  **Float and Weighted Average Delay**  Every month your neighbour receives two cheques, one for €16,000 and one for €3,000. The larger cheque takes four days to clear after it is deposited; the smaller one takes five days.

(a)  What is the total float for the month?

(b)  What is the average daily float?

(c)  What are the average daily receipts and weighted average delay?

22  **NPV and Collection Time**  Your firm has an average receipt size of £80. A bank has approached you concerning a new service that will decrease your total collection time by two days. You typically receive 12,000 cheques per day. The daily interest rate is 0.016 per cent. If the bank charges a fee of £190 per day, should the new service be accepted? What would the net annual savings be if the service were adopted?

23  **Using Weighted Average Delay**  A mail-order firm processes 5,000 cheques per month. Of these, 65 per cent are for €50 and 35 per cent are for €70. The €50 cheques are delayed two days on average; the €70 cheques are delayed three days on average.

(a)  What is the average daily collection float? How do you interpret your answer?

(b)  What is the weighted average delay? Use the result to calculate the average daily float.

(c)  How much should the firm be willing to pay to eliminate the float?

(d)  If the interest rate is 7 per cent per year, calculate the daily cost of the float.

(e)  How much should the firm be willing to pay to reduce the weighted average float by 1.5 days?

24  **Value of Lockboxes**  Paper Submarine Manufacturing is investigating a lockbox system to reduce its collection time. It has determined the following:

Average number of payments per day: 400
Average value of payment: £1,400
Variable lockbox fee (per transaction): £0.75
Daily interest rate on money market securities: 0.02%

The total collection time will be reduced by three days if the lockbox system is adopted.

(a)   What is the PV of adopting the system?

(b)   What is the NPV of adopting the system?

(c)   What is the net cash flow per day from adopting? Per cheque?

25   **Collections**   It takes Modular Homes AB about six days to receive and deposit cheques from customers. Modular Homes' management is considering a new system to reduce the firm's collection times. It is expected that the new system will reduce receipt and deposit times to three days total. Average daily collections are NKr140,000, and the required rate of return is 9 per cent per year.

(a)   What is the reduction in outstanding cash balances as a result of implementing the new system?

(b)   What monetary return could be earned on these savings?

(c)   What is the maximum monthly charge Modular Homes should pay for this new system?

26   **Value of Delay**   No More Pencils plc disburses cheques every two weeks that average £70,000 and take seven days to clear. How much interest can the company earn annually if it delays transfer of funds from an interest-bearing account that pays 0.02 per cent per day for these seven days? Ignore the effects of compounding interest.

27   **NPV and Reducing Float**   No More Books SA has an agreement with National Bank whereby the bank handles €8 million in collections a day and requires a €500,000 compensating balance. No More Books is contemplating cancelling the agreement and dividing its Belgian activities so that two other banks will handle its business. Banks A and B will each handle €4 million of collections a day, and each requires a compensating balance of €300,000. No More Books' financial management expects that collections will be accelerated by one day if the Belgian activities are divided between two banks. Should the company proceed with the new system? What will be the annual net savings? Assume that the T-bill rate is 5 per cent annually.

28   **Determining Optimal Cash Balances**   The Tommy Byrne Company is currently holding €700,000 in cash. It projects that over the next year its cash outflows will exceed cash inflows by €360,000 per month. How much of the current cash holding should be retained, and how much should be used to increase the company's holdings of marketable securities? Each time these securities are bought or sold through a broker, the company pays a fee of €500. The annual interest rate on money market securities is 6.5 per cent. After the initial investment of excess cash, how many times during the next 12 months will securities be sold?

29   **Using Miller–Orr**   SlapShot plc has a fixed cost associated with buying and selling marketable securities of £100. The interest rate is currently 0.021 per cent per day, and the firm has estimated that the standard deviation of its daily net cash flows is £75. Management has set a lower limit of £1,100 on cash holdings. Calculate the target cash balance and upper limit using the Miller–Orr model. Describe how the system will work.

30   **Using Miller–Orr**   The variance of the daily cash flows for the Pele Bicycle Shop is €960,000. The opportunity cost to the firm of holding cash is 7 per cent per year. What should be the target cash level and the upper limit if the tolerable lower limit has been established as €150,000? The fixed cost of buying and selling securities is €500 per transaction.

31    **Using Baumol**    All Night Ltd has determined that its target cash balance if it uses the Baumol model is €2,200. The total cash needed for the year is €21,000, and the order cost is €10. What interest rate must All Night be using?

32    **Lockboxes and Collection Time**    Bird's Eye Treehouses Ltd, a Scottish company, has determined that a majority of its customers are located in the Highlands area. It therefore is considering using a lockbox system offered by a bank located in Inverness. The bank has estimated that use of the system will reduce collection time by two days. Based on the following information, should the lockbox system be adopted?

> Average number of payments per day: 600
> Average value of payment: £1,100
> Variable lockbox fee (per transaction): £0.35
> Annual interest rate on money market securities: 6.0%

How would your answer change if there were a fixed charge of £1,000 per year in addition to the variable charge?

**CHALLENGE**

**33 – 35**

33    **Calculating Transactions Required**    Leon Dung SA, a large fertilizer distributor based in the north of Spain, is planning to use a lockbox system to speed up collections from its customers located in the Castille y Leon region. A Vallidolid-area bank will provide this service for an annual fee of €25,000 plus 10 cents per transaction. The estimated reduction in collection and processing time is one day. If the average customer payment in this region is €5,500, how many customers each day, on average, are needed to make the system profitable for Leon Dung? Treasury bills are currently yielding 5 per cent per year.

34    **Baumol Model**    Lisa Tylor, CFO of Purple Rain Co., concluded from the Baumol model that the optimal cash balance for the firm is $10 million. The annual interest rate on marketable securities is 5.8 per cent. The fixed cost of selling securities to replenish cash is $5,000. Purple Rain's cash flow pattern is well approximated by the Baumol model. What can you infer about Purple Rain's average weekly cash disbursement?

35    **Miller–Orr Model**    Gold Star Ltd and Silver Star Ltd both manage their cash flows according to the Miller–Orr model. Gold Star's daily cash flow is controlled between £95,000 and £205,000, whereas Silver Star's daily cash flow is controlled between £120,000 and £230,000. The annual interest rates Gold Star and Silver Star can get are 5.8 per cent and 6.1 per cent, respectively, and the costs per transaction of trading securities are £2,800 and £2,500, respectively.

   (a)    What are their respective target cash balances?

   (b)    Which firm's daily cash flow is more volatile?

**MINI CASE**

# Cash Management at Seglem Ltd

Seglem Ltd was founded 20 years ago by its president, Trygve Seglem. The company originally began as a mail-order company but has grown rapidly in recent years, in large part thanks to its website. Because of the wide geographical dispersion of the company's customers, it currently employs a lockbox system with collection centres in Trondheim, Stavanger, Hammerfest, Molde and Tromsø.

Arne Austreid, the company's treasurer, has been examining the current cash collection policies. On average, each lockbox centre handles NKr130,000 in payments each day. The company's current policy is to invest these payments in short-term marketable securities daily at the collection centre banks. Every two weeks the investment accounts are swept, and the proceeds are wire-transferred to Seglem's headquarters in Oslo to meet the company's payroll. The investment accounts each pay 0.015 per cent per day, and the wire transfers cost 0.15 per cent of the amount transferred.

Arne has been approached by Third National Bank, located just outside Oslo, about the possibility of setting up a concentration banking system for Seglem Ltd. Third National will accept the lockbox centres' daily payments via automated clearing house (ACH) transfers in lieu of wire transfers. The ACH-transferred funds will not be available for use for one day. Once cleared, the funds will be deposited in a short-term account, which will also yield 0.015 per cent per day. Each ACH transfer will cost NKr700. Trygve has asked Arne to determine which cash management system will be the best for the company. Arne has asked you, his assistant, to answer the following questions:

1  What is Seglem's total net cash flow from the current lockbox system available to meet payroll?

2  Under the terms outlined by Third National Bank, should the company proceed with the concentration banking system?

3  What cost of ACH transfers would make the company indifferent between the two systems?

## Additional Reading

The following papers consider the cash management function in firms.

Almeida, H., M. Campello and M.S. Weisbach (2004) 'The cash flow sensitivity of cash', *Journal of Finance*, vol. 59, no. 4, pp. 1777–1804. **US**.

Bates, T.W., K.M. Kahle and R.M. Stulz (2009) 'Why do US firms hold so much more cash than they used to?', *Journal of Finance* (forthcoming). **US**.

Dittmar, A. and J. Mahrt-Smith (2007) 'Corporate governance and the value of cash holdings', *Journal of Financial Economics*, vol. 83, no. 3, pp. 599–634. **US**.

Foley, C.F., J.C. Hartzell, S. Titman and G. Twite (2007) 'Why do firms hold so much cash? A tax based explanation', *Journal of Financial Economics*, vol. 86, no. 4, pp. 579–607. **US**.

Kalcheva, I. and K.V. Lins (2007) 'International evidence on cash holdings and expected managerial agency problems', *Review of Financial Studies*, vol. 20, no. 4, pp. 1087–1112. **International**.

Klasa, S., W.F. Maxwell and H. Ortiz-Molina (2009) 'The strategic use of corporate cash holdings in collective bargaining with labor unions', *Journal of Financial Economics* (forthcoming). **US**.

Pinkowitz, L., R. Stulz and R. Williamson (2007) 'Cash holdings, dividend policy, and corporate governance: a cross-country analysis', *Journal of Applied Corporate Finance*, vol. 19, no. 1, pp. 81–87. **International**.

## Endnotes

1  W.S. Baumol, 'The transactions demand for cash: an inventory theoretic approach', *Quarterly Journal of Economics*, vol. 66 (November 1952).

2  M.H. Miller and D. Orr, 'A model of the demand for money by firms', *Quarterly Journal of Economics* (August 1966).

3  D. Mullins and R. Hamonoff discuss tests of the Miller–Orr model in 'Applications of inventory cash management models', in *Modern Developments in Financial Management*, ed. by S. C. Myers (New York: Praeger, 1976). They show that the model works very well when compared with the actual cash balances of several firms. However, simple rules of thumb do as good a job as the Miller–Orr model.

To help you grasp the key concepts of this chapter check out the extra resources posted on the Online Learning Centre at **www.mcgraw-hill.co.uk/textbooks/hillier**

Among other helpful resources there are PowerPoint presentations, chapter outlines and mini-cases.

# Chapter 28

# Credit Management

In any sale, one of the most important decisions made by the seller is whether to grant credit and, if credit is granted, the terms of the credit sale. As with many other decisions, there is variation from company to company, but credit policies tend to be similar within industries.

One way to examine a company's credit policy is to look at the days' sales in receivables, or the length of time from the sale until the company is paid. In 2009 the receivables period for a typical firm in Europe was about 35 days, or a little over a month. For some firms the period is much shorter. For example, British retailer Sainsbury's was about five days and Tesco's was about nine days. Although both firms have operations in several industries, neither routinely grants credit to its customers, and so these numbers come as no surprise. In contrast, in the pharmaceutical business, credit periods are longer. Sanofi-Aventis, for example, had a credit period of about 65 days in 2007 (see Chapter 26).

In this chapter we examine how a firm sets its credit policy, including when to grant credit and for how long.

## 28.1 Terms of the Sale

The *terms of sale* refer to the period for which credit is granted, the cash discount, and the type of credit instrument. For example, suppose a customer is granted credit with terms of 2/10, net 30. This means that the customer has 30 days from the **invoice** date within which to pay.[1] In addition, a cash discount of 2 per cent from the stated sales price is to be given if payment is made in 10 days. If the stated terms are net 60, the customer has 60 days from the invoice date to pay, and no discount is offered for early payment.

When sales are seasonal, a firm might use seasonal dating. O.M. Scott and Sons is a manufacturer of lawn and garden products with a seasonal dating policy that is tied to the growing season. Payments for winter shipments of fertilizer might be due in the spring or summer. A firm offering 3/10, net 60, 1 May dating, is making the effective invoice date 1 May. The stated amount must be paid on 30 June, regardless of when the sale is made. The cash discount of 3 per cent can be taken until 10 May.

A trade or account receivable is created when credit is granted; a trade or account payable is created when a firm receives credit. These accounts are illustrated in Fig. 28.1. The term 'trade credit' refers to credit granted to other firms.

### Credit Period

**Credit periods** vary between different industries. For example, a jewellery store may sell diamond engagement rings for 5/30, net 4 months. A food wholesaler, selling fresh fruit and produce, might use net 7. Generally, a firm must consider three factors in setting a credit period:

**Figure 28.1** Trade credit

Trade credit extended to a customer by a firm appears as a trade receivable.
Trade credit extended by the firm's supplier to the firm appears as a trade payable.

**Figure 28.2** The cash flows of granting credit

1  *The probability that the customer will not pay*: A firm whose customers are in high-risk businesses may find itself offering restrictive credit terms.

2  *The size of the account*: If the account is small, the credit period will be shorter. Small accounts are more costly to manage, and small customers are less important.

3  *The extent to which the goods are perishable*: If the collateral values of the goods are low and cannot be sustained for long periods, less credit will be granted.

Lengthening the credit period effectively reduces the price paid by the customer. Generally, this increases sales. Figure 28.2 illustrates the cash flows from granting credit.

## Cash Discounts

Cash discounts are often part of the terms of sale. One reason for offering them is to speed up the collection of receivables. The firm must trade this off against the cost of the discount.

---

**EXAMPLE 28.1**

## Credit Policy

Edward Manalt, the chief financial officer of Ruptbank, is considering the request of the company's largest customer, who wants to take a 3 per cent discount for payment within 20 days on a £10,000 purchase. In other words, he intends to pay £9,700 [= £10,000 × (1 − 0.03)]. Normally, this customer pays in 30 days with no discount. The cost of debt capital for Ruptbank is 10 per cent. Edward has worked out the cash flow implications illustrated in Fig. 28.3. He assumes that the time required to cash the cheque when the customer receives it is the same under both credit arrangements. He has calculated the present value of the two proposals:

**Figure 28.3** Cash flows for different credit terms

Current policy:

$$PV = \frac{£10,000}{1 + (0.1 \times 30/365)}$$
$$= £9,918.48$$

Proposed policy:

$$PV = \frac{£9,700}{1 + (0.1 \times 20/365)}$$
$$= £9,647.14$$

His calculation shows that granting the discount would cost Ruptbank £271.34 (= £9,918.48 – £9,647.14) in present value. Consequently, Ruptbank is better off with the current credit arrangement.

In the previous example we implicitly assumed that granting credit had no side effects. However, the decision to grant credit may generate higher sales and involve a different cost structure. The next example illustrates the impact of changes in the level of sales and costs in the credit decision.

## EXAMPLE 28.2 More Credit Policy

Suppose that Ruptbank has variable costs of £0.50 per £1 of sales. If offered a discount of 3 per cent, customers will increase their order size by 10 per cent. This new information is shown in Fig. 28.4. That is, the customer will increase the order size to £11,000 and, with the 3 per cent discount, will remit £10,670 [= £11,000 × (1 – 0.03)] to Ruptbank in 20 days. It will cost more to fill the larger order because variable costs are £5,500. The net present values are worked out here:

Current policy:

$$NPV = -£5,000 + \frac{£10,000}{1 + (0.1 \times 30/365)}$$
$$= £4,918.48$$

**Figure 28.4** Cash flows for different credit terms: the impact of new sales and costs

Proposed policy:

$$\text{NPV} = -£5,500 + \frac{£10,670}{1 + (0.1 \times 20/365)}$$

$$= £5,111.85$$

Now it is clear that the firm is better off with the proposed credit policy. This increase is the net effect of several different factors, including the larger initial costs, the earlier receipt of the cash inflows, the increased sales level, and the discount.

## Credit Instruments

Most credit is offered on *open account*. This means that the only formal credit instrument is the invoice, which is sent with the shipment of goods, and which the customer signs as evidence that the goods have been received. Afterwards, the firm and its customers record the exchange on their accounting books.

At times, the firm may require that the customer sign a *promissory note* or IOU. This is used when the order is large and when the firm anticipates a problem in collections. Promissory notes can eliminate controversies later about the existence of a credit agreement.

One problem with promissory notes is that they are signed after delivery of the goods. One way to obtain a credit commitment from a customer before the goods are delivered is through the use of a *commercial draft*. The selling firm typically writes a commercial draft calling for the customer to pay a specific amount by a specified date. The draft is then sent to the customer's bank with the shipping invoices. The bank has the buyer sign the draft before turning over the invoices. The goods can then be shipped to the buyer. If immediate payment is required, it is called a *sight draft*. Here, funds must be turned over to the bank before the goods are shipped.

Frequently, even a signed draft is not enough for the seller. In this case she might demand that the banker pay for the goods and collect the money from the customer. When the banker agrees to do so in writing, the document is called a *banker's acceptance*. That is, the banker *accepts* responsibility for payment. Because banks generally are well-known and well-respected institutions, the banker's acceptance becomes a liquid instrument. In other words, the seller can then sell (*discount*) the banker's acceptance in the secondary market.

A firm can also use a *conditional sales contract* as a credit instrument. This is an arrangement where the firm retains legal ownership of the goods until the customer has completed payment. Conditional sales contracts are usually paid off in instalments and have interest costs built into them.

## 28.2 The Decision to Grant Credit: Risk and Information

Locust Industries has been in existence for two years. It is one of several successful firms that develop computer programs. The present financial managers have set out two alternative credit strategies: the firm can offer credit, or the firm can refuse credit.

Suppose Locust has determined that if it offers no credit to its customers, it can sell its existing computer software for €50 per program. It estimates that the costs to produce a typical computer program are €20 per program.

The alternative is to offer credit. In this case customers of Locust will pay one period later. With some probability, Locust has determined that if it offers credit, it can charge higher prices and expect higher sales.

**Strategy 1: Refuse Credit**   If Locust refuses to grant credit, cash flows will not be delayed, and period 0 net cash flows, NCF, will be

$$P_0 Q_0 - C_0 Q_0 = \text{NCF}$$

The subscripts denote the time when the cash flows are incurred, where $P_0$ is the price per unit received at time 0, $C_0$ is the cost per unit paid at time 0, and $Q_0$ is the quantity sold at time 0.

The net cash flows at period 1 are zero, and the net present value to Locust of refusing credit will simply be the period 0 net cash flow:

$$\text{NPV} = \text{NCF}$$

For example, if credit is not granted and $Q_0 = 100$, the NPV can be calculated as

$$(\text{€}50 \times 100) - (\text{€}20 \times 100) = \text{€}3{,}000$$

**Strategy 2: Offer Credit**   Alternatively, let us assume that Locust grants credit to all customers for one period. The factors that influence the decision are listed here:

|  | Strategy 1: Refuse credit | Strategy 2: Offer credit |
|---|---|---|
| Price per unit | $P_0 = \text{€}50$ | $P_0' = \text{€}50$ |
| Quantity sold | $Q_0 = 100$ | $Q_0' = 200$ |
| Cost per unit | $C_0 = \text{€}20$ | $C_0' = \text{€}25$ |
| Probability of payment | $h = 1$ | $h = 0.90$ |
| Credit period | 0 | 1 period |
| Discount rate | 0 | $\bar{R}_B = 0.01$ |

The prime (') denotes the variables under the second strategy. If the firm offers credit and the new customers pay, the firm will receive revenues of $P_0' Q_0'$ one period hence, but its costs, $C_0' Q_0'$, are incurred in period 0. If new customers do not pay, the firm incurs costs $C_0' Q_0'$ and receives no revenues. The probability that customers will pay, $h$, is 0.90 in the example. Quantity sold is higher with credit because new customers are attracted. The cost per unit is also higher with credit because of the costs of operating a credit policy.

The expected cash flows for each policy are set out as follows:

|  | Expected Cash Flows | |
|---|---|---|
|  | **Time 0** | **Time 1** |
| Refuse credit | $P_0Q_0 - C_0Q_0$ | 0 |
| Offer credit | $-C_0'Q_0'$ | $h \times P_0'Q_0'$ |

Note that granting credit produces delayed expected cash inflows equal to $h \times P_0'Q_0'$. The costs are incurred immediately and require no discounting. The net present value if credit is offered is

$$\text{NPV(offer)} = \frac{h \times P_0'Q_0'}{1 + R_B} - C_0'Q_0'$$

$$= \frac{0.9 \times \text{€}50 \times 200}{1.01} - \text{€}5{,}000$$

$$= \text{€}3{,}910.89$$

Locust's decision should be to adopt the proposed credit policy. The NPV of granting credit is higher than that of refusing credit. This decision is very sensitive to the probability of payment. If it turns out that the probability of payment is 81 per cent, Locust Software is indifferent to whether it grants credit or not. In this case the NPV of granting credit is €3,000, which we previously found to be the NPV of not granting credit:

$$\text{€}3{,}000 = h \times \frac{\text{€}50 \times 200}{1.01} - \text{€}5{,}000$$

$$\text{€}8{,}000 = h \times \frac{\text{€}50 \times 200}{1.01}$$

$$h = 80.8\%$$

The decision to grant credit depends on four factors:

1   The delayed revenues from granting credit, $P_0'Q_0'$.

2   The immediate costs of granting credit, $C_0'Q_0'$.

3   The probability of payment, $h$.

4   The appropriate required rate of return for delayed cash flows, $R_B$.

## The Value of New Information about Credit Risk

Obtaining a better estimate of the probability that a customer will default can lead to a better decision. How can a firm determine when to acquire new information about the creditworthiness of its customers?

It may be sensible for Locust to determine which of its customers are most likely not to pay. The overall probability of non-payment is 10 per cent. But credit checks by an independent firm show that 90 per cent of Locust's customers (computer stores) have been profitable over the last five years, and that these customers have never defaulted on payments. The less profitable customers are much more likely to default. In fact, 100 per cent of the less profitable customers have defaulted on previous obligations.

Locust would like to avoid offering credit to the deadbeats. Consider its projected number of customers per year of $Q_0' = 200$ if credit is granted. Of these customers, 180 have been profitable over the last five years and have never defaulted on past obligations. The remaining 20 have not been profitable. Locust Software expects that all of these less profitable customers will default. This information is set out here:

| Type of customer | Number | Probability of non-payment (%) | Expected number of defaults |
|---|---|---|---|
| Profitable | 180 | 0 | 0 |
| Less profitable | 20 | 100 | 20 |
| Total customers | 200 | 10 | 20 |

The NPV of granting credit to the customers who default is

$$\frac{hP_0'Q_0'}{1 + R_B} - C_0'Q_0' = \frac{0 \times €50 \times 20}{1.01} - €25 \times 20$$
$$= -€500$$

This is the cost of providing them with the software. If Locust can identify these customers without cost, it would certainly deny them credit.

In fact, it actually costs Locust €3 per customer to figure out whether a customer has been profitable over the last five years. The expected pay-off of the credit check on its 200 customers is then

$$\begin{array}{ccc} \text{Gain from not} & & \text{Cost of} \\ \text{extending credit} & - & \text{credit checks} \\ €500 & - & €3 \times 200 & = -€100 \end{array}$$

For Locust, credit is not worth checking. It would need to pay €600 to avoid a €500 loss.

## Future Sales

Up to this point Locust has not considered the possibility that offering credit will permanently increase the level of sales in future periods (beyond next month). In addition, payment and non-payment patterns in the current period will provide credit information that is useful for the next period. These two factors should be analysed.

In the case of Locust, there is a 90 per cent probability that the customer will pay in period 1. But, if payment is made, there will be another sale in period 2. The probability that the customer will pay in period 2, if the customer has paid in period 1, is 100 per cent. Locust can refuse to offer credit in period 2 to customers that have refused to pay in period 1. This is diagrammed in Fig. 28.5.

**FIGURE 28.5**

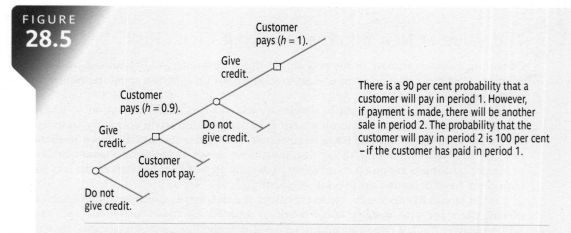

Figure 28.5 Future sales and the credit decision

## 28.3 Optimal Credit Policy

So far, we have discussed how to compute net present value for two alternative credit policies. However, we have not discussed the optimal amount of credit. At the optimal amount of credit, the incremental cash flows from increased sales are exactly equal to the carrying costs from the increase in accounts receivable.

Consider a firm that does not currently grant credit. This firm has no bad debts, no credit department, and relatively few customers. Now consider another firm that grants credit. This firm has lots of customers, a credit department, and a bad debt expense account.

It is useful to think of the decision to grant credit in terms of carrying costs and opportunity costs:

1   *Carrying costs* are the costs associated with granting credit and making an investment in receivables. Carrying costs include the delay in receiving cash, the losses from bad debts, and the costs of managing credit.

2   *Opportunity costs* are the lost sales from refusing to offer credit. These costs drop as credit is granted.

We represent these costs in Fig. 28.6.

The sum of the carrying costs and the opportunity costs of a particular credit policy is called the *total credit cost curve*. A point is identified as the minimum of the total credit cost curve. If the firm extends more credit than the minimum, the additional net cash flow from new customers will not cover the carrying costs of this investment in receivables.

The concept of optimal credit policy in the context of modern principles of finance should be somewhat analogous to the concept of the optimal capital structure discussed earlier in the text. In perfect financial markets there should be no optimal credit policy. Alternative amounts of credit for a firm should not affect the value of the firm. Thus the decision to grant credit would be a matter of indifference to financial managers.

Just as with optimal capital structure, we could expect taxes, monopoly power, bankruptcy costs and agency costs to be important in determining an optimal credit policy in a world of imperfect financial markets. For example, customers in high tax brackets would be better off borrowing and taking advantage of cash discounts offered by firms than would customers in low tax brackets. Corporations in low tax brackets would be less able to offer credit, because borrowing would be relatively more expensive than for firms in high tax brackets.

In general, a firm will extend trade credit if it has a comparative advantage in doing so. Trade credit is likely to be advantageous if the selling firm has a cost advantage over other

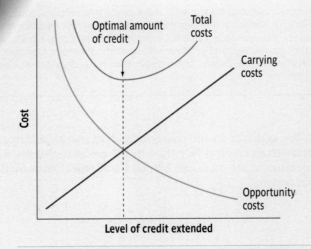

Carrying costs are the costs that must be incurred when credit is granted. They are positively related to the amount of credit extended.

Opportunity costs are the lost sales from refusing credit. These costs drop when credit is granted.

**Figure 28.6** The costs of granting credit

potential lenders, if the selling firm has monopoly power it can exploit, if the selling firm can reduce taxes by extending credit, and if the product quality of the selling firm is difficult to determine. Firm size may be important if there are size economies in managing credit.

---

## The Decision to Grant Credit

**Trade credit is more likely to be granted by the selling firm if**

1. The selling firm has a cost advantage over other lenders.

   *Example:* York Manufacturing Ltd produces widgets. In a default, it is easier for York Manufacturing Ltd to repossess widgets and resell them than for a finance company to arrange for it with no experience in selling widgets.

2. The selling firm can engage in price discrimination.

   *Example:* National Motors can offer below-market interest rates to lower-income customers who must finance a large portion of the purchase price of cars. Higher-income customers pay the list price and do not generally finance a large part of the purchase.

3. The selling firm can obtain favourable tax treatment.

   *Example:* AB Production offers long-term credit to its best customers. This form of financing may qualify as an instalment plan and allow AB Production to book profits of the sale over the life of the loan. This may save taxes, because the present value of the tax payments will be lower if spread over time.

4. The selling firm has no established reputation for quality products or services.

   *Example:* Advanced Micro Instruments (AMI) manufactures sophisticated measurement instruments for controlling electrical systems on commercial airplanes. The firm was founded by two engineering graduates from the University of Amsterdam in 2002. It became a public firm in 2009. To hedge their bets, aircraft manufacturers will ask for credit from AMI. It is very difficult for customers of AMI to assess the quality of its instruments until the instruments have been in place for some time.

5. The selling firm perceives a long-term strategic relationship.

   *Example:* Food.com is a fast-growing, cash-constrained Internet food distributor. It is currently not profitable. Fantastic Food will grant Food.com credit for food purchased because Food.com will generate profits in the future.

*Source*: S.I. Mian and C.W. Smith, 'Extending trade credit and financing receivables', *Journal of Applied Corporate Finance* (Spring 1994); M. Deloof and M. Jegers, 'Trade credit, product quality, and intragroup trade: some European evidence', *Financial Management* (Autumn 1996); M. Long, I.B. Malitz and S.A. Ravid, 'Trade credit, quality guarantees, and product marketability', *Financial Management* (Winter 1993); and M.A. Petersen and R.G. Rajan, 'Trade credit: theories and evidence', *The Review of Financial Studies*, vol. 10 (1997).

---

The optimal credit policy depends on the characteristics of particular firms. Assuming that the firm has more flexibility in its credit policy than in the prices it charges, firms with excess capacity, low variable operating costs, high tax brackets and repeat customers should extend credit more liberally than others.

## 28.4 Credit Analysis

When granting credit, a firm tries to distinguish between customers that will pay and customers that will not pay. There are a number of sources of information for determining creditworthiness.

## Credit Information

Information commonly used to assess creditworthiness includes the following:

- *Financial statements*: A firm can ask a customer to supply financial statements. Rules of thumb based on calculated financial ratios can be used.

- *Credit reports on customer's payment history with other firms*: Many organizations sell information on the credit strength of business firms. Firms such as Experian, Equifax and Dun & Bradstreet provide subscribers with credit reports on individual firms.

- *Banks*: Banks will generally provide some assistance to their business customers in acquiring information on the creditworthiness of other firms.

- *The customer's payment history with the firm*: The most obvious way to obtain an estimate of a customer's probability of non-payment is whether he or she has paid previous bills.

## Credit Scoring

Once information has been gathered, the firm faces the hard choice of either granting or refusing credit. Many firms use the traditional and subjective guidelines referred to as the 'five Cs of credit':

1 *Character*: The customer's willingness to meet credit obligations.

2 *Capacity*: The customer's ability to meet credit obligations out of operating cash flows.

3 *Capital*: The customer's financial reserves.

4 *Collateral*: A pledged asset in the case of default.

5 *Conditions*: General economic conditions.

Conversely, firms such as credit card issuers have developed elaborate statistical models (called **credit scoring** models) for determining the probability of default. Usually, all the relevant and observable characteristics of a large pool of customers are studied to find their historic relation to default. Because these models determine who is and who is not creditworthy, not surprisingly they have been the subject of government regulation. For example, if a statistical model were to find that women default more than men, it might be used to deny women credit. Regulation removes such models from the domain of the statistician and makes them the subject of politicians.

# 28.5 Collection Policy

Collection refers to obtaining payment of past-due accounts. The credit manager keeps a record of payment experiences with each customer.

## Average Collection Period

Paragon Blu-Ray Disc Players sells 100,000 Blu-Ray disc players a year at €300 each. All sales are for credit with terms of 2/20, net 60.

Suppose that 80 per cent of Paragon's customers take the discounts and pay on day 20; the rest pay on day 60. The **average collection period (ACP)** measures the average amount of time required to collect a trade or account receivable. The ACP for Paragon is 28 days:

$$0.8 \times 20 \text{ days} + 0.2 \times 60 \text{ days} = 28 \text{ days}$$

(The average collection period is frequently referred to as *days' sales outstanding* or *days in receivables*.)

Of course, this is an idealized example where customers pay on either one of two dates. In reality, payments arrive in a random fashion, so the average collection period must be calculated differently.

To determine the ACP in the real world, firms first calculate average daily sales. The average daily sales (ADS) equal annual sales divided by 365. The ADS of Paragon are

$$\text{Average daily sales} = \frac{\text{€300} \times 100{,}000}{365 \text{ days}}$$

$$= \text{€82,192}$$

If receivables today are €2,301,376, the average collection period is

$$\text{Average collection period} = \frac{\text{Accounts receivable}}{\text{Average daily sales}}$$

$$= \frac{\text{€2,301,376}}{\text{€82,192}}$$

$$= 28 \text{ days}$$

In practice, firms observe sales and receivables daily. Consequently, an average collection period can be computed and compared with the stated credit terms. For example, suppose Paragon had computed its ACP at 40 days for several weeks, versus its credit terms of 2/20, net 60. With a 40-day ACP, some customers are paying later than usual. Some accounts may be overdue.

However, firms with seasonal sales will often find the *calculated* ACP changing during the year, making the ACP a somewhat flawed tool. This occurs because receivables are low before the selling season and high after the season. Thus firms may keep track of seasonal movement in the ACP over past years. In this way, they can compare the ACP for today's date with the average ACP for that date in previous years. To supplement the information in the ACP, the credit manager may make up an accounts receivable ageing schedule.

## Ageing Schedule

The ageing schedule tabulates receivables by age of account. In the following schedule, 75 per cent of the accounts are on time, but a significant number are more than 60 days past due. This signifies that some customers are in arrears.

| Age of account | Percentage of total value of accounts receivable |
|---|---|
| 0–20 days | 50 |
| 21–60 days | 25 |
| 61–80 days | 20 |
| Over 80 days | 5 |
| | 100 |

The ageing schedule changes during the year. Comparatively, the ACP is a somewhat flawed tool because it gives only the yearly average. Some firms have refined it so that they can examine how it changes with peaks and valleys in their sales. Similarly, the ageing schedule is often augmented by the payments pattern. The *payments pattern* describes the lagged collection pattern of receivables. Like a mortality table that describes the probability that a 23-year-old will live to be 24, the payments pattern describes the probability that a 67-day-old account will still be unpaid when it is 68 days old.

## Collection Effort

The firm usually employs the following procedures for customers that are overdue:

1  Send a delinquency letter informing the customer of the past-due status of the account.

2  Make a telephone call to the customer.

3  Employ a collection agency.

4  Take legal action against the customer.

At times, a firm may refuse to grant additional credit to customers until arrears are paid. This may antagonize a normally good customer, and points to a potential conflict of interest between the collections department and the sales department.

## Factoring

**Factoring** refers to the sale of a firm's trade receivables to a financial institution known as a *factor*. The firm and the factor agree on the basic credit terms for each customer. The customer sends payment directly to the factor, and the factor bears the risk of non-paying customers. The factor buys the receivables at a discount, which usually ranges from 0.35 to 4 per cent of the value of the invoice amount. The average discount throughout the economy is probably about 1 per cent.

One point should be stressed. We have presented the elements of credit policy as though they were somewhat independent of each other. In fact, they are closely interrelated. For example, the optimal credit policy is not independent of collection and monitoring policies. A tighter collection policy can reduce the probability of default, and this in turn can raise the NPV of a more liberal credit policy.

## 28.6 How to Finance Trade Credit

In addition to the unsecured debt instruments described earlier in this chapter, there are three general ways of financing accounting receivables: secured debt, a captive finance company, and securitization.

Use of secured debt is usually referred to as *asset-based receivables financing*. This is the predominant form of receivables financing. Many lenders will not lend without security to firms with substantive uncertainty or little equity. With secured debt, if the borrower gets into financial difficulty, the lender can repossess the asset and sell it for its fair market value.

Many large firms with good credit ratings use *captive finance companies*. The captive finance companies are subsidiaries of the parent firm. This is similar to the use of secured debt, because the creditors of the captive finance company have a claim on its assets and, as a consequence, the accounts receivable of the parent firm. A captive finance company is attractive if economies of scale are important, and if an independent subsidiary with limited liability is warranted.

*Securitization* occurs when the selling firm sells its accounts receivable to a financial institution. The financial institution pools the receivables with other receivables and issues securities to finance items.

## Summary and Conclusions

1  The components of a firm's credit policy are the terms of sale, the credit analysis, and the collection policy.

2  The terms of sale describe the amount and period of time for which credit is granted, and the type of credit instrument.

3  The decision to grant credit is a straightforward NPV decision that can be improved by additional information about customer payment characteristics. Additional information about the customer's probability of defaulting is valuable, but this value must be traded off against the expense of acquiring the information.

4  The optimal amount of credit the firm offers is a function of the competitive conditions in which it finds itself. These conditions will determine the carrying costs associated with granting credit and the opportunity costs of the lost sales from refusing to offer credit. The optimal credit policy minimizes the sum of these two costs.

5   We have seen that knowledge of the probability that customers will default is valuable. To enhance its ability to assess customers' default probability, a firm can score credit. This relates the default probability to observable characteristics of customers.

6   The collection policy is the method of dealing with past-due accounts. The first step is to analyse the average collection period and to prepare an ageing schedule that relates the age of accounts to the proportion of the accounts receivable they represent. The next step is to decide on the collection method and to evaluate the possibility of factoring – that is, selling the overdue accounts.

## connect **Questions and Problems**

**CONCEPT 1 – 5**

1   **Terms of the Sale**   Explain what is meant by the credit terms of a sale. Provide an example of a typical trade credit agreement.

2   **The Decision to Grant Credit**   Review the factors that are commonly considered when deciding to offer credit to a customer.

3   **Optimal Credit Policy**   Is it possible to have an optimal credit policy? In this context, discuss what the total credit curve is, and its impact on a firm's approach to trade credit.

4   **Credit Analysis**   What are the five 'C's of credit? Are there any other factors a firm should consider?

5   **Collection Policy**   How can a firm use an ageing schedule of payments to maximize its total collection of outstanding debtors?

**REGULAR 6 – 35**

6   **Credit Instruments**   Describe each of the following:

(a)   Sight draft.

(b)   Time draft.

(c)   Banker's acceptance.

(d)   Promissory note.

(e)   Trade acceptance.

7   **Trade Credit Forms**   In what form is trade credit most commonly offered? What is the credit instrument in this case?

8   **Receivables Costs**   What are the costs associated with carrying receivables? What are the costs associated with not granting credit? What do we call the sum of the costs for different levels of receivables?

9   **Credit Period Length**   What are some factors that determine the length of the credit period? Why is the length of the buyer's operating cycle often considered an upper bound on the length of the credit period?

10   **Credit Period Length**   In each of the following pairings, indicate which firm would probably have a longer credit period, and explain your reasoning.

(a)   Firm A sells a miracle cure for baldness; firm B sells toupees.

(b)   Firm A specializes in products for landlords; firm B specializes in products for renters.

(c)   Firm A sells to customers with an inventory turnover of 10 times; firm B sells to customers with an inventory turnover of 20 times.

(d)   Firm A sells fresh fruit; firm B sells canned fruit.

(e)   Firm A sells and installs carpeting; firm B sells rugs.

11   **Credit Analysis**   When performing an NPV analysis for the decision to grant credit, what cost of debt should be used?

12   **Granting Credit**   Suppose we have a new customer who will buy from our company if we grant credit. In calculating the default rate, it is likely to be high. Why is this so? How does this compare with the decision to grant credit to a previous, cash-paying customer?

13   **Granting Credit**   Suppose we are considering granting credit to a new customer who will make a one-time purchase. If we compare the default rate from this analysis with the default rate for a customer who will become a repeat customer, which default rate will be higher? Why?

14   **Granting Credit**   What is the relationship between the decision to grant credit and the gross margin of the product?

15   **Cash Discounts**   You place an order for 200 units of inventory at a unit price of £95. The supplier offers terms of 2/10, net 30.

   (a)   How long do you have to pay before the account is overdue? If you take the full period, how much should you remit?

   (b)   What is the discount being offered? How quickly must you pay to get the discount? If you take the discount, how much should you remit?

   (c)   If you don't take the discount, how much interest are you paying implicitly? How many days' credit are you receiving?

16   **Size of Accounts Receivable**   Zidane SA has annual sales of €65 million. The average collection period is 48 days. What is Zidane's average investment in accounts receivable as shown on the balance sheet?

17   **ACP and Accounts Receivable**   Dalglish plc sells earnings forecasts for British securities. Its credit terms are 2/10, net 30. Based on experience, 65 per cent of all customers will take the discount.

   (a)   What is the average collection period for Dalglish?

   (b)   If Dalglish sells 1,200 forecasts every month at a price of £2,200 each, what is its average balance sheet amount in accounts receivable?

18   **Size of Accounts Receivable**   Vitale, Baby! Ltd has weekly credit sales of £18,000, and the average collection period is 29 days. The cost of production is 80 per cent of the selling price. What is Vitale's average accounts receivable figure?

19   **Terms of Sale**   A firm offers terms of 2/9, net 40. What effective annual interest rate does the firm earn when a customer does not take the discount? Without doing any calculations, explain what will happen to this effective rate if:

   (a)   The discount is changed to 3 per cent.

   (b)   The credit period is increased to 60 days.

   (c)   The discount period is increased to 15 days.

20   **ACP and Receivables Turnover**   Muziek Stad NV has an average collection period of 52 days. Its average daily investment in receivables is €46,000. What are annual credit sales? What is the receivables turnover?

21   **Size of Accounts Receivable**   Fragrances Ltd sells 4,000 units of its perfume collection each year at a price per unit of £400. All sales are on credit with terms of 2/15, net 40. The discount is taken by 60 per cent of the customers. What is the amount of the company's accounts receivable? In reaction to sales by its main competitor, Sentiment Spray plc, Fragrances is considering a change in its credit policy to terms of 4/10, net 30 to preserve its market share. How will this change in policy affect accounts receivable?

22   **Size of Accounts Receivable**   Baker Ginger Ltd sells on credit terms of net 25. Its accounts are, on average, nine days past due. If annual credit sales are £8 million, what is the company's balance sheet amount in accounts receivable?

23 **Evaluating Credit Policy** Air Spares is a wholesaler that stocks engine components and test equipment for the commercial aircraft industry. A new customer has placed an order for eight high-bypass turbine engines, which increase fuel economy. The variable cost is €1.5 million per unit, and the credit price is €1.8 million each. Credit is extended for one period, and based on historical experience, payment for about 1 out of every 200 such orders is never collected. The required return is 2.5 per cent per period.

(a) Assuming that this is a one-time order, should it be filled? The customer will not buy if credit is not extended.

(b) What is the break-even probability of default in part (a)?

(c) Suppose that customers who don't default become repeat customers and place the same order every period for ever. Further assume that repeat customers never default. Should the order be filled? What is the break-even probability of default?

(d) Describe in general terms why credit terms will be more liberal when repeat orders are a possibility.

24 **Credit Policy Evaluation** Champions SA is considering a change in its cash-only sales policy. The new terms of sale would be net one month. Based on the following information, determine whether Champions should proceed. Describe the build-up of receivables in this case. The required return is 1.5 per cent per month.

| | Current policy | New policy |
|---|---|---|
| Price per unit (€) | 800 | 800 |
| Cost per unit (€) | 475 | 475 |
| Unit sales per month | 1,130 | 1,195 |

25 **Evaluating Credit Policy** Bruce Jacks plc is in the process of considering a change in its terms of sale. The current policy is cash only; the new policy will involve one period's credit. Sales are 70,000 units per period at a price of £530 per unit. If credit is offered, the new price will be £552. Unit sales are not expected to change, and all customers are expected to take the credit. Bruce Jacks estimates that 2 per cent of credit sales will be uncollectable. If the required return is 2 per cent per period, is the change a good idea?

26 **Credit Policy Evaluation** Clapton Erich GmbH sells 3,000 pairs of running shoes per month at a cash price of €90 per pair. The firm is considering a new policy that involves 30 days' credit and an increase in price to €91.84 per pair on credit sales. The cash price will remain at €90, and the new policy is not expected to affect the quantity sold. The discount period will be 10 days. The required return is 1 per cent per month.

(a) How would the new credit terms be quoted?

(b) What is the investment in receivables required under the new policy?

(c) Explain why the variable cost of manufacturing the shoes is not relevant here.

(d) If the default rate is anticipated to be 10 per cent, should the switch be made? What is the break-even credit price? The break-even cash discount?

27 **Factoring** The factoring department of Inter Scandinavian Bank (ISB) is processing 100,000 invoices per year with an average invoice value of €1,500. ISB buys the accounts receivable at 3.5 per cent off the invoice value. Currently 2.5 per cent of the accounts receivable turns out to be bad debt. The annual operating expense of this department is €400,000. What are the EBIT for the factoring department of ISB?

28 **Factoring Receivables** Your firm has an average collection period of 34 days. Current practice is to factor all receivables immediately at a 2 per cent discount. What is the effective cost of borrowing in this case? Assume that default is extremely unlikely.

29 **Credit Analysis** Silicon Wafers plc (SW) is debating whether to extend credit to a particular customer. SW's products, used primarily in the manufacture of semiconductors, currently sell for £1,850 per unit. The variable cost is £1,200 per unit. The order under consideration is for 12 units today; payment is promised in 30 days.

(a) If there is a 20 per cent chance of default, should SW fill the order? The required return is 2 per cent per month. This is a one-time sale, and the customer will not buy if credit is not extended.

(b) What is the break-even probability in part (a)?

(c) This part is a little harder. In general terms, how do you think your answer to part (a) will be affected if the customer will purchase the merchandise for cash if the credit is refused? The cash price is £1,700 per unit.

30 **Credit Analysis** Consider the following information about two alternative credit strategies:

| | Refuse credit | Grant credit |
|---|---|---|
| Price per unit (£) | 51 | 55 |
| Cost per unit (£) | 29 | 31 |
| Quantity sold per quarter | 3,300 | 3,500 |
| Probability of payment | 1.0 | 0.90 |

The higher cost per unit reflects the expense associated with credit orders, and the higher price per unit reflects the existence of a cash discount. The credit period will be 90 days, and the cost of debt is 0.75 per cent per month.

(a) Based on this information, should credit be granted?

(b) In part (a), what does the credit price per unit have to be to break even?

(c) In part (a), suppose we can obtain a credit report for £2 per customer. Assuming that each customer buys one unit, and that the credit report correctly identifies all customers who will not pay, should credit be extended?

31 **NPV of Credit Policy Switch** Suppose a corporation currently sells $Q$ units per month for a cash-only price of $P$. Under a new credit policy that allows one month's credit, the quantity sold will be $Q'$ and the price per unit will be $P'$. Defaults will be $\pi$ per cent of credit sales. The variable cost is $v$ per unit and is not expected to change. The percentage of customers who will take the credit is $\alpha$, and the required return is $R$ per month. What is the NPV of the decision to switch? Interpret the various parts of your answer.

32 **Credit Policy** Walloon NV operates a mail-order running shoe business. Management is considering dropping its policy of no credit. The credit policy under consideration is this:

| | Current policy | New policy |
|---|---|---|
| Price per unit (€) | 35 | 40 |
| Cost per unit (€) | 25 | 32 |
| Quantity sold | 2,000 | 3,000 |
| Probability of payment (%) | 100 | 85 |
| Credit period | 0 | 1 |

(a) If the interest rate is 3 per cent per period, should the company offer credit to its customers?

(b) What must the probability of payment be before the company would adopt the policy?

33  **Credit Policy**   The Silver Spokes Bicycle Shop has decided to offer credit to its customers during the spring selling season. Sales are expected to be 400 bicycles. The average cost to the shop of a bicycle is £280. The owner knows that only 97 per cent of the customers will be able to make their payments. To identify the remaining 3 per cent, she is considering subscribing to a credit agency. The initial charge for this service is £500, with an additional charge of £4 per individual report. Should she subscribe to the agency?

34  **Credit Policy Evaluation**   Dschungel AG is considering a change in its cash-only policy. The new terms would be net one period. Based on the following information, determine whether Dschungel should proceed. The required return is 3 per cent per period.

| | Current policy | New policy |
|---|---|---|
| Price per unit (€) | 75 | 80 |
| Cost per unit (€) | 43 | 43 |
| Unit sales per month | 3,200 | 3,500 |

35  **Credit Policy Evaluation**   Happiness Systems currently has an all-cash credit policy. It is considering making a change in the credit policy by going to terms of net 30 days. Based on the following information, what do you recommend? The required return is 2 per cent per month.

| | Current policy | New policy |
|---|---|---|
| Price per unit (£) | 340 | 345 |
| Cost per unit (£) | 260 | 265 |
| Unit sales per month | 1,800 | 1,850 |

**CHALLENGE**
**36–39**

36  **Break-Even Quantity**   In Problem 34, what is the break-even quantity for the new credit policy?

37  **Credit Mark-up**   In Problem 34, what is the break-even price per unit that should be charged under the new credit policy? Assume that the sales figure under the new policy is 3,300 units and all other values remain the same.

38  **Credit Mark-up**   In Problem 35, what is the break-even price per unit under the new credit policy? Assume all other values remain the same.

39  **Credit Policy**   Netal Ltd has annual sales of 50 million rand, all of which are on credit. The current collection period is 45 days, and the credit terms are net 30. The company is considering offering terms of 2/10, net 30. It anticipates that 70 per cent of its customers will take advantage of the discount. The new policy will reduce the collection period to 28 days. The appropriate interest rate is 6 per cent. Should the new credit policy be adopted? How does the level of credit sales affect this decision?

**MINI CASE**

# Credit Policy at Schwarzwald AG

Dagmar Bamberger, the president of Schwarzwald AG, has been exploring ways of improving the company's financial performance. Schwarzwald manufactures and sells office equipment to retailers. The company's growth has been relatively slow in recent years, but with an expansion in the economy it appears that sales may increase more quickly in the future. Dagmar has asked Johann Rüstow, the company's treasurer, to examine Schwarzwald's credit policy to see whether a different credit policy can help increase profitability.

The company currently has a policy of net 30. As with any credit sales, default rates are always of concern. Because of Schwarzwald's screening and collection process, the default rate on credit is currently only 1.5 per cent. Johann has examined the company's credit policy in relation to other vendors, and he has determined that three options are available.

The first option is to relax the company's decision on when to grant credit. The second option is to increase the credit period to net 45, and the third option is a combination of the relaxed credit policy and the extension of the credit period to net 45. On the positive side, each of the three policies under consideration would increase sales. The three policies have the drawbacks that default rates would increase, the administrative costs of managing the firm's receivables would increase, and the receivables period would increase. The credit policy change would impact on all four of these variables in different degrees. Johann has prepared the following table outlining the effect on each of these variables:

| | Annual sales (€ millions) | Default rate (% of sales) | Administrative costs (% of sales) | Receivables period (days) |
|---|---|---|---|---|
| Current policy | 120 | 1.5 | 2.1 | 38 |
| Option 1 | 140 | 2.4 | 3.1 | 41 |
| Option 2 | 137 | 1.7 | 2.3 | 51 |
| Option 3 | 150 | 2.1 | 2.9 | 49 |

Schwarzwald's variable costs of production are 45 per cent of sales, and the relevant interest rate is a 6 per cent effective annual rate. Which credit policy should the company use? Also, notice that in option 3 the default rate and administrative costs are below those in option 2. Is this plausible? Why or why not?

## Additional Reading

In the aftermath of the global credit crunch in 2007, the study of trade credit, and credit in general, has taken on much more importance. See below for some relevant reading.

Atanasova, C. (2007) 'Access to institutional finance and the use of trade credit', *Financial Management*, vol. 36, no. 1, pp. 49–67. **UK**.

Cunat, V. (2007) 'Trade credit: suppliers as debt collectors and insurance providers', *Review of Financial Studies*, vol. 20, no. 2, 491–527. **UK**.

Garcia-Teruel, P.J. and P. Martinez-Solano (2009) 'A dynamic approach to accounts receivable: a study of Spanish SMEs', *European Financial Management* (forthcoming). **Spain**.

Love, I., L.A. Preve and V. Sarria-Allende (2007) 'Trade credit and bank credit: evidence from recent financial crises', *Journal of Financial Economics*, vol. 83, no. 2, pp. 453–469. **International**.

Howorth, C. and B. Reber (2003) 'Habitual late payment of trade credit: an empirical examination of UK small firms', *Managerial and Decision Economics*, vol. 24, nos 6/7, pp. 471–482. **UK**.

Sufi, A. (2009) 'Bank lines of credit in corporate finance: an empirical analysis', *Review of Financial Studies*, vol. 22, no. 3, pp. 1057–1088. **UK**.

Wilner, B.S. (2000) 'The exploitation of relationships in financial distress: the case of trade credit', *Journal of Finance*, vol. 55, no. 1, pp. 153–178. **US**.

## Endnote

1  An *invoice* is a bill written by a seller of goods or services and submitted to the buyer. The invoice date is usually the same as the shipping date.

To help you grasp the key concepts of this chapter check out the extra resources posted on the Online Learning Centre at **www.mcgraw-hill.co.uk/textbooks/hillier**

Among other helpful resources there are PowerPoint presentations, chapter outlines and mini-cases.

# Chapter 29

# Mergers and Acquisitions

The 2009 consolidation of two British banks, Halifax Bank of Scotland (HBOS) plc and Lloyds TSB plc, was just one of many corporate restructurings that took place as a result of the major downturn in developed economies. To understand the importance of the HBOS–Lloyds TSB consolidation it is necessary to consider both banks in the context of the larger British banking sector. HBOS was Britain's largest mortgage lender, with a market share of 20 per cent. Lloyds TSB was in a similar position, but slightly smaller, having a market share of 9 per cent. Combining both companies resulted in the largest bank in the UK.

The consolidation also led to the British government owning 43.4 per cent of the shares of the new entity, Lloyds Banking Group plc. This was later increased to 65 per cent because of the disastrous state of HBOS's bad debts. So why did Lloyds TSB merge with HBOS? HBOS was in serious difficulty resulting from significant exposures to short-term funding requirements and bad loan portfolios. Hindsight has shown that Lloyds would have been far better off without the 'toxic assets' they inherited from the consolidation.

The main reason given by both firms for the merger was cost savings, which were estimated to be £1.5 billion per annum. Of course, the cost savings were only an estimate, and often these estimates are incorrect. Unfortunately for the new Lloyds Banking Group, the markets did not respond well, and in the first week of trading the share price collapsed. How do companies like Lloyds and HBOS determine whether an acquisition or merger is a good idea? This chapter explores the reasons why corporate restructurings, such as mergers, should take place – and, just as important, the reasons why they should not.

## 29.1 The Basic Forms of Acquisition

Acquisitions follow one of three basic forms: (a) merger or consolidation; (b) acquisition of shares; and (c) acquisition of assets.

### Merger or Consolidation

A merger refers to the absorption of one firm by another. The acquiring firm retains its name and identity, and it acquires all of the assets and liabilities of the acquired firm. After a merger, the acquired firm ceases to exist as a separate business entity.

A consolidation is the same as a merger except that an entirely new firm is created. In a consolidation both the acquiring firm and the acquired firm terminate their previous legal existence and become part of the new firm.

# Merger Basics

Suppose firm A acquires firm B in a merger. Further, suppose firm B's shareholders are given one share of firm A's equity in exchange for two shares of firm B's equity. From a legal standpoint, firm A's shareholders are not directly affected by the merger. However, firm B's shares cease to exist. In a consolidation, the shareholders of firm A and firm B exchange their shares for shares of a new firm (e.g. firm C).

Because of the similarities between mergers and consolidations, we shall refer to both types of reorganization as mergers. Here are two important points about mergers and consolidations:

1   A merger is legally straightforward, and does not cost as much as other forms of acquisition. It avoids the necessity of transferring title of each individual asset of the acquired firm to the acquiring firm.

2   The shareholders of each firm must approve a merger.[1] Typically, votes of the owners of two-thirds of the shares are required for approval. In addition, shareholders of the acquired firm have *appraisal rights*. This means that they can demand that the acquiring firm purchase their shares at a fair value. Often the acquiring firm and the dissenting shareholders of the acquired firm cannot agree on a fair value, which results in expensive legal proceedings.

## Acquisition of Shares

A second way to acquire another firm is to purchase the firm's voting shares in exchange for cash, or shares of equity and other securities. This process may start as a private offer from the management of one firm to another. At some point the offer is taken directly to the selling firm's shareholders, often by a tender offer. A tender offer is a public offer to buy shares of a target firm. It is made by one firm directly to the shareholders of another firm. The offer is communicated to the target firm's shareholders by public announcements such as newspaper advertisements. Sometimes a general mailing is used in a tender offer. However, a general mailing is difficult, because the names and addresses of the shareholders of record are not usually available.

The following factors are involved in choosing between an acquisition of shares and a merger:

•   In an acquisition of shares, shareholder meetings need not be held and a vote is not required. If the shareholders of the target firm do not like the offer, they are not required to accept it and need not tender their shares.

•   In an acquisition of shares, the bidding firm can deal directly with the shareholders of a target firm via a tender offer. The target firm's management and board of directors are bypassed.

•   Target managers often resist acquisition. In such cases, acquisition of shares circumvents the target firm's management. Resistance by the target firm's management often makes the cost of acquisition by shares higher than the cost by merger.

•   Frequently a minority of shareholders will hold out in a tender offer, and thus the target firm cannot be completely absorbed.

•   Complete absorption of one firm by another requires a merger. Many acquisitions of shares end with a formal merger.

## Acquisition of Assets

One firm can acquire another by buying all of its assets. The selling firm does not necessarily vanish, because its 'shell' can be retained. A formal vote of the target shareholders is required in an acquisition of assets. An advantage here is that although the acquirer is often left with minority shareholders in an acquisition of shares, this does not happen in an acquisition of

**Figure 29.1** Varieties of takeover

assets. Minority shareholders often present problems, such as holdouts. However, asset acquisition involves transferring title to individual assets, which can be costly.

## A Classification Scheme

Financial analysts have typically classified acquisitions into three types:

1   *Horizontal acquisition*: Here, both the acquirer and acquired are in the same industry. Lloyds TSB's merger with HBOS in 2009 is an example of a horizontal merger in the banking industry.

2   *Vertical acquisition*: A vertical acquisition involves firms at different steps of the production process. The acquisition by an airline company of a travel agency would be a vertical acquisition.

3   *Conglomerate acquisition*: The acquiring firm and the acquired firm are not related to each other. The acquisition of a food products firm by a computer firm would be considered a conglomerate acquisition.

## A Note about Takeovers

*Takeover* is a general and imprecise term referring to the transfer of control of a firm from one group of shareholders to another.[2] A firm that has decided to take over another firm is usually referred to as the **bidder**. The bidder offers to pay cash or securities to obtain the equity or assets of another company. If the offer is accepted, the **target** firm will give up control over its equity or assets to the bidder in exchange for *consideration* (i.e. its equity, its debt, or cash).

Takeovers can occur by acquisition, proxy contests, and going-private transactions. Thus takeovers encompass a broader set of activities than acquisitions, as depicted in Fig. 29.1.

If a takeover is achieved by acquisition, it will be by merger, tender offer for shares of equity, or purchase of assets. In mergers and tender offers the acquiring firm buys the voting ordinary shares of the acquired firm.

*Proxy contests* can result in takeovers as well. Proxy contests occur when a group of shareholders attempts to gain seats on the board of directors. A *proxy* is written authorization for one shareholder to vote for another shareholder. In a proxy contest an insurgent group of shareholders solicits proxies from other shareholders.

In *going-private transactions* a small group of investors purchases all the equity shares of a public firm. The group usually includes members of incumbent management and some outside investors. The shares of the firm are delisted from the stock exchange, and can no longer be purchased in the open market.

## 29.2  Synergy

The previous section discussed the basic forms of acquisition. We now examine why firms are acquired. (Although the previous section pointed out that acquisitions and mergers have different definitions, these differences will be unimportant in this, and many of the following, sections. Thus, unless otherwise stated, we shall refer to acquisitions and mergers synonymously.)

Much of our thinking here can be organized around the following four questions:

1   Is there a rational reason for mergers? Yes – in a word, *synergy*.

Suppose firm A is contemplating acquiring firm B. The value of firm A is $V_A$ and the value of firm B is $V_B$. (It is reasonable to assume that, for public companies, $V_A$ and $V_B$ can be determined by observing the market prices of the outstanding securities.) The difference between the value of the combined firm ($V_{AB}$) and the sum of the values of the firms as separate entities is the synergy from the acquisition:

$$\text{Synergy} = V_{AB} - (V_A + V_B)$$

In words, synergy occurs if the value of the combined firm after the merger is greater than the sum of the value of the acquiring firm and the value of the acquired firm before the merger.

2   Where does this magic force, synergy, come from?

Increases in cash flow create value. We define $\Delta CF_t$ as the difference between the cash flows at date $t$ of the combined firm and the sum of the cash flows of the two separate firms. From the chapters about capital budgeting, we know that the cash flow in any period $t$ can be written as

$$\Delta CF_t = \Delta Rev_t - \Delta Costs_t - \Delta Taxes_t - \Delta Capital\ Requirements_t$$

where $\Delta Rev_t$ is the incremental revenue of the acquisition, $\Delta Costs_t$ is the incremental costs of the acquisition, $\Delta Taxes_t$ is the incremental acquisition taxes, and $\Delta Capital\ Requirements_t$ is the incremental new investment required in working capital and fixed assets.

It follows from our classification of incremental cash flows that the possible sources of synergy fall into four basic categories: revenue enhancement, cost reduction, lower taxes, and lower capital requirements. Improvements in at least one of these four categories create synergy. Each of these categories will be discussed in detail in the next section.

In addition, reasons are often provided for mergers where improvements are not expected in any of these four categories. These 'bad' reasons for mergers will be discussed in Section 29.4.

3   How are these synergistic gains shared? In general, the acquiring firm pays a premium for the acquired, or target, firm. For example, if the equity of the target is selling for €50, the acquirer might need to pay €60 a share, implying a premium of €10 or 20 per cent. The gain to the target in this example is €10. Suppose that the synergy from the merger is €30. The gain to the acquiring firm, or bidder, would be €20 (= €30 − €10). The bidder would actually lose if the synergy were less than the premium of €10. A more detailed treatment of these gains or losses will be provided in Section 29.6.

4   Are there other motives for a merger besides synergy? Yes.

As we have said, synergy is a source of benefit to shareholders. However, the *managers* are likely to view a potential merger differently. Even if the synergy from the merger is less than the premium paid to the target, the managers of the acquiring firm may still benefit. For example, the revenues of the combined firm after the merger will almost certainly be greater than the revenues of the bidder before the merger. The managers may receive higher compensation once they are managing a larger firm. Even beyond the increase in compensation, managers generally experience greater prestige and power when managing a larger firm. Conversely, the managers of the target could lose their jobs after the acquisition, and they might very well oppose the takeover even if their shareholders would benefit from the premium. These issues will be discussed in more detail in Section 29.9.

# 29.3 Sources of Synergy

In this section, we discuss sources of synergy.

## Revenue Enhancement

A combined firm may generate greater revenues than two separate firms. Increased revenues can come from marketing gains, strategic benefits, or market power.

**Marketing Gains** It is frequently claimed that, because of improved marketing, mergers and acquisitions can increase operating revenues. Improvements can be made in the following areas:

- Previously ineffective media programming and advertising efforts

- A weak existing distribution network

- An unbalanced product mix

**Strategic Benefits** Some acquisitions promise a *strategic* benefit, which is more like an option than a standard investment opportunity. For example, imagine that a sewing machine company acquires a computer company. The firm will be well positioned if technological advances allow computer-driven sewing machines in the future.

Michael Porter has used the word *beachhead* to denote the strategic benefits from entering a new industry.[3] He uses the example of Procter & Gamble's acquisition of the Charmin Paper Company as a beachhead that allowed Procter & Gamble to develop a highly interrelated cluster of paper products – disposable nappies, paper towels, feminine hygiene products, and bathroom tissue.

**Market or Monopoly Power** One firm may acquire another to reduce competition. If so, prices can be increased, generating monopoly profits. However, mergers that reduce competition do not benefit society, and the government regulators may challenge them.

## Cost Reduction

A combined firm may operate more efficiently than two separate firms. This was the primary reason for the Lloyds TSB–HBOS merger. A merger can increase operating efficiency in the following ways.

**Economies of Scale** An economy of scale means that the average cost of production falls as the level of production increases. Figure 29.2 illustrates the relation between cost per unit and size for a typical firm. As can be seen, average cost first falls and then rises. In other words, the firm experiences economies of scale until optimal firm size is reached. Diseconomies of scale arise after that.

Though the precise nature of economies of scale is not known, it is one obvious benefit of horizontal mergers. The phrase *spreading overhead* is frequently used in connection with economies of scale. This refers to sharing central facilities such as corporate headquarters, top management, and computer systems.

**Economies of Vertical Integration** Operating economies can be gained from vertical combinations as well as from horizontal combinations. The main purpose of vertical acquisitions is to make co-ordination of closely related operating activities easier. This is probably why most forest product firms that cut timber also own sawmills and hauling equipment. Because petroleum is used to make plastics and other chemical products, the DuPont–Conoco merger was motivated by DuPont's need for a steady supply of oil. Economies from vertical integration probably explain why most airline companies own airplanes. They may also explain why some airline companies have purchased hotels and car rental companies.

**Technology Transfer** Technology transfer is another reason for merger. An automobile manufacturer might well acquire an aircraft company if aerospace technology can improve

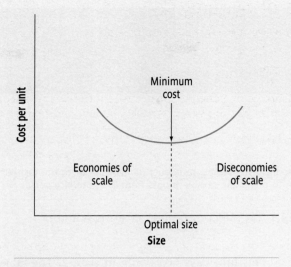

**Figure 29.2** Economies of scale and the optimal size of the firm

automotive quality. This technology transfer was the motivation behind the merger of General Motors and Hughes Aircraft.

**Complementary Resources**   Some firms acquire others to improve usage of existing resources. A ski equipment store merging with a tennis equipment store will smooth sales over both the winter and summer seasons, thereby making better use of store capacity.

**Elimination of Inefficient Management**   A change in management can often increase firm value. Some managers overspend on perquisites and pet projects, making them ripe for take-over. Alternatively, incumbent managers may not understand changing market conditions or new technology, making it difficult for them to abandon old strategies. Although the board of directors should replace these managers, the board is often unable to act independently. Thus a merger may be needed to make the necessary replacements.

Mergers and acquisitions can be viewed as part of the labour market for top management. Michael Jensen and Richard Ruback have used the phrase 'market for corporate control', in which alternative management teams compete for the rights to manage corporate activities.[4]

## Tax Gains

Tax reduction may be a powerful incentive for some acquisitions. This reduction can come from:

- The use of tax losses
- The use of unused debt capacity
- The use of surplus funds

**Net Operating Losses**   A firm with a profitable division and an unprofitable one will have a low tax bill, because the loss in one division offsets the income in the other. However, if the two divisions are actually separate companies, the profitable firm will not be able to use the losses of the unprofitable one to offset its income. Thus, in the right circumstances, a merger can lower taxes.

Consider Table 29.1, which shows pre-tax income, taxes and after-tax income for firms A and B. Firm A earns €200 in state 1 but loses money in state 2. The firm pays taxes in state 1 but is not entitled to a tax rebate in state 2. Conversely, firm B turns a profit in state 2 but

TABLE
29.1

| | Before merger | | | | After merger | |
|---|---|---|---|---|---|---|
| | **Firm A** | | **Firm B** | | **Firm AB** | |
| | If state 1 | If state 2 | If state 1 | If state 2 | If state 1 | If state 2 |
| Taxable income (€) | 200 | −100 | −100 | 200 | 100 | 100 |
| Taxes (€) | 68 | 0 | 0 | 68 | 34 | 34 |
| Net income (€) | 132 | −100 | −100 | 132 | 66 | 66 |

Neither firm will be able to deduct its losses prior to the merger. The merger allows the losses from A to offset the taxable profits from B – and vice versa.

**Table 29.1** Tax effect of merger of firms A and B

not in state 1. This firm pays taxes only in state 2. The table shows that the combined tax bill of the two separate firms is always €68, regardless of which state occurs.

However, the last two columns of the table show that, after a merger, the combined firm will pay taxes of only €34. Taxes drop after the merger, because a loss in one division offsets the gain in the other.

The message of this example is that firms need taxable profits to take advantage of potential losses. These losses are often referred to as *net operating losses* or *NOL* for short. Mergers can sometimes bring losses and profits together. However, there are two qualifications to the previous example:

1    Many countries' tax laws permit firms that experience alternating periods of profits and losses to equalize their taxes by carry-back and carry-forward provisions. For example, a firm that has been profitable but has a loss in the current year may be able to get refunds of income taxes paid in *three previous years* and can carry the loss *forward for 15 years*. Thus a merger to exploit unused tax shields must offer tax savings over and above what can be accomplished by firms via carry-overs.[5]

2    Tax authorities in many countries are likely to disallow an acquisition if its principal purpose is to avoid the payment of taxes.

**Debt Capacity**    There are at least two cases where mergers allow for increased debt and a larger tax shield. In the first case the target has too little debt, and the acquirer can infuse the target with the missing debt. In the second case both target and acquirer have optimal debt levels. A merger leads to risk reduction, generating greater debt capacity and a larger tax shield. We treat each case in turn.

**Case 1: Unused Debt Capacity**    In Chapter 16 we pointed out that every firm has a certain amount of debt capacity. This debt capacity is beneficial, because greater debt leads to a greater tax shield. More formally, every firm can borrow a certain amount before the marginal costs of financial distress equal the marginal tax shield. This debt capacity is a function of many factors, perhaps the most important being the risk of the firm. Firms with high risk generally cannot borrow as much as firms with low risk. For example, a utility or a supermarket – both firms with low risk – can have a higher debt-to-value ratio than can a technology firm.

Some firms, for whatever reason, have less debt than is optimal. Perhaps the managers are risk-averse, or perhaps they simply don't know how to assess debt capacity properly. Is it bad for a firm to have too little debt? The answer is yes. As we have said, the optimal level of debt occurs when the marginal cost of financial distress equals the marginal tax shield. Too little debt reduces firm value.

This is where mergers come in. A firm with little or no debt is an inviting target. An acquirer could raise the target's debt level after the merger to create a bigger tax shield.

**Case 2: Increased Debt Capacity**    Let us move back to the principles of modern portfolio theory, as presented in Chapter 10. Consider two equities in different industries, where both equities have the same risk or standard deviation. A portfolio of these two equities has lower risk than that of either equity separately. In other words, the two-equity portfolio is somewhat diversified, whereas each equity by itself is completely undiversified.[6]

Now, rather than considering an individual buying both equities, consider a merger between the two underlying firms. Because the risk of the combined firm is less than that of either one separately, banks should be willing to lend more money to the combined firm than the total of what they would lend to the two firms separately. In other words, the risk reduction that the merger generates leads to greater debt capacity.

For example, imagine that each firm can borrow £100 on its own before the merger. Perhaps the combined firm after the merger will be able to borrow £250. Debt capacity has increased by £50 (= £250 − £200).

Remember that debt generates a tax shield. If debt rises after the merger, taxes will fall. That is, simply because of the greater interest payments after the merger, the tax bill of the combined firm should be less than the sum of the tax bills of the two separate firms before the merger. In other words, the increased debt capacity from a merger can reduce taxes.

To summarize, we first considered the case where the target had too little leverage. The acquirer could infuse the target with more debt, generating a greater tax shield. Next, we considered the case where both target and acquirer began with optimal debt levels. A merger leads to more debt even here. That is, the risk reduction from the merger creates greater debt capacity and thus a greater tax shield.

**Surplus Funds**    Another quirk in the tax laws involves surplus funds. Consider a firm that has *free cash flow*. That is, it has cash flow available after payment of all taxes, and after all positive net present value projects have been funded. In this situation, aside from purchasing securities, the firm can either pay dividends or buy back shares.

We have already seen in our previous discussion of dividend policy that an extra dividend will increase the income tax paid by some investors. Investors pay lower taxes in a share repurchase.[7] However, a share repurchase is not normally a legal option if the sole purpose is to avoid taxes on dividends.

Instead, the firm might make acquisitions with its excess funds. Here, the shareholders of the acquiring firm avoid the taxes they would have paid on a dividend.[8]

## Reduced Capital Requirements

Earlier in this chapter we stated that, owing to economies of scale, mergers can reduce operating costs. It follows that mergers can reduce capital requirements as well. Accountants typically divide capital into two components: fixed capital and working capital.

When two firms merge, the managers will probably find duplicate facilities. For example, if both firms had their own headquarters, all executives in the merged firm could be moved to one headquarters building, allowing the other headquarters to be sold. Some plants might be redundant as well. Or two merging firms in the same industry might consolidate their research and development, permitting some R&D facilities to be sold.

The same goes for working capital. The inventory-to-sales ratio and the cash-to-sales ratio often decrease as firm size increases. A merger permits these economies of scale to be realized, allowing a reduction in working capital.

## 29.4    Two 'Bad' Reasons for Mergers

### Earnings Growth

An acquisition can create the appearance of earnings growth, perhaps fooling investors into thinking that the firm is worth more than it really is. Let's consider two companies, Global Resources and Regional Enterprises, as depicted in the first two columns of Table 29.2. As can

TABLE
**29.2**

| | Global Resources before merger | Regional Enterprises before merger | Global Resources after merger | |
| --- | --- | --- | --- | --- |
| | | | The market is 'smart' | The market is 'fooled' |
| Earnings per share (€) | 1.00 | 1.00 | 1.43 | 1.43 |
| Price per share (€) | 25.00 | 10.00 | 25.00 | 35.71 |
| Price–earnings ratio | 25 | 10 | 17.5 | 25 |
| Number of shares | 100 | 100 | 140 | 140 |
| Total earnings (€) | 100 | 100 | 200 | 200 |
| Total value (€) | 2,500 | 1,000 | 3,500 | 5,000 |

Exchange ratio: 1 share in Global for 2.5 shares in Regional.

**Table 29.2** Financial positions of Global Resources and Regional Enterprises

be seen, earnings per share are €1 for both companies. However, Global sells for €25 per share, implying a price–earnings (P/E) ratio of 25 (= 25/1). By contrast, Regional sells for €10, implying a P/E ratio of 10. This means that an investor in Global pays €25 to get €1 in earnings, whereas an investor in Regional receives the same €1 in earnings on only a €10 investment. Are investors getting a better deal with Regional? Not necessarily. Perhaps Global's earnings are expected to grow faster than Regional's earnings. If this is the case, an investor in Global will expect to receive high earnings in later years, making up for low earnings in the short term. In fact, Chapter 5 argues that the primary determinant of a firm's P/E ratio is the market's expectation of the firm's growth rate in earnings.

Now let's imagine that Global acquires Regional, with the merger creating no value. If the market is smart, it will realize that the combined firm is worth the sum of the values of the separate firms. In this case, the market value of the combined firm will be €3,500, which is equal to the sum of the values of the separate firms before the merger.

At these values Global will acquire Regional by exchanging 40 of its shares for 100 shares of Regional, so that Global will have 140 shares outstanding after the merger.[9] Global's share price remains at €25 (= €3,500/140). With 140 shares outstanding and €200 of earnings after the merger, Global earns €1.43 (= €200/140) per share after the merger. Its P/E ratio becomes 17.5 (= 25/1.43), a drop from 25 before the merger. This scenario is represented by the third column of Table 29.2. Why has the P/E dropped? The combined firm's P/E will be an average of Global's high P/E and Regional's low P/E before the merger. This is common sense once you think about it. Global's P/E should drop when it takes on a new division with low growth.

Let us now consider the possibility that the market is fooled. As we just said, the acquisition enables Global to increase its earnings per share from €1 to €1.43. If the market is fooled, it might mistake the 43 per cent increase in earnings per share for true growth. In this case, the price–earnings ratio of Global may not fall after the merger. Suppose the price–earnings ratio of Global remains at 25. The total value of the combined firm will increase to €5,000 (= 25 × €200), and the share price of Global will increase to €35.71 (= €5,000/140). This is reflected in the last column of the table.

This is earnings growth magic. Can we expect this magic to work in the real world? Managers of a previous generation certainly thought so, with firms such as LTV Industries, ITT and Litton Industries all trying to play the P/E-multiple game in the 1960s. However, in hindsight it looks as if they played the game without much success. These operators have all dropped out, with few, if any, replacements. It appears that the market is too smart to be fooled this easily.

## Diversification

Diversification is often mentioned as a benefit of one firm acquiring another. However, we argue that diversification, by itself, cannot produce increases in value. To see this, recall that a business's variability of return can be separated into two parts: (a) what is specific to the business, and called *unsystematic*; and (2) what is *systematic*, because it is common to all businesses.

Systematic variability cannot be eliminated by diversification, so mergers will not eliminate this risk at all. By contrast, unsystematic risk can be diversified away through mergers. However, the investor does not need widely diversified companies such as Unilever to eliminate unsystematic risk. Shareholders can diversify more easily than corporations by simply purchasing equity in different corporations. For example, instead of Air France and KLM merging to form Air France-KLM, the shareholders of Air France could have purchased shares in KLM if they believed there would be diversification gains in doing so. Thus diversification through merger may not benefit shareholders.[10]

Diversification can produce gains to the acquiring firm only if one of two things is true:

1   Diversification decreases the unsystematic variability at a lower cost than by investors' adjustments to personal portfolios. This seems very unlikely.

2   Diversification reduces risk and thereby increases debt capacity. This possibility was mentioned earlier in the chapter.

## 29.5  A Cost to Shareholders from Reduction in Risk

In Chapter 22 we used option pricing theory to show that pure financial mergers are bad for shareholders. In this section we shall revisit this idea from an alternative perspective and show that the diversification effects of mergers can benefit bondholders at the expense of shareholders.

### The Base Case

Consider an example where firm A acquires firm B. Panel I of Table 29.3 shows the net present values of firm A and firm B prior to the merger in the two possible states of the economy. Because the probability of each state is 0.50, the market value of each firm is the average of its values in the two states. For example, the market value of firm A is

$$0.5 \times £80 + 0.5 \times £20 = £50$$

Now imagine that the merger of the two firms generates no synergy. The combined firm AB will have a market value of £75 (= £50 + £25), the sum of the values of firm A and firm B. Further imagine that the shareholders of firm B receive equity in AB equal to firm B's stand-alone market value of £25. In other words, firm B receives no premium. Because the value of AB is £75, the shareholders of firm A have a value of £50 (= £75 − £25) after the merger − just what they had before the merger. Thus the shareholders of both firms A and B are indifferent to the merger.

### Both Firms Have Debt

Alternatively, imagine that firm A has debt with a face value of £30 in its capital structure, as shown in Panel II of Table 29.3. Without a merger, firm A will default on its debt in state 2, because the value of firm A in this state is £20, less than the face value of the debt of £30. As a consequence, firm A cannot pay the full value of the debt claim: the bondholders receive only £20 in this state. The creditors take the possibility of default into account, valuing the debt at £25 (= 0.5 × £30 + 0.5 × £20).

Firm B's debt has a face value of £15. Firm B will default in state 1 because the value of the firm in this state is £10, less than the face value of the debt of £15. The value of firm B's debt is £12.50 (= 0.5 × £10 + 0.5 × £15). It follows that the sum of the value of firm A's debt and the value of firm B's debt is £37.50 (= £25 + £12.50).

TABLE
**29.3**

| | NPV | | |
|---|---|---|---|
| | State 1 | State 2 | Market value |
| Probability | 0.5 | 0.5 | |
| **I. Base case (no debt in either firm's capital structure)** | | | |
| Values before merger (£): | | | |
| Firm A | 80 | 20 | 50 |
| Firm B | 10 | 40 | 25 |
| Values after merger (£):* | | | |
| Firm AB | 90 | 60 | 75 |
| **II. Debt with face value of £30 in firm A's capital structure; debt with face value of £15 in firm B's capital structure** | | | |
| Values before merger (£): | | | |
| Firm A | 80 | 20 | 50 |
| Debt | 30 | 20 | 25 |
| Equity | 50 | 0 | 25 |
| Firm B | 10 | 40 | 25 |
| Debt | 10 | 15 | 12.50 |
| Equity | 0 | 25 | 12.50 |
| Values after merger (£):† | | | |
| Firm AB | 90 | 60 | 75 |
| Debt | 45 | 45 | 45 |
| Equity | 45 | 15 | 30 |

Values of both firm A's debt and firm B's debt rise after merger. Values of both firm A's equity and firm B's equity fall after merger.
*Shareholders in firm A receive £50 of equity in firm AB. Shareholders in firm B receive £25 of equity in firm AB. Thus shareholders in both firms are indifferent to the merger.
†Shareholders in firm A receive equity in firm AB worth £20. Shareholders in firm B receive equity in firm AB worth £10. Gains and losses from merger are

    Loss to equity-holders in firm A: £20 − £25 = −£5
    Loss to equity-holders in firm B: £10 − £12.50 = −£2.50
    Combined gain to bondholders in both firms: £45.00 − £37.50 = £7.50

**Table 29.3** Equity-swap mergers

Now let's see what happens after the merger. Firm AB is worth £90 in state 1 and £60 in state 2, implying a market value of £75 (= 0.5 × £90 + 0.5 × £60). The face value of the debt in the combined firm is £45 (= £30 + £15). Because the value of the firm is greater than £45 in either state, the bondholders always get paid in full. Thus the value of the debt is its face value of £45. This value is £7.50 greater than the sum of the values of the two debts before the merger, which we just found to be £37.50. Therefore the merger benefits the bondholders.

What about the shareholders? Because the equity of firm A was worth £25 and the equity of firm B was worth £12.50 before the merger, let's assume that firm AB issues two shares to firm A's shareholders for every share issued to firm B's shareholders. Firm AB's equity is £30, so firm A's shareholders get shares worth £20 and firm B's shareholders get shares worth £10. Firm A's shareholders lose £5 (= £20 − £25) from the merger. Similarly, firm B's shareholders lose £2.50 (= £10 − £12.50). The total loss to the shareholders of both firms is £7.50, exactly the gain to the bondholders from the merger.

There are a lot of numbers in this example. The point is that the bondholders gain £7.50 and the shareholders lose £7.50 from the merger. Why does this transfer of value occur? To see what is going on, notice that when the two firms are separate, firm B does not guarantee firm A's debt. That is, if firm A defaults on its debt, firm B does not help the bondholders of firm A. However, after the merger the bondholders can draw on the cash flows from both A and B. When one of the divisions of the combined firm fails, creditors can be paid from the profits of the other division. This mutual guarantee, which is called the *co-insurance effect*, makes the debt less risky and more valuable than before.

There is no net benefit to the firm as a whole. The bondholders gain the co-insurance effect, and the shareholders lose the co-insurance effect. Some general conclusions emerge from the preceding analysis:

1  Mergers usually help bondholders. The size of the gain to bondholders depends on the reduction in the probability of bankruptcy after the combination. That is, the less risky the combined firm is, the greater are the gains to bondholders.

2  Shareholders of the acquiring firm are hurt by the amount that bondholders gain.

3  Conclusion 2 applies to mergers without synergy. In practice, much depends on the size of the synergy.

## How Can Shareholders Reduce their Losses from the Co-Insurance Effect?

The co-insurance effect raises bondholder values and lowers shareholder values. However, there are at least two ways in which shareholders can reduce or eliminate the co-insurance effect. First, the shareholders in firm A could retire its debt *before* the merger announcement date and reissue an equal amount of debt after the merger. Because debt is retired at the low pre-merger price, this type of refinancing transaction can neutralize the co-insurance effect to the bondholders.

Also, note that the debt capacity of the combined firm is likely to increase, because the acquisition reduces the probability of financial distress. Thus the shareholders' second alternative is simply to issue more debt after the merger. An increase in debt following the merger will have two effects, even without the prior action of debt retirement. The interest tax shield from new corporate debt raises firm value, as discussed in an earlier section of this chapter. In addition, an increase in debt after the merger raises the probability of financial distress, thereby reducing or eliminating the bondholders' gain from the co-insurance effect.

## 29.6  The NPV of a Merger

Firms typically use NPV analysis when making acquisitions. The analysis is relatively straightforward when the consideration is cash. The analysis becomes more complex when the consideration is equity.

### Cash

Suppose firm A and firm B have values as separate entities of £500 and £100, respectively. They are both all-equity firms. If firm A acquires firm B, the merged firm AB will have a combined value of £700 due to synergies of £100. The board of firm B has indicated that it will sell firm B if it is offered £150 in cash.

Should firm A acquire firm B? Assuming that firm A finances the acquisition out of its own retained earnings, its value after the acquisition is[11]

$$\text{Value of firm A after the acquisition} = \text{Value of combined firm} - \text{Cash paid}$$
$$= £700 - £150$$
$$= £550$$

Because firm A was worth £500 prior to the acquisition, the NPV to firm A's equity-holders is

$$£50 = £550 - £500 \tag{29.1}$$

TABLE
**29.4**

| | Before acquisition | | | After acquisition: firm A | |
| | (1) | (2) | (3) | (4) | (5) |
|---|---|---|---|---|---|
| | | | | Equity† exchange ratio (0.75:1) | Equity† exchange ratio (0.6819:1) |
| | Firm A | Firm B | Cash* | | |
| Market value ($V_A$, $V_B$) (£) | 500 | 100 | 550 | 700 | 700 |
| Number of shares | 25 | 10 | 25 | 32.5 | 31.819 |
| Price per share (£) | 20 | 10 | 22 | 21.54 | 22 |

*Value of firm A after acquisition: cash
$$V_A = V_{AB} - \text{Cash}$$
$$£550 = £700 - £150$$
†Value of firm A after acquisition: equity
$$V_A = V_{AB}$$
$$£700 = £700$$

**Table 29.4** Cost of acquisition: cash versus equity

Assuming that there are 25 shares in firm A, each share of the firm is worth £20 (= £500/25) prior to the merger and £22 (= £550/25) after the merger. These calculations are displayed in the first and third columns of Table 29.4. Looking at the rise in equity price, we conclude that firm A should make the acquisition.

We spoke earlier of both the synergy and the premium of a merger. We can also value the NPV of a merger to the acquirer:

$$\text{NPV of a merger to acquirer} = \text{Synergy} - \text{Premium}$$

Because the value of the combined firm is £700 and the pre-merger values of A and B were £500 and £100, respectively, the synergy is £100 [= £700 − (£500 + £100)]. The premium is £50 (= £150 − £100). Thus the NPV of the merger to the acquirer is

$$\text{NPV of merger to firm A} = £100 - £50 = £50$$

One caveat is in order. This textbook has consistently argued that the market value of a firm is the best estimate of its true value. However, we must adjust our analysis when discussing mergers. If the true price of firm A *without the merger* is £500, the market value of firm A may actually be above £500 when merger negotiations take place. This happens because the market price reflects the possibility that the merger will occur. For example, if the probability is 60 per cent that the merger will take place, the market price of firm A will be

| | Market value of firm A with merger | Probability of merger | | Market value of firm A without merger | Probability of no merger |
|---|---|---|---|---|---|
| £530 = | £550 | × 0.60 | + | £500 | × 0.40 |

The managers would underestimate the NPV from the merger in Eq. (29.1) if the market price of firm A is used. Thus managers face the difficult task of valuing their own firm without the acquisition.

## Equity

Of course, firm A could purchase firm B with equity instead of cash. Unfortunately, the analysis is not as straightforward here. To handle this scenario we need to know how many shares are outstanding in firm B. We assume that there are 10 shares outstanding, as indicated in column 2 of Table 29.4.

Suppose firm A exchanges 7.5 of its shares for the entire 10 shares of firm B. We call this an exchange ratio of 0.75:1. The value of each share of firm A's equity before the acquisition is £20. Because $7.5 \times £20 = £150$, this exchange *appears* to be the equivalent of purchasing firm B in cash for £150.

This is incorrect: the true cost to firm A is greater than £150. To see this, note that firm A has 32.5 (= 25 + 7.5) shares outstanding after the merger. Firm B shareholders own 23 per cent (= 7.5/32.5) of the combined firm. Their holdings are valued at £161 (= 23% × £700). Because these shareholders receive equity in firm A worth £161, the cost of the merger to firm A's shareholders must be £161, not £150.

This result is shown in column 4 of Table 29.4. The value of each share of firm A's equity after an equity-for-equity transaction is only £21.54 (= £700/32.5). We found out earlier that the value of each share is £22 after a cash-for-equity transaction. The difference is that the cost of the equity-for-equity transaction to firm A is higher.

This non-intuitive result occurs because the exchange ratio of 7.5 shares of firm A for 10 shares of firm B was based on the *pre-merger* prices of the two firms. However, because the equity of firm A rises after the merger, firm B equity-holders receive more than £150 in firm A equity.

What should the exchange ratio be so that firm B equity-holders receive only £150 of firm A's equity? We begin by defining $\alpha$, the proportion of the shares in the combined firm that firm B's shareholders own. Because the combined firm's value is £700, the value of firm B shareholders after the merger is

Value of firm B shareholders after merger:

$$\alpha \times £700$$

Setting $\alpha \times £700 = £150$, we find that $\alpha = 21.43\%$. In other words, firm B's shareholders will receive equity worth £150 if they receive 21.43 per cent of the firm after merger.

Now we determine the number of shares issued to firm B's shareholders. The proportion, $\alpha$, that firm B's shareholders have in the combined firm can be expressed as follows:

$$\alpha = \frac{\text{New shares issued}}{\text{Old shares + New shares issued}}$$
$$= \frac{\text{New shares issued}}{25 + \text{New shares issued}}$$

Plugging our value of $\alpha$ into the equation yields

$$0.2143 = \frac{\text{New shares issued}}{25 + \text{New shares issued}}$$

Solving for the unknown, we have

$$\text{New shares} = 6.819 \text{ shares}$$

Total shares outstanding after the merger are 31.819 (= 25 + 6.819). Because 6.819 shares of firm A are exchanged for 10 shares of firm B, the exchange ratio is 0.6819:1.

Results at the exchange ratio of 0.6819:1 are displayed in column 5 of Table 29.4. Because there are now 31.819 shares, each share of equity is worth £22 (= £700/31.819), exactly what it is worth in the equity-for-cash transaction. Thus, given that the board of firm B will sell its firm for £150, this is the fair exchange ratio, not the ratio of 0.75:1 mentioned earlier.

## Cash versus Equity

In this section we have examined both cash deals and equity-for-equity deals. Our analysis leads to the following question: When do bidders want to pay with cash and when do they want to pay with equity? There is no easy formula: the decision hinges on a few variables, with perhaps the most important being the price of the bidder's equity.

In the example of Table 29.4, firm A's market price per share prior to the merger was £20. Let's now assume that at the time firm A's managers believed the 'true' price was £15. In other words, the managers believed that their equity was overvalued. Is it likely for managers to have a different view than that of the market? Yes – managers often have more information than the market does. After all, managers deal with customers, suppliers and employees daily, and are likely to obtain private information.

Now imagine that firm A's managers are considering acquiring firm B with either cash or equity. The overvaluation would have no impact on the merger terms in a cash deal; firm B would still receive £150 in cash. However, the overvaluation would have a big impact on a share-for-share deal. Although firm B receives £150 worth of A's equity as calculated at market prices, firm A's managers know that the true value of the equity is less than £150.

How should firm A pay for the acquisition? Clearly, firm A has an incentive to pay with equity, because it would end up giving away less than £150 of value. This conclusion might seem rather cynical, because firm A is, in some sense, trying to cheat firm B's shareholders. However, both theory and empirical evidence suggest that firms are more likely to acquire with equity when their own equities are overvalued.[12]

The story is not quite this simple. Just as the managers of firm A think strategically, firm B's managers are likely to think this way as well. Suppose that in the merger negotiations firm A's managers push for a share-for-share deal. This might tip off firm B's managers that firm A is overpriced. Perhaps firm B's managers will ask for better terms than firm A is currently offering. Alternatively, firm B may resolve to accept cash or not to sell at all. And just as firm B learns from the negotiations, the market learns also. Empirical evidence shows that the acquirer's equity price generally falls upon the announcement of a equity-for-equity deal.[13]

## 29.7 Valuation of Mergers in Practice

The previous section provided the tools of merger valuation. However, in practice the approach to valuation is significantly more complex and subjective. Mergers and acquisitions have two distinct differences from the typical investment project that a firm will undertake. First, the size of a merger will be significantly larger, which means that the risks of mis-evaluation are substantially higher. If an acquiring firm arrives at the wrong value of a target it may destroy both companies. A good example of this is the Royal Bank of Scotland acquisition of the Dutch bank ABN AMRO in 2007, when the Royal Bank of Scotland (with Fortis Bank and Banco Santander) bought ABN AMRO for £49 billion. The acquisition took place just before the collapse in bank valuations because of the global credit crunch. Two years later, in 2009, the Royal Bank of Scotland revalued the acquisition and reported a resultant £28 billion loss. The bank was subsequently bailed out by the British government, and most of the directors lost their jobs.

The second difference is that if the target company is listed on a stock exchange, the share price can be used as an indicator of the value of the target's equity. While this makes things intuitively easier, because of the run-up in target valuations when takeover bids are rumoured, share price valuations may be too high if the current share price is used. As the previous section shows, this may lead to the wrong bid price being tabled.

When considering a potential target for acquisition or merger, both firms should evaluate a variety of scenarios and consider the various embedded options that exist in most firms (see Chapter 8). We suggest that acquiring firms take the following steps to evaluate prospective targets.

## Stage 1: Value the Target as a Stand-Alone Firm

The first stage in the valuation process is to consider the target as a stand-alone entity. This is the base-case valuation upon which the merger can be assessed. To value a company requires estimates of future cash flows and the appropriate rates for discounting the cash flows. The initial valuation should then be compared with the current share price of the target to form an initial opinion of the merger.

## Stage 2: Calibrate the Valuation

It is very unlikely that your initial valuation of the target firm will be equal to its share price, and any differential in valuations needs to be explained. As mentioned in the previous section, share prices may also reflect takeover probabilities and potential takeover premiums. In addition, the share price may not incorporate private information that has been gained as a result of your in-depth analysis. For example, private information could be provided by the management of the target firm if the merger is friendly and fully supported by the target's board. Alternatively, new information may have been discovered in the course of your investigations. Because the effort in this phase is so great, and the analysis so extensive, it is possible that your valuation may be better than the share price of the market. This is especially true if the target firm is listed on a small exchange or emerging market, where valuations may not be so accurate.

If you do not have more information than the market, and there is still a difference between your valuation and the share price, it is highly probable that your valuation is incorrect. In other words, your estimate of future cash flows and discount rates will be different from that of the market. At this point it is strongly recommended that you revisit your assumptions to see whether anything can be improved. It is imperative that you get your assumptions right, because they are the building blocks for the rest of your analysis.

## Stage 3: Value the Synergies

Whereas stages 1 and 2 focus on your initial valuation of the target, stage 3 concerns your assessment of the benefits of a possible merger or acquisition. To do this, you must value the synergies associated with combining the target and the acquirer. In the same way as you initially valued the target firm, you value synergies by estimating the cash flows generated by the synergies along with the appropriate discount rates. Some synergies are easier to predict, but others are considerably more difficult. For example, synergies that come from tax savings or reductions in fixed costs are easier to predict than increased sales or reductions in variable costs.

The future cash flows and the discount rates used in the base-case valuation are likely to be used in valuing risky synergies. For example, you may believe that the proposed merger will lead to a 10 per cent increase in the target's cash flows in the five years after the merger. Valuing this synergy will require both the pre-acquisition discount rate and the cash flows of the target. In addition, valuing synergies may also require an estimate of the acquiring firm's cost of capital and expected cash flows. Hence the acquiring firm will want to use the procedures outlined in stages 1 and 2 to value its own equity and calibrate its cost of capital and cash flows.

When synergies are valued, it is important to discount cash flows arising from the synergy using the weighted average of both firms' cost of capital. For example, as a result of the disastrous conditions in the automobile market in 2009, Fiat entered into merger talks with Chrysler. The reason for the merger was that Fiat would have access to the North American car market and Chrysler would be able to increase its presence in Europe. Assume that, as a result of the merger, both companies would increase their pre-tax profits by 10 per cent per year. Given that the gain in each year is proportional to the pre-acquisition cash flows of both firms, the appropriate discount rate would be an equally weighted average of the two firm's costs of capital.

The Fiat–Chrysler example illustrates a case where synergies affect both parties to the merger equally. However, this will not always be the case. If the merger was expected to result in a proportional increase in Fiat's profits, but not Chrysler's, then you would use Fiat's cost of capital to value the synergy.

Because the major gain from the merger is Fiat's penetration of the North American market, there will be many strategic options open to the company once it starts operations. Consequently, it might be better to consider valuing the synergy as a strategic option, using the real options methodology in Chapters 8 and 22, instead of the risk-adjusted discount rate method. When a firm expands into a new market, it has the option to expand further if prospects turn out to be more favourable than originally anticipated, and to exit if the situation turns out to be unfavourable. In these situations an investment may be substantially undervalued when such options are ignored.

### Stage 4: Value the Merger

The final part of the analysis is to add the base-case valuation of the target to the value of the synergies from the merger or acquisition. The rule of thumb is that the merger or acquisition should go ahead if the costs of the merger, which include the bid premium as well as all transaction costs, are lower than the combined value of the merger.

## 29.8 Friendly versus Hostile Takeovers

Mergers are generally initiated by the acquiring, not the acquired, firm. Thus the acquirer must decide to purchase another firm, select the tactics to effect the merger, determine the highest price it is willing to pay, set an initial bid price, and make contact with the target firm. Often the CEO of the acquiring firm simply calls on the CEO of the target and proposes a merger. Should the target be receptive, a merger eventually occurs. Of course, there may be many meetings, with negotiations over price, terms of payment, and other parameters. The target's board of directors generally has to approve the acquisition. Sometimes the bidder's board must also give its approval. Finally, an affirmative vote by the shareholders is needed. But when all is said and done, an acquisition that proceeds in this way is viewed as *friendly*.

Of course, not all acquisitions are friendly. The target's management may resist the merger, in which case the acquirer must decide whether to pursue the merger and, if so, what tactics to use. Facing resistance, the acquirer may begin by purchasing some of the target's equity in secret. This position is often called a *toehold*. Regulation in almost every country requires that an institution or individual disclose their holding in a company once a specific percentage ownership threshold is passed. For example, in the UK, an acquiring company must disclose any holdings above 3 per cent and provide detailed information, including its intentions and its position in the target. Secrecy ends at this point, because the acquirer must state that it plans to acquire the target. The price of the target's shares will probably rise after the disclosure, with the new equity price reflecting the possibility that the target will be bought out at a premium.

Although the acquirer may continue to purchase shares in the open market, an acquisition is unlikely to be effected in this manner. Rather, the acquirer is more likely at some point to make a *tender offer* (an offer made directly to the shareholders to buy shares at a premium above the current market price). The tender offer may specify that the acquirer will purchase all shares that are tendered – that is, turned in to the acquirer. Alternatively, the offer may state that the acquirer will purchase all shares up to, say, 50 per cent of the number of shares outstanding. If more shares are tendered, pro-rating will occur. For example, if, in the extreme case, all of the shares are tendered, each shareholder will be allowed to sell one share for every two shares tendered. The acquirer may also say that it will accept the tendered shares only if a minimum number of shares have been tendered.

National regulators normally require that tender offers be held open for a minimum period. This delay gives the target time to respond. For example, the target may want to notify its shareholders not to tender their shares. It may release statements to the press criticizing the offer. The target may also encourage other firms to enter the bidding process.

At some point the tender offer ends, at which time the acquirer finds out how many shares have been tendered. The acquirer does not necessarily need 100 per cent of the shares to obtain control of the target. In some companies a holding of 20 per cent or so may be enough for control. In others the percentage needed for control is much higher. *Control* is a vague term, but you might think of it operationally as control over the board of directors. Shareholders elect members of the board, who, in turn, appoint managers. If the acquirer receives enough equity to elect a majority of the board members, these members can appoint the managers whom the acquirer wants. And effective control can often be achieved with less than a majority. As long as some of the original board members vote with the acquirer, a few new board members can gain the acquirer a working majority.

Sometimes, once the acquirer gets working control, it proposes a merger to obtain the few remaining shares that it does not already own. The transaction is now friendly, because the board of directors will approve it. Mergers of this type are often called *clean-up* mergers.

A tender offer is not the only way to gain control of a *hostile* target. Alternatively, the acquirer may continue to buy more shares in the open market until control is achieved. This strategy, often called a *street sweep*, is infrequently used, perhaps because of the difficulty of buying enough shares to obtain control. Also, as mentioned, tender offers often allow the acquirer to return the tendered shares if fewer shares than the desired number are tendered. By contrast, shares purchased in the open market cannot be returned.

Another means to obtain control is a *proxy fight* – a procedure involving corporate voting. Elections for seats on the board of directors are generally held at the annual shareholders' meeting, perhaps four to five months after the end of the firm's fiscal year. After purchasing shares in the target company, the acquirer nominates a slate of candidates to run against the current directors. The acquirer generally hires a proxy solicitor, who contacts shareholders prior to the shareholders' meeting, making a pitch for the insurgent slate. Should the acquirer's candidates win a majority of seats on the board, the acquirer will control the firm. And as with tender offers, effective control can often be achieved with less than a majority. The acquirer may just want to change a few specific policies of the firm, such as the firm's capital budgeting programme or its diversification plan. Or it may simply want to replace management. If some of the original board members are sympathetic to the acquirer's plans, a few new board members can give the acquirer a working majority.

Whereas mergers end up with the acquirer owning all of the target's equity, the victor in a proxy fight does not gain additional shares. The reward to the proxy victor is simply share price appreciation if the victor's policies prove effective. In fact, just the threat of a proxy fight may raise share prices, because management may improve operations to head off the fight.

## 29.9 Defensive Tactics

Target firm managers frequently resist takeover attempts. Actions to defeat a takeover may benefit the target shareholders if the bidding firm raises its offer price or another firm makes a bid. Alternatively, resistance may simply reflect self-interest at the shareholders' expense. That is, the target managers might fight a takeover to preserve their jobs. Sometimes management resists while simultaneously improving corporate policies. Shareholders can benefit in this case, even if the takeover fails.

In this section we describe various ways in which target managers resist takeovers. A company is said to be 'in play' if one or more suitors are currently interested in acquiring it. It is useful to separate defensive tactics before a company is in play from tactics after the company is in play.

### Deterring Takeovers before Being in Play

**Corporate Charters** The corporate charter refers to the articles of incorporation and corporate by-laws governing a firm. Among other provisions, the charter establishes conditions allowing a takeover. Firms frequently amend charters to make acquisitions more difficult. As examples, consider the following two amendments:

1   *Classified or staggered board*: In an unclassified board of directors, shareholders elect all of the directors each year. In a staggered board, only a fraction of the board is elected each year, with terms running for multiple years. For example, one-third of the board might stand for election each year, with terms running for three years. Staggered boards increase the time an acquirer needs to obtain a majority of seats on the board. In the previous example, the acquirer can gain control of only one-third of the seats in the first year after acquisition. Another year must pass before the acquirer is able to control two-thirds of the

seats. Therefore the acquirer may not be able to change management as quickly as it would like. However, some argue that staggered boards are not necessarily effective, because the old directors often choose to vote with the acquirer.

2  *Supermajority provisions*: Corporate charters determine the percentage of voting shares needed to approve important transactions such as mergers. A supermajority provision in the charter means that this percentage is above 50 per cent. Two-thirds majorities are common, though the number can be much higher. A supermajority provision clearly increases the difficulty of acquisition in the face of hostile management. Many charters with supermajority provisions have what is known as a *board out* clause as well. Here supermajority does not apply if the board of directors approves the merger. This clause makes sure that the provision hinders only hostile takeovers.

**Golden Parachutes**  This colourful term refers to generous severance packages provided to management in the event of a takeover. The argument is that golden parachutes will deter takeovers by raising the cost of acquisition. However, some authorities point out that the deterrence effect is likely to be unimportant, because a severance package, even a generous one, is probably a small part of the cost of acquiring a firm. In addition, some argue that golden parachutes actually *increase* the probability of a takeover. The reasoning here is that management has a natural tendency to resist any takeover because of the possibility of job loss. A large severance package softens the blow of takeover, reducing management's inclination to resist.

Golden parachutes are very controversial in economic downturns, as there is nothing the media likes more than to splash an incredibly generous severance package all over the front pages when the company is in financial distress. This has been the case in recent years, when many outgoing executives bowed to public pressure and rescinded their golden parachutes. A good example concerns the chief executives of the Royal Bank of Scotland and HBOS, the big British banks that succumbed to the credit crisis in 2009. Fred Goodwin (RBS) and Andy Hornby (HBOS) gave up their golden parachutes of £1.2 million and £1 million respectively when they left their banks, after intense political and public criticism.

**Poison Pills**  The poison pill is a sophisticated defensive tactic that is common in the US but illegal in Europe. In the event of a hostile bid, a poison pill allows the target firm to issue new shares at a deep discount to every shareholder *except the bidder*.

Perhaps the example of PeopleSoft (PS) will illustrate the general idea. At one point in 2005 PS's poison pill provision stated that once a bidder acquired 20 per cent or more of PeopleSoft's shares, all shareholders except the acquirer could buy new shares from the corporation at half price. At the time PS had about 400 million shares outstanding. Should some bidder acquire 20 per cent of the company (80 million shares), every shareholder *except the bidder* would be able to buy 16 new shares for every one previously held. If all shareholders exercised this option, PeopleSoft would have to issue 5.12 billion (= 0.8 × 400 million × 16) new shares, bringing its total to 5.52 billion. The share price would drop, because the company would be selling shares at half price. The bidder's percentage of the firm would drop from 20 per cent to 1.45 per cent (= 80 million/5.52 billion). Dilution of this magnitude causes some critics to argue that poison pills are insurmountable.

Since poison pills are illegal in many countries, this has led to greater frequency of hostile takeovers, especially by hedge funds looking to take over a company quickly and sell it on at a profit. Outlawing poison pills has also led to some criticism, because acquiring firms can quickly take control of a target firm before other, possibly better, bids are being prepared by other firms.

## Deterring a Takeover after the Company Is in Play

**Greenmail and Standstill Agreements**  Managers may arrange a *targeted repurchase* to forestall a takeover attempt. In a targeted repurchase a firm buys back its own equity from a potential bidder, usually at a substantial premium, with the proviso that the seller promises not to acquire the company for a specified period. Critics of such payments label them *greenmail*.

A *standstill agreement* occurs when the acquirer, for a fee, agrees to limit its holdings in the target. As part of the agreement the acquirer often promises to offer the target a right of first refusal in the event that the acquirer sells its shares. This promise prevents the block of shares from falling into the hands of another would-be acquirer.

Greenmail has been a colourful part of the financial lexicon since its first application in the late 1970s. Since then, pundits have commented numerous times on either its ethical or unethical nature. Greenmail is predominantly a strategy undertaken by US firms, and is not common in the rest of the world.

**White Knight and White Squire**   A firm facing an unfriendly merger offer might arrange to be acquired by a friendly suitor, commonly referred to as a *white knight*. The white knight might be favoured simply because it is willing to pay a higher purchase price. Alternatively, it might promise not to lay off employees, fire managers, or sell off divisions.

Management instead may wish to avoid any acquisition at all. A third party, termed a *white squire*, might be invited to make a significant investment in the firm, under the condition that it vote with management and not purchase additional shares. White squires are generally offered shares at favourable prices. Billionaire investor Warren Buffett has acted as a white squire to many firms, including Champion International and Gillette.

**Recapitalizations and Repurchases**   Target management will often issue debt to pay out a dividend – a transaction called a *leveraged recapitalization*. A *share repurchase*, where debt is issued to buy back shares, is a similar transaction. The two transactions fend off takeovers in a number of ways. First, the equity price may rise, perhaps because of the increased tax shield from greater debt. A rise in share price makes the acquisition less attractive to the bidder. However, the price will rise only if the firm's debt level before the recapitalization was below the optimum, so a levered recapitalization is not recommended for every target. Consultants point out that firms with low debt but with stable cash flows are ideal candidates for 'recaps'. Second, as part of the recapitalization, management may issue new securities that give management greater voting control than it had before the recap. The increase in control makes a hostile takeover more difficult. Third, firms with a lot of cash are often seen as attractive targets. As part of the recap, the target may use this cash to pay a dividend or buy back equity, reducing the firm's appeal as a takeover candidate.

**Exclusionary Self-Tenders**   An *exclusionary self-tender* is the opposite of a targeted repurchase. Here the firm makes a tender offer for a given amount of its own equity while excluding targeted shareholders.

In a particularly celebrated case Unocal, a large integrated oil firm, made a tender offer for 29 per cent of its shares while excluding its largest shareholder, Mesa Partners II (led by T. Boone Pickens). Unocal's self-tender was for $72 per share, which was $16 over the prevailing market price. It was designed to defeat Mesa's attempted takeover of Unocal by transferring wealth, in effect, from Mesa to Unocal's other equity-holders. This type of activity is almost non-existent in most countries outside the United States because of the existence of pre-emptive rights. Notable examples are Barclays Bank plc and Unicredit Bank, who attempted in 2008 to bypass the pre-emptive rights of existing shareholders in order to raise cash quickly. Not surprisingly, the management of both companies came under intense pressure from institutional shareholders to change their decisions.

**Asset Restructurings**   In addition to altering capital structure, firms may sell off existing assets or buy new ones to avoid takeover. Targets generally sell, or divest, assets for two reasons. First, a target firm may have assembled a hotchpotch of assets in different lines of business, with the various segments fitting together poorly. Value might be increased by placing these divisions into separate firms. Academics often emphasize the concept of *corporate focus*. The idea here is that firms function best by focusing on those few businesses that they really know. A rise in equity price following a divestiture will reduce the target's appeal to a bidder.

The second reason is that a bidder might be interested in a specific division of the target. The target can reduce the bidder's interest by selling off this division. Although the strategy may fend off a merger, it can hurt the target's shareholders if the division is worth more to the target than to the division's buyer. Authorities frequently talk of selling off the *crown jewels* or pursuing a *scorched earth policy*.

While some targets divest existing assets, others buy new ones. Two reasons are generally given here. First, the bidder may like the target as is. The addition of an unrelated business makes the target less appealing to the acquirer. However, a bidder can always sell off the new business, so the purchase is probably not a strong defence. Second, antitrust legislation is designed to prohibit mergers that reduce competition. Antitrust law is enforced at both country level and regional level. For example, in the UK, mergers are governed by the Takeover Panel (UK regulator) and the European Commission (Europe). A target may purchase a company, knowing that this new division will pose antitrust problems for the bidder. However, this strategy might not be effective because, in its filings with the respective regulatory authorities, the bidder can state its intention to sell off the unrelated business.

## 29.10 The Diary of a Hostile Takeover: Ryanair plc and Aer Lingus Group plc

At the end of 2008 the budget airline Ryanair plc announced a cash offer for its rival, Aer Lingus Group plc. On the date of the announcement, 1 December 2008, Ryanair's share price was €2.95 and the Aer Lingus share price was €1.105. The following is a timeline of events in the takeover bid.

### 1 December 2008: Ryanair Announces a Cash Offer for Aer Lingus Group

Prior to the cash offer, Ryanair already owned 29.82 per cent of Aer Lingus shares from an earlier takeover attempt. The cash offer was €1.40/share for 100 per cent of Aer Lingus shares, and the proposal was to form one airline group, but with the two companies operating separate brands in a similar way to Air France-KLM.

In its opening gambit, Ryanair argued that the offer would benefit Aer Lingus shareholders in the following ways:

- The offer was a cash offer and not shares.

- The bid premium was 28 per cent over the average Aer Lingus price (€1.09) in the previous 30 days, and it represented a 25 per cent premium over the closing price of €1.12 on 28 November 2008.

The benefits to Aer Lingus employees were given as follows:

1   The Aer Lingus executive share option scheme would receive €137 million in cash.

2   The size of the fleet would double within five years, and 1,000 jobs would be created.

3   The growth prospects of the combined firm would improve promotion prospects and increase job security. The size of the new firm would be comparable to Europe's big three airlines: Air France-KLM, British Airways Group, and Lufthansa-Swiss.

Ryanair also went on the offensive and criticized the performance of Aer Lingus management:

- The Aer Lingus share price had collapsed from €3.00 in December 2006 to less than €1.00 in November 2008.

- Aer Lingus long-haul customers had fallen by 7 per cent and short-haul customers had fallen by 2 per cent in 2008.

- Ryanair forecast that Aer Lingus would have operating losses of €20 million for 2008 and 2009.

- The firm had wasted €24 million on its defence of Ryanair's previous offer of €2.80 in December 2006.

- The basic directors' fee in Aer Lingus had tripled in three years from €17,500 to €45,000 and the non-executive chairman's fee had increased fivefold from €35,000 to €175,000.

- Short-haul fares had increased by 7 per cent and fuel surcharges were increased five times to an average of €75 per sector.

- Aer Lingus had suffered repeated strike threats, closed its Shannon base, and opened a poorly performing Belfast base in 2007. It also ordered new A330 aircraft in 2007 when they were at their most expensive, and then deferred delivery of these to November 2008.

In response to the offer, the Aer Lingus board released a statement on the same day arguing that Ryanair's previous offer for their shares in 2006 failed to achieve antitrust clearance and, as a result, the new offer was not possible. They also stated that Aer Lingus had a strong business, with significant cash reserves, and the Ryanair offer of €1.40 per share significantly undervalued the company.

The share price of Aer Lingus jumped 16.7 per cent to €1.29 from €1.105 and Ryanair's share price fell nearly 5 per cent from €2.9225 to €2.7825 on the day of the announcement. Holding all else constant, the market estimated the probability of success of the takeover as:

$$€1.29 = \underset{\substack{\text{Share price} \\ \text{of Aer Lingus} \\ \text{with merger}}}{€1.40} \times \underset{\substack{\text{Probability} \\ \text{of} \\ \text{merger}}}{p} + \underset{\substack{\text{Share price of} \\ \text{Aer Lingus} \\ \text{without merger}}}{€1.105} \times \underset{\substack{\text{Probability} \\ \text{of no} \\ \text{merger}}}{(1-p)}$$

Solving for $p$ gives an initial probability of success as 62.7 per cent.

## 11 December 2008: Aer Lingus Discusses Ryanair Offer with the Irish Minister for Transport

The Aer Lingus board announced that it had met with the Irish Minister of Transport, Noel Dempsey, and made clear that they had unanimously rejected the offer because it would lead to a monopoly in Ireland and contravene competition laws. The Irish government held 25 per cent of Aer Lingus shares and thus was a major shareholder. The chief executive of Aer Lingus, Dermot Mannion, said in a statement afterwards:

> "We had a productive meeting with the Minister today and have committed to give the Government, as well as all other shareholders, a comprehensive rebuttal of Ryanair's offer after the publication of its Offer Document. Ryanair cannot spin away the fact that Aer Lingus is and will continue to be its fiercest competitor into and out of Ireland. It is offering other Aer Lingus shareholders a mere €525 million, a pathetic sum in the context of the €1.3 billion in cash on the Group's balance sheet, the substantial value of our fleet and the value of the Heathrow slots. Aer Lingus remains a strong business with significant cash reserves and a robust long-term future. Despite all of Ryanair's insincere promises, this Offer, if accepted, would be bad for Irish consumers, for Aer Lingus' shareholders and for everyone who works in the airline."

The share price of Aer Lingus at close of day was €1.4975, and the Ryanair share price was €2.925. Why would the Aer Lingus share price be above the bid amount of €1.40? The basic reason is that the market anticipated that Ryanair would have to make an increased bid for the company if it was to be successful in the takeover attempt.

## 15 December 2008: Ryanair Issues a 184-page Formal Offer Document for Aer Lingus Shares

The formal offer document contained essentially the same information as the original announcement. However, Ryanair also personally attacked the management of Aer Lingus. As the offer became increasingly hostile, the chairman of Aer Lingus, Colm Barrington, released the following statement:

*"This document contains nothing new. It is the usual stream of invective, spin and misrepresentation that we expect from the people at Ryanair. It also fails to address the recent EU prohibition decision which found emphatically that Ryanair wants to destroy consumer choice. It is a desperate last effort to create an airline monopoly in Ireland, and is clearly not in the interests of Aer Lingus shareholders and the travelling public. Aer Lingus is and will continue to be a strong independent airline. Ryanair clearly needs Aer Lingus but we do not need Ryanair."*

The Aer Lingus share price at close of day was now €1.4725 and the Ryanair share price was €2.77, a further fall from its starting value of €2.95.

## 22 December 2008: Aer Lingus Releases a 64-page Defence Document

The board of Aer Lingus presented a vigorous argument as to why the €1.40 cash offer from Ryanair was not good for Aer Lingus shareholders. The points they made were as follows:

* The Aer Lingus business model was successful. Short-haul business had low prices, high return on capital, and a growing business base. Moreover, its expansion into Gatwick airport provided significant growth opportunities in short haul.

* Aer Lingus was and will be profitable in the future. In contrast to Ryanair's predictions, the Aer Lingus management argued that it would make a profit for 2008.

* The balance sheet of Aer Lingus was one of the strongest in the industry. It had €1.3 billion of cash reserves and €803 million of net cash. They argued that Ryanair wanted to spend €525 million to acquire Aer Lingus in order to gain access to the €1.3 billion cash.

* Ryanair was opportunistically using the dreadful market conditions of late 2008 to profit from the Aer Lingus business model and access its cash resources and assets at a discounted price.

* The Ryanair offer was flawed, because the previous offer in 2006 fell foul of European antitrust laws, and the current offer was no different.

The Aer Lingus share price was now €1.50 and Ryanair's had grown to €3.085!

## 6 January 2009: Ryanair Seeks Aer Lingus Shareholder Meeting

In a dramatic twist to the saga, Ryanair sought an extraordinary meeting of Aer Lingus shareholders to block changes in the employment contract of the Aer Lingus chairman, Colm Barrington. The company had changed his contract at the turn of the year so that, in the event that Aer Lingus was bought over, he would be due a €2.8 million golden parachute payment if he resigned.

Ryanair also announced that only 0.01 per cent of Aer Lingus shareholders (excluding Ryanair itself, which owned 29.82 per cent of Aer Lingus shares) had accepted the cash offer of €1.40 per share. As a result of the extraordinary meeting call, the offer period was extended to 13 February 2009.

Aer Lingus's share price now closed at €1.49, and Ryanair closed even higher at €3.20!

## 22 January 2009: The Irish Government Announces that it Will not Support the Ryanair Bid

One of Aer Lingus's major shareholders was the Irish government, which owned 25 per cent of the company's shares. It made a statement that the Ryanair offer

*"greatly undervalues Aer Lingus and a merger on the basis proposed would be likely to have a significant negative impact on competition in the market. Because we live on an island, Irish*

*consumers depend heavily on air transport. A monopoly in this area would not be in the best interests of Irish consumers. The offer by Ryanair did not include any proposed remedies for the virtual monopoly that would result if the offer was accepted."*

Reluctantly, the chief executive of Ryanair, Michael Dempsey, conceded that the offer was no longer feasible:

*"We respect that decision. It means our offer won't be successful since our 90 per cent acceptance condition can't be satisfied. Sadly it means the government won't receive €200m, and there won't be 1,000 new jobs created in Aer Lingus over the next five years."*

The closing share price of Aer Lingus on 23 January 2009, was €1.15 and that of Ryanair was €3.11. Clearly, the market felt that the proposed takeover was bad for Ryanair's shareholders and good for Aer Lingus shareholders. As the probability of the proposed merger became zero, the price of Aer Lingus fell back to its pre-announcement value.

The Ryanair–Aer Lingus takeover bid provides many insights into the process of a hostile takeover. First, the bidder will criticize the company in terms of its performance, value, or management. Second, the target firm's management, if they do not wish to be taken over, will respond in a negative manner and defend their business model and performance. Third, the market will have its own view on the viability and likelihood of a merger. Finally, it is clear that much effort on the part of both management teams was expended over the period. This time could have been spent elsewhere improving the value of each firm's business operations.

## 29.11 Do Mergers Add Value?

In Section 29.2 we stated that synergy occurs if the value of the combined firm after the merger is greater than the sum of the value of the acquiring firm and the value of the acquired firm before the merger. Section 29.3 provided a number of sources of synergy in mergers, implying that mergers *can* create value. We now want to know whether mergers actually create value in practice. This is an empirical question, and must be answered by empirical evidence.

There are a number of ways to measure value creation, but many academics favour *event studies*. These studies estimate abnormal equity returns on, and around, the merger announcement date. An *abnormal return* is usually defined as the difference between an actual equity return and the return on a market index or control group of equities. This control group is used to net out the effect of market-wide or industry-wide influences.

Consider Table 29.5, where returns around the announcement days of mergers in the US are reported. The average abnormal percentage return across all mergers from 1980 to 2001 is 0.0135. This number combines the returns on both the acquiring company and the acquired company. Because 0.0135 is positive, the market believes that mergers on average create value. The other three returns in that column are positive as well, implying value creation in the different subperiods. Many other academic studies have provided similar results. Thus it appears from this column that the synergies we mentioned in Section 29.3 show up in the real world.

However, the next column tells us something different. Across all mergers from 1980 to 2001 the aggregate dollar change around the day of merger announcement is –$79 billion. This means that the market is, on average, *reducing* the combined equity value of the acquiring and acquired companies around the merger announcement date. Though the difference between the two columns may seem confusing, there is an explanation. Although most mergers have created value, mergers involving the very largest firms have lost value. The abnormal percentage return is an unweighted average in which the returns on all mergers are treated equally. A positive return here reflects all those small mergers that created value. However, losses in a few large mergers cause the aggregate dollar change to be negative.

But there is more. The rest of the third column indicates that the aggregate dollar losses occurred only in the 1998 to 2001 period. While there were losses of –$134 billion in this period, there were gains of $12 billion from 1980 to 1990. And interpolation of the table indicates that there were gains of $44 billion (= $134 – $90) from 1991 to 1997. Thus it appears that some large mergers lost a great deal of value from 1998 to 2001.

TABLE
**29.5**

| Time period | Gain or loss to merger (both acquired and acquiring firms) | | Gain or loss to acquiring firms | |
|---|---|---|---|---|
| | Abnormal percentage return | Aggregate dollar gain or loss | Abnormal percentage return | Aggregate dollar gain or loss |
| 1980–2001 | 0.0135 | −$79 billion | 0.0110 | −$220 billion |
| 1980–1990 | 0.0241 | $12 billion | 0.0064 | −$4 billion |
| 1991–2001 | 0.0104 | −$90 billion | 0.0120 | −$216 billion |
| 1998–2001 | 0.0029 | −$134 billion | 0.0069 | −$240 billion |

*Source*: Modified from S. Moeller, F. Schlingemann and R. Stulz, 'Wealth destruction on a massive scale? A study of acquiring-firm returns in the recent merger wave', *Journal of Finance* (April 2005), Table 1.

**Table 29.5** Percentage and dollar returns for mergers

The analysis presented in Table 29.5 considers the effect of mergers on shareholders. It does not consider the effect of mergers on the whole firm, that is, equity and debt. Recall from Section 29.5 that mergers may transfer value from equity-holders to debtholders because of the reduction in risk of the combined company. Doukas and Kan[14] show this to be the case for cross-border mergers involving US firms, and find that overall firm value is not reduced from this activity.

Most research on mergers and acquisitions has focused on US firms. This is largely because the activity has not been particularly common elsewhere. For example, in Europe, merger activity grew significantly only after the introduction of the euro. The exception to this is the UK, where mergers have been commonplace, and come in waves in a similar way to the US. Figure 29.3 presents the total market value of UK mergers over time. There was a massive spike in the late 20th century as the high-tech boom took hold, which then fell after the bubble burst. In recent years mergers across the world have dropped drastically with the disappearance of credit in the financial markets. Admittedly, there has been a consolidation of companies that were forced to merge as a result of financial distress or economic necessity (for example, HBOS with Lloyds TSB, and Merrill Lynch with Bank of America), but on the whole there has been very little interest in acquisitions.

When one considers the value benefits of mergers and acquisitions, it is important to remember that every country has a different regulatory and legal framework for dealing with acquisitions. In some places, foreign ownership is allowed only up to a certain pre-specified percentage of shares. This can significantly affect the success of merger bids. Europe is particularly interesting, because although it operates under a cohesive regulation system, corporate cultures are very different across the area. Campa and Hernando[15] show that differences in the institutional environment can affect the benefits of mergers and acquisitions. They found that European mergers in regulated industries or those that were under government control were significantly less successful than in unregulated industries.

The results in a table such as Table 29.5 should have important implications for public policy, because regulators are always wondering whether mergers are to be encouraged or discouraged. However, the results in that table are, unfortunately, ambiguous. On the one hand, you could focus on the first column, saying that mergers create value on average. Proponents of this view might argue that the great losses in the few large mergers were flukes, not likely to occur again. On the other hand, we cannot easily ignore the fact that, over the entire period, mergers destroyed more value than they created.

Mergers and acquisitions are often driven by different agenda. For example, the mergers and acquisitions of recent times have been in response to the economic woes facing

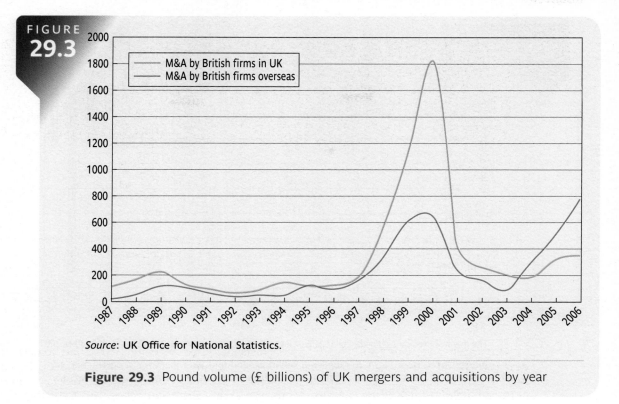

FIGURE
**29.3**

Source: UK Office for National Statistics.

**Figure 29.3** Pound volume (£ billions) of UK mergers and acquisitions by year

world economies. Economies of scale and risk reduction are the main factors underlying the mergers of 2008 and later. If you go several years back in time, the mergers and acquisitions were largely a result of growth into new markets and exploitation of different synergies. Naturally, the performance of mergers after 2008 will be very different from earlier periods.

Before we move on, some final thoughts are in order. Readers may be bothered that abnormal returns are taken only around the time of the acquisition, well before all of the acquisition's impact is revealed. Academics look at long-term returns, but they have a special fondness for short-term returns. If markets are efficient, the short-term return provides an unbiased estimate of the total effect of the merger. Long-term returns, while capturing more information about a merger, also reflect the impact of many unrelated events.

## Returns to Bidders

The preceding results combined returns on bidders and targets. Investors want to separate the bidders from the targets. Columns 4 and 5 of Table 29.5 provide returns for acquiring companies alone. The fourth column shows that abnormal percentage returns for bidders have been positive for the entire sample period and for each of the individual subperiods – a result similar to that for bidders and targets combined. The fifth column indicates aggregate losses, suggesting that large mergers did worse than small ones. The time pattern for these aggregate losses to bidders is presented in Fig. 29.4. Again, the large losses occurred from 1998 to 2001, with the greatest loss in 2000.

Let's fast-forward a few decades and imagine that you are the CEO of a company. In that position you will certainly be faced with potential acquisitions. Does the evidence in Table 29.5 and Fig. 29.3 encourage you to make acquisitions or not? Again, the evidence is ambiguous. On the one hand, you could focus on the averages in column 4 of the table, probably increasing your appetite for acquisitions. On the other hand, column 5 of the table, as well as the figure, might give you pause.

The graph shows the aggregate dollar gain or loss across all acquiring firms each year from 1980 to 2001.

*Source*: Taken from Fig. 1, S. Moeller, F. Schlingemann and R. Stulz, 'Wealth destruction on a massive scale? A study of acquiring-firm returns in the recent merger wave', *Journal of Finance* (April 2005).

**Figure 29.4** Yearly aggregate dollar gain or loss for the shareholders of acquiring firms

## Target Companies

Although the evidence just presented for both the combined entity and the bidder alone is ambiguous, the evidence for targets is crystal-clear. Acquisitions benefit the target's equity-holders. Consider the following chart, which shows the median merger *premium* over different periods in the United States:[16]

| Time period | 1973–1998 | 1973–1979 | 1980–1989 | 1990–1998 |
|---|---|---|---|---|
| Premium | 42.1% | 47.2% | 37.7% | 34.5% |

The premium is the difference between the acquisition price per share and the target's pre-acquisition share price, divided by the target's pre-acquisition share price. The average premium is quite high for the entire sample period and for the various subsamples. For example, a target company selling at $100 per share before the acquisition that is later acquired for $142.1 per share generates a premium of 42.1 per cent. The results are similar in other countries. For example, in the UK, the average premium is 45 per cent.[17]

Though other studies may provide different estimates of the average premium, all studies show positive premiums. Thus we can conclude that mergers benefit the target shareholders. This conclusion leads to at least two implications. First, we should be somewhat sceptical of target managers who resist takeovers. These managers may claim that the target's share price does not reflect the true value of the company. Or they may say that resistance will induce the bidder to raise its offer. These arguments could be true in certain situations, but they may also provide cover for managers who are simply scared of losing their jobs after acquisition. Second, the premium creates a hurdle for the acquiring company. Even in a merger with true synergies, the acquiring shareholders will lose if the premium exceeds the value of these synergies.

# The Managers versus the Shareholders

**Managers of Bidding Firms**    The preceding discussion was presented from the shareholders' point of view. Because, in theory, shareholders pay the salaries of managers, we might think that managers would look at things from the shareholders' point of view. However, it is important to realize that individual shareholders have little clout with managers. For example, the typical shareholder is simply not in a position to pick up the phone and give the managers a piece of her mind. It is true that the shareholders elect the board of directors, which monitors the managers. However, an elected director has little contact with individual shareholders.

Thus it is fair to ask whether managers are held fully accountable for their actions. This question is at the heart of what economists call *agency theory*. Researchers in this area often argue that managers work less hard, get paid more, and make worse business decisions than they would if shareholders had more control over them. And there is a special place in agency theory for mergers. Managers frequently receive bonuses for acquiring other companies. In addition, their pay is often positively related to the size of their firm. Finally, managers' prestige is also tied to firm size. Because firm size increases with acquisitions, managers are disposed to look favourably on acquisitions, perhaps even ones with negative NPV.

A fascinating study[18] compared companies where managers received a lot of options on their own company's equity as part of their compensation package with companies where the managers did not. Because option values rise and fall in tandem with the firm's equity price, managers receiving options have an incentive to forgo mergers with negative NPVs. The paper reported that the acquisitions by firms where managers receive lots of options (termed *equity-based compensation* in the paper) create more value than the acquisitions by firms where managers receive few or no options.

Agency theory may also explain why the biggest merger failures have involved large firms. Managers owning a small fraction of their firm's equity have less incentive to behave responsibly, because the great majority of any losses are borne by other shareholders. Managers of large firms probably have a smaller percentage interest in their firm's equity than do managers of small firms (a large percentage of a large firm is too costly to acquire). Thus the merger failures of large acquirers may be due to the small percentage ownership of the managers.

An earlier chapter of this text discussed the free cash flow hypothesis. The idea here is that managers can spend only what they have. Managers of firms with low cash flow are likely to run out of cash before they run out of good (positive NPV) investments. Conversely, managers of firms with high cash flow are likely to have cash on hand even after all the good investments are taken. Managers are rewarded for growth, so managers with cash flow above that needed for good projects have an incentive to spend the remainder on bad (negative NPV) projects. A paper tested this conjecture, finding that 'cash-rich firms are more likely than other firms to attempt acquisitions. . . . cash-rich bidders destroy seven cents in value for every dollar of cash reserves held. . . . consistent with the equity return evidence, mergers in which the bidder is cash-rich are followed by abnormal declines in operating performance.'[19]

The previous discussion has considered the possibility that some managers were knaves – more interested in their own welfare than in the welfare of their shareholders. However, a recent paper entertained the idea that other managers were more fools than knaves. Malmendier and Tate[20] classified certain CEOs as overconfident, either because they refused to exercise equity options on their own company's equity when it was rational to do so, or because the press portrayed them as confident or optimistic. The authors find that these overconfident managers are more likely to make acquisitions than are other managers. In addition, the equity market reacts more negatively to announcements of acquisitions when the acquiring CEO is overconfident.

**Managers of Target Firms**    Our discussion has just focused on the managers of acquiring firms, finding that these managers sometimes make more acquisitions than they should. However, that is only half of the story. Shareholders of target firms may have just as hard a time controlling their managers. While there are many ways in which managers of target firms can put themselves ahead of their shareholders, two seem to stand out. First, we said earlier that because premiums are positive, takeovers are beneficial to the target's shareholders.

However, if managers may be fired after their firms are acquired, they may resist these takeovers.[21] Tactics employed to resist takeover, generally called defensive tactics, were discussed in an earlier section of this chapter. Second, managers who cannot avoid takeover may bargain with the bidder, getting a good deal for themselves at the expense of their shareholders.

Consider Wulf's fascinating work on *mergers of equals* (MOEs).[22] Some deals are announced as MOEs, primarily because the two firms have equal ownership in and equal representation on the board of directors of the merged entity. AOL and Time Warner, Daimler-Benz and Chrysler, Morgan Stanley and Dean Witter, and Fleet Financial Group and BankBoston are generally held out as examples of MOEs. Nevertheless, authorities point out that in any deal one firm is typically 'more equal' than the other. That is, the target and the bidder can usually be distinguished in practice. For example, Daimler-Benz is commonly classified as the bidder and Chrysler as the target in their merger.

Wulf finds that targets get a lower percentage of the merger gains, as measured by abnormal returns around the announcement date, in MOEs than in other mergers. And the percentage of the gains going to the target is negatively related to the representation of the target's officers and directors on the post-merger board. These and other findings lead Wulf to conclude, 'They [the findings of the paper] suggest that CEOs trade power for premium in merger of equals transactions.'

## 29.12 Accounting and Tax Considerations

Many mergers involve companies in two different countries, which presents many difficulties in assessing the value of acquisitions. This is because accounting and tax rules can be very different across countries. In recent years there has been a concerted effort by accounting standard-setters and regulatory authorities to streamline the administrative and bureaucratic challenges that face merging firms. In the subsequent discussion we shall try to be as generic as possible about the accounting and tax considerations without losing the necessary important detail. However, given the heterogeneity of regulations across countries, it is impossible to be specific about every regulation in place regarding mergers.

Accounting systems differ in the US from the rest of the world. In Europe, and many other countries, International Financial Reporting Standards govern the way that companies account for transactions. To improve the efficiency of the accounting treatment of cross-border mergers, the International Accounting Standards Board (IASB) and the US Financial Accounting Standards Board (FASB) have been working together to converge the standards of the two systems. This is an ongoing project, and developments will continue in the future.

The main guidance provided by both bodies is that the accounting treatment of any acquisition or merger recognizes the fair value of all assets and liabilities on the acquisition date. The guidance, which is given in IFRS3 *Business Combinations*, states that these be presented in such a way as to allow stakeholders to understand the true value of the acquisition or merger. The only exceptions to this rule are leases and insurance contracts, which are valued using the contractual terms at inception of the contract (see Chapter 20).

The accounting impact of the merger is evaluated using the acquisition method proposed by IFRS3. Specifically, the following must be done:

- *Step 1: Identify the acquirer.* A separate accounting standard, IAS27 *Consolidated and Separate Financial Statements*, is used to identify the party that has gained control in the merger transaction. This can be quite difficult, especially when the merger is a merger of equals (MOE).

- *Step 2: Determine the acquisition date.* The acquirer must identify the date on which it gains control of the target. This is normally the date of legal transfer or consolidation of assets and liabilities between the two parties.

- *Step 3: Recognize and measure the identifiable assets that have been acquired, the liabilities assumed, and any non-controlling interest in the acquiree.* The acquirer must recognize all assets and liabilities (excluding goodwill) at fair value. In 2008 an exceptionally important change in this standard was introduced. In a break with previous practice, the costs of a merger or acquisition must now be treated as an expense in the financial accounts. Before this, the acquirer would lump the merger costs into the value of the target company, and this would be represented in the statement of financial position. Now, the costs affect the income statement, and this clearly impacts upon the profitability of the acquirer in the period after the acquisition takes place. It has been argued that this accounting change will reduce the frequency of mergers and acquisitions in countries that employ International Financial Reporting Standards.

- *Step 4: Recognize and measure goodwill or a gain from a bargain purchase as of the acquisition date.* In a purchase, an accounting term called *goodwill* is created. Goodwill is the excess of the purchase price over the sum of the fair market values of the individual assets acquired. The goodwill of a target company will normally be taken from its financial accounts. In some cases a merger or acquisition will take place because the target is in financial distress and the acquiring company is able to get the target's assets at a discount. This happened during the credit crunch of 2008, when JP Morgan bought Bear Stearns for a deeply discounted price. In such a situation IFRS would require that the acquirer reassess the value of the assets of the target at fair value.

## Acquisitions and Accounting

EXAMPLE
**29.2**

Suppose firm A acquires firm B, creating a new firm, AB. Firm A's and firm B's financial positions at the date of the acquisition are shown in Table 29.6. The book value of firm B on the date of the acquisition is £10 million. This is the sum of £8 million in buildings and £2 million in cash. However, an appraiser states that the sum of the fair market values of the individual buildings is £14 million. With £2 million in cash, the sum of the market values of the individual assets in firm B is £16 million. This represents the value to be received if the firm is liquidated by selling off the individual assets separately. However, the whole is often worth more than the sum of the parts in business. Firm A pays £19 million in cash for firm B. This difference of £3 million (= £19 million – £16 million) is goodwill. It represents the increase in value from keeping the firm as an ongoing business. Firm A issued £19 million in new debt to finance the acquisition.

| Firm A (£m) | | | | Firm B (£m) | | | | Firm AB (£m) | | | |
|---|---|---|---|---|---|---|---|---|---|---|---|
| Cash | 4 | Equity | 20 | Cash | 2 | Equity | 10 | Cash | 6 | Debt | 19 |
| Land | 16 | | | Land | 0 | | | Land | 16 | Equity | 20 |
| Buildings | 0 | | | Buildings | 8 | | | Buildings | 14 | | |
| | | | | | | | | Goodwill | 3 | | |
| Total | 20 | | 20 | Total | 10 | | 10 | Total | 39 | | 39 |

When the acquisition method is used, the assets of the acquired firm (firm B) appear in the combined firm's books at their fair market value.

**Table 29.6** Accounting for acquisitions: purchase (in £ millions)

The total assets of firm AB increase to £39 million. The buildings of firm B appear in the new statement of financial position at their current market value. That is, the market value of the assets of the acquired firm becomes part of the book value of the new firm. However, the assets of the acquiring firm (firm A) remain at their old book value. They are not revalued upwards when the new firm is created.

The excess of the purchase price over the sum of the fair market values of the individual assets acquired is £3 million. This amount is reported as goodwill. Financial analysts generally ignore goodwill, because it has no cash flow consequences. Each year the firm must assess the value of its goodwill. If the value goes down (this is called *impairment* in accounting speak), the amount of goodwill on the statement of financial position must be decreased accordingly. Otherwise no amortization is required.

In a similar way that the accounting treatment of mergers and acquisitions is converging to one basic standard across the world, governments have also attempted to integrate country-level tax laws. The taxation of mergers and acquisitions across national borders can be extremely complex and prohibitive in cost, and this deters many corporations from pursuing cross-border mergers. Each national tax system is different, but in recent years there have been a number of treaties that smooth out these differences.

In Europe the main treaty is the Cross-Border Merger Directive, which was fully implemented at the end of 2007 (with the exception of Belgium, which the Commission reported had not fully met the requirements of the Directive). As Chapter 2 attests, the governance systems across Europe are quite varied, and employee participation is stronger in some countries (e.g. Germany, France and Belgium) than in others (e.g. the United Kingdom). Amalgamating the operations of corporations that are based in countries with different governance cultures and taxation systems presents some difficulty. The EU Merger Directive presents a cohesive framework that allows European national taxation systems to operate fully within a broader international context.

## 29.13 Going Private and Leveraged Buyouts

Going-private transactions and leveraged buyouts have much in common with mergers, and it is worth while to discuss them in this chapter. A publicly traded firm *goes private* when a private group, usually composed of existing management, purchases its equity. As a consequence, the firm's equity is taken off the market (if it is an exchange-traded equity, it is delisted) and is no longer traded. Thus, in going-private transactions, shareholders of publicly held firms are forced to accept cash for their shares.

Going-private transactions are frequently *leveraged buyouts* (LBOs). In a leveraged buyout the cash offer price is financed with large amounts of debt. Part of the appeal of LBOs is that the arrangement calls for little equity capital. This equity capital is generally supplied by a small group of investors, some of whom are likely to be managers of the firm being purchased.

The selling shareholders are invariably paid a premium above market price in an LBO, just as in a merger. As with a merger, the acquirer profits only if the synergy created is greater than the premium. Synergy is quite plausible in a merger of *two* firms, and we delineated a number of types of synergy earlier in the chapter. However, it is more difficult to explain synergy in an LBO because only *one* firm is involved.

Two reasons are generally given for value creation in an LBO. First, the extra debt provides a tax deduction, which, as earlier chapters suggested, leads to an increase in firm value. Most LBOs are on firms with stable earnings and with low to moderate debt. The LBO may simply increase the firm's debt to its optimum level.

The second source of value comes from increased efficiency, and is often explained in terms of 'the carrot and the stick'. Managers become owners under an LBO, giving them an incentive to work hard. This incentive is commonly referred to as the carrot. Interest payments from the high level of debt constitute the stick. Large interest payments can easily turn a profitable firm before an LBO into an unprofitable one after the LBO. Management must make changes, either through revenue increases or through cost reductions, to keep the firm in the black. Agency theory, a topic mentioned earlier in this chapter, suggests that managers can be wasteful with a large free cash flow. Interest payments reduce this cash flow, forcing managers to curb the waste.

Though it is easy to measure the additional tax shields from an LBO, it is difficult to measure the gains from increased efficiency. Nevertheless, this increased efficiency is considered at least as important as the tax shield in explaining the LBO phenomenon.

Academic research suggests that LBOs have, on average, created value. First, premiums are positive, as they are with mergers, implying that selling shareholders benefit. Second, studies indicate that LBOs that eventually go public generate high returns for the management group. Finally, other studies show that operating performance increases after the LBO. However, we cannot be completely confident of value creation, because researchers have difficulty obtaining data about LBOs that do not go public. If these LBOs generally destroy value, the sample of firms going public would be a biased one.

Regardless of the average performance of firms undertaking an LBO, we can be sure of one thing: because of the great leverage involved, the risk is huge. On the one hand, LBOs have created many large fortunes. On the other hand, a number of bankruptcies and near-bankruptcies have occurred as well.

## 29.14 Divestitures

This chapter has been concerned primarily with acquisitions, but it is also worth while to consider their opposite – divestitures. Divestitures come in a number of different varieties, the most important of which we discuss next.

### Sale

The most basic type of divestiture is the *sale* of a division, business unit, segment, or set of assets to another company. The buyer generally, but not always, pays in cash. A number of reasons are provided for sales. First, in an earlier section of this chapter we considered asset sales as a defence against hostile takeovers. It was pointed out in that section that sales often improve corporate focus, leading to greater overall value for the seller. This same rationale applies when the selling company is not in play. Second, asset sales provide needed cash to liquidity-poor firms. Third, it is often argued that the paucity of data about individual business segments makes large, diversified firms hard to value. Investors may discount the firm's overall value because of this lack of transparency. Sell-offs streamline a firm, making it easier to value. However, this argument is inconsistent with market efficiency, because it implies that large, diversified firms sell below their true value. Fourth, firms may simply want to sell unprofitable divisions. However, unprofitable divisions are likely to have low values to everyone. A division should be sold only if its value is greater to the buyer than to the seller.

There has been a fair amount of research on sell-offs, with academics reaching two conclusions. First, event studies show that returns on the seller's equity are positive around the time of the announcement of sale, suggesting that sell-offs create value to the seller. Second, acquisitions are often sold off down the road. For example, Kaplan and Weisbach[23] found that over 40 per cent of acquisitions were later divested, a result that does not reflect well on mergers. The average time between acquisition and divestiture was about seven years.

### Spin-Off

In a spin-off a parent firm turns a division into a separate entity and distributes shares in this entity to the parent's shareholders. Spin-offs differ from sales in at least two ways. First, the parent firm receives no cash from a spin-off: shares are sent for free to the shareholders. Second, the initial shareholders of the spun-off division are the same as the parent's shareholders. By contrast, the buyer in a sell-off is most likely another firm. However, because the shares of the division are publicly traded after the spin-off, the identities of the shareholders will change over time.

At least four reasons are generally given for a spin-off. First, as with a sell-off, the spin-off may increase corporate focus. Second, because the spun-off division is now publicly traded, stock exchange regulators require additional information to be disseminated – so investors may find it easier to value the parent and subsidiary after the spin-off. Third, corporations often compensate executives with shares of equity in addition to cash. The equity acts as an incentive: good performance from managers leads to share price increases. However, prior to the spin-off, executives can receive equity only in the parent company. If the division is small relative to the entire firm, price movement in the parent's equity will be related less to the performance of the manager's division than to the performance of the rest of the firm. Thus divisional managers may see little relation between their effort and equity appreciation. However, after the spin-off the manager can be given equity in the subsidiary. The manager's effort should directly impact on price movement in the subsidiary's equity. Fourth, the tax consequences from a spin-off are generally better than from a sale, because the parent receives no cash from a spin-off.

## Carve-Out

In a carve-out the firm turns a division into a separate entity and then sells shares in the division to the public. Generally the parent retains a large interest in the division. This transaction is similar to a spin-off, and the first three benefits listed for a spin-off apply to a carve-out as well. However, the big difference is that the firm receives cash from a carve-out, but not from a spin-off. The receipt of cash can be both good and bad. On the one hand, many firms need cash. Michaely and Shaw[24] find that large, profitable firms are more likely to use carve-outs, whereas small, unprofitable firms are more likely to use spin-offs. One interpretation is that firms generally prefer the cash that comes with a carve-out. However, small and unprofitable firms have trouble issuing equity. They must resort to a spin-off, where equity in the subsidiary is merely given to their own equity-holders.

Unfortunately, there is also a dark side to cash, as developed in the free cash flow hypothesis. That is, firms with cash exceeding that needed for profitable capital budgeting projects may spend it on unprofitable ones. Allen and McConnell[25] find that the equity market reacts positively to announcements of carve-outs if the cash is used to reduce debt. The market reacts neutrally if the cash is used for investment projects.

## Summary and Conclusions

1   One firm can acquire another in several different ways. The three legal forms of acquisition are merger and consolidation, acquisition of equity, and acquisition of assets. Mergers and consolidations are the least costly from a legal standpoint, but they require a vote of approval by the shareholders. Acquisition by equity does not require a shareholder vote, and is usually done via a tender offer. However, it is difficult to obtain 100 per cent control with a tender offer. Acquisition of assets is comparatively costly, because it requires more difficult transfer of asset ownership.

2   The synergy from an acquisition is defined as the value of the combined firm ($V_{AB}$) less the value of the two firms as separate entities ($V_A$ and $V_B$):

$$\text{Synergy} = V_{AB} - (V_A + V_B)$$

The shareholders of the acquiring firm will gain if the synergy from the merger is greater than the premium.

3   The possible benefits of an acquisition come from the following:

   (a)   Revenue enhancement

   (b)   Cost reduction

   (c)   Lower taxes

   (d)   Reduced capital requirements

4   Shareholders may not benefit from a merger that is done only to achieve diversification or earnings growth. And the reduction in risk from a merger may actually help bondholders and hurt shareholders.

5   A merger is said to be friendly when the managers of the target support it. A merger is said to be hostile when the target managers do not support it. Some of the most colourful language of finance stems from defensive tactics in hostile takeover battles. *Poison pills*, *golden parachutes*, *crown jewels* and *greenmail* are terms that describe various anti-takeover tactics.

6   The empirical research on mergers and acquisitions is extensive. On average, the shareholders of acquired firms fare very well. The effect of mergers on acquiring shareholders is less clear.

7   In a *going-private* transaction, a buyout group, usually including the firm's management, buys all the shares of the other equity-holders. The equity is no longer publicly traded. A *leveraged buyout* is a going-private transaction financed by extensive leverage.

**Questions and Problems**

CONCEPT

1–13

1   **The Basic Forms of Acquisition**   Describe the three main types of acquisition. Provide a real-life example of each type.

2   **Synergy**   Explain the concept of synergy. Provide a non-financial example of a synergy.

3   **Sources of Synergy**   Where does synergy come from? Is it possible that costs of new synergies may be more than the benefits? Discuss.

4   **Bad Reasons for Mergers**   Many explanations and justifications are made by acquiring (and sometimes target) managers for a merger. Review these justifications and discuss whether they are good or bad for shareholders.

5   **A Cost to Shareholders in Risk**   An argument has been made that financial mergers are bad for shareholders, because bondholders benefit from the reduction in risk. However, are there situations where a financial merger can be good for shareholders?

6   **NPV of a Merger**   Describe the main uncertainties that are involved in a merger analysis. Are mergers an ideal activity in which to use real option valuation? Discuss some of the ways in which a real option analysis could be used to value a merger.

7   **Merger Valuation in Practice**   Discuss the main steps that are involved in a merger analysis.

8   **Friendly versus Hostile Takeovers**   What types of action might the management of a firm take to fight a hostile acquisition bid from an unwanted suitor? How do the target firm shareholders benefit from the defensive tactics of their management team? How are the target firm shareholders harmed by such actions? Explain.

9   **Defensive Tactics**   Review the various tactics that a target firm's management may use when trying to deter a hostile takeover attempt. For each tactic provide a balanced discussion of whether they are good or bad for the target's shareholders.

10   **The Diary of a Takeover**   Why do you think the Ryanair takeover of Aer Lingus failed? Do you feel that a Ryanair takeover would have been a good thing or a bad thing for Aer Lingus shareholders? Explain.

11   **Do Mergers Add Value?**   Given the evidence, do you think mergers add value? If so, why do we observe merger waves? If not, why do we see mergers at all?

12   **Accounting for Mergers and Takeovers**   Explain the acquisition method of accounting for mergers and acquisitions. What effect does expensing merger costs have on the viability of a potential merger or acquisition?

13   **Divestitures**   Why would a firm wish to sell off its assets? If the sold divisions are so bad, why are buyers found for them?

REGULAR

14–35

14   **Mergers**   Indicate whether you think the following claims regarding takeovers are true or false. In each case, provide a brief explanation for your answer.

(a)   By merging competitors, takeovers have created monopolies that will raise product prices, reduce production, and harm consumers.

(b)   Managers act in their own interests at times, and in reality may not be answerable to shareholders. Takeovers may reflect runaway management.

(c)   In an efficient market takeovers would not occur, because market prices would reflect the true value of corporations. Thus bidding firms would not be justified in paying premiums above market prices for target firms.

(d)   Traders and institutional investors, having extremely short time horizons, are influenced by their perceptions of what other market traders will be thinking of equity prospects, and do not value takeovers based on fundamental factors. Thus they will sell shares in target firms despite the true value of the firms.

(e) Mergers are a way of avoiding taxes, because they allow the acquiring firm to write up the value of the assets of the acquired firm.

(f) Acquisitions analysis frequently focuses on the total value of the firms involved. An acquisition, however, will usually affect relative values of equities and bonds, as well as their total value.

15 **Merger Rationale** Explain why diversification *per se* is probably not a good reason for merger.

16 **Corporate Split** In May 2005 high-end retailer Nieman Marcus announced plans to sell off its private label credit card business. Unlike other credit cards, private label credit cards can be used only in a particular merchant's store. Why might a company do this? Is there a possibility of reverse synergy?

17 **Poison Pills** Are poison pills good or bad for equity-holders? How do you think acquiring firms are able to get around poison pills? What effect do you think the illegality of poison pills in Europe has had on hostile takeovers?

18 **Merger and Taxes** Discuss why it is important for the tax treatment of mergers to be cohesive across countries.

19 **Economies of Scale** What does it mean to say that a proposed merger will take advantage of available economies of scale? Suppose Eastern Power and Western Power are located in different time zones. Both operate at 60 per cent of capacity, except for peak periods, when they operate at 100 per cent of capacity. The peak periods begin at 9:00 a.m. and 5:00 p.m. local time and last about 45 minutes. Explain why a merger between Eastern and Western might make sense.

20 **Merger Offers** Suppose a company in which you own equity has attracted two takeover offers. Would it ever make sense for your company's management to favour the lower offer? Does the form of payment affect your answer at all?

21 **Merger Profit** Acquiring firm shareholders seem to benefit little from takeovers. Why is this finding a puzzle? What are some of the reasons offered for it?

22 **Calculating Synergy** Evan plc has offered £740 million cash for all of the equity in Tanner plc. Based on recent market information, Tanner is worth £650 million as an independent operation. If the merger makes economic sense for Evan, what is the minimum estimated value of the synergistic benefits from the merger?

23 **Balance Sheets for Mergers** Consider the following pre-merger information about firm X and firm Y:

| | Firm X | Firm Y |
|---|---|---|
| Total earnings (£) | 40,000 | 15,000 |
| Shares outstanding | 20,000 | 20,000 |
| Per-share values (£): | | |
|   Market | 49 | 18 |
|   Book | 20 | 7 |

Assume that firm X acquires firm Y by paying cash for all the shares outstanding at a merger premium of £5 per share. Assuming that neither firm has any debt before or after the merger, construct the post-merger balance sheet for firm X.

24 **Balance Sheets for Mergers** Assume that the following balance sheets are stated at book value. Construct a post-merger balance sheet assuming that Jurion SE purchases Johan GmbH, and both sets of accounts are presented according to International Financial Reporting Standards.

| JURION SE | | | |
|---|---|---|---|
| | **(€)** | | **(€)** |
| Current assets | 10,000 | Current liabilities | 3,100 |
| Non-current assets | 14,000 | Non-current liabilities | 1,900 |
| | | Equity | 19,000 |
| Total | 24,000 | Total | 24,000 |
| JOHAN GmbH | | | |
| | **(€)** | | **(€)** |
| Current assets | 3,400 | Current liabilities | 1,600 |
| Non-current assets | 5,600 | Non-current liabilities | 900 |
| | | Equity | 6,500 |
| Total | 9,000 | Total | 9,000 |

The fair market value of Johan's non-current assets is €12,000 versus the €5,600 book value shown. Jurion pays €17,000 for Johan and raises the needed funds through an issue of long-term debt. Construct the post-merger balance sheet, assuming that the acquisition method of accounting is used.

25 **Balance Sheets for Mergers**  Silver Enterprises has acquired All Gold Mining in a merger transaction. Construct the balance sheet for the new corporation. The following balance sheets represent the pre-merger book values for both firms:

| SILVER ENTERPRISES | | | |
|---|---|---|---|
| | **(€)** | | **(€)** |
| Current assets | 2,600 | Current liabilities | 1,800 |
| Goodwill | 800 | Non-current liabilities | 900 |
| Net non-current assets | 3,900 | Equity | 4,600 |
| Total | 7,300 | Total | 7,300 |
| ALL GOLD MINING | | | |
| | **(€)** | | **(€)** |
| Current assets | 1,100 | Current liabilities | 900 |
| Goodwill | 350 | Non-current liabilities | 0 |
| Non-current assets | 2,800 | Equity | 3,350 |
| Total | 4,250 | Total | 4,250 |

The market value of All Gold Mining's non-current assets (excluding goodwill) is €2,800; the market values for current assets and goodwill are the same as the book values. Assume that Silver Enterprises issues €8,400 in new long-term debt to finance the acquisition.

26 **Cash versus Equity Payment**  Penn NV is analysing the possible acquisition of Teller NV. Both firms have no debt. Penn believes the acquisition will increase its total after-tax annual cash flows by €3.1 million indefinitely. The current market value of Teller is €78 million, and that of Penn is €135 million. The appropriate discount rate for the incremental cash flows is 12 per cent. Penn is trying to decide whether it should offer 40 per cent of its equity or €94 million in cash to Teller's shareholders.

(a)  What is the cost of each alternative?

(b)  What is the NPV of each alternative?

(c)  Which alternative should Penn choose?

27 **EPS, P/E and Mergers** The shareholders of Flannery SA have voted in favour of a buyout offer from Stultz Corporation. Information about each firm is given here:

|  | Flannery | Stultz |
|---|---|---|
| Price – earnings ratio | 5.25 | 21 |
| Shares outstanding | 60,000 | 180,000 |
| Earnings (€) | 300,000 | 675,000 |

Flannery's shareholders will receive one share of Stultz equity for every three shares they hold in Flannery.

(a) What will the EPS of Stultz be after the merger? What will the P/E ratio be if the NPV of the acquisition is zero?

(b) What must Stultz feel is the value of the synergy between these two firms? Explain how your answer can be reconciled with the decision to go ahead with the takeover.

28 **Merger Rationale** Ziff Electrics (ZE) is a public utility that provides electricity to the whole Yorkshire region. Recent events at its Mile-High Nuclear Station have been discouraging. Several shareholders have expressed concern over last year's financial statements.

| Income statement last year (£ millions) | | Balance sheet end of year (£ millions) | |
|---|---|---|---|
| Revenue | 110 | Assets | 400 |
| Fuel | 50 | Debt | 300 |
| Other expenses | 30 | Equity | 100 |
| Interest | 30 |  |  |
| Net income | 0 |  |  |

Recently, a wealthy group of individuals has offered to purchase half of ZE's assets at fair market price. Management recommends that this offer be accepted, because 'We believe our expertise in the energy industry can be better exploited by ZE if we sell our electricity generating and transmission assets and enter the telecommunication business. Although telecommunications is a riskier business than providing electricity as a public utility, it is also potentially very profitable.'

Should the management approve this transaction? Why or why not?

29 **Cash versus Equity as Payment** Consider the following pre-merger information about a bidding firm (firm B) and a target firm (firm T). Assume that both firms have no debt outstanding.

|  | Firm B | Firm T |
|---|---|---|
| Shares outstanding | 1,500 | 900 |
| Price per share (£) | 34 | 24 |

Firm B has estimated that the value of the synergistic benefits from acquiring firm T is £3,000.

(a) If firm T is willing to be acquired for £27 per share in cash, what is the NPV of the merger?

(b) What will the price per share of the merged firm be assuming the conditions in (a)?

(c)   In part (a), what is the merger premium?

(d)   Suppose firm T is agreeable to a merger by an exchange of equity. If B offers three of its shares for every one of T 's shares, what will the price per share of the merged firm be?

(e)   What is the NPV of the merger assuming the conditions in (d)?

30   **Cash versus Equity as Payment**   In problem 29, are the shareholders of firm T better off with the cash offer or the equity offer? At what exchange ratio of B shares to T shares would the shareholders in T be indifferent between the two offers?

31   **Effects of an Equity Exchange**   Consider the following pre-merger information about firm A and firm B:

|                       | Firm A | Firm B |
|-----------------------|--------|--------|
| Total earnings (DKr)  | 900    | 600    |
| Shares outstanding    | 550    | 220    |
| Price per share (DKr) | 40     | 15     |

Assume that firm A acquires firm B via an exchange of equity at a price of DKr20 for each share of B's equity. Both A and B have no debt outstanding.

(a)   What will the earnings per share (EPS) of firm A be after the merger?

(b)   What will firm A's price per share be after the merger if the market incorrectly analyses this reported earnings growth (that is, the price–earnings ratio does not change)?

(c)   What will the price–earnings ratio of the post-merger firm be if the market correctly analyses the transaction?

(d)   If there are no synergy gains, what will the share price of A be after the merger? What will the price–earnings ratio be? What does your answer for the share price tell you about the amount A bid for B? Was it too high? Too low? Explain.

32   **Merger NPV**   Show that the NPV of a merger can be expressed as the value of the synergistic benefits, $\Delta V$, less the merger premium.

33   **Merger NPV**   Fly-By-Night Couriers is analysing the possible acquisition of Flash-in-the-Pan Restaurants. Neither firm has debt. The forecasts of Fly-By-Night show that the purchase would increase its annual after-tax cash flow by £600,000 indefinitely. The current market value of Flash-in-the-Pan is £20 million. The current market value of Fly-By-Night is £35 million. The appropriate discount rate for the incremental cash flows is 8 per cent. Fly-By-Night is trying to decide whether it would offer 25 per cent of its equity or £25 million in cash to Flash-in-the-Pan.

(a)   What is the synergy from the merger?

(b)   What is the value of Flash-in-the-Pan to Fly-By-Night?

(c)   What is the cost to Fly-By-Night of each alternative?

(d)   What is the NPV to Fly-By-Night of each alternative?

(e)   Which alternative should Fly-By-Night use?

34   **Merger NPV**   Harrods plc has a market value of £600 million and 30 million shares outstanding. Selfridge Department Store has a market value of £200 million and 20 million shares outstanding. Harrods is contemplating acquiring Selfridge. Harrods's CFO concludes that the combined firm with synergy will be worth £1 billion, and Selfridge can be acquired at a premium of £100 million.

(a) If Harrods offers 15 million shares of its equity in exchange for the 20 million shares of Selfridge, what will the equity price of Harrods be after the acquisition?

(b) What exchange ratio between the two equities would make the value of equity offer equivalent to a cash offer of £300 million?

35 **Mergers and Shareholder Value** Bentley plc and Rolls Manufacturing are considering a merger. The possible states of the economy and each company's value in that state are shown here:

| State | Probability | Bentley | Rolls |
|---|---|---|---|
| Boom | 0.70 | £300,000 | £260,000 |
| Recession | 0.30 | £110,000 | £80,000 |

Bentley currently has a bond issue outstanding with a face value of £140,000. Rolls is an all-equity company.

(a) What is the value of each company before the merger?

(b) What are the values of each company's debt and equity before the merger?

(c) If the companies continue to operate separately, what are the total value of the companies, the total value of the equity, and the total value of the debt?

(d) What would be the value of the merged company? What would be the value of the merged company's debt and equity?

(e) Is there a transfer of wealth in this case? Why?

(f) Suppose that the face value of Bentley's debt was £100,000. Would this affect the transfer of wealth?

**CHALLENGE**
**36 – 37**

36 **Calculating NPV** Plant AG is considering making an offer to purchase Palmer AG. Plant's vice-president of finance has collected the following information:

| | Plant | Palmer |
|---|---|---|
| Price – earnings ratio | 12.5 | 9 |
| Shares outstanding | 1,000,000 | 550,000 |
| Earnings (€) | 2,000,000 | 580,000 |
| Dividends (€) | 600,000 | 290,000 |

Plant also knows that securities analysts expect the earnings and dividends of Palmer to grow at a constant rate of 5 per cent each year. Plant management believes that the acquisition of Palmer will provide the firm with some economies of scale that will increase this growth rate to 7 per cent per year.

(a) What is the value of Palmer to Plant?

(b) What would be Plant's gain be from this acquisition?

(c) If Plant were to offer €18 in cash for each share of Palmer, what would the NPV of the acquisition be?

(d) What is the most Plant should be willing to pay in cash per share for the equity of Palmer?

(e) If Plant were to offer 100,000 of its shares in exchange for the outstanding equity of Palmer, what would the NPV be?

(f) Should the acquisition be attempted? If so, should it be as in (c) or as in (e)?

(g) Plant's outside financial consultants think that the 7 per cent growth rate is too optimistic, and a 6 per cent rate is more realistic. How does this change your previous answers?

37 **Mergers and Shareholder Value** The Chocolate Ice Cream Company and the Vanilla Ice Cream Company have agreed to merge and form Fudge Swirl Consolidated. The two companies are exactly alike except that they are located in different towns. The end-of-period value of each firm is determined by the weather, as shown below. There will be no synergy to the merger.

| State | Probability | Value (£) |
|---|---|---|
| Rainy | 0.1 | 100,000 |
| Warm | 0.4 | 200,000 |
| Hot | 0.5 | 400,000 |

The weather conditions in each town are independent of those in the other. Furthermore, each company has an outstanding debt claim of £200,000. Assume that no premiums are paid in the merger.

(a) What are the possible values of the combined company?

(b) What are the possible values of end-of-period debt values and equity values after the merger?

(c) Show that the bondholders are better off and the equity-holders are worse off in the combined firm than they would have been if the firms had remained separate.

## The Birdie Golf–Hybrid Golf Merger

**MINI CASE**

Birdie Golf has been in merger talks with Hybrid Golf Company for the past six months. After several rounds of negotiations, the offer under discussion is a cash offer of €550 million for Hybrid Golf. Both companies have niche markets in the golf club industry, and the companies believe a merger will result in significant synergies due to economies of scale in manufacturing and marketing, as well as significant savings in general and administrative expenses.

Bryce Bichon, the financial officer for Birdie, has been instrumental in the merger negotiations. Bryce has prepared the following pro forma financial statements for Hybrid Golf assuming the merger takes place. The financial statements include all synergistic benefits from the merger:

| | 2010 (€) | 2011 (€) | 2012 (€) | 2013 (€) | 2014 (€) |
|---|---|---|---|---|---|
| Sales | 800,000,000 | 900,000,000 | 1,000,000,000 | 1,125,000,000 | 1,250,000,000 |
| Productions costs | 562,000,000 | 630,000,000 | 700,000,000 | 790,000,000 | 875,000,000 |
| Depreciation | 75,000,000 | 80,000,000 | 82,000,000 | 83,000,000 | 83,000,000 |
| Other expenses | 80,000,000 | 90,000,000 | 100,000,000 | 113,000,000 | 125,000,000 |
| EBIT | 83,000,000 | 100,000,000 | 118,000,000 | 139,000,000 | 167,000,000 |
| Interest | 19,000,000 | 22,000,000 | 24,000,000 | 25,000,000 | 27,000,000 |
| Taxable income | 64,000,000 | 78,000,000 | 94,000,000 | 114,000,000 | 140,000,000 |
| Taxes (40%) | 25,600,000 | 31,200,000 | 37,600,000 | 45,600,000 | 56,000,000 |
| Net income | 38,400,000 | 46,800,000 | 56,400,000 | 68,400,000 | 84,000,000 |

Bryce is also aware that the Hybrid Golf division will require investments each year for continuing operations, along with sources of financing. The following table outlines the required investments and sources of financing:

| | 2010 (€) | 2011 (€) | 2012 (€) | 2013 (€) | 2014 (€) |
|---|---|---|---|---|---|
| **Investments:** | | | | | |
| Net working capital | 20,000,000 | 25,000,000 | 25,000,000 | 30,000,000 | 30,000,000 |
| Non-current assets | 15,000,000 | 25,000,000 | 18,000,000 | 12,000,000 | 7,000,000 |
| Total | 35,000,000 | 50,000,000 | 43,000,000 | 42,000,000 | 37,000,000 |
| **Sources of financing:** | | | | | |
| New debt | 35,000,000 | 16,000,000 | 16,000,000 | 15,000,000 | 12,000,000 |
| Profit retention | 0 | 34,000,000 | 27,000,000 | 27,000,000 | 25,000,000 |
| Total | 35,000,000 | 50,000,000 | 43,000,000 | 42,000,000 | 37,000,000 |

The management of Birdie Golf feels that the capital structure at Hybrid Golf is not optimal. If the merger take place, Hybrid Golf will immediately increase its leverage with a €110 million debt issue, which would be followed by a €150 million dividend payment to Birdie Golf. This will increase Hybrid's debt-to-equity ratio from 0.50 to 1.00. Birdie Golf will also be able to use a €25 million tax loss carry-forward in 2011 and 2012 from Hybrid Golf's previous operations. The total value of Hybrid Golf is expected to be €900 million in five years, and the company will have €300 million in debt at that time.

Equity in Birdie Golf currently sells for €94 per share, and the company has 18 million shares of equity outstanding. Hybrid Golf has 8 million shares of equity outstanding. Both companies can borrow at an 8 per cent interest rate. The risk-free rate is 6 per cent, and the expected return on the market is 13 per cent. Bryce believes the current cost of capital for Birdie Golf is 11 per cent. The beta for Hybrid Golf equity at its current capital structure is 1.30.

Bryce has asked you to analyse the financial aspects of the potential merger. Specifically, he has asked you to answer the following questions:

1   Suppose Hybrid shareholders will agree to a merger price of €68.75 per share. Should Birdie proceed with the merger?

2   What is the highest price per share that Birdie should be willing to pay for Hybrid?

3   Suppose Birdie is unwilling to pay cash for the merger, but will consider an equity exchange. What exchange ratio would make the merger terms equivalent to the original merger price of €68.75 per share?

4   What is the highest exchange ratio Birdie would be willing to pay and still undertake the merger?

## Practical Case Study

The HBOS–Lloyds TSB merger was one of the biggest in European banking history. Both banks had been hit hard by the global banking crisis in 2008, and the British government strongly encouraged them to merge in order to be safe enough to ride out the forthcoming recession. Both companies argued that there would be cost savings, and the merger would be good for both sets of shareholders. However, within months of the merger the British government had to bail out the new Lloyds Banking Group and effectively nationalize it.

Carry out your own research into the merger and use the merger techniques in this chapter to ascertain, from an *ex ante* perspective, whether the merger was good for either set of shareholders. Write a brief report on your analysis.

# Relevant Accounting Standards

The main accounting standard for mergers and acquisitions is IFRS3 *Business Combinations*. For restructuring activities the relevant standard is IAS37 *Provisions, Contingent Liabilities and Contingent Assets*.

# Additional Reading

As the size of this chapter attests, the study of mergers, acquisitions and corporate restructuring is huge. Below is a list of recent papers in the area. Naturally, the categorization of papers is not mutually exclusive, and papers do overlap categories. However, hopefully the groupings will aid the reading effort.

## The Merger, Acquisition and Corporate Restructuring Process

Antoniou, A., P. Arbour and H. Zhao (2008) 'How much is too much: are merger premiums too high?', *European Financial Management*, vol. 14, no. 2, pp. 268–287. **UK**.

Betton, S., B.E. Eckbo and K.S. Thorburn (2009) 'Merger negotiations and the toehold puzzle', *Journal of Financial Economics*, vol. 91, no. 2, pp. 158–178. **US**.

Boone, A.L. and J.H. Mulherin (2007) 'How are firms sold?', *Journal of Finance*, vol. 62, no. 2, pp. 847–875. **US**.

Bouwman, C., K. Fuller and A. Nain (2009) 'Market valuation and acquisition quality: empirical evidence', *Review of Financial Studies*, vol. 22, no. 2, pp. 633–679. **US**.

Dittmann, I., E. Maug and C. Schneider (2008) 'How Preussag became TUI: a clinical study of institutional blockholders and restructuring in Europe', *Financial Management*, vol. 37, no. 3, pp. 571–598. **Germany**.

Eckbo, B.E. (2009) 'Bidding strategies and takeover premiums: a review', *Journal of Corporate Finance*, vol. 15, no. 1, pp. 10–29. **International**.

Ekkayokkaya, M., P. Holmes and K. Paudyal (2009) 'The euro and the changing face of European banking: evidence from mergers and acquisitions', *European Financial Management*, vol. 15, no. 2, pp. 451–476. **Europe**.

Faccio, M. and R. Masulis (2005) 'The choice of payment method in European mergers and acquisitions', *Journal of Finance*, vol. 60, no. 3, pp. 1345–1388. **Europe**.

Harford, J. (2005) 'What drives merger waves?', *Journal of Financial Economics*, vol. 77, no. 3, pp. 529–560. **US**.

Hodgkinson, L. and G.H. Partington (2008) 'The motivation for takeovers in the UK', *Journal of Business Finance and Accounting*, vol. 35, nos. 1/2, pp. 102–126. **UK**.

Holmen, M. and J. Knopf (2004) 'Minority shareholder protection and private benefits of control for Swedish mergers', *Journal of Financial and Quantitative Analysis*, vol. 39, 167–191. **Sweden**.

Laeven, L. and R. Levine (2007) 'Is there a diversification discount in financial conglomerates?', *Journal of Financial Economics*, vol. 85, no. 2, pp. 331–367. **US**.

Lambrecht, B.M. and S.C. Myers (2007) 'A theory of takeovers and disinvestment', *Journal of Finance*, vol. 62, no. 2, pp. 809–845. **Theoretical paper**.

Luo, Y. (2005) 'Do insiders learn from outsiders? Evidence from mergers and acquisitions', *Journal of Finance*, vol. 60, no. 3, pp. 1951–1982. **US**.

Maksimovic, V. and G. Phillips (2008) 'The industry life cycle, acquisitions and investment: does firm organisation matter?', *Journal of Finance*, vol. 62, no. 2, pp. 673–708. **US**.

Martynova, M. and L. Renneboog (2008) 'A century of corporate takeovers: what have we learned and where do we stand?', *Journal of Banking and Finance*, vol. 32, no. 10, pp. 2148–2177. **Review paper**.

Martynova, M. and L. Renneboog (2009) 'What determines the financing decision in corporate takeovers: cost of capital, agency problems, or the means of payment?', *Journal of Corporate Finance* (forthcoming). **Europe**.

Rhodes-Kropf, M., D.T. Robinson and S. Viswanathan (2005) 'Valuation waves and merger activity: the empirical evidence', *Journal of Financial Economics*, vol. 77, no. 3, pp. 561–603. **US**.

Rossi, S. and P.F. Volpin (2005) 'Cross-country determinants of mergers and acquisitions', *Journal of Financial Economics*, vol. 74, no. 2, pp. 277–304. **International**.

Wright, M., L. Renneboog, T. Simons and L. Scholes (2006) 'Leveraged buyouts in the UK and continental Europe: retrospect and prospect', *Journal of Applied Corporate Finance*, vol. 18, no. 3, pp. 38–55. **Europe**.

### Pre-Restructuring

Botsari, A. and G. Meeks (2008) 'Do acquirers manage earnings prior to a share for share bid?', *Journal of Business Finance and Accounting*, vol. 35, nos. 5/6, pp. 633–670. **UK**.

Dong, M., D. Hirshleifer, S. Richardson and S.H. Teoh (2006) 'Does investor misvaluation drive the takeover market?', *Journal of Finance*, vol. 61, no. 2, pp. 725–762. **US**.

Field, L.C. and J.M. Karpoff (2002) 'Takeover defenses of IPO firms', *Journal of Finance*, vol. 57, no. 5, pp. 1857–1889. **US**.

Jenkinson, T. and H. Jones (2004) 'Bids and allocations in European IPO bookbuilding', *Journal of Finance*, vol. 59, no. 5, pp. 2309–2338. **Europe**.

Kisgen, D.J., J. Qian and W. Song (2009) 'Are fairness opinions fair? The case of mergers and acquisitions', *Journal of Financial Economics*, vol. 91, no. 2, pp. 179–207. **US**.

Veld, C. and Y.V. Veld-Merkoulova (2008) 'An empirical analysis of the stockholder–bondholder conflict in corporate spin-offs', *Financial Management*, vol. 37, no. 1, pp. 103–124. **US**.

### Post-Restructuring

Devos, E., P. Kadapakkam and S. Krishnamurthy (2009) 'How do mergers create value? A comparison of taxes, market power, and efficiency improvements as explanations for synergies', *Review of Financial Studies*, vol. 22, no. 3, pp. 1179–1211. **US**.

Draper, P. and K. Paudyal (2008) 'Information asymmetry and bidders' gains', *Journal of Business Finance and Accounting*, vol. 35, nos. 3/4, pp. 376–405. **UK**.

Hagendorff, J., M. Collins and K. Keasey (2008) 'Investor protection and the value effects of bank merger announcements in Europe and the US', *Journal of Banking and Finance*, vol. 32, no. 7, pp. 1333–1348. **Europe**.

Masulis, R.W., C. Wang and F. Xie (2007) 'Corporate governance and acquirer returns', *Journal of Finance*, vol. 62, no. 4, pp. 1851–1889. **US**.

Moeller, S.B., F.P. Schlingemann and R.M. Stulz (2005) 'Wealth destruction on a massive scale? A study of acquiring-firm returns in the recent merger wave', *Journal of Finance*, vol. 60, no. 2, pp. 757–782. **US**.

Paul, D.L. (2007) 'Board composition and corrective action: evidence from corporate responses to bad acquisition bids', *Journal of Financial & Quantitative Analysis*, vol. 42, no. 3, pp. 759–778. **US**.

Rajan, R., H. Servaes and L. Zingales (2000) 'The cost of diversity: the diversification discount and inefficient investment', *Journal of Finance*, vol. 55, no. 1, pp. 35–80. **US**.

Renneboog, L. and P.G. Szilagyi (2008) 'Corporate structuring and bondholder wealth', *European Financial Management*, vol. 14, no. 4, pp. 792–819. **Review**.

Santalo, J. and M. Becerra (2008) 'Competition from specialized firms and the diversification–performance linkage', *Journal of Finance*, vol. 62, no. 2, pp. 851–883. **US**.

Wang, C. and F. Xie (2009) 'Corporate governance transfer and synergistic gains from mergers and acquisitions', *Review of Financial Studies*, vol. 22, no. 2, pp. 829–858. **US**.

## Endnotes

1 Mergers between corporations require compliance with government laws. In virtually all countries the shareholders of each corporation must give their assent.

2 *Control* can usually be defined as having a majority vote on the board of directors.

3 M. Porter, *Competitive Advantage* (New York: Free Press, 1998).

4  M.C. Jensen and R.S. Ruback, 'The market for corporate control: the scientific evidence', *Journal of Financial Economics*, vol. 11 (1983).

5  Every country's tax system is different, and almost always complex. The best way to find up-to-date information is by visiting the website of a country's tax authority. A good site with summary information on many countries' tax systems is www.worldwide-tax.com.

6  Although diversification is most easily explained by considering equities in different industries, the key is really that the returns on the two equities are less than perfectly correlated – a relationship that should occur even for equities in the same industry.

7  A dividend is taxable to all tax-paying recipients. A repurchase creates a tax liability only for those who choose to sell (and do so at a profit).

8  The situation is actually a little more complex: The target's shareholders must pay taxes on their capital gains. These shareholders will probably demand a premium from the acquirer to offset this tax.

9  This ratio implies a fair exchange, because a share of Regional is selling for 40 per cent (= €10/€25) of the price of a share of Global.

10  In fact, a number of scholars have argued that diversification can *reduce* firm value by weakening corporate focus, a point to be developed in a later section of this chapter.

11  The analysis will be essentially the same if new equity is issued. However, the analysis will differ if new debt is issued to fund the acquisition, because of the tax shield to debt. An adjusted present value (APV) approach would be necessary here.

12  The basic theoretical ideas are presented in S. Myers and N. Majluf, 'Corporate financing and investment decisions when firms have information that investors do not have', *Journal of Financial Economics* (1984).

13  For example, see G. Andrade, M. Mitchell and E. Stafford, 'New evidence and perspectives on mergers', *Journal of Economic Perspectives* (Spring 2001); and R. Heron and E. Lie, 'Operating performance and the method of payment in takeovers', *Journal of Financial and Quantitative Analysis* (2002).

14  J. Doukas and O.B. Kan, 'Does global diversification destroy firm value?', *Journal of International Business Studies* (2006).

15  See J.M. Campa and I. Hernando, 'Shareholder value creation in European M&As', *European Financial Management* (2004).

16  Taken from G. Andrade, M. Mitchell and E. Stafford, 'New evidence and perspectives on mergers', *Journal of Economic Perspectives* (Spring 2001), Table 1.

17  A. Antonios, P. Arbour and H. Zhang, 'How much is too much? Are merger premiums too high?', *European Financial Management* (2008).

18  S. Datta, M. Iskandar-Datta and K. Raman, 'Executive compensation and corporate acquisition decisions', *Journal of Finance* (December 2001).

19  From J. Harford, 'Corporate cash reserves and acquisitions', *Journal of Finance* (December 1999), p. 1969.

20  U. Malmendier and G. Tate, 'Who makes acquisitions? CEO overconfidence and the market's reaction', *Journal of Financial Economics* (2008).

21  However, as stated earlier, managers may resist takeovers to raise the offer price, not to prevent the merger.

22  J. Wulf, 'Do CEOs in mergers trade power for premium? Evidence From "mergers of equals"', *Journal of Law, Economics, and Organization* (Spring 2004).

23  S. Kaplan and M. Weisbach, 'The success of acquisitions: evidence from divestitures', *Journal of Finance* (March 1992).

24  R. Michaely and W. Shaw, 'The choice of going public: spinoffs vs. carveouts', *Financial Management* (Autumn 1995).

25  J. Allen and J. McConnell, 'Equity carve-outs and managerial discretion', *Journal of Finance* (February 1998).

Online LearningCentre

To help you grasp the key concepts of this chapter check out the extra resources posted on the Online Learning Centre at **www.mcgraw-hill.co.uk/textbooks/hillier**

Among other helpful resources there are PowerPoint presentations, chapter outlines and mini-cases.

# Chapter 30

# Financial Distress

| | |
|---|---|
| APR | Absolute priority rule |
| CVA | Company voluntary agreement |
| DIP | Debtor in possession (debt) |
| Z | Index of bankruptcy |

If there is one thing that has characterized recent times, it is that many firms have become financially distressed. Because of the global credit crunch, which led to the worldwide recession in 2009, corporations have never been in such difficulty. In most industries demand for services and goods has plummeted, and at the time of writing the International Monetary Fund has predicted that global economic growth will be only 0.5 per cent in 2009. This is the worst economic performance since World War Two.

A firm that does not generate enough cash flow to make a contractually required payment, such as an interest payment, will experience financial distress. A firm that defaults on a required payment may be forced to liquidate its assets. More often, a defaulting firm will reorganize its financial structure. Financial restructuring involves replacing old financial claims with new ones, and takes place with private workouts or legal bankruptcy. Private workouts are voluntary arrangements to restructure a company's debt, such as postponing a payment or reducing the size of the payment. If a private workout is not possible, formal bankruptcy is usually required.

## 30.1 What Is Financial Distress?

Financial distress is surprisingly hard to define precisely. This is true partly because of the variety of events befalling firms under financial distress. The list of events is almost endless, but here are some examples:

- Dividend reductions
- Plant closings
- Losses
- Layoffs
- CEO resignations
- Plummeting share prices

Financial distress is a situation where a firm's operating cash flows are not sufficient to satisfy current obligations (such as trade credits or interest expenses), and the firm is forced to take corrective action.[1] Financial distress may lead a firm to default on a contract, and it may involve financial restructuring between the firm, its creditors, and its equity investors. Usually the firm is forced to take actions that it would not have taken if it had sufficient cash flow.

Our definition of financial distress can be expanded somewhat by linking it to insolvency. Insolvency is defined in *Black's Law Dictionary* as[2]

> Inability to pay one's debts; lack of means of paying one's debts. Such a condition of a woman's (or man's) assets and liability that the former made immediately available would be insufficient to discharge the latter.

TABLE
30.1

| Company | Country | Year |
|---|---|---|
| Ssangyong Motor Company | South Korea | 2009 |
| Nortel Networks | United States | 2009 |
| Washington Mutual | United States | 2008 |
| Sterling Airlines | Denmark | 2008 |
| Sanlu Group | China | 2008 |
| Lehman Brothers Holdings Inc. | United States | 2008 |
| Kaupthing Bank | Iceland | 2008 |
| Hypo Real Estate | Germany | 2008 |
| Yukos | Russia | 2006 |
| MG Rover | United Kingdom | 2005 |
| Delta Air Lines, Inc. | United States | 2005 |
| Parmalat | Italy | 2004 |
| Worldcom Inc. | United States | 2002 |
| Sabena | Belgium | 2001 |
| Enron Corp. | United States | 2001 |

**Table 30.1** Large corporate bankruptcies since 2001

This definition has two general themes: value and flows.[3] These two ways of thinking about insolvency are depicted in Fig. 30.1. Value-based insolvency occurs when a firm has negative net worth, so the value of assets is less than the value of its debts. Flow-based insolvency occurs when operating cash flow is insufficient to meet current obligations. Flow-based insolvency refers to the inability to pay one's debts.

## 30.2 What Happens in Financial Distress?

There are many responses to financial distress that a firm can make. These include one or more of the following turnaround strategies.

- Asset expansion policies
- Operational contraction policies
- Financial policies
- External control activity
- Changes in managerial control
- Wind up company

### Asset Expansion Policies

If a firm finds itself in difficulty, it may try to reduce the risk of its operations by increasing the size of its business or assets. Asset expansion policies include the full acquisition of another firm, a partial acquisition, setting up a new joint venture, increasing capital expenditure, higher levels of production, or expansion of existing facilities.

The joint venture between Fiat and Chrysler is a good example of an asset expansion policy. In 2009 carmakers were facing a bleak prospect, with sales down across the world. The US and British governments had already bailed out their own automobile industries, and many carmakers had reduced production to only part of the year. By entering into a joint venture, Fiat and Chrysler were able to expand their sales revenue at a time when they needed it the most.

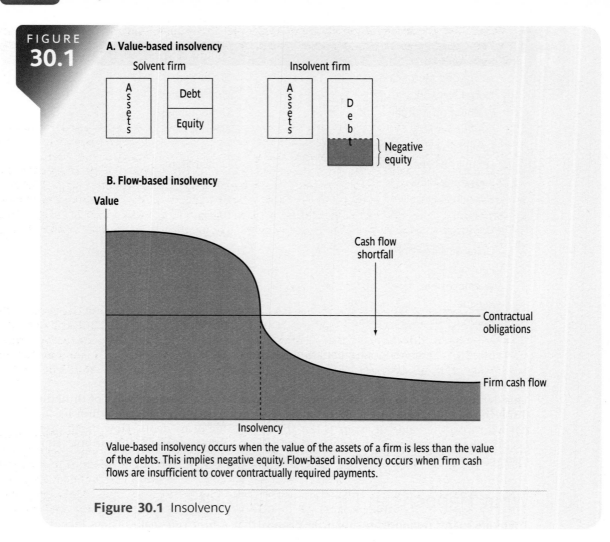

**FIGURE 30.1**

**A. Value-based insolvency**

Value-based insolvency occurs when the value of the assets of a firm is less than the value of the debts. This implies negative equity. Flow-based insolvency occurs when firm cash flows are insufficient to cover contractually required payments.

**Figure 30.1** Insolvency

## Operational Contraction Policies

The opposite of expansion is contraction, and many firms choose to focus on their most profitable businesses during a downturn. Operational contraction policies include asset sales, spin-offs and divestitures (see Chapter 29). Plants may also be closed, production can be cut, and employees made redundant. Redundancies are politically very sensitive, and many countries have very strong trade unions that can dramatically constrain the flexibility of firms when dealing with their own workforce.

Honda is a good example of following a contraction policy. First quarter results for 2009 were absolutely dire. Car sales had dropped by 10 per cent, and 400,000 fewer cars were sold than in the same period in 2008. There was also the very strong possibility that the company would make an annual loss for the first time since it was founded in 1948. In response, Honda cut global production by 420,000 units and closed its UK plant for four months in order to reduce inventory levels. The employees of the British plant were still paid during this period and, as a result, no redundancies were made.

## Financial Policies

Financially distressed firms will definitely face some type of cash liquidity problem. Several remedies are available. One, the company can reduce its annual dividend. Another option is to restructure existing debt facilities so that less interest is paid. The equity and debt markets may also be tapped to raise further funding.

During the global credit crunch many banks had to be bailed out by their governments with loan guarantees and equity share issues. In addition, almost every bank slashed its dividends to zero.

## External Control Activity

External control activity means that the firm has been taken over, or an outside investor takes a significant stake in the firm. A change in external control means that one or more major shareholders sell their shares to another investor with a larger capital base and greater access to capital.

The European football industry has seen many deals of this type. One notable example is Glasgow Celtic, which was days away from bankruptcy when investor Fergus McCann purchased the shares of the club, imposed a very strict turnaround strategy, and reduced debt to almost zero. The team subsequently went on to dominate Scottish football, reached the UEFA cup final in 2003, and was one of only a few major British clubs to make a profit during the economic recession.

## Changes in Managerial Control

The ultimate penalty for poor performance is losing your job, and many firms opt to remove their chairman, chief executive or other directors when they are in financial distress. This will normally go hand in hand with other forms of restructuring. Examples include Fred Goodwin, the former chief executive of Royal Bank of Scotland, who had to step down after the bank found itself in serious financial difficulty as a result of the acquisition of Dutch bank ABN AMRO in 2007.

## Wind up Company

The final and least desirable strategy a financially distressed firm will follow is to wind up its operations and go into some form of bankruptcy. Bankruptcy laws differ on a country-by-country basis, and even within the United Kingdom bankruptcy law is different in Scotland from the rest of the country. At the time of writing (2009), growth in corporate bankruptcies had rocketed as a result of the harsh economic conditions facing businesses. Bankruptcy may not always end in the disappearance of a company, and firms may be split up, sold on to a new buyer, or restructured during the process.

Figure 30.2 shows how large public firms move through financial distress in the US. Approximately half of the financial restructurings have been effected via private workouts. Most large public firms (approximately 70 per cent) that file for bankruptcy are able to reorganize and continue to do business.[4]

Firms in Europe follow a very similar process when they are financially distressed. For example, Table 30.2 presents the turnaround strategies of British firms that faced financial distress during the 1990s. The majority of firms reduced their scope of operations and underwent some form of financial restructuring.

Financial distress can serve as a firm's 'early warning' system for trouble. Firms with more debt will experience financial distress earlier than firms with less debt. However, firms that experience financial distress earlier will have more time for private workouts and reorganization. Firms with low leverage will experience financial distress later and, in many instances, be forced to liquidate.

# 30.3 Bankruptcy Liquidation and Reorganization

Firms that cannot or choose not to make contractually required payments to creditors have two basic options: liquidation or reorganization.

Liquidation means termination of the firm as a going concern; it involves selling the assets of the firm for salvage value. The proceeds, net of transactions costs, are distributed to creditors in order of established priority.

FIGURE
**30.2**

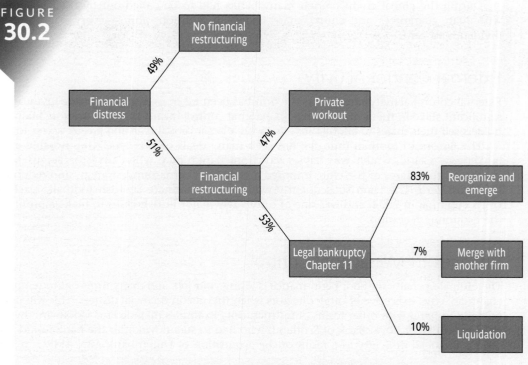

*Source*: K.H. Wruck, 'Financial distress: reorganization and organizational efficiency', *Journal of Financial Economics*, vol. 27 (1990), Figure 2. See also S.C. Gilson, K. John and L.N.P. Lang, 'Troubled debt restructuring: an empirical study of private reorganization of firms in defaults', *Journal of Financial Economics*, vol. 27 (1990); and L.A. Weiss, 'Bankruptcy resolution: direct costs and violation of priority of claims', *Journal of Financial Economics*, vol. 27 (1990).

**Figure 30.2** What happens in financial distress

**Reorganization** is the option of keeping the firm as a going concern; it sometimes involves issuing new securities to replace old securities.

Liquidation and formal reorganization may be done by bankruptcy. *Bankruptcy* is a legal proceeding, and can be done voluntarily, with the corporation filing the petition, or involuntarily, with the creditors filing the petition.

## Bankruptcy Law

Bankruptcy law across the world is converging to a similar process. However, there are important country-level differences. The European Union introduced its bankruptcy regulation in 2002, 'Regulation on Insolvency Proceedings', which is followed by all EU countries, with the exception of Denmark. As European bankruptcy law is very similar, the regulations facing British bankruptcy will be discussed in detail, followed by an overview of the salient differences in other countries.

Financially distressed firms in the UK can be voluntarily or compulsorily dissolved or liquidated. Liquidation means that the firm's assets are sold to allow payment of the outstanding liabilities of the firm. However, this is the very last and least desirable option, and it will be considered only when all other strategies have been exhausted. An alternative is to appoint an administrator, who will attempt to restructure the firm's outstanding claims, introduce a viable business model, or look for a potential buyer. It is important to note that when a firm is in administration, it will continue business until a solution (which may be liquidation) is found.

| TABLE 30.2 | Reported action | Percentage of firms |
|---|---|---|
| | *Asset expansion policies* | |
| | Full acquisition | 32.46 |
| | Partial acquisition | 4.55 |
| | Joint venture | 8.44 |
| | Increase investment expenditures | 0.65 |
| | Increase output / expand production facilities | 2.60 |
| | Total | 40.26 |
| | *Asset contraction policies* | |
| | Asset sale / spin-off / divestiture | 29.87 |
| | Plant closure | 1.30 |
| | Withdrawal from line of business | 7.14 |
| | Unspecified cost-cutting programme | 16.23 |
| | Cut in employment | 13.64 |
| | Total | 65.58 |
| | *Financial policies* | |
| | Cut dividend | 45.45 |
| | Debt restructuring / renegotiation | 1.95 |
| | Issue debt | 4.55 |
| | Rights issue | 3.90 |
| | Placing | 6.49 |
| | Total | 54.55 |
| | *External control activity* | |
| | Non-financial block purchase | 0.65 |
| | Negotiations | 4.55 |
| | Unsuccessful offer | 0 |
| | Total | 4.55 |
| | *Change in managerial control* | |
| | CEO turnover | 20.78 |
| | Forced CEO turnover | 8.44 |
| | Total | 20.78 |

*Source*: D. Hillier and P. McColgan, 'Managerial discipline and firm responses to a decline in operating performance', Working Paper (2007).

**Table 30.2** Turnaround strategies of financially distressed UK firms 1992–1998

**Liquidation** For a firm to be liquidated or made insolvent, a creditor, the directors or shareholders must petition a court for a winding-up order. If a judge decides that there is a case for liquidation, an official receiver will be appointed, who liquidates the assets of the firm and distributes the proceeds to all creditors. Normally, creditors will not be paid all that they are due, because of direct bankruptcy costs from legal and administration fees.

**Priority of Claims** Once a corporation is determined to be bankrupt, liquidation takes place. The distribution of the proceeds of the liquidation occurs according to the following general priority:

1   Administration expenses associated with liquidating the bankrupt's assets

2   Unsecured claims arising after the filing of an involuntary bankruptcy petition

3   Wages, salaries, and commissions

4   Contributions to employee benefit plans arising within a set period before the filing date

5   Consumer claims

6   Tax claims

7   Secured and unsecured creditors' claims

8   Preference shareholder claims

9   Ordinary shareholder claims

The priority rule in liquidation is known as the absolute priority rule (APR).

One qualification to this list concerns secured creditors. Liens on property are outside APR ordering. However, if the secured property is liquidated and provides cash insufficient to cover the amount owed them, the secured creditors join with unsecured creditors in dividing the remaining liquidating value. In contrast, if the secured property is liquidated for proceeds greater than the secured claim, the net proceeds are used to pay unsecured creditors and others.

## EXAMPLE 30.1    APR

The B.O. Deodorant Company is to be liquidated. Its liquidating value is £2.7 million. Bonds worth £1.5 million are secured by a mortgage on the B.O. Deodorant Company corporate headquarters building, which is sold for £1 million; £200,000 is used to cover administrative costs and other claims (including unpaid wages, pension benefits, consumer claims, and taxes). After paying £200,000 to the administrative priority claims, the amount available to pay secured and unsecured creditors is £2.5 million. This is less than the amount of unpaid debt of £4 million.

Under APR, all creditors must be paid before shareholders, and the mortgage bondholders have first claim on the £1 million obtained from the sale of the headquarters building.

The trustee has proposed the following distribution:

| Type of claim | Prior claim (£) | Cash received under liquidation (£) |
|---|---|---|
| Bonds (secured by mortgage) | 1,500,000 | 1,500,000 |
| Subordinated debentures | 2,500,000 | 1,000,000 |
| Ordinary shareholders | 10,000,000 | 0 |
| Total | 14,000,000 | 2,500,000 |

| **Calculation of the distribution** | (£) |
|---|---|
| Cash received from sale of assets available for distribution | 2,500,000 |
| Cash paid to secured bondholders on sale of mortgaged property | 1,000,000 |
| Available to bond and debenture holders | 1,500,000 |
| Total claims remaining (£4,000,000 less payment of £1,000,000 on secured bonds) | 3,000,000 |
| Distribution of remaining £1,500,000 to cover total remaining claims of £3,000,000 | |

| Type of claim remaining | Claim on liquidation | |
|---|---|---|
| | Proceeds (£) | Cash received (£) |
| Bonds | 500,000 | 500,000 |
| Debentures | 2,500,000 | 1,000,000 |
| Total | 3,000,000 | 1,500,000 |

**Administration**  When a company enters administration, the administrator will attempt to restructure the company's liabilities, look for a buyer, or break up the company into viable parts. Possible strategies also include exchanging debt for equity, which allows the financially distressed firm to dispense with paying interest on debt, and at the same time gives the creditor a stake in the company should it recover.

The legal agreement that details how the firm's liabilities are to be restructured is known as a company voluntary agreement (CVA). If creditors reject the CVA, or the company does not submit a CVA to the court, the judge can give the corporation an extension, during which it must come up with an acceptable plan or ask the creditors to come up with their own reorganization plan. In most cases at least one extension is granted. Under UK bankruptcy law a CVA will be accepted if at least 75 per cent of the company's claimholders, including shareholders, vote in favour of it. Once accepted, the agreement is legally binding.

In Scotland bankruptcy law is slightly more complex. In addition to administration and insolvency procedures, firms may also go into receivership. This is also a characteristic of bankruptcy law in England and Wales for firms that have outstanding securities issued before 2003. The differences between administration and receivership are important. When in administration, the financially distressed firm is legally protected from its creditors while a CVA is prepared. An insolvency practitioner, such as an accounting firm, is normally appointed to run the business while the agreement is being drawn up. A firm will go into receivership if its creditors do not believe that the company can recover and repay its liabilities. A receiver, again normally an accounting firm, will thus be appointed to sell the assets of the firm so that the creditors can be paid.

---

**EXAMPLE 30.2**

Suppose B.O. Deodorant Co. decides to go into administration and reorganize. Generally, senior claims are honoured in full before various other claims receive anything. Assume that the 'going concern' value of B.O. Deodorant Co. is £3 million, and that its statement of financial position is as shown:

|  | (£) |
|---|---|
| Assets | 3,000,000 |
| Liabilities |  |
| Mortgage bonds | 1,500,000 |
| Subordinated debentures | 2,500,000 |
| Shareholders' equity | −1,000,000 |

The firm has proposed the following reorganization plan:

| Old security | Old claim (£) | New claim with reorganization plan (£) |
|---|---|---|
| Mortgage bonds | 1,500,000 | 1,500,000 |
| Subordinated debentures | 2,500,000 | 1,500,000 |

and a distribution of new securities under a new claim with this reorganization plan:

| Old security | Received under proposed reorganization plan |
|---|---|
| Mortgage bonds | £1,000,000 in 9% senior debentures |
|  | £500,000 in 11% subordinated debentures |
| Debentures | £1,000,000 in 8% preference shares |
|  | £500,000 in ordinary shares |

▶ However, it will be difficult for the firm to convince secured creditors (mortgage bonds) to accept unsecured debentures of equal face value. In addition, the firm may wish to allow the old shareholders to retain some participation in the firm. Needless to say, this would be a violation of the absolute priority rule, and the holders of the debentures would not be happy.

**Bankruptcy in Other Countries**   Bankruptcy procedures in most countries follow the same model as that in the United Kingdom. In the United States financially distressed firms may file for Chapter 11 bankruptcy (equivalent to administration) or for Chapter 7 bankruptcy (equivalent to liquidation). All other aspects of the system are practically the same.

Countries in the European Union follow the 2002 'Regulation on Insolvency Proceedings'. Some country level differences do exist, however. Under Spanish insolvency law a creditors' meeting is organized to form a CVA, and if it is not possible to come to an agreement, the firm will be liquidated. France has a three-stage process. The first stage involves pre-insolvency hearings, which can occur if the firm's auditor is concerned about the financial health of the firm. If the hearings cannot resolve the auditor's concerns, a petition will be made to a commercial court. The firm may at this point request a three-month window to draw up a CVA that will be acceptable to all parties. If this is unsuccessful, the firm will be wound up. Finally, although South Africa follows a similar system to other countries, there is no administration process. Thus creditors, shareholders, or the company itself will go directly to the South African High Court to request that the firm be placed in liquidation. The process is then worked through the system, and restructuring or winding-up may be an outcome of this process.

# In Their Own Words

## Edward I. Altman* on Corporate Financial Distress and Bankruptcy

As we entered the new millennium, corporate distress and bankruptcy were no longer a niche area of corporate evolution. The average company is far riskier today than it was just two decades ago, and the roles of the bankruptcy courts and restructuring specialists have never been more important. Financial distress of private and public entities throughout the world is a frequent occurrence with important implications to their many stakeholders. While the role of corporate bankruptcy laws is clear – either to provide a legal procedure that permits firms, which have temporary liquidity problems, to restructure and successfully emerge as continuing entities or to provide an orderly process to liquidate assets for the benefit of creditors before asset values are dissipated – bankruptcy laws differ markedly from country to country.

It is generally agreed that the US Chapter 11 provisions under the Bankruptcy Reform Act of 1978 provide the most protection for bankrupt firms' assets and result in a greater likelihood of successful reorganization than is found in other countries where liquidation and sale of the assets for the benefit of creditors is more likely the result. But the US code's process is usually lengthy (averaging close to two years, except where a sufficient number of creditors agree in advance via a prepackaged Chapter 11) and expensive, and the reorganized entity is not always successful in avoiding subsequent distress. If the reorganization is not successful, then liquidation under Chapter 7 will usually ensue.

Bankruptcy processes in the industrialized world outside the United States strongly favour senior creditors who obtain control of the firm and seek to enforce greater adherence to debt contracts. The UK process, for example, is speedy and less costly, but the reduced costs can result in undesirable liquidations, unemployment, and underinvestment. The new bankruptcy code in Germany attempts to reduce the considerable power of secured creditors but it is still closer to the UK system.

Regardless of the location, one of the objectives of bankruptcy and other distressed workout arrangements is that creditors and other suppliers of capital clearly know their rights and expected recoveries in the event of a distressed situation. When these are not transparent and/ or are based on outdated processes with arbitrary and possibly corrupt outcomes, then the entire economic system suffers and growth is inhibited. Such is the case in several emerging-market countries. Revision of these outdated systems should be a priority.

*\* Edward I. Altman is Max L. Heine Professor of Finance, NYU Stern School of Business. He is widely recognized as one of the world's experts on bankruptcy and credit analysis, as well as the distressed debt and high-yield bond markets.*

## 30.4 Private Workout or Bankruptcy: Which Is Best?

A firm that defaults on its debt payments will need to restructure its financial claims. The firm will have two choices: formal bankruptcy or private workout. The previous section described two types of formal bankruptcy: bankruptcy liquidation and bankruptcy reorganization. This section compares private workouts with bankruptcy reorganizations. Both types of financial restructuring involve exchanging new financial claims for old financial claims. Usually senior debt is replaced with junior debt, and debt is replaced with equity. Much recent academic research has described what happens in private workouts and formal bankruptcies.[5]

- Historically, half of financial restructurings have been private, but recently formal bankruptcy has dominated.

- Firms that emerge from private workouts experience share price increases that are much greater than those for firms emerging from formal bankruptcies.

- The direct costs of private workouts are much less than the costs of formal bankruptcies.

- Top management usually loses pay and sometimes jobs in both private workouts and formal bankruptcies.

These facts, when taken together, seem to suggest that a private workout is much better than a formal bankruptcy. We then ask: Why do firms ever use formal bankruptcies to restructure?

### The Marginal Firm

For the average firm a formal bankruptcy is more costly than a private workout, but for some firms formal bankruptcy is better. Formal bankruptcy allows firms to issue debt that is senior to all previously incurred debt. This new debt is 'debtor in possession' (DIP) debt. For firms that need a temporary injection of cash, DIP debt makes bankruptcy reorganization an attractive alternative to a private workout. There are some tax advantages to bankruptcy. Firms do not lose tax carry-forwards in bankruptcy, and the tax treatment of the cancellation of indebtedness is better in bankruptcy. Also, interest on pre-bankruptcy unsecured debt stops accruing in formal bankruptcy.

### Holdouts

Bankruptcy is usually better for the equity investors than it is for the creditors. Using DIP debt and stopping pre-bankruptcy interest on unsecured debt helps the shareholders and hurts the creditors. As a consequence, equity investors can usually hold out for a better deal in bankruptcy. The absolute priority rule, which favours creditors over equity investors, is usually violated in formal bankruptcies. One recent study found that in 81 per cent of recent bankruptcies the equity investor obtained some compensation.[6] When a firm is in administration, the creditors are often forced to give up some of their seniority rights to get management and the equity investors to agree to a deal.

## Complexity

A firm with a complicated capital structure will have more trouble putting together a private workout. Firms with secured creditors and trade creditors will usually use formal bankruptcy, because it is too hard to reach an agreement with many different types of creditor.

## Lack of Information

There is an inherent conflict of interest between equity investors and creditors, and the conflict is accentuated when both have incomplete information about the circumstances of financial distress. When a firm initially experiences a cash flow shortfall, it may not know whether the shortfall is permanent or temporary. If the shortfall is permanent, creditors will push for a formal reorganization or liquidation. However, if the cash flow shortfall is temporary, formal reorganization or liquidation may not be necessary. Equity investors will push for this viewpoint. This conflict of interest cannot easily be resolved.

These last two points are especially important. They suggest that financial distress will be more expensive (cheaper) if complexity is high (low) and information is incomplete (complete). Complexity and lack of information make cheap workouts less likely.

## Institutional Factors

Most research on corporate bankruptcies has looked at single countries, such as the United States and United Kingdom. However, an examination of only one country can mask the effect of important institutional factors that relate to the legal and corporate system. Davydenko and Franks (2008) look at the French, German and British systems of bankruptcy, and investigate whether their country-specific regulations impact upon the likelihood of firms going into and surviving formal administration.[7]

The legal bankruptcy systems in France, Germany and the UK fall under the umbrella of EU regulation. However, France and the UK represent two extremes in their approaches to resolving bankruptcy. Whereas France's approach focuses on the debtor or borrowing firm, the UK is very much creditor- or lender-friendly. In France lenders have no input, beyond an advisory role, into the reorganization plan. This contrasts with the situation in the UK, where creditors can veto any reorganization plan that is put forward by the company. Germany is somewhere in between these two extremes.

Davydenko and Franks found that banks required higher levels of collateral when lending to French companies to offset the lower likelihood of receiving outstanding debts in the event of a default. Moreover, recovery rates (i.e. the percentage of outstanding debts that are received by creditors) are significantly higher in the United Kingdom (92 per cent) than in Germany (67 per cent) or France (56 per cent). Interestingly, British firms are more likely to survive administration, because their creditors, normally banks, are more likely to work with the financially distressed company to see it through the administration period.

# 30.5 Predicting Financial Distress: The *Z*-Score Model[8]

Many potential lenders use credit scoring models to assess the creditworthiness of prospective borrowers. The general idea is to find statistical factors that enable the lenders to discriminate between good and bad credit risks. To put it more precisely, lenders want to identify attributes of the borrower that can be used to predict default or bankruptcy.

Edward Altman has developed a model using financial statement ratios and multiple discriminant analyses to predict bankruptcy for publicly traded manufacturing firms. The resultant model for US companies is of the form:

| TABLE 30.3 | Bankrupt firms | Non-bankrupt firms |
|---|---|---|
| Net working capital / Total assets | −6.1% | 41.4% |
| Accumulated retained earnings / Total assets | −62.6% | 35.5% |
| EBIT / Total assets | −31.8% | 15.4% |
| Market value of equity / Total liabilities | 40.1% | 247.7% |
| Sales / Assets | 150% | 190% |

*Source*: E.I. Altman, *Corporate Financial Distress and Bankruptcy* (New York: John Wiley & Sons, 1993), Table 3.1, p. 109.

**Table 30.3** Financial statement ratios one year before bankruptcy: manufacturing firms

$$Z = 3.3 \times \frac{\text{EBIT}}{\text{Total assets}} + 1.2 \times \frac{\text{Net working capital}}{\text{Total assets}}$$
$$+ 1.0 \times \frac{\text{Sales}}{\text{Total assets}} + 0.6 \times \frac{\text{Market value of equity}}{\text{Book value of debt}}$$
$$+ 1.4 \times \frac{\text{Accumulated retained earnings}}{\text{Total assets}}$$

where *Z* is an index of bankruptcy.

A score of *Z* less than 2.675 indicates that a firm has a 95 per cent chance of becoming bankrupt within one year. However, Altman's results show that in practice scores between 1.81 and 2.99 should be thought of as a grey area. In actual use, bankruptcy would be predicted if $Z \le 1.81$ and non-bankruptcy if $Z \ge 2.99$. Altman shows that bankrupt firms and non-bankrupt firms have very different financial profiles one year before bankruptcy. These different financial profiles are the key intuition behind the *Z*-score model, and are depicted in Table 30.3.

Altman's original *Z*-score model requires a firm to have publicly traded equity and be a manufacturer. He uses a revised model to make it applicable for private firms and non-manufacturers. The resulting model is this:

$$Z = 6.56 \times \frac{\text{Net working capital}}{\text{Total assets}} + 3.26 \times \frac{\text{Accumulated retained earnings}}{\text{Total assets}}$$
$$+ 1.05 \times \frac{\text{EBIT}}{\text{Total assets}} + 6.72 \times \frac{\text{Book value of equity}}{\text{Total liabilities}}$$

where $Z < 1.23$ indicates a bankruptcy prediction, $1.23 \ge Z \le 2.90$ indicates a grey area, and $Z > 2.90$ indicates no bankruptcy.

**EXAMPLE 30.3**

Consider the financial accounts of Sanofi-Aventis SA from Chapter 26. The company is publicly traded, but not a manufacturer, and so the modified *Z*-score model will be used. The alert reader will notice that the model uses accounting variables that are found in US accounting statements. International Financial Reporting Standards (IFRS) have slightly different ways of presenting the information. For example, net working capital appears as current assets less current liabilities, and accumulated retained earnings appears in notes to the statement of financial position.

The first step is to determine the value of each of the financial statement variables and apply them in the Z-score model. In € millions:

$$\frac{\text{Net working capital}}{\text{Total assets}} = \frac{\text{Current assets } - \text{ Current liabilities}}{\text{Total assets}}$$

$$= \frac{12,553 - 9,669}{71,994} = 0.040$$

$$\frac{\text{Accumulated retained earnings}}{\text{Total assets}} = \frac{47,275}{71,994} = 0.657$$

$$\frac{\text{EBIT}}{\text{Total assets}} = \frac{5,911}{71,994} = 0.082$$

$$\frac{\text{Book value of equity}}{\text{Total liabilities}} = \frac{44,719}{27,195} = 1.644$$

The next step is to calculate the revised Z-score:

$$Z = 6.56 \times 0.040 + 3.26 \times 0.657 + 1.05 \times 0.082 + 6.72 \times 1.644$$
$$= 11.05$$

Finally we determine that the Z-score is above 2.9, and we conclude that Sanofi-Aventis is a good credit risk.

The same alert reader will also wonder why US Z-score coefficients can be used for a firm that is based in Europe. This would be a very good observation. In practice, banks use a variety of propriety prediction models when assessing the credit-worthiness of potential borrowers, and Altman's Z-score model is just one of these. Another approach is to use neural networks to predict failure in borrowers. Irrespective of the model used, good-quality data on credit defaults is required in order to calibrate the coefficients. The coefficients in any model will clearly be a function of the borrower and lender demographics, institutional factors, and the quality of data that the analyst has in her possession. In practice, each country will have its own set of important variables and coefficients. All Altman's model does is provide a prediction of failure, which is not a perfect prediction of the future. As a general indicator, the US coefficients can be used to provide some insight into the bankruptcy risk of corporations in other countries – only don't take the outcome as particularly precise.

## Summary and Conclusions

This chapter examined what happens when firms experience financial distress.

1   Financial distress is a situation where a firm's operating cash flow is not sufficient to cover contractual obligations. Financially distressed firms are often forced to take corrective action and undergo financial restructuring. Financial restructuring involves exchanging new financial claims for old ones.

2   Financial restructuring can be accomplished with a private workout or formal bankruptcy. Financial restructuring can involve liquidation or reorganization. However, liquidation is not common.

3   Corporate bankruptcy involves liquidation or reorganization. An essential feature of bankruptcy codes is the absolute priority rule. The absolute priority rule states that senior creditors are paid in full before junior creditors receive anything. However, in practice the absolute priority rule is often violated.

# Questions and Problems

1  **Financial Distress**  Define *financial distress* using the value-based and flow-based approaches.

2  **What Happens in Financial Distress**  Review the turnaround strategies that firms can follow when in financial distress. Which do you think are most effective? Why?

3  **Bankruptcy Liquidation and Administration**  What is the difference between administration and reorganization? What are some benefits of financial distress?

4  **Private Workouts and Bankruptcy**  Do you think country-level institutional factors affect the turnaround strategies financially distressed firms may adopt? Explain.

5  **Predicting Financial Distress**  Review the variables in Altman's Z-score model. Why do you think these variables are important in predicting financial distress?

6  **Financial Distress**  Why doesn't financial distress always cause firms to die?

7  **APR**  What is the absolute priority rule?

8  **DIP Loans**  What are DIP loans? Where do DIP loans fall in the APR?

9  **Bankruptcy Ethics**  Firms sometimes use the threat of a bankruptcy filing to force creditors to renegotiate terms. Critics argue that in such cases the firm is using bankruptcy laws 'as a sword rather than a shield'. Is this an ethical tactic?

10  **Bankruptcy Ethics**  Several firms have entered bankruptcy, or threatened to enter bankruptcy, at least in part, as a means of reducing labour costs. Whether this move is ethical, or proper, is hotly debated. Is this an ethical use of bankruptcy?

11  **Bankruptcy versus Private Workouts**  Why do so many firms file for legal bankruptcy when private workouts are so much less expensive?

12  **Administration**  When Beacon Computers entered insolvency, it had the following balance sheet information:

| Liquidating value | (£) | Claims | (£) |
|---|---|---|---|
| | | Trade credit | 3,000 |
| | | Secured mortgage notes | 6,000 |
| | | Senior debentures | 5,000 |
| | | Junior debentures | 9,000 |
| Total assets | 15,500 | Book equity | −7,500 |

Assuming there are no legal fees associated with the bankruptcy, as trustee, what distribution of liquidating value do you propose?

13  **Administration**  When Masters Printing filed for bankruptcy, it entered administration. Key information is shown here:

| Assets | (£) | Claims | (£) |
|---|---|---|---|
| | | Mortgage bonds | 10,000 |
| | | Senior debentures | 6,000 |
| | | Junior debentures | 4,000 |
| Going concern value | 15,500 | Book equity | −5,000 |

As trustee, what reorganization plan would you accept?

## Practical Case Study

It is not difficult to find firms that are in financial distress. Download the financial accounts for five firms in your country that have performed poorly over the last year. Carry out a Z-score analysis for these companies. Now download the financial accounts for five firms that performed strongly in the past year and carry out a similar analysis. Are the Z-scores for the poor performance sample different from the good performance sample? Write a report on your analysis.

## Relevant Accounting Standards

Many financially distressed firms choose to restructure their assets and sell off poorly performing divisions. An important standard in this regard is IAS37 *Provisions, Contingent Liabilities and Contingent Assets*. If firms wish to sell off divisions or non-current assets, they should also be familiar with IFRS5 *Non-Current Assets Held for Sale and Discontinued Operations*.

## Additional Reading

Financial distress is another topic that has taken on a new lease of life in recent years because of the unprecedented events in the world economy. The literature can be separated into factors that influence financial distress and turnaround strategies once a company is in trouble.

**Predictors of Distress**

Acharya, V.V., S.T. Bharath and A. Srinivasan (2007) 'Does industry-wide distress affect defaulted firms? Evidence from credit recoveries', *Journal of Financial Economics*, vol. 85, no. 3, pp. 787–821. **US.**

Agarwal, V. and R. Taffler (2008) 'Comparing the performance of market-based and accounting-based bankruptcy prediction models', *Journal of Banking and Finance*, vol. 32, no. 8, pp. 1541–1551. **UK.**

Braun, M. and B. Larrain (2005) 'Finance and the business cycle: international, inter-industry evidence', *Journal of Finance*, vol. 60, no. 3, pp. 1097–1127. **International.**

Campbell, J.Y., J. Hilscher and J. Szilagyi (2008) 'In search of distress risk', *Journal of Finance*, vol. 63, no. 6, pp. 2899–2939. **US.**

Yang, L. (2008) 'The real determinants of asset sales', *Journal of Finance*, vol. 63, no. 5, pp. 2231–2262. **US.**

**Turnaround Strategies and the Bankruptcy Process**

Bates, T.W. (2005) 'Asset sales, investment opportunities, and the use of proceeds', *Journal of Finance*, vol. 60, no. 1, pp. 105–135. **US.**

Bris, A., I. Welch and N. Zhu (2006) 'The costs of bankruptcy: Chapter 7 liquidation versus Chapter 11 reorganization', *Journal of Finance*, vol. 61, no. 3, pp. 1253–1303. **US.**

Brown, D.T., B.A. Ciochetti and T.J. Riddiough (2006) 'Theory and evidence on the resolution of financial distress', *Review of Financial Studies*, vol. 19, no. 4, pp. 1357–1397. **US.**

Davydenko, S.A. and J.R. Franks (2008) 'Do bankruptcy codes matter? A study of defaults in France, Germany and the UK', *Journal of Finance*, vol. 62, no. 2, pp. 565–608. **Europe.**

Eckbo, B.E. and K. Thorburn (2009) 'Creditor financing and overbidding in bankruptcy auctions: theory and tests', *Journal of Corporate Finance*, vol. 15, no. 1, pp. 10–29. **Sweden.**

Eisdorfer, A. (2008) 'Empirical evidence of risk shifting in financially distressed firms', *Journal of Finance*, vol. 62, no. 2, pp. 609–637. **US.**

Faccio, M., R.W. Masulis and J.J. McConnell (2006) 'Political connections and corporate bailouts', *Journal of Finance*, vol. 16, no. 6, pp. 2597–2635. **International.**

Hillier, D., A. Marshall, P. McColgan and S. Werema (2007) 'Employee layoffs, shareholder wealth and firm performance: evidence from the UK', *Journal of Business Finance and Accounting*, vol. 34, nos. 3/4, pp. 467–494. **UK.**

Jostarndt, P. and Z. Sautner (2008) 'Financial distress, corporate control, and management turnover', *Journal of Banking and Finance*, vol. 32, no. 10, pp. 2188–2204. **Germany.**

Lee, E. and S. Lin (2008) 'Corporate sell-offs in the UK: use of proceeds, financial distress and the long-run impact on shareholder wealth', *European Financial Management*, vol. 14, no. 2, pp. 222–242. **UK.**

**Other Relevant Research**

Ongena, S., D.C. Smith and D. Michalsen (2003) 'Firms and their distressed banks: lessons from the Norwegian banking crisis', *Journal of Financial Research*, vol. 67, no. 1, pp. 81–112. **Norway.**

# Endnotes

1  This definition is close to the one used by K. Wruck, 'Financial distress: reorganization and organization efficiency', *Journal of Financial Economics*, vol. 27 (1990), p. 425.

2  *Black's Law Dictionary*, 5th ed. (St. Paul, MN: West Publishing Company), p. 716.

3  Edward Altman was one of the first to distinguish between stock-based insolvency and flow-based insolvency. See E. Altman, *Corporate Financial Distress: A Complete Guide to Predicting, Avoiding, and Dealing with Bankruptcy*, 2nd ed. (New York: John Wiley & Sons, 1993).

4  However, only less than 20 per cent of all firms (public or private) going through a bankruptcy are successfully reorganized.

5  For example, see S. Gilson, 'Managing default: some evidence on how firms choose between workouts and bankruptcy', *Journal of Applied Corporate Finance* (Summer 1991); and S.C. Gilson, K. John and L.N.P. Lang, 'Troubled debt restructuring: an empirical study of private reorganization of firms in defaults', *Journal of Financial Economics*, vol. 27 (1990).

6  L.A. Weiss, 'Bankruptcy dissolution: direct costs and violation of priority and claims', *Journal of Financial Economics*, vol. 23 (1990). However, W. Beranek, R. Boehmer and B. Smith, in 'Much ado about nothing: absolute priority deviations in Chapter 11', *Financial Management* (Autumn 1996), find that 33.8 per cent of bankruptcy reorganizations leave shareholders with nothing.

7  S.A. Davydenko and J. Franks, 'Do bankruptcy codes matter? A study of defaults in France, Germany and the UK', *Journal of Finance*, vol. 63 (2008).

8  E.I. Altman, *Corporate Financial Distress and Bankruptcy* (New York: John Wiley & Sons, 1993), Chapter 3.

**Online LearningCentre**

To help you grasp the key concepts of this chapter check out the extra resources posted on the Online Learning Centre at **www.mcgraw-hill.co.uk/textbooks/hillier**

Among other helpful resources there are PowerPoint presentations, chapter outlines and mini-cases.

# Chapter 31

# International Corporate Finance

Relatively few large companies operate in a single country. As a financial manager in a corporation, even if your sales are not overseas, it is very likely that your competitors or suppliers are from overseas. In most industries, raw materials and components are sourced and imported from overseas, and many services and products are sold to different countries.

For example, an analysis of 2007 import and export revenue for the United Kingdom shows that most of Britain's export revenue comes from the US (14.2 per cent), Germany (11.1 per cent), France (8.1 per cent), Ireland (8 per cent), the Netherlands (6.8 per cent), Belgium (5.3 per cent), Spain (4.5 per cent) and Italy (4.1 per cent). Similarly, the United Kingdom's main import partners are Germany (14.2 per cent), the US (8.7 per cent), China (7.3 per cent), the Netherlands (7.3 per cent), France (6.9 per cent), Belgium (4.7 per cent), Norway (4.7 per cent) and Italy (4.2 per cent). Table 31.1 presents the main import and export partners for selected countries in 2007.

Currency fluctuations will clearly have an impact on firms. For example, if the euro strengthens against the British pound, British exports become more competitive in Europe. Similarly, raw materials sourced from Europe will become more expensive, and British corporations will look elsewhere for cheaper inputs. One of the reasons why European monetary union was adopted in 2000 was precisely because many countries in the Eurozone traded heavily with each other. With a single currency the risk of fluctuations is eradicated. In this chapter we explore the roles played by currencies and exchange rates, along with a number of other key topics in international corporate finance.

Corporations with significant foreign operations are often called *international corporations* or *multinationals*. Such corporations must consider many financial factors that do not directly affect purely domestic firms. These include foreign exchange rates, differing interest rates from country to country, different and possibly more complex accounting methods for foreign operations, foreign tax rates, and foreign government intervention.

The basic principles of corporate finance still apply to international corporations: like domestic companies, these firms seek to invest in projects that create more value for the shareholders than they cost, and to arrange financing that raises cash at the lowest possible cost. In other words, the net present value principle holds for both foreign and domestic operations, although it is usually more complicated to apply the NPV rule to foreign investments.

**TABLE 31.1**

| | Top three export partners | Top three import partners |
|---|---|---|
| Australia | Japan (19.1%), China (14.7%), South Korea (8%) | China (14.3%), US (12.9%), Japan (9.6%) |
| Austria | Germany (29.8%), Italy (8.8%), US (4.9%) | Germany (45.5%), Italy (5%), Netherlands (4.3%) |
| Belgium | Germany (19.5%), France (16.7%), Netherlands (11.9%) | Germany (17.7%), Netherlands (17.6%), France (11.2%) |
| China | US (19.1%), Hong Kong (15.1%), Japan (8.4%) | Japan (14%), South Korea (10.9%), Taiwan (10.5%) |
| Denmark | Germany (17.4%), Sweden (14.5%), UK (8%) | Germany (21.7%), Sweden (14.4%), Netherlands (7.1%) |
| Finland | Germany (10.9%), Sweden (10.7%), Russia (10.3%) | Germany (15.8%), Russia (14%), Sweden (13.7%) |
| France | Germany (14.9%), Spain (9.3%), Italy (8.9%) | Germany (18.9%), Belgium (11.4%), Italy (8.4%) |
| Germany | France (9.7%), US (7.5%), UK (7.3%) | Netherlands (12%), France (8.6%), Belgium (7.8%) |
| Greece | Germany (11.4%), Italy (10.7%), Cyprus (6.5%) | Germany (12.9%), Italy (11.7%), Russia (5.6%) |
| India | US (15%), China (8.8%), UAE (8.7%) | China (10.7%), US (7.8%), Germany (4.5%) |
| Ireland | UK (18.7%), US (17.9%), Belgium (14.5%) | UK (38.2%), US (11.3%), Germany (9.7%) |
| Italy | Germany (12.9%), France (11.4%), Spain (7.4%) | Germany (16.9%), France (9%), China (5.9%) |
| Japan | US (20.4%), China (15.3%), South Korea (7.6%) | China (20.5%), US (11.6%), Saudi Arabia (5.7%) |
| Netherlands | Germany (24.4%), Belgium (13.5%), UK (9.1%) | Germany (17.6%), China (10.5%), Belgium (9.3%) |
| Norway | UK (26.3%), Germany (12.3%), Netherlands (10.2%) | Sweden (14.7%), Germany (13.6%), UK (6.9%) |
| Poland | Germany (25.9%), Italy (6.8%), France (6%) | Germany (28.9%), Russia (8.8%), Italy (6.5%) |
| Portugal | Spain (27.1%), Germany (12.9%), France (12.3%) | Spain (29.5%), Germany (12.9%), France (8.4%) |
| Russia | Germany (9.5%), Netherlands (7.5%), Turkey (6%) | Germany (16.2%), China (12.7%), Italy (5.5%) |
| South Africa | US (11.9%), Japan (11.1%), Germany (8%) | Germany (10.9%), China (10%), Spain (8.2%) |
| Spain | France (18.8%), Germany (10.8%), Portugal (8.6%) | Germany (15.7%), France (12.7%), Italy (8.4%) |
| Sweden | Germany (10.4%), Norway (9.4%), US (7.6%) | Germany (18.4%), Denmark (9.2%), Norway (8.3%) |
| Switzerland | Germany (22%), Italy (8.4%), France (8.4%) | Germany (27.7%), Italy (10.2%), US (9.4%) |
| Tanzania | China (9.9%), India (9.3%), Netherlands (6.2%) | China (11.9%), Kenya (7.9%), South Africa (7.6%) |
| Thailand | US (12.6%), Japan (11.9%), China (9.7%) | Japan (20.3%), China (11.6%), US (6.8%) |
| Turkey | Germany (11.2%), UK (8.1%), Italy (7%) | Russia (13.8%), Germany (10.3%), China (7.8%) |
| United Arab Emirates | Japan (23.4%), South Korea (10.2%), Thailand (4.9%) | China (12.9%), India (10%), US (8.8%) |
| United Kingdom | US (14.2%), Germany (11.1%), France (8.1%) | Germany (14.2%), US (8.7%), China (7.3%) |
| United States | Canada (21.4%), Mexico (11.7%), China (5.6%) | China (16.9%), Canada (15.7%), Mexico (10.6%) |

*Source: CIA World Factbook*

**Table 31.1** Main import and export partners of selected countries

One of the most significant complications of international finance is foreign exchange. The foreign exchange markets provide important information and opportunities for an international corporation when it undertakes capital budgeting and financing decisions. As we shall discuss, international exchange rates, interest rates and inflation rates are closely related. We shall spend much of this chapter exploring the connection between these financial variables.

We shan't have much to say here about the role of cultural and social differences in international business. Nor shall we be discussing the implications of differing political and economic systems. These factors are of great importance to international businesses, but it would take another book to do them justice. Consequently we shall focus only on some purely financial considerations in international finance, and on some key aspects of foreign exchange markets.

# 31.1 Terminology

A common buzzword for the student of business finance is *globalization*. The first step in learning about the globalization of financial markets is to conquer the new vocabulary. As with any specialized field, international finance is rich in jargon. Accordingly, we get started on the subject with a highly eclectic vocabulary exercise.

The terms that follow are presented alphabetically, and they are not all of equal importance. We choose these particular ones because they appear frequently in the financial press, or because they illustrate the colourful nature of the language of international finance.

- An American depositary receipt (ADR) is a security issued in the United States that represents shares of a foreign equity, allowing that equity to be traded in the United States. Foreign companies use ADRs, which are issued in US dollars, to expand the pool of potential US investors. ADRs are available in two forms for a large and growing number of foreign companies: company sponsored, which are listed on an exchange; and unsponsored, which usually are held by the investment bank that makes a market in the ADR. Both forms are available to individual investors, but only company-sponsored issues are quoted daily in newspapers. A global depositary receipt (GDR) is an equivalent security denominated in sterling or euros, and issued and traded in financial centres such as London or Frankfurt.

- The cross-rate is the implicit exchange rate between two currencies (usually an emerging or transitional economy) when both are quoted in some third currency, usually the US dollar, euro, or British pound.

- A Eurobond is a bond issued in multiple countries but denominated in a single currency, usually the issuer's home currency. Such bonds have become an important way to raise capital for many international companies and governments. Eurobonds are issued outside the restrictions that apply to domestic offerings, and are syndicated and traded mostly from London. Trading can and does take place anywhere there are buyers and sellers.

- Eurocurrency is money deposited in a financial centre outside the country whose currency is involved. For instance, Eurodollars – the most widely used eurocurrency – are US dollars deposited in banks outside the US banking system. Eurosterling and Euroyen are British and Japanese equivalents.

- Foreign bonds, unlike Eurobonds, are issued in a single country and are usually denominated in that country's currency. Often, the country in which these bonds are issued will draw distinctions between them and bonds issued by domestic issuers – including different tax laws, restrictions on the amount issued, and tougher disclosure rules.

  Foreign bonds are often nicknamed for the country where they are issued: Yankee bonds (United States), Samurai bonds (Japan), Rembrandt bonds (the Netherlands), and Bulldog bonds (Britain). Partly because of tougher regulations and disclosure requirements, the foreign bond market hasn't grown in past years with the vigour of the Eurobond market.

**TABLE 31.2**

| Country | Currency | Symbol |
|---|---|---|
| Australia | Australian dollar | A$ |
| Canada | Canadian dollar | C$ |
| Denmark | Danish krone | DKr |
| Eurozone | Euro | € |
| Hungary | Forint | Ft |
| India | Indian rupee | Rs |
| Iran | Rial | IR |
| Japan | Yen | ¥ |
| Kuwait | Kuwaiti dinar | KD |
| Norway | Norwegian krone | NKr |
| Saudi Arabia | Saudi riyal | SR |
| South Africa | Rand | R |
| Sweden | Swedish krona | SKr |
| Switzerland | Swiss franc | SwFr |
| Tanzania | Tanzanian shilling | TSh |
| United Kingdom | Pound/sterling | £ |
| United States | Dollar | $ |

**Table 31.2** International currency symbols

## 31.2 Foreign Exchange Markets and Exchange Rates

The foreign exchange market is undoubtedly the world's largest financial market. It is the market where one country's currency is traded for another's. Most of the trading takes place in a few currencies: the US dollar ($), the British pound sterling (£), the Japanese yen (¥), and the euro (€). Table 31.2 lists some of the more common currencies and their symbols.

The foreign exchange market is an over-the-counter market, so there is no single location where traders get together. Instead, market participants are located in the major commercial and investment banks around the world. They communicate using computers, telephones, and other telecommunications devices. For example, one communications network for foreign transactions is maintained by the Society for Worldwide Interbank Financial Telecommunications (SWIFT), a Belgian not-for-profit co-operative. Using data transmission lines, a bank in Berlin can send messages to a bank in London via SWIFT regional processing centres.

The many different types of participants in the foreign exchange market include the following:

- Importers who pay for goods using foreign currencies

- Exporters who receive foreign currency and may want to convert to the domestic currency

- Portfolio managers who buy or sell foreign equities and bonds

- Foreign exchange brokers who match buy and sell orders

- Traders who 'make a market' in foreign currencies

- Speculators who try to profit from changes in exchange rates

### Exchange Rates

An exchange rate is simply the price of one country's currency expressed in terms of another country's currency. In practice, almost all trading of currencies takes place in terms of the US dollar, the yen, or the euro.

**Exchange Rate Quotations**    Figure 31.1 reproduces exchange rate quotations as they appeared in the *Financial Times* in 2009. The three main columns give the number of units of foreign currency it takes to buy one dollar, euro or pound, respectively. Because this is the price in foreign currency with respect to dollars, euros or pounds, it is called an *indirect* quote. For example, the Thai baht (Bt) is quoted at 50.4235 against the pound, which means that you can buy one British pound with 50.4235 Thai baht.

If you were a Thai person and the quote was Bt50.4235/£, the quote would be a *direct* quote because it is in the home currency (baht) with respect to the foreign currency (£).

You can also find exchange rates on a number of websites. Suppose you have just returned from your dream vacation to Zimbabwe, and feel rich because you have 1,000,000 Zimbabwean dollars left over. You now need to convert these to euros. How much will you have? We went to www.xe.com and used the currency converter on the site to find out. This is what we found:

| Universal Currency Converter © Results | Using live mid-market rates. More currencies… |
|---|---|

Live rates at 2009.02.01 15:01:57 UTC

Notice: The Zimbabwe government redenominated the ZWD on August 1, 2008 at a rate of 10,000,000,000 old ZWD to 1 new ZWD. No new currency code has been issued, but the old ZWD currency remains legal tender until December 31, 2008. More info (PDF)

**1,000,000.00 ZWD    =    0.0002277266 EUR**

| Zimbabwe Dollars | Euro |
|---|---|
| 1 ZWD = 0.00000000022773 EUR | 1 EUR = 4,391,230,955.17 ZWD |

**Trade Currencies.**

Looks like you left Zimbabwe just before you ran out of money!

**EXAMPLE 31.1**

## Rand for Euros

Suppose you have £1,000. Based on the rates in Fig. 31.1, how many South African rand can you get? Alternatively, if a Porsche costs €100,000, how many pounds will you need to buy it?

The exchange rate in terms of rand per pound is 14.7090. Your £1,000 will thus get you

$$£1,000 \times 14.7090 \text{ rand per } £1 = 14,709 \text{ rand}$$

Because the exchange rate in terms of pound per euro is 0.8889, you will need

$$€100,000 \times £0.8889 \text{ per } € = £88,890$$

**Cross-Rates and Triangle Arbitrage**    The *Financial Times* quotes exchange rates in terms of the US dollar, euro and British pound. Using any of these currencies as the common denominator in quoting exchange rates greatly reduces the number of possible cross-currency quotes. For example, with five major currencies, there would potentially be 10 exchange rates instead of just 4.[1] Also, the fact that the one currency (dollar, euro or pound) is used throughout cuts down on inconsistencies in the exchange rate quotations.

Earlier, we defined the cross-rate as the exchange rate for a foreign currency expressed in terms of another foreign currency. For example, suppose we observe the following for the Russian rouble (Rb) and the Bahraini dinar (BD):

FIGURE
31.1

| Jan 30 | Currency | DOLLAR Closing Mid | DOLLAR Day's Change | EURO Closing Mid | EURO Day's Change | POUND Closing Mid | POUND Day's Change |
|---|---|---|---|---|---|---|---|
| Argentina | (Peso) | 3.4865 | 0.0003 | 4.4680 | -0.0919 | 5.0265 | 0.0331 |
| Australia | (A$) | 1.5726 | 0.0544 | 2.0153 | 0.0296 | 2.2672 | 0.0928 |
| Bahrain | (Dinar) | 0.3770 | – | 0.4831 | -0.0100 | 0.5435 | 0.0035 |
| Bolivia | (Boliviano) | 7.0200 | – | 8.9962 | -0.1857 | 10.1208 | 0.0660 |
| Brazil | (R$) | 2.3233 | 0.0380 | 2.9773 | -0.0117 | 3.3495 | 0.0763 |
| Canada | (C$) | 1.2399 | 0.0242 | 1.5889 | -0.0011 | 1.7875 | 0.0463 |
| Chile | (Peso) | 616.900 | 4.7500 | 790.557 | -10.1043 | 889.385 | 12.6023 |
| China | (Yuan) | 6.8380 | – | 8.7629 | -0.1809 | 9.8584 | 0.0643 |
| Colombia | (Peso) | 2435.55 | 55.2500 | 3121.16 | 7.8441 | 3511.33 | 102.029 |
| Costa Rica | (Colon) | 560.000 | 0.1600 | 717.641 | -14.6025 | 807.353 | 5.4931 |
| Czech Rep. | (Koruna) | 21.8623 | 0.7739 | 28.0165 | 0.4340 | 31.5189 | 1.3140 |
| Denmark | (DKr) | 5.8171 | 0.1199 | 7.4546 | 0.0029 | 8.3865 | 0.2264 |
| Egypt | (Egypt £) | 5.5665 | -0.0005 | 7.1335 | -0.1480 | 8.0253 | 0.0516 |
| Estonia | (Kroon) | 12.2134 | 0.2506 | 15.6514 | 0.0048 | 17.6080 | 0.4738 |
| Hong Kong | (HK$) | 7.7547 | -0.0022 | 9.9376 | -0.2079 | 11.1799 | 0.0699 |
| Hungary | (Forint) | 232.844 | 11.2189 | 298.390 | 8.5150 | 335.692 | 18.2576 |
| India | (Rs) | 48.8800 | -0.1100 | 62.6397 | -1.4367 | 70.4703 | 0.3019 |
| Indonesia | (Rupiah) | 11380.0 | 65.0000 | 14583.5 | -215.983 | 16406.5 | 200.073 |
| Iran | (Rial) | 9695.50 | – | 12424.8 | -256.445 | 13978.0 | 91.1377 |
| Israel | (Shk) | 4.0673 | 0.0205 | 5.2122 | -0.0807 | 5.8638 | 0.0676 |
| Japan | (Y) | 89.8100 | -0.1050 | 115.092 | -2.5128 | 129.479 | 0.6938 |
| One Month | | 89.7701 | 0.0043 | 114.988 | 0.0150 | 129.370 | 0.0226 |
| Three Month | | 89.6321 | -0.0035 | 114.751 | 0.0443 | 129.130 | 0.0224 |
| One Year | | 88.9360 | -0.0830 | 113.867 | 0.1447 | 128.199 | -0.0090 |
| Kenya | (Shilling) | 79.6500 | 0.2300 | 102.072 | -1.8059 | 114.831 | 1.0781 |
| Kuwait | (Dinar) | 0.2898 | 0.0005 | 0.3713 | -0.0070 | 0.4178 | 0.0034 |
| Malaysia | (M$) | 3.6075 | 0.0085 | 4.6230 | -0.0844 | 5.2010 | 0.0461 |
| Mexico | (New Peso) | 14.3710 | 0.1900 | 18.4165 | -0.1316 | 20.7187 | 0.4072 |
| New Zealand | (NZ$) | 1.9724 | 0.0426 | 2.5276 | 0.0036 | 2.8436 | 0.0796 |
| Nigeria | (Naira) | 148.750 | 2.3500 | 190.623 | -0.8607 | 214.453 | 4.7642 |
| Norway | (NKr) | 6.9114 | 0.1634 | 8.8569 | 0.0309 | 9.9641 | 0.2990 |
| Pakistan | (Rupee) | 79.0500 | 0.0800 | 101.303 | -1.9863 | 113.966 | 0.8577 |
| Peru | (New Sol) | 3.1750 | 0.0075 | 4.0688 | -0.0742 | 4.5774 | 0.0405 |
| Philippines | (Peso) | 47.3700 | 0.1750 | 60.7047 | -1.0240 | 68.2933 | 0.6959 |
| Poland | (Zloty) | 3.4780 | 0.1203 | 4.4570 | 0.0652 | 5.0142 | 0.2049 |
| Romania | (New Leu) | 3.3518 | 0.1048 | 4.2953 | 0.0485 | 4.8322 | 0.1817 |
| Russia | (Rouble) | 35.7411 | 0.8164 | 45.8022 | 0.1224 | 51.5279 | 1.5052 |
| Saudi Arabia | (SR) | 3.7526 | 0.0001 | 4.8090 | -0.0992 | 5.4102 | 0.0355 |
| Singapore | (S$) | 1.5108 | 0.0059 | 1.9361 | -0.0322 | 2.1782 | 0.0228 |
| South Africa | (R) | 10.2025 | 0.2600 | 13.0745 | 0.0702 | 14.7090 | 0.4683 |
| South Korea | (Won) | 1379.60 | 0.8500 | 1767.96 | -35.3786 | 1988.97 | 14.1857 |
| Sweden | (SKr) | 8.2952 | 0.2447 | 10.6303 | 0.1007 | 11.9592 | 0.4286 |
| Switzerland | (SFr) | 1.1607 | 0.0155 | 1.4875 | -0.0104 | 1.6734 | 0.0331 |
| Taiwan | (T$) | 33.5875 | – | 43.0424 | -0.8884 | 48.4231 | 0.3157 |
| Thailand | (Bt) | 34.9750 | 0.0650 | 44.8205 | -0.8401 | 50.4235 | 0.4219 |
| Tunisia | (Dinar) | 1.4256 | 0.0206 | 1.8269 | -0.0108 | 2.0552 | 0.0428 |
| Turkey | (Lira) | 1.6446 | 0.0221 | 2.1075 | -0.0146 | 2.3710 | 0.0470 |
| UAE | (Dirham) | 3.6728 | -0.0007 | 4.7067 | -0.0980 | 5.2950 | 0.0335 |
| UK (0.6936)* | (£) | 1.4417 | 0.0094 | 0.8889 | -0.0243 | – | – |
| One Month | | 1.4411 | 0.0002 | 0.8888 | -0.0001 | – | – |
| Three Month | | 1.4407 | 0.0003 | 0.8886 | 0.0001 | – | – |
| One Year | | 1.4415 | 0.0013 | 0.8882 | 0.0010 | – | – |
| Ukraine | (Hrywnja) | 7.6850 | -0.0600 | 9.8484 | 9.8484 | 11.0795 | -0.0137 |
| Uruguay | (Peso) | 22.6500 | -0.0500 | 29.0260 | 29.0260 | 32.6545 | 0.1412 |
| USA | ($) | – | – | 1.2815 | -0.0265 | 1.4417 | 0.0094 |
| One Month | | – | – | 1.2809 | 0.0001 | 1.4411 | 0.0002 |
| Three Month | | – | – | 1.2803 | 0.0005 | 1.4407 | 0.0003 |
| One Year | | – | – | 1.2803 | 0.0026 | 1.4415 | 0.0013 |
| Venezuela †(Bolivar Fuerte) | | 2.1473 | – | 2.7518 | -0.0568 | 3.0958 | 0.0202 |
| Vietnam | (Dong) | 17483.5 | 6.5000 | 22405.1 | -453.938 | 25206.0 | 173.654 |
| Euro (0.7803)* | (Euro) | 1.2815 | -0.0265 | – | – | 1.1250 | 0.0299 |
| One Month | | 1.2809 | 0.0001 | – | – | 1.1251 | 0.0001 |
| Three Month | | 1.2803 | 0.0005 | – | – | 1.1253 | -0.0001 |
| One Year | | 1.2803 | 0.0026 | – | – | 1.1259 | -0.0011 |
| SDR | – | 0.6701 | 0.0044 | 0.8587 | -0.0120 | 0.9660 | 0.0125 |

*Source: Financial Times, 30 January 2009, www.ft.com*

**Figure 31.1** Exchange rate quotations

$$\text{Russian rouble per €1} = 45.8022$$
$$\text{Bahraini dinar per €1} = 0.4831$$

Suppose the cross-rate is quoted as:

$$\text{Dinar per rouble} = 0.01$$

What do you think?

The cross-rate here is inconsistent with the exchange rates. To see this, suppose you have €100. If you convert this to Russian roubles, you will receive:

$$\text{€100} \times 45.8022 \text{ roubles per €1} = 4,580.22 \text{ roubles}$$

If you convert this to dinar at the cross-rate, you will have

$$4,580.22 \text{ roubles} \times 0.01 \text{ per rouble} = 45.8022 \text{ dinar}$$

However, if you just convert your euros to dinar without going through Russian roubles, you will have

$$\text{€100} \times 0.4831 \text{ dinar per €1} = 48.31 \text{ dinar}$$

What we see is that the dinar has two prices, 0.4831 dinar per €1 and 0.4580 dinar per €1, with the price we pay depending on how we get the dinar.

To make money, we want to buy low and sell high. The important thing to note is that dinar are cheaper if you buy them with euros, because you get 0.4831 dinar instead of just 0.4580 dinar. You should proceed as follows:

1 Buy 48.31 dinar for €100.

2 Use the 48.31 dinar to buy Russian roubles at the cross-rate. Because it takes 0.01 dinar to buy a Russian rouble, you will receive 48.31 dinar/0.01 roubles = 4,831 roubles.

3 Use the 4,831 roubles to buy euros. Because the exchange rate is 45.8022 roubles per euro, you receive 4,831 roubles/45.8022 = €105.48, for a round-trip profit of €5.48.

4 Repeat steps 1 to 3.

This particular activity is called *triangular arbitrage*, because the arbitrage involves moving through three different exchange rates:

To prevent such opportunities, it is not difficult to see that because a euro will buy you either 45.8022 Russian roubles or 0.4831 Bahraini dinar, the cross-rate must be

$$\text{(€1/0.4831 dinar)/(45.8922 rouble/€1)} = 0.010527 \text{ dinar/rouble}$$

That is, the cross-rate must be 0.010527 Bahraini dinar per 1 Russian rouble. If it were anything else, there would be a triangular arbitrage opportunity.

## Shedding Some Pounds

EXAMPLE
31.2

According to Fig. 31.1, the exchange rates for the British pound against the euro and dollar are:

$$€/£ = 1.1250$$
$$\$/£ = 1.4417$$

The cross-rate is $1.2815/€. Show that the exchange rates are consistent.

**Types of Transaction**   There are two basic types of trades in the foreign exchange market: spot trades and forward trades. A *spot trade* is an agreement to exchange currency 'on the spot', which actually means that the transaction will be completed or settled within two business days. The exchange rate on a spot trade is called the *spot exchange rate*. Implicitly, all of the exchange rates and transactions we have discussed so far have referred to the spot market.

A *forward trade* is an agreement to exchange currency at some time in the future. The exchange rate that will be used is agreed upon today and is called the *forward exchange rate*. A forward trade will normally be settled some time in the next 12 months.

If you look back at Fig. 31.1 you will see forward exchange rates quoted for the dollar, euro and pound. For example, the spot €/£ exchange rate is €1.1250/£. The one-year forward exchange rate is €1.1259/£. This means that you can buy a pound today for €1.1250, or you can agree to take delivery of a pound in one year and pay €1.1259 at that time.

Notice that the British pound is more expensive in the forward market (€1.1259 versus €1.1250). Because the British pound is more expensive in the future than it is today, it is said to be selling at a *premium* relative to the euro. For the same reason, the euro is said to be selling at a *discount* relative to the British pound.

Why does the forward market exist? One answer is that it allows businesses and individuals to lock in a future exchange rate today, thereby eliminating any risk from unfavourable shifts in the exchange rate.

## Looking Forward

EXAMPLE
31.3

Suppose you are a British business and are expecting to receive a million euros in three months, and you agree to a forward trade to exchange your euros for pounds. Based on Fig. 31.1, how many pounds will you get in three months? Is the euro selling at a discount or a premium relative to the pound?

In Fig. 31.1 the spot exchange rate and the three-month forward rate in terms of pounds per euros are £0.8889 = €1 and £0.8886 = €1, respectively. If you expect €1 million in three months, then you will get €1 million × 0.8886 per pound = £888,600. Because it is more expensive to buy a pound in the forward market than in the spot market (£0.8889 versus £0.8886), the pound is said to be selling at a premium relative to the euro.

As we mentioned earlier, it is standard practice around the world (with a few exceptions) to quote exchange rates in terms of the dollar, euro and pound. This means that rates are quoted as the amount of currency per dollar, euro or pound. For the remainder of this chapter, we shall stick with this form. Things can get extremely confusing if you forget this. Thus, when we say things like 'the exchange rate is expected to rise', it is important to remember that we are talking about the exchange rate quoted as units of foreign currency per dollar, euro or pound.

# 31.3 Purchasing Power Parity

Now that we have discussed what exchange rate quotations mean, we can address an obvious question: What determines the level of the spot exchange rate? In addition, because we know that exchange rates change through time, we can ask the related question: What determines the rate of change in exchange rates? At least part of the answer in both cases goes by the name of **purchasing power parity (PPP)**, the idea that the exchange rate adjusts to keep purchasing power constant among currencies. As we discuss next, there are two forms of PPP, *absolute* and *relative*.

## Absolute Purchasing Power Parity

The basic idea behind *absolute purchasing power parity* is that a commodity costs the same, regardless of what currency is used to purchase it or where it is selling. This is a very straight-forward concept. If a beer costs 50 kroner in Oslo, and the exchange rate is NKr10 per pound, then a beer costs NKr50/10 = £5 in London. In other words, absolute PPP says that £1 or €1 will buy you the same number of, say, cheeseburgers anywhere in the world.

More formally, let $S_0$ be the spot exchange rate between the euro and the dollar today (time 0), and we are quoting exchange rates as the amount of foreign currency per euro. Let $P_{US}$ and $P_{euro}$ be the current US and euro prices, respectively, on a particular commodity, say, apples. Absolute PPP simply says that

$$P_{US} = S_0 \times P_{euro}$$

This tells us that the US price for something is equal to the euro price for that same something multiplied by the exchange rate.

The rationale behind PPP is similar to that behind triangle arbitrage. If PPP did not hold, arbitrage would be possible (in principle) if apples were moved from one country to another. For example, suppose apples are selling in Milan for €2 per bushel, whereas in New York the price is $3 per bushel. Absolute PPP implies that

$$P_{US} = S_0 \times P_{euro}$$
$$\$3 = S_0 \times €2$$
$$S_0 = \$3/€2 = \$1.50/€$$

That is, the implied spot exchange rate is $1.50 per euro. Equivalently, a dollar is worth €1/$1.5 = €0.667/$.

Suppose instead that the actual exchange rate is $1.2815/€. Starting with €2, a trader could buy a bushel of apples in Madrid, ship it to New York, and sell it there for $3. Our trader could then convert the $3 into euros at the prevailing exchange rate, $S_0 = \$1.2815/€$, yielding a total of $3/€1.2815 = €2.34. The round-trip gain would be 34 cents.

Because of this profit potential, forces are set in motion to change the exchange rate and/or the price of apples. In our example, apples would begin moving from Madrid to New York. The reduced supply of apples in Madrid would raise the price of apples there, and the increased supply in the US would lower the price of apples in New York.

In addition to moving apples around, apple traders would be busily converting dollars back into euros to buy more apples. This activity would increase the supply of dollars and simultaneously increase the demand for euros. We would expect the value of a dollar to fall. This means that the euro would be getting more valuable, so it would take more dollars to buy one euro. Because the exchange rate is quoted as dollars per euro, we would expect the exchange rate to rise from $1.2815/£.

For absolute PPP to hold absolutely, several things must be true:

1 The transaction costs of trading apples – shipping, insurance, spoilage, and so on – must be zero.

2 There must be no barriers to trading apples – no tariffs, taxes, or other political barriers.

3    Finally, an apple in New York must be identical to an apple in Madrid. It won't do for you to send red apples to Madrid if the Spanish eat only green apples.

Given the fact that the transaction costs are not zero, and that the other conditions are rarely met exactly, it is not surprising that absolute PPP is really applicable only to traded goods, and then only to very uniform ones.

For this reason, absolute PPP does not imply that a Mercedes costs the same as a Ford, or that a nuclear power plant in France costs the same as one in New York. In the case of the cars, they are not identical. In the case of the power plants, even if they were identical, they are expensive and would be very difficult to ship. On the other hand, we would be very surprised to see a significant violation of absolute PPP for gold.

Violations of PPP are actually sought out by corporations. For example, in the middle of 2004 Alcoa announced that it would build a $1 billion aluminium smelter plant on the Caribbean island of Trinidad. At the same time the company was breaking ground on another $1 billion plant in Iceland, and looking into other locations including China, Brunei, Bahrain, Brazil and Canada. In all cases low energy costs were the attraction (aluminium smelting is very energy-intensive). Meanwhile, the company had several plants in the Pacific North-west that were closed, because higher electricity prices in this region made the plants unprofitable.

One of the more famous violations of absolute PPP is the Big Mac Index constructed by *The Economist*. To construct the index, prices for a Big Mac in different countries are gathered from McDonald's. Below you will find the January 2009 Big Mac index from www.economist.com. (We shall leave it to you to find the most recent index.)

**Big Mac index**
Local currency under (–)/over (+) valuation against the dollar, %

Big Mac price*, $

|  | 60 | 40 | 20 | – 0 + | 20 | 40 | 60 |  |
|---|---|---|---|---|---|---|---|---|
| Switzerland |  |  |  |  |  |  |  | 5.75 |
| Norway |  |  |  |  |  |  |  | 5.74 |
| Sweden |  |  |  |  |  |  |  | 4.59 |
| Euro area† |  |  |  |  |  |  |  | 4.50 |
| Brazil |  |  |  |  |  |  |  | 3.39 |
| Britain |  |  |  |  |  |  |  | 3.33 |
| Japan |  |  |  |  |  |  |  | 3.21 |
| Turkey |  |  |  |  |  |  |  | 3.13 |
| Mexico |  |  |  |  |  |  |  | 2.36 |
| Australia |  |  |  |  |  |  |  | 2.31 |
| Poland |  |  |  |  |  |  |  | 2.14 |
| Russia |  |  |  |  |  |  |  | 1.87 |
| China |  |  |  |  |  |  |  | 1.83 |
| South Africa |  |  |  |  |  |  |  | 1.68 |

*At market exchange rate (January 19th)
†Weighted average of member countries

Source: *The Economist* using McDonald's price data

As you can see from the index, absolute PPP does not seem to hold, at least for the Big Mac. In fact, in only 4 of the 14 currencies surveyed by *The Economist* is the exchange rate within 20 per cent of that predicted by absolute PPP. The largest disparity is in Switzerland, where the currency is apparently overvalued by about 60 per cent. And 5 of the 14 currencies are 'incorrectly' priced by more than 40 per cent. Why?

There are several reasons. First, a Big Mac is not really transportable. Yes, you can load a ship with Big Macs and send it to Norway, where the currency is supposedly overvalued by more than 60 per cent. But do you really think people would buy your Big Macs? Probably not. Even though it is relatively easy to transport a Big Mac, it would be relatively expensive, and the hamburger would suffer in quality along the way.

Also, if you look, the price of the Big Mac is the average price from each of the countries in the Eurozone. The reason is that Big Macs do not sell for the same price in Europe, where presumably they are all purchased with the euro. The cost of living and competition are only two of the factors that affect the price of a Big Mac in Europe. If Big Macs are not priced the same in the same currency, would we expect absolute PPP to hold across currencies?

Finally, differing tastes can account for the apparent discrepancy. In the United States, hamburgers and fast food have become a staple of the American diet. In other countries, hamburgers have not become as entrenched. We would expect the price of the Big Mac to be lower in the United States, because there is much more competition.

Having examined the Big Mac, we can say that absolute PPP should hold more closely for more easily transportable items. For instance, there are many companies with equity listed on exchanges in more than one country. If you examine the share prices on the two exchanges you will find that the price of the shares is almost exactly what absolute PPP would predict. The reason is that a share of equity in a particular company is (usually) the same wherever you buy it and whatever currency you use.

## Relative Purchasing Power Parity

As a practical matter, a relative version of purchasing power parity has evolved. *Relative purchasing power parity* does not tell us what determines the absolute level of the exchange rate. Instead, it tells us what determines the *change* in the exchange rate over time.

**The Basic Idea**    Suppose the British pound–US dollar exchange rate is currently $S_0 = \$1.30$. Further suppose that the inflation rate in the US is predicted to be 10 per cent over the coming year, and (for the moment) the inflation rate in the United Kingdom is predicted to be zero. What do you think the exchange rate will be in a year?

If you think about it, you see that a pound currently costs $1.30 in the US. With 10 per cent inflation, we expect prices in the US to generally rise by 10 per cent. So we expect that the price of a pound will go up by 10 per cent, and the exchange rate should rise to $\$1.30 \times 1.1 = \$1.43$.

If the inflation rate in the United Kingdom is not zero, then we need to worry about the *relative* inflation rates in the two countries. For example, suppose the UK inflation rate is predicted to be 4 per cent. Relative to prices in the United Kingdom, prices in the US are rising at a rate of 10 per cent – 4 per cent = 6 per cent per year. So we expect the price of the pound to rise by 6 per cent, and the predicted exchange rate is $\$1.30 \times 1.06 = \$1.378$.

**The Result**    In general, relative PPP says that the change in the exchange rate is determined by the difference in the inflation rates of the two countries. To be more specific, we shall use the following notation:

- $S_0$ = Current (Time 0) spot exchange rate (foreign currency per home currency)

- $E(S_t)$ = Expected exchange rate in $t$ periods

- $h_{HC}$ = Inflation rate in the home currency

- $h_{FC}$ = Foreign country inflation rate

Based on our discussion just preceding, relative PPP says that the expected percentage change in the exchange rate over the next year, $[E(S_1) - S_0]/S_0$, is

$$\frac{E(S_1) - S_0}{S_0} = h_{FC} - h_{HC} \qquad (31.1)$$

In words, relative PPP simply says that the expected percentage change in the exchange rate is equal to the difference in inflation rates. If we rearrange this slightly, we get

$$E(S_1) = S_0 \times [1 + (h_{FC} - h_{HC})] \qquad (31.2)$$

This result makes a certain amount of sense, but care must be used in quoting the exchange rate.

In our example involving United States and Britain, relative PPP tells us that the exchange rate will rise by $h_{FC} - h_{HC} = 10$ per cent – 4 per cent = 6 per cent per year. Assuming the difference in inflation rates doesn't change, the expected exchange rate in two years, $E(S_2)$, will therefore be

$$E(S_2) = E(S_1) \times (1 + 0.06)$$
$$= 1.378 \times 1.06$$
$$= 1.461$$

Notice that we could have written this as

$$E(S_2) = 1.378 \times 1.06$$
$$= 1.30 \times (1.06 \times 1.06)$$
$$= 1.30 \times (1.06)^2$$

In general, relative PPP says that the expected exchange rate at some time in the future, $E(S_t)$, is

$$E(S_t) = S_0 \times [1 + (h_{FC} - h_{HC})]^t \tag{31.3}$$

As we shall see, this is a very useful relationship.

Because we don't really expect absolute PPP to hold for most goods, we shall focus on relative PPP in our following discussion. Henceforth, when we refer to PPP without further qualification, we mean relative PPP.

EXAMPLE
31.4

## It's All Relative

From Fig. 31.1, the Turkish lira–euro exchange rate is 2.1705 lira per euro. The inflation rate in Turkey over the next three years will run at, say, 10 per cent per year, whereas the Eurozone inflation rate will be 2 per cent. Based on relative PPP, what will the exchange rate be in three years?

Because the Eurozone inflation rate is lower, we expect that a euro will become more valuable. The exchange rate change will be 10 per cent – 2 per cent = 8 per cent per year. Over three years the exchange rate will rise to

$$E(S_3) = S_0 \times [1 + (h_{FC} - h_{HC})]^3$$
$$= 2.1705 \times [1 + (0.08)]^3$$
$$= 2.7342$$

**Currency Appreciation and Depreciation**   We frequently hear things like 'the euro strengthened (or weakened) in financial markets today' or 'the euro is expected to appreciate (or depreciate) relative to the pound.' When we say that the euro strengthens or appreciates, we mean that the value of a euro rises, so it takes more foreign currency to buy a euro.

What happens to the exchange rates as currencies fluctuate in value depends on how exchange rates are quoted. Because we are quoting them as units of foreign currency per home currency, the exchange rate moves in the same direction as the value of the home currency: It rises as the home currency strengthens, and it falls as the home currency weakens.

Relative PPP tells us that the exchange rate will rise if the home currency inflation rate is lower than the foreign country's inflation rate. This happens because the foreign currency depreciates in value, and therefore weakens relative to the home currency.

## 31.4 Interest Rate Parity, Unbiased Forward Rates, and the International Fisher Effect

The next issue we need to address is the relationship between spot exchange rates, forward exchange rates, and interest rates. To get started, we need some additional notation:

$$F_t = \text{Forward exchange rate for settlement at time } t$$
$$R_{HC} = \text{Home currency nominal risk-free interest rate}$$
$$R_{FC} = \text{Foreign country nominal risk-free interest rate}$$

As before, we shall use $S_0$ to stand for the spot exchange rate. You can take the home currency nominal risk-free rate, $R_{HC}$, to be the home country T-bill rate.

### Covered Interest Arbitrage

From Fig. 31.1 we observe the following information about the British pound and the US dollar in the market:

$$S_0 = \$1.4417$$
$$F_1 = \$1.4415$$
$$R_{HC} = 2.13\%$$
$$R_{FC} = 0.27\%$$

where $R_{FC}$ is the nominal risk-free rate in the United States. The period is one year, so $F_1$ is the 360-day forward rate.

Do you see an arbitrage opportunity here? Suppose you have £10,000 to invest, and you want a riskless investment. One option you have is to invest the £10,000 in a riskless UK investment such as a 360-day T-bill. If you do this, then in one period your £1 will be worth

$$£ \text{ value in 1 period} = £1 \times (1 + R_{HC})$$
$$= £10,213$$

Alternatively, you can invest in the US risk-free investment. To do this, you need to convert your £10,000 to US dollars and simultaneously execute a forward trade to convert dollars back to pounds in one year. The necessary steps would be as follows:

1   Convert your £10,000 to £10,000 × $S_0$ = $14,417.

2   At the same time, enter into a forward agreement to convert US dollars back to pounds in one year. Because the forward rate is $1.4415, you will get £1 for every $1.4415 that you have in one year.

3   Invest your $14,417 in the United States at $R_{FC}$. In one year, you will have

$$\$ \text{ value in 1 year} = \$14,417 \times (1 + R_{FC})$$
$$= \$14,417 \times 1.0027$$
$$= \$14,456$$

4   Convert your $14,456 back to pounds at the agreed-upon rate of $1.4415 = £1. You end up with

$$£ \text{ value in 1 year} = \$14,456/1.4415$$
$$= £10,028$$

Notice that the value in one year resulting from this strategy can be written as

$$£ \text{ value in 1 year} = £10{,}000 \times S_0 \times (1 + R_{FC})/F_1$$
$$= £10{,}000 \times 1.4417 \times 1.0027/1.4415$$
$$= £10{,}028$$

The return on this investment is apparently 0.28 per cent. This is lower than the 2.13 per cent we get from investing in the United Kingdom. Because both investments are risk-free, there is an arbitrage opportunity.

To exploit the difference in interest rates, you need to borrow, say, $10 million at the lower US rate and invest it at the higher British rate. What is the round-trip profit from doing this? To find out, we can work through the steps outlined previously:

1   Convert the $10 million at $1.4417/£ to get £6,936,256.

2   Agree to exchange dollars for pounds in one year at $1.4415 to the pound.

3   Invest the £6,936,256 for one year at $R_{UK} = 2.13$ per cent. You end up with £7,083,998.

4   Convert the £7,083,998 back to dollars to fulfil the forward contract. You receive £7,083,998 × $1.4415/£ = $10,211,583.

5   Repay the loan with interest. You owe $10 million plus 0.27 per cent interest, for a total of $10,027,000. You have $10,211,583, so your round-trip profit is a risk-free $184,583.

The activity that we have illustrated here goes by the name of *covered interest arbitrage*. The term *covered* refers to the fact that we are covered in the event of a change in the exchange rate, because we lock in the forward exchange rate today.

## Interest Rate Parity

If we assume that significant covered interest arbitrage opportunities do not exist, then there must be some relationship between spot exchange rates, forward exchange rates, and relative interest rates. To see what this relationship is, note that in general strategy 1 from the preceding discussion, investing in a riskless home currency investment, gives us $1 + R_{HC}$ for every unit of home currency we invest. Strategy 2, investing in a foreign risk-free investment, gives us $S_0 \times (1 + R_{FC})/F_1$ for every unit of home currency we invest. Because these have to be equal to prevent arbitrage, it must be the case that:

$$1 + R_{HC} = S_0 \times \frac{1 + R_{FC}}{F_1}$$

Rearranging this a bit gets us the famous interest rate parity (IRP) condition:

$$\frac{F_1}{S_0} = \frac{1 + R_{FC}}{1 - R_{HC}} \tag{31.4}$$

There is a very useful approximation for IRP that illustrates clearly what is going on, and is not difficult to remember. If we define the percentage forward premium or discount as $(F_1 - S_0)/S_0$, then IRP says that this percentage premium or discount is *approximately* equal to the difference in interest rates:

$$\frac{F_1 - S_0}{S_0} = R_{FC} - R_{HC} \tag{31.5}$$

Loosely, what IRP says is that any difference in interest rates between two countries for some period is just offset by the change in the relative value of the currencies, thereby eliminating any arbitrage possibilities. Notice that we could also write

$$F_1 = S_0 \times [1 + (R_{FC} - R_{HC})] \tag{31.6}$$

In general, if we have $t$ periods instead of just one, the IRP approximation is written like this:

$$F_t = S_0 \times [1 + (R_{FC} - R_{HC})]^t \tag{31.7}$$

## Parity Check

**EXAMPLE 31.5**

From Fig. 31.1, suppose the exchange rate for the South African rand, $S_0$, is currently R13.0745 = €1. If the interest rate in the Eurozone is $R_{\text{euro}} = 2.12$ per cent and the interest rate in South Africa is $R_{\text{SA}} = 10.95$ per cent, then what must the forward rate be to prevent covered interest arbitrage?

From IRP, we have

$$
\begin{aligned}
F_1 &= S_0 \times [1 + (R_{\text{SA}} - R_{\text{euro}})] \\
&= \text{R}13.0745 \times [1 + (0.1095 - 0.0212)] \\
&= \text{R}13.0745 \times 1.0883 \\
&= \text{R}14.2290
\end{aligned}
$$

Notice that the rand will sell at a discount relative to the euro. (Why?)

## Forward Rates and Future Spot Rates

In addition to PPP and IRP, there is one more basic relationship we need to discuss. What is the connection between the forward rate and the expected future spot rate? The **unbiased forward rates (UFR)** condition says that the forward rate, $F_1$, is equal to the *expected* future spot rate, $E(S_1)$:

$$F_1 = E(S_1)$$

With $t$ periods, UFR would be written as

$$F_t = E(S_t)$$

Loosely, the UFR condition says that, on average, the forward exchange rate is equal to the future spot exchange rate.

If we ignore risk, then the UFR condition should hold. Suppose the forward rate for the South African rand is consistently lower than the future spot rate by, say, 10 rand. This means that anyone who wanted to convert euros to rand in the future would consistently get more rand by not agreeing to a forward exchange. The forward rate would have to rise to get anyone interested in a forward exchange.

Similarly, if the forward rate were consistently higher than the future spot rate, then anyone who wanted to convert rand to euros would get more euros per rand by not agreeing to a forward trade. The forward exchange rate would have to fall to attract such traders.

For these reasons, the forward and actual future spot rates should be equal to each other, on average. What the future spot rate will actually be is uncertain, of course. The UFR condition may not hold if traders are willing to pay a premium to avoid this uncertainty. If the condition does hold, then the one-year forward rate that we see today should be an unbiased predictor of what the exchange rate will actually be in one year.

## Putting it All Together

We have developed three relationships – PPP, IRP, and UFR – that describe the interactions between key financial variables such as interest rates, exchange rates, and inflation rates. We now explore the implications of these relationships as a group.

**Uncovered Interest Parity** To start, it is useful to collect our international financial market relationships in one place:

$$
\begin{aligned}
\text{PPP:} \quad & E(S_1) = S_0 \times [1 + (h_{\text{FC}} - h_{\text{HC}})] \\
\text{IRP:} \quad & F_1 = S_0 \times [1 + (R_{\text{FC}} - R_{\text{HC}})] \\
\text{UFR:} \quad & F_1 = E(S_1)
\end{aligned}
$$

We begin by combining UFR and IRP. Because we know that $F_1 = E(S_1)$ from the UFR condition, we can substitute $E(S_1)$ for $F_1$ in IRP. The result is

$$\text{UIP: } E(S_1) = S_0 \times [1 + (R_{FC} - R_{HC})] \tag{31.8}$$

This important relationship is called **uncovered interest parity (UIP)**, and it will play a key role in our international capital budgeting discussion that follows. With $t$ periods, UIP becomes

$$E(S_t) = S_0 \times [1 + (R_{FC} - R_{HC})]^t \tag{31.9}$$

**The International Fisher Effect**   Next we compare PPP and UIP. Both of them have $E(S_1)$ on the left side, so their right sides must be equal. We thus have

$$S_0 \times [1 + (h_{FC} - h_{HC})] = S_0 \times [1 + (R_{FC} - R_{HC})]$$
$$h_{FC} - h_{HC} = R_{FC} - R_{HC}$$

This tells us that the difference in returns between the home country and a foreign country is just equal to the difference in inflation rates. Rearranging this slightly gives us the **international Fisher effect (IFE)**:

$$\text{IFE: } R_{HC} - h_{HC} = R_{FC} - h_{FC} \tag{31.10}$$

The IFE says that *real* rates are equal across countries.[2] The conclusion that real returns are equal across countries is really basic economics. If real returns were higher in, say, Britain than in the Eurozone, money would flow out of Eurozone financial markets and into British markets. Asset prices in Britain would rise and their returns would fall. At the same time, asset prices in Europe would fall and their returns would rise. This process acts to equalize real returns.

Having said all this, we need to note a couple of things. First, we haven't explicitly dealt with risk in our discussion. We might reach a different conclusion about real returns once we do, particularly if people in different countries have different tastes and attitudes towards risk. Second, there are many barriers to the movement of money and capital around the world. Real returns might be different in two different countries for long periods if money can't move freely between them.

Despite these problems, we expect that capital markets will become increasingly internationalized. As this occurs, any differences in real rates will probably diminish. The laws of economics have little respect for national boundaries.

# 31.5 International Capital Budgeting

Kihlstrom Equipment, a US-based international company, is evaluating an overseas investment. Kihlstrom's exports of drill bits have increased to such a degree that it is considering building a distribution centre in France. The project will cost €2 million to launch. The cash flows are expected to be €0.9 million a year for the next three years.

The current spot exchange rate for euros is €0.5/$. Recall that this is euros per dollar, so a euro is worth $1/0.5 = $2. The risk-free rate in the United States is 5 per cent, and the risk-free rate in France is 7 per cent. Note that the exchange rate and the two interest rates are observed in financial markets, not estimated.[3] Kihlstrom's required return on dollar investments of this sort is 10 per cent.

Should Kihlstrom take this investment? As always, the answer depends on the NPV; but how do we calculate the net present value of this project in US dollars? There are two basic methods:

1  *The home currency approach*: Convert all the euro cash flows into dollars, and then discount at 10 per cent to find the NPV in dollars. Notice that for this approach we have to come up with the future exchange rates to convert the future projected euro cash flows into dollars.

2  *The foreign currency approach*: Determine the required return on euro investments, and then discount the euro cash flows to find the NPV in euros. Then convert this euro NPV to a dollar NPV. This approach requires us to somehow convert the 10 per cent dollar required return to the equivalent euro required return.

The difference between these two approaches is primarily a matter of when we convert from euros to dollars. In the first case we convert before estimating the NPV. In the second case we convert after estimating NPV.

It might appear that the second approach is superior, because for it we have to come up with only one number, the euro discount rate. Furthermore, because the first approach requires us to forecast future exchange rates, it probably seems that there is greater room for error with this approach. As we illustrate next, however, based on our previous results, the two approaches are really the same.

## Method 1: The Home Currency Approach

To convert the project future cash flows into dollars, we shall invoke the uncovered interest parity, or UIP, relation to come up with the projected exchange rates. Remember that the euro is the foreign currency in this example. Based on our earlier discussion, the expected exchange rate at time $t$, $E(S_t)$, is

$$E(S_t) = S_0 \times [1 + (R_{\epsilon} - R_{US})]^t$$

where $R_{\epsilon}$ stands for the nominal risk-free rate in France. Because $R_{\epsilon}$ is 7 per cent, $R_{US}$ is 5 per cent, and the current exchange rate ($S_0$) is €0.5:

$$E(S_t) = 0.5 \times [1 + (0.07 - 0.05)]^t$$
$$= 0.5 \times 1.02^t$$

The projected exchange rates for the drill bit project are thus as shown here:

| Year | Expected exchange rate |
|------|------------------------|
| 1 | €0.5 × $1.02^1$ = €0.5100 |
| 2 | €0.5 × $1.02^2$ = €0.5202 |
| 3 | €0.5 × $1.02^3$ = €0.5306 |

Using these exchange rates, along with the current exchange rate, we can convert all of the euro cash flows to dollars (note that all of the cash flows in this example are in millions):

| Year | (1) Cash flow in € millions | (2) Expected exchange rate | (3) Cash flow in $ millions (1)/(2) |
|------|------------------------------|----------------------------|--------------------------------------|
| 0 | −2.0 | 0.5000 | −4.00 |
| 1 | 0.9 | 0.5100 | 1.76 |
| 2 | 0.9 | 0.5202 | 1.73 |
| 3 | 0.9 | 0.5306 | 1.70 |

To finish off, we calculate the NPV in the ordinary way:

$$NPV_{\$} = -\$4 + \$1.76/1.10 + \$1.73/1.10^2 + \$1.70/1.10^3$$
$$= \$0.3 \text{ million}$$

So, the project appears to be profitable.

## Method 2: The Foreign Currency Approach

Kihlstrom requires a nominal return of 10 per cent on the dollar-denominated cash flows. We need to convert this to a rate suitable for euro-denominated cash flows. Based on the international Fisher effect, we know that the difference in the nominal rates is

$$R_{\epsilon} - R_{US} = h_{\epsilon} - h_{US}$$
$$= 7\% - 5\% = 2\%$$

The appropriate discount rate for estimating the euro cash flows from the drill bit project is approximately equal to 10 per cent plus an extra 2 per cent to compensate for the greater euro inflation rate.

If we calculate the NPV of the euro cash flows at this rate, we get

$$NPV_\in = -\in2 + \in0.9/1.12 + \in0.9/1.12^2 + \in0.9/1.12^3$$
$$= \in0.16 \text{ million}$$

The NPV of this project is €0.16 million. Taking this project makes us €0.16 million richer today. What is this in dollars? Because the exchange rate today is €0.5, the dollar NPV of the project is

$$NPV_\$ = \in NPV_\in/S_0 = \in0.16/0.5 = \$0.3 \text{ million}$$

This is the same dollar NPV that we previously calculated.

The important thing to recognize from our example is that the two capital budgeting procedures are actually the same, and will always give the same answer.[4] In this second approach, the fact that we are implicitly forecasting exchange rates is simply hidden. Even so, the foreign currency approach is computationally a little easier.

## Unremitted Cash Flows

The previous example assumed that all after-tax cash flows from the foreign investment could be remitted to (paid out to) the parent firm. Actually, substantial differences can exist between the cash flows generated by a foreign project and the amount that can be remitted, or 'repatriated', to the parent firm.

A foreign subsidiary can remit funds to a parent in many forms, including the following:

- Dividends

- Management fees for central services

- Royalties on the use of trade names and patents

However cash flows are repatriated, international firms must pay special attention to remittances, because there may be current and future controls on remittances. Many governments are sensitive to the charge of being exploited by foreign national firms. In such cases governments are tempted to limit the ability of international firms to remit cash flows. Funds that cannot currently be remitted are sometimes said to be *blocked*.

# 31.6 Exchange Rate Risk

**Exchange rate risk** is the natural consequence of international operations in a world where relative currency values move up and down. Managing exchange rate risk is an important part of international finance. As we discuss next, there are three different types of exchange rate risk or exposure: short-term exposure, long-term exposure, and translation exposure.

## Short-Term Exposure

The day-to-day fluctuations in exchange rates create short-term risks for international firms. Most such firms have contractual agreements to buy and sell goods in the near future at set prices. When different currencies are involved, such transactions have an extra element of risk.

For example, imagine that you are importing imitation pasta from Italy and reselling it in the United Kingdom under the Impasta brand name. Your largest customer has ordered 10,000 cases of Impasta. You place the order with your supplier today, but you won't pay until the goods arrive in 60 days. Your selling price is £6 per case. Your cost is €8.4 per case, and the exchange rate is currently €1.50, so it takes 1.50 euros to buy £1.

At the current exchange rate your cost in pounds of filling the order is €8.4/1.5 = £5.60 per case, so your pre-tax profit on the order is 10,000 × (£6 − 5.60) = £4,000. However, the exchange rate in 60 days will probably be different, so your profit will depend on what the future exchange rate turns out to be.

For example, if the rate goes to €1.6, your cost is €8.4/1.6 = £5.25 per case. Your profit goes to £7,500. If the exchange rate goes to, say, €1.4, then your cost is €8.4/1.4 = £6, and your profit is zero.

The short-term exposure in our example can be reduced or eliminated in several ways. The most obvious way is by entering into a forward exchange agreement to lock in an exchange rate. For example, suppose the 60-day forward rate is €1.58. What will be your profit if you hedge? What profit should you expect if you don't?

If you hedge, you lock in an exchange rate of €1.58. Your cost in pounds will thus be €8.4/1.58 = £5.32 per case, so your profit will be 10,000 × (£6 − 5.32) = £6,800. If you don't hedge, then, assuming that the forward rate is an unbiased predictor (in other words, assuming the UFR condition holds), you should expect that the exchange rate will actually be €1.58 in 60 days. You should expect to make £6,800.

Alternatively, if this strategy is not feasible, you could simply borrow the pounds today, convert them into euros, and invest the euros for 60 days to earn some interest. Based on IRP, this amounts to entering into a forward contract.

## Long-Term Exposure

In the long term, the value of a foreign operation can fluctuate because of unanticipated changes in relative economic conditions. For example, imagine that we own a labour-intensive assembly operation located in another country to take advantage of lower wages. Through time, unexpected changes in economic conditions can raise the foreign wage levels to the point where the cost advantage is eliminated or even becomes negative.

The impact of changes in exchange rate levels can be substantial. During 2008 the euro continued to strengthen against other currencies, in particular the British pound. This meant that British manufacturers took home more for each euro's worth of sales they made, which can lead to big profit swings. For example, during 2007 Barclays lost £654 million as a result of exchange rate changes. This compares with a gain of £552 million in 2006.

Hedging long-term exposure is more difficult than hedging short-term risks. For one thing, organized forward markets don't exist for such long-term needs. Instead, the primary option that firms have is to try to match up foreign currency inflows and outflows. The same thing goes for matching foreign-currency-denominated assets and liabilities. For example, a firm that sells in a foreign country might try to concentrate its raw material purchases and labour expense in that country. In that way the home currency values of its revenues and costs will move up and down together. Probably the best examples of this type of hedging are the so-called transplant auto manufacturers such as BMW, Honda, Mercedes and Toyota, which now build a substantial portion of the cars they sell in the United States at plants located in the United States, thereby obtaining some degree of immunization against exchange rate movements.

For example, the German firm BMW produces 160,000 cars in South Carolina, USA, and exports about 100,000 of them. The costs of manufacturing the cars are paid mostly in dollars, and when BMW exports the cars to Europe it receives euros. When the dollar weakens, these vehicles become more profitable for BMW. At the same time, BMW exports about 217,000 cars to the United States each year. The costs of manufacturing these imported cars are mostly in euros, so they become less profitable when the dollar weakens. Taken together, these gains and losses tend to offset each other, and give BMW a natural hedge.

Similarly, a firm can reduce its long-term exchange rate risk by borrowing in the foreign country. Fluctuations in the value of the foreign subsidiary's assets will then be at least partially offset by changes in the value of the liabilities.

## Translation Exposure

When a British company calculates its accounting net income and EPS for some period, it must translate everything into pounds. Similarly, a Eurozone firm must translate all overseas income into euros. This can create some problems for the accountants when there are significant foreign operations. In particular, two issues arise:

1   What is the appropriate exchange rate to use for translating each account in the statement of financial position?

2   How should accounting gains and losses from foreign currency translation be handled?

To illustrate the accounting problem, suppose we started a small foreign subsidiary in Lilliputia a year ago. The local currency is the gulliver, abbreviated GL. At the beginning of the year the exchange rate was GL2 = €1, and the statement of financial position for gulliver looked like this:

| | (GL) | | | (GL) |
|---|---|---|---|---|
| Assets | 1,000 | | Liabilities | 500 |
| | | | Equity | 500 |

At 2 gullivers to the euro, the beginning statement of financial position in euros was as follows:

| | (€) | | | (€) |
|---|---|---|---|---|
| Assets | 500 | | Liabilities | 250 |
| | | | Equity | 250 |

Lilliputia is a quiet place, and nothing at all actually happened during the year. As a result, net income was zero (before consideration of exchange rate changes). However, the exchange rate did change to 4 gullivers = €1, purely because the Lilliputian inflation rate is much higher than the Eurozone inflation rate.

Because nothing happened, the ending statement in financial position in gullivers is the same as the beginning one. However, if we convert it to euros at the new exchange rate, we get these figures:

| | (€) | | | (€) |
|---|---|---|---|---|
| Assets | 250 | | Liabilities | 125 |
| | | | Equity | 125 |

Notice that the value of the equity has gone down by €125, even though net income was exactly zero. Despite the fact that absolutely nothing happened, there is a €125 accounting loss. How to handle this €125 loss has been a controversial accounting question.

The current approach to handling translation gains and losses is based on rules set out in the International Accounting Standards Board (IASB) International Accounting Standard no. 21 (IAS 21). For the most part, IAS 21 requires that all assets and liabilities be translated from the subsidiary's currency into the parent's currency using the exchange rate that currently prevails. Income and expenses are treated differently, and these are translated at the exchange rate that prevails at the time of the transaction, or at the average rate for the period when this is a reasonable approximation. In contrast to US accounting rules, the impact of translation gains and losses is explicitly recognized in net income. In the US the translation gain or loss is not recognized until the underlying assets and liabilities are sold or otherwise liquidated.

## Managing Exchange Rate Risk

For a large multinational firm the management of exchange rate risk is complicated by the fact that there can be many different currencies involved in many different subsidiaries. It is likely that a change in some exchange rate will benefit some subsidiaries and hurt others. The net effect on the overall firm depends on its net exposure.

For example, suppose a firm has two divisions. Division A buys goods in Italy for euros and sells them in Britain for pounds. Division B buys goods in Britain for pounds and sells them in Italy for euros. If these two divisions are of roughly equal size in terms of their inflows and outflows, then the overall firm obviously has little exchange rate risk.

In our example, the firm's net position in pounds (the amount coming in less the amount going out) is small, so the exchange rate risk is small. However, if one division, acting on its own, were to start hedging its exchange rate risk, then the overall firm's exchange rate risk would go up. The moral of the story is that multinational firms have to be conscious of the overall position that the firm has in a foreign currency. For this reason, management of exchange rate risk is probably best handled on a centralized basis.

## 31.7 Political Risk

One final element of risk in international investing is political risk – that is, changes in value that arise as a consequence of political actions. This is not a problem faced exclusively by international firms. For example, changes in British tax laws and regulations may benefit some British firms and hurt others, so political risk exists nationally as well as internationally.

Some countries have more political risk than others, however. When firms have operations in these riskier countries, the extra political risk may lead the firms to require higher returns on overseas investments to compensate for the possibility that funds may be blocked, critical operations interrupted, and contracts abrogated. In the most extreme case the possibility of outright confiscation may be a concern in countries with relatively unstable political environments.

Political risk also depends on the nature of the business: Some businesses are less likely to be confiscated because they are not particularly valuable in the hands of a different owner. An assembly operation supplying subcomponents that only the parent company uses would not be an attractive takeover target, for example. Similarly, a manufacturing operation that requires the use of specialized components from the parent is of little value without the parent company's co-operation.

**TABLE 31.3**

| Country | Score | Country | Score |
|---------|-------|---------|-------|
| Denmark | 9.3 | United Arab Emirates | 5.9 |
| New Zealand | 9.3 | South Africa | 4.9 |
| Sweden | 9.3 | Italy | 4.8 |
| Finland | 9.0 | Greece | 4.7 |
| Switzerland | 9.0 | China | 3.6 |
| Iceland | 8.9 | Thailand | 3.5 |
| Netherlands | 8.9 | India | 3.4 |
| Australia | 8.7 | Tanzania | 3.0 |
| Austria | 8.1 | Nigeria | 2.7 |
| Germany | 7.9 | Vietnam | 2.7 |
| Norway | 7.9 | Pakistan | 2.5 |
| Ireland | 7.7 | Iran | 2.3 |
| United Kingdom | 7.7 | Kenya | 2.1 |
| Belgium | 7.3 | Russia | 2.1 |
| USA | 7.3 | Zimbabwe | 1.8 |
| France | 6.9 | Iraq | 1.3 |
| Spain | 6.5 | Somalia | 1.0 |

*Source*: Transparency International. Countries with lower numbers are more corrupt.

**Table 31.3** Perceptions of Corruption Index 2008

Natural resource developments, such as copper mining or oil drilling, are just the opposite. Once the operation is in place, much of the value is in the commodity. The political risk for such investments is much higher for this reason. Also, the issue of exploitation is more pronounced with such investments, again increasing the political risk.

Corruption is a very big issue in many countries, and the payment of kickbacks or 'business facilitation fees' is the norm in many areas. Government officials, petty bureaucrats and cumbersome administrative regulations can significantly restrict the efficiency of international operations.

Many organizations present rankings of political risk in countries, and it is paramount that these are considered before any foreign direct investment takes place. *Transparency International*'s 'perceptions of corruption' ranking is an example of such an assessment, and is presented in Table 31.3.

Political risk can be hedged in several ways, particularly when confiscation or nationalization is a concern. The use of local financing, perhaps from the government of the foreign country in question, reduces the possible loss because the company can refuse to pay the debt in the event of unfavourable political activities. Based on our discussion in this section, structuring the operation in such a way that it requires significant parent company involvement to function is another way to reduce political risk.

# Summary and Conclusions

The international firm has a more complicated life than the purely domestic firm. Management must understand the connection between interest rates, foreign currency exchange rates, and inflation, and it must become aware of many different financial market regulations and tax systems. This chapter is intended to be a concise introduction to some of the financial issues that come up in international investing.

Our coverage has been necessarily brief. The main topics we discussed are the following:

1 *Some basic vocabulary*: We briefly defined some exotic terms in international finance.

2 *The basic mechanics of exchange rate quotations*: We discussed the spot and forward markets and how exchange rates are interpreted.

3 *The fundamental relationships between international financial variables*:

 (a) Absolute and relative purchasing power parity, PPP

 (b) Interest rate parity, IRP

 (c) Unbiased forward rates, UFR

 Absolute purchasing power parity states that a currency, such as the euro, should have the same purchasing power in each country. This means that an orange costs the same whether you buy it in Brussels or in Oslo.

 Relative purchasing power parity means that the expected percentage change in exchange rates between the currencies of two countries is equal to the difference in their inflation rates.

 Interest rate parity implies that the percentage difference between the forward exchange rate and the spot exchange rate is equal to the interest rate differential. We showed how covered interest arbitrage forces this relationship to hold.

 The unbiased forward rates condition indicates that the current forward rate is a good predictor of the future spot exchange rate.

4 *International capital budgeting*: We showed that the basic foreign exchange relationships imply two other conditions:

 (a) Uncovered interest parity

 (b) The international Fisher effect.

By invoking these two conditions, we learned how to estimate NPVs in foreign currencies, and how to convert foreign currencies into the home currency to estimate NPV in the usual way.

5   *Exchange rate and political risk*: We described the various types of exchange rate risk, and discussed some common approaches to managing the effect of fluctuating exchange rates on the cash flows and value of the international firm. We also discussed political risk and some ways of managing exposure to it.

## connect  Questions and Problems

CONCEPT
1 – 7

1   **Terminology**   Explain the difference between a domestic bond, a foreign bond and a Eurobond.

2   **Foreign Exchange Markets and Exchange Rates**   What is meant by triangular arbitrage? Is this likely to occur in real life? Explain.

3   **Purchasing Power Parity**   Do you think purchasing power parity exists in the world economies? As country barriers fall, is purchasing power parity likely to become more prevalent? Discuss.

4   **Interest Rate Parity, Unbiased Forward Rates and the International Fisher Effect**   Review the international parity conditions. Which ones do you think are likely to exist, and which are less likely to be valid? During a global recession, do you think they are less or more likely to be valid? Explain.

5   **International Capital Budgeting**   What are the main factors that differentiate international capital budgeting decisions from ones that are focused in the domestic market?

6   **Exchange Rate Risk**   Are exchange rate changes necessarily good or bad for a particular company?

7   **Political Risk**   How can developed countries be viewed as being politically risky?

REGULAR
8 – 38

8   **Spot and Forward Rates**   Suppose the exchange rate for the Norwegian krone is quoted as NKr9.96/£ in the spot market and NKr10/£ in the 90-day forward market.

   (a)   Is the British pound selling at a premium or a discount relative to the krone?

   (b)   Does the financial market expect the krone to weaken relative to the pound? Explain.

   (c)   What do you suspect is true about relative economic conditions in the United Kingdom and Norway?

9   **Purchasing Power Parity**   Suppose the rate of inflation in the Eurozone will run at about 3 per cent higher than the UK inflation rate over the next several years. All other things being the same, what will happen to the euro versus pound exchange rate? What relationship are you relying on in answering?

10   **Exchange Rates**   The exchange rate for the Australian dollar is currently A$2.02/€. This exchange rate is expected to rise by 10 per cent over the next year.

   (a)   Is the Australian dollar expected to get stronger or weaker?

   (b)   What do you think about the relative inflation rates in the Eurozone and Australia?

   (c)   What do you think about the relative nominal interest rates in the Eurozone and Australia? About relative real rates?

11   **Yankee Bonds**   Which of the following most accurately describes a Bulldog bond?

   (a)   A bond issued by Vodafone in Frankfurt with the interest payable in British pounds.

   (b)   A bond issued by Vodafone in Frankfurt with the interest payable in euros.

(c)  A bond issued by BMW in Germany with the interest payable in British pounds.

(d)  A bond issued by BMW in London with the interest payable in British pounds.

(e)  A bond issued by BMW worldwide with the interest payable in British pounds.

12  **International Risks**  At one point, Duracell International confirmed that it was planning to open battery-manufacturing plants in China and India. Manufacturing in these countries allows Duracell to avoid import duties of between 30 and 35 per cent that have made alkaline batteries prohibitively expensive for some consumers. What additional advantages might Duracell see in this proposal? What are some of the risks to Duracell?

13  **Multinational Corporations**  Given that many multinationals based in many countries have much greater sales outside their domestic markets than within them, what is the particular relevance of their domestic currency?

14  **Exchange Rate Movements**  Are the following statements true or false? Explain why.

(a)  If the general price index in Great Britain rises faster than that in the United States, we would expect the pound to appreciate relative to the dollar.

(b)  Suppose you are a German machine tool exporter, and you invoice all of your sales in foreign currency. Further suppose that the European Central Bank begins to undertake an expansionary monetary policy. If it is certain that the easy money policy will result in higher inflation rates in Germany relative to those in other countries, then you should use the forward markets to protect yourself against future losses resulting from the deterioration in the value of the euro.

(c)  If you could accurately estimate differences in the relative inflation rates of two countries over a long period while other market participants were unable to do so, you could successfully speculate in spot currency markets.

15  **Exchange Rate Movements**  Some countries encourage movements in their exchange rate relative to those of some other country as a short-term means of addressing foreign trade imbalances. For each of the following scenarios, evaluate the impact the announcement would have on a Danish importer and a Danish exporter doing business with the foreign country:

(a)  Officials in the Danish government announce that they are comfortable with a rising krone relative to the euro.

(b)  The Bank of England announces that it feels the krone has been driven too low by currency speculators relative to the British pound.

(c)  The European Central Bank announces that it will print billions of new euros and inject them into the economy in an effort to reduce the country's unemployment rate.

16  **International Capital Market Relationships**  We discussed five international capital market relationships: relative PPP, IRP, UFR, UIP, and the international Fisher effect. Which of these would you expect to hold most closely? Which do you think would be most likely to be violated?

17  **Exchange Rate Risk**  If you are an exporter who must make payments in foreign currency three months after receiving each shipment, and you predict that the domestic currency will appreciate in value over this period, is there any value in hedging your currency exposure?

18  **International Capital Budgeting**  Suppose it is your task to evaluate two different investments in new subsidiaries for your company, one in your own country and the other in a foreign country. You calculate the cash flows of both projects to be identical after exchange rate differences. Under what circumstances might you choose to invest in the foreign subsidiary? Give an example of a country where certain factors might influence you to alter this decision and invest at home.

19 **International Capital Budgeting** An investment in a foreign subsidiary is estimated to have a positive NPV after the discount rate used in the calculations is adjusted for political risk and any advantages from diversification. Does this mean the project is acceptable? Why or why not?

20 **International Borrowing** If a South African firm raises funds for a foreign subsidiary, what are the disadvantages to borrowing in South Africa? How would you overcome them?

21 **International Investment** If financial markets are perfectly competitive and the Eurodollar rate is above that offered in the US loan market, you would immediately want to borrow money in the United States and invest it in Eurodollars. True or false? Explain.

22 **Eurobonds** What distinguishes a Eurobond from a foreign bond? Which particular feature makes the Eurobond more popular than the foreign bond?

23 **Using Exchange Rates** Take a look back at Fig. 31.1 to answer the following questions:

(a) If you have €100, how many British pounds can you get?

(b) How much is one pound worth?

(c) If you have £5 million, how many euros do you have?

(d) Which is worth more, a New Zealand dollar or a Singapore dollar?

(e) Which is worth more, a Mexican peso or a Chilean peso?

(f) How many Mexican pesos can you get for an Israeli shekel? What do you call this rate?

(g) Per unit, which is the most valuable currency of those listed? The least valuable?

24 **Using the Cross-Rate** Use the information in Fig. 31.1 to answer the following questions:

(a) Which would you rather have, €100 or £100? Why?

(b) Which would you rather have, 100 Swiss francs (SFr) or 100 Norwegian kroner (NKr)? Why?

(c) What is the cross-rate for Swiss francs in terms of Norwegian kroner? For Norwegian kroner in terms of Swiss francs?

25 **Forward Exchange Rates** Use the information in Fig. 31.1 to answer the following questions:

(a) What is the three-month forward rate for the US dollar per euro? Is the dollar selling at a premium or a discount? Explain.

(b) What is the three-month forward rate for British pounds in euros per pound? Is the euro selling at a premium or a discount? Explain.

(c) What do you think will happen to the value of the euro relative to the dollar and the pound, based on the information in the figure? Explain.

26 **Using Spot and Forward Exchange Rates** Suppose the spot exchange rate for the South African rand is R15/£ and the six-month forward rate is R16/£.

(a) Which is worth more, the British pound or the South African rand?

(b) Assuming absolute PPP holds, what is the cost in the United Kingdom of a Castle beer if the price in South Africa is R20? Why might the beer actually sell at a different price in the United Kingdom?

(c) Is the British pound selling at a premium or a discount relative to the South African rand?

(d) Which currency is expected to appreciate in value?

(e)   Which country do you think has higher interest rates – the United Kingdom or South Africa? Explain.

27   **Cross-Rates and Arbitrage**   Use Fig. 31.1 to answer the following questions:

(a)   What is the cross-rate in terms of Iranian rial per Thai baht?

(b)   Suppose the cross-rate is 279 rial = 1 Thai baht. Is there an arbitrage opportunity here? If there is, explain how to take advantage of the mispricing.

28   **Interest Rate Parity**   Use Fig. 31.1 to answer the following questions. Suppose interest rate parity holds, and the current one year risk-free rate in the Eurozone is 3.8 per cent. What must the one year risk-free rate be in Great Britain? In the US?

29   **Interest Rates and Arbitrage**   The treasurer of a major British firm has £30 million to invest for three months. The annual interest rate in the United Kingdom is 0.45 per cent per month. The interest rate in the United Kingdom is 0.6 per cent per month. The spot exchange rate is €1.12/£, and the three-month forward rate is €1.15/£. Ignoring transaction costs, in which country would the treasurer want to invest the company's funds? Why?

30   **Inflation and Exchange Rates**   Suppose the current exchange rate for the Polish zloty is Z5/£. The expected exchange rate in three years is Z5.2/£. What is the difference in the annual inflation rates for the United Kingdom and Poland over this period? Assume that the anticipated rate is constant for both countries. What relationship are you relying on in answering?

31   **Exchange Rate Risk**   Suppose your company, which is based in Nantes, imports computer motherboards from Singapore. The exchange rate is given in Fig. 31.1. You have just placed an order for 30,000 motherboards at a cost to you of 168.5 Singapore dollars each. You will pay for the shipment when it arrives in 90 days. You can sell the motherboards for €100 each. Calculate your profit if the exchange rate goes up or down by 10 per cent over the next 90 days. What is the break-even exchange rate? What percentage rise or fall does this represent in terms of the Singapore dollar versus the euro?

32   **Exchange Rates and Arbitrage**   Suppose the spot and six-month forward rates on the Swedish krona are SKr11.95/£ and SKr12.00/£, respectively. The annual risk-free rate in the United Kingdom is 2.5 per cent, and the annual risk-free rate in Sweden is 1.13 per cent.

(a)   Is there an arbitrage opportunity here? If so, how would you exploit it?

(b)   What must the six-month forward rate be to prevent arbitrage?

33   **The International Fisher Effect**   You observe that the inflation rate in the United Kingdom is 3.5 per cent per year and that T-bills currently yield 3.9 per cent annually. What do you estimate the inflation rate to be in:

(a)   Australia if short-term Australian government securities yield 5 per cent per year?

(b)   Canada if short-term Canadian government securities yield 7 per cent per year?

(c)   Taiwan if short-term Taiwanese government securities yield 10 per cent per year?

34   **Spot versus Forward Rates**   Suppose the spot and three-month forward rates for the Indian rupee are Rs62.5/€ and Rs61.8/€, respectively.

(a)   Is the rupee expected to get stronger or weaker?

(b)   What would you estimate is the difference between the inflation rates of the Eurozone and India?

35   **Expected Spot Rates**   Suppose the spot exchange rate for the Tanzanian shilling is TSh2000/£. The inflation rate in the United Kingdom is 3.5 per cent, and it is 8.6 per cent in Tanzania. What do you predict the exchange rate will be in one year? In two years? In five years? What relationship are you using?

36  **Forward Rates**  The spot rate of foreign exchange between the United States and the United Kingdom is \$1.50/£. If the interest rate in the United States is 13 per cent, and it is 8 per cent in the United Kingdom, what would you expect the one-year forward rate to be if no immediate arbitrage opportunities exist?

37  **Capital Budgeting**  The Dutch firm ABS Equipment has an investment opportunity in the United Kingdom. The project costs £12 million, and is expected to produce cash flows of £2.7 million in year 1, £3.5 million in year 2, and £3.3 million in year 3. The current spot exchange rate is €1.12/£ and the current risk-free rate in the Eurozone is 2.12 per cent, compared with that in the United Kingdom of 2.13 per cent. The appropriate discount rate for the project is estimated to be 13 per cent, the Eurozone cost of capital for the company. In addition, the subsidiary can be sold at the end of three years for an estimated £7.4 million. What is the NPV of the project?

38  **Capital Budgeting**  As a German company, you are evaluating a proposed expansion of an existing subsidiary located in Switzerland. The cost of the expansion would be SFr27.0 million. The cash flows from the project would be SFr7.5 million per year for the next five years. The euro required return is 13 per cent per year, and the current exchange rate is SFr1.48/€. The going rate on EURIBOR is 8 per cent per year. It is 7 per cent per year on Swiss francs.

  (a)  What do you project will happen to exchange rates over the next four years?

  (b)  Based on your answer in (a), convert the projected franc flows into euro cash flows and calculate the NPV.

  (c)  What is the required return on franc cash flows? Based on your answer, calculate the NPV in francs and then convert to euros.

39  **Using the Exact International Fisher Effect**  From our discussion of the Fisher effect in Chapter 7, we know that the actual relationship between a nominal rate, $R$, a real rate, $r$, and an inflation rate, $h$, can be written as follows:

$$1 + r = (1 + R)/(1 + h)$$

This is the *domestic* Fisher effect.

  (a)  What is the non-approximate form of the international Fisher effect?

  (b)  Based on your answer in (a), what is the exact form for UIP? (*Hint*: Recall the exact form of IRP and use UFR.)

  (c)  What is the exact form for relative PPP? (*Hint*: Combine your previous two answers.)

  (d)  Recalculate the NPV for the Kihlstrom drill bit project (discussed in Section 31.5) using the exact forms for the UIP and the international Fisher effect. Verify that you get precisely the same answer either way.

# West Coast Yachts Goes International

Larissa Warren, the owner of West Coast Yachts, has been in discussions with a yacht dealer in Monaco about selling the company's yachts in Europe. Jarek Jachowicz, the dealer, wants to add West Coast Yachts to his current retail line. Jarek has told Larissa that he feels the retail sales will be approximately €5 million per month. All sales will be made in euros, and Jarek will retain 5 per cent of the retail sales as commission, which will be paid in euros. Because the yachts will be customized to order, the first sales will take place in one month. Jarek will pay West Coast Yachts for the order 90 days after it is filled. This payment schedule will continue for the length of the contract between the two companies.

Larissa is confident the company can handle the extra volume with its existing facilities, but she is unsure about any potential financial risks of selling yachts in Europe. In her discussion with Jarek she found that the current exchange rate is €1.12/£. At this exchange rate the company would spend 70 per cent of the sales income on production costs. This number does not reflect the sales commission to be paid to Jarek.

Larissa has decided to ask Dan Ervin, the company's financial analyst, to prepare an analysis of the proposed international sales. Specifically she asks Dan to answer the following questions:

1    What are the pros and cons of the international sales plan? What additional risks will the company face?

2    What will happen to the company's profits if the British pound strengthens? What if the British pound weakens?

3    Ignoring taxes, what are West Coast Yachts' projected gains or losses from this proposed arrangement at the current exchange rate of €1.12/£? What will happen to profits if the exchange rate changes to €1.20/£? At what exchange rate will the company break even?

4    How can the company hedge its exchange rate risk? What are the implications for this approach?

5    Taking all factors into account, should the company pursue international sales further? Why or why not?

## Practical Case Study

Search on Google for the price of a specific model of car (your choice) that is sold in the United Kingdom, Ireland, France, Italy, Spain, and Germany. Does absolute purchasing power parity hold?

## Relevant Accounting Standards

When investing or doing business overseas, companies need to be sure of the accounting standards to which the target country adheres. Although over 100 countries follow international accounting standards, many countries do not follow these standards, including the US. Foreign currency earnings need to be translated according to IAS21 *The Effects of Changes in Foreign Exchange Rates*. Further, if a company is carrying out business in countries with a hyperinflationary environment (examples are Zimbabwe, Angola and Myanmar) they may have to adhere to IAS29 *Financial Reporting in Hyperinflationary Economies*. Sometimes overseas investments are in the form of joint ventures. If this is the case, IAS31 *Interests in Joint Ventures* is also important.

## Additional Reading

A good paper that links the financial markets and foreign exchange movements is Brennan and Xia (2006). However, it is very technical, so beware!

Brennan, M.J. and Y. Xia (2006) 'International capital markets and foreign exchange risk', *Review of Financial Studies*, vol. 19, no. 3, pp. 753–795. **International**.

## Endnotes

1 There are four exchange rates instead of five because one exchange rate would involve the exchange of a currency for itself. More generally, it might seem that there should be 25 exchange rates with five currencies. There are 25 different combinations, but, of these, five involve the exchange of a currency for itself. Of the remaining 20, half are redundant, because they are just the reciprocals of another exchange rate. Of the remaining 10, six can be eliminated by using a common denominator.

2 Notice that our result here is in terms of the approximate real rate, $R - h$ (see Chapter 7), because we used approximations for PPP and IRP. For the exact result, see Problem 39 at the end of the chapter.

3 For example, the interest rates might be the short-term LIBOR and EURIBOR rates offered by large banks.

4 Actually, there will be a slight difference, because we are using the approximate relationships. If we calculate the required return as $1.10 \times (1 + 0.02) - 1 = 12.2\%$, then we get exactly the same NPV. See Problem 39 for more detail.

Online **LearningCentre**

**To help you grasp the key concepts of this chapter** check out the extra resources posted on the Online Learning Centre at www.mcgraw-hill.co.uk/textbooks/hillier

Among other helpful resources there are PowerPoint presentations, chapter outlines and mini-cases.

# Appendix A   Mathematical Tables

**Table A.1** Present Value of £1 or €1 to Be Received after $T$ Periods $= 1/(1 + r)^T$

**Table A.2** Present Value of an Annuity of £1 or €1 per Period for $T$ Periods $= [1 - 1/(1 + r)^T]/r$

**Table A.3** Future Value of £1 or €1 at the End of $T$ Periods $= (1 + r)^T$

**Table A.4** Future Value of an Annuity of £1 or €1 per Period for $T$ Periods $= [(1 + r)^T - 1]/r$

**Table A.5** Future Value of £1 or €1 with a Continuously Compounded Rate $r$ for $T$ Periods: Values of $e^{rT}$

**Table A.6** Present Value of £1 or €1 with a Continuous Discount Rate $r$ for $T$ Periods: Values of $e^{-rT}$

TABLE A.1

| Period | 1% | 2% | 3% | 4% | 5% | 6% | 7% | 8% | 9% |
|--------|------|------|------|------|------|------|------|------|------|
| | | | | | Interest rate | | | | |
| 1 | 0.9901 | 0.9804 | 0.9709 | 0.9615 | 0.9524 | 0.9434 | 0.9346 | 0.9259 | 0.9174 |
| 2 | 0.9803 | 0.9612 | 0.9426 | 0.9246 | 0.9070 | 0.8900 | 0.8734 | 0.8573 | 0.8417 |
| 3 | 0.9706 | 0.9423 | 0.9151 | 0.8890 | 0.8638 | 0.8396 | 0.8163 | 0.7938 | 0.7722 |
| 4 | 0.9610 | 0.9238 | 0.8885 | 0.8548 | 0.8227 | 0.7921 | 0.7629 | 0.7350 | 0.7084 |
| 5 | 0.9515 | 0.9057 | 0.8626 | 0.8219 | 0.7835 | 0.7473 | 0.7130 | 0.6806 | 0.6499 |
| 6 | 0.9420 | 0.8880 | 0.8375 | 0.7903 | 0.7462 | 0.7050 | 0.6663 | 0.6302 | 0.5963 |
| 7 | 0.9327 | 0.8706 | 0.8131 | 0.7599 | 0.7107 | 0.6651 | 0.6227 | 0.5835 | 0.5470 |
| 8 | 0.9235 | 0.8535 | 0.7894 | 0.7307 | 0.6768 | 0.6274 | 0.5820 | 0.5403 | 0.5019 |
| 9 | 0.9143 | 0.8368 | 0.7664 | 0.7026 | 0.6446 | 0.5919 | 0.5439 | 0.5002 | 0.4604 |
| 10 | 0.9053 | 0.8203 | 0.7441 | 0.6756 | 0.6139 | 0.5584 | 0.5083 | 0.4632 | 0.4224 |
| 11 | 0.8963 | 0.8043 | 0.7224 | 0.6496 | 0.5847 | 0.5268 | 0.4751 | 0.4289 | 0.3875 |
| 12 | 0.8874 | 0.7885 | 0.7014 | 0.6246 | 0.5568 | 0.4970 | 0.4440 | 0.3971 | 0.3555 |
| 13 | 0.8787 | 0.7730 | 0.6810 | 0.6006 | 0.5303 | 0.4688 | 0.4150 | 0.3677 | 0.3262 |
| 14 | 0.8700 | 0.7579 | 0.6611 | 0.5775 | 0.5051 | 0.4423 | 0.3878 | 0.3405 | 0.2992 |
| 15 | 0.8613 | 0.7430 | 0.6419 | 0.5553 | 0.4810 | 0.4173 | 0.3624 | 0.3152 | 0.2745 |
| 16 | 0.8528 | 0.7284 | 0.6232 | 0.5339 | 0.4581 | 0.3936 | 0.3387 | 0.2919 | 0.2519 |
| 17 | 0.8444 | 0.7142 | 0.6050 | 0.5134 | 0.4363 | 0.3714 | 0.3166 | 0.2703 | 0.2311 |
| 18 | 0.8360 | 0.7002 | 0.5874 | 0.4936 | 0.4155 | 0.3503 | 0.2959 | 0.2502 | 0.2120 |
| 19 | 0.8277 | 0.6864 | 0.5703 | 0.4746 | 0.3957 | 0.3305 | 0.2765 | 0.2317 | 0.1945 |
| 20 | 0.8195 | 0.6730 | 0.5537 | 0.4564 | 0.3769 | 0.3118 | 0.2584 | 0.2145 | 0.1784 |
| 21 | 0.8114 | 0.6598 | 0.5375 | 0.4388 | 0.3589 | 0.2942 | 0.2415 | 0.1987 | 0.1637 |
| 22 | 0.8034 | 0.6468 | 0.5219 | 0.4220 | 0.3418 | 0.2775 | 0.2257 | 0.1839 | 0.1502 |
| 23 | 0.7954 | 0.6342 | 0.5067 | 0.4057 | 0.3256 | 0.2618 | 0.2109 | 0.1703 | 0.1378 |
| 24 | 0.7876 | 0.6217 | 0.4919 | 0.3901 | 0.3101 | 0.2470 | 0.1971 | 0.1577 | 0.1264 |
| 25 | 0.7798 | 0.6095 | 0.4776 | 0.3751 | 0.2953 | 0.2330 | 0.1842 | 0.1460 | 0.1160 |
| 30 | 0.7419 | 0.5521 | 0.4120 | 0.3083 | 0.2314 | 0.1741 | 0.1314 | 0.0994 | 0.0754 |
| 40 | 0.6717 | 0.4529 | 0.3066 | 0.2083 | 0.1420 | 0.0972 | 0.0668 | 0.0460 | 0.0318 |
| 50 | 0.6080 | 0.3715 | 0.2281 | 0.1407 | 0.0872 | 0.0543 | 0.0339 | 0.0213 | 0.0134 |

TABLE
A.1

| Period | 10% | 12% | 14% | 15% | 16% | 18% | 20% | 24% | 28% | 32% | 36% |
|--------|-----|-----|-----|-----|-----|-----|-----|-----|-----|-----|-----|
| | | | | | | | Interest rate | | | | |
| 1 | 0.9091 | 0.8929 | 0.8772 | 0.8696 | 0.8621 | 0.8475 | 0.8333 | 0.8065 | 0.7813 | 0.7576 | 0.7353 |
| 2 | 0.8264 | 0.7972 | 0.7695 | 0.7561 | 0.7432 | 0.7182 | 0.6944 | 0.6504 | 0.6104 | 0.5739 | 0.5407 |
| 3 | 0.7513 | 0.7118 | 0.6750 | 0.6575 | 0.6407 | 0.6086 | 0.5787 | 0.5245 | 0.4768 | 0.4348 | 0.3975 |
| 4 | 0.6830 | 0.6355 | 0.5921 | 0.5718 | 0.5523 | 0.5158 | 0.4823 | 0.4230 | 0.3725 | 0.3294 | 0.2923 |
| 5 | 0.6209 | 0.5674 | 0.5194 | 0.4972 | 0.4761 | 0.4371 | 0.4019 | 0.3411 | 0.2910 | 0.2495 | 0.2149 |
| 6 | 0.5645 | 0.5066 | 0.4556 | 0.4323 | 0.4104 | 0.3704 | 0.3349 | 0.2751 | 0.2274 | 0.1890 | 0.1580 |
| 7 | 0.5132 | 0.4523 | 0.3996 | 0.3759 | 0.3538 | 0.3139 | 0.2791 | 0.2218 | 0.1776 | 0.1432 | 0.1162 |
| 8 | 0.4665 | 0.4039 | 0.3506 | 0.3269 | 0.3050 | 0.2660 | 0.2326 | 0.1789 | 0.1388 | 0.1085 | 0.0854 |
| 9 | 0.4241 | 0.3606 | 0.3075 | 0.2843 | 0.2630 | 0.2255 | 0.1938 | 0.1443 | 0.1084 | 0.0822 | 0.0628 |
| 10 | 0.3855 | 0.3220 | 0.2697 | 0.2472 | 0.2267 | 0.1911 | 0.1615 | 0.1164 | 0.0847 | 0.0623 | 0.0462 |
| 11 | 0.3505 | 0.2875 | 0.2366 | 0.2149 | 0.1954 | 0.1619 | 0.1346 | 0.0938 | 0.0662 | 0.0472 | 0.0340 |
| 12 | 0.3186 | 0.2567 | 0.2076 | 0.1869 | 0.1685 | 0.1372 | 0.1122 | 0.0757 | 0.0517 | 0.0357 | 0.0250 |
| 13 | 0.2897 | 0.2292 | 0.1821 | 0.1625 | 0.1452 | 0.1163 | 0.0935 | 0.0610 | 0.0404 | 0.0271 | 0.0184 |
| 14 | 0.2633 | 0.2046 | 0.1597 | 0.1413 | 0.1252 | 0.0985 | 0.0779 | 0.0492 | 0.0316 | 0.0205 | 0.0135 |
| 15 | 0.2394 | 0.1827 | 0.1401 | 0.1229 | 0.1079 | 0.0835 | 0.0649 | 0.0397 | 0.0247 | 0.0155 | 0.0099 |
| 16 | 0.2176 | 0.1631 | 0.1229 | 0.1069 | 0.0930 | 0.0708 | 0.0541 | 0.0320 | 0.0193 | 0.0118 | 0.0073 |
| 17 | 0.1978 | 0.1456 | 0.1078 | 0.0929 | 0.0802 | 0.0600 | 0.0451 | 0.0258 | 0.0150 | 0.0089 | 0.0054 |
| 18 | 0.1799 | 0.1300 | 0.0946 | 0.0808 | 0.0691 | 0.0508 | 0.0376 | 0.0208 | 0.0118 | 0.0068 | 0.0039 |
| 19 | 0.1635 | 0.1161 | 0.0829 | 0.0703 | 0.0596 | 0.0431 | 0.0313 | 0.0168 | 0.0092 | 0.0051 | 0.0029 |
| 20 | 0.1486 | 0.1037 | 0.0728 | 0.0611 | 0.0514 | 0.0365 | 0.0261 | 0.0135 | 0.0072 | 0.0039 | 0.0021 |
| 21 | 0.1351 | 0.0926 | 0.0638 | 0.0531 | 0.0443 | 0.0309 | 0.0217 | 0.0109 | 0.0056 | 0.0029 | 0.0016 |
| 22 | 0.1228 | 0.0826 | 0.0560 | 0.0462 | 0.0382 | 0.0262 | 0.0181 | 0.0088 | 0.0044 | 0.0022 | 0.0012 |
| 23 | 0.1117 | 0.0738 | 0.0491 | 0.0402 | 0.0329 | 0.0222 | 0.0151 | 0.0071 | 0.0034 | 0.0017 | 0.0008 |
| 24 | 0.1015 | 0.0659 | 0.0431 | 0.0349 | 0.0284 | 0.0188 | 0.0126 | 0.0057 | 0.0027 | 0.0013 | 0.0006 |
| 25 | 0.0923 | 0.0588 | 0.0378 | 0.0304 | 0.0245 | 0.0160 | 0.0105 | 0.0046 | 0.0021 | 0.0010 | 0.0005 |
| 30 | 0.0573 | 0.0334 | 0.0196 | 0.0151 | 0.0116 | 0.0070 | 0.0042 | 0.0016 | 0.0006 | 0.0002 | 0.0001 |
| 40 | 0.0221 | 0.0107 | 0.0053 | 0.0037 | 0.0026 | 0.0013 | 0.0007 | 0.0002 | 0.0001 | * | * |
| 50 | 0.0085 | 0.0035 | 0.0014 | 0.0009 | 0.0006 | 0.0003 | 0.0001 | * | * | * | * |

*The factor is zero to four decimal places.

Table A.1 Present Value of £1 or €1 to Be Received after $T$ Periods $= 1/(1 + r)^T$

TABLE
**A.2**

| Number of Periods | 1% | 2% | 3% | 4% | 5% | 6% | 7% | 8% | 9% |
|---|---|---|---|---|---|---|---|---|---|
| | | | | | Interest rate | | | | |
| 1 | 0.9901 | 0.9804 | 0.9709 | 0.9615 | 0.9524 | 0.9434 | 0.9346 | 0.9259 | 0.9174 |
| 2 | 1.9704 | 1.9416 | 1.9135 | 1.8861 | 1.8594 | 1.8334 | 1.8080 | 1.7833 | 1.7591 |
| 3 | 2.9410 | 2.8839 | 2.8286 | 2.7751 | 2.7232 | 2.6730 | 2.6243 | 2.5771 | 2.5313 |
| 4 | 3.9020 | 3.8077 | 3.7171 | 3.6299 | 3.5460 | 3.4651 | 3.3872 | 3.3121 | 3.2397 |
| 5 | 4.8534 | 4.7135 | 4.5797 | 4.4518 | 4.3295 | 4.2124 | 4.1002 | 3.9927 | 3.8897 |
| 6 | 5.7955 | 5.6014 | 5.4172 | 5.2421 | 5.0757 | 4.9173 | 4.7665 | 4.6229 | 4.4859 |
| 7 | 6.7282 | 6.4720 | 6.2303 | 6.0021 | 5.7864 | 5.5824 | 5.3893 | 5.2064 | 5.0330 |
| 8 | 7.6517 | 7.3255 | 7.0197 | 6.7327 | 6.4632 | 6.2098 | 5.9713 | 5.7466 | 5.5348 |
| 9 | 8.5660 | 8.1622 | 7.7861 | 7.4353 | 7.1078 | 6.8017 | 6.5152 | 6.2469 | 5.9952 |
| 10 | 9.4713 | 8.9826 | 8.5302 | 8.1109 | 7.7217 | 7.3601 | 7.0236 | 6.7101 | 6.4177 |
| 11 | 10.3676 | 9.7868 | 9.2526 | 8.7605 | 8.3064 | 7.8869 | 7.4987 | 7.1390 | 6.8052 |
| 12 | 11.2551 | 10.5753 | 9.9540 | 9.3851 | 8.8633 | 8.3838 | 7.9427 | 7.5361 | 7.1607 |
| 13 | 12.1337 | 11.3484 | 10.6350 | 9.9856 | 9.3936 | 8.8527 | 8.3577 | 7.9038 | 7.4869 |
| 14 | 13.0037 | 12.1062 | 11.2961 | 10.5631 | 9.8986 | 9.2950 | 8.7455 | 8.2442 | 7.7862 |
| 15 | 13.8651 | 12.8493 | 11.9379 | 11.1184 | 10.3797 | 9.7122 | 9.1079 | 8.5595 | 8.0607 |
| 16 | 14.7179 | 13.5777 | 12.5611 | 11.6523 | 10.8378 | 10.1059 | 9.4466 | 8.8514 | 8.3126 |
| 17 | 15.5623 | 14.2919 | 13.1661 | 12.1657 | 11.2741 | 10.4773 | 9.7632 | 9.1216 | 8.5436 |
| 18 | 16.3983 | 14.9920 | 13.7535 | 12.6593 | 11.6896 | 10.8276 | 10.0591 | 9.3719 | 8.7556 |
| 19 | 17.2260 | 15.6785 | 14.3238 | 13.1339 | 12.0853 | 11.1581 | 10.3356 | 9.6036 | 8.9501 |
| 20 | 18.0456 | 16.3514 | 14.8775 | 13.5903 | 12.4622 | 11.4699 | 10.5940 | 9.8181 | 9.1285 |
| 21 | 18.8570 | 17.0112 | 15.4150 | 14.0292 | 12.8212 | 11.7641 | 10.8355 | 10.0168 | 9.2922 |
| 22 | 19.6604 | 17.6580 | 15.9369 | 14.4511 | 13.1630 | 12.0416 | 11.0612 | 10.2007 | 9.4424 |
| 23 | 20.4558 | 18.2922 | 16.4436 | 14.8568 | 13.4886 | 12.3034 | 11.2722 | 10.3741 | 9.5802 |
| 24 | 21.2434 | 18.9139 | 16.9355 | 15.2470 | 13.7986 | 12.5504 | 11.4693 | 10.5288 | 9.7066 |
| 25 | 22.0232 | 19.5235 | 17.4131 | 15.6221 | 14.0939 | 12.7834 | 11.6536 | 10.6748 | 9.8226 |
| 30 | 25.8077 | 22.3965 | 19.6004 | 17.2920 | 15.3725 | 13.7648 | 12.4090 | 11.2578 | 10.2737 |
| 40 | 32.8347 | 27.3555 | 23.1148 | 19.7928 | 17.1591 | 15.0463 | 13.3317 | 11.9246 | 10.7574 |
| 50 | 39.1961 | 31.4236 | 25.7298 | 21.4822 | 18.2559 | 15.7619 | 13.8007 | 12.2335 | 10.9617 |

TABLE
**A.2**

| Number of Periods | 10% | 12% | 14% | 15% | 16% | 18% | 20% | 24% | 28% | 32% |
|---|---|---|---|---|---|---|---|---|---|---|
| | | | | | Interest rate | | | | | |
| 1 | 0.9091 | 0.8929 | 0.8772 | 0.8696 | 0.8621 | 0.8475 | 0.8333 | 0.8065 | 0.7813 | 0.7576 |
| 2 | 1.7355 | 1.6901 | 1.6467 | 1.6257 | 1.6052 | 1.5656 | 1.5278 | 1.4568 | 1.3916 | 1.3315 |
| 3 | 2.4869 | 2.4018 | 2.3216 | 2.2832 | 2.2459 | 2.1743 | 2.1065 | 1.9813 | 1.8684 | 1.7663 |
| 4 | 3.1699 | 3.0373 | 2.9137 | 2.8550 | 2.7982 | 2.6901 | 2.5887 | 2.4043 | 2.2410 | 2.0957 |
| 5 | 3.7908 | 3.6048 | 3.4331 | 3.3522 | 3.2743 | 3.1272 | 2.9906 | 2.7454 | 2.5320 | 2.3452 |
| 6 | 4.3553 | 4.1114 | 3.8887 | 3.7845 | 3.6847 | 3.4976 | 3.3255 | 3.0205 | 2.7594 | 2.5342 |
| 7 | 4.8684 | 4.5638 | 4.2883 | 4.1604 | 4.0386 | 3.8115 | 3.6046 | 3.2423 | 2.9370 | 2.6775 |
| 8 | 5.3349 | 4.9676 | 4.6389 | 4.4873 | 4.3436 | 4.0776 | 3.8372 | 3.4212 | 3.0758 | 2.7860 |
| 9 | 5.7590 | 5.3282 | 4.9464 | 4.7716 | 4.6065 | 4.3030 | 4.0310 | 3.5655 | 3.1842 | 2.8681 |
| 10 | 6.1446 | 5.6502 | 5.2161 | 5.0188 | 4.8332 | 4.4941 | 4.1925 | 3.6819 | 3.2689 | 2.9304 |
| 11 | 6.4951 | 5.9377 | 5.4527 | 5.2337 | 5.0286 | 4.6560 | 4.3271 | 3.7757 | 3.3351 | 2.9776 |
| 12 | 6.8137 | 6.1944 | 5.6603 | 5.4206 | 5.1971 | 4.7932 | 4.4392 | 3.8514 | 3.3868 | 3.0133 |
| 13 | 7.1034 | 6.4235 | 5.8424 | 5.5831 | 5.3423 | 4.9095 | 4.5327 | 3.9124 | 3.4272 | 3.0404 |
| 14 | 7.3667 | 6.6282 | 6.0021 | 5.7245 | 5.4675 | 5.0081 | 4.6106 | 3.9616 | 3.4587 | 3.0609 |
| 15 | 7.6061 | 6.8109 | 6.1422 | 5.8474 | 5.5755 | 5.0916 | 4.6755 | 4.0013 | 3.4834 | 3.0764 |
| 16 | 7.8237 | 6.9740 | 6.2651 | 5.9542 | 5.6685 | 5.1624 | 4.7296 | 4.0333 | 3.5026 | 3.0882 |
| 17 | 8.0216 | 7.1196 | 6.3729 | 6.0472 | 5.7487 | 5.2223 | 4.7746 | 4.0591 | 3.5177 | 3.0971 |
| 18 | 8.2014 | 7.2497 | 6.4674 | 6.1280 | 5.8178 | 5.2732 | 4.8122 | 4.0799 | 3.5294 | 3.1039 |
| 19 | 8.3649 | 7.3658 | 6.5504 | 6.1982 | 5.8775 | 5.3162 | 4.8435 | 4.0967 | 3.5386 | 3.1090 |
| 20 | 8.5136 | 7.4694 | 6.6231 | 6.2593 | 5.9288 | 5.3527 | 4.8696 | 4.1103 | 3.5458 | 3.1129 |
| 21 | 8.6487 | 7.5620 | 6.6870 | 6.3125 | 5.9731 | 5.3837 | 4.8913 | 4.1212 | 3.5514 | 3.1158 |
| 22 | 8.7715 | 7.6446 | 6.7429 | 6.3587 | 6.0113 | 5.4099 | 4.9094 | 4.1300 | 3.5558 | 3.1180 |
| 23 | 8.8832 | 7.7184 | 6.7921 | 6.3988 | 6.0442 | 5.4321 | 4.9245 | 4.1371 | 3.5592 | 3.1197 |
| 24 | 8.9847 | 7.7843 | 6.8351 | 6.4338 | 6.0726 | 5.4509 | 4.9371 | 4.1428 | 3.5619 | 3.1210 |
| 25 | 9.0770 | 7.8431 | 6.8729 | 6.4641 | 6.0971 | 5.4669 | 4.9476 | 4.1474 | 3.5640 | 3.1220 |
| 30 | 9.4269 | 8.0552 | 7.0027 | 6.5660 | 6.1772 | 5.5168 | 4.9789 | 4.1601 | 3.5693 | 3.1242 |
| 40 | 9.7791 | 8.2438 | 7.1050 | 6.6418 | 6.2335 | 5.5482 | 4.9966 | 4.1659 | 3.5712 | 3.1250 |
| 50 | 9.9148 | 8.3045 | 7.1327 | 6.6605 | 6.2463 | 5.5541 | 4.9995 | 4.1666 | 3.5714 | 3.1250 |

**Table A.2** Present Value of an Annuity of £1 or €1 per Period for $T$ Periods = $[1 - 1/(1 + r)^T]/r$

TABLE
**A.3**

|  | | | | Interest rate | | | | |
| Period | 1% | 2% | 3% | 4% | 5% | 6% | 7% | 8% | 9% |
|---|---|---|---|---|---|---|---|---|---|
| 1 | 1.0100 | 1.0200 | 1.0300 | 1.0400 | 1.0500 | 1.0600 | 1.0700 | 1.0800 | 1.0900 |
| 2 | 1.0201 | 1.0404 | 1.0609 | 1.0816 | 1.1025 | 1.1236 | 1.1449 | 1.1664 | 1.1881 |
| 3 | 1.0303 | 1.0612 | 1.0927 | 1.1249 | 1.1576 | 1.1910 | 1.2250 | 1.2597 | 1.2950 |
| 4 | 1.0406 | 1.0824 | 1.1255 | 1.1699 | 1.2155 | 1.2625 | 1.3108 | 1.3605 | 1.4116 |
| 5 | 1.0510 | 1.1041 | 1.1593 | 1.2167 | 1.2763 | 1.3382 | 1.4026 | 1.4693 | 1.5386 |
| 6 | 1.0615 | 1.1262 | 1.1941 | 1.2653 | 1.3401 | 1.4185 | 1.5007 | 1.5869 | 1.6771 |
| 7 | 1.0721 | 1.1487 | 1.2299 | 1.3159 | 1.4071 | 1.5036 | 1.6058 | 1.7138 | 1.8280 |
| 8 | 1.0829 | 1.1717 | 1.2668 | 1.3686 | 1.4775 | 1.5938 | 1.7182 | 1.8509 | 1.9926 |
| 9 | 1.0937 | 1.1951 | 1.3048 | 1.4233 | 1.5513 | 1.6895 | 1.8385 | 1.9990 | 2.1719 |
| 10 | 1.1046 | 1.2190 | 1.3439 | 1.4802 | 1.6289 | 1.7908 | 1.9672 | 2.1589 | 2.3674 |
| 11 | 1.1157 | 1.2434 | 1.3842 | 1.5395 | 1.7103 | 1.8983 | 2.1049 | 2.3316 | 2.5804 |
| 12 | 1.1268 | 1.2682 | 1.4258 | 1.6010 | 1.7959 | 2.0122 | 2.2522 | 2.5182 | 2.8127 |
| 13 | 1.1381 | 1.2936 | 1.4685 | 1.6651 | 1.8856 | 2.1329 | 2.4098 | 2.7196 | 3.0658 |
| 14 | 1.1495 | 1.3195 | 1.5126 | 1.7317 | 1.9799 | 2.2609 | 2.5785 | 2.9372 | 3.3417 |
| 15 | 1.1610 | 1.3459 | 1.5580 | 1.8009 | 2.0789 | 2.3966 | 2.7590 | 3.1722 | 3.6425 |
| 16 | 1.1726 | 1.3728 | 1.6047 | 1.8730 | 2.1829 | 2.5404 | 2.9522 | 3.4259 | 3.9703 |
| 17 | 1.1843 | 1.4002 | 1.6528 | 1.9479 | 2.2920 | 2.6928 | 3.1588 | 3.7000 | 4.3276 |
| 18 | 1.1961 | 1.4282 | 1.7024 | 2.0258 | 2.4066 | 2.8543 | 3.3799 | 3.9960 | 4.7171 |
| 19 | 1.2081 | 1.4568 | 1.7535 | 2.1068 | 2.5270 | 3.0256 | 3.6165 | 4.3157 | 5.1417 |
| 20 | 1.2202 | 1.4859 | 1.8061 | 2.1911 | 2.6533 | 3.2071 | 3.8697 | 4.6610 | 5.6044 |
| 21 | 1.2324 | 1.5157 | 1.8603 | 2.2788 | 2.7860 | 3.3996 | 4.1406 | 5.0338 | 6.1088 |
| 22 | 1.2447 | 1.5460 | 1.9161 | 2.3699 | 2.9253 | 3.6035 | 4.4304 | 5.4365 | 6.6586 |
| 23 | 1.2572 | 1.5769 | 1.9736 | 2.4647 | 3.0715 | 3.8197 | 4.7405 | 5.8715 | 7.2579 |
| 24 | 1.2697 | 1.6084 | 2.0328 | 2.5633 | 3.2251 | 4.0489 | 5.0724 | 6.3412 | 7.9111 |
| 25 | 1.2824 | 1.6406 | 2.0938 | 2.6658 | 3.3864 | 4.2919 | 5.4274 | 6.8485 | 8.6231 |
| 30 | 1.3478 | 1.8114 | 2.4273 | 3.2434 | 4.3219 | 5.7435 | 7.6123 | 10.063 | 13.268 |
| 40 | 1.4889 | 2.2080 | 3.2620 | 4.8010 | 7.0400 | 10.286 | 14.974 | 21.725 | 31.409 |
| 50 | 1.6446 | 2.6916 | 4.3839 | 7.1067 | 11.467 | 18.420 | 29.457 | 46.902 | 74.358 |
| 60 | 1.8167 | 3.2810 | 5.8916 | 10.520 | 18.679 | 32.988 | 57.946 | 101.26 | 176.03 |

**TABLE A.3**

Interest rate

| Period | 10% | 12% | 14% | 15% | 16% | 18% | 20% | 24% | 28% | 32% | 36% |
|---|---|---|---|---|---|---|---|---|---|---|---|
| 1 | 1.1000 | 1.1200 | 1.1400 | 1.1500 | 1.1600 | 1.1800 | 1.2000 | 1.2400 | 1.2800 | 1.3200 | 1.3600 |
| 2 | 1.2100 | 1.2544 | 1.2996 | 1.3225 | 1.3456 | 1.3924 | 1.4400 | 1.5376 | 1.6384 | 1.7424 | 1.8496 |
| 3 | 1.3310 | 1.4049 | 1.4815 | 1.5209 | 1.5609 | 1.6430 | 1.7280 | 1.9066 | 2.0972 | 2.3000 | 2.5155 |
| 4 | 1.4641 | 1.5735 | 1.6890 | 1.7490 | 1.8106 | 1.9388 | 2.0736 | 2.3642 | 2.6844 | 3.0360 | 3.4210 |
| 5 | 1.6105 | 1.7623 | 1.9254 | 2.0114 | 2.1003 | 2.2878 | 2.4883 | 2.9316 | 3.4360 | 4.0075 | 4.6526 |
| 6 | 1.7716 | 1.9738 | 2.1950 | 2.3131 | 2.4364 | 2.6996 | 2.9860 | 3.6352 | 4.3980 | 5.2899 | 6.3275 |
| 7 | 1.9487 | 2.2107 | 2.5023 | 2.6600 | 2.8262 | 3.1855 | 3.5832 | 4.5077 | 5.6295 | 6.9826 | 8.6054 |
| 8 | 2.1436 | 2.4760 | 2.8526 | 3.0590 | 3.2784 | 3.7589 | 4.2998 | 5.5895 | 7.2058 | 9.2170 | 11.703 |
| 9 | 2.3579 | 2.7731 | 3.2519 | 3.5179 | 3.8030 | 4.4355 | 5.1598 | 6.9310 | 9.2234 | 12.166 | 15.917 |
| 10 | 2.5937 | 3.1058 | 3.7072 | 4.0456 | 4.4114 | 5.2338 | 6.1917 | 8.5944 | 11.806 | 16.060 | 21.647 |
| 11 | 2.8531 | 3.4785 | 4.2262 | 4.6524 | 5.1173 | 6.1759 | 7.4301 | 10.657 | 15.112 | 21.199 | 29.439 |
| 12 | 3.1384 | 3.8960 | 4.8179 | 5.3503 | 5.9360 | 7.2876 | 8.9161 | 13.215 | 19.343 | 27.983 | 40.037 |
| 13 | 3.4523 | 4.3635 | 5.4924 | 6.1528 | 6.8858 | 8.5994 | 10.699 | 16.386 | 24.759 | 36.937 | 54.451 |
| 14 | 3.7975 | 4.8871 | 6.2613 | 7.0757 | 7.9875 | 10.147 | 12.839 | 20.319 | 31.691 | 48.757 | 74.053 |
| 15 | 4.1772 | 5.4736 | 7.1379 | 8.1371 | 9.2655 | 11.974 | 15.407 | 25.196 | 40.565 | 64.359 | 100.71 |
| 16 | 4.5950 | 6.1304 | 8.1372 | 9.3576 | 10.748 | 14.129 | 18.488 | 31.243 | 51.923 | 84.954 | 136.97 |
| 17 | 5.0545 | 6.8660 | 9.2765 | 10.761 | 12.468 | 16.672 | 22.186 | 38.741 | 66.461 | 112.14 | 186.28 |
| 18 | 5.5599 | 7.6900 | 10.575 | 12.375 | 14.463 | 19.673 | 26.623 | 48.039 | 86.071 | 148.02 | 253.34 |
| 19 | 6.1159 | 8.6128 | 12.056 | 14.232 | 16.777 | 23.214 | 31.948 | 59.568 | 108.89 | 195.39 | 344.54 |
| 20 | 6.7275 | 9.6463 | 13.743 | 16.367 | 19.461 | 27.393 | 38.338 | 73.864 | 139.38 | 257.92 | 468.57 |
| 21 | 7.4002 | 10.804 | 15.668 | 18.822 | 22.574 | 32.324 | 46.005 | 91.592 | 178.41 | 340.45 | 637.26 |
| 22 | 8.1403 | 12.100 | 17.861 | 21.645 | 26.186 | 38.142 | 55.206 | 113.57 | 228.36 | 449.39 | 866.67 |
| 23 | 8.9543 | 13.552 | 20.362 | 24.891 | 30.376 | 45.008 | 66.247 | 140.83 | 292.30 | 593.20 | 1178.7 |
| 24 | 9.8497 | 15.179 | 23.212 | 28.625 | 35.236 | 53.109 | 79.497 | 174.63 | 374.14 | 783.02 | 1603.0 |
| 25 | 10.835 | 17.000 | 26.462 | 32.919 | 40.874 | 62.669 | 95.396 | 216.54 | 478.90 | 1033.6 | 2180.1 |
| 30 | 17.449 | 29.960 | 50.950 | 66.212 | 85.850 | 143.37 | 237.38 | 634.82 | 1645.5 | 4142.1 | 10143. |
| 40 | 45.259 | 93.051 | 188.88 | 267.86 | 378.72 | 750.38 | 1469.8 | 5455.9 | 19427. | 66521. | * |
| 50 | 117.39 | 289.00 | 700.23 | 1083.7 | 1670.7 | 3927.4 | 9100.4 | 46890. | * | * | * |
| 60 | 304.48 | 897.60 | 2595.9 | 4384.0 | 7370.2 | 20555. | 56348. | * | * | * | * |

*FVIV 99,999.

**Table A.3** Future Value of £1 or €1 at the End of $T$ Periods = $(1 + r)^T$

TABLE
**A.4**

| Number of Periods | 1% | 2% | 3% | 4% | 5% | 6% | 7% | 8% | 9% |
|---|---|---|---|---|---|---|---|---|---|
| | | | | | Interest rate | | | | |
| 1 | 1.0000 | 1.0000 | 1.0000 | 1.0000 | 1.0000 | 1.0000 | 1.0000 | 1.0000 | 1.0000 |
| 2 | 2.0100 | 2.0200 | 2.0300 | 2.0400 | 2.0500 | 2.0600 | 2.0700 | 2.0800 | 2.0900 |
| 3 | 3.0301 | 3.0604 | 3.0909 | 3.1216 | 3.1525 | 3.1836 | 3.2149 | 3.2464 | 3.2781 |
| 4 | 4.0604 | 4.1216 | 4.1836 | 4.2465 | 4.3101 | 4.3746 | 4.4399 | 4.5061 | 4.5731 |
| 5 | 5.1010 | 5.2040 | 5.3091 | 5.4163 | 5.5256 | 5.6371 | 5.7507 | 5.8666 | 5.9847 |
| 6 | 6.1520 | 6.3081 | 6.4684 | 6.6330 | 6.8019 | 6.9753 | 7.1533 | 7.3359 | 7.5233 |
| 7 | 7.2135 | 7.4343 | 7.6625 | 7.8983 | 8.1420 | 8.3938 | 8.6540 | 8.9228 | 9.2004 |
| 8 | 8.2857 | 8.5830 | 8.8932 | 9.2142 | 9.5491 | 9.8975 | 10.260 | 10.637 | 11.028 |
| 9 | 9.3685 | 9.7546 | 10.159 | 10.583 | 11.027 | 11.491 | 11.978 | 12.488 | 13.021 |
| 10 | 10.462 | 10.950 | 11.464 | 12.006 | 12.578 | 13.181 | 13.816 | 14.487 | 15.193 |
| 11 | 11.567 | 12.169 | 12.808 | 13.486 | 14.207 | 14.972 | 15.784 | 16.645 | 17.560 |
| 12 | 12.683 | 13.412 | 14.192 | 15.026 | 15.917 | 16.870 | 17.888 | 18.977 | 20.141 |
| 13 | 13.809 | 14.680 | 15.618 | 16.627 | 17.713 | 18.882 | 20.141 | 21.495 | 22.953 |
| 14 | 14.947 | 15.974 | 17.086 | 18.292 | 19.599 | 21.015 | 22.550 | 24.215 | 26.019 |
| 15 | 16.097 | 17.293 | 18.599 | 20.024 | 21.579 | 23.276 | 25.129 | 27.152 | 29.361 |
| 16 | 17.258 | 18.639 | 20.157 | 21.825 | 23.657 | 25.673 | 27.888 | 30.324 | 33.003 |
| 17 | 18.430 | 20.012 | 21.762 | 23.698 | 25.840 | 28.213 | 30.840 | 33.750 | 36.974 |
| 18 | 19.615 | 21.412 | 23.414 | 25.645 | 28.132 | 30.906 | 33.999 | 37.450 | 41.301 |
| 19 | 20.811 | 22.841 | 25.117 | 27.671 | 30.539 | 33.760 | 37.379 | 41.446 | 46.018 |
| 20 | 22.019 | 24.297 | 26.870 | 29.778 | 33.066 | 36.786 | 40.995 | 45.762 | 51.160 |
| 21 | 23.239 | 25.783 | 28.676 | 31.969 | 35.719 | 39.993 | 44.865 | 50.423 | 56.765 |
| 22 | 24.472 | 27.299 | 30.537 | 34.248 | 38.505 | 43.392 | 49.006 | 55.457 | 62.873 |
| 23 | 25.716 | 28.845 | 32.453 | 36.618 | 41.430 | 46.996 | 53.436 | 60.893 | 69.532 |
| 24 | 26.973 | 30.422 | 34.426 | 39.083 | 44.502 | 50.816 | 58.177 | 66.765 | 76.790 |
| 25 | 28.243 | 32.030 | 36.459 | 41.646 | 47.727 | 54.865 | 63.249 | 73.106 | 84.701 |
| 30 | 34.785 | 40.568 | 47.575 | 56.085 | 66.439 | 79.058 | 94.461 | 113.28 | 136.31 |
| 40 | 48.886 | 60.402 | 75.401 | 95.026 | 120.80 | 154.76 | 199.64 | 259.06 | 337.88 |
| 50 | 64.463 | 84.579 | 112.80 | 152.67 | 209.35 | 290.34 | 406.53 | 573.77 | 815.08 |
| 60 | 81.670 | 114.05 | 163.05 | 237.99 | 353.58 | 533.13 | 813.52 | 1253.2 | 1944.8 |

TABLE
**A.4**

| Number of Periods | Interest rate | | | | | | | | | | |
|---|---|---|---|---|---|---|---|---|---|---|---|
| | 10% | 12% | 14% | 15% | 16% | 18% | 20% | 24% | 28% | 32% | 36% |
| 1 | 1.0000 | 1.0000 | 1.0000 | 1.0000 | 1.0000 | 1.0000 | 1.0000 | 1.0000 | 1.0000 | 1.0000 | 1.0000 |
| 2 | 2.1000 | 2.1200 | 2.1400 | 2.1500 | 2.1600 | 2.1800 | 2.2000 | 2.2400 | 2.2800 | 2.3200 | 2.3600 |
| 3 | 3.3100 | 3.3744 | 3.4396 | 3.4725 | 3.5056 | 3.5724 | 3.6400 | 3.7776 | 3.9184 | 4.0624 | 4.2096 |
| 4 | 4.6410 | 4.7793 | 4.9211 | 4.9934 | 5.0665 | 5.2154 | 5.3680 | 5.6842 | 6.0156 | 6.3624 | 6.7251 |
| 5 | 6.1051 | 6.3528 | 6.6101 | 6.7424 | 6.8771 | 7.1542 | 7.4416 | 8.0484 | 8.6999 | 9.3983 | 10.146 |
| 6 | 7.7156 | 8.1152 | 8.5355 | 8.7537 | 8.9775 | 9.4420 | 9.9299 | 10.980 | 12.136 | 13.406 | 14.799 |
| 7 | 9.4872 | 10.089 | 10.730 | 11.067 | 11.414 | 12.142 | 12.916 | 14.615 | 16.534 | 18.696 | 21.126 |
| 8 | 11.436 | 12.300 | 13.233 | 13.727 | 14.240 | 15.327 | 16.499 | 19.123 | 22.163 | 25.678 | 29.732 |
| 9 | 13.579 | 14.776 | 16.085 | 16.786 | 17.519 | 19.086 | 20.799 | 24.712 | 29.369 | 34.895 | 41.435 |
| 10 | 15.937 | 17.549 | 19.337 | 20.304 | 21.321 | 23.521 | 25.959 | 31.643 | 38.593 | 47.062 | 57.352 |
| 11 | 18.531 | 20.655 | 23.045 | 24.349 | 25.733 | 28.755 | 32.150 | 40.238 | 50.398 | 63.122 | 78.998 |
| 12 | 21.384 | 24.133 | 27.271 | 29.002 | 30.850 | 34.931 | 39.581 | 50.895 | 65.510 | 84.320 | 108.44 |
| 13 | 24.523 | 28.029 | 32.089 | 34.352 | 36.786 | 42.219 | 48.497 | 64.110 | 84.853 | 112.30 | 148.47 |
| 14 | 27.975 | 32.393 | 37.581 | 40.505 | 43.672 | 50.818 | 59.196 | 80.496 | 109.61 | 149.24 | 202.93 |
| 15 | 31.772 | 37.280 | 43.842 | 47.580 | 51.660 | 60.965 | 72.035 | 100.82 | 141.30 | 198.00 | 276.98 |
| 16 | 35.950 | 42.753 | 50.980 | 55.717 | 60.925 | 72.939 | 87.442 | 126.01 | 181.87 | 262.36 | 377.69 |
| 17 | 40.545 | 48.884 | 59.118 | 65.075 | 71.673 | 87.068 | 105.93 | 157.25 | 233.79 | 347.31 | 514.66 |
| 18 | 45.599 | 55.750 | 68.394 | 75.836 | 84.141 | 103.74 | 128.12 | 195.99 | 300.25 | 459.45 | 700.94 |
| 19 | 51.159 | 64.440 | 78.969 | 88.212 | 98.603 | 123.41 | 154.74 | 244.03 | 385.32 | 607.47 | 954.28 |
| 20 | 57.275 | 72.052 | 91.025 | 102.44 | 115.38 | 146.63 | 186.69 | 303.60 | 494.21 | 802.86 | 1298.8 |
| 21 | 64.002 | 81.699 | 104.77 | 118.81 | 134.84 | 174.02 | 225.03 | 377.46 | 633.59 | 1060.8 | 1767.4 |
| 22 | 71.403 | 92.503 | 120.44 | 137.63 | 157.41 | 206.34 | 271.03 | 469.06 | 812.00 | 1401.2 | 2404.7 |
| 23 | 79.543 | 104.60 | 138.30 | 159.28 | 183.60 | 244.49 | 326.24 | 582.63 | 1040.4 | 1850.6 | 3271.3 |
| 24 | 88.497 | 118.16 | 158.66 | 184.17 | 213.98 | 289.49 | 392.48 | 723.46 | 1332.7 | 2443.8 | 4450.0 |
| 25 | 98.347 | 133.33 | 181.87 | 212.79 | 249.21 | 342.60 | 471.98 | 898.09 | 1706.8 | 3226.8 | 6053.0 |
| 30 | 164.49 | 241.33 | 356.79 | 434.75 | 530.31 | 790.95 | 1181.9 | 2640.9 | 5873.2 | 12941. | 28172.3 |
| 40 | 442.59 | 767.09 | 1342.0 | 1779.1 | 2360.8 | 4163.2 | 7343.9 | 22729. | 69377. | * | * |
| 50 | 1163.9 | 2400.0 | 4994.5 | 7217.7 | 10436. | 21813. | 45497. | * | * | * | * |
| 60 | 3034.8 | 7471.6 | 18535. | 29220. | 46058. | * | * | * | * | * | * |

*FVIFA 99,999.

**Table A.4** Future Value of an Annuity of £1 or €1 per Period for T Periods $= [(1 + r)^T - 1]/r$

TABLE
A.5

| Period (T) | Continuously compounded rate (r) | | | | | | | | | | | | | |
|---|---|---|---|---|---|---|---|---|---|---|---|---|---|---|
| | 1% | 2% | 3% | 4% | 5% | 6% | 7% | 8% | 9% | 10% | 11% | 12% | 13% | 14% |
| 1 | 1.0101 | 1.0202 | 1.0305 | 1.0408 | 1.0513 | 1.0618 | 1.0725 | 1.0833 | 1.0942 | 1.1052 | 1.1163 | 1.1275 | 1.1388 | 1.1503 |
| 2 | 1.0202 | 1.0408 | 1.0618 | 1.0833 | 1.1052 | 1.1275 | 1.1503 | 1.1735 | 1.1972 | 1.2214 | 1.2461 | 1.2712 | 1.2969 | 1.3231 |
| 3 | 1.0305 | 1.0618 | 1.0942 | 1.1275 | 1.1618 | 1.1972 | 1.2337 | 1.2712 | 1.3100 | 1.3499 | 1.3910 | 1.4333 | 1.4770 | 1.5220 |
| 4 | 1.0408 | 1.0833 | 1.1275 | 1.1735 | 1.2214 | 1.2712 | 1.3231 | 1.3771 | 1.4333 | 1.4918 | 1.5527 | 1.6161 | 1.6820 | 1.7507 |
| 5 | 1.0513 | 1.1052 | 1.1618 | 1.2214 | 1.2840 | 1.3499 | 1.4191 | 1.4918 | 1.5683 | 1.6487 | 1.7333 | 1.8221 | 1.9155 | 2.0138 |
| 6 | 1.0618 | 1.1275 | 1.1972 | 1.2712 | 1.3499 | 1.4333 | 1.5220 | 1.6161 | 1.7160 | 1.8221 | 1.9348 | 2.0544 | 2.1815 | 2.3164 |
| 7 | 1.0725 | 1.1503 | 1.2337 | 1.3231 | 1.4191 | 1.5220 | 1.6323 | 1.7507 | 1.8776 | 2.0138 | 2.1598 | 2.3164 | 2.4843 | 2.6645 |
| 8 | 1.0833 | 1.1735 | 1.2712 | 1.3771 | 1.4918 | 1.6161 | 1.7507 | 1.8965 | 2.0544 | 2.2255 | 2.4109 | 2.6117 | 2.8292 | 3.0649 |
| 9 | 1.0942 | 1.1972 | 1.3100 | 1.4333 | 1.5683 | 1.7160 | 1.8776 | 2.0544 | 2.2479 | 2.4596 | 2.6912 | 2.9447 | 3.2220 | 3.5254 |
| 10 | 1.1052 | 1.2214 | 1.3499 | 1.4918 | 1.6487 | 1.8221 | 2.0138 | 2.2255 | 2.4596 | 2.7183 | 3.0042 | 3.3201 | 3.6693 | 4.0552 |
| 11 | 1.1163 | 1.2461 | 1.3910 | 1.5527 | 1.7333 | 1.9348 | 2.1598 | 2.4109 | 2.6912 | 3.0042 | 3.3535 | 3.7434 | 4.1787 | 4.6646 |
| 12 | 1.1275 | 1.2712 | 1.4333 | 1.6161 | 1.8221 | 2.0544 | 2.3164 | 2.6117 | 2.9447 | 3.3201 | 3.7434 | 4.2207 | 4.7588 | 5.3656 |
| 13 | 1.1388 | 1.2969 | 1.4770 | 1.6820 | 1.9155 | 2.1815 | 2.4843 | 2.8292 | 3.2220 | 3.6693 | 4.1787 | 4.7588 | 5.4195 | 6.1719 |
| 14 | 1.1503 | 1.3231 | 1.5220 | 1.7507 | 2.0138 | 2.3164 | 2.6645 | 3.0649 | 3.5254 | 4.0552 | 4.6646 | 5.3656 | 6.1719 | 7.0993 |
| 15 | 1.1618 | 1.3499 | 1.5683 | 1.8221 | 2.1170 | 2.4596 | 2.8577 | 3.3201 | 3.8574 | 4.4817 | 5.2070 | 6.0496 | 7.0287 | 8.1662 |
| 16 | 1.1735 | 1.3771 | 1.6161 | 1.8965 | 2.2255 | 2.6117 | 3.0649 | 3.5966 | 4.2207 | 4.9530 | 5.8124 | 6.8210 | 8.0045 | 9.3933 |
| 17 | 1.1853 | 1.4049 | 1.6653 | 1.9739 | 2.3396 | 2.7732 | 3.2871 | 3.8962 | 4.6182 | 5.4739 | 6.4883 | 7.6906 | 9.1157 | 10.8049 |
| 18 | 1.1972 | 1.4333 | 1.7160 | 2.0544 | 2.4596 | 2.9447 | 3.5254 | 4.2207 | 5.0531 | 6.0496 | 7.2427 | 8.6711 | 10.3812 | 12.4286 |
| 19 | 1.2092 | 1.4623 | 1.7683 | 2.1383 | 2.5857 | 3.1268 | 3.7810 | 4.5722 | 5.5290 | 6.6859 | 8.0849 | 9.7767 | 11.8224 | 14.2963 |
| 20 | 1.2214 | 1.4918 | 1.8221 | 2.2255 | 2.7183 | 3.3201 | 4.0552 | 4.9530 | 6.0496 | 7.3891 | 9.0250 | 11.0232 | 13.4637 | 16.4446 |
| 21 | 1.2337 | 1.5220 | 1.8776 | 2.3164 | 2.8577 | 3.5254 | 4.3492 | 5.3656 | 6.6194 | 8.1662 | 10.0744 | 12.4286 | 15.3329 | 18.9158 |
| 22 | 1.2461 | 1.5527 | 1.9348 | 2.4109 | 3.0042 | 3.7434 | 4.6646 | 5.8124 | 7.2427 | 9.0250 | 11.2459 | 14.0132 | 17.4615 | 21.7584 |
| 23 | 1.2586 | 1.5841 | 1.9937 | 2.5093 | 3.1582 | 3.9749 | 5.0028 | 6.2965 | 7.9248 | 9.9742 | 12.5535 | 15.7998 | 19.8857 | 25.0281 |
| 24 | 1.2712 | 1.6161 | 2.0544 | 2.6117 | 3.3201 | 4.2207 | 5.3656 | 6.8210 | 8.6711 | 11.0232 | 14.0132 | 17.8143 | 22.6464 | 28.7892 |
| 25 | 1.2840 | 1.6487 | 2.1170 | 2.7183 | 3.4903 | 4.4817 | 5.7546 | 7.3891 | 9.4877 | 12.1825 | 15.6426 | 20.0855 | 25.7903 | 33.1155 |
| 30 | 1.3499 | 1.8221 | 2.4596 | 3.3204 | 4.4817 | 6.0496 | 8.1662 | 11.0232 | 14.8797 | 20.0855 | 27.1126 | 36.5982 | 49.4024 | 66.6863 |
| 35 | 1.4191 | 2.0138 | 2.8577 | 4.0552 | 5.7546 | 8.1662 | 11.5883 | 16.4446 | 23.3361 | 33.1155 | 46.9931 | 66.6863 | 94.6324 | 134.2898 |
| 40 | 1.4918 | 2.2255 | 3.3201 | 4.9530 | 7.3891 | 11.0232 | 16.4446 | 24.5235 | 36.5982 | 54.5982 | 81.4509 | 121.5104 | 181.2722 | 270.4264 |
| 45 | 1.5683 | 2.4596 | 3.8574 | 6.0496 | 9.4877 | 14.8797 | 23.3361 | 36.5982 | 57.3975 | 90.0171 | 141.1750 | 221.4064 | 347.2344 | 544.5719 |
| 50 | 1.6487 | 2.7183 | 4.4817 | 7.3891 | 12.1825 | 20.0855 | 33.1155 | 54.5982 | 90.0171 | 148.4132 | 244.6919 | 403.4288 | 665.1416 | 1096.633 |
| 55 | 1.7333 | 3.0042 | 5.2070 | 9.0250 | 15.6426 | 27.1126 | 46.9931 | 81.4509 | 141.1750 | 244.6919 | 424.1130 | 735.0952 | 1274.106 | 2208.348 |
| 60 | 1.8221 | 3.3201 | 6.0496 | 11.0232 | 20.0855 | 36.5982 | 66.6863 | 121.5104 | 221.4064 | 403.4288 | 735.0952 | 1339.431 | 2440.602 | 4447.067 |

TABLE
A.5

| Period (T) | Continuously compounded rate (r) | | | | | | | | | | | | | |
|---|---|---|---|---|---|---|---|---|---|---|---|---|---|---|
| | 15% | 16% | 17% | 18% | 19% | 20% | 21% | 22% | 23% | 24% | 25% | 26% | 27% | 28% |
| 1 | 1.1618 | 1.1735 | 1.1853 | 1.1972 | 1.2092 | 1.2214 | 1.2337 | 1.2461 | 1.2586 | 1.2712 | 1.2840 | 1.2969 | 1.3100 | 1.3231 |
| 2 | 1.3499 | 1.3771 | 1.4049 | 1.4333 | 1.4623 | 1.4918 | 1.5220 | 1.5527 | 1.5841 | 1.6161 | 1.6487 | 1.6820 | 1.7160 | 1.7507 |
| 3 | 1.5683 | 1.6161 | 1.6653 | 1.7160 | 1.7683 | 1.8221 | 1.8776 | 1.9348 | 1.9937 | 2.0544 | 2.1170 | 2.1815 | 2.2479 | 2.3164 |
| 4 | 1.8221 | 1.8965 | 1.9739 | 2.0544 | 2.1383 | 2.2255 | 2.3164 | 2.4109 | 2.5093 | 2.6117 | 2.7183 | 2.8292 | 2.9447 | 3.0649 |
| 5 | 2.1170 | 2.2255 | 2.3396 | 2.4596 | 2.5857 | 2.7183 | 2.8577 | 3.0042 | 3.1582 | 3.3201 | 3.4903 | 3.6693 | 3.8574 | 4.0552 |
| 6 | 2.4596 | 2.6117 | 2.7732 | 2.9447 | 3.1268 | 3.3201 | 3.5254 | 3.7434 | 3.9749 | 4.2207 | 4.4817 | 4.7588 | 5.0351 | 5.3656 |
| 7 | 2.8577 | 3.0649 | 3.2871 | 3.5254 | 3.7810 | 4.0552 | 4.3492 | 4.6646 | 5.0028 | 5.3656 | 5.7546 | 6.1719 | 6.6194 | 7.0993 |
| 8 | 3.3201 | 3.5966 | 3.8962 | 4.2207 | 4.5722 | 4.9530 | 5.3656 | 5.8124 | 6.2965 | 6.8210 | 7.3891 | 8.0045 | 8.6711 | 9.3933 |
| 9 | 3.8574 | 4.2207 | 4.6182 | 5.0531 | 5.5290 | 6.0496 | 6.6194 | 7.2427 | 7.9248 | 8.6711 | 9.4877 | 10.3812 | 11.3589 | 12.4286 |
| 10 | 4.4817 | 4.9530 | 5.4739 | 6.0496 | 6.6859 | 7.3891 | 8.1662 | 9.0250 | 9.9742 | 11.0232 | 12.1825 | 13.4637 | 14.8797 | 16.4446 |
| 11 | 5.2070 | 5.8124 | 6.4883 | 7.2427 | 8.0849 | 9.0250 | 10.0744 | 11.2459 | 12.5535 | 14.0132 | 15.6426 | 17.4615 | 19.4919 | 21.7584 |
| 12 | 6.0496 | 6.8210 | 7.6906 | 8.6711 | 9.7767 | 11.0232 | 12.4286 | 14.0132 | 15.7998 | 17.8143 | 20.0855 | 22.6464 | 25.5337 | 28.7892 |
| 13 | 7.0287 | 8.0045 | 9.1157 | 10.3812 | 11.8224 | 13.4637 | 15.3329 | 17.4615 | 19.8857 | 22.6464 | 25.7903 | 29.3708 | 33.4483 | 38.0918 |
| 14 | 8.1662 | 9.3933 | 10.8049 | 12.4286 | 14.2963 | 16.4446 | 18.9158 | 21.7584 | 25.0281 | 28.7892 | 33.1155 | 38.0918 | 43.8160 | 50.4004 |
| 15 | 9.4877 | 11.0232 | 12.8071 | 14.8797 | 17.2878 | 20.0855 | 23.3361 | 27.1126 | 31.5004 | 36.5982 | 42.5211 | 49.4024 | 57.3975 | 66.6863 |
| 16 | 11.0232 | 12.9358 | 15.1803 | 17.8143 | 20.9052 | 24.5325 | 28.7892 | 33.7844 | 39.6464 | 46.5255 | 54.5982 | 64.0715 | 75.1886 | 88.2347 |
| 17 | 12.8071 | 15.1803 | 17.9933 | 21.3276 | 25.2797 | 29.9641 | 35.5166 | 42.0980 | 49.8990 | 59.1455 | 70.1054 | 83.0963 | 98.4944 | 116.7459 |
| 18 | 14.8797 | 17.8143 | 21.3276 | 25.5337 | 30.5694 | 36.5982 | 43.8160 | 52.4573 | 62.8028 | 75.1886 | 90.0171 | 107.7701 | 129.0242 | 154.4700 |
| 19 | 17.2878 | 20.9052 | 25.2797 | 30.5694 | 36.9661 | 44.7012 | 54.0549 | 65.3659 | 79.0436 | 95.5835 | 115.5843 | 139.7702 | 169.0171 | 204.3839 |
| 20 | 20.0855 | 24.5325 | 29.9641 | 36.5982 | 44.7012 | 54.5982 | 66.6863 | 81.4509 | 99.4843 | 121.5104 | 148.4132 | 181.2722 | 221.4064 | 270.4264 |
| 21 | 23.3361 | 28.7892 | 35.5166 | 43.8160 | 54.0549 | 66.6863 | 82.2695 | 101.4940 | 125.2110 | 154.4700 | 190.5663 | 235.0974 | 290.0345 | 357.8092 |
| 22 | 27.1126 | 33.7844 | 42.0980 | 52.4573 | 65.3659 | 81.4509 | 101.4940 | 126.4694 | 157.5905 | 196.3699 | 244.6919 | 304.9049 | 379.9349 | 473.4281 |
| 23 | 31.5004 | 39.6464 | 49.8990 | 62.8028 | 79.0436 | 99.4843 | 125.2110 | 157.5905 | 198.3434 | 249.6350 | 314.1907 | 395.4404 | 497.7013 | 626.4068 |
| 24 | 36.5982 | 46.5255 | 59.1455 | 75.1886 | 95.5835 | 121.5104 | 154.4700 | 196.3699 | 249.6350 | 317.3483 | 403.4288 | 512.8585 | 651.9709 | 828.8175 |
| 25 | 42.5211 | 54.5982 | 70.1054 | 90.0171 | 115.5843 | 148.4132 | 190.5663 | 244.6919 | 314.1907 | 403.4288 | 518.0128 | 665.1416 | 854.0588 | 1096.633 |
| 30 | 90.0171 | 121.5104 | 164.0219 | 221.4064 | 298.8674 | 403.4288 | 544.5719 | 735.0952 | 992.2747 | 1339.431 | 1808.042 | 2440.602 | 3294.468 | 4447.067 |
| 35 | 190.5663 | 270.4264 | 383.7533 | 544.5719 | 772.7843 | 1096.633 | 1556.197 | 2208.348 | 3133.795 | 4447.067 | 6310.688 | 8955.293 | 12708.17 | 18033.74 |
| 40 | 403.4288 | 601.8450 | 897.8473 | 1339.431 | 1998.196 | 2980.958 | 4447.067 | 6634.244 | 9897.129 | 14764.78 | 22026.47 | 32859.63 | 49020.80 | 73130.44 |
| 45 | 854.0588 | 1339.431 | 2100.646 | 3294.468 | 5166.754 | 8103.084 | 12708.17 | 19930.37 | 31257.04 | 49020.80 | 76879.92 | 120571.7 | 189094.1 | 296558.6 |
| 50 | 1808.042 | 2980.958 | 4914.769 | 8103.084 | 13359.73 | 22026.47 | 36315.50 | 59874.14 | 98715.77 | 162754.8 | 268337.3 | 442413.4 | 729416.4 | 1202604. |
| 55 | 3827.626 | 6634.244 | 11498.82 | 19930.37 | 34544.37 | 59874.14 | 103777.0 | 179871.9 | 311763.4 | 540364.9 | 936589.2 | 1623346. | 2813669. | 4876801. |
| 60 | 8103.084 | 14764.78 | 26903.19 | 49020.80 | 89321.72 | 162754.8 | 296558.6 | 540364.9 | 984609.1 | 1794075. | 3269017. | 5956538. | 10853520. | 19776403. |

Table A.5  Future Value of £1 or €1 with a Continuously Compounded Rate r for T Periods: Values of $e^{rT}$

TABLE A.6

**Continuous discount rate (r)**

| Period (T) | 1% | 2% | 3% | 4% | 5% | 6% | 7% | 8% | 9% | 10% | 11% | 12% | 13% | 14% | 15% | 16% | 17% |
|---|---|---|---|---|---|---|---|---|---|---|---|---|---|---|---|---|---|
| 1 | 0.9900 | 0.9802 | 0.9704 | 0.9608 | 0.9512 | 0.9418 | 0.9324 | 0.9231 | 0.9139 | 0.9048 | 0.8958 | 0.8869 | 0.8781 | 0.8694 | 0.8607 | 0.8521 | 0.8437 |
| 2 | 0.9802 | 0.9608 | 0.9418 | 0.9231 | 0.9048 | 0.8869 | 0.8694 | 0.8521 | 0.8353 | 0.8187 | 0.8025 | 0.7866 | 0.7711 | 0.7558 | 0.7408 | 0.7261 | 0.7118 |
| 3 | 0.9704 | 0.9418 | 0.9139 | 0.8869 | 0.8607 | 0.8353 | 0.8106 | 0.7866 | 0.7634 | 0.7408 | 0.7189 | 0.6977 | 0.6771 | 0.6570 | 0.6376 | 0.6188 | 0.6005 |
| 4 | 0.9608 | 0.9231 | 0.8869 | 0.8521 | 0.8187 | 0.7866 | 0.7558 | 0.7261 | 0.6977 | 0.6703 | 0.6440 | 0.6188 | 0.5945 | 0.5712 | 0.5488 | 0.5273 | 0.5066 |
| 5 | 0.9512 | 0.9048 | 0.8607 | 0.8187 | 0.7788 | 0.7408 | 0.7047 | 0.6703 | 0.6376 | 0.6065 | 0.5769 | 0.5488 | 0.5220 | 0.4966 | 0.4724 | 0.4493 | 0.4274 |
| 6 | 0.9418 | 0.8869 | 0.8353 | 0.7866 | 0.7408 | 0.6977 | 0.6570 | 0.6188 | 0.5827 | 0.5488 | 0.5169 | 0.4868 | 0.4584 | 0.4317 | 0.4066 | 0.3829 | 0.3606 |
| 7 | 0.9324 | 0.8694 | 0.8106 | 0.7558 | 0.7047 | 0.6570 | 0.6126 | 0.5712 | 0.5326 | 0.4966 | 0.4630 | 0.4317 | 0.4025 | 0.3753 | 0.3499 | 0.3263 | 0.3042 |
| 8 | 0.9231 | 0.8521 | 0.7866 | 0.7261 | 0.6703 | 0.6188 | 0.5712 | 0.5273 | 0.4868 | 0.4493 | 0.4148 | 0.3829 | 0.3535 | 0.3263 | 0.3012 | 0.2780 | 0.2576 |
| 9 | 0.9139 | 0.8353 | 0.7634 | 0.6977 | 0.6376 | 0.5827 | 0.5326 | 0.4868 | 0.4449 | 0.4066 | 0.3716 | 0.3396 | 0.3104 | 0.2837 | 0.2592 | 0.2369 | 0.2165 |
| 10 | 0.9048 | 0.8187 | 0.7408 | 0.6703 | 0.6065 | 0.5488 | 0.4966 | 0.4493 | 0.4066 | 0.3679 | 0.3329 | 0.3012 | 0.2725 | 0.2466 | 0.2231 | 0.2019 | 0.1827 |
| 11 | 0.8958 | 0.8025 | 0.7189 | 0.6440 | 0.5769 | 0.5169 | 0.4630 | 0.4148 | 0.3716 | 0.3329 | 0.2982 | 0.2671 | 0.2393 | 0.2144 | 0.1920 | 0.1720 | 0.1541 |
| 12 | 0.8869 | 0.7866 | 0.6977 | 0.6188 | 0.5488 | 0.4868 | 0.4317 | 0.3829 | 0.3396 | 0.3012 | 0.2671 | 0.2369 | 0.2101 | 0.1864 | 0.1653 | 0.1466 | 0.1300 |
| 13 | 0.8781 | 0.7711 | 0.6771 | 0.5945 | 0.5220 | 0.4584 | 0.4025 | 0.3535 | 0.3104 | 0.2725 | 0.2393 | 0.2101 | 0.1845 | 0.1620 | 0.1423 | 0.1249 | 0.1097 |
| 14 | 0.8694 | 0.7558 | 0.6570 | 0.5712 | 0.4966 | 0.4317 | 0.3753 | 0.3263 | 0.2837 | 0.2466 | 0.2144 | 0.1864 | 0.1620 | 0.1409 | 0.1225 | 0.1065 | 0.0926 |
| 15 | 0.8607 | 0.7408 | 0.6376 | 0.5488 | 0.4724 | 0.4066 | 0.3499 | 0.3012 | 0.2592 | 0.2231 | 0.1920 | 0.1653 | 0.1423 | 0.1225 | 0.1054 | 0.0907 | 0.0781 |
| 16 | 0.8521 | 0.7261 | 0.6188 | 0.5273 | 0.4493 | 0.3829 | 0.3263 | 0.2780 | 0.2369 | 0.2019 | 0.1720 | 0.1466 | 0.1249 | 0.1065 | 0.0907 | 0.0773 | 0.0659 |
| 17 | 0.8437 | 0.7118 | 0.6005 | 0.5066 | 0.4274 | 0.3606 | 0.3042 | 0.2567 | 0.2165 | 0.1827 | 0.1541 | 0.1300 | 0.1097 | 0.0926 | 0.0781 | 0.0659 | 0.0556 |
| 18 | 0.8353 | 0.6977 | 0.5827 | 0.4868 | 0.4066 | 0.3396 | 0.2837 | 0.2369 | 0.1979 | 0.1653 | 0.1381 | 0.1153 | 0.0963 | 0.0805 | 0.0672 | 0.0561 | 0.0469 |
| 19 | 0.8270 | 0.6839 | 0.5655 | 0.4677 | 0.3867 | 0.3198 | 0.2645 | 0.2187 | 0.1809 | 0.1496 | 0.1237 | 0.1023 | 0.0846 | 0.0699 | 0.0578 | 0.0478 | 0.0396 |
| 20 | 0.8187 | 0.6703 | 0.5488 | 0.4493 | 0.3679 | 0.3012 | 0.2466 | 0.2019 | 0.1653 | 0.1353 | 0.1108 | 0.0907 | 0.0743 | 0.0608 | 0.0498 | 0.0408 | 0.0334 |
| 21 | 0.8106 | 0.6570 | 0.5326 | 0.4317 | 0.3499 | 0.2837 | 0.2299 | 0.1864 | 0.1511 | 0.1225 | 0.0993 | 0.0805 | 0.0652 | 0.0529 | 0.0429 | 0.0347 | 0.0282 |
| 22 | 0.8025 | 0.6440 | 0.5169 | 0.4148 | 0.3329 | 0.2671 | 0.2144 | 0.1720 | 0.1381 | 0.1108 | 0.0889 | 0.0714 | 0.0573 | 0.0460 | 0.0369 | 0.0296 | 0.0238 |
| 23 | 0.7945 | 0.6313 | 0.5016 | 0.3985 | 0.3166 | 0.2516 | 0.1999 | 0.1588 | 0.1262 | 0.1003 | 0.0797 | 0.0633 | 0.0503 | 0.0400 | 0.0317 | 0.0252 | 0.0200 |
| 24 | 0.7866 | 0.6188 | 0.4868 | 0.3829 | 0.3012 | 0.2369 | 0.1864 | 0.1466 | 0.1153 | 0.0907 | 0.0714 | 0.0561 | 0.0442 | 0.0347 | 0.0273 | 0.0215 | 0.0169 |
| 25 | 0.7788 | 0.6065 | 0.4724 | 0.3679 | 0.2865 | 0.2231 | 0.1738 | 0.1353 | 0.1054 | 0.0821 | 0.0639 | 0.0498 | 0.0388 | 0.0302 | 0.0235 | 0.0183 | 0.0143 |
| 30 | 0.7408 | 0.5488 | 0.4066 | 0.3012 | 0.2231 | 0.1653 | 0.1225 | 0.0907 | 0.0672 | 0.0498 | 0.0369 | 0.0273 | 0.0202 | 0.0150 | 0.0111 | 0.0082 | 0.0061 |
| 35 | 0.7047 | 0.4966 | 0.3499 | 0.2466 | 0.1738 | 0.1225 | 0.0863 | 0.0608 | 0.0429 | 0.0302 | 0.0213 | 0.0150 | 0.0106 | 0.0074 | 0.0052 | 0.0037 | 0.0026 |
| 40 | 0.6703 | 0.4493 | 0.3012 | 0.2019 | 0.1353 | 0.0907 | 0.0608 | 0.0408 | 0.0273 | 0.0183 | 0.0123 | 0.0082 | 0.0055 | 0.0037 | 0.0025 | 0.0017 | 0.0011 |
| 45 | 0.6376 | 0.4066 | 0.2592 | 0.1653 | 0.1054 | 0.0672 | 0.0429 | 0.0273 | 0.0174 | 0.0111 | 0.0071 | 0.0045 | 0.0029 | 0.0018 | 0.0012 | 0.0007 | 0.0005 |
| 50 | 0.6065 | 0.3679 | 0.2231 | 0.1353 | 0.0821 | 0.0498 | 0.0302 | 0.0183 | 0.0111 | 0.0067 | 0.0041 | 0.0025 | 0.0015 | 0.0009 | 0.0006 | 0.0003 | 0.0002 |
| 55 | 0.5769 | 0.3329 | 0.1920 | 0.1108 | 0.0639 | 0.0369 | 0.0213 | 0.0123 | 0.0071 | 0.0041 | 0.0024 | 0.0014 | 0.0008 | 0.0005 | 0.0003 | 0.0002 | 0.0001 |
| 60 | 0.5488 | 0.3012 | 0.1653 | 0.0907 | 0.0498 | 0.0273 | 0.0150 | 0.0082 | 0.0045 | 0.0025 | 0.0014 | 0.0007 | 0.0004 | 0.0002 | 0.0001 | 0.0001 | 0.0000 |

TABLE
A.6

**Continuous discount rate ($r$)**

| Period (T) | 18% | 19% | 20% | 21% | 22% | 23% | 24% | 25% | 26% | 27% | 28% | 29% | 30% | 31% | 32% | 33% | 34% | 35% |
|---|---|---|---|---|---|---|---|---|---|---|---|---|---|---|---|---|---|---|
| 1 | 0.8353 | 0.8270 | 0.8187 | 0.8106 | 0.8025 | 0.7945 | 0.7866 | 0.7788 | 0.7711 | 0.7634 | 0.7558 | 0.7483 | 0.7408 | 0.7334 | 0.7261 | 0.7189 | 0.7118 | 0.7047 |
| 2 | 0.6977 | 0.6839 | 0.6703 | 0.6570 | 0.6440 | 0.6313 | 0.6188 | 0.6065 | 0.5945 | 0.5827 | 0.5712 | 0.5599 | 0.5488 | 0.5379 | 0.5273 | 0.5169 | 0.5066 | 0.4966 |
| 3 | 0.5827 | 0.5655 | 0.5488 | 0.5326 | 0.5169 | 0.5016 | 0.4868 | 0.4724 | 0.4584 | 0.4449 | 0.4317 | 0.4190 | 0.4066 | 0.3946 | 0.3829 | 0.3716 | 0.3606 | 0.3499 |
| 4 | 0.4868 | 0.4677 | 0.4493 | 0.4317 | 0.4148 | 0.3985 | 0.3829 | 0.3679 | 0.3535 | 0.3396 | 0.3263 | 0.3135 | 0.3012 | 0.2894 | 0.2780 | 0.2671 | 0.2567 | 0.2466 |
| 5 | 0.4066 | 0.3867 | 0.3679 | 0.3499 | 0.3329 | 0.3166 | 0.3012 | 0.2865 | 0.2725 | 0.2592 | 0.2466 | 0.2346 | 0.2231 | 0.2122 | 0.2019 | 0.1920 | 0.1827 | 0.1738 |
| 6 | 0.3396 | 0.3198 | 0.3012 | 0.2837 | 0.2671 | 0.2516 | 0.2369 | 0.2231 | 0.2101 | 0.1979 | 0.1864 | 0.1755 | 0.1653 | 0.1557 | 0.1466 | 0.1381 | 0.1300 | 0.1225 |
| 7 | 0.2837 | 0.2645 | 0.2466 | 0.2299 | 0.2144 | 0.1999 | 0.1864 | 0.1738 | 0.1620 | 0.1511 | 0.1409 | 0.1313 | 0.1225 | 0.1142 | 0.1065 | 0.0993 | 0.0926 | 0.0863 |
| 8 | 0.2369 | 0.2187 | 0.2019 | 0.1864 | 0.1720 | 0.1588 | 0.1466 | 0.1353 | 0.1249 | 0.1153 | 0.1065 | 0.0983 | 0.0907 | 0.0837 | 0.0773 | 0.0714 | 0.0659 | 0.0608 |
| 9 | 0.1979 | 0.1809 | 0.1653 | 0.1511 | 0.1381 | 0.1262 | 0.1153 | 0.1054 | 0.0963 | 0.0880 | 0.0805 | 0.0735 | 0.0672 | 0.0614 | 0.0561 | 0.0513 | 0.0469 | 0.0429 |
| 10 | 0.1653 | 0.1496 | 0.1353 | 0.1225 | 0.1108 | 0.1003 | 0.0907 | 0.0821 | 0.0743 | 0.0672 | 0.0608 | 0.0550 | 0.0498 | 0.0450 | 0.0408 | 0.0369 | 0.0334 | 0.0302 |
| 11 | 0.1381 | 0.1237 | 0.1108 | 0.0993 | 0.0889 | 0.0797 | 0.0714 | 0.0639 | 0.0573 | 0.0513 | 0.0460 | 0.0412 | 0.0369 | 0.0330 | 0.0296 | 0.0265 | 0.0238 | 0.0213 |
| 12 | 0.1154 | 0.1023 | 0.0907 | 0.0805 | 0.0714 | 0.0633 | 0.0561 | 0.0498 | 0.0442 | 0.0392 | 0.0347 | 0.0308 | 0.0273 | 0.0242 | 0.0215 | 0.0191 | 0.0169 | 0.0150 |
| 13 | 0.0963 | 0.0846 | 0.0743 | 0.0652 | 0.0573 | 0.0503 | 0.0442 | 0.0388 | 0.0340 | 0.0299 | 0.0263 | 0.0231 | 0.0202 | 0.0178 | 0.0156 | 0.0137 | 0.0120 | 0.0106 |
| 14 | 0.0805 | 0.0699 | 0.0608 | 0.0529 | 0.0460 | 0.0400 | 0.0347 | 0.0302 | 0.0263 | 0.0228 | 0.0198 | 0.0172 | 0.0150 | 0.0130 | 0.0113 | 0.0099 | 0.0086 | 0.0074 |
| 15 | 0.0672 | 0.0578 | 0.0498 | 0.0429 | 0.0369 | 0.0317 | 0.0273 | 0.0235 | 0.0202 | 0.0174 | 0.0150 | 0.0129 | 0.0111 | 0.0096 | 0.0082 | 0.0071 | 0.0061 | 0.0052 |
| 16 | 0.0561 | 0.0478 | 0.0408 | 0.0347 | 0.0296 | 0.0252 | 0.0215 | 0.0183 | 0.0156 | 0.0133 | 0.0113 | 0.0097 | 0.0082 | 0.0070 | 0.0060 | 0.0051 | 0.0043 | 0.0037 |
| 17 | 0.0469 | 0.0396 | 0.0334 | 0.0282 | 0.0238 | 0.0200 | 0.0169 | 0.0143 | 0.0120 | 0.0102 | 0.0086 | 0.0072 | 0.0061 | 0.0051 | 0.0043 | 0.0037 | 0.0031 | 0.0026 |
| 18 | 0.0392 | 0.0327 | 0.0273 | 0.0228 | 0.0191 | 0.0159 | 0.0133 | 0.0111 | 0.0093 | 0.0078 | 0.0065 | 0.0054 | 0.0045 | 0.0038 | 0.0032 | 0.0026 | 0.0022 | 0.0018 |
| 19 | 0.0327 | 0.0271 | 0.0224 | 0.0185 | 0.0153 | 0.0127 | 0.0105 | 0.0087 | 0.0072 | 0.0059 | 0.0049 | 0.0040 | 0.0033 | 0.0028 | 0.0023 | 0.0019 | 0.0016 | 0.0013 |
| 20 | 0.0273 | 0.0224 | 0.0183 | 0.0150 | 0.0123 | 0.0101 | 0.0082 | 0.0067 | 0.0055 | 0.0045 | 0.0037 | 0.0030 | 0.0025 | 0.0020 | 0.0017 | 0.0014 | 0.0011 | 0.0009 |
| 21 | 0.0228 | 0.0185 | 0.0150 | 0.0122 | 0.0099 | 0.0080 | 0.0065 | 0.0052 | 0.0043 | 0.0034 | 0.0028 | 0.0023 | 0.0018 | 0.0015 | 0.0012 | 0.0010 | 0.0008 | 0.0006 |
| 22 | 0.0191 | 0.0153 | 0.0123 | 0.0099 | 0.0079 | 0.0063 | 0.0051 | 0.0041 | 0.0033 | 0.0026 | 0.0021 | 0.0017 | 0.0014 | 0.0011 | 0.0009 | 0.0007 | 0.0006 | 0.0005 |
| 23 | 0.0159 | 0.0127 | 0.0101 | 0.0080 | 0.0063 | 0.0050 | 0.0040 | 0.0032 | 0.0025 | 0.0020 | 0.0016 | 0.0013 | 0.0010 | 0.0008 | 0.0006 | 0.0005 | 0.0004 | 0.0003 |
| 24 | 0.0133 | 0.0105 | 0.0082 | 0.0065 | 0.0051 | 0.0040 | 0.0032 | 0.0025 | 0.0019 | 0.0015 | 0.0012 | 0.0009 | 0.0007 | 0.0006 | 0.0005 | 0.0004 | 0.0003 | 0.0002 |
| 25 | 0.0111 | 0.0087 | 0.0067 | 0.0052 | 0.0041 | 0.0032 | 0.0025 | 0.0019 | 0.0015 | 0.0012 | 0.0009 | 0.0007 | 0.0006 | 0.0004 | 0.0003 | 0.0003 | 0.0002 | 0.0002 |
| 30 | 0.0045 | 0.0033 | 0.0025 | 0.0018 | 0.0014 | 0.0010 | 0.0007 | 0.0006 | 0.0004 | 0.0003 | 0.0002 | 0.0002 | 0.0001 | 0.0001 | 0.0001 | 0.0001 | 0.0000 | 0.0000 |
| 35 | 0.0018 | 0.0013 | 0.0009 | 0.0006 | 0.0005 | 0.0003 | 0.0002 | 0.0002 | 0.0001 | 0.0001 | 0.0001 | 0.0000 | 0.0000 | 0.0000 | 0.0000 | 0.0000 | 0.0000 | 0.0000 |
| 40 | 0.0007 | 0.0005 | 0.0003 | 0.0002 | 0.0002 | 0.0001 | 0.0001 | 0.0000 | 0.0000 | 0.0000 | 0.0000 | 0.0000 | 0.0000 | 0.0000 | 0.0000 | 0.0000 | 0.0000 | 0.0000 |
| 45 | 0.0003 | 0.0002 | 0.0001 | 0.0001 | 0.0001 | 0.0000 | 0.0000 | 0.0000 | 0.0000 | 0.0000 | 0.0000 | 0.0000 | 0.0000 | 0.0000 | 0.0000 | 0.0000 | 0.0000 | 0.0000 |
| 50 | 0.0001 | 0.0001 | 0.0000 | 0.0000 | 0.0000 | 0.0000 | 0.0000 | 0.0000 | 0.0000 | 0.0000 | 0.0000 | 0.0000 | 0.0000 | 0.0000 | 0.0000 | 0.0000 | 0.0000 | 0.0000 |
| 55 | 0.0001 | 0.0000 | 0.0000 | 0.0000 | 0.0000 | 0.0000 | 0.0000 | 0.0000 | 0.0000 | 0.0000 | 0.0000 | 0.0000 | 0.0000 | 0.0000 | 0.0000 | 0.0000 | 0.0000 | 0.0000 |
| 60 | 0.0000 | 0.0000 | 0.0000 | 0.0000 | 0.0000 | 0.0000 | 0.0000 | 0.0000 | 0.0000 | 0.0000 | 0.0000 | 0.0000 | 0.0000 | 0.0000 | 0.0000 | 0.0000 | 0.0000 | 0.0000 |

**Table A.6** Present Value of £1 or €1 with a Continuous Discount Rate $r$ for $T$ Periods: Values of $e^{-rT}$

# Index